T0291301

MACROECONOMICS

MACROECONOMICS

Institutions, Instability, and Inequality

WENDY CARLIN
Professor of Economics, University College London
Fellow of the British Academy

&

DAVID SOSKICE
Emeritus Professor, The London School of Economics and Political Science
Fellow of the British Academy

With contributions from

JAMES CLOYNE, co-author of Chapter 18
Associate Professor of Economics, University of California, Davis

STANISLAS LALANNE, co-author of Chapter 5
University of Oxford

JAVIER LOZANO, author of *The Macroeconomic Simulator*
Lecturer in Economics, University of the Balearic Islands

ANDREW MCNEIL, co-author of Chapter 17
The London School of Economics and Political Science, International Inequalities Institute

OXFORD
UNIVERSITY PRESS

OXFORD
UNIVERSITY PRESS

Great Clarendon Street, Oxford, OX2 6DP,
United Kingdom

Oxford University Press is a department of the University of Oxford.
It furthers the University's objective of excellence in research, scholarship,
and education by publishing worldwide. Oxford is a registered trade mark
of Oxford University Press in the UK and certain other countries

Published in the United States of America by Oxford University Press
198 Madison Avenue, New York, NY 10016, United States of America

British Library Cataloguing in Publication Data
Data available

Library of Congress Control Number: 2023935831

ISBN 978–0–19–883866–1 (pbk.)

Printed in Great Britain by
Bell & Bain Ltd., Glasgow

To Niki and in memory of Andrew
and to the new generation, Poppy and Florence, and Gus and Fordie

REVIEWS

'This enlightening book is a wonderful guide to the key topics of macroeconomics: inflation, monetary policy, including at the zero lower bound, growth and innovation, inequality, exchange rates and more. Very closely connected to the real world, Carlin and Soskice's book brings a wealth of data and historical examples into the discussion in a very pedagogical way. It covers extremely well the links between risk taking, financial cycles and crises which are at the heart of our modern economies. It has also an essential and very timely chapter on commodity price shocks. This is what macroeconomics is about: first order questions, affecting the lives of billions of people, clear modelling and rigorous thinking informed by data and history. Very exciting!'

Hélène Rey, Professor of Economics, London Business School

'This wonderful textbook achieves a rare feat: the material is consistent with work at the current research frontier but nevertheless remains highly accessible. I first learned macroeconomics from an earlier volume of this textbook, when I was an undergraduate student twenty years ago. Now as then the core of the book is its simple 3-equation model for studying business cycles and stabilization policy. But this latest volume also takes on board many of the key developments over the last two decades. Specifically, this is the first textbook to integrate the lessons of the exploding literature on heterogeneous-agent macroeconomics and of the new HANK models. As Carlin and Soskice write: "it's time for 'inequality' to have a place in the title of a macroeconomics textbook"—I couldn't agree more!'

Benjamin Moll, Professor of Economics, London School of Economics

'Beautifully written and rich in data and historical examples, Macroeconomics sets out the building blocks of macroeconomic modelling and guides readers to the frontier of the discipline. The book underscores the crucial role played by institutions, inequality and innovation in contemporary economies. Once you start reading it, you cannot stop it!'

Silvana Tenreyro, Professor of Economics, Department of Economics, London School of Economics and External Member of the Monetary Policy Committee, Bank of England

'Carlin and Soskice have written a masterful treatise on modern macroeconomics. The authors bring to life the fundamental importance of balance for the healthy functioning of an economy—not only the balance between supply and demand, but also in terms of equitable distribution of income. They carefully walk us through when finance is useful, and when its excesses can be harmful for the economy. Most importantly, the authors explain why institutions, i.e. the manner in which a society chooses to govern itself, are central to how far an economy prospers.'

Atif Mian, Professor of Economics, Princeton University, Co-author of House of Debt (2014, The University of Chicago Press)

'Wendy Carlin and David Soskice have once more achieved a pedagogical tour de force, bringing frontier research to the undergraduate level. The increased focus on inequality, its sources and its implications, is a particularly welcome addition.'

Olivier Blanchard, formerly Chief Economist, IMF, Professor of Economics, MIT, Senior Fellow, Peterson Institute

'This remarkable new macroeconomics text brings upper-level undergraduates to the frontier of research and policy. The exposition is at the same time accessible, engaging, and relevant to current concerns about the broad consequences of policies—intended and unintended. The book's attention to historical and institutional context, as well as its treatment of innovation and technical change, set it apart from other textbooks at this level.'

Maurice Obstfeld, Professor of Economics, University of California Berkeley, Co-author of Foundations of International Macroeconomics (1996, MIT Press)

'Austerity, financial crises, quantitative easing, artificial intelligence: this book has it all. A macroeconomics text that explains the data and logic that policymakers really do use. Read this book and understand the world.'

Jonathan Haskel, Professor of Economics, Imperial College London and External Member of the Bank of England's Monetary Policy Committee

'This is the only undergraduate macroeconomics textbook that weaves a serious treatment of inequality into a core 3-equation model, and, at the same time, it also includes an unparalleled introduction to incorporating the financial system in this framework. As such, it marks a serious departure from most macroeconomics textbooks, which tend to relegate distribution and finance to the secondary status of extensions or special topics. The accompanying simulation tool also makes the book exceptionally classroom friendly, not only by providing instructors a visual way to summarize comparative statics, but also by giving students a tool with which they can independently explore extensions of classroom discussions.'

Leila E. Davis, Associate Professor of Economics, University of Massachusetts Boston

'Economics students want to understand the world we live in, and no other macroeconomics textbook satisfies this desire to engage with the world's most significant issues quite like Carlin and Soskice. With its intuitive, tractable, and realistic approach, their textbook equips students to easily comprehend even the most complex macroeconomic concepts and their relationship to real-world problems like inequality and economic shocks. The 3-equation model helps students grasp how economic shocks affect the economy, while the new book's analysis of inequality gives a more thorough understanding of how policy responses can impact people's lives. The book equips the next generation of economics graduates to make a meaningful impact in the world.

The new book also links to the CORE Econ Project, enabling programme leaders to create a more integrated curriculum in macroeconomics across years.'

Stefania Paredes Fuentes, Associate Professor, University of Warwick

'The coverage on environmental and social sustainability of production is much appreciated.'

Christina Wolf, Senior Lecturer in Economics, University of Hertfordshire

'Employers value graduates comfortable to deal with real world issues, using appropriate theory and data skills. Using this textbook will be an ideal way to foster such a graduate.'

Marco Gundermann, Head of Economics, International Relations and Development, University of Northampton

'Carlin and Soskice offer a clear, balanced, engaging, and forward-looking perspective on a wide range of topics, from short-term monetary policy to growth and innovation. Students will appreciate the authors' crystal-clear exposition, along with the careful balance of technical detail and intuitive real-world examples presented.'

Ceri Davies, Associate Professor in Economics, University of Birmingham

'The book's development and applications of the 3-equation model make it easy to introduce students to more advanced theoretical ideas and current policy issues. It is straightforward to pick chunks of the book and incorporate other material. Resources provided to instructors and students are very helpful.'

Jennifer Smith, Associate Professor of Economics, University of Warwick

REVIEWS OF MACROECONOMICS: INSTITUTIONS, INSTABILITY, AND THE FINANCIAL SYSTEM

'Carlin and Soskice have produced a gem of a book. The teaching of macroeconomics after the crisis has changed surprisingly little, limiting itself to incorporating "frictions" into otherwise standard models that failed during the crisis. Carlin and Soskice embark on a much more ambitious venture. They show how the financial cycle and macroeconomics are inextricably linked, with the risk-taking channel as the linchpin. Their exposition is refreshingly original and yet lucid and accessible. This book will appeal to serious students of economics and to all inquiring minds who have wondered about the role of the financial cycle in macroeconomics.'

Hyun Song Shin, Economic Adviser and Head of Research, Bank for International Settlements and Hughes-Rogers Professor of Economics, Princeton University

'This is, I believe, the first macro-economic textbook effectively to incorporate the lessons of the Great Financial Crisis and to describe how financial frictions can impact the macro-economy. The authors weave together the old, mainstream, 3-equation model with the newer account of potential financial disturbances in a lucid and efficient manner. As such, it has a major advantage over almost all other extant textbooks, and will be a boon not only for undergraduates, but also for graduates and those wishing to understand the current working of our macroeconomic system, beset as it has been with financial strains.'

Professor Charles Goodhart, Director of the Financial Regulation Research Programme, The London School of Economics and Political Science

'This illuminating book introduces the reader to macroeconomics in a revolutionary fashion. Namely, by means of very elegant and accessible models that are always based on sound microfoundations and developed against a narrative of the performance and policy regimes of the advanced economies over the post war period. Unlike most other macro textbooks, this book builds on the most recent research and debates to teach macroeconomics the way it should now be taught: by emphasizing the interplay between macro and finance; by linking growth to innovation, market structure and firm dynamics; and more generally by taking institutions seriously into account when looking at growth, business cycles, and unemployment and the interplay between them. This book is an absolute must read for students and policy makers, even those with little initial background, who need to be fully acquainted with modern macroeconomics.'

Philippe Aghion, Robert C. Waggoner Professor of Economics, Harvard

'This is an exciting new textbook. It offers a clear and cogent framework for understanding not only the traditional macroeconomic issues of business cycles, inflation and growth, but also the financial crisis and ensuing Great Recession that have recently shaken the world economy. The paradigm it offers is highly accessible to undergraduates. Yet at the same time it is consistent with what goes on at the frontiers of the field. Overall, the book confirms my belief that macroeconomics is alive and well!'

Mark Gertler, Henry and Lucy Moses Professor of Economics, New York University

'To be relevant, economics need to help society understand those phenomena which do it greatest harm—unemployment, inflation and deflation, financial instability, fiscal and banking crisis. Pre-crisis, mainstream economic models failed that societal test and therefore failed society. Wendy Carlin and David Soskice's important new book is the first step towards redemption, providing students and scholars with a rigorous but accessible framework for understanding what troubles society most.'

Andrew G Haldane, Chief Economist, Bank of England

'The Carlin and Soskice book does a wonderful job of covering the economics behind macroeconomics and the financial system, alongside presenting the latest research on this and the drivers of the great recession. It also has an impressive array of data and examples woven in with theory explained in a beautifully intuitive way. For any student interested in a refreshingly modern take on the financial crisis and the economics that underlie this, this book is invaluable.'

Nicholas Bloom, Professor of Economics, Stanford University

'One of the first macro textbooks to integrate the lessons of the crisis. An elegant bridge between introductory undergraduate and graduate macro texts.'

Olivier Blanchard, Chief Economist, IMF, and Professor of Economics, MIT

'In the light of the events of the past decade, it is important that a new macroeconomics text attempts to satisfy the demands of those learning and using macroeconomics to be able to access relatively simple models which reflect the ways in which the financial sector interacts with the real economy. This is by no means an easy task. The new Carlin and Soskice book represents a significant step forward in this regard. Consequently undergraduates, post-graduates and their teachers should be grateful that they can now access teaching materials which have something useful to say about the financial crisis.'

Professor Stephen Nickell, CBE, FBA. Honorary Fellow of Nuffield College, Oxford

PREFACE

This is the fourth book on intermediate macroeconomics that we have written and reflects our teaching of economics undergraduates since the mid-1980s, and of political science graduate students in the last 20 years. The Introduction sets out our goals; the most important of which is to develop a relatively simple, internally coherent, and tractable way of modelling contemporary economies.

Through the four books, institutions have remained central to our analysis of how macroeconomies function, even when the relative importance of different ones has varied greatly. Each decade has thrown up major new issues, together with changes in institutions to go with them. Our last book, published in 2015, was strongly influenced by the global financial crisis and had a major focus on finance and financial institutions. That book underlined the instability of advanced capitalism, an issue which we need to be highly sensitive to in analysing the macroeconomics of the 21st century.

In this volume we bring into the macro model a focus on inequality and innovation, reflecting new research in both economics and political science. From economics, the final chapter of the book covers current research on inequality and macroeconomic modelling. In the new HANK (Heterogeneous Agent New Keynesian) models, households can end up in quite unequal positions in terms of income and wealth, which matters in its own right, and also for the transmission of monetary policy. From political science, there is a chapter on the institutional determinants of innovation encapsulated by the ICT revolution and how they vary across countries to produce different varieties of innovation and diffusion in the high-income countries and China.

Through the decades in which we have been teaching macroeconomics, a great number of topical and sometimes hotly debated issues have arisen. These have captured the interest of students. Our goal has been to build a 'transparent and tractable'—but also realistic—model of the macroeconomy, which students could use to understand and explain these issues. We call the business cycle component the 3-equation model (Carlin and Soskice 2015). The first equation, the *Aggregate Demand* or *IS* equation, states that output is determined by aggregate demand (including monetary and fiscal policy, and other exogenous components of demand). Second is the *Phillips curve*, showing how inflation increases when output is above equilibrium. And third, the *Monetary Rule* (or *Taylor Rule*), explaining how the central bank uses the interest rate to guide inflation back to its target rate. A significant part of the book adapts the model from the closed to the open economy, with the addition of the *Uncovered Interest Parity* condition to the 3-equation model.

We have changed and adapted the 3-equation model over the years to focus, for example, on firms rather than unions as wage-setters given the diminishing role of unions in many economies. We cover the move in the last decade to an environment in which central banks cannot actively use interest rates for macroeconomic management. Together with the integration of a realistic financial sector into the model, we believe that the underlying modelling approach has retained its usefulness through the very large institutional, financial, and technological changes of the last four decades.

We hope it remains sufficiently transparent in the mechanisms producing the general equilibrium results and intuitive that the reader—student or other—who is not an academic macroeconomist can deploy it to address questions that particularly interest them.

The book is geared primarily to the intermediate-level economics undergraduate. Hopefully it will be useful to graduate students in the other social sciences who increasingly want or need to understand aspects of macroeconomics. It is also written for the many professional (non-academic) economists in the public and private sectors for whom the research frontier of modern macroeconomic research is often inaccessible. And we hope, too, it will function as a useful reference for economics graduate students, providing sound foundations and an integrated perspective as they grapple with the rigors of leading-edge academic research in growth theory as well as in macro-finance and business cycle analysis.

What we call here 'leading-edge research' in business cycle modelling is presented in some detail in the final chapter of the book, co-authored with James Cloyne. James learnt macroeconomics from earlier volumes of Carlin and Soskice and taught using it. He worked as a research economist at the Bank of England, is now an economics professor at the University of California Davis and an active researcher in contemporary quantitative macroeconomics. Macroeconomists build general equilibrium models that solve the forward-looking optimization problems of the agents. The complexity arises from having to solve for the future path of the economy in response to a shock in an environment that combines rational (i.e. model-consistent) expectations of agents, intertemporal optimization, frictions of various kinds such as sticky prices, and general equilibrium. As indicated above, we welcome the growing prominence of the new heterogeneous agent (or HANK) versions of these models that introduce inequality, which, as a result, reproduce many of the core predictions of our simpler 3-equation model.

Olivier Blanchard's career has—at the highest level—straddled academic macroeconomics and policy making, where he was chief economist at the IMF from 2008 to 2015 through the period of the global financial and Eurozone crises. From that vantage point, his reflections on the use of models in macroeconomics are of particular interest. He argues (Blanchard 2018) that different kinds of general equilibrium models of the business cycle are required for different purposes and would benefit from open-minded interaction among practitioners. For those interested in a non-technical birds-eye view of the debates about modelling the business cycle, Blanchard's article is a good place to begin.

One of the five types of model he sees as valuable he calls 'toy models'. This is not to disparage them. He has in mind the 'IS/LM' and Mundell-Fleming models, as well as our 3-equation model. In Blanchard's words: 'I have found, for example, that I could often, as a discussant, summarize the findings of a DSGE (Dynamic Stochastic General Equilibrium) paper in a simple graph. I had learned something from the formal model, but I was able (and allowed as the discussant) to present the basic insight more simply than the author of the paper.'

Building economic intuition about the macroeconomy is essential both for creating the next generation of curious and thoughtful researchers as well as for educating the great majority of readers who will remain consumers rather than producers of economics research as citizens, commentators, professional economists, think-tankers and policy makers. Our goal in this book, by developing the 3-equation approach to the business cycle, augmenting it with the financial system model and connecting it to growth theory is to make a contribution to this important work.

Wendy Carlin and David Soskice,
London, January 2023

ACKNOWLEDGEMENTS

Hundreds of colleagues and thousands of students have contributed to the preceding volumes of *Macroeconomics* since we began the project in the mid-1980s. The current book rests on those contributions.

Two outstanding young researchers have made it possible to complete the new book. Stanislas Lalanne is co-author of Chapter 5 and has worked to clarify the treatment of money, banks, monetary policy and financial stability. His incisive mind and attention to detail are reflected throughout the book. Alessandro Guarnieri has contributed and improved many of the appendices, organized and suggested insights from a large body of new research for many of the chapters, managed the manuscript, and completed the major task of systematizing and updating the data and charts. It's been a real highlight of the past couple of years for Wendy to work so closely with Stan and Alessandro.

James Cloyne (University of California, Davis), joined the writing team, leading on Chapter 18. This chapter takes the book to the research frontier in heterogeneous agent macroeconomics.

Andrew McNeil is co-author of Chapter 17, working primarily with David to bring recent research in political economy on the ICT revolution to an audience of macro-economists. This has also greatly benefitted from work with Torben Iversen, as well as Cathy Boone, Anke Hassel, David Hope, Ciaran Driver, Lucio Baccaro, Jonas Pontusson, Bruno Palier, Paul Pierson, Kathy Thelen, and Frieder Mitsch.

The macroeconomic simulator (available at www.oup.com/he/carlin-soskice) built by Javier Lozano is a centre-piece of the learning resources for the book. It is such a pleasure working with Javier and benefiting from his sure sense of how the simulator can be refined to heighten students' learning opportunities. There is a lot of feedback from students on how they use the simulator to explore questions of their own.

The CORE Econ project, now generously supported by and based in the James M. and Cathleen D. Stone Centre on Wealth Concentration, Inequality, and the Economy at UCL, has provided rich intellectual input to Wendy's work on the book. Margaret Stevens and Samuel Bowles have led the work on building a new model of wage-setting that combines search and matching with the labour discipline approach. That model is set out in Chapter 15. The derivation of the Lorenz curve from the wage- and price-setting model in Chapter 2 is drawn from CORE Econ's *The Economy* and is an important contribution to the book's ability to connect measures of inequality to the macroeconomic model.

Other collaborations in the CORE project have borne fruit for the book. Claudia Buch co-authored a CORE Insight on 'Too big to fail' (https://www.core-econ.org/selection/too-big-to-fail-lessons-from-a-decade-of-financial-sector-reforms/), which has influenced the treatment of financial stability in the book, prompting the inclusion of a new chapter on financial stability policy. Another CORE Insight authored by Barry Eichengreen and Ugo Panizza on public debt (https://www.core-econ.org/selection/public-debt-threat-or-opportunity/) has contributed to the coverage of debt dynamics in the book. Work with Kevin O'Rourke, Samuel Bowles, Suresh Naidu, and other members of the CORE community to address the role played by colonies and slavery in the economic development of the high-income countries is reflected in Chapter 16. Jack Blundell, Tzvetan Moev, and Tina Rozsos have produced the inequality 'skyscraper' visualizations in the Introduction.

For Wendy, teaching intermediate macroeconomics at UCL has meant collaborating with co-teachers and graduate teaching assistants as well as with students. In recent years, much has been learnt from Wei Cui and the chapters on Demand, the Financial System, Monetary Policy and Fiscal Policy have benefited especially from this. Former TAs have become colleagues and co-workers, including in the CORE Econ project—James Cloyne (UC Davis), David Hope (KCL), and Davide Melcangi (New York Fed). More recently, Alejandro Estefan Davila (Notre Dame), Gherardo Caracciolo (Birmingham) and Thomas Lazarowicz as lead TAs on the macroeconomics module, have improved the pedagogy. Working with them to refine exercises and problems, and to learn from their interactions with students is part of the great privilege of teaching very talented undergraduates. Two of them, Antara Roy and Adam Butlin, took on the task of creating the animated powerpoints to help students understand the dynamics of the models. Madigan Dockrill's skill in the questions to quiz students on within the chapters is greatly appreciated, as is Eduard Krkoska's work checking the maths and the multiple-choice questions, and Haruka Shuei's slides for instructors.

Over previous volumes, as well as this one, Philippe Aghion, Andrea Boltho, Matt Harding, Javier Lozano, Thomas Michl, John Muellbauer, Bob Rowthorn, Hyun Shin, Stephen Wright, and David Vines have been consistent and generous in their help and encouragement, for which we are very grateful.

The expert assistance of Claudio Borio and Mathias Drehmann from the BIS, and of Michael McLeay, Amar Radia, and Ryland Thomas from the Bank of England has been invaluable. Wendy has benefited from discussions at the meetings of the Resolution Foundation's Macroeconomic Policy Unit with James Smith, Greg Thwaites, Torsten Bell, and Kate Barker, Jason Furman, Toby Nangle, Jumana Saleheen, Silvana Tenreyro, Jan Vlieghe, and Tony Yates. The meetings of the Expert Advisory Panel of the UK's Office for Budget Responsibility have also provided much stimulation and input to the book. Thanks to Charlie Bean, Robert Chote, Richard Hughes, Andy King, David Miles, and Kevin Daly, Carl Emmerson, Jonathan Gillham, John Llewellyn, Andrew Scott, Peter Spencer, Coen Teulings, and Simon Wren Lewis.

James Cloyne and Wendy were encouraged by the feedback and suggestions of many colleagues on Chapter 18: Olivier Blanchard, Riccardo Cioffi, Alessandro Guarnieri, Franck Portier, Greg Kaplan, Thomas Lazarowicz, Ralph Luetticke (who also contributed a box on Toolkits), Alisdair McKay, Davide Melcangi, Ben Moll, Łukasz Rachel, Allen Shen, Jón Steinsson, and Gianluca Violante.

For their generous help and support (not already acknowledged above), we are grateful to Yann Algan, Angus Armstrong, Orazio Attanasio, Roger Backhouse, Saleem Bahaj, Eric Beinhocker, Nick Bloom, Richard Blundell, Javier Boncompte Guarda, Chris Bowdler, Lennart Brandt, Steve Broadberry, Antonio Cabrales, John Campbell, Luis Candiota, Pedro Carneiro, Jagjit Chadha, Parama Chaudhury, David Cobham, Nick Crafts, Kenneth Creamer, Chiara Criscuolo, Luka Crnjakovic, Silvia Dal Bianco, Michel de Vroey, Arin Dube, John Duca, Christian Dustmann, Jan Eeckhout, Asmaa El-Ganainy, Doyne Farmer, Vikram Gandhi, Ian Goldin, Bishnupriya Gupta, Mihir Gupta, Frederick Guy, Simon Halliday, Michael Jacobs, Arjun Jayadev, Cloda Jenkins, Paul Klemperer, Niki Lacey, Philip Lane, Christopher Lee, Dunli Li, Steve Machin, Neil Majithia, Costas Meghir, Michael McMahon, Meg Meyer, Atif Mian, Ramin Nassehi, Houda Nait El Barj, Yuval Ofek-Shanny, Martha Omolo, Andrew Oswald, Stefania Paredes Fuentes, Christina Patterson, Enrico Perotti, Giacomo Piccoli, Ian Preston, Matthias Pum, Morten Ravn, Jonathan Rée, Marc Resinek, Jamie Rush, Ellen Ryan, Amarjit Sagoo, Mark Schaffer, Franziska Schobert, Uta Schoenberg, Paul Seabright, Paul Segal, Yael Selfin, Dooho Shin, Sahana Subramanyam, Sophia Sun, Adelson Teh, Eileen Tipoe, Peter Trubowitz, David Tuckett, Miguel Urquiola, John Van Reenen, John Vickers, Snjezana Voloscuk, Georg von Graevenitz, Elisabeth Wood, Martin Wolf, Francesco Zanetti, and Fabrizio Zilibotti.

Wendy is grateful for the support from colleagues and the professional services staff in the Department of Economics at UCL. Summer visits to the Santa Fe Institute, where Wendy is External Professor, have brought new ideas from those in other disciplines working on complex systems, and greatly facilitated joint work with Sam Bowles, which has found its way into many parts of the book.

David would like to thank the friendly and warm support over nearly a decade of the International Inequalities Institute at the LSE, where he was for many years Research Director, and particularly Lisa Ryan, Armine Ishkanian, Mike Savage, Chico Ferreira, and the sadly gone John Hills. Also Chandran Kukathas, Cheryl Schonhardt Bailey, Emily Crook, and Karen Dickenson.

The OUP reviewers have alerted us to some pitfalls, and Felicity Boughton and Jon Crowe at OUP have been flexible, and allowed time for this new book to evolve. The final writing has taken place in a period of renewed turmoil and crisis in the world economy, which is a good test for a macroeconomics textbook. We thank Karen Moore for her careful handling of the editorial and production process.

We would finally like to thank Tessa, Jonny, Juliet, and William, and especially Niki Lacey, for providing contributions beyond macroeconomics.

COPYRIGHT ACKNOWLEDGEMENTS

Grateful acknowledgement is made to all the authors and publishers of copyright material which appears in this book, and in particular to the following for permission to reprint material from the sources indicated:

American Economic Review and the authors for Table 5, Figure 2(b), and Figure 4(b) from Kaplan, G., Moll, B., and Violante, G. L. (2018), Monetary Policy According to HANK. *American Economic Review*, 108(3), 697–743 (https://doi.org/10.1257/aer.20160042). Reproduced using the replication package of Kaplan, Moll, and Violante (2018).

Bank of England Chart 1.4 from page 22 of *Bank of England Monetary Policy Report*, November 2022 and figure from page 2 of Joyce, M., Tong, M., and Woods, R. (2011), The United Kingdom's Quantitative Easing Policy: Design, Operation and Impact, *Bank of England Quarterly Bulletin*, 2011 Q3.

Cambridge University Press for four panels from Figure 3 in Elkjær, M. A. and Iversen, T. (2022), The Democratic State and Redistribution: Whose Interests Are Served? *American Political Science Review*, 1–16 (doi:10.1017/S0003055422000867).

Oxford University Press for Figure 1 from Farber, H. S., Herbst, D., Kuziemko, I., and Naidu, S. (2021), Unions and Inequality over the Twentieth Century: New Evidence from Survey Data, *The Quarterly Journal of Economics*, 136(3), August 2021, 1325–1385 (https://doi.org/10.1093/qje/qjab012).

Elsevier for Figure 4 reprinted from Heathcote, J., Perri, F., and Violante, G. L. (2020), The rise of US earnings inequality: Does the cycle drive the trend? *Review of Economic Dynamics*, 37(1), S181–S204 (https://doi.org/10.1016/j.red.2020.06.002) and Table 1 and Figure 3 from Patel, D., Sandefur, J., and Subramanian, A. (2021), The new era of unconditional convergence. *Journal of Development Economics*, 152, 102687 (https://doi.org/10.1016/j.jdeveco.2021.102687).

S&P Dow Jones Indices LLC for S&P Dow Jones Indices LLC, S&P 500 [SP500], retrieved from FRED, Federal Reserve Bank of St Louis (https://fred.stlouisfed.org/series/SP500) 12 January 2023.

Springer Nature for Figure 4 from Mourre, G. and Poissonnier, A. (2019), What Drives the Responsiveness of the Budget Balance to the Business Cycle in EU Countries? *Intereconomics*, 2019(4), 237–240.

Professor Gianluca Violante for figure from Violante, G. (29 October 2021), What have we learned from HANK models, thus far? [Conference presentation]. Proceedings of the ECB Forum on Central Banking 2021 (https://www.ecb.europa.eu/pub/conferences/html/20210928_ecb_forum_on_central_banking.en.html).

CONTENTS

DETAILED CONTENTS

INTRODUCTION

Students and non-experts ask questions like these: 'what effect does the rise in inequality over the past four decades have on macroeconomic performance and policy', 'what caused the global financial crisis and why has growth since then been so weak', 'was the increase in government debt in the pandemic necessary and how should it be managed', 'has the extensive use of monetary policy in the form of quantitative easing to support the economy since the financial crisis created new risks to financial stability', 'what threats to macroeconomic performance and challenges for policy does the climate crisis pose', 'why does an energy price hike raise the rate of inflation', and 'what affects the pace and direction of innovation (green innovation, automation) and its effects on the future of work'.

Providing a framework for answering these questions and connecting them to the best contemporary research is one of the objectives of this book (and of the CORE Econ project, www.core-econ.org, with which Carlin is associated). This book provides intermediate level macroeconomics in a framework consistent with the CORE approach in *The Economy*: real-world problem-motivated, actor-centred, and research-connected. It shares the foundations of principal-agent modelling in the labour and credit markets and the emphasis on Nash equilibrium thinking. It is a very good complement to the intermediate microeconomics textbook authored by Samuel Bowles and Simon Halliday, *Microeconomics: Competition, Conflict, and Coordination* (OUP: 2022). They share the new benchmark for economics, which replaces complete information, atomistic agents and clearing markets by information problems, strategic interactions and incomplete contracts (Bowles and Carlin 2020).

This is the fourth volume of *Macroeconomics* since 1990, each of which has a different slant, explained by the historical context in which it was written and the research frontier at the time (see Section 2).

The subtitle of this book, 'Institutions, instability, and inequality' reflects continuity with the previous volumes. Inequality finds its way into the title this time because macroeconomic research over the past decade has turned its attention to inequality. There has been a wave of work in macro-finance on the role of household balance sheets in the transmission of the financial crisis and increased interest in the market power of firms and its effect on the macroeconomy and inequality. In business cycle macroeconomics, the research frontier has shifted under the label 'heterogeneous agent models'. Recent empirical work in endogenous growth theory has produced new results on the relationship between innovation and inequality. Although the model in *Macroeconomics* has always had inequality at its heart, the research base was not there to connect the model to empirical findings. This has changed and it's time for 'inequality' to have a place in the title of a macroeconomics textbook.

The wage-setting/price-setting (WS-PS) model first set out in *Macroeconomics and the Wage Bargain* in 1990 constitutes the supply-side model in the subsequent volumes. This is a 'whole economy' model in which the actors are distinguished by their

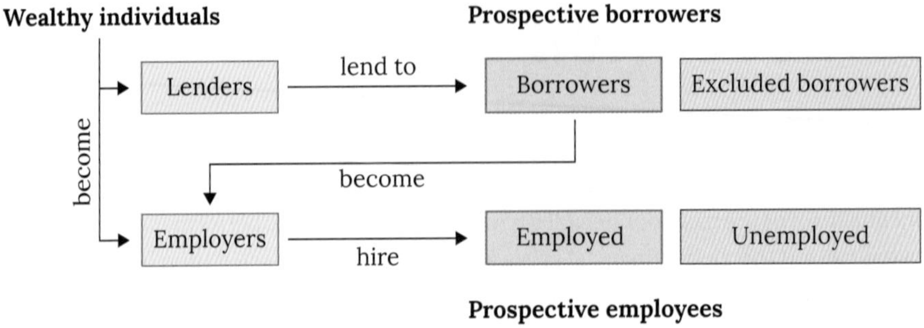

Figure 1 The credit and labour markets shape the relationships between groups with different endowments.

endowments. In the labour market, owners/employers are distinct from employees. More generally, the actors in both the two key markets—labour and credit—differ in their endowments and in the economic opportunities available to them. By anchoring the modelling in principal-agent problems in those markets, the model of the macroeconomy builds in problems of incomplete and asymmetric information, which means the equilibria are characterized by involuntary unemployment and credit rationing.

As Figure 1 illustrates, wealthy individuals (owners) participate in the economy as lenders and employers. Borrowers can also become employers. Individuals lacking wealth have many fewer choices. They are prospective employees but because the labour market does not clear in equilibrium, some will be unemployed. These differences in endowments and the relationships between the actor types affect the way macroeconomic shocks and policies are transmitted through the economy.

Incomplete and asymmetric information between employers and employees means it is impossible to write a complete employment contract covering the worker's effort. This unobservable effort gives rise to an employment rent, which means that there is a cost to job loss: a worker fired for supplying inadequate effort will not be able immediately to find an equivalent job as is the case in a clearing labour market. It is this cost of losing a job (i.e. the employment rent received by the worker in their current job that they stand to lose), which incentivizes the supply of adequate effort and entails the existence of involuntary unemployment in equilibrium. The labour market does not clear and when unemployment is low, the employer has to set a high wage in order to secure effort on the job. When job seekers differ in their reservation wage, the employer faces a recruitment problem as well. Both are brought together in a model of wage setting in Chapter 15, which allows for the analysis of the employer's monopsony power.

There is a similar information problem in the credit market that leads to credit rationing. Because it is impossible to ensure via a contract that a borrower exerts effort in their use of borrowed funds, some borrowers with good projects are excluded from the credit market. Whereas a higher interest rate can be charged to cover default due to factors outside the control of the borrower, it cannot address the problem that the lender is not able to observe the effort the borrower exerts to repay the loan. Charging a higher interest rate will have the effect of deterring borrowers more likely to repay. The consequence is that having something to offer as collateral is often essential to access credit, with the result that there will always be some borrowers who will be excluded from the market. This will not only affect investment projects but also consumption behaviour as some households will not be able to smooth fluctuations in their income by borrowing.

There is no chapter on inequality in the book—the data, measurement and analysis are integrated throughout. For example, by assuming as the benchmark that firms have market power and are price-setters in the product market, there is a direct link to inequality from the WS-PS model. In equilibrium, income inequality is affected by the markup of price over marginal cost, which is the profit share, and by the rate of unemployment. Credit constraints reflect wealth inequality and affect the nature and transmission of business cycle fluctuations. For a concise introduction to the historical evolution, measurement and causes of economic inequality, we recommend CORE Econ's *The Economy* Unit 19 (https://www.core-econ.org/the-economy/book/text/19.html).[1]

'Instability' refers to the importance of positive feedback processes in markets that are central to the way the macroeconomy works. The major innovation in the previous volume (2015) was to show how financial accelerator processes work in the housing market and in investment banks. We introduced a model with two stable and one unstable equilibria, which we apply to the housing market and to leverage in investment banks. This is used to illustrate the concept of a tipping point and the genesis of a financial crisis.

In addressing questions about the climate crisis, instability refers to environmental feedback processes. The tipping point model of instability can be applied to the human-physical climate interaction with positive feedbacks that lies behind global warming. Parallels can be drawn between the model of financial instability and climate instability (or similarly, between the financial and the global climate accelerator).[2]

'Institutions' refers to the rules of the game through which actors interact in the economy. The two principal-agent problems are defined by the rules by which the owners/workers and lenders/borrowers interact. Rules of the game affect union bargaining, the entry and exit of firms, and competition in markets, which affects the markup. The shifts from Bretton Woods to floating exchange rates and for some

---

[1] The CORE Insight on 'Persistent racial inequality in the US' provides a model of intergenerational mobility, which is of broad applicability. (https://www.core-econ.org/insights/persistent-racial-inequality-in-the-united-states/text/01.html)

[2] See The CORE Team (2017) *The Economy*, Unit 17 (the house price tipping point) and Unit 20 (the climate tipping point). Muellbauer and Aron (2022), 'The global climate accelerator and the financial accelerator: Clarifying the commonalities, and implications for Putin's war', VoxEU, 24 March 2022. (https://cepr.org/voxeu/columns/global-climate-accelerator-and-financial-accelerator-clarifying-commonalities-and.) See also in CORE: (https://www.core-econ.org/the-economy/book/text/17.html#figure-17-23) (housing) and (https://www.core-econ.org/the-economy/book/text/20.html#figure-20-23) (environmental).

countries in Europe to a common currency area are changes in the rules of the game, as was the adoption of explicit fiscal rules, central bank independence and inflation targeting. Missing from the title but an important theme is the role of innovation and technological change. Innovation plays a part in the analysis of the evolution of firm markups and in the Schumpeterian model of endogenous growth. The book also addresses the fourth industrial—ICT—revolution and productivity puzzle.

1. FROM THE 'RATIONAL EXPECTATIONS' TO THE 'INEQUALITY' REVOLUTION IN MACROECONOMICS

Just as the rational expectations revolution transformed macroeconomic research in the 1980s, a new revolution has taken hold in the last decade and a half: the inequality revolution. The world itself looks very different in 2020 as compared with 1980 as the charts on the global distribution of income in Figure 2 vividly illustrate. Global wealth inequality has also been transformed (shown in Figure 3 using the available data from 1995 onwards).

The countries of the world are lined up from left to right with the poorest measured by GDP per capita on the left and richest on the right. The width of each country's bar reflects its population—the broad bars for China and India are notable. For each country, average income for each decile is shown from the poorest decile at the front to the richest at the back. The same visualization is provided for wealth inequality. The change in the shape of the world distributions of income and wealth is immediately evident in the steeper profiles of within-country inequality in 2020 as compared with the earlier year: the 'skyscrapers' at the back of each country's income profile became more prominent. China's transformation from a very poor country with little inequality to a much more unequal richer one is clear. The accumulation of wealth and its uneven distribution in China since 1995 is strikingly illustrated in Figure 3. The other side of China's story is its leapfrogging across countries as it moved to the higher GDP per capita side of the chart, which reflected its success in taking much of its population out of extreme poverty.

The attention of macroeconomists and policy makers was drawn to income and wealth inequality in high-income countries by the global financial crisis. Those studying its causes focused on the weak growth of median wages, household, and in particular, housing debt, and the behaviour of banks.

At the same time, at the research frontier, the toolkit of business cycle macroeconomists expanded to allow them to study a model economy that features income and wealth inequality, arising from the fact that households have different experiences with unemployment and are unable to insure themselves against its impact on their income. This implies that there are low-income households who are unable to borrow when hit by a bad shock like unemployment. And even better-off households, who share ownership of their house with a mortgage provider, do not borrow when they experience a temporary hit to their income. Introducing this kind of inequality into a macro model has an important effect on how business cycle fluctuations are propagated through the economy.

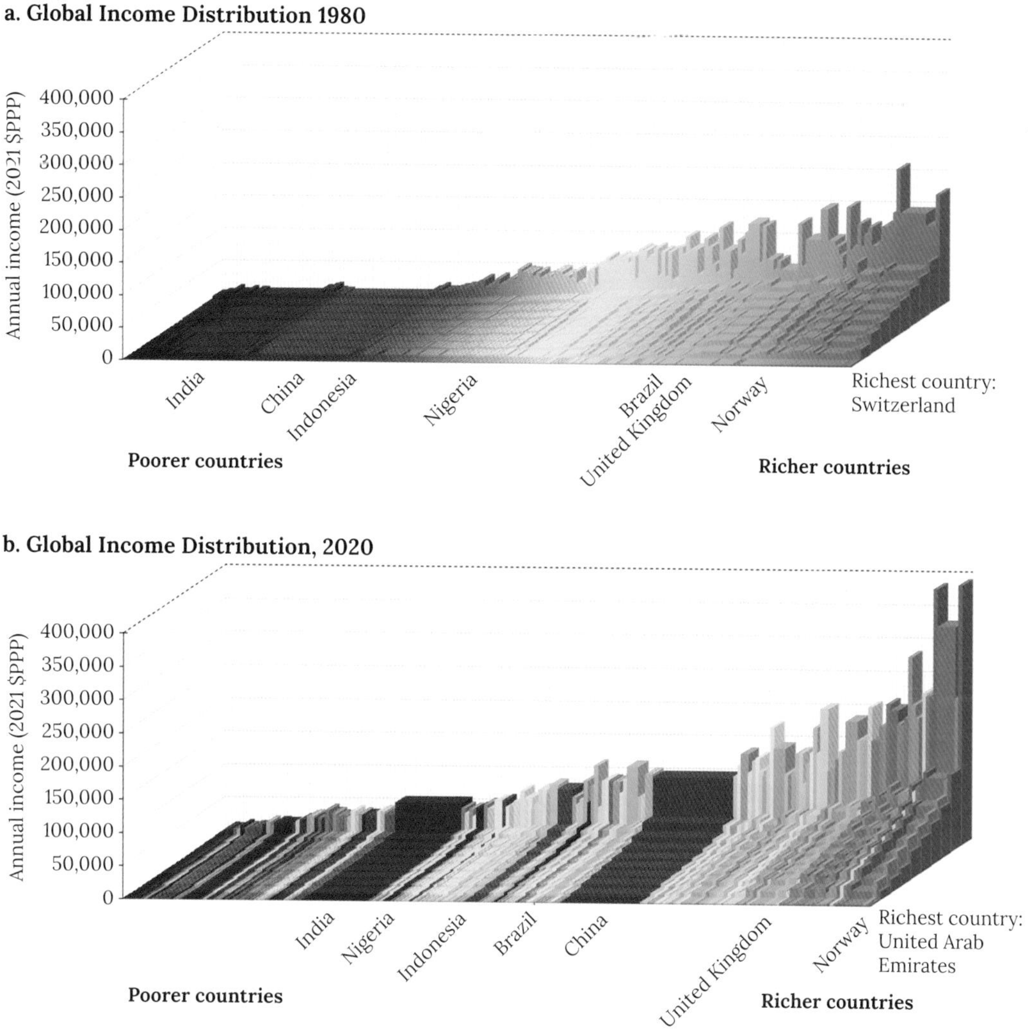

Figure 2 Global (market) income distribution.

Notes: Market income refers to annual earnings of individuals before taking account of taxes and government transfers such as benefits. Within-country inequality is represented by 10 decile blocks with the lowest at the front and the taller ones corresponding to higher market income. Wider blocks correspond to higher population. Colours correspond to how rich the country was in 1980. Countries are ordered from left to right according to their average income per capita in the year shown; colours are fixed from the initial year ordering.

Source: (https://www.core-econ.org/visualisations/) Data source: World Inequality Database.

The oil shock of 2022 and the return of the dynamics of a wage–price spiral as firms seek to defend their profit margins, and workers their living standards, has led economists at the research frontier to embrace the conflict theory of inflation (Lorenzoni and Werning 2023). From the first volume of *Macroeconomics* (1990), we have modelled inflation that way (following the pioneering paper of Rowthorn 1977).

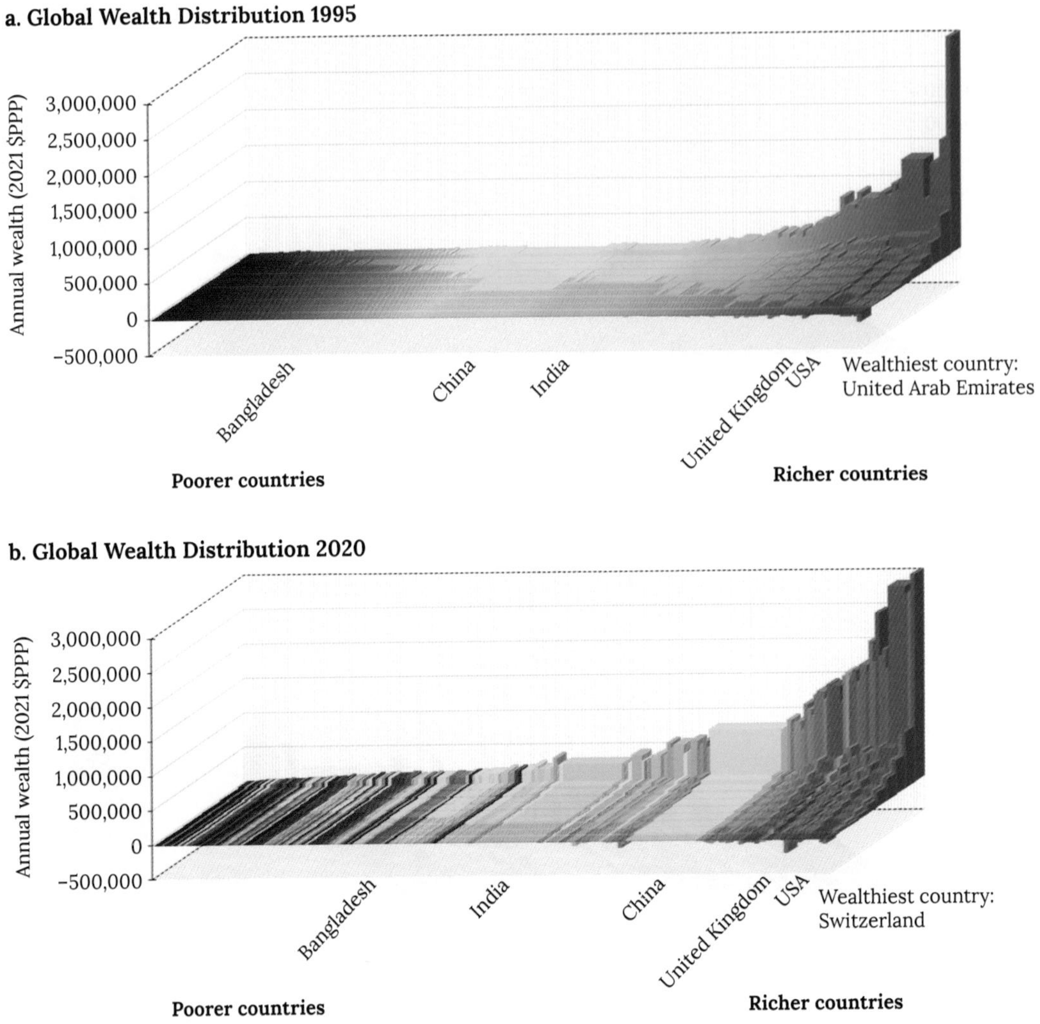

Figure 3 Global wealth distribution.

Notes: Wealth refers to the total value of the assets held by a household such as savings, bonds and houses, minus its debts. Countries are ordered by their per capita market income, with colours fixed by the 1995 ordering.

Source: (https://www.core-econ.org/visualisations/) Data source: World Inequality Database.

In the field of economic growth, while growth economists had always sought to explain changes in the *cross-country* income distribution, the attention of those working on endogenous growth models turned to how inequality affects growth through the innovation process.

The route from the rational expectations revolution in macro, which was located in its historical and history of thought context in Chapter 4 of Carlin and Soskice (1990), to the inequality or heterogeneous agent revolution of the 2000s went via representative agent dynamic general equilibrium models, starting with the real business cycle (RBC) model and later the New Keynesian Dynamic Stochastic General Equilibrium (DSGE) model. Although dominating microeconomics research from the 1980s,[3] information problems and heterogeneity did not generally take centre stage in macro models prior to the global financial crisis. Rather, a key objective was to develop a method of quantitative modelling of intertemporal optimization in general equilibrium. The logic of this methodology, as well as its benefits, limitations and legacy in the new generation of heterogeneous agent models, are explained and discussed in Chapter 18.

As we shall see, many of the research results arising from heterogeneous agent macro are very useful in understanding the macroeconomy and it turns out that they are often aligned with the transmission mechanisms in the simpler models taught in this book. Unlike earlier representative agent New Keynesian models where inequality is absent, the new HANK models, for example, have sizeable multipliers arising from credit-constrained low-wealth households as well as from wealthy ones with mortgages and low liquid assets.

2. LEARNING MACROECONOMICS IN HISTORICAL CONTEXT

From the perspective of 2022–23, a war in Europe and an accompanying energy price shock are a reminder that an essential component of a macroeconomics education is an awareness of 100 years of economic history. Macroeconomic theory evolves in response to the problems policy makers are called on to address. In turn, when new macroeconomic theory becomes embedded in policy making, economic outcomes are affected.

The key developments over the last 100 years are:

- the Great Depression and the development of Keynes' model, able to account for the persistence of mass unemployment;
- a proactive role for government in supporting aggregate demand in Roosevelt's New Deal;
- a new post-WWII architecture for economic policy in the West, with larger automatic stabilizers reflecting an expanded role of government and use of countercyclical monetary and fiscal policy;
- a new post-war international economic policy regime based on decisive abandonment of the Gold Standard and adoption of the Bretton Woods arrangements of pegged but adjustable exchange rates;
- the golden age of the 1950s and 1960s, during which continental European economies and Japan experienced unprecedentedly high rates of capital accumulation, caught up to levels of GDP per capita in the US through the adoption of US technology and management practices;

[3] See Bowles (2006) for a graduate level treatment.

- the decline in within-country income inequality as the benefits of rapid productivity growth were widely shared;
- the beginning of the slow collapse of the high productivity growth associated with the third industrial revolution (so-called Fordism), causing manufacturing job loss over the next three decades in the high-income economies, and the growing dominance of services;
- the stagflation of the 1970s triggered by the slowdown in productivity growth and the exercise of increased bargaining power by workers, and exacerbated by the oil and commodity shocks;
- non-accommodating macroeconomic policy in the 1980s and the experience of wide variation in unemployment rates across countries; a focus on supply-side reforms to reduce equilibrium unemployment;
- widespread adoption of central bank independence and inflation targeting in the 1990s, including in the mandate of the European Central Bank, as part of the constitution of the Eurozone;
- years of the Great Moderation in the high-income countries, with moderate growth, falling unemployment and low inflation, accompanied by rapid export-led growth in China; in the background, income and wealth inequality surged and global imbalances, including between the US and China, emerged;
- the global financial crisis, caused by the excessive leverage of banks arising from a business model that was shattered when house prices began to fall right across the US; lessons of the Great Depression were used to prevent the collapse of the banking system and to stabilize the global economy; a sovereign debt crisis occurred in Europe highlighting the inadequacies of the governance structure of the Eurozone (and echoing problems of the Gold Standard);
- weak recovery from the financial crisis across the high-income economies, characterized by low productivity growth, inflation below target, low real interest rates and policy operating at the zero lower bound;
- quantitative easing used by central banks in an attempt to stimulate aggregate demand; their balance sheets increased dramatically and they shifted to a new operational regime of ample reserves setting the policy rate as the interest rate paid on reserves;
- the implications of climate change for the macroeconomy, including the potential for shocks to aggregate demand and the supply side, stranded assets, spillovers to financial instability and consequences for central bank mandates and operations came to the attention of economic policy makers;
- the global Covid-19 pandemic produced behavioural and policy responses to limit face to face economic interactions and led central banks to support the liquidity of banks and firms, and governments to support household incomes and business solvency;
- supply-chain and labour market disruption due to the pandemic along with war in Ukraine confirmed the shift from fear of deflation to fear of inflation and brought

back to centre stage analysis of the implications of an oil shock, credibility of central banks and anchoring of inflation expectations.

The economic challenges and advances in economic theory and policy in the initial eight bullet points informed the supply side macro model with wage- and price-setting curves, in the first volume of *Macroeconomics* published in 1990. To model inflation targeting, the framework was expanded in the 2006 volume to include a policy maker with an explicit optimization problem to solve—this is the 3-equation model. The model was extended in the third volume (2015) to the open economy, showing how decisions in a forward-looking foreign exchange market interact with those of an inflation-targeting central bank to produce its interest rate response to a range of shocks.

Reacting to the financial crisis, we took on the task of integrating the macroeconomic model with a model of the financial system. Banks and leverage-based financial cycles are modelled using a Value at Risk model of shadow (investment) bank behaviour. A model of house price bubbles is based on the financial accelerator with multiple equilibria and a tipping point.

In the current book, the operation of monetary policy at the zero lower bound, including quantitative easing, is explained. The potential supply-side effects of weak growth following the financial crisis brought to the fore the phenomenon of hysteresis and the question of how policy makers should take account of it. Chapter 4 develops a model to show how hysteresis interacts with anchored inflation expectations. On the monetary side, the new operational regime of inflation targeting under ample reserves, where the policy rate is the rate paid on reserves, is contrasted to the previous regime of scarce reserves (Chapter 5).

In the period after 1990, weak growth in the high-income countries in combination with the low frequency of policy disasters in low-income countries and rapid growth in some middle-income ones has led to reporting new results on absolute convergence using the Solow model (Chapter 16).

A chapter titled 'The ICT revolution, productivity puzzle, and political economy of uneven growth' (Chapter 17) brings into the book a conceptual framework for understanding the sources of American leadership of the ICT revolution, and of the varieties of diffusion of the new technology and management practices observed among high-income economies, and in China. It looks as well at the consequences for polarization of jobs, places, and politics. Chapter 18 is a guide to modern business cycle macroeconomics, including heterogeneous agent (HANK) models. This chapter provides a bridge from the models considered in this book to contemporary quantitative macroeconomics research. The chapter aims to equip the reader with a critical appreciation of the modern macroeconomist's toolkit, as well as the benefits and limitations of these methods.

PART

1

BASICS: DEMAND SIDE, SUPPLY SIDE, AND POLICY MAKER

CHAPTER 1

THE DEMAND SIDE

1.1 OVERVIEW

In the late 2000s, households and firms across the world cut back their spending and the global economy went into recession. There is little disagreement among economists that the dramatic fall in global GDP in 2008–09, which is now known as the global financial crisis, was a negative shock to aggregate demand. The Covid-19 pandemic led to a much larger contraction of global economic activity in the first half of 2020 than had occurred during the financial crisis. A combination of government mandated lock-downs of businesses and travel, and decisions by citizens to reduce their face-to-face interactions produced a collapse in demand for goods and services.

This chapter begins the task of building a macroeconomic model with the demand side of the economy, which concerns the spending decisions of households, firms and government. As we shall see in Chapter 2, the supply side refers to the production activities in the economy. Dramatic changes in aggregate demand—that is, spending in the economy as a whole—as occurred in 2020 or in 2008–09 are unusual. In more normal times, shifts in aggregate spending decisions are the main sources of the irregular fluctuations from recession to boom that form the business cycle.

If a period of depressed spending is forecast, there is much discussion in the financial media about whether the central bank will intervene and offset the likely recession by loosening monetary policy, for example, by cutting the interest rate. The central bank would cut the interest rate because it expects this to encourage spending and help return the economy to stability. Similarly, if a boom in spending were forecast, the central bank would try to dampen it down by raising the interest rate. As well as the central bank, the government also needs to know how spending patterns are likely to evolve and affect output. A recession will depress tax revenue and increase spending on unemployment benefits. Forecasting patterns of spending is therefore a priority, not only for businesses, but also for the monetary and fiscal policy makers.

Aggregate demand and spending decisions

In this chapter, we focus on what lies behind the spending decisions in the economy and how they influence the level of economic activity. By the level of activity, we mean output or income. When output changes, employment also changes. For example, when output rises, more workers or longer hours are needed to produce the higher level of output. With more hours worked, the wage bill is larger and with higher sales, total profits are higher. This is why changes in economic activity are thought of as both changes in output and in income (i.e. wages and profits). When we think of a real-world economy, output is normally growing and recessions and booms produce fluctuations around a trend growth rate. However, we will often simplify by working with levels of output rather than its rate of growth.

Spending decisions are complex and forward-looking. For consumers they involve questions like 'how do I allocate my spending over time given my current income and wealth, and how I expect my income to evolve in the future?'. Firms make decisions to purchase machinery and equipment and to build new premises based on a business plan that includes forecasts about how input costs and demand for their products will evolve over time. The government must also forecast demographic trends when making plans for building new schools and hospitals.

Decisions about spending by the entities that make up the economy—firms, families and government bodies—lie behind the demand side of the economy. Macroeconomics is concerned with the aggregate sum of spending decisions of these groups, and the consequences of those decisions for economy-wide outcomes such as the rate of unemployment or inflation. Household spending decisions add up to aggregate consumption, C; firms' investment decisions add up to aggregate investment, I (note that I refers to spending on machinery, equipment and new houses and other buildings); and government spending on different goods and services adds up to a single number, G.

Including the purchase of new business premises as part of investment highlights the difference between on the one hand, aggregate demand, which refers to spending on goods and services and on the other hand, the purchase of assets such as company shares or second-hand property. Buying a second-hand factory building does not contribute to aggregate demand. It is the transfer of the ownership of an asset from one business to another. In contrast, the sale of new business premises reflects the goods and services used in its construction and sale.

Although the first chapters in the book concentrate on a closed economy (a single nation without links with others) as noted above, in the fuller model (set out in Chapters 11 and 12) the demand side includes foreign spending on home goods and services, exports (X), and domestic spending on foreign goods and services, imports (M). Aggregate demand is real expenditure on goods and services produced in the home economy. This can be summarized by an equation relating real expenditure, which is called y^D, to its individual components:

$$y^D = C + I + G + (X - M), \qquad \text{(aggregate demand)}$$

where we add to the trio of C, I and G, the expenditure of foreigners on home output, X and subtract the spending of home agents on output produced abroad, M.

Aggregate demand and government policy

Two of the major tools of macroeconomic policy, monetary and fiscal policy, work by influencing different elements on the demand side. Policy makers worry about fluctuations in aggregate demand because they affect household wellbeing via unemployment and inflation.

Monetary policy seeks to stabilize aggregate demand by changing interest rates, which affect the investment decisions of firms and the purchase of new houses and durable goods like new cars and furniture by households. A rise in the interest rate increases the cost of financing investment projects, and projects that would have gone ahead with lower interest rates are postponed or cancelled. Monetary policy also has indirect effects because the interest rate affects incentives to save and therefore shifts spending decisions over time. For example, by making new borrowing more expensive and increasing the return on saving, a higher interest rate will encourage households to postpone consumption.

Through changes in government spending on goods and services (G), fiscal policy affects aggregate demand directly. Fiscal policy can also be used to affect demand indirectly through its influence on household incomes and through that channel, on household spending. Changes in taxation and in the transfers made by the government to households in the form of pensions, disability and unemployment benefits feed through into the spending decisions of households, i.e. into C, to affect aggregate demand.

An important reason to study the demand side is to construct a model of the transmission mechanism by which monetary and fiscal policy, via the spending decisions of households, firms and the government, affect the economy. Before explaining the first building block of the macro model, which is the IS curve, we provide some facts about the demand side.

1.1.1 Facts about the demand side and business cycles

Shares of GDP

Table 1.1 sets out the average composition of gross domestic product (GDP) in five major economies for the period between the financial crisis and the pandemic, from 2010 to 2018. GDP is the national accounts measure of national output. We discuss the calculation of GDP in the next subsection. Table 1.1 shows that consumption makes up the largest proportion of GDP in all the economies with the exception of China. In particular, the importance of consumption in GDP ranges from 37% in China to 68% in the US. A large part of this cross-country variation can be explained by differences in the contribution of investment. For example, an exceptionally high proportion of Chinese GDP arises from investment spending; the UK's share is low. The table also

	Consumption	Investment incl. gov.	Government cons. spending	Net exports
China	36.7	44.9	15.9	2.4
Germany	53.6	20.5	19.6	6.3
Japan	57.3	23.2	19.9	−0.4
United Kingdom	64.7	16.7	19.9	−1.4
United States	67.9	20.2	15.0	−3.1

Table 1.1 Shares of GDP (in %), current prices, average 2010–18.

Note: GDP in current prices is a measure of nominal GDP; shares might not add up to 100% due to statistical discrepancies.

Source: OECD National Accounts (data accessed July 2020).

highlights the variation across countries in the contribution to GDP from net exports. On average, between 2010 and 2018, the US, the UK and Japan ran trade deficits with imports in excess of exports, whereas Germany and China were in trade surplus (see Chapter 12 for further discussion and definitions).

The upper panel of Figure 1.1 shows how the shares of consumption, investment and government spending in GDP changed over time for the UK from 1948 to 2019. From 1948 until the end of the 1960s the share of consumption falls and is mirrored by a rise in the share of investment. The share of investment peaks in 1989, falls sharply in the

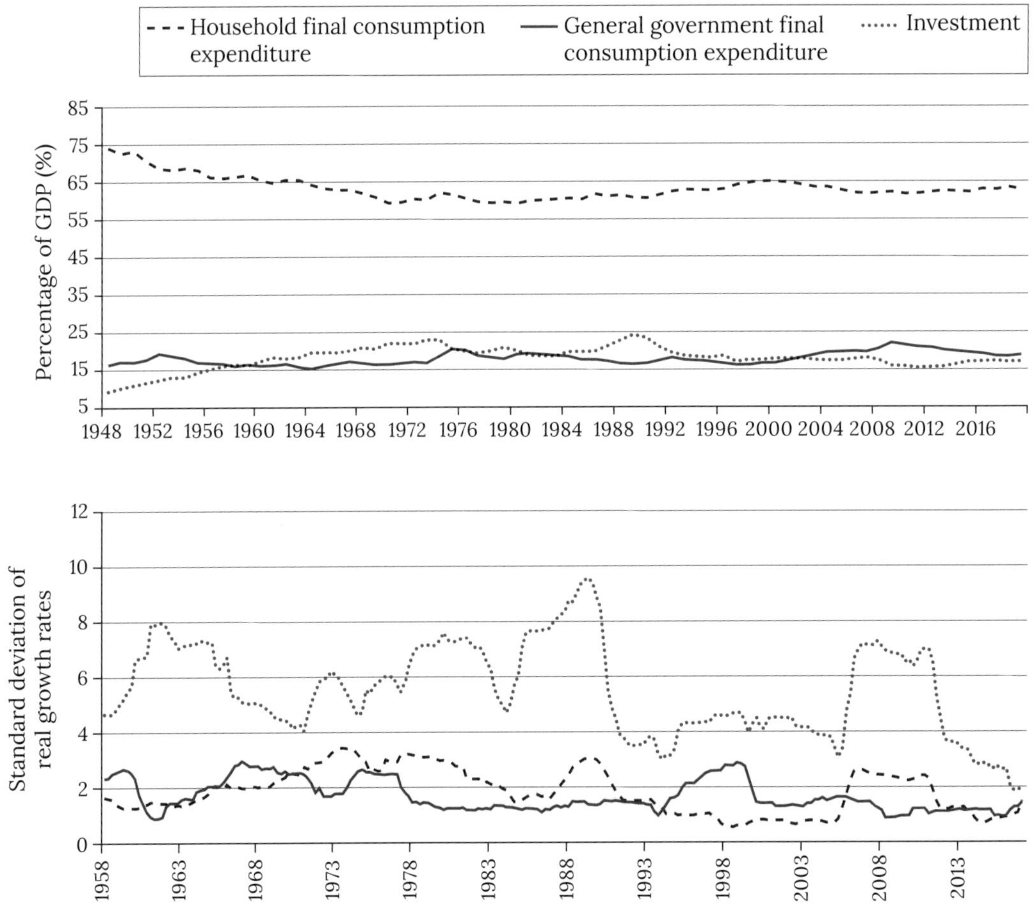

Figure 1.1 Components of GDP in the UK: as a percentage of GDP between 1948 and 2019 (upper panel) and volatility of growth rates between 1958 Q3 and 2017 Q3 (lower panel).

Note: Volatility has been calculated as the standard deviation of the GDP growth rate over a rolling 21-quarter period. The upper graph uses data from the series 'Gross Domestic Product by category of expenditure, current prices' and the lower graph uses data from the series 'Gross Domestic Product by category of expenditure, chained volume measures'.

Source: UK Office for National Statistics (data accessed July 2020).

financial crisis and recovers only weakly thereafter. The government's consumption spending increases sharply in the crisis but then declines as austerity policies were introduced from 2010.

National accounts

The national accounts are used to measure the output of an economy. The most commonly used measure for calculating national output is gross domestic product, or GDP. GDP can be measured in three different ways. All three equations for calculating GDP are identities, which means that because of the way the variables are defined, the left-hand side must always equal the right-hand side. This special feature of an identity is signalled by the use of the equals sign with three bars.

First, is the *expenditure* method, which is the one we use in the model of the demand side. This method measures GDP as the total expenditure on the economy's output of goods and services:

$$y \equiv C + I + G + (X - M), \qquad \text{(GDP identity, expenditure method)}$$

where $y \equiv$ output (or GDP), $C \equiv$ consumption, $I \equiv$ investment (including changes in stocks of raw materials and finished goods), $G \equiv$ government spending and $(X - M)$ $\equiv$ net exports. This is an identity, as it simply breaks down GDP into its constituent components. A fall in one of the components on the right-hand side, for example consumption, will therefore always result in an equivalent reduction in measured GDP on the left-hand side.

When a *new house* is bought, just like a new piece of machinery, this is an investment decision—the house provides a flow of services to the household over many years—and is included in the national accounts under the term, I. The house and the piece of machinery form part of the economy's capital stock. National accountants have to make many tricky classification decisions: although households buy a variety of durable goods that provide services over many years, by convention it is only housing that is considered as investment in the national accounts. Cars and furniture, for example, are treated in the national accounts as consumption.

It is important to recall that only government spending on goods and services is part of aggregate demand; G does not include government expenditure on transfers (e.g. pensions or social security payments). When the recipients of transfers spend their income from benefits or pensions, this is then recorded as consumption.

The expenditure method only includes *final goods*. For example, during the production process, firms buy raw materials and *intermediate goods* to make their final goods. The only purchases that are counted in GDP are when the firm sells the finished goods to the consumer. This avoids any double counting. In this way, GDP captures only the *value added* created in the economy. This leads onto the second approach for calculating GDP; the *value added method*. This method measures GDP as the value added created in all sectors of the economy, such that:

$$y \equiv \text{value of output sold} - \text{cost of raw materials and intermediate goods}$$

(GDP identity, value added method)

The third and final approach for calculating GDP is the *income method*. This method measures GDP as the total income of all agents in the economy, such that:

$$y \equiv \text{salaries of workers} + \text{profits of the owners of capital} \quad \text{(GDP identity, income method)}$$

The three methods of calculating GDP are all identities and each holds at each point in time. It makes intuitive sense that the total income in the economy is equal to the total expenditure on goods and services produced at home, because for every transaction there is both a buyer and a seller. What is expenditure for the buyer is income to the seller. In practice, however, GDP calculated using the three methods may differ. This is a matter of *measurement error*, which can arise for several reasons. Measurement error may be more serious for one rather than another of the three methods. For example, tax evasion or the existence of a substantial black market are likely to produce a greater problem of underestimation of GDP when measured by incomes than for the other methods. If the underlying components could be measured completely accurately, then each of the three approaches would yield exactly the same estimate of GDP.

Relative volatility

The lower panel of Figure 1.1 shows the relative volatility of growth rates for the three components of aggregate demand: a higher standard deviation means higher volatility. We can see that investment is much more volatile than consumption and government spending: the line showing the standard deviation for investment lies above that for consumption and government spending. Investment depends on expected post-tax profits and is very dependent on how optimistic firms are, so it tends to flourish in boom periods and collapse in recessions, making it more volatile than the other components of GDP, or GDP itself. In addition to this, investment can also be postponed in recessions, whereas government current spending and consumption cannot be as easily delayed. For example, a household still has to spend money on food and drink in a recession, whereas a firm may choose to wait until the economy has recovered before it undertakes investment. We shall also see—in Section 1.2.6—that fixed investment decisions are often bunched, further accounting for the greater volatility of investment.

Growth and cycles

The idea that economies fluctuate between phases of boom and recession is confirmed by looking at the data for the US. Figure 1.2 illustrates the long-run growth and business cycles in the US economy. In the top panel, the log of GDP in constant prices is plotted and shows the rather steady growth rate of GDP over the long run. Using the log scale, a straight line would represent a constant growth rate from 1948 to 2022.[1] In fact, average annual growth rates in each decade from 1948 were: 4.3%, 4.5%, 3.2%, 3.1%, 3.2%, 1.9%, 2.3%, and 1.5% between 2020 and the first quarter of 2022.

---

[1] See Section 16.7.1 of Chapter 16 for a detailed discussion of growth concepts, and the use and interpretations of natural logs.

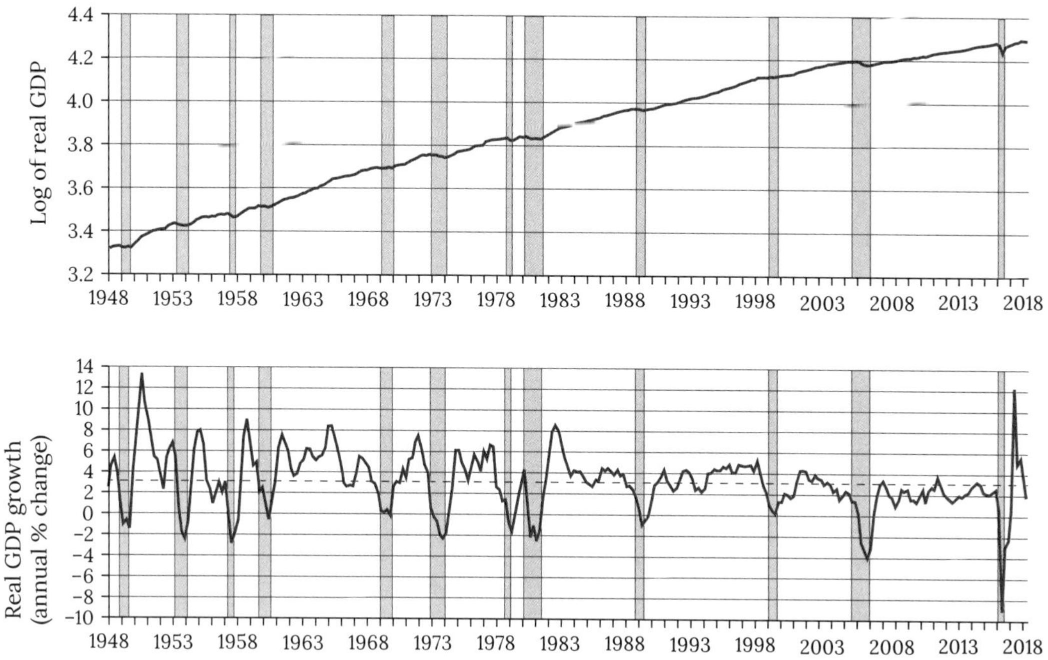

Figure 1.2 Business cycles in the United States between 1948 and 2022: Log of real GDP (upper panel) and real GDP growth (lower panel).

Note: The shaded grey areas represent recessions as defined by NBER. Both graphs use data from the series 'Real GDP, chained dollars, billions of chained (2012) dollars.'

Source: US Bureau of Economic Analysis (data accessed September 2022).

By plotting the *annual* growth rate of GDP in the lower panel, the fluctuations of the economy around the long-run trend are highlighted. The dotted line represents the average growth rate between 1948 and 2019 of 3.2%. Peaks and troughs of growth occur about twice a decade. In the US, an independent body called the National Bureau of Economic Research (NBER) establishes the dates of US business cycles and states there have been twelve separate contractions (i.e. recessions) over this period, which are represented by the shaded grey areas on the graphs. Recessions start at the peak of a business cycle and end at the trough: during recessions, economic activity is contracting. In the period we are analysing, the recessions range from 6 to 18 months in duration. This is why the *annual* GDP growth rate shown in Figure 1.2 is not negative in all of the recessions (e.g. the 2001 recession). The longest of these recessions was the 2007–09 global financial crisis, which spanned a year and a half.

Before the global financial crisis many macroeconomists claimed that better policy making had improved macro stability. This led to the use of the term 'the Great Moderation' to describe the calmer macroeconomic conditions from the mid-1980s (fewer and shorter recessions as illustrated in Figure 1.2).

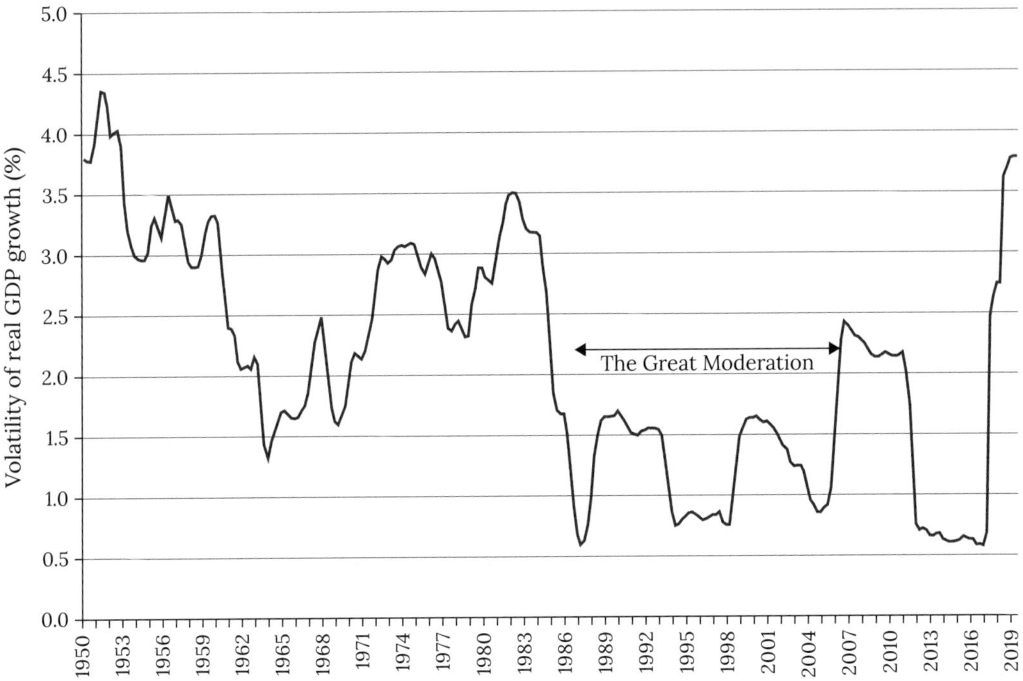

Figure 1.3 Volatility of real GDP growth in the United States: 1950 Q3 to 2019 Q4.

Note: Volatility has been calculated as the standard deviation of the GDP growth rate over a rolling 21-quarter period. Graph uses data from the series 'Real GDP, chained dollars, billions of chained (2012) dollars.'

Source: US Bureau of Economic Analysis (data accessed September 2022).

A more precise way to document the Great Moderation is to look at the volatility of GDP growth. Figure 1.3 shows the volatility of US GDP growth since the late 1950s. By plotting the moving average of the standard deviation of the growth rate, changes in volatility can be seen easily. Figure 1.3 uses a 21-quarter moving average of the standard deviation of the annual growth rate. There is a noticeable fall in the volatility of GDP growth from the mid 1980s. However, the spike in volatility experienced during the recession brought the era of the Great Moderation to an end. Volatility was low again between the end of the financial crisis and the Covid-19 crisis.

1.1.2 **Introducing the *IS* curve**

In this chapter, we begin to capture essential elements of the complex real-world macro-economy in a model. The model is called the 3-equation model because there are three core elements, representing the demand side, the supply side and the policy maker. The IS is the curve that represents the demand side. It is called the IS curve because it refers to planned investment and savings decisions; hence the *I* and the S.

It was originally formulated as a simple shorthand version of John Maynard Keynes's description of the demand side in his General Theory.[2]

By modelling the goods market we can answer interesting questions about the demand side that we might otherwise struggle with, such as the following:

1. If you give an individual a $100 bonus, how much of it will they spend?
2. How much will output increase following a rise in government spending or a boost in the confidence of households and firms about their future prospects?
3. To what extent will a rise in the interest rate curtail investment in new housing, machinery and equipment?

The IS curve summarizes how aggregate output in the economy is affected by changes in the spending decisions of families, firms and government bodies. For example, when firms increase their spending on new equipment, this triggers increased production in the capital goods producing sector of the economy. More people are employed to produce the extra capital goods and as they spend their wages, demand for consumer goods goes up and employment and output expand in those sectors as well. As a result of this process, the economy will move to a higher level of output and employment. We shall see that in response to the initial expansion of spending, output will grow until the extra saving households want to make just balances the extra spending on investment. At that point, the process by which the impact of the initial increase in aggregate demand is multiplied through the economy in subsequent rounds of higher employment, spending by newly employed workers, higher demand for consumer goods, etc. comes to an end.

Aggregate demand in the private sector

Focusing attention on decisions by the private sector, the level of aggregate demand will be affected by current income and by the following factors.

1. **Expectations about the future**: The plans of firms to invest in new IT, equipment and premises depend on their expectations of *future post-tax profits*. If firms experience high levels of capacity utilization and strong order books, they will increase investment in new capacity. Households prefer to have smooth rather than fluctuating consumption, which means they need to save and borrow in order to spread their consumption more evenly over time. To make their saving and borrowing decisions, they must form a view about the future growth of their income. The *life-cycle motive* for saving refers to the planning of saving as the person takes into account the projected pattern of income during their working life and retirement. Households will revise upward their estimate of how much they can spend each period if they have new information that leads them to expect their income to grow more strongly. Firms and households form their expectations in

[2] See Keynes (1936). The IS curve underlies the famous IS-LM model, which was introduced by John Hicks (Hicks 1937). For a concise and interesting discussion of its origins and impact, see Durlauf and Hester's article entitled 'IS-LM' in the *New Palgrave Dictionary of Economics* (Durlauf and Hester 2008).

the face of uncertainty. For example, an increase in the unemployment rate in the economy could be a signal to households that *uncertainty* about their future income has risen, which would trigger an increase in saving for *precautionary* reasons.

2. **The extent of credit constraints**: These arise because of problems faced by banks in assessing the creditworthiness of households and firms. It is impossible for banks to have full information about borrowers' projects and actions. Borrowing by households and by small and medium-sized firms is therefore often restricted by banks. Households and business that cannot borrow as much money as they would like are said to be *credit constrained*. The information problems inherent in bank lending mean that access to credit is often highly dependent on the amount of *collateral* the borrower has with which to secure the loan. The most common form of collateral for households is the value of their house. This means that changes in the value of collateral, which occur when house prices change, affect consumption and investment because they either tighten or relax credit constraints. People with higher wealth have more collateral and are less likely to be credit-constrained.
3. **The interest rate**: There are a number of channels through which the interest rate will affect aggregate demand. When interest rates go up, households find it more expensive to get a mortgage. This reduces the demand for new houses and for furnishings and other consumer durables that go along with moving house. A higher interest rate will lead firms to rein in their spending plans on new capital equipment and buildings. Finally, households will tend to postpone consumption spending because of the improved returns from saving, which we call the substitution effect. However, creditor and debtor households would be expected to react differently due to income changes. A creditor household will find their income has gone up when the interest rate rises and this will boost consumption spending through the income effect. For debtor households, the effect will be the opposite. The first and third effects (substitution effects, and income effect for debtors) are normally stronger than the second one (income effect for creditors) and thus a higher interest rate is associated with postponed consumption.

The *IS* curve

The IS curve summarizes in an equation and diagram the demand side in the macroeconomic model. It shows the combinations of the interest rate and output at which aggregate demand (i.e. spending) in the economy is equal to output.

Figure 1.4 shows the IS curve. This is a downward-sloping relationship. To see this, think of the combination of a high interest rate and low output. When the interest rate is high, spending on housing, consumer durables, machinery and equipment will be low. This means aggregate demand is low and a low level of output will satisfy the low demand. Hence, we have the first point on the IS curve at A. Now, take a combination of a low interest rate and high output. Here the situation is the opposite: buoyant spending on new houses, consumer durables and investment goods generates a high level of output and high incomes for households. This second point gives us the downward-sloping IS curve at B.

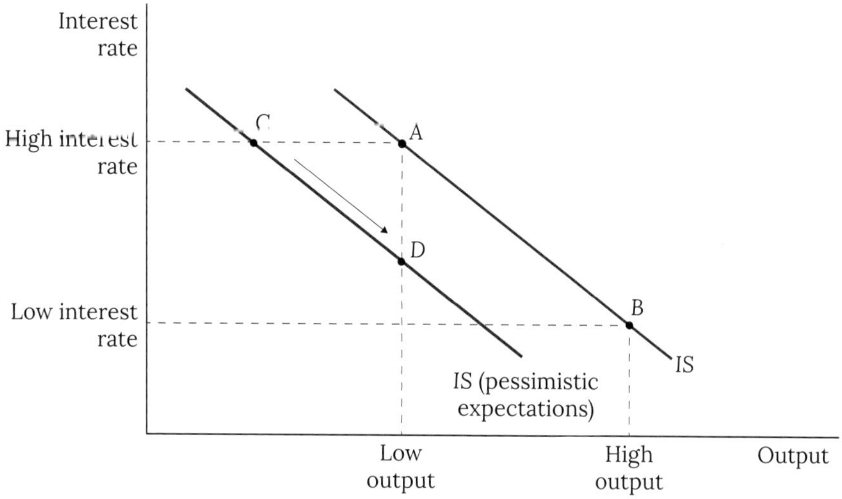

Figure 1.4 The IS curve—the effects of changes in optimism and economic policy. Visit www.oup.com/he/carlin-soskice to explore the IS curve with Animated Analytical Diagram 1.4.

To show how changes in profit or income growth expectations, uncertainty and the value of collateral can be captured in the diagram, we hold the interest rate constant and look at shifts in the IS curve. As an example, in a situation of depressed profit expectations, we would expect firms to postpone new investment. The result is lower investment spending at any interest rate. The IS curve shifts to the left (shown by the curve labelled IS (pessimistic expectations)).

Using the IS diagram, we can show how the central bank or the government can affect the demand side. Following up the situation where the business environment becomes more pessimistic, the central bank could lower the interest rate to stimulate investment. This would be shown as a move *along* the IS curve from point C to point D. As an example, there was much discussion about the decision by the US central bank, the Federal Reserve, to reduce the policy interest rate and keep it low as a way of stimulating investment in the aftermath of the collapse of the Dotcom bubble in 2001. The long period of low interest rates stimulated investment in new house construction and we shall see in Chapter 9 the role this played in the background to the global financial crisis of 2008.

Another response to a leftward shift of the IS curve due to pessimistic profit expectations could be action by the government rather than central bank. If the government decides to launch a major expenditure programme, such as to improve healthcare provision or to install an information super-highway, this will *shift* the IS curve to the right: at a given interest rate, the government purchases a larger amount of goods and services. Under our assumption that suppliers will respond to the higher demand, the economy moves to a higher level of output and employment. In the diagram, this would shift the IS curve to the right back towards its initial position.

The demand side is only part of the macroeconomic model. To understand how the spending decisions of households, firms and the government fit into the bigger picture, we need to include the supply side and the motivations and behaviour of the policy makers. Chapter 2 addresses the supply side and Chapter 3 brings in the policy maker. Before moving on, we set out the modelling of the demand side in more detail.

1.2 MODELLING

The Modelling sections of the chapters in the book provide more details of the models and their components introduced in the Overview sections. Detailed derivations of some of the results are available in the appendix.

As a first step in this chapter, we introduce the concept of goods market equilibrium and the definition and mechanics of the multiplier process. Throughout this section, we assume that firms are willing to meet the higher demand for their goods and services and workers are willing to take the extra jobs or work the extra hours that are offered.

1.2.1 Goods market equilibrium

We begin our modelling of the goods market by considering each component of aggregate demand in the closed economy. The aggregate—or economy-wide—demand for goods and services consists of:

- **consumption:** Expenditure by individuals on goods and services. Spending is on both *durable* products such as a car, laptop or sofa and on *non-durable* products such as a theatre show, child-care services or groceries.
- **investment:** Expenditure on goods that produce a stream of utility in the form of future services. When discussing investment as a component of aggregate demand, it includes spending on capital goods (machinery, equipment, and buildings). In addition, most spending on R&D is treated as investment in national accounts. Spending is by households on new houses, by firms on new capital goods, including structures, and building up inventories of materials or finished goods, and by government (on public infrastructure projects, such as building a new high speed rail line).
- **demand stemming from government purchases:** Government expenditure on salaries, goods and services. Spending includes public sector wages (e.g. civil servants, teachers), purchases of goods (e.g. educational supplies, ammunition for the army) and purchases of services (e.g. waste disposal and contract cleaning).

The model of goods market equilibrium

We now set out a model of the goods market. In the closed economy, aggregate demand, y^D, is given by

$$y^D = C + I + G, \tag{1.1}$$

and we ignore imports and exports. All variables are in real terms, which is also referred to as constant price terms. Equilibrium in the goods market requires that planned real expenditure on goods and services (i.e. aggregate demand) is equal to real output

$$y^D = y, \qquad \text{(goods market equilibrium)}$$

where y is output. y is also income: spending on the output of the economy in turn becomes the income of those producing it (wages and profits). This circular flow of income to expenditure and output, and back to the incomes of producers means we can use the terms output, income and expenditure interchangeably. We shall come back to the goods market equilibrium condition after providing some more detail about consumption and investment behaviour.

To start, we assume that aggregate consumption is a simple linear function of after-tax or disposable aggregate income

$$C = c_0 + c_1(y - T), \tag{1.2}$$

where T is total taxes.

To get the consumption function we make the additional assumption that taxes are a fixed proportion of income; i.e. $T = ty$, where $0 < t < 1$. The consumption function then becomes

$$C = c_0 + c_1(1 - t)y. \qquad \text{(Keynesian consumption function)}$$

This is a Keynesian consumption function. It consists of a constant term, c_0, which is referred to as autonomous consumption because it does not depend on current income, and the other component of consumption, $c_1(1-t)y$, which fluctuates with the level of disposable income. Since we assume a proportional tax rate, t, $c_1(1-t)y$ is a fixed proportion of disposable income. c_1 is referred to as the marginal propensity to consume and lies between zero and one ($0 < c_1 < 1$).

Note that the marginal propensity to consume (MPC) shows the change (where change is denoted by a triangle symbol) in consumption as the result of a change in post-tax or disposable income:

$$MPC \equiv \frac{\Delta C}{\Delta y^{disp}} = c_1, \qquad \text{(marginal propensity to consume)}$$

where $y^{disp} \equiv (1-t)y$.

In this model of consumption, private saving is $S \equiv y^{disp} - C$ and adds to one's assets. Income is the amount that can be consumed without reducing one's assets. The corresponding marginal propensity to save is s_1 and $c_1 + s_1 = 1$ (i.e. disposable income can be either saved or spent).

If disposable income is zero, the Keynesian consumption function predicts consumption equal to c_0. For this to be the case, households have savings and/or are able to borrow. A more satisfactory model of consumption must therefore include forward-looking behaviour in order to account for savings and we build this in to the model of consumption later in the chapter.

1.2.2 **The multiplier**

We use the Keynesian consumption function to introduce in the simplest way the concept of how equilibrium in the goods market is determined and how the multiplier process works. If we substitute the consumption function into the equation for aggregate demand, then we get a relation between aggregate demand,

$$y^D = c_0 + c_1(1-t)y + I + G, \qquad \text{(aggregate demand)}$$

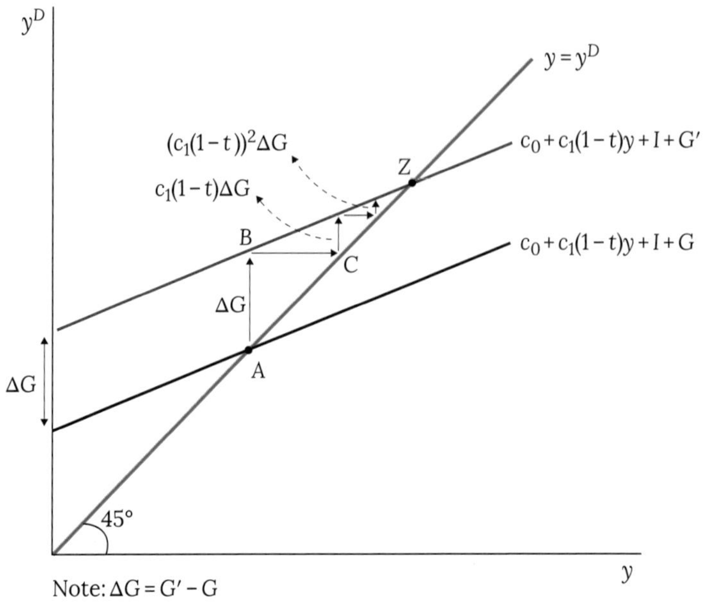

Figure 1.5 Keynesian cross–increase in government spending. Visit www.oup.com/he/carlin-soskice to explore the Keynesian cross with Animated Analytical Diagram 1.5.

and output, y, which we can draw on a diagram with output on the x-axis and aggregate demand on the y-axis (Figure 1.5). The intercept of the curve will be $(I + G + c_0)$ and the slope $c_1(1-t)$ which, given the assumption that both c_1 and t are between 0 and 1, will itself be between zero and one. We can also draw the goods market equilibrium condition on the same graph, which will be a 45° line, because in equilibrium

$$y = y^D.$$

The point at which the two curves intersect shows the level of output where planned real expenditure on goods (and services) by firms, households and government is exactly equal to the level of goods being supplied in the economy. Above the 45° line, the demand for goods is greater than the supply.

To understand the model, we disturb the initial equilibrium at point A. Suppose there is an increase in government spending. From the aggregate demand equation, we can see that this shifts the aggregate demand curve upwards by the change in government spending, ΔG. Aggregate demand now exceeds output (Point B). As the government increases its purchases of goods (e.g. of office equipment) the stocks of these goods in warehouses decline. The inventory management software records the fall in stocks and triggers an increase in production: output rises. This is the move from B to C, where once again $y = y^D$. The higher output in turn raises incomes (in the form of wages of the additional workers employed and the profits of the owners of the firms making higher sales) and according to the consumption function, some proportion of the higher income is spent on goods and services in the economy, raising aggregate demand further. The process continues until the new goods market equilibrium is reached at point Z, where output and aggregate demand are equal.

Adjustment to shifts in aggregate demand via inventory accumulation and decumulation shows how a purely quantity based adjustment to a new goods market equilibrium can take place. For the goods market to be in equilibrium it must be the case that $y = y^D$. If we substitute y into the aggregate demand equation we can rearrange to define equilibrium output in terms of the *exogenous variables*. Exogenous variables are those that are determined outside the model. In the model of goods market equilibrium, the exogenous variables are autonomous consumption (c_0), investment (I) and government spending (G), the marginal propensity to consume (c_1) and the tax rate (t). If we know the value of these five variables, we can work out the level of equilibrium output,

$$y = c_0 + c_1(1-t)y + I + G \tag{1.3}$$

$$y - c_1(1-t)y = c_0 + I + G$$

$$y = \underbrace{\frac{1}{1-c_1(1-t)}}_{\text{multiplier}} \underbrace{(c_0 + I + G)}_{\text{autonomous demand}}. \tag{1.4}$$

Because c_1 and t are between 0 and 1, this simplified model implies that the *multiplier* is greater than 1. This means that a 1% increase in autonomous demand would be predicted to lead to an increase in output of more than 1%. This is referred to as the short-run multiplier as we hold the interest rate and all other policy responses constant—i.e. output is the only variable allowed to change. Note that if consumption was not a function of current income, i.e. if the marginal propensity to consume, c_1, is equal to zero, then the aggregate demand line is horizontal and there is no multiplier process amplifying the impact on the economy of the rise in government spending. A rule of thumb is that the multiplier in 'normal times' is between one and 1.5; higher values are estimated for recessions.

In the consumption function, c_0 is an exogenous variable, meaning that it is not influenced by any other variables in the equation (i.e. it is determined outside the model). The second part of the equation, $c_1(1-t)y$, is *endogenous*. In order to calculate the level of aggregate consumption in equilibrium, we therefore need to first work out the equilibrium value of y and then compute the level of consumption.

We now combine algebra and geometry to deepen our understanding of the multiplier process. We return to the previous example shown in Figure 1.5 where the government uses fiscal policy to increase activity in the economy. Since the AD curve is flatter than the market-clearing condition, equilibrium output will increase by more than the increase in government expenditure, i.e. the multiplier is larger than one. The initial boost in government spending increases aggregate demand by ΔG. This increases output, and income, and so aggregate consumption increases by $c_1(1-t)\Delta G$. The increase in aggregate consumption increases aggregate demand by the same amount, and, given that the goods market clears, increases output and income too. Aggregate consumption increases again by $[c_1(1-t)]^2 \Delta G$, and so on to infinity. The total increase in output is given by the sum of these changes:

$$\Delta y = \Delta G + [c_1(1-t)]\Delta G + [c_1(1-t)]^2 \Delta G.... \tag{1.5}$$

$$= \left(1 + [c_1(1-t)] + [c_1(1-t)]^2 + ...\right)\Delta G. \tag{1.6}$$

This is a geometric progression and its sum to infinity is given by[3]

$$\Delta y = \underbrace{\frac{1}{1 - c_1(1-t)}}_{\text{multiplier}} \Delta G = k\Delta G, \tag{1.7}$$

where k is the multiplier.

Application: The paradox of thrift

Imagine the economy is in a recession and the following question is put to an economist: should a policy be introduced to encourage or to discourage private saving in order to help the economy recover? On the one hand, the idea of encouraging more saving sounds helpful—if more is saved and invested in new capital stock, that would seem a good recipe for recovery. On the other hand, if more saving just means less consumption and there is no increase in investment, won't aggregate demand fall and the recession get worse?

To answer this question requires spelling out how agents are assumed to behave. In an economic model, these decisions are summarized by behavioural equations. In macroeconomics, it is aggregate behaviour that is captured by these equations. In the very simple model we have set out, the behavioural equation for consumption is the Keynesian consumption function. Investment and government spending are assumed to remain constant: in the model so far, they are not affected by other variables (i.e. they are exogenous). The behavioural equations are as follows:

$$C = c_0 + c_1(1-t)y;\ G = \overline{G};\ \text{and}\ I = \overline{I}, \qquad \text{(behavioural equations)}$$

where we put a bar over the G and the I to emphasize that these are both exogenous. From the behavioural equations, we can write planned real expenditure (aggregate demand) as

---

[3] This is the sum of a geometric series. We want to find an expression for the series $1 + [c_1(1-t)] + [c_1(1-t)]^2 + [c_1(1-t)]^3 + \cdots$, which we call x. If we put

$$x = 1 + [c_1(1-t)] + [c_1(1-t)]^2 + [c_1(1-t)]^3 + \cdots,$$

and multiply both sides by the common factor, $[c_1(1-t)]$, then

$$[c_1(1-t)] \cdot x = [c_1(1-t)] + [c_1(1-t)]^2 + [c_1(1-t)]^3 + \cdots$$

and if we subtract the bottom equation from the one above, we have

$$x(1 - [c_1(1-t)]) = 1$$

$$\Rightarrow x = \frac{1}{1 - [c_1(1-t)]}.$$

$$y^D = c_0 + c_1(1-t)y + \bar{I} + \overline{G} \quad (1.8)$$

As usual, the goods market equilibrium condition is $y^D = y$, and if we substitute equation 1.8 into this, then in equilibrium, planned private savings are equal to planned investment plus government spending:

$$\underbrace{(1-c_1(1-t))y - c_0}_{\text{Planned private saving}} = \underbrace{\bar{I}+\overline{G}}_{\text{Planned I and G}} \quad \text{(equilibrium condition)}$$

We model the proposal to encourage savings by a fall in autonomous consumption from c_0 to c_0'. Aggregate demand falls initially by $(c_0 - c_0')$ and the multiplier process works in the downwards direction. Using the same logic as illustrated in Figure 1.5 in reverse, this process continues until we get to the new equilibrium at lower output. At the new lower output level, y', planned savings on the left-hand side of equation 1.9 is equal to planned investment plus government spending on the right-hand side, which have not changed:

$$(1-c_1(1-t))y' - c_0' = \bar{I} + \overline{G}. \quad (1.9)$$

An important insight emerges from this example. The initial equilibrium was disturbed by a fall in autonomous consumption as households sought to increase their savings. However, the intention to save more did not lead to higher aggregate savings because *income fell* ($\Delta y = k(c_0 - c_0')$). This must be the case for equation 1.9 to hold.[4] This is called the *paradox of thrift* because if greater thriftiness is not matched by higher investment in fixed capital or some other increase in spending, income will fall and there will be no overall increase in savings in the economy.

To summarize, the answer to the question of whether saving should be encouraged in a recession depends on the model of the economy the economist is using—and of course, on how well that model matches the real economy under study. Using the model we have developed so far in this chapter, the answer is clear: encouragement to save more will not help the economy to exit recession. The reason is that there is no mechanism in *this* model through which higher saving is translated into higher investment. Investment remains at $\bar{I}$ throughout. Hence the result is that aggregate demand falls, output falls and the recession is deepened.

By contrast, if the model included a central bank, then the recession could be averted by the central bank cutting the interest rate and boosting investment to offset the fall in consumption. In Section 1.2.3, we remove the simplifying assumption of exogenous investment to show the impact on the demand side when investment is responsive to changes in the interest rate and in expected post-tax profits.

---

[4] We can confirm that the change in aggregate saving is equal to zero. Using equation 1.7:

$$\Delta y = \frac{1}{1-c_1(1-t)}\Delta c_0,$$

$$\Delta S = \left[(1-c_1(1-t))\frac{1}{1-c_1(1-t)}\Delta c_0\right] - \Delta c_0 = 0.$$

1.2.3 The *IS* curve

Deriving the IS equation

Throughout this book, we use the IS curve to represent the demand side of the economy. In this subsection, we derive the IS curve and use it as a starting point to think about how monetary and fiscal policy work. As we discussed in Section 1.1.2, the IS curve shows the combinations of output and the real interest rate at which the goods market is in equilibrium.

We first set out the relationship between the real interest rate, r, and the nominal interest rate, i. This relationship is shown by the Fisher equation:

$$r = i - \pi^{E}. \qquad \text{(Fisher equation)}$$

This equation says that the real interest rate is simply the nominal interest adjusted for expected inflation. Inflation is denoted by π and E is used to represent expectations. It is the real interest rate that is most important for investment and saving decisions, as it represents the true cost of borrowing (and the true return on saving). This interest rate is therefore the one used in the investment equation and in the IS curve. When the central bank sets the nominal interest rate, it does this with the intention of achieving a particular real interest rate since it aims to affect interest-sensitive spending. In Section 1.5.1 of the Appendix, we show how the Fisher equation is derived.

At this stage, we assume there is just one interest rate in the economy that applies to all borrowing and saving. We make the assumption to keep the maths as simple as possible. In reality, there is a spectrum of interest rates. For example, the interest rate on bank lending will typically be higher than the interest rate set by the central bank (see Chapter 5).

The transmission of monetary policy will work through its effect on investment spending, including on new houses and on other durable goods. Up to this point, we have assumed that investment is determined by expected future profits, which we have assumed to be exogenous. We now incorporate the interest rate into the investment function as follows:

$$I = a_0 - a_1 r, \qquad \text{(investment function)}$$

where r is the real interest rate, a_0 and a_1 are constants and $a_1 > 0$. The main determinant of investment is expected future post-tax profits, which is captured by the term, a_0.

We derive the IS curve as follows. Substituting the investment function into equation 1.4 gives us a relationship between the real interest rate and output, which is the IS curve. We can then use k to denote the multiplier and simplify to achieve a simple equation for the IS curve:

$$y = \underbrace{\frac{1}{1 - c_1(1-t)}}_{\text{multiplier}}[c_0 + (a_0 - a_1 r) + G] \qquad (1.10)$$

$$= k[c_0 + (a_0 - a_1 r) + G] \qquad (1.11)$$

$$= k(c_0 + a_0 + G) - k a_1 r \qquad (1.12)$$

$$= A - ar, \qquad \text{(IS curve)}$$

where $A \equiv k(c_0 + a_0 + G)$ and $a \equiv k a_1$.

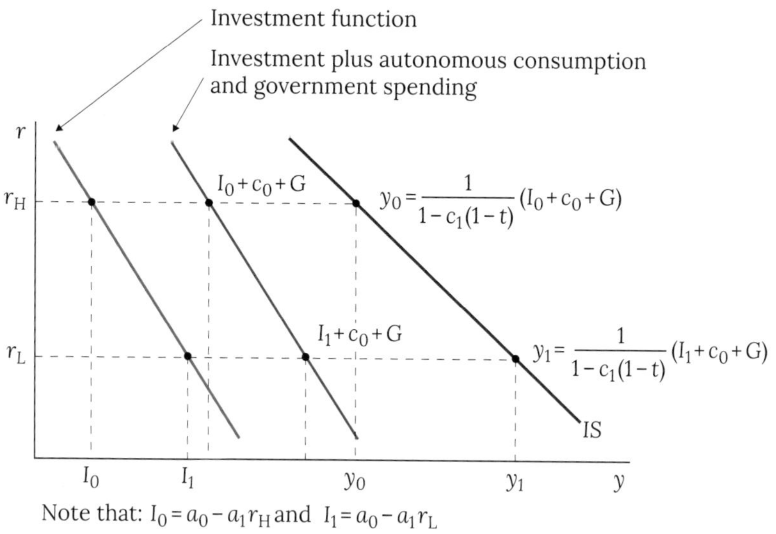

Figure 1.6 Deriving the IS curve. Visit www.oup.com/he/carlin-soskice to explore deriving the IS curve with Animated Analytical Diagram 1.6.

The derivation of the equation for the IS curve highlights the fact that given r, equilibrium output, y, is found by multiplying autonomous consumption and investment, and government spending by the multiplier $k = \frac{1}{1-c_1(1-t)}$. This fixes an r–y combination on the IS curve. It is clear from equation 1.12 that a higher multiplier, k, or higher interest-sensitivity of spending to the interest rate, a_1, increases the effect of a change in the interest rate on output, making the IS curve flatter.

The IS curve is derived graphically in Figure 1.6 using the IS curve equation shown above. Three curves are shown on the figure: the investment function, the investment function plus autonomous consumption and government spending, and the IS curve. Two real interest rates are shown in the figure: a high real interest rate, r_H, and a low real interest rate, r_L. At r_H, investment is more costly, so the level of planned investment is low, whereas the opposite is true at r_L. This leads to a downward-sloping investment function. Autonomous consumption and government spending are unaffected by the interest rate, so when added on, the curve shifts out parallel. The last step to derive the IS curve is to multiply $I_0 + c_0 + G$ by the multiplier. This gives output equal to planned expenditure, y, on the IS curve. The IS curve shows all the combinations of output and real interest rate where the goods market is in equilibrium.

Using the IS curve equation and the diagram, we can summarize its properties.

1. The IS curve is downward sloping because a low interest rate generates high investment and consumer durables spending, which will be associated with high output. By contrast, when the interest rate is high, investment and consumer durable spending, and consequently equilibrium output, are low.
2. The slopc of the IS:
   a. Any change in the size of the *multiplier* will change the slope of the IS curve. For example, a rise in the marginal propensity to consume, c_1, or a fall in the

tax rate, t, will increase the multiplier, making the IS flatter: it rotates counter clockwise from the intercept on the vertical axis.

b. Any change in the *interest sensitivity of investment* (a_1) will lead to a consequential change in the slope of the IS curve: a more interest-sensitive investment function (i.e. $\uparrow a_1$) will be reflected in a flatter IS curve.

3. Shifts in the IS curve: Any change in *autonomous consumption*, *autonomous investment* or *government expenditure* (c_0, a_0, G) will cause the IS curve to shift by the change in autonomous spending times the multiplier (i.e., the intercept of the IS curve on the vertical axis shifts).

1.2.4 **Forward-looking behaviour**

The spending decisions of agents in the present are influenced by their expectations of the future. This means there is an intertemporal component to both consumption and investment.

1. Households adjust their current spending based on their expected income in the future. For example, a final year economics undergraduate who secures a lucrative job contract (which is set to commence after university), has low current income, but high expected future income. Having got the job, this individual may borrow in the present, consume more and pay back the money when they start their job. This behaviour is referred to as *consumption smoothing*.
2. Firms make decisions (e.g. purchasing machinery, equipment and premises) based on a business plan that includes forecasts about future demand for their products and input costs. For example, a firm selling cars to Vietnam might choose to build a new factory (i.e. undertake investment) based on forecasts that Vietnamese incomes (and therefore their demand for cars) will continue to rise rapidly over the next 20 years. Investment is intrinsically forward looking, as it incurs a cost today, but the stream of benefits occurs in the future.

Present value calculation

We can calculate the present value of a flow of income or profits received in future periods in the following way. We take the example of a firm making an investment decision.

We assume that firms aim to maximize profits, so they undertake investment projects if these offer a return that is higher than costs. The outlay on investment typically precedes the returns, which may be lumpy and spread over a number of years. The way to deal with this is to calculate the 'Present Value' (V) of the expected flow of profits Π, where $\Pi_t, \Pi_{t+1}, \ldots$ is the flow of profits in period t, $t+1$ etc. Suppose the interest rate is 10%. Then if I save €100 today I will have €110 in a year's time (100 (1 + 10%)). Expressed the other way around, we could say that €110 in a year's time has the same value as €100 today—its present value is €100.

More generally, if interest rates are constant at r, the value of X in n years' time is the same as that of $X/(1+r)^n$ today. We can calculate the present value of our stream of expected profits, Π^E, from an investment project with profits over T years by:

$$V_t^E = \Pi_t^E + \frac{\Pi_{t+1}^E}{(1+r)} + \frac{\Pi_{t+2}^E}{(1+r)^2} + \cdots + \frac{\Pi_{t+T}^E}{(1+r)^T} = \sum_{i=0}^{T} \frac{1}{(1+r)^i} \Pi_{t+i}^E.$$

(expected present value calculation)

We use the superscript E to denote the expected value of a variable.

If the cost of the machine is greater than the present value of the flow of profits from the machine, then it would be more profitable not to buy the machine but instead put the money in the bank or in bonds (which earn interest of r). Similarly, if the money to purchase the machine is being borrowed, then if the cost of the machine is greater than the present value, buying the machine will be unprofitable. On the other hand, if the present value is greater than the cost, then this investment is profitable, and a profit-maximizing firm will go ahead with it.

We can apply the same logic to model consumption decisions. We can account for the fact that the future will affect consumption decisions by calculating the present value of the stream of expected income over a person's lifetime. If we assume that individuals live forever, we can use the formula for calculating present value to calculate the expected present value of lifetime wealth (Ψ^E, pronounced 'sigh'), which is defined at time t as follows,

$$\Psi_t^E = (1+r)A_{t-1} + \sum_{i=0}^{\infty} \frac{1}{(1+r)^i} y_{t+i}^E,$$

(expected present value of lifetime wealth)

where $\sum_{i=0}^{\infty} \frac{1}{(1+r)^i} y_{t+i}^E$ is the present value of expected post-tax lifetime labour income and $(1+r)A_{t-1}$ are the resources available in period t from the assets the individual held in the previous period.[5]

The present value calculation says that a rise in the interest rate reduces the present value of future expected income flows, which is one determinant of current investment and consumption decisions.

1.2.5 **Consumption**

People's income fluctuates over the life cycle; it also changes when they lose their job, move to a different job or get a promotion. Given that people prefer to smooth out

---

[5] The assumption that individuals 'live forever' can be thought of as assuming that households have children or heirs and that they incorporate the utility of their children or heirs into their consumption function. In other words, households behave 'as if' they last forever. The assumption is clearly unrealistic, but it greatly simplifies the mathematical derivation of the PIH. From this point onward, however, we will refer to lifetime income and earnings in the text, as it is more intuitive to think about forward-looking behaviour in terms of a household maximizing utility over their lifetime.

the fluctuations in their income in their spending behaviour, they take account of the future and would like to be able to save and borrow. The modelling of consumption should include how households form expectations about the future and how they borrow and save.

The desire to smooth consumption in the face of fluctuations in income is captured by the assumption of diminishing marginal utility of consumption. A simple way of visualizing this is to consider the choice of consumption in a world of just two periods. If we know income will be higher next period, how does that affect consumption now? Consider the choice between either low consumption equal to income in the first period and high consumption equal to income in the second period, or having the average of the two consumption levels in each period. If there is diminishing marginal utility of consumption, more consumption always increases utility, but successive increases in consumption deliver smaller and smaller benefits. Therefore, households will make the second choice, because consuming the average in both periods offers higher utility than the first choice.

The two-period model also provides insight about the effect of a change in the rate of interest on consumption. A rise in the interest rate increases the opportunity cost of consumption this period and incentivizes moving consumption to the future by saving more of the current period's income. This is called the *intertemporal substitution* effect. As with any change in relative prices, there is also an income effect. For a creditor, the income effect is positive and could outweigh the substitution effect, raising current consumption. However, for debtor households (making interest payments), the income effect will dampen consumption, reinforcing the substitution effect. To work through the 2-period model, see Unit 9 in CORE Econ's *The Economy* (https://www.core-econ.org/the-economy/book/text/09.html).

The permanent income hypothesis (PIH)

The permanent income hypothesis (PIH) states that individuals optimally choose how much to consume by allocating their resources across their lifetimes.[6] Their resources include their assets and their current and future income. This is a forward-looking decision and will depend on interest rates, asset values, expectations of future income and of future taxes. The PIH predicts that optimal consumption is smooth as compared to income. For example, when individuals start work, their income is low and they borrow to consume more; when income increases, they keep consumption constant and use the excess income to pay off debts and save for retirement; then at retirement, their income falls and they draw down their savings. Figure 1.7 shows how consumption and income change over the life cycle in this simplified example. The important point is that the PIH predicts that households will borrow and save in order to smooth consumption over their lifetimes. Likewise, over the business cycle, if an individual becomes unemployed, the model predicts that they borrow in order to sustain consumption during the spell of unemployment. As we shall see in Chapter 7

[6] This view of the consumption function was first developed by Modigliani and Brumberg (1954). See also Friedman (1957). For a review of Friedman's theory, its influence on modern economics and the relevant empirical literature, see Meghir (2004).

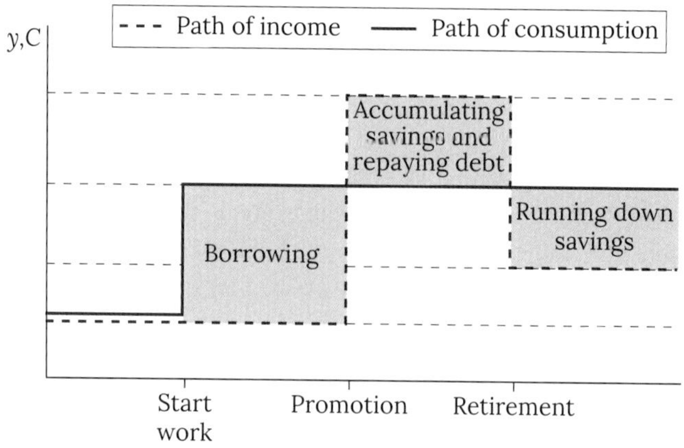

Figure 1.7 The permanent income hypothesis over the life cycle.

on fiscal policy, the government plays an important role in smoothing consumption through the provision of unemployment benefits.

The PIH model of consumption provides a stark contrast with the Keynesian consumption function where there is no explicit consideration of the future. Aggregate consumption of households is modelled there as the consumption of a fixed amount, c_0 and a fixed proportion of the current period's disposable income.

The PIH model is derived in more detail in Section 1.5.2 of the Appendix, but it is useful to set out the intuition and predictions of the model here, as it provides a framework for thinking about forward-looking consumption decisions. Given that income will fluctuate over a person's lifetime, the starting point of the PIH is their desire to smooth out fluctuations in consumption and their ability to save and borrow in order to achieve this.

The next question is whether an individual prefers their smooth consumption path to be one of constant consumption each period or of rising or falling consumption. This will depend on the relationship between the interest rate on saving and borrowing and the rate at which the individual trades off consumption in the future for consumption in the present. The latter is the *subjective discount rate* ρ, which is a measure of an individual's impatience.

The household chooses a path of consumption to maximize its lifetime utility subject to its lifetime budget constraint, which is

$$\Psi_t^E = (1+r)A_{t-1} + \sum_{i=0}^{\infty} \frac{1}{(1+r)^i} y_{t+i}^E. \quad \text{(lifetime budget constraint, expected lifetime wealth)}$$

Note that when considering the PIH, income, y is defined as post-tax income. The key to solving this problem can be thought about over just two periods, since the same considerations will apply to every subsequent pair of periods.[7] The answer is a simple

[7] See Hall (1978) for a full derivation of the PIH and an empirical test of the main implications of the theory.

relationship between consumption this period and next period, which is called an Euler equation (the derivation is in Section 1.5.2 of the Appendix):

$$C_t = \frac{1+\rho}{1+r} C^E_{t+1}. \qquad \text{(Euler equation)}$$

The intuition about consumption smoothing is clearest if we take the case where the interest rate, r, and the subjective discount rate, ρ, are the same. This means the household gets the same (objective) return from saving, r, as their (subjective) willingness to trade off consumption in the present for consumption in the future, ρ. In this case, the agent prefers a constant level of consumption each period, $C_t = C^E_{t+1}$.

We can see that if the discount rate is above the interest rate, then $C_t > C^E_{t+1}$ and consumption is falling over time, reflecting the 'impatience' of the household. The opposite is the case if the discount rate is below the interest rate; a patient household will have a path in which consumption rises over time, i.e. $C_t < C^E_{t+1}$. The crucial point to note is that whichever of these consumption patterns is chosen, it is independent of the period-by-period changes in income.

From now on we focus on the PIH where the subjective discount rate is equal to the real rate of interest, i.e. ($\rho = r$). To implement a lifetime consumption plan like this, given each period's income the household must do whatever saving and borrowing is called for in order to deliver the constant level of consumption each period. If current income is above permanent income, individuals save and if it is below, they borrow.

The next step is to use the Euler equation to find out how much individuals consume each period (the derivation is in Section 1.5.2 of the Appendix). When $\rho = r$, consumption is

$$C_t = \frac{r}{1+r} \Psi^E_t. \qquad \text{(PIH consumption function)}$$

The intuition is easy to understand: an individual with this consumption function will borrow and save to deliver a perfectly smooth consumption path (in expectation). The amount they consume each period is equal to the annuity value of expected lifetime wealth and is called 'permanent income'. The individual consumes their permanent income and the formula ensures that in expectation, they will be able to do this forever.

Predictions of the PIH

How does consumption react to a change in the interest rate? If the change in the interest rate is expected to persist in the long run, then a rise in the interest rate reduces the expected present value of lifetime income flows and therefore, permanent income and consumption. On the other hand, if the central bank raises the interest rate as a policy measure, this is a temporary change. Since a higher interest rate increases the opportunity cost of current consumption, it leads to a fall in C_t (the 'intertemporal substitution effect').

How does consumption react when a change in income occurs? The answer depends on the nature of the change in income. According to the PIH,

1. *Anticipated* or foreseen changes in income should have no effect on consumption when they occur. The reason is that anticipated changes will already have been incorporated into consumption through the recalculation of permanent income.

Hence, when the change in current income is recorded, the marginal propensity to consume is predicted to be zero (the multiplier is equal to one). A finding of '*excess sensitivity*' to anticipated income changes would contradict the full smoothing behaviour predicted by the PIH.

2. *News or unanticipated* changes in income should affect consumption because they require the recalculation of future lifetime wealth, Ψ_t^E.
   a. News of a temporary increase in income. If current income y_t increases unexpectedly by one unit, consumption increases by the extent to which this raises permanent income. Since the increase in one unit will be spread over the entire future, the PIH consumption function tells us that permanent income and hence consumption rise very little, just by $\frac{r}{1+r}$ times the increase in lifetime wealth. The marginal propensity to consume out of temporary income is $\frac{r}{1+r}$. (For example, if the real interest rate is 4 per cent, the MPC is 0.038, which implies a multiplier barely above one.) A finding of '*excess sensitivity*' of consumption to a temporary change in income would contradict the simple PIH.
   b. News of a permanent increase in income. If there is news that income y_t is higher from now and for every future period by one unit, then permanent income and hence consumption rise by the full one unit.[8] This means the marginal propensity to consume out of post-tax permanent income is one. A finding of '*excess smoothness*' of consumption in response to news of permanent income changes would contradict the simple PIH.

We shall see that the predictions of the simple PIH in relation to income changes are not supported by the facts.

Excess sensitivity to anticipated changes in income

The first testable hypothesis suggests that if the change in income was known in advance, there should be no change in consumption at the time income changes. This is because consumption should already have adjusted as soon as the news arrived of the change in future income. An influential study by Campbell and Mankiw (1989) tested this hypothesis econometrically using aggregate data on consumption and income from the G7 countries. The study rejected a model in which all consumers were following PIH and could not reject a model in which half of all consumers were simply following the 'rule of thumb' of spending their current income. In other words, they found that current consumption was overly sensitive to expected changes in income across the G7.

A study used the 2001 federal income tax rebates in the US as a testing ground: according to the PIH, the one-off (temporary) tax rebate should have very little effect on spending and if there is any effect, it should occur when the announcement was made and not when the cheques arrived. Johnson et al. (2006) were able to identify

---

[8] This can be derived using the PIH consumption function: $\Delta C_t = \frac{r}{1+r}\sum_{i=0}^{\infty}\left(\frac{\Delta y}{(1+r)^i}\right) = \frac{r}{1+r}\left(\frac{\Delta y}{1-\frac{1}{1+r}}\right) = \frac{r}{1+r}\frac{1+r}{r}\Delta y = \Delta y$

the causal effect of the tax rebate by using household data and the fact that the timing of the sending of cheques was based on the taxpayer's social security number, which is random. They found that the average household spent between 20–40% of the (predictable) tax rebate in the 3-month period when the cheque was received rather than when the programme was announced. They also found that it was households with low income and wealth that responded most, underlining the likely role of limits on the ability of households to borrow, i.e. credit constraints. This is referred to as the *excess sensitivity* of consumption and is evidence against the predictions of the PIH.[9]

A study by Ganong and Noel (2019) provides powerful evidence about consumption behaviour in forward-looking models even when they include credit constraints. This evidence suggests that the predictions of the PIH fail not only because many households are unable to borrow to smooth their consumption but also because of the cognitive trait of present-bias (also referred to as myopia or short-sightedness). A trait of present-bias means that the desire for consumption in the present outweighs the desire to smooth consumption.

We can learn from this study due to its focus on what happens to consumption when unemployment benefits run out. The setting is the US and centres on 17 states where entitlement to unemployment insurance benefits is exhausted after six months. The authors use bank account data for households where someone had a single spell of unemployment between September 2013 and June 2016 and observe what happens to consumption when the spell of unemployment begins and when it ends.

They find that consumption is highly sensitive to unemployment benefits. At the beginning of the spell of unemployment when wage income is replaced by unemployment benefit, consumption falls indicating an inability or unwillingness to smooth the drop in income while unemployed. For those still unemployed when eligibility to unemployment benefits ends at six months, consumption falls again. Since the termination of unemployment benefits is predictable, the sharp further drop in consumption at that time reflects a failure to save and build up a buffer stock in a run-up to the end date that would have enabled some smoothing. The drops in consumption are largest for households with the fewest liquid assets. They find that the MPC of unemployed households (0.8) is substantially higher than for employed households.

Responsiveness to news

Contrary to the PIH, studies have found that consumption responds strongly to temporary income shocks. An early example of this was the large consumption response of US veterans after the Second World War to an unexpected windfall payout of the National Service Life Insurance. This evidence questions the assumption in the PIH that households make optimizing decisions over a time horizon stretching a long way into the future and use a low discount rate (equal to the interest rate) to compare consumption at near and far horizons. The fact that people respond to a windfall by raising spending suggests that discount rates are higher than assumed in the simple

[9] For a detailed summary of the early literature on excess sensitivity see Deaton (1992). An excellent overview of the empirical testing of the excess sensitivity and excess smoothness hypotheses is provided by Jappelli and Pistaferri (2010).

PIH: people appear to be more *impatient* than the hypothesis assumes: they display 'present-bias'.

It is also likely that uncertainty about whether observed income changes are temporary or permanent prevents households from acting exactly as PIH would predict. For example, if a household mistakenly thought a temporary change in their current income was permanent, then they would consume more of the income change than would be consistent with PIH behaviour. Jappelli and Pistaferri (2010) review the evidence and suggest that it shows that consistent with the PIH, consumption responds more to permanent than transitory income shocks, but that households do not revise their consumption fully into line with permanent shocks.

Credit constraints, present-bias, and uncertainty

The evidence presented suggests there are four reasons for the failure of the simple PIH to provide an adequate model of aggregate consumption:

1. The presence of credit constraints, which prevent borrowing by households who lack wealth or collateral
2. Present-bias, which explains why some households do not smooth their consumption even when they could
3. Uncertainty about future income, which explains precautionary saving over and above the level predicted by the PIH
4. The particular role of house price increases and of house price bubbles (this is covered in Chapters 8 and 9)

Credit constraints

If people prefer to smooth their consumption, but are prevented from doing so because they cannot borrow to bring forward consumption when their current income is below their expected permanent income, they are said to face credit constraints. Because of information problems facing banks in assessing creditworthiness, banks are not always willing to lend to households without the wealth or collateral to secure a loan in order that they can smooth their consumption (see Chapter 5). Figure 1.8 shows the consumption response for PIH and credit-constrained households to an anticipated rise in income. The PIH households borrow to raise consumption as soon as the news of the future income increase is received, whereas the credit-constrained households do not have this option, so consumption can only rises when income does.

Estimates from studies using household data have found that around 20% of the population in the United States is credit constrained.[10] A much higher estimate of closer to two-thirds comes from a study of the way people respond to automatic increases in the limits on their credit cards: if spending responds to such automatic increases, it suggests the card-owner was credit constrained.[11]

---

[10] See Jappelli (1990), Mariger (1986) and Hall and Mishkin (1982).
[11] See Gross and Souleles (2002).

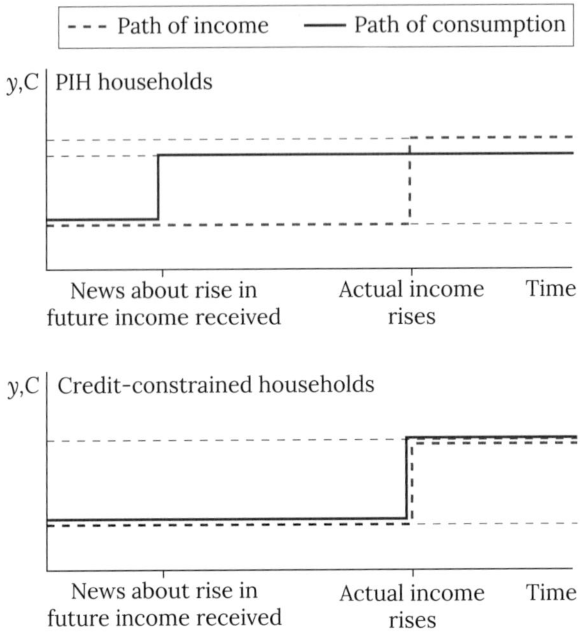

Figure 1.8 The consumption response of PIH and credit-constrained households to an anticipated rise in income.

Another explanation is that some households with wealth have few *liquid* assets, namely assets that can be easily sold and converted into money to use for consumption. Their spending would be expected to respond to higher credit card limits. These so-called wealthy hand-to-mouth own wealth in the form of equity in their house but the wealth is illiquid. This results in behaviour akin to that of low-income households without wealth: both have a high marginal propensity to consume (see the end of this section for a hybrid consumption function incorporating this phenomenon, and Chapter 18 for further details about recent research on this behaviour).

Present-bias

The observation that consumption of a substantial fraction of households changes one-for-one with their current income (i.e. very little borrowing or saving) reflects two features of the real world. One is the presence of credit constraints, which can prevent households from borrowing to smooth their consumption. This seems to especially affect young and low wealth households. Faced with a spell of unemployment, for example, constraints on borrowing will prevent a household from maintaining its level of consumption.

Whereas credit constraints can explain the inability of households to borrow to smooth consumption, it cannot explain the failure of some households to save, which would allow for some consumption smoothing without relying on access to loans.[12]

[12] For instance see Ganong and Noel (2019), which was described earlier in this chapter.

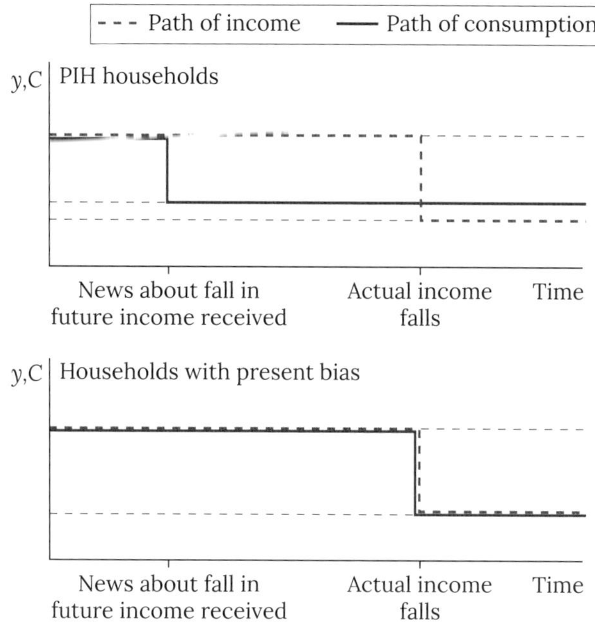

Figure 1.9 The consumption response of PIH and myopic households to an anticipated fall in income.

It seems that there are households who are not only credit constrained, but who also experience present-bias. Figure 1.9 shows the consumption response for PIH and myopic (i.e. present-bias) households to an anticipated fall in income. The PIH households start saving as soon as the news of the fall in future income is received, which allows them to smooth consumption over the two periods. In contrast, the households with present-bias fail to reduce current consumption upon receipt of the news, meaning consumption falls dramatically when income actually falls.

Experimental evidence on present-bias

The short-sightedness of households is represented in a model of consumption by a higher discount rate for the short run than the longer run. A simple illustration of what this means is to consider the following experiment: if you were choosing today for eating *next week*, would you choose fruit or chocolate? About three-quarters of experimental subjects choose fruit. When asked whether they would choose fruit or chocolate to eat *today*, 70% choose chocolate. From this, we can see that preferences are not consistent over time, because if we run time forward to next week, the three quarters who said they would prefer fruit would have shrunk to 30%. When next week comes, they would in fact, choose chocolate.[13]

[13] See Read and van Leeuwen (1998).

Present-bias is also documented in experiments related to consumption and saving behaviour. For example, subjects have a budget and can choose between two accounts paying the same interest rate: a 'freedom account' with no constraints on withdrawal or a 'commitment account' where there are restrictions on withdrawal before a date chosen by the participant. From a purely economic point of view the freedom account is preferable because it imposes no constraints on withdrawal. In spite of this, more than half of investment was put in the commitment account (no withdrawal before the goal date), which reveals the desire of the experimental subjects to commit themselves to saving.[14]

Very large differences between a high short-run and a low long-run discount rate help explain why people simultaneously save in illiquid assets such as housing (where the interest rate is low) and borrow on credit cards, paying a very high interest rate. Although a person can agree that their expected wellbeing is higher if they save more now, they are unable to resist consuming and blowing a hole in their saving plan when they get an unexpected increase in their income. One way of committing to saving is to take out a mortgage. Another is for the government to automatically enrol people in schemes for saving for retirement (from which they can opt out) such as pensions.

Uncertainty and precautionary saving

If there is uncertainty about future job opportunities or about health, then the household may want to save to insure themselves against future contingencies. For example, having a 'buffer stock of savings' could be important to sustain consumption in the event of job loss for a credit-constrained household.[15] In the face of uncertainty, households would tend to save more early in life than the PIH predicts with the result that consumption rises with income (not by more than income) early in the life cycle. If saving for a rainy day is important, then the utility provided by having assets to tide the household over if need be outweighs the utility that would have come from higher consumption in the early years.

House price changes and house price bubbles

Changes in the price of houses affects the consumption spending of credit-constrained home owners, including those with mortgages. A rise in house prices increases the owner's equity in the house, which means the value of their collateral is higher and banks will lend them more, enabling them to make purchases that had previously been constrained due to lack of credit. Home equity, banks and collateral are explained in Chapter 5, a model of house price bubbles and the collateral channel of consumption is developed in Chapter 8, and the role played by the impact on consumption of the house price boom and bust in the global financial crisis is covered in Chapter 9.

---

[14] See Ashraf et al. (2006).

[15] See Carroll (1997) for an exposition of the buffer-stock savings model.

An empirical consumption function

We now consider a consumption function estimated on macroeconomic data for the UK, US and Japan.[16] The empirical model allows for *permanent income considerations* to affect consumption; households will have a notion of sustainable consumption constrained by their budget, which includes their income forecasts. They will therefore know that they cannot spend their existing assets now without impairing future consumption and that future income affects their sustainable consumption.

In addition to permanent income considerations based on forecasts, the consumption function that is estimated includes the following factors.

1. Consumption is predicted to respond more strongly to current income than the PIH predicts due to the presence of *credit constraints and present-bias*. This is modelled by a high discount rate on future income.
2. Because of income uncertainty, households save for *precautionary reasons*. Income uncertainty is measured by the change in the unemployment rate; an increase is predicted to reduce consumption.
3. *Credit conditions* matter. Higher house prices interact with increased credit availability to increase consumption. The presence of this *collateral effect* depends on the institutional arrangements for mortgage borrowing in the country in question. In some countries, home equity loans are available: this is a loan secured against the equity in an individual's home. (Home equity is the difference between the current market value of the house and the remaining mortgage, hence it increases as house prices rise.) When credit conditions are eased, the collateral effect operates to boost consumption. In countries where it is not possible to get a home equity loan, as in France, Germany, Japan and China, this channel does not operate. In fact, if home equity loans are unavailable and high down-payments are required to get a mortgage (as in Japan), then higher house prices can actually dampen consumer spending as young people have to save more to accumulate the required down-payment.
4. The current *real interest rate*. There are many interest rate channels, some of which point to a negative and some to a positive effect of a higher real interest rate on consumption.
5. Increases in households' *wealth to income ratio* are expected to increase consumption.

The empirical consumption function includes the housing and financial variables that are at the centre of the discussion in Chapters 5, 8, and 9, where the banking system, financial cycles and financial crises are brought into the macro model.

For the UK and US, the estimated consumption functions suggest that roughly 50 per cent of household consumption is accounted for by permanent income considerations. Current income has an important positive effect on consumption and the real interest

---

[16] See Aron et al. (2012). Muellbauer (2022) provides a guide to how the ECB and European central banks model the consumption function to include the role of housing.

rate has a negative effect. The wealth to income ratio has a positive effect but different types of wealth have different effects. For example, *liquid wealth* in the form of cash in a bank or savings account is more spendable than pension wealth. And the evidence is that for a given degree of access to new credit, higher debt of \$100 reduces consumer spending more than higher pension or stock market wealth of \$100 increases spending.

For the US and UK, where home equity loans are important, increased credit availability and house prices interact to raise consumption through the collateral effect. A house price boom in conditions where access to credit is easier, boosts consumption.

Aggregate consumption and current income: A hybrid consumption function

For the macroeconomic model, we bring together insights from the PIH with the evidence on credit constraints and present-bias to derive a hybrid aggregate consumption function. This has the same form as the Keynesian consumption function, ($c_t = c_0 + c_1(1-t)y_t$) and both provides a realistic average marginal propensity to consume and associated multiplier for use in the IS curve and matches the empirical evidence that is accruing about so-called hand-to-mouth household consumption behaviour.

When income increases, hand-to-mouth (HTM) households consume all of this so their MPC is equal to one. This behaviour is characteristic of households without wealth and with present-bias. Moreover, there are also richer households who display the same hand-to-mouth behaviour. These are typically households with mortgages and although they have some home equity wealth, this is illiquid. They could save and borrow to smooth fluctuations in income but are observed not to do so, preferring as discussed above to put their savings into illiquid wealth and as a result to experience a less smooth consumption path (for further detail, see Chapter 18).

To derive a hybrid consumption function, we assume that the share of PIH households is σ (sigma) and of HTM households is $(1-\sigma)$. Then:

$$c_t = \sigma c_t^{PIH} + (1-\sigma)c_t^{HTM}$$

$$\text{Using} \quad c_t^{PIH} = \frac{r}{1+r}\Psi_t^E + \frac{r}{1+r}y_t \quad \text{and}$$

$$c_t^{HTM} = y_t, \quad \text{we have}$$

$$\begin{aligned} c_t &= \sigma\frac{r}{1+r}\Psi_t^E + \sigma\frac{r}{1+r}y_t + (1-\sigma)y_t \\ &= \sigma\hat{c}_0 + \underbrace{\left[\sigma\frac{r}{1+r} + (1-\sigma)\right]}_{c_1} y_t, \quad \text{where} \end{aligned}$$

$$\hat{c}_0 \equiv \frac{r}{1+r}\Psi_t^E \quad \text{and } \sigma \text{ is the share of PIH households} \tag{1.13}$$

Note that since the first term in the square brackets is small, the MPC is closely approximated by the share of HTM households.

From the hybrid consumption function, we see that changes in expected lifetime wealth shift the consumption function through the 'autonomous consumption' term, as does a change in the share of PIH households. The marginal propensity to consume increases with the proportion of hand-to-mouth households, which may rise in a recession when the risk of unemployment goes up.

The Keynesian consumption function is a simplified version of the hybrid consumption function; both imply the presence of a multiplier above one in the macro model. There is one point to clarify: the y_t in the Keynesian consumption function is pre-tax income whereas in the PIH, y_t, refers to post tax income.

To make the hybrid consumption function consistent with notation in the rest of the macro model, we write it as:

$$c_t = \sigma \hat{c}_0 + \left[\sigma \frac{r}{1+r} + (1-\sigma)\right](1-t)y_t, \quad \text{where}$$

$$\hat{c}_0 = \frac{r}{1+r}\Psi_t^E \quad \text{and } \Psi_t^E \text{ now refers to expected post-tax lifetime wealth}$$

(hybrid consumption function)

1.2.6 **Investment**

The decision a firm makes of whether to invest or not will depend on their expectations about future after tax profits. The role of expectations helps explain the excess volatility of investment over the other components of GDP visible in Figure 1.1. In developing the IS equation, we used a simple linear relation to model investment in Section 1.2.3, where the amount of investment depended positively on expected future profits (captured by the constant term, a_0) and negatively on the real interest rate (a measure of firms' borrowing costs). In this subsection we introduce a more sophisticated forward-looking modelling approach—the q theory of investment.

Tobin's *q* theory of investment

This theory was developed by Nobel Prize winner James Tobin.[17] Like the PIH, Tobin's q theory of investment is forward looking. Firms choose the amount of investment to undertake with a view to maximizing the expected discounted profits over the lifetime of the project. The q theory amounts to comparing the benefits from investment in an increase in the capital stock with the costs of doing so: if the expected benefits exceed the costs, investment should take place.

Marginal and average q models

The theory is derived explicitly in Section 1.5.3 of the Appendix, but it is useful to set out the equation for *marginal* q here, as it provides a framework for thinking about forward-looking investment decisions:

$$q = \frac{\text{Marginal benefit of investment}}{\text{Marginal cost of investment}} = \frac{Af_K}{\delta + r}. \qquad \text{(marginal } q \text{ model of investment)}$$

The firm's production function is $y_t = Af(N_t, Kt)$ with the inputs of labour and capital and the level of technology, A, which will rise with technological progress. The marginal product of capital is denoted by f_k, δ is the rate at which capital depreciates and r is the rate of interest.

The model is intrinsically forward looking since the firm is considering the future benefits from investment spending now. Before looking at the expression on the right,

[17] See Tobin (1969) and Tobin and Brainard (1977).

we note that the optimal amount of investment occurs when $q = 1$. This is where the expected marginal benefit of investment is equal to the expected marginal cost. Thus, if $q > 1$, the marginal benefit of investment exceeds the marginal cost, so firms should invest to increase the capital stock until $q = 1$. If $q < 1$ firms should reduce their capital stock.

It is important to note that the q theory of investment optimizes firms' investment decisions (a flow) by pinning down the optimal capital stock. Small changes in the desired capital stock can therefore translate into large changes in the flow of investment. This is one reason why investment is more volatile than GDP (see Figure 1.1).

The marginal benefits from investment are higher and a firm should undertake more investment if there is:

1. an improvement in technology, A,
2. an increase in the marginal productivity of capital, f_K which, once multiplied by A, indicates the increase in output produced by the new capital equipment,
3. a reduction in the rate of interest, r; or
4. a reduction in the rate of depreciation, δ. For example, a rise in the expected rate of depreciation (e.g. as a result of uncertainty about future legislation banning fossil-fuel-using cars) would lead to a reduction in the level of current investment because it would reduce the expected benefits to the firm from additional investment in the auto industry.

Is q theory a good way to represent real-world investment behaviour? Marginal q implies firms adjust their level of investment in each period to equate the marginal benefits and marginal costs of investment. This does not fit with the real-world data on investment. When economists looked at detailed microeconomic data for very large numbers of plants, they found that contrary to the idea of a smooth investment flow, investment was in fact very bunched.[18] For example, a growing manufacturing firm might build a new factory once every 10 years.

The share price as indicator of expected profits

Testing q theory directly is difficult because q itself is difficult to measure. This is because it depends on the marginal product of capital and a measure of technology, which cannot be observed. In the real world, firms do not know their production functions and do not think explicitly in terms of marginal products. To operationalize the theory, the market value of the firm as reflected in its stock market valuation is compared with the replacement cost of the capital stock. If the market value is higher then this signals that the firm should increase investment. On the other hand if the market value is below the replacement cost, then the firm would not want to build a *new* factory because it could buy an existing one more cheaply.

---

[18] See the survey chapter on 'Investment' by Caballero (1999).

We can define average Q as follows:

$$Q = \frac{\text{Market value of firm}}{\text{Replacement cost of capital}}. \qquad \text{(average Q model of investment)}$$

This is often called *average* Q to distinguish it from marginal q. Whereas q is the ratio of the marginal benefit of a unit of investment to its marginal cost, Q depends on the total expected return from the firm's capital divided by the total cost. For publicly listed companies, the stock market provides a forward-looking measure of the market value of the firm, which can be used in the numerator of the Q equation: when a firm's market value rises relative to its replacement cost firm, as reflected in a rise in the price of its shares, the model suggests that investment should go up. A higher interest rate and depreciation rate will raise the replacement cost of capital.

The idea is that the market value incorporates information about how well the firm is expected to be able to implement the investment, whether new competitors will enter the market, whether there are new technological innovations likely to affect the firm's value, the state of the macroeconomy and the labour market; and the future path of the interest rate. Since investing in a firm is a wager on this uncertain future, investors continuously evaluate these factors and, under certain conditions, the share price and hence the market value of the firm will reflect all the information available.

The stock market is notoriously volatile. For example, in 2008 as the financial crisis gathered pace, the UK's leading share index—the FTSE 100—fell 31% and GDP contracted by just 1.1%. The following year, the FTSE 100 rose 22%, while GDP continued to contract, but this time by 4.4%.[19] In times of extreme uncertainty, the share price may not reflect the fundamental value of a firm. Large movements in share prices heavily affect market capitalization, which is the measure used to proxy for the market value of the firm in the calculation of average Q. As the stock market is volatile and subject to bubbles, fads and herd behaviour, it may not be a good indicator of the firm's prospects.

However, a study using US micro data (over 1,000 firms from 1982 to 1999) shows that a Q model of investment can be successfully estimated when analysts' forecasts of a firm's profits are used instead of the stock market price to measure the numerator in the Q equation.[20]

Empirical evidence on investment

The empirical evidence on the q theory is that Q helps to explain investment but it is not the only influence. In particular, just as was the case for consumption, credit constraints play an important role in explaining investment spending.

Credit constraints—the role of cash flow

A testable prediction of q theory is that current cash flow should have no impact on investment. The reason is that forward-looking firms should take into account

---

[19] GDP data from IMF World Economic Outlook database, April 2012. Stock market data from Bloomberg News articles.

[20] See Bond and Cummins (2001).

any credit constraints that they face: these should already be incorporated into the stock market valuation, Q. However, the role of cash flow in empirical studies of investment suggests that *capital market imperfections* are important. The importance of cash flow variables in estimated investment equations is reminiscent of the role of current income in consumption functions. As we have seen, the presence of credit-constrained households causes excess sensitivity of consumption to predictable changes in income. Similarly, the presence of cash flow terms in estimated investment functions strongly suggests that firms are credit constrained. Although some firms are able to borrow as much or sell as much equity as they would like in order to finance their investment plans, for others, their investment will be limited by their internal funds. This is referred to as the *excess sensitivity of investment to internal funds*. For firms like this, cash flow is an important determinant of investment.[21]

A study using UK company data for the period 1975–86 found that company investment was significantly influenced by Q and by credit constraints.[22] However, the impact of Q was found to be very small: a 10% rise in the stock market value of a company was associated with an immediate rise in the investment rate of only 2.5%. Cash flow, on the other hand, was very important. The sample period was divided into two and it was found that the impact of Q was lower and the impact of cash flow higher in the first part of the sample during which the UK economy was in a deep recession. This is consistent with the idea of credit constraints biting especially hard in a recession.

Uncertainty—the option value of waiting

The decision of firms of whether to invest or not is also influenced by uncertainty about the future. Under certain circumstances, there can be a value to waiting to undertake an investment project. With the passing of time, more information arrives, which means that the costs of delay in lost profits may be outweighed by more secure information on the balance between the costs (including those sunk in the project) and the benefits of undertaking it. The upshot of such considerations is that an expected rate of return considerably higher than the cost of capital will be required to trigger investment. Dixit (1992) gives examples to show that including the so-called 'option value of waiting' can double the hurdle rate (i.e. the return required to trigger investment) for an investment project to proceed.

Because there is a limited second-hand market in capital goods, net investment decisions are largely irreversible. For those decisions to be taken, management must have strong positive views about the future growth of the markets for its products. In the absence of such positive expectations, the firm will invest little so as to reduce its risk.[23] In recessions, uncertainty about market growth is high and the 'wait and see' behaviour prevails keeping investment depressed. The Covid-19 crisis in 2020 created great uncertainty about when businesses would be able to trade again. The effect on investment extended well beyond large firms. A survey of self-employed workers in

[21] See, for example, Chirinko (1993).

[22] See Blundell et al. (1992).

[23] See Bloom (2014) and Bloom et al. (2007).

the UK in April 2020 found that 44% of respondents reported delaying or cancelling investment in work equipment.[24]

Investment and animal spirits

Tobin's q theory suggests that new, smaller firms should invest more because their marginal benefit from additional investment usually outweighs the marginal cost. However, a harsh truth is that the majority of new firms fail; according to the Bureau of Labor Statistics, approximately 20% of small businesses fail within the first year, and around 70% fail by the end of the first decade.[25] Investment requires some form of 'spontaneous optimism' on the side of firms. John Maynard Keynes referred to such spontaneity in his General Theory as 'animal spirits':[26]

> Most, probably, of our decisions to do something positive, the full consequences of which will be drawn out over many days to come, can only be taken as the result of animal spirits—a spontaneous urge to action rather than inaction, and not as the outcome of a weighted average of quantitative benefits multiplied by quantitative probabilities.

Therefore, we often fail to explain a firm's decision to invest by looking at the ratio of its stock market value to replacement cost of capital. Jack Welch, former General Electric CEO, said he had little use for analytical projections and rational business plans. He said the most important business decisions come 'straight from the gut'.[27]

Using survey data to understand aggregate investment

Fresh insights into the determinants of aggregate investment come from survey data in which managers in German manufacturing firms were asked about the importance of sales, expected returns, financial and technological factors in their investment decisions in a given year (Bachmann and Zorn 2020). Economists have traditionally been sceptical about the value of survey data but well-designed econometric techniques are able to make this 'soft' data interpretable.

The main findings are that financial factors such as borrowing costs are unimportant in explaining both the level and fluctuations in investment. The bulk of the explanation for what drives aggregate investment is 'the sales situation and expectations'—expected demand for the firm's output. This is consistent with the importance of uncertainty in investment decisions: managers look for signals about the strength of demand before committing to irreversible investment.

These findings underline the limited role in explaining the pattern of investment in Figure 1.1 played by changes in the interest rate: it is the expected returns from expanding capacity to meet additional demand for their output that lie behind the troughs and peaks of business investment.

---

[24] See Blundell and Machin (2020).
[25] Statistics extracted from the BLS—Establishment Age and Survival Data, updated 2020.
[26] Excerpt from page 161–162 of Keynes (1936).
[27] Quote from Welch and Byrne (2003).

1.3 APPLICATIONS

1.3.1 The demand side and inequality

One of the challenges for students of macroeconomics is to understand how the rising inequality that has characterized the high-income countries over the past forty years affects business cycles and growth.

Research confirms that rising inequality in the distribution of income is reproduced in rising consumption inequality. This means that a proportion of households are unable to fully insure themselves so as to smooth their consumption through borrowing and by building up 'buffer stocks' for use in hard times.[28]

Inequality matters for the business cycle because low-income workers are both credit constrained and more exposed to the risk of unemployment in a downturn. This interaction has the effect of increasing the size of the multiplier in the economy as a whole, making recessions deeper and booms stronger than would otherwise be the case. As we shall see when we introduce the policy maker, this makes the need for policy intervention to dampen a recession more important and boosts its effectiveness.

Figure 1.10 illustrates how the marginal propensity to consume varies across categories of workers in the US. It is highest among young, black and low-income workers. Research by Patterson (2020) provides evidence for the conjecture that demographic groups with higher marginal propensities to consume are more exposed to recessions. For example, black men between the ages of 25 and 35 with earnings less than \$22,000 have an average MPC of above 1 and their earnings are very sensitive to fluctuations in the economy as a whole because of their high risk of unemployment (a fall in GDP by 1 percent sees their earnings fall by 2 percent). By contrast, non-black women with earnings of \$48,000 to \$65,000 have a much lower MPC and their earnings hardly change when GDP does because they have a low risk of losing their job in a recession.

As wealth becomes more unequally distributed, so too do marginal propensities to consume. At the same time, inequalities in the labour market measured by the probability of job loss affect those with low wealth. These two effects interact to deepen recessions.

The empirical evidence of variations in the MPC across households is captured in a simple way in the model of consumption by the presence of hand-to-mouth households in the hybrid consumption function in Section 1.2.5.

1.3.2 Consumption, investment, and the *IS* curve

In Section 1.2.4, we introduced models of consumption and investment that took account of forward-looking behaviour. Expectations of future income and of future profits play a key role in the spending decisions of households and firms. We also reported empirical evidence on aggregate consumption and investment, which highlighted the role of credit constraints for households and firms. What are the implications for the IS curve?

---

[28] See Attanasio and Pistaferri (2016) for an overview of the relationship between income inequality and consumption inequality.

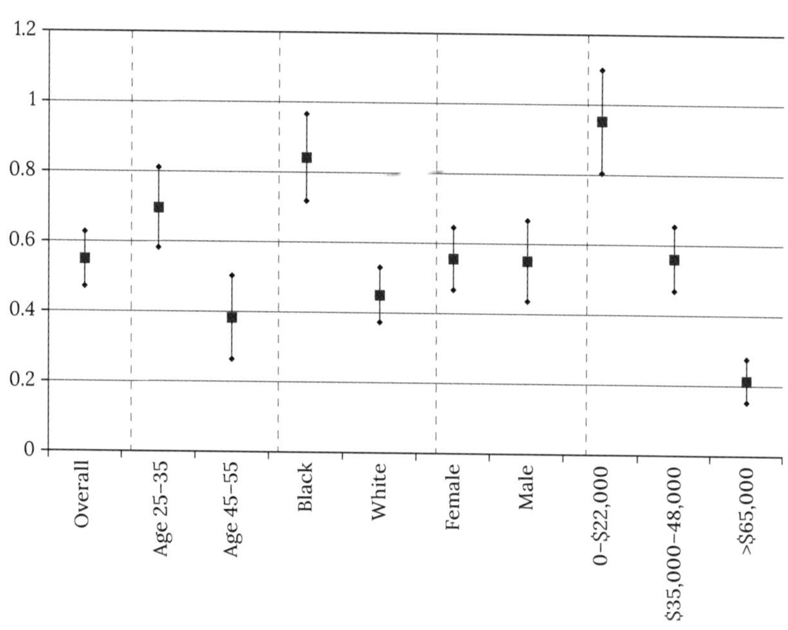

Figure 1.10 Marginal Propensity to Consume (MPC) for different groups in the United States.

Note: Uses data from the PSID. Each estimate is derived from a separate regression including only the stated demographic group. The author used unemployment to instrument for income changes. The squares denote estimated MPC, while the lines show the 5% to 95% confidence interval.

Source: Patterson, C. (2020) The Matching Multiplier and the Amplification of Recessions. The Washington Center for Equitable Growth 040820-WP.

The basic form of the IS curve was presented in Section 1.2.3 and we shall see that we can bring together the additional insights about consumption and investment by focusing on the factors that affect the slope of the IS curve and which shift it.

The IS equation is:

$$y = k(c_0 + a_0 + G) - ka_1 r \quad (1.14)$$

$$= A - ar, \quad \text{(IS curve)}$$

where $A \equiv k(c_0 + a_0 + G)$ and $a \equiv ka_1$; k is the multiplier, which in the hybrid consumption function is increased by the proportion of hand-to-mouth households. Remember that the MPC in the hybrid consumption function is approximately equal to the proportion of HTM households.

A larger multiplier makes the IS curve flatter, which increases the impact on output of a change in the interest rate; it also increases the impact on output of a shift in c_0, a_0 or G for a given interest rate. Thus, the size of the multiplier is important for understanding the effectiveness of both fiscal and monetary policy.

As we shall see in Chapter 7 on fiscal policy, there was much debate about the empirical size of the multiplier in the context of the use of fiscal stimulus to respond to global financial crisis. In the context of policy making, the answers to questions about the size of the government spending multiplier depend on characteristics of the economy and on the context in which a fiscal stimulus is being applied.

The slope of the IS curve is affected by the interest sensitivity of investment and of consumption. The theoretical prediction on the impact of the interest rate on consumption is ambiguous; a reduction in interest rates boosts consumption through some channels and dampens it through others. From the Euler equation (or indeed, the 2-period model of intertemporal substitution), we know that the substitution effect of a rise in the interest rate leads households to shift consumption to the future thereby cutting consumption in the current period. The income effect (for savers) goes in the opposite direction, raising current consumption, whereas for borrowers, for whom a rise in the interest rate reduces their income, the substitution effect is reinforced. The empirical evidence on the consumption function suggests that national institutional structures, particularly in relation to the housing market, are important for determining the strength and direction of the relationship. Aron et al. (2012) find a negative relationship between consumption and the real interest rate in the financially liberalized UK and US economies, but they find a positive relationship in Japan, where households' huge liquid deposits (on which interest is paid) far outweigh household debt.

Looking first at consumption, the PIH (and hybrid consumption function) predict that the IS curve is shifted by anything that changes expected lifetime wealth, Ψ_t^E, such as changes in asset prices or in perceptions about future earnings arising, for example, from widespread fears about skill obsolescence. The empirical findings about consumption highlight three other factors that can shift the IS curve:

1. The role of uncertainty: a rise in the rate of unemployment will raise savings for precautionary purposes, shifting the IS to the left.
2. A boom in house prices will boost consumption in a country with home equity loans by loosening credit constraints, shifting the IS to the right. However, a house price boom could also shift the IS to the left in countries where home equity loans are unobtainable and large down-payments are needed to get a mortgage.
3. A shift in credit market architecture that increases household access to credit, such as financial innovation or deregulation, will shift the IS to the right (at least until the effect of the accumulation of debt eventually offsets some of the shift).

Turning our attention to investment, Tobin's marginal q predicts that the following factors will shift the IS curve to the right:

1. An improvement in technology, A,
2. An increase in the marginal productivity of capital, f_K; and
3. A reduction in the rate of depreciation, δ.

Lastly, the average Q equation highlights the role of expectations of future profits as a shift factor for the IS curve: a rise in the stock market tends to boost fixed investment as it signals a rise in the value of companies relative to their replacement cost. Research emphasizes the importance of expectations of future market growth for investment given that much investment is irreversible.

1.4 CONCLUSIONS

This chapter has provided the first building block in the model of the macroeconomy. We have set out the IS curve, which is used to model the demand side of the economy and is one of the three equations that underpin the 3-equation model that will form the core model of this textbook.

The IS curve allows us to think systematically about how changes in the spending behaviour of firms, households and governments can influence output and drive business cycles. The IS curve shows the combinations of the real interest rate and output where the goods market is in equilibrium. It slopes downwards to account for the fact that households' consumption and new housing decisions respond negatively to the interest rate; firms will also undertake fewer investment projects as the cost of borrowing increases.

We return to the questions at the start of the modelling section (1.2) and see how the model we have developed helps us work towards an answer. This acts as an exercise to summarize what we have learnt in this chapter.

1. If you give an individual a \$100 bonus, how much of it will they spend? This depends on the model of household spending we are using. If consumer behaviour is well modelled by a Keynesian consumption function (i.e. $C_t = c_0 + c_1(1-t)y_t$) then households will spend a fixed proportion of any extra income they receive. In the case of a \$100 bonus, they will spend everything left over once they have paid tax and put some money into savings. However, if consumer behaviour is better modelled by the permanent income hypothesis (PIH), then individuals' current consumption is a function of their expected lifetime wealth (i.e. $C_t = \left(\frac{r}{1+r}\right)\Psi_t^E$). As the bonus is a one-off, it will only increase expected lifetime wealth by a small amount, resulting in a small increase in consumption in this and all future periods. This leads the individual to save the majority of the bonus in the current period. The hybrid consumption function provides a useful basis for the consumption component of the IS curve as illustrated in Section 1.3.2, where we showed how the relative proportions HTM and PIH households in the economy affect the multiplier and the IS curve. From Section 1.3.1, we know that inequality affects the multiplier through its effect on the average marginal propensity to consume.
2. How much will output increase following a rise in autonomous demand, such as higher government spending or a boost in the confidence of households and firms? The multiplier will determine the extent to which an €x increase in autonomous demand will increase output. In the simple model presented in Section 1.2.1 and the one based on the hybrid consumption function in Section 1.2.5, the multiplier is always greater than 1, as both c_1 and t are between zero and one. This means that in the short run, an injection of autonomous demand will always boost output more than one for one. The extent of the boost of output will depend on the size of the

multiplier. The multiplier will be larger if the tax rate (t) is low and there is a high average marginal propensity to consume (c_1).

The PIH draws attention to the difference between temporary and permanent changes in income and that distinction will become important in the analysis of tax changes.

3. To what extent will a rise in the interest rate curtail investment? In the simple model in Section 1.2.3, where $I = a_0 - a_1 r$, a rise in the interest rate of Δr will reduce investment by $a_1 \Delta r$. In the marginal q theory of investment (with $q = \frac{Af_K}{\delta + r}$), an increase in the interest rate will increase the marginal cost of investment. If we assume that q is initially equal to one (i.e. the marginal cost and marginal benefit of carrying out the investment project are equal) then an increase in r will lead firms to reduce investment. The extent to which investment will fall depends on how quickly the marginal productivity of capital (f_K) rises as investment falls to bring q back toward a value of 1.

   From the empirical evidence, business investment is not very sensitive to the interest rate. This focuses attention on shifts in the IS curve.

This chapter has provided a model of the demand side which can shed light on macroeconomic questions. We have discussed how the models of consumption and investment relate to characteristics of the real world. For example, the greater volatility of investment as compared with consumption observed in the data can be partly explained by the factors that influence investment spending decisions and by consumers borrowing and saving to smooth their consumption over the economic cycle. Households vary—some are myopic and find it difficult to save whereas others are prudent and save for precautionary reasons. Inequality is a major determinant of the variation in household consumption behaviour. Credit constraints facing both households and firms help better align the models of consumption and investment with the empirical data.

Although the demand side is an important influence on economic activity, it is only part of the story of how the macroeconomy works. To develop our understanding of economic fluctuations and longer-run trends, we need to introduce the supply side. This will provide a framework for thinking about how wages and prices are set and what determines the unemployment rate. The supply side is the subject of Chapter 2.

1.5 APPENDIX

1.5.1 Real and nominal interest rates, and the Fisher equation

To clarify why it is the real rather than the nominal interest rate that affects real expenditure decisions in the economy, think about a firm considering an investment project. A higher money or nominal rate of interest will not impose a greater real burden on the firm if it is balanced by correspondingly higher inflation because the expected profits from the investment project will be higher in money terms and the balance between the real cost and the real return on the project will not have changed.

The real interest rate is defined in terms of *goods* and the nominal interest rate, in terms of *money*. Thinking of a consumer good, the real rate of interest, r, is how much extra in terms of this good—namely $(1+r)$ units—would have to be paid in the future in order to borrow one unit of the goods today. The nominal rate of interest is how much extra in euros would have to be paid in the future in order to have one euro today. If goods prices remain constant then it is clear that the real and nominal interest rates are the same: if you lent one euro today, you would be able to buy $(1+r)$ goods in the future. In general,

$$1 + r_t = (1 + i_t) \cdot \frac{P_t}{P^E_{t+1}},$$

where it is the expected price level in the future (P^E_{t+1}) that comes into play since at time t, we do not know what the price level will be at $t+1$. If we use the following definition of expected inflation:

$$\pi^E_{t+1} = \frac{P^E_{t+1} - P_t}{P_t},$$

then

$$\frac{P_t}{P^E_{t+1}} = \frac{1}{1 + \pi^E_{t+1}}.$$

By rearranging the above expression, it follows that

$$(1 + r_t) = \frac{(1 + i_t)}{(1 + \pi^E_{t+1})},$$

and therefore that

$$r_t = \frac{i_t - \pi^E_{t+1}}{1 + \pi^E_{t+1}}.$$

When expected inflation is low, the denominator of this expression is close to 1 and we have the standard approximation for the relationship between the real and the nominal rate of interest:

$$i_t \approx r_t + \pi^E_{t+1}. \qquad \text{(Fisher equation)}$$

Inflation expectations will drive the divergence between the real and nominal interest rates. It should be noted that only one of these three terms is observable: the nominal interest rate, i. The real interest rate can be estimated from historical data on the nominal interest rate and the rate of inflation: this gives a measure of the so-called *ex post* real rate of interest. Alternatively, an *ex ante* measure can be derived from a model that is able to predict inflation. Finally, if bonds have been issued in the economy that are protected against inflation because the face value is indexed by the rate of inflation, then the yield on such a bond is a real rate of interest and can provide a third measure. But there are only a few countries that have issued index-linked or inflation-proof bonds (UK in 1981, the US in 1997, France in 1998).

1.5.2 Deriving the Euler equation and the PIH consumption function

Deriving the Euler equation

The first step in deriving the Euler equation is to set out an expression for the present value of a consumer's utility:

$$V_t^E = U(C_t) + \frac{U(C_{t+1}^E)}{1+\rho} + \frac{U(C_{t+2}^E)}{(1+\rho)^2} + \ldots \qquad \text{(expected present value of consumption)}$$

The present value equation uses the expectations operator (i.e. C_{t+i}^E for all $i > 0$) to show that future consumption is uncertain in the present period. In addition, the utility of consumption is discounted to the present period by the consumer's rate of time preference. Future consumption will be worth less in the current period to more impatient consumers.

To derive the Euler equation we need to assume a specific functional form for the utility function. We choose $U(C_t) = \log C_t$ because it exhibits diminishing marginal returns and is easy to work with. We can take the first differential of the utility function to find the marginal utility of consumption, which is $U'(C_t) = \frac{1}{C_t}$.

The Euler equation shows the optimal C_t in relation to C_{t+1}^E. If we just think about these two periods, then it is easy to derive the Euler equation. In period t the consumer must weigh up the gain from consuming more in this period, against the discounted loss of consuming less in the next period. The expected present value of consumption is effectively a discounted sum of within-period utilities. We may call this an 'additive utility function'. Clearly, an optimal consumption path is one that maximizes the additive utility function subject to the individual's budget constraint. In the case of just two periods, this is the same as saying that the marginal utility from consuming an additional unit of wealth today is equal to the marginal utility of consuming (1+r) units of wealth in the following period; this is because saving one unit of wealth today means having (1+r) units to spend in the following period; we can think of (1+r) as being the ratio of the price of consumption in period t and its price in period (t+1). However, marginal utility from consumption in the next period must be discounted by the individual's rate of impatience. Therefore, the additive utility function is maximized when:

$$U'(C_t) = \frac{1+r}{1+\rho} U'(C_{t+1}^E). \qquad \text{(Euler equation)}$$

Setting $U(C) = \log C$, the Euler equation becomes:

$$\frac{1}{C_t} = \frac{1+r}{1+\rho} \frac{1}{C_{t+1}^E}$$

$$\rightarrow C_t = \frac{1+\rho}{1+r} C_{t+1}^E. \qquad (1.15)$$

Deriving the permanent income hypothesis consumption function

The simplest case of the Euler equation is when the rate of interest is equal to the consumer's subjective discount rate $r = \rho$. This is the case we have focused on throughout this chapter. We can see from the Euler equation that this implies $C_t = C_{t+1}^E$. In other words, it implies that consumption is constant in expectation in all future periods.

In order to derive the permanent income hypothesis, we make the additional assumption that future consumption is known with certainty, so that $C_t = C_{t+1} = .. = C_{t+i} = C$. To calculate C we need to set out the expression for the present value of consumption, $\overline{C_t}$:

$$\overline{C_t} = C_t + \frac{C_{t+1}}{1+r} + ... + \frac{C_{t+i}}{(1+r)^i} + .. = C\left(1 + \frac{1}{1+r} + ... + \frac{1}{(1+r)^i} + ...\right)$$

$$= C\left(\frac{1}{1-\frac{1}{1+r}}\right) = C\left(\frac{1+r}{r}\right). \qquad \text{(present value of consumption)}$$

The permanent income hypothesis implies that the present value of consumption has to be equal to the present value of income, Ψ_t^E, so that:

$$\overline{C_t} = C\left(\frac{1+r}{r}\right) = \Psi_t^E$$

$$C_t = C = \left(\frac{r}{1+r}\right)\Psi_t^E, \qquad \text{(PIH consumption function)}$$

where C_t is the amount the consumer consumes in each period. It is their permanent income and is equal to the annuity value of their expected lifetime wealth.

1.5.3 Tobin's *q* theory of investment

Just as households choose consumption to maximize the present value of their expected utility, firms choose investment to maximize the present value of their expected profits V_t, such that

$$V_t = E_t \sum_{i=0}^{\infty} \frac{1}{(1+r)^i} \Pi_{t+i}, \qquad (1.16)$$

where Π is the profit the firm makes in any period and r is the real interest rate. To choose the level of investment that maximizes the present value of their expected profits, firms will want to invest up until the point where the marginal benefits (MB) of investment are equal to the marginal costs (MC).

The simplest way of thinking about this problem is to take the case where a company invests 1 unit. We assume that it pays 1 for the investment immediately. We then need to work out the marginal benefits and costs to the company of this extra unit of investment. The marginal benefit is the present value of the resultant stream of profits (i.e. the additional profits the investment will allow the company to make over its lifetime, discounted to the present period).

The production function of a firm shows how much output the firm can produce from a given amount of inputs. If we denote the firm's output as y_t, then we can write the production function as $y_t = Af(N_t, K_t)$, where N and K are the inputs of production—labour and capital, and A is a measure of technology. The within-period benefit of investing an additional unit of capital is given by its marginal product, i.e. the partial derivative of output y_t with respect to capital, which gives us Af_K. If the investment is made in period t, the company will receive this benefit in every future period. We also need to take account of interest payments and depreciation to calculate the present value marginal benefit of the investment.

We assume the output from the investment comes at the end of each period, as does the payment of interest r, which the company could have got from investing 1 elsewhere; and that the investment depreciates by δ each period, which is paid at the beginning of the following period; these assumptions imply that the marginal benefits (MB) are given by:

$$\begin{aligned} MB &= Af_K\left(\frac{1}{1+r}+\frac{1-\delta}{(1+r)^2}+\frac{(1-\delta)^2}{(1+r)^3}+\ldots\right) \\ &= Af_K\left(\frac{1}{1+r}\right)\left(1+\frac{1-\delta}{1+r}+\frac{(1-\delta)^2}{(1+r)^2}+\ldots\right). \end{aligned} \tag{1.17}$$

The last term in equation 1.17 is a geometric series with a first term of 1 and a ratio of $\frac{1-\delta}{1+r}$, so its sum to infinity is $\left(\frac{1}{1-\frac{1-\delta}{1+r}}\right)=\left(\frac{1+r}{r+\delta}\right)$. This means equation 1.17 becomes

$$MB = \frac{Af_K}{r+\delta}. \qquad \text{(marginal benefit of investment)}$$

The marginal benefits need to be equal to the marginal costs for the firm to maximize their lifetime profits. The marginal cost of the investment is 1 in this simple case. The firm has invested 1 unit, which could instead have been distributed as current profits to shareholders. Hence, equating marginal benefits and marginal costs of 1 extra unit of investment:

$$\frac{Af_K}{\delta+r} = 1 = \frac{MB}{MC}. \qquad \text{(first order condition for the optimal capital stock)}$$

The first order condition for the optimal capital stock says that a company should invest until this condition holds. The numerator is the value of the marginal product of an extra unit of investment and is the marginal benefit of investing another unit. The denominator is often referred to as the user cost of capital. If you invest a unit today, δ is lost in depreciation and the remainder only generates profits tomorrow, which are worth r less per unit in the next period.

We will now define *marginal q* as

$$q = \frac{Af_K}{\delta+r}. \qquad \text{(marginal q)}$$

If $q > 1$, the marginal benefit of investment exceeds the marginal cost, so firms should invest to increase the capital stock until $q = 1$. If $q = 1$ the capital stock is optimal. If $q < 1$ the firms should reduce their capital stock. The assumption of diminishing marginal productivity of capital is required for this system to move towards the optimal level of investment. For $q > 1$, the firm is investing and the benefit of each additional unit of investment falls if the production function exhibits diminishing marginal productivity of capital. Hence they will invest until the marginal benefit of investment has fallen to a level where it equals the marginal cost of investment.

This is often referred to as Tobin's q, after James Tobin, the Nobel Prize-winning economist, and it tells us how investment depends on the four factors on the right-hand side of the equation. The table below shows how increases in these variables affect q and consequently I:

Variable	Effect on q	Effect on I
r	↓	↓
δ	↓	↓
A	↑	↑
f_K	↑	↑

The marginal q equation is a condition for the optimal capital stock and the quantity of investment in any period will be whatever is needed to bring the capital stock to this optimal level.

QUESTIONS AND PROBLEMS FOR CHAPTER 1

CHECKLIST QUESTIONS

1. What is the IS curve? Why does it slope downwards?
2. Use the equation for the IS curve shown in Section 1.2.3 to answer the following questions:
   a. If we assume that $0 < c_1, t < 1$, then what can we say about the size of the multiplier?
   b. If there is a decrease in government spending of ΔG, by how much does this decrease output?
   c. Describe the feedback process that means a decrease in government spending can decrease output by more than 1 : 1.
3. Use the Keynesian cross to show the effect of a decrease in autonomous investment on the economy. Discuss the path of the economy as it adjusts to the new medium-run equilibrium. Why does the economy not continue to contract?
4. Use the Keynesian cross to illustrate the paradox of thrift. Model the change in savings behaviour as an increase in the marginal propensity to save, s_1 (remember that $c_1 + s_1 = 1$). Show how a rise in investment can counteract the reduction in output associated with the rise in savings.
5. Use the equation for the IS curve shown in Section 1.2.3 and Figure 1.6 to discuss what happens to the IS curve in response to the following shocks. In each case provide a real-world example of what might cause the shock.
   a. An increase in autonomous consumption (i.e. $\uparrow c_0$)
   b. A reduction in the interest sensitivity of investment (i.e. $\downarrow a_1$)
   c. An increase in the marginal rate of taxation (i.e. $\uparrow t$)

6. According to the permanent income hypothesis, how will the paths of borrowing and consumption change in response to:
   a. a temporary decrease in income when it occurs
   b. a permanent decrease in income when it occurs
   c. are the answers different if the changes in income are unanticipated, i.e. if they are 'news'? Comment on the size of the marginal propensity to consume and the size of the multiplier.
7. Assuming the real interest rate is 4 per cent, calculate how, according to the PIH, consumption and borrowing would change in each of the following cases:
   a. A stock market crash permanently reduces the value of an individual's assets by 1,000.
   b. Households are told that in a year's time, they will receive a one-off bonus of 1000. Then in one year's time, it is not paid.
   c. Comment briefly on your results.
8. Explain the concepts of excess sensitivity and excess smoothness that arise from the empirical literature on the permanent income hypothesis. What could explain these findings?
9. What does Tobin's q tell us firms' investment decisions depend upon? According to Tobin's q, when should a firm invest?
10. What is the key problem with measuring marginal q? Is there an alternative measurement that can be used instead? Is this alternative measurement likely to be an accurate proxy for marginal q?
11. Use Section 1.3.2 to discuss what is expected to happen to the IS curve in response to the following shocks:
    a. A crash in the stock market
    b. An increase in the retirement age
    c. A decrease in the rate of depreciation
    d. An increase in the cost of oil
    e. An increase in the rate of technological progress

PROBLEMS

1. The IS curve represents the relationship between the real interest rate and output.
   a. Explain how the intuition behind the PIH model is captured in the IS curve. You will need to explain the relevant equations.
   b. Explain how the intuition behind Tobin's q theory is captured in the IS curve. You will need to explain the relevant equations.

2. This question involves collecting data from national statistics agencies (e.g. the UK Office for National Statistics) and/or international organizations (e.g. the OECD or the IMF). First, select an emerging and a developed economy.

   a. Collect annual data on real GDP as far back as it is available for both countries. Convert the data to the log scale and plot on a graph. Comment on your findings. Calculate the growth rates of GDP for the two countries over the period and plot them on a graph. How do the business cycles of the two countries compare? To what extent do they appear synchronized?

   b. Collect current price data on GDP and its components for the two countries. Calculate the percentage of GDP according to each of the four main types of expenditure—i.e. household consumption, government consumption, gross fixed capital formation and net exports (i.e. exports minus imports) and plot the series. How does the composition of GDP and changes over time in the two countries compare? Discuss possible reasons for the differences.

3. We start this question with a simple version of the aggregate demand function, where to keep the maths simple, we omit taxation and government spending:

$$y^D = c_0 + c_1 y + \bar{I} \tag{1.18}$$

Now, assume that $c_0 = 200$ and $\bar{I} = 200$. In addition, assume that $c_1 = 0.8$, such that:

$$y^D = 200 + 0.8y + 200 \tag{1.19}$$

   a. What is the level of output in goods market equilibrium?

   b. Assume there is a fall in the marginal propensity to consume, c_1, to 0.6—i.e. there is a rise in the savings rate, as $s_1 + c_1 = 1$. If we assume that the rise in planned savings leads to the accumulation of unplanned inventories of goods and does not increase planned investment ($\bar{I}$), then what is the level of output that satisfies the new goods market equilibrium?

   c. Compare the level of savings in the new and old goods market equilibria. Note that in goods market equilibrium; $S = s_1 y - c_0$ and $I = \bar{I}$.

   d. Comment on your findings in (c) in response to the question of whether it is advisable for the policy maker to encourage households to increase their savings to help escape a recession. Describe in words a mechanism, which is not included in this model, that could provide a connection from a policy encouraging households to save more and exit from a recession.

4. Use Section 1.2.4 and appropriate readings from beyond this book to decide whether the following statements (S1 and S2) are both true, or whether one of them is false. Justify your answer.

   S1: According to Tobin's q theory, the path of investment is independent of current cash flow (and profits).

   S2: The empirical evidence shows that current cash flow is an important determinant of investment.

5. Aggregate consumption varies less than GDP and aggregate investment varies more. Can you reconcile these observations with the assumption that consumption and investment decisions are taken by rational, forward-looking agents?

6. Read the following short article 'The distribution of wealth and the MPC: implications of new European data', *American Economic Review: Papers and Proceedings*, **104**(5), 107–111. Explain the implications of the findings about consumption and inequality reported in the paper for aggregate consumption behaviour. Use the model of the hybrid consumption function presented in this chapter.

INTERESTED IN EXPLORING THESE TOPICS FURTHER?

Visit www.oup.com/he/carlin-soskice to consolidate and extend your learning with the multiple-choice questions and Animated Analytical Diagrams accompanying this chapter.

CHAPTER

2

THE SUPPLY SIDE

2.1 OVERVIEW

2.1.1 Unemployment

Unemployment is a characteristic feature of a market economy. There are unemployed people looking for work who would be prepared to take a job at the going wage but cannot get a job offer. This is involuntary unemployment and it reflects the fact that the labour market does not clear.

Figure 2.1 illustrates how unemployment varies over time and across countries. We can see that there is a large amount of heterogeneity in unemployment across the high-income economies; following the global financial crisis, average unemployment between 2009 and 2012 ranged from 5.0% in the Netherlands to 21.0% in Spain. In addition, the figure highlights that an individual country can experience large changes in unemployment; Irish unemployment fell from 16% in the late 1980s to just above 4% in the early 2000s, before rising again to 15% in the wake of the economic crises of 2009–12.

All countries in Figure 2.1 saw unemployment decline after having reached a peak during the 2009–12 crisis, with some countries (for instance, Germany, the UK and the US) recording their lowest unemployment rates since the 1970s. The next five years unemployment (2020-24, of which 2020-21 are shown in the figure) will be affected by the pandemic, policies to protect incomes and employment during the pandemic, and the effects of the war in Ukraine.

Unemployment is costly to the economy since it represents a waste of resources, and it is associated with unhappiness and psychological distress to those affected. It is a major source of concern for policy makers.

In this chapter, we develop the supply side of the macroeconomic framework to provide a model of structural, or equilibrium, unemployment. Whereas the demand side refers to spending decisions, the supply side refers to production activities in the economy. Although both capital and labour are inputs to the production process, we concentrate on the input of labour. The supply side refers to both the supply of labour by workers and the demand for labour by firms. We return to discuss capital accumulation when we look at long-run growth in Chapter 16. On the supply side, we ask how firms decide how much output to produce, how many workers to employ and what prices to set. We want to know what determines the wage an employer offers and how the employer solves the problems of recruiting and motivating workers.

2.1.2 **Why the labour market does not clear**

When a market clears, the price is such that there is neither excess supply of, nor demand for, the good. If the market is for 'labour', then the wage would rise in response to excess demand and fall in response to excess supply, with the result that there would be no 'unsold' labour. As we shall see, this is not a good way of thinking about the labour market. The data in Figure 2.1 covers many countries over more than five decades. It reveals unemployment as characteristic of capitalist economies. In Chapter 15, we explore reasons for the variations in unemployment over time and across countries. Here we are drawing attention to the general case in which there are workers who are willing to work at the going wage but cannot find a job. Consistent with the term 'involuntary' to describe the unemployment is the large amount of evidence that workers are unhappy when they are unemployed. For example, in an early study, Clark and Oswald (1994) use data for a sample of six thousand British workers in 1991 and find that the unemployed have twice the level of mental distress of the employed.[1]

To understand why the labour market does not clear, we ask the obvious question of why an employer would not offer a job to a worker who is willing to work at a lower wage. This draws attention to the crucial difference between recruiting a worker and

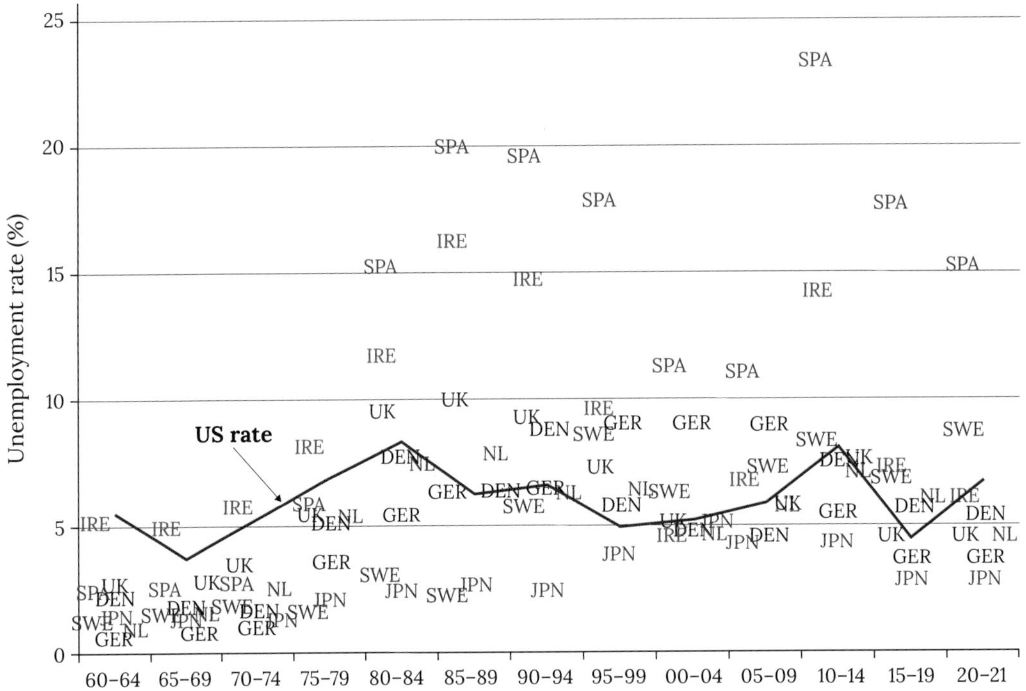

Figure 2.1 Trends and heterogeneity in unemployment for selected OECD economies, 1960–2021.

Source: Howell et al. (2007), Figure 1.1, used until 1995. Updated to 2021 using OECD harmonized unemployment rates (data accessed June 2022).

[1] For a review of the literature on unemployment and happiness, see Oswald (1997). More recent results can be found in Clark and Oswald (2002) and in the Annual World Happiness Reports (https://worldhappiness.report/).

motivating them to work hard and effectively on the job. The employer needs both problems to be solved for output to be produced and profits maximized.

To recruit a worker, the lowest wage the employer can pay is called the reservation wage. And to get the worker to exert adequate effort on the job, the employer must pay more than the reservation wage. We will explain more about these two problems shortly, but it should already be clear that someone offering to work at the reservation wage, i.e., below the wage required to motivate effort, will not be hired.

Thinking of the labour market through the eyes of the potential employee highlights the factors that will influence the wage the employer sets.

1. **The recruitment problem and the reservation wage:** The wage at which an unemployed person can be hired depends on:
   - the unemployment benefit and any other income from family support or other activities that the person receives;
   - the net utility of being unemployed (on the positive side of the ledger is the free time for leisure or study, and on the negative are the stigma and mental health consequences of unemployment);
   - or, if recruited from another firm, the wage and net utility of that job.
2. **The motivation problem and the no-shirking wage:** The wage that needs to be paid to motivate workers to exert effort is higher than the reservation wage and is called the no-shirking wage. The no-shirking wage depends on:
   - the cost of effort, i.e., how onerous it is for the employee to provide the required level of effort;
   - the probability that the employer can detect shirking and fires the worker; and
   - the expected duration of unemployment if the worker loses his job. This will depend on the rate of unemployment in the economy.

Workers experience the effort of working hard as costly and would rather shirk if they could do so without being caught. From the employer's point of view, when hiring the worker at an hourly wage or a monthly or annual salary, they would like to specify the supply of effort in an employment contract, but this is not possible. A contract in which, for example, a server in a restaurant was obliged to be courteous to guests could not be verified in a court of law. The contract is intrinsically incomplete.

The employer can only monitor the worker imperfectly (in the case of a white-collar worker, for example, using keystroke surveillance technology), and if finding he is shirking, can fire him. To incentivize the worker to supply the required effort, the employer sets the wage above the reservation wage so that the worker faces the cost of job loss if he is caught shirking and fired. When the wage is set above the reservation wage, it is called an 'efficiency wage'. This model of wage-setting is called the labour discipline model and the efficiency wage is called the 'no shirking wage'.[2]

---

[2] The efficiency wage model was first formalized in Shapiro and Stiglitz' landmark 1984 paper 'Equilibrium unemployment as a worker discipline device.' See also Bowles (1985), which provides a more general treatment. For an earlier model that derives results for inflation as well as unemployment, see Rowthorn (1977).

Innovation in information technology makes detection of shirking workers easier in some occupations and industries. For example, truck drivers can be tracked by in-cab monitoring devices and GPS navigation equipment in a way that was impossible before such technologies became low cost. Accelerated by widespread 'working from home' in the pandemic, surveillance to detect shirking has expanded to many more occupations, including senior management ones. Key-stroke activity is monitored remotely and web cams are used to track 'time on task' by photos taken randomly in each 10-minute interval. These developments bring to the fore the problem the employer faces of ensuring the worker exerts effort.[3] But ICT may also enable more productive autonomous work.

There are other efficiency wage models that explain why the employer chooses to set the wage above the reservation wage. In a separate contribution, Akerlof (1982) uses a psychological or behavioural rather than a purely rational explanation for efficiency wages, which he refers to as a gift exchange. This amounts to the employee saying to herself: this firm treats me well since my wage is above my reservation wage so I will respond in kind by working hard. This highlights that a worker paid efficiency wages has something to lose by quitting. Turnover is also costly to the employer so this is another reason for observing efficiency wages.

In the labour discipline model, this problem is ignored—the worker either works hard enough to be valuable to the employer or not and if paid the no-shirking wage, the worker remains with the employer. A model focusing on the costs of turnover and the need to incentivize retention would predict that the employer will pay a wage above the reservation wage and she will pay a higher 'retention' wage, the higher are the costs incurred when recruiting and training employees, which will rise in a tighter labour market.

Figure 2.2 is a diagram with employment on the horizontal axis and the real wage on the vertical axis. The reservation wage is horizontal and the wage-setting curve is upward sloping. The no-shirking wage is set above the reservation wage and it rises as unemployment falls. At point A, unemployment is high and a low wage is set: the cost of job loss is relatively high. At point B, unemployment is low. Given the relatively low cost of job loss, a higher wage is set.[4] A rise in the unemployment benefit will shift the wage-setting curve upwards and vice versa.

The labour supply curve is shown as vertical. This is a simplification reflecting two reasons for an inelastic supply of labour at the level of the aggregate economy. We assume the outcome of these factors is a perfectly inelastic labour supply. For those employed, a rise in the wage has both an income and a substitution effect.

---

[3] See Thiel et al. (2021) for a view of worker surveillance from a management studies perspective.

[4] Sometimes students are puzzled by the statement that it is easier to find a job when unemployment is low. Surely at low unemployment, they reason, all the jobs are filled and it would be hard to get one. This reasoning is incorrect because it assumes that there are a fixed number of jobs: but the number of jobs and the economy's unemployment rate are the *outcome* of the interaction of workers and firms. Keeping in mind that vacancies are high when unemployment is low reinforces the point that the number of jobs is not fixed and that it will indeed be easier to find one when unemployment is low.

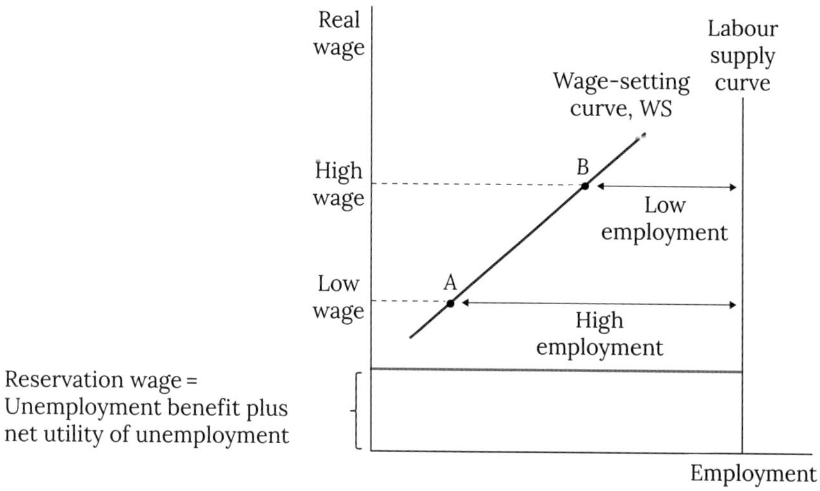

Figure 2.2 The wage-setting curve, WS.

The substitution effect suggests that labour supply rises with the wage because working becomes more worthwhile. The income effect suggests the opposite: since it is assumed that there is a disutility of working, if the same income can be earned in fewer hours of work, labour supply will fall. It is even possible for the labour supply curve to be backward bending if the income effect outweighs the substitution effect. The second factor concerns the decision to participate in the labour market. As the wage increases, participation goes up. There will be a steep aggregate labour supply curve if the tendency of workers to enter the labour force when the wage rises is offset by a fall in hours of work of those who are employed.

A point on the wage-setting curve is an answer to the question: what wage has to be paid to secure adequate worker effort (effective labour input) at a given level of unemployment (and associated level of employment)?

A point on the labour supply curve is an answer to the question: if a given wage were to be offered, how much labour would workers be willing to supply?

The horizontal gap between the wage-setting curve and the labour supply curve is therefore involuntary unemployment, because it shows the extra supply of labour that would be offered at that wage but is not employed when wages are set on the wage-setting curve. The vertical gap between the wage-setting curve and the horizontal part of the labour supply curve is inversely related to the cost of job loss at the relevant level of employment: a higher efficiency wage has to be paid when the labour market is tight and it is relatively easy to get another job.

The explanation in the labour discipline model of why the labour market does not clear is based on the nature of the relationship between employer and worker. The WS curve represents the wage the employer pays to deter shirking. Since worker effort is necessary for production, it is the wage-setting curve and not the labour supply curve that is relevant for how wages are set in the economy, and, as we shall see, for pinning down the unemployment rate consistent with constant inflation. The outcome of any efficiency wage model is that involuntary unemployment is a permanent feature of the economy.

Since involuntary unemployment is characteristic of the economy in this model, it cannot be the case that the level of employment is determined by *labour market clearing*. A market clears when the price adjusts so that there is neither excess demand nor excess supply. The typical textbook diagram with a downward-sloping labour demand curve intersecting an upward-sloping labour supply curve is a model of a clearing labour market. So we are led to ask the question: what fixes employment and the real wage when the economy is on the WS curve? To answer, we introduce firms to the model in the next section.

It might be suggested that the employer use piece rates rather than an hourly wage to pay workers. By paying for the worker's output rather than the worker's time, the problem of not being able to observe effort is solved. But taking a look at any economy quickly reveals that very little economic activity is organized around piece rates for labour. This is particularly true of modern service-based economies, where output is less easily quantifiable. In addition, much of the production activity in the economy is based on team production, where the contribution of an individual worker is hard to determine. The exception is the gig economy where workers complete tasks and are paid per task. In this case, the contract is complete and gig workers are not employees; they do not receive an efficiency wage.

Efficiency wage setting

There is a large body of empirical evidence documenting the existence of a 'wage curve', which is represented in the model by the WS curve.[5] Microeconomic data on local labour markets is used to uncover the relationship between a change in the unemployment rate at the local level and the wage that is paid. A comprehensive meta-study of more than 200 estimates from a large number of countries points toward the existence of a wage curve with an elasticity of −0.07. This means that a 10% rise in the unemployment rate (for example, an increase in the rate of unemployment from 10% to 11%) would, holding everything else constant, is associated with a real wage lower by 0.7%.[6]

The empirical wage curve is non-linear. The linear WS used in the model in this book is a simplification. The logic of the labour discipline model fits the convex wage curve in Figure 2.3: as unemployment goes toward zero, the cost of job loss does so too and as a result, the wage that would have to be set to incentivize effort increases without limit.

A vivid example of efficiency wage setting from the early years of mass manufacturing in the US is documented by Raff and Summers (1987): this is Henry Ford's introduction of a $5 wage per day for his production workers in 1914. This represented a 240% pay increase for workers at his plant. Worker turnover fell from 370% in 1913 to

[5] For an introduction to the empirical literature on using microeconomic evidence to estimate wage curves, see Blanchflower and Oswald (1995). For a full exposition of 'The Wage Curve', see Blanchflower and Oswald (2003).

[6] See Nijkamp and Poot (2005).

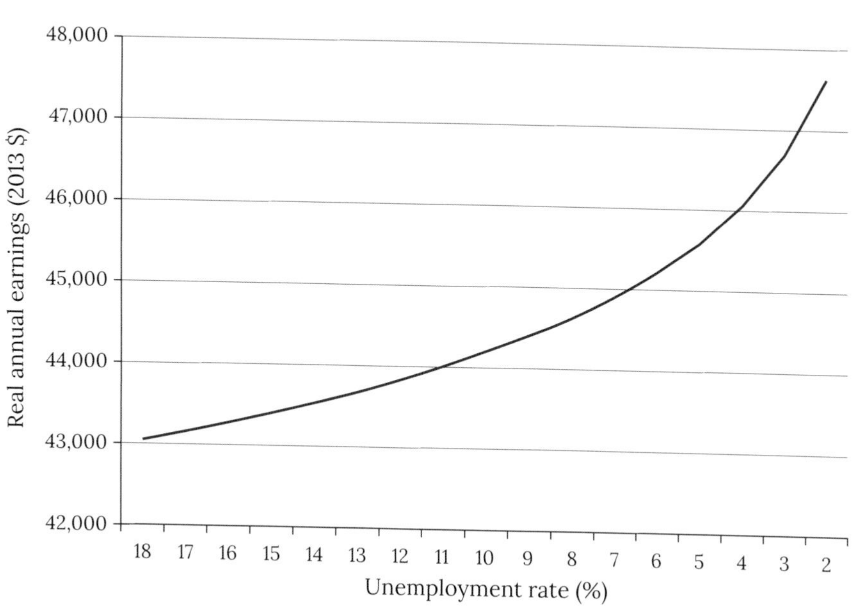

Figure 2.3 A wage-setting curve estimated for the US economy (1979–2013).
Note: The unemployment rate is measured from high on the left to low on the right.
Source: Estimated by Stephen Machin (UCL 2015) from Current Population Survey microdata from the Outgoing Rotation Groups for 1979 to 2013.

only 16% in 1915 and absenteeism was reduced from 10% to 2.5% in just one year.[7] The authors conclude that in this case, wage increases resulted in significant productivity benefits and higher profits.

It is important to understand that Henry Ford's decision to increase wages was not a response to labour shortage. On the contrary, there were queues of workers wanting to work in the factory and yet instead of allowing the wage to fall to 'clear the market', Ford did the opposite, raising wages substantially.[8] This is taken as a famous illustration of the payment of efficiency wages.

Examples of other studies documenting the employer's motivation problem and the relationship between wages and effort include:

- Agell and Lundborg (1995) undertook interviews with senior wage negotiators and personnel managers and found that they believed work effort would increase if local unemployment increased.
- Fleisher and Wang (2001) provide evidence for the effects of higher wages on worker effort and the prevalence of shirking. The paper uses data from Chinese urban

[7] Turnover is measured as the total amount of workers hired in a year divided by the average workforce for that year. For example, Ford had to hire 50,448 workers in 1913 to maintain an average workforce of just 13,623. This equates to annual turnover of 370%. All figures from Raff and Summers (1987).

[8] See Raff and Summers (1987).

and rural nonagricultural firms to investigate efficiency-wage effects for technical, managerial and production workers. They report strong evidence of productivity-enhancing wage-setting behaviour in both state, collectively and privately owned companies. The survey also collected data from workers on how frequently they observe shirking amongst their co-workers. These data were included in the regression models, and the results show that employees are less liable to shirk if they are paid higher wages.

- Evidence to support the existence of efficiency wages comes from econometric studies that measure the loss of earnings of an employee when they lose their job as a result of a plant closure.[9] Interestingly, the loss of earnings is not restricted to those who fail to find another job after plant closure. For example, Farber (2005, p. 25) finds that 'counting foregone earnings increases enjoyed by non-losers, full-time job losers who find new full-time jobs earn up to 17% less on average in their new jobs than they would have had they not been displaced'.
- Other evidence comes from studies that compare productivity under different compensation schemes. The evidence shows that workers exert more effort and produce more output when they are on piece-rates (i.e. a payment per unit of output). For example, Foster and Rosenzweig (1994) use longitudinal data from rural farming households in the Philippines to investigate the relationship between effort and contractual arrangements. They find that work effort was substantially higher under piece-rates than under time-wage (i.e. a fixed wage per hour) contracts.
- In related work, Lazear, Shaw and Stanton (2016) use data from 20,000 workers in a single large firm to investigate the cause of the rise in productivity observed in the United States during the global financial crisis. They find that the productivity increase was mainly driven by workers putting in more effort during the recession. This fits with the idea of firms 'making do with less'; workers are laid off, but instead of output falling equivalently, the existing workers are made to take on the extra workload. What makes the existing workers willing to put in extra effort for the same wage? An interpretation using the efficiency wage model is that the recession increased unemployment and lowered the probability of finding another job if dismissed. The research found that productivity increased as the recession proceeded and the duration of unemployment spells went up and that the productivity effect was stronger where increases in local unemployment were higher. The efficiency wage model predicts that the employer would cut wages: with higher unemployment, the employment rent rises and a lower wage can be paid without damaging effort. This did not happen perhaps for reasons suggested in research carried out by Truman Bewley (Bewley 1999). He found that the reluctance to cut wages in recessions arises from the fear that the damage to morale would be sufficient to nullify any cost savings.

The literature has also provided evidence for the role of efficiency wages in addressing the firm's retention problem. Campbell and Kamlani (1997) find that:

---

[9] See, for example, Farber (2005).

[F]irms fear the loss of firm-specific human capital when experienced workers quit almost as much as they fear the cost of hiring and training replacements.

Union wage setting

In efficiency wage models, the employer sets the wage. However, in many economies, unions play a central role in wage setting, as shown by Figure 2.4. In some European countries, wages set by unions cover virtually the entire workforce (e.g. 98% in Austria). In the US, by contrast, only 12% of workers are covered. As the observations close to 100% on the vertical axis in Figure 2.4 show, not all countries in which union wages cover almost all workers have high union membership. France is an extreme case with the data showing union density of just 9% but coverage by union-negotiated wages of 98%.

In general, we can think of the labour market comprising two parts: a unionized sector and a non-unionized sector. In the latter, wages are not covered by union agreements and employers set efficiency wages; in the unionized sector, wages are set by unions. When unions set wages, they can use their bargaining power to achieve a so-called union premium above the wage for non-union workers. In the model, this is represented by an upward shift in the WS curve.

The variation in the presence and organization of unions across countries is interesting because it gives a hint at one of the reasons unemployment rates may differ across countries for lengthy periods of time. Types of union bargaining vary widely. In some countries with very high coverage of the workforce by union wage bargains, unemployment is lower than the OECD average (e.g. in Austria and the

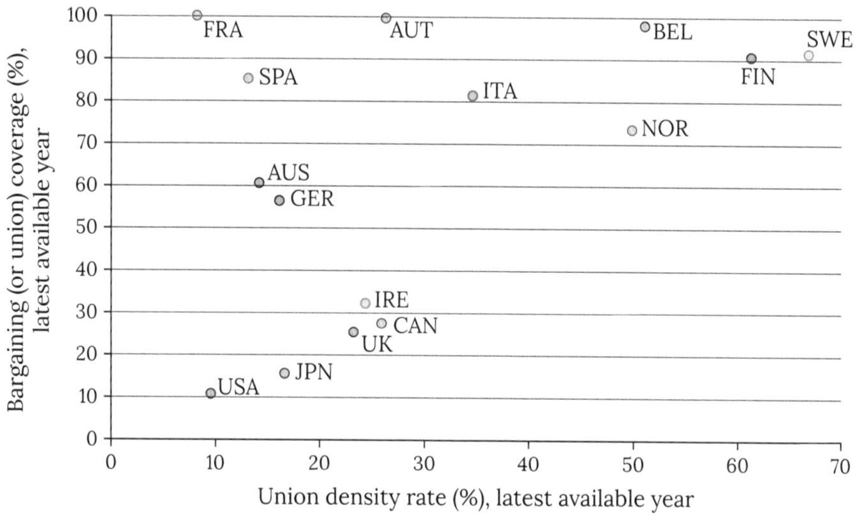

Figure 2.4 The importance of unions in wage setting: selected OECD countries.

Source: OECD Statistics (data accessed July 2020).

AUS Australia, AUT Austria, BEL Belgium, CAN Canada, DEU Germany, ESP Spain, FIN Finland, FRA France, IRL Ireland, ITA Italy, JPN Japan, NOR Norway, SWE Sweden, UK United Kingdom, US United States. See footnote 9.

Nordic countries) whereas in others, such as France or Italy, unemployment rates are relatively high.

This suggests that the answer to the question of the role of unions in unemployment is more complex than we might think at first. It turns out that in institutional situations where unions are powerful and recognize their influence on the whole economy, they tend to exercise bargaining restraint, which is compatible with low unemployment (represented by a downward shift in the WS curve relative to the one with unrestrained union bargaining). In other settings, powerful unions take a narrower perspective and do not exercise restraint. Their bargaining power allows them to set higher nominal wages and the economy ends up with higher unemployment. Such institutional differences in wage-setting are one element in explaining the patterns of unemployment in Figure 2.1. A model that links wage-setting institutions to unemployment outcomes is set out in Chapter 15.

2.1.3 Equilibrium (structural) unemployment

The wage-setting curve relates to the decisions of workers to accept jobs. Given the rate of unemployment, a firm will offer the wage shown on the WS curve and the worker will accept for the reasons explained in Section 2.1.2. To pin down the economy's real wage and employment level, we need a second curve. This one arises from the behaviour of firms as they interact with customers in markets for goods and services. Firms employ workers in order to produce output, which they sell to maximize their profits. They produce differentiated goods and services (think of the different brands and specifications of bicycles) and face competition from other producers. Each firm faces a downward-sloping demand curve and sets the profit-maximizing price given the extent of competition it faces (reflected in the elasticity of the demand curve) and their marginal cost curve.

We assume that the production function is very simple with constant average and therefore marginal productivity. The upper horizontal line in Figure 2.5 shows output per worker (i.e. the average and marginal product of labour). When the firm sets its profit-maximizing price, this results in profits per worker as shown in the figure. The residual amount of output per worker is the real wage, which the worker gets.

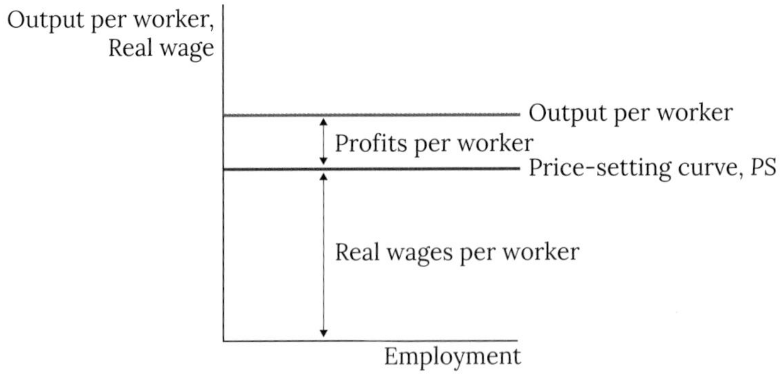

Figure 2.5 The price-setting curve, PS.

This gives the second curve that we need. It is called the *price-setting curve* and where it intersects with the wage-setting curve fixes the equilibrium real wage and employment in the economy.

Figure 2.6 shows the wage-setting and price-setting curves. This is called the WS–PS model. The intersection of the price-setting (PS) curve and the upward-sloping wage-setting (WS) curve determines the real wage, employment and unemployment when the supply side is in equilibrium. At the equilibrium, the real wage is consistent with what is needed to secure sufficient labour (on the WS curve) and for firms to be maximizing their profits given the competitive conditions in the economy (on the PS curve). As we shall see later in the chapter, a feature of the equilibrium level of employment at which the WS and PS curves intersect is that inflation is constant. With any higher employment, inflation rises; with lower employment, inflation falls.

We can use Figure 2.6 to show how the unemployment rate is defined. The labour force is shown by a vertical line. This is the total number of people reported by the statistical agency who are working or looking for work. The unemployment rate is defined as unemployment divided by the sum of employment and unemployment, that is, the numbers unemployed divided by the labour force:

$$\text{Unemployment rate} \equiv \frac{\text{unemployed}}{\text{employed} + \text{unemployed}} \equiv \frac{\text{unemployed}}{\text{labour force}}.$$

Equilibrium or structural unemployment is the difference between employment at the WS–PS intersection and the labour force. From Figure 2.7, it is clear that equilibrium unemployment will rise if the wage-setting curve shifts up or if the price-setting curve shifts down. Taking the case of a higher unemployment benefit first, we have seen that a higher unemployment benefit will shift the WS curve up because it raises the reservation wage. In Figure 2.7a, this shifts the WS curve up to WS′. The new WS–PS intersection is at a lower level of employment.

The economics behind this can be explained as follows. For equilibrium, a profit-maximizing firm has to be on the price-setting curve. At point C above the PS curve, the higher wage that has to be paid would reduce its profits so the firm will raise its price in

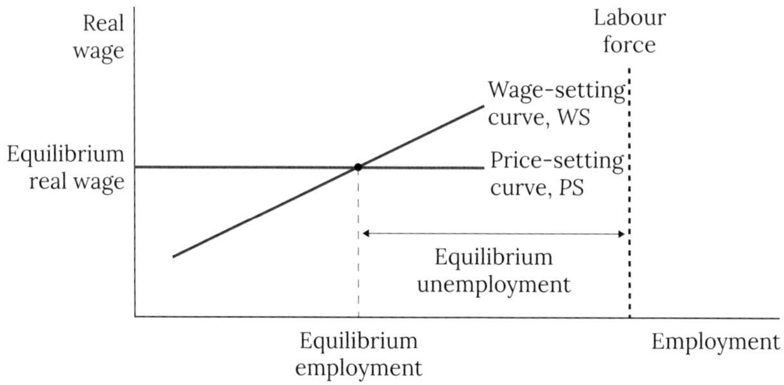

Figure 2.6 Supply-side equilibrium: the intersection of the wage-setting and price-setting curves.

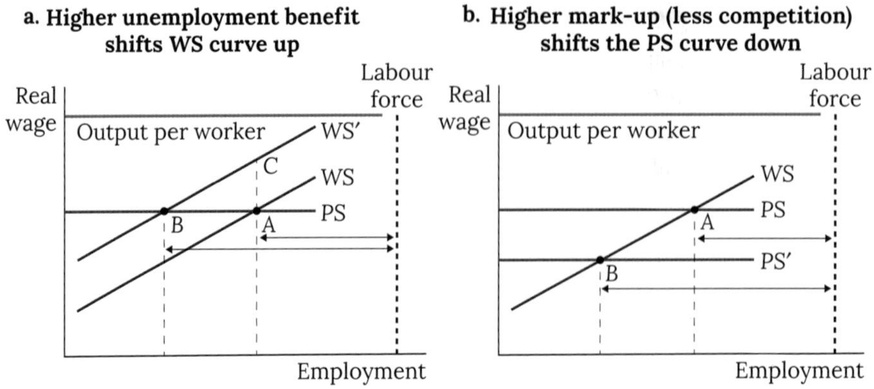

Figure 2.7 The impact on equilibrium unemployment of shifts in the WS and PS curves. Visit www.oup.com/he/carlin-soskice to explore the effect of shifting the WS and PS curves on unemployment with Animated Analytical Diagram 2.7.

Note: the double-headed arrows show equilibrium unemployment for each case.

response. Point C is not a supply-side equilibrium. From the diagram, we see that only at higher unemployment will this economy be in equilibrium. Higher unemployment increases the cost of job loss and lowers the wage the firm needs to set. The new equilibrium is at point B. Given the higher out-of-work benefits, a higher risk of job loss is necessary to make the unchanged real wage required by price-setters consistent with wage setters' behaviour.

Equilibrium unemployment will also be higher if the PS curve shifts down (from PS to PS′ in Figure 2.7b). If there is a reduction in the extent of competition in the goods market, which allows the markup of price over unit labour costs to rise, the price-setting real wage will be reduced: under the new conditions, firms are able to raise their prices and the real wage workers end up with after prices have been set is reduced. In terms of Figure 2.5, a higher markup increases the share of output per worker that goes to profits and reduces the share to wages. The new equilibrium is at a lower real wage and higher unemployment. For the wage-setting real wage to be reduced to the new equilibrium level, there must be higher unemployment in the economy. With a higher cost of job loss, the efficiency real wage is lower.

The concept of equilibrium or structural unemployment is a medium to long-run concept. It tells us the unemployment rate at which both wage and price setters are content with the prevailing real wage. The kinds of policies that can be implemented to affect equilibrium unemployment are those that shift the WS or the PS curve. These are *supply-side policies*.

In the modelling section and in Chapter 15 on supply-side policies, we enrich the model of the supply side by introducing additional institutions and policies that shift the wage- and price-setting curves. These include the role of taxes, workplace policies that affect the cost of effort, labour market regulations that affect the ease of firing, and competition policy. These factors help explain both the cross-country variation and the changes over time in the 5-year average unemployment rates shown in Figure 2.1.

2.1.4 Nominal rigidities, demand-side shocks, and policy

When discussing equilibrium unemployment, the focus is on the medium run when the economy is at a WS–PS intersection, and hence on the effect of supply-side policies and institutions on unemployment. In this subsection, we introduce *nominal rigidities* and the role of *demand-side* shocks and policies. The term nominal rigidity refers to the fact that nominal wages (in dollars or euros) and prices do not adjust immediately to fluctuations in aggregate demand to keep the economy at equilibrium unemployment.

In Chapter 1, we assumed an extreme form of this rigidity, namely that prices and wages don't change at all in response to shifts in demand. This meant that when aggregate demand shifted, as a result, for example of an investment boom, output and employment in the economy responded fully to bring supply into line with the higher demand. We used the multiplier process to model the response of output and employment based on the assumption that wages and prices remained unchanged. An alternative extreme assumption is that the economy is always at the medium-run equilibrium, i.e. at a WS–PS intersection, and therefore that fluctuations in aggregate demand do not affect output and employment. The terms 'fixed price' and 'flex price' are sometimes used to label these two extreme cases.

In building a model suitable for analysing real-world economies, we recognize that wages are changed at intervals, for example, at an annual wage review and that there are good reasons why firms do not change their prices continuously. A vivid illustration of wage and price rigidity is the very limited extent to which they were changed in response to the massive disruption of economies caused by Covid-19. Output and employment both fell dramatically but wages and prices remained virtually unchanged. Price-gouging as firms sought to take advantage of specific spikes in demand for items like toilet paper and hand sanitizer were the exception and not the rule. More detailed arguments and evidence are provided in the modelling section. Here we summarize the main points. Before doing so, it is important to distinguish between real and nominal wages.

Nominal wages, real wages, and inflation

To this point, all of the discussion about the supply side has been in terms of the *real* wage. This is because it is the real wage that workers care about (i.e. how much their dollar or euro wage buys in goods and services). This is therefore the employer's concern when setting the wage to secure the worker's effort. For firms, the profitability of production depends on the cost of labour in terms of the price they set for their output. Yet workers are paid a wage in money terms: this is the *nominal* wage. And although firms set prices, it is the consumer price index rather than the price of their employer's product that employees have in mind when agreeing on a wage offer.

We can see how real and nominal wages are related in the model as follows. Given the unemployment rate, employers set the nominal wage so as to achieve their desired real wage on the wage-setting curve. This means that when they set the nominal wage, they must make an assumption about the *consumer price level*, which is the outcome of price-setting by firms across the economy. Firms set their profit-maximizing *product price* based on the wage set in their firm.

Note that when wages are set by the employer, it would be the firm's human resources division that sets the nominal wage taking account of the consumer price level to ensure workers supply adequate effort for the firm's operations. Given the nominal wage, the marketing and strategy divisions set the price for the firm's product.

Modern economies are typically characterized by a positive rate of inflation. Central banks often target an inflation rate of 2%. If nominal wages rise by 2% per annum and prices rise by 2% per annum, the real wage is unchanged. At a WS–PS intersection, the real wage is constant, which means nominal wages and prices are rising at the same rate. This is a constant inflation equilibrium.

Rigidities in wage setting

Nominal wages are set periodically, usually at an annual wage round or review. They are not continuously adjusted by the wage setter. Barattieri et al. (2014) analyse US survey data and find that wages are indeed very 'sticky'; they are most likely to be adjusted just once every year. The authors also find that there is little variation in the frequency of wage changes across different industries and occupations.

An important reason for the stickiness of wages relates to the interactions between employers and workers, where considerations of fairness and morale play an important role. Campbell and Kamlani (1997) surveyed 184 firms and find strong support for two explanations of wage rigidity (in this case, why wages are not cut as much as possible in a recession). First, firms were concerned that wage cuts would lead their most productive workers to quit, whereas layoffs could target the least productive workers. Second, respondents linked wage cuts to reduced worker effort, particularly when wage cuts were viewed as being 'unfair'. Bewley (2007) reviews the empirical literature on fairness and wage rigidity and finds that fairness considerations are one of the primary determinants of company morale. He also finds that wage cuts are only viewed as being fair when they are seen as saving a large number of jobs.

Rigidities in price setting

The frequency of price changes varies a great deal across industries. However, for large parts of the economy, firms are cautious about frequent price adjustments in response to fluctuations in demand because of their concern about their competitors' and customers' reactions.

A detailed survey of how firms set prices using a structured questionnaire of a random sample of 330 US firms found that almost half of all prices were changed no more than annually. The survey identified the following major reasons for price stickiness: firms are deterred from raising prices because of concerns their competitors will not follow suit; cost increases are generally industry-wide and can serve as convenient signals that other firms are probably under pressure to raise prices; implicit contracts with customers deter price hikes when demand rises but permit them when costs rise; and firms hold prices steady until the next regularly scheduled price review.[10]

---

[10] See Blinder et al. (1998).

Aggregate demand shocks and the role of nominal rigidities

In the macroeconomic model, we make simplifying assumptions about how wage and price rigidities operate. The simplifying assumptions reflect the arguments presented about why wages and prices are adjusted infrequently. We assume that wage contracts are reviewed annually at the 'wage round'. This means that if an aggregate demand shock occurs in the interval between wage rounds, the wage is not adjusted. We assume that prices are not adjusted in response to shifts in aggregate demand; however, prices are adjusted immediately following the wage round. Since the adjustment in wages will reflect changes in aggregate demand, prices respond to changes in aggregate demand with a lag.

The timeline for wage and price setting, shocks and changes in output and employment can be summarized as follows:

Aggregate demand shock → output and employment change
Next wage round → nominal wages change
Immediately after the wage round → prices change

Before looking at an aggregate demand shock, we look at what happens when the economy is at supply-side equilibrium in an environment of constant inflation. The equilibrium is where the WS and PS curves intersect in Figure 2.8. Inflation in the previous year was 2%.

At the next annual wage round, wage setters observe that prices have risen 2% over the previous year and they will set a 2% nominal wage increase to keep the real wage constant. After the wage round, firms will observe that the 2% increase in wages has increased their costs by 2%. If they raise their prices by 2%, this will keep their profit margin constant (and the real wage will remain on the PS curve). As long as the economy remains at the equilibrium level of employment, wage and price inflation will remain unchanged at 2% per year and the real wage will remain constant.

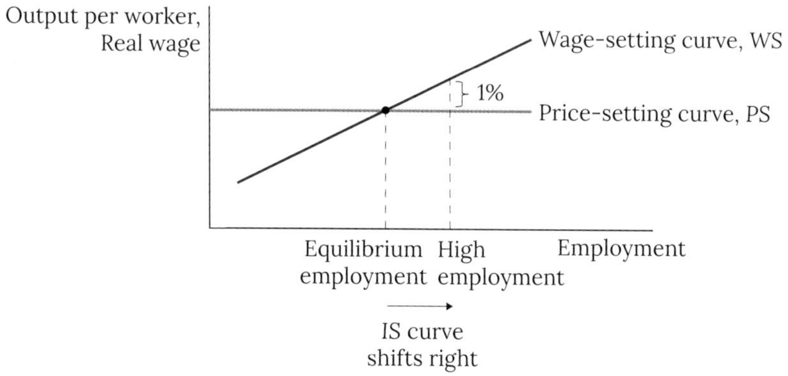

Figure 2.8 The response of wages and prices to a cyclical upswing.

We now look at what happens when there is an aggregate demand shock of the kind discussed in Chapter 1: for example, an investment boom raises output. Since the investment boom does not affect the WS or the PS curve, it has no effect on equilibrium unemployment. The investment boom raises output and employment in the short run: we assume output per worker is constant. As Figure 2.8 shows, the economy is no longer in medium-run equilibrium.

What happens the next time there is an opportunity for wages to be adjusted? At the next wage round, employment is higher and wage setters will respond by setting a nominal wage increase to take the real wage up to the point on the WS curve at the higher level of employment. They will need a 2% nominal wage increase as usual, plus an additional increase. In the example shown in Figure 2.8, this is an extra 1%. Nominal wages go up by 3%. How do price setters respond to the higher wages? Their costs have risen by 3% (rather than the usual 2%), so they mark up this cost increase in their prices and price inflation goes up from 2% to 3%. Firms are likely to feel comfortable about raising their prices at this point, because they can observe that wages have gone up during the annual wage round for their competitors as well. We have the result that an expansion of aggregate demand that pushes output and employment above the equilibrium level is followed by a rise in wage and price inflation.

This behaviour of the economy, which is called an upswing or downswing of the *business cycle*, creates a role for a policy maker who aims to improve welfare by keeping the economy close to the medium-run equilibrium unemployment rate. The involuntary unemployment characteristic of the economy when it is at the constant inflation equilibrium (i.e. WS–PS intersection) is raised in a business cycle downswing and lowered in an upswing. A policy maker who focuses on stabilization and uses demand-side policy is introduced in Chapter 3.

The inflation-stabilizing rate of unemployment

In the model, actual unemployment will deviate from the equilibrium rate of unemployment over the economic cycle as a result of fluctuations in aggregate demand due to shifts in the IS curve as discussed in Chapter 1. In Figure 2.9, we show actual unemployment rates and estimates made by the OECD of constant inflation unemployment rates in four advanced economies.

The inflation-stabilizing, structural, or equilibrium rate of unemployment is sometimes called the NAIRU—the Non-Accelerating Inflation Rate of Unemployment. This is an estimate of the unemployment rate at which inflation would be constant. The figures show, as expected, that the NAIRU is much less volatile than actual unemployment in all four countries. Actual unemployment is measured in a comparable way across countries using labour market surveys (the so-called harmonized rate of unemployment published by the OECD).

Patterns of unemployment differ over time and across countries (Figure 2.9). The UK and US both saw trend declines in the NAIRU, with the decline in the UK particularly noteworthy. This suggests that structural change has taken place in the labour market since the 1980s. The comparison with France's stability is stark. The rise in French unemployment in the early 1990s appears to have pulled the NAIRU up from 7% to

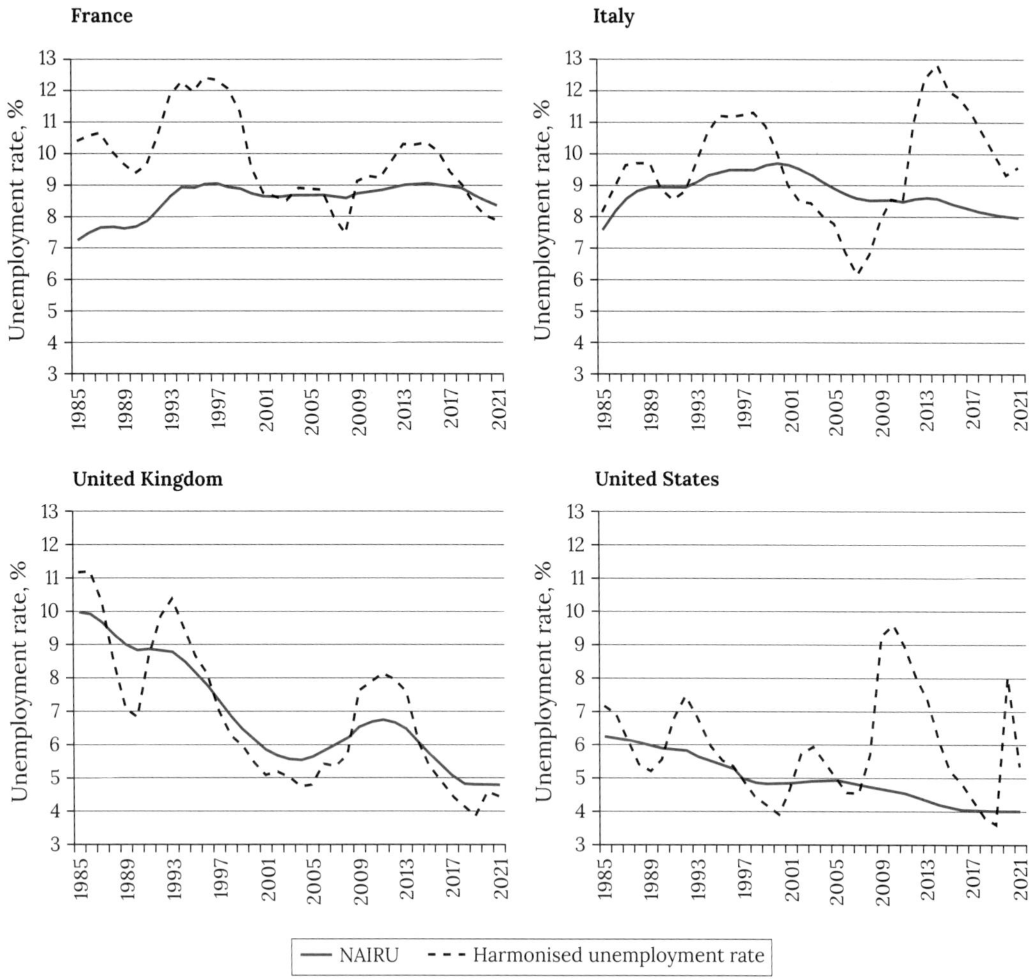

Figure 2.9 Non-Accelerating Inflation Rate of Unemployment (NAIRU) and harmonized unemployment rates in France, Italy, the United Kingdom, and the United States: 1983–2021.

Source: OECD Economic Outlook (May 2021 edition).

around 9%. In spite of strong fluctuations in unemployment before and after the financial crisis, the NAIRU in Italy was trending down from around 2000.

In Figure 2.9, we saw that unemployment differs from equilibrium unemployment over the economic cycle. In the WS–PS model, when output is above equilibrium (i.e. when unemployment is below equilibrium), this creates upward inflationary pressure and vice versa.

Figure 2.10 displays the inflation rates in selected OECD countries from the 1960s to 2021: while inflation in the past decade has been low at 2% to 3% in many of the OECD countries, it was much higher, and often at rates of between 10% and 20% in the 1970s. By comparing Figure 2.9 and Figure 2.10, we can see that the decline in inflation in France and Italy from high rates at the end of the 1970s to very low rates in the

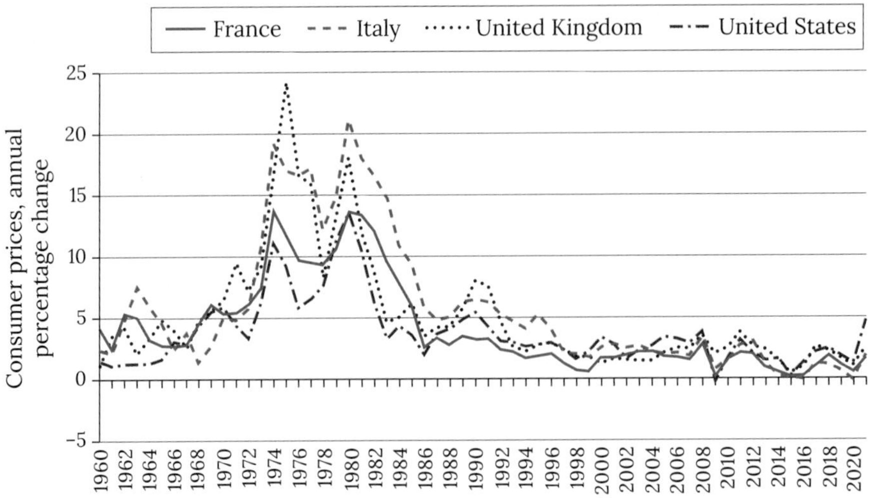

Figure 2.10 Consumer price inflation rates in France, Italy, the United Kingdom, and the United States: 1960–2021.

Source: OECD Monthly Economic Indicators (accessed July 2022).

mid 2000s is consistent with the persistence of unemployment above the estimated inflation-stabilizing rate during this period.

In Chapter 3, we look at the costs of getting inflation down from its high levels in the 1970s in terms of prolonged high unemployment. The years of so-called 'stagflation'—a combination of high unemployment and high inflation—imposed heavy costs on economies. As a consequence, policy makers sought to find better ways of managing the economy. One outcome was a move to inflation targeting and central bank independence.

2.2 MODELLING

We cover three aspects of the supply-side model in this section. We begin by setting out a more complete version of the model of equilibrium unemployment (the WS–PS model), highlighting the supply-side features that determine the medium-run level of output around which the economy fluctuates over the course of the business cycle. Next, we show how unemployment and the distribution of income between wages and profits determine income inequality in a model with three groups comprising the unemployed, employed and owners of firms. There is a mapping from the WS–PS diagram to the Lorenz curve diagram and to the Gini coefficient as a measure of inequality. In the third section, we extend the analysis of nominal rigidities and aggregate-demand driven cycles and introduce Phillips curves.

2.2.1 Supply-side determinants of equilibrium (structural) unemployment

The logic of both the wage- and price-setting curves and equilibrium unemployment was presented in Sections 2.1.2 and 2.1.3.

The wage-setting curve

In Chapter 15, we set out a formal model of the WS curve based on the twin problems of recruitment and motivation in a labour market in which workers have different valuations of the utility of unemployment. These differences arise from variations in how nearby the job opening is, the hours of work, and the like. This introduces the problem of search and matching, where job seekers search for a good match with a vacancy. In the model with search and matching in Chapter 15, because the employer must pay the marginal hire a higher wage, the reservation wage curve is upward sloping (see Figure 15.6). The no-shirking wage is above the reservation wage and there is a convex wage-setting curve in the aggregate economy.

For the workhorse model of the WS curve we use in the rest of the book, we simplify by assuming that the utility of unemployment does not vary across job seekers, with the implication that the reservation wage is constant. Figure 2.11 shows the model of the WS curve:

- The reservation wage curve is horizontal.
- The WS curve is upward sloping. This linear WS curve is a simplification of the convex WS curve, which steepens as (involuntary) unemployment approaches zero.
- Involuntary unemployment refers to those seeking jobs at a given wage to the left of the labour supply curve.
- The labour force represents the total number of people able to work. The difference between the labour force, those *able* to work, and the labour supply, those *willing* to work at a particular wage, represents voluntary unemployment.

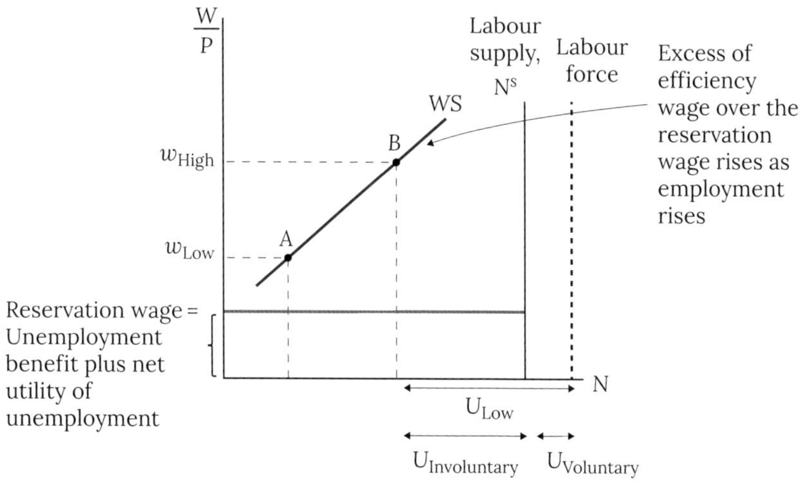

Figure 2.11 The WS curve, the reservation wage, voluntary and involuntary unemployment. Visit www.oup.com/he/carlin-soskice to explore the WS curve, the reservation wage, voluntary and involuntary unemployment with Animated Analytical Diagram 2.11.

A worker's decision to accept a job offer and to exert effort on the job depends on the real wage they expect to receive measured in terms of what they can consume with the wage. And when the employer sets the nominal wage making the 'take it or leave it' offer, she has to take the same perspective. Since the price level that will prevail over the course of the contract, for example, in the year ahead until the wage can be renegotiated is not known, wage setting takes place using the expected real wage and is written as:

$$W = P^E \cdot B(N, \mathbf{z}_w),$$

where P^E is the expected price level and B is a positive function of the level of employment, N, and a set of wage-push variables, $\mathbf{z}_w$. Workers will evaluate *nominal* (i.e. money) wage offers, W, in terms of the *real* wage it is expected to deliver—i.e. it is the nominal wage relative to the expected consumer price level that affects workers' standard of living and hence their utility.

The wage equation can be written in terms of real wages to define the upward-sloping wage-setting curve:

$$w^{WS} = \frac{W}{P^E} = B(N, \mathbf{z}_w). \qquad \text{(wage-setting real wage equation, WS)}$$

The wage-setting curve is explained for simplicity as though all workers in a firm are treated identically. Of course that is a simplification in the contemporary world where many employees will be graduates with whom pay will be negotiated individually, reflecting their different bargaining power and contributions. But the basic principles (including usually annual wage-setting and cost of living increases) are well captured in the simplified wage-setting curve.

Shifts in the WS curve and wage-push factors

The wage-push factors in the wage-setting curve (the $\mathbf{z}_w$'s) include institutional, policy, structural and shock variables.

Holding all else constant, the WS curve shifts up and unemployment increases when:

1. there is a rise in the unemployment benefit or its duration or a fall in costs of applying for it or in the eligibility criteria. These factors are summarized by '*b*', an increase in which raises the reservation wage
2. there is a rise in the net utility of unemployment. Anything that shifts the balance from work toward unemployment such as less flexible working hours, better opportunities for acquiring income from non-employment sources or a lessening of the stigma of being unemployed shifts the reservation wage up
3. there is a rise in the cost of effort. When providing the level of effort required to avoid being fired if caught shirking becomes more onerous, this shifts the WS curve up
4. monitoring of work effort or firing a worker who shirks becomes more difficult or costly.

When unions are present in the workplace, the following factors will shift the WS curve (showing the wage set by the union) up relative to the non-union WS curve:

1. Unions are given more legal protection.
2. Unions are stronger, for example, as measured by a higher proportion of employees belonging to a union (density) or by a higher proportion of employees covered by a union wage (coverage). See Figure 2.4.
3. Unions cease exercising bargaining restraint.

Price setting and the price-setting real wage curve

Firms face downward-sloping demand curves in the product market and *set a price* to maximize their profits. The markup on marginal cost will depend on the elasticity of demand, which is the responsiveness of output demanded to a change in price and reflects the extent of competition, reflecting in turn the importance the consumer attaches to the product in question. As the elasticity of demand rises, the markup falls until we get to the special case of perfect competition, where the elasticity of demand is infinite and the price is the one that clears the market.

When a firm faces a downward-sloping demand curve, it maximizes profits when marginal revenue is equal to marginal cost. If the (absolute value of the) elasticity of demand is η, (called eta), then the price is set as a markup over marginal cost of $\left(\frac{1}{\eta-1}\right)$ and we have the price-setting formula (derived in Appendix 2.5.2):

$$\begin{aligned} P &= \left(1+\frac{1}{\eta-1}\right)\left(\frac{W}{MPL}\right) \equiv (1+\text{markup on MC})\left(\frac{W}{MPL}\right) \\ &= (1+\mu^C)\left(\frac{W}{MPL}\right). \end{aligned} \quad \text{(pricing formula)}$$

For example, if the elasticity of demand is 8, the price is set at a markup of 14% above marginal cost. The markup with superscript 'C' is called the cost-based markup.

The next step is to recognize that setting the profit-maximizing price defines the real wage as a residual, which is the price-setting real wage. From the pricing formula:

$$\begin{aligned} \frac{W}{P} &= \frac{MPL}{(1+\text{markup on MC})} \\ &= \frac{MPL}{(1+\mu^C)}. \end{aligned} \quad \text{(price-setting real wage, in terms of markup on MC)}$$

By rearranging the profit maximizing condition, we can also derive the price-setting real wage in terms of the markup on the price (see the Appendix):

$$\frac{W}{P} = MPL(1-\text{markup on P}) = MPL(1-\mu). \quad \text{(price-setting real wage)}$$

where μ is the markup on price. The markup without a superscript is the price-based markup.

Figure 2.12 illustrates the PS curve: the price-setting real wage is a fraction of the marginal product of labour. For the example of the elasticity of demand of 5, the price-setting real wage is 75% of the level of the marginal product of labour.

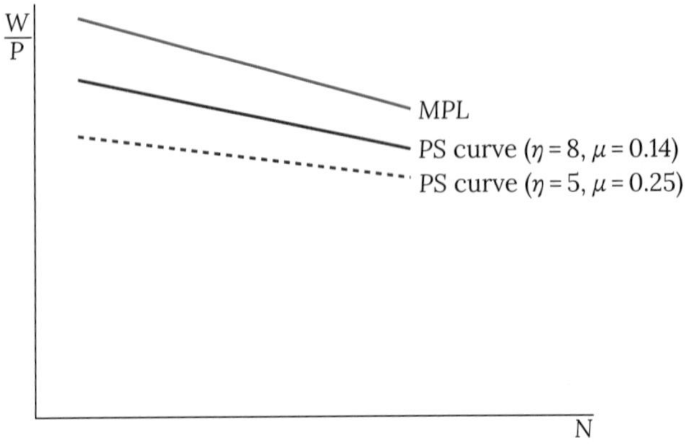

Figure 2.12 Relationship between the MPL, the price elasticity of demand (η), and the PS curve.

The real wage on the PS curve is below that on the marginal product of labour curve at any level of employment by the amount of the supernormal profits per worker (in real terms) associated with imperfect competition in the product market.

For simplicity in working with the macro model, we normally use a horizontal rather than a downward-sloping PS curve.

Two alternative sets of assumptions to get a horizontal PS curve are:

1. if the marginal product of labour is constant (which implies that it is equal to the average product) and the markup is constant, the price-setting real wage is equal to a constant fraction of labour productivity
2. if firms set their prices using a rule of thumb, basing their price on their average costs over the business cycle (i.e. as the economy moves from recession to boom and vice versa) the PS curve would also flatten. Such a 'normal cost pricing' rule might result from firms wishing to limit the extent to which they modify their prices in response to changes in costs associated with changes in demand.

Taking the simplest case, to derive a flat PS curve, we assume constant productivity and a constant markup. We define $\frac{y}{N}$ (output per worker) as λ (lambda, labour productivity). Given these assumptions, if firms set prices to deliver a specific profit margin, then the fixed amount of output per worker is split into two parts: profits per worker and real wages per worker. The real wage implied by pricing behaviour is therefore constant and the PS curve is flat. Price setting can then be summarized as the marking up of unit labour costs by a fixed percentage, μ,[11]

$$P = (1 + \mu^C)\left(\frac{W}{\lambda}\right), \tag{2.1}$$

[11] Note that:

$$\frac{1}{1+\mu^C} = 1 - \mu$$

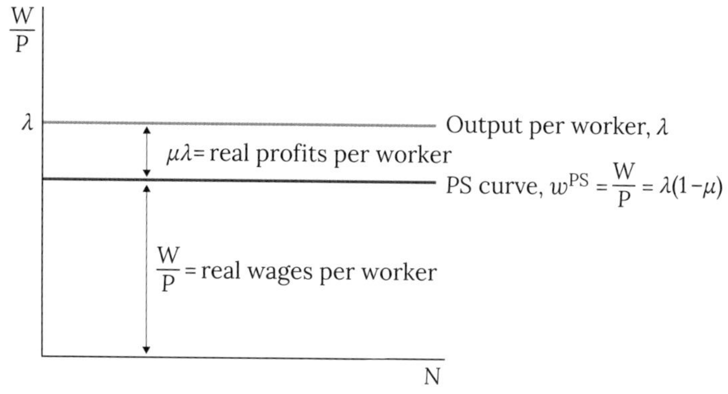

Figure 2.13 The price-setting real wage curve: PS.

where unit labour costs are the cost of labour per unit of output; i.e. $W \times N$ divided by y. We write the price setting real wage equation in terms of the markup on price:

$$w^{PS} = \frac{W}{P} = \lambda(1-\mu). \qquad \text{(PS, price-setting real wage equation)}$$

In other words, given the markup, the level of labour productivity, and the nominal wage, the price level set by firms implies a specific value of the real wage.

A rearrangement of the PS equation shows how output per worker is decomposed into real profits per worker and the real wage as a result of the firm's price-setting decision and this is illustrated in Figure 2.13:

$$\lambda = \mu\lambda + \frac{W}{P} \qquad (2.2)$$

output per worker = real profits per worker + real wages per worker.

Of course, as with the WS curve, the PS curve is inevitably derived in a simplified way. It takes no account of the cost of capital, since output is simply employment times labour productivity. Much competition in the real world takes place through product innovation (see Chapters 16 and 17).

Shifts in the *PS* curve

The tax wedge: How are W and P measured?

Before providing examples of the price-shift variables, one clarification is needed. Once income taxes, labour taxes such as social security contributions and indirect taxes such as VAT are introduced, we have to be clear about what W and P measure and which measure we show on the axis in the labour market diagram. This is a matter of choosing a convention, and we find it convenient to show the real *consumption* wage in the labour market diagram. This entails measuring W as the post-tax money wage paid to the employee and to measure P_c as the consumer price index, i.e. inclusive of indirect taxes, t_v.

$$P_c = P(1 + t_v).$$

This means that when we show $w = W/P_c$ on the axis of the labour market diagram, this is the real consumption wage—the concept relevant from the perspective of the utility of the worker.

By contrast, the real wage that is of relevance to the employer is the real product wage, which is the full cost of labour to firms—inclusive of income tax and non-wage labour costs such as social security contributions paid by employers and employees—divided by the price the firm gets for its product (i.e. excluding indirect taxes). This is called the producer price. The difference between the real consumption wage and the real product wage is called the *tax wedge*. Given the way we have defined the labour market diagram in terms of W and P_c, the wedge shows up as a price-push factor. Any increase in either direct or indirect taxation reduces the price-setting real wage and therefore shifts the PS curve downwards. The derivation of the PS curve including the tax wedge is shown in the Appendix.

The oil price wedge

Another 'wedge' between the real consumption wage and the real product wage arises in the open economy from the presence of imported raw materials. A rise in the price of imported raw materials (e.g. a hike in the oil price on global markets) shifts the PS curve downwards. The real consumption wage on the PS curve, W/P_c, is reduced by the increase in the unit cost of imported materials. The analysis of oil shocks and the derivation of the PS curve incorporating imported raw materials is covered in Chapter 13. In this chapter, we refer to the price-push factor as the 'oil price wedge'.

Price-push factors

We incorporate the tax and oil price wedges as two of the price-push factors, and write the PS curve compactly as:

$$w^{PS} = \lambda F(\mu, \mathbf{z}_p), \qquad \text{(PS curve including price-push factors)}$$

where $\mathbf{z}_p$ is a set of price-push variables.

The PS curve shifts down, raising equilibrium unemployment, when there is:

1. a rise in the tax or oil price wedge, which are included in $\mathbf{z}_p$,
2. a rise in the markup, μ, due, for example, to a change in competitive conditions such as weaker competition policy rules or enforcement, or
3. a fall in productivity, λ.

It is important to note that what matters for shifting the PS curve and therefore for affecting equilibrium unemployment is the tax wedge as a whole: a rise in income tax or in indirect tax will push equilibrium unemployment up. There is nothing special about the effect of the so-called payroll taxes, i.e. the employer and employee social security contributions.

Other factors included in $\mathbf{z}_p$ may be regulations that increase the cost of employment, such as business registration and some employment regulations. However, such regulations do not necessarily have the effect of increasing price push and therefore

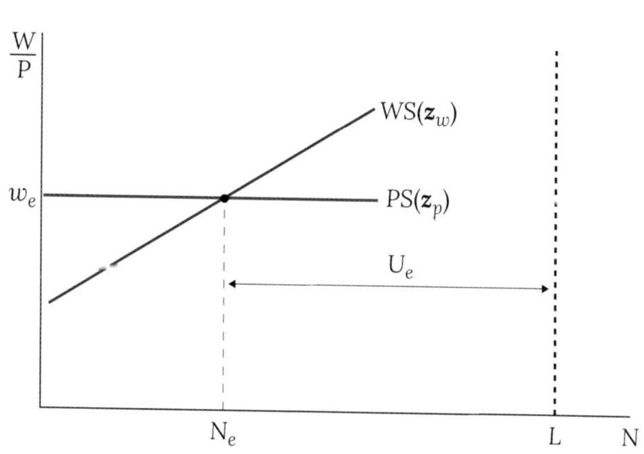

Figure 2.14 Equilibrium employment and unemployment: N_e and U_e.

raising the equilibrium rate of unemployment. For example, although regulations enforcing health and safety standards impose costs on firms, they may have a compensating positive effect on productivity.

Equilibrium in the labour market

The labour market is characterized by an upward-sloping WS curve and a flat or downward-sloping PS curve. The labour market is in equilibrium where the curves cross (see Figure 2.14):

$$w^{WS} = w^{PS}$$

$$B(N, \mathbf{z}_w) = \lambda F(\mu, \mathbf{z}_p), \qquad \text{(labour market equilibrium)}$$

and this defines the unique equilibrium level of employment N_e. The associated equilibrium rate of unemployment is U_e/L, where L is the labour force.

Unemployment in equilibrium

The equilibrium rate of unemployment is the outcome of the structural or supply-side features of the economy that lie behind the wage-setting and price-setting curves. It can therefore in principle be changed by supply-side policies or structural changes that affect either the wage-push or price-push factors.

An increase in the degree of product market competition—as a result, say, of changes in the application of tougher competition policy or because the internet makes it easier to compare prices—would produce a lower profit margin (μ) and a higher real wage at each level of employment (the PS curve would shift up). Similarly, any government policy change that affects wage- and price-setting outcomes will shift equilibrium unemployment. Policies related to the cost of job loss such as unemployment benefits, changes in taxation, labour, and product market regulation and incomes accords are all relevant. It is thus easy to imagine that international differences in policy and in institutional structures produce differences in equilibrium unemployment. We return to analyse supply-side shifts and the evidence regarding their role in explaining cross-country unemployment trends in Chapter 15.

2.2.2 Supply-side equilibrium and inequality

To this point, we have concentrated on the implications for equilibrium unemployment of supply side factors. We now turn explicitly to inequality. Since those who are unemployed have lower income, inequality is higher when unemployment rises. A direct connection to inequality arises from the firm's market power vis-à-vis its customers. When firms acquire more monopoly power in the product market reflected by a higher markup over its costs, the share of profits in the economy goes up, and this, too, raises inequality.

A simple graphical model enables us to translate changes in the labour market equilibrium (due to shifts in the WS and PS curves) into changes in inequality through their effect on equilibrium unemployment. We can also show the effect of changes in the markup on inequality via the profit share. The model uses the Lorenz curve (and associated Gini coefficient) as the measure of inequality. We assume there are three groups of income recipients in the economy: the unemployed (who may receive unemployment benefits), the employed (who receive wages) and owners of firms (who receive profits).

The Gini coefficient and Lorenz curve

The Gini coefficient[12] is a measure of economic inequality based on differences in incomes between people. It uses the income information about everyone (and not just for example the 'top' and 'bottom' of the distribution in familiar rich/poor ratio measures or top 1% measures). The Gini coefficient is calculated from two pieces of information:

- The average of the differences between people (e.g. in Figure 2.15, $(10 + 8 + 2)/3 = 20/3 = 6.67$).
- The average income of people: $(12 + 4 + 2)/3 = 6$.

The Gini is equal to one-half the average of the differences divided by the average income, $0.5(6.67/6) = 0.56$. The Gini coefficient is equal to 1 if a single person owns everything and 0 if everyone has the same income, and therefore lies between

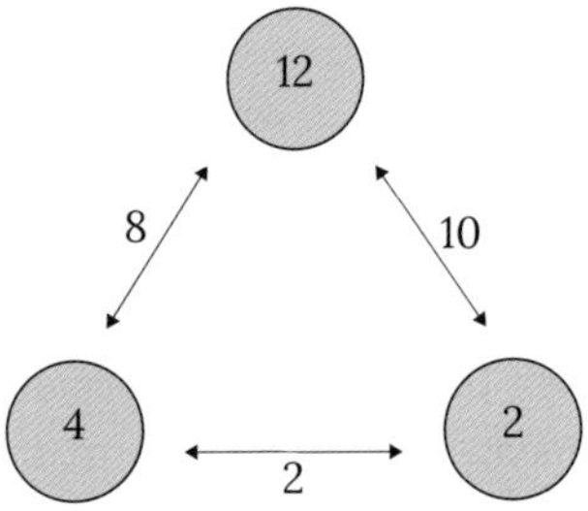

Figure 2.15 Income differences among pairs of households.

[12] This analysis and the examples come from the CORE Team's *The Economy*, Unit 9.8.

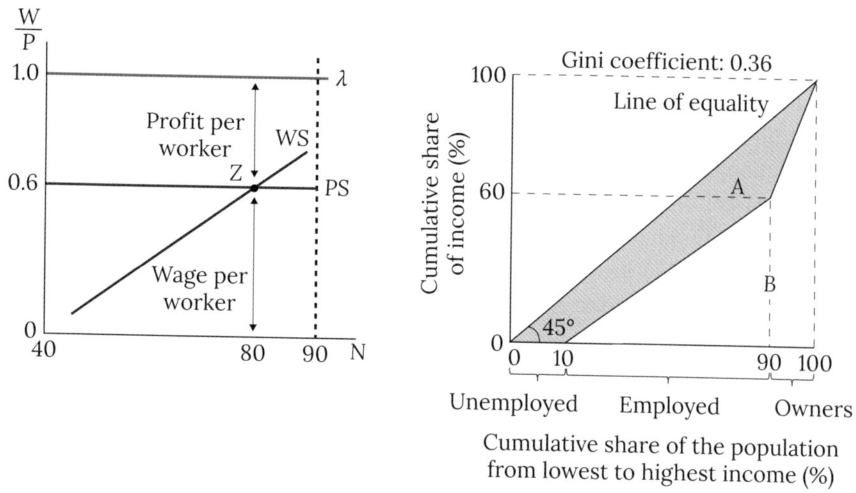

Figure 2.16 The distribution of income at labour and product market equilibrium. Visit www.oup.com/he/carlin-soskice to explore distribution of income at labour and product market equilibrium with Animated Analytical Diagram 2.16.

0 and 1. Figure 2.15 illustrates the differences in income between the households in a 3-household population on the basis of which the Gini coefficient is calculated.[13]

We now apply the Gini coefficient to a population divided into the three relevant groups for the macro model: unemployed, employed and owners. This will also enable us to represent inequality in the Lorenz curve, which is a visualization of the Gini coefficient. The usual WS–PS diagram is shown in the left-hand panel of Figure 2.16.[14] In this economy, there are 90 workers, of whom 10 are unemployed. Labour is the only input in production and we can see that the wage share is 60% and the profit share, 40%. In the right-hand panel is a Lorenz curve diagram, where for simplicity we have assumed the unemployed do not receive unemployment benefit so they are shown with zero income.

To show the level of inequality in a Lorenz curve diagram, people are ordered from left to right according to their income along the horizontal axis. The vertical axis shows the cumulative share of income from zero to 100%. The line of equality is the 45 degree line, which shows the hypothetical situation in which each person has the same income: along that line, the 10% of the population on the left of the horizontal axis has the same share of income as the 'top' 10% in the extreme right.

---

[13] See Bowles and Carlin (2020a) for a more detailed analysis of the Gini coefficient (and the Lorenz curve) as a measure of experienced inequality.

[14] See the CORE Team's *The Economy* for an explanation of how to compute the Gini coefficient from the Lorenz curve (https://www.core-econ.org/the-economy/book/text/09.html?query=Lorenz+curve#einstein-the-lorenz-curve-and-the-gini-coefficient-in-an-economy-with-unemployed-employed-and-employers-owners).

In the example shown, the 10 unemployed have zero income and the next 80 (who are all identical) have wage income amounting to 60% of income. Finally, the owners are the remaining 10 people going from 90 to 100 along the horizontal axis. The income of each (identical) owner is higher than that of each worker and is reflected in the steep section of the Lorenz curve. The 40% of income, which is profits, is divided equally between the 10 owners. The segments of the Lorenz curve are linear because there are no differences in income between members of a group such as employees. To calculate the Gini measure of inequality, the area between the line of equality and the Lorenz curve (area A) is divided by A + B, where B is the area below the Lorenz curve.

To summarize, in the WS-PS model, a rise in the markup (higher profit share) and structural changes that raise equilibrium unemployment raise inequality and can be mapped into the Lorenz curve diagram. Note that in this model, an upward shift in the WS curve due to an increase in union bargaining power *raises* inequality because its only effect on income distribution is through the effect of increasing equilibrium unemployment. The reason that higher union bargaining power does not result in an increase in labour's share of income is that in this model, firms are always able to pass on higher nominal wage increases in their prices, preserving their markup and therefore the share of profits in income.

2.2.3 **Nominal rigidities, the Phillips curve, and the business cycle**

Demand-driven cycles

In Section 2.1 we explained that the economy will be shifted away from the medium-run equilibrium (where the WS and PS curves intersect) by fluctuations in aggregate demand. Wages and prices do not adjust spontaneously to keep the economy at equilibrium unemployment. We reported the survey evidence that wages are set periodically and that employers do not usually cut nominal wages when unemployment goes up.

What about prices? Fluctuations in aggregate demand lead to business cycle upswings and downswings because firms respond to changes in demand by altering output and employment. One explanation for demand-driven cycles is that imperfectly competitive firms find it profitable to respond to shifts in demand by changing their output.[15] Price stickiness refers to the reluctance of firms to change prices in the face of changes in aggregate demand.

The demand curve faced by an imperfectly competitive firm is shifted by shocks to aggregate demand in the economy of the kind introduced in Chapter 1. It is clear from the markup equation that when profits are maximized, the price will be above marginal cost: the firm will make super-normal profits.

The key point is that because price-setting firms are making super-normal profits when maximizing profits, they will continue to make profits on sales when demand fluctuates above and below equilibrium. They can respond to fluctuations in demand

---

15 See Solow (1998) for further discussion of this point.

by changing output rather than by changing their price. There are two reasons why they are likely to choose to respond this way:

1. It may be profit-maximizing not to change the price (in the case of a linear demand curve, constant marginal cost and a percentage change in demand). If the demand curve rotates relative to the vertical axis so that demand increases or decreases by a percentage, delta, then the elasticity and therefore the markup is unaffected at a given price because the percentage increase in quantity in the case of a boom is exactly offset by a flattening of the slope of the demand curve (see the Appendix for the details). Thus fluctuations in demand do not affect the markup and, with constant costs, the profit-maximizing price is therefore unchanged. Firms will respond to demand fluctuations by changing output, not price.
2. If the assumptions required in (1) do not hold, keeping the price unchanged in the face of demand fluctuations may still be the firm's preferred strategy because of other costs associated with changing prices.

One type of cost is the so-called menu cost. The term comes from the idea that there are costs involved in changing the prices on menus in restaurants. This is a relevant consideration for those firms that operate with posted prices like restaurants, or firms with printed price catalogues. However, these costs seem much less relevant for firms where prices can be changed at the touch of a button. Yet, even when the technology is available to adjust prices at low cost, a firm may worry that it will lose customers if it changes its price when other firms producing similar products do not. Given that the benefits of changing price are likely to be modest under imperfect competition (since firms continue to make profits when output fluctuates), the costs do not have to be large to outweigh the benefits.

A large study has used firm level (i.e. micro) data sources and surveys to investigate price stickiness in the euro area.[16] The authors find that firms change their prices infrequently, on average once a year. They also found that the main sources of price stickiness are strategic interactions between competing firms and implicit or explicit contracts with their customers, with menu costs being judged less important. Older survey evidence found that firms coordinate their price increases around industry-wide wage rounds.

We can summarize by saying that in the model, prices are sticky in response to shifts in demand and flexible in response to changes in costs.

Business cycles and inflation: The Phillips curve

As we saw in the previous subsection, there is a unique unemployment rate at which the labour market is in equilibrium. At this equilibrium, the WS and PS curves intersect, which means both wage and price setters are content with the prevailing real wage and have no incentive to alter their behaviour. In this section, we focus on nominal rigidities and how fluctuations in aggregate demand produce business cycle upswings and downswings around the equilibrium rate of unemployment.

---

16 See Álvarez et al. (2006).

To simplify the modelling, we have assumed that labour productivity is constant. This implies that changes in output are reflected one-for-one in changes in employment. When drawing diagrams, it means that the horizontal shift in output is the same as in employment. In the real world, there is not a one-for-one relationship between changes in output and employment. Okun's law refers to the empirical relationship between a change in aggregate demand, output and the unemployment rate.

BOX 2.1 **Okun's Law**

When output rises, workers who have been kept on the pay-roll but have not been fully employed (e.g. those working shorter than normal hours) may be fully utilized, with the result that higher output does not—at least initially—entail a rise in employment. This is called labour hoarding. Also even if employment rises, unemployment does not necessarily fall if the new jobs are taken by those who were not previously in the labour force. People of working age who are neither employed nor unemployed are called economically inactive and the decision of whether or not to participate in the labour market is dependent on economic conditions.

The combination of labour hoarding and changes in the labour force mean that a 1% change in output growth above or below its trend tends to be associated with respectively a fall or rise in the unemployment rate of less than 0.5 percentage points. This empirical relationship between changes in the growth rate relative to its trend and changes in the unemployment rate is called Okun's Law (an Okun coefficient of −0.5). The responsiveness of unemployment to changes in growth is lower in countries with tighter regulations on hiring and firing (as observed in many continental European countries) and with stronger traditions of lifetime employment (as observed in Japan).

Ball, Leigh, and Loungani (2017) examine data for 20 advanced economies, and find that Okun's Law has been a 'strong relationship in most countries, and one that is fairly stable over time.' They argue that this relationship did not change substantially in the financial crisis of 2008–09, but that there is a large variation across countries in the coefficient in the relationship (i.e. the degree of responsiveness of the unemployment rate to output). They find an Okun's coefficient of −0.48 for the US, −0.17 for Japan and a much higher coefficient (in absolute value) of −0.82 for Spain, where temporary employment contracts are prevalent. They do however argue that since 2011 Okun's Law has been violated in the US, with the unemployment rate falling without the expected corresponding increases in output growth.

A second study by the same authors has shown that on average, Okun's coefficient in developing countries is half the size of that in developed countries (Ball et al. 2019). One possible explanation is that countries which have a high share of services, usually a characteristic of developed countries, see greater responses in employment to fluctuations in output.

A positive aggregate demand shock increases employment above the equilibrium level, and inflation rises. The timing of events is summarized as before:

$$\begin{aligned}\text{Aggregate demand shock} &\rightarrow \text{output and employment change}\\ \text{Next wage round} &\rightarrow \text{nominal wages change}\\ \text{Immediately after the wage round} &\rightarrow \text{prices change}\end{aligned}$$

This behaviour is modelled by the Phillips curve. We now need to formalize that relationship to develop the model of inflation and unemployment.

The WS curve says that the real wage increases with employment. It simplifies the modelling to express this in terms of the *output gap*, $(y_t - y_e)$, and to write the WS curve in linear form:

$$w^{WS}(y_t) = (W/P)^{WS} = B + \underbrace{\alpha \underbrace{(y_t - y_e)}_{\text{output gap}}}_{\text{bargaining gap}} + \mathbf{z}_w, \qquad \text{(WS curve; linear form)}$$

where B is a constant reflecting the unemployment benefit and the net utility of unemployment , $\alpha(y_t - y_e)$ is the *bargaining gap* and $\mathbf{z}_w$ is the set of wage-push factors.

Because price setting always restores the real wage to its pre-existing level, w_1, forward-looking wage setters will attempt to increase the expected real wage by the bargaining gap:

$$w^{WS}(y_t) - w_{-1} = w^{WS}(y_t) - w_e = (B + \alpha(y_t - y_e) + \mathbf{z}_w) - (B + \mathbf{z}_w) = \alpha(y_t - y_e). \qquad (2.3)$$

If wage-setters expect prices to increase by $(\Delta P/P)_{t-1}$, we use the approximation $(\Delta W/W)_t - (\Delta P/P)_{t-1} \approx w^{WS}(y_t) - w_{-1}$. Thus we have $(\Delta W/W)_t - (\Delta P/P)_{t-1} = \alpha(y_t - y_e)$ or

$$(\Delta W/W)_t \approx (\Delta P/P)_{t-1} + \alpha(y_t - y_e). \qquad \text{(wage inflation)}$$

This says that wage setters set the percentage increase in the nominal wage to cover the previous period's price increase and to reflect any positive or negative output gap at the time of the wage round.

Turning to price setters, we use the pricing formula, and noting from the timeline that firms set prices immediately after wages have been set, we have:[17]

---

[17] The conversion of the price-setting equation into the price inflation equation is carried out as follows. If you are unfamiliar with logs and their properties, see Appendix 16.7.1 in Chapter 16. We assume that μ^C remains constant over time. In continuous time, we find an expression for the growth rate of $P = (1 + \mu^C)W/\lambda$ by first taking logs, then differentiating with respect to time and using the fact that $\frac{d\log x}{dx} = \frac{1}{x}$:

$$\log(P(t)) = \log(1 + \mu^C) + \log(W(t)) - \log(\lambda(t))$$

Differentiate each term with respect to time recalling that we assumed $d\log(1 + \mu^C)/dt = 0$.

$$\frac{d[\log(P(t))]}{dt} = \frac{d[\log(W(t))]}{dt} - \frac{d[\log(\lambda(t))]}{dt}.$$

By the chain rule for composite functions, the equation above becomes:

$$\frac{d\log P}{dP}\frac{dP}{dt} = \frac{d\log W}{dW}\frac{dW}{dt} - \frac{d\log \lambda}{d\lambda}\frac{d\lambda}{dt}$$

$$P = (1+\mu^C)\frac{W}{\lambda}, \text{ and}$$

$$(\Delta P/P)_t = (\Delta W/W)_t - (\Delta\lambda/\lambda)_t. \qquad \text{(price inflation)}$$

Substituting the expression for wage inflation into the equation for price inflation gives the following equation for inflation when productivity is constant. This is called the Phillips curve:

$$(\Delta P/P)_t = (\Delta P/P)_{t-1} + \alpha(y_t - y_e) \qquad (2.4)$$

$$\underbrace{\pi_t}_{\text{current inflation}} = \underbrace{\pi_{t-1}}_{\text{lagged inflation}} + \underbrace{\alpha\underbrace{(y_t - y_e)}_{\text{output gap}}}_{\text{bargaining gap}} \qquad \text{(Phillips curve, PC)}$$

where π_t is the rate of inflation. If P_t is today's price level and P_{t-1} is last period's price level, then the rate of inflation over the past year is π_t:

$$\pi_t \equiv \frac{P_t - P_{t-1}}{P_{t-1}} = \Delta P/P.$$

Graphical derivation of the Phillips curve

In Figure 2.17, we assume that an investment boom because of more optimistic business expectations shifts the IS curve to the right. Output and employment rise to the 'high' levels shown. The fall in unemployment shifts the balance of power in the labour market towards workers as reflected in the positively sloped WS curve. At the next wage round, wage setters respond to the positive output gap: they will need to set a 2% nominal wage increase to cover last period's inflation plus an additional increase equal to the bargaining gap, which is α times the output gap (see the wage inflation equation). In the example shown in Figure 2.8, this is an extra 2%. Nominal wages go up by 4%.

How do price setters respond to the higher wages? Their labour costs have risen by 4%, so they mark up this cost increase in their prices, and price inflation goes up from 2% to 4% (see the price inflation equation). We have the result that an expansion of aggregate demand that pushes output and employment above the equilibrium level is followed by a rise in wage and price inflation. By joining together points A and B, we have an upward-sloping line in the inflation–output diagram. This is a Phillips curve.

Will inflation stay at 4%? Let us assume that employment remains at its high level until the next wage round. How do wage setters respond? The first thing to notice is that employees will be disappointed with their real wage over the past year: they had expected a high real wage in line with the tighter labour market. This did not eventuate because firms passed on the labour cost increase immediately in higher prices. With this behaviour generalized across the economy, the consumer price index will have risen by 4%. As shown by the WS curve, wage setters (the firm's HR department) will now have to set a wage increase to make good the erosion of the real wage over the

---

Using the fact that $d\log x/dx = 1/x$:

$$\frac{dP/dt}{P} = \frac{dW/dt}{W} - \frac{d\lambda/dt}{\lambda}$$

$$\pi = \frac{dW/dt}{W} - \frac{d\lambda/dt}{\lambda}.$$

Writing this in discrete time, gives the expression in the text.

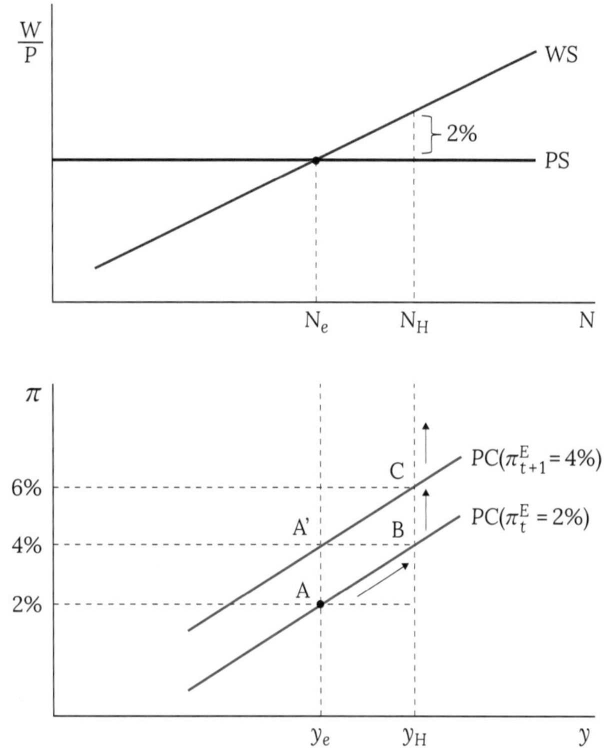

Figure 2.17 The derivation of the Phillips curve. Visit www.oup.com/he/carlin-soskice to explore the derivation of the Phillips curve with Animated Analytical Diagram 2.17.

past year (an increase of 4%) plus another 2% to take the expected real wage to its high level on the WS curve. Firms will follow by putting prices up by 6%. A new Phillips curve is defined by joining up point A′ and C. Each Phillips curve is labelled by lagged inflation. Case 2 in Table 2.1 shows the output and inflation outcomes following a positive demand shock in period 0.

Any positive gap between the PS and the WS curves signals a conflict between the claims of firms for profits and of workers for wages. The conflict produces rising prices and wages and is known as the conflict theory of inflation (Rowthorn 1977, Lorenzoni and Werning 2023).

If we take the converse case of an equal size negative demand shock that moves employment below the equilibrium rate such that output is reduced to $y_L < y_e$, the same reasoning gives the result that inflation is falling. The process will be the exact reverse of that set out above for the positive demand shock. The summary of the output and inflation outcomes for this example is shown as Case 3 in Table 2.1. This example shows that employment below the equilibrium is accompanied by falling inflation.

Summary of the Phillips curve (*PC*)

We have shown that the Phillips curve (PC) is derived from the wage-setting and price-setting curves. In the formulation of the PC that underlies the core 3-equation model,

Inflation (% per year) and employment					
Period	Output	Lagged inflation	Bargaining gap	Wage inflation	Price inflation
−1	y_e	2	0	2	2
Case 1: constant inflation					
0	y_e	2	0	2	2
1	y_e	2	0	2	2
2	y_e	2	0	2	2
Case 2: rising inflation					
0	y_H	2	2	4	4
1	y_H	4	2	6	6
2	y_H	6	2	8	8
Case 3: falling inflation					
0	y_L	2	−2	0	0
1	y_L	0	−2	−2	−2
2	y_L	−2	−2	−4	−4

Table 2.1 Constant, rising, and falling inflation.

each Phillips curve shows a feasible set of output and inflation pairs for a given rate of lagged inflation. The Phillips curves are pinned down by lagged inflation because of the presence of lagged inflation in the wage inflation equation. Wage setters are interested in the real wage. When setting the nominal wage increase, they take a view about the way the consumer price index is likely to evolve over the course of the wage contract. A simple rule for doing this uses consumer price inflation over the previous period.

In modelling inflation and Phillips curves, it is usual to express the role of lagged inflation in terms of inflation expectations. We use this language and return in Chapter 4 to a detailed investigation of how expectations are formed. Thus, we can write:

$$\pi_t^E = \pi_{t-1}, \qquad \text{(adaptive inflation expectations)}$$

where π_t^E is expected inflation in period t and π_{t-1} is actual inflation in period $t-1$. When we model wage setters' behaviour in this manner, then we say that they have *adaptive expectations*. This is because they update their expectations every period based on their best guess for how prices will evolve over the year ahead and they use the outturn for inflation in the last period as their forecast. As shown in Figure 2.17, we pin down the vertical height of the Phillips curve by expected inflation. Throughout this book, we will denote the Phillips curve by PC($\pi_t^E = x\%$). In the adaptive expectations case, x is simply last period's inflation rate.

The Phillips curves are upward sloping, reflecting the effect of the output gap, $(y_t - y_e)$, on wages and prices through the wage- and price-setting curves, and hence on inflation. As we saw in the previous subsection, if output is above equilibrium, then inflation will be higher than last period's inflation and vice versa. In the model, workers get a base wage increase equal to lagged inflation, and they also get an additional wage change to reflect the position of the economy relative to equilibrium. A positive output gap will result in a positive additional wage change and a negative output gap the opposite. This reflects the positively sloped wage-setting curve.

We can see from Figure 2.17 that each adaptive expectations Phillips curve is defined by two characteristics:

1. The lagged inflation rate (π_{t-1}), which fixes the height of the Phillips curve on a vertical line above the level of output associated with the equilibrium rate of unemployment; and
2. The slope of the WS curve, which fixes its slope.[18] The Phillips curves will be steeper if the WS curve is steeper and vice versa.

In equation form, the Phillips curve is:

$$\pi_t = \pi_t^E + \alpha(y_t - y_e)$$

$$\underbrace{\pi_t}_{\text{current inflation}} = \underbrace{\pi_{t-1}}_{\text{lagged inflation}} + \underbrace{\alpha(y_t - y_e)}_{\text{output gap}}. \qquad \text{(adaptive expectations Phillips curve)}$$

We can see from this expression that the Phillips curve shifts up or down whenever lagged inflation changes and that its slope depends on α, which in turn reflects the slope of the WS curve.

Evidence on inflation dynamics in many countries over the past few decades suggests that changes in output (and employment) are followed by changes in inflation, which is summarized by saying that output leads inflation; and that inflation is persistent.[19] Consistent with this evidence, the Phillips curve states that inflation depends on past inflation, π_{t-1} and the output gap, which reflects the difference between current unemployment and the equilibrium rate of unemployment.

The assumption that prices are adjusted immediately to cost increases means that the real wage remains on the PS curve and is constant over the business cycle. Empirically, at the aggregate level, real wages are mildly pro-cyclical. In the model, if lags in price setting are introduced (in addition to the lag in wage-setting due to the annual wage round), then the real wage would lie in between the WS and PS curves. This could also be the case if only some fraction of firms adjusted their price immediately after the wage round. Real wages would then be pro-cyclical reflecting the upward-sloping wage-setting curve. Real wages would rise in business cycle upswings and fall in downswings.

2.3 APPLICATIONS

2.3.1 Shocks in the absence of a stabilizing policy maker

We shall see in Chapter 3 that an inflation-targeting central bank will diagnose the nature of a shock and then respond by adjusting the interest rate. To motivate the

[18] Note that if the PS curve was downward sloping, the slope of the Phillips curve would be steeper, reflecting the slope of both the WS and the PS curves. At output above equilibrium, for example, there would not only be the 'gap' due to the slope of the WS curve but there would be a second 'gap' between the existing real wage and that on the PS curve. Firms would push up prices further to reduce the real wage down to the lower real wage on the PS curve.

[19] For evidence, see for instance Christiano et al. (2005); Estrella and Fuhrer (2002); or Fuhrer and Moore (1995).

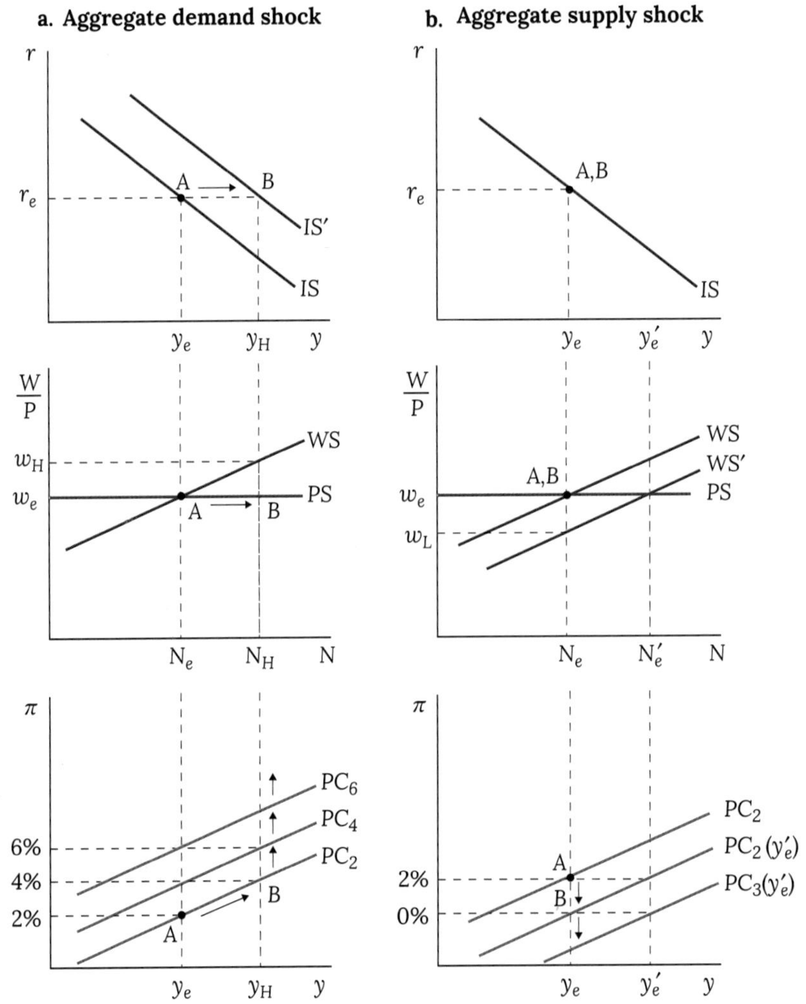

Figure 2.18 World without a stabilizing policy maker: inflationary implications of aggregate demand and supply-side shocks. Visit www.oup.com/he/carlin-soskice to explore shocks without a stabilizing policy maker with Animated Analytical Diagram 2.18.
Note: PC_x is used as short form for $PC(\pi_t^E = x\%)$, where x is the level of lagged inflation and t is the time period.

introduction of a policy maker who seeks to stabilize the economy, we show what happens to the economy when it is disturbed by a demand or supply shock in the absence of such a policy maker. We look in turn at demand shocks, represented in the model by a shift of the IS curve or a shift along it due to a change in the interest rate, and at supply shocks, represented by shifts in the WS and or the PS curves.

An aggregate demand shock

By drawing the IS diagram above the labour market diagram we show the positive aggregate demand shock explicitly in the left-hand panel of Figure 2.18. Our assumption that there is no stabilizing policy maker is reflected in the fact that the IS curve remains at IS' following the shock and the real interest rate is kept constant at its initial level, r_e.

We assume the economy begins at equilibrium output y_e with lagged inflation of 2%. A positive aggregate demand shock shifts the IS curve to IS′. An example of such a shock would be the US economic boom associated with higher government spending (on military and non-military goods and services) that coincided with the start of the Vietnam war in 1965. US GDP growth was 6.4% in 1965 and 6.5% in 1966, compared to an average of just 3.9% for the other years in that decade.[20]

As shown in Figure 2.18a, the shock is accompanied by ever-increasing inflation: with output above equilibrium at y_H, there is a gap between the WS and the PS every period, wages and prices are adjusted first as wage setters try to achieve the real wage w_H and second as firms push up prices to restore their profit margin (which implies the real wage is kept at w_e). The process is exactly the same as in the example used to derive the Phillips curve in the last section (see Figure 2.17 and Case 2 in Table 2.1).

With the real interest rate kept constant at r_e, a positive demand shock is associated with higher employment and rising inflation. In Chapter 3, we address the question of why the policy maker will not be happy with a situation of ever-increasing inflation and what they could do to stabilize the demand shock, and get inflation back to the initial level of 2%.

A supply-side shock

We now turn to the implications of a supply-side shock, which we can model as a shift in:

1. the production function, i.e. a technology or productivity shock (change in λ)
2. the WS curve, e.g. a shift in bargaining power from workers to employers or in any of the other wage-push factors (i.e. $\mathbf{z}_w$)
3. the PS curve, e.g. more intense competition in the product market (i.e. $\downarrow \mu$) or a shift in any of the price-push factors (i.e. $\mathbf{z}_p$).

To illustrate the implications for output, employment and inflation, we take the example of a downward shift in the WS curve. An example of such a shock would be the Dutch supply-side reforms of the 1980s. The Netherlands was seen as one of Europe's 'employment miracles'. In 1983, unemployment stood at 8.3%, whereas the average for the 1990–2008 period was just 4.6%. The Dutch reforms included reduced unemployment benefit generosity, increased expenditure on active labour market policies to make workers more employable and closer coordination in the wage bargaining process.[21]

We analyse the adjustment of the economy to the supply shock using Figure 2.18b. We assume the economy begins at equilibrium output y_e with lagged inflation of 2%. A positive supply shock shifts the WS curve downward to WS′. This raises the equilibrium

[20] Figures calculated using data on real GDP from the US Bureau of Economic Analysis.
[21] See Nickell and van Ours (2000) and Nickell et al. (2000).

level of employment from N_e to N'_e and the equilibrium level of output from y_e to y'_e. Again, we assume there is no stabilizing policy maker, so the real interest rate is kept constant at its initial level of r_e following the shock.

At the original output level, y_e, there is now a negative gap between the WS and PS curves shown by the downward-shifted WS curve. Workers will now be willing to supply adequate effort at the lower wage w_L, because there is a higher cost of job loss (as a result of lower benefit generosity). We assume that the negative output gap is such that $\alpha(y_e - y'_e) = -2\%$. The wage inflation equation derived earlier gives that the increase in nominal wages is equal to:

$$(\Delta W/W)_t = (\Delta P/P)_{t-1} + \alpha\left(y_t - y'_e\right) = 2\% - 2\% = 0\% \tag{2.5}$$

Hence, nominal wages are not increased at all in this wage round. There have been no changes in competition in the product market and with no change in their costs and workers' productivity, firms keep prices unchanged. This follows from the price inflation equation:

$$(\Delta P/P)_t = (\Delta W/W)_t - (\Delta\lambda/\lambda)_t = 0\% - 0\% = 0\% \tag{2.6}$$

Inflation therefore falls from 2% to 0% and the Phillips curve shifts down.

In the following periods, the adjustment of the economy is similar to that of a negative demand shock (see Case 3 in Table 2.1). Inflation falls in each period. This process will carry on indefinitely, as long as output is kept below the new equilibrium—i.e. unemployment cannot be kept at a level above equilibrium without falling inflation.

A positive supply shock is defined as one that raises equilibrium output and employment. We have shown that a positive supply shock is associated with falling inflation *at the initial output level* $y = y_e$. If the supply shock is permanent, then the economy is capable of operating with lower unemployment and constant inflation. As we shall see in Chapter 3, the policy maker is likely to respond to the shock by reducing the interest rate to allow the economy to operate at the new equilibrium output level of y'_e with constant inflation.

2.3.2 **The supply side and inequality: Markups**

Using the mapping from the WS-PS diagram to the Lorenz curve, we consider the impact on inequality of a decline in the extent of competition faced by firms. A rise in the markup shifts the PS curve down and equilibrium unemployment rises. Also, the profit share rises, increasing inequality directly through a second channel as the owners making up a small proportion of the population share a larger slice of output. In the example in Figure 2.19, the PS shifts down as the markup rises from 24% to 40%. This increases the number unemployed in the new equilibrium at C from 7 to 10. The increase in the profit share translates directly into the downward shift in the kink in the Lorenz curve. Both changes are reflected in the outward shift in the Lorenz curve away from the line of equality; the Gini coefficient rises from 0.19 to 0.36.

Figure 2.20 shows the evolution of average markups in the US since 1980 in the left panel and of the Gini coefficient for market (i.e. pre tax and transfer) income in

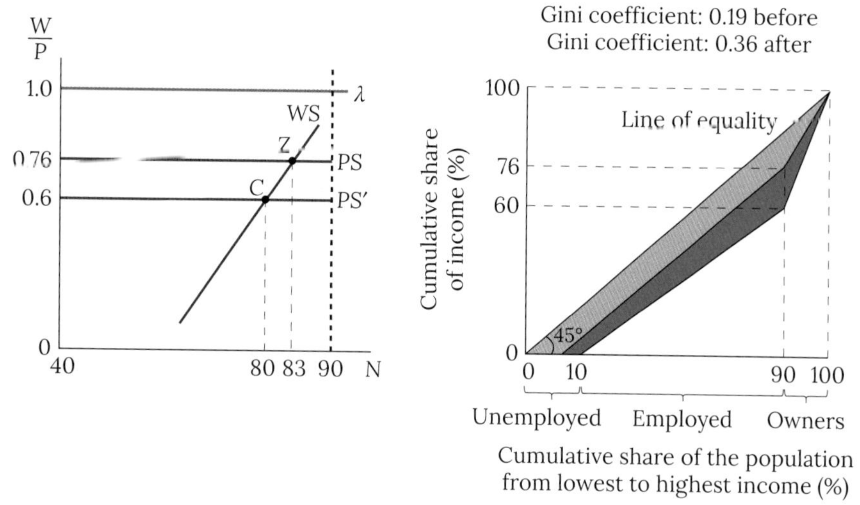

Figure 2.19 The effect of a fall in the extent of competition faced by firms: the PS curve shifts down and inequality rises.

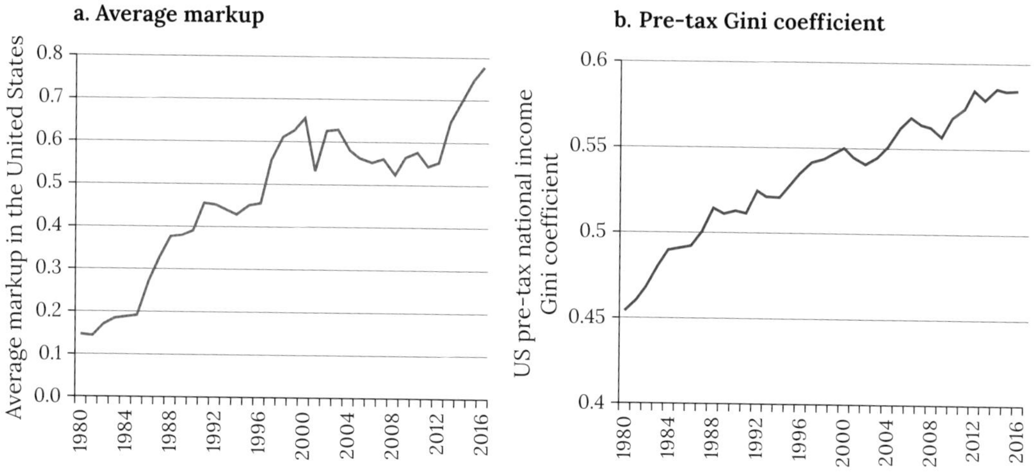

Figure 2.20 Average Markups and pre-tax Gini coefficient in the United States: 1980–2016.
Source: De Loecker and Eeckhout (2018) (left panel) and World Inequality Database (right panel).

the right panel. In the period during which household income inequality increased, average markups also rose.

The growth in market dominance in key industries is evident—we experience daily the influence of five firms (Alphabet (Google), Amazon, Apple, Meta (Facebook), Microsoft). Although for some of these firms, prices are ostensibly low, marginal costs are even lower and profit margins high. Measures of the difference between price and cost in firms across the thousands of sectors in the economy provide a better insight into trends in product market power.

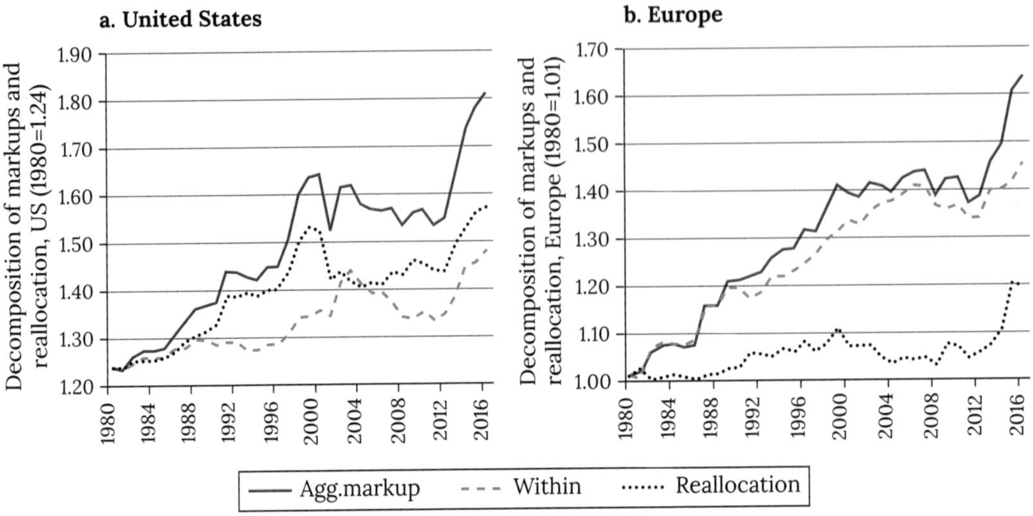

Figure 2.21 Comparison of markups in the United States and Europe: 1980–2016.

Source: De Loecker and Eeckhout (2018) (left panel) and World Inequality Database (right panel).

Figure 2.21 presents the data on average markups for the US and also for Europe from 1980. The patterns shown in the upper series (average markup) for both are remarkably similar. Markups grew rapidly from 1980 to 2000, then plateaued and resumed their rise from 2010. An interesting hypothesis is that the entry of Chinese suppliers in the first decade of China's membership of the World Trade Organization (WTO), which it joined in 2001—often referred to as the 'China shock'—coincided with the pause in the upward trend of markups among firms in the US and Europe. These new entrants increased competition via imports and could have placed a temporary check on the rise in average markups in the markets of domestic firms, where they entered. Evidence supporting this conjecture comes from the finding that following the China shock, markups in the US declined in industries (like furniture and clothing) that experienced the largest import competition (Autor, Dorn, and Hanson 2013).

Although the trends in average markups are similar for the US and Europe, there is an interesting difference between them. Figure 2.21 decomposes the change in the average markup across firms into two components. The first is the 'reallocation' effect reflecting the shift in industry sales from lower to higher markup firms and the second is the 'within' effect, which measures the growth in markups within firms.

In the US, the bulk of the rise in markups is accounted for by the reallocation of market share from low to high markup firms (without changes in markups). The increasingly dominant so-called 'superstar' firms in each industry are those with large market shares and high productivity.[22] By contrast, in Europe, rising average markups reflected increases in markups across the population of firms rather than reallocation

[22] See Autor et al. (2020); a shorter treatment is also available at https://www.aeaweb.org/articles?id=10.1257/aer.p20171102.

of sales toward initially high markup ones. Figure 2.21 shows these contrasting patterns for the US and Europe (Eeckhout 2021). Exploring these trends across countries and uncovering the role of technology, globalization and competition policy, as well as the implications for unemployment and inequality is a lively area of research.

Other hypotheses that may have contributed to rising profit margins and the shift in income distribution from wages to profits are connected with technological change. The application of new technology—the ICT revolution—across the economy is often characterized by scale economies and sometimes also by network effects.[23] Along with the growing role of intangible capital, these act as barriers to entry to the market. See Chapter 17 for analysis of the ICT revolution.

2.3.3 The supply side and inequality: Unions

In the WS-PS model, a rise in union bargaining power does not affect the wage share. If it shifts the WS curve up, this raises equilibrium unemployment, and inequality. If strong unions exercise bargaining restraint as in some northern European countries, then this reduces equilibrium unemployment and lowers inequality. The wage share is determined entirely by the markup.

Increased attention to inequality since the financial crisis reignited interest in the role of unions. In the US, the rise in inequality since the 1970s coincided with a decline in union density (union members as a proportion of employees) and research has shown that weaker unions contributed to rising inequality (Farber et al. 2021). The authors show that over the period from 1940 to the present unions raised the wages of workers covered by union wage agreements, producing a union wage premium. The US is well-suited to this analysis because union density and coverage are closely related in level and trend (unlike the case of some other countries, illustrated in Figure 2.4).

Figure 2.22 shows that the hump-shaped rise and fall in union density in the US was mirrored in the U-shaped path of two measures of inequality: the share of the top 1% in income and the Gini coefficient of earnings.

In the US, the union wage premium remained relatively constant over time as union strength increased in the post-war decades, stabilized in the 1960s and declined from the 1970s. The union wage premium is higher for less educated and non-white workers, which means that as unions became weaker and covered fewer workers, those (lower wage) workers lost the union premium and inequality increased. Estimating how much of the fall in inequality between 1940 and 1960 when union density increased (by 11 percentage points) and of the rise in inequality between 1970 and 2004 when density fell by 12 percentage points is due to union strength is complicated. Farber et al. use a variety of methods to show that about 10% of the initial fall and 5% of the subsequent rise in household income inequality in the US was due to the waxing and waning of union strength. These effects on the household distribution of income are not captured in the WS-PS model.

---

[23] See Unit 21 of CORE's *The Economy* for modelling of network effects and winner-takes-all competition (https://www.core-econ.org/the-economy/book/text/21.html#214-economies-of-scale-and-winner-take-all-competition).

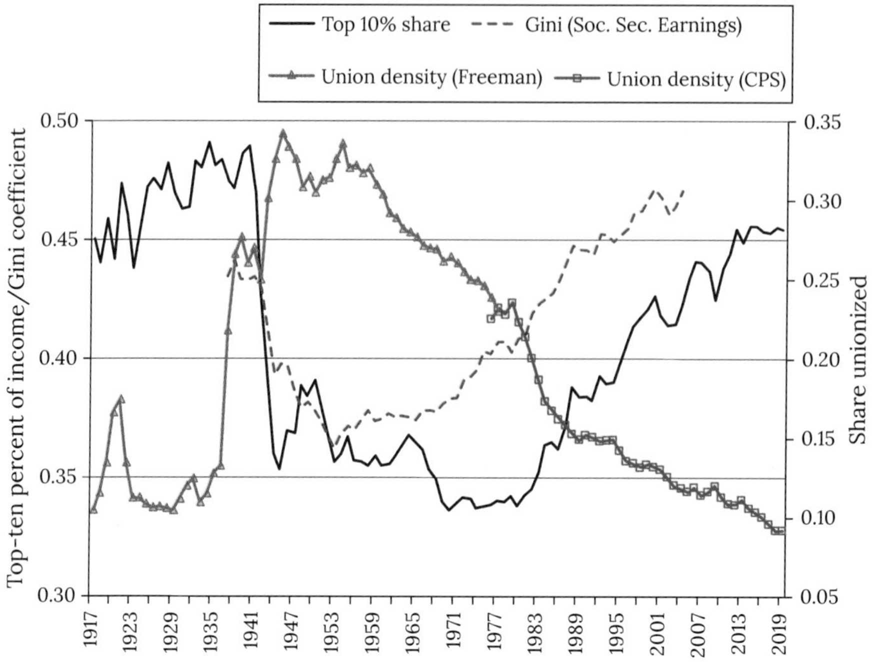

Figure 2.22 Union density and inequality over time in the United States.

Source: Replicates Figure 1 in Farber, H., Herbst, D., Kuziemko, I., and Naidu, S. (2021) Unions and inequality over the Twentieth Century: new evidence from survey data. *The Quarterly Journal of Economics*, **136**(3), 1325–1385. https://doi.org/10.1093/qje/qjab012. By permission of Oxford University Press.

2.4 CONCLUSIONS

This chapter has provided the second building block for the model of the macroeconomy. We have set out the WS–PS model, which is used to determine the equilibrium level of output in the economy. From the WS–PS model, we derived the Phillips curve, or PC, which we use to model wage and price inflation and is one of three equations that underpins the 3-equation model of the macroeconomy that will be set out in Chapter 3.

In the WS–PS model, the wage at equilibrium unemployment is higher than the reservation wage, which means there is involuntary unemployment. With monopolistic (or equivalently imperfect) competition in goods markets, firms charge a markup on their goods and make supernormal profits. At the supply-side equilibrium, the rate of unemployment is such that both wage and price setters are content with the prevailing real wage. Workers accept job offers and provide the required work effort, and firms receive the markup consistent with the competitive conditions in the product market. The real wage is constant, which implies that wages and prices are rising at the same rate: inflation is constant. Inflation could be constant at a rate of zero, in which case, nominal wages and prices would remain unchanged. Modern economies are typically characterized by positive inflation. In Chapter 3, we explain what determines the rate of inflation when the economy is at equilibrium unemployment.

By combining the analysis of aggregate demand summarized in the IS curve with the supply side (WS and PS curves), we can analyse current and historical episodes of unemployment and inflation. For example, we can model both the rapid growth of unemployment following the global financial crisis and the Covid-19 pandemic and the gradual increases in equilibrium unemployment that characterized many European economies from the 1970s. In the first two cases, there was a large negative aggregate demand shock, which pushed economies below their inflation-stabilizing unemployment rates. In the third, negative supply shocks pushed up equilibrium unemployment, leaving it higher, even when stable inflation was restored.

Given the economy's supply-side characteristics, the Phillips curve shows the feasible set of inflation and output pairs for a given rate of lagged inflation. We can interpret the lagged inflation term as agents forming expectations about how prices will evolve in the future using as their best guess, last period's consumer price inflation. Another interpretation of the lagged term is that the wage increase is set in the annual wage round to compensate workers for the erosion of their real wages associated with last period's inflation. We shall show in Chapter 3 that the Phillips curve acts as a constraint on the policy maker, limiting their choice of viable inflation-output combinations in each period.

The modelling undertaken in Sections 2.2 and 2.3 has provided a framework with which we can shed light on important questions concerning the supply side of the economy. As a summary of the chapter, we return to each of the key questions posed in these sections:

1. **Supply-side effects on equilibrium unemployment**: What determines the medium-run equilibrium level of output and unemployment around which the economy fluctuates? The equilibrium rate of unemployment is pinned down by the intersection of the WS and PS curves. Structural features of the economy, such as unionization, along with policy choices, such as the generosity of unemployment benefits, the evolution of market power and the stringency of competition policy, will affect equilibrium unemployment. Swings in demand will move the economy away from equilibrium, resulting in actual unemployment deviating from equilibrium (see Figure 2.9 for the comparison of trends for unemployment and the NAIRU in four countries). Unemployment below equilibrium is associated with output above equilibrium, i.e. a positive output gap ($y > y_e$).
2. **Nominal rigidities, inflation and the business cycle**: What happens to inflation when the economy is away from equilibrium? Our model of monopolistically competitive firms explains why fluctuations in aggregate demand cause output and employment to change. When output is above equilibrium, the increased tightness of the labour market is reflected in a higher wage on the WS curve. There is a lower cost of job loss and workers will expect higher real wages in order to exert effort. These are expected real wages because the real wage outturn depends on what happens to inflation in the economy as a whole over the period of the wage contract. In this case WS > PS, and workers will get a nominal wage increase that more than compensates them for the erosion in real wage due to last period's

inflation. However, firms protect their profit margins and will immediately raise prices following the wage round. This means that workers' real wage expectations are repeatedly frustrated when output is above equilibrium. The only way in which output can remain above equilibrium is with rising inflation, as shown in Figure 2.17. The opposite is true for output below equilibrium. The relationship between output and inflation can be summed up by the Phillips curve: $\pi_t = \pi_{t-1} + \alpha(y_t - y_e)$. This equation shows that the current period's inflation (π_t) depends positively on both last period's inflation (π_{t-1}) and the output gap ($y_t - y_e$).

3. **Demand shocks, supply shocks, and the Phillips curve**: How does the economy respond to demand or supply shocks in a world without a policy maker who aims to stabilize the economy? The economy reacts differently to supply and demand shocks. We can highlight these differences by seeing how they are captured by different parts of the model. Demand shocks affect the IS curve and supply shocks affect the WS or PS curves and consequently the Phillips curve, PC. A positive demand shock leads to a movement along the PC and subsequently to ever-increasing inflation if aggregate demand is kept at a level where there is a positive output gap. In contrast, a positive supply shock increases equilibrium output and is associated with falling inflation as long as output is kept at the initial equilibrium rate of output. In this case, falling inflation signals that the economy is capable of operating at a higher equilibrium level of output.
4. **The supply side and inequality**: The WS—PS model helps us to understand trends in inequality by highlighting two direct channels from the supply side to household income inequality. Shifts in the PS curve change the distribution of income between profits and wages; and shifts in both the PS and WS curves affect inequality through their effects on structural unemployment. A model with three groups of 'unemployed', 'employed', and 'owners' provides a method of calculating the effect on pre-tax income inequality when there is a supply-side shock or policy change. The measure of inequality is the Gini coefficient and the Lorenz curve translates shifts in equilibria in the WS-PS diagram into changes in the Lorenz curve diagram, from which the change in the Gini coefficient can be calculated.

Having a framework of the kind set out in Chapters 1 and 2 is essential in understanding how policy makers assess the state of the economy and whether intervention is required. This sets the stage for the introduction of the policy maker with stabilization objectives in the next chapter. In Chapter 3, we show why governments introduced inflation-targeting central banks in a bid to improve economic performance.

2.5 APPENDIX

2.5.1 The textbook model: Competitive markets and complete contracts

To help bring out the way the labour market works and to clarify the notion of involuntary unemployment, it is useful to provide a comparison with a simple textbook model. In the textbook model, the intrinsic feature of the labour market of variable effort is neglected. It is assumed that the wage buys a specific amount of work.

What would a market for labour mean when employment contracts are complete? The image to have in mind is of a hiring hall where employers and workers gather. In the hall, employers shout out job offers and workers respond. Since the textbook model assumes that what the employer gets in exchange for a particular hourly wage offered is unambiguous, he will be happy to hire labour on this basis. In the hiring hall, a wage is posted and workers respond by accepting or declining to work.

As discussed in Section 2.1, we assume the labour supply curve to be quite inelastic. This reflects the offsetting income and substitution effects of a wage change, as well as the effects of changes in labour force participation. Imagine the wage offers are being broadcast outside the hiring hall and people are drawn in to participate in the labour market by higher wage offers.

Turning to the labour demand side, in the textbook model, there is a downward-sloping labour demand curve, which shows the labour demanded at a given real wage. Assuming for simplicity that the capital stock (K) is fixed, output is a positive function of the level of employment (N), i.e.

$$y = f(N; K),$$

where f is the production function. It is assumed that the production function is characterized by diminishing returns, which means that as more workers are employed—holding capital constant—the extra output produced by each additional worker declines. Another way of putting this is that the marginal product of labour, which can be written as $\frac{\partial y}{\partial N}$ or *MPL*, declines as employment rises. The labour demand curve (N^D) is often referred to as the MPL curve since under perfect competition, firms take the real wage as given and employ labour up to the point at which the marginal product of labour is equal to the exogenously given real wage (the wage shouted out in the hiring hall).

The market clears at the real wage where the labour demand curve intersects the labour supply curve. Bringing together the labour demand and labour supply schedules as in Figure 2.23, the labour market clears with the real wage w_0 and employment, N_{CECC} (for Competitive Equilibrium Complete Contracts).

Any temporary displacement of the economy from equilibrium is assumed to be eliminated by a movement in real wages. For example, if the real wage rises above the market-clearing level (due say, to an unexpected fall in the price level), then labour supply exceeds labour demand at that real wage (w_1). The excess supply of labour will result in falling nominal wages until the unique competitive equilibrium is re-established with the real wage at w_0 and employment at N_{CECC}. In this model, the only people who will be unemployed will be those *voluntarily* unemployed in the sense that at the going real wage, they prefer searching for a job or leisure over the goods and services obtainable through working.

In Figure 2.23, the rate of unemployment in the market-clearing equilibrium is U_{CECC}/L, where L is the labour force, i.e. the sum of the employed and the unemployed. It is important to remember that in the textbook model, the economy is at a welfare optimum in the market-clearing equilibrium, so the voluntary unemployment that exists does not signify a problem. Rather, it reflects the choice by workers about

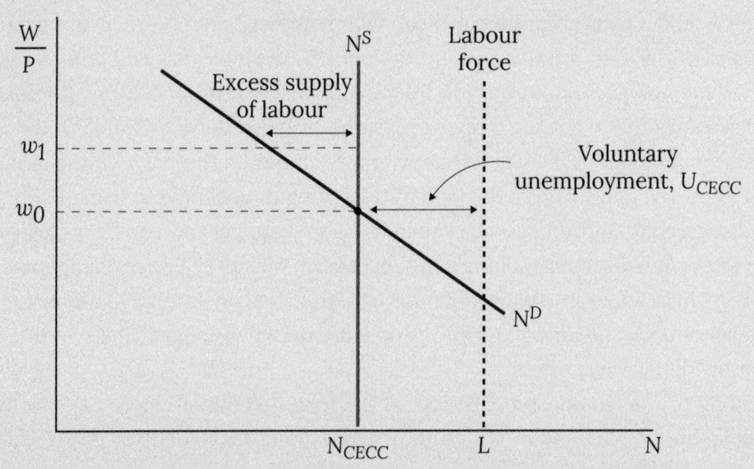

Figure 2.23 Market clearing equilibrium in a textbook labour market with complete employment contracts.

whether and how much to work at the existing real wage. It is difficult to motivate the study of supply-side institutions and policies and of demand-side (that is, stabilization) policy in this model.

2.5.2 The markup and the elasticity of demand

Firms' profits are computed as the difference between revenue and costs. In particular, we define revenue as:

$$R = Py \qquad \text{(total revenue)}$$

where P is the selling price of a firm's product and y is the quantity of output sold. Firms' profits can then be written as:

$$\pi(P, y) = P(y)y - C(y) \qquad \text{(profit function)}$$

where both prices and costs depend on the quantity of output produced.

To maximize profits with respect to output, we take the partial derivative and set it equal to zero:

$$\frac{\partial \pi}{\partial y} = P + y\frac{dP}{dy} - \frac{dC}{dy} = 0. \tag{2.7}$$

This implies that a firm facing a downward-sloping demand curve maximizes profits when marginal revenue $\left(MR = P + y\frac{dP}{dy}\right)$ equals marginal cost $\left(MC = \frac{dC}{dy}\right)$. From equation 2.7 we then notice that:

$$P\left(1 + \frac{y}{P}\frac{dP}{dy}\right) = \frac{dC}{dy} = MC. \tag{2.8}$$

Given that the elasticity of demand η is defined by:

$$\eta = -\frac{dy}{dP}\frac{P}{y}. \qquad \text{(elasticity of demand)}$$

Substituting this in equation 2.8 gives:

$$P = \frac{MC}{1-\frac{1}{\eta}}, \qquad (2.9)$$

$$\rightarrow P\left(1-\frac{1}{\eta}\right) = \frac{W}{MPL}. \qquad (2.10)$$

Dividing both sides by P, we get:

$$\left(1-\frac{1}{\eta}\right) = \frac{W}{P\ \ MPL},$$

$$\rightarrow \frac{W}{P} = MPL\left(1-\frac{1}{\eta}\right). \qquad \text{(price-setting real wage, in terms of elasticity, } \eta\text{)}$$

Finally, we note from equation 2.9 that:

$$\frac{P-MC}{P} = \frac{\frac{\eta MC}{\eta-1} - MC}{\frac{\eta MC}{\eta-1}} = 1-\frac{\eta-1}{\eta} = \frac{1}{\eta}. \qquad \text{(markup on price)}$$

Hence, the markup on price (which we denote by μ) is actually equal to $\frac{1}{\eta}$. Therefore, substituting in the price-setting real wage equation above gives:

$$\frac{W}{P} = MPL(1-\mu). \qquad \text{(price-setting real wage, in terms of markup on price, } \mu\text{)}$$

However, the markup is often computed over marginal cost rather than price, in which case:

$$\mu^C = \frac{1}{\eta-1}. \qquad \text{(markup on marginal cost)}$$

Substituting in the price-setting real wage in terms of η gives:

$$\frac{W}{P} = \frac{1}{1+\mu^C} MPL. \qquad \text{(price-setting real wage, in terms of markup on marginal cost)}$$

Note also that:

$$\frac{1}{1+\mu^C} = 1-\mu.$$

In the case of perfect competition $\eta = \infty$ and the markup is zero. As the demand curve becomes more inelastic, the markup rises. If, for example, $\eta = 6$, the firm will mark up marginal costs by 20%; $\mu^C = \frac{1}{\eta-1} = \frac{1}{6-1} = 0.2$.

2.5.3 **The rationale for treating demand shifts and the markup as separable**

We show here a simple and plausible model in which shifts in demand facing a firm, for example due to a shift in aggregate demand, do not affect the elasticity of demand, so that we can accommodate demand shifts without having to take account of possibly associated changes in the markup.

To study the effect of a proportional change in demand (by δ percent) we let x be sales and p be the price at which goods are sold.

The linear demand curve incorporating the demand shift parameter δ is:

$$p = \bar{p} - \left(\frac{\beta}{1+\delta}\right)x$$

You can see that $\bar{p}$ is the y-axis intercept of the demand curve (or the maximum willingness to pay), $-\beta$ is the slope of the inverse demand curve in the initial situation and $-\beta/1+\delta$ is the 'effective slope of the inverse demand curve' following a demand shift.

Suppose the initial situation is one in which we have price $\underline{p}$ and sales $\underline{x}$, and there is a change in sales to $\hat{x}$, with no change in price. The price elasticity of demand following this change is:

$$\eta(\delta) = \frac{dx}{dp}\frac{\underline{p}}{\hat{x}} = \frac{-(1+\delta)}{\beta}\frac{\underline{p}}{\underline{x}(1+\delta)} = -\frac{1}{\beta}\frac{\underline{p}}{\underline{x}}$$

which shows that with a constant price, the elasticity of demand is unaffected by a proportional change in demand and its associated change in sales, i.e. the price elasticity of demand is independent of δ.

The reason is that the change in demand is exactly offset by a change in the slope of the demand curve, so for example, an increase in demand (increasing x) is exactly offset by a flattening of the demand curve (decrease in the absolute value of the 'effective slope'). This is why the δ terms cancel out.

In this model, a proportional increase in demand leaves the elasticity of demand and hence the markup unchanged at a given price. With constant marginal costs, the firm's profit-maximizing price is therefore unchanged when demand fluctuates this way.

Other (also plausible) ways of representing a (non-proportional) change in demand—an increase in $\bar{p}$ for example—would not have this feature.

2.5.4 Deriving the *PS* curve to include the tax and oil price wedge

The wage element of costs for firms is the full cost of labour to firms—i.e. the gross wage paid to the worker (which includes the income tax and social security payments that have to be made by the worker) plus the employer's social security contributions. All direct taxes are summarized in the tax rate, t_d. This is shown in the pricing formula, where P is the producer price:

$$P = (1+\mu^C)\frac{W^{gross}}{\lambda} = (1+\mu^C)\frac{W(1+t_d)}{\lambda}. \qquad \text{(pricing formula)}$$

But to get the PS curve we need the price-setting equation in terms of the consumption price, $P_c = (1+t_v)P$, so that:

$$P_c = (1+t_v)P = (1+t_v)(1+\mu^C)\frac{W(1+t_d)}{\lambda},$$

which implies

$$\frac{W}{P_c} = \frac{1}{(1+\mu^C)}\frac{\lambda}{(1+t_d)(1+t_v)}$$

and switching to using μ as the markup on price, we have:

$$w^{PS} = \frac{W}{P_c} = \frac{\lambda(1-\mu)}{(1+t_d)(1+t_v)}. \quad \text{(PS equation including tax wedge)}$$

We can see that:

1. Any fall in the wedge, for example, a fall in income tax, implies an upward shift in the PS curve, indicating that the real wage is higher at any level of employment since the tax take is smaller.
2. The smaller wedge means that WS and PS curves cross at higher employment: there is a lower equilibrium rate of unemployment because a higher real consumption wage on the WS curve is consistent with equilibrium for price setters (on the new higher PS curve).

The expression for the PS curve incorporating the oil price wedge is provided in Chapter 13 (equation 13.6). It is:

$$w^{PS} = \frac{W}{P_c} = \frac{\lambda(1-\mu)}{1+\nu\frac{P^*_{rm}e}{P}} \quad (2.11)$$

where the denominator is the unit imported material requirement (ν) and P^*_{rm} is the world price of raw materials (i.e. oil in our example). A rise in the price of raw materials relative to home's price level implies a fall in (W/P_C) and hence downward shift in the PS curve.

QUESTIONS AND PROBLEMS FOR CHAPTER 2

CHECKLIST QUESTIONS

1. Why is the wage-setting curve upward sloping? If there is a disutility of working, why are workers unhappy when they are unemployed? Why do firms not offer to hire involuntarily unemployed workers at slightly lower wages?
2. Derive the price-setting curve. What does the equation for the PS curve tell us about the ability of firms to make supernormal profits? Explain in words why the decisions of firms about what price to set has implications for the real wage in the economy. Provide two different explanations for why the PS curve might be flat.
3. Explain in words and using a diagram what is meant by labour market clearing (refer to Appendix 2.5.1). Why is labour market clearing not observed in real-world labour markets?

4. What is being assumed about the timing of wage setting and price setting that enables us to say that the economy is always on the PS curve but only on the WS curve in a medium-run equilibrium? What timing assumptions would deliver the result that the economy is always on the WS curve but only on the PS curve in a medium-run equilibrium?

5. Explain in words the inflationary consequences of an upswing in aggregate demand. Assume the economy is initially at equilibrium and make sure you adequately explain the transmission mechanisms as well as the final result.

6. Evaluate the following statement:
'When the economy is in equilibrium in the WS–PS model, there is only voluntary unemployment, because no agent has an incentive to change their behaviour.'

7. Equation 2.1 in Section 2.2.1 shows that firms set prices as a markup over unit labour costs. Use this equation to show the relationship between wage growth and price growth in the economy. What assumptions (ignoring taxes and imported oil) do we have to make for wage changes to translate one-for-one into price changes? In this case, how will a rise in wages impact on a firm's profit margin?

8. Assess the following statements S1 and S2. Are they both true, both false or is only one true? Justify your answer.
   S1. When output is above equilibrium, wage setters will secure wage increases that reflect the tightness of the labour market.
   S2. If output is consistently above equilibrium, then wage-setters' real wage expectations are constantly frustrated.

9. Use the WS–PS model to graphically derive a set of Phillips curves. Explain the intuition behind the diagram. Provide an explanation of how a situation of deflation could occur (deflation is a situation in which inflation is negative so that prices are falling). What are you assuming about the real interest rate?

10. Giving in each case an example of what could have caused it, explain how unemployment can be above equilibrium due to the following. Use diagrams, such as those in Figure 2.18, to show the inflationary implications of each shock (assume there is no stabilizing policy maker).
    a. Aggregate demand being too low
    b. A wage-setting shock

11. Consider the combination of an increase in the average market power of firms and a fall in union strength. Use the WS-PS and Lorenz curve diagrams to illustrate any expected change in inequality.

PROBLEMS

1. Collect an inflation report from the central bank website of an OECD economy (e.g. the Bank of England, the ECB, the Federal Reserve etc.) and answer the following questions:
   a. What factors do they view as important drivers of inflation (or the outlook for inflation)?
   b. Divide these factors into supply-side and demand-side factors.
   c. For each factor, provide a plausible explanation for which curve of the model they affect (e.g. IS, WS or PS).
   d. For each factor, in which direction would you expect the affected curve to shift?
2. Read the following statement and then answer the questions below: 'Just by looking at real-world labour markets, it is obvious they are far too complex to be accurately modelled by either the efficiency wage model or the textbook model with complete contracts'. [Hint: the textbook model is set out in the Appendix.]
   a. Does the statement provide a good justification for not using a model when thinking about the supply side of the economy?
   b. What are the key predictions of the efficiency wage model and the textbook model with complete contracts?
   c. The predictions of which model more closely match what we observe by analysing real-world data? Provide examples to justify your answer.
3. Consider two key events; the credit crunch that plunged the world into recession in 2008 and the Fukushima nuclear disaster that struck Japan in 2011. Find data on the path of the monthly harmonized unemployment rate from the start of 2007 onwards for both the US and Japan using OECD.Stat. Answer the following questions:
   a. Plot the evolution of the Gini coefficient for post-tax household income (you may want to use data from the World Inequality Database (WID)).
   b. Describe (i) how US unemployment reacted to the credit crunch; and (ii) how Japanese unemployment reacted to the Fukushima nuclear disaster.
   c. Using the material in this chapter and Chapter 1, make an assessment of which curves were likely to have been affected by these economic shocks—i.e. was it the *IS*, *WS*, or *PS* curve that was affected (or some combination of them)? Make sure you justify your answer.
   d. Given your answer to part (c), do you predict that the equilibrium level of unemployment shifted in response to these shocks? Justify your answers.

4. Consider the Covid-19 pandemic in 2020. Find data on the path of the monthly harmonized unemployment rate from the start of 2019 onwards for Germany and the UK using OECD.Stat. Answer the following questions:
   a. Describe how German and UK unemployment reacted to the Covid-19 shock.
   b. Using the material in this chapter and the previous chapter, make an assessment of which curves were likely to have been affected by this shock—i.e. was it the IS, WS, or PS curve that were affected (or some combination of them)? Make sure you justify your answer.
   c. Given your answer to part (b), do you predict that the equilibrium level of unemployment shifted in response to these shocks? Justify your answers.
5. Collect data for GDP and the unemployment rate for OECD economies between 2007 and 2010 from OECD.Stat. Produce a scatterplot of percentage point changes in GDP and the unemployment rate (from peak to trough) over the course of the Great Recession. Answer the following questions:
   a. Describe briefly what the graph shows.
   b. Does the data support Okun's Law (i.e. an Okun coefficient of −0.5)?
   c. If not, then suggest some factors that might account for the differences in Okun coefficients observed across the OECD economies for this period.

INTERESTED IN EXPLORING THESE TOPICS FURTHER?

Visit www.oup.com/he/carlin-soskice to consolidate and extend your learning with the multiple-choice questions and Animated Analytical Diagrams accompanying this chapter.

CHAPTER

3

THE 3-EQUATION MODEL AND MACROECONOMIC POLICY

3.1 OVERVIEW

In Chapter 1, we focused on the way shocks to aggregate demand produce fluctuations in output and employment. In Chapter 2, we looked at how supply-side features of the economy determine the inflation-stabilizing equilibrium. Then, at the end of Chapter 2, we put these supply- and demand-side elements together. This produced a picture of an economy affected by both demand- and supply-side shocks, which are amplified by the multiplier process and dampened by households' ability to tide themselves over through borrowing or drawing on their precautionary savings when their current income falls. In contrast to the generally slow-moving shifts in equilibrium unemployment, actual unemployment rises and falls in accordance with business cycles largely driven by fluctuations in aggregate demand.

In the model as laid out in Chapter 2, there was no policy intervention to prevent the gap between the real wage workers require in order to supply effort (on the WS curve) and the real wage consistent with firms maximizing profits (on the PS curve) from producing ever-increasing inflation when unemployment is lower than the equilibrium rate, or falling inflation in the case unemployment is above equilibrium. In the first case, this incompatibility between the claims of workers and firms—and hence the inflationary pressure in the economy—could in principle be resolved in two ways:

1. First, by supply-side institutional change or policies to raise equilibrium output by either shifting the WS curve downwards or shifting the PS curve upwards. Examples of this include policies to weaken the bargaining power of workers by worsening the living conditions they would face if they lost their jobs (brought about, for instance, by lowering unemployment benefits). Another example is an institutional change which increases bargaining restraint by unions. One policy which might shift the PS curve upwards would be the promotion of more competition, thus reducing the markup on product prices.
2. Second, by the use of demand management policy to reduce employment and output to the level consistent with a WS–PS equilibrium, where inflation will be constant. This policy lever takes supply-side institutions and policies as given.

In this chapter, the focus is on the second set of policies mentioned above. This means that we do not deal here with supply-side policies that aim to influence equilibrium unemployment. These were introduced in Chapter 2 and are explored further in Chapter 15, which can be read immediately after this chapter. Here, we begin with unemployment at its equilibrium rate (the WS–PS intersection), where the output gap is zero and inflation is constant. If, at this point, the economy suffers a shock, how would the policy maker respond so as to stabilize it at its inflation-stabilizing level?

Shortly, we will look in more detail at how demand management policy is implemented to stabilize the economy (for example by raising aggregate demand in the face of a negative demand shock or dampening it in the face of a positive demand shock). But, before that, we need a little more background information about the policy regime and its history. During the 1990s, many countries around the world adopted a new macroeconomic policy regime known as inflation targeting. It means that the government gives responsibility to the central bank to stabilize the economy by adopting a specific target for the annual rate of inflation, the most commonly adopted rate being 2%. To help clarify the reasons why these changes in regime and policy have taken place it would be useful to answer three related background questions:

1. Why do governments often define the central bank's responsibility as the control of inflation?
2. Why, in any case do governments regard inflation as a problem which needs to be controlled?
3. Why do governments hand over the problem of keeping inflation low and stable to the makers of monetary policy (the central banks) rather than keeping it themselves?

Regarding the first of these questions, we have already seen that the rate of unemployment at which inflation is constant depends on structural features of the labour market and the goods market. It is these structural features which determine the positions of the WS and PS curves in the supply-side model. But, since the central bank does not have policy instruments with which it can change these supply-side economic features, it is clearly not the right policy maker to be charged with reducing equilibrium unemployment. The government will have to do this, in ways that are discussed in Chapter 15.

We shall see, however, that there is one important way in which the central bank's behaviour does affect unemployment. A central bank that is given responsibility for maintaining high employment as well as keeping inflation close to its target level would be less inclined to support policies of rapidly cutting inflation through pushing unemployment up sharply. In Chapter 6, we return to the question of how differences in the mandates of central banks around the world can be represented in the model.

The second preliminary question is why policy makers are concerned about inflation at all. One reason why governments might pursue low inflation is that the level of inflation is a key priority for voters. Governments might have to pay a large electoral price if they fail to control inflation. The importance the US general public gives to inflation is highlighted in a 1997 paper by Robert Shiller, who surveys both economists

	1 Fully agree	2 Somewhat agree	3 Undecided	4 Somewhat disagree	5 Completely disagree	
US all	52%	32%	4%	8%	4%	n = 117
Economists	18%	28%	11%	26%	18%	n = 80

Table 3.1 Public attitudes on the importance of preventing high inflation. Do you agree that preventing high inflation is an important national priority, as important as preventing drug abuse or deterioration in the quality of our schools?

Source: Survey data from Shiller (1997).

and members of the public in the US about their views. Table 3.1 shows that the general public (more than economists) see controlling inflation as a national priority. We shall look in more detail at the factors that lie behind voters' concerns with inflation in the next subsection.

This leaves the third preliminary question: why, in the inflation-targeting regime, is stabilization policy placed in the hands of the central bank rather than the government? This question is best broken down into two separate parts.

The first part is: why is monetary policy chosen over fiscal policy as the primary tool for stabilization policy? There are both practical and political economy reasons why monetary policy is the preferred stabilizer even when both monetary and fiscal policy are available. Firstly, changing public expenditure or taxation normally involve lengthy parliamentary processes, and there is no equivalent to the gradual adjustment possible through quarter-point changes in the interest rate at monthly intervals. Secondly, fiscal policy is inherently political since it involves the use of tax revenue, a fact which is captured by the classic refrain of struggles for democracy: 'No taxation without representation'. Monetary policy is viewed as more neutral and not so obviously associated in the mind of the public with creating winners and losers, making it a less contentious policy instrument for use in short-run demand management.

The second part is: why does the government cede control of monetary policy to an independent central bank? The government can potentially gain an electoral advantage by controlling monetary policy. For example, they could raise output above the equilibrium or change politically sensitive mortgage interest rates in the run-up to an election. In light of this, why have governments around the world chosen to delegate control of monetary policy to a committee of independent experts? It is because governments lack low inflation credibility, which translates into higher inflation. The political pressures to manipulate interest rates for electoral gain are the source of this credibility deficit. Independent central banks are free from these pressures so are more likely to deliver low and stable inflation. To the extent that voters care about inflation and sound macroeconomic management, this provides the incentive for the government to relinquish control of this policy lever. These arguments have been persuasive among both left- and right-wing policy makers, as illustrated by the fact that one of the very first acts of the British Labour Party when it came to power in 1997, after 18 years in opposition, was to make the Bank of England independent.

The discussion in Chapter 1 brought out the extent to which households are able to limit the costs to them of fluctuations in income that arise from shocks to the economy through smoothing their consumption. Nevertheless volatility remains and the policy maker aims to provide additional stabilization. We shall see in the course of this chapter how the central bank responds to a range of shocks: its interest rate decisions affect aggregate demand and the output gap, guiding the economy back to the medium-run equilibrium with low steady inflation as its objective.

3.1.1 The role of the central bank in stabilization

Since the early 1990s a growing number of central banks have been assigned the task of stabilizing the macroeconomy around a low target rate of inflation. This is known as an inflation-targeting monetary policy regime. In response to a surge in inflation, we would expect to see the central bank raise the interest rate; this would lower interest-sensitive spending, such as spending on housing, machinery and equipment, due to the increase in the interest rate (in other words, in the cost of borrowing). The cut-back in investment and spending on consumer durables would lead in turn to lower aggregate demand and a fall in output. Unemployment would go up and inflationary pressure would diminish.

In 1997, the year in which the Bank of England was made independent, the Bank's Chief Economist, Mervyn King, who later became Governor, explained:[1]

> [M]onetary policy can be described in terms of two policy variables—a medium-term inflation target and a response of interest rates to shocks that create fluctuations in inflation and output. The overriding objective of monetary policy is to ensure that on average inflation is equal to the target. But such a target is not sufficient to define policy. There is a subordinate decision on how to respond to shocks as they occur.

Figure 3.1 provides a schematic overview of the macro model, including the policy maker. On the left-hand side, the role of the demand and supply sides are summarized.

The components of aggregate demand determine the level of output and employment in the goods market equilibrium. The structural features of the economy on the supply side determine the equilibrium rate of unemployment at which inflation is constant. The third panel shows the implications for inflation: if unemployment is at the equilibrium rate, then inflation will remain constant and the central bank will do nothing. If unemployment is below the equilibrium rate, inflation is rising and vice versa for unemployment above it. An increase in inflation above the central bank's target will trigger intervention by the central bank: it will raise the interest rate. Equivalently, a fall in inflation below target will trigger an easing of monetary policy with a lower interest rate.

The outside arrows depict the feedback from the central bank's monetary policy rule to aggregate demand. This illustrates how a central bank uses a monetary policy rule to hold inflation close to a low target value.

---

[1] Excerpt taken from King (1997*b*). King was the Governor of the Bank of England 2003–13.

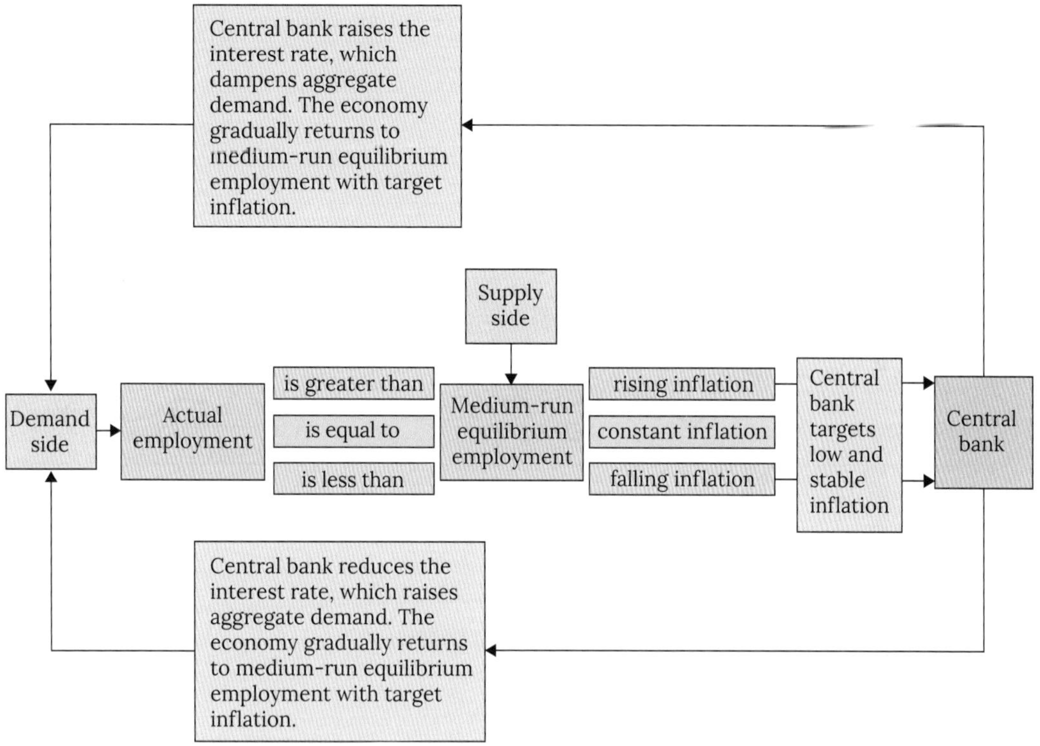

Figure 3.1 Schematic overview of the macro model.

Figure 3.2 shows the course of inflation in a selection of developed economies since 1980. The chart shows that a period of high and volatile inflation was followed by one in which inflation was lower and more stable. The introduction of inflation-targeting regimes was part of the evolution of the policy framework, where from the end of the 1970s, governments used macroeconomic policy to squeeze inflation out of the economy by depressing aggregate demand.

The shift from high to low inflation shown in the chart began before the large fall in the oil price in 1986 and the gradual emergence of low-cost (especially Chinese) manufacturers into world markets, which subsequently also had a significant effect on inflation. Although formal inflation targeting was adopted later in the US compared to other countries, its inflation behaviour was similar to the other countries shown in Figure 3.2, where its date of introduction in New Zealand, Australia, Sweden, and the US is shown. The move towards formal or informal inflation targeting is frequently identified with the beginning of the 'Great Moderation' (the period of unprecedented macroeconomic stability shown in Figure 1.3 in Chapter 1).

There are, however, two very important situations in which the central bank cannot be relied on to stabilize shocks by changing the interest rate as described above. The first is when the economy experiences such a large negative demand shock that even when the central bank cuts the nominal interest rate all the way to zero this is not low enough to stimulate a revival of aggregate demand. With a nominal interest rate of

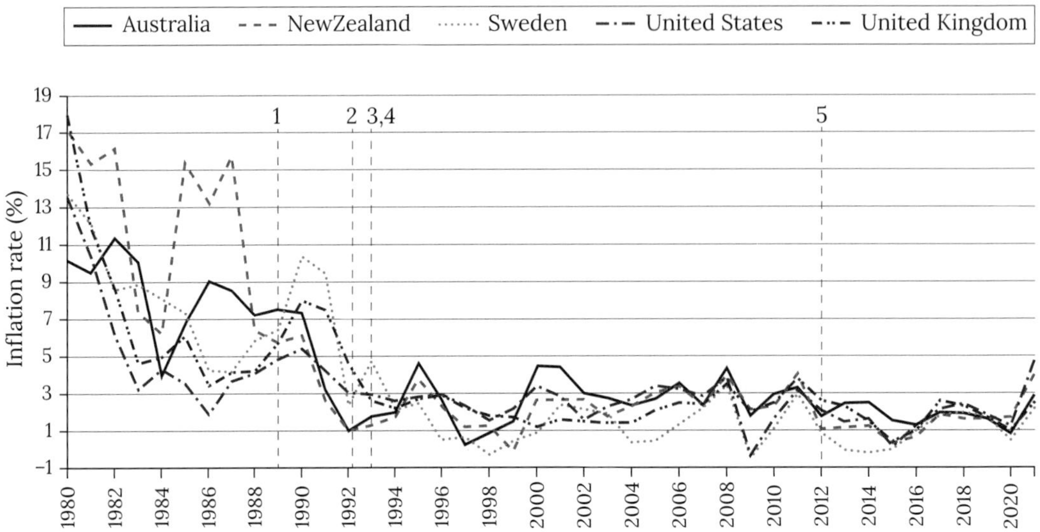

Dates inflation targeting was first adopted:

1. Reserve Bank of New Zealand—April 1988
2. Bank of England—September 1992
3. Sveriges Riksbank (the Swedish central bank)—January 1993
4. Reserve Bank of Australia—March 1993
5. US Federal Reserve—January 2012

Figure 3.2 Inflation rates—before and after the adoption of inflation targeting: 1980–2021.

Source: OECD CPI complete database (accessed July 2022).

zero, the real interest rate, which is the one relevant to spending decisions of firms and households, is not low enough to stimulate interest-sensitive spending. This problem of the *zero lower bound* is closely related to the possibility that the economy can become caught in a *deflation trap*, where it enters a vicious cycle of falling output and prices. Once the usual channel of monetary stabilization is shut down, the central bank can try to stimulate the economy using other policies, such as quantitative easing, or it can share responsibility for stabilization with fiscal policy. The cases of the zero lower bound and the role of fiscal policy as stabilizer are addressed later in this chapter. We leave a discussion of quantitative easing until Chapters 5, 6, and 9.

The second case in which monetary policy cannot be used to achieve stabilization is when the economy has a fixed exchange rate. This is easy to see in the setting of a common currency area such as the Eurozone: member countries of the Eurozone all use the euro as their currency and they share a single central bank, the European Central Bank (ECB). As a result, these countries do not have their own monetary policy maker which could stabilize shocks that are specific to their country. Because all Eurozone countries have the same monetary policy, any stabilization of shocks to a particular country would have to be achieved by the use of fiscal policy (a case explained in Chapter 14).

3.1.2 Inflation and deflation

Rising inflation and distributional conflict

Rising inflation reflects distributional conflict as different social groups (employees and the owners of firms) seek to protect their interests.

There is a conflict of interest between the two sides of the labour market because the wage employers need to pay to get workers to work sufficiently hard (given the state of the labour market) may differ from the wage that is consistent with the profit margin firms seek given conditions of competition in markets for goods and services. A situation of rising inflation reflects inconsistent claims by these groups on the output per head produced in the economy.

When unemployment is below the equilibrium rate, the gap between the real wage on the WS curve and on the PS curve reflects the conflict of interest over the shares of output and causes inflation to rise. As shown in Chapter 2, as unemployment falls, workers become more powerful in the labour market and are able to secure a higher expected real wage: this is the reason the WS curve is upward-sloping. But firms will seek to secure their profit margin by setting prices accordingly—leaving a gap, which we call the 'bargaining gap', between the higher real wage workers expect on the WS curve and the unchanged real wage on the PS curve. This pushes inflation up.

Rising inflation produces social tension as frustration mounts. As we shall see, inflationary episodes of this kind have frequently been followed by painful periods of disinflation, where years with output below equilibrium (accompanied by high unemployment) were required to bring inflation down.[2]

The empirical evidence suggests that periods of disinflation to bring down inflation from high rates (up to double digit rates per annum) have involved significant costs in OECD economies where this has occurred. Figure 3.3 shows the path of inflation and unemployment in the UK between the early 1970s and 2021. The high level of inflation in the 1970s was tackled by tight monetary policy from 1979. The process of getting inflation down from a higher level to the targeted one is known as disinflation. It is likely to be a costly process, involving a period of high unemployment to squeeze inflation out of the system. The costs of high unemployment include the direct waste of resources, the erosion of skills and increased vulnerability to mental illness that comes with long spells of unemployment, and the damage to the functioning of families and communities. Figure 3.3 shows that reducing inflation from rates above 20 to below 5% was associated in the British economy with a rise in unemployment from 4 to 12% during the disinflationary episode.

The costs of high and unstable inflation

The survey on public attitudes to inflation summarized in Table 3.2 shows that the main reason the US public dislike inflation is due to the erosion of living standards that are believed to accompany high inflation. We can relate this to an aspect of

[2] An early formal model of equilibrium unemployment and of the inflation process as one of conflicting distributional claims is in Rowthorn (1977). A new related literature on 'Inflation is conflict' arose in 2023, see Lorenzoni and Werning (2023).

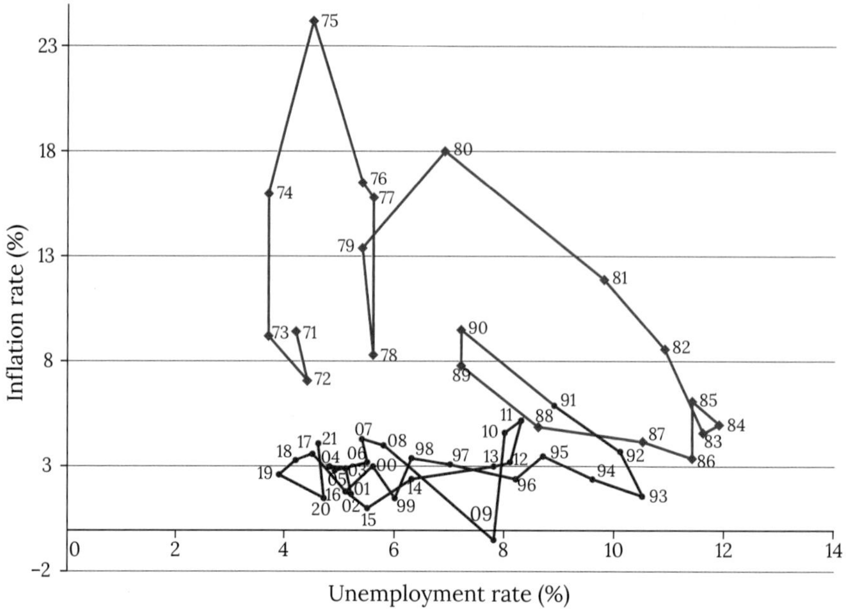

Figure 3.3 UK inflation and unemployment: 1971–2021. The Bank of England adopted inflation targeting in 1992 and was made independent in 1997.

Source: UK Office for National Statistics (data accessed June 2022).

the dynamics of the WS–PS model. The US public's biggest complaint about inflation accords with the outcome of the WS–PS model in an inflationary environment, in the sense that rising inflation leads to the persistent frustration of workers' real wage expectations.

In the model in Chapter 2, we used the simplest case regarding the timing of wage and price setting. If firms are able to adjust prices immediately after wages have been set, rising inflation reflects a situation in which the real wage wage setters require is systematically frustrated (in other words, the expected real wage of workers as indicated by the WS curve is above the real wage on the PS curve). In this case, the real wage outcome is on the PS curve, not on the WS curve. If there are lags in price setting as well as in wage setting, then the real wage lies between the PS and WS curves and neither wage nor price setters are fully satisfied. This case is more realistic because the empirical evidence suggests that real wages are mildly pro-cyclical, which means that when there is a positive output gap the real wage ends up between the WS curve and the PS curve (that is, higher than at the inflation-stabilizing equilibrium) and vice versa for a negative output gap.

Table 3.2 reveals a divergence between what the public and the economists view as the most significant costs of inflation. Whereas the public appear to worry about their real incomes being eroded by inflation, economists do not see this as much of a concern and place more stress on the interference that high inflation creates for the ability of prices to convey information. Periods of high inflation are also often ones with volatile inflation. To see why this matters, consider an economy with technical progress in which innovation takes place unevenly across sectors. In sectors with rapid

	1	2	3	
US all	7%	77%	15%	n = 110
Economists	49%	12%	40%	n = 78

Table 3.2 What is people's biggest gripe with inflation? Which of the following comes closest to your biggest grip about inflation:
1. Inflation causes a lot of inconveniences: I find it harder to comparison shop, I feel I have to avoid holding too much cash, etc.
2. Inflation hurts my real buying power, it makes me poorer.
3. Other.

Source: Survey data from Shiller (1997).

innovation, prices will be falling relative to prices in other sectors where technology is more stagnant (think of the falling prices of computing power). These are economically significant changes in *relative prices* and should lead to a reallocation of resources in the economy. Volatile inflation can distort resource allocation to the extent that it masks these relative price changes. In short, volatile inflation has adverse real effects on the economy that are hard to avoid.

When inflation is high, people also want to hold less money. This is because inflation acts as a tax on holding money balances, eroding their real value over time. The so-called inflation tax imposes inefficiencies because it distorts behaviour: people spend more time managing their financial assets incurring what are referred to as 'shoe-leather costs'. Other firms incur costs as a consequence of the need for frequent price changes ('menu costs').

The 'optimal' rate of inflation

Given the costs associated with high inflation can we infer that the 'optimal' rate of inflation is zero or even negative? Think about the following: the return on holding notes and coins is zero so with any positive inflation rate, the return in real terms, i.e. after controlling for inflation, is negative. The negative real return leads people to waste effort economizing on their money holdings (shoe leather costs again) and this is inefficient given that it is virtually costless to produce money.

If we follow the logic of this argument and use the Fisher equation, then with a positive real rate of interest, for the *nominal* interest rate to be zero, inflation would have to be negative (i.e. prices falling, which is called deflation). This was Milton Friedman's view of the optimal rate of inflation: the rate of deflation should equal the real rate of interest, leaving the nominal interest rate equal to zero.[3] Friedman's rule ensures that people avoid shoe leather costs, but is this a good reason to say that deflation is optimal?

The danger of deflation

An important reason why central banks target a low but positive inflation rate is that they wish to prevent the economy from falling into a deflation trap, a problem which can emerge when weak aggregate demand leads inflation to fall and eventually

[3] See Friedman (1969).

become negative. When aggregate demand is very weak, the central bank will want to reduce interest rates in order to stimulate interest-sensitive spending like investment. This can push the nominal interest rate close to its lower bound of zero. But when a nominal interest rate close to zero is combined with falling prices (deflation), the Fisher equation tells us that this implies a positive real interest rate which may be too high to stimulate private sector demand and get the economy back to equilibrium. Continued weak demand will make inflation more negative, thereby pushing the real interest rate up. This is exactly the opposite of what the central bank wants, which is to reduce the interest rate sufficiently to escape the deflation trap.

In addition, deflation increases real debt burdens. Debts are typically denominated in nominal terms, with borrowers having to pay back a fixed amount each period. If wages (and prices) are falling every period then the burden of the debt increases as a proportion of income. This will lower households' disposable income and squeeze firms' profits, exerting a drag on economic growth and slowing down recovery.

Deflation poses a third problem related to the apparent difficulty in cutting nominal wages. If workers are particularly resistant to *nominal* wage cuts, then a positive rate of inflation creates the flexibility needed to achieve changes in *relative* wages. For example, if, due to a fall in demand for one kind of labour, a real wage cut is required it can be achieved with an inflation rate of, say, 2% p.a. with the nominal wage left unchanged in the sector where the real wage cut is necessary. This argument is referred to as inflation's role in 'oiling the wheels of the labour market'.

Central bank independence and inflation targeting coincided with the achievement of a low and stable inflation environment as reflected in Figure 3.2. This helped to reinforce the virtues of a 2% inflation target and central banks have not seriously considered changing to a higher target. In fact, the US Federal Reserve, which has historically avoided having an official inflation target, announced at the start of 2012 that it was joining other developed economies in targeting 2% inflation.[4] The Bank of Japan did likewise, announcing a 2% inflation target in January 2013.[5]

3.1.3 **Introduction to the 3-equation model**

Figure 3.1 puts together the demand and supply sides of the economy and shows the role an inflation-targeting central bank can play in responding to a shock that takes the economy away from equilibrium. What the inflation-targeting central bank does is to raise the interest rate in response to inflation which is above the target rate in order to dampen aggregate demand and vice versa.

A crucial characteristic of an inflation-targeting monetary policy regime is that the central bank is forward looking. The central bank forecasts inflation by analysing what is going on in the economy and it must take into account the lags between changes in the interest rate it uses for policy purposes and the impact of that rate on

---

[4] Federal Reserve FOMC *Statement on Longer-Run Goals and Monetary Policy Strategy*, January 25th 2012.

[5] Bank of Japan *The 'Price Stability Target' under the Framework for the Conduct of Monetary Policy*, January 22nd 2013. The 2% target replaced an earlier 'price stability goal in the medium to long term' of 1%.

economic activity. The importance of forecasting and lags for the work of central banks is highlighted in the monetary policy strategy document of the Sveriges Riksbank (the Swedish central bank):[6]

> It takes time before monetary policy has a full impact on inflation and the real economy. Monetary policy is therefore guided by forecasts for economic developments.

When three things are known—what the central bank is trying to achieve, how it thinks about the constraints it faces arising from the behaviour of the private sector, and how it implements its policy—this information will provide a skeletal model enabling an analysis of how the bank will respond to a variety of shocks to the economy. These responses to shocks can then be summarized in the form of a simple monetary policy rule. This rule sits at the heart of the 3-equation model, which is produced by adding the Monetary Rule (MR) curve to the IS curve from the demand side and the Phillips curve (PC) from the supply side.

Taking each question in turn:

1. What is the central bank trying to achieve? It is assumed that its aim is to use monetary policy to stabilize the economy, which means keeping the economy close to equilibrium output and keeping inflation close to its targeted rate. The central bank may be penalized if it fails to meet its inflation target. In the UK, for example, if the inflation rate diverges more than one percentage point above or below the 2% target then the Governor of the Bank of England is obliged to write an open letter to the Chancellor of the Exchequer explaining the reasons for the bank's failure and a plan for returning inflation to target. This is, at the least, embarrassing for the Governor and costly in terms of the central bank's reputation. The closer is the economy to having output at equilibrium and inflation on its target, the lower is the reputational cost to the bank.
2. What forces prevent the central bank from achieving its target? As seen in Chapters 1 and 2, the economy is affected by shocks to demand and supply, which affect output and inflation. An unforeseen boom, for example, which takes output above equilibrium, will increase inflation above the target as the position of workers in the labour market strengthens. This aspect of wage behaviour is captured in the Phillips curve (PC). The central bank has to take into account behaviour, including the persistence of inflation, when it designs its response to the initial shock to the economy.
3. How does the central bank translate its objectives into monetary policy? It uses a monetary policy rule. This can be represented in the same diagram as the Phillips curves, that is, in a diagram with output on the horizontal axis and inflation on the vertical axis. This will demonstrate how the central bank will choose its preferred policy response given the constraint it faces from the behaviour of wage and price setters, which is captured by a particular Phillips curve.

---

[6] Excerpt taken from: Sveriges Riksbank, 2010, *Monetary Policy in Sweden*.

To implement its preferred policy response in practice, the central bank diagnoses the shock and its forecast effect on inflation and output. It uses this, together with its preferences for stabilization, to estimate the output gap it is trying to achieve. The *MR* curve illustrates the central bank's best response to the shock. It then uses the relationship between the interest rate and output in the *IS* curve to implement that choice.

An example—a consumption boom

The example of a consumption boom is used to show how the model works. Figure 3.4 shows how the central bank analyses a shock of this kind.

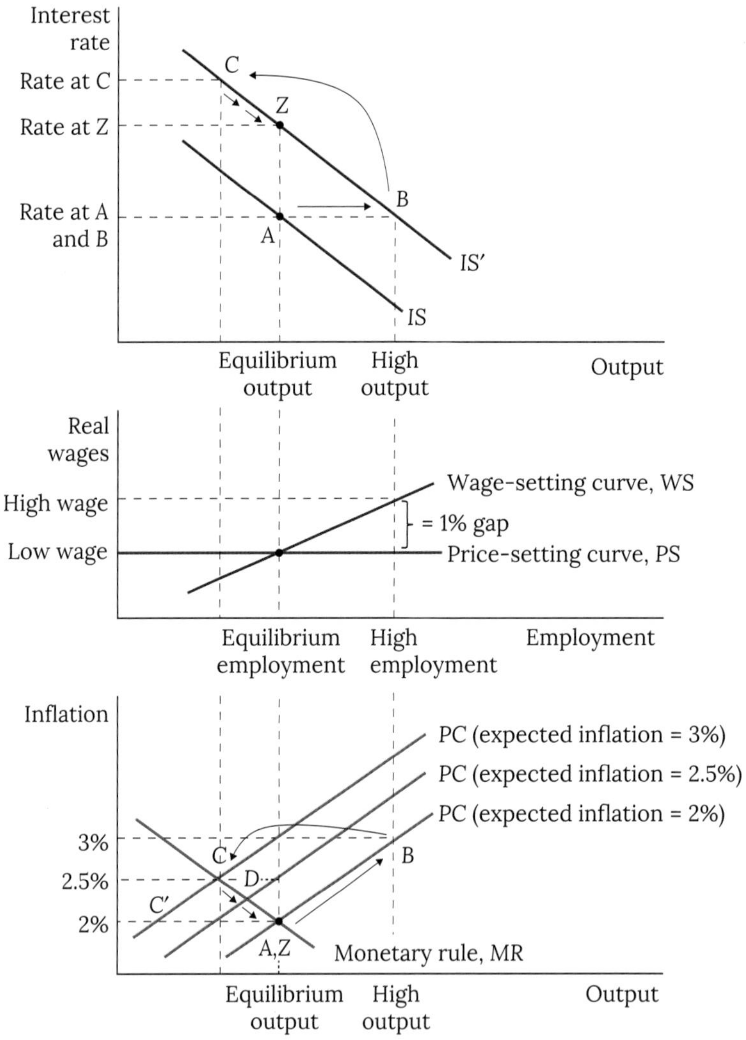

Figure 3.4 The 3-equation model: the adjustment of the economy to a permanent demand shock.

The shock has its initial positive impact on output and employment (shown by the rightward shift of the *IS* curve and the movement from A to B in the *IS* diagram). By following the diagrams in Figure 3.4 from top to bottom, we can see that the labour market impact of the consumption boom is reflected in a disturbance of the initial constant-inflation equilibrium. At the first wage-setting round following the fall in unemployment, wage and price inflation will rise above the target inflation rate of 2%. As illustrated in the wage-setting and price-setting diagram, the shock has opened up a bargaining gap of 1% between the prevailing (low) real wage and the (high) real wage consistent with the tighter labour market following the consumption boom. This means that workers will get a 2% wage rise to compensate them for the erosion of their real wages due to last period's inflation and an additional 1% increase to bring their real wage up to the level indicated by the wage-setting curve. In this case, wages rise by 3% and firms automatically raise their prices by 3% to protect their profit margins; in other words, inflation rises to 3%.

The increase in inflation from 2% to 3% is shown by the movement along the Phillips curve from A to B. Here, we need to take into account the fact that the higher inflation of 3% will become embedded in the expectations of wage setters. For the next wage-setting round—the one the central bank must anticipate in taking its stabilization decision—expected inflation of 3% will mean that the relevant Phillips curve facing the central bank is the one labelled 'PC (expected inflation = 3%)'. Given this forecast of inflationary behaviour, the central bank chooses its best response to the situation—the place on the new PC where it would like to locate. Its preference is likely to be for a balanced response—making progress in getting inflation back toward target but not imposing a harsh recession—such as at point C. This is a point on the *MR*, which shows the central bank's optimal output-inflation pair for any Phillips curve it faces.

In the top panel of the diagram is the *IS* curve. If the central bank takes the view that in the absence of any response on its part the consumption boom would persist, it will need to choose the interest rate shown by point C in order to dampen aggregate demand sufficiently to move the economy onto the path which leads to the inflation target. Once the economy is on the *MR* curve at point C, inflation will come down as forecast. Lower inflation will then shift expected inflation down. We can see this in the shift of the Phillips curve downwards to 'PC (expected inflation = 2.5%)'. The central bank will choose point D as its best response to the new inflation environment it faces and will adjust the interest rate down from its peak. In the subsequent periods, the central bank will continue to guide the economy along the *MR* curve by reducing the interest rate as inflation returns to the target rate. The adjustment process finishes when the economy is back at equilibrium output and target inflation (point Z). There will, however, be a higher interest rate at the new equilibrium, as shown in the *IS* diagram (the top panel of Figure 3.4). A reduced level of investment is needed to offset the persistent consumption boom.

A summary of modern inflation-targeting central banking

Central bank thinking on monetary policy in the era of inflation targeting was succinctly summarized by Glenn Stevens, the Assistant Governor of the Reserve Bank of

Australia in a speech in 1999, in which he lists the six key things that have been learnt about monetary policy after 200 years of thought by economists and others:[7]

1. Monetary policy affects principally, or only, prices [and not economic activity] in the medium term;
2. It affects activity in the short term;
3. Because of lags, policy has to look forward;
4. But the future is uncertain, as is the impact of policy changes on the economy;
5. Expectations matter, so giving people some idea of what you are trying to do, and acting consistently, is useful; and
6. An adequate degree of operational independence for the central bank [from the government] in the conduct of monetary policy is important.

3.2 **MODELLING**

The primary aim of this chapter is to add the policy maker to the models of the demand and supply sides of the economy that we have built in Chapters 1 and 2. This adds the third curve, the MR in the graphical model based on the three equations that give the model its name:

1. *IS* curve
2. *PC* curve
3. *MR* curve

We extend the introduction to the 3-equation model by setting out in more detail how the central bank goes about achieving its objective of keeping inflation at target. This gives the *monetary rule*, or MR curve, which determines the output gap the central bank should set in order to stabilize the economy following an economic shock. We go on to use the 3-equation model to analyse a range of shocks in Section 3.3.

3.2.1 **The 3-equation model**

The first task of this section is to derive the MR curve, which shows the chosen output gap of the central bank in response to any economic shock. The MR curve shows the path along which the central bank seeks to guide the economy back to target inflation (and equilibrium output). The mathematical derivation of the model is provided in Appendix 3.5.1.

The basic method for deriving a monetary policy rule involves the following steps:

1. Define the central bank's preferences in terms of a utility (or loss) function to capture the costs it incurs of being away from the inflation target and from equilibrium output. This produces the policy maker's indifference curves in output-inflation

[7] Excerpt taken from Stevens (1999). Square brackets indicate additions to the text made by the authors.

space and shows what the policy maker would like to do—i.e. to be close to the inflation target at equilibrium output.

2. Define the constraints faced by the policy maker from the supply side of the economy: these are the Phillips curves, which are also shown in output-inflation space. These show the 'objective' trade-off between inflation and unemployment in the short run and pin down what it is feasible for the central bank to achieve.
3. Derive the best response *monetary rule* in output-inflation space: this is the MR curve. For a given Phillips curve that it faces, the MR shows the central bank's desired output–inflation combination.
4. Once the central bank knows where it wants to be by using the MR curve, it uses the IS curve to implement that choice, since the IS curve shows the interest rate that will deliver the central bank's chosen level of output. The interest rate is the central bank's policy lever for influencing aggregate demand.

Note that the IS curve plays a twin role in the model: it represents the goods market equilibrium condition and is the implementation curve for monetary policy. In the second half of the book, when we introduce the open economy, we will instead use the open economy RX curve for the implementation of monetary policy.

The central bank's preferences

Where do the central bank's preferences come from? A pragmatic way of thinking about how to model these is to infer their preferences from their behaviour. From the empirical analysis of the behaviour of the US central bank, the Federal Reserve, the economist John Taylor inferred a monetary policy rule. The famous Taylor Rule can be derived from a model in which the central bank minimizes fluctuations from the inflation target and the size of the output gap. Since our aim is to throw light on the way central banks behave, we use this loss function.

In this subsection, we use the central bank's loss function (i.e their utility function) to derive indifference curves representing the trade-off in its preferences between inflation being away from its target and output being away from equilibrium. Looking first at inflation, we assume that it wants to minimize fluctuations around the inflation target π^T:

$$(\pi_t - \pi^T)^2.$$

A loss function is just like a utility function except that the higher the loss, the worse it is for the central bank. This loss function has two implications. First, the central bank is as concerned to avoid inflation below its target as it is inflation above its target. If $\pi^T = 2\%$, the loss from $\pi_t = 4\%$ is the same as the loss from $\pi_t = 0\%$. In both cases $(\pi_t - \pi^T)^2 = 4$. Second, it attaches increased importance to bringing inflation back to its target the further it is away from π^T; the loss from $\pi_t = 6\%$ is 16, compared to the loss of 4 from $\pi_t = 4\%$.

We turn now to the central bank's second concern of keeping output close to equilibrium. We assume the central bank seeks to minimize the gap between y_t and y_e—remembering that it has no way of controlling y_e itself—in order to aid it in achieving its inflation target. The central bank's loss as a result of output being different from its target of y_e is

$$(y_t - y_e)^2.$$

Note that this loss function also assumes a symmetrical attitude to positive and negative deviations–in this case, from the equilibrium level of output. The most straightforward way of thinking about this is that the central bank understands the model and realizes that inflation is only constant at $y_t = y_e$. If $y_t < y_e$ then this represents unnecessary unemployment that should be eliminated. If $y_t > y_e$, this is unsustainable and will require costly increases in unemployment to bring the associated inflation back down. Whenever the economy is disturbed, the central bank sees its task as steering the economy back to this constant-inflation output level.

Adding the two loss functions together, the central bank's loss function is:

$$L = (y_t - y_e)^2 + \beta(\pi_t - \pi^T)^2, \qquad \text{(central bank loss function)}$$

where β is the relative weight attached to the loss from inflation. This is a critical parameter: a $\beta > 1$ will characterize a central bank that places less weight on deviations in employment from its target than on deviations in inflation, and vice versa. A more inflation-averse central bank is characterized by a higher β.[8]

With $\beta = 1$, the central bank is equally concerned about inflation and output deviations from its targets. The loss function is simple to draw: each indifference curve is a circle with (y_e, π^T) at its centre (see Figure 3.5a). The loss declines as the circle gets smaller. When $\pi_t = \pi^T$ and $y_t = y_e$, the circle shrinks to a single point (called the 'bliss point') and the loss is at a minimum, which is zero. With $\beta = 1$, the central bank is indifferent between inflation 1% above (or below) π^T and output 1% below (or above) y_e. They are on the same loss circle.

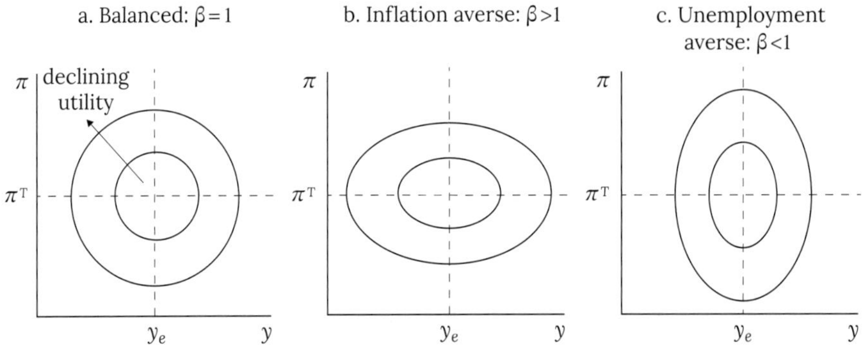

Figure 3.5 Central bank loss functions: utility declines with distance from the 'bliss point'.

[8] The central bank's preferences can be presented in this simple way if we assume that the central bank's discount rate is infinite. This means that it only considers one period at a time when making its decision. We look at the implications of dropping this assumption in Section 3.5.2.

If $\beta > 1$, the central bank is called inflation-averse: it is indifferent between (say) inflation 1% above (or below) π^T and output 2% above (or below) y_e. They are on the same loss curve. This makes the indifference curves ellipsoid as in Figure 3.5b. They are flat because the central bank is willing to trade off a small fall in inflation for a large rise in unemployment above equilibrium. A central bank with less aversion to inflation ($\beta < 1$) will have ellipsoid indifference curves with a vertical rather than a horizontal orientation (Figure 3.5c). In that case, the indifference curves are steep, reflecting that the central bank is only willing to trade off a given fall in inflation for a smaller fall in output than in the other two cases. If the central bank cares only about inflation then the loss ellipses become one dimensional along the line at $\pi_t = \pi^T$.

The value of β does not reflect whether the central bank focuses on achieving an inflation target or an output target. Rather, a central bank with lower β is willing to trade off a longer period during which inflation is away from target to reduce the impact on unemployment of the adjustment path back to equilibrium than would a more inflation-averse central bank with a higher β. Central bank preferences are discussed in more detail in Chapter 6.

The Phillips curve constraint

As discussed in Chapter 2, output affects inflation via the (adaptive expectations) Phillips curve:

$$\pi_t = \pi_t^E + \alpha(y_t - y_e) \quad (3.1)$$

$$= \pi_{t-1} + \alpha(y_t - y_e), \quad \text{(Phillips curve, PC)}$$

where $\pi_t^E = \pi_{t-1}$.

The Phillips curve is a constraint for the central bank because it shows all the output and inflation combinations from which the central bank can choose for a given level of expected inflation. In other words, in any period, the central bank can only choose to locate the economy at a point on the Phillips curve it faces. In the Phillips curve used in this chapter, expected inflation is simply lagged inflation—other methods of forming inflation expectations will be discussed in Chapter 4.

This is shown in Figure 3.6, where the upward-sloping lines are the Phillips curves we worked with in Chapter 2. In the diagram, it is assumed that $\alpha = 1$, so that each Phillips curve has a slope of 45°. Each Phillips curve is labelled by a given level of expected inflation. Assume that $\pi_t^E = \pi_{t-1} = \pi^T = 2$ (remember that this PC must go through point A at which $y = y_e$ and $\pi = 2$). The central bank is in the happy position of being able to choose bliss point A or (π^T, y_e) at which its loss is zero.

What happens if there has been a shock to inflation and it is not equal to the inflation target? Suppose, for example, that inflation was 4%. The central bank is faced with the constraint of the Phillips curve shown by PC($\pi_t^E = 4$) and can only choose among points along it. The bliss point is no longer obtainable. The central bank faces a trade-off: if it wants a level of output of y_e next period, then it has to accept an inflation rate above its target, i.e. $\pi_t = 4 \neq \pi^T$ (i.e. point B). On the other hand, if it wishes to hit the inflation target next period, it must accept a much lower level of output next period (point C). Point B corresponds to a fully accommodating monetary policy in which the objective

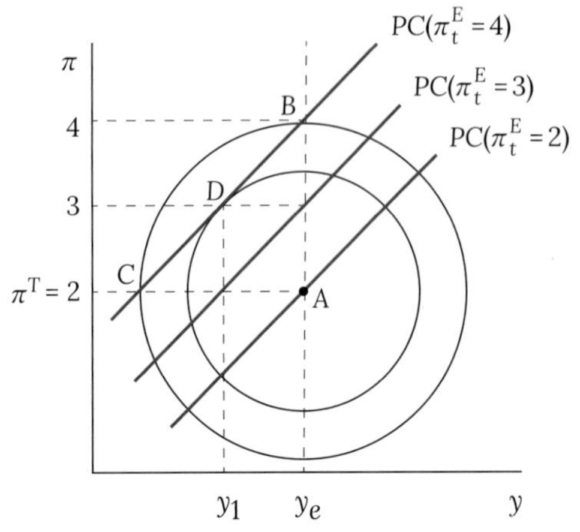

Figure 3.6 Loss circles and Phillips curves.

is purely to hit the output target ($\beta = 0$), and point C corresponds to a completely non-accommodating policy, in which the objective is purely to hit the inflation target.

It is clear from Figure 3.6 that given its preferences, if the central bank is faced by $PC(\pi_t^E = 4)$, then it can do better (achieve a loss circle closer to A) than either point B or point C. It minimizes its loss function by choosing point D, where the $PC(\pi_t^E = 4)$ line is tangential to the indifference curve of the loss function closest to the bliss point. Thus if is it on $PC(\pi_t^E = 4)$ it will choose an output level y_1 which will in turn imply an inflation rate of 3% and a Phillips curve the following period of $PC(\pi_t^E = 3)$.

Deriving the monetary rule (*MR*) curve graphically

The MR curve shows the central bank's preferred output-inflation combination for any Phillips curve it faces. It can be derived graphically by finding the points of tangency between the Phillips curves and the loss circles. As shown in Figure 3.7a, points A, B and C all minimize the loss function of the central bank for their given Phillips curve. For example, take point B, which is on $PC(\pi_t^E = 3)$. If the central bank were to choose any other point on that Phillips curve, then the economy would be on a loss circle further from the bliss point and hence at a lower level of utility.

If we join up the points of tangency as shown in Figure 3.7b, this gives us the MR curve. This shows the output and inflation combination that the central bank will choose to minimize its loss function for any given Phillips curve it is faced with.

In the Appendix, we derive the monetary rule using the equations for the central bank's loss function and the Phillips curve. The equation for the MR curve shown in Figure 3.7 is:

$$(y_t - y_e) = -\alpha\beta(\pi_t - \pi^T). \qquad \text{(monetary rule, MR)}$$

The MR tells the central bank what output gap it should choose when it observes that inflation is away from its target. The monetary policy rules used by central banks are often described as Taylor Rules. The difference between the MR and a Taylor Rule is

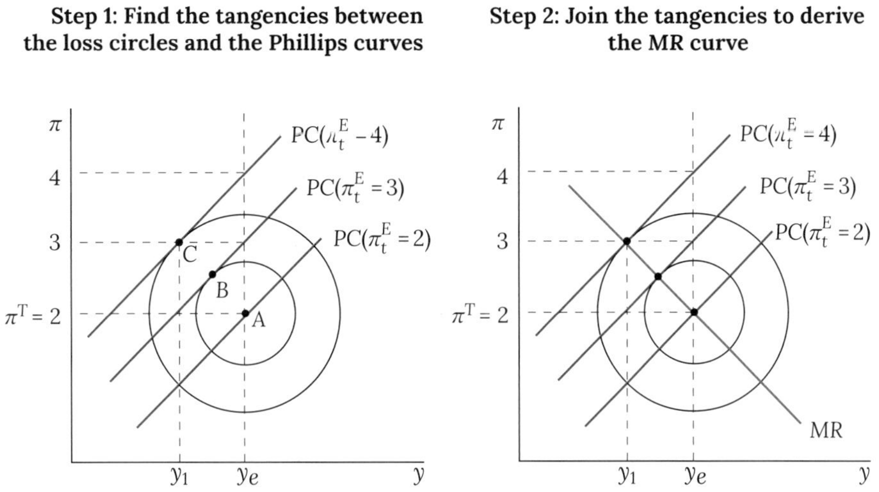

Figure 3.7 Deriving the MR curve. Visit www.oup.com/he/carlin-soskice to explore deriving the MR curve with Animated Analytical Diagram 3.7.

that the latter is expressed in terms of the interest rate the central bank should choose to implement its chosen output gap. Taylor Rules used by central banks are discussed in Chapter 6. To find out the interest rate the central bank should choose once it has decided on its preferred output gap using the MR we need to introduce the IS curve. In addition to the Phillips curve (PC) and the monetary rule (MR), the IS is the third equation in the 3-equation model.

Implementing central bank policy—the *IS* curve

In the previous subsection, we set out the process by which the central bank pins down its preferred output gap in response to an economic shock. The instrument the central bank uses to implement its policy is the real interest rate, r. The fact that the central bank must adjust the *nominal* interest rate that it sets in order to achieve a particular *real* interest rate on the IS curve is called the Taylor Principle. As mentioned above, the so-called Taylor rule for monetary policy is explained in Chapter 6.

The real interest rate is chosen to secure the appropriate level of aggregate demand and hence output. The central bank chooses the best point along the Phillips curve that it faces and in order to deliver the right level of aggregate demand, it must set the interest rate at the level shown by the IS curve. The IS curve shows the effect of changes in the interest rate on aggregate demand and was introduced in the following form in Chapter 1:

$$y = k(c_0 + a_0 + G) - ka_1 r \quad (3.2)$$

$$= A - ar, \quad \text{(IS curve)}$$

BOX 3.1 Summary of the 3-equation model

We now have all the components to set out the central bank's decision-making process:

1. The central bank minimizes its loss function, which expresses its objective of keeping inflation close to target, π^T

$$L = (y_t - y_e)^2 + \beta(\pi_t - \pi^T)^2, \qquad \text{(central bank loss function)}$$

2. subject to the constraint from the supply side, which is the Phillips curve (PC).

$$\pi_t = \pi_{t-1} + \alpha(y_t - y_e). \qquad \text{(Phillips curve, PC)}$$

3. Together these produce the monetary rule function (MR), which fixes the best response output gap $(y_t - y_e)$,

$$(y_t - y_e) = -\alpha\beta(\pi_t - \pi^T). \qquad \text{(monetary rule, MR)}$$

4. which is implemented through the central bank's choice of r using the dynamic IS equation, incorporating the lag from the interest rate to output

$$y_t = A - ar_{t-1}. \qquad \text{(dynamic IS curve)}$$

where $A \equiv k(c_0 + a_0 + G)$, $a \equiv ka_1$ and k is the multiplier. The term A includes the multiplier and the demand shift variables such as government spending and both the autonomous and forward-looking components of consumption and investment.

In the 3-equation model, we will use a 'dynamic' IS curve to represent the demand side, which captures the fact that aggregate demand responds negatively to the real interest rate (r) with a one period lag. Central banks emphasize that the impact of interest rates on output may take around two years.[9]

The dynamic IS curve is the policy implementation rule and is defined as follows:

$$y_t = A - ar_{t-1}. \qquad \text{(dynamic IS curve)}$$

To deliver y_t (the best-response output gap) from the MR curve, the central bank sets r_{t-1} from the IS curve.

Visit www.oup.com/he/carlin-soskice to explore the 3-equation model further with Animated Analytical Diagram: A guide to deriving the 3-equation model.

3.2.2 Using the 3-equation model

This section shows how to use the 3-equation model to explain the response of the central bank to a shock. The economy is initially at the central bank's 'bliss point'—output is at equilibrium and inflation is at target. This is the medium-run equilibrium, y_e, where the WS and PS curves intersect and there is therefore no pressure on inflation to change. The interest rate that is associated with equilibrium is known as the *stabilizing rate of interest*, or r_S.

[9] See for instance the *Monetary Policy* section of the Bank of England's website.

Inflation shock

An inflation shock is the simplest to analyse and serves to highlight the dynamic behaviour of the model. The term inflation shock is used to refer to an exogenous shift in the Phillips curve. This could be caused, for example, by a natural disaster such as a drought that reduces agricultural output and raises food prices, or by a temporary burst of union militancy, which pushes up wages. It could also be caused by a shock to expected inflation, unrelated to lagged inflation.

In the 3-equation model framework, the central bank follows two main steps to stabilize the economy after an inflation shock:

1. The inflation shock shifts the Phillips curve upwards. The central bank must choose the position on the new Phillips curve that minimizes their loss. This will be where the *MR* curve intersects the new Phillips curve. As inflation is above target, the central bank will have to reduce output below equilibrium to squeeze inflation out of the system.
2. The central bank uses the IS in its role as the *policy-implementation curve* to find the increase in the real interest rate required to get the economy back onto the *MR* curve. The higher interest rate depresses output and inflation starts to fall. The central bank then gradually reduces the interest rate until output rises back to equilibrium and inflation falls back at target.

Figure 3.8 provides a summary of the dynamic adjustment of the economy to an inflation shock (start at the top and follow round). Figure 3.9a shows the typical fashion in which shocks can be modelled graphically in the 3-equation model, with the *IS* diagram at the top and the *PC*–*MR* diagram directly below it. This allows the position of the economy to be shown simultaneously on both diagrams. As shown in Figure 3.9a, the adjustment of the economy to the inflation shock is as follows:

Period 0: The economy starts at A, where the central bank's utility is highest. The economy is then hit by an inflation shock which shifts the *PC* to *PC*(inflation shock) in the lower panel and the economy moves from A to B. Point B is not on the central bank's *MR* curve. The central bank forecasts the *PC* in the next period. We denote next period's *PC* as $PC(\pi_1^E = \pi_0)$. Faced with this *PC* and the one period lag in output responding to its interest rate decision, the best the central bank can do is to locate at point C, back on the *MR* curve next period. They therefore set the interest rate at r_0 using the *IS* curve. The economy ends period 0 with inflation at π_0, output at y_e and the interest rate at r_0.

Period 1: The new interest rate has had time to reduce aggregate demand by dampening investment. The economy moves to point C, with output below equilibrium at y_1 and inflation at π_1. The central bank forecasts the *PC* in the next period. The Phillips curve shifts when inflation expectations are updated: hence the *PC* will change in the next period, moving to $PC(\pi_2^E = \pi_1)$. Faced with this *PC*, the central bank would like to locate at point D, back on their *MR* curve. They therefore reduce the interest rate to r_1. The interest rate can only affect economic output with a one period lag, however, so the economy ends period 1 with inflation at π_1, output at y_1 and the interest rate at r_1.

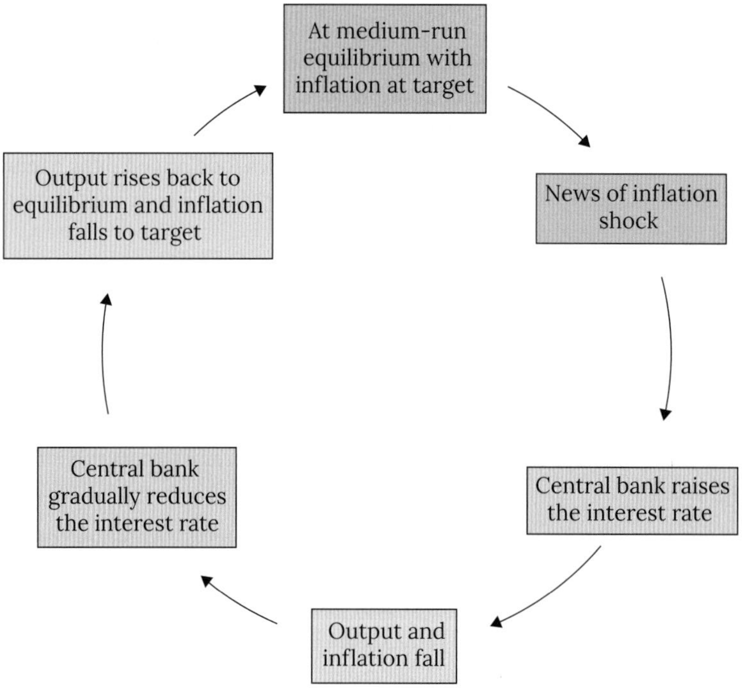

Figure 3.8 Dynamic adjustment to an inflation shock.

Period 2 onwards: In period 2, the economy moves to point D, as the lower interest rate stimulates demand. This increases output to y_2 and inflation falls to π_2. The same process now repeats itself until the economy is back at equilibrium at Z. This involves the central bank forecasting next period's PC and setting the interest rate in the current period to ensure they stay on the MR curve in the following period. The adjustment from D to Z will take a number of periods. The economy will move gradually down the MR curve, as the central bank slowly adjusts the interest rate down from r_1 to r_S. This causes output to rise slowly from y_2 to y_e and inflation to fall slowly from π_2 to π^T. The economic adjustment to the inflation shock ends when the economy is back at point Z, with output at y_e, inflation at π^T and the interest rate at r_S.

Figure 3.9b shows the path of the key macroeconomic variables over time following the inflation shock. These types of graphs are called *impulse response functions* and are useful for visualizing the adjustment path of the economy following an economic shock. In this case, we can see that inflation has risen after the shock and is then slowly brought back to target. The interest rate follows a similar path, rising as soon as the shock takes place and then slowly being reduced to target. The path of output is slightly different, in that it does not change until one period after the shock. This is because the higher interest rate takes one period to affect output, as shown by the IS relation underlying the model, $y_t = A - ar_{t-1}$.

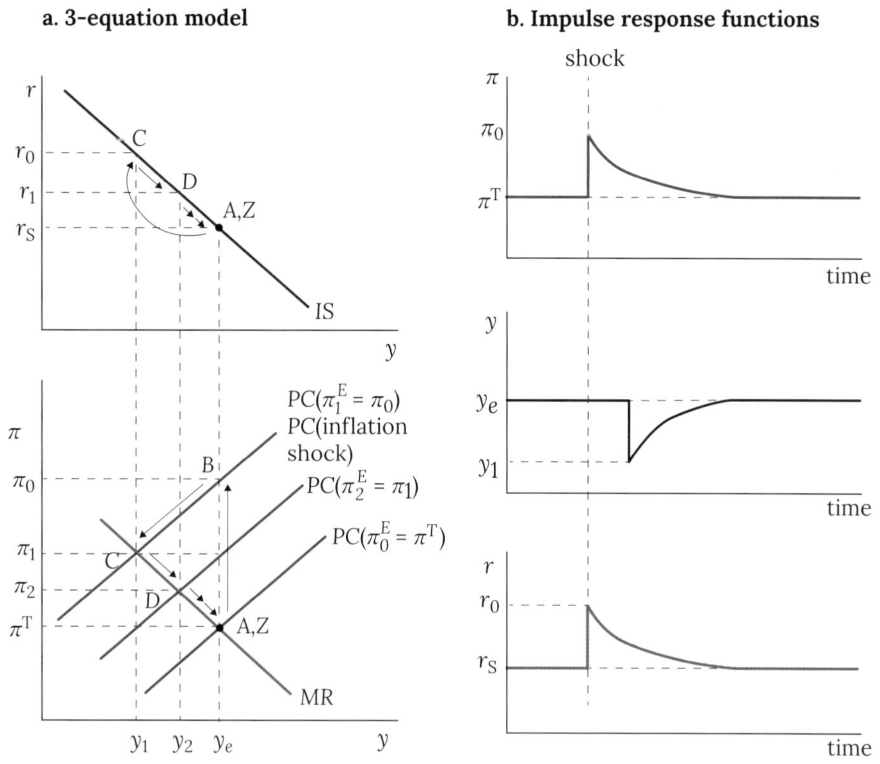

Figure 3.9 Inflation shock and the monetary rule. Visit www.oup.com/he/carlin-soskice to explore an inflation shock and the monetary rule with Animated Analytical Diagram 3.9.

The 3-equation model can be used to analyse a wide range of situations faced by the central bank. In Section 3.3, it is used to analyse demand and supply shocks and to examine the special case of a deflation trap.

Visit www.oup.com/he/carlin-soskice to push your understanding of the 3-equation model further with Animated Analytical Diagram: A guide to drawing and understanding the 3-equation model.

3.3 **APPLICATIONS**

In this section, we show more examples of the 3-equation model at work, focusing on demand- and supply-side shocks. We highlight the integral role played by central bank forecasting in identifying the best response interest rate to ensure medium-run economic stability. We go on to analyse the special case of a deflation trap, where a sizeable negative demand shock pushes the economy into a vicious cycle of falling inflation and output. We provide some escape routes from a deflation trap, while noting their potential pitfalls. We end this section by looking at a supply shock, which is a shift in either the wage- or price-setting curve. In this case, the central bank acts to stabilize the economy at the new equilibrium level of output fixed by the new intersecton of the WS and PS curves.

3.3.1 A temporary demand shock

We assume that the economy starts off in equilibrium with output at the equilibrium and inflation at the target rate of π^T (see Figure 3.10). The economy is then disturbed by a temporary positive aggregate demand shock. By a temporary aggregate demand shock, we mean that the shock shifts the *IS* curve to *IS′*, but it only remains at *IS′* for one period. The economy is shifted from A to B in Figure 3.10 as a result of the aggregate demand shock. This rise in output builds a rise in inflation above target into the economy. Because of inflation inertia, this can only be eliminated by pushing output below (and unemployment above) the equilibrium. The central bank therefore raises the interest rate in response to the aggregate demand shock because it can work out the consequences for inflation. It must raise the interest rate in order to depress interest-sensitive demand and reduce output. The central bank is forward looking and takes all available information into account.

The adjustment to the shock is shown in Figure 3.10.

Period 0: The economy starts at A—the central bank's bliss point. Following the demand shock, the economy moves from A to B. The shock has increased both output ($y_0 > y_e$) and inflation ($\pi_0 > \pi^T$). Point B is not on the central bank's *MR* curve. The central bank forecasts the *PC* in the next period. The Phillips curve shifts when inflation expectations are updated: hence the *PC* will change in the next period, moving

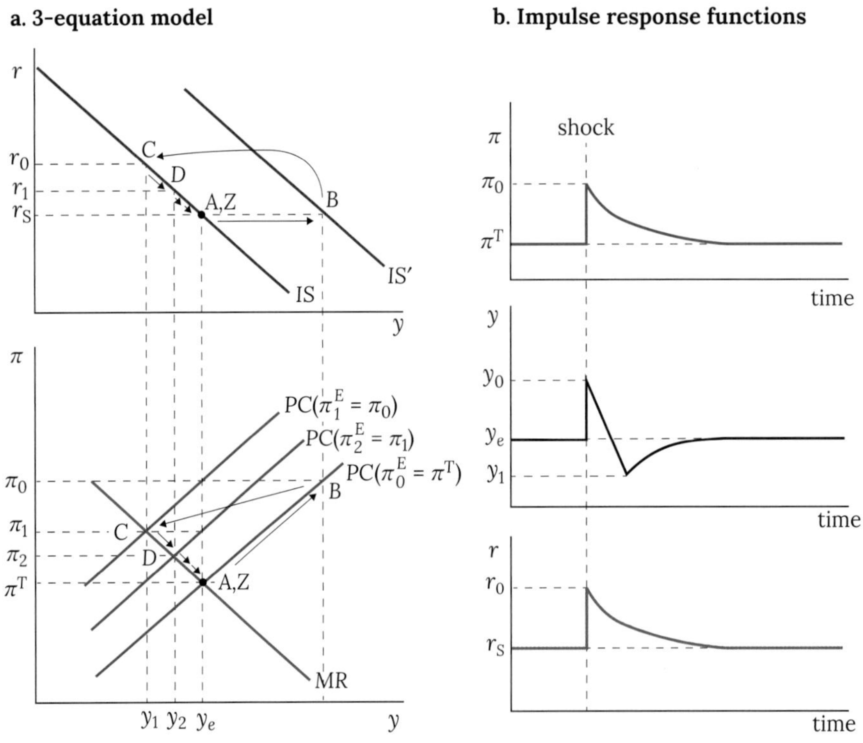

Figure 3.10 Adjustment of the economy to a temporary positive aggregate demand shock. Visit www.oup.com/he/carlin-soskice to explore the central bank's response to a temporary demand shock with Animated Analytical Diagram 3.10.

to PC($\pi_1^E = \pi_0$). Faced with this PC, the central bank would like to locate at point C, back on their MR curve. They therefore set the interest rate at r_0.The central bank expects the demand shock to be temporary, so that the IS curve will shift back in the next period. This is the reason they use the original IS as the implementation curve to set the interest rate. The interest rate can only affect economic output with a one period lag, however, so the economy ends period 0 with inflation at π_0, output at y_0 and the interest rate at r_0.

Period 1: The new interest rate has had time to affect aggregate demand. The higher rate of interest depresses investment. This reduces output and the economy moves to point C, with output below equilibrium at y_1 and inflation at π_1. The central bank forecasts the PC in the next period: the PC will move to PC($\pi_2^E = \pi_1$). Faced with this PC, the central bank would like to locate at point D, on their MR curve. They therefore reduce the interest rate to r_1. The interest rate can only affect economic output with a one period lag, however, so the economy ends period 1 with inflation at π_1, output at y_1 and the interest rate at r_1.

Period 2 onwards: In period 2, the economy moves to point D, as the lower interest rate stimulates demand. This increases output to y_2 and inflation falls to π_2. The same process now repeats itself until the economy is back at equilibrium at Z. The economic adjustment to the temporary demand shock ends when the economy is back at point Z, with output at y_e, inflation at π^T and the interest rate at r_S.

We can use a Reserve Bank of Australia press release from March 2005 to provide an example of a case where an inflation-targeting central bank increased interest rates by 25 basis points to 5.5% in response to rising demand pressures:[10]

> In Australia, there are high levels of confidence in both the business and household sectors, credit growth is providing ample support for spending, employment is growing strongly and national income and spending will continue to be boosted this year by the rising terms of trade. In these circumstances, the Board judged that an increase in the cash rate was warranted in order to reduce the risk of an unacceptable rise in inflation in the medium term.

3.3.2 **Forecasting and lags**

The example of the central bank's reaction to a demand shock can be used to highlight the role played by forecasting and lags in the effect of monetary policy on aggregate demand and output. In the previous subsection, we discussed the adjustment of the economy to a temporary positive demand shock (Figure 3.10). We now use Figure 3.11 to compare this to the case of a permanent demand shock. It is left as an exercise for the reader to set out the detailed period-by-period adjustment for the permanent shock.

The examples highlight two important points about the central bank's reaction to an aggregate demand shock:

---

[10] Excerpt taken from: Ian Macfarlane, 2nd March 2005, *Statement by the Governor, Mr Ian Macfarlane: Monetary Policy*.

1. The central bank has to forecast both the PC and IS curves. The forecasting of the IS curve means predicting the persistence of the shock—is it temporary or permanent?
2. The reason that the central bank must forecast the IS is that the persistence of the shock affects the central bank's preferred reaction. In Figure 3.11, where the shock is permanent, the IS curve *remains* at IS′ and this is the policy implementation curve. The initial increase in the interest rate (i.e. from r_S to r_0) is much greater in the case of a permanent shock. This is because a permanent shock leads to a higher stabilizing rate of interest in the new equilibrium—r'_S. The higher autonomous aggregate demand (for example, due to improved consumer confidence) needs to be offset by lower interest-sensitive aggregate demand (e.g. investment) if output is to return to its equilibrium level y_e.

What happens if the central bank is uncertain about whether the shock is temporary or permanent? In this case, the central bank would be likely to set an interest rate somewhere in between the interest rates it would set in the cases presented in Figures 3.10 and 3.11. In reality, central banks are unlikely to be able to tell (in the period of the shock) whether shocks will be temporary or permanent, so use their best judgement to respond to shocks and often have to adjust interest rates as new information arrives.

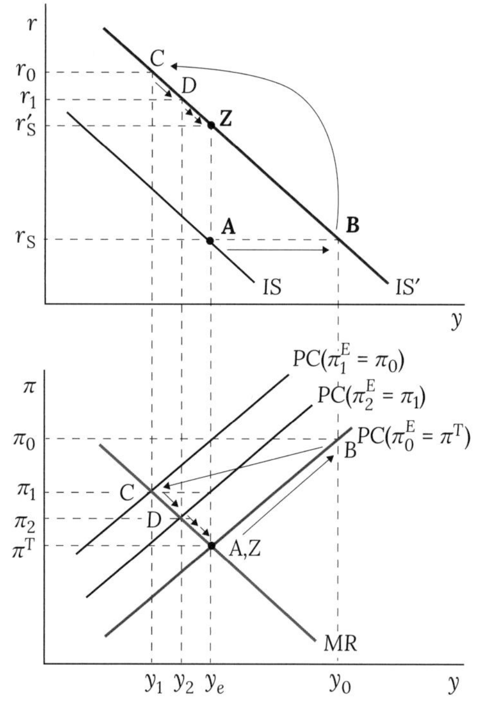

Figure 3.11 Adjustment of the economy to a permanent positive aggregate demand shock. Visit www.oup.com/he/carlin-soskice to explore the central bank's response to a permanent demand shock with Animated Analytical Diagram 3.11.

In the benchmark 3-equation model, the interest rate affects output with a one period lag: $y_t = A - ar_{t-1}$. However, it is interesting to see what happens if the central bank could affect output immediately, i.e. if $y_t = A - ar_t$. In this case, as soon as the IS shock is diagnosed, the central bank would raise the interest rate to r'_S. The economy then goes directly from A to Z in the IS diagram (in Figure 3.11) and it remains at A in the PC–MR diagram, i.e. points A and Z coincide. Since the aggregate demand shock is fully and immediately offset by the change in the interest rate, there is no chance for inflation to rise.

This underlines the crucial role of lags and hence of forecasting for the central bank: the more timely and accurate are forecasts of shifts in aggregate demand (and of other kinds of shock), the greater is the chance that the central bank can offset them and limit their impact on inflation. Once inflation has been affected, the presence of inflation inertia means that the central bank must change the interest rate and get the economy onto the MR curve in order to steer it back to the inflation target.

Inflation-targeting monetary policy responds to the paradox of the thrift

In Section 1.2.2, the paradox of thrift was explained. In the modern inflation-targeting framework, the paradox of thrift can be resolved through active monetary policy. Faced with a fall in aggregate demand due to higher desired household saving (i.e. a negative aggregate demand shock which shifts the IS curve to the left), inflation falls below the central bank's target. It is obliged by its mandate to cut the interest rate and guide the economy back to equilibrium output at a lower stabilizing real interest rate. Interest-sensitive spending rises, offsetting the effect on aggregate demand of the fall in autonomous consumption. The desire to save more at a given level of income does not result in persistent lower output because the central bank intervenes to prevent it. In terms of equation 1.9 (Chapter 1), this could be thought of as boosting $\bar{I}$, allowing c_0 to fall without requiring a corresponding fall in income.

3.3.3 The deflation trap

Problems arise for using monetary policy along the lines of the 3-equation model when the real rate of interest needed to stabilize demand cannot be achieved because the nominal interest rate cannot be reduced further.

The zero lower bound on nominal interest rates

In Chapter 1, we set out the Fisher equation, which shows the relationship between the real and nominal interest rates and the expected rate of inflation:

$$i = r + \pi^E. \qquad \text{(Fisher equation)}$$

When responding to an economic shock, the central bank adjusts the nominal interest rate (i), in order to affect the real interest rate (r) which in turn affects aggregate demand through the IS relation. To do this, it must take into account expected inflation as shown by the Fisher equation. In this regard, we can model the central bank as setting the real interest rate.

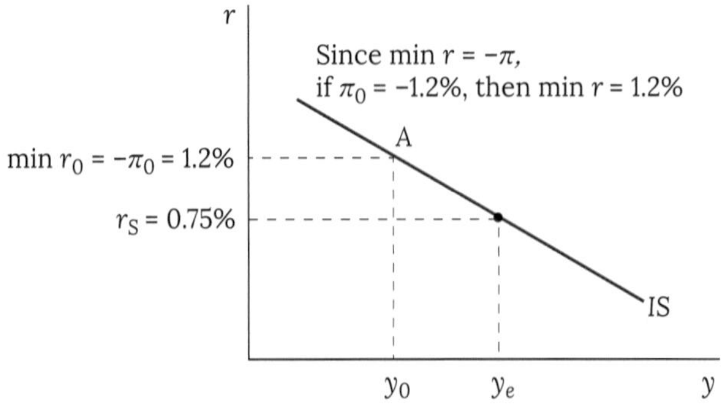

Figure 3.12 The zero lower bound on the nominal interest rate.

We saw in Figure 3.1, that the central bank will respond to falling inflation by reducing the interest rate to stimulate aggregate demand. There is, however, a limit to the extent to which the central bank can reduce the nominal interest rate. The lowest nominal interest rate the central bank can set is zero (see the Box 3.2 for more detail, including about negative interest rates). From the Fisher equation, we can see that if the real interest rate that is needed to achieve the central bank's chosen output gap on the MR curve is, for example, 0.75%, and expected inflation is –1.2%, then a nominal interest rate of –0.45% would be required.

With a *zero lower bound* (or *ZLB*) on the nominal interest rate, the minimum real interest rate that can be achieved is set as follows.

If the ZLB holds, $i \geq 0$ and using the Fisher equation,

$$r + \pi^E \geq 0$$

$$\rightarrow \min r = -\pi^E$$

This means that in our example, the minimum real interest rate achievable is 1.2%, which is not low enough get the economy on to the MR (0.75%) and on the path back to equilibrium. This condition is shown in Figure 3.12 where the stabilizing real interest rate is below the minimum feasible rate of 1.2%. Given the depressed state of aggregate demand depicted by the position of the IS curve, if inflation has fallen to –1.2%, then it will be impossible to achieve the equilibrium level of output using conventional monetary policy. The economy is stuck at point A on the IS curve.

BOX 3.2 The zero lower bound and negative nominal interest rates

There is no technical reason why nominal interest rates cannot be negative. The central bank could, for example, set the interest rate at −5%. In this environment, an individual who deposited £100 in the bank at the start of the year could withdraw £95 at the end of the year. This is not beneficial for savers, but this could be the interest rate required to get the economy onto the MR curve and back to equilibrium. It would certainly be expected to stimulate borrowing, by making the cost of obtaining credit cheaper.

There is, however, a major practical implication to negative interest rates arising from the presence of notes and coins. When nominal interest rates are negative, there is nothing to stop people simply holding their savings in cash, which has a nominal interest rate of zero. Anecdotal evidence of this behaviour comes from the sales director of Germany's largest safe manufacturer who the *Financial Times* reported as saying that the sale of safes increased by one-third after the deposit rate at the ECB went below zero. However, more systematic research by the ECB doesn't support this[a].

Several central banks including the Swedish Riksbank, the Bank of Japan, and the Swiss and Danish National Banks as well as the ECB used negative interest rates as a monetary policy tool as they sought to get stubbornly low inflation back up toward target following the financial crisis. Sweden abandoned the policy after five years. Since holding more money at the central bank is costly, the aim is to encourage banks to make more loans. In practice this policy has meant that some individuals in Europe have had to pay to deposit large sums in banks and instead of paying interest, some mortgage borrowers in Denmark (i.e. households) have received money from their lenders (banks).

Whilst noting its adverse effects on the profitability of banks and the limits to how negative the policy rate can go, the ECB assesses the use of modestly negative interest rates as contributing to easing monetary policy, see Boucinha and Burlon (2020). However during the Covid-19 pandemic when powerful deflationary forces emerged, central banks tended to use asset purchases (so-called quantitative easing) rather than moving the policy interest rate further into negative territory[b].

[a] For a thorough assessment of negative interest rates see Boucinha and Burlon (2020).
[b] See the speech by Philip Lane, Member of the Executive Board of the ECB (Lane 2020*a*).

The deflation trap and the 3-equation model

We can use the 3-equation model to provide a period-by-period explanation of how a negative aggregate demand shock can lead to the economy becoming stuck in a deflation trap, where output and inflation are falling without limit. We assume that the economy starts off with output at equilibrium and inflation at the target rate of π^T as shown in Figure 3.13. The economic adjustment to the shock is as follows:

Period 0: The economy starts at A—the central bank's bliss point. The economy is hit by a large permanent negative aggregate demand shock which shifts the IS curve to IS′ and the economy moves from A to B. The shock has reduced both output ($y_0 < y_e$) and inflation ($\pi_0 < \pi^T$). In fact, inflation has become negative—i.e. there is deflation. Point B is not on the central bank's MR curve. The central bank forecasts the PC in the next period. Inflation is currently below equilibrium at π_0, which means the PC will shift in the next period, moving to PC($\pi_1^E = \pi_0$). Faced with this PC, the central bank would like to locate at point C′, back on their MR curve. This would require setting an interest

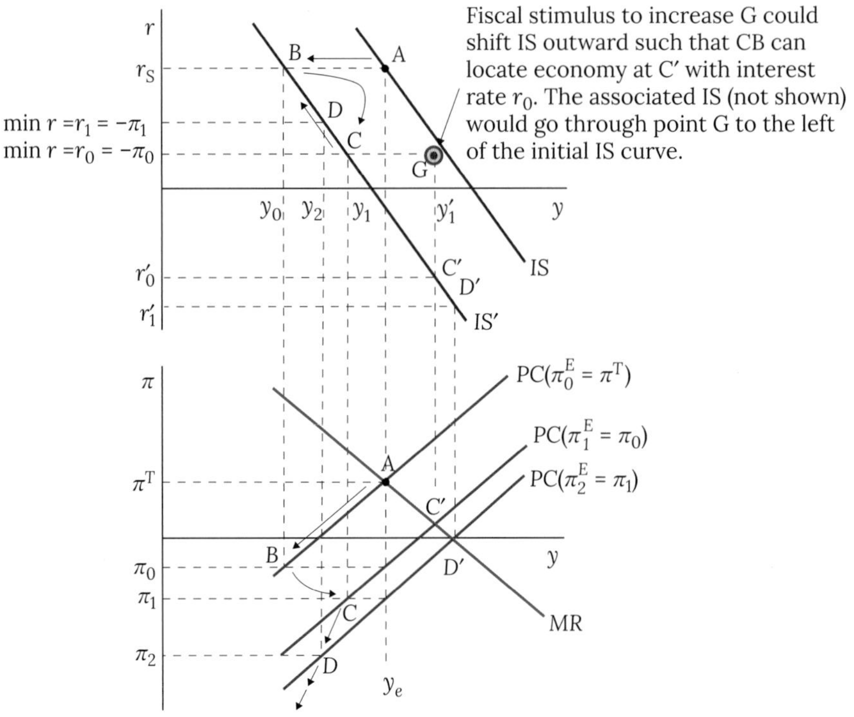

Figure 3.13 How a large negative permanent aggregate demand shock can lead to the economy entering a deflation trap. Visit www.oup.com/he/carlin-soskice to explore a deflation trap with Animated Analytical Diagram 3.13.

rate of r_0'. However, this is below the minimum real interest rate the central bank can achieve (by setting nominal interest rates to zero). The lowest interest rate they can achieve is $r_0 = -\pi_0$. The central bank expects the demand shock to be permanent, so that the IS curve will stay at IS′ in the next period. This is the reason they use the new IS curve to set the interest rate. The interest rate can only affect economic output with a one period lag, however, so the economy ends period 0 with inflation at π_0, output at y_0 and the interest rate at r_0.

Period 1: The new interest rate has had time to affect aggregate demand. The lower rate of interest boosts investment. This increases output and the economy moves to point C, with output still below equilibrium at y_1. This level of output is far below the central bank's best response level of y_1', which causes inflation to fall further to π_1. The central bank forecasts the PC in the next period. The PC will move to $PC(\pi_2^E = \pi_1)$. Faced with this PC, the central bank would like to locate at point D′, back on their *MR* curve. This would require setting an interest rate of r_1'. However, this is below the minimum real interest rate the central bank can achieve (by setting nominal interest rates to zero). The lowest interest rate they can achieve is $r_1 = -\pi_1$. The interest rate can only affect economic output with a one period lag, however, so the economy ends period 1 with inflation at π_1, output at y_1 and the interest rate at r_1.

Period 2 onwards: In period 2, the economy moves to point D, as the higher interest rate dampens demand. This reduces output to y_2 and inflation falls further to π_2. The economy has entered a deflation trap—both output and inflation are falling every period and conventional monetary policy is powerless to stop them. In each future period, inflation becomes more negative, which increases the minimum real interest rate the central bank can achieve. The higher interest rate dampens demand, which further reduces inflation. In other words, the economy is caught in a vicious cycle. The arrows on Figure 3.13 show that the economy will not revert to medium-run equilibrium in this case, but rather it will diverge, with ever-falling inflation and output.

The potential for a downward spiral of the economy in a deflation trap explains why policy makers are so keen to avoid this situation. We have shown in Figure 3.13 that conventional monetary policy (e.g. adjusting interest rates) is insufficient to escape a deflation trap. There are, however, two policies which could be initiated to pull the economy out of this downward spiral:

1. The *IS* curve could be shifted to the right (to go through point G) in the period after the initial demand shock (the shifted curve is not shown). This would allow the central bank to achieve their desired output level of y_1' by setting the minimum achievable interest rate of r_0. This could result from a spontaneous recovery of autonomous investment or a recovery of autonomous consumption. Alternatively, the government can step in and implement the desired output gap shown by the *MR* curve by using fiscal policy. In this case, the *MR* becomes a more general policy rule and would be labelled *PR*, for 'policy rule'.
2. Creating more positive inflation expectations. If expected inflation becomes less negative, the min r line shifts down and the *PC* curve shifts up. This may allow the central bank to use the interest rate based monetary rule in the usual way to move the economy to the south-east along the *IS* curve.

However, the idea of escaping from the deflation trap by creating positive inflation expectations may not work in practice. One possible way to create expectations of inflation in the future is to create expectations of future higher aggregate demand: if the authorities do not take measures to create the demand, there is no reason to think that people will expect higher inflation.

Another potential option for central banks stuck at the zero lower bound is to introduce unconventional monetary policies, such as quantitative easing. We leave a discussion of this policy option until Chapters 5 and 6, however, as it is easier to explain once we have introduced the banking system into the model.

To extend this model to explain how an economy can get stuck at the zero lower bound without continuously falling prices, and explore its relevance to high-income countries following the financial crisis, see Carlin and Soskice (2018).

3.3.4 **A supply shock**

At the end of Chapter 2, we looked at the implications for inflation of a positive aggregate supply shock. This was modelled as a downward shift of the WS curve, which could be the result of a number of factors, such as a decrease in union bargaining

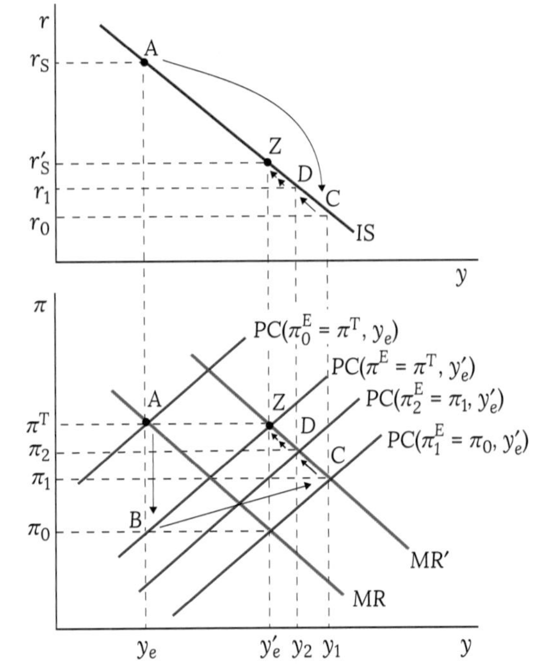

Figure 3.14 The adjustment of the economy to a positive permanent aggregate supply shock. Visit www.oup.com/he/carlin-soskice to explore a positive supply shock with Animated Analytical Diagram 3.14.

power or a reduction in unemployment benefits. The initial effect of this supply shock is a downward shift of the Phillips curve. We will now go on to explain how the central bank stabilizes the economy in the event of a supply shock and the characteristics of the new medium-run equilibrium (see Figure 3.14).

The stabilizing interest rate is lower (at r'_S) in the new medium-run equilibrium. Since equilibrium output is higher as a consequence of the supply-side shift, a lower real interest rate is required to provide the appropriate level of aggregate demand. This example highlights that supply shocks differ from inflation and demand shocks in three key ways:

1. Firstly, a supply shock changes the equilibrium level of output (i.e. y'_e in Figure 3.14).
2. As a result, a supply shock shifts the MR schedule so that it goes through the point where inflation is at target and output at the new equilibrium (i.e. MR′ in Figure 3.14).
3. Thirdly, the consequence is that the Phillips curves need to be redrawn: each PC curve must now go through the intersection of π^E and y'_e.

The period-by-period adjustment of the economy to a positive supply shock and the central bank's intervention is illustrated in Figure 3.14 and described below.

Period 0: The economy starts at A—the central bank's bliss point. The economy is hit by a permanent positive aggregate supply shock. This fundamentally changes the equilibrium level of output in the economy, increasing it from y_e to y'_e. At A, the economy is now below equilibrium output and there is pressure on inflation to fall (as WS < PS, see Chapter 2). The Phillips curve shifts down from $PC(\pi_0^E = \pi^T, y_e)$ to $PC(\pi_0^E = \pi^T, y_e')$, reflecting the change in the equilibrium level of output. The economy moves from A to B, where output is still at its original level, but inflation has fallen to π_0.

The central bank predicts that the shock is a permanent supply shock, so they shift the MR curve outwards to ensure their bliss point is now where output is equal to y_e' and inflation is equal to π^T. Point B is not on the central bank's new MR curve, MR′. The central bank forecasts the PC in the next period. Output is currently below the new equilibrium level of y_e', which means the PC will shift in the next period, moving to $PC(\pi_1^E = \pi_0, y_e')$. Faced with this PC, the central bank would like to locate at point C, on their new MR curve, MR'. They therefore set the interest rate at r_0. The interest rate can only affect economic output with a one period lag, however, so the economy ends period 0 at with inflation at π_0, output at y_e and interest rates at r_0.

Period 1: The new interest rate has had time to affect aggregate demand. The lower rate of interest boosts investment. This increases output and the economy moves to point C, with output above the new equilibrium at y_1 and inflation at π_1. The central bank forecasts the PC in the following period. Output is still away from the new equilibrium, so the PC will change again in the next period, moving to $PC(\pi_2^E = \pi_1, y_e')$. Faced with this PC, the central bank would like to locate at point D, on the MR' curve. They therefore increase the interest rate to r_1. The interest rate can only affect economic output with a one period lag, however, so the economy ends period 1 with inflation at π_1, output at y_1 and interest rates at r_1.

Period 2 onwards: In period 2, the economy moves to point D, as the higher interest rate depresses demand. This reduces output to y_2 and inflation rises to π_2. The same process now repeats itself in the usual way until the economy is back at equilibrium at Z. Adjustment to the supply shock ends when the economy is back at point Z, with output at y_e', inflation at π^T and the interest rate at r_S'.[11]

A positive supply shock can be the result of a shift in the WS or PS curves. We have shown the example of a downward shift in the WS curve above, but equally a positive supply shock could reflect an upward shift of the PS curve, due to increased product market competition or productivity gains. This latter case applies to the United States in the late 1990s, where the ICT revolution spurred productivity increases (see Chapters 16 and 17). The Federal Reserve correctly identified this as a positive supply shock and took into account its role in moderating inflation:[12]

> Responding to the availability of new technologies at increasingly attractive prices, firms have been investing heavily in new capital equipment; this

[11] Note that the Phillips curve in the new equilibrium is denoted by $PC(\pi^E = \pi^T, y_e')$. This does not include a time subscript because the Phillips curve is in this position in two periods—in period 0 straight after the supply shock and then in the period when the economy completes its adjustment to the new equilibrium at point Z.

[12] Excerpt taken from: The Federal Reserve Board, July 22nd 1999, *Monetary Policy Report submitted to the Congress.*

investment has boosted productivity and living standards while holding down the rise in costs and prices.

3.4 CONCLUSIONS

This chapter has provided the final building block for the 3-equation model of the macroeconomy by setting out the monetary rule, or MR curve, which shows the central bank's chosen combination of output gap and inflation rate relative to target for any given Phillips curve they face. The equations of the 3-equation model are:

1. IS curve: $y_t = A - ar_{t-1}$.
2. PC curve: $\pi_t = \pi_{t-1} + \alpha(y_t - y_e)$.
3. MR curve: $(y_t - y_e) = -\alpha\beta(\pi_t - \pi^T)$.

The policy maker is modelled as an inflation-targeting central bank not because this is necessarily the best policy-making arrangement, but because it most closely resembles how modern stabilization policy is undertaken. We noted the economic and political reasons that have been used to explain why, in the more than two decades running up to the global financial crisis, stabilization policy was put in the hands of the monetary policy maker.

In Chapter 1, we introduced the IS curve to model the demand side of the economy. In Chapter 2, we introduced the Phillips curve (PC) to model the supply side of the economy. In this chapter, we have introduced the MR curve to model the policy maker and showed how the IS curve is used to implement monetary policy. These are the three components of the 3-equation model. The modelling section of this chapter set out the 3-equation model in full; the Appendix shows the mathematical derivation. Putting them together provides a framework in which to answer a variety of questions about the macroeconomy and stabilization policy in particular:

1. Why target low and stable inflation? Central banks target low and stable inflation to minimize the negative effects of inflation on the economy—such as price distortions, shoe leather costs, menu costs—and to avoid high and rising (or volatile) inflation. The lag of wage increases behind price increases reduces real wages and fuels discontent about falling living standards. Does that mean it is optimal to target 0% inflation? No, because central banks also want to guard against the threat of deflation (i.e. falling prices). Deflation is particularly problematic for the economy due to the possibility of entering a deflation trap. In light of this, the majority of central banks in high-income economies have chosen to target 2% inflation.
2. How do modern central banks go about achieving their inflation target? How do they react to economic shocks? The central bank's best response position—their 'bliss point'—is to be in medium-run equilibrium, with inflation equal to target (π^T) and output equal to equilibrium (y_e). The *monetary rule* (or MR) curve of a central bank shows the output and inflation combinations that minimize their *loss function* (i.e. maximize their utility) for any given Phillips curve they face. In response to an economic shock, the central bank finds the relevant Phillips

curve and uses the *MR* curve to find their preferred output gap. The real interest rate (r) is the policy lever they use to achieve their desired output gap. It affects aggregate demand via the *IS* relation, which, in the closed economy, is the *policy implementation curve*. The central bank then continues to adjust the interest rate along the policy implementation curve (the *IS*) to guide the economy to the new medium-run equilibrium. The use of the interest rate to implement monetary policy is sometimes called a Taylor rule based monetary policy. Demand shocks will cause the economy to diverge from its initial equilibrium level of output for a number of periods, whereas permanent supply shocks will cause the economy to move to a new equilibrium level of output.

3. What role do lags and forecasting play in monetary policy? The model reflects the real-world phenomenon that it takes time for the real interest rate to affect aggregate demand. This means that forecasting plays a large role in the central bank's setting of interest rates. For a shock in period zero, the central bank has to forecast where the Phillips curve will be next period and then set the appropriate interest rate (using the *MR* curve) to minimize their loss function. The Phillips curve also contains a backward-looking component, which means that if inflation is above target, a period of output below equilibrium (i.e. high unemployment) is required to reduce inflation back to target (and vice versa).

At this point, you may want to learn about the use of quantitative easing, which central banks used to support their monetary policy objectives in the low interest rate environment following the financial crisis. To do this, go to Section 6.4.3 in Chapter 6. And to see how the 3-equation model is extended to the open economy, go to Chapter 11. An important component of the core 3-equation model is the equilibrium rate of unemployment: it is possible to go straight from here to the analysis of the supply-side institutions and policies that determine equilibrium unemployment in Chapter 15.

In this part of the book, we go on to consider a number of extensions to the model. In Chapter 4, we look in more depth at the way in which expectations about the future are formed. The role played by the banking system and how this can lead to instability and financial crises is integrated in the model in Chapters 5 and 8 and monetary and fiscal policy are the focus of Chapters 6 and 7.

3.5 APPENDIX

3.5.1 The 3-equation model in more detail

In the chapter, graphical analysis was used to provide a simple and intuitive explanation of the 3-equation model. In this section, we set out more carefully how the model works, focusing on the mathematical derivation of the *MR* curve. We start by deriving a more general form of the central bank's monetary rule. In setting out the equations that form the basis of the 3-equation model, we need to make explicit the timing structure. By choosing the interest rate in period zero, the central bank affects output and inflation in period 1. We assume it is only concerned with what happens in period 1.

This is the reason that its loss function is defined in terms of y_1 and π_1. If we let β and α take any positive values, the central bank chooses y to minimize

$$L = (y_1 - y_e)^2 + \beta(\pi_1 - \pi^T)^2, \qquad \text{(central bank loss function)}$$

subject to

$$\pi_1 = \pi_0 + \alpha(y_1 - y_e). \qquad \text{(Phillips curve)}$$

By substituting the equation for the Phillips curve into the central bank loss function we can rewrite the loss function as:

$$L = (y_1 - y_e)^2 + \beta((\pi_0 + \alpha(y_1 - y_e)) - \pi^T)^2.$$

If we now differentiate this with respect to y_1 (since this is the variable the central bank can control via its choice of the interest rate), we have:

$$\frac{\partial L}{\partial y_1} = (y_1 - y_e) + \alpha\beta(\pi_0 + \alpha(y_1 - y_e) - \pi^T) = 0. \qquad (3.3)$$

Rearranging the Phillips curve to find π_0 and substituting this back into equation 3.3 gives:

$$(y_1 - y_e) = -\alpha\beta(\pi_1 - \pi^T). \qquad \text{(monetary rule, MR)}$$

The *monetary rule* shows the central bank's best response to a shock; it is the relationship between the inflation rate chosen indirectly and the level of output chosen directly by the central bank to maximize its utility (minimize its loss) given its preferences and the constraints it faces. The monetary rule is an inverse relation between π and y with a negative slope, which shows that the central bank must reduce aggregate demand and output, y, below y_e so as to reduce π below π^T.

In the general form of the MR curve shown above, it can be seen directly that the larger is α (i.e. the more responsive are wages to employment) or the larger is β (i.e. the more inflation averse is the central bank), the flatter will be the slope of the monetary rule.

In the first case this is because any reduction in aggregate demand achieves a bigger cut in inflation, i.e. whatever its preferences, the central bank gets a 'bigger bang (i.e. fall in inflation) for its buck (i.e. fall in aggregate demand)'.

In the second case, this is because, whatever the labour market it faces, a more inflation-averse central bank will wish to reduce inflation by more than a less 'hard-nosed' one.

Figure 3.15 shows the 3-equation model when the economy is in medium-run equilibrium—i.e. output is at equilibrium and inflation is constant at target. In the PC–MR diagram, the economy is at the central bank's 'bliss point'—the levels of output and inflation that minimize the loss function (i.e. y_e and π^T). In the IS diagram, we can use the IS curve to read off the interest rate the central bank must set to keep inflation constant and output at y_e. This is the *stabilizing rate of interest*, r_S.

In the case when output is at equilibrium (i.e. y_e) and the interest rate is at its stabilizing level (i.e. r_S), we can rewrite the IS curve as:

$$y_e = A - ar_S. \qquad \text{(IS curve, in medium-run equilibrium)}$$

We can use the two versions of the IS equation to find a relationship between deviations of output from equilibrium and the interest rate from its stabilizing level. We do this by subtracting one from the other, such that:

$$y_t - y_e = -a(r_{t-1} - r_S). \qquad \text{(IS equation, in deviations)}$$

In period zero, this becomes,

$$y_1 - y_e = -a(r_0 - r_S), \qquad \text{(IS equation, in deviations, in period zero)}$$

which takes into account the fact that interest rate changes in period zero do not affect output until period one (i.e. the lag structure of the model). This is the IS curve used for policy implementation. It can be useful to think of the IS equation in deviations form in the 3-equation model and particularly for deriving interest rate rules, which will be discussed in detail in Chapter 6.

Figure 3.15 can also give us an insight into how varying the underlying targets or parameters will affect the 3-equation model. There are six key parameters that affect the underlying curves in the 3-equation model and the central bank's best response to economic shocks:[13]

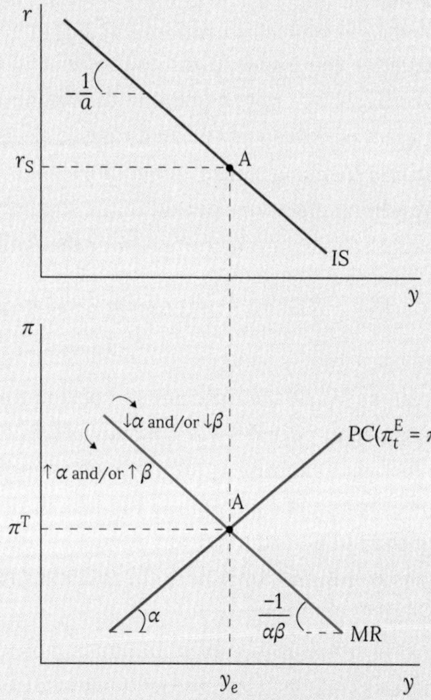

Figure 3.15 The 3-equation model in medium-run equilibrium.

[13] The Macroeconomic Simulator (available at www.oup.com/he/carlin-soskice) can be used to test the effects of varying key parameters on the adjustment path of the economy following an economic shock. See Questions 3 and 4 in the Problems section.

1. The central bank's inflation target, π^T: this affects the position of the MR line;
2. The central bank's preferences, β: this determines the shape of the loss ellipses and affects the slope of the MR line;
3. The slope of the Phillips curve, α: this also affects the slope of the MR line;
4. The interest sensitivity of aggregate demand, a: this determines the slope of the IS curve;
5. The equilibrium level of output, y_e: this determines the level of output at which there is no pressure on inflation to change and affects the position of the MR line;
6. The stabilizing interest rate, r_S: the central bank adjusts the interest rate relative to r_S so it must always analyse whether this has shifted, e.g. as a result of a shift in the IS or due to a change in the equilibrium level of output, y_e.

3.5.2 A more forward-looking central bank

In the 3-equation model, the central bank looks ahead when responding to new information such as inflation, demand, or supply shocks. It works out the Phillips curve constraint it will face next period as a consequence of inflation today and, recognizing that its decision takes a period to feed through to output (via the IS equation), sets r_0 to produce y_1 so as to achieve its best-response output gap in t_1.

It is interesting to consider the implications of the central bank taking a longer horizon into account. Intuitively, we might imagine that a more far-sighted central bank would think at the outset of how to minimize its losses along the entire path back to equilibrium rather than just focusing on the immediate loss. To investigate, we make the simplest extension by adding one more period to the loss function. Since this loss occurs in the future, we apply a discount factor to lower the weight on it.

$$L = (y_t - y_e)^2 + \beta(\pi_t - \pi^T)^2 + \frac{1}{1+\delta}((y_{t+1} - y_e)^2 + \beta(\pi_{t+1} - \pi^T)^2),$$

(central bank dynamic loss function)

where δ represents the rate at which the outcomes in period $t+1$ are discounted (i.e. weighted less) relative to those in period t when making decisions. Specifically when the CB sets r_0 to deliver its best-response y_1, what weight does it place on the loss in the following period? For example, if $\delta = 0.1$, then the loss in period $t+1$ is weighted 10 percent less important than in period t. If $\delta = 0$, period $t+1$ has the same weight as period t and as δ increases to infinity, only period t matters (as in the standard loss function used in the chapter).

We can illustrate the difference this makes in Figure 3.16. Consider an inflation shock that happens in period $t-1$. In our standard analysis, in $t-1$ the central bank chooses its best response output gap for period t at point C where the loss contour is tangential to the PC constraint it faces. At point C, any deviation from its policy is costly: the marginal benefit of raising the interest rate in lowering inflation is more than offset by the cost in terms of lower output. Meanwhile in period t, the bank would choose its best response output gap for period $t+1$ at point D for similar reasons.

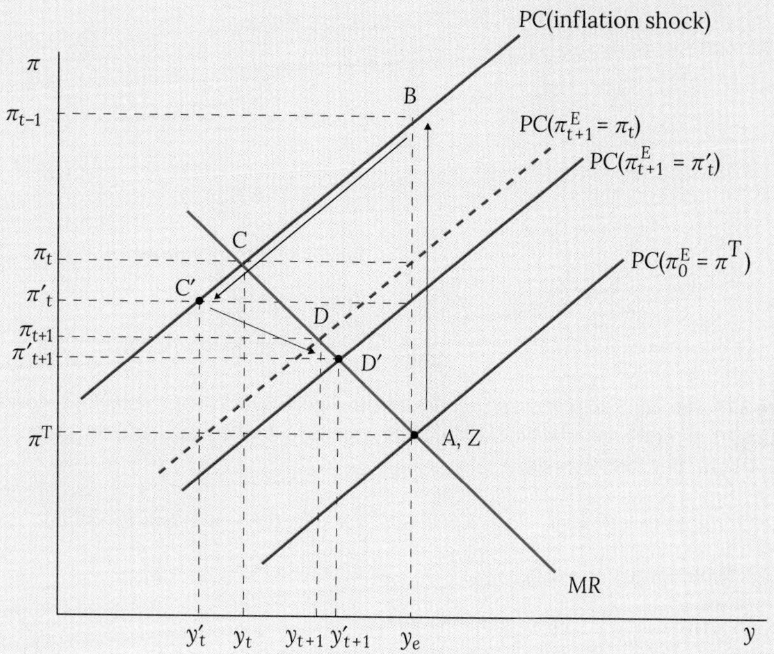

Figure 3.16 Comparing the response of a more forward-looking central bank with the baseline model.

Now consider what would happen if the central bank chose point C′, instead of C. The combination of inflation and output at C′ would generate a higher loss for the central bank in period t than point C. However, by choosing C′, the central bank would face a Philips curve constraint in period t + 1, $PC(\pi^E_{t+1} = \pi'_t)$, which is closer to the bliss point than $PC(\Pi^E_{t+1} = \Pi_t)$, allowing the bank to achieve D′. D′ strictly dominates D, as it has lower inflation and output that is closer to equilibrium.[14] Thus by choosing C′ over C, a central bank would increase losses in period t but decrease losses in period t + 1. A non-forward looking central bank would never choose to do this, but a forward-looking bank that already cares about t + 1 while in t − 1 might (depending on the parameters). Figure 3.17 shows the impulse response functions, highlighting that the forward-looking central bank trades off a deeper initial cut in output for the benefit of a faster adjustment back to equilibrium.

Using the equation for the central bank dynamic loss function, we can see that if $\delta \to \infty$ the weight on the second term disappears; only then is C its best response.

We can find point C′ exactly by solving the central bank's problem mathematically by means of a Lagrangian.

The forward-looking central bank minimizes its loss function subject to two supply-side constraints (two Phillips curves). We can write the central bank's problem as:

[14] Although shown in Figure 3.16 on the original MR curve (for simplicity), the precise location of point D′ will be to the left of the MR curve on $PC(\pi^E_{t+1} = \pi'_t)$ and with a loss lower than at point D. Unlike the standard case, there is not a linear MR curve.

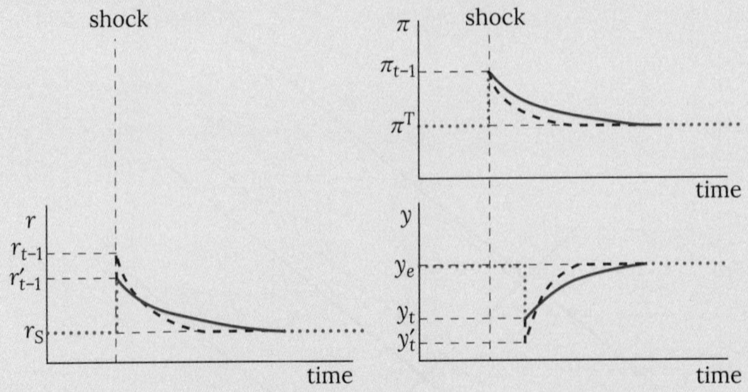

Figure 3.17 The impulse response functions from Figure 3.16. The red solid line represents a 'standard' central bank, the blue dashed line a forward-looking one, and the green dotted line is where they have overlap.

$$\text{minimize} \quad L = (y_1 - y_e)^2 + \beta(\pi_1 - \pi^T)^2 + \frac{1}{1+\delta}((y_2 - y_e)^2 + \beta(\pi_2 - \pi^T)^2)$$

$$\text{subject to} \quad \pi_1 - \alpha(y_1 - y_e) = \pi_0 \quad \text{and} \quad \pi_2 - \alpha(y_2 - y_e) = \pi_1$$

We then write down a Lagrangian:

$$\begin{aligned}\mathcal{L} =& (y_1 - y_e)^2 + \beta(\pi_1 - \pi^T)^2 + \frac{1}{1+\delta}((y_2 - y_e)^2 + \beta(\pi_2 - \pi^T)^2) \\ & - \mu[\pi_1 - \alpha(y_1 - y_e) - \pi_0] - \lambda[\pi_2 - \alpha(y_2 - y_e) - \pi_1].\end{aligned}$$

And find the first order conditions by differentiating with respect to each endogenous variable and the multipliers, and setting each derivative equal to zero:

$$\text{FOC} : \left\{ \frac{\partial \mathcal{L}}{\partial y_1} = 0, \quad \frac{\partial \mathcal{L}}{\partial y_2} = 0, \quad \frac{\partial \mathcal{L}}{\partial \pi_1} = 0, \quad \frac{\partial \mathcal{L}}{\partial \pi_2} = 0, \quad \frac{\partial \mathcal{L}}{\partial \mu} = 0, \quad \frac{\partial \mathcal{L}}{\partial \lambda} = 0 \right\} \tag{3.4}$$

In particular, the first order conditions are:

1. $2(y_1 - y_e) + \alpha\mu = 0$
2. $\dfrac{2(y_2 - y_e)}{1+\delta} + \alpha\lambda = 0$
3. $\lambda - \mu + 2\beta(\pi_1 - \pi^T) = 0$
4. $\dfrac{2\beta(\pi_2 - \pi^T)}{1+\delta} - \lambda = 0$
5. $\alpha(y_1 - y_e) + \pi_0 - \pi_1 = 0$
6. $\alpha(y_2 - y_e) + \pi_1 - \pi_2 = 0$

We now have a system of 6 equations in 6 unknowns $(y_1, y_2, \pi_1, \pi_2, \mu, \lambda)$. Solving the system allows us to find the sequence of optimal output gaps for the forward-looking central bank.

We focus on the output gap in the period following the inflation shock. Solving the system for y_1 gives:

$$(y_1 - y_e) = -\frac{\alpha\beta\left[2+\delta+\alpha^2\beta(1+\delta)\right](\pi_0-\pi^T)}{1+\delta+\alpha^2\beta\left[3+2\delta+\alpha^2\beta(1+\delta)\right]}. \tag{3.5}$$

To simplify the expression, we assume $\alpha = \beta = 1$. Equation 3.5 then becomes:

$$(y_1 - y_e) = -\frac{(3+2\delta)(\pi_0-\pi^T)}{5+4\delta}. \tag{3.6}$$

It is now easy to see that the smaller is δ (i.e. the more weight is given to the second period), the larger is the output gap in period 1. Conversely, if we take the limit of equation 3.6 as δ tends to infinity, so that only the current period matters, we get:

$$\lim_{\delta\to+\infty} -\frac{(3+2\delta)(\pi_0-\pi^T)}{5+4\delta} = -\frac{1}{2}(\pi_0-\pi^T). \tag{3.7}$$

Which is exactly equal to the optimal gap in period 1 for the baseline central bank when $\alpha = \beta = 1$. To see this, we simply take the standard monetary rule equation and substitute in the Phillips curve equation:

$$\begin{aligned}(y_1 - y_e) &= -(\pi_1 - \pi^T)\\ &= -(\pi_0 + (y_1 - y_e) - \pi^T)\\ &= -\frac{1}{2}(\pi_0 - \pi^T).\end{aligned} \tag{3.8}$$

This shows that as δ tends to infinity (i.e. the less weight is given to the second period), the gap in period one converges to that of the baseline model.

This result can be generalized using a loss function that places weight on all future periods as follows:

$$L = \sum_{i=0}^{\infty} \frac{1}{(1+\delta)^i} L_{t+i}, \qquad \text{(intertemporal central bank loss function)}$$

The implications of this extension are clear: the greater the weight placed on its future losses (lower δ), the more will the central bank tighten monetary policy in response to a shock that increases inflation. By deviating from its choice of point C in the standard case toward C′, it will choose a higher r_0, i.e. a tighter monetary policy response. When comparing central banks across countries and over time, in the standard case, the central bank's best-response output gap is higher, and therefore monetary policy tighter, the more inflation-averse it is (higher β). A greater weight on future losses (lower δ) is an additional factor that can differ across central banks and vary over time and help explain monetary policy choices.

In the next chapter we introduce the phenomenon of hysteresis in which low output (and associated high unemployment) can have scarring effects on the supply side of the economy that reduce equilibrium output. The risk of hysteresis effects would reduce future gains from lower inflation arising from implementing a deeper initial recession.

QUESTIONS AND PROBLEMS FOR CHAPTER 3

CHECKLIST QUESTIONS

1. Why is monetary policy chosen over fiscal policy as the preferred tool for stabilization policy? What does the government gain from controlling monetary policy? Why would they choose to delegate responsibility for monetary policy to an independent central bank?

2. 'If the economy has high but stable inflation, the government has much to lose and little to gain by reducing inflation to a low rate.' Explain and assess this statement.

3. What are the advantages and disadvantages of a target inflation rate of 4% as compared with one of 0% per annum? Use the 3-equation model to explain the adjustment process for the case where the central bank adopts a higher inflation target.

4. Explain what is meant by the central bank's loss function. How are the central bank's preferences reflected in the loss function? Draw the loss 'circles' for the cases where:

   a. $\beta = 1$;

   b. $\beta < 1$;

   c. $\beta > 1$.

   In which of the three cases will the central bank reduce inflation back to target quickest after an inflation shock? Is there any downside to adopting this policy stance?

5. Assume that $\alpha = \beta = 1$, derive the MR curve graphically using the tangencies between the loss circles and the Phillips curves. With reference to the diagrams, explain the effect of the following (in each case, assume all other parameters are held constant):

   a. An increase in the slope of the Phillips curve, α

   b. An increase in central bank's inflation aversion, β.

6. Following an inflation shock, explain why unemployment goes up before the economy returns to medium-run equilibrium.

7. Draw the 3-equation model and give a detailed period-by-period description of the adjustment process for the case where the economy is hit by a permanent negative aggregate demand shock.

8. With reference to the scenario in Question 7, explain the behaviour of the central bank and the economy in a situation where there is no lag in the IS curve.

9. Draw the impulse response functions for output, inflation and the real interest rate after a permanent positive aggregate demand shock and a permanent positive supply shock. [Hint: the 3-equation model diagrams for these two cases are shown in Figures 3.11 and 3.14 respectively.]

10. Use the 3-equation model diagrams to show how the economy can fall into a deflation trap. Explain, with reference to the diagram, how the central bank/government can intervene to escape the trap. Show the relevant IS curve and re-label the MR as the PR to indicate that fiscal policy is being used. Are there any reasons why these policies might not work? Now, assume that nominal wage inflation cannot fall below 3%. What does this imply for the deflation trap? What could explain this behaviour of wages? Show the implications for the WS/PS diagram.

PROBLEMS

1. Pick one developed economy and one emerging or developing economy. Use the latest version of the IMF World Economic Outlook Database to download inflation data for each of the countries from 1980 to the latest available data. Plot the data in a graph. Answer the following:
   a. Describe the evolution of inflation in each country.
   b. Do the countries have independent central banks?
   c. If the country does have an independent central bank, did inflation fall when the central bank gained independence? Propose some reasons why.
   d. If the country does not have an independent central bank, have they managed to find other mechanisms to establish a low inflation monetary policy regime? Propose some reasons why.

2. Select two out of the following central banks: Bank of England, Reserve Bank of New Zealand, Bank of Canada, and the Swedish Riksbank. Each of these central banks has adopted explicit 'inflation targeting'. For each of your chosen banks, answer the following questions:
   a. What is their target level of inflation and how do they justify choosing that level?
   b. What actions did it take following the collapse of Lehman Brothers in September 2008 and how did it explain these actions?
   c. Did they hit the zero lower bound on nominal interest rates during the global financial crisis? If so, how could they adjust their inflation target to reduce the likelihood of this happening again in the future? Check for evidence of a public debate about this issue.

3. This question uses the Macroeconomic Simulator (available at www.oup.com/he/carlin-soskice) to model a negative temporary aggregate demand shock. Start by opening the simulator and choosing the closed economy version. Then reset all shocks by clicking the appropriate button on the left-hand side of the main page. Use the simulator and the content of this chapter to work through the following:

   a. Apply a temporary 5% negative demand shock. Save your data.
   b. Use the impulse response functions from the simulator to help explain the path of the economy following the shock.
   c. Draw the IS – PC – MR diagrams for this scenario.
   d. Adjust the central bank preferences (i.e. β) to 0.5 and save your data. Now, adjust the central bank preferences to 1.5 and save your data again.
   e. How has varying β affected the impulse response functions? Relate this to the effect that changing β has on the MR curve.

4. This question uses the Macroeconomic Simulator (available at www.oup.com/he/carlin-soskice) to show how the economy can get stuck in a deflation trap and what it can do to escape it. Start by opening the simulator and choosing the closed economy version. Then reset all shocks by clicking the appropriate button on the left-hand side of the main page. Use the simulator and the content of this chapter to work through the following:

   a. Apply a temporary 8% negative demand shock. Save your data.
   b. Use the impulse response functions to help explain the path of the economy following the shock.
   c. Apply a temporary increase in public expenditure of 7% alongside the original demand shock. Save your data.
   d. Comment on the changes to the impulse response functions. [Hint: it might be necessary to view the second case in isolation to accurately view the movements in the impulse response functions.]
   e. Has fiscal policy been effective at stabilizing the economy? If so, explain why using the 3-equation model framework.

INTERESTED IN EXPLORING THESE TOPICS FURTHER?

Visit www.oup.com/he/carlin-soskice to consolidate and extend your learning with the multiple-choice questions and Animated Analytical Diagrams accompanying this chapter.

Additionally, visit https://tinyco.re/inflationtool to find CORE Econ's Interactive Learning Tool which features further content related to this chapter.

CHAPTER

4

EXPECTATIONS AND MONETARY POLICY

4.1 INTRODUCTION

In this chapter, we focus on how households, firms and policy makers form expectations about the future, how this is modelled by economists and the implications for macroeconomic policy. In Chapters 1–3, we touched on the importance of uncertainty and expectations in the macroeconomy. We introduced forward-looking theories of consumption and investment in Chapter 1, where expectations about the future influence decision making in the current period. In Chapter 2, we discussed the role of inflation expectations in wage setting.

In Chapter 3, we introduced the dynamic macroeconomic model, which showed how a forward-looking central bank seeks to keep the economy close to its inflation target. The 3-equation model of the macroeconomy emphasizes the importance of forecasting: in order to stabilize the economy the central bank must diagnose the nature of shocks and forecast their effects on the output gap and inflation. In the light of these forecasts, the central bank judges how best to set the interest rate. It continuously updates its forecasts and adjusts its policy as new information is received.

We begin this chapter by highlighting the role of expectations in the core elements of the macro model we have developed by considering in turn the three components: the IS curve, the Phillips curve, and the monetary rule.

4.1.1 The *IS* curve

In the models of consumption and investment in Chapter 1, expectations about the future influence the spending decisions of households and firms. Tobin's Q theory is a clear example of a model of investment in which there is an institutional mechanism—the stock market—that aggregates information about the views of those outside the firm about the firm's expected future profits. When Tobin's Q is greater than one, the model predicts positive investment because the expected value of the firm based on expected future profits from expanding the capital stock is greater than its replacement cost.

For the household, the permanent income hypothesis encapsulates the idea that consumption decisions today reflect all the available information about expected future income: the household prefers a smooth path of consumption so it is in its interest to aggregate the available information and—if it can—consume close to its permanent income.

The economist Nick Bloom suggests that periods of high stock market volatility occur when economic agents are very unclear about the future. There is evidence that the effects of this type of uncertainty on fixed investment decisions can be so severe that they can actually cause the economy to go into recession (as occurred for example, after the 9/11 terrorist attacks). Another example was the extreme *policy uncertainty* in late 2012, when the US was described as coming to the edge of a fiscal cliff. It was unclear whether the Republican-dominated Congress and the re-elected Democrat president would be able to agree on fiscal measures that would prevent tax rises and spending cuts from automatically coming into force. As a result, private agents faced serious policy uncertainty.

In July 2020, Bloom and co-authors published near real-time indicators of uncertainty in the context of the pandemic. The indices included stock market volatility, newspaper- or Twitter-based measures counting the frequency of the use of terms 'economic', 'uncertainty', and 'policy'; an indicator of the uncertainty business executives put on sales growth; and measures based on the extent of disagreement among professional forecasters about GDP growth.[1] Covid-19 triggered historically high levels of uncertainty according to several of these indices, as can be seen by the global Economic Policy Uncertainty (EPU) index almost doubling between February and April 2020 as the pandemic spread and countries implemented lockdown measures.

Bloom (2009) finds that when agents are uncertain about the future they wait and do nothing. For example, firms uncertain about future demand do not invest or hire. Similarly, consumers do not make large purchases of consumer durables if they are in doubt about their next paycheck. In times of acute uncertainty the economy therefore comes to a standstill as agents 'wait and see'. The complicated nature of forming expectations in the face of uncertainty is well articulated by John Maynard Keynes, one of the most influential economists of the twentieth century:[2]

> We are merely reminding ourselves that human decisions affecting the future, whether personal or political or economic, cannot depend on strict mathematical expectation, since the basis for making such calculations does not exist; and that it is our innate urge to activity which makes the wheels go round, our rational selves choosing between the alternatives as best we are able, calculating where we can, but often falling back for our motive on whim or sentiment or chance.

Keynes highlighted the implications for economic decisions of the distinction between risk and uncertainty (see Box 4.1).

---

[1] The live *Economic Policy Uncertainty Index* can be seen on http://www.policyuncertainty.com/ accessed August 2020.

[2] See Chapter 12: *The State of Long-Term Expectation* in Keynes (1936).

BOX 4.1 Expectations, risk, and uncertainty

While we can never know exactly what will happen in the future, in some cases we can make a much more informed prediction than in others. This matters when thinking about how households, firms and policy makers form expectations. An important distinction is between *risk* and *uncertainty*.

Risk exists when individuals make decisions about the future based on *known* probabilities. In such conditions agents can work out an expected outcome. For example, a group of ten people all put £10 into a pot and a winner is randomly selected to receive the total contents of £100. Before the random selection is made, the expected payoff to each participant is 0.1 (their probability of winning) multiplied by £100 (the prize for winning), which is equal to £10. In this example there is risk, given that each individual will receive either £0 or £100 after the random selection is made. But they know beforehand the probability with which each possible outcome (winning or not winning) will occur.

Uncertainty differs from risk in two important ways: first, uncertainty exists where it is impossible to assign probabilities to known outcomes and, second, where there are some outcomes which may be unknown.

Keynes believed some things were inherently uncertain and that we could not attach any meaningful probabilities to them.[a] He summed up uncertainty in this widely cited excerpt from a journal article that he wrote in 1937:[b]

> The prospect of a European war is uncertain, or the price of copper and the rate of interest twenty years hence, or the obsolescence of a new invention, or the position of private wealth owners in the social system of 1970. About these matters there is no scientific basis on which to form any calculable probabilities whatever. We simply do not know.

Whether we are considering risk or uncertainty matters greatly for the way we analyse how expectations are formed. Households facing risk can accurately attach probabilities to different future states of the world, which makes it much easier for them to evaluate in the present, decisions which affect the future. But in the case of uncertainty, this is not possible, because unforeseen events, such as the Arab Spring of 2010–11 or the war in Ukraine in 2022, or a major natural disaster or a global pandemic, may occur.[c]

---

[a] This view was first emphasized by Frank Knight (1921) and John M. Keynes (1921).
[b] Excerpt from page 214 of Keynes (1937).
[c] See Wakker's article on Uncertainty in *The New Palgrave Dictionary of Economics* (2008) for a summary of the evolution of economic thinking on risk and uncertainty. It contains a discussion of a number of decision models that can be used under unknown probabilities.

4.1.2 **The Phillips curve**

As in the case of those who make spending decisions, it is highly likely that wage setters think about the future when forming their expectations of how prices will evolve. After all when firms set the wage, they know that workers evaluate the offer in terms of the *real consumption* wage, which means that the future movement of the prices of goods in the consumption basket is of concern. To this point, however, we have assumed that the best that workers can expect is to get nominal wage increases that compensate them for any erosion of the real wage that occurred due to unanticipated inflation over the previous period. Wage setters use a rule of thumb that says the best forecast for the change in the consumer price index in the year ahead is last year's inflation.[3]

We can model the behaviour of wage setters as that of rational forward-looking agents who are prevented from implementing their forecast of inflation in their wage bargain because of institutional arrangements such as wage indexation or because the costs of coming to an agreement over how inflation will evolve over the coming year are too high. Alternatively, we can model the behaviour as building compensation for last period's inflation into the wage bargain. There are several reasons why compensation is frequently used in wage setting: it captures the idea of being rewarded for the work done—the employee does not feel cheated. Second actual price increases (as opposed to expectations of future ones) are generally easily verified from official data. And third, since compensation is a widespread practice, employees are unlikely to feel they are losing out in comparison with their peers in other companies or workplaces.

One indicator of the range of forecasts for future inflation can be found in central bank publications. Figure 4.1 is a fan chart for the annual change in the Consumer

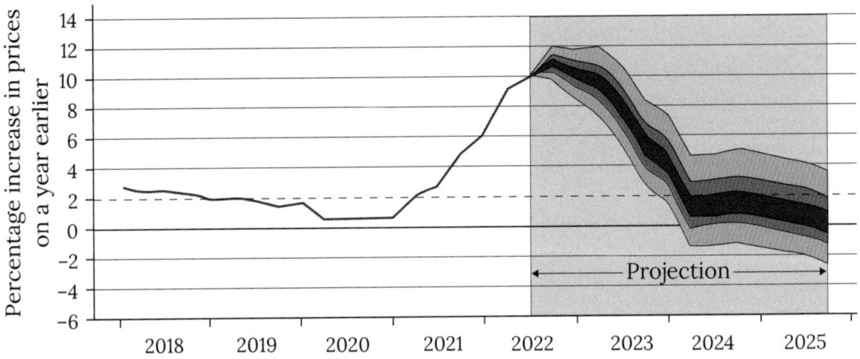

Figure 4.1 Bank of England's CPI inflation projection.

Note: If economic circumstances identical to today's were to prevail on 100 occasions, the inflation rate is expected to lie within the darkest central band on only 30 of those occasions. Outturns are expected to lie within each pair of the lighter areas on 30 occasions and to lie somewhere within the fan on 90 occasions.

Source: Chart 1.4 (page 22), *Bank of England Monetary Policy Report*, November 2022.

[3] Du Caju et al. (2008) provide detailed evidence on how expected and unexpected price increases are incorporated through formal indexation and informal practices in the wage bargains of 23 European countries, the US, and Japan.

Price Index (CPI), the Bank's chosen measure of inflation. The fan chart shows the Bank's judgement of the probability of various outcomes for inflation in the future. The Monetary Policy Committee (MPC) is mandated to target an inflation rate of 2%, two years ahead. The shaded bands refer to the likelihood of observing inflation of that level if the economic conditions at the time of publication were to prevail on 100 different occasions. It shows that even for one year ahead, the Bank's Monetary Policy Committee sees a wide range of possible inflation outcomes.

Inflation forecasts by central banks and private sector forecasters have become a common feature of economies and can provide insight into how individuals form expectations. The macroeconomic implications of inflation forecasts are limited, however, unless we know whether agents incorporate inflation forecasts into their expectations formation and the extent to which they act on their expectations.

Armentier et al. (2012) attempt to answer this question in a particular context by carrying out a financially incentivized investment experiment to see if agents' forecasts of inflation feed into their behaviour. The experimental subjects stand to win money if they use forecast inflation when choosing between two kinds of financial investment. The authors find that most individuals tend to act on their expectations, but that the less financially and numerically literate respondents had most trouble doing so.

4.1.3 The *MR* curve

The policy maker in the 3-equation model (the inflation-targeting central bank from Chapter 3) is a forward-looking actor. As we have seen, the central bank makes a forecast about inflation in the next period and, based on this, decides the interest rate to set. This is an example of rational expectations behaviour: we have assumed that the central bank knows the model of the macroeconomy and that having diagnosed the nature of any shock, it chooses its best response interest rate.

However, as we have seen, forecasting inflation is by no means easy for the central bank, due to the inherent uncertainty surrounding macroeconomic developments (and their effects on inflation). This point was echoed by Charles Bean of the UK Monetary Policy Committee (MPC) in a speech in 2005:[4]

> Uncertainty is an ever-present feature of the economic landscape that monetary policy makers cannot escape. Broadly speaking, there are three types of uncertainty that confront us on the MPC: uncertainty about the data; uncertainty about the nature and persistence of shocks; and uncertainty about the structure of the economy [in other words, uncertainty about what is the correct model and what size are the key parameters].

In the next section, the focus is on how the use of different specifications for the Phillips curve has evolved with the changing behaviour of inflation and policy makers over the course of the past seventy years. A major theoretical development in macroeconomics dating from the 1970s was the introduction of insights from

[4] Excerpt taken from Bean (2005).

game theory. This produced the so-called rational expectations revolution with strong predictions for the Phillips curve and policy effectiveness.

The unique inflation-stabilizing level of output (and associated rate of unemployment) pinned down by the supply side WS and PS relationships is an important feature of the 3-equation model. Later in the chapter, we look at the implications of moving away from the assumption that the loss function of the central bank includes the deviation of output from its *equilibrium* level. It is replaced by the deviation of output from an *output target*. We shall see in Section 4.3 that if the model is otherwise unchanged, having the central bank target an output level above equilibrium leads to 'inflation bias'. The economy comes to rest at an equilibrium with output at the equilibrium level (not the higher target level) and with inflation above target.

But this result does not always hold if the model is modified in two ways, which we introduce in Section 4.4, for which there is supportive empirical evidence. The first modification is to use a model of anchored inflation expectations in the Phillips curve. In that case, inflation expectations are a weighted average of past inflation and the central bank's inflation target. The second modification is to allow equilibrium output to be affected by past output levels. The possibility that equilibrium output is affected by the path of actual output instead of being purely determined by the supply side is known as path-dependence or *hysteresis*. The presence of hysteresis means that a deep recession can cause a fall in equilibrium output. One of the most common hysteresis mechanisms is the effect that a prolonged spell of unemployment has in eroding a worker's skills. In the model, this implies an upward shift in the WS curve and lower equilibrium output. By targeting the original (higher) equilibrium output level rather than the contemporaneous one as in the standard model, the central bank can restore this higher output level while also hitting the inflation target. This would prevent the scarring caused by a period of persistent high unemployment.

The results about inflation bias are important in understanding why central bank independence and inflation targeting were adopted in the 1990s following the so-called 'great inflation' of the 1970s and the heavy costs incurred in bringing inflation down in the 1980s. The results about anchored inflation expectations and hysteresis shed light on the functioning of economies with inflation-targeting central banks in the long recession following the global financial crisis, as well as on monetary policy responses to the Covid-19 pandemic. A model with anchored expectations and hysteresis highlights the opportunities for policy makers to mitigate the scarring effects that can arise from a deep recession; however the inflation bias results point to the dangers if inflation expectations were to become unanchored. An output target cannot be freely chosen by the policy maker without running the risk of losing the anchoring of inflation expectations to the central bank's target.

4.2 PHILLIPS CURVES, EXPECTATIONS, AND INFLATION

This section investigates in more detail how economists model the way agents in the macroeconomy form inflation expectations. In the 3-equation model of Chapter 3, we used a specific assumption about inflation expectations, from which we derived the

Phillips curve, and in turn, the MR equation. As we shall see, the Phillips curve will take different forms depending on the way inflation expectations are modelled.

Notation and timing

We start by setting out the notation that will be used throughout the remainder of this chapter. We are primarily concerned with how agents at the beginning of period t form expectations of the current period's inflation. The current period is denoted by a t subscript. These expectations will be formed on the basis of the information available at the beginning of period t—we say expected inflation in period t, conditional on the information set (denoted by Ω) dated $t-1$, is therefore:

$$E_t(\pi_t \mid \Omega_{t-1}) \equiv \pi_t^E.$$

We use π_t^E to denote expected inflation in period t throughout the rest of the chapter as it makes the notation simpler. The information set in period t includes the outturn of all the macroeconomic variables up to and including period $t-1$. This means that, in period t, agents know the actual rate of inflation for every period up to and including period $t-1$ (i.e. the last period).

As we shall see, when agents in an economic model have so-called rational expectations, they make use of their knowledge of the model and of all available information to work out the implications for inflation of the shocks that have occurred up to and including period $t-1$. As a result, apart from a shock that occurs in period t itself, they are able to correctly predict that period's inflation.

Phillips curves

The term Phillips curve is used for the relationship between inflation and output arising from the supply side of the economy. There is no single form for the Phillips curve, but rather, it depends on the way we model inflation expectations. To allow us to discuss different hypotheses about expectations, we write the Phillips curve like this:

$$\pi_t = \pi_t^E + \alpha(y_t - y_e). \qquad \text{(standard Phillips curve)}$$

We shall call this a standard Phillips curve.

In this chapter, we investigate four ways in which inflation expectations are modelled.

1. ***Static* expectations**—agents expect inflation to remain unchanged. Inflation then varies only with the output gap.
2. ***Adaptive* expectations**—agents expect inflation to be what it was in the previous period. This is a simple form of what is called error correction behaviour. Agents set aside their forecast of inflation last period and take last period's outturn as their best guess of inflation this period. In the 3-equation model, we assume wage setters use this rule. As noted earlier, this can equally be thought of as compensation for past inflation.
3. ***Rational* expectations**—This implies expectations are forward looking, all available information is used and systematic errors are avoided. In the 3-equation model

used most of the time in this book, the central bank is assumed to have rational expectations. It knows the model and uses that knowledge to design its monetary policy responses. We shall investigate in this chapter how the conduct of monetary policy in the 3-equation model is affected if private sector actors as well as the central bank have rational expectations. Their behaviour is modelled by a rational expectations Phillips curve.[5]

4. ***Anchored* expectations**—agents expect inflation to be a weighted average of the central bank's inflation target and lagged inflation. The more credible the reputation of the central bank, the higher the weight on the inflation target.

In this section, the first three expectations hypotheses are introduced using the historical context of the inflation experience of high-income countries and in particular, the UK since the end of the Second World War. We return to anchored expectations later in the chapter.

4.2.1 Inflation in the post-war period

We can see from Figure 4.2, that inflation in the UK fluctuated around zero between 1801 and the end of World War II (WWII). In the 1950s and 1960s, however, inflation was positive in almost every year but there was no trend. This was followed by a period of high inflation from the end of the 1960s through to the early 1980s. Disinflation

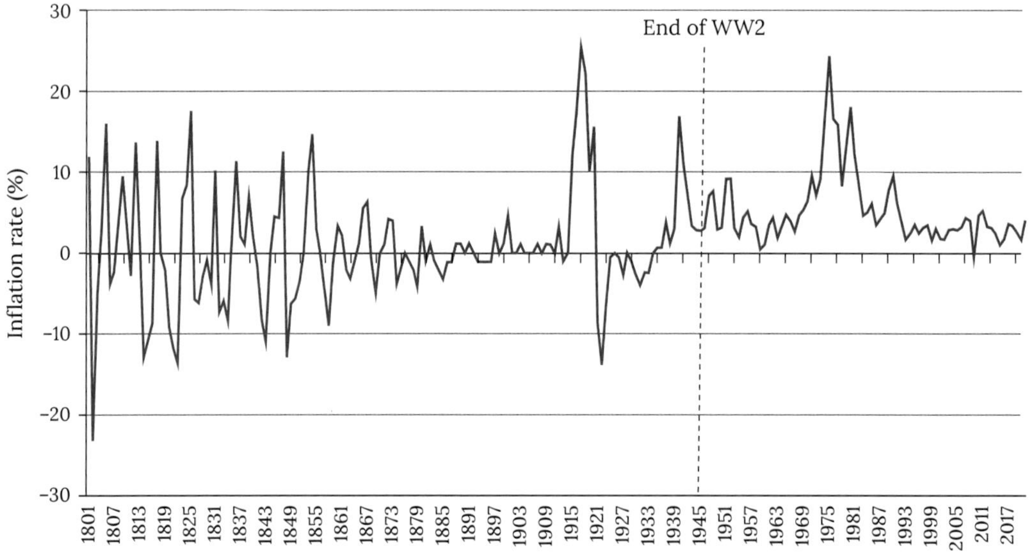

Figure 4.2 UK inflation: 1801–2021.

Note: Variable shown is the annual percentage change of the long-term indicator of prices of consumer goods and services.

Source: UK Office for National Statistics (July 2022 release).

[5] We do not discuss the so-called New Keynesian Phillips curve in this chapter. See Chapter 18.

followed. Apart from volatility around the financial crisis (and later, the Covid-19 crisis), inflation fluctuated in a narrow range around the Bank of England's inflation target after the inflation-targeting policy was adopted in 1992.

One interpretation of the period of stable but positive inflation in the 1950s and 1960s is that governments were pursuing activist demand management policies and were happy to achieve low rates of unemployment even if there was some positive inflation. This can be understood against the background of the Great Depression in the 1930s and the awareness of policy makers of the dangers of deflation. At the time, policy makers feared unemployment and deflation more than inflation. Their policies reflected this, yielding consistently positive, although fairly stable, inflation.

The hypothesis of *static* expectations is applied to this period. Simply put, inflation is expected to remain unchanged. The outturn for inflation then depends only on the state of the business cycle. This can be expressed in the following equation:

$$\begin{aligned}\pi_t &= \pi_t^E + \alpha(y_t - y_e)\\ &= \bar{\pi} + \alpha(y_t - y_e), \qquad \text{(static expectations Phillips curve)}\end{aligned}$$

where $\bar{\pi}$ is a constant, resulting in a unique Phillips curve that always goes through the point $(y_e, \bar{\pi})$. This tells us that the Phillips curve under *static* expectations would only shift if equilibrium output were to change (a supply-side shock). Otherwise, as demand-side factors cause fluctuations in current output, we would move *along* the single Phillips curve. An economic upswing would result in inflation above $\bar{\pi}$, while a recession would result in inflation falling below.

Toward the end of the 1960s, inflation began to rise year after year. One part of the explanation is that important developments on the supply side of the economy in the late 1960s and the 1970s led to a rise in equilibrium unemployment, which meant that conventional measures of 'high employment' implied more inflationary pressure. In this period, there was a shift in bargaining power toward workers reflected in a wave of strikes across Europe referred to as the 'hot autumn' of 1968 (an upward shift in the WS curve) and a fall in the rate of productivity growth (which implies a downward shift in the PS curve, assuming wage-setting behaviour does not adjust quickly to the slower productivity growth).[6] As well as this, there was a series of commodity price shocks (which imply downward shifts in the PS curve) preceding the first oil shock of 1973. The oil shocks are discussed in detail in Chapter 13. Upward pressure on inflation arises when policy makers fail to respond to negative supply shocks like the ones described by tightening policy; it also arises from expansionary demand policies. Both are documented for the period preceding the 'great inflation'.[7]

---

[6] Productivity growth slowed for two reasons. First because the gains from the widespread adoption of so-called Fordist mass production methods in the catching-up countries of Western Europe and Japan were becoming exhausted. And second, the limits to further productivity gains based on Fordism were being reached even in the technology leader, the US.

[7] For instance, see Bernanke (2003).

Let us compare the new inflationary behaviour with the predictions of the models of static and adaptive inflation expectations. We begin by using the equation of the static expectations Phillips curve.

Static expectations Phillips curve and a negative supply shock

The economy is initially at point A in the left panel of Figure 4.3, with inflation at 2%. Suppose the economy experiences a negative supply shock as described above. The supply-side shock reduces equilibrium output to y_e'. At the existing output level equal to previous equilibrium output of y_e, the economy is now 'overheating'. The PC will therefore shift up to a new position and stay there. With the output level unchanged, inflation will rise from A to B: inflation is higher but stable. The hypothesis of static expectations can explain higher inflation but not the rising inflation that was experienced in the 1970s.

Adaptive expectations Phillips curve and a negative supply shock

In this example, we take an economy where wage setters use adaptive expectations, which is initially at point A in Figure 4.3 with inflation stable at 2% and output at equilibrium, y_e. The supply-side shock reduces equilibrium output to y_e'. If the government continues to pursue an unchanged level of output, inflation will rise continuously.

Inflation expectations are updated to correct for the erosion of the expected real wage.[8] Under this hypothesis, wage setters observe that the real wage needed to elicit effort at the prevailing output and unemployment level has been eroded by the higher than expected inflation. They update their expectations based on the outturn of inflation. The PC therefore shifts upwards and is labelled in (Figure 4.3) with the new higher expected rate of inflation.

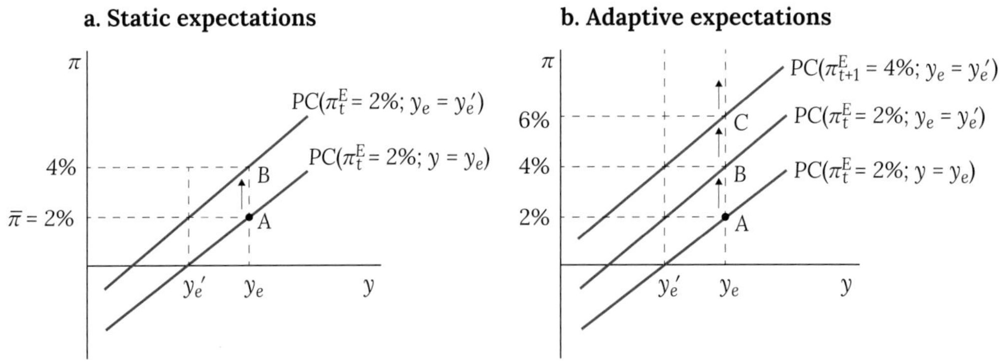

Figure 4.3 Static and adaptive expectations: the government attempts to maintain low unemployment after a negative supply-side shock.

[8] The pioneering work on adaptive expectations was carried out by Nobel Prize winners Edmund Phelps and Milton Friedman in the late 1960s and early 1970s. See, for example, Phelps (1967) and Friedman (1968).

As long as the government keeps $y > y_e'$, inflation expectations will adjust upwards as wage setters see the expected real wage eroded. With $y = y_e$, the shifted PC results in inflation of 4%. The only outcome of the government continuing to pursue an output target above equilibrium will be ever-increasing inflation, as shown by the movement from B to C (and onwards) in Figure 4.3. A government policy of this kind is referred to as an accommodating policy; effectively, there is a vertical MR curve through points A, B and C. It contrasts sharply with the behaviour of an inflation-targeting central bank as set out in the 3-equation model in Chapter 3.

4.2.2 Expectations and the output—inflation trade-off

In the adaptive expectations framework, workers respond to their forecasting errors—i.e. they update their expectations based on the outturn for inflation last period. We modify the standard Phillips curve to get the adaptive expectations Phillips curve as follows:

$$\begin{aligned} \pi_t &= \pi_t^E + \alpha(y_t - y_e) \\ &= \pi_{t-1} + \alpha(y_t - y_e), \end{aligned} \qquad \text{(adaptive expectations Phillips curve)}$$

where $\pi_t^E = \pi_{t-1}$.

The equation can be rearranged to show how inflation changes over time:

$$\pi_t - \pi_{t-1} = \Delta\pi_t = \alpha(y_t - y_e). \qquad (4.1)$$

Equation 4.1 shows that inflation will continue to increase as long as output remains above equilibrium, which matches the outcome shown in Figure 4.3. The prediction that if output is above equilibrium, inflation will be rising, can be contrasted with the prediction from the static expectations hypothesis:

$$\pi_t - \bar{\pi} = \alpha(y_t - y_e). \qquad (4.2)$$

Equation 4.2 with static expectations shows that inflation will be *higher* when there is a positive output gap but it will not be rising.

Unlike the static expectations model, the adaptive expectations one predicts there is no long-run trade-off between inflation and unemployment. The presence of a trade-off would mean that policy makers could choose to operate the economy at a level of output above equilibrium if they were willing to accept a higher level of inflation. In other words, they could choose their preferred point on the static expectations Phillips curve. In the model with adaptive expectations, this is not possible because there is always pressure on inflation to rise (and the PC to shift upwards) if output is above equilibrium.

Using these two models of how expectations are formed, we could say that the low and stable inflation of the 1950s and 1960s shown in Figure 4.2 only held as long as inflation expectations were static. Once the supply shocks pushed up inflation, wage setters are likely to have switched to adaptive expectations as workers realized that their real wages were being eroded by higher inflation. As we have stressed, the switch to incorporating past inflation in the current wage agreement as occurred at this time could be interpreted either as 'compensation for past inflation', or as wage setters incorporating expectations over future inflation and using last period's inflation as their expectation. The Phillips curve equation is the same regardless of the interpretation.

Meanwhile, governments continued to run the economy with levels of aggregate demand that produced a positive output gap. Nobel Prize winner Milton Friedman described the prevailing postwar policy stance in his famous 1968 Presidential Address:[9]

> Today, primacy is assigned to the promotion of full employment, with the prevention of inflation a continuing but definitely secondary objective.

He sums up the inflationary consequences of pursuing this policy and acknowledges that there is no long-run trade-off between unemployment and inflation:[10]

> In order to keep unemployment at its target level of three per cent [which in this hypothetical example is below the 'natural' rate], the monetary authority would have to raise monetary growth still more . . . the 'market' rate [of unemployment] can be kept below the 'natural' rate only by inflation . . .
>
> To state this conclusion differently, there is always a temporary trade-off between inflation and unemployment; there is no permanent trade-off.

Figure 4.4a uses US data to illustrate the reasonably stable relationship between inflation and output in the 1950s and 1960s. The relationship completely fell apart during the following 15 years (see Figure 4.4b).

In many developed economies, the 1970s were characterized by 'stagflation'—a combination of high unemployment and high inflation—which destroyed any notion of a long-run trade-off between inflation and output. The experiences of this decade marked the end of a period where macroeconomic policy had been guided by the principles of Keynesian demand management, which accorded priority to avoiding deflation. Friedman pointed to the displacement of static by adaptive expectations and the disappearance of a long-run trade-off between inflation and unemployment. At the frontiers of macroeconomic research a further step was taken: it ushered in the era where models were built based on agents using rational expectations to form their forecasts and guide their actions.

The adaptive expectations hypothesis states that wage setters respond to their forecasting errors but they do this in a purely mechanical way. This involves them making *systematic errors* because as long as $y > y_e$, for example, the real wage outcome is below what had been expected since the inflation outturn is higher than expected (see Figure 4.3). This suggests we investigate the implications of wage setters not just updating their *expectations* but changing their *forecasting rule*. This is the basis of

[9] These excerpts are from Friedman (1968).

[10] Friedman uses slightly different terminology than we have so far in this chapter. The 'natural rate' of unemployment is equivalent to the equilibrium rate of unemployment. The 'market' rate is equivalent to the actual unemployment rate.

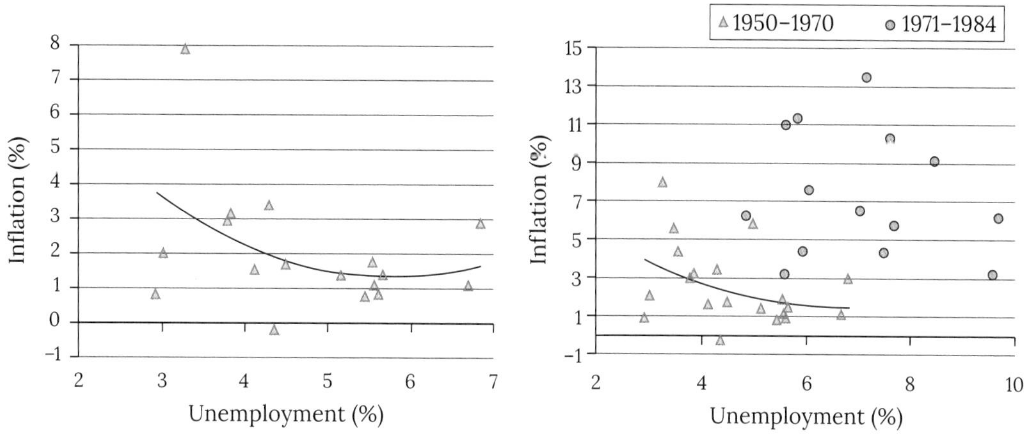

Figure 4.4 US empirical Phillips curves: (left) 1950–70, (right) 1950–70 and 1971–84.
Note: The black curves on the graphs are quadratic regression lines.
Source: US Bureau of Labor Statistics (accessed July 2020).

the next expectations hypothesis, rational expectations, which can be summarized like this:

> The *rational expectations hypothesis* or REH refers to a choice by the economist about how to model the behaviour of economic agents. It implies that *agents in the model* use the model and all available information to forecast and therefore do not make systematic errors. The term model-consistent expectations can be used instead of rational expectations.

In the 3-equation model so far, we have only one actor with rational expectations—the central bank. We now look at how the model changes when the private agents also have rational expectations.

4.2.3 Rational and adaptive expectations in the 3-equation model

The defining assumption of the rational expectations hypothesis is that the actors have full knowledge of the model. The MR curve has already been defined in such a way: the central bank minimizes its loss function subject to the constraint of the Phillips curve, which summarizes the behaviour of the private sector wage and price setters, and it implements its 'best-response' output gap on the MR curve by choosing the interest rate on the IS curve. We now investigate what happens if wage and price setters have rational expectations but wages and prices do not adjust immediately after the unexpected shock. As we shall see at the end of the section, the *combination* of REH and fully flexible wages and prices produces different results.

Returning to the equation

$$E_t(\pi_t \mid \Omega_{t-1}) \equiv \pi_t^E,$$

the information set Ω that agents are assumed to have at the beginning of period t includes full knowledge of the model. In the rational expectations framework, therefore, it is only unanticipated shocks that result in inflation being different from its expected value. We now set out how actors with rational expectations respond to an inflation shock, which we will assume is an unanticipated change in product market conditions. The economy is initially in equilibrium at $t = 0$. Then product market conditions change for all firms simultaneously, allowing them to increase their markup from μ_0 to μ_1, where $\mu_1 > \mu_0$. As before, the actors are the price setters, the wage setters and the Central Bank. The actors discover simultaneously that this change has taken place: it is 'common knowledge'.

We assume wage setting in the current period ($t = 1$) has occurred before the change in product market conditions was evident. Having set wages, they are constrained not to change wage inflation again this period, and this is also common knowledge, so that

$$(\Delta W/W)_1 = (\Delta W/W)_0 = \pi^T.$$

Since the wage setters cannot respond to the news about the markup, we can now leave them out of the calculation, and the two key actors are the price setters and the central bank.

The central bank's MR curve is common knowledge to both the price setters and the central bank and shows its best response y_1 to π_1.

The Phillips curve shifts up reflecting the ability of price setters to raise the markup from μ_0 to μ_1. The higher markup shifts the price-setting curve, the PS, downwards and we can write this explicitly as a fall in the price-setting real wage from $\lambda(1-\mu_0)$ to $\lambda(1-\mu_1)$. As usual, this opens up a positive bargaining gap between the unchanged WS curve and the lower PS curve at equilibrium output, which gives a percentage boost to inflation of

$$\frac{\lambda(1-\mu_0)-\lambda(1-\mu_1)}{\lambda(1-\mu_0)} = \frac{\mu_1-\mu_0}{1-\mu_0} = \varepsilon_1. \qquad (4.3)$$

Hence, π_1, the new rate of inflation, is given by the new Phillips curve of

$$\pi_1 = \pi^T + \alpha(y_1 - y_e) + \frac{\mu_1-\mu_0}{1-\mu_0}$$

$$\pi_1 = \pi^T + \alpha(y_1 - y_e) + \varepsilon_1. \qquad \text{(rational expectations Phillips curve; 3-equation model)}$$

As is clear from the equation, to find out the rate of inflation, π_1, we need to know y_1.

But at this initial moment, neither the central bank nor the price setters know π_1 or y_1. Here is the rational expectations problem: both the central bank and price setters move simultaneously (the CB to choose y_1 and the price setters to choose π_1). The problem is that the price setters need to know y_1 to set π_1 and the CB needs to know π_1 to set y_1, while neither know y_1 or π_1.

However, this is not a difficult problem to solve: the price setters know that if they set π_1 on the new Phillips curve, it will be optimal for the CB to choose y_1 where its MR intersects the PC; and if CB chooses that y_1 the optimal choice for the price setters is to choose the corresponding π_1. This pair of strategies is thus a Nash equilibrium. The CB and the price setters simultaneously choose point C, the combination of (y_1, π_1).

In Figure 4.5a, with rational expectations, in response to the temporary shock to the markup, we have shown that the economy moves initially from A to C. Once the markup shock has gone, we can use the same argument in reverse to show that in

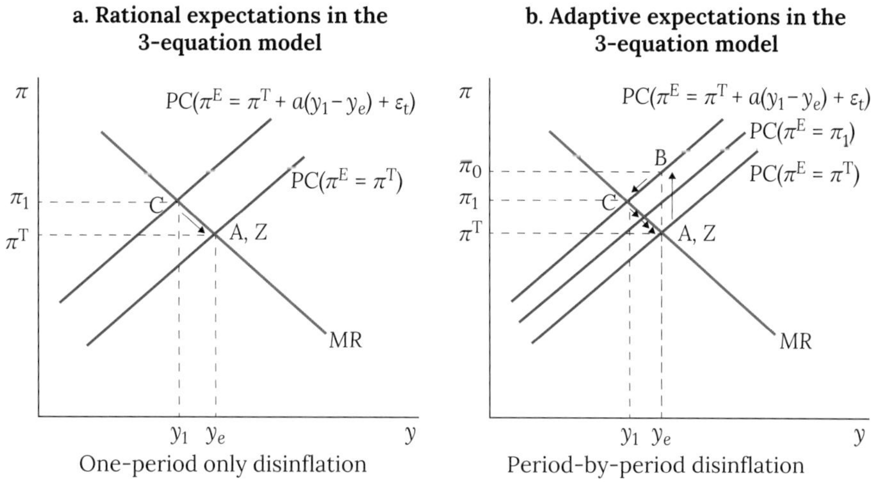

Figure 4.5 Adjustment to an inflation (markup) shock in the 3-equation model under rational and adaptive expectations. Visit www.oup.com/he/carlin-soskice to explore ration and adaptive expectations with Animated Analytical Diagram 4.5.

the next period the economy goes straight back to Z (i.e., A). So, *all* the disinflation associated with the shock takes place in one period. (Note that whereas a permanent change in the markup would shift the MR curve, this is not the case for a temporary shock.)

We can compare the one-period REH disinflation with the disinflation that occurs with adaptive expectations. This is shown in the right-hand panel, Figure 4.5b.

The two panels have many things in common: first, the central bank's MR curve is the same whether we are talking about rational or adaptive expectations. The same is true of the pre-shock and final Phillips curves, which go through the point labelled A and Z. We now show that they also share the new Phillips curve, which arises because of the shock to product market conditions and enables firms to raise their markups.

Before the shock, the Phillips curve is given by

$$\pi_0 = \pi^T + \alpha(y_0 - y_e),$$

where inflation has the two regular components, the rate of wage inflation (equal to target inflation, its pre-existing rate) plus the bargaining gap due to any deviation of output from equilibrium, which is zero initially.

The shock enables price setters to raise the markup, and we assume they do so. Inflation goes up by the percentage increase as in equation (4.3). In the adaptive expectations case, the central bank cannot change output until a period later, so since the economy starts with output at equilibrium, and moves vertically up to B in the right panel with

$$\pi_0 = \pi^T + \alpha(y_0 - y_1) + \varepsilon_1$$

as shown.

By contrast, in the rational expectations case, as we have seen, price setters and the central bank jointly solve the PC and the MR equations, which takes the economy directly to point C, with $y = y_1$ and $\pi = \pi_1$, where the PC and the MR curves intersect. As compared with the AEH case, price setters do not push prices up by as much because they know the central bank will want to restrict output below equilibrium.

In the REH case, the economy goes back to its initial position (A, Z) in the next period, but in the adaptive expectations case it goes back step by step in the usual way set out in Chapter 3.

Another notable difference between the 3-equation model with rational and adaptive expectations is that under rational expectations, if the central bank decides to reduce the inflation target, it can announce it before the wage-setting round and there will be a costless move to the new equilibrium with both the MR_{REH} and Phillips curve shifting down when the announcement is made. This contrasts with the protracted and costly period-by-period adjustment to a lower inflation target under adaptive expectations.

Finally, it is important to point out that if we supplement the assumption of rational expectations with the assumption of *perfectly flexible wages and prices*, then there is no role at all for active monetary policy to stabilize fluctuations. Under these conditions once a shock happens, nominal variables adjust immediately. There would be a transitory adjustment of nominal wages to reflect the inflation shock; all real variables would remain unchanged, including output. Because the entire adjustment to a temporary nominal shock (an inflation shock) occurs immediately, the only role for the central bank is to set the inflation target and there is no MR curve.

4.3 EXPECTATIONS HYPOTHESES, INFLATION BIAS, AND TIME INCONSISTENCY

4.3.1 The Lucas critique

The stagflation of the 1970s coincided with the development of *New Classical Macroeconomics*. This school of economics was influential in policy-making circles in the 1980s, and fundamentally changed the course of macroeconomic modelling. The underlying principle of New Classical Economics is that macroeconomic models should be based on rigorous microeconomic foundations, and in particular, on forward-looking optimizing agents with model-consistent expectations. The real business cycle model was developed in this tradition. It is set out in Chapter 18.

Such models were thought necessary to address the so-called *Lucas critique*, which highlighted the dangers of using models for forecasting that rely on the relationships found in historical data. Such forecasting methods will be unreliable if those relationships are conditional on the policy regime that was in place during the historical period being analysed. If the policy regime changes, then the relationships found in historical data could well break down. Why? Because economic agents will change their behaviour in response to the new policy regime.[11] This is an application of the

---

[11] See Lucas Jr (1976). For a definition of the Lucas critique see Lars Ljungqvist's definition in *The New Palgrave Dictionary of Economics*, 2nd Edition (2008).

concept of the Nash equilibrium. For a simple example, see Section 3.9 of CORE's *Economy, Society, and Public Policy*.[12]

The Lucas critique was directed at the widespread use of large econometric models for forecasting. Such models dominated governments and central banks from the 1950s to the mid-1970s. A well-known example was the MPS model designed by Modigliani and his collaborators in the late 1960s. This model was used for quantitative forecasting and macroeconomic analysis by the Federal Reserve Board.[13] Lucas was very sceptical that these models, which were based on relationships from historical data, could provide meaningful forecasts. He made a powerful critique of the policy mistakes that can arise from this practice.

To explain this, we begin with an example where the government uses fiscal policy (tax or spending giveaways) to get a pre-election boost in its popularity.

Suppose the government sneaks in such a spending increase after the central bank has set the interest rate for the period. Hence from the central bank's point of view there has been an unexpected increase in aggregate demand, engineered by fiscal policy so that $y_t > y_e$. However, the central bank cannot do anything about it until next period.

What now happens to inflation during the current period? Assume that wage and price setters set prices with the same information as the central bank, that is before the government had increased expenditure. If wage and price setters have rational expectations, they assume that $\pi_t^E = \pi^T$ and they believe that $y_t = y_e$, so inflation remains at target despite output being boosted beyond y_e. The next period the central bank reacts to the higher level of government spending and raises the interest rate because the stabilizing interest rate, r^S, is higher. Inflation is therefore at π^T in the next period (because with rational expectations, the higher inflation does not get built into next period's expected inflation) and output falls back to equilibrium.

Hence if wage and price setters have rational expectations, the best that the government can do is to get a one-period gain in output. Nevertheless *in the data*, one would observe a one period rise in output without a rise in inflation above target.

The next step is to introduce a government that is suspicious of independent central banks. It believes, for example, that central banks are 'conservative' and are simply concerned to keep output and employment low. The central bank defends its behaviour and, using the Phillips curve with rational expectations, explains that increased government expenditure is incompatible with inflation remaining at its target.

In spite of the advice of the central bank, the evidence the new government uses is that the old government increased government expenditure and output increased, without any change in inflation. Hence the new government thinks the central bank is simply conservative. It therefore takes away the independence of the central bank and says that the central bank must not raise interest rates when it increases government expenditure. The new government then increases government expenditure. Since

---

12 https://www.core-econ.org/espp/book/text/03.html#39-unintended-consequences-of-a-redistributive-tax.

13 See Brayton et al. (1997).

the central bank is forbidden from reacting by raising interest rates, inflation will jump upward in the period after the shock. There is no trade-off consistent with the behaviour of wage and price setters that can be exploited by the government, permitting lower unemployment (higher output) to be gained at the expense of higher inflation. Inflation would rise without limit.

This example illustrates how the use of historical data, which showed an association between a fiscal expansion, higher output and no increase in inflation, was used to forecast the outcome of a fiscal policy intervention and produced a poor economic outcome. In this example, the correct model of behaviour is one with rational expectations of wage and price setters: this can account both for the data observed from the pre-election episode and for the poor outcome of the new government's policy of abolishing central bank independence and pursuing fiscal expansion.

4.3.2 **Target output, inflation bias, and macroeconomic policy**

In this section, we explore what happens when the policy maker seeks to run the economy with output higher than equilibrium. We shall see that the outcome is that the economy's medium-run equilibrium is at equilibrium output (not at the higher target level) and that inflation is above target. The failure of inflation-targeting policy under these conditions is called inflation bias. Why does inflation bias arise and what determines its size?

The difference between this problem and the ones discussed in the previous section and in Chapter 3 is the structure of the policy maker's loss function. Previously, the loss function was defined in terms of deviations from the inflation target and *equilibrium* output, y_e. The policy maker's new loss function is defined in terms of deviations from the inflation target and *target* output, which we assume is higher than equilibrium.

$$L = (y_t - y^T)^2 + \beta(\pi_t - \pi^T)^2, \qquad \text{(central bank loss function; target output)}$$

where $y^T > y_e$.

The choice of an output target in excess of the equilibrium defined by the intersection of the WS and PS curves may be the result of political pressure arising from the idea that a government able to deliver higher employment would be rewarded in the polls for its economic competence.

But it may also reflect the policy maker's desire to move closer to the welfare optimum. We know that although the WS–PS intersection is a Nash equilibrium because none of the actors has any incentive to change their behaviour given what others are doing, it is not a Pareto equilibrium. There are other allocations—at higher employment—at which some of those currently unemployed would be better off and no-one else worse off. The source of the Pareto-inefficiency is signalled by the presence of involuntary unemployment at equilibrium.

We illustrate this case in Figure 4.6, where the central bank's MR curve goes through the new output target, y^T, where the new loss contours are centred. The central bank's bliss point is now at A′, where output is at y^T and inflation is at target.

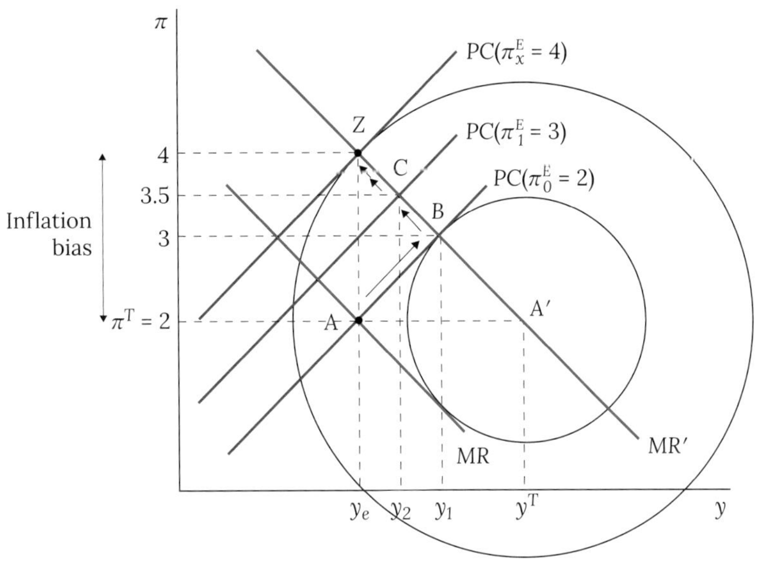

Figure 4.6 The inflation bias. Visit www.oup.com/he/carlin-soskice to explore inflation bias with Animated Analytical Diagram 4.6.

Using the 3-equation model with adaptive expectations and the modified central bank loss function, the adjustment of the economy after the change in policy stance is as follows:

1. The central bank forecasts that the Phillips curve will not move next period, because actual inflation has not changed as a result of the change in output target and agents form expectations in a backward-looking manner (i.e. $\pi_t^E = \pi_{t-1}$). The central bank therefore minimizes its loss by lowering the interest rate, which stimulates aggregate demand and moves the economy to point B. Given the new MR curve, point B is the central bank's optimal point on the original Phillips curve. At point B, the central bank is closer to their new bliss point than they were at point A; they are willing to accept the rise in inflation, because output is closer to their new output target.
2. At point B, however, output is above equilibrium, so there is pressure on inflation to change. Inflation rises, the Phillips curve shifts upward and the central bank reoptimizes by raising the interest rate and moving the economy to point C.
3. At point C, output is still above equilibrium, so there is still pressure on inflation to change. Again, inflation rises, the Phillips curve shifts upward and the central bank reoptimizes by raising the interest rate. This adjustment process continues over a number of periods until the economy reaches the new medium-run equilibrium at point Z.

Figure 4.6 shows the inflation bias result. When the central bank targets a level of output above equilibrium the outcome is that inflation is higher than its target. Output in the medium run must always be at the equilibrium level, as only at y_e is there is no pressure on inflation to change. On the new MR curve in Figure 4.6, the medium-run equilibrium is at point Z. At Z, the central bank is further from its bliss point than if it had stuck with the original output target of y_e and remained at point A. The example highlights that under adaptive expectations, there is only a short-run benefit from targeting a level of output above equilibrium.

We can quantify the inflation bias by taking the difference between the equilibrium rate of inflation and target inflation: the inflation bias in the example is equal to $4\% - 2\% = 2\%$. The next step is to pin down its size. The loss function the central bank now wants to minimize is

$$L = (y_t - y^T)^2 + \beta(\pi_t - \pi^T)^2, \tag{4.4}$$

where $y^T > y_e$. This is subject as before to the Phillips curve constraint,

$$\pi_t = \pi_{t-1} + \alpha(y_t - y_e). \tag{4.5}$$

Minimizing the central bank's loss function (equation 4.4) subject to the Phillips curve (equation 4.5) implies the first order condition:

$$y_t - y^T + \alpha\beta(\pi_{t-1} + \alpha(y_t - y_e) - \pi^T) = 0$$
$$y_t - y^T + \alpha\beta(\pi_t - \pi^T) = 0.$$

So the new monetary rule equation is:

$$y_t - y^T = -\alpha\beta(\pi_t - \pi^T).$$

This equation is indeed for a line that goes through (π^T, y^T). Since equilibrium requires that there is no pressure on inflation to change, it must be the case that $y_t = y_e$ and that $\pi_t = \pi_{t-1}$. If we substitute this back into the monetary rule we have:

$$y_e = y^T - \alpha\beta(\pi_{t-1} - \pi^T)$$
$$\Rightarrow \pi_t = \pi^T + \underbrace{\frac{(y^T - y_e)}{\alpha\beta}}_{\text{inflation bias}}. \qquad \text{(inflation bias, adaptive expectations)}$$

In equilibrium, inflation will exceed the target by $\frac{(y^T - y_e)}{\alpha\beta}$. This is called the inflation bias and it will be positive whenever $y^T > y_e$.[14] The steeper is the central bank's monetary rule (i.e. the less inflation averse it is, lower β), the greater will be the inflation bias. A lower α also raises the inflation bias. A lower α implies that inflation is less responsive to changes in output. Therefore, any given reduction in inflation is more expensive in lost output; so, in cost-benefit terms for the central bank, it pays to allow a little more inflation and a little less output loss.

When wage and price setters in the 3-equation model have rational expectations, inflation bias also arises. We can use Figure 4.6 to illustrate that under rational expectations, the announcement by the central bank of the output target, y^T will see a jump from point A to point Z. This is because the forward-looking, rational agents in the

[14] For an early model of inflation bias with backward-looking inflation expectations, see Phelps (1967).

economy can see that given the new loss function, the new medium-run equilibrium will be at point Z. There is only one tangency between the loss contours and the Phillips curves when output is at y_e, and it is at point Z. It is clear from the diagram that the size of the inflation bias will be the same as under adaptive expectations.

When comparing the outcomes under adaptive and rational expectations in the 3-equation model, the only outcome that can occur under the REH is point Z. Under the AEH, we observe points A, B, C and Z due to the period-by-period adjustment in which the optimal choice in each period is a point on the MR curve.

Returning to the REH and a central bank output target above equilibrium, could the central bank offer to set policy so as to achieve point A in Figure 4.6 where its losses are lower than at Z? The answer is 'no' because the private sector's only expected rate of inflation consistent with the central bank's loss function is $\pi^E = \pi_Z$, the inflation rate incorporating the inflation bias. If it were to set its expected inflation instead at $\pi^E = \pi_A = \pi^T$, then the central bank would minimize its loss by choosing higher output. Its stated policy of sticking to output of y_e is 'time inconsistent'. Given that its goal is target output above equilibrium, the commitment to the 'low' output policy is not credible. In the next section, we discuss how a policy maker can establish a reputation for toughness, which in this case, means an output target at equilibrium.

Note that, in contrast to the REH case, problems of time-consistency and credibility do not arise under adaptive expectations because the private sector agents in that model are not forward-looking (they use lagged inflation to form their expectations).

4.3.3 Approaches to mitigating inflation bias in the 3-equation model

As we have shown, under both adaptive and rational expectations, a more inflation-averse central bank (a higher β in the CB's loss function) would reduce the extent of inflation bias and it can be eliminated if the central bank's output target is the equilibrium level of output.

Debates about inflation bias arose during the stagflationary 1970s and 1980s and contributed to the emergence of inflation-targeting as an explicit responsibility of central banks, and of central bank independence.

Delegation

The problem of inflation bias can be solved if the monetary policy maker gives up their over-ambitious output target. This logic lies behind the idea of delegating monetary policy to an independent central bank, which has no incentive to target output above equilibrium. Put another way, the independent central bank can credibly commit to targeting output of y_e. Delegation is socially beneficial; welfare is higher if a body with different preferences from the government (and the private sector who elect them) has control over monetary policy.

Whereas governments are likely to be characterized by myopia as a consequence of the electoral cycle, an independent monetary policy committee will take account of the consequences of inflation this period for next period's inflation (and their chances of meeting the inflation target). In order to encourage independent central bankers to take a medium-term view of policy, chairmen and committee members typically have long tenures that extend over multiple electoral cycles. In Appendix 4.6.1, we show how to model a more far-sighted central bank. It is also argued that central bankers are more inflation averse than the government, which is modelled by a greater weight on the inflation deviation in the loss function.

The empirical evidence supports the argument that delegation reduces inflation bias. Klomp and de Haan (2010) use 59 previous studies that examine the relationship between inflation and central bank independence to carry out a meta-regression analysis. The authors find that the overall body of empirical evidence suggests that central bank independence reduces inflation. They find a 'true effect' of central bank independence on inflation, even when they control for publication bias, which makes it harder to publish results that do not show a 'statistically significant' effect. The literature also suggests that adopting an inflation-targeting regime with an *explicit* inflation target improves macroeconomic performance in terms of both inflation and output stability by anchoring the public's inflation expectations to the central bank's objectives.[15]

In many OECD economies, inflation bias lapsed as a significant problem, because control of monetary policy was delegated to an independent central bank that is run by officials who are motivated by concern about their professional reputations. This point is summarized neatly by the economist Peter Howitt, who highlights the role of foreign exchange market operators in containing any tendency of domestic policy makers to try to boost output above equilibrium. We return to the role of the foreign exchange market in Chapter 11:[16]

> The 'temptation' to raise the level of economic activity with some surprise inflation might exist if society were indeed locked into expectations. In reality, however, the temptation just doesn't arise, as practitioners of central banking have long maintained. Central bankers are keenly aware that although there are long and variable lags between monetary stimulus and any resulting rise in the level of economic activity, there are no lags at all between such a stimulus and the currency depreciation and capital flight that will occur if the stimulus is taken by investors as a signal of future weakness in the currency. Because of this, there is no reason for believing that discretionary central banks have the inflationary bias that the game-theoretic [time-inconsistency] view attributes to them. . . .
>
> Responsible people entrusted with such important and delicate jobs as the management of a country's central bank are typically motivated by the desire

[15] For example, Orphanides and Williams (2005). See also Masciandaro and Romelli (2019) for an interesting history of central bank independence, and possible macroeconomic factors that have driven independence trends.

[16] Howitt (2009). Howitt refers to the useful paper by Mervyn King, then Deputy Governor of the Bank of England; from 2003 until 2013, Governor of the Bank of England: King (1997*a*). Another useful source is the short book of three lectures by Alan Blinder reflecting on how he used academic research when he was Vice-Chairman of the Federal Reserve Board: Blinder (1999).

to be seen as having done a good job, to have acquitted themselves well. They pursue this objective by doing everything possible to avoid major inflations, financial panics and runs on the currency, while carrying out the day-to-day job of making available the base money needed for the financial system to function.

Reputation building

Another solution to the problem of inflation bias lies with the government or central bank building a reputation for being tough on inflation. Suppose that the government has delegated monetary policy to the central bank but wage setters remain unsure of just how independent the central bank is. They only know that there is a probability p that the central bank is independent and a probability $(1-p)$ that it is a puppet of the government. The only way that they can find out is by observing the decisions taken by the central bank. If this is the case, how should the central bank behave? This problem can be analysed in detail using game theory.[17] Here we convey the flavour of the solution.

The situation is one in which the central bank interacts with wage setters more than once. Will a 'weak' central bank with an output target above the equilibrium find it rational to behave as if it were tough—i.e. with an output target closer to the equilibrium? If so, then we can say that it is possible to build a reputation for toughness as a method of solving the inflation bias problem.

Let us begin with the case in which the interaction between the central bank and wage setters occurs twice: in period one, wage setters choose π_1^E with no knowledge of whether the central bank is weak or tough (but they know there is a probability of p that it is tough); the central bank then chooses output in period one, y_1 knowing π_1^E. In period two, the wage setters choose π_2^E knowing y_1; the central bank then chooses y_2 knowing π_2^E.

The result is that a weak central bank will choose to act like a tough one in the first period, which will establish a low expected inflation rate in the second period, thereby providing bigger gains from boosting output in the second period. The central bank gains because in the first period, the outcome is inflation at its target (no inflation bias) and output at the equilibrium (instead of the time inconsistency outcome of inflation above the target and output at equilibrium) while in the second period, it can gain by setting output above the equilibrium (i.e. by exploiting the short-run trade-off between inflation and unemployment by a surprise increase in inflation).

When the game is extended from two to many periods, the benefits to the central bank from behaving as if it were tough increase. This is because the situation in period one (where inflation bias is avoided) is repeated again and again until the last period. This type of model provides an explanation for the process by which a reputation for toughness can be built in the face of public scepticism.

---

[17] See Vickers (1986). For a simplified version of the central bank signalling game presented in Vickers' paper see Carlin and Soskice (2006), Chapter 16.

4.4 ANCHORED INFLATION EXPECTATIONS AND HYSTERESIS

4.4.1 Central bank communication and anchored inflation expectations

The modern, inflation-targeting central bank spends a large amount of time and effort on communication. Central banks do not limit their communication to informing the public and the financial markets of their interest rate decisions. They will typically also provide: macroeconomic commentary and forecasts, a monthly or quarterly inflation/monetary policy report, which sets out the detailed reasoning behind interest rate decisions, minutes from committee meetings, transcripts of speeches by prominent members of the central bank, a statistics hub containing data on historic interest rates, exchange rates and the banking sector, in-house economic research on monetary economics and financial markets; and games and competitions involving monetary policy.[18]

One interpretation of the investment in communications is that the central bank's objective is to keep inflation expectations anchored at the inflation target. This is explained by economist Benoît Cœuré, a member of the Executive Board of the European Central Bank (ECB):[19]

> Stable inflation expectations at levels consistent with price stability provide an important nominal anchor for the economy. They reduce inflation persistence and curb harmful macroeconomic volatility.
>
> There is compelling empirical evidence suggesting that increased clarity about central banks' mandates, their reaction functions and inflation aims has helped anchor inflation expectations and reduce their variability around the communicated inflation aim despite significant shocks to inflation in both directions.

We can capture the idea of anchoring in a simple way by modifying the adaptive expectations Phillips curve so that expected inflation is a weighted average of the inflation target and lagged inflation, where the weight on the inflation target is called χ (chi, for credibility):

$$\pi_t = \left[\chi\pi^T + (1-\chi)\pi_{t-1}\right] + \alpha(y_t - y_e) \qquad \text{(anchored expectations Phillips curve)}$$

where

$$\pi_t^E = \chi\pi^T + (1-\chi)\pi_{t-1}. \qquad \text{(anchored expectations)}$$

In this model, the central bank's credibility is incorporated directly in the Phillips curve. For a fully credible central bank, $\chi = 1$ and the Phillips curve is anchored to π^T. This is a special case of the static expectations Phillips curve in which $\bar{\pi} = \pi^T$. For $\chi = 0$, expected inflation is last period's inflation as in the case with adaptive expectations.

---

18 For more detail on central bank communication, including a summary of the different methods employed to inform the public and a case study of the Federal Open Market Committee's (FOMC) public statements, please see the Part III chapters in Mayes et al. (2019).

19 Excerpt taken from Cœuré (2019).

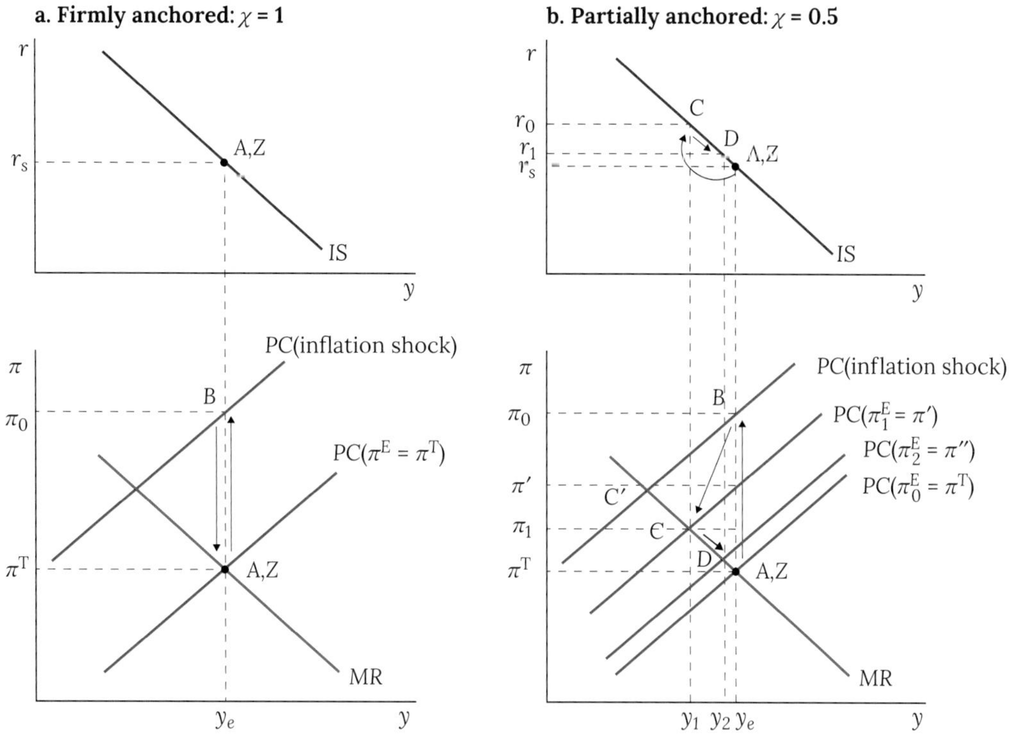

Figure 4.7 Varying the level of central bank credibility, using the example of an inflation shock:
a. Fully anchored: $\chi = 1$
b. Partially anchored: $\chi = 0.5$.

Anchored expectations can be visualized in the Phillips curve diagram. In Figure 4.7, the firmly anchored case (i.e. $\chi = 1$) is shown in the left-hand panel and the partially anchored case with $\chi = 0.5$ is shown on the right. Using this figure, we compare the response to an inflation shock.

$\chi = 1$: *firmly anchored at* π^T

After the inflation shock, there is just one period of high inflation. In the second period, the Phillips curve reverts to its original position (i.e. PC($\pi^E = \pi^T$)), as inflation expectations are firmly anchored to the target. This means that the central bank does not have to change interest rates and hence output does not deviate from equilibrium—the disinflation is costless (Figure 4.7a). At the next wage round, expected inflation is at the target. This explains the return of the economy directly from point B to point A.

$\chi = 0.5$: *partially anchored at* π^T

After the inflation shock, the central bank has to raise interest rates, but to a lesser extent than when expectations are fully backward looking. The fall in output is lower, and adjustment back to the initial equilibrium is quicker than when $\chi = 0$. If $\chi = 0.5$, then in the period following the shock, the Phillips curve moves down to intersect the

y_e line at a level of inflation which is an average of inflation last period (i.e. π_0) and target inflation (i.e. π^T). In Figure 4.7b this is shown as the inflation level π', and on this new Phillips curve the central bank chooses a level of inflation π_1 at point C. Using the same logic, the next move is to point D.

$\chi = 0$: *fully backward-looking*

This is the familiar case analysed in Chapter 3. The full analysis is shown in Figure 3.9. In Figure 4.7b, the central bank's best response to the shock is shown by point C′ in the lower panel. It is obvious from the figure that as compared with adaptive expectations, any degree of anchoring of inflation expectations improves welfare (as measured by the central bank's loss function).

This modification of the 3-equation model shows that the central bank can reduce the costs of stabilizing a shock if it is able to increase the weight on its inflation target in the Phillips curve. More firmly anchored inflation expectations reduce the negative impact of stabilization policy on the economy by restoring output and inflation to target more rapidly. This model of expectations formation helps explain why central banks place a lot of emphasis on transparency and communication.

Kicking off a regular review of Canada's inflation-targeting policy in 2018, Lawrence Schembri, Deputy Governor of the Bank of Canada, highlighted the importance of transparency for the anchoring of inflation expectations:[20]

> It's not often that a policy performs better than expected. Our inflation-control target did just that, and continues to do so. Over the past 27 years, we have reduced inflation as measured by the CPI and maintained it at a level close to our 2 per cent target, with no persistent episodes outside our control range. Because inflation has been so close to the 2 per cent target, it has served as an anchoring and coordinating mechanism, allowing Canadians to make better economic decisions and achieve better economic outcomes. In addition, there has been much less volatility in interest rates and output growth.
>
> We have learned some key lessons from this experience.
>
> First, the clarity and simplicity of the 2 per cent target has facilitated its communication and broad acceptance, and that has helped enhance the target's credibility.
>
> Second, as inflation expectations have become firmly anchored at the 2 per cent target, the effectiveness of the policy has increased. For example, during the global financial crisis of 2007–08, the Bank was able to aggressively reduce its policy rate and provide substantial monetary stimulus because inflation expectations were so well anchored. As a consequence, a reduction in the policy rate translated directly into a similar reduction in the real interest rate, which is necessary for stimulating demand.
>
> Third, the more successful we are at hitting the target, the more credible the policy is and the more confident Canadians are that inflation will remain on

[20] Excerpt taken from Schembri (2018).

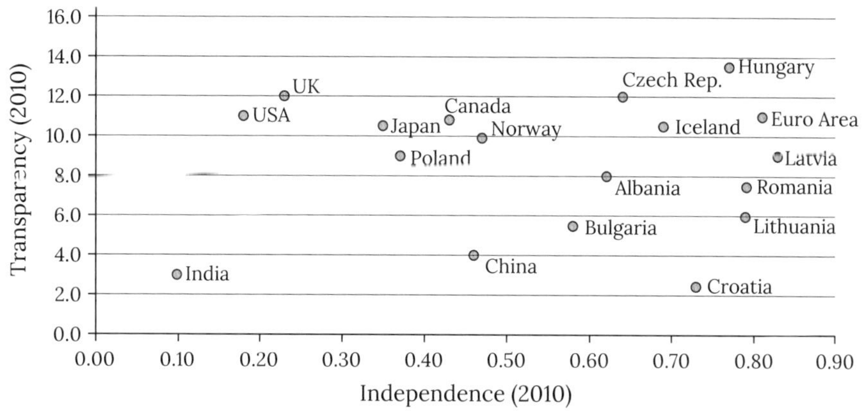

Figure 4.8 Central bank independence and transparency (in 2010).
Source: Dincer and Eichengreen (2014).

target. This self-reinforcing feedback loop has been instrumental in our ability to keep inflation on target.

The understanding of how monetary policy should be operated evolved rapidly in the wake of the failure of attempts to use money supply targets to bring inflation down in the late 1970s and early 1980s. By the end of the 1990s, central banks across the developed world had realized the importance of independence, transparency and credibility for successfully maintaining low and stable inflation. Figure 4.8 shows the relative levels of transparency and independence of global central banks in 2010.

Evidence

The academic literature on central bank communication has two distinct strands. The first strand uses constructed indices of transparency to test the empirical relationships between transparency and macroeconomic variables, such as inflation and output. The second strand focuses more explicitly on communication, trying to assess whether communication leads to better predictions of central bank behaviour and therefore has a desirable effect on economic stability.

Demertzis and Hallett (2007) and Dincer and Eichengreen (2014) are two papers from the first strand. They both find that central bank transparency reduces inflation variability, but has no effect on the level of inflation, using standard cut-offs for statistical significance.

Sturm and de Haan (2011) is a paper in the second strand, which identifies five indicators of European Central Bank communication that are based on the ECB President's introductory statement at the press conference following the ECB policy meetings. The authors find that although the indicators are often quite different from one another, they add information that helps predict the next policy decision of the ECB. This finding is backed up by Blinder et al. (2008), which provides a review of the available literature on central bank communication. The paper comes to the conclusion that more and better central bank communication improves the predictability of monetary policy decisions.

Evidence on how well anchored inflation expectations are as a measure of monetary policy credibility is provided in a study of advanced and emerging economies from 1996–2019 (Moessner and Takáts 2020). As their measure of anchoring, they use the effects of short-term inflation expectations on long-term expectations in survey data (the consensus of professional forecasters). They find that inflation expectations are well-anchored in advanced economies (better than in emerging economies) and that this has not been affected during the post financial crisis period in which interest rates have been at the zero lower bound.

The sharp rise in inflation to double digit rates throughout the world from 2021–22 stimulated a new debate about inflation expectations and their importance for monetary policy.[21]

4.4.2 **Anchoring, hysteresis, and output targeting: Policy following a deep recession**

In the chapter so far, we have shown that when the central bank's loss function is defined in terms of deviations from an output target higher than equilibrium as well as from an inflation target, it can at best get a temporary gain in output above equilibrium. The analysis of inflation bias shows that the case for having an output target higher than equilibrium is weak. In this section, we introduce assumptions that modify this result. We show the circumstances in which an output target above equilibrium is both attainable and desirable from a welfare point of view. As we shall see, this is not a general result but depends on the state of the economy. Specifically, it refers to an economy that has experienced a deep recession.

The explanation rests on some features of a post-recession world that can be incorporated in the model, namely that a deep recession can cause a fall in *equilibrium* output. This is called *hysteresis* and it is an example of *path dependence*. If monetary policy targets the higher pre-recession equilibrium level of output, it is possible, under some conditions, to improve outcomes with higher output and with inflation at the central bank's target. If a long recession damages the supply-side of the economy and *if the damage can be reversed by higher economic activity*, then a policy that targets the *initial* equilibrium level of output has merit.

Experience during the early 2010s suggests that hysteresis indeed accompanies a prolonged downturn. One indicator of this is the repeated downgrading since the deep recessions following the financial crisis 2008–09 of estimates of 'potential GDP', which is an indicator of the concept of equilibrium output in the model (Ball 2014). Figure 4.9 shows this downgrading of potential output estimates for Spain and Canada. The upper solid blue lines indicate the path of potential output as estimated in the December 2007 OECD *Economic Outlook*, published before the financial crisis. The lower dashed orange line indicates the path of potential output as estimated in the May 2014 OECD *Economic Outlook*, providing a measure of the best that could have happened following the crisis; finally, the black dashed line represents actual GDP, thus showing what actually happened. Spain, which was amongst the countries particularly

[21] For insight, see Reis (2021) and the comments and discussion that follow.

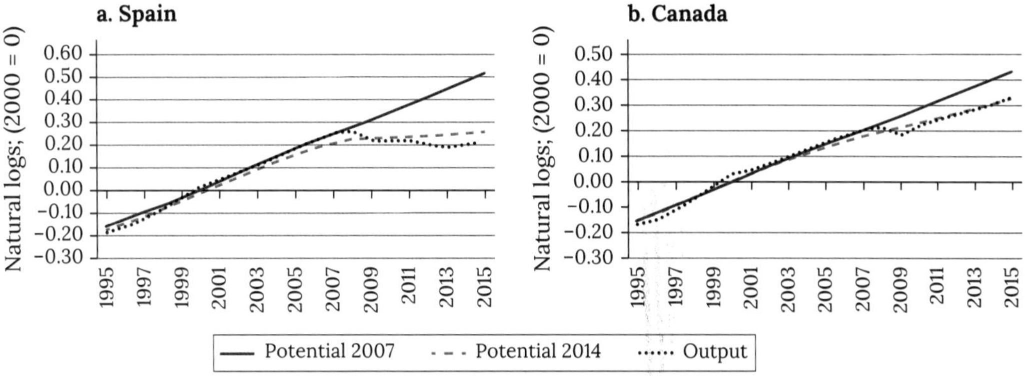

Figure 4.9 This replicates 2 panels of Figure 2 from Ball (2014). Data on potential output was used from the 2007 OECD *Economic Outlook*, and the 2015 OECD *Economic Outlook* was used to measure actual output. This uses log of potential output, normalizing the year 2000 to 0. The 2007 projections were extended beyond 2009 by using average growth of log potential output in previous years, as in Ball (2014).

affected by the recession, shows a very significant divergence between the projected path of equilibrium output and the actual path. However, it is interesting to notice that the hysteresis effect, although less prominent, was also present in less affected countries such as Canada.

Remember that in the standard model, the equilibrium rate of unemployment (or equivalently, of output) is only shifted by supply-side factors. This implies that aggregate demand shocks have a short-run effect on output and unemployment but no effect in the medium run. However, several different mechanisms have been proposed through which recession itself shifts either the WS curve upward or the PS curve downward thereby reducing equilibrium output (for models, see Chapter 15). One such mechanism with strong empirical support relates to the effect of recession in leading to the decay of the human capital of laid-off workers (e.g. by losing touch with new technologies and work practices or erosion of habits such as punctuality) and consequently on their ability to compete in the labour market (Yagan 2019).

By comparing local areas in the US which experienced more severe employment shocks in the post-financial crisis recession than others, Yagan is able to quantify the long-term scarring effects of the recession. The long-term scarring reflected in increased rates of withdrawal from participation in the labour market can be represented in the model by an upward shift in the WS curve, producing lower equilibrium output via hysteresis.

Consistent with the findings of Yagan, Heathcote et al. (2020) report that the scarring effects of recessions increase inequality. For the US, it is shown that the main driver of the widening inequality in the bottom half of the earnings distribution for men is declining hours of work. This is sharply concentrated in recessions and the jobs are not regained in the recovery. Low-skilled men are more likely to experience job loss in a recession; their skills deteriorate reducing their ability to compete for jobs in the recovery; and finally, they give up job search producing a rise in non-participation in the labour force.

Hysteresis mechanisms help to explain the extensive policies introduced across high-income economies during the Covid-19 crisis to subsidize wages and keep workers attached to their employers. They are explored in more detail in Chapter 15.

We begin by introducing anchored inflation expectations and then incorporate hysteresis. It is the presence of *both* that produces the result that monetary policy can deliver output at a target higher than the current equilibrium, while keeping inflation at target as well. Keeping in mind the Lucas critique, we return to ask whether this result is 'too good to be true', and specifically, how might inflation expectations become unanchored.

Anchored inflation expectations

In the Appendix 4.6.1, we show mathematically that if we use the Phillips curve with anchored expectations, and change nothing else in the model, then we get a result that is similar to the one under static expectations. Specifically, there is a long-run trade-off between inflation and output, and the scale of trade-off depends on the weight on the inflation anchor in the Phillips curve.

This is illustrated for the 3-equation model using a modified version of the Carlin-Soskice Macroeconomic Simulator (available at www.oup.com/he/carlin-soskice). In the example in Figure 4.10, the economy begins at equilibrium output of 98 and with inflation at the target of 2%. In period 5, the central bank adopts an output target of 100. This replaces equilibrium output in its loss function. The simulation in Figure 4.10, Case 1, shows the outcome for output and inflation in three different experiments: with $\chi=0$, i.e. no inflation anchoring, which is the standard adaptive expectations hypothesis, and with two levels of anchoring, $\chi = 0.3$ and $\chi = 0.7$. In line with the predictions of the model in the Appendix, the simulation in Figure 4.10 shows that the economy has higher output and inflation above target in the new equilibrium. The larger the value of χ—more firmly anchored expectations—the smaller the increase in medium-run inflation above the target. Hence, there is a long-run trade-off, with a higher output level achieved at the cost of higher inflation.

However, there is a paradox in these results: as Case 1 shows, when the central bank's inflation target is more credible because a higher proportion of agents anchor their expectations (higher χ), the trade-off improves and yet the central bank is exploiting it. One would predict that over time, confidence in the central bank's inflation target would fade away and the unpalatable outcome of inflation bias would reappear. As shown with $\chi = 0$, output returns to 98 in the new equilibrium and inflation is constant at a higher level than the target.

Anchored inflation expectations and hysteresis

If the level of past output (and employment) affects equilibrium output, then a central bank targeting output higher than equilibrium will be able to achieve both its output and inflation targets. This result is shown mathematically in Appendix 4.6.2. In Figure 4.10, Case 2, we can see that following the adoption of the higher output target in period 5, the economy converges to a new equilibrium in which inflation is at target and output is at the new target, above the initial equilibrium level of 98.

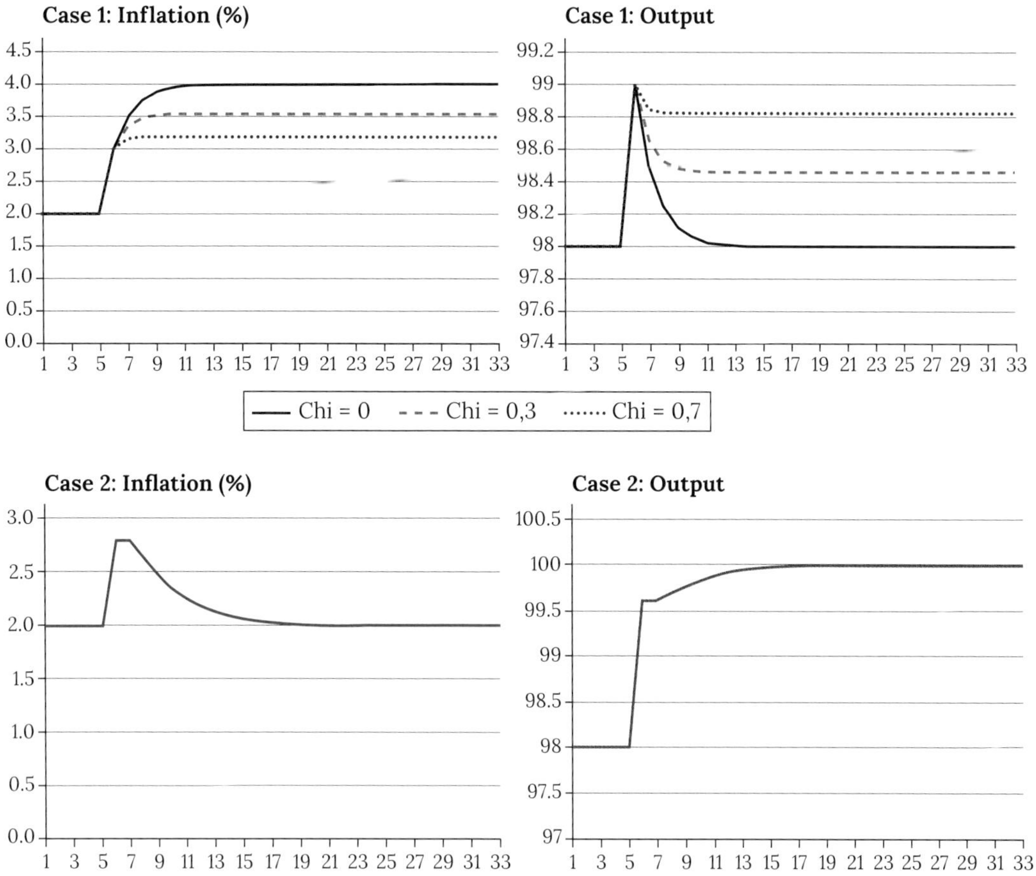

Figure 4.10 Case 1 (comparing the degree of expectation anchoring) and Case 2 (the basic hysteresis case) are described in the text. The x-axis represents the number of periods elapsed, starting in period 1. The y axis on the left-hand side graphs represents inflation in the model, in percent increase in prices per period, while the y-axis on the right-hand side graphs represents output per period relative to initial output of 98.

Because of hysteresis, higher economic activity improves the supply side (for example, by reactivating people who had withdrawn from the labour force), which permits equilibrium output to rise. An important difference between Case 1 and Case 2 is that the economy with hysteresis (Case 2) returns to the inflation target in the new equilibrium at higher output.[22]

Thus, if expectations are anchored to the central bank's inflation target and there is hysteresis, the implementation of the central bank's policy using the *MR* equation will produce convergence of the economy to the target inflation rate and the target output. This means that the equilibrium output level is not determined purely on the supply-side and aggregate demand policy can be effective in raising it. The economy

[22] Further analysis of this case extending the 3-equation model can be found in Michl and Oliver (2019).

shown in Case 2 is clearly better off following the adoption of the higher output target. We discuss the implications of this result for macroeconomic policy in situations of depressed aggregate demand below. But first we ask if this result is too good to be true.

4.4.3 The Lucas critique, anchoring, and hysteresis

Taken literally, the result we have just seen is striking: it shows that in the presence of anchoring and hysteresis, it is possible to achieve central bank targets for *both* output and inflation. However, the Lucas critique cautions against interpreting this result as resurrecting the ability of the policy maker to choose *any* level of output while maintaining inflation at target. The Lucas critique prompts us to ask the question: is it in the interest of the private sector to continue to adopt anchored inflation expectations if the policy maker seeks to exploit its apparent ability to raise output to its target? Will inflation expectations become unanchored?

In the simulation in Figure 4.10, Case 2, recall that in period 5, the central bank raises its output target and keeps the inflation target unchanged, which produces convergence to a new equilibrium with higher output and with inflation at target. The economy experiences a temporary 'inflation surprise' as shown in the figure where for a number of periods, inflation is above target. It appears that only a temporary cost is incurred to achieve a lasting gain in a higher output level. Adopting the higher output target is welfare-improving.

There are two potential problems with this. The first is whether the 'inflation surprise' serves to de-anchor inflation expectations. The private sector may have adopted anchored expectations because it believed the central bank would not take advantage of this possibility in order to achieve its output target.

The second problem is revealed when we reconsider the supply-side of the 3-equation model. For simplicity, we normally model the wage-setting curve as linear. However, as the discussion of the model of wage-setting in Chapter 2 makes clear, as unemployment becomes very low, the WS curve becomes steeper as it approaches the labour supply curve (which may be vertical). At very low unemployment, vacancies are high and the cost of job loss becomes very small so employers have to offer high wages to elicit effort from workers. This reminds us that the supply-side will impose a limit on the extent to which a higher output level can be targeted. Placing a limit on the maximum equilibrium output level attainable, which we call y_e^{max} restricts the hysteresis process from operating: it reintroduces a trade-off with higher output possible but at the cost of a higher rate of inflation in the new equilibrium.[23] This trade-off is shown in Figure 4.11, Case 3. The permanent discrepancy between inflation and the target raises a problem for the credibility of the inflation target as an anchor for expectations.

[23] Once a maximum level of equilibrium output is introduced, equilibrium output is modelled as $y_e = \min(y_e^{max}, \theta y_t + (1-\theta)y_{e,t-1})$.

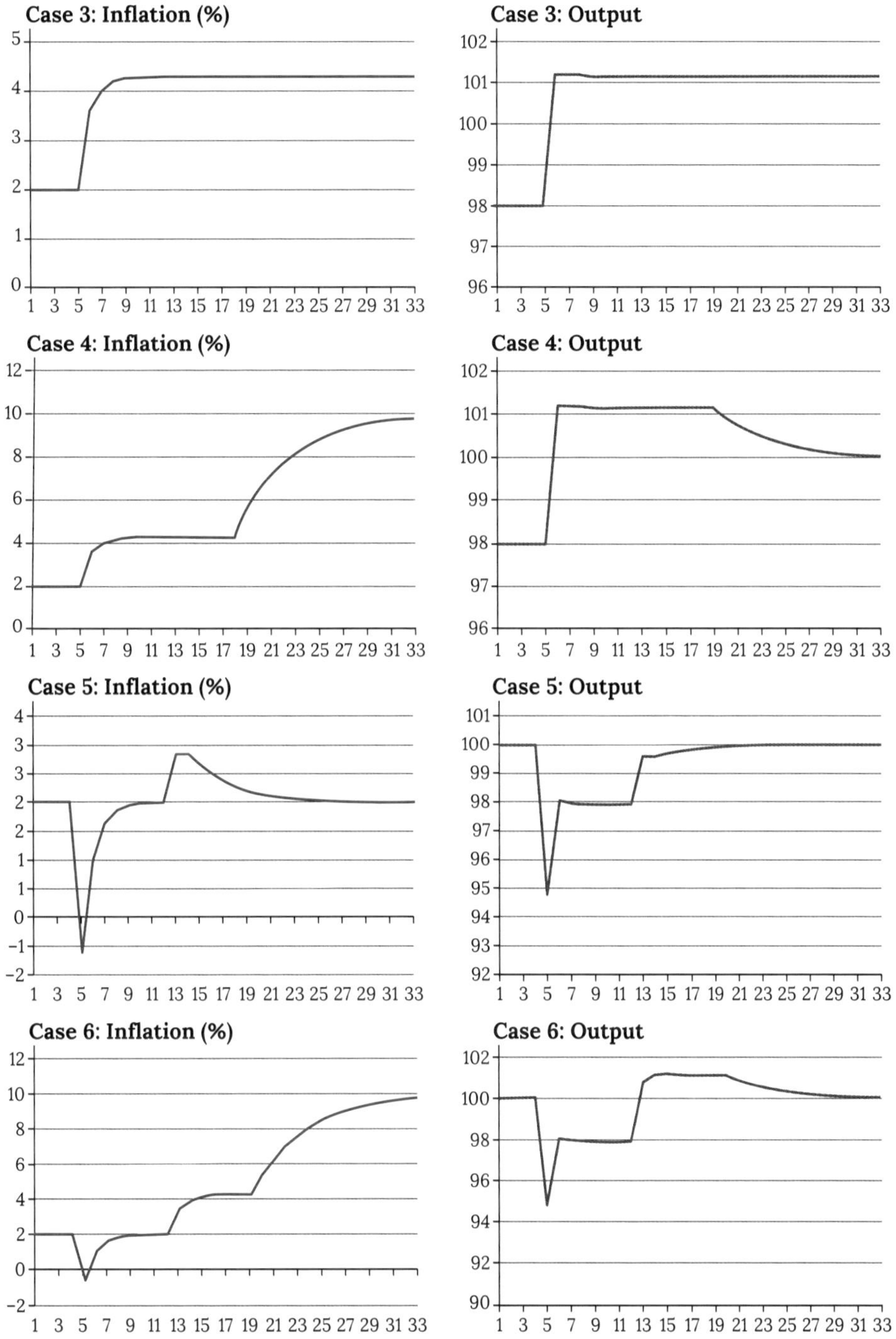

Figure 4.11 Case 3 (supply-side constraints on maximum equilibrium output), Case 4 (expectations becoming unanchored), Case 5 (responding to a recession), and Case 6 (an overly ambitious response to a recession) are described in the text. The x-axis represents the number of periods elapsed, starting in period 1. The y axis on the left-hand side graphs represents inflation in the model, in percent increase in prices per period, while the y-axis on the right-hand side graphs represents output per period relative to initial output (98 in Case 3 and 4, 100 in Case 5 and 6).

The Lucas critique warns that if inflation is persistently higher than target, the assumption that inflation expectations are anchored will become untenable. Sooner or later, wage setters will cease to believe in the inflation target and the credibility factor, χ, will fall to zero. This is shown in Figure 4.11, Case 4, which is identical to Case 3 until period 20 when expectations become unanchored. The inflation bias result re-emerges and inflation converges to a yet higher rate. A policy maker would then be faced with the problem of implementing costly disinflation and rebuilding its reputation as an inflation-targeting central bank. This echoes the problems of the 1980s.

A negative demand shock

To focus attention for policy analysis on the contribution as well as the limitations of the model with anchoring and hysteresis, we return to the scenario of a deep recession caused by a contraction of aggregate demand.

Result 1: In the absence of output targeting, the economy experiences a permanently lower level of output in the new equilibrium with inflation at target. This results from hysteresis—the supply side damage caused by the recession lowers output and raises unemployment, which become the new established equilibrium levels. This is shown in the evolution of the economy up to period 12 in Figure 4.11, Case 5, where the negative demand shock occurs in period 5.

Result 2: The previous outcome can be avoided if the policy maker targets the *pre-recession* equilibrium output level (which, by assumption, is less than the maximum output level determined by the supply-side). As illustrated in the simulation, the economy experiences a temporary overshooting of the inflation target on the path back to equilibrium. This is shown from period 12 in Case 5. The policy announced in 2020 by the US Federal Reserve of 'average inflation targeting' would be consistent with this approach.

Result 3: If the policy maker were to choose an over-ambitious output target above the maximum determined by the supply side, i.e. $y^T > y_e^{max}$, then following a period in which inflation is persistently above target, it is likely that inflation expectations become unanchored. This is shown in Figure 4.11, Case 6. In the new equilibrium, output would be at equilibrium (not at target, i.e. $y = y_e < y_e^{max} < y^T$) and inflation would be higher than target, replicating the result of inflation bias.

These three results are combined in two simulations (Case 5 and Case 6) that provide a narrative to illuminate post financial crisis macroeconomic performance and policy options. Both simulations begin with the economy in a deep recession caused by a contraction of aggregate demand that hits in period 5. In each case, the economy experiences hysteresis and can be observed 5 periods after the shock with inflation back at target after an initial decline but with output at a new lower equilibrium below the initial level of 100.

In Case 5, in period 12, the central bank recognizes the damage caused by hysteresis and changes its behaviour replacing the contemporaneous equilibrium output level in its loss function by the pre-recession equilibrium level. This becomes its target level of output. By adopting this target, the central bank guides the economy back to its initial equilibrium. As noted in Result 2 above, this path sees a temporary blip of inflation above target.

The situation in Case 6 is the same until period 12. However, the central bank then decides on an output target that is more ambitious. It sets $y^T > y_e^{max}$. Result 3 plays out: after many periods in which inflation is persistently above target, in period 20, wage setters drop the inflation anchor in forming their expectations of inflation. The central bank has lost credibility and expectations are unanchored. As shown, inflation rises to a new higher level, where it stabilizes (above 10% in the simulation) and output drops to the original equilibrium level (100). Costly disinflation would be necessary. It is clear the outcome in Case 6 is undesirable. We now summarize the lessons of the model and the simulations.

Constraints on the policy maker in the model with anchoring and hysteresis

First, it is clear that the policy maker is not free to choose any arbitrary output target. There is a supply-side constraint. Second, if there are errors in expectations in equilibrium, we predict the de-anchoring of inflation expectations.

The model provides insight about the past forty years of macroeconomic performance and policy. The high unemployment in the 1980s produced hysteresis. In the absence of anchored inflation expectations, high costs of disinflation were experienced in many OECD economies. Inflation targeting was adopted in the 1990s and inflation expectations of wage setters became anchored to the inflation target. The large negative aggregate demand shock following the financial crisis of 2008–09 produced hysteresis. The model predicts that the combination of anchored expectations and hysteresis leaves economies with output permanently lower and with inflation at target (rather than with a deflationary spiral as modelled in Chapter 3). Had central banks targeted the pre-recession output level and been willing to accept a temporary rise in inflation above target (along the lines of the Fed's proposal of average inflation targeting), the model predicts a less costly outcome: output at the pre-recession level and inflation at target (as in Figure 4.11, Case 5).

This narrative has implications for economic management in other deep recessions such as the one associated with Covid-19 and the war in Ukraine. It encourages the policy maker to be aware of the implications of hysteresis for the application of its policy rule. It also warns against proposals that fail to take account of the maximum output level determined by the supply side and of the likely de-anchoring of inflation expectations that comes with overambitious output targeting. The negative supply-side shock due to the Ukrainian war highlights the dangers. Central banks are hesitant to acknowledge the implications of hysteresis for their optimal monetary policy decisions because of the uncertainty that surrounds estimates of equilibrium output, or as it is often referred to in the policy discussion, potential output. The model considered here suggests that the costs that are associated with failing to take account of hysteresis following a negative demand shock can be considerable. The Fed's average inflation targeting approach is one way for central banks to help communicate a policy that takes account of hysteresis, allowing for a temporary inflation surprise as the economy returns to its pre-existing level of equilibrium output.

4.5 CONCLUSIONS

This chapter has taken a closer look at inflation and monetary policy.

We set out four ways in which inflation expectations are commonly modelled, each of which implies a different form of the Phillips curve and provides insight for a specific historical period of policy making. They are: *static* expectations, where expected inflation is constant; *adaptive* expectations, where expected inflation is equal to last period's inflation; *rational* expectations, where agents form their forecasts using the model and taking into account all available information; and *anchored expectations*, where expectations incorporate the central bank's inflation target.

Amending the 3-equation model by using the different Phillips curves allows us to answer some interesting questions about the part played by expectations in the macroeconomy:

1. When inflation expectations are formed rationally, how does this change the role of the central bank in the 3-equation model of the economy? The central bank's job is easier under rational expectations. It can directly influence the public's inflation expectations, which means that adopting a lower or higher inflation target is not accompanied by a costly adjustment process. If there is an inflation shock, then under REH, the central bank implements a one-period tightening to minimize its losses. Unlike the standard case of adaptive inflation expectations, inflation does not get built into the economy, requiring a prolonged period of negative output gaps as the economy moves along the *MR* curve to equilibrium.
2. Why do modern central banks communicate to the public and financial markets about monetary policy? Central bank communication is directly related to transparency and credibility. If the rational expectations hypothesis does not hold, it is more likely that inflation expectations will stay close to target if the public are better informed about monetary policy. This was one of the key reasons for central banks introducing explicit inflation targets in the first place. Anchored expectations incorporate the inflation target and when firms and households have more confidence in the credibility of the central bank, this acquires a higher weight in the Phillips curve equation. A consequence is that the adjustment to shocks is less costly.
3. What is the Lucas critique? What dangers does it highlight for economic policy making? The Lucas critique concerns the problems of basing policy decisions on forecasting models that rely on relationships found in historical data. If the relationships in the models are conditional on the historical policy regime, then the models are rendered obsolete when the policy regime changes. There is a danger that constructing policy using these models will fail to produce the intended policy response due to the fact that economic agents change their behaviour when the new policy regime is introduced. More generally, the Lucas critique alerts us to the risks of assuming invariant behaviour when formulating policy. The de-anchoring of inflation expectations is a good example.
4. What happens when the monetary policy maker with an inflation target, targets output above equilibrium? How do expectations affect this process? The outcome

is that in the medium run, while output is at equilibrium, inflation is above target. This is called inflation bias. Whether expectations are adaptive or rational does not influence the equilibrium, only the pace of adjustment. Under adaptive expectations the process of adjustment takes time, under rational expectations there is not protracted adjustment to the new medium-run equilibrium. Inflation bias is most likely to occur when the government is able to exert control over monetary policy. A government with an over-ambitious output target would actually be better off targeting y_e, but cannot credibly commit to that output target. The problem can be alleviated by delegating control of monetary policy to an independent central bank.

5. With anchored inflation expectations and when equilibrium output is path-dependent (or equivalently, subject to hysteresis), monetary policy can successfully achieve target output above equilibrium with inflation remaining at target. The logic is that a deep recession drives output down and unemployment up. Workers become displaced from the labour force as their skills erode and this pushes the WS curve up, raising equilibrium unemployment. There is a new lower path-dependent equilibrium level of output. As long as inflation expectations are anchored (i.e. with some weight on the inflation target), the central bank can target the pre-recession (equilibrium) level of output above the new low equilibrium and guide the economy back to higher output, which is consistent with stable inflation at the central bank's target. However, targeting too high a level of output could cause the anchored expectations to unravel, leading to inflation bias.

Until the last chapter of the book, which introduces the real business cycle model and the New Keynesian DSGE model, we use as the base case a hybrid model where the central bank is forward-looking and has model-consistent expectations. The behaviour of wage and price setters is modelled by a Phillips curve with lagged inflation (where fully anchored expectations is a special case). These choices reflect features of real-world economies (inflation is persistent, disinflations are costly in terms of unemployment and there are lags in monetary transmission) and provide a reasonable match to the way central banks describe their decision-making. Nevertheless, the Lucas critique needs to be kept in mind when designing and evaluating economic policy. Likewise, although the workhorse model does not exhibit hysteresis, this phenomenon—explored further in Chapter 15—is an important part of understanding contemporary macroeconomic problems.

4.6 APPENDIX

4.6.1 Inflation bias extensions

Inflation bias: Adaptive expectations and a dynamic loss function

What happens to inflation bias when the central bank places weight on losses due to inflation above target in future periods? Intuitively, we would expect this to reduce the bias. In this case, the central bank minimizes the loss function, where L is defined as above in terms of deviations from target output and target inflation:

$$L = \sum_{i=0}^{\infty} \frac{1}{(1+\delta)^i} L_{t+i}, \qquad \text{(intertemporal central bank loss function)}$$

As before the economy begins at point A in medium-run equilibrium. From Figure 4.12, it is clear that losses accumulate as the economy moves to point Z. The greater the weight placed on those future losses, the more costly is the inflation bias and the less attractive to the central bank is the adoption of the output target above equilibrium. In the example shown in Figure 4.12, we compare two paths for the economy starting from the initial equilibrium at point A, where $\pi^E = \pi^T$. In the path $A', B', \ldots$, the policy maker chooses to minimize the current loss function, disregarding the long-term consequences of its choices for inflation, i.e. it implements the policy shown by the MR curve, ending up at Z′ with inflation bias. In the second path, denoted by $A, B, C, \ldots$, the policy maker chooses to apply a policy consistent with the inflation target and remain at the same point for all periods. This eliminates inflation surprises caused by the policy maker. From the loss contours in the example shown, losses are smaller at B′ than at B, they are the same at C and C′ and for every period thereafter, losses are lower with the second strategy.

Returning to the equation, at one extreme, with $\delta \to \infty$, the central bank's loss function reverts to the static one where the future losses don't count and the economy ends up at Z′. At the other extreme, $\delta = 0$ and the losses ahead are never worth it and the economy remains at point A. For other values of δ, the equilibrium will lie on the line between A and Z′.

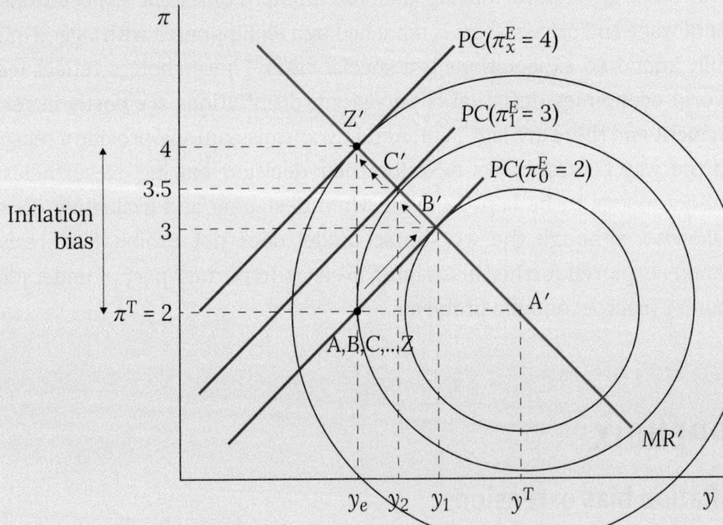

Figure 4.12 Inflation bias under two extremes: a fully forward-looking central bank ($\delta = 0$) and one with a static loss function ($\delta \to \infty$).

Inflation bias: Deriving a solution under anchored expectations

We will show how to derive a solution for the inflation bias and output levels, under anchored expectations. First, we begin with the anchored expectations Phillips curve equation,

$$\pi_t = \left[\chi\pi^T + (1-\chi)\pi_{t-1}\right] + \alpha(y_t - y_e) \qquad \text{(anchored expectations Phillips curve)}$$

This is equivalent to,

$$\pi_t - \pi^T = (1-\chi)(\pi_{t-1} - \pi^T) + \alpha(y_t - y_e)$$

Now consider the central bank loss function, and substitute in the Phillips curve from above,

$$L = (y_t - y^T)^2 + \beta(\pi_t - \pi^T)^2 \qquad \text{(loss function)}$$

$$L = (y_t - y^T)^2 + \beta[(1-\chi)(\pi_{t-1} - \pi^T) + \alpha(y_t - y_e)]^2 \qquad \text{(substituting in Phillips curve)}$$

Minimizing the loss function by setting $\frac{\partial L}{\partial y_t} = 0$ then rearranging, gives,

$$2(y_t - y^T) + 2\alpha\beta(\pi_t - \pi^T) = 0$$

$$y_t = y^T - \alpha\beta(\pi_t - \pi^T) \qquad (4.6)$$

Finally, substituting this into the Phillips curve equation gives:

$$\pi_t - \pi^T = (1-\chi)(\pi_t - \pi^T) + \alpha(y^T - y_e) - \alpha^2\beta(\pi_t - \pi^T)$$

Notice that π_t appears on the right-hand side instead of π_{t-1}; this is because at equilibrium it must be the case that $\pi_t = \pi_{t-1}$. We can now try to find the solution for inflation and output. First, expand all brackets,

$$\pi_t - \pi^T = \pi_t - \chi\pi_t - \pi^T + \chi\pi^T + \alpha y^T - \alpha y_e - \alpha^2\beta\pi_t + \alpha^2\beta\pi^T$$

Note that there are π_t and π^T terms on both sides which cancel out. Now rearrange:

$$\alpha^2\beta\pi_t + \chi\pi_t = \alpha^2\beta\pi^T + \chi\pi^T + \alpha y^T - \alpha y_e$$

The first two terms on either side have a common factor of $(\alpha^2\beta + \chi)$. We divide both sides by this term to get an expression for inflation bias,

$$\pi_t = \pi^T + \frac{\alpha(y^T - y_e)}{\alpha^2\beta + \chi} \qquad \text{(inflation bias with anchored expectations, inflation)}$$

We consider the meaning of this equation at the end of the section.

We can now substitute this expression into equation 4.6, immediately cancelling out the two π^T terms,

$$y_t = y^T - \alpha\beta\left(\frac{\alpha(y^T - y_e)}{\alpha^2\beta + \chi}\right)$$

We can rearrange further by first multiplying the right-hand side by $\frac{\alpha^2\beta+\chi}{\alpha^2\beta+\chi}$,

$$y_t = \frac{1}{\alpha^2\beta + \chi}(\alpha^2\beta y^T + \chi y^T - \alpha^2\beta y^T + \alpha^2\beta y_e)$$

The $\alpha^2\beta y^T$ terms cancel. Finally, we can add and subtract χy_e on the right-hand side, which allows us to take out a y_e term, yielding an expression for output:

$$y_t = y_e + \frac{\chi(y^T - y_e)}{\alpha^2\beta + \chi} \qquad \text{(inflation bias with anchored expectations, output)}$$

Using the two inflation bias equations above, if we assume the economy moves to an equilibrium where $\pi = \pi_{t-1} = \pi^*$, then

$$\pi_t \to \pi^* = \pi^T + \frac{\alpha(y^T - y_e)}{\alpha^2\beta + \chi} \tag{4.7}$$

$$y_t \to y^* = y_e + \frac{\chi(y^T - y_e)}{\alpha^2\beta + \chi} \tag{4.8}$$

As we would expect, when the central bank's output target coincides with equilibrium output (in other words, $y^T - y_e = 0$), the results for equilibrium inflation and output are inflation at target and output at the equilibrium level. In that case, the anchoring coefficient, χ affects the path to equilibrium (as shown in Figure 4.7b), but not the equilibrium itself.

However, if the output target of the central bank is higher than equilibrium, we get an inflation bias term that is modified by the extent to which inflation expectations are anchored. In equation 4.7, a higher value of χ (more firmly anchored expectations) reduces the size of the last term, meaning that the extent to which inflation exceeds target inflation falls for any given y^T. Meanwhile the implications for equilibrium output depend on χ as follows:

1. $\chi = 0$. In this case, $y^* = y_e$
2. $\chi > 0$. In this case, $y^* > y_e$.

A larger value of χ implies a smaller increase in medium-run inflation *and* a higher level of output above equilibrium. This means there is a 'permanent' trade-off between inflation and output. Using equations 4.7 and 4.8, we can express the trade-off as follows:

$$\pi^* - \pi^T = \frac{\alpha}{\chi}(y^* - y_e). \tag{4.9}$$

4.6.2 **Anchored expectations and hysteresis**

In this final section we show that if there is a tendency for past output to affect equilibrium output a central bank targeting output higher than equilibrium will be able to achieve both its output and inflation targets. This is a potentially important result for understanding how the long-lasting effect of recession on the economy (as appears to have occurred in the Great Recession) could be mitigated through aggregate demand policy.[24]

---

[24] Further analysis of this case extending the 3-equation model can be found in Michl and Oliver (2019).

As before, the Phillips curve is

$$\pi_t^E = \chi\pi^T + (1-\chi)\pi_{t-1}, \quad (4.10)$$

where $0 \leq \chi < 1$.

Hysteresis is given by

$$y_e = \theta y_t + (1-\theta)y_{e,t-1}, \quad (4.11)$$

where $0 < \theta < 1$. This means that current equilibrium output is a weighted average of last period's equilibrium output and this period's realized output. Whenever y_t is less than $y_{e,t-1}$, equilibrium output will be falling.

The loss function is as before with the output target above equilibrium:

$$L = (y_t - y^T)^2 + \beta(\pi_t - \pi^T)^2 \quad (4.12)$$

$$= (y_t - y^T)^2 + \beta[(1-\chi)(\pi_{t-1} - \pi^T) + \alpha(1-\theta)(y_t - y_{e,t-1})]^2. \quad (4.13)$$

Setting $\frac{\partial L}{\partial y_t} = 0$ gives

$$2(y_t - y^T) + 2\alpha\beta(1-\theta)(\pi_t - \pi^T) = 0. \quad (4.14)$$

And the optimum policy rule is:

$$y_t - y^T = -\alpha\beta(1-\theta)(\pi_t - \pi^T). \quad (4.15)$$

We show in the web appendix to this chapter (www.oup.com/he/carlin-soskice) that if $\chi > 0$ and $\theta > 0$, the optimum policy ensures that

$$\pi_t \rightarrow \pi^T \quad (4.16)$$

$$y_t \rightarrow y^T \quad (4.17)$$

QUESTIONS AND PROBLEMS FOR CHAPTER 4

CHECKLIST QUESTIONS

1. What role do expectations play in the IS curve that underpins the 3-equation model? Provide an example of a situation where a change in expectations of the future can influence households' behaviour in the current period and shift the IS curve.

2. What is meant by agents making 'systematic errors' under adaptive expectations? Prepare a diagram and a table to illustrate the size of the errors.

3. Describe the difference between risk and uncertainty. Provide an example of each case.

4. Assess the following statements S1 and S2. Are they both true, both false or is only one true? Justify your answer.

   S1. Rational expectations means agents do not to make systematic errors.

   S2. Rational, forward-looking central banks' forecasts are often wrong.

5. When we add rational expectations to wage and price setting in the 3-equation model keeping the model otherwise unchanged, how does that change the predictions of the model? How is the result affected if wages are fully flexible?

6. Explain what is meant by the following statement: 'disinflation can be costless if the central bank is perfectly credible'. Draw the impulse response functions for output, inflation and the real interest rate following an inflation shock and interpret your results, when:

   a. inflation expectations are fully backward looking

   b. inflation expectations are firmly anchored to the inflation target.

7. Assess the following statements S1 and S2. Are they both true, both false or is only one true? Justify your answer.

   S1. Better communication by central banks can influence the path the economy takes after an economic shock.

   S2. Better communication by central banks does not affect how economic agents react to interest rate changes (which is the main tool used by monetary policy makers to achieve their inflation target).

8. Provide a definition of the Lucas critique. What is the relevance of the critique to (a) the stagflation of the 1970s and (b) to proposals for expansionary macroeconomic policy post-pandemic?

9. Imagine the government is able to exert control over monetary policy. What happens under adaptive expectations when the government targets a level of output above equilibrium? Is there a short-run trade-off between inflation and unemployment? How about under rational expectations? What difference, if any, does it make if inflation expectations are anchored to the inflation target and there is hysteresis?

10. Can a government with an overly ambitious output target credibly commit to targeting equilibrium output? If not, then how can they solve the inflation bias problem?

PROBLEMS

1. Use this chapter and your own knowledge and further research to answer the following questions:

   a. Is Keynes' treatment of expectations consistent with the rational expectations hypothesis?

b. Do you think the inflationary trends following the Covid-19 recovery are consistent with the Adaptive Expectations Hypothesis?

2. Collect data on inflation and unemployment for the UK and the US during the 1970s and 1980s using OECD.Stat. The 1980s was a period of significant disinflation for the two economics. Use the data gathered and the content of this chapter to answer the following questions:

a. Was the disinflation costly (in terms of rising unemployment)?

b. Does the data provide evidence that inflation expectations were being formed rationally during this period?

c. How can the concepts of anchored expectations and hysteresis be used to suggest what the UK and US governments could have done to reduce the costs associated with disinflation.

3. Assume that inflation expectations are formed rationally. Use the 3-equation model to show the adjustment of the economy to a permanent demand and a permanent supply shock. Provide a period-by-period explanation of the adjustment process (as done in Chapter 3). How does the central bank reaction differ from the cases where we assumed adaptive inflation expectations (as shown in the Chapter 3)?

4. This question uses the Macroeconomic Simulator (available at www.oup.com/he/carlin-soskice) to show how central bank credibility affects the adjustment of the economy following an inflation shock. Start by opening the simulator and choosing the closed economy version. Then reset all shocks by clicking the appropriate button on the left-hand side of the main page. Use the simulator and the content of this chapter to work through the following:

a. Apply a 2% positive inflation shock. Save your data.

b. Adjust the degree of inflation inertia/credibility of the central bank to zero (i.e. full credibility, which is equivalent to setting $\chi = 1$ in the anchored expectations Phillips curve equation). Save your data.

c. Use the impulse response functions in your saved data and Section 4.4.1 to compare the adjustment path of the economy following the shock in each case. Use the 3-equation model to explain any differences in the adjustment paths.

d. Set the degree of inflation inertia/credibility of the central bank to 0.5 (i.e. partial credibility). Save your data.

e. What do our answers to parts a. to d. tell us about the benefit to a central bank of increasing their credibility?

f. How might a central bank go about increasing their credibility?

5. Extend the data in Figure 3.3 to the present. Use the insights from the simulations in Figure 4.11 to discuss the path of inflation and unemployment in the UK following the pandemic and the war in Ukraine.

INTERESTED IN EXPLORING THESE TOPICS FURTHER?

Visit www.oup.com/he/carlin-soskice to consolidate and extend your learning with the multiple-choice questions, Animated Analytical Diagrams, and web appendix accompanying this chapter.

Additionally, visit https://tinyco.re/inflationtool to find CORE Econ's Interactive Learning Tool which features further content related to this chapter.

PART

2

MONEY, BANKING, MONETARY AND FISCAL POLICY

CHAPTER

5

MONEY, BANKING, AND THE MACROECONOMY

This chapter has been co-authored by Wendy Carlin, Stanislas Lalanne, and David Soskice.

5.1 INTRODUCTION

If the banking system is working well its presence is hardly noticed. Despite its role in providing essential services in the modern economy, it is treated as part of the background infrastructure much like the electricity grid. When the financial crisis erupted in 2008, economists and the public were suddenly made much more aware of the banking system: the system's primary function is to intermediate between borrowers and lenders and, although at the time it was one of the most regulated industries in the economy, it became the site of a crisis that touched households and firms across the high-income world.

This chapter is the first of four in this book that focus on the interaction of the financial system and the macroeconomy. In this one, the building blocks of the financial system are set out with particular emphasis on understanding the banking system—a subset of the wider financial system. Chapters 8, 9, and 10 return to the theme of financial instability. To make the chapters easier to navigate, we start by briefly outlining the content each will cover:

Chapter 5: This chapter explains the role the banking system plays in the macroeconomy both as a conduit through which the central bank responds to shocks originating elsewhere and as a source of macroeconomic shocks itself. The chapter opens by highlighting the difference between the policy interest rate and the lending rate and illustrates how a shock to the banking system as occurred in the credit crunch of 2007–08 can have macroeconomic effects.

Introducing banks to the model raises a series of questions that are addressed in the rest of the chapter. What determines the margin between the lending rate and the policy interest rate? What is the business model of a commercial bank in a fractional reserve banking system and specifically, what services does it provide, and what are the risks it faces and that it poses to the wider economy? What is the relationship between commercial banks and the central bank and how does that relationship enable the central bank to implement monetary policy?

Understanding this relationship helps us better understand how monetary policy is used to stabilize the economy, as well as understanding whether or not there is a causal connection between central bank reserves, the money supply, and inflation

(**Chapter 6**). A different tool available to policy makers, fiscal policy, is introduced in **Chapter** 7.

Chapter 8: In Chapter 8, we reevaluate the usual assumption in macroeconomics that the financial system runs smoothly by looking at potentially destabilizing features, such as the financial accelerator and asset price bubbles. We introduce the concept of a *financial cycle*, distinct from the *business cycle*, which can be fuelled by a house price bubble and amplified by the risk-taking behaviour of investment banks. When the bubble bursts, a financial crisis can ensue. We show how financial cycle upswings can occur despite successful inflation targeting.

Chapter 9: We apply the framework developed in Chapters 5 and 8 to the global financial crisis of 2008–09, and its aftermath in the Great Recession of the next decade. This allows the financial crisis and the macroeconomic policy and banking regulation responses it provoked to be explained and analysed within a coherent macroeconomic framework.

Chapter 10: This chapter focuses on the lessons for financial stability policy arising both from the financial crisis and from new challenges, including those associated with FinTech and Big Tech firms and digital currencies.

In the first of these chapters, we begin by setting out a simple way of incorporating banks in the 3-equation model introduced in Chapter 3. This extension highlights the vital importance of banks in facilitating borrowing and lending in the economy and in the transmission of monetary policy. Continuity of banking services lies behind the IS curve. Whenever we use the IS curve, we assume households and firms can implement their planned spending decisions by using money, credit and the payments system.

The new elements we introduce are as follows:

1. A distinction between the policy interest rate, which is set by the central bank through its monopoly over the supply of *central bank* or *base money*, and the lending rate, which is the cost of borrowing the private sector faces.
2. Commercial banks, also simply called banks in this chapter, which set the lending rate, make loans to the private sector, thereby creating *bank money* (deposits for households and firms), borrow and lend in the money market, and keep reserve accounts (base money) at the central bank.[1] In addition to setting the lending rate, we shall see why banks impose credit rationing with the result that some households (and small and medium-sized firms) face credit constraints. This explains the origin of credit constraints that are incorporated in the IS curve.
3. The money market, which in our simplified representation of the financial system includes the interbank market, is where borrowing and lending *among* commercial banks takes place and also where saver households can buy and sell government bonds.

---

[1] Apart from setting a lending rate, banks also set a deposit rate. We simplify our model, both in the loan creation example in Section 5.4.1, and in the deposit part of Appendix 5.7.1, to assume the deposit rate is zero. This is often the case for *demand deposit* accounts, which will be introduced in Section 5.3.1.

4. Balance sheets of commercial banks help clarify the concepts of liquidity, solvency and the importance of a bank's equity for financial stability. The central bank's balance sheet has come into prominence since the financial crisis when they purchased large quantities of bonds (the policy of *quantitative easing*).
5. The contrast between how inflation-targeting central banks set the policy interest rate before and after the financial crisis. Before the crisis, the central bank adjusted the policy interest rate up and down in the so-called *scarce reserves* regime by announcing the rate and allowing the supply of reserves to adjust to the demand at the new rate. Since the financial crisis, the policy interest rate is the rate the central bank pays on reserve accounts. This is known as the *ample reserves* regime.

5.2 INTEREST RATES, BANKS, AND FINANCIAL MARKETS

5.2.1 Two interest rates: Shocks from the banking system

In the 3-equation model up to this point, we have assumed that the central bank stabilizes the economy by setting the *policy* interest rate. When we introduce the banking system, however, we need to distinguish between the policy rate set by the central bank and the *lending* rate, which is the rate relevant for the spending decisions of households and firms represented by the IS curve. For the central bank to implement its policy decisions, there needs to be a predictable relationship between the policy and lending rates.

A shock to the banking system

We shall see in Section 5.3 that the lending rate is a markup on the policy rate, which reflects the optimizing behaviour of banks. In simple terms, to make a profit, the bank must cover its operational costs including assessing creditworthiness of borrowers, and the cost of bad loans, from the margin between their lending rate and the cost of their borrowing.

We can represent this in the 3-equation model by explicitly labelling the vertical axis in the IS diagram 'Lending interest rate, r', since this is the one relevant for the spending decisions of households and firms shown in the IS curve. Figure 5.1a (the left-hand panel) shows the decision-making of the central bank in the usual way in the lower panel. Once it has decided on the optimal output gap (here, a zero output gap), the central bank works out from the IS curve the associated lending rate, labelled 'Desired lending interest rate, r_S'. The banking markup (also referred to in this book using the terms 'margin', 'spread' or 'wedge') is indicated as the vertical gap between the lending rate and the policy rate—in other words the profit the bank is making on lending if we ignore operating costs and risks of default. Using its knowledge of the banking system, specifically knowledge about the size of the markup, the central bank sets the policy rate to deliver the desired lending rate. The policy rate that delivers the lending rate r_S is labelled 'Policy rate, r^P'.

We can now look at the implications for the economy of a shock to the banking system. Let us use as an example a situation where banks suddenly take the view

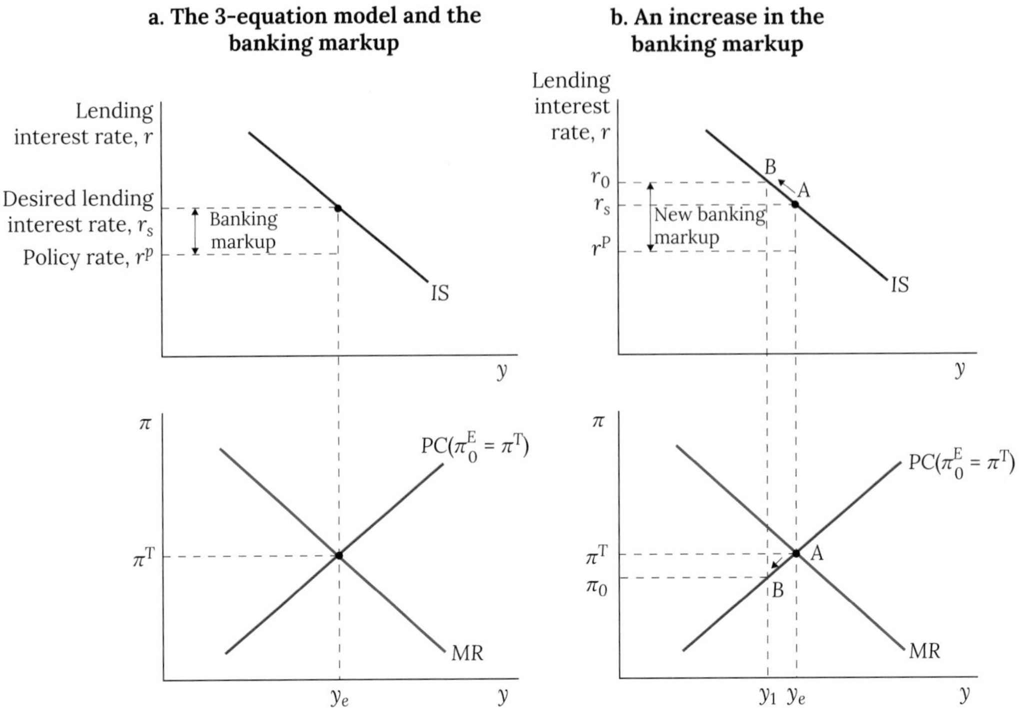

Figure 5.1 The 3-equation model and the banking markup.

that the loans they have made are riskier than previously thought. This leads them to increase the margin of the lending rate above the policy rate to cover the greater expected losses on loans. In this example, the increase in the lending rate is a shock unanticipated by the central bank so the policy rate is unchanged. Figure 5.1b shows the macroeconomic consequences: the unexpected rise in the lending rate, from a higher markup but an unchanged policy rate, leads to a contraction of aggregate demand to the north-west along the IS curve. Output falls to y_1, while inflation falls to π_0.

From our analysis in Chapter 3, an inflation-targeting central bank would react to the fall in output as a consequence of the negative shock to aggregate demand (the move along the IS curve to point B) by forecasting a fall in inflation expectations next period to π_0. It would then find its desired position on the MR curve, work out the lending rate that would deliver this positive output gap and lower the policy rate accordingly to get the economy on the path back to medium-run equilibrium.

We can summarize the causal chain of central bank decision-making as follows:

→ a negative shock to banks

→ rise in interest rate margin (banking markup) and a higher lending rate

→ fall in output

→ fall in inflation, and therefore in forecast inflation, shifts the PC

→ the central bank (CB) finds desired output gap on MR

→ CB calculates the lending rate on IS to achieve this output gap

→ CB sets new lower policy rate to achieve this lending rate and reach the MR.

The important point to take away from this example is that shocks to the banking system that change the interest rate margin influence aggregate demand—i.e. they have real economic effects. Note that we use a stylized framework, where the central bank has precise information on the size of the markup. In reality, there is likely to be much uncertainty over the markup, and the central bank must constantly monitor a range of data to understand the markup.

5.2.2 A simplified representation of the financial system

There are many different financial markets, assets and interest rates in the economy. To cut through the complexity, we greatly simplify and leave to one side concepts that are not directly relevant to understanding the behaviour of banks and the operation of fiscal, monetary and macro-prudential policy. Some additional assets and markets will be introduced as needed in Chapters 8 and 9 when explaining the financial cycle and the behaviour of investment banks, and their significance for the financial crisis.

We define the banking system as consisting of commercial banks and investment banks (investment banks are not covered in this chapter), while the financial system is broader and includes institutions such as stock and bond markets and pension funds.

Three interest rates

In practice, there are many different interest rates ranging from the policy rate set by the central bank, to the two-week lending rate in the interbank market, to the yield on short-term and longer term government bonds, to the lending rate on mortgages and the interest rate on credit card debt and pay-day loans. We will simplify this to just considering three interest rates:

1. **The lending rate:** As seen previously, this is the cost of borrowing to the private sector, and together with the IS curve, determines current output.
2. **Money market rate:** Another important interest rate is the rate at which banks can borrow from and lend to other banks, which determines their cost of borrowing, also called the *funding cost*. This is one determinant of the lending rate banks will offer. The lending rate and money market rates are set by market conditions, meaning that the central bank does not directly control them. For much of this chapter, we can use the term 'money market rate' to refer to the several interest rates set in different parts of the money market. When differences between them matter (e.g. between the interbank rate and the repo rate), we will explain why.
3. **The policy rate:** This is controlled directly by central banks. In Sections 5.5.1 and 5.5.2, we look at how central banks' definitions of the policy rate have changed over time. The Bank of England is a useful example. Prior to May 2006, the policy rate was a stated target for the money market rate, and the Bank's operations ensured that the money market rate remained close to the policy rate target. Since May 2006 the Bank of England began to pay interest on reserves deposited by commercial banks, and the policy rate is the interest rate on reserves.

Assuming perfect arbitrage, the central bank can influence the funding cost of banks (the money market rate) using the policy rate. To explain why arbitrage holds, we introduce the money market in the next subsection. We will continue to denote the

<table>
<tr><th colspan="3">The model</th><th colspan="3">The UK in 2016 (annual average nominal rates)</th></tr>
<tr><td colspan="2">The lending rate</td><td>r</td><td colspan="2">Rate on 5 year fixed rate mortgages</td><td>2.50</td></tr>
<tr><td rowspan="3">Capital and money market rate</td><td rowspan="2">Short-term interbank lending rates</td><td rowspan="2">r^p</td><td rowspan="3">Capital and money market rates</td><td>Sterling 2 week mean interbank lending rate</td><td>0.38</td></tr>
<tr><td>Sterling overnight mean interbank lending rate</td><td>0.36</td></tr>
<tr><td>Short- and medium-term government bond yields</td><td>r^p</td><td>5 year government bond yield</td><td>0.65</td></tr>
<tr><td colspan="2">The policy rate</td><td>r^p</td><td colspan="2">Official Bank Rate</td><td>0.40</td></tr>
</table>

Figure 5.2 The assumptions made in the model about real interest rates and the associated nominal interest rates from the UK in 2016.

Source: Bank of England (data accessed September 2020). Unfortunately the relevant interbank lending rate series were discontinued at the end of 2016. Similar series are available, for example from the *Financial Times*.

lending rate as r. The arbitrage assumption allows us to further simplify the model to just two rates, r^p and r, and we can treat the lending rate r simply as a markup over the policy rate r^p.

The right-hand side of Figure 5.2 provides some data on UK interest rates in 2016. We can see that there is a spectrum of interest rates in the money and capital markets. In line with our model, the average short-term money market rates, represented by the overnight and 2 week interbank rates, were almost identical to the policy rate. We use an indicator of the mortgage rate as an example of what the lending rate represents in practice. Again in line with our model, the lending rate exceeds the funding cost of banks.

Throughout this chapter, we will largely ignore the distinction between the nominal interest rate and the real interest rate. In Chapter 1, we introduced the Fisher equation, which relates the two rates directly:

$$i \approx r + \pi^E. \qquad \text{(Fisher equation)}$$

In practice the policy rate is a nominal rate, as is the money market rate and the rate that banks charge on loans, while the lending rate that actually matters for the IS curve in the 3-equation model is a real rate, r. Under normal economic conditions, the Fisher equation means that holding inflation expectations constant, reducing the nominal interest rates in the economy is the same as reducing the real interest rate, and vice versa. This allows us to simplify by calling the policy rate r^P, a real rate, and ignore how the nominal policy rate translates into the real policy rate. An example of where the distinction matters, due to zero lower bound issues, is provided at the end of this section.

The simplified financial system

Figure 5.3 shows the relation between the non-financial sector, commercial banks, and the central bank. It contains many terms that may be unfamiliar and a full understanding of how the model works will only be possible after studying the chapter. Nevertheless the diagram gives a preliminary overview, and will provide a useful point of reference as we construct the model.

The non-financial private sector

This group comprises households and non-financial firms. For a given lending rate, households and firms will choose spending and investment levels, determining current output—this relationship is the IS curve from Chapter 1. To implement their spending plans, including shifting consumption over time and borrowing to invest, they use banks. Households and firms also determine the supply side, which as we saw in Chapter 2, sets equilibrium output. Together with the IS curve, this fixes the stabilizing interest rate, r_S.

Commercial banks

Commercial banks are profit-maximizing firms. They make (risky) loans to the private sector, setting the lending rate as a markup on their funding cost. The derivation of the markup is left until Section 5.3.2. However, the determinants are intuitively plausible. The markup over the funding costs will be greater, the riskier are loans, the less the

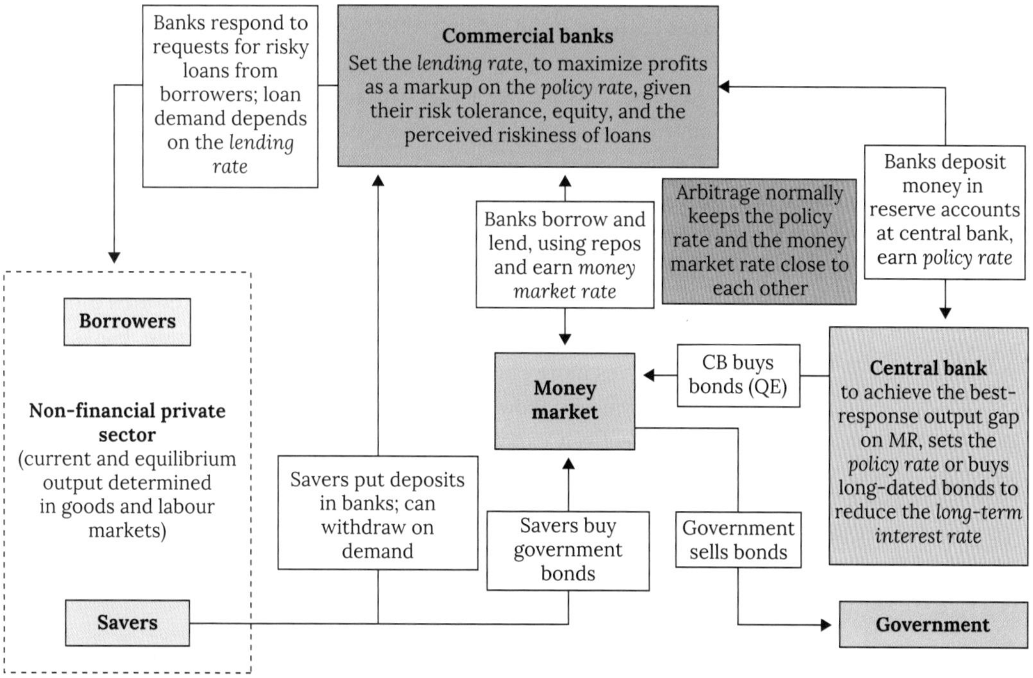

Figure 5.3 A simplified representation of the banking system.

bank is willing to bear risk, and the lower is the bank's capacity to absorb losses, which as we shall see, depends on the bank's equity.

Banks create deposits when making loans to the private sector, and can also try to attract deposits from new customers, but deposits can be withdrawn from the bank at any time. Banks also hold reserves, a type of money, at the central bank—we will explore how this works in later sections. To fund their operations, and avoid being unable to meet withdrawal demands of depositors, banks must either use reserves in their accounts at the central bank, or borrow reserves from other banks in the money market. Section 5.3.4 will provide an overview of the risk associated with customers withdrawing their deposits, which we call liquidity risk.

The central bank

Commercial banks hold deposits at the central bank, known as reserves, and earn an interest rate equal to the policy rate. In our explanation of the money market, we show why this gives the central bank indirect control over the funding costs of commercial banks. The central bank aims to minimize a loss function, as in Chapter 3. To ensure that the economy is on the MR curve, the central bank will choose a desired lending rate, and assuming knowledge of the markup, will set a policy rate to achieve this lending rate.

The money market

When we look at a typical bank balance sheet in Section 5.4.1, we see that banks do a lot of borrowing and lending in the money market. In addition to funding their lending, their money market borrowing and lending reflects the flows between different banks in the interbank market as money is transferred between the accounts of households and firms. The reason for this activity is that banks must always have enough liquidity to satisfy demand from depositors.

The option of holding balances in reserve accounts at the central bank and earning the policy rate means that there will be arbitrage between the money market rate and the policy rate. If the money market rate was below the policy rate, banks could borrow reserves on the money market and deposit them at the central bank, earning a guaranteed positive return. This would drive the money market rate up towards the policy rate.[2] Meanwhile if the money market rate was above the policy rate, banks might be able to borrow reserves more cheaply from the central bank than from the money market. Central banks typically allow banks to borrow reserves at a rate slightly higher than the policy rate, effectively capping how far money market rates can go above the policy rate. We will now look in more detail at how the money market operates.

Collateral, bonds, and repos

Before explaining how banks borrow and lend on the money market, we need to introduce collateral, bonds and repos.

1. **Collateral:** Making a loan is risky—if the borrowing individual or institution is unable to repay ('defaults' on the loan), the lender will have lost some or even all of the

[2] In practice, the money market rate is often slightly below the interest rate on reserves, as not all financial institutions are able to deposit reserves at the central bank.

money they lent out. Many types of loans will specify collateral, an asset that the lender will receive should the borrower default. Borrowing with collateral is sometimes called secured borrowing, or collateralized borrowing. One example introduced in Section 5.3.2 is the housing market, where in the event of default the lender can claim ownership of the borrower's house.

2. **Bonds:** A bond is a financial instrument sold by an institution wishing to borrow, such as a government or a company, to an investor wishing to lend. The key difference between a bond and a bank loan is that the bond can be bought by any willing investor in the bond market, and the initial buyer can sell the bond to another investor through the same market at the prevailing price. Bank loans could not traditionally be sold in the same way, but in Chapter 9 we will explore how a process known as securitization turned loans into tradeable assets in the build-up to the financial crisis. Box 5.1 provides further information about how payments on bonds are calculated, and the relationship between the market price of a bond and the interest rate.
3. **Repos:** The main way that banks borrow and lend to each other in the money market is through repos (or repurchase agreements). The term 'repo' is shorthand for sale and repurchase agreement and is a form of very short-term secured borrowing by banks. To fund their everyday activities they borrow by selling a bond in the repo market (i.e. part of the money market in our model) and promising to buy it back the next day (or 14 days later) at a slightly higher price. The difference between the prices is the interest paid on the loan, which is the repo rate. Because the borrowing takes place using the temporary transfer of ownership of the bond itself, the loan is secured. One benefit is that in times of market stress borrowers can raise funding without having to sell their bonds outright, making the 'fire sale' scenario in Section 5.3.4 less likely.

The collateral assets used for repo transactions are typically government bonds. This creates a demand for government bonds, which under most circumstances are deemed a safe asset since the government is assumed not to default on payments due. The supply of bonds by the government is shown in the bottom right-hand corner of Figure 5.3. Households and firms who wish to save can also buy government bonds in the money market as an alternative to deposits; as we shall see in Section 5.3.1, the ability of households and firms to purchase these bonds influences money demand.[3] The availability of alternative savings opportunities (equivalent in terms of risk) keeps the interest rates close together under normal market conditions and we simplify the discussion by only talking about money market rates.[4]

---

[3] In reality, some of these government bonds will be bought in the capital markets, which are markets that house financial securities with longer maturities than the money markets. In addition households rarely purchase bonds directly, and will usually use intermediaries such as pension funds. For simplicity we assume that this all falls under what we called the money market and that households purchase bonds.

[4] This equivalence does not always hold: for a case study of a disruption in the US repo market in 2019, which caused repo rates to temporarily diverge from interbank rates, see Cheng and Wessel (2020), which we also return to at the end of Section 5.5.

BOX 5.1 How are interest rates and bond prices related?

Bonds vary according to the period over which they promise a fixed nominal payment per period and are classified in the UK as short-dated (up to a maturity of 7 years), medium (between 7 and 15 years), and long (over 15 years). US Treasury Bills are short-dated bonds, often with a one-month maturity. At the other extreme is a famous type of bond, the 'consol' or perpetuity, which has no maturity date. In the UK, no consols have been issued by the government since 1946. We look at three different cases below. What unites all of these is the promise to pay a stream of fixed payments into the future, which is why bonds are considered 'fixed income securities', and there is always an inverse relation between market prices and interest rates.

Consols

In the simple case of a consol, the nominal interest rate, i, on a bond, often known as the 'yield', is given by

$$i = \frac{\text{coupon}}{\text{price}}, \qquad \text{(bond yield; consol)}$$

where 'coupon' is a fixed payment made to the bondholder every period forever, unless the bond issuer defaults. The word coupon is used to refer to the fixed payment on the bond because this used to be a physical paper coupon which bondholders would detach and present to claim their periodic payment. The 'price' is the price at which the bond *currently trades* on the bond market, which we can call the *market price*. The market price generally differs from the price at which the bond was initially sold, but gives an indication of the price at which new bonds would sell. Consider the following numerical example. If the market price of the bond is £100, and the coupon is £5, then the interest rate is 5%. If interest rates in the market fall to 2.5%, to prevent arbitrage the rate on the bond should also fall to 2.5%. Since the coupon is fixed, it is the market price of the bond that determines the interest rate paid on such bonds. The price of the bond would rise to £200, at which point with a £5 coupon the yield becomes 2.5%. This shows that the market price of the bond and the interest rate are inversely related.

A one-year maturity bond

To explain a negative interest rate it is necessary to move away from the pure coupon bond that never matures described above because it is not possible to have a negative interest rate on a consol. We therefore go to the other extreme and look at another simple bond, one that matures in one year. On maturity, the holder of the bond will receive the 'face value' of the bond, plus a one-off coupon payment. Let the fixed amount which the bond returns on maturity be called $\overline{P}$ (for instance, if the bond has a face value of £100, and the coupon is £5, it has a $\overline{P}$ of £105, also called the redemption value). If the bond's current market price P is less than $\overline{P}$, it is called a *discount bond*, as it is selling 'at a discount.'

Formally, we can define the yield or interest rate, i, by this formula: $i = (\overline{P} - P)/P$. If we rearrange, we have an equation that expresses the yield/price relationship transparently.

$$P = \frac{\overline{P}}{1+i}, \qquad \text{(bond price; discount bond)}$$

Clearly an increase in the interest rate is associated with a decline in the market price of this bond, just as it was for a consol. From the bond pricing equation, we can now see what a negative interest rate entails. The yield on this bond becomes negative when the current market price is *greater* than the redemption value, $P > \overline{P}$. Investing in this bond yields a negative return. One reason why investors will sometimes purchase a bond with a negative return is that when interest rates are low and there is a high level of uncertainty in the economy, buying a safe bond such as a government bond will protect the investor from being exposed to risk, and can justify accepting a small loss.

This equation also says that the market price of the bond is the *present discounted value* of its future pay-outs, discounted by the current nominal rate in the market, i. We can now consider a bond with a maturity between one year and infinity, and the logic of the market price being equal to the present discounted value of payouts will still apply.

Consider a bond issued on 1 January 2020, with a face value of £100, a coupon of £5, and a maturity of 4 years. The issuer of the bond will pay the holder a £5 coupon payment on 1 January 2021, 1 January 2022, 1 January 2023, and 1 January 2024. In addition at maturity on 1 January 2024, the holder of the bond will receive the face value of £100. If the nominal interest rate i in the market is 3%, the present discounted value of payouts would be:

$$P = \frac{5}{(1.03)^1} + \frac{5}{(1.03)^2} + \frac{5}{(1.03)^3} + \frac{5}{(1.03)^4} + \frac{100}{(1.03)^4}$$
$$= 4.85 + 4.71 + 4.58 + 4.44 + 88.85 = 107.43$$

This tells us that despite the bond paying £120 over the next four years, an investor would be willing to pay at most £107.43 today. As before, the market price is inversely related to the interest rate. For instance if the nominal interest rate increased to 4%, the above calculations would give a new price of £103.63. The price of the bond may be lower than this due to default risk, but we focus on government bonds, which are typically considered a safe asset.

Repo transactions are also the main way the central bank fine tunes the supply of reserves as explained in Section 5.5 when the central bank's monetary policy operations are set out.

The yield curve, a negative demand shock, and quantitative easing

The final new element introduced in Figure 5.3 is the option of a quantitative easing policy instrument, under which the central bank buys bonds when the economy is at the zero lower bound. Understanding why an unconventional monetary policy such as quantitative easing can be required takes us back to the situation of the zero lower bound set out in Chapter 3. We must first consider the relationship between bond maturities (i.e. the time remaining before the face value of the bond must be repaid to the buyer) and their yield.

Panel a. of Figure 5.4 shows a simplified yield curve. In this example, we focus on just two kinds of bonds: short-term (S) and long-term (L), with corresponding nominal interest rates i_S and i_L. The curve slopes upwards because investors demand a premium over short-term interest rates to hold long-term bonds. This is due to the higher level of uncertainty associated with the long term. If an investor buys a ten year bond, they cannot know whether or not interest rates will rise over the next decade. If rates rise during this period this will reduce the value of their bond, and as such the investor will require a term premium to compensate for this risk (while the investor could just hold the bond to maturity, the opportunity cost will have been missing out on purchasing new bonds at the higher interest rates). Another example of uncertainty

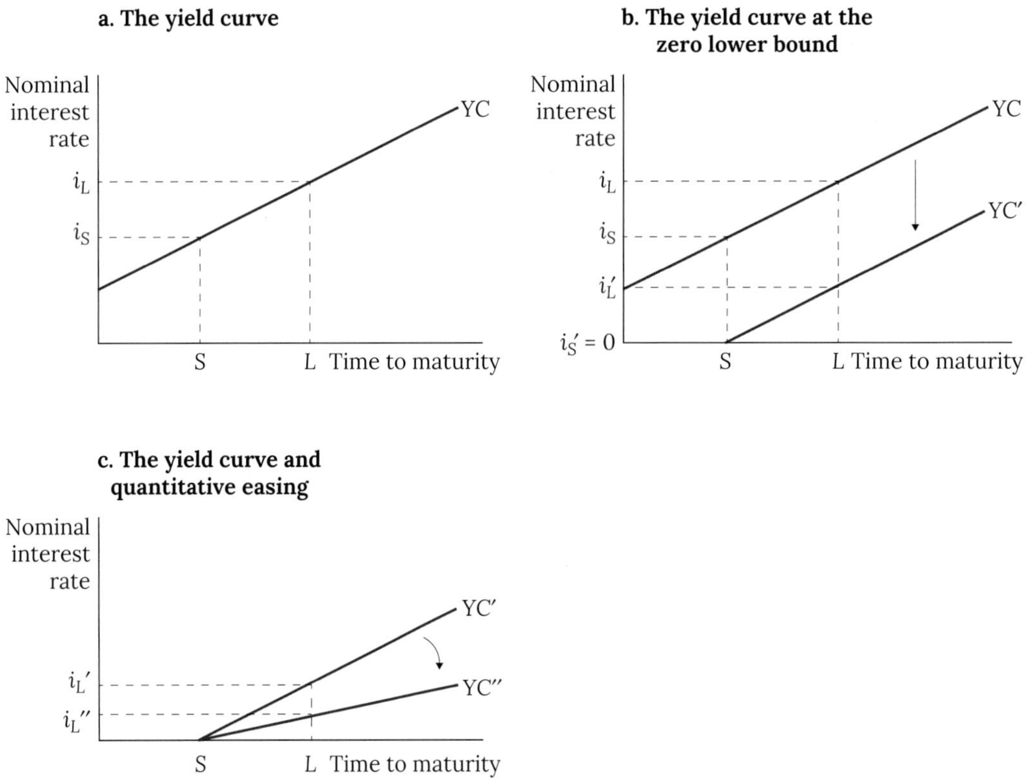

Figure 5.4 Monetary policy and the yield curve.

Note: In reality, the yield curve may not have a monotonic relationship with time to maturity. For instance if short-term rates are high but investors expect a recession in the near future, this suggests that interest rates will be cut soon to stimulate growth. Investors may therefore be happy to lock in a lower yield on long-term debt than on short-term debt, as they know that the relatively high short-term yields will not last long. This is known as 'yield curve inversion.'

is that an investor might be fairly certain whether or not there will be a recession in the next two years, but is likely to be much less certain whether there will be one in the next twenty years.

Next we consider the central bank's response to a negative demand shock. We know from the 3-equation model that the central bank will want to reduce the interest rate. Using our simplified financial system, we can see that first the central bank will lower the policy rate, which due to arbitrage will lower the money market rate, meaning a lower funding cost for banks, and in turn commercial banks will lower the lending rate. However, as seen in the zero lower bound example introduced in Chapter 3, nominal rates cannot fall below zero, which restricts feasible real policy rates r^P that the central bank can set (recall the Fisher relationship in Section 5.2.2 above). To add further complication, the policy rate is a short-term rate, while the lending rate that determines economic activity depends on both short-term and long-term rates.

Panel b. of Figure 5.4 shows a conventional monetary policy response to a large negative demand shock—the central bank lowers the policy rate to zero, which shifts the yield curve down to YC′, lowering the long-term nominal rate to i'_L.[5] The combination of both short-term and long-term nominal rates falling means that the real lending rate in the economy will have fallen as well, boosting aggregate demand by encouraging more spending and investment. As the short-term rate cannot fall below zero, this means that the long-term rate cannot fall below i'_L. For a large negative demand shock, this may be insufficient to stabilize the economy.

The central bank could respond to this by implementing a policy instrument known as quantitative easing, which involves buying large quantities of long-dated government bonds.[6] This increases the price of government bonds, and in turn decreases their yield following the inverse relation described in Box 5.1. Given the long maturity of the bonds purchased, we can model this as a pivoting of the yield curve. In panel c. of Figure 5.4 the reduction in longer term yields reduces the long-term rate from i'_L to i''_L.

Quantitative easing therefore operates by reducing interest rates at the long end of the yield curve once the central bank is no longer able to reduce the policy rate further. We will consider in more detail how quantitative easing is implemented in terms of the central bank's balance sheet in Section 5.4.2. Chapter 6 includes a more detailed discussion of QE, including its transmission mechanisms.

5.2.3 **Transmission of a shock through the banking system**

Now that we have a bird's-eye view of the financial system, it is helpful to work through an example of the extended 3-equation model incorporating banks. We use an investment boom that permanently shifts the IS curve, first examined in Chapter 3.

---

[5] Assuming the spread between short- and long-term rates remains the same.

[6] Other types of bonds could also be purchased—we have simplified by ignoring bonds issued by other institutions. This holds well for the United Kingdom, as at the end of 2020 the Bank of England's quantitative easing program held £725 billion of government bonds, and only £20 billion of corporate bonds. The United States Federal Reserve did purchase large quantities of mortgage-backed securities as part of its quantitative easing program, but government bonds still accounted for around 65% of securities held at the end of 2020.

Much investment by non-financial firms is borrowed from commercial banks, and that is what we assume in this section. But of course financing also comes from retained earnings and from venture capitalists, as well as from private equity, share issues, and from the sale of corporate bonds.

How does the investment boom affect the economy?

In response to the improvement in business sentiment, firms wish to undertake new investment projects. Given the lending rate, r_S, they will borrow more from commercial banks to be able to increase investment. In Figure 5.5 this is shown as a shift of the IS curve from IS to IS′, raising current output from y_e to y_0, and inflation from π^T to π_0.

How will the central bank respond to the investment boom?

The central bank will realize that inflation expectations next period will have increased to π_0 (we assume adaptive expectations). To minimize the loss function, the central bank will aim to bring the economy next period to point C, where output is y_1 and inflation π_1. A lending rate of r_0 would be required to dampen aggregate spending and the demand for loans sufficiently to achieve the central bank's goal. Using knowledge

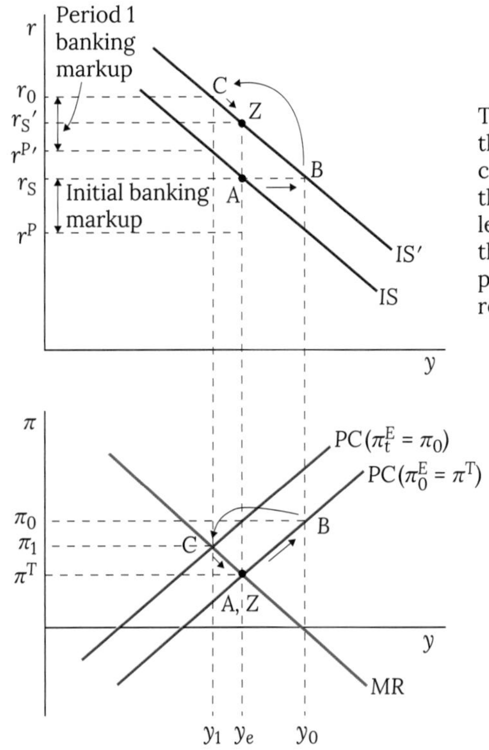

The increase in investment shifts the IS curve to the right. The central bank responds by raising the policy rate to $r^{P\prime}$ to achieve a lending rate of r_0. Policy rate then lowered over following periods until the lending rate reaches r_S'.

Figure 5.5 A permanent investment boom in the 3-equation model with the banking system. This is similar to the analysis done in Chapter 3, except that the central bank now sets the policy rate, targeting a desired lending rate.

about the markup of the lending rate above the policy rate, the central bank will raise the policy rate to $r^{P'}$, knowing that this will result in a lending rate of r_0 next period.

How will banks and the money market react?

Due to arbitrage, the increase in the policy rate will lead to an increase in the money market rate. This increases the funding cost of banks and, due to profit-maximizing behaviour, they will increase the lending rate that they charge households and firms for loans. In Section 5.5 we will see that under some circumstances banks would also decrease the amount of reserves they hold, for instance by purchasing bonds from the central bank.

How will the non-financial private sector react?

The increase in the lending rate will choke off the demand for loans from the private sector because even with the buoyant sentiment, some investment projects that were expected to be profitable at the original lending rate will no longer be profitable at the higher rate. This causes output to fall to y_1, bringing the economy to point C. In subsequent periods the central bank then gradually reduces the policy rate until the lending rate reaches its new stabilizing rate at r_S', and inflation has returned to target.

5.3 THE BUSINESS OF BANKING

Most commercial banks in OECD economies are privately owned and it is reasonable to model them as maximizing profits like other private sector firms. Creating bank money is integral to their business model since it occurs whenever they make loans. It is important to be clear about the difference between a bank's objective of 'making profits' on the one hand and, on the other, the way it 'creates money' as a by-product of its loans business. We begin the section by exploring the distinction between bank money and base money, and the factors influencing the supply and demand of bank money.

As we shall see, a bank's ability to make profits is constrained by competition (as in other industries), its success in identifying creditworthy loans, the cost of funding its lending, including its ability to attract deposits, and by the regulatory environment, which will affect the amount of equity it has. Banks make profits from their lending, but they do not bear the full cost of the risks that are entailed. The extent of their lending in relation to the equity they have, which is available to absorb losses, is therefore regulated.

The potential effect of bank lending on financial stability helps explain why banks are the most heavily regulated industry in the economy. This is because of the centrality of the functioning of the banking system for the operation of the rest of the economy. Banks not only provide essential services but are highly interconnected. Interruptions to the payments system or panic about a bank's ability to pay out its depositors on demand are highly contagious. The original reason for bank regulation was to prevent such liquidity driven bank runs. Government deposit insurance schemes are designed to prevent them.

Banks impose external costs on the whole economy. And unlike firms facing bankruptcy in the rest of the economy, failing banks are often bailed out. When making their business decisions they do not internalize the effects of bank failure on the rest of the economy and as a result, they take on a level of risk that is too high from the viewpoint of society. Excessive risk-taking is examined in Chapter 8 and its role in the financial crisis and the regulatory response that followed in Chapters 9 and 10.

5.3.1 **Central bank and commercial bank money**

In a decentralized economy with many different kinds of goods and services, money allows transactions to occur without requiring the 'double coincidence of wants' where two parties each have a good or service that the other party wants. This requirement of a 'barter' or 'moneyless' economy is very restrictive and drastically cuts down the amount of viable trades each person can make. Two parties could print out their own IOUs ('I Owe You', a promise to repay someone at a later date) to settle up their trades but for an entire economy, there would need to be trust between each pair in every chain of transactions.

Money functions as a *medium of exchange* when trust can be established in the issuer of IOUs. Money also allows for the comparison of the value of all goods and services in terms of a common standard—the *unit of account* function. And thirdly, money provides a *store of value* allowing the shifting of consumption over time. The special quality of money is that it fulfils all three of these functions. Money enables specialization and promotes efficiency.[7]

In the modern economy, money is created by both the central bank and commercial banks.

1. *Base money*, also called central bank money, is created by the central bank. Its IOUs are currency (banknotes and coins, which we will refer to as banknotes) and the reserves held by commercial banks in their accounts at the central bank. We shall see in Section 5.5 that it is their monopoly on the supply of base money that gives central banks their ability to implement monetary policy.
2. *Bank money* is created by commercial banks when they make loans. When a bank makes a loan, money appears as a deposit in the bank account of the household or firm receiving the loan. Like banknotes, this IOU can be used to purchase goods and services.

While households and firms hold some base money (banknotes), most of the money they hold is bank money in their bank accounts. Commercial banks create bank money when making loans, and will do so when it is profitable, depending on their funding cost and expected returns. They use base money from their reserve accounts at the central bank to clear their accounts with other banks on a daily basis. We provide an

[7] For an interesting discussion of barter, money and trust, see the two short chapters (8 and 9) in Seabright (2010). In Chapter 10, we discuss digital currencies and the way that large amounts of 'work' in the form of energy consumed in 'mining' is the substitute for the trust in the currencies supplied by central banks at virtually zero cost.

example of how reserves are used to clear transactions with other banks in Section 5.4.1, once balance sheets have been introduced. In addition commercial banks need to maintain some base money in their vaults, in case households or firms decide to withdraw their deposits at the bank in the form of banknotes. Base money is also referred to as 'liquidity'. Later in this section we will look at what happens if there are concerns that a commercial bank has insufficient liquidity.

Money supply

The money supply is measured from narrow to broad aggregates and normally refers to the quantity of money in the hands of the non-bank public, i.e. households and firms. Money supply measures typically do not include base money held by banks, whether banknotes in their vaults or their reserve accounts at the central bank.[8] Defining money supply in this way means that it can be compared with the demand for money by households and firms.

There are many different ways to measure the money supply, which vary depending on the definition of bank money used. In the narrowest form, money supply is limited to banknotes in the hands of the non-bank public, and easily accessible deposits, which we will call demand deposits.[9] In a modern economy, currency (banknotes) can account for less than 5% of the narrow money supply, for instance in the UK; even in the US, where payments by banknotes are relatively more common, currency represents just 12% of narrow money supply, with the majority accounted for by demand deposits.

Broader definitions include term deposits, which pay more interest than demand deposits but place restrictions on how the money can be used, for instance requiring periods of notice before the money can be withdrawn and converted to a different form or used for a transaction. In practice these products will be marketed with various names, for example 'fixed rate accounts' and 'notice accounts' in the United Kingdom. Term deposits and similar safe assets sacrifice liquidity (the ease with which a form of money can be used for a transaction, with base money being the most liquid asset in the economy) for higher returns than deposits. The central role of money in facilitating transactions can explain why people are still willing to hold it in its narrowest form, banknotes and demand deposits, even though in terms of return this is dominated by other safe assets that pay interest.

Central banks monitor a range of narrow money monetary aggregates as an indicator of spending in the economy, for instance the MZM (zero maturity money) measure. They also use a measure of broad money as an indicator of future spending and of the transmission mechanism of monetary policy. For example, the Bank of England uses $M4^{ex}$. This includes all demand and term deposits, and other liquid assets with a maturity of less than 5 years held by the non-bank private sector. The 'ex' highlights

---

[8] An important exception of historical interest is the Bank of England's measure M0, which was discontinued in 2006. M0 was notes and coins plus central bank reserves, i.e. a measure of the base money in the economy.

[9] In the United Kingdom these will usually be marketed as a 'current account.' Some sources refer to them as 'sight deposits.'

the difficulty of defining broad money. As financial institutions and instruments evolve the definitions are refined—in this case to exclude deposits of 'intermediate and other financial corporations', which are viewed as reflecting interbank lending rather than being directly related to spending in the economy.

In our treatment of money in the macro model, it is unnecessary to get into the technicalities of how central banks define the different measures of the money supply. The precise definitions can be found on the central banks' websites.[10]

Money demand

As we have seen, money is created directly by both banks and the central bank, and can be used to buy goods and services, assets, or repay debts. This takes us to the demand for money.

We assume households choose to hold their financial assets as money (either banknotes or demand deposits—they are not eligible to hold them in reserve accounts at the central bank) or as government bonds. Government bonds are not money because they cannot be used to pay for goods or services, or to service or pay down debts (they are 'less liquid' than deposits), though as we saw in Section 5.2.2 they can be used as collateral when borrowing money. They can also lose value when the interest rate goes up, which does not happen with deposits, meaning that they are more risky than deposits.

For simplicity, we assume demand deposits do not pay interest and we ignore other types of bank accounts, as well as financial assets such as company bonds and shares. Households' and firms' choice of how much money to hold—whether in banknotes or in demand deposits—will depend positively on income (or output) and negatively on the nominal interest rate as follows:

1. The level of income. As their income increases, they will want to carry out more transactions, so will hold greater quantities of money.
2. The nominal interest rate paid on non-money financial assets, which in our model are government bonds. A higher interest rate will make buying government bonds more attractive, thus reducing the demand for money—in other words, the interest rate is the opportunity cost of holding money, which always has a nominal return of zero.

This is called the demand for money function and is written:

$$\frac{M}{P}^{D} = f(y, i; \Phi)$$

where y is output, i is the nominal interest rate, and Φ (Phi, pronounced like hi) are factors explained below. The demand for money function is shown in Figure 5.6 with money in real terms on the horizontal axis and the nominal interest rate on the vertical axis. The money demand curve is downward sloping as a lower nominal interest rate

[10] For instance see Table 1 in McLeay et al. (2014) for an overview of measures used in the UK.

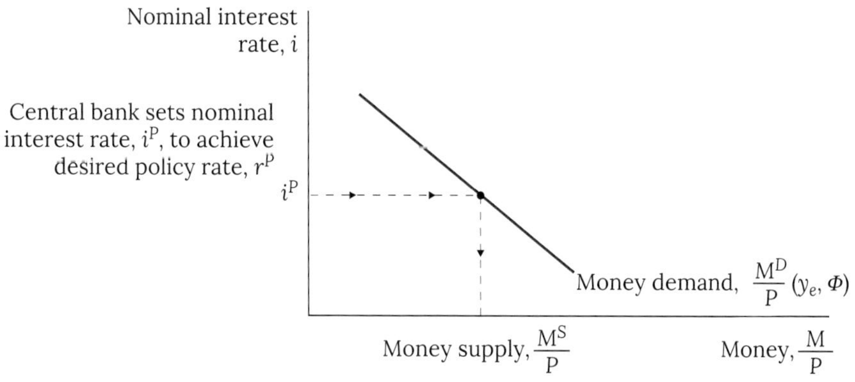

Figure 5.6 The central bank policy rate and the demand for money.

means a lower opportunity cost of holding money. It shifts as output rises and falls, and also shifts when factors Φ change.

The Fisher equation, $i = r + \pi^E$ reveals the two components of the nominal interest rate: the real interest rate and expected inflation. If either expected inflation or the real interest rate goes up, the nominal interest rate will rise in line. This increases the opportunity cost of money and demand will be lower, which is a movement along the curve in Figure 5.6. On the other hand a rise in *unanticipated* inflation will not be reflected in the nominal interest rate but it will, nevertheless, reduce the demand for money. This would shift the money demand curve to the left, implying lower demand for money at any given nominal interest rate.

The demand for money function is also shifted by a range of structural changes in the financial sector, which are captured by the variable, Φ. One such factor is innovation in payments technology. Examples include the diffusion of mobile phones with the capability of making payments and transferring money between different types of accounts, as well as the introduction of 'sweep' options, which would automatically transfer balances from the demand deposit to a higher interest earning account when the balance was above a certain level—or vice versa. Both of these examples led to a fall in the demand for more narrowly defined money, by making it easier to transfer money to and from term deposits.

Another important factor influencing Φ is confidence. All over the world, the demand for money went up in 2008–09 in the face of the fear associated with the global financial crisis and credit crunch. The fear that the financial system might malfunction led households and firms to want to hold more of their financial assets in liquid form, i.e. as money. Looking across the spectrum of money from banknotes to the broadest definition, people wanted to hold more of the narrower forms of money like banknotes and demand deposits.

The policy rate is indicated in Figure 5.6. Given the demand for money function, the supply of money will adjust to match the demand at this interest rate. If the central bank sets a higher policy rate to dampen economic activity, the demand for money will decline (a movement to the north-west along the function) and the supply will fall in line. If the demand for money shifts because of a new technology or a shock to confidence, then at a given policy interest rate, the supply will adjust.

These examples illustrate that changes in the supply of money in the economy are the outcome of changes in the demand for money. Over the business cycle, as the policy rate, income and inflation vary, the desire of households and firms to hold money (rather than bonds) changes. However, since it is the central bank that controls the policy rate, the movements in the demand and supply of money are entirely reactive. They do not cause changes in any of the key variables in the economy, and are not relevant to the transmission of monetary policy to the wider economy, which we will see in Section 5.5 depends on the demand for reserves from commercial banks, rather than the demand for money from households and firms.

The next step is to understand the determinants of the banks' markup over the policy interest rate.

5.3.2 The markup of the lending rate over the policy rate

We begin by asking how an individual bank behaves. A bank faces a demand for new loans from the private sector. It also faces a cost of funding, the cost of borrowing from the money market, which we previously assumed is the same as the policy rate due to arbitrage. The bank's problem is to set the lending rate to maximize profits.

To model the markup of the lending rate over the policy rate, we simplify on a number of counts. In particular, we ignore the administration costs to banks of providing loans, such as bank salaries and expertise for assessing loans and certain external costs such as advertising and renting and maintaining a network of branches. Some of these costs are fixed, at least in the short run, and so do not affect marginal lending decisions.

A simple formal model is set out in the appendix to this chapter. In the model, the profits of banks depend on:

1. the expected return on the loans they make;
2. the rate they pay for borrowing in the money market;
3. their ability to absorb losses, which depends on their equity (or equivalently, their capital adequacy, as it is referred to by regulators).

A bank's core business, lending, is necessarily risky. There is no guarantee that interest payments on a loan will be repaid or that the principal will be paid back in full when repayment is due. In maximizing their expected rate of return, banks must take this risk, which is called *credit risk*, into account. As explained below, even bank lending that is backed by collateral carries credit risk. The spillover effects of bank lending require regulation of its lending relative to its loss-absorbing capacity.

Collateral and credit risk

Collateral, introduced in Section 5.2.2, plays a key role in the banking system. For most households, their biggest investment is in purchasing a house. One of the reasons why banks are prepared to lend the large amounts of money needed to buy a house is that the loan is secured against the value of the house: if the borrower fails to meet her loan repayments, the bank can repossess the house and sell it.[11]

However if house prices have fallen since the mortgage was made, the value of the house may be lower than the value of the loan, meaning that in the event of default the bank has made a loss. This means the bank bears credit risk even on loans with collateral. This was a serious issue for banks in the United States, Spain and Ireland during the global financial crisis, where severe recessions and falling house prices led to many banks taking heavy losses on collateralized real estate loans.

To make matters worse, as became clear in the financial crisis, foreclosure (or repossession) is costly in terms of transactions and legal costs, and the house falls into disrepair when foreclosure is anticipated. Recovery is normally a fraction of the value of well-maintained properties. Losses on mortgage loans can therefore occur even if the underlying house value has not fallen. The use of collateral reduces but does not eliminate credit risk because an asset's value depends on the state of both the market and the asset itself when the asset has to be sold.

The banking markup

Given that lending is risky, even with collateral, banks will charge a markup or margin above the rate at which they can borrow money (in our model, r^P). The more risky are the loans it makes, the higher will be the margin of the lending rate r above r^P. In addition to the riskiness of the loans, banks vary in their willingness to take on risk. We call this the bank's risk tolerance. A bank with a lower risk tolerance will require a higher margin of r above r^P to compensate it for a given riskiness of loans. As we will see in the next section, a bank's perception of how risky an individual is will often depend on how much wealth they can post as collateral.

Finally, the ability of the bank to bear risk depends on its loss-absorbing capacity. This depends on how much capital or equity it has. In Section 5.4.1, we will see that the bank's equity (capital) buffer is the difference between the value of its assets and its other liabilities. Equity is a liability owed to the bank's shareholders but unlike other liabilities, it absorbs losses when assets fall in value. A smaller equity buffer means it is less able to bear risk because a smaller fall in the value of its assets (holding liabilities constant) would wipe out its equity, leaving liabilities greater than assets. A bank with lower equity is less able to absorb losses and therefore to bear credit risk and it will choose a higher interest rate margin and make fewer loans.

These three elements: risk, risk tolerance and bank equity, explain the gap between the interest rate set by banks, r, and the policy rate, r^P. An increase in the riskiness of projects or a fall in risk tolerance or lower equity will increase the lending rate for a given policy rate. In fact, the profit-maximizing bank chooses to respond to these changes by both raising the price they charge for loans (i.e. the lending rate) and by making fewer loans—we look at credit rationing in Section 5.3.3.

---

[11] A second reason is that banks require people buying a house to invest some of their own money, called a down payment or mortgage deposit depending on the country. This is to ensure that the borrower has some of their own 'skin in the game'.

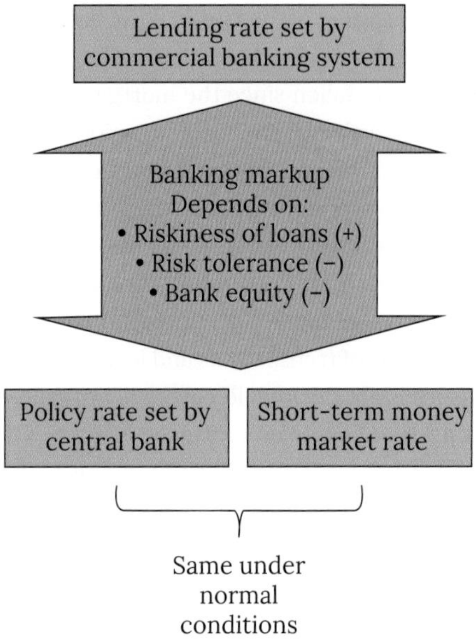

Figure 5.7 The relationship between the policy interest rate, the short-term money market rate, and the lending interest rate.

We add one more equation to the 3-equation model:

$$r = (1 + \mu^B)r^P, \qquad \text{(interest rate margin; banking markup equation)}$$

where μ^B is the banking markup that depends positively on risk, and negatively on risk tolerance and the equity buffer.

Figure 5.7 shows the relationship between the key interest rates in the model. As discussed in Section 5.2.2, under normal conditions, the policy interest rate and the money market rate are very similar (in the model, they are identical). The lending rate is higher than the policy and money market rate. The size of the gap between the lending and the other rates (i.e. the margin or markup) is determined by the factors in the double-headed arrow.

If the banking sector is not competitive, a further factor will affect the markup of the lending rate over the policy rate. In a parallel fashion to the goods market in Chapter 2, in which the markup of the price above unit labour costs rises with the extent of market power, a bank with market power will set a higher profit-maximizing margin of the lending rate above the policy rate.

Typically the pass-through of the policy rate to lending rates is slower when the policy rate is being cut than when it is being raised. In addition, the markup can increase significantly during a crisis. Figure 5.8 shows the spread between the Bank of England policy rate and the mortgage lending rate being charged by UK banks. The chart suggests that the stable relationship in 'normal times' was disrupted by the financial crisis. Before the crisis the typical spread was roughly one percentage point, while in the immediate aftermath of the crisis the spread increased to four percentage

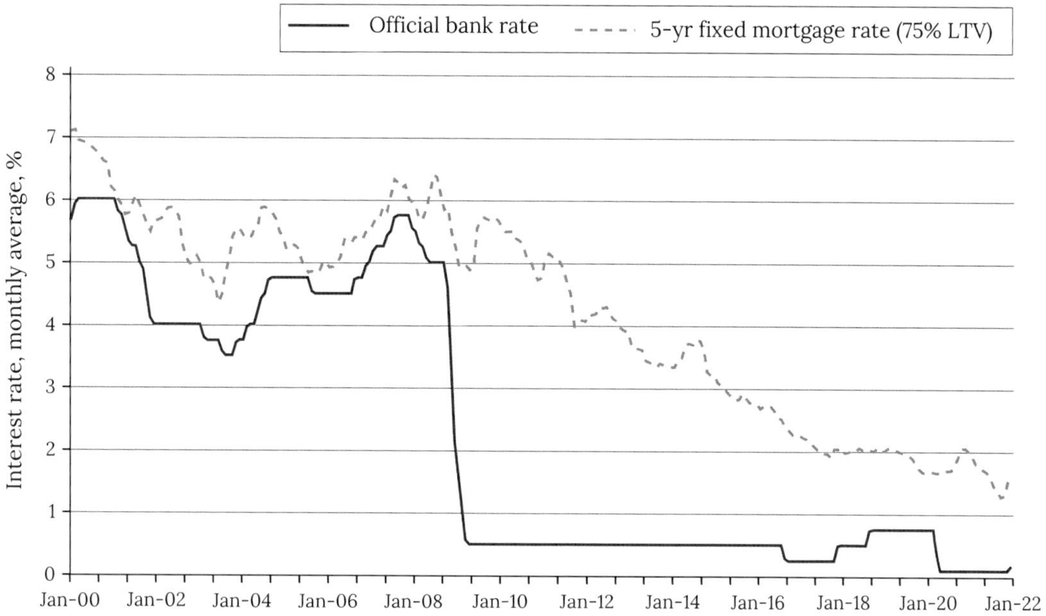

Figure 5.8 UK Official Bank Rates and 5-year fixed mortgage rates (75% Loan to Value ratio): Jan 2000–Dec 2021. A 75% Loan to Value mortgage is where the borrower has borrowed up to 75% of the value of the house, with the remainder coming from a deposit.

Source: Bank of England (data accessed June 2022).

points. Even ten years after the crisis, the gap remained greater than one percentage point. This highlights that the key transmission mechanism of monetary policy (i.e. that changes in r^P by the central bank alter the long-term borrowing costs for households and firms) broke down in the post-crisis world.

5.3.3 **Credit risk and credit constraints**

When modelling bank behaviour and its effects on the macroeconomy, we need to understand the determinants of the margin of the lending rate over the policy rate and why banks ration credit. Credit rationing and the associated credit constraints faced by households play an important role in the macroeconomic model. In analysing household behaviour in Chapter 1, the size of the multiplier is higher and the slope of the IS curve consequently flatter when the share of credit-constrained households is higher: shocks to aggregate demand are amplified. As argued in Chapter 1, the share of credit-constrained households rises in a recession. This increases the size of the government expenditure multiplier and has been relevant in the past decade in light of the importance of fiscal policy for stabilization when the economy has been at the zero lower bound.

For firms, credit rationing is a reason why Tobin's Q model of investment fails. As discussed in Chapter 1, affected firms rely on cash flow to finance investment. Just as for households, this makes investment spending more highly dependent on current income. A simple extension of the investment function to incorporate this would include a term dependent on current income (i.e. the marginal propensity to invest in new machinery, equipment and structures out of income). If credit constraints on firms are more pervasive, this channel would increase the size of the multiplier.

A separate question is the effect of credit constraints on the slope of the investment function itself. Credit-excluded households or firms will not be able to respond to a fall in the interest rate and the response of credit-constrained ones will be muted. This reduces the interest sensitivity of the investment curve, making it steeper. By extension, holding the multiplier constant, a steeper IS curve reduces the power of a given cut in the interest rate by the central bank to stimulate spending. For any given level of the lending rate, there will be fewer potential investments that can secure funding, and hence lower output in goods market equilibrium. In Chapter 8, we shall extend the model further to show how higher house prices can relax the borrowing constraint for credit-constrained households by increasing the value of their collateral, and the role this plays in financial booms and busts.

As we have seen, managing credit risk is a major part of a bank's business and the markup of the lending rate over the policy rate varies positively with credit risk. We now explain why banks will not only adjust their markup to reflect the average credit risk of their loan portfolio but will also impose credit rationing. This involves two kinds of information problem: moral hazard and adverse selection.

Information problems

Credit risk is ever-present: will the investment project be the success it is forecast to be in the firm's business plan? Will household members remain in employment and will their salaries grow in the way that was expected when they took out a mortgage to allow them to buy their house?

But even more important than the fact that the future is unknown is the way that differences in the information available to borrowers and lenders can affect behaviour. This is known as the problem of *asymmetric information*. For example, if I want to borrow money from you to launch a new venture and it turns out that I am unable to repay, you don't know if that is because I was unlucky or because, given that you lent me the money, I exerted less effort than I would have done if all the funding had been my own. It may be difficult for you to find this out and to find out the returns generated by the project.

The problem of possible default by the borrower for reasons other than bad luck is an example of asymmetric information, specifically *moral hazard*, and it affects the willingness of banks to lend, as well as explaining why that willingness is affected by the wealth of the borrower. As the example above suggests, the more of your own wealth you are able (and prepared) to invest in your project, the easier it is to borrow. When your own funds are at stake, your incentives are better aligned with those of the lender. Borrowers with insufficient wealth to invest in their project may be denied credit.

In addition to the problem of moral hazard, there is another pervasive information problem. In the permanent income hypothesis of Chapter 1, it is assumed that households are able to borrow to carry out their consumption plans in line with their expected permanent income. However, to make you a loan so that you can consume your permanent income implies the lender can observe your expected future earning capacity.

Given it does not have this information, it might seem obvious for the bank to simply charge a higher interest rate to cover the risk that your self-reported future earning plans fail to materialize. However, because you have better information about your expected future earnings than the bank, this is another situation of asymmetric information. It means that if the bank were to charge a higher interest rate, individuals with stronger prospects (known to themselves but difficult to signal credibly to the bank) would self-select away from bank credit; the cost of borrowing is viewed as too high by individuals with a high probability of success. The self-selection leaves the weaker applicants dominating the pool seeking bank credit, as these applicants believe there is a chance they will default and not have to pay the debt back. Since banks will not want to be left with the lower quality applicants as a consequence of their choice of a higher lending rate, they will respond by refusing or rationing credit. This type of asymmetric information is called *adverse selection* and provides a second explanation for credit rationing by banks.

The pervasiveness of information problems and the response of banks to them explains why the macroeconomic model includes credit-constrained households and firms. Figure 5.9 provides a visual representation of the causal chain in the bank's decision-making process in regard to making loans. It highlights the importance of borrower wealth and hence, inequality, in both aligning the incentives of banks and borrowers and in signalling to the bank the quality of the project. An unfortunate effect of the problems of moral hazard and adverse selection is that borrowers who do not possess the wealth to provide an equity stake or the collateral to secure a loan will be

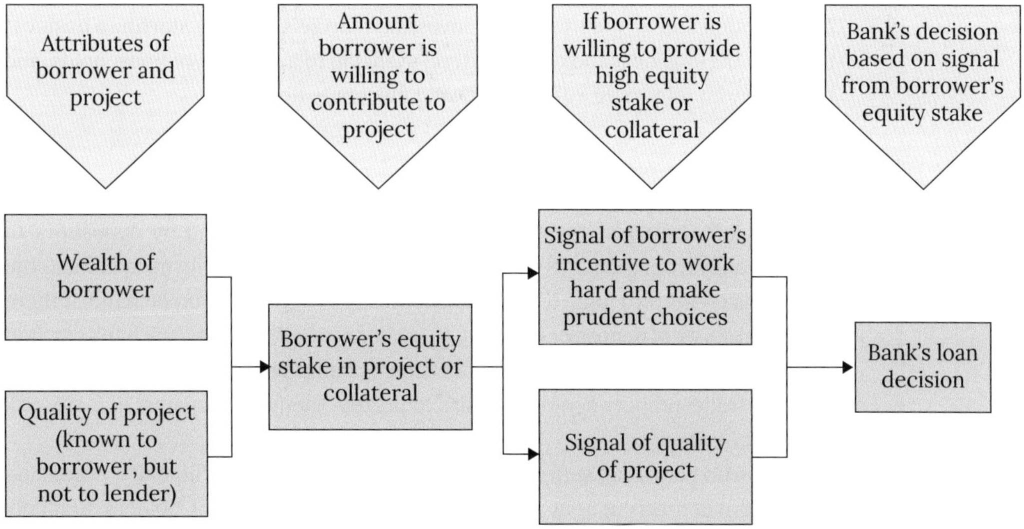

Figure 5.9 Credit constraints: the role of borrower wealth in the lending decisions of banks.

denied credit, even if they have a high quality project. The outcome is inefficient as well as unfair.

5.3.4 **Banks in a fractional reserve system**

From the perspective of macroeconomics, we have focused on the interaction between banks and the central bank, and how monetary policy works by affecting the demand for loans. However, we should not lose sight of why a banking system exists in the first place. Banks fulfil a number of vital functions, many of which can be categorized as facilitating 'intermediation' between borrowers and lenders. We summarize those roles and then turn to the more problematic issues of liquidity risk and solvency.

1. **Maturity transformation:** On the bank lending side, savers want access to their savings at short notice, but borrowers want to finance long-term projects including mortgages. Banks assist in this maturity transformation in the economy. Banks hold only a fraction of deposits in liquid form in their reserve accounts at the central bank, which explains why this is called a *fractional reserve banking system.*
2. **Aggregation:** Typical savings quantities (e.g. regular savings by households) are much smaller than typical loan requirements (e.g. for lumpy investment projects such as house purchase or building a new production facility) and banks provide the service of aggregating the small savings and making larger loans.
3. **Risk pooling:** Some borrowers will default, which reflects the *credit risk* discussed previously. Whereas this might bankrupt individual lenders, larger institutions, such as banks, can withstand a certain proportion of defaults, and hence offer little or no risk to savers.
4. **Access to collateral:** The information problems highlighted earlier (adverse selection and moral hazard) explain why households without wealth are excluded from borrowing unless they have access to collateral. This limits their ability to smooth consumption and to undertake risky investment projects such as starting a business (Chapter 1). Housing is the only collateral available to a majority of households, and banks play an important role in supplying mortgage finance.

Liquidity risk

Liquidity risk is the risk that a bank in a fractional reserve system has inadequate reserves in its account at the central bank to meet the demand by depositors to withdraw money from their accounts. The risk arises from a maturity mismatch, as the bank extends credit on a long-term basis but must pay depositors on demand. If there is an unusual surge of depositors wishing to withdraw their deposits, the bank can find itself unable to meet this demand. The decision by banks about their reserve holdings reflects the trade-off between their desire to protect themselves against liquidity risk and the cost of doing so.

Even well-run banks can suffer from an unexpected shortage of liquidity. A 'banking panic' arises when throughout the banking system, bank deposit holders suddenly demand either that banks convert their deposits into banknotes or move them to other 'safer' banks, to such an extent that the affected banks' reserve holdings are depleted before all savers have managed to withdraw their deposits. Although in normal times, bank money (deposits) and base money (here, banknotes) are perfect substitutes for fulfilling transactions, fear of a bank run makes customers doubt that bank money is a perfect substitute for base money and they want to withdraw their deposits. The money issued by the central bank in the form of notes and coins is legal tender, which means it cannot legally be refused in settlement of debt, but the money created by commercial banks in the form of deposits is not legal tender. In a fractional reserve system, a bank will be unable to pay out to everyone if all its depositors try to withdraw their funds at once. The Nobel Prize in 2022 was awarded to economists Ben Bernanke, Douglas Diamond, and Philip Dybvig for work in banking and financial crises. Diamond and Dybvig modelled the vulnerabilities of banks to a bank run.[12]

One way of explaining a banking panic is using a 'coordination problem' model: if there is a panic trigger, it can create a self-fulfilling belief that banks will fail. The argument is simple: because the depositor at the front of the queue will certainly get back all his funds, there is an incentive to be the first to withdraw if there is a danger that everyone might withdraw (even if the bank is essentially sound) and produce a bank run.

This explains why central banks provide insurance in the form of a back-stop provision of central bank (base) money through the Lender of Last Resort facility (LOLR). The lender of last resort steps in to provide liquidity, normally at a penalty interest rate, to (otherwise solvent) banks who do not have sufficient reserves in their reserve accounts to meet their short-term liabilities. This was implemented on a large scale in 2008 by central banks in many countries, as will be discussed later in this chapter when we look at central bank balance sheets.

Governments provide deposit insurance schemes as a further means to reduce the likelihood of a banking panic. We will see this in more detail in Section 9.2, and will also examine the trade-offs that governments and central banks face when designing schemes to prevent banking panics.

Solvency

Another potential danger for banks is insolvency. A bank is insolvent or bankrupt when the value of its assets (i.e. what it owns) is less than the value of what it owes (its debts or liabilities). At this point, the bank will go out of business if it does not find a buyer or is not bailed out by the government. Insolvency has immediate and direct negative effects for the bank's depositors, creditors including bondholders, and shareholders. Having a large equity buffer makes insolvency less likely, as the value of assets exceeds the value of liabilities by a large proportion.

Liquidity and insolvency risk can interact and aggravate each other. An illiquid bank that has to borrow at the central bank's penalty rate is adding to its liabilities and worsening its solvency problems. Note that a bank has to pay depositors on demand

---

[12] See Press release. NobelPrize.org. Nobel Prize Outreach AB 2023. Wed. 15 Feb 2023. https://www.nobelprize.org/prizes/economic-sciences/2022/press-release/ Last accessed February 2023.

but makes long-term loans. This maturity mismatch between its liabilities and its assets leaves the bank facing liquidity risk. If there is a run on liabilities by depositors, as described in the previous subsection, the bank may have to sell assets at short notice, often at discounted prices. This would cause the value of the bank's assets to fall, potentially leaving the bank insolvent. If a liquidity problem in one bank causes asset sales this lowers the value of other banks' assets in turn generating losses. If this occurs to multiple banks simultaneously, the forced sale of assets is known as a 'fire sale.' Central banks are equipped to deal with liquidity issues but as explained further in Chapter 10, rebuilding capital is more problematic.

When insolvency threatens a bank that is interconnected with other banks through chains of lending and borrowing, the functioning of the money market comes under pressure and the flow of credit freezes up. A solvency problem for a small number of banks can quickly become a widespread liquidity problem in a modern banking system, because no bank can be sure whether it is safe to lend to another. Such freezing of credit is sometimes referred to as a 'credit crunch' or 'credit squeeze', and will be explored further in Chapter 9 in the context of the global financial crisis. The spillover effect from the failure of a systemically important bank to the functioning of the banking system and its supply of core banking services lies behind the behaviour of governments in stepping in to save or 'bail out' insolvent banks.

5.4 BALANCE SHEETS

Balance sheets allow us to keep track of changes in the assets and liabilities of banks that take place through lending and borrowing, as well as through changes in asset prices. They are central to understanding liquidity and solvency. Just as the relationship between the non-financial sector (households and firms) and banks is illuminated through connections between their balance sheets, so is the relationship between the central bank and commercial banks. As we shall see, every financial asset has some corresponding liability; for instance reserves are an asset for banks but a liability for the central bank, deposits are an asset for households and firms but a liability for banks, and loans are an asset for banks but a liability for households and firms. Studying central bank balance sheets can also shed light on why the economy moved to an 'ample reserves' situation since the financial crisis, which is a key feature of the operation of contemporary monetary policy.

5.4.1 The balance sheet of a commercial bank

Figure 5.10 provides a simplified illustration of the balance sheet of a commercial bank designed to bring out the important elements for economic analysis. The figure records the balance sheet identity, which holds for all economic entities, such as the entire banking system, households, and the central bank.

The balance sheet identity is

$$\begin{aligned}&\text{Net worth (equity), owed to shareholders}\\&\quad\equiv \text{Assets} - \text{Liabilities}\\&\quad\equiv \text{what you own or is owed to you} - \text{what you owe others.}\end{aligned}$$

Assets	% of balance sheet	Liabilities	% of balance sheet
1. Banknotes and reserve account balances at the central bank	2	1. Deposits	50
2. Government bonds, which can be used as collateral for repo borrowing	10	2. Wholesale repo borrowing secured with collateral	30
3. Bonds and other financial assets issued by the private sector, some of which can be used as collateral for repo borrowing	20	3. Unsecured borrowing	16
4. Wholesale reverse repo lending	11		
5. Loans (e.g. mortgages)	55		
6. Fixed assets (e.g. buildings, equipment)	2		
Total assets	100	Total liabilities	96
		Net worth	
		Equity	4

Memorandum item: Leverage (Total assets/Net worth)	100/4 = 25

Figure 5.10 The balance sheet of a typical commercial bank before the financial crisis.
Note: All items in the balance sheet are expressed as a percentage of total assets.

The net worth of an entity is equal to what is owed to the shareholders, as it is equal to the amount of money left over if all assets are liquidated and all debts paid off. This explains why net worth is on the liabilities side of the balance sheet. If the value of your assets is less than the value of what you owe others then you are insolvent.

The balance sheet identity can be reorganized as follows:

$$\text{Assets} \equiv \text{Liabilities} + \text{Net worth (equity)}.$$

The second way of writing the identity highlights the funding of the bank: it funds its assets through a combination of debt (liabilities) and equity (net worth).

On the *asset* side of the simplified bank balance sheet in Figure 5.10 are six main items, which are things owned by or owed to the bank:

1. **Banknotes and reserve account balances at the central bank:** These are the bank's highly liquid assets, and are components of what we earlier called 'base money'. Banknotes in its vaults (and in ATMs) and the bank's reserve account balance provide the liquidity the bank needs to operate. Even when central banks pay the policy rate of interest on bank reserves, these do not earn as much as bonds or loans, so a bank will not want to hold higher reserves than it considers prudent to meet its liquidity needs or its legal obligation, if a minimum level of reserves is required. We return to the presence of so-called 'excess reserves' after explaining the central bank's balance sheet.

2. **Government bonds:** Banks hold these assets as they are interest-earning and relatively safe. Note that the price of bonds varies inversely with the interest rate so they are not 'capital-safe'—although this risk is small for very short-dated bonds. Government bonds in advanced economies are normally considered to be free of sovereign default risk, i.e. the risk that the government defaults by failing to make interest payments or to repay the principal when the bond matures. Because they are low risk, they can be used as high-quality collateral when the bank itself borrows.
3. **Bonds and other financial assets issued by the private sector:** These include asset-backed securities (ABS), which are financial assets constructed from bundles of loans, including mortgages (MBS) and car loans. Credit rating agencies rate the riskiness of these assets and those rated low risk can be used as collateral for the bank's own borrowing.
4. **Wholesale reverse repo lending**: This makes more sense to explain in the context of the related item on the liabilities side, wholesale repo borrowing. See item 2 in the following text.
5. **Loans:** This is the largest item on the asset side of the balance sheet and includes all loans made by the bank, such as mortgages, business and car loans. This is the bank's core activity and is why the banking system is so crucial to the functioning of the economy.
6. **Fixed assets:** The physical assets of the bank, such as its buildings and equipment.

To the right of the assets column, we have indicated the approximate proportions of the different assets in a typical bank balance sheet in the pre-crisis period. The bank holds very low amounts of banknotes and reserves at the central bank. Government bonds make up about 10% of its balance sheet and about the same proportion comes from wholesale loans. The bank holds 20% of its assets in asset-backed securities, as they typically offer a higher rate of return than government bonds or money market lending. By far the largest part of the asset side of the bank's balance sheet is made up of loans to households and firms: this is the bank's core business. As we have seen, it makes profits by lending at a higher interest rate than the cost of its funds.

Turning to the liability side there are three main items:

1. **Deposits:** The largest item on the liabilities side are deposits by households and firms. In our example, they comprise over half of the bank's liabilities, and constitute what we earlier called 'bank money.'
2. **Wholesale repo borrowing secured with collateral**: As seen in Section 5.2.2, repo borrowing is the way banks fund their everyday activities—they borrow reserves by selling assets to another bank (the lending bank) and promising to buy them back the next day, or in a few weeks or months. The repurchase price is higher than the sale price, providing interest for the lending bank. The loans are secured (or collateralized), which means that if the bank selling the assets is not able to buy them back, then the lender will keep the assets. High-quality assets are typically required for repo transactions, such as government bonds or highly-rated privately

issued securities (e.g. asset-backed securities, ABS or mortgage-backed securities, MBS).[13] Item 4 on the asset side shows the reverse repos held by the bank. These are reserves which the bank has lent out in return for assets, which they will then sell back. Large banks typically engage in both lending and borrowing in the repo market. This function is sometimes referred to as the *market maker* function. The important point is that large volumes of short-term reserve borrowing and lending take place among banks.

3. **Unsecured borrowing:** Banks can borrow reserves in the money market from other banks. Unlike repo borrowing, this is not secured with collateral, which means that the lender would not be repaid if the borrowing bank were to become insolvent. As a consequence the money market rate is usually above the repo rate in practice, especially in times when there are high levels of uncertainty about solvency.[14] Banks can also sell bonds as a way of raising funds through unsecured borrowing.

The balance sheet helps us to see how banks can make loans without impacting reserves. When a bank makes a loan, its assets increase by the value of the loan, while its liabilities increase by the size of the deposit it has just created, without any impact on reserves. However banks do need to maintain a minimum level of reserves relative to their balance sheet for liquidity purposes, which might come from a binding reserve requirement from the country's financial authorities, or from the bank's own internal liquidity management requirements. Regulatory liquidity requirements mean that a portion of the bank's lending has to be matched by holding reserves and or bonds. These liquid assets yield lower returns, which effectively lowers the profitability of lending since for every £1 lent, an extra £x is invested in something with a lower return.

Whenever a customer of Bank A spends money at a business that has an account at Bank B, the customer's bank money (deposit) is transferred from Bank A to Bank B, along with a corresponding amount of reserves. In addition to having enough reserves to clear transactions with other banks at the end of every day (and through real time settlement services), a bank must also retain sufficient reserves to be able to meet withdrawal demands of depositors, which involves transferring banknotes from its reserve account at the central bank to the bank's vaults.

The above also explains why banks seek to attract new deposits when making loans. While new deposits are not required to make loans, which are created 'out of nothing,' they help the bank meet liquidity needs. Take for instance a bank that has £10 in base money assets (either banknotes or reserves at the central bank, most likely reserves), £100 in loan assets, and £100 in deposit liabilities, leaving £10 as equity (Column 1 in Table 5.1). The bank currently has enough reserves to cover 10% of its deposits in

---

[13] In the financial crisis, the quality of the so-called private label securities (ABS and MBS) was called into question when their price fell sharply. This was an important factor in the credit crunch of 2009, which is explained in Chapter 9.

[14] However while some institutions can carry out transactions in both the money market and the repo market, such as Federal Home Loan Banks in the US, many institutions are restricted to just the repo market. This means that the repo rate can sometimes be observed above the money market rate due to imperfect arbitrage.

	Column 1: initial situation	Column 2: £10 of new loans	Column 3: The £10 are spent at a different bank	Column 4: £10 of new deposits are attracted
Loans (asset)	100	110	110	110
Reserves (asset)	10	10	0	10
Deposits (liability)	100	110	100	110
Equity (liability)	10	10	10	10
Reserve to deposit ratio	10%	9.1%	0%	9.1%

Table 5.1 Why banks require deposits. Visit www.oup.com/he/carlin-soskice to explore Table 5.1 in more detail.

Source: Based on McLeay et al. (2014).

case customers withdraw money, either physically or by transferring to another bank. Imagine that the bank creates £10 of new loans, which are an asset, and this is matched by £10 of new deposit liabilities (Column 2). After a borrower has taken out a loan, they are likely to spend it at a business that has an account with a different bank, leading to deposits and reserves flowing out to the other bank (Column 3). This has left the bank without base money. In case of outflows, the bank could borrow reserves on the money market, which could be expensive depending on the money market rate. A second option would be to attract new deposits from customers, which we assume banks do not pay interest on.[15] Whenever a customer makes a new deposit, either by physically paying in banknotes or making a transfer from another bank, the bank gains corresponding reserves (Column 4).

Since the advent of ample reserves, which we explore in detail later, many central banks have found that setting minimum reserve ratio requirements is redundant as banks already hold significantly more reserves than legally required. The US Federal Reserve and the Bank of England are two examples where there are no reserve requirements at the time of writing. A major constraint on bank lending seems to be expected profitability of loans, rather than needing to raise reserves further—this becomes important in Section 6.5 when looking at the link between reserves and inflation. A second constraint is that banks are often required to have a minimum level of equity relative to risky assets, to act as a loss absorber in case of solvency issues as described in Section 5.3. In the example above, the ratio of equity to loans fell when new loans were made. Banks can raise equity by paying fewer dividends, in other words retaining a greater share of profits for themselves, or in extreme circumstances they could issue new equity, as we will now see was the case for Barclays.

An important concept for a bank is its *leverage*: this is the ratio of its assets to its equity. In the example shown in Figure 5.10, the bank has a leverage ratio of 100/4 = 25.

[15] In reality, demand deposits will often pay some low level of interest to customers. However banks will charge fees such as overdraft services or monthly costs in return.

Assets		Liabilities	
1. Banknotes and reserve account balances at the central bank	7,345	1. Deposits	336,316
2. Wholesale reverse repo lending	174,090	2. Wholesale repo borrowing secured with collateral	136,956
3. Loans (e.g. mortgages)	313,226	3. Unsecured borrowing	111,137
4. Fixed assets (e.g. buildings, equipment)	2,492	4. *Trading portfolio liabilities*	71,874
5. *Trading portfolio assets, including government bonds*	177,867	5. *Derivative financial instruments*	140,697
6. *Derivative financial instruments*	138,353	6. *Other liabilities*	172,417
7. *Other assets*	183,414		
Total assets	996,787	Total liabilities	969,397
		Net worth	
		Equity	27,390

Memorandum item: Leverage (Total assets/Net worth)	996,787/27,390 = 36.4

Figure 5.11 The consolidated balance sheet of Barclays PLC in 2006, £m.

Source: Barclays PLC Annual Report 2006.

This is the inverse of the ratio of equity to assets, and as such a higher leverage ratio implies a smaller equity buffer. As we shall see in Chapters 8 and 9, leverage played a central role in the build-up to the financial crisis of 2008.

Figure 5.11 shows the balance sheet of the British bank Barclays just before the financial crisis. It is more complicated than the simple balance sheet in Figure 5.10, because Barclays combines in the activities of a commercial bank those of a retail bank and an investment bank.

On the asset side of the Barclays balance sheet we can see entries for banknotes and reserves, loans, reverse repos, and fixed assets (e.g. buildings, equipment) just as in Figure 5.10. The remaining assets in Figure 5.11 (which do not appear in our simple model and are shown in italics) relate to Barclays' investment banking activities. Barclays' holdings of government bonds are contained within the trading portfolio assets and other assets categories. On the liabilities side of the Barclays balance sheet, we can see entries for deposits, repos and unsecured lending, exactly as in Figure 5.10. The other items on the liabilities side of Barclays' balance sheet (in italics) refer to items that mainly relate to investment banking. Lastly, Barclays' equity was around £27.4bn in 2006 and their leverage ratio, calculated as the value of assets divided by equity, was 36.4. Figure 5.12 shows that the bank's leverage ratio grew rapidly in the years leading up to the financial crisis, peaking in 2008. Between 2008 and 2009 Barclays experienced rapid de-leveraging.

The value of Barclays' assets fell sharply in the financial crisis, which put it at risk of insolvency. At the same time, the regulatory authority increased the required ratio of equity to assets, the inverse of the leverage ratio in Figure 5.12. To achieve this, Barclays

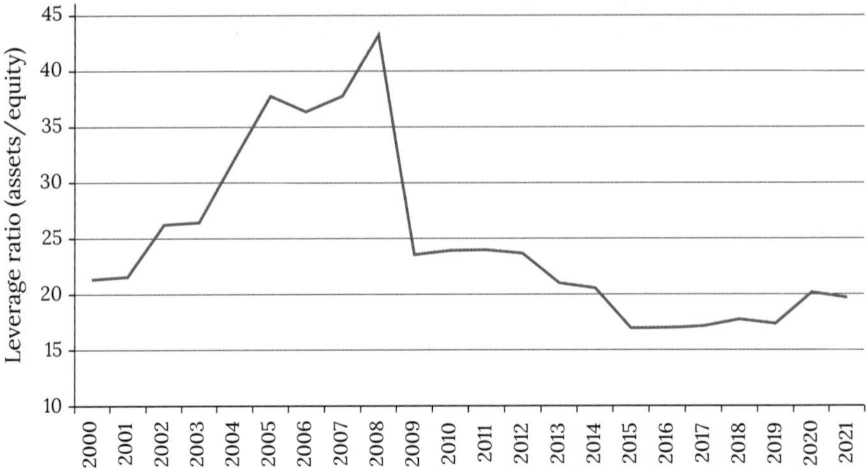

Figure 5.12 The leverage ratio of Barclays PLC from 2000 to 2021 (defined as total assets/equity).

Source: Barclays PLC Annual Reports.

sold off parts of its portfolio of loans.[16] Barclays also sold new shares to the public to raise money, increasing its equity directly. The latter is very unpopular with existing shareholders because it dilutes the value of their existing shares.

5.4.2 The balance sheet of the central bank

Whereas the IOUs of commercial banks are the deposit accounts of households and firms, the central bank's IOUs are banknotes plus the balances in the reserve accounts of commercial banks, namely, the base money in the economy.[17] As noted previously, while most transactions in the economy are conducted using bank money, it is base money that is the ultimate means of settlement of all transactions. The connection to monetary policy is that because the central bank has a monopoly on the supply of base money, it can control its price (the policy interest rate). If the interest rate is at the zero lower bound, the central bank operates monetary policy by creating base money to purchase other assets like government bonds in an attempt to influence longer term interest rates. In both cases, the aim is to affect the spending decisions of households and firms by affecting the cost of finance.

The inflation-targeting regimes introduced in the 1990s were operated using the interest rate as the policy instrument while the period since the financial crisis has seen quantitative easing used to loosen monetary policy. Central bank balance sheets

[16] 'Assets', when calculating equity to asset ratios, are risk-weighted. Government bonds are considered risk-free and have a weight of zero, meaning that they do not contribute towards total assets when calculating the equity ratio. As such, if a bank sells loans in exchange for government bonds, or some other safe asset, it reduces the equity to asset ratio despite total assets as measured on the balance sheet not changing.

[17] This section draws on Rule (2015) and Vlieghe (2020).

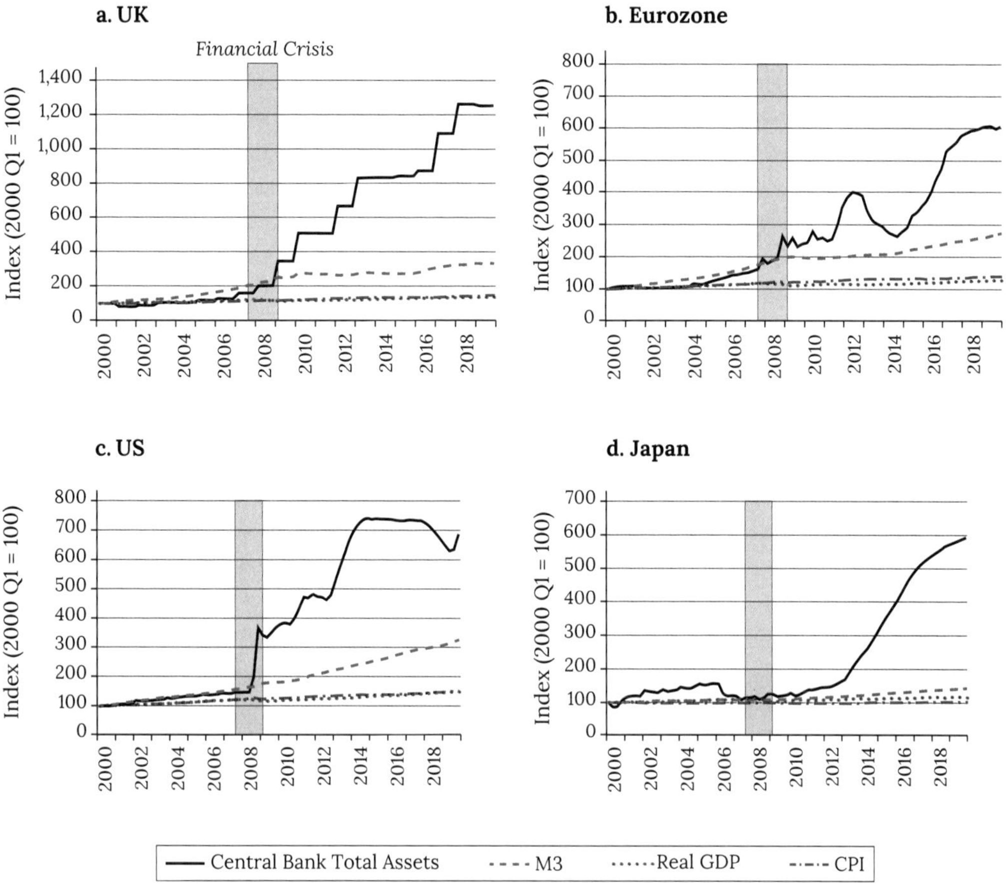

Figure 5.13 The total central bank assets, real GDP, M3 money supply and Consumer Price Index for the UK, the Eurozone, the US and Japan.

Source: Federal Reserve Bank of St Louis, Bank of Japan, European Central Bank, Economic Statistics Centre of Excellence, and the OECD.

have come to public attention under QE because the purchase of assets has seen a massive expansion in their size as shown in Figure 5.13 for the US Federal Reserve, the Bank of Japan, the European Central Bank and the Bank of England.[18] The growth in central bank assets has significantly outstripped growth in either real GDP, the consumer price index, or the money supply, suggesting that it has not been driven purely by economic fundamentals.

[18] The Japanese economy has followed a different path. The country's economic woes began much earlier, experiencing low economic growth and low or negative inflation since around 1992. The large expansion in central bank assets around 2013 followed the election of Shinzo Abe in December 2012. As Prime Minister, Abe launched a range of stimulus measures, including a significant expansion of the quantitative easing program by the Bank of Japan.

When the financial crisis first hit, money (interbank) markets dried up as commercial banks stopped lending to each other. Many commercial banks started to hoard reserves instead of lending in money markets, partly to self-insure against potential adverse shocks to themselves such as bank runs, and partly out of heightened credit risk fears with regard to potential counterparties. To ensure that banks could have sufficient liquidity to settle all transactions, central banks increased the supply of reserves, leading to *liability driven* increases in central bank balance sheets. Subsequent poor economic growth led central banks to focus on stimulating the economy, leading to *asset driven increases* in balance sheets as central banks purchased government and corporate assets. The liability- and asset-driven changes are explained toward the end of the section.

A stylized central bank balance sheet can be seen in Figure 5.14. The balance sheets of central banks have the same structure as for private firms. This means that the excess of assets over liabilities is the central bank's equity, which allows the central bank to absorb losses.[19]

The majority of a central bank's liabilities come from reserve account balances of commercial banks. Commercial bank reserve accounts are the demand deposits

Assets	% of balance sheet	Liabilities	% of balance sheet
1. Bond holdings	3	1. Reserve account balances	81
2. Open market operations, assets	2	2. Open market operations, liabilities	1
3. Foreign currency, reserves	1	3. Notes in circulation	14
4. Asset Purchase Facility (QE)	75	4. Foreign currency, liabilities	1
5. Other assets	19		
Total assets	100	Total liabilities	97
		Net worth	
		Equity	3

Figure 5.14 An example Central Bank balance sheet, loosely based on the Bank of England's balance sheet in January 2020. The Asset Purchase Facility is used by the Bank to implement quantitative easing (QE).

[19] This is sometimes called *equity capital*.

of commercial banks and are used to settle the transactions between banks. Like banknotes, they are the most liquid and low-risk assets in the economy. Although an individual bank can choose the level of reserves to hold (over and above any minimum requirement), the total amount of reserves in the economy is fixed by the central bank. If a commercial bank uses some reserves to buy other assets, the bank which sells the assets will acquire the reserves in return. The total reserves remain fixed—they can only be changed by the decision of the central bank.

The other liabilities in Figure 5.14 are Open Market Operations liabilities, which are explained below, banknotes in circulation, and foreign currency liabilities. Meanwhile, the asset side consists of bond holdings, Open Market Operations assets, foreign currency assets, assets acquired through quantitative easing, and miscellaneous assets. The choice of exchange rate regime, discussed in Chapter 14, is the key determinant of how many foreign currency liabilities and assets a central bank will hold; in fixed exchange rate regimes central banks require foreign exchange reserves to enable direct intervention, while in floating exchange rate regimes central banks have a reduced need for foreign exchange reserves. The stylized example is based on the Bank of England, which operates in a floating exchange rate setting.

The central bank uses Open Market Operations to make collateralized loans of reserves to banks, i.e. using repos, when loosening monetary policy. With the launch of quantitative easing, the new Asset Purchase Facility (APF) was used to buy bonds. The main distinctions between Open Market Operations and quantitative easing are that the central bank:

- uses OMOs to adjust the quantity of reserves so as to meet a specific money market rate, i.e. it is targeting the price (the policy rate)
- uses QE to try to influence long-term interest rates by buying a specific quantity of assets.

The former primarily targets short-term rates, such as the repo rate, while quantitative easing targets long-term ones and is typically implemented on a larger scale.

One way to understand the balance sheet is to look separately at the liabilities and assets side for a specific central bank. The charts in Figure 5.15 are for the Bank of England for the period from May 2006 to the summer of 2022.

The liabilities in Figure 5.15 exactly match the categories we described in Figure 5.14. The asset categories are very similar, except that the Asset Purchase Facility (used to buy long-term government bonds to implement quantitative easing) is included under 'other assets'. Quantitative easing assets have consistently accounted for around 80% of the Bank of England's 'other assets'. The final item on the balance sheet, which may seem confusing, is *Ways and Means*. The *Ways and Means* facility functions as the government's overdraft account, helping the UK government manage cashflows. Its usage has declined over time and by 2020 it represented a negligible fraction of the balance sheet.

The Bank's cash liabilities, representing banknotes in the hands of the public, in ATM machines and in the vaults of commercial banks, have grown slowly over time in line with the economy. Demand for banknotes is relatively stable over the business cycle, although there are typically daily and seasonal fluctuations, such as increases in demand around public holidays. Under the UK's floating exchange rate regime, foreign currency assets and liabilities are small.

There was little volatility in the composition of the Bank of England's balance sheet prior to the financial crisis, which reflected the successful operation of inflation targeting through the setting of the policy rate. This changed in the financial crisis, and the balance sheet over the entire post-crisis period looks very different from before.

One dramatic feature of Figure 5.15 is the huge growth in 'other assets' since the financial crisis, driven almost entirely by quantitative easing. Away from the zero lower bound, the central bank sets the policy rate as its monetary policy tool, adjusting the supply of reserves to support its chosen price (i.e. the chosen policy rate). Under these conditions, the central bank's balance sheet changes rather little since its role is to respond to the ebb and flow in demand for reserves (see Figure 5.15 before the crisis, and Figure 5.16). The effect on the central bank's balance sheet arises from its willingness to meet the demand for reserves (its liabilities) at the price it sets and is referred to as 'liability-driven'.

One application of this is when interbank lending markets dried up at the start of the financial crisis, leading to a liquidity shortage. To meet the demand for liquidity, central banks around the world increased the supply of reserves to commercial banks.

Beginning in March 2009 the Bank began to use newly issued base money (reserves) to purchase bonds and other assets, with the intent of reducing long-term interest rates. This represents asset-driven expansion as described previously. The expansion of assets was matched by an increase in reserve balance liabilities, which were being used to fund the scheme, and has resulted in a situation of 'excess reserves'.

As already explained, excess reserves are those in reserve accounts over and above any reserves held for prudential reasons. Under this monetary policy framework, commercial banks hold involuntary excess reserves. There will continue to be excess reserves until the central bank decides to unwind quantitative easing, which would involve the central bank selling acquired assets back to commercial banks (reducing 'other assets' on its balance sheet), in return for reserve balances (reducing reserve liabilities on its balance sheet). We discuss the issues with this process at the end of Section 5.5.

To summarize, before the financial crisis, monetary policy was operated in a scarce reserves framework (the interest rate was the policy instrument); since the financial crisis, it has been operated in an ample reserves framework (where QE is the policy instrument at the zero lower bound, and monetary tightening takes place using the interest rate on reserves and quantitative tightening). The change in the structure of the central bank's balance sheet reveals this change vividly. We now turn to the operation of each of these regimes.

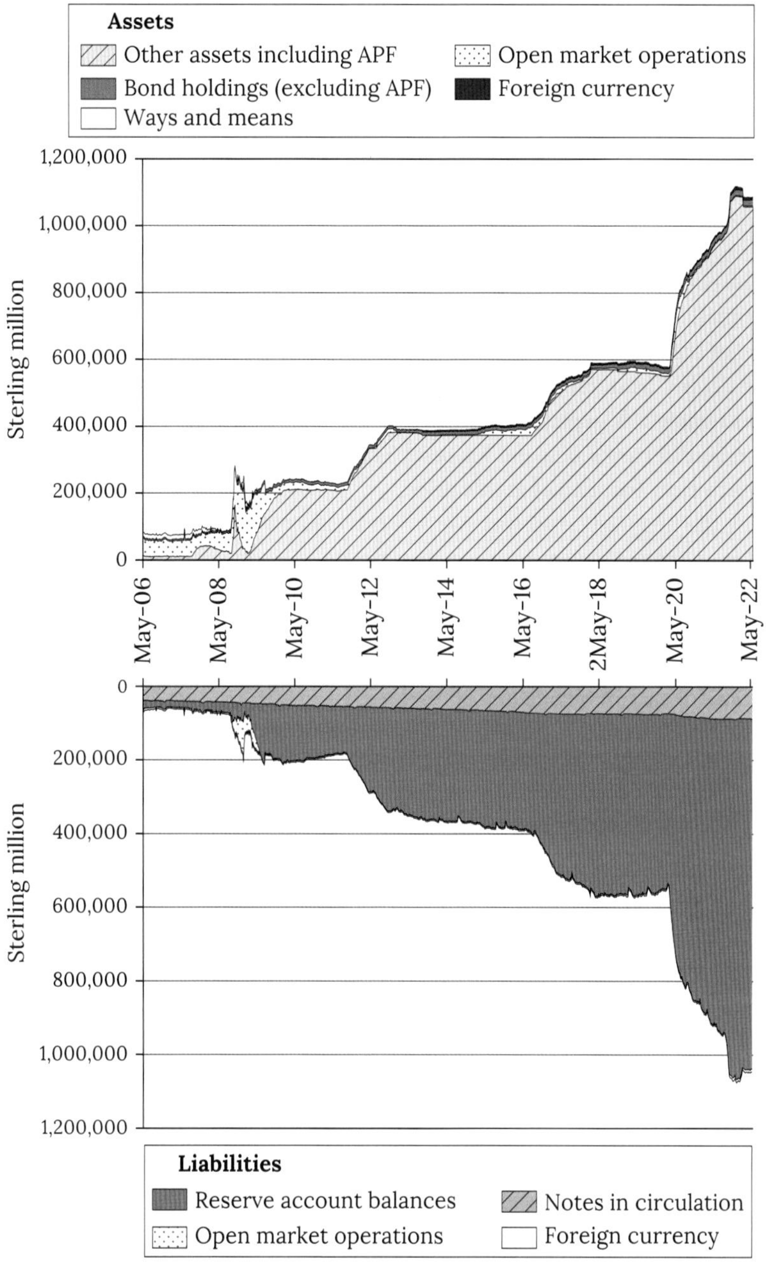

Figure 5.15 The Bank of England's (BofE) Weekly Report accounts for around 90% of the BofE's balance sheet. The data only extends backwards to September 2013. Before September 2013, we use the Bank Return for assets (which existed until September 2014, allowing us to verify overlap). Several asset series can be matched pre- and post-September 2013, but this is imperfect. Not all OMO series were reported before December 2008. We constructed post-September 2013 'other assets' to match the pre-September 2013 'other assets' as closely as possible. Prior to September 2013, foreign currency assets were counted under 'other assets,' and it is not possible to separate these. We assumed that the post-September 2013 series for bond holding assets would have been 60% of the pre-September 2013 equivalent when extending backwards, based on the overlap period.

Source: Bank of England's Weekly Report (data accessed June 2022).

5.5 MONETARY POLICY OPERATIONS

The logic of inflation-targeting policy is that the central bank influences aggregate demand through the lending interest rate; the way it does this is by announcing its policy rate. Central bank policy depends on clear signalling of its intentions. For instance, announcing a lower policy rate signals to households and firms that the lending rate will soon be reduced by banks and they begin to alter their spending plans accordingly.

In this section, we shall see the way that monetary policy was loosened and tightened under inflation-targeting both before and after the financial crisis. To do this, we use a model of the supply and demand for reserves. Commercial banks demand reserves and the central bank supplies them. Prior to the financial crisis, the so-called scarce reserves regime was in place. Given the chosen policy rate (the 'price' of reserves) and the commercial banks' demand for reserves, the central bank adjusted the supply of reserves to clear the market at this price.

During the financial crisis, however, central banks were constrained in their ability to loosen monetary policy because they hit the zero lower bound on the nominal interest rate. Loosening policy by cutting the policy rate further was not possible and the channel to influence spending plans of households and firms became quantitative easing. As the evolution of the Bank of England's balance sheet in the previous section vividly illustrates, reserves ceased being scarce. As a result, it was necessary for central banks to switch from a regime in which their chosen policy rate cleared the market for reserves to a new one, known as the ample reserves regime.[20]

5.5.1 The scarce reserves regime

To understand this regime, we will consider the case where the central bank decides to raise its output target, from y_1 to y_2. On the lower panel of Figure 5.16 we show the IS curve, which gives a relationship between output and the lending rate. Initially, the central bank required a lending rate of r_H, which it achieved by setting the policy rate r^P_H. To raise output to y_2, the central bank announces that the policy rate will be r^P_L. Commercial banks react to this new policy rate by reducing the lending rate to r_L, a consequence of their funding costs falling. Note that the interest rates shown in that diagram are real interest rates since that is the basis on which the IS curve is defined, but the Fisher equation can be used to translate these into nominal rates.

The upper panel shows the market for reserves. The demand for reserves by commercial banks is downward sloping. This is an indirect, or derived demand, arising from the bank's funding decisions. When the central bank announces a lower interest rate, the lending rate of commercial banks also falls. This leads to an increased demand for loans from households and firms shown by the IS. When commercial banks make these loans, they create more deposits. To ensure that they are able to settle transactions, the banks will seek to hold more reserves at the central bank; in other words, banks

[20] For more detailed explanation see Ihrig and Wolla (2020) and Vlieghe (2020) from which this section draws. Note that it is in theory possible to have a scarce reserves regime which pays interest on reserves but for clarity in explaining the two regimes, we assume this is not the case.

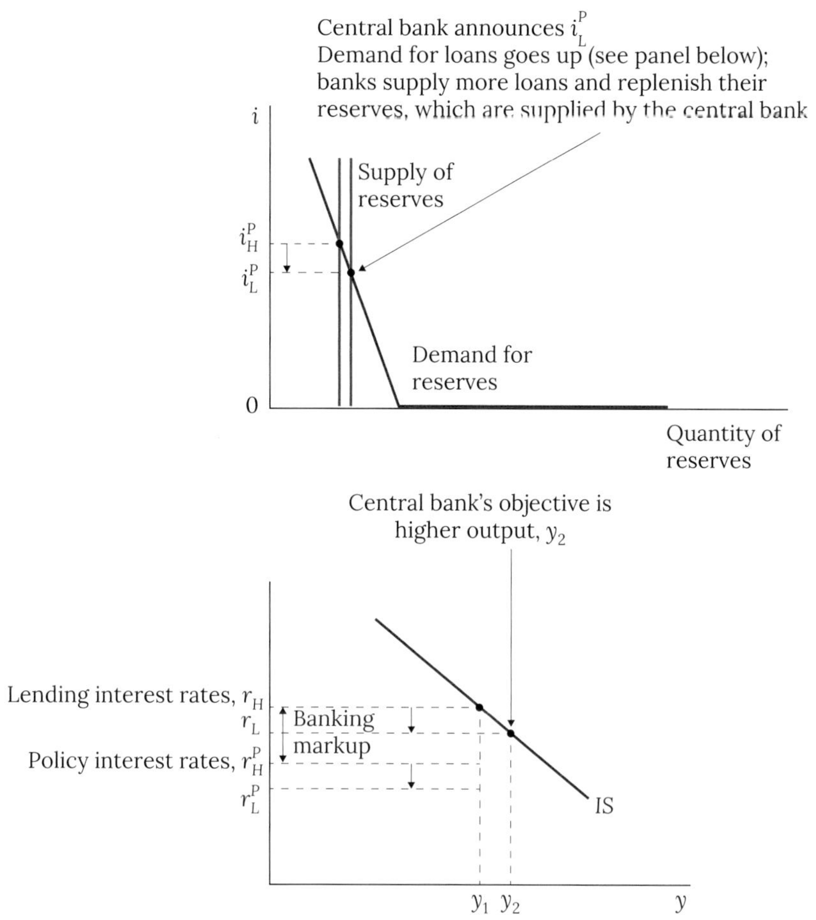

Figure 5.16 The scarce reserves regime. The central bank implements a cut in the policy rate. Visit www.oup.com/he/carlin-soskice to explore the scarce reserves regime with Animated Analytical Diagram 5.16.

require reserves for liquidity purposes. An additional effect is that the lower the money market interest rate, the lower the opportunity cost of holding reserves (the rate at which a bank could have lent out its reserves to another bank). The central bank will supply additional reserves to meet this extra demand. In our example, the fall of the policy rate from i_H^P to i_L^P is associated with the central bank increasing the supply of reserves.

The central bank uses some combination of open market operations and repos, to increase (or decrease) the supply of reserves by the correct amount. In the scarce reserves regime, banks are continuously engaged in short-term transactions in the money market to ensure they have positive balances at the central bank at the end of each day. As we saw in Section 5.2.2, the lending and borrowing is done using repos. The central bank lends to the banking system using repos to provide additional liquidity.[21] When the central bank announces a lower policy rate, the demand for reserves increases as explained in the previous paragraph. The central bank can then increase the scale of its repo lending to ensure that the supply of reserves intersects the demand for reserves at the new target policy rate.

There are three things to note about the market for reserves: first, the demand curve is very inelastic because only small changes in desired reserves arise in response to a change in the policy rate and second, this implies that the fluctuations in the supply of reserves will be modest. Third, the demand for reserves is flat when the interest rate is at the zero lower bound, beyond which the central bank is not able to stimulate interest-sensitive spending by announcing a lower policy rate. Once interest rates are at zero, there are no opportunity costs for commercial banks to hold reserves instead of lending them out, and as such they are potentially willing to hold very large amounts.

After reaching the zero lower bound following the financial crisis, central banks embarked on quantitative easing programmes, which led to the dramatic expansion of central bank balance sheets that we saw in Figure 5.13 (and more specifically, an expansion in reserve liabilities, as seen for the Bank of England in Figure 5.15). This led to a situation of ample reserves, which we shall now turn to.

5.5.2 The ample reserves regime

In the upper panel of Figure 5.17, the situation of ample reserves is shown with an interest rate of zero on reserves. Should the central bank wish to tighten monetary policy, it would have to shift the supply of reserves all the way to where the downward-sloping part of the demand for reserves curve intersects the horizontal axis. In other words, the central bank would have to completely unwind its programme of bond buying under quantitative easing before it could use the policy rate again as a tool of monetary policy. Such a large sale of bonds could disrupt the financial market, as we will see later in this section.

This is the reason why when faced with a situation of ample reserves, central banks pay interest on reserve accounts as shown in the lower panel of Figure 5.17. This means that while in the scarce reserves regime the policy rate was the central bank's target in the money market, under ample reserves it is the *rate paid on reserves*, a directly administered rate. Note that the demand for reserves becomes flat at whatever is the interest rate paid on reserves, for a similar reason to why it was flat at zero when no interest was paid. The opportunity cost of holding reserves is the difference between the rate at which a bank could have lent out its reserves to another bank (the money market rate) and the interest they could get from holding the reserves. When the money market rate is the same as the interest being paid on reserves, there is no opportunity cost of reserves, and banks are willing to hold even very large amounts. The interest on reserves therefore provides a floor to the 'willingness to accept' price and the demand curve is horizontal. Due to arbitrage the money market

[21] For instance, a commercial bank hands over a government bond to the central bank and agrees to repurchase it fourteen days later.

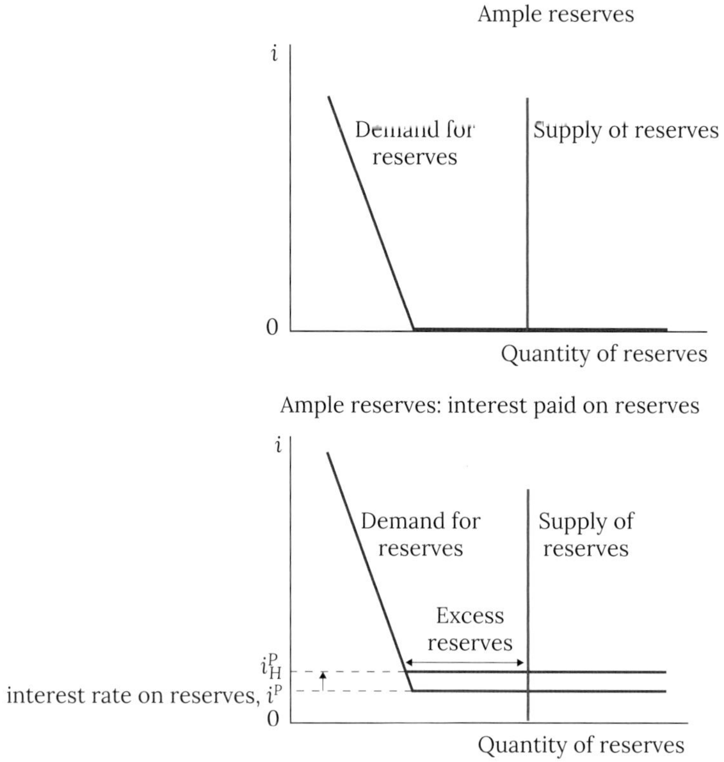

Figure 5.17 The ample reserves regime. The central bank implements a rise in the interest rate on reserves (lower panel).

rate will continue to be very close to the policy rate, for the same reasons explained in Section 5.2.2.

The key feature is that by paying interest on reserves, a central bank can either tighten or loosen monetary policy without changing quantitative easing assets—as we shall see in Chapter 6, this means that a central bank could expand assets to provide emergency liquidity to maintain financial stability at the same time as it tightens monetary policy. Should the central bank wish to tighten monetary policy in the ample reserves regime, it has two choices. It can either embark on quantitative tightening (QT) by selling some of the bonds purchased during quantitative easing, or it can simply raise the interest rate paid on reserves. Similarly, should the central bank wish to loosen monetary policy, it could either embark on further quantitative easing, or simply lower the interest rate paid on reserves.

In the example where the central bank chooses to tighten by raising the policy rate, namely, the interest rate on reserves, the process of arbitrage will imply that the interest rate in the money market rises in line with the policy rate. Faced with this increase in funding costs, commercial banks will raise their lending rates. The demand for loans coming from the non-bank private sector will decline. An example is given on the lower panel of Figure 5.17, where the central bank has raised rates paid on reserves from i^P to i^P_H. Note that the supply of reserves did not need to change during this process—this means that under ample reserves, central banks no longer need to precisely match the supply and demand for reserves. In summary, a higher interest paid on reserves raises the bar for the minimum rate at which commercial banks are willing to lend to the private economy. Therefore, the interest paid on reserves could also be interpreted as the opportunity cost of lending to the private economy faced by commercial banks (the higher the interest, the higher the opportunity cost).

To implement quantitative tightening, the central bank sells bonds to primary dealers. The dealers' banks act as intermediaries, and reduce the dealers' deposits by the amount they paid for the bonds, while reducing their own reserve holdings by the same amount. QT would be expected to push up the yield on long-dated bonds (when the central bank sells them, the price falls and the yield rises), steepening the yield curve and dampening spending plans. This would also shift the supply of reserves line to the left as the balances in reserve accounts decline.[22]

However due to uncertainty regarding the shape of the demand curve for reserves from commercial banks, any monetary tightening performed using QT would have to be a gradual process, to avoid moving too rapidly into scarce reserves territory and losing control of the interest rate. This occurred in the United States in September 2019. The US Federal Reserve (US central bank) underestimated the desired reserve holdings of commercial banks, and performed QT too rapidly. This reduced the supply of reserves being lent out on the repo market. At the same time, reserves fell because of two different payments to the government (quarterly corporate tax payments and the proceeds of a government debt auction). Any payment to the government must necessarily reduce the supply of reserves held by banks as long as the treasury takes payment to an account at the central bank. As we have seen, this would not happen if the deposits were to government accounts at commercial banks. This caused the repo rate to temporarily spike at over 5%, up from 2% a few days earlier, and the money market (interbank) rate began to follow, as institutions started to reduce lending on the money market to profit from lending at higher rates on the repo market. Figure 5.18 shows that while the interest on reserves, the money market rate and the repo rate usually remain close due to arbitrage, there was a significant divergence in mid-September 2019.

The crisis was resolved after the Federal Reserve injected reserves into the system by purchasing more Treasury securities, effectively reversing QT, and expanded repo trading activities. When the Covid-19 pandemic hit a few months later, the Federal Reserve once again expanded its quantitative easing programme by purchasing more Treasury securities, and increased the amount of reserves it could lend using repos from US$ 120 billion to US$ 2 trillion. In July 2021 the central bank created a domestic standing repo facility (SRF), effectively a permanent commitment to offer repo lending to commercial banks in times of low liquidity. A second example of when QT may need

[22] See Hauser (2019) for a discussion of quantitative tightening; the conclusion, pre-dating Covid-19, was that even after QT, reserves will remain at a much higher level than before the financial crisis. The September 2019 US repo example below is based on Cheng and Wessel (2020) and Anbil et al. (2020).

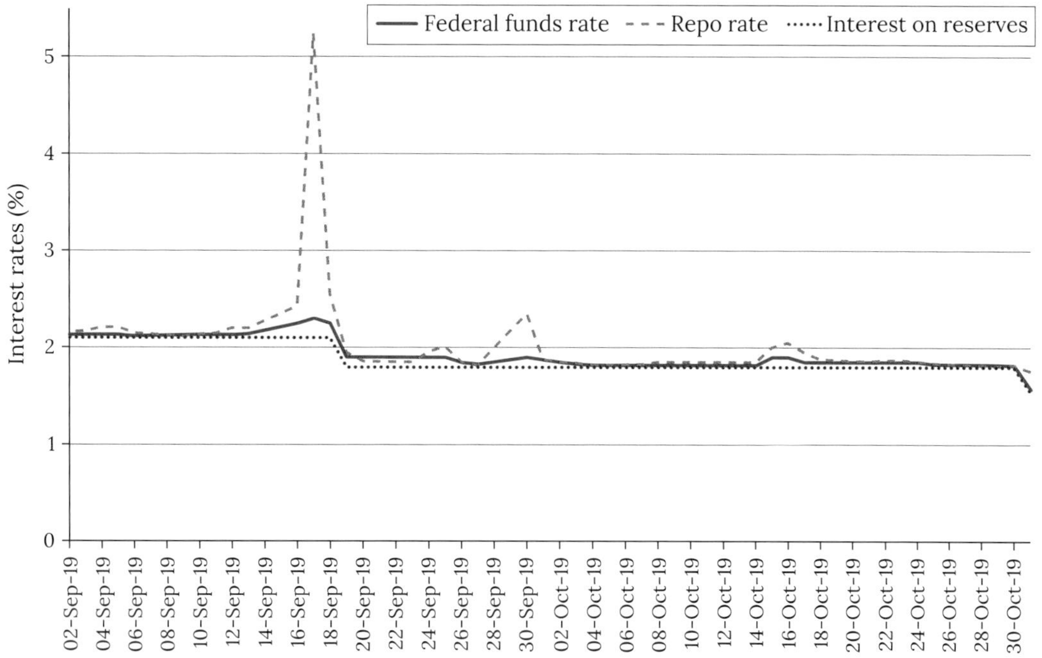

Figure 5.18 United States interest rates in September and October 2019. We have used the effective federal funds rate as the money market (interbank) rate, the interest on excess reserves as the policy rate, and the Secured Overnight Financing Rate (SOFR) as a measure of the repo rate.

Source: Federal Reserve Bank of St. Louis (data accessed August 2021).

to be rapidly undone to prevent distress in financial markets is the United Kingdom government bond market in September 2022, which is covered in Chapter 6.

5.6 CONCLUSIONS

In this chapter, we have provided a simple way of representing a modern financial system, which highlights its essential role in the macroeconomy. The financial system facilitates economic transactions, allows households and firms to implement their planned spending decisions and is the transmission mechanism for inflation-targeting monetary policy.

We have also introduced the concept of a balance sheet, which documents what an economic agent owes against what it is owed and shows their net worth. This is a useful framework for discussing the two major problems in the banking sector; insufficient liquidity and solvency. In a modern banking system, these problems are the joint responsibility of the central bank and the government (i.e. taxpayers). The spillover effects to the rest of the economy from these problems explain why banking is the most regulated industry in the economy. The balance sheets also illuminate the relationship between the central bank and commercial banks, which has come to the fore with the advent of quantitative easing policy.

The main focus of the chapter has been to extend the core 3-equation model set out in Chapter 3 to include the banking system. We have added more flesh to the bones of monetary policy transmission by making the distinction between the *policy rate of interest* (the rate set by the central bank) and the *lending rate of interest* (the rate that influences the spending and investment decisions of households and firms). The lending rate is determined by the profit-maximizing decisions of banks and is set as a markup on the policy rate of interest.

The 3-equation model including the banking system provides a framework in which we can answer interesting questions about the role of the banking system and money in the macroeconomy, such as:

1. What factors affect the banking markup? There are three key factors that influence the markup of the lending rate (r) over the policy rate (r^P) in the model. The markup will increase as banks' loans are perceived to be riskier, and will fall the more risk tolerant are the banks and the larger the equity buffer they have with which to absorb losses. The central bank has to monitor each of these potential sources of disturbance to macroeconomic stability. Financial stability requires adequate loss-absorbing capacity and this is explained further in Chapters 8, 9, and 10.
2. How does the central bank react to economic shocks when banks are included in the model? The central bank analyses shocks in the same way as it does in the core 3-equation model. The objective is to affect the spending decisions of households and firms primarily by affecting the cost of borrowing, but also by affecting agents' expectations of future aggregate demand-stabilizing monetary policy. The mechanism through which this takes place is more thoroughly explained once we include the banking system. The central bank sets the policy interest rate. The lending rate is then determined as a markup on the policy rate. Following an economic shock, the central bank uses the *MR* curve to determine its desired output gap, then sets the policy rate that will deliver that output gap next period (taking into account the banking markup). Unlike the simple 3-equation model, the extended model can address the question of the implications for the economy of shocks to the banking system itself.
3. How has the use of quantitative easing affected the operation of inflation-targeting monetary policy? Rather than a brief episode at the zero lower bound, many economies experienced this for more than a decade. The adoption of quantitative easing as the monetary policy instrument to target the central bank's best response output gap has resulted in the huge expansion of the central bank's balance sheet. This means that commercial banks have excess reserves in their accounts at the central bank. This has changed the monetary policy framework from one of scarce to one of ample reserves. Under the latter, it is the interest rate on reserves that is the policy interest rate.

This chapter provides a theoretical framework for thinking about the interaction between the banking system and the macroeconomy. Chapter 8 moves away from the case where the system functions smoothly to analyse the darker side of financial markets: financial cycles and banking crises.

5.7 APPENDIX

5.7.1 Modelling the banking markup (r-r^P)

This Appendix formally sets out a simple model of the banking markup. We assume a competitive banking system. The main conclusions of the model would be unchanged if we moved to a monopolistic banking system. The difference between the two models is the assumptions around pricing. Banks are 'price takers' in the competitive case—they take the lending rate as given and maximize profits based on the amount of loans they provide. In contrast, in the model used in the chapter, the monopoly bank is a 'price setter'—it chooses the lending rate in order to maximize its profits.

In reality, banking systems are usually oligopolistic, an intermediate case between monopolistic and competitive. For example, the UK banking system has a handful of firms that dominate the market. The important point to note is that for all types of market structure, the factors influencing the banking markup are the same and work in the same direction. The market structure affects the size of the markup. When banks have market power they are able to charge a higher lending rate, holding everything else constant.

The supply of loans by banks

The first step in setting out the banking model is to define the key variables: $r =$ the lending rate, $r^P =$ the policy rate, which we assume due to perfect arbitrage is equal to the money market rate, $\tau =$ is a bank's risk tolerance, and $v =$ the riskiness of loans, for instance the variance of the expected return on loans.

The lending rate is decided by the interaction of the supply and demand for loans. We will first solve a competitive (price-taking) bank's profit maximization problem to derive the supply of loans, before solving the household problem to find the demand for loans. The interaction of supply and demand will give us the equilibrium lending rate.

Consider the case of a bank which has pre-existing loans L^{Old}, reserves R^{Old}, and deposits D^{Old}. We use a simple static model where the bank has to make a one-off decision over how many new loans to make, $L^{New} \geq 0$, which will be the 'supply' of loans. Section 5.4.1 explains why banks need to attract reserves when lending, to ensure that they have sufficient liquidity to settle transactions. We will call the amount of reserves the bank has to raise after making new loans as R^{Raised}. We begin by assuming that we are in a **scarce reserves** framework, where the bank always holds exactly how many reserves it needs to fulfil a reserve to deposit ratio rd, which could be a legal requirement or a self-imposed prudential requirement to ensure sufficient liquidity.

The profit function, ignoring any terms related to previous loan decisions, which cannot be modified, is:

$$V_B = \underbrace{\frac{rL^{New} - r^P R^{Raised}}{e}}_{\text{expected return}} - \frac{1}{2\tau}\underbrace{(v)\left(\frac{L^{New}}{e}\right)^2}_{\text{total risk}}. \qquad \text{(bank profit function)}$$

The first term shows the return on loans (rL^{New}) minus the cost of borrowing new reserves on the money market. In reality banks will raise part of their funding using longer term rates, such as the three-month LIBOR rate in the UK,[23] which we will simplify by considering a single rate, r^P. The first term is divided by equity to get a measure of the bank's profit relative to equity (return on equity). The second term includes a measure of the riskiness of loans (v) and a measure of the bank's leverage ($\left(\frac{L}{e}\right)^2$), which represents its equity buffer. The negative impact of total risk on the bank's profits then reduces the more risk tolerant the bank is (i.e. $\uparrow \tau$), the less risky the loans are ($\downarrow v$) and the lower the leverage ratio ($\downarrow \frac{L}{e}$) is. The specific functional form of the negative part of the profit function was chosen for computational ease.

Before making the loan, the bank was operating exactly at its reserve requirement, meaning that $rd = \frac{R^{Old}}{D^{Old}}$. We assume that when new loans and hence deposits are made, a proportion $0 \le \alpha \le 1$ of the new deposits stay at the bank, with the borrower spending the rest at a company that has an account with a different bank. This means that new reserves will be $R^{Old} - (1-\alpha)L^{New} + R^{Raised}$, while new deposits will be $D^{Old} + \alpha L^{New}$. On the assumption that the bank continues to operate at its reserve requirement, the ratio of new reserves to new deposits must be equal to rd.

Equating the two measures for rd, we can rearrange to find $R^{Raised} = \alpha L^{New} rd + L^{New} - \alpha L^{New} = L^{New}(1+(rd-1)\alpha)$. This means that the amount of reserves to be raised depends on three things. Firstly, as rd and α are both between zero and one, a higher L means that the bank must raise more reserves. Secondly, as $rd-1$ is negative a higher α means that there is a smaller need to raise reserves, all else equal; intuitively, if more of the newly created deposits stay with the bank, there is less need to fill the outflow of reserves. Thirdly, a higher rd means that the bank has to raise more reserves, all else equal.

Let us consider the simple case where $\alpha = 0$, meaning that all new deposits created when lending are spent at a different bank. From the point of view of an individual bank, which we are considering, this makes sense. However from the point of view of the banking system as a whole it might not, as if banks are creating loans at the same time they will receive inflows of deposits from borrowers at other banks. When $\alpha = 0$, the profit function can be re-written as,

$$V_B = \underbrace{\frac{rL^{New} - r^P L^{New}}{e}}_{\text{expected return}} - \frac{1}{2\tau}\underbrace{(v)\left(\frac{L^{New}}{e}\right)^2}_{\text{total risk}}. \qquad \text{(bank profit function)}$$

To find the supply of bank loans, we simply need to differentiate the profit function with respect to L^{New}, then set it equal to zero and rearrange for optimal L^{New},

$$\frac{\partial V_B}{\partial L^{New}} = \frac{r - r^P}{e} - \tau^{-1}(v)\frac{L^{New}}{e^2} = 0$$

$$r - r^P = \tau^{-1}(v)\frac{L^{New}}{e}$$

$$\rightarrow L^S = \left(\frac{e\tau}{v}\right)(r - r^P). \qquad \text{(the optimal supply of bank loans)}$$

[23] See Button et al. (2010) for a more detailed breakdown of the marginal funding cost.

The optimal supply of banks loans increases with the banking markup $r - r^p$, the equity of the bank e and its risk tolerance τ, and falls with the riskiness of loans v. We can also rewrite this equation to give the bank's desired leverage:

$$\lambda^S = \frac{L^S}{e} = \left(\frac{\tau}{v}\right)(r - r^P). \qquad \text{(optimal bank leverage)}$$

Raising deposits

Instead of borrowing new reserves on the money market, a bank could try to attract new deposits from customers. Regardless of whether customers pay in physically by depositing banknotes, or electronically by making a transfer, the inflow of a new deposit will come with new reserves. Thus new reserves will be $R^{Old} - (1-\alpha)L^{New} + R^{Raised} + D^{Raised}$, while new deposits will be $D^{Old} + \alpha L^{New} + D^{Raised}$, where D^{Raised} is the amount of new deposits. Making the ratio equal to rd, and equating it to the initial rd, we find that $R^{Raised} = L^{New}(1 + (rd-1)\alpha + D^{Raised}(rd-1))$. This has the same interpretation as before, but in addition, given that $rd - 1$ is negative, the result shows that raising more deposits reduces the need to raise reserves by borrowing, all else given.

As we assume there is no interest paid on deposits, this may be an attractive way to gain reserves relative to borrowing. However savers are slow to react by changing banks,[24] and there may be other costs involved in attracting new customers such as advertising or welcome bonuses, which is why banks typically make decisions using the marginal cost of borrowing rather than the cost of attracting deposits. In a competitive marketplace, all banks will be simultaneously competing for new deposits, reducing the ease of attracting them.

Ample reserves

In a situation of ample reserves we can drop the assumption that banks need to meet an exact reserve requirement rd. For simplicity, we will instead assume that banks have a certain amount of reserves, and want to maintain this level of reserves. When making new loans, $(1-\alpha)L^{New}$ reserves will flow out as before. The bank can replenish this either by borrowing reserves, R^{Raised}, or attracting deposits, D^{New}, thus giving $(1-\alpha)L^{New} = R^{Raised} + D^{New}$. Under the assumption that α is zero as before, this gives us a profit function,

$$V_B = \underbrace{\frac{rL^{New} - r^P(L^{New} - D^{New}) - cD^{New}}{e}}_{\text{expected return}} - \underbrace{\frac{1}{2\tau}(v)\left(\frac{L^{New}}{e}\right)^2}_{\text{total risk}}. \qquad \text{(ample reserves profit function)}$$

where c is the cost of attracting new deposits, and may be increasing in the amount of deposits raised. If we simplify by assuming that banks are always trying to attract deposits regardless, in other words D^{New} is exogenous, the only decision being made is over the amount of new loans L^{New}. We can then differentiate and follow the exact same steps as under scarce reserves. The amount $L^{New} - D^{New}$ represents how many reserves

[24] See Collinson, P. (2013, September 07). Switching banks: Why are we more loyal to our bank than to a partner? *The Guardian*. Retrieved from https://www.theguardian.com/money/2013/sep/ 07/switching-banks-seven-day

need to be raised by borrowing, and is sometimes called the 'customer funding gap,' as it represents reserves which are not raised directly from customers (depositors).

The demand for loans by households

The next stage in the model of the banking markup is to set out an equation for the demand for loans. Recall this form of the IS curve introduced in Chapter 3:

$$y = A - ar. \qquad \text{(IS curve)}$$

In using this equation here, we radically simplify by assuming that A is the non-interest-sensitive demand for loans. We can see from the IS equation that aggregate demand depends inversely on the lending rate. We can therefore write the aggregate demand for loans as:

$$L^D = \bar{L} - ar. \qquad \text{(demand for loans by households)}$$

We can break this equation down further by splitting the autonomous loan demand, $\bar{L}$, into demand from credit-constrained households (A_C) and from unconstrained households (A_U), such that,

$$\bar{L} = A_C + A_U = A$$
$$\rightarrow L^D = A_C + A_U - ar.$$

(demand for loans by credit-constrained and unconstrained households)

The credit-constrained households are able to borrow $A_C \leq lW$, where W is a measure of their wealth and l is the fraction of wealth that banks are willing to lend to households. These households are credit constrained if they wish to borrow $A_C > lW$. The unconstrained households demand $A_U - ar$ of loans; their demand for loans falls as the interest rate rises. This is in contrast to the credit-constrained households who are completely insensitive to changes in the lending rate, for instance due to asymmetric information issues which prevent banks from ever lending more than lW to these households.

Equilibrium in the loan market

We now have all the components to derive the lending rate. It is simply determined by equating supply and demand in the loan market:

$$L^S = L^D$$
$$\rightarrow \left(\frac{e\tau}{v}\right)(r - r^P) = \bar{L} - ar. \qquad \text{(equilibrium in the loan market)}$$

To simplify the equilibrium equation we define $\omega \equiv \frac{v}{e\tau}$. We now rearrange to find the equilibrium lending rate:

$$\left(\frac{e\tau}{v}\right)(r - r^P) = \bar{L} - ar$$
$$\frac{1}{\omega}(r - r^P) = \bar{L} - ar$$
$$r(1 + a\omega) = r^P + \omega\bar{L}$$
$$r = \frac{r^P + \omega\bar{L}}{1 + a\omega}. \qquad \text{(equilibrium lending rate)}$$

We can see that, holding the policy rate constant, the banking markup increases when:

1. the autonomous demand for loans, $\bar{L}$, increases;
2. the riskiness of loans, v, increases;
3. the risk tolerance of banks, τ, falls;
4. equity, e, falls.[25]

We can also rewrite the equilibrium lending rate to show the impact of credit constraints on the markup. We know that $\bar{L} = A_C + A_U$ and that A_C is a positive function of the wealth of credit-constrained households. If we assume that credit-constrained households borrow up to their maximum (i.e. $A_C = lW$), then the equilibrium lending rate becomes

$$r = \frac{r^P + \omega(A_C + A_U)}{1 + a\omega}$$

$$r = \frac{r^P + \omega(lW + A_U)}{1 + a\omega}.$$

(equilibrium lending rate for credit-constrained and unconstrained households)

This equation shows that the higher the wealth of credit-constrained households, the higher the banking markup.

Central bank's choice of r^P in equilibrium

In equilibrium, the central bank will set r^P such that the lending rate is at the stabilizing rate of interest, r_S. This is the lending rate at which output is at equilibrium, y_e. We can substitute r_S into the lending rate equation and y_e into the demand for loans equation and rearrange to find an equation for the policy rate:

$$r_S = \frac{r^P + \omega\bar{L}}{1 + a\omega}.$$

$$r^P = r_S(1 + a\omega) - \omega\bar{L}$$

$$r^P = r_S - \omega(\bar{L} - ar_S)$$

$$L = \bar{L} - ar_S$$

$$r^P = r_S - \omega y_e. \qquad \text{(the policy rate in equilibrium)}$$

---

[25] We can take the composite risk term, ω, and show that unless r is so high that L^D is negative, the three final results hold. They follow from:

$$r = \frac{r^P + \omega\bar{L}}{1 + a\omega}.$$

$$\frac{\partial r}{\partial \omega} = \frac{\bar{L}}{1 + a\omega} - \frac{r^P + \omega\bar{L}}{(1 + a\omega)^2}a.$$

$$\frac{\partial r}{\partial \omega} > 0 \rightarrow \frac{1}{1 + a\omega}\left(\bar{L} - a\left(\frac{r^P + \omega\bar{L}}{1 + a\omega}\right)\right) > 0$$

$$\rightarrow \bar{L} - ar > 0$$

So long as this holds, an increase in ω increases the markup; this implies that anything which increases ω (fall in equity, fall of risk tolerance, increase in risk) increases the markup.

The equation shows that the central bank first needs to know the lending rate that will stabilize output at equilibrium. The next step is to take account of all the factors that influence the markup. Lastly, they subtract the markup from the stabilizing lending rate to find the equilibrium policy rate.

QUESTIONS AND PROBLEMS FOR CHAPTER 5

CHECKLIST QUESTIONS

1. Why do saver households not lend directly to borrower households? How can banks help solve this problem?
2. Why are loans to households and firms considered risky? Make sure you refer to and explain the following terms in your answer:
   a. Uncertainty.
   b. Moral hazard.
   c. Adverse selection.
3. Are the following two statements both true or is only one of them true? Justify your answer.
   S1. The bank lending rate will increase the riskier loans are perceived to be.
   S2. Given S1, the more risk that banks can tolerate, the higher the bank lending rate will be.
4. The following four borrowers are categorized according to their level of wealth and the quality of their proposed investment project. Which of the borrowers is likely to receive a loan from the bank for their project and why?
   a. Low wealth, low quality project
   b. Low wealth, high quality project
   c. High wealth, low quality project
   d. High wealth, high quality project
5. The interest rate in the economy is 3%. The government plans to sell a bond with a maturity in five years, a face value of 100 pounds, and an annual coupon payment of 5 pounds. Assuming there is no default risk, how much would this bond sell for?
6. Set out a simple balance sheet for a single commercial bank (as in Figure 5.11). Define each item in turn and discuss why that item has been labelled as an asset or a liability. Why is net worth on the liabilities side of the balance sheet?

7. What are the channels through which banks can fund their lending? In the model presented in this chapter, can banks influence the level of aggregate demand in the economy?

8. What are the key differences between the way that monetary policy is conducted in the 3-equation model (from Chapter 3) and in the 3-equation model with the banking system? Does this change the policy implemented by the central bank following economic shocks? Consider both the scarce reserves and the ample reserves frameworks.

9. Use the 3-equation model to show the impact of a reduction in consumer confidence on the economy. Make sure you show the period 1 markup on your diagram and discuss what happens to both the policy rate and the lending rate (as in Figure 5.5).

10. Use yield curve diagrams to explain how conventional (i.e. adjusting short-term interest rates) and unconventional (i.e. quantitative easing) monetary policies aim to influence the level of aggregate demand in the economy.

11. Explain using the material from this chapter how commercial banks *create* money, and why.

12. In a situation of ample reserves, are there constraints on the supply of loans by commercial banks?

13. Suppose the policy rate and the money market rate are equal. Answer the following:
    a. If the policy rate is the interest paid on reserves, why would banks be willing to hold large reserve holdings?
    b. If a single bank now decides to hold more reserves, has the total supply of reserves in the economy increased?

14. Why does paying interest on reserves allow a central bank to tighten monetary policy without unwinding quantitative easing assets? What risks might be associated with unwinding quantitative easing?

PROBLEMS

1. Collect the annual report of a US commercial bank from a recent year. Find the consolidated balance sheet and condense it into a form similar to the Barclays' balance sheet shown in Figure 5.11. Answer the following questions:
    a. What proportion of customer deposits does the bank hold with the central bank as reserves?
    b. How much of the bank's loans are funded through customer deposits?
    c. What is the bank's leverage?

2. Use central bank websites to collect data on monthly policy rates and mortgage rates in two developed economies between 2005 and 2020. Plot the data on graphs, as per Figure 5.8. Answer the following:
   a. How do the banking markups compare in the two countries?
   b. Do the banking markups change over time?
   c. Use the chapter and Appendix 5.7.1 to discuss possible reasons for any differences observed over time and between countries.

3. In the wake of the global financial crisis, there has been a lot of discussion about whether banking is 'socially useful'. Use the simple model of the macroeconomy and the financial system to explain the benefits to the economy of the banking system and its role in stabilization policy. What factors are not considered in the basic model which could lead to the banking system destabilizing the economy? Could these activities be considered socially useful?

4. The UK government introduced lending targets (encouraging more lending to households and firms) for the five major UK banks after the global financial crisis. Use the model of the macroeconomy and the financial system to discuss this policy. Make sure you refer to the following:
   a. Whether you think the policy makes economic sense.
   b. Are there any potential pitfalls with the policy?
   c. How could it affect stabilization policy?

INTERESTED IN EXPLORING THESE TOPICS FURTHER?

Visit www.oup.com/he/carlin-soskice to consolidate and extend your learning with the multiple-choice questions and Animated Analytical Diagrams accompanying this chapter.

CHAPTER

6

MONETARY POLICY

6.1 INTRODUCTION

In previous chapters, we have built up a macroeconomic model with the following structure:

1. Supply-side institutions and policies pin down the equilibrium level of output and unemployment in the economy.
2. Wages and prices do not adjust flexibly so as to keep the economy at equilibrium output in the presence of shocks. This implies there is a role for stabilization policy and that disinflation is costly in terms of higher unemployment.
3. When available, monetary rather than fiscal policy is the preferred stabilization policy.
4. The economy's nominal anchor (the inflation rate in medium-run equilibrium) is established by the adoption of an inflation target by a credible central bank.

In this chapter, we look in more depth at the reasoning and evidence behind the central role that monetary policy plays in contemporary macroeconomic management.

Grappling with high inflation, policy makers in the late 1970s and 1980s introduced money supply targets ('monetary targeting'). The 'Monetarist' policy of the UK's Thatcher government provides a striking example of the failure of monetary targeting. This experience contributed to the shift toward the inflation-targeting monetary policy regime, which combines explicit targets for inflation with the use of the interest rate as the policy instrument. The 3-equation model is based on this framework.

In Section 6.3, we extend the modelling of the inflation-targeting framework from Chapter 3. We firstly look at the underlying determinants of the sacrifice ratio, which is the unemployment cost of reducing inflation. This is followed by a subsection in which we combine the central bank's MR equation with the IS equation to derive the interest rate setting rule of the central bank. This is the best-response interest rate rule and is sometimes referred to as the optimal Taylor rule.

The practice of central banks that operate within the inflation-targeting monetary policy regime is the subject of Section 6.4, which begins with the Bank of England's explanation of the transmission mechanism of monetary policy. This is followed by a comparison of central bank mandates and interest rate rules across countries.

Section 6.4 goes on by focusing on monetary policy and the global financial crisis. Section 6.4.2 begins with the debate, which began before the crisis, about whether central banks should intervene to burst asset price bubbles such as the dot-com bubble of the late 1990s. The general approach taken by central bankers before the crisis was to refrain from targeting asset price bubbles, to wait until they burst and then to 'mop up' after them by providing liquidity. We use this section to set out both sides of the debate.

The remainder of Section 6.4 analyses the use of unorthodox monetary policy during the Great Recession. With interest rates at or close to the zero lower bound, central banks across the world reached for other instruments to keep inflation close to target and to prevent a deflation trap. As discussed in Chapter 5 on the operational shift from the scarce to the ample reserves regime, they engaged in large-scale asset purchases (known as quantitative easing, or QE) in an attempt to boost asset prices. As we saw previously, higher bond prices reduce their yield. The aim of QE is to reduce the cost of long-term borrowing and to boost wealth, both of which are expected to stimulate spending and close the output gap. The focus here is on the transmission mechanism of QE, the evidence of its effectiveness and how central banks exit from QE. An example from the UK in September 2022 demonstrates that unwinding QE can be difficult, as the need to support financial stability can clash with inflation-targeting goals. At the end of the section, we discuss distributional consequences of monetary policy. The final section of the chapter considers the relationship between the central bank's balance sheet and inflation.

6.2 ESTABLISHING THE ECONOMY'S NOMINAL ANCHOR

6.2.1 Money supply

In the early 1970s, after the end of the era of the Bretton Woods system of fixed exchange rates, the choice of nominal anchor reverted to national authorities. The German and Swiss National Banks chose to adopt targets for the growth rate of the money supply as their nominal anchor. The German Bundesbank was successful in using the language of monetary targeting to communicate to the public the orientation of monetary policy toward the long-run stability of inflation at a low rate.[1] One way of expressing this is to say that by describing its behaviour in terms of monetary targeting, the Bundesbank succeeded in establishing a value close to one for the coefficient on the inflation target, χ, in the Phillips curve with anchored inflation expectations introduced in Chapter 4:

$$\pi_t = [\chi\pi^T + (1-\chi)\pi_{t-1}] + \alpha(y_t - y_e). \tag{6.1}$$

As we saw in Chapter 4, a higher level of anchoring of expectations reduces the costs of disinflation in this model.

In Chapter 4, we also explained that in a model economy where agents have rational expectations and there are fully flexible wages and prices, the announcement of a lower inflation target would lead to an immediate fall in inflation to the new target without cost. Applying those assumptions to the use of the growth rate of the money supply as the nominal anchor, the announcement of a lower target for money growth would reduce inflation at no unemployment cost.

In the absence of fully flexible wages and prices, a policy of tighter money has its effects through raising the real interest rate, creating a negative output gap

[1] See Mishkin (1999).

and bearing down on inflation in the usual way via the Phillips curve. Under these conditions, for a policy of monetary targeting to be successful in its objective of controlling inflation, two conditions must hold: (1) the central bank must be able to control the chosen monetary aggregate and (2) the relationship between inflation and the targeted monetary aggregate must be reliable.

Problems can arise at both points. These problems undermined monetary targeting in the US, Canada and the UK. The UK provides a nice case study because both of the above problems were present. Although the central bank can control a narrow money aggregate (such as the quantity of banknotes in the hands of the public), the relationship between narrow money and inflation is weak, undermining the role of the target in shaping inflation expectations, which we can model as limiting the maximum value of the χ term to below 1 in equation 6.1.

In the UK, it was argued that whenever the monetary authority attempted to control a particular monetary aggregate as its target, there would be a response by the financial system in the form of the emergence of close substitutes or near-moneys that would lie outside the target and therefore serve to undermine it.[2] This phenomenon is referred to as Goodhart's law.

In relation to the second condition, shifts in the demand for money (called velocity instability) will alter the relationship between the targeted money supply aggregate and inflation, making monetary targeting an inaccurate way of controlling aggregate demand.

The failed Thatcher experiment with money supply targeting

Economic policy making in the United Kingdom from the end of the Second World War to the late 1970s focused on achieving multiple objectives. Governments used all the policy levers at their disposal to pursue low inflation, high employment, economic growth and a sustainable external balance.

The Conservative government that came to power under Margaret Thatcher in June 1979 broke from this framework, choosing instead to concentrate its macroeconomic policy on reducing inflation. At the same time, the government introduced a range of supply-side policies to reduce equilibrium unemployment, which are discussed in Chapter 15.

The path of inflation and unemployment over the Thatcher years is shown in Figure 3.3 in Chapter 3. The year that Thatcher took office, retail price inflation stood at 13.4%, which was very high for the post WWII period.

The Conservatives attempted to achieve their desired disinflation by setting 'intermediate financial targets'. In practice, this translated into fixed targets for the growth rate of the money supply and public sector borrowing in each of the next four years, as set out in Thatcher's Medium-Term Financial Strategy (MTFS).[3] As discussed in Chapter 3, the Thatcher disinflation entailed large costs in terms of higher unemployment. Table 6.1 shows that inflation in the UK fell dramatically from 18% to 4.6% between 1980 and 1983, but unemployment rose from 6.9% to 11.6% over the same period.

---

[2] For details, see Goodhart (1989).

[3] The key papers used in this subsection are: Buiter and Miller (1981 and 1983) and Goodhart (1986 and 1989).

The government targeted the growth of broad money, M3, which consists of currency, central bank reserves, demand deposits, savings deposits and time deposits. It can be argued that the central bank cannot directly control broad money, but rather only narrow money, M0, which consists of just currency and central bank reserves. This can translate into control of M3, but only when the relationship between M0 and M3 is stable over time.

What the government had not anticipated was that the early 1980s would see substantial shifts in the demand for money. This primarily came through two channels. One was the outcome of regulatory changes which removed restrictions on bank lending behaviour and liberalized the scope for building societies to attract deposits. The second was related to the government's own anti-inflation policy. The severity of the recession in the early 1980s and the sharp appreciation of sterling (see Chapter 12 for a discussion of the associated exchange rate overshooting) had squeezed the non-bank financial sector (particularly in manufacturing, see Table 6.1). This led to an increase in the demand for loans from these companies as they fought to stay in business.

The Thatcher government missed its targets for M3 during the early years of the MTFS, with M3 expanding faster than intended (see Table 6.1). Changes in economic policy, financial innovation and the severe economic downturn had changed the relationship between M0 and M3, leading to the government losing control of M3 just as Goodhart's law suggested it would.

The outcome was the perverse combination of money supply growth above target (which would suggest policy was looser than intended) with an overall effect on the economy of a tighter squeeze than the one targeted by the MTFS.

The Thatcher experiment was over-optimistic about the anticipated effects of the announced money growth target on inflation expectations: the unemployment cost of disinflation was much higher than anticipated. In the British case, use of a money supply target as the anchor for inflation was flawed. Both problems tarnished the image of Monetarism as a practical policy doctrine. In debates about British economic policy, the Thatcher experiment was referred to by its proponents and opponents as 'Monetarist'. Box 6.1 explores what is meant by Monetarism and how it affected macroeconomic thinking.

	1980	1981	1982	1983
M3 growth target range (%)	7–11	6–10	8–12	7–11
M3 growth outturn (%)	19.4	13	11.1	9.5
RPI inflation (%)	18	11.9	8.6	4.6
Unemployment (%)	6.9	9.8	10.9	11.6
Manufacturing output growth (%)	-8.7	-6.2	0	2.1

Table 6.1 Money supply targets vs. outturn and UK macroeconomic performance: 1980–83.

Note: Money supply targets and outturn run from February to April—e.g. 1980 refers to the period from February 1980 to April 1981.

Source: Goodhart (1986); UK Office for National Statistics.

BOX 6.1 Monetarism, inflation, and monetary policy

The term 'Monetarism' is defined by *The New Palgrave Dictionary of Economics* as:[a]

> Monetarism is the view that the quantity of money has a major influence on economic activity and the price level and that the objectives of monetary policy are best achieved by targeting the rate of growth of the money supply.

This definition echoes Milton Friedman's famous quote that 'inflation is always and everywhere a monetary phenomenon'.[b] A core tenet of Monetarism (following the Quantity Theory of Money, see Section 6.5) is that inflation arises when there is a more rapid increase in the quantity of money than in output.

Friedman's Monetarism proposed that monetary policy be conducted through targeting the growth of the *money supply*. This approach is very different to what has become the mainstream view today—i.e. central banks adjusting interest rates to achieve a fixed inflation target. In its heyday in policy circles in the early 1980s, Monetarism was also associated with policies of reducing the size of the state and limiting the scope for government intervention in the economy.

Monetarism came to be very closely associated with the policies of the Thatcher government in the UK, including the willingness of the government to accept a high sacrifice ratio in terms of unemployment to get inflation down (see Figure 3.3 in Chapter 3 and Section 6.3.2), supply-side policies of privatization and labour market reforms (see Table 12.3 in Chapter 12) and the broad objective of reducing the size of government. Monetarism also placed stress on the potential of credibility and expectations to reduce the costs associated with disinflation, as reflected in Thatcher's famous 'the lady's not for turning' speech.[c]

Monetarist ideas have not all stood the test of time. The experience of the US, the UK and Canada in the 1980s clearly discredited monetary targeting. In fact, it was discredited to such an extent that Milton Friedman himself admitted in 2003 that it had 'not been a success' and that he would no longer advocate the policy as strongly as he once did.[d] Monetarism has, however, had an enduring influence on the evolution of macroeconomics and economic policy. For example, in contrast to other major central banks the ECB still retains a target for the growth rate of money (see Chapter 14). More generally, Monetarism played a part in the shift in mainstream economic analysis toward the following ideas:

1. At least in the closed economy and leaving aside the possibility of hysteresis (see Chapter 4), the constant inflation rate of unemployment is pinned down by the supply-side of the economy, and systematic attempts by policy makers to run the economy at lower unemployment would lead to rising inflation. This was one of the central ideas put forward by Milton Friedman in his influential 1968 presidential address on Monetarism.[e]

(continued)

2. When available, monetary rather than fiscal policy is the instrument of choice to stabilize the economy. This was partly a reflection of the shift at the time from fixed exchange rates under the Bretton Woods system to flexible exchange rates, where monetary policy gains effectiveness.
3. It follows that if the central bank is the policy maker and there is a unique equilibrium rate of unemployment, then achieving low and stable inflation at least cost is the appropriate policy goal.

---

[a] See Phillip Cagan's entry on 'Monetarism' in *The New Palgrave Dictionary of Economics*, Second Edition (2008).

[b] See Friedman (1970).

[c] This refers to Margaret Thatcher's speech at the Conservative Party Conference on October 10th 1980.

[d] Excerpt taken from an interview with Milton Friedman published in the *Financial Times* in June 2003.

[e] See Friedman (1968).

6.2.2 Inflation target

The failure of the British experiment with money supply targeting helps to explain the emergence of the inflation-targeting monetary policy framework, where the nominal anchor is the inflation target and the central bank uses a monetary rule as modelled by the *MR* curve in the 3-equation model to keep the economy close to target. Instead of using the intermediate target of the money supply, the modern framework uses an announced inflation target to anchor inflation expectations and chooses the desired degree of tightening by setting the interest rate directly. This sidesteps the problems of the instability of the demand for money that can undermine a money supply target.

6.3 MODELLING MONETARY POLICY

6.3.1 Active rule-based policy

At the end of Chapter 2, we saw that a passive monetary policy that keeps the nominal interest rate fixed in the face of shocks will not stabilize the economy around the constant inflation equilibrium. This motivated the analysis in Chapter 3 of the 3-equation model and the *MR* curve, where the central bank actively intervenes to guide the economy back to the constant inflation equilibrium. We have now filled in a piece of economic history and doctrine by looking at the attempt to respond to the problem of rising inflation in the 1970s by adopting money supply targets.

Under inflation targeting, frequent adjustments are made to the interest rate as the central bank seeks to achieve its inflation objective at least cost. It is therefore quite consistent to think of the central bank as following a 'rule-based' approach to monetary policy yet having to be very active. Figure 6.1 shows central bank interest rates in key high-income economies between 1999 and 2022. The chart shows that during the years running up to the global financial crisis central banks regularly made adjustments to interest rates to keep inflation close to target. This active central bank behaviour

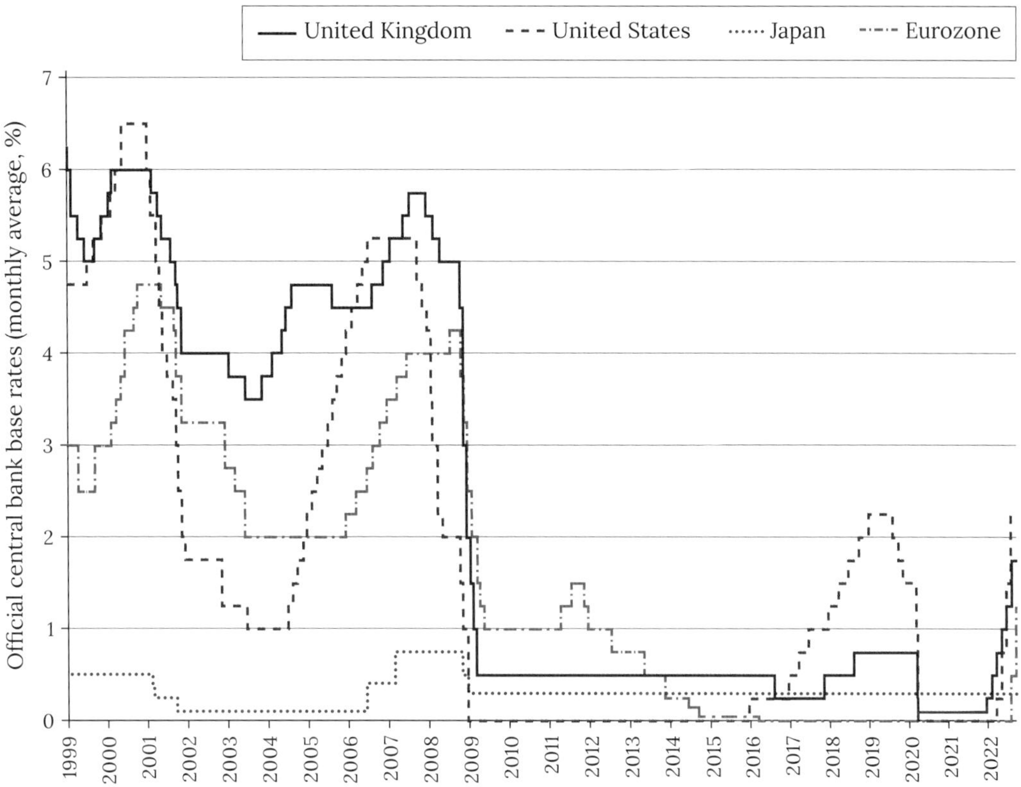

Figure 6.1 Official central bank interest rates, monthly averages, %: 1999–2022.

Source: Bank of England; Board of Governors of the Federal Reserve System (US); Bank of Japan; European Central Bank (data accessed September 2022).

was witnessed between 1999–2007, which corresponded to a period of unprecedented macroeconomic stability—the Great Moderation.

As we saw in Chapter 5, a new mode of active intervention was required once interest rates hit the zero lower bound: the use of quantitative easing. Irrespective of the monetary policy instrument (interest rate or QE), the rule-based framework remains intact. When economic conditions eventually began to normalize, signalled by forecast inflation rising above its target, the US Federal Reserve implemented a sequence of interest rate rises (from December 2015) shown in Figure 6.1.

The data in Table 6.2 for the UK, show that if the five years from the start of the financial crisis are excluded, then the volatility of inflation and growth is much lower in the period since inflation targeting was adopted than it was previously. This provides some support for the rule-based policy when success is judged by the central bank's loss function.

	Average annual CPI inflation	Inflation volatility	Four-quarter GDP growth	Four-quarter GDP growth volatility	Unemployment rate
Pre-inflation targeting (1972–92)	9.0	5.4	2.2	2.9	7.8
Start of inflation targeting to MPC independence (1993–97Q2)	2.3	0.4	2.9	0.7	9.0
MPC independence to crisis (1997Q3–2007)	1.6	0.5	3.0	0.9	5.4
2008–end 2012	3.3	1.0	0.0	2.7	7.4
2013–March 2020	1.7	1.0	2.0	0.5	5.2

Table 6.2 Inflation lower and less volatile since MPC independence.
Source: Carney (2020).

6.3.2 Central bank preferences

This section looks at the role of central bank preferences, investigating how different preferences affect the slope of the MR curve and what this implies for the trade-off between inflation and unemployment deviations on the path to the new equilibrium. We will also set out the two approaches to disinflation, the so-called 'cold-turkey' and the 'gradualist' approaches, which can be seen as descriptions of how inflation averse the central bank is.

Central bank preferences and the slope of the *MR*

To begin with, we recall the results from Chapter 3, where we derived the MR curve by minimizing the central bank's loss function subject to the Phillips curve constraint. The key equations are:

$$L = (y_t - y_e)^2 + \beta(\pi_t - \pi^T)^2. \qquad \text{(Central bank loss function)}$$

$$\pi_1 = \pi_0 + \alpha(y_1 - y_e). \qquad \text{(Phillips curve (PC))}$$

$$(y_1 - y_e) = -\alpha\beta(\pi_1 - \pi^T). \qquad \text{(monetary rule (MR) curve)}$$

We saw in the Modelling section in Chapter 3 that the central bank's preferences influence its chosen adjustment path for the economy after a shock. The degree of inflation aversion of the central bank is captured by β in the central bank loss function.[4] If $\beta > 1$, the central bank attaches more importance to being away from the inflation

[4] The central bank's preferences can be presented in this simple way if we assume that the central bank's discount rate is infinite. This means that it only considers one period at a time when making its decision. In a more realistic model, the central bank would minimize its losses over the whole adjustment path as set out in Appendix 3.5.2. A simple way to capture this is to use a larger weight for β since lower inflation this period, reduces it in the next period via the Phillips curve.

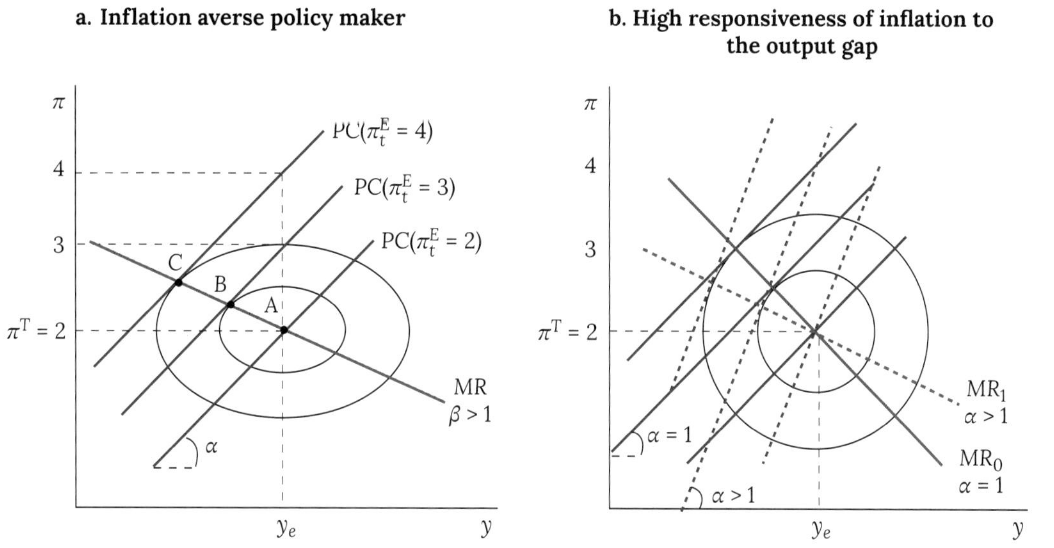

Figure 6.2 How varying the parameters in the 3-equation model affects the MR curve:
a. Inflation-averse policy maker ('flattened' ellipses): flat MR line ($\beta > 1$)
b. High responsiveness of inflation to output (steep Phillips curves): flat MR line ($\alpha > 1$).

Note: The angle marked α in the diagrams is in fact the angle whose tangent is α. We adopt this convention throughout.

target than from equilibrium output. This results in a flatter monetary rule, as shown in Figure 6.2a. Given these preferences, any inflation shock that shifts the Phillips curve upward implies that the optimal position for the central bank will involve a more significant output reduction and hence a sharper cut in inflation along that Phillips curve than in the neutral case.

The second factor that determines the slope of the monetary rule is the responsiveness of inflation to output (i.e. the slope of the Phillips curve). Intuitively, the higher the value of α, the steeper the Phillips curves, so that any given cut in output has a greater effect in reducing inflation. As we can see from Figure 6.2b, a higher value of α makes the MR curve flatter.

Our intuition tells us that steeper Phillips curves make things easier for the central bank, since a smaller rise in unemployment (fall in output) is required to achieve any desired fall in inflation. We can show this in a diagram. In Figure 6.3a we compare two economies, one with steeper Phillips curves (dashed) and one with flatter ones. As we have already shown, the MR line is flatter for the economy with steeper Phillips curves: this is MR_1. Suppose there is a rise in inflation in each economy that shifts the Phillips curves up: each economy is at point B. We can see that a *smaller* cut in aggregate demand is best response in the economy with the steeper Phillips curves. Point D is in fact much closer to the central bank's bliss point compared to point C. In particular, in the economy with the flatter Phillips curve ($\alpha = 1$), inflation remains

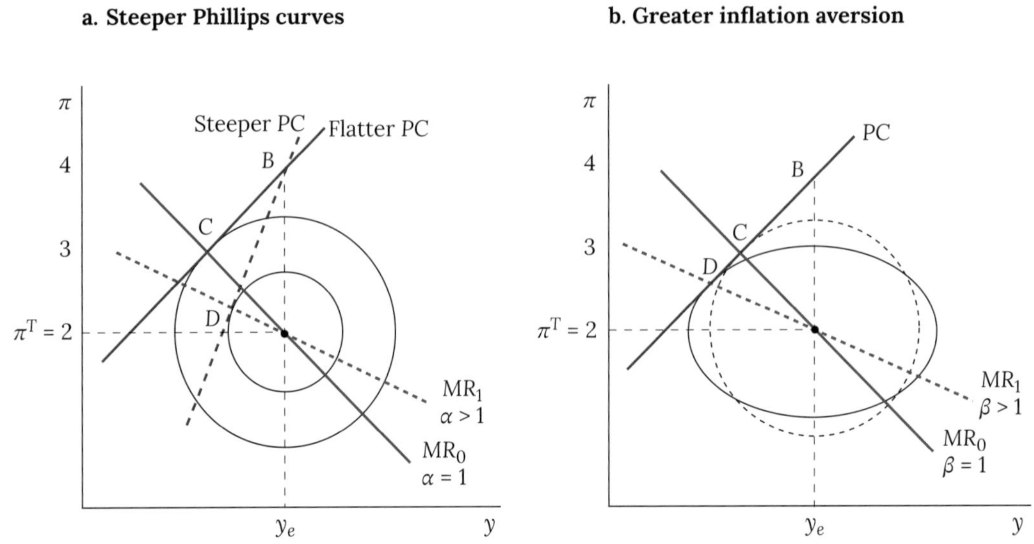

Figure 6.3 Comparing the response of the central bank in two cases: steeper Phillips curves and a more inflation-averse central bank.

significantly further away from target despite a larger cut in output. This reflects our intuitive argument above.[5]

The slope of the Phillips curve has been on the minds of central bankers for some time. The economist, Lael Brainard (a member of the US Federal Reserve Board of Governors) said in January 2021 that 'price inflation is much less sensitive to labour market tightness than historically—that is, a flat Phillips curve.' The scatterplot in Figure 6.4 shows the flattening of the slope of the Phillips curve in the second decade of inflation-targeting.

There are two important responses to this observation. The first is that when the Phillips curve is plotted using wage growth, the flattening disappears.[6]

The second response highlights a problem with expecting the Phillips curve to be visible in the outturns for inflation and unemployment in the presence of successful inflation targeting. The 3-equation model tells us that if we observed an inflation-targeting central bank implementing its best response output gap following inflation, or demand shocks, the correlation between inflation and the output gap would be the opposite from that shown by the Phillips curve. The Phillips curve is upward sloping but the MR curve along which the economy would move on the path back to equilibrium

[5] For those who are curious, with $\beta \geq 1$, the output cut in response to a given inflation shock is always less when $\alpha > 1$ as compared with $\alpha = 1$. For $\beta < 1$, the output cut is less as long as $\alpha > (1/\beta)^{\frac{1}{2}}$.

[6] Research by the National Bank of Canada indicates that if an indicator more representative of labour market tightness (namely, underemployment) is used as a substitute for unemployment and the growth of median wages is used rather than average wages, then the Phillips curve relationship is less flat.

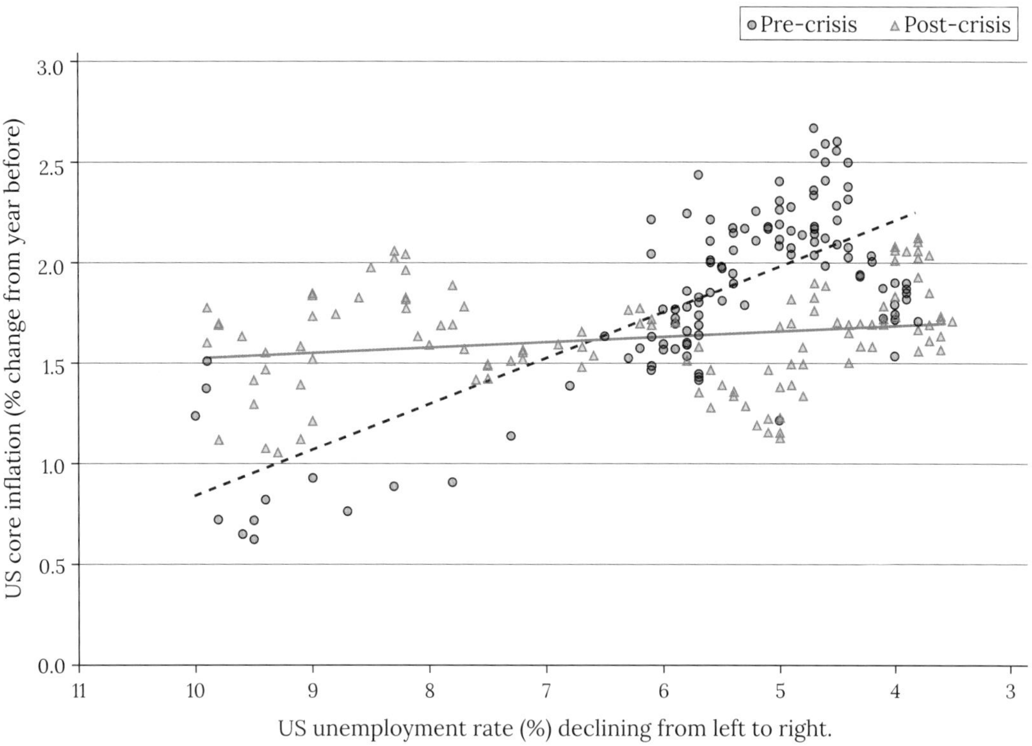

Figure 6.4 Flattening of the Phillips curve in the United States from the second decade of inflation-targeting.

Notes: The chart plots core inflation (personal consumption expenditure excluding food and energy) against the unemployment rate, which declines from left to right. Pre-crisis data covers the period 2000–09, Post-crisis data covers the period 2010–19.

Source: FRED Economic Data (accessed November 2021).

is downward sloping.[7] In the case of a supply shock, the MR curve shifts, adding a further reason for the difficulty in observing the underlying Phillips curve relationship between inflation and the output gap.

Turning to Figure 6.3b, we compare two economies with identical Phillips curves but in which one has an inflation-averse central bank (the oval-shaped indifference ellipse), and show the central bank's reaction to inflation at point B. The more inflation-averse central bank always responds to this shock by cutting aggregate demand (and output) more (point D).

Disinflation strategies

Disinflation is costly whenever a negative output gap has to be created to bring inflation down. This is captured by the concept of a sacrifice ratio. This ratio represents

[7] For a similar argument, presented explicitly in terms of the difficulty in identifying the underlying structural Phillips curve in the observed data when the central bank uses a best-response monetary policy rule, see McLeay and Tenreyro (2019).

the percentage point rise in unemployment experienced for a one percentage point reduction in inflation during a disinflationary episode.

To get an empirical feel for the costs of disinflation, Lawrence Ball examines 28 episodes of disinflation in nine OECD countries and finds that with only one exception, disinflation was contractionary, with sacrifice ratios ranging from 2.9 in Germany (i.e. for a one percentage point reduction in inflation, the increase in unemployment was 2.9 percentage points for a year) to 0.8 in the United Kingdom and France.[8]

A study by Carvalho and Gonçalves extends the empirical research on disinflation, showing that amongst the OECD countries, countries with inflation targeting central banks have suffered smaller output losses during disinflations when compared to non-targeters.[9]

We have also seen that the immediate response of a more inflation-averse central bank to an inflation shock is to dampen output by more than would a less inflation-averse one. It is willing to see a sharper rise in unemployment to get a faster fall in inflation. And this means that unemployment can consequently return more rapidly to equilibrium. The terms 'cold turkey'[10] or 'shock therapy' are sometimes applied to this strategy and are contrasted with a more 'gradualist' approach in which unemployment rises by less, but the process of disinflation takes longer.

An interesting question is whether cumulative unemployment is higher under the cold turkey or gradualist approach: in other words, if we add up the unemployment rates in every period after the inflation shock until inflation returns to target and unemployment to equilibrium, with which strategy will there have been a higher total amount of unemployment?

If the Phillips curves are linear and parallel, the cumulative amount of unemployment to achieve the reduction of inflation to target is the same under both strategies. In other words, in this case, the sacrifice ratio (cumulative unemployment to achieve a given reduction in inflation) is independent of the degree of inflation aversion of the central bank. But if the Phillips curves are flatter at higher unemployment (i.e. convex), then cumulative unemployment will be higher under the cold turkey strategy. The intuition is that the strategy of a very inflation-averse central bank to reduce inflation down to the target fast will be more costly than a gradualist one if it is the case that inflation responds less to a rise in unemployment when unemployment is high.[11]

These results depend on the persistence of adaptive inflation expectations. It could be the case that 'shock therapy' strategies are perceived as more credible given that inflation is reduced more quickly. If so, this could help anchor expectations and reduce the employment losses resulting from reducing inflation.

---

[8] See Ball (1994).

[9] See Gonçalves and Carvallo (2009). This association does not of course prove that inflation targeting caused less costly disinflation.

[10] The analogy is to the treatment of alcohol or drug addiction: a cold turkey strategy reduces drug intake dramatically at the outset whereas a gradualist treatment reduces it slowly. The choice thus ranges between severe discomfort for a short time or less pain for a longer period of time.

[11] Section 2.6 of Chapter 3 (p. 89) of Carlin and Soskice (2006) provides a simple geometric proof of these results.

6.3.3 The *MR* equation and Taylor rules

In the 3-equation model, the MR equation shows the central bank's response to a shock. The IS curve is used by the central bank in a closed economy to find out what interest rate to set given its best response output–inflation combination in the Phillips diagram, i.e. once it has located the best available position on the MR line. We now show how to derive a best response *interest rate rule*, which directly expresses the interest rate the central bank should choose to achieve its objectives in terms of the current state of the economy.

The behaviour of central banks is often described by an interest rate rule of this kind. These rules have come to be known as Taylor rules, because of John Taylor's original claim in his landmark 1993 paper that the historical behaviour of the US Federal Reserve was well described by the following rule:[12]

$$r_0 - r_S = 0.5(\pi_0 - \pi^T) + 0.5(y_0 - y_e), \tag{6.2}$$

where π^T is the central bank's inflation target, y_e is the equilibrium level of output, and r_S is the stabilizing interest rate. The Taylor rule states that if output is 1% above equilibrium and inflation is at the target, the central bank should raise the interest rate by 0.5 percentage points relative to stabilizing interest rate. As above we interpret the difference between y and y_e as the percentage gap; this is the equivalent of defining y as the log of output. And if inflation is one percentage point above the target and output is at equilibrium, then the Taylor rule says that the real interest rate needs to be 0.5 percentage points higher.

We return to the question of how well a Taylor rule describes real-world central bank behaviour in Section 6.3. First, we show how the best response or optimal Taylor rule for the interest rate is derived in the 3-equation model.

The best response Taylor rule in the 3-equation model

We can reorganize the 3-equation model to derive a rule for the interest rate the central bank *should* set if it is minimizing its loss function. This is called a best response Taylor rule because it is derived from a model of optimizing behaviour of the central bank. In contrast, the original Taylor rule (equation 6.2) was an empirical relationship inferred from historical data.

To derive a simple version of the best response Taylor rule, we bring together the three equations of the model:[13]

$$\pi_1 = \pi_0 + \alpha(y_1 - y_e) \qquad \text{(Phillips curve)}$$

$$y_1 - y_e = -a(r_0 - r_S) \qquad \text{(IS)}$$

$$(y_1 - y_e) = -\alpha\beta(\pi_1 - \pi^T). \qquad \text{(MR)}$$

---

[12] See Taylor (1993). Taylor assumed that $r_S = 2\%$ but we write the Taylor rule in the more general form, which allows r_S to vary.

[13] We use the three equations as derived in the appendix to Chapter 3. We use the deviations form of the IS curve.

From these equations, we can derive a formula for the interest rate, r_0, in terms of the period zero observation of inflation in the economy. If we substitute for π_1 using the Phillips curve in the MR, we get

$$\pi_0 + \alpha(y_1 - y_e) - \pi^T = -\frac{1}{\alpha\beta}(y_1 - y_e)$$
$$\pi_0 - \pi^T = -\left(\alpha + \frac{1}{\alpha\beta}\right)(y_1 - y_e)$$

and if we now substitute for $(y_1 - y_e)$ using the IS, and rearrange, we get the interest-rate rule:

$$r_0 - r_S = \frac{1}{a\left(\alpha + \frac{1}{\alpha\beta}\right)}(\pi_0 - \pi^T). \qquad \text{(best response Taylor rule)}$$

We can see that

$$r_0 - r_S = 0.5(\pi_0 - \pi^T), \qquad (6.3)$$

if $a = \alpha = \beta = 1$.

All the parameters of the 3-equation model matter for the central bank's response to a rise in inflation. If each parameter is equal to one, the coefficient on the inflation deviation is one half. This says that if inflation is one percentage point above the target, then the real interest rate needs to be 0.5 percentage points higher than the stabilizing rate. Since inflation is higher by one percentage point, the *nominal* interest rate must be raised by $1 + 0.5$, i.e. by 1.5 percentage points in order to secure a rise in the *real* interest rate of 0.5 percentage points. This follows from the Fisher equation set out in Chapter 1:

$$r_0 = i_0 - \pi_1^E \qquad (6.4)$$

Recall that under adaptive expectations $\pi_1^E = \pi_0$. Hence, equation 6.3 can be rewritten as:

$$(i_0 - \pi_0) - (i_s - \pi^T) = 0.5(\pi_0 - \pi^T)$$
$$\rightarrow (i_0 - i_s) = 1.5(\pi_0 - \pi^T)$$

The requirement—if the central bank's response is to be stabilizing—that the nominal interest rate has to be raised sufficiently to push up the real interest rate is called the *Taylor principle.*

The central bank should respond to any deviation of inflation from target as follows:

1. As β increases to reflect a more inflation-averse central bank, its best response output gap goes up, and from the best response Taylor rule equation, this means the central bank will respond to an inflation shock with a larger rise in the interest rate.
2. As α increases, i.e. as the Phillips curve gets steeper, the MR gets flatter, and as shown in Figure 6.3, the central bank's desired output gap in response to an inflation shock falls (as long as $\beta \geq 1$). Hence the central bank's interest rate response to an inflation shock will be smaller.[14]

[14] This follows from the 'best response Taylor rule' equation given that: $\lim_{\alpha \to \infty}\left(\alpha + \frac{1}{\alpha\beta}\right) = \infty$.

3. As a increases, i.e. as the IS curve gets flatter, reflecting greater interest-sensitivity of aggregate demand, the central bank's best response change in the interest rate to an inflation shock is reduced.

6.4 MONETARY POLICY TRANSMISSION

In the inflation-targeting framework, the central bank adjusts the interest rate to keep inflation on target. For example, Figure 6.5 shows how the Bank of England sees the transmission mechanism of monetary policy to inflation when the economy is away from the zero lower bound.[15]

Domestic inflationary pressure occurs when aggregate expenditure exceeds equilibrium (or potential) output. In a growing economy, it is when aggregate expenditure grows more rapidly than potential output. The central bank aims to affect the level of

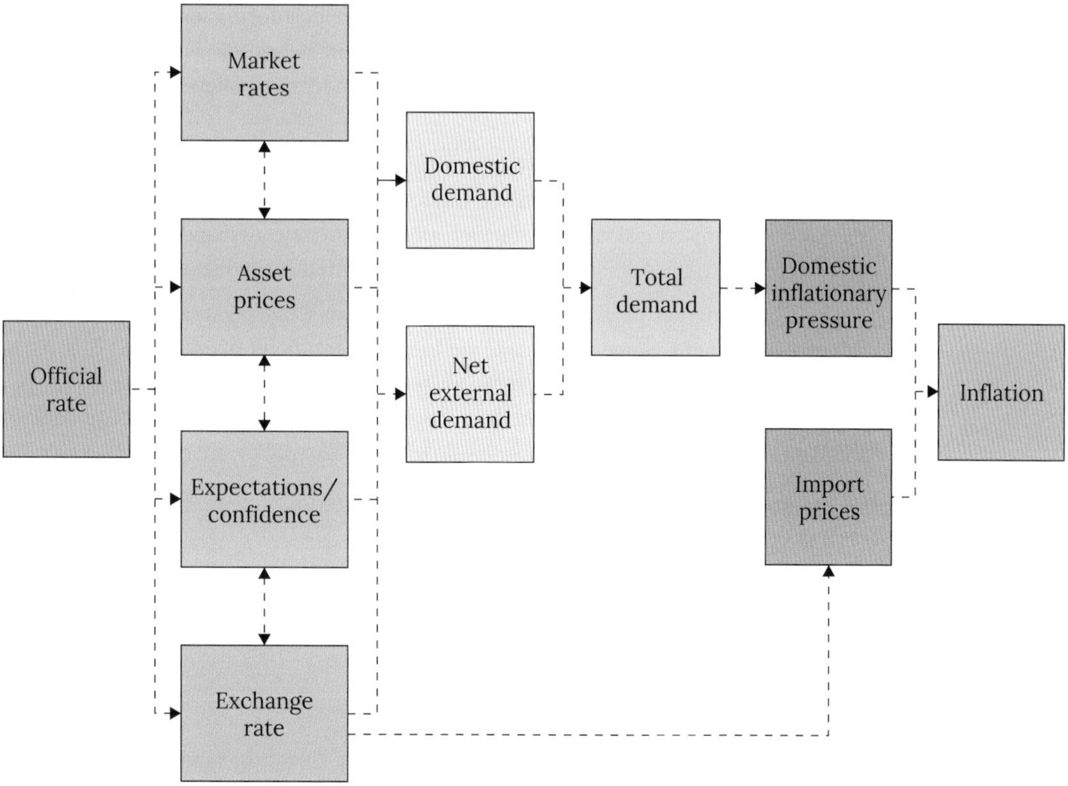

Figure 6.5 Monetary policy transmission mechanisms.
Source: Bank of England (accessed June 2012).

[15] This subsection is based on the 'How Monetary Policy Works' section of the Bank of England website (as of June 2012). For the ECB's 2023 equivalent chart, see https://www.ecb.europa.eu/mopo/intro/transmission/html/index.en.html.

expenditure in the economy (i.e. aggregate demand) by setting interest rates. There are four main channels through which interest rates can affect expenditure:

Market rates: Official rates directly influence market and lending interest rates (as discussed in Chapter 5), which affects the funding cost of banks and therefore the lending rate. Lower interest rates will stimulate aggregate demand (i.e. consumption and investment) as banks lower their lending rates, thereby making borrowing more desirable and savings less desirable. The opposite is true of a rate rise.

Asset prices: Market interest rates can affect asset prices, such as equities and house prices. For example, lower interest rates encourage borrowing that can be spent on assets, pushing up their prices. Higher household wealth viewed as permanent pushes up consumption via the permanent income hypothesis (see Chapter 1). In some countries, higher house prices will also allow households to undertake additional borrowing by refinancing their mortgage (home equity loans, as explained in Chapter 8). This practice was widespread in the US in the mid-2000s as discussed in Chapter 9.

Expectations/confidence: Interest rate changes provide information about the central bank's future policy stance, which can affect current behaviour. For example, a rate reduction could signal a commitment to an accommodative policy stance and help to bring expenditure plans forward.

Exchange rate: As we shall see in Chapter 11, in a globally integrated financial market, interest rates directly affect exchange rates. Exchange rates affect both net external demand and import prices. The former affect aggregate demand, while the latter directly feed into the calculation of consumer price inflation as discussed in Chapter 12.

The labour market plays a key role in this process. Changes in aggregate demand affect employment, wage costs and workers' expectations of inflation. This feeds through to producer prices and eventually to consumer price inflation.

The magnitude and timing of the four channels can vary considerably. The Bank of England estimates lags in the transmission of monetary policy, such that:[16]

- the impact of interest rates on output is estimated to take up to (a maximum of) one year; and
- the impact of interest rates on inflation is estimated to take up to (a maximum of) two years.

6.4.1 Taylor rules in practice

Central bank mandates: Cross-country differences

In high-income countries, not all inflation-targeting central banks have the same mandate. What the mandates have in common is that they tend to concentrate on the objectives of price stability (low and stable inflation) and supporting full employment and economic growth. Where the central banks differ is on the weight they place on each of these objectives.

[16] This excerpt is taken from the 'How Monetary Policy Works' section of the Bank of England website (as of June 2012).

The primary focus of the Bank of Japan until its change of course in early 2013 was on keeping inflation on target:[17]

> The Bank of Japan Act states that the Bank's monetary policy should be 'aimed at achieving price stability, thereby contributing to the sound development of the national economy'.

The fact that price stability will help create a favourable environment for economic growth and employment was taken as a given by the Bank of Japan.

At the other end of the scale are a number of central banks that have objectives to achieve both price stability and full employment, such as the Sveriges Riksbank (the Swedish central bank), the Reserve Bank of Australia and the Federal Reserve (the US central bank). The Federal Reserve is said to have a *dual mandate* for monetary policy, as set out by the Board of Governors of the Federal Reserve System:[18]

> The Congress established the statutory objectives for monetary policy—maximum employment, stable prices and moderate long-term interest rates—in the Federal Reserve Act.

The dual mandate refers to the Federal Reserve's goals of achieving stable prices and maximum employment. The Federal Reserve under Alan Greenspan (1987–2006) did not have an official inflation target. This set it apart from other central banks, which saw having an explicit target as the cornerstone of a credible inflation-targeting monetary regime. A target of 2% (in line with other developed economies) was, however, introduced by Ben Bernanke in January 2012 in order to help keep long-term inflation expectations firmly anchored.[19]

In August 2020, Fed Chair Jerome Powell announced a shift from the explicit commitment to an inflation rate of 2% to a longer-term target of 2% to be achieved on average over time. This decision partly reflected growing awareness of structural transformations of the economy as well as the challenges posed by the proximity of interest rates to the zero lower bound.[20]

It is important to clarify that central banks that have a dual mandate are not targeting both output and inflation. They operate under the assumption that there is a unique equilibrium rate of unemployment, such that in the medium run, targeting a level of unemployment lower than the equilibrium will only lead to higher inflation (and no output gain). For instance, the Federal Reserve defines its maximum employment mandate as 'the highest level of employment or lowest level of unemployment that the

---

[17] Excerpt taken from the 'Monetary Policy Outline' on the Bank of Japan's website (accessed May 2012).

[18] Excerpt taken from the Federal Reserve website's Current FAQs section: What are the Federal Reserve's objectives in conducting monetary policy? (accessed May 2012).

[19] See Federal Open Market Committee (FOMC) statement of *Longer-run goals and policy strategy*, January 25th, 2012.

[20] See Martínez-García et al. (2021) for a more comprehensive review of the Federal Reserve's strategy to achieve price stability.

economy can sustain while maintaining a stable inflation rate'.[21] It can be said however, that central banks that put more focus on output (a smaller β in the loss function) experience bigger welfare losses when output deviates from target than those that focus more on inflation. This means they are less willing to accept large reductions in output to bring inflation back to target quickly after an economic shock—i.e. they would prefer a 'gradualist' to a 'cold turkey' approach to disinflation (see Section 6.3.2).

Lastly, some central banks fall somewhere in the middle, such as the ECB and the Bank of England. These two central banks have a primary objective of price stability, and a secondary objective of full employment. This is highlighted in the monetary policy framework of the Bank of England:[22]

> The Bank's monetary policy objective is to deliver price stability–low inflation–and, subject to that, to support the Government's economic objectives including those for growth and employment. Price stability is defined by the Government's inflation target of 2%.

Taylor rules: Cross-country differences

We have seen that central banks have different stated objectives, but how is this reflected in their actual behaviour? For example, does the ECB care less about deviations in the output gap than the Federal Reserve, as would be implied by their mandates? In this subsection, we present evidence on empirical Taylor rules for the Federal Reserve, the ECB and the Bank of England during the inflation-targeting period to try and answer these questions.

A paper by Castro (2011) uses econometric techniques to estimate Taylor rules for the periods through to the onset of the global financial crisis:

- **Bank of England: 1992–2007:** The starting point is when the Bank of England began inflation targeting.
- **ECB: 1999–2007:** This covers the period since the formation of the ECB (i.e. when they assumed responsibility for Eurozone monetary policy).
- **Federal Reserve: 1982–2007:** This starts when the so-called Volcker disinflation began.

The basic form of the Taylor rule uses contemporaneous output and inflation gaps to determine the nominal interest rate the central bank should set in this period:

$$r_t = r_S + 0.5(\pi_t - \pi^T) + 0.5(y_t - y_e). \qquad \text{(TR for the real interest rate)}$$

This is the rule from Taylor's landmark 1993 paper in real terms.[23] The coefficients were chosen as they fitted US historic data well. In more general models, the coefficients

[21] https://www.federalreserve.gov/faqs/what-economic-goals-does-federal-reserve-seek-to-achieve-through-monetary-policy.htm (accessed January 2023).

[22] Excerpt taken from the 'Monetary Policy Framework' on the Bank of England's website.

[23] Unlike the optimal Taylor rule derived above, the empirical Taylor rule has a term for the output gap as well as for inflation. As shown in Carlin and Soskice (2006) pp. 153–7, if in the Phillips curve, inflation responds to the output gap with a lag, the optimal Taylor rule will also have a term for the output gap.

on the output and inflation gaps will vary depending on the preferences of the central bank, and the rule is often expressed in terms of the nominal interest rate (as this is the interest rate central banks actually control). A general Taylor rule in nominal terms would be:

$$i_t = \bar{i} + \gamma_1(\pi_t - \pi^T) + \gamma_2(y_t - y_e), \qquad \text{(TR for the nominal interest rate)}$$

where $\bar{i}$ represents the nominal interest rate that prevails when output is at equilibrium and inflation is at target (it is the nominal counterpart to the stabilizing real rate of interest, r_S). The coefficients γ_1 and γ_2 will vary depending on the relative weight the central bank assigns to stabilizing deviations of inflation and output from target.

In order for monetary policy to be stabilizing, the *Taylor principle* states that the coefficient on the inflation gap, γ_1, has to exceed one, such that an increase in inflation (above target) leads to an increase in the *real* interest rate. Monetary policy is said to be destabilizing if a rise in inflation above target leads to a reduction in the real interest rate.[24]

Table 6.3 shows the coefficients on the output and inflation gap for forward-looking Taylor rules for the Bank of England, the ECB and the Federal Reserve:[25]

The coefficients show that all three central banks react to deviations in both inflation and output. In line with the central bank mandates, the ECB and the Bank of England react more strongly to inflation gaps than output gaps, whereas the US has a more balanced response (as per the dual mandate). However, perhaps unexpectedly, the results suggest that it is the ECB (in the short period of observation) and not the Federal Reserve that reacts most strongly to movements in the output gap.[26]

Central bank (time period)	Inflation gap coefficient	Output gap coefficient
Bank of England (1992–2007)	1.87 (4.89)	0.91 (2.8)
ECB (1999–2007)	2.77 (2.85)	1.99 (5.84)
Federal Reserve (1982–2007)	1.53 (5.18)	1.40 (2.77)

Table 6.3 Estimated coefficients for linear Taylor rules prior to the global financial crisis.
Note: T-statistics using robust standard errors are shown in brackets, all coefficients are significant at the 1% level.
Source: Castro (2011).

---

[24] Equivalently, in a general Taylor rule in real terms, the Taylor principle dictates that the coefficient on inflation has to be greater than zero, such that an increase in inflation (above target) leads to an increase in the real interest rate.

[25] Castro (2011) bases his modelling on forward-looking Taylor rules that take into account expected output and inflation gaps for 6 to 12 months into the future. This matches how modern central banks operate.

[26] Not all macroeconomic models produce a best response Taylor rule in which the coefficients γ_1 and γ_2 vary depending on the central bank's preferences (as captured by β, their level of inflation aversion). However, in line with much of the applied and policy literature, we assume this interpretation in our discussion of the estimates from Table 6.3. For further discussion, see Carlin and Soskice (2006): pp. 153–7.

6.4.2 Asset price bubbles and central bank intervention

An asset price bubble occurs when financial market valuations become unrealistic—i.e. when the market price of an asset far exceeds its fundamental value. It is a source of much contention in macroeconomic and policy circles as to whether central banks should intervene to burst asset prices bubbles, such as the dot-com boom in the late 1990s or the sub-prime mortgage boom in the mid-2000s.[27] In both those cases, central bankers made little attempt to prick the bubbles and instead chose to 'mop up' after they burst. As we shall see in Chapter 9, the mopping up after the mortgage-based boom turned into crisis-management on an unprecedented scale.

Asset price bubbles distort resource allocation, affect the central bank's target variables (e.g. inflation and output) both now and in the future and can cause financial instability.

However, for the central bank to effectively and wisely intervene to burst asset price bubbles, it must:

1. be able to identify bubbles before a financial crash occurs,
2. refrain from identifying bubbles that do not exist; and
3. burst bubbles without causing excessive damage to the wider economy.

The former Federal Reserve Chairman Alan Greenspan believed that central banks were unable to fulfil these criteria, so he strongly advocated *ex post* rather than *ex ante* intervention. This position is known as the 'Greenspan doctrine'. Bubbles are inherently hard to identify *ex ante*. There is a significant risk that a central bank could intervene to burst a bubble that turned out not to be one. For example, Greenspan thought a bubble was forming in the US stock market as early as 1995–96. In reality, the bubble didn't emerge until 1998–99. If rates had been raised in 1995–96 this could have wiped out the significant economic gains that accrued to the US economy between 1995–96 and the onset of the dot-com boom.

Let's assume for a moment that the central bank could correctly identify bubbles. How would they then go about bursting them? The main tool they have at their disposal is the interest rate. This is a very blunt instrument, and would be unable to deflate a bubble without also harming the rest of the economy (by dampening consumption and investment in sectors not affected by the inflated asset prices). It is also not clear that a moderate rise in interest rates would be sufficient to burst a bubble. For example, investors were expecting returns of up to 100% per annum during the height of the dot-com boom. It seems fanciful that a small rise in interest rates would have had a major effect on the decisions made by these investors.

The debate on central bank intervention to stop bubbles forming returned to the agenda of policy makers following the global financial crisis. Chapter 9 provides a detailed discussion of the causes and consequences of the global financial crisis.

The most consistent voice among central bankers to argue for leaning against the asset price bubble forming in the 2000s was the Bank for International Settlements in

[27] This section is based on the discussion and analysis in Blinder and Reis (2005).

Basel.[28] Unlike national central banks, the BIS's mandate is to establish international standards to promote financial stability through policies to regulate banks.[29]

The near meltdown of the global banking system that caused the global financial crisis was precipitated by the high level of interconnectedness of major banks, meaning that a problem in one bank—if it was systemically important—could potentially compromise the integrity of the entire system.

Central banks admitted that their pre-recession regulatory frameworks overlooked *systemic risk* in the banking system. For an explanation and evaluation of reforms in financial regulation, see Section 10.2.

6.4.3 **Policy transmission at the zero lower bound**

Taylor rules and the Great Recession

As background to looking at monetary policy transmission at the zero lower bound, we show the nominal interest rate that is implied if a simple Taylor rule is applied to the output gaps and inflation deviations for the US, Japan, UK and the Eurozone.[30] As we shall see, the Taylor rule can call for negative nominal interest rates. The zero lower bound means that the central bank cannot always choose the interest rate that would produce the desired output gap (as determined by the MR curve) to stabilize the economy. In extreme cases, this can lead to a deflation trap, in which the economy becomes stuck in a downward spiral of deflation and falling output. This highlights the motivation of central banks to adopt other instruments to stimulate aggregate demand.

The Taylor rule for the nominal interest rate introduced in the equation labelled 'TR for the nominal interest rate' is:

$$i_t = \bar{i} + \gamma_1(\pi_t - \pi^T) + \gamma_2(y_t - y_e),$$

where the following assumptions are made for setting the parameter values:

1. $\bar{i}$, to the average policy rate between 1999 and 2018,
2. π_t, to core consumer price inflation (i.e. excluding energy and food prices) in period t,[31]
3. π^T, to the core consumer price inflation target for each central bank—assumed to be 2% for the Fed, the BoE and the ECB. For the BoJ, a target of 1% is assumed until 2013 Q1, while this rises to 2% from 2013 Q2 onwards (see break line for Japan in Figure 6.6),

---

[28] See for example, Borio and White (2004).

[29] See Section 5.3.4 in Chapter 5 for a more detailed discussion on the role played by equity buffers in reducing risks to banks' solvency.

[30] Using the same method as Sheets and Sockin (2012).

[31] Core inflation was used instead of headline inflation, because using headline inflation produced large variations in the implied policy rate due to the big swings in commodity prices over this period. We did not see these large movements in the policy rate in reality, suggesting that central banks were more focused on core inflation when making their monetary policy decisions. The Eurozone measure is for the Harmonized Index of Consumer Prices (HICP). All the others are for the Consumer Price Index (CPI). The Eurozone and UK indices of core inflation also exclude alcohol and tobacco on top of energy and food.

4. $(y_t - y_e)$, to the output gap (i.e. the difference between actual and potential GDP) in period t as a percentage of potential GDP,
5. γ_1, to 1.5 and
6. γ_2, equal to either 0.5 or 1, to show the effect on implied policy rates of two different levels of unemployment aversion.[32]

The results of the analysis are shown in Figure 6.6. The solid black lines show the central bank interest rates in the four countries between 1999 and 2022, the red lines show the interest rates implied by the Taylor rule when the coefficient on the output gap is set to 1 (dashed line) and 0.5 (dotted line). The important points to take away from the charts are explained in the following paragraphs.

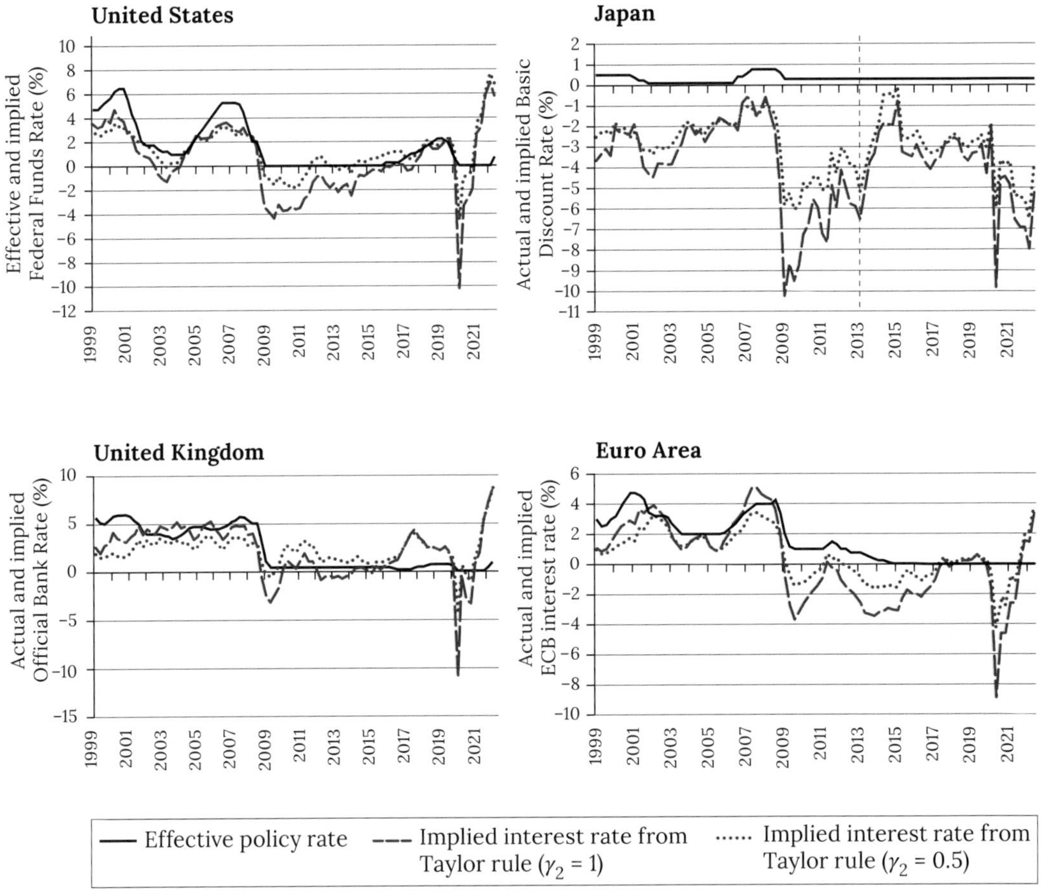

Figure 6.6 Nominal interest rates implied by Taylor rules vs. observed central bank policy rates: 1999 Q1–2022 Q2.

Source: National statistical offices, national central banks, OECD, Eurostat (data accessed October 2022); Oxford Economics (October 2022). Note that the vertical line for 2013 Q1 for Japan indicates a break in the series.

32 These rules follow Taylor (1993) and Taylor (1999).

In Japan, the black line indicates that the policy interest rate has been virtually at the lower bound throughout. There are large negative gaps to the two series that indicate the interest rate proposed by the Taylor rule. This means that conventional monetary policy has been an ineffective tool for stabilizing the Japanese economy in response to economic shocks for more than two decades.

In the Eurozone and the US, the zero lower bound on interest rates was hit during the global financial crisis and again in the pandemic. The Taylor rule predicts negative nominal interest rates for these periods. This is important for discussions of the optimal level of the inflation target in Chapter 3 and the deflation trap in Chapters 3 and 9. However, in 2021–22, the policy interest rates in both the US and the Eurozone lagged behind the rate proposed by the Taylor Rule. According to the Taylor Rule, these two central banks raised interest rates too little and too late.

The UK experienced CPI inflation above target during the recovery phase of the global financial crisis, which leads the Taylor rule to predict interest rates higher than those that prevailed. However, the above target CPI inflation was mainly the result of two factors: (1) increases in Value Added Tax (VAT), and (2) the depreciation of the sterling exchange rate (markedly following the Brexit vote in 2016). In both these cases, the Bank of England took the view that these were one-off sources of inflation and given the weakness of the economy over this period, would not translate into persistent inflation via wage increases. Indeed, wage growth was modest throughout. As elsewhere, the ZLB was hit once more during the pandemic. And along with the Fed and the ECB, the Bank of England's response to rising inflation from 2021 was not matched by tighter monetary policy in accordance with the Taylor rule.

Figure 6.6 shows that in many high-income economies, monetary policy hit the zero lower bound during the Great Recession, rendering conventional monetary policy an ineffective tool for macroeconomic stabilization.

6.4.4 **Quantitative easing**

As discussed in Chapter 5, at the zero lower bound, the central bank can still stimulate aggregate demand if it is able to convince borrowers that the cost of borrowing is going to remain low in the future. The key transmission mechanism is through the effect of asset purchases by the central bank in lowering long-term interest rates, illustrated by the flattening of the yield curve (Figure 5.4). The central bank uses its ability to create central bank money to buy financial assets. In the UK, these assets were mainly government bonds (bought from non-financial companies in secondary markets), whereas in the US, the Fed bought a mixture of mortgage-backed securities from financial institutions, but also some government bonds.

The objective of unconventional policies is to help central banks to stabilize demand and avoid undershooting their inflation targets when conventional policies are constrained by the zero lower bound. This point is captured by the Federal Reserve's announcement of larger asset purchases in response to the Covid-19 pandemic in December 2020:[33]

[33] Excerpt from the FOMC statement on December 16th 2020.

> The Federal Reserve will continue to increase its holdings of Treasury securities by at least \$80 billion per month and of agency mortgage-backed securities by at least \$40 billion per month until substantial further progress has been made toward the Committee's maximum employment and price stability goals.

Quantitative easing: Transmission mechanisms

Conventional monetary policy has a clear transmission mechanism (see Figure 6.5). In a simplified form, the central bank sets the interest rate, which then influences the level of aggregate demand (and hence the output gap and inflation) through its effects on interest-sensitive spending in the economy and on the exchange rate in the open economy. Unconventional monetary policy does not have such a clear transmission mechanism. In theory, it could potentially affect the economy through a number of channels.

Figure 6.7 is taken from the *Bank of England Quarterly Bulletin* (2011 Q3) and shows the ways in which the Bank believes that their asset purchases can affect the real

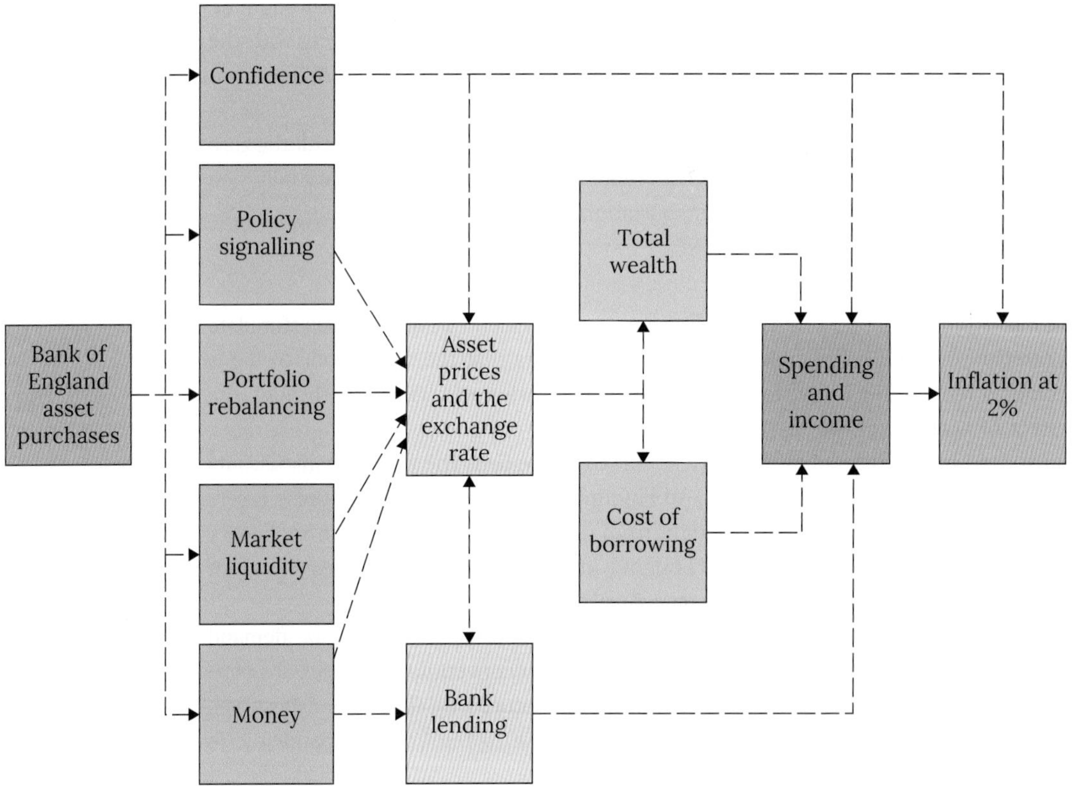

Figure 6.7 Quantitative easing transmission channels.

Source: Joyce et al. (2011).

economy.[34] The majority of the channels work through raising asset prices. This will lead to a reduction in the cost of borrowing (as bond prices are inversely related to the interest rate), which could potentially raise consumption and investment.

We have seen that QE was introduced as a result of interest rates being limited by the zero lower bound. How then can QE reduce interest rates when we are already at the ZLB? Firstly, QE is not aimed at affecting short-term policy rates, which are set by the central bank, but long-term interest rates, which are set in financial markets as discussed in Section 5.2.2. As explained in Chapter 5 (see Section 5.2.2), QE is aimed at altering the term structure of interest rates and flattening the yield curve.

Secondly, in times of financial distress, interest rates on assets previously viewed as very safe (e.g. interbank loans) can diverge from the policy rate, increasing the cost of borrowing. QE can help reduce the interest rate wedge by boosting market confidence and increasing market liquidity (see below).

In Figure 6.7, there are five transmission channels, which can be summarized as follows:

- **Confidence:** Improved confidence over the economic outlook raises perceptions of permanent income, which in turn could have a direct effect on increasing spending.
- **Policy signalling:** The introduction of QE signals the central bank's commitment to meeting the inflation target and might help to anchor inflation expectations at target. If inflation expectations were allowed to fall below the target, this would raise the real interest rate (via the Fisher equation: $r = i - \pi^e$) and depress activity. Central banks are also very scared of falling into the deflation trap and unconventional policies send a strong signal that the central bank is willing to do whatever is necessary in terms of supporting asset prices to avoid this situation. The deflation trap is modelled using the 3-equation model in Chapters 3 and 9.
- **Portfolio rebalancing:** The purchases of government bonds by the central bank will directly push up the price of government bonds, but it will also indirectly increase the price of other assets. Firms that sell their bonds to the central bank will be left with money. To the extent that money and assets are not perfect substitutes, sellers will rebalance their portfolios, buying other financial assets and pushing up their prices. This will reduce the interest rates on financial assets, lowering borrowing costs for households and firms and stimulating demand. In a situation in which banks are re-building their balance sheets, this channel seeks to facilitate borrowing by firms through the issue of bonds.
- **Market liquidity:** QE can actively encourage trading in times of financial market distress, which increases liquidity in temporarily dysfunctional markets. This can influence asset prices by reducing the premia associated with illiquidity (see Section 9.5.2 for an example). This channel is likely to be most prominent when the actual asset purchases are taking place.

---

[34] See Joyce et al. (2011).

- **Money:** The sellers of government bonds to the central bank will be left with higher deposits while their banks will be left with higher reserves. A higher level of liquid assets could induce the financial institutions to lend more, stimulating activity, and also raising asset prices. This route is less likely to take place during financial crises when financial institutions are under pressure to reduce the size of their balance sheets.

The Covid-19 crisis has highlighted the distinction between 'Wall Street QE' and 'Main Street QE' in the transmission mechanism from QE to aggregate demand. QE implemented following the financial crisis was 'Wall Street QE' (Sims and Wu 2020). It was directed at easing the constraints on bank lending by improving bank liquidity and by increasing the value of the long-dated bonds in their asset portfolios, which would reduce their leverage constraint. The objective was to help banks rebuild their balance sheets, as a pre-cursor to their ability to resume lending to the non-financial sector. More generally, as we saw in Section 5.7.1, the supply of loans by banks is positively correlated with the bank's equity so the increase in the value of bonds and other assets on their balance sheet arising from the QE purchases will make banks more willing to lend (Kuttner 2018).

During the pandemic, governments mandated the closure of entire sectors of the economy, which meant that businesses' cash flow dried up. In these conditions, what holds back spending by non-financial firms is not the willingness of banks to lend to them as was the case after the financial crisis, but rather, their weak cash flow. This calls for a different form of QE: with 'Main St QE', the central bank lends directly to firms facing a cash flow constraint, who rely on debt finance for investment. Equivalently, in the US, the central bank purchases bonds issued by non-financial firms. The use of 'Wall St QE' under these circumstances is ineffective because making the banks' balance sheets healthier will not make them more willing to lend to cash-flow constrained firms.

The explanation of QE here is in terms of a closed economy. In an open economy an important effect is via a depreciation of the exchange rate as explained in Chapter 11.

Quantitative easing: Does it work?

The key difficulty in measuring the impact of quantitative easing on the economy is the lack of a counterfactual—i.e. we do not know what would have happened in the absence of the policy. There are, however, some impacts that are easier to measure than others such as the effect of QE on government bond yields. The empirical evidence for the UK and the US suggests that QE brought down long-term government bond yields by up to 100 basis points (i.e. 1 percentage point). In addition, the use of the policy in the financial crisis had wide-ranging effects on the markets for housing agency debt and mortgage-backed securities in the US.[35]

It is more difficult to predict the effect of QE on output and inflation, as there were so many other factors affecting these variables during the Great Recession. Kapetanios

[35] See Joyce et al. (2011) and Gagnon et al. (2011).

et al. (2012) attempt to isolate the impact of QE by using advanced modelling techniques to construct counterfactuals for output and inflation in the UK. They find that QE may have had a peak effect on the level of real GDP of around 1.5% and a peak effect on annual consumer price inflation of about 1.25 percentage points. Hohberger et al. (2017) use a New-Keynesian open economy model to evaluate the impact of QE on real GDP growth and CPI inflation in the Eurozone over the period 2015Q1–2016Q2. Their model predicts that when the zero-bound constraint is binding, the peak effects on GDP growth and inflation are up to 1 and 0.7 percentage points respectively.

We can see from Figure 6.6 that the best response nominal interest rate was negative in a number of developed economies during the global financial crisis (i.e. conventional monetary policy was constrained by the ZLB). QE was used as a substitute for conventional monetary policy during the crisis. The impact of QE can also be quantified by looking at what the equivalent effect would be on the central bank policy rate. In the UK, Joyce et al. (2011) summarize several previous studies and find that QE was equivalent to a 150–300 basis points cut in the policy rate. Similarly in the US, Chung et al. (2012) find that the Fed's QE during the crisis was equivalent to a 200 basis points reduction in the federal funds rate. These studies suggest that QE made some contribution to bridging the gap between the ZLB and the central banks' best response interest rate during the crisis.

However, it is important to note that longer-term yields, which are targeted by QE strategies, also have a lower bound. This is a consequence of arbitrage opportunities arising whenever the yield on long-term bonds becomes too low. Investors can borrow at long-term rates and use the proceeds to re-invest at short-term rates (they bear no risk of loss since short-term rates are at the ZLB).[36] To illustrate the point by means of Figure 5.4, this effect can be thought of in terms of a lower bound on the flattening of the yield curve that is achievable from quantitative easing.

An alternative policy: Yield curve control

Dell'Ariccia et al. (2018) point out that quantitative easing has traditionally been implemented by announcing a specific amount of asset purchases rather than a target on longer-term bond yields. In 2016 the Bank of Japan adopted a more 'radical' 'yield curve control' approach, specifically pegging yields on 10-year Japanese Government Bonds at zero percent. One potential advantage of such an approach is in the credibility of the long-term target. If markets believe the central bank's objective is credible, then the yields on long-term bonds may fall without requiring substantial purchases by the central bank (similarly to how anchoring inflation expectations at target renders the adjustment process following an inflation shock costless). A second is that yield curve control gets around the uncertainty of the impact on long-term interest rates of a given amount of QE.

---

[36] See Gertjan Vlieghe's presentation 'Revisiting the 3D Perspective on Low Long Term Interest Rates' at the London School of Economics and Political Sciences on July 26th 2021.

Quantitative easing: What are the risks?

In Figure 5.13 of Chapter 5, we showed the magnitude of QE undertaken since its widespread use during the global financial crisis and explained how it had led to the development of a new operational regime for monetary policy of 'ample reserves'. In this section, we consider a set of concerns that have been raised about QE. A major concern relates to the impact of QE on inequality, to which we return shortly in Section 6.4.5.

- **Central bank independence and credibility:** The movement towards central bank independence has been one of the key trends of the inflation-targeting era, but this has been compromised by the extended role taken on by central banks during the Great Recession, and the Covid-19 pandemic. If the extension of the central bank remit into areas previously deemed off-limits (e.g. large purchases of financial assets by the Fed) and higher levels of political interference (e.g. the political pressure the ECB came under during the Eurozone sovereign debt crisis) lead to a perceived reduction in credibility, then inflation expectations could become less firmly anchored to the inflation target and stabilization policy could become more costly (in terms of unemployment fluctuations).[37] The interdependence of fiscal and monetary policy arises at the zero lower bound and we return to the potential problems that poses for central bank independence and credibility in Chapter 7.
- **Inflation expectations:** As discussed in Chapter 5, quantitative easing represents a huge expansion of central bank balance sheets. Although some observers view this as representing a potential future danger of higher inflation (along the lines of the Quantity Theory of Money (see Section 6.5.2)), under conditions of a deep recession, it was intended to boost inflation expectations. This was viewed as a necessary step to guard against deflation in the midst of the financial crisis.
- **Financial stability:** Central banks resorted to QE because the collapse of the upswing of the financial cycle (see Chapters 8 and 9) was so serious that it rendered conventional interest rate-based monetary policy inoperative. The problem is that under conditions of prolonged low interest rates and official asset purchases, the so-called search for yield reemerges to inflate housing and other asset price bubbles. There is the further danger that financial markets come to expect liquidity support from the central bank when tensions in financial markets occur, which increases their risk-taking. This points not only to problematic design issues in monetary policy but also to the importance of financial and macro-prudential regulation, which is discussed in Section 10.2.
- **Excess reserves:** Banks are required to hold reserves at their national (or supranational) central bank. Since the advent of QE, banks have built up large excess reserves in their central bank accounts (i.e. reserves over and above any required amount). A high level of excess reserves means that banks can quickly create large amounts of new loans and deposits without putting pressure on deposit rates and without

---

[37] See the modelling in Chapter 4, Sections 4.4.2 and 4.4.3.

any change in central bank policy. This carries inflationary risks if the central bank does not respond by raising the interest rate on reserves or is slow to react.[38] It is also important to note that when the central bank raises the policy rate, this is the interest rate it pays on reserves. It will have to pay the additional interest bill on the large stock of outstanding debt on its balance sheet.

- **Pressure on commercial banks' profitability:** As pointed out in Chapter 5, commercial banks issue short-term liabilities (i.e. deposits) and invest in long-term assets such as mortgages to make a profit. QE flattens the yield curve, thus lowering returns on long-term loans and hence shrinking banks' profit margins.

Quantitative easing: Exit strategies

The policy of quantitative easing is not unwound when the central bank stops purchasing assets, but rather when the assets accumulated on the central bank's balance sheet mature or are sold back into the market. The sheer scale of asset purchases by central banks has led to concerns over the *exit strategy*—how central banks plan to unwind their positions and reduce the size of their balance sheets. In theory, the selling of assets by the central bank will have the exact opposite effects to those mentioned earlier, such that it will depress asset prices and raise long-term yields. This would be expected to have a contractionary effect on the economy and exert downward pressure on inflation. As mentioned earlier, part of the exit strategy and the move back to 'normal' monetary policy includes raising the policy interest rate on reserves. Concerns about the timing of quantitative tightening were overtaken by events in 2022 when central banks began raising the policy rate belatedly (according to the Taylor rule) in response to rapidly rising inflation (see Figure 6.6).

The role of forward guidance

As we have seen, central bank communication stretches far beyond the publishing of current interest rate decisions. A key reason that central banks invest so heavily in communication is to help households and firms to form more accurate expectations about the future paths of inflation and interest rates. *Forward guidance* is one method of achieving this objective and is based on the expectations hypothesis linking the short-term policy interest rate and long-term rates along the yield curve. The idea is that greater confidence about the path of the policy rate produces greater confidence about the long-term rate, which is relevant to investment decisions. The term forward guidance is used to describe any communication by a central bank aimed at signalling the likely future path of policy rates.[39]

The Reserve Bank of New Zealand pioneered the publication of the interest rate path it intended implementing in 1997; the central banks of Norway and Sweden followed in 2005 and 2007. Alan Greenspan (Fed Chairman from 1987–2006) was initially sceptical of the advantages of transparency, claiming it could add to market instability. Monetary policy for the majority of his tenure was characterized by little

[38] See Ennis and Wolman (2010).
[39] See Woodford (2008).

indication of the future path of policy rates.[40] The Fed became more transparent over time, however, and now provides calendar-date guidance—i.e. communicating the amount of time that the current policy stance is expected to be maintained for. The Federal Open Market Committee (FOMC) started taking this approach in 2003, with the Committee's assertion that 'policy accommodation can be maintained for a considerable period'.[41]

Forward guidance became particularly important during and after the global financial crisis, when conventional monetary policy was constrained by the zero lower bound. In an environment of near zero interest rates and a weak recovery, it becomes very important for the central bank to signal its commitment to accommodative policy. In December 2012, the Fed committed not to raise interest rates until unemployment fell below 6.5% (assuming inflation projections were close to target).[42] In contrast to the *quantitative guidance* provided by the FOMC and by the Bank of England, qualitative criteria are also used (e.g. the Bank of Japan announced in October 2010 that it would keep rates low until 'price stability is in sight') (Dell'Arricia et al. 2018).

The policy of forward guidance fits into the trend of central banks moving towards greater levels of transparency and communication. Forecasts of future policy rates will of course often be wrong, as interest rate decisions are highly dependent on the latest economic developments. Nevertheless, the forecasts are valuable because they set out explicitly the policy stance of the central bank, giving a clear indication of the speed with which rates are expected to be returned to 'normal' levels. The forecasts should therefore benefit household and firm decision making, aid the anchoring of inflation expectations and help ensure that policy is as tight or loose as the central bank intends. In principle, this helps to educate the public about the central bank's best response function. As a practical matter however, given the extent of uncertainty facing policy makers and market participants (see Chapter 4), it may be difficult for policy makers to achieve a consensus on the interest rate path. This may limit the feasibility of forward guidance.

Evidence of the importance of the forward guidance provided by the central bank relative to the release of information about its interpretation of economic conditions comes from the application of machine learning (using topic modelling) to the statements made by the FOMC between 2008 and 2014 (Hansen and McMahon 2016). The algorithm produces a series of topics that are most likely to have 'written' the paragraphs along with the time spent covering the topic in each paragraph. Concentrating on the paragraphs identified as dealing with economic conditions, the authors then construct an index of how positive the Fed is about the economy. The second task is to manually identify the paragraphs dealing with forward guidance, picking out for example conditional statements about the extent of monetary support going forward or any date-based guidance provided by the Fed in recent years. From this analysis, they construct a forward guidance index. When confronting the two

---

[40] See Blinder and Reis (2005).

[41] Excerpt taken from the *Federal Open Market Committee Statement*, August 12th 2003.

[42] See the question *What is forward guidance, and how is it used in the Federal Reserve's monetary policy?* in the Current FAQs section of the Federal Reserve website.

indices with the variation in bond prices, forward guidance explains three to four times as much as does communication about economic conditions, which explains little.

The end of a uniform central banking model?

With the adoption of inflation targeting from the early 1990s, central banks in high-income countries converged on an inflation target of 2%. The implementation of QE following the financial crisis introduced differentiation across central banks in terms of the composition of assets purchased but the objectives of the policy were communicated in similar ways. The Bank of Japan and the ECB experienced the most difficulty in raising inflation up to the target in the decade following the financial crisis.

Prompted by the Covid-19 pandemic, monetary policy makers reviewed their policy rules. The Fed decided that it would no longer pre-emptively slow the economy by tightening monetary policy on a given degree of tightness of the labour market. Moreover, it decided formally to embrace *average inflation targeting*, looking to allow inflation to be above 2% for a period to counterbalance years with inflation persistently below 2%.

The data in Figure 6.8 for the US suggests that as economies emerged from the pandemic, bond markets were more concerned about a reversion to the situation of 'too low' inflation that characterized the pre-Covid decade than they were about an inflation threat. The observations for 2021–22 appear to be outliers relative to the long-

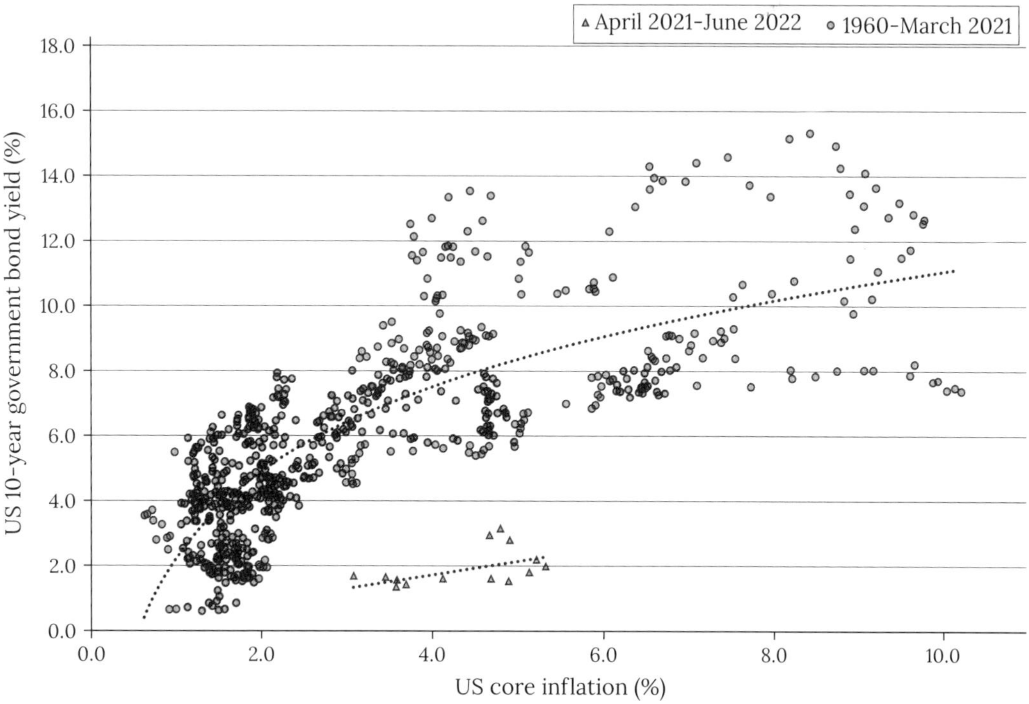

Figure 6.8 US inflation ('core' inflation) and 10-year US bond yields at monthly frequency (January 1960–June 2022).

Source: Extended from TS Lombard using data from FRED, accessed June 2022.

run relationship between a measure of underlying or 'core' inflation and 10 year bond yields. If traders in the bond market expected inflation to 'take off', then they would expect the Fed to tighten monetary policy, with higher interest rates pushing down the price of bonds and imposing a capital loss on their bond holdings. Anticipating this, there 'should' be a sell-off in bond markets, sending prices down and yields up. The data points for 2021–22 are not a good fit with the earlier pattern. One interpretation is that prior to mid-2022, bond markets had altered their interpretation of Fed policy to correspond to the adoption of average inflation targeting. The situation changed dramatically thereafter as bond prices dropped in late 2022 and early 2023.

The ECB shifted from its traditional position of an inflation target of below 2% to adopt a symmetric target, accepting that persistent inflation below 2% was to be interpreted as costly to the economy.

Meanwhile, the Bank of Japan and the Reserve Bank of Australia adopted explicit *yield curve control* targeting long-term interest rates close to zero.

Although central banks chose somewhat different modifications of their previous 'Taylor rule' approaches, there was a common theme of recognizing the damage caused by weak growth and too low inflation during the post-financial crisis years.

The September 2022 UK gilt crisis and conflicting central bank objectives

One of the objectives of quantitative easing (QE) is to raise inflation when at the zero lower bound, by lowering long-term rates. However, as we will see in Section 9.2, central banks typically also assume some responsibility for financial stability, for instance by acting as a Lender of Last Resort to provide emergency liquidity when there is a bank run. By influencing the demand for bonds, both Quantitative Easing and quantitative tightening (QT) have direct effects on financial stability.

Expanding QE will both lower long-term rates, and provide more liquidity. During the 2008 financial crisis, which saw a simultaneous shortage of liquidity and a need to lower rates below the zero lower bound, these goals aligned. An example of when the goals conflict occurred in September 2022 in the United Kingdom.

During the summer of 2022 the Bank of England announced that it would be both raising interest rates and reducing the size of its QE programme (i.e. QT) to tackle rising inflation. On 22 September 2022 the Bank's Monetary Policy Committee voted to reduce QE assets by £80 billion as part of actions intended to bring inflation down.

The following day the UK Government announced a mini-budget which included £45 billion of unfunded tax cuts, the largest tax cuts in a generation, a refusal to allow independent forecasts from the official Office for Budget Responsibility, and significant spending increases. The uncertainty about funding these commitments and about the likely future path of interest rates led to a sell-off of UK government bonds (gilts). As we have seen in Chapter 5, falling bond prices imply rising yields. Within a few days the yield on the 30-year gilt, long-term government debt, had risen from 3.5 percent to over 5 percent.[43]

[43] https://www.ft.com/content/156682c1-1fb9-42d1-aac3-de531e266d68.

Since UK government bonds are considered low risk, and thus widely used as collateral, falling prices meant that a number of institutions, in particular pension funds, faced so-called margin calls causing them to sell gilts, further depressing prices. As demonstrated dramatically in this case, when the value of a financial institution's assets used as collateral falls below a threshold, it will be required to provide cash to cover the 'margin' or gap (this is a margin call). Concerns over the solvency of pension funds caused the Bank of England to announce on 28 September 2022 it was ready to increase its gilt purchases to stabilize the price, effectively an increase in the size of QE, six days after it had voted for QT.

Monetary policy and QE/QT with excess reserves

Using the model developed in Section 5.5 and represented in Figure 5.17, where there are excess reserves and interest is paid on reserves, it should be possible to vary the size of QE without affecting the policy interest rate. The UK September 2022 episode illustrates this. In effect, the Bank of England shifted the supply of reserves to the right, by expanding QE to boost liquidity, while remaining committed to raising the policy interest rate (i^P) to tackle inflation. So long as the central bank's commitment to keep raising (i^P) remains credible despite expanding QE, this should not affect the central bank's monetary policy.

The Bank of England's communications regarding the situation highlight the importance of this credibility. In a statement accompanying the decision, the central bank assured the public that:

> These purchases will be strictly time limited. They are intended to tackle a specific problem in the long-dated government bond market... The purchases will be unwound in a smooth and orderly fashion once risks to market functioning are judged to have subsided.
>
> The Monetary Policy Committee has been informed of these temporary and targeted financial stability operations... The MPC will not hesitate to change interest rates by as much as needed to return inflation to the 2% target sustainably in the medium term, in line with its remit.
>
> The MPC's annual target of an £80bn stock reduction [QT] is unaffected and unchanged.[44]

Similarly, a few days later the Bank of England chief economist reiterated that,

> These operations do not create central bank money on a lasting basis. As a result they will not shift the underlying macroeconomically-relevant monetary trends in the economy, which ultimately pin down developments in the price level.... So yesterday's intervention was not a monetary policy operation. The temporary and targeted character of the Bank's intervention

[44] https://www.bankofengland.co.uk/news/2022/september/bank-of-england-announces-gilt-market-operation.

is key to the distinction between financial stability and monetary policy that I have emphasized here.[45]

Operating in an excess reserves regime, the central bank can respond as the Bank of England did above, intervening to ensure financial stability without having to backtrack on inflation targets. This would not have been possible in a scarce reserves regime.

6.4.5 Effect on income and wealth inequality

When the monetary policy maker seeks to implement its inflation-targeting mandate, its decisions are transmitted to inequality through two channels. To illustrate this, take the case of a recession in which in response to forecast inflation below target, the central bank cuts the interest rate or engages in QE (at the ZLB). The 'earnings' channel arises from the increase in employment: income inequality falls because as we saw in Chapter 1, lower income households are typically worse hit in a recession (Coibion et al. 2017). By implementing policy consistent with its mandate, the central bank reduces income inequality through this channel.

However, a second channel operates through the effect of easier monetary policy on asset prices. A lower interest rate raises asset prices (bond prices, directly, and of other financial assets, indirectly). Given the concentration of asset holdings among higher income households, this 'asset price' channel increases wealth inequality (Kaplan, et al. 2018 and further discussion in Chapter 18). Lower interest rates also boost house prices. When monetary policy is operated using QE, the major transmission channel is via asset prices so the effect of raising wealth inequality is 'baked in' to the policy (Bernanke 2020). But note that the channel through which the policy of QE is supposed to boost aggregate demand and employment by raising consumption as higher asset prices raise wealth, will be limited by the low marginal propensity to consume of the rich, who do not fall into the wealthy 'hand-to-mouth' category discussed in Chapter 1. As noted below, the effect on consumption depends on whether the increase in wealth is interpreted as permanent or temporary.

An important question is the relative size of these effects. Interesting evidence comes from a study of the distributional consequences of monetary policy for racial inequality. Research using US data quantifies the earnings and asset price channels (Bartscher et al. 2021). They find that a loosening of monetary policy raises the employment of black households relative to white ones but that this is by far outweighed by the larger wealth gains of white households. This indicates that the policy maker in pursuit of its mandate—and especially if QE is used—is likely to reduce income inequality but raise wealth inequality. The relative size of the estimated effects in this case point to an unambiguous dis-equalizing effect of expansionary monetary policy.

Specifically, the earnings channel produces an estimated \$97 increase in annual earnings for the median black as compared to a white household. The same shock increases share prices by 5% and house prices by 2% (together with the intended effects of lower yields on government and corporate bonds, which is what produces

---

[45] https://www.bis.org/review/r220930i.htm.

the earnings channel effect). This flows through to capital gains for white families of at least $25,000 (about a quarter of their annual income) and of only $5,000 for black families (5% of their annual income). Shares are mainly owned by white households and although house ownership is more equal, it is white households that benefit more from house price rises.

The increase in wealth inequality produces further macroeconomic effects, which are likely to be permanent. Consumption increases in households benefiting from higher wealth, suggesting it is interpreted as permanent. The estimates suggest that a $20,000 capital gain would translate into $600 of additional household consumption—much larger than the relative earnings gain of black households. Another sizeable effect is the feedback from higher asset prices to household collateral. Predominantly white households benefit from the enhanced ability to borrow and to start a business, for example, with potential long-term effects on inequality.

This highlights the danger of ignoring the asset price channel of monetary policy that arises from the skewed distribution of portfolios across households. The earnings channel works to lower inequality in concert with the central bank's mandate but the asset price channel does the opposite.

Returning to the central bank's mandate, we conclude by noting how contractionary policy implemented to reduce inflation affects inequality.[46] As we have seen in Chapter 5, inflation is a 'tax' on assets denominated in nominal terms. This includes banknotes and deposit accounts, which are the only financial assets of the lowest income households, which means they are disproportionately affected by inflation. In situations of rapid nominal exchange rate depreciation, which accompany high inflation, such households are also unable to protect themselves by transferring assets abroad. Finally, low-income households rely on wages and pensions, which are set in nominal terms (although some pensions are linked to the rate of inflation, as is the case in the UK). A central bank's success in keeping inflation low and stable prevents these effects on inequality from arising.

6.5 CENTRAL BANK BALANCE SHEET, MONEY, AND INFLATION

Central bank reserve liabilities, and the corresponding reserve account balances on the asset side of the balance sheets of commercial banks, expanded substantially for a second time this century in the wake of the Covid-19 crisis. To the extent that banks make additional loans, the quantitative easing programmes will ultimately be reflected in higher deposits in commercial banks. Through this mechanism, the expanded central bank balance sheet can result in a rise in the money supply. Figure 5.13 shows that money supply, if defined by M3, has been rising across countries at the same time as central bank assets expanded. However, the money supply was rising before quantitative easing began, and there does not seem to have been any notable acceleration in the decade following the financial crisis.

---

[46] Borio (2021).

Questions arise about whether or not rising money supply will cause rising inflation, or even hyperinflation. Hyperinflation has traditionally been defined as referring to a situation in which inflation rates rise to above 50% per month. This was more common in the first half of the 20th century than either in earlier epochs, or since. Situations of very high inflation or hyperinflation are normally the result of governments being unable to finance their expenditure through the normal means (borrowing or taxation), and therefore resort to monetary financing, which is the creation of reserves by the central bank to finance government debt. This is known as seigniorage. The Appendix to this chapter develops a model of seigniorage and hyperinflation.

From the perspective of economic theory, the answer depends on the model of money and banking being used. We can set out the circumstances that would have to prevail according to the models developed in Chapters 1–5 for the situation described to turn into one of rising inflation or hyperinflation. It is interesting to also do the same exercise for a completely different set of models.

As we have seen, the models of Chapters 1–5 incorporate inflation targeting, and profit-maximizing banks that respond to the demand for loans coming to them from a mixture of credit unconstrained and constrained households and firms, in the context of aggregate demand-driven business cycles around an equilibrium with involuntary unemployment. In the alternative set of models, the macroeconomy works very differently. Money is exogenous and controlled by the central bank, banks are passive intermediaries between borrowers and savers and have a fixed reserve-deposit ratio. Households and firms have a stable demand for money and a fixed banknote to deposit ratio. Information is complete and prices are flexible so there is neither involuntary unemployment at equilibrium nor aggregate demand-driven business cycles.

6.5.1 **The models of Chapters 1–5**

We first explain what has to happen for the expansion of central bank balance sheets to result in a situation of ever-increasing inflation, or the extreme case of hyperinflation, using the models of Chapters 1–5. We consider a scenario of a boom in spending, which pushes unemployment down below the equilibrium rate, and in which inflation expectations become unanchored from the inflation target. The first two conditions show what must happen for this to trigger continually rising inflation, while the third is an additional requirement to generate hyperinflation. This section spells out why, despite the great increase in the size of the central bank's balance sheet, we do not think hyperinflation is remotely likely to occur in any high-income country.

1. Suppose that the central bank either does not care about a process of rising inflation above its target, does not have any effective tools to implement inflation-targeting policy, or is prevented from acting against rising inflation. One example of the latter is where the government has authority over the central bank, *and* given the tradeoffs it faces does not respond to rising inflation. This is referred to as *fiscal dominance*. As we saw in Chapter 3, reducing inflation leads to temporarily rising unemployment, which is politically unpopular. Consider for instance the positive demand shock in Figure 3.4. Once the economy has reached point B, the central bank should raise the interest rate, bringing the economy to point C the following period, then gradually returning the economy to the medium-run equilibrium: the

movement from B to C involves a significant rise in unemployment. If the central bank is not independent, the government could prevent it from raising the interest rate in order to keep the electorate happy. With adaptive (i.e. unanchored) inflation expectations, a situation of rising inflation of the kind shown in Figure 2.18 would occur, so long as the central bank continues to avoid intervention.

2. However, the situation in Figure 2.18 requires that a combination of the non-bank private sector as a whole and the government wishes to spend at a level that keeps output *persistently* above equilibrium (i.e. there is a bargaining gap), *and* banks believe that the private spending plans are sufficiently soundly based as to enable bank loans to be repaid. As we have seen, bank lending is constrained by demand for loans by the non-bank private sector, the expected profitability of the lending (credit risk) and the adequacy of the bank's equity buffer (solvency risk). If the conditions for lending are not met, the banks will not make the loans, and, unless the government permanently spends to sustain the bargaining gap, we would not get continued rising inflation.
3. In order for the rising inflation from conditions one and two to escalate into hyperinflation (defined as inflation above 50% per month), the empirical evidence suggests that the annual inflation rate would have to rise to well over 100% (Fischer et al. 2002). The mechanism suggested in a famous model of hyperinflation (Cagan 1956) is that once inflation rises to a high level for a prolonged amount of time, the demand for money suddenly collapses and hyperinflation ensues.[47] It is notable that after 2000, almost no country in the world has had inflation above 50% per annum, and less than 10% of countries have recorded inflation of above 15% (Kremer et al. 2021).

A concern over the expansion of central bank reserves is that it could facilitate condition two; commercial banks now hold sufficient reserves to be able to significantly expand lending, while still meeting reserve requirements. In addition, governments may have greater motivation to prevent the policy rate from rising even if inflation increases.

Since the financial crisis, holdings of government debt by central banks have increased significantly, a form of monetary financing. When a government bond is held by the private sector, the cost to the government is the interest rate on bonds. When the bond is held by the central bank, the government pays the central bank the interest rate on bonds, while the central bank pays out to banks the policy rate on the reserves it created to purchase the bond. As the government owns the central bank, the 'net' cost of the debt is the interest paid on reserves. This means that a rise in the policy rate, in the presence of excess reserves and interest on reserves, leads to greater costs for the government.[48]

The hypothetical causal chain can be summarized using the following scenario, beginning from a situation in which the central bank has expanded its balance sheet (post-Covid, for example).

---

[47] See Appendix 6.7.2 for further discussion of hyperinflation.

[48] Vlieghe (2020).

a. Households and firms plan to spend such that aggregate demand is greater than is consistent with equilibrium output y_e, and

b. banks decide that loan requests are creditworthy, and

c. because they are not constrained by reserves and assuming their capital requirements are adequate, banks are able to extend new loans (which, we note, by creating additional bank money, increase the measured money supply), and

d. although forecasting a rise in inflation, the central bank does not raise the interest rate, for instance due to political pressure from the government, then:

output and employment expand and inflation rises; unanchored inflation expectations adjust upwards according to the adaptive expectations process; inflation rises further.

Without the entire sequence (a) to (d), the causal chain is interrupted, and the process of rising inflation is halted. Note that condition (a) could arise from a negative supply shock, including an external one such as an energy price shock modelled in Chapter 2 and in more detail in Chapter 13. The monetary policy framework provides theoretical and evidence-based reasons to doubt the completion of this causal chain. The energy price shock triggered by the war in Ukraine provides a test. The scenario in Figure 2.18 would involve continually rising inflation, without any further gains in employment—it is unlikely that any government or central bank could tolerate this for an extended period. We saw in Chapter 3 that central banks have increasingly adopted inflation-targeting as a stated policy, while in Chapter 4 we saw that there has been a trend towards central bank independence.

Note that if the chain were to be completed, then *ex-post*, the rise in a measure of broad money supply, which is money in the hands of the non-bank public, will be correlated with higher inflation but in this model there is no causal relationship. Likewise, the expanded central bank balance sheets which are a feature of the post-crisis world would be correlated with higher inflation, but again without a causal relationship. If the correlation is observed, the causes lie with the profit-seeking behaviour of banks, the regulatory environment, the mandate of the central bank, its relationship with the government, and the government's objectives and its accountability to voters.

6.5.2 The Quantity Theory of Money and monetary-base multiplier models

Before comparing how an alternative conceptual framework can be used to interpret a connection between an expanded central bank balance sheet and rising inflation, it is necessary to introduce the relevant models and concepts. In the first model, we show how the Quantity Theory of Money provides a causal model from the money supply to the price level and inflation. In the second model, we show how the monetary-base multiplier concept provides a causal model from the monetary base (closely related to reserves) to the money supply. Putting these together, we have a causal model that predicts that a change in reserves leads to a change in the money supply, which in turn directly affects the price level and inflation.

The classical dichotomy and the nominal anchor

The classical dichotomy refers to the possibility of identifying different factors that pin down the real (output, employment) and the nominal sides (price level, inflation rate) in a model of the economy. In a textbook economy with complete information and contracts, and price-taking in all markets, the labour market clears and there are no credit constraints (see Section 2.5.1). Under these conditions, the classical dichotomy holds at *all points in time*. This means that prices and wages always adjust immediately to keep the economy at equilibrium output.

On the real side, technology and preferences (the most basic supply-side building blocks of household and firm behaviour) pin down output while on the nominal side, the money supply pins down the price level. The Quantity Theory of Money encapsulates the classical dichotomy:

$$Py = MV, \qquad \text{(Quantity Theory of Money)}$$

where P is the price level, y, the level of output, M, the money supply and V is called the velocity of circulation of money. In the Quantity Theory, y is the outcome of goods and labour market clearing. The growth rate of the money supply is exogenous and controlled by the central bank. To gain policy insights from the Quantity Theory of Money it is necessary to convert the equation into growth rates. Using discrete time notation, we have:

$$\frac{\Delta P}{P} + \frac{\Delta y}{y} \approx \frac{\Delta M}{M} + \frac{\Delta V}{V}. \tag{6.5}$$

Equation 6.5 shows that the growth rate of prices plus the growth rate of output is approximately equal to the growth rate of the money supply plus the growth rate of the velocity of circulation. To make the maths as simple as possible, we make the assumptions that output growth is zero and that the velocity of circulation is constant. This gives us a simple expression for inflation:

$$\frac{\Delta P}{P} \approx \frac{\Delta M}{M} \tag{6.6}$$

$$\rightarrow \pi \approx \left[\frac{\Delta M}{M}\right]. \tag{6.7}$$

Under these assumptions, the rate of inflation is determined by the choice of the growth rate of the money supply by the policy maker, shown in square brackets to highlight that it is exogenous.

To summarize, since the assumption that wages and prices are perfectly flexible means the economy is always in the medium-run equilibrium (or steady state, that is, $y = y_e$), the choice by the policy maker of M, pins down the price level, P; the choice of the growth rate of M pins down inflation, π.

The next step is to introduce the banking system in order to provide a connection between the central bank's balance sheet, bank lending, the money supply M, and inflation.

The monetary-base multiplier

The monetary-base multiplier is a model of fractional reserve banking that works differently from the model presented in Chapter 5. The key assumption is that a bank holds a fixed proportion of its deposits as reserves, called the 'reserve to deposit ratio' (*rd*). By also assuming that the public wish to hold a fixed ratio of banknotes, denoted by '*c*' for cash, to deposits (*cd*), we show in the appendix that a rise in the monetary base (e.g. a rise in reserves) implies a $\varkappa$-fold rise in the money supply (the money held by the non-bank public), where $\varkappa = \frac{1+cd}{cd+rd}$. The intuition is that when the public receive an injection of base money, for instance from the central bank buying bonds, only a proportion of the money is held as banknotes because of households' and firms' desired banknote to deposit ratio. The rest is deposited with banks, which raises their reserves. As banks' reserve to deposit ratio is now above the desired one, they will lend out part of this money to the public, who in turn will store some as banknotes and deposit the rest. A multiplier process is therefore assumed to occur until both the reserve deposit and cash deposit ratios are stable at the desired levels.

The conditions required for rising inflation in this alternative model, given a situation in which the central bank has expanded its balance sheet (post-Covid, for example), can be summarized as,

a. Households and firms have a fixed banknote to deposit ratio, and

b. banks have a fixed reserve to deposit ratio, and

c. the velocity of circulation is fixed (i.e. the demand for money is stable), and

d. the level of output is determined by the clearing of the labour market at full employment.

Given these conditions, the increased supply of reserves leads to rising inflation.

However, the assumptions of the model are at odds with a modern economy and banking system. There is no fixed monetary-base multiplier (banks decide whether to extend loans based on their business model, as we have seen); the evidence shows that at least in some countries, there is no fixed relationship between the money supply and nominal output (i.e. the velocity of circulation is not constant); and the evidence contradicts the assumptions that credit and labour markets clear, and that disequilibria are transitory. Central banks have tried to clarify some of these misconceptions, for instance by criticizing the idea that banks are simply intermediaries who lend out deposits.[49]

6.6 CONCLUSIONS

Building on the foundations of previous chapters, this one has deepened the analysis of monetary policy. We can summarize the main conclusions as follows:

1. Monetary policy has evolved dramatically over the last 30 years. Monetary targeting was used with mixed success in the 1980s, but was ultimately replaced by the inflation-targeting framework with central banks that display Taylor rule-type

49 See McLeay et al. (2014).

behaviour to set interest rates. This sea-change in approach to monetary policy and the movement away from Monetarist ideas was partly the result of the failure of monetary targeting in the UK and North America in the 1980s. The Monetarist version of inflation targeting was undermined by the inability of monetary authorities to control their chosen monetary aggregate and the instability of the relationship between monetary growth and inflation.

2. The inflation-targeting central bank has preferences over output and inflation deviations, as represented in a loss function by the parameter for the degree of inflation aversion, β. The level of β affects the slope of the *MR* and consequently the central bank's best policy response to shocks. A more inflation-averse central bank will be more aggressive in raising interest rates in response to an inflation shock. This type of central bank would prefer an adjustment path that reduced inflation quickly, even if this caused a large rise in unemployment ('cold turkey'), as opposed to an adjustment path that entailed a smaller initial reduction in unemployment, but brought inflation back to target more slowly ('gradualist'). The *MR* curve is also flatter if inflation is more responsive to changes in output (i.e. if α in the Phillips curve is higher). Figure 6.4 showed that there is some evidence of a decreasing positive correlation between output and inflation starting from the second half of the inflation-targeting system. However, this does not necessarily represent a flattening of the Phillips curve; indeed, the dynamics of the 3-equation model show that inflation-targeting triggers a downward-sloping relationship between inflation and output (MR curve) following an economic shock. Hence, Figure 6.4 may reflect a period of successful inflation-targeting on the part of central banks rather than lower sensitivity of inflation to output.

3. The best response or optimal Taylor rule is derived from the 3-equation model and shows the interest rate the central bank should set to minimize its loss function. The size of the best response to an economic shock in the closed economy will depend on the inflation aversion of the central bank (β), the supply-side structure as reflected in the slope of the Phillips curve (α) and the interest-sensitivity of aggregate demand (a). Central banks around the world have different preferences, which are reflected in their mandates. The nominal interest rates implied by simple Taylor rules in some countries were negative during the financial crisis, suggesting that conventional monetary policy had reached its limits.

4. We have seen a number of times in the past that asset price bubbles arise in financial markets, such as the tech boom of the late 1990s and the sub-prime mortgage-backed securities boom in the mid 2000s. Should central banks intervene to burst these bubbles by pre-emptively raising the interest rate? The interest rate is the main policy tool of modern inflation-targeting central banks and raising it may not cool the asset market in question, where returns are typically extremely high (while the bubble is inflating). There is also little evidence that central bankers are better placed to identify bubbles than financial markets and a significant risk they might make errors. In light of this, the central banks' preferred approach has been to wait until bubbles burst and then mop up after them. As argued in Chapters 8 and 9, the severe recession following the global financial crisis highlighted the dangers of leverage-fuelled bubbles in a highly interdependent banking system. Central banks

and other regulatory authorities have been tasked with design and implementation of improved financial stability regulation to reduce risk-taking behaviour and to preempt the formation of bubbles that threaten financial stability (see Chapter 10). This includes macro-prudential regulation such as adjusting loan to value ratios for mortgage loans and structural reforms to the banking system such as caps on leverage to reduce the scale of leverage-fuelled financial cycles (modelled in Chapter 8).

5. The global financial crisis saw a number of countries introduce unconventional monetary policies in response to interest rates being stuck at the zero lower bound. Quantitative easing—the central bank using newly created reserves to buy financial assets—was the most commonly used of these policies. The early research suggests this policy had some limited success against its objectives: increasing asset prices, reducing long-term interest rates, boosting GDP and putting upward pressure on inflation. The policy is not without its dangers, however, such as its impact on central bank credibility and independence, medium-term inflation and the as yet unknown macroeconomic effects of exiting the policy (i.e. selling the assets purchased back into the market). With bounded-below interest rates, the monetary response to the Covid-19 pandemic relied on unconventional policies aimed at reducing longer term rates (quantitative easing and forward guidance). Contrary to conventional interest rate changes, policies of QE and yield curve control have a direct effect on asset prices (i.e. via higher demand); this triggered concerns regarding the distributional consequences of monetary policy given salient differences in the portfolio composition of richer and poorer households. Although QE can reduce income inequality through its effect on employment, the effect in redistributing wealth toward the rich is substantially larger.

6. What is the relationship between the expansion of central bank balance sheets that has resulted from quantitative easing and inflation? The models presented in Chapters 1 to 5 can be combined to provide guidance in answering this question. There is no direct causal connection between the growth in the size of central bank balance sheets—which were the outcome of policies to prevent *deflation* from taking hold—and a problem of persistently rising inflation. A different set of models (the Quantity Theory of Money, the monetary-base multiplier, and clearing labour and product markets) can be used to show a direct link from the growth of reserves to inflation. However, the assumptions underlying these models do not capture the way contemporary high-income economies work.

6.7 APPENDIX

6.7.1 The monetary-base multiplier

In this model, money is created through the operation of the monetary-base multiplier. Suppose the central bank's actions use open market operations to buy bonds from the public by 'printing' money. The public holds only, say, one-third of this as banknotes and deposits the rest in banks to maintain their banknote (cash) to deposit ratio of 1:2. The banks keep say 10% of the deposits in their reserve accounts to maintain their desired reserve to deposit ratio and make new loans to the public with the rest. Eventually this process of credit creation will raise the money supply by 2.5 times the original increase in base money by the central bank.

This works as follows. If the initial injection was $100, the initial increase in the money supply is $100. Given the public's *cd* of 1:2, they will hold on to one-third of the cash and place two-thirds of it on deposit in a bank ($66.7). The rise in deposits in the bank means that it will increase how many reserves it holds by $6.67. This leaves it free to make loans to the public using the extra $60. This ends up in the hands of the public as firms and households borrow from banks. This process continues until the public's *cd* ratio is stable at 1:2 and the banks' reserve ratio, *rd*, is stable at 10%.

The new base money in the economy will end up partly in the hands of the public (banknotes) and partly as reserves of the banks. Because $cd = 0.5$ (from 1:2) and $rd = 0.1$, $cd + rd$ = (banknotes + reserves)/deposits = base money/deposits = 0.6. In our example, deposits will have increased by 100/0.6 = 166.7, which is from rearranging the previous equation of base money/deposits = 0.6 and having an injection of 100 base money. Banknotes in the hands of the public will now be higher by $0.5 \times 166.7 = 83.3$. The remainder of the new base money ends up as reserves, hence $100 - 83.3 = 16.7$. The money supply, which is measured by banknotes held by the public plus their deposits with banks, will have increased by $250, implying a monetary-base multiplier of 2.5. More generally, the monetary-base multiplier is $\varkappa = \frac{1+cd}{cd+rd}$, derived below, and in this example we have $\varkappa = \frac{1+cd}{cd+rd} = \frac{1+0.5}{0.5+0.1} = 2.5$.

In the example, the increase in the money supply of $250 can be thought of as being made up of the 100 units of base money created by the central bank (sometimes called 'outside' money) and 150 units of 'inside money' created by the banks when they make loans to the public. The asset side of the banks' balance sheet shows $16.66 of new assets in the form of reserves and $150 loans to the public. This adds up to $166.7, which is exactly equal to the increase in the banks' deposits, i.e. their new liabilities.

Deriving the monetary-base multiplier

The result for $\varkappa$ is derived as follows. Let B be the initial injection of base money by the central bank to the public. We assume that B must be equal to deposits plus cash, as the public store the money as one of the two. We also assume that cash is equal to deposits multiplied by *cd*. Hence we know that $B = \text{deposits} + cd * \text{deposits}$, which can be solved to find that deposits equal $\frac{B}{1+cd}$. The remainder of the base money injection, $\frac{B*cd}{1+cd}$, is held as cash.

Of the new deposits, a proportion $1-rd$ is then lent out, as rd represents what proportion of the new deposits are kept as reserves rather than being lent out. This means that the second round injection of money to households and firms is $\frac{B(1-rd)}{1+cd}$. Of this, a proportion $\frac{1}{1+cd}$ is deposited to banks, of which a proportion $(1-rd)$ is lent out. This cycle continues, and we can write the total injection of money as an infinite geometric series,

$$\Delta\text{Money supply} = B + B\frac{(1-rd)}{1+cd} + B\left(\frac{(1-rd)}{1+cd}\right)^2 + \ldots \tag{6.8}$$

Using the formula for the sum of an infinite geometric series, this adds up to $B\frac{1+cd}{cd+rd}$ with the fraction representing the monetary-base multiplier, κ.

6.7.2 **Monetizing government debt, seigniorage, and hyperinflation**

If the government has high debt and wishes to continue to maintain or expand its spending, how can it do this if it cannot borrow more from the public and it is unwilling or unable to raise taxes? A reason the public may be unwilling to continue to lend to the government is because they believe there is a high risk of the government defaulting, i.e. not paying interest and principal on outstanding bonds. We explore in more detail how governments finance their spending in Chapter 7 on fiscal policy. For now, we rule out borrowing or taxation being adequate to finance the government's spending plans.

To see how the direct financing of government spending by money creation can play a role, we begin by assuming we are in the model described in Section 6.5, with a constant monetary-base multiplier κ, which implies that the growth rate of base money and the growth rate of money supply are equal, and the medium-run equilibrium growth rate of money supply is equal to the rate of inflation. Hence we have, $\gamma_M = \gamma_H = \pi$, where γ_M is the growth rate of money supply, γ_H is the growth rate of base money, and π is inflation. If the central bank prints base money to finance government spending, $\gamma_H = \pi > 0$, implying that prices P are rising. The monetary-base multiplier model assumes that markets always clear at full employment, and as such output y is constant as long as supply factors are unchanged. This means that as the central bank creates base money, nominal output Py rises at rate $\pi(= \gamma_H)$, and the value of existing government debt falls relative to nominal output. The higher is γ_H, the faster the debt burden will fall.

Since $\gamma_H = \pi$, this has led to the use of the term *inflation tax* to refer to this method of financing government spending. It takes us to the related term *seigniorage revenues*, which refers to the amount of real expenditure the government is able to finance through its ability to create base money. Seigniorage revenue is defined as:

$$S = \frac{\Delta H}{P} = \frac{\Delta H}{H}\frac{H}{P} = \gamma_H \frac{H}{P} \tag{6.9}$$

Seigniorage revenue is the amount of new money printed to finance spending, ΔH, normalized by the price level P. In medium-run equilibrium, therefore,

$$S = \pi \frac{H}{P} \tag{6.10}$$

Let $h = \frac{H}{Py}$, the ratio of base money H to nominal output Py. We know from the above assumptions that h remains constant, as the numerator and denominator both grow at the same rate. If calculated as a proportion of real output, seigniorage is,

$$\frac{S}{y} = \pi \frac{H}{Py} = \gamma_H h \tag{6.11}$$

which is the contribution to the fall in the government's debt ratio. The equation for seigniorage above suggests that the government can finance more of its expenditure through seigniorage by raising the growth rate of base money and hence by raising inflation.

However, there is a limit to the extent to which seigniorage can be used as a source of revenue (and therefore as a method of reducing the debt ratio). The limit arises because as inflation goes up, the public becomes less willing to hold money. If we substitute the demand for money into the seigniorage equation, where money demand M^D is equal to base money H times the multiplier $\varkappa$, we get,

$$S = \pi\frac{H}{P} = \pi\frac{M^D}{P}\frac{1}{\varkappa} \tag{6.12}$$

While higher money growth (and inflation) pushes up seigniorage via the first term in the equation, it pushes it down via the second term, $\frac{M^D}{P}$, maintaining our assumption of a constant $\varkappa$ for the third term. To use the tax analogy, pushing up the rate of taxation (in this case, π), has the effect of reducing the tax base (which in this case are real money balances, M/P, as we saw in Section 5.3.1 higher inflation reduces money demand).

Empirical studies suggest that the second effect begins to outweigh the first effect when inflation rates go above about 175% p.a.;[47] this suggests that the maximum amount of revenue the government could raise in this way is about 10% of GDP. These estimates indicate that governments typically curtail their use of seigniorage not because they are near the maximum amount that can be collected but rather because the costs of higher inflation outweigh the benefits.

This raises the question of how hyperinflation with inflation at 50% per month comes about. If the government is using inflation to finance its spending, why would it let inflation rise above the seigniorage maximizing rate? One answer is that the seigniorage equation holds in equilibrium. Hence if it takes time for people to adjust their demand for money to inflation (i.e. the demand for money reacts to inflation slowly), then the government can push up its revenue beyond the revenue-maximizing level that holds in equilibrium by raising the growth rate of base money fast enough. However, as inflation continues to persistently rise, there will come a point when the demand for money suddenly collapses as people lose confidence in the prospect of inflation coming under control, and hyperinflation ensues. This mechanism lies behind the theory of hyperinflation developed by Phillip Cagan (1956).

[47] See Fischer et al. (2002).

QUESTIONS AND PROBLEMS FOR CHAPTER 6

CHECKLIST QUESTIONS

1. Section 6.2.1 sets out two conditions that must hold if monetary targeting is going to succeed in controlling inflation. Briefly explain these two conditions and why they were violated during the Thatcher experiment with monetary targeting in the UK.

2. Margaret Thatcher started an aggressive disinflationary policy when she came to office as the UK's prime minister in 1979. In October 1980, she delivered her famous 'the lady's not for turning' speech. What was the aim of this speech and how was it influenced by Monetarist views on the importance of credibility and managing inflation expectations?

3. Use the central bank's loss ellipses and Phillips curves to derive the MR curve in the following cases:
   a. When $\alpha = 1$ and $\beta = 1$
   b. When $\alpha = 1$ and $\beta < 1$
   c. When $\alpha < 1$ and $\beta = 1$.

4. Use a PC–MR diagram to show that the cumulative unemployment caused by disinflation is independent of the degree of inflation aversion (β) of the central bank. How does this finding change if:
   a. The Phillips curves are convex
   b. The Phillips curves are steeper (i.e. $\uparrow \alpha$)?

5. Use the IS–PC–MR diagram to show the logic behind the equation

$$r_0 - r_S = \frac{1}{a\left(\alpha + \frac{1}{\alpha\beta}\right)}\left(\pi_0 - \pi^T\right). \qquad \text{(best response Taylor rule)}$$

   Approach the question as follows:
   a. Use the diagrams to show how the initial interest rate response to an inflation shock varies with the slope of the MR.
   b. What parameters affect the slope of the MR?
   c. Are your findings consistent with the best response Taylor rule equation?

6. Assess the following statement: 'asset price bubbles played a major role in the global financial crisis, so central banks should have stepped in to burst them in their early stages'. Refer to Chapter 9 for details about bubbles and the financial crisis.

7. Explain how the Taylor rule could find the best response nominal interest rate to be negative.

8. Compare the transmission mechanisms of conventional monetary policy with quantitative easing. Can the two policies be viewed as substitutes?

9. Is there any reason why an inflation-targeting central bank should be concerned with inequality?

10. Assess the following statement: 'during the financial crisis, central banks significantly expanded their balance sheets through quantitative easing and this did not cause inflation expectations to become less firmly

anchored to the inflation target, thus we can say that QE does not pose a danger to macroeconomic stability'.

PROBLEMS

1. Pick a high-income economy (outside of the UK) that experimented with money supply targeting in the 1980s. Use the concepts in this chapter and the available academic literature to answer the following questions:
   a. Was the policy successful?
   b. What were the reasons that led to the policy being successful or unsuccessful?
   c. How do these reasons relate to the Quantity Theory of Money?

2. A central bank has the following loss function:

$$L = -(y_t - y_e) + \beta(\pi_t - \pi^T)^2. \tag{6.13}$$

   Use the information in this chapter to answer the following questions:
   a. What can we interpret about the central bank's preferences from this loss function (equation 6.13)?
   b. Briefly explain how this loss function compares to the standard loss function and to a loss function with $y^T > y_e$.
   c. Find the inflation bias for a central bank with this loss function (equation 6.13). [Hint: see Section 4.6.2 in Chapter 4.]

3. Pick an economy (outside of the US, the Eurozone, the UK and Japan) with an inflation-targeting central bank. Use their central bank's website to gather information on interest rates and total assets for the period from 2006 to 2011. Present the data in a graph. Use the graph to answer the following questions:
   a. Did the central bank hit the zero nominal bound during the Great Recession? If so, did they employ quantitative easing?
   b. Use your own knowledge and macroeconomic indicators (e.g. from the IMF World Economic Outlook Database) to provide a picture of your chosen economy before and during the crisis. Does this help to shed light on why it did or did not reach the ZLB during the global financial crisis? [Hint: think about your chosen economy's strength entering the recession, the severity of their recession, other policies used to stimulate demand (e.g. fiscal policy), their reliance on exports etc.]

4. Use this chapter and your own research to answer the following questions. Why might the factors listed below have compounded Japan's macroeconomic problems in its so-called 'lost decades'? Do Japan's lost decades provide strong evidence for the impotence of conventional and unconventional monetary policy at the zero lower bound?

a. The refusal to adopt an explicit inflation target.

b. Tightening monetary policy too soon in the 1990s.

c. Banks continuing to lend to firms in severe financial distress (so-called zombie firms) in order to avoid recognizing bad loans on their own books.

5. This question uses the Macroeconomic Simulator (available at www.oup.com/he/carlin-soskice). Open the simulator in the closed economy version, and select a permanent positive aggregate demand shock of magnitude 5% (you may change the shock magnitude as you wish). Run the simulator and go to the numerical results. On a different worksheet, copy the values for 'Inflation' and the 'Output gap' from period 6 (this is the period after the shock) to period 20. Finally, produce a scatter plot with inflation on the vertical axis and the output gap on the horizontal axis with the more negative values of the output gap on the left. Now answer the following questions:

   a. Is the trendline in your scatter plot upward or downward sloping? Is this trend consistent with the value of the 'Sensitivity of inflation wrt output gap' you see in the simulator's (see www.oup.com/he/carlin-soskice) settings (note that this value represents the slope of the Phillips curve)? Explain.

   b. Would your scatter plot look different if there was no central bank working to stabilize the economy? Explain.

   c. Given your answers to parts (a) and (b), which curve in the 3-equation model does your trendline represent?

INTERESTED IN EXPLORING THESE TOPICS FURTHER?

Visit www.oup.com/he/carlin-soskice to consolidate and extend your learning with the multiple-choice questions accompanying this chapter.

CHAPTER

7

FISCAL POLICY

7.1 INTRODUCTION

Fiscal policy refers to decisions by governments about raising revenue through taxation and distributing that revenue as public expenditure including transfers such as pensions. The 3-equation model places primary responsibility for macroeconomic stabilization on monetary policy. In the model, the best-response output gap of the policy maker to shocks is implemented by a change in the interest rate, if it is available as a policy instrument. Fiscal policy is important for three reasons:

1. *Discretionary* fiscal policy in the form of government purchases of goods and services, transfers, and taxation is used as a stabilization tool by governments around the world, as shown, for example, by the coordinated fiscal stimulus programmes implemented during the global financial crisis and the response to the pandemic. This policy lever was particularly important in those circumstances because conventional monetary policy was constrained by the zero lower bound. In the face of ordinary business cycle fluctuations, countries that do not have an independent monetary policy, because of fixed exchange rates or membership of a common currency area (see Chapter 14), use fiscal policy to stabilize aggregate demand.
2. Fiscal policy provides *automatic stabilizers*, which insulate the economy to some extent from shocks to aggregate demand, even in the absence of changes in the fiscal policy stance. For example, in a recession, automatic stabilizers will help boost the economy, by increasing social security spending (e.g. unemployment benefits) and reducing tax burdens.
3. A government's ability to borrow enables it to provide *insurance* to citizens in the face of bad shocks, like a war or a pandemic. Fiscal policy is used to *manage the debt*. The accumulation of public debt in the global financial crisis reflected the consequences of bank bail-outs, and of the fiscal stabilization measures necessitated by the deep recessions that followed. The Covid-19 pandemic highlighted the value of a government having the scope to borrow to support incomes when its public health priorities led to the shutdown of many economic activities. By borrowing at a time when the private sector is unable or unwilling to support aggregate demand and incomes, the government can improve welfare. However, the borrowing accumulates as government debt. High-income countries with governments able to borrow could benefit from fulfilling the role of the 'insurer of last resort'; low- and middle-income countries could not.

The macroeconomic policy framework based on delegating stabilization policy to the central bank was in its heyday between the early 1990s and the financial crisis—a

Models and policies	Objectives	
	Stabilization	Public debt management
3-equation model macro policy framework, widely adopted	Monetary policy	Fiscal policy
Modern Monetary Theory (MMT)	Fiscal policy	Monetary policy
Policies implemented at the zero lower bound 2008–2021	Fiscal and monetary	Fiscal and monetary

Table 7.1 The assignment of monetary and fiscal policy to the objectives of stabilization and public debt management.

period lasting a decade and a half. In Table 7.1, this framework is summarized in the top row: stabilization was the job of monetary policy. Given that monetary policy set the interest rate, fiscal policy had to manage the trajectory of the public debt through its influence on the gap between its expenditure and revenue from taxation, i.e. the budget deficit excluding interest payments. The pandemic both extended the zero lower bound period and required governments to borrow to stabilize. This shines the spotlight on the relationship between fiscal and monetary policy, and on the assignment of policy instruments to objectives, which was brought to prominence in so-called Modern Monetary Theory.[1]

The second row of the table highlights how Modern Monetary Theory reverses the responsibility for stabilization and public debt management as compared with the conventional assignment of policy instruments to targets (row 1). Because the central bank is able to create reserves with which to purchase government bonds, MMT proposes that monetary policy be used to manage the public debt. Meanwhile, fiscal policy—the choice of government spending and taxation—should be used to stabilize the level of aggregate demand to ensure that employment is high. In the event of inflationary pressure, MMT advocates that fiscal, rather than monetary, policy be used to reduce aggregate demand. For more details, see Box 7.1 on MMT.

The third row in the table indicates that, in the years after 2008, with many economies stuck at the zero lower bound, a combination of fiscal and monetary policy was deployed in relation to the two objectives of stabilization and public debt management. For stabilization, quantitative easing (monetary policy) has been combined with discretionary fiscal policy. And through QE, monetary policy has influenced the long-term interest rate on bonds, which has reduced the cost of servicing the public debt. At the research frontier, work in the so-called HANK framework, which is explained in Chapter 18, highlights that when we recognize the redistributive effects of monetary policy (see Chapter 6), the superiority of monetary policy for stabilization is no longer as clear as it appears in the 3-equation model, even when the economy is away from the ZLB.

[1] For a discussion of MMT from the perspective of the assignment of monetary and fiscal policy to targets, see Jayadev, A. and Mason, J. W. (2018), 'Mainstream macroeconomics and modern monetary theory: what really divides them', *Institute for New Economic Thinking*. https://www.ineteconomics.org/perspectives/blog/mainstream-macroeconomics-and-modern-monetary-theory-what-really-divides-them or Mason and Jayadev (2018).

BOX 7.1 Modern Monetary Theory

Modern Monetary Theory (MMT) is a variant of Keynesian economics that has its roots in Abba Lerner's theory of functional finance published in 1943.[a] It rose to prominence in the 21st century, as it gained a significant following in the US on the left of the Democratic Party. Despite its name, MMT contains little that is genuinely new (Mankiw 2020). It emphasizes certain ideas that were already present in the macroeconomic literature, but downplayed by more mainstream economists, who saw them as appropriate to extreme circumstances like the zero lower bound rather than a guide to policy in 'normal times'. Its main theoretical drawback is a tendency to minimize the dangers involved in some of its policies if they are pushed too far.

The main propositions of MMT are as follows:

1. A government with its own sovereign currency has no budget constraint.
2. Such a government can always finance expenditure by 'printing' money.
3. The only constraint is inflation arising from excess demand.
4. To restrain demand, the government can raise taxes or sell interest-bearing bonds. The former will directly reduce the spending power of the public; the latter will choke off investment demand by raising the interest rate.
5. Government debt that is held by the central bank should not be included in the national debt.
6. The national debt, properly measured, can always be reduced by purchasing outstanding government bonds using money created by the central bank.
7. Apart from technical details, it makes no difference whether government expenditure (for example, citizens are sent a cheque or a bank transfer, as happened in the US in the pandemic and in Australia in the financial crisis) is directly financed by the central bank (e.g. so-called helicopter money), or is financed using money obtained from the central bank in exchange for bonds.

Objections:

1. Inflation. In MMT, there is no inflation due to excess demand until the economy is at 'full' employment. In reality there may be undesirable—and rising—inflation as expectations adjust before this point, as illustrated by the Phillips curve.
2. Political economy. Once the public gets used to financing expenditure by 'printing money' this may be difficult to reverse if inflation starts to take off. Although MMT advocates recognize this danger, they downplay it.
3. Exchange rate depreciation. Excessive creation of money by the central bank may cause the national currency to depreciate, leading to a terms of trade loss and imported inflation (Chapters 12 and 13).

---

[a] See in particular p.471 of Lerner (1943 *Social Research*) 'Functional finance and the federal debt', reprinted in *Readings in Fiscal Policy* (1955) published for the American Economic Association by Richard D. Irwin. For an introduction to MMT, see Lavoie (2013). For a textbook exposition, see Mitchell et al. (2019).

In this chapter, we set out some more formal modelling of fiscal policy and government finances. We provide the reasoning and evidence behind the use of fiscal policy in macroeconomic management, as well as assessing the necessary conditions for government debt to be kept on a sustainable path. The rest of the chapter is organized as follows.

In Section 7.2, we analyse the use of fiscal policy for stabilization in the economy. There are two key components to fiscal policy—*automatic stabilizers* and *discretionary* fiscal policy. The former refers to the changes in the budget deficit that occur automatically as a response to the economic cycle (e.g. unemployment benefits) imparting a stabilizing effect, whereas the latter refers to changes in the fiscal policy stance of the government, typically to reinforce the automatic stabilizers.

Section 7.3 focuses on a key downside of using discretionary fiscal policy—the build-up of public debt. We use a simple model of debt dynamics to show how government debt (as a percentage of GDP) evolves, and the factors that can influence its path. The section ends by discussing debt reduction—what is the impact of high debt on GDP growth? What methods can governments employ to reduce their debt ratios? Is it possible for contractionary fiscal policy introduced to reduce public debt, known as austerity policy, to have expansionary effects on the economy contrary to the predictions of the model?

Section 7.4 introduces the concept of *Ricardian equivalence*. This links back to the discussion of the permanent income hypothesis in Chapter 1. We show how the impact of fiscal policy on the economy differs when households are rational and fully forward-looking, and where they incorporate the government's budget constraint into their own saving decisions. These are the PIH households who face no credit constraints and don't have cognitive biases. We also use this framework to look at the difference between tax- and bond-based financing, and temporary and permanent changes to fiscal policy.

In Section 7.5, we report a number of explanations for the tendency of governments to run budget deficits and for debt ratios to rise—the so-called *deficit bias*. We also look into why the extent of deficit bias varies across countries. We end the section by discussing the two approaches commonly used to tackle deficit (and austerity) bias: *fiscal rules* and *fiscal policy councils*.

7.2 FISCAL POLICY'S ROLE IN STABILIZATION

7.2.1 The scope of fiscal policy

In addition to its role in stabilization, fiscal policy is used to meet a distinct set of government objectives related to income redistribution, resource allocation, and the provision of public goods.

Income redistribution: Fiscal policy involves raising revenue through taxation and redistributing it through government expenditure on purchases, transfers, and interest payments on its debt. Tax and transfer systems in high-income economies are normally designed to redistribute income from those with higher incomes to those with lower incomes. This can be embedded in the structure of taxes, such as an income tax where tax rates increase as income increases (i.e. a progressive tax). Social security transfers, such as unemployment and housing benefits, also redistribute income towards those with lower income. There are substantial cross-country differences in the extent of redistribution. For example, redistribution is a much higher political priority in Continental Europe and the Nordic countries than it is in the United States, Korea or Japan.

Resource reallocation: Fiscal policy can be used to intervene and alter the market allocation of resources. The government could do this by providing subsidies to a particular industry. This would encourage more of the economy's resources to be devoted to that industry than would otherwise be the case. Taxing undesirable activities is the other side of this coin. This approach has been widely used to discourage the consumption of goods that harm the environment or public health, such as petrol and cigarettes. The implementation of a carbon tax is a good example of how fiscal policy may be used to successfully reallocate resources towards environmentally sustainable activities. Using the tax revenues to provide a 'carbon dividend' to citizens has been proposed as a method of addressing the increase in inequality associated with a carbon tax.

Provision of public and merit goods: Governments have an obligation to provide public goods, as they would not be provided by the market. These goods are said to be non-excludable and non-rivalrous, such as clean air and defence.[2] The government typically also provides some merit goods, such as health, education and libraries. These are goods and services that should be available to everyone, independently of their ability to pay. Merit goods are politically contested. Left-leaning governments generally prefer a higher government provision of these goods than right-leaning governments. For example, the provision of merit goods, particularly universal healthcare, was a driving force behind the creation of the modern welfare state in the United Kingdom by the Labour government following the Second World War.

Insurer of last resort: The fiscal response to Covid-19 illustrates the insurance role of government when it had deliberately reduced economic activity by public messaging and regulation to contain the transmission of the virus.[3] Research shows that the stimulus packages introduced in the US following Covid-19 redistributed income towards low-income households. The largest welfare costs of the pandemic accrued to households in the middle of the income distribution, who gained little from the stimulus packages, and will bear the burden of higher future taxes as the pandemic public debt is repaid (Kaplan et al. 2020). While disposable income inequality fell,

---

[2] Non-excludable means that no one can be excluded from using the good once it has been provided. Non-rivalrous means that consumption of the good by one person does not diminish the availability of that good to others. For example, if the government cleans up the air in a city, none of the city's inhabitants can be excluded from breathing that air. In addition, if one person breathes the clean air it does not diminish the amount of air available for others to breathe.

[3] To familiarize yourself with the modelling of the transmission of the virus through social contact and its impact on the economic value of face to face interactions, see CORE's Covid-19 transmission simulation at https://www.core-econ.org/covid-simulation/

evaluation of the effects on inequality of the pandemic in the UK suggest that, in the longer term, the loss of work experience and training for those with less education, and the missed schooling that disproportionately affected children from more deprived families, will increase inequality and reduce social mobility (Blundell et al. 2022).

7.2.2 Effects of discretionary fiscal policy

To understand debates about the likely effectiveness of fiscal policy, we need to know (1) the initial state of the economy (e.g. recession or equilibrium output), (2) the model that is being used, and (3) the timescale (e.g. short- or medium-run). The scenario analysis is done using the closed economy model. Extension to the open economy is left as an exercise for the reader after studying the model in Chapter 11. To compare outcomes in the closed with the open economy, use the Macroeconomic Simulator (available at www.oup.com/he/carlin-soskice).

Fiscal scenarios

We shall restrict the use of the term discretionary fiscal policy to stabilization-oriented fiscal policy measures. And in the discussion of discretionary fiscal policy, we are going to focus on government spending changes that solely affect the demand side of the economy. We discuss the implications of government policies that affect the supply side in Chapter 15. Supply-side government policies are those that can be modelled as shifting the WS and PS curves, such as changes in the tax wedge or unemployment benefits.

Multipliers: short- and medium-run

A great deal of discussion about fiscal policy is couched in terms of 'the multiplier'. The use of fiscal policy in the financial crisis revived interest.[4] In Chapter 1, we defined the multiplier in the simple Keynesian model and showed how it can be reinterpreted by introducing more sophisticated forward-looking behaviour of households and firms, and distinguishing between credit-constrained and unconstrained households in the hybrid consumption function (Section 1.2.5). We use the simple multiplier formula to clarify an important distinction, namely between the short-run multiplier in the IS curve, which assumes everything else remains unchanged and the medium-run multiplier, which tells us by how much output increases once we take into account any monetary policy response.

The short-run multiplier tells us the *partial equilibrium* effect of a change in government spending: i.e. holding everything else constant, by how much does a change in government spending affect output? We derived the short-run multiplier in Chapter 1 and we can use it to calculate how much a change in government spending (ΔG) will change output (Δy):

---

[4] See, for example, Paul Krugman's blog post from November 10th 2009 entitled *Depression multipliers* or John Cochrane's blog post from March 21st 2012 entitled *Austerity, stimulus, or growth now?*

$$\Delta y = \underbrace{\frac{1}{1 - c_1(1-t)}}_{\text{multiplier}} \Delta G = k \Delta G. \quad (7.1)$$

The short-run multiplier is equal to k or $\frac{1}{1-c_1(1-t)}$ and since c_1 and t are between zero and one, the multiplier is always greater than one. The change in output (keeping everything else constant) that is associated with a change in government spending is $k\Delta G$, which means that output increases by more than the initial change in government spending. In diagrammatic terms, any positive multiplier shifts the IS curve to the right when G increases; a multiplier greater than 1 shifts the IS curve further than the effect of the increase in government spending itself.

We are generally interested not only in the short-run multiplier—i.e. what happens before wages, prices and policy respond to the stimulus—but in the 'full effect' of the increase in government spending. As we shall see, the full effect depends on the model (and what is being assumed e.g. about monetary policy) and on the initial conditions of the economy. This is because the general equilibrium outcome of a rise in government spending will be different depending on the way other elements of the economy are assumed to respond. In the two scenarios below, we shall see that although we assume the short-run multiplier is the same in each case, i.e. $k = \frac{1}{1-c_1(1-t)}$, the medium-run multiplier showing the full effect of the change in government spending on output differs. To preview the conclusion, the context in which the increase in government spending occurs is critical to its full (general equilibrium) effect in the 3-equation model.

We compare two different scenarios where a fiscal stimulus is used by the government. In the first, the economy is affected by a severe negative demand shock. In the normal course of events, the central bank would respond by cutting interest rates. However, in this scenario, monetary policy is disabled because of the zero lower bound and stabilization therefore falls to fiscal policy. In the second scenario, the economy is at equilibrium but the government wishes to run the economy at lower unemployment. To pursue its objective, it prevents the central bank from independently targeting inflation. The fiscal policy maker takes charge and we look at the consequences. In both cases, to emphasize the fiscal channel, we fix the interest rate at the stabilizing rate.

Scenario 1: Deep recession

The economy is in a deep recession—a negative demand shock has pushed output below equilibrium (i.e. the IS has shifted leftwards and the economy has moved from point A to point B in Figure 7.1a). Fiscal policy comes to the fore as a policy instrument in a deep recession because of the ZLB. A more detailed discussion of the ZLB is provided in Chapters 3, and 9, where the policy rule curve, PR, is introduced and applied to the financial crisis.

With output below equilibrium, inflation will have fallen below target and the government will have to increase government spending to G_1 to shift the IS curve to $IS(A', G_1)$, and get the economy back onto the policy rule curve labelled PR (as shown by the movement from point B to point C in Figure 7.1a). From point C on the PR, the policy maker then gradually eases the fiscal stimulus to guide the economy back to A, with output at equilibrium and inflation at target.

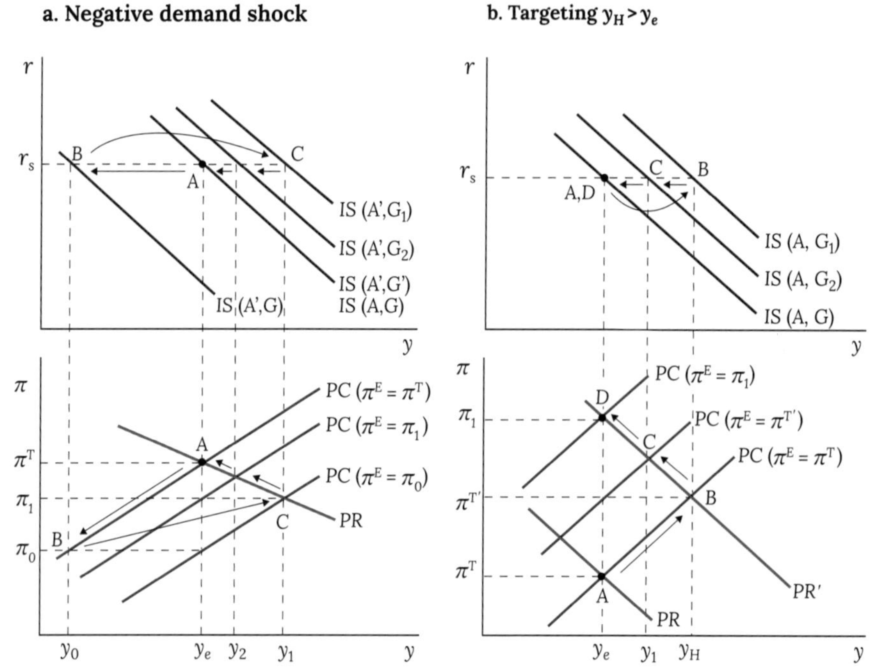

Figure 7.1 Using fiscal policy to:
a. stabilize the economy following a negative demand shock.
b. target a level of output greater than equilibrium output (i.e. $y_H > y_e$).
Visit www.oup.com/he/carlin-soskice to explore using fiscal policy after a demand shock, and to target a higher output level with Animated Analytical Diagram 7.1.

In the new medium-run equilibrium (MRE), inflation is at target and the real interest rate is at r_S, so interest-sensitive private spending will be at its pre-recession level. The new MRE is, however, characterized by higher government and lower private spending. Autonomous private spending remains depressed at A′, so government spending must be higher in the new MRE to make up the shortfall: $\Delta G = G' - G = (y_e - y_0)/k = \Delta y/k$.

Once the negative demand shock begins to recede, the policy maker will reverse the fiscal stimulus to keep the economy at the MRE. One argument for the use of stabilization policy (whether monetary or fiscal) is that, by making clear its objective of keeping output close to equilibrium, private sector expectations are stabilized, and less intervention is required following economic shocks.

Scenario 2: An over-ambitious output target

In this scenario, the economy is initially at equilibrium output (point A in Figure 7.1b). The government decides to introduce an expansionary fiscal policy. This means that the PR curve goes through $y_H > y_e$. Under inflation targeting, the central bank would respond to the fiscal expansion by pushing up the interest rate and squeezing the inflation caused by the government's policy out of the system in the usual way. However, to bring out the consequences of a government using fiscal policy to target output above equilibrium, we have to assume it is able to prevent the central bank from responding to its expansionary policy by tightening monetary policy. In this scenario, fiscal policy is dominant.

The government decides to try and take advantage of the short-run trade-off between output and inflation by increasing output to y_H, which is above equilibrium output. This move to target a higher level of output ($y_H > y_e$) and accept a higher inflation target $\pi^{T'}$ reflects the new bliss point at B. As a consequence, the PR curve shifts rightwards to PR′ in Figure 7.1b. To implement its new objectives, the government undertakes a fiscal expansion ($G_1 > G$) to increase output and the economy moves to point B, where output is at y_H.

However, point B is not a medium-run equilibrium as workers' inflation expectations are not being fulfilled as is evident in Figure 7.1b. The Phillips curve shifts upwards in the next period. Faced with $PC(\pi^E = \pi^{T'})$, the government will re-optimize (and minimize its loss function) by part reversing the expansionary policy in order to get the economy on to the PR′ curve at point C in Figure 7.1b. At point C, output is still above equilibrium, so there is positive pressure on inflation, and the Phillips curve shifts up again. This process will continue until the economy arrives at point D—the new MRE.

What is the overall outcome of the fiscal expansion? At the new MRE, output is back at y_e, but inflation has risen to π_1. Given its new bliss point, the government is no better off at point D than it would have been by staying at point A. This is reminiscent of the inflation bias outcome from Chapter 4 and highlights the limitations of using a fiscal stimulus in Scenario 2—unless the government is seeking a short-term gain, for example prior to an election, or is content with establishing a higher inflation target. The medium-run multiplier in this case is zero because once the dynamic adjustment of the economy is complete, there is no increase in output.

The lessons from these scenarios are the following:

1. For a given size of $k = \frac{1}{1-c_1(1-t)}$, the short-run multiplier, the change in y ultimately associated with the change in G depends on the model, the context, the objectives of the government, its relationship with the central bank, and the behaviour of the central bank.
2. In an economy with spare capacity, i.e. with output below potential, the government can boost aggregate demand and raise output. This is welfare-enhancing.
3. In an economy initially with output at equilibrium, a fiscally dominant government targeting output higher than equilibrium produces an outcome in which the economy ends up at a new MRE at point D in Figure 7.1b, with inflation bias and higher government debt.

Tax finance and the balanced budget multiplier

In the two scenarios discussed above, we implicitly assumed that the government financed its expenditure plans by borrowing, i.e. by selling bonds. Later in the chapter, we look in more detail at the special case in which a bond- and a tax-financed expansion have the same effects on consumption behaviour (so-called Ricardian equivalence). However, before doing so, it is useful to calculate the short-run multiplier when government expenditure is tax-financed.

Suppose the government increases taxation by enough to finance its increased government spending so that there is no deficit at the new short-run equilibrium. We assume that the interest rate is fixed throughout. What is the effect on the economy of a *fully* tax-financed expenditure programme? The argument is transparent when taxation is lump-sum—i.e. it does not depend on the level of income. Firstly, we need to restate the aggregate demand equation that underlies the *IS* equation introduced in Chapter 1, but using a lump-sum tax instead of a proportional tax rate:

$$y^D = c_0 + c_1(y - T) + (a_0 - a_1 r) + G. \tag{7.2}$$

Next, let us consider the impact on output of the change in G:

$$\Delta y = \Delta G + c_1 \Delta G + c_1(c_1 \Delta G) + \cdots \tag{7.3}$$

and then, the impact on output of the equal and opposite change in T:

$$\Delta y = -c_1 \Delta T - c_1(c_1 \Delta T) - \cdots \tag{7.4}$$

We add the two effects together to get the total effect on output and use $\Delta G = \Delta T$:

$$\begin{aligned} \Delta y &= \Delta G + c_1 \Delta G + c_1(c_1 \Delta G) + \cdots - c_1 \Delta T - c_1(c_1 \Delta T) - \cdots \\ &= \Delta G, \end{aligned} \tag{7.5}$$

$$\text{i.e. } \frac{\Delta y}{\Delta G} = 1. \qquad \text{(balanced budget multiplier)}$$

The balanced budget multiplier result is interesting: it does not depend on the assumption that taxes are lump sum. It hinges on the fact that the government spending on goods and services (ΔG) generates extra output and income (Equation 7.3), whereas the increase in taxation *redistributes* spending power from taxpayers to those who provide the goods and services (Equation 7.4). If these two groups have the *same* marginal propensity to consume (as is assumed here, i.e. c_1 is the same in Equation 7.3 and Equation 7.4), then the balanced budget multiplier is equal to one. Why? Because *aggregate consumption* remains unchanged as a consequence of the redistribution of spending power. The only impact on output comes from the first round effect of the government's purchases of goods and services, ΔG. All the other terms cancel out.

The balanced budget multiplier result is important for practical policy purposes: a government that is unable or unwilling to use debt financing can still raise the level of *aggregate demand* in the economy by engaging in a balanced budget expenditure programme. In the 3-equation model, if the economy is in a deep recession where monetary policy is ineffective and if the government does not want to increase its deficit, a balanced budget expansion is a potentially valuable policy option.

Empirical evidence on the size of the multiplier

The debate on the size of the multiplier as a matter of importance for policy makers intensified due to the widespread use of stimulus packages during the global financial crisis and the subsequent adoption of austerity policies. The issue returned to the spotlight due to the unprecedented fiscal stimulus implemented by governments in response to the Covid-19 outbreak.

There is no firm consensus in the empirical literature on the size of the multiplier. Studies on this topic face the problem that it is very difficult to isolate the impact of changes in fiscal policy on output when other economic variables are changing at the same time (as is always the case in the real world). There is a specific problem when trying to estimate the size of the multiplier. The aim is to find the effect of a change in government spending or taxation on output, but the data will also include episodes where a change in output (such as a recession) led to a change in government spending or taxation. When looking for the size of the causal effect *from* a change in fiscal policy *to* output in the data, the estimated size of the effect will be contaminated by the presence of the reverse causal effect from a weaker economy to the use of looser fiscal policy. A variety of econometric techniques have been used to address these problems and to provide an estimate of the size of the multiplier. They have led to a range of estimates.

The empirical evidence supports the idea that the size of the multiplier is dependent on context. This is consistent with the modelling approach taken in this book. The two scenarios shown earlier in this section highlighted the importance of the state of the economy and the behaviour of the central bank for the impact of discretionary government spending on output. We showed that in the 3-equation model, fiscal stimulus can help boost aggregate demand and return the economy to medium-run equilibrium in a recession. We also discussed how fiscal policy is one of the only tools available to policy makers to stabilize the economy when monetary policy is constrained by the zero lower bound.

The first strand of this literature assesses whether the size of the multiplier is dependent on the economic characteristics of individual countries. Ilzetzki, Mendoza and Végh (2013) use data on government expenditures across 44 countries and find that the multiplier is:

1. larger in high-income than low- or middle-income countries (in developing countries there may be more waste or diversion of the fiscal stimulus from its intended purpose because of weaker governance);
2. larger in closed than open economies (due to leakages of aggregate demand to imports in a more open economy);
3. zero in economies operating under a flexible exchange rate regime, but relatively large for countries with fixed exchange rates (monetary policy can offset the effects of fiscal stimulus in flexible but not in fixed exchange rate regimes); and
4. negative in high-debt countries (due to its anticipated effects on macroeconomic stability such as provoking a sovereign debt or exchange rate crisis).

The latter two results are noted here but will make more sense once the modelling is extended to the open economy in Part 4.

Ramey (2011) summarizes the empirical literature on the size of the multiplier in the US for a temporary, deficit-financed increase in government purchases (e.g. a fiscal stimulus).[5] Looking at around 30 aggregate level and cross-state studies for the US, she concludes that the multiplier is probably between 0.8 and 1.5.

---

[5] There is also a literature on the multiplier effect of tax cuts. For studies that use narrative information on policy changes to uncover the causal effect of a tax cut on GDP, see Romer and Romer (2010) for the US and Cloyne (2013) for the UK.

The second strand of this literature assesses whether the size of the multiplier differs over the economic cycle. In other words, is the multiplier different during recessions and expansions?

A number of empirical studies have found that the multiplier is larger during recessions.[6] For example, the IMF (2012) study analysed data on 28 economies during the Great Recession and found multipliers for that period in the range of 0.9 to 1.7. There is also some contrasting evidence that multipliers are not bigger in times of economic slack. Ramey's view of the evidence from the global financial crisis contrasts with that of many others. She suggests multipliers of one or below during recessions.

Relevant to the contrast between fixed and flexible exchange rate regimes (point 3 above), there is some evidence that fiscal multipliers for the Euro Area (see Chapter 14) are particularly large at the ZLB. For example, work by Amendola et al. (2020) finds that the average three-year multiplier for the Eurozone is about 1 in normal times and between 1.6 and 2.8 at the ZLB.

7.2.3 The automatic stabilizers

From the formula for the short-run multiplier, it is clear that taxes related to the level of income reduce the size of the multiplier and hence dampen the impact on aggregate demand of a demand shock. Similarly, because unemployment benefit payments vary with the numbers unemployed, transfers increase as the level of output falls and this, too, reduces the size of the short-run multiplier. Note that government spending on unemployment benefits is a transfer payment and shows up in the model in T, which is taxes less transfers, and not in G, which is government spending on goods and services.

Recall that a smaller multiplier is reflected in a steeper IS curve that rotates less around the vertical intercept in response to a change in exogenous expenditure (see Chapter 1). This inbuilt dampening of shocks is what is meant by the 'automatic stabilizer' role of the tax and social security system. A consequence of this feature of the fiscal structure is that the budget deficit rises (automatically) when activity falls and declines when activity rises.

To interpret the significance of the budget deficit recorded at any particular time, it is necessary to know whether output is below, at, or above equilibrium. To assist policy makers, the cyclically-adjusted budget deficit is calculated. This is the budget deficit that would prevail given existing tax and transfer commitments if the economy was operating at equilibrium output. The concept of the cyclically-adjusted deficit indicates whether fiscal policy is expansionary or contractionary. One practical problem with using the cyclically-adjusted deficit as a measure of fiscal stance is in estimating the level of equilibrium or *potential* output, as it is often called.

Let us define the relationship between the different concepts of the fiscal balance as follows.

$$\begin{aligned} \text{cycl. adj. or structural budget deficit} &\equiv \text{budget deficit} - \text{impact of aut. stabilizers} \\ \text{discret. fiscal impulse} &\equiv \text{budget deficit} - \text{impact of aut. stabilizers} \\ G(y_e) - T(y_e) &\equiv [G(y_t) - T(y_t)] - a(y_e - y_t), \end{aligned} \quad (7.6)$$

[6] See also Auerbach and Gorodnichenko (2013) and Fazzari, Morley, and Panovska (2012).

where a is a constant and the term $a(y_e - y_t)$ captures the impact on the budget deficit of the automatic stabilizers. Note that here we are only concerned with the budget deficit *excluding* interest payments on the outstanding government debt. This is known as the *primary* budget deficit.

If current output, y_t, is below equilibrium output, y_e, the economy is in a recession. The automatic stabilizers will automatically help to stabilize the economy by raising government expenditure on transfers and depressing tax revenue $(a(y_e - y_t) > 0)$, thereby pushing up the deficit $[G(y_t) - T(y_t) > 0]$. If these two effects on the right-hand side of Equation 7.6 cancel out, then the change in the deficit simply reflects the automatic stabilizers: there is no discretionary fiscal impact on aggregate demand and the cyclically-adjusted deficit is zero.

By definition, the impact on the budget deficit of the automatic stabilizers is zero when output is at its equilibrium level. A cyclically-adjusted budget deficit $(G(y_e) - T(y_e) > 0)$ implies an expansionary fiscal impulse, and a surplus, implies a contractionary impact on aggregate demand.

If the economy is in recession with output below the equilibrium and the cyclically-adjusted deficit or surplus is zero, then the observed deficit simply reflects the automatic stabilizers, and will disappear once the economy returns to the equilibrium. In this case, fiscal policy is providing no additional discretionary stimulus to push the economy back toward the equilibrium (i.e. in 3-equation model terminology, there is no rightward shift of the IS curve).

Figure 7.2 provides a picture of UK government finances since the 1970s. Recessions are highlighted by the light grey shaded areas.[7] The top panel shows observed and cyclically adjusted primary budget balances as a percentage of GDP (a negative value implies a budget deficit). The dark bars show the observed government primary budget balance, which has been in deficit for the majority of the four decades shown. It worsened sharply during (and after) recessions, such as in the early 1990s and the late 2000s. The light bars show the cyclically-adjusted government budget balance, for which a deficit represents the use of discretionary fiscal expansion. There were large cyclically-adjusted deficits in those recessions, suggesting that the UK government undertook discretionary fiscal stimulus on top of the stabilization provided by automatic stabilizers. Procyclical fiscal policy is also observed: exacerbating the downturn in the 1980–81 recession and reinforcing the upturn in the years of growth directly preceding the global financial crisis. The cyclically-adjusted deficit was larger than the observed deficit in all bar one of the years between 2002 and 2008. This suggests that the Labour government ran a potentially destabilizing, pro-cyclical fiscal policy during their second and third terms in power.

The lower panel of Figure 7.2 shows the evolution of UK government debt as a percentage of GDP between 1970 and 2021. We can see that periods of high budget deficits usually translate into increases in the government debt burden (e.g. during the Great Recession). This was not the case however in the 1970s: the government ran persistent deficits, but the debt ratio followed a downwards trend.

---

[7] We define recessions as periods of two or more consecutive quarters of negative GDP growth. The data on real GDP used to calculate the series is from the UK Office for National Statistics (accessed October 2022).

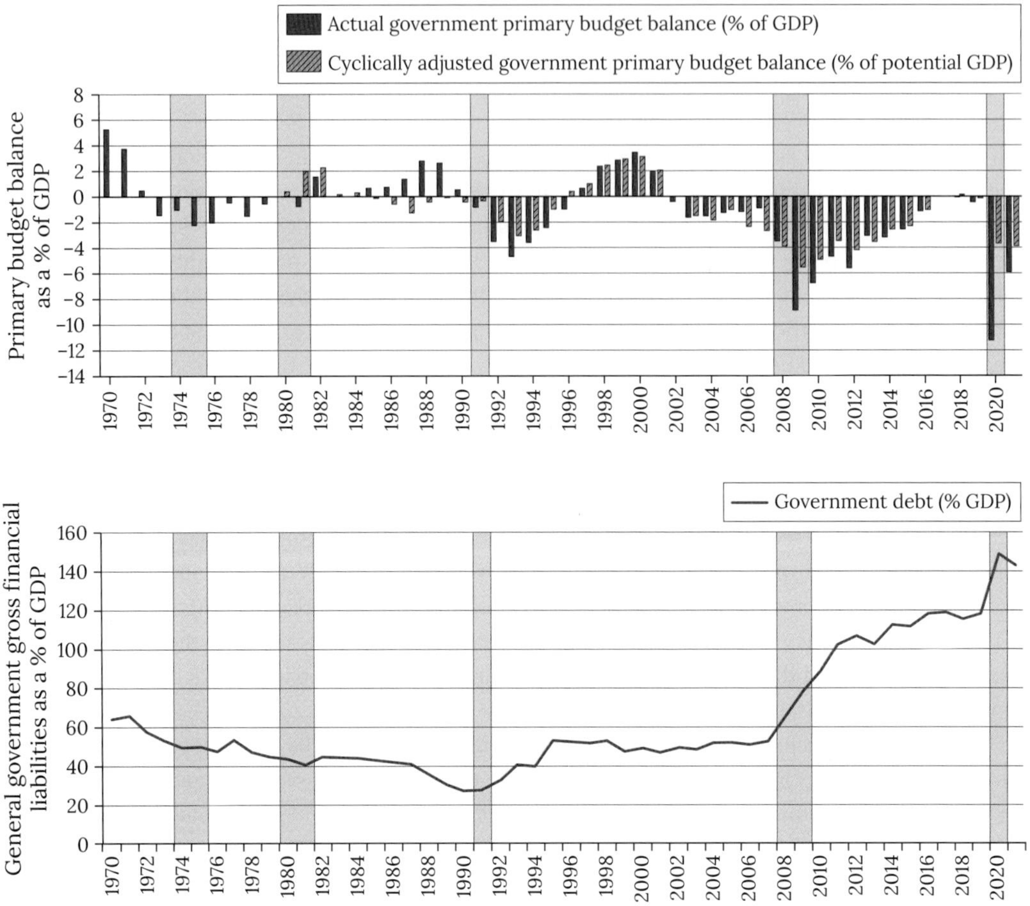

Figure 7.2 UK government debt and primary budget balance as a percentage of GDP: 1970–2021.

Note: The primary balance has been calculated by adding net interest payments back onto the government budget balance. Data for the cyclically-adjusted primary balance is only available from 1980 onwards.

Source: OECD Economic Outlook, June 2022.

This can be explained by the high inflation, which reduced the real burden of debt, and is discussed in more detail in Section 7.3.3.

How effective are the automatic stabilizers?

This question was investigated for the US at the turn of the century. Auerbach and Feenberg (2000) focus on the stabilization role of federal taxes and unemployment compensation. They find that the US tax system offsets about 8%, and unemployment benefits about 2%, of any initial shock to GDP. This is rather modest, and the effects are greater in Central and Northern European countries, which typically have higher taxation and more generous unemployment benefits.[8]

[8] See Dolls et al. (2011). This paper also includes a useful summary of the academic literature on automatic stabilizers.

Cross-country research highlights the importance of the size of government in accounting for the role of the automatic stabilizers.[9] A mental experiment helps clarify this. Let us take a simple example where the tax system is proportional, i.e. a 1% fall in income leads to a 1% fall in tax revenue. If consumption depends on current disposable income, this means that the tax system provides no stabilization in the face of the shock. The assumption of a proportional tax system highlights the role in stabilization played by the size of government. Under the assumption that government spending is acyclical, i.e. it does not change with a fall in GDP, then following a fall in income, the budget deficit increases and helps to dampen the impact of the fall in income. The larger is G, the larger is this dampening or counter-cyclical effect.

From their study of 23 OECD countries over the period 1960–2010, Fatás and Mihov (2012) report two interesting empirical results:

1. As expected, countries with larger government sectors (i.e. G/Y) have larger automatic stabilizers. Figure 7.3 illustrates this by plotting general government expenditure as a share of GDP as the indicator of government size on the horizontal axis, and the change in the budget balance induced by a 1% change in GDP on the vertical axis.

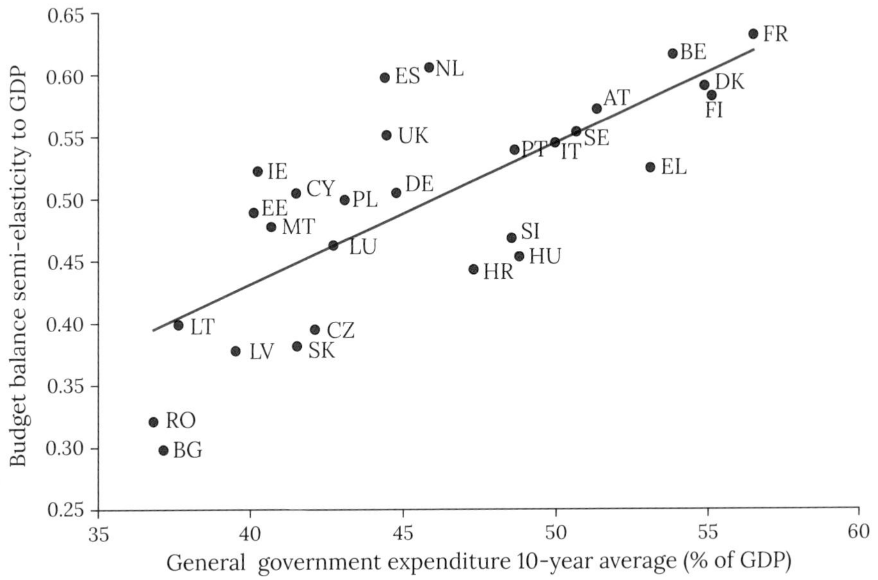

Figure 7.3 Automatic stabilizers in 2018 against 10-year average general government expenditure for EU countries (and UK).

Note: Automatic stabilizers are measured as the change in the cyclically adjusted budget balance induced by a 1% change in GDP.

Source: Figure 4 from Mourre, G. and Poissonnier, A. (2019). What drives the responsiveness of the budget balance to the business cycle in EU countries. *Intereconomics*, **2019**(4), 237–240. With permission of Springer Nature. For country codes, see https://en.wikipedia.org/wiki/List_of_ISO_3166_country_codes.

[9] See Fatás and Mihov (2012).

2. Countries with larger governments, and hence larger automatic stabilizers, undertake less discretionary fiscal policy.

One interpretation of the second result is that, even if governments place similar weight on the benefits of stabilization, their ability to achieve it is affected by the size of government—hence, discretionary and automatic stabilizers substitute for each other. The authors contrast the US and Germany. In the US, the share of government in GDP is 37% and in Germany it is 48%.[10] For the US, they find that counter-cyclical discretionary policy is almost as large as the automatic stabilizer effect; in Germany, with its much larger government and larger automatic stabilizers, the counter-cyclical behaviour comes from the automatic stabilizers.

7.3 MODELLING: DEBT DYNAMICS

7.3.1 The government's budget identity

Each period, the government must finance its expenditure plans and also pay interest on the outstanding government debt. Government debt is the stock of government bonds that have been sold to the private sector in the past. The government can use taxation, the sale of new bonds, or the 'printing of money' to finance its expenditure. The sources of funds are on the right-hand side of the identity and the uses of funds are on the left-hand side. The government's budget identity in each period is:

$$\underbrace{G_t}_{\text{govt. exp.}} + \underbrace{i_t B_{t-1}}_{\text{interest}} \equiv \underbrace{T_t}_{\text{tax revenue}} + \underbrace{\Delta B_t}_{\text{new bonds}} + \underbrace{\Delta M_t}_{\text{new reserves}},$$

where G_t is government expenditure on goods, services, and transfers in nominal terms, i_t is the nominal interest rate, B_{t-1} is the outstanding stock of bonds, and hence the value of the national debt at the beginning of the period, T_t is tax revenues, ΔB_t is the value of the new bonds issued in the current period, and ΔM_t is the new central bank money (reserves) used by the government for its spending. Note the definition of G to include transfers and that we use G_t and T_t to represent nominal values in this section. This is different from the use of G_t and T_t elsewhere in the book, where they represent real values. We do this to make the notation of the debt dynamics model simpler, which will become apparent as we derive the model. The t subscript denotes that value of the variable in period t, $\Delta B_t = B_t - B_{t-1}$ and $\Delta M_t = M_t - M_{t-1}$.

A time subscript will only be shown when referring to the variable in a period other than t. For example, G_t becomes G, but the value of G in period $t-1$ would be written as G_{t-1}.

As we saw in Chapter 5 and in Box 7.1 on MMT, when the government finances public expenditure through creating reserves, this is called *monetary financing*. In this case, the government requires that the central bank credits it with new reserves in its account at the central bank. Those funds are used for the fiscal programme (transfers,

[10] The variable used is: total disbursements, general government, as a percentage of GDP. These values are an average for the period 1991–2010. The data is from the OECD Economic Outlook, June 2012.

tax credits, new spending). In the government's budget constraint, this is represented by the term ΔM; there is no increase in government debt.

It is important to maintain the distinction between (a) monetary financing (no increase in government debt, $\Delta B = 0$) and a situation in which (b) the government funds its stimulus programme by selling bonds to the public (debt-financed, ΔB). At the same time, the central bank (in pursuit of its inflation-targeting mandate) undertakes QE purchasing bonds in the secondary market with newly created reserves. In the latter case, government debt increases and the bonds are owned by the central bank.[11]

In Chapter 6, we discussed a different context for monetary financing: one in which the government is unable to raise sufficient revenue for its expenditure plans through taxation or borrowing. It is in that quite different scenario that monetary financing can in extreme cases produce hyperinflation (see Section 6.7.2).

In what follows, we exclude the possibility that the government can borrow directly from the independent central bank (i.e. that it can routinely use the creation of central bank reserves to finance its deficit). This assumption implies that $\Delta M = 0$.

7.3.2 **Debt dynamics**

What determines the path of the government's debt over time? If the debt is rising, will it continue rising indefinitely? To answer these questions, we need to move beyond the government's single-period budget identity.

The budget identity is:

$$\underbrace{G}_{\text{govt. exp.}} + \underbrace{iB_{t-1}}_{\text{interest}} \equiv \underbrace{T}_{\text{tax revenue}} + \underbrace{\Delta B}_{\text{new bonds}}.$$

We begin by distinguishing between the budget deficit, which is the difference between total expenditure and revenue (i.e. observed deficit $\equiv G + iB_{t-1} - T$), and the primary deficit, which excludes the interest payments on the debt (i.e. primary deficit $\equiv G - T$). It is important to note that the stock of bonds in the economy (held by the public) is equal to the stock of government debt. Whenever expenditure, including on interest payments, is above revenue, the government has to borrow by selling more bonds, thereby increasing its debt by this amount. By rearranging the budget identity we can see that the government's deficit, which is a flow that has to be financed, adds to the stock of government debt:

$$\Delta B \equiv (G - T) + iB_{t-1} \tag{7.7}$$

$$\text{change in debt} \equiv \text{primary deficit} + \text{interest on outstanding debt}$$

$$\text{change in debt} \equiv \text{budget deficit.}$$

[11] For a detailed explanation of monetary financing, with particular focus on the role played by 'helicopter' money, see Ben Bernanke's article 'What tools does the Fed have left? Part 3: Helicopter money', published online at Brookings on April 11th, 2016. (Available online at: https://www.brookings.edu/blog/ben-bernanke/2016/04/11/what-tools-does-the-fed-have-left-part-3-helicopter-money/)

The burden of government debt is measured relative to GDP and below we derive the expression for how the debt to GDP ratio moves over time. The intuition is straightforward: the primary deficit (relative to GDP) adds to the debt burden as new bonds have to be issued to cover the gap between the (non-interest) spending and revenue flows. In terms of the existing stock of debt, if the interest rate that has to be paid is higher than the rate at which the economy is growing, then that will add to the stock of debt relative to GDP. A different but equivalent way of putting the logic of the debt dynamics is this: think of a government that is running a balanced budget excluding interest payments. In this case, the increase in debt and hence, the extra bonds that have to be sold, is equal to the rate of interest on the debt. Meanwhile, a higher growth rate of GDP means the debt ratio falls without the need for higher future taxes.

The change in the ratio of debt to GDP, b, is equal to the primary deficit (G-T) as a share of GDP, d, plus the stock of debt inherited from last period multiplied by the interest rate minus the growth rate.

This is the expression for the debt dynamics:

$$\Delta b = d + (r - \gamma_y)b_{t-1}. \tag{7.8}$$

where d is the primary deficit ratio, r is the real interest rate, γ_y is the growth rate of real GDP, and b_{t-1} is the existing ratio of government debt to GDP.

Before working through the maths (set out in Box 7.2), it may be helpful to look at a series of historical episodes to see how changes in the debt ratio can be decomposed to show the role of the budget balance and the interest rate/growth rate differential. A great variety of patterns can be observed (see Tables 7.2 and 7.4).

BOX 7.2 Deriving the debt dynamics equation

Let us start by defining the ratio of debt outstanding to GDP as:

$$\text{debt ratio} \equiv b_{t-1} \equiv \frac{B_{t-1}}{Py},$$

where P is the price level and y is real national income, which means that Py is nominal GDP. We derive the debt dynamics equation in three very simple steps which also develop the intuition:

1. Suppose that there is no primary deficit (or surplus); i.e. $d = 0$. Moreover, assume that GDP growth (denoted by $\gamma_y \approx \Delta y_t / y_{t-1}$) is also zero. It then follows that the change in debt-to-GDP ratio Δb will the sum of two terms: the interest payments on outstanding debt plus the change in the value of debt due to inflation. Hence:

$$\begin{aligned}\Delta b &= ib_{t-1} + \left(\frac{B_{t-1}}{P_t y_{t-1}} - \frac{B_{t-1}}{P_{t-1} y_{t-1}}\right) \\ &= ib_{t-1} + \frac{B_{t-1}}{P_{t-1} y_{t-1}}\left(\frac{P_{t-1}}{P_t} - 1\right) \\ &= ib_{t-1} - \pi b_{t-1} = rb_{t-1}.\end{aligned}$$

2. Now allow for some new primary debt—i.e. $d \neq 0$—but keep assuming no economic growth ($\gamma_y = 0$). Intuitively, the debt-to-GDP ratio will be given by (real) interest payments on old debt plus the newly created primary debt. Hence:

$$\Delta b = rb_{t-1} + d.$$

3. Finally, we relax the assumption of no economic growth and assume $\gamma_y > 0$. We now assume no primary deficit, a nominal interest rate equal to zero, as well as zero inflation (i.e. $i = 0$, $P_t = P_{t-1}$, and $d = 0$). It follows that the debt-to-GDP ratio will decrease by an amount proportional to the outstanding debt ratio multiplied by the growth rate of GDP:

$$\Delta b = \frac{B_{t-1}}{P_{t-1}y_t} - \frac{B_{t-1}}{P_{t-1}y_{t-1}} = B_{t-1}\left(\frac{1}{P_{t-1}y_t} - \frac{1}{P_{t-1}y_{t-1}}\right) = \frac{B_{t-1}}{P_{t-1}y_{t-1}}\left(\frac{y_{t-1}}{y_t} - 1\right) = -b_{t-1}\gamma_y.$$

Putting the three components together, we get:

$$\Delta b = rb_{t-1} + d - b_{t-1}\gamma_y$$

$$\rightarrow \Delta b = d + (r - \gamma_y)b_{t-1} \tag{7.9}$$

Equation 7.9 provides a framework for understanding how the debt ratio evolves. It also provides guidance on the fiscal rules that governments have introduced or may consider introducing. To interpret the equation, let us consider two cases:

Case 1: The real interest rate is above the growth rate (i.e. $r > \gamma_y$): the arithmetic of Equation 7.9 says that in this case, the debt to GDP ratio will be rising unless d is negative, i.e. unless there is a primary budget surplus. The explanation is straightforward: with the real interest rate above the growth rate, the interest payments on the existing debt are rising faster than is GDP. Hence servicing the debt interest is pushing up the debt burden. The only way that this can be offset so that the debt ratio does not rise (i.e. for $\Delta b = 0$) is for the government to run a primary budget surplus.

Case 2: The real interest rate is below the growth rate (i.e. $r < \gamma_y$): this case represents a benign scenario from the perspective of the government's finances. Since the growth of the economy is sufficient to reduce the impact of interest payments on the debt burden, some level of primary deficit is consistent with a constant ratio of debt to GDP. Indeed, if the government were to run a primary surplus in this scenario, it would eventually end up with negative public debt. The *public* sector would own financial assets issued by the *private* sector.

A diagram helps to clarify the relationship between the primary deficit, the real interest rate, the growth rate and the debt ratio and to highlight the difference between Case 1 and Case 2. We use a diagram with the existing debt to GDP ratio (b_{t-1}) on the horizontal axis and the change in the debt to GDP ratio (Δb) on the vertical axis. The primary deficit, d, is the intercept term, and the relationship between the real interest rate and the growth rate determines the slope of the line showing the growth of the debt ratio. For any economy, in order to draw the appropriate 'phase line' (the name for the line showing Δb as a function of b_{t-1}), we need to know the

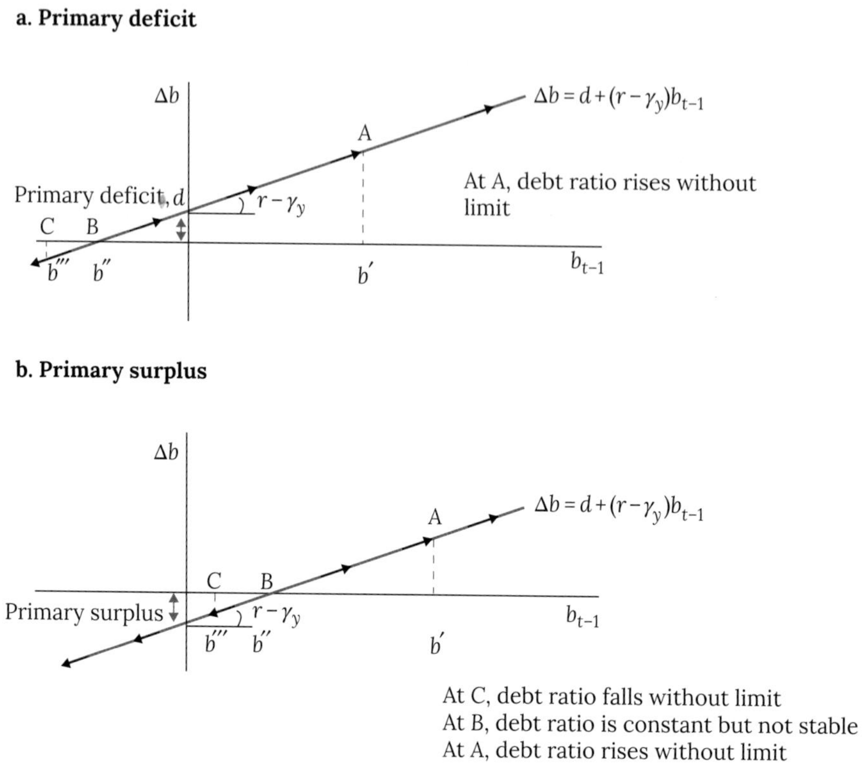

Figure 7.4 The government debt ratio. Case 1: the real interest rate exceeds the growth rate.
Visit www.oup.com/he/carlin-soskice to explore the government debt ratio further with Animated Analytical Diagram 7.4.

current primary deficit, the real interest rate and the growth rate. The existing level of debt, b_{t-1}, then tells us where we are on the phase line. Of course, unless the initial position of the economy is on the horizontal axis with $\Delta b = 0$, the debt ratio will have changed if we look at the economy at a later time.

Figure 7.4 illustrates Case 1: the real interest rate exceeds the growth rate (i.e. $r > \gamma_y$), so the phase line is upward sloping. Figure 7.4a shows an economy with a primary deficit ($d \geq 0$). Once we know the existing level of debt (e.g. b'), we can fix the economy's position on the phase line. But note that the economy will not remain stationary: it will be moving north-east along the phase line as shown by the arrows. In particular, net interest payment on outstanding debt is pinned down by the gradient of the phase line multiplied by existing debt (i.e. $(r - \gamma_y)b'$).

Note that if the existing debt ratio is negative, then the public sector earns interest on the assets issued by the private sector. If such interest payments are greater than the primary deficit (as at point C in Figure 7.4a), then the debt ratio falls without limit. The government has an overall budget surplus at C (i.e. $\Delta b < 0$).

Figure 7.4b shows an economy with exactly the same interest rate and growth rate as in Figure 7.4a, but with a primary surplus (hence the intercept is below the horizontal axis). Here, we note the situation with three different initial debt ratios. If an economy happens to have an initial debt ratio shown by point C, its debt ratio will be falling (as shown by the arrows in the south-westerly direction). Why is this? This is because it is a situation in which the primary surplus is sufficiently large to offset the $(r > \gamma_y)$ effect so that the debt ratio declines. If the debt ratio is at point B, then the debt ratio will remain constant: the primary surplus (reducing the debt ratio) and the $(r > \gamma_y)$ effect (raising it) exactly offset each other. But, note that point B is not *stable*: a slight increase in the debt ratio triggers an ever-increasing debt ratio and a slight fall triggers an ever-falling debt ratio. An appropriate primary surplus can hold the debt ratio constant, but it cannot mitigate the underlying dynamics of the debt, which are determined by the relationship between r and γ_y. An economy with a debt ratio as at point A is characterized by an ever-increasing debt ratio.

The case in Figure 7.4b can also be illustrated by means of the price dynamic equations, which are also used in Chapter 8 to describe house price behaviour. In this case, we rewrite equation 7.9 to show the relationship between the debt ratio last period and this period:

$$\Delta b = d + (r - \gamma_y)b_{t-1},$$

$$\rightarrow b_t = d + (1 + r - \gamma_y)b_{t-1}. \qquad \text{(Debt dynamics equation (DDE))}$$

To illustrate the instability where the change in the debt ratio is zero (point B in Figure 7.4b), Figure 7.5 shows that, if the slope of the debt dynamic equation (DDE) is above 1 (i.e. $r > \gamma_y$), any positive deviation from point B implies an even higher debt ratio

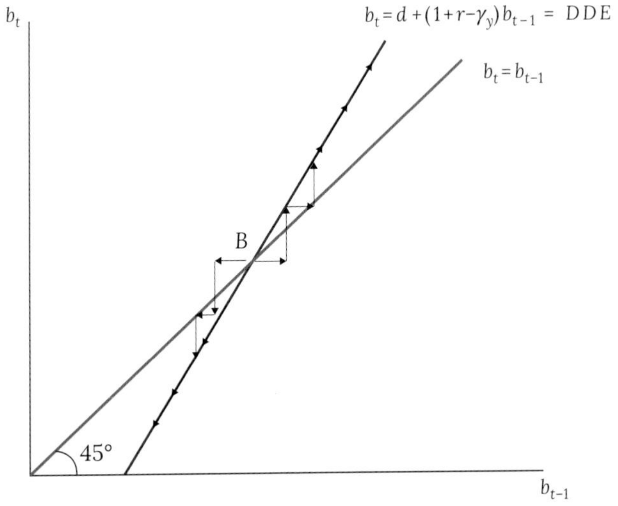

Figure 7.5 The government debt ratio. Case 1: the debt dynamics equation. Point B is from Figure 7.4b.

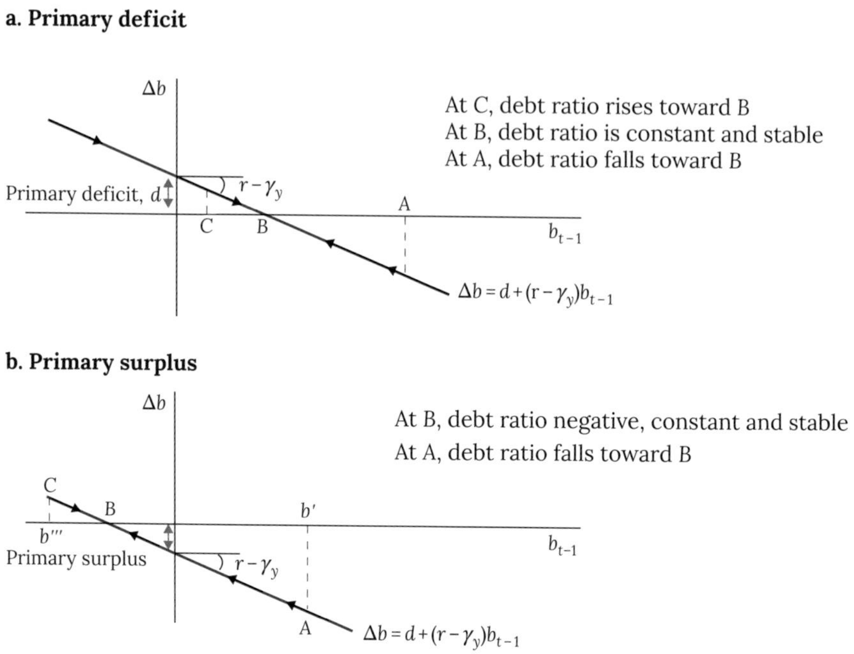

Figure 7.6 The government debt ratio. Case 2: the growth rate exceeds the real interest rate. Visit www.oup.com/he/carlin-soskice to explore the government debt ratio further with Animated Analytical Diagram 7.6.

in the future. Similarly, any small decrease in existing debt (from B), leads to an ever falling debt ratio. The debt ratio at Point B is therefore not stable.

Figure 7.6 illustrates Case 2: the growth rate exceeds the real interest rate (i.e. $r < \gamma_y$). In this case, the phase line has a negative slope. At point C in Figure 7.6a, the debt ratio is rising as shown by the arrows to the south-east; this is because the debt-reducing effect accruing from $r < \gamma_y$ is not enough to offset the debt-increasing effect of a primary budget in deficit. But what happens when we observe this economy some time later and the debt ratio has risen to the level shown by point B? As long as the primary deficit and interest and growth rates remain unchanged, the economy will remain at point B. Moreover, unlike point B in Figure 7.4b, this debt ratio is *stable*: a slight increase in the debt ratio will put the economy on to the segment with the north-westerly arrows taking it back to the equilibrium (and vice versa). How can we explain this? Let us compare point B in Figure 7.4b with point B in Figure 7.6a. In Figure 7.4b, the fact that $r > \gamma_y$ means that, when there is a small increase in the debt ratio, the interest burden of the debt reinforces the increase in the debt ratio. By contrast, in Figure 7.6a, the fact that $r < \gamma_y$ means that the increase in the debt is dampened because output grows faster than the interest cost of the debt. The task of illustrating this case using the DDE as in Figure 7.5 is left as an exercise for the reader. (Hint: the DDE line has a slope of less than 45 degrees.)

The lower panel of Figure 7.6 shows the case where a primary surplus ($d < 0$) characterizes an economy in which the growth rate exceeds the real interest rate. As the diagram shows, such an economy will converge toward a negative debt ratio. In particular, at point A in the diagram, a primary surplus combined with growth rate of GDP above the real interest rate implies that $\Delta b = d + (r - \gamma_y)b'$ is unambiguously negative. When observed at a later time, the government will be a net holder of private sector financial assets. Note that at point C the debt ratio is increasing because the primary surplus is not large enough to offset the erosion of interest receipts on net assets; in other words, the growth rate of GDP is greater than the interest payments owed to the government on its net asset holdings, implying that, as a percentage of GDP, debt becomes less negative until it stabilizes at point B.

We can use the debt diagram to explore some interesting examples. In the first example (Figure 7.7a), the initial situation is one in which there is a primary deficit, the growth rate exceeds the real interest rate, and the debt ratio is declining (at time $t-1$, the economy is at point A); we assume that the economy suddenly experiences a rise in the interest rate and/or a fall in the growth rate so that $r > \gamma_y$. What happens? The new phase line is shown by the upward-sloping line and the economy jumps from point A to point B. The debt ratio begins to rise and will rise without limit unless the interest rate, growth rate or the primary deficit changes.

In the second example (Figure 7.7b), we follow the same economy but this time, as soon as the switch in $r - \gamma_y$ occurs, the government immediately tightens fiscal policy

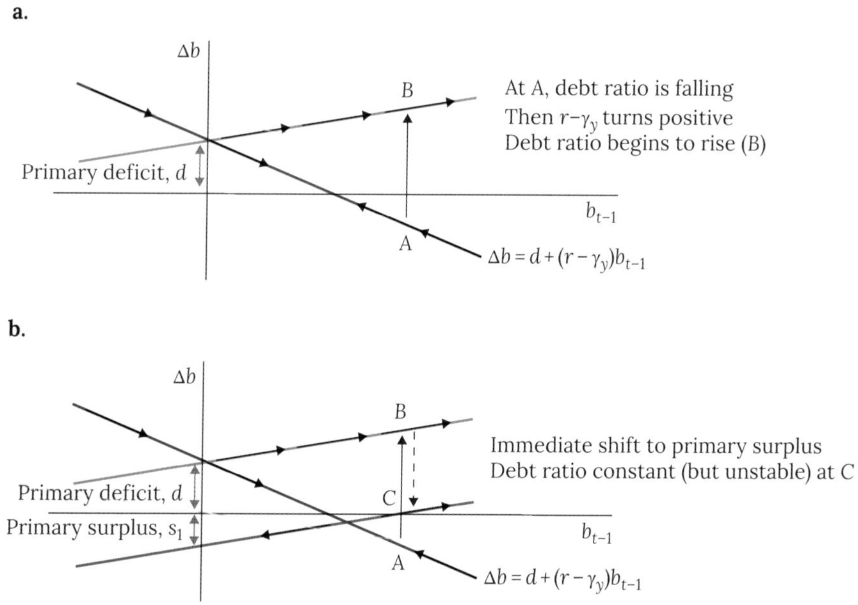

Figure 7.7 Switch from the case where the growth rate exceeds the real interest rate to the case where the growth rate is less than the real interest rate.
Visit www.oup.com/he/carlin-soskice to explore debt dynamics with Animated Analytical Diagram 7.7.

so that the primary deficit is replaced by a primary surplus (s_1). This would require a dramatic cut in government spending and/or a rise in taxation. If this could be done instantaneously, then the economy would move from point A to point C and the debt ratio would be constant (although unstable).

Sovereign default risk

Until the global financial crisis, it was customary in discussions of debt dynamics for the high-income economies to assume that there was essentially no risk that the government would not honour its bonds, i.e. pay the interest and repay the principal. This is no longer the case, as vividly demonstrated by the crisis in the Eurozone in 2010.[12] A positive default risk alters the debt dynamics since the risk premium, ρ, is added to $r^{\text{risk-free}}$, the risk-free real interest rate. (Note that the symbol ρ has previously been used for the subjective discount rate. These two concepts are unrelated.) A non-zero risk of sovereign default affects the path of the debt ratio:

$$r = r^{\text{risk-free}} + \rho$$

$$\Delta b = d + (r^{\text{risk-free}} + \rho - \gamma_y)b_{t-1}. \tag{7.10}$$

From Equation 7.10, it is clear that a positive risk premium worsens the debt dynamics.

Gross and net measures of public debt

Two concepts are relevant for measuring the public debt—gross and net. Net public debt is calculated by subtracting government assets from the gross debt. Most references to public debt are to the gross concept. There are several reasons for this.

- From an economic viewpoint, the most important reason to focus on gross debt is that many of the government's assets such as land are illiquid and would be difficult to sell if the government needed to raise cash quickly in order to buy back bonds. The question of liquidity is especially relevant for countries in which the central bank cannot operate as the lender of last resort to the government, as is the case when borrowing is in a foreign currency (or, as shown in Chapter 14, in the case of Eurozone countries, in euros, which the national central bank cannot issue).
- In addition to liquidity considerations, government assets are often difficult to value.
- Note also that the holdings of public debt (bond-holdings) by the central bank are not netted out. The reason is that, as we saw in Chapter 5, when the central bank buys government bonds as part of QE, the counterpart liability is reserves in banks held at the central bank on which it pays interest.

In the data presented in this chapter, all measures of public debt are gross.

7.3.3 Case studies of debt dynamics

Case 1: The UK over the long run

By looking over a long historical period, the different ways in which debt dynamics operate are visible in Table 7.2. The decomposition uses the debt dynamics equation,

---

12 See Chapter 14 for an explanation of why the sovereign debt crisis affected member countries of the Eurozone.

separating out the contribution of the change in the primary balance (a positive number indicates the increase of government spending relative to tax revenues) and to the interest-rate growth rate differential (a positive number indicates the greater burden of interest payments on outstanding debt relative to the economy's growth rate). The final column is titled 'Stock-flow adjustment'. This is a residual category in the calculation and includes the effect of valuation changes on the stock of debt.[13]

Starting with the most recent period shown in the table, i.e. from the financial crisis and into the very weak recovery period, the debt ratio in the UK more than doubled. Three-quarters of the increase is attributable to the primary balance effect, namely the persistent excess of expenditure over revenue. Both the unfavourable relationship between the real interest rate and the growth rate, and the 'residual' component, contributed to the increase. In the model, the phase line has a small positive slope but was shifted up by the primary deficit. This can be shown using Figure 7.4b.

The comparison of the first period, which covered much of the 19th century and up to the first world war with the post second world war period from 1946 to 1975 is instructive. In both episodes, the debt ratio fell to less than one-fifth of its initial level, in the second, at a much faster rate. In the first case, the fall in the primary deficit, i.e. so-called fiscal effort or austerity, was so large that it outweighed the unfavourable effect of a real interest rate in excess of the growth rate. This is an example of the case shown in Figure 7.4a in which the phase line has to be shifted down by contractionary

	Debt/GDP ratio			Decomposition		
Period	Starting level	Ending level	Increase	Primary balance effect	Interest-growth differential	Stock-flow adjustment
1822–1913	194.1	28.3	−165.8	−299.3	158.5	25.0
1923–1929	195.5	170.5	−25.0	−52.2	25.6	−1.7
1929–1933	170.5	186.6	16.1	−35.0	40.5	10.6
1946–1975	269.8	46.7	−223.1	−95.2	−182.8	54.9
1980–1992	48.7	39.5	−6.6	−2.7	4.2	−5.1
1992–1997	39.5	57.9	18.3	12.7	2.2	3.5
1997–2007	57.9	43.9	−14.0	−7.5	−2.7	−3.8
2007–2013	41.7	85.2	43.4	33.1	5.4	4.8

Table 7.2 Debt dynamics in the UK: 1822-2013.

Note: The first two columns are in per cent; the other columns are percentage points. This interest rate–growth rate differential is multiplied by the outstanding debt-to-GDP ratio, since the magnitude of this effect depends on the level of inherited debt. Episodes are selected so that the decomposition of changes in government debt is roughly consistent within an episode.

Source: Raw data were provided by the authors of Eichengreen et al. 2021; own calculations.

[13] Valuation changes are due to a number of factors including capital gains or losses on foreign currency denominated debt due to changes in the exchange rate, debt restructurings which write down the value of outstanding debt, and other financial operations. For a more detailed explanation see the appendix to Chapter 7 in Eichengreen et al. (2021).

fiscal policy (an increase in the primary surplus). In the second case, the fiscal effort was reinforced by a very large contribution from the high growth rate relative to the real interest rate. In the model, the phase line for a case like this is downward-sloping (Figure 7.6).

Case 2: The role of inflation

The link between inflation and the government debt ratio is given by:

$$\Delta b = d + (i - \pi - \gamma_y)b_{t-1}. \tag{7.11}$$

We can see from the equation that inflation contributes to reducing the change in the debt ratio.[14] This is intuitive, as we can think of inflation as reducing the real value of debt. When the debt level is high, governments may be tempted to allow inflation to rise and erode the real debt burden. This highlights the fact that the equation showing the relation between inflation and the change in debt does not express causality. Causality can clearly go in either direction: for a given debt burden, higher inflation will reduce it; but higher inflation may be a consequence of a policy response to a higher debt burden.

In Germany, hyperinflation from around 1918 completely liquidated the debt (shown in black in Figure 7.8b using the right vertical axis), leading to disruptive economic consequences. From 1923, inflation was brought to a halt through political compromises and an international loan (the Dawes Loan). After that, investors demanded a higher risk premium when lending to the German government, leading to a positive interest-growth rate differential. Consequently, the German debt started to rise again.

The extent to which inflation can influence government debt ratios can be shown over nearly two centuries of British economic history, focusing on four historical episodes.[15] Figure 7.8 compares the observed government debt to GDP ratio to that which would have prevailed had prices been held constant in four different time periods; 1830–1909, 1910–39, 1946–79 and 1980–2021.[16] We can study each period in turn to highlight the importance of inflation to the path of the debt ratio. In each case, it is interesting to keep in mind the possibility of reverse causality and to think about what lay behind the very different behaviour of inflation. These cases show that a high debt ratio was not always followed by high inflation.

1830–1909: The debt ratio started the period at 182% due to the large amount of debt the British government built up during the Napoleonic wars. The ratio had fallen to 35% by the end of the period. The evolution of the constant price debt ratio almost exactly matches the observed debt ratio, as the price level stayed roughly constant

---

[14] For a discussion of the impact of inflation on other fiscal policy factors, such as revenue, expenditure and debt interest costs, see Box 4.3 in the Office for Budget Responsibility's *Economic and Fiscal Outlook*, March 2011.

[15] Hall and Sargent (2010) undertake a similar analysis for the United States in the post-WWII period. The authors ascertain the contributions to changes in the US debt ratio from both inflation and the other variables in the debt dynamics equation (e.g. the interest rate, economic growth and the primary deficit).

[16] This section uses the same methodology as the analysis presented in Chapter 4 of Eichengreen et al. (2011).

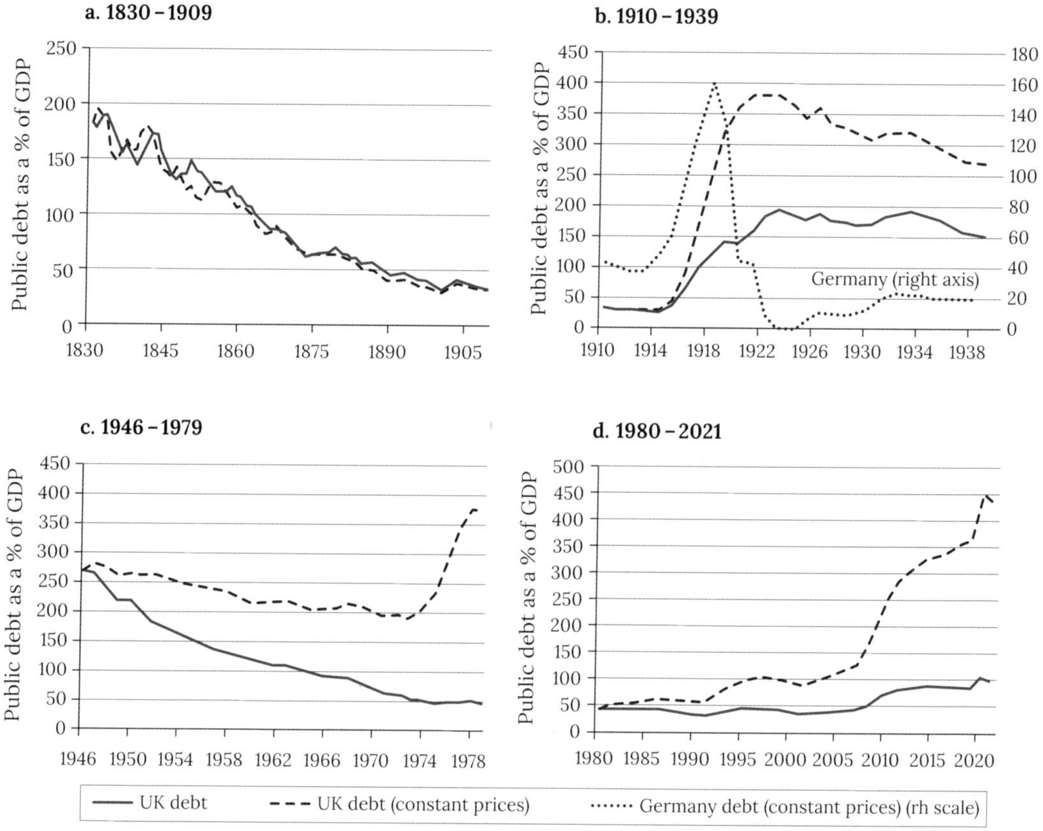

Figure 7.8 UK government debt to GDP ratios: current vs. constant prices 1830–2010.

Note: The constant price data was calculated by multiplying the nominal debt data (from the IMF) by the consumer price index in the current year relative to that in the base year (for each chart separately). The right axis of panel b shows the scale for the debt ratio in Germany.

Source: Debt data from the IMF Historical Public Debt Database (see Abbas et al. 2010) and the IMF Datamapper. Consumer prices data from the ONS (accessed October 2022). Public debt data for Germany between 1914–24 were taken from estimates by Schularick and made available by Burret et al. (2013).

throughout this period (i.e. inflation was zero on average). In other words, inflation did not contribute to the fall in the debt burden. As discussed in the context of Table 7.2, most of the debt reduction was due to fiscal effort, or what would be referred to now as austerity.

1910–39: Following the start of World War I, the debt ratio rose sharply, to 196% by 1923 (UK debt in Figure 7.8b is shown on the left axis). On the other hand, public debt would have been much higher had it not been for dramatic inflationary pressure during the War. However, the debt ratio did not fall substantially until the years directly preceding World War II. It would have fallen much faster had the price level not fallen. This period (starting from the 1920s) was, however, characterized by deflation, which made debt reduction more difficult.

1946–79: The post-World War II period was one of inflation; prices were over eight times higher in 1979 than they were in 1946. This aided the government in reducing the burden of the substantial debt incurred during WWII. The debt ratio started the period at 270% and fell to around 50% by 1973. In the absence of the effects of inflation, debt would have only fallen to 189% by this time. The period from 1974–79 was one of very high inflation (partly as a result of the OPEC oil shocks discussed in Chapter 13) and poor economic performance. The debt ratio would have risen sharply to over 400% of GDP in this period without this rapid increase in prices, as it was, the observed debt ratio finished the period just below the 50% mark.

1980–2021: The four decades from 1980 were also characterized by positive inflation, albeit typically at much lower levels than those seen in the 1970s. In this period, the debt ratio hovered around 50% of GDP before climbing to 75% in the second half of the 2000s as a result of the global financial crisis, and to 104.5% in 2020 as a result of the fiscal measures implemented in response to the Covid-19 pandemic. The constant price series shows that the debt ratio would have risen to over 458% in 2020 had there been no inflation over the post-1980 period.

This analysis highlights two important points. Firstly, high levels of government debt decline slowly. In the absence of hyperinflation such as the German interwar case, it can take years to reduce debt to sustainable levels. Secondly, the path of the debt ratio is influenced by inflation. High inflation may also be a response to high debt.

7.3.4 The costs of high and rising government debt

The interest rate–growth rate differential

In the examples we have discussed, it is clear that the cost of high public debt differs according to whether the real interest rate (including the risk premium) is higher or lower than the growth rate. If the growth rate is higher than the interest rate, then the economy is converging to a stable debt ratio—there is no problem with solvency. The problematic situation is one in which the real interest rate exceeds the growth rate. Although the latter was typical of high-income economies in the 1980s and 1990s, the former was characteristic of the 1960s and 1970s. Table 7.3 provides data for the US and Germany for the 1960s to the 1990s. It is interesting to note that in the years when the growth rate exceeded the real interest rate, it was nevertheless the case that the real rate of return on capital remained above the growth rate. However, for the evolution of the debt ratio, it is the relationship between the real growth rate and real interest rate on government debt that matters. In the high-income countries, it is typically the case that the real interest rate on government bonds is risk free. This means that it is well below the real rate of return on fixed investment, as illustrated in the data for Germany and the US.

As we have seen, with $r > \gamma_y$, a substantial primary *surplus* may be required to stop the debt ratio rising further and an even larger primary surplus is required to reduce the debt burden. This is likely to create problems for the economy for a number of reasons. Increasing the primary surplus either requires painful cuts in expenditure or politically unpopular increases in taxation. Because of their supply-side effects,

	US			Germany		
	1960s & 1970s	1980s	1990s	1960s & 1970s	1980s	1990s
Growth rate (% p.a.)	3.7	3.2	3.1	3.5	1.4	1.8
Real interest rate (%)	0.9	5.4	4.5	2.7	4.5	4.2
Real profit rate (%)	10.0	7.8	8.6	14.1	8.9	10.3

Table 7.3 Growth rates, real interest rates, and real rates of return.

Note: Prior to 1995, Germany is West Germany.

Source: OECD, Historical Statistics (various years); the real profit rate is for the business sector and calculated for the US from Bureau of Economic Analysis National Income and Product Accounts and for Germany from the Statistisches Bundesamt, Volkswirtschaftliche Gesamtrechnungen.

increases in taxation are also likely to raise equilibrium unemployment (PS shifts down) and make macroeconomic management more difficult (see Chapter 15).

Default risk

A high level of debt that is rising without limit may trigger concerns that the government may default on its debt. If so, the government will face a higher interest rate on its borrowing to incorporate the premium for default risk, ρ. A higher interest rate will in turn feed back to worsen the debt burden as shown in Equation 7.10, as well as dampening investment. In addition, at some point, credit to the government may be cut off. To continue to finance its expenditure the government may resort to monetizing the debt.

In explaining the mechanics of debt dynamics, we have assumed that the interest rate and the growth rate are exogenous. However, we have now highlighted the potential feedback from the debt ratio to the interest rate via the risk premium.

Vulnerability arising from a high debt ratio

To see why this matters, let us consider the case of a government operating in the benign regime in which the growth rate exceeds the real interest rate. As we have seen, in this regime, a primary budget deficit is consistent with a stable debt ratio, and a larger primary deficit is associated with a larger stable debt ratio.

However, the higher is the debt ratio, the more vulnerable is the government in the event that the relationship between the growth rate and the real interest rate becomes adverse: it has to undertake greater fiscal tightening in order to stem the rise in the debt ratio. Moreover, this possibility may in turn lead to a rise in the risk premium and trigger such an adverse shift. This provides an argument for the government to be concerned about the *size* of the debt ratio even when there is no immediate threat of an ever-increasing debt ratio because the growth rate is above the real interest rate.

Next, to look more carefully at a government's vulnerability, we use Equation 7.9, assume there is positive government debt (i.e. $b_{t-1} > 0$) and focus on the conditions necessary for the debt ratio not to increase, i.e. for $\Delta b \leq 0$:

$$\text{Since } \Delta b = d + (r - \gamma_y)b_{t-1},$$

$$\text{this implies that for } \Delta b \leq 0,$$

$$b_{t-1} \leq \frac{-d}{r - \gamma_y}$$

$$\text{i.e. pre-existing debt/GDP} \leq \frac{\text{primary surplus/GDP}}{(r - \gamma_y)}.$$

The expression can be interpreted as showing the size of the primary surplus that is required to stabilize the debt ratio at its existing level given an expectation that, over the long run, the interest rate will exceed the growth rate.

Alternatively, there may from a political point of view be a maximum size of primary surplus that is deemed feasible in the sense that any greater squeeze on expenditure relative to revenue or 'more austerity' would lead to the government losing power. In this case, it is the size of '$-d$' that is fixed. The equation then pins down the maximum amount of debt consistent with this political constraint on the amount of 'bearable' austerity for a given interest rate and growth rate.

As an example, let $-\bar{d} = 3\%$. Then if $r - \gamma_y = 3\%$, it follows that $\bar{b} = 100\%$, where $-\bar{d}$ and $\bar{b}$ denote the maximum size of the primary surplus and government debt respectively.

Case 3: The Eurozone sovereign debt crisis

The Eurozone provides a good example of how government (or sovereign) debt can become unsustainable (see also Chapter 14). Figure 7.9 shows the difference between nominal GDP growth and the long-term interest rate for selected Eurozone members from 2000 to 2021. When this difference is positive, we know from Section 7.3.2 that sovereign debt is converging to a stable ratio.

During the global financial crisis, all selected countries experienced a sharp decline in GDP growth, leading to a dramatic worsening in the sustainability of public debt. Although fiscal conditions improved rapidly in Germany and France, in Italy and Spain the rising interest rates on their government bonds during the sovereign debt crisis kept public debt on an unsustainable path (the situation was even worse in Greece and Ireland). For more detail, see Chapter 14. We can use the debt dynamics equation including the risk premium on sovereign debt (equation 7.10), to trace the cause of this increase in debt burdens:

$$\Delta b = d + (r^{\text{risk-free}} + \rho - \gamma_y)b_{t-1}.$$

The severity of the recession caused by the global financial crisis and the need to bail out banking systems meant these countries all ran large primary budget deficits between 2008 and 2011, that is, $d > 0$ (see Figure 7.7). The collapse in aggregate demand that accompanied the global financial crisis (and the subsequent debt crisis) negatively affected economic growth, reducing γ_y. The risk premium on sovereign bonds issued by the governments in Portugal, Italy, Ireland, Greece, and Spain increased substantially upon fears of default, that is, $\uparrow \rho$.

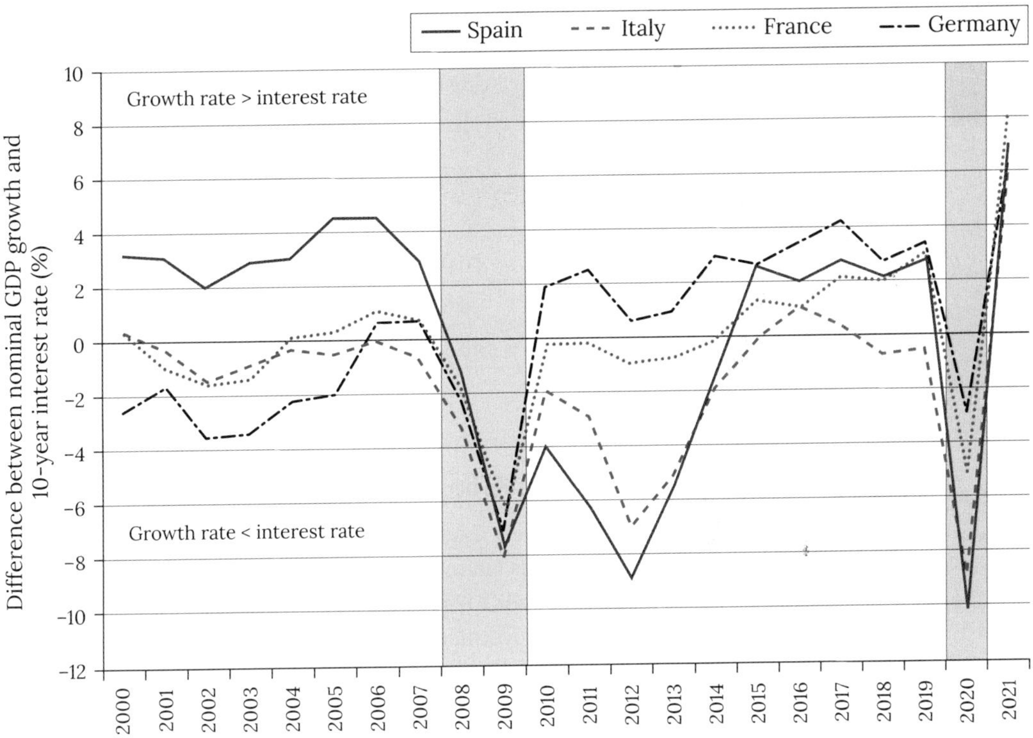

Figure 7.9 Difference between the nominal GDP growth and the interest rate on 10-year government bonds yield in selected Eurozone countries, 2000–21. Above the zero line, the growth rate exceeds the interest rate; below the opposite is the case.

Source: OECD Economic Outlook, June 2022.

Table 7.4 focuses on the decomposition of the changes in the debt ratio of a sample of Eurozone countries from 2007 to 2013 following the method in Table 7.2 earlier in the chapter. The collapse of growth and rise of interest rates (due to the high-risk premia) account for almost all of the increase in the debt ratios of Greece and Italy. By contrast, in the Irish and Spanish cases, where banking crises were driven by the bursting of housing bubbles, the principal driver of the increase in the debt ratio was the increase in government spending, including to rescue banks, and the collapse in tax revenue, especially from the construction and housing related sectors.

The experience of these countries shows that even low and stable government debt ratios are inherently vulnerable to negative economic shocks and a sudden increase in $(r^{\text{risk-free}} + \rho)$ relative to γ_y. This can put debt on an explosive path. Figure 7.9 shows that the impact of the Covid-19 pandemic on public finances was of similar (or even greater) magnitude than that of the financial crisis. However, as discussed in Chapter 14 (see Section 14.5.4), the policy response to the pandemic was deemed credible by financial markets, leading to a reduction in sovereign debt spreads despite the presence of dramatically increased government deficits and debt.

Country	Debt/GDP ratio			Decomposition		
	Starting level	Ending level	Increase	Primary balance effect	Interest-growth differential	Stock-flow adjustment
Germany	64.0	78.6	14.6	−3.7	4.9	13.4
Greece	103.1	177.9	74.8	24.9	75.9	−25.9
Ireland	23.9	120.0	96.1	66.0	17.3	12.8
Italy	99.8	129.0	29.2	−5.6	28.7	6.1
Spain	35.5	95.5	59.9	40.5	18.2	1.3

Table 7.4 Debt dynamics in the Eurozone 2007–2013.

Source: Eichengreen et al. 2021.

Empirical evidence on the relationship between high debt and GDP growth

The rise in government debt levels associated with the global financial crisis and the Eurozone sovereign debt crisis led to much research activity on the relationship between high government debt and GDP growth. The literature has primarily focused on the question of whether high government debt acts as a drag on economic growth. An influential paper by Reinhart and Rogoff (2010) ignited this debate. The authors analysed historical episodes of debt overhang and reported that periods in which government debt to GDP ratios exceeded 90% were associated with roughly 1% lower growth annually.

Economists have questioned the direction of causality in the association between high debt and slow growth found in the data. Reinhart and Rogoff claim that high debt causes low growth; other economists claim that it is more likely to be slow growth causing the build-up of debt.[17] It is important to establish the true direction of causation, as the two potential explanations imply very different policy recommendations (for example, on austerity).

The use of appropriate statistical techniques can help disentangle the causal effect of higher debt on growth from the reverse effect of weaker growth leading to higher debt. The academic literature has taken a number of different approaches to this, such as using instrumental variables and distributed lag models. However, the literature has yet to come to a consensus.

Policy makers in Europe used Reinhart and Rogoff's paper as evidence to justify the implementation of frontloaded fiscal consolidations (i.e. austerity measures) in the wake of the sovereign debt crisis. However, even a finding that high debt is bad for long-run growth does not necessarily lead to this policy recommendation. Cottarelli and Jaramillo (2013) find that fiscal consolidation is bad for short-term growth and can delay improvements in fiscal indicators, particularly when frontloaded. In the case where there is no immediate market pressure, the authors therefore recommend a more gradual pace of consolidation to balance the short-term costs of consolidation against the long-term gains.

[17] See for example, Irons and Bivens (2010) and Paul Krugman's blog post from August 11th 2010 entitled *Reinhart and Rogoff are confusing me*.

The discussion about the possible cost a high debt ratio imposes on the economy in limiting the government's ability to use fiscal policy to stabilize a recession has been questioned by research that followed the financial crisis. Countries with larger pre-existing debt ratios tended to do less fiscal stimulus in response to the financial crisis. At first sight, this could be interpreted as reinforcing the 'vulnerability' argument: high debt constrained borrowing in the next crisis by raising the risk premium and making borrowing prohibitively expensive (increase in ρ) or even causing the government to be shut out of the market due to the fear of default.

However, there is an alternative interpretation to the one of bond-market imposed austerity. The correlation between prior debt and size of fiscal stimulus could be the result of the *belief of policy-makers* that higher borrowing would damage growth. Another possibility is that EU rules or IMF conditions of lending require governments that accept assistance to implement austerity. These hypotheses are tested by Romer and Romer (2019) using data on the financial crisis and associated fiscal stimulus policies. The authors find that policy makers' choices were important as a channel separate from market access.

This is an important argument and consistent with other research that highlights the dangers of premature austerity in the aftermath of a recession when fiscal multipliers are large and hysteresis (as discussed in Chapters 4 and 15) is present.[18] Interestingly Rogoff wrote in 2019 in the *Sunday Times* that the UK government should not worry about the debt ratio (84% at the time) and should instead prioritize investment, reassure the markets, and protect vulnerable households from the adverse effects of Brexit.

Section 7.3.5 looks more closely at the debate surrounding austerity policies aimed at reducing government debt ratios, asking whether there are circumstances under which fiscal consolidation can be positive for GDP growth.

7.3.5 The austerity/fiscal consolidation debate

Fiscal consolidation in the 1980s

In the cost/benefit analysis of fiscal consolidation (or equivalently, austerity), it has been assumed so far that an increase in the primary budget surplus (i.e. a cut in government expenditure on transfers, consumption or investment and/or a rise in taxation) will have the short-run consequence of reducing the level of aggregate demand and output (because the IS curve shifts to the left). However, arguments have been developed—partly in response to the experience of fiscal consolidation in the 1980s of a number of European countries—that a contractionary short-run effect may not necessarily occur. Denmark (1983–86) and Ireland (1987–89) in the 1980s provide two examples of periods where fiscal consolidations ran alongside expansions in consumption, investment and GDP.[19]

If the economy is already in a state of so-called fiscal stress (defined by an unsustainable fiscal position), then because of the risk premium (ρ) imposed in the bond market,

[18] See for example Auerbach and Gorodnichenko (2012) and Christiano et al. (2011).

[19] See Giavazzi and Pagano (1990).

the interest rate will be higher than it otherwise would be. This will depress interest-sensitive spending. In addition, in the expectation of some kind of crisis, households may have lowered their estimates of their wealth and cut back on consumption. Uncertainty about future economic developments will typically depress investment and spending more generally.

Under these conditions, a fiscal consolidation that was viewed by the public as credible may boost both investment and consumption by resolving uncertainty as well as by reducing the risk premium and restoring optimism about expected wealth.

Other arguments may also hold weight. If the government announces a fiscal consolidation plan that is based on cutting government consumption (e.g. the public sector wage bill) rather than cutting government investment or raising taxation, the public may believe that this signals a commitment to long-term fiscal reform. In an economy in which beliefs are widespread that there are too many bureaucrats with low productivity and high wages, this policy may lift households' expectations of lifetime wealth because they believe that taxes in the future will be lower (see Section 7.4.1). For households that are not credit constrained and behave according to the permanent income hypothesis, consumption spending should rise.

The idea that the *composition* rather than simply the size of a fiscal consolidation programme matters centres on the expectational effects of the programmes. It is argued that given the strength of vested interests such as public sector unions in some countries, cutting government consumption may be perceived as more costly in political terms than is either cutting government investment or raising taxes. This may therefore more effectively signal the government's seriousness about fiscal reform and hence have a stronger effect on expectations in the private sector.

The insights from the macro model highlight the need to take account when analysing the impact of a fiscal consolidation programme of (1) the supply-side impact of the consolidation policy (e.g. an increase in tax would shift the PS curve down and prompt monetary policy tightening whereas a consolidation based on cuts in public sector pay would shift the WS curve down permitting an easing of monetary policy), (2) the stance of monetary policy, (3) other supply-side policies, and (4) the presence of hysteresis.

An analysis of the details of fiscal consolidation programmes that were implemented in the 1980s and 1990s suggests that the impact on output in the short run was influenced by the balance between expenditure cuts and tax increases, the associated stance of monetary policy and by wage accords. In particular, features of policy in countries observed to have expansionary fiscal consolidations were the following: expenditure-based consolidations, implementation of a devaluation of the exchange rate and a wage accord at the same time as the consolidation.[20] The first lent credibility to the government's intention, the second counteracted the contractionary fiscal policy, and the third reduced equilibrium unemployment, allowing output to rise.

[20] See, for example, Alesina and Ardagna (1998 and 2010). For a summary of the evidence, see Briotti (2004). For a reevaluation of four cases originally thought to support the idea of expansionary fiscal consolidation see Perotti (2013).

Alesina and Ardagna (2010) analyse 107 fiscal consolidations in OECD economies between 1970 and 2007. The authors find that 26 of these episodes (roughly a quarter of the total) were expansionary and that all episodes were mostly associated with spending cuts rather than tax increases.

Later research does not support the expansionary fiscal consolidation hypothesis. Guajardo et al. (2014) argue that the earlier studies mismeasured fiscal consolidation episodes. They use official documents to identify tax hikes or spending cuts that were explicitly undertaken to improve the public finances. In this way, by using the so-called narrative approach, Guajardo et al. identify episodes when fiscal policy actions were motivated by deficit reduction, irrespective of their success. In contrast, Alesina and co-authors identified consolidation by outcomes measured by an improvement in the cyclically adjusted primary budget balance. The problem is that the CAPB is affected by non-policy developments such as the collapse of house prices (and of associated tax revenues), which increases the budget deficit in spite of the government implementing tighter fiscal policy. Straightforward reverse causality is also a problem: tighter fiscal policy to temper a boom will produce a positive correlation between consolidation and growth, which will bias against finding that tightening dampens growth.[21]

Using the more reliable narrative approach to identify fiscal consolidation episodes produces the result that tighter fiscal policy has a substantial negative effect on GDP, with the result lasting up to five years. The analysis finds that fiscal consolidation reduces GDP even if it is spending-based, although the effects are even more contractionary with a tax-increase-based policy.

Moreover, consolidation will be most painful when undertaken simultaneously in economies with fixed exchange rates and little scope for monetary stimulus. This provided a bleak picture for the Eurozone economies that embarked on austerity in the wake of the global financial crisis and the Eurozone debt crisis. Fiscal consolidation is especially damaging to GDP in circumstances in which monetary policy is either constrained by membership of a common currency area (see Chapter 14) or the economy is at the zero lower bound.

Austerity and hysteresis

Pessimism about the level of potential output and the effectiveness of fiscal policy can produce a self-fulfilling reduction in potential output.[22]

Following the financial crisis, pessimism about potential GDP in 2008 and 2009 along with the elevated levels of public debt arising from the crisis came together

[21] Figure 3 in Guajardo et al. (2014) vividly illustrates the divergent predictions about the effect of a fiscal shock using the CAPB versus the narrative shocks measure. Note that Alesina and co-authors return to the analysis of austerity in a book published in 2019 (Princeton University Press). They adopt a narrative approach to identifying fiscal consolidation. Their findings are less supportive of the phenomenon of expansionary fiscal consolidation than Alesina's earlier work but contrary to other research continue to find evidence of expenditure-based consolidation occasionally having a positive effect on GDP.

[22] See Antonio Fatás' article 'Self-fulfilling pessimism: The fiscal policy doom loop' published on *Vox.eu* (September 28th 2018).

with beliefs about both the necessity of fiscal consolidation and the possibility of its expansionary effect to produce a first wave of fiscal consolidation from 2010 to 2011. Having underestimated the negative effect of such policies on GDP (possibly because hysteresis effects modelled in Chapter 4 were ignored), policy makers adjusted their estimates of potential GDP downward. In turn, pessimism about potential GDP raised greater concerns about debt sustainability, thus triggering a second wave of austerity between 2012 and 2013 (the data shows that countries whose economic conditions deteriorated more from 2010 to 2011 engaged in larger consolidations between 2012 and 2013). The process, driven by self-fulfilling pessimism, would continue until the economy ends up with potential output significantly lower because of successive downward revisions to the forecast level.

7.4 MODELLING: THE GOVERNMENT'S BUDGET CONSTRAINT AND RICARDIAN EQUIVALENCE

In Section 7.3, we used the government's budget identity to investigate the determinants of the path of the debt to GDP ratio. Here we show the connection between that discussion and the analysis of household consumption behaviour using the permanent income hypothesis (PIH) set out in Chapter 1. In the RE–PIH (Ricardian equivalence-permanent income hypothesis), the government's intertemporal optimization problem is set up in the same way as the household's, i.e. maximizing utility subject to an intertemporal budget constraint. Households and government are connected through their budget constraints.

Looked at in this light, and recalling the permanent income hypothesis from Chapter 1, we can see that the household will take into account the consequences for its budget constraint of how the government finances its expenditure. The model assumes there are no credit-constrained households. If the government sells bonds (to households) to fund its spending, the household will figure out that higher taxes will be required later on to service the debt and repay the principal. Under some circumstances, therefore, deficit-financed spending will be viewed as identical to tax-financed spending. The term Ricardian equivalence is used to refer to this case.

We address the following questions:

1. Under what conditions is the household indifferent between taxes now and in the future, i.e. when does Ricardian equivalence hold?
2. Is there empirical evidence for this behaviour?
3. If the world is Ricardian in this way, what does it imply for the effectiveness of fiscal policy; in particular, what are the implications of a tax cut or a rise in government spending for aggregate demand and output?

7.4.1 Ricardian equivalence and the PIH

The core idea of the RE–PIH, is that households will fully internalize the consequences for them over an infinite time horizon of government spending and financing decisions.[23] Any increase in the government deficit will be analysed by households for its consequences for their permanent income and they will behave accordingly. As we shall see, this may or may not mean that aggregate demand changes in response to a change in the government deficit. The answer depends on the implications for household permanent income. This argument has a pedigree stretching back to the nineteenth-century classical economist David Ricardo and was revived in the 1970s by Robert Barro, and is known as 'Ricardian equivalence'.[24]

It is simplest to think about the Ricardian equivalence hypothesis by modelling the economy over an infinite time horizon as in Chapter 1. We assume that the permanent income hypothesis describes consumption behaviour. As we showed in Chapter 1, households prefer a smooth path of consumption independent of current income and since it is assumed that they can borrow at the interest rate r, they will be able to implement this.

We begin by writing the households' intertemporal budget constraint (in the absence of government) as follows:

$$\sum_{i=0}^{\infty} \frac{y_{t+i}}{(1+r)^i} = \sum_{i=0}^{\infty} \frac{C_{t+i}}{(1+r)^i} \qquad \text{(HH intertemporal budget constraint)}$$

where $\sum_{i=0}^{\infty} \frac{1}{(1+r)^i} y_{t+i}$ is total lifetime labour income and noting that in this model, consumption is the only type of expenditure. To simplify, we omit the expectation operator, assume a constant real rate of interest r, and ignore assets held at the beginning of the period. This says that the present value of the income of the household sector, which is assumed to live forever, is equal to the present value of its spending.

Households maximize their utility subject to the intertemporal budget constraint. As discussed in Chapter 1, the solution to the maximization problem takes the form of the Euler equation,

$$C_t = \frac{1+\rho}{1+r} C_{t+1}, \qquad \text{(Euler equation)}$$

which highlights the consumption smoothing result of the PIH.[25] In this model, ρ is the subjective discount rate of the households (not the risk premium on government bonds) and when $\rho = r$, households consume the same in every period. We will assume $\rho = r$.[26]

Step 1: Introduce the government with tax-financed spending

We now introduce the government. It is assumed that the government undertakes spending in each period and that the spending is financed through lump-sum taxation, i.e. there is a balanced budget in each period ($T = G$). It is assumed that government spending does not provide utility to households. How does this affect our results for

---

23 See Appendix 7.7.1 for a mathematical derivation of the government's intertemporal budget constraint and to see how it relates to the debt dynamics equation.

24 Barro (1974).

25 As discussed in Appendix 1.5.2 of Chapter 1, the Euler equation takes this form if and only if we assume a log utility function of the form: $U(C_{t+i}) = \frac{\log C_{t+i}}{(1+\rho)^i}$.

26 Appendix 7.7.2 shows how the results in this section can be confirmed mathematically.

consumption? We modify the intertemporal budget constraint for the households by explicitly including the tax that has to be paid each period to finance the government spending:

$$\sum_{i=0}^{\infty} \frac{y_{t+i} - T_{t+i}}{(1+r)^i} = \sum_{i=0}^{\infty} \frac{C_{t+i}}{(1+r)^i}. \qquad \text{(HH intertemporal budget constraint with government)}$$

We compare the housholds' intertemporal budget constraint with and without the government, noting the following: the tax is lump-sum, so it cannot affect incentives; and government spending does not affect either future income (e.g. via infrastructure spending) or utility. The latter leaves the household utility function unaffected by government spending.

Given this set-up, when households maximize utility, they will smooth consumption, just as in the case without government. Their behaviour is captured by the Euler equation and the only difference is that the *level* of consumption in the Euler equation will be *lower* because taxation reduces permanent income. Consumption will therefore be constant over time, but at a lower level than in the case without government.

We have assumed that $r = \rho$, such that the household's optimal comsumption path is to consume the same amount in each period. How much do they consume when government spending is tax financed? When the economy is in equilibrium, they will consume their permanent disposible income, which is equal to $y_e - T$ (or equivalently $y_e - G$).

Step 2: *What happens if the government switches to financing government spending through borrowing rather than taxation?*

We now assume that the government reduces tax in period 0 to zero and finances government spending through borrowing. The government borrows $B = G$ in each period by selling a bond of value B and must then pay interest of rB in perpetuity on that period's borrowing. We assume that the government has to raise taxes to pay the interest and that they do this as the interest comes due (i.e. tax in period 1 is rB, tax in period 2 is $2rB$, and so on). The interest bill (and hence taxation) increases in each period because the government has to pay interest of rB for every bond of value B it sells and it sells one every period from period 0 onwards.

How much disposible income do households have in each period in this scenario? Again assuming the economy starts at equilibrium, they will have y_e minus the tax in each period. Hence, disposible income in period 0 is equal to y_e, disposible income in period 1 is equal to $y_e - rB$, disposible income in period 2 is equal to $y_e - 2rB$, and so on.

In our model, we have assumed that $r = \rho$, so that households want to consume the same amount in each period. How much would the household need to save in each period in order to earn interest that would exactly cover the amount they will be required to pay in taxation in the future? The answer is obvious, they would need to save B in each period, in effect buying the bond the government has sold. The stream of income from the bonds bought by the households will then exactly cover their tax bill and as B is the same in each period, consumption smoothing is preserved.

What is the permanent disposible income of households in this scenario? It is simply $y_e - B = y_e - G = y_e - T$. Hence, the permanent consumption of households is the same whether government spending is financed by taxes or by borrowing. Under the RE-PIH, households do not take advantage of the higher disposable income they have in period 0 to increase consumption, because they want to smooth consumption in order to maximize their utility.

In short, the household takes action in period 0 to completely neutralize the effect of the shift from tax to bond finance. Once the interdependence between the government and the household sector is made transparent, the strong result of Ricardian equivalence can be clearly seen.

The Ricardian equivalence result depends on the following assumptions:

1. the absence of credit constraints on households, i.e. households are able to borrow against expected future income at the current interest rate (permanent income hypothesis);
2. the interest rate and time horizon faced by households and the government are the same; and
3. households have children or heirs and incorporate the utility of their heirs into their consumption behaviour, i.e. households behave 'as if' they live forever.

Let us take each of these in turn. If households are credit constrained, then as we saw in Chapter 1, they are unable to implement consumption smoothing. If this is the case, Ricardian equivalence will not hold, because being unable to borrow, the household will *not* be indifferent to the timing of changes in its income.

Unlike the Ricardian equivalence assumption that the government is just the aggregate of all the households in the economy, in the real world, governments can often borrow more cheaply than households. This makes government borrowing more attractive to the household than higher current taxation. This is also the case if households are more myopic or short-sighted than governments, or if they care more about their own welfare than that of their children or of other new households, including those who arrive as immigrants and enter the economy in the future. In all these cases, households will prefer to defer taxes and hence will raise consumption by more in the first period in the case of the bond-financed spending programme.

After a clear statement of the nature of the assumptions required to deliver Ricardian equivalence, John Seater, in a survey in the *Journal of Economic Literature*, concludes:[27]

> Finite horizons, non-altruistic or inoperative bequest motives, childless couples, credit constraints, and uncertainty can all lead to failure of Ricardian equivalence and it seems virtually certain that some of these sources of non-equivalence are operative. It appears likely that the world is not Ricardian.

The consensus view is that changes in fiscal policy are only partly offset by changes in private sector savings: the sources of 'non-equivalence' in the real world mean that Ricardian equivalence is not a good representation of macroeconomic behaviour.[28]

---

[27] Seater (1993: 155–6).

[28] For evidence on the real world being only partially Ricardian see Holmes (2006) and Brittle (2010).

Research has shown that standard macroeconomic models fit the empirical data better by allowing for the presence of some hand-to-mouth consumers alongside the PIH ones as in the hybrid consumption function. At the research frontier in the HANK models, Ricardian equivalence does not hold (see Chapter 18).

In addition, research has found that Ricardian-type effects are stronger the more developed are financial markets.[29] This finding not only suggests that credit constraints are a salient source of 'non-equivalence', but also that the global trend towards financial development could see the world economy becoming more Ricardian over time. This could have important implications for stabilization policy, as we shall see in Section 7.4.2.

7.4.2 Ricardian equivalence and fiscal policy effectiveness

We turn our attention to the implications of the RE-PIH for the effectiveness of fiscal stimulus packages, i.e. the use of *temporary* changes in taxation or government spending to boost aggregate demand.

Temporary tax cuts

In the RE-PIH framework, a temporary tax cut entails a tax increase later in order that the intertemporal budget constraint is met. Because the tax cut is saved (as in Step 2 above), consumption and hence aggregate demand do not change at all. Attempting to stimulate the economy by increasing aggregate demand via a temporary tax cut like this is completely ineffective if the economy is characterized by Ricardian equivalence (remember that this is a lump-sum tax cut so it has no effect on incentives).

Temporary rise in government spending financed by borrowing

The case of a temporary rise in government spending financed by borrowing is different. If we return to Step 1 above, we can easily see that higher government spending in period 0 reduces permanent income for households. They will therefore re-optimize and reduce consumption in every period. To calculate the net impact of the increased government spending on aggregate demand in period 0, we therefore need to add together the extra government spending and the reduced level of consumption. Since the impact of the higher government spending on the household's budget constraint is spread across all periods (saving goes up in all periods to pay the higher taxes in order to satisfy the intertemporal budget constraint), the fall in consumption must be less than the rise in government spending: hence there is a positive boost to aggregate demand in period 0. This assumes that the real interest rate remains unchanged.

To summarize, if Ricardian equivalence (and hence the PIH) holds:

1. Temporary tax cuts have no impact on aggregate demand (and cannot therefore affect output).
2. Temporary higher government spending financed by borrowing boosts aggregate demand, because the offsetting effect on consumption is spread over future periods

[29] See Röhn (2010).

whereas all of the government spending affects aggregate demand in period 0. Note that the increase in government spending is partially offset by lower consumption, so the multiplier must be less than 1.

3. Combining the first and second results, a temporary increase in government spending financed by higher taxes (i.e. a balanced budget spending boost) will have the same effect as the case where the spending is financed by borrowing.

These results contrast with a model with Keynesian (or hybrid) consumption behaviour, where holding the interest rate constant, the multiplier is greater than 1 in the case of a temporary rise in government spending financed by borrowing and equal to 1 when it is a balanced budget fiscal expansion.

7.5 DEFICIT BIAS AND THE POLITICAL ECONOMY OF DEBT

Setting aside the specific conditions following the financial crisis and the pandemic, Figure 7.2 for the UK highlights what is called 'deficit bias'. This is the tendency for budget deficits to rise in recessions, but not to fall in a sufficiently offsetting way in booms. The bias leads to a preference for financing government spending through borrowing rather than taxation.

The result is the upward trend in debt ratios reported in Section 7.3. Relating these data to the debt dynamics equation in the form that includes inflation (see equation 7.11), we can infer that a tendency toward deficit bias has been mainly interrupted by bursts of inflation (e.g. the UK in the 1970s; see Figure 7.8) or especially rapid GDP growth relative to the real interest rate (e.g. Spain in the early 2000s; see Figure 7.9).

In this section, we set out briefly some of the hypotheses that have been proposed to explain deficit bias behaviour.[30] Some of the explanations help to account for a general tendency for deficit bias and others are more helpful in explaining why the problem appears to be more severe in some countries than in others. We end the section by discussing fiscal rules and fiscal policy councils; two commonly used approaches to tackle deficit bias.

7.5.1 Causes of deficit bias

Over-ambitious output target

At the beginning of this chapter, we looked at the case of a government with an over-ambitious output target (e.g. it seeks to achieve unemployment below the equilibrium rate). The medium-run impact of this policy stance is that the economy returns to equilibrium output at constant inflation, but the new medium-run equilibrium is characterized by both inflation bias and higher government debt.

---

[30] Calmfors and Wren-Lewis (2011) provide a very useful summary and relate the different explanations for deficit bias to the role of a fiscal council.

Uncertainty about growth forecasts

This explanation is related to the previous one. In the previous example, we assumed that the government knows potential output and chooses to ignore this by opting for a higher output target—possibly for reasons of electoral gain. The government can implement its favourite spending plans or provide tax cuts to its target voters prior to an election. However, even if neither the government nor the voters have these preferences, it is still possible, given the extent of uncertainty about the future evolution of the economy, that they believe growth will be higher than it turns out to be. Since more optimistic forecasts for growth will produce higher estimates for tax revenue, this may encourage the government to adopt tax and spending plans that raise the debt level if the outturn for growth is lower than expected.

Intergenerational conflict

The current generation of voters may take insufficient account of the future burden that will arise, for example, if current fiscal policy places too low a weight on the higher future spending that will be associated with an ageing population. This effect will be exacerbated to the extent that politicians have even shorter time horizons than voters.

7.5.2 Variation across countries

A number of theories have been put forward to explain why some countries are more affected by deficit bias than others.

Different preferences for public goods

Song et al. (2012) propose a theory in which there are differences across countries in the extent to which public goods are valued relative to private consumption. They point to the stylized fact that in Scandinavian countries, where public goods are highly valued and quality is high, governments run *tighter* fiscal policies than do those in countries like Greece and Italy where public goods are provided less efficiently. The idea is that when young and old members of the current generation vote and when there is no intergenerational altruism, the current generation is tempted to pass on the cost of public spending to the next generation (non-voters). This can only be avoided in countries where the current young voters are sufficiently confident about the quality of the public goods supply in the future (i.e. in their lifetime) that they vote to restrict spending and debt accumulation in the short term in order to secure the supply of valued public goods later on.

Another application of this idea is the impact on the debt ratio of partisan politics, where political parties have different preferences for public goods. The following quote from the *New York Times* about President Reagan's State of the Union address in January 1987 captures this:[31]

---

[31] *New York Times*, January 25th 1987, 'The State of the President' (accessed online June 2012).

> This deficit is no despised orphan. It's President Reagan's child, and secretly, he loves it... The deficit rigorously discourages any idea of spending another dime for social welfare.

Since parties of the right are typically associated with small government, at first it seems paradoxical that this preference might contribute to deficit bias. The explanation is as follows: if one party, the right, values public goods less than does the left, and if there is uncertainty about who will win the next election, it is in the interests of the right leaning party to cut taxes, increase the deficit and thereby make it harder for a left leaning government if it wins the next election to spend on public goods. This strategy is sometimes referred to as 'starve the beast'. Song et al. (2012) find empirical evidence for this prediction. In a panel of OECD countries from 1980 to 2005, the authors find that a political shift from left to right increases the debt to GDP ratio by 0.7 percentage points per year.

Common pool problems and budgetary processes

These explanations centre on the political process and suggest, for example, that countries with systems of government based on proportional representation, where coalitions are common, may face different pressures in budget making from countries with majoritarian systems. The core idea is that public spending projects or tax cuts may favour particular groups in the economy and ministers of spending departments may fail to fully internalize the costs to the current and future budget. Proportional representation electoral systems are more likely to lead to the fragmented governments that will exacerbate this overspending problem.

7.5.3 Mitigating deficit bias

Two commonly used approaches to mitigating deficit bias are fiscal rules and fiscal policy councils. Deficit bias and the approaches used to mitigate it can be seen as analogous to inflation bias in Chapter 4. In that case, government control over monetary policy led to a sub-optimal equilibrium, providing the motivation for the adoption of monetary policy rules, independent central banks, and the delegation of monetary policy to monetary policy committees.

Fiscal rules

Fiscal rules set out a guideline for how fiscal policy should be conducted. The aim of the rules is to keep the public finances sustainable in the medium and long term. In practice the rules are typically numerical limits for fiscal aggregates such as government debt to GDP ratios and budget deficit to GDP ratios. Fiscal rules are normally written into government legislation and viewed as long term (i.e. they are not changed when governments change hands). The adoption of rules can help limit deficit bias by constraining the government's ability to use discretionary fiscal policy and by providing a benchmark against which the government's management of the public finances can be judged.

There are two sides to our discussion of fiscal rules. The first looks at an optimal fiscal policy rule and the second looks at how fiscal policy rules have been used in practice. This comparison parallels the discussion of the optimal Taylor rule in monetary policy and the monetary policy rules that are used in practice.

What is the optimal fiscal policy rule?

In thinking about the optimal fiscal policy rule, we begin with the debt dynamics equation set out in the Section 7.3.[32] An optimal or prudent fiscal policy rule (PFPR) is to set the share of tax in GDP at a constant level equal to the 'permanent' or long-run level required to satisfy the constraint:

$$\overline{(T/Py)} = (T/Py)^{\mathbf{P}} \geq (G/Py)^{\mathbf{P}} + (r^{\mathbf{P}} - \gamma_y^{\mathbf{P}})b_{t-1}, \qquad \text{(prudent fiscal policy rule)}$$

where the superscript P refers to the long-run or permanent value. The derivation of the PFPR is set out in the Appendix (Section 7.7.3).

The PFPR has a number of key implications for fiscal policy:

1. Any permanent increase in government expenditure, such as a rise in long-run government pension obligations, should be financed through a rise in taxation.
2. Any temporary increase in government expenditure, such as rising government transfers in a recession, should be financed through borrowing.
3. Any major government infrastructure investment programme that could take government expenditure above its permanent level for years (or even decades), such as renewing the transportation system, should be financed through borrowing.
4. Borrowing should be permitted to rise if the interest rate is confidently known to be temporarily higher than its permanent value or if growth is depressed relative to its long-run value.
5. Government expenditure must be reduced below its permanent level in upswings. Averaged over the cycle there is no case for divergence between G/Py and $(G/Py)^{\mathbf{P}}$.

The PFPR advocates a constant tax share. This is because taxes are distortionary and the distortions are assumed to increase with the amount of taxation raised. Hence, the optimal way for the government to behave is to smooth tax revenue collection over time by borrowing and saving. This is analogous to the household smoothing consumption through borrowing and saving under the permanent income hypothesis that we saw in Chapter 1. The government's optimal tax share therefore only changes when there is a permanent change to the government's intertemporal budget constraint. Temporary and/or unforeseen fluctuations in expenditure (due to the business cycle, wars, natural disasters, etc.) are dealt with solely by changes in borrowing. This analysis puts to one side the pressures likely to require a rising tax share over time due to demographic pressure and the climate transition, and to the tendency for unit costs to increase more rapidly in government funded services than in the rest of the economy.

---

[32] This discussion of fiscal rules relies heavily on the work of Willem Buiter. See for example Buiter (2001) and Buiter and Grafe (2004).

Fiscal policy rules in practice

We begin with the Stability and Growth Pact (SGP) of the European Union because it applied across so many countries and diverges from the PFPR introduced in the previous subsection. As discussed further in Chapter 14, the original SGP contained two central rules: the budget deficit to GDP ratio must be less than 3%, and the government debt to GDP ratio must be less than 60%. A major drawback of these rules is that they might not allow adequate room for stabilization in a deep recession. The PFPR indicates that there is no economic reason that the deficit ratio should be limited to a fixed number. In contrast to the SGP, the PFPR advocates as much borrowing as is necessary after a temporary shock, even if this exceeds 3% of GDP.

The SGP is widely viewed as a failure. The deficit ceiling was broken by the Eurozone's two largest economies, Germany and France, in the early 2000s. Under the rules, the breaches should have been met with repercussions (e.g. fines) but were not, which undermined the legitimacy of the Pact. As explained in Chapter 14, the Pact did nothing to discourage destabilizing pro-cyclical fiscal policy during the first ten years of the single currency. Lastly, the SGP was shown to be too restrictive for stabilization in a deep recession, with 10 out of the 11 core economies exceeding the deficit ceiling during the global financial crisis (see Figure 7.10). Under the pressure of the pandemic the EU stepped away from the constraints of the Stability and Growth Pact in order to prevent the rules-based pro-cyclical fiscal policy from destabilizing the national economies.

Fiscal policy councils

A fiscal policy council (FPC) is an independent (or semi-independent) body whose main role is to be a *fiscal watchdog*—i.e. to make sure government fiscal policy is sustainable over the long term.[33] It is the FPC's mandate to guard against deficit bias by providing independent forecasts of the evolution of the public finances and calling the government to account when their tax and spending plans are unsustainable.[34]

FPCs have been in operation in some countries for many years, such as the Central Planning Bureau (CPB) in The Netherlands (established in 1947) and the Congressional Budget Office (CBO) in the US (established in 1975), but they were not widespread before the global financial crisis. Sweden, the UK and Slovenia have all set up FPCs since 2007, highlighting the renewed interest in fiscal watchdogs in the wake of the Great Recession.

There are three main reasons for the re-emergence of FPCs as an approach to limiting deficit bias following the global financial crisis:

1. The success of independent inflation-targeting central banks during the 1990s and 2000s.

---

[33] For more information on fiscal policy councils (e.g. definitions, international examples and relevant academic literature) see Simon Wren-Lewis' website (https://sites.google.com/site/sjqwrenlewis/fiscal-councils).

[34] This subsection relies heavily on the work of Lars Calmfors. See for example Calmfors (2010) and Calmfors and Wren-Lewis (2011).

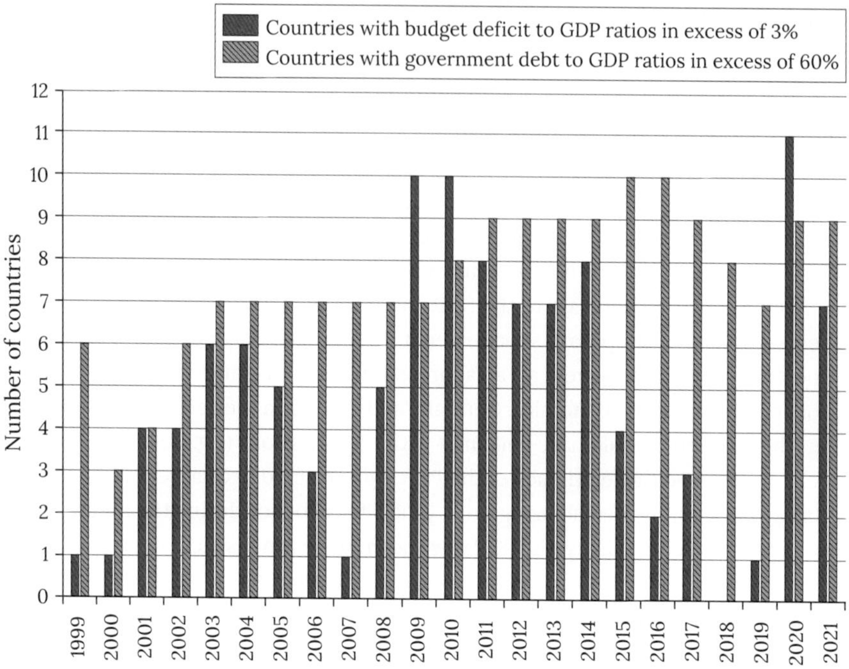

Figure 7.10 Breaches of the Stability and Growth Pact by Eurozone members: 1999–2021.
Note: The Eurozone members are Austria, Belgium, Finland, France, Germany, Greece, Ireland, Italy, Netherlands, Portugal and Spain. The measure used for budget balances is net lending (+)/net borrowing (-) under the EDP (Excessive Deficit Procedure). The measure used for debt is gross public debt, Maastricht criterion, as a percentage of GDP. Greek data is included from 2001 onwards.

Source: Budget balance data from Eurostat (accessed October 2022). Public debt data from OECD Economic Outlook, June 2022.

2. Fiscal rules proved insufficient to ensure prudent management of the public finances in the years preceding the crisis.
3. Politically unpopular austerity packages were introduced to repair the damage done to the public finances by the Great Recession. FPCs can boost the credibility of fiscal consolidation packages and act as a commitment device for successive governments when consolidation is spread over a number of years. They can also identify instances of unnecessary or damaging austerity.

The mandates of existing fiscal policy councils

There is currently no consensus 'best-practice' framework for FPCs. The list below shows some of the features of existing FPCs, starting with those with the narrowest remits.

1. To produce forecasts for growth, the output gap and the public finances on which the government's fiscal decisions conforming to their targets must be made (e.g. the UK's Office for Budget Responsibility (OBR)).
2. To carry out *positive* policy analysis—i.e. to assess the fiscal cost of different policies, but to remain objective and non-partisan (e.g. the US CBO and The Netherland's CPB).
3. To make *normative* recommendations based on the government's stated economic objectives—i.e. the FPC is actively engaged in the public debate about fiscal policy decisions (e.g. the Swedish Fiscal Policy Council and the Economic Council in Denmark).

It is important to note that even the FPC with the widest remit does not have the power to set fiscal policy in the same way that an independent central bank sets monetary policy. Fiscal policy has largely remained in the hands of elected politicians and has tended to be more discretionary than rules based. It has more policy levers than monetary policy and different winners and losers are created depending on which lever is pulled. For example, raising duties on cigarettes and alcohol disproportionately affects the poor, whereas raising capital gains tax disproportionately affects the rich. Recent research highlights the distributional consequences of monetary policy—for example, lower interest rates redistribute income from savers to borrowers and QE delivers capital gains on assets that accrue to the wealthy. Nevertheless, monetary policy continues to be perceived as more neutral, so in contrast to fiscal policy, the public and politicians are happier to see it put in the hands of an independent expert council.

The future of fiscal policy councils

An unprecedented fiscal expansion was required to avoid the collapse of banking systems and economies in the high-income world during the financial crisis and then, as a result of the pandemic. Fiscal consolidation and the sustainability of the public finances are likely to be central to macroeconomic debate and policy over the medium term. This may enhance the visibility and influence of existing fiscal councils; and lead to the establishment of more fiscal councils (as advocated by international organizations, such as the IMF and the OECD; and European policy makers, such as the ECB and the European Commission (EC)).

Proposals for a new fiscal policy architecture

One feature of fiscal reform proposals is the objective of limiting discretionary policy.[35] This entails shifting more of the burden of stabilization on to automatic features of the tax and transfer system, along with managing the structure of public debt by selling bonds of longer maturity.

---

[35] This section draws on Orszag, Rubin, and Stiglitz (2021).

1. *Strengthen automatic stabilizers.* As shown earlier in the chapter, automatic stabilizers reduce the need for discretionary policy. For example, the duration of eligibility for unemployment insurance could be extended until triggered by recovery from recession. This would reduce precautionary savings during a spell of unemployment, helping to stabilize aggregate demand. The disadvantage is the potential increase in equilibrium unemployment via a higher reservation wage. The trade-off will be affected by the degree of hysteresis in the economy.
2. *Create a new infrastructure automatic stabilizer.* In many countries, infrastructure spending is pro-cyclical because it is a relatively easy target for spending cuts when governments are worried about rising public debt. Orszag et al. (2021) call for 'a new infrastructure funding program that would expand during recessions and focus on projects that could be quickly completed (or meaningfully accelerated) during periods of economic weakness. This new infrastructure program should be in the mandatory, rather than discretionary, component of the budget.' Such a scheme worked well in Sweden from 1955 to the early 1970s (Taylor 1982).
3. *Extend the maturities of bonds.* The most straightforward way to provide insurance against the risk of interest rate spikes is to shift the maturity structure of bond issues, increasing the issuance of 30-years bonds and creating new, longer-date instruments (e.g., 50- or 100-year bonds or even perpetual bonds). Over time, as the proportion of long-dated bonds increases, any interest rate shock would have a smaller overall effect on the interest bill of the government.

7.6 CONCLUSIONS

This chapter on fiscal policy is a counterpart to the previous one on monetary policy. In combination with the analysis of the special features of the Eurozone set out in Chapter 14, they provide an analytical framework for thinking about the role of stabilization policy in contemporary economies. We can summarize the main findings of this chapter as follows:

1. The predicted effects of *discretionary* fiscal policy and the size of the short- and medium-run multipliers are highly dependent on the initial conditions in the economy and the modelling framework being used. In the 3-equation model, fiscal stimulus can be effective in raising output and welfare, if the economy is hit by a negative demand shock and monetary policy is unavailable (i.e. nominal rates have reached the zero lower bound). The other side of fiscal policy is its role in *automatically stabilizing* the economy—the presence of the government as a major source of injections and withdrawals of spending power in the economy helps to mitigate aggregate demand shocks. The stabilization provided by the automatic stabilizers is largely a by-product of the structure of the tax and social security systems. Although these systems are typically designed to meet the government's income distribution and microeconomic goals rather than its macroeconomic objectives, they nevertheless play an important role in stabilization. We also show

that economies with larger government sectors have, on average, larger automatic stabilizers (see Figure 7.3).

2. We set out a model to determine the path of government debt over time. The evolution of the government debt ratio is influenced by the primary budget deficit (d), the differential between the interest rate and the growth rate ($r - \gamma_y$) and the existing stock of government debt (b_{t-1}). We use the model of *debt dynamics* to show that public debt ratios can be reduced by shrinking d, ($r - \gamma_y$) or (b_{t-1}). Inflation induces significant variations in the dynamics of debt. Moreover, as we can see in the Eurozone, austerity is one method of reducing d, but it is likely to have detrimental effects on economic growth. In some cases, fiscal consolidation has taken place alongside economic expansion, but economists are divided whether this was due to the expectations effects of consolidation or because of the complementary policies enacted in parallel (i.e. monetary stimulus, exchange rate depreciation and wage accords). It is largely agreed, however, that consolidations that rely on spending cuts instead of tax rises exert less contractionary effects on output.
3. As a theoretical exercise, it is useful to spell out the conditions under which it does not matter whether permanent changes in government spending are financed by taxation or by borrowing; the consumption response will be the same—this is the *Ricardian equivalence* result. The result relies on households being rational and forward looking so that they *internalize* the government's intertemporal budget constraint when making decisions (see Section 7.7.2 in the Appendix). This theory also implies that temporary fiscal stimulus packages will have no effect on consumption and hence on aggregate demand and output if they are based on tax cuts. In contrast, we show that they will boost output in the current period, although with a multiplier of less than one, if they are based on government spending; this is the case regardless of whether they are financed by taxation or borrowing.
4. *Deficit bias* is the tendency for budget deficits to rise in recessions, but not to fall in a sufficiently offsetting way in booms. The bias leads to a preference for financing government spending through borrowing rather than taxation. Common causes of deficit bias are: governments targeting a level of output above equilibrium, uncertainty around economic growth forecasts, and intergenerational conflict. The extent of deficit bias can also vary across countries depending on preferences for public goods, political systems and partisan politics. *Fiscal rules* and *fiscal policy councils* are two methods of guarding against deficit bias. The optimal fiscal rule is a *prudent fiscal policy rule*, which is analogous to the optimal Taylor rule for monetary policy introduced in Chapter 6. This rule is preferable to existing rules, such as the original Stability and Growth Pact of the EU, as it ensures the long-term sustainability of the public finances, while allowing for stabilization in downturns and for long-term public investment projects. Fiscal policy councils (FPCs) have re-emerged as a method to tackle deficit bias in the wake of the global financial crisis. Although the mandates of existing FPCs vary across countries, their central role is to be a *fiscal watchdog*—i.e. to make sure the government's fiscal policy is sustainable over the long term.

7.7 APPENDIX

7.7.1 Deriving the government's intertemporal budget constraint

In Section 7.4 we explained that rational PIH households will fully internalize the consequences for their permanent income of the government's spending and funding decisions over an infinite time horizon. Clearly, this requires knowledge of the government's intertemporal budget constraint. In this Appendix[36] we pin down mathematically the intertemporal constraint on a government's spending.

We begin by recalling the government's budget identity presented in Section 7.3. For simplicity, we neglect monetary financing as a source of revenue:

$$\begin{aligned} G_t + i_t B_{t-1} &\equiv T_t + \Delta B_t \\ &= T_t + (B_t - B_{t-1}). \end{aligned}$$

Bringing B_{t-1} to the LHS gives:

$$G_t + (1 + i_t)B_{t-1} = T_t + B_t.$$

We divide through by price level in period t in order to have values in real terms:

$$\frac{G_t}{P_t} + (1 + i_t)\frac{B_{t-1}}{P_t} = \frac{T_t}{P_t} + \frac{B_t}{P_t}.$$

We now use the 'precise' form of the Fisher equation (i.e. $1 + r = \frac{1+i}{1+\pi}$) to rewrite the above as:

$$\frac{G_t}{P_t} + (1 + r_t)(1 + \pi^E_{t+1})\frac{B_{t-1}}{P_t} = \frac{T_t}{P_t} + \frac{B_t}{P_t}. \tag{7.12}$$

Assuming backward-looking inflation expectations we let $\pi^E_{t+1} = \pi_t$.

Notice that:

$$\begin{aligned} (1 + \pi_t) &= 1 + \frac{P_t - P_{t-1}}{P_{t-1}} \\ &= \frac{P_t}{P_{t-1}} \end{aligned}$$

We can then rewrite equation 7.12 as:

$$\frac{G_t}{P_t} + (1 + r_t)\frac{P_t}{P_{t-1}}\frac{B_{t-1}}{P_t} = \frac{T_t}{P_t} + \frac{B_t}{P_t}.$$

$$\rightarrow g_t + (1 + r)\tilde{b}_{t-1} = t_t + \tilde{b}_t$$

where $\tilde{b}$ is the real value of debt (i.e. debt divided by the price level); note that this is not the same as debt-to-GDP ratio defined in Section 7.3. We assume $r_t = r$ for all t.

Solving for $\tilde{b}_{t-1}$ gives:

$$\tilde{b}_{t-1} = \frac{1}{1 + r}(t_t - g_t + \tilde{b}_t), \tag{7.13}$$

[36] This Appendix is written by Alessandro Guarnieri and draws on notes by Wei Cui.

Similarly, for the next period:

$$\tilde{b}_t = \frac{1}{1+r}(t_{t+1} - g_{t+1} + \tilde{b}_{t+1}), \tag{7.14}$$

And the next:

$$\tilde{b}_{t+1} = \frac{1}{1+r}(t_{t+2} - g_{t+2} + \tilde{b}_{t+2}), \tag{7.15}$$

Substituting 7.15 for $\tilde{b}_{t+1}$ into 7.14, and then for $\tilde{b}_t$ into 7.13, we get:

$$\tilde{b}_{t-1} = \frac{1}{1+r}(t_t - g_t)\frac{1}{(1+r)^2}(t_{t+1} - g_{t+1}) + \frac{1}{(1+r)^3}(t_{t+2} - g_{t+2} + \tilde{b}_{t+2}). \tag{7.16}$$

Proceeding in the same way over infinite periods gives:

$$\tilde{b}_{t-1} = \sum_{i=0}^{\infty} \frac{1}{(1+r)^{i+1}}(t_{t+i} - g_{t+i}). \tag{7.17}$$

Or, equivalently:

$$(1+r)\tilde{b}_{t-1} = \sum_{i=0}^{\infty} \frac{1}{(1+r)^{i}}(t_{t+i} - g_{t+i}). \qquad \text{(Government's intertemporal budget constraint)}$$

This expression has an intuitive interpretation: the real value of the existing stock of debt must be equal to the real present value of future primary surpluses.

7.7.2 The PIH under Ricardian equivalence: The effect of changes in tax and spending

In this Appendix[37] we provide a mathematical derivation of the results presented in Section 7.4. As highlighted in Section 7.4.1, provided that the assumptions behind the permanent income hypothesis hold, knowledge of the government's intertemporal budget constraint will be internalized in households' calculations of their permanent income, thus affecting their consumption path.

We start by recalling the expression for the expected present value of lifetime wealth presented in Chapter 1:

$$\psi_t^E = (1+r)a_{t-1} + \sum_{i=0}^{\infty} \frac{y_{t+i}^E - t_{t+i}^E}{(1+r)^i}. \tag{7.18}$$

Where y_{t+i}^E is expected pre-tax income and t_{t+i}^E is the expected lump-sum tax imposed by the government.

The government's intertemporal budget constraint, derived in Appendix 7.7.1, can be rearranged to show that:

$$\sum_{i=0}^{\infty} \frac{t_{t+i}^E}{(1+r)^i} = (1+r)\tilde{b}_{t-1} + \sum_{i=0}^{\infty} \frac{g_{t+i}}{(1+r)^i} \tag{7.19}$$

Substituting in equation 7.18 gives:

$$\psi_t^E = (1+r)a_{t-1} - (1+r)\tilde{b}_{t-1} + \sum_{i=0}^{\infty} \frac{y_{t+i}^E - g_{t+i}}{(1+r)^i},$$

---

[37] This Appendix is written by Alessandro Guarnieri and draws on notes by Wei Cui.

For simplicity, we assume government bonds are the only asset in the economy. This implies $a_{t-1} = \tilde{b}_{t-1}$. Therefore:

$$\psi_t^E = \sum_{i=0}^{\infty} \frac{y_{t+i}^E}{(1+r)^i} - \sum_{i=0}^{\infty} \frac{g_{t+i}}{(1+r)^i} \tag{7.20}$$

We can use this equation to verify the results presented in Sections 7.4.1 and 7.4.2. In particular:

(i) *Temporary tax cuts.* Equation 7.20 clearly shows permanent income, and hence consumption, is unaffected by the time path of taxes.

(ii) *Temporary rise in government spending.* This is shown in equation 7.20 by a one-off increase, say Δg, in g_t. The present value of lifetime wealth then becomes:

$$\psi_t^E = \sum_{i=0}^{\infty} \frac{y_{t+i}^E}{(1+r)^i} - \Delta g - \sum_{i=0}^{\infty} \frac{g_{t+i}}{(1+r)^i},$$

$$\rightarrow \Delta\psi_t^E = -\Delta g.$$

Using the PIH consumption function derived in Chapter 1, this implies that households' consumption is permanently lowered by an amount:

$$\Delta C = \frac{r}{1+r}\Delta\psi_t^E = -\frac{r}{1+r}\Delta g.$$

So that the increase in government spending is partially offset by lower consumption. Whether the increase in spending is financed by taxes or by borrowing clearly has no effect on households' consumption path.

(iii) *Permanent rise in government spending.* If government spending increases permanently (i.e. each period) by an amount Δg, this implies that:

$$\psi_t^E = \sum_{i=0}^{\infty} \frac{y_{t+i}^E}{(1+r)^i} - \sum_{i=0}^{\infty} \frac{\Delta g}{(1+r)^i} - \sum_{i=0}^{\infty} \frac{g_{t+i}}{(1+r)^i}$$

$$\rightarrow \Delta\psi_t^E = -\frac{1+r}{r}\Delta g,$$

which implies:

$$\Delta C = \frac{r}{1+r}\Delta\psi_t^E = -\frac{r}{1+r}\frac{1+r}{r}\Delta g = -\Delta g.$$

So that the increase in government spending is completely offset by lower consumption, thus reducing the fiscal multiplier all the way to zero.

7.7.3 Deriving the prudent fiscal policy rule (PFPR)

It is useful to restate the government's budget constraint in terms of the change in the debt to GDP ratio focusing first on the role of the real interest rate (equation 7.22) and then on the role of the nominal interest rate and the rate of inflation (equation 7.24):

$$\Delta b = d + (r - \gamma_y)b_{t-1} \tag{7.21}$$

$$= (G/Py - T/Py) + (r - \gamma_y)b_{t-1} \tag{7.22}$$

$$\Delta b = d + (i - \pi - \gamma_y)b_{t-1} \tag{7.23}$$

$$= (d + ib_{t-1}) - (\pi + \gamma_y)b_{t-1}. \tag{7.24}$$

Given the pre-existing level of the debt ratio, b, the second form (equation 7.24) highlights the fact that the debt ratio is raised by the budget deficit $(d + ib_{t-1})$ and reduced by the growth of nominal GDP $((\pi + \gamma_y)b_{t-1})$. The first form (equation 7.22) highlights the fundamental determinants of the change in the debt ratio as the primary deficit (d) and the difference between the real interest rate and the real growth rate $((r - \gamma_y)b_{t-1})$. It is also useful to write equation 7.24 in terms of the budget deficit:

$$\frac{\text{deficit}}{\text{GDP}} = (d + ib_{t-1}) = \Delta b + (\pi + \gamma_y)b_{t-1}. \qquad (7.25)$$

Deriving a rule for prudent fiscal policy begins from the condition $\Delta b \leq 0$ for the debt ratio not to increase. This implies:

$$b_{t-1} \leq \frac{(T/Py)^{\mathbf{P}} - (G/Py)^{\mathbf{P}}}{r^{\mathbf{P}} - \gamma_y^{\mathbf{P}}}, \qquad (7.26)$$

where the superscript **P** refers to the long-run or 'permanent' value. Let us assume that there is a given public expenditure programme that entails a long-run ratio of government expenditure to GDP, $(G/y)^{P}$. The question is, how should this best be financed? For the debt ratio not to increase, rewriting (equation 7.26) implies:

$$(T/Py)^{\mathbf{P}} \geq (G/Py)^{\mathbf{P}} + (r^{\mathbf{P}} - \gamma_y^{\mathbf{P}})b_{t-1}.$$

A prudent fiscal rule is to set the share of tax in GDP at a constant level equal to the 'permanent' or long-run level required to satisfy the constraint:

$$\overline{(T/Py)} = (T/Py)^{\mathbf{P}} \geq (G/Py)^{\mathbf{P}} + (r^{\mathbf{P}} - \gamma_y^{\mathbf{P}})b_{t-1}.$$

Substituting the PFPR into equation 7.22 implies that the debt ratio moves as follows:

$$\Delta b \leq (G/Py - (G/Py)^{\mathbf{P}}) + [(r - r^{\mathbf{P}}) - (\gamma_y - \gamma_y^{\mathbf{P}})]b_{t-1}. \qquad (7.27)$$

Sticking to the rule ensures solvency—although it relies on the government making public its forecasts about the real interest rate and growth rate and about expenditure programmes well into the future. The rule implies that, if government expenditure is *temporarily* above its permanent level, borrowing should finance this—this entails a rise in the debt ratio and is consistent with the rule. This would be the case if there is a recession so that government transfers are higher than normal (i.e. the automatic stabilizers are working).

It would also be the case if a major programme of exceptional government infrastructure investment is planned that would take government spending as a share of GDP above its long-run level for many years (or decades). An example of this might be the investment requirements associated with German reunification in the 1990s. If the real interest rate is confidently known to be temporarily higher than its 'permanent' value or if growth is depressed relative to its long-run value, the rule says that the deficit can safely be allowed to widen (and the debt ratio to rise). Equally, the rule says that an expected rise in *permanent* government spending, for example, as a consequence of long-run government pension obligations must be funded by a rise in taxation.

QUESTIONS AND PROBLEMS FOR CHAPTER 7

CHECKLIST QUESTIONS

1. What are the automatic stabilizers? How could the method of local income-based or property-value based government taxation affect the automatic stabilizers?

2. Explain the logic of the balanced budget multiplier result. Investigate whether this result continues to hold if there is a proportional income tax (rather than a lump sum tax).

3. What is meant by the cyclically-adjusted primary budget deficit? How can it be calculated? Why is it conceptually equivalent to the discretionary fiscal impulse? Is such a deficit sustainable?

4. Is the view that automatic stabilizers are effective consistent with the view that discretionary fiscal policy is not?

5. Explain in words the intuition behind the debt dynamics equation: $\Delta b = d + (r - \gamma_y)b_{t-1}$.

6. Discuss how each of the following can help to reduce the debt burden on governments. What are the problems and potential negative consequences associated with each method?

   a. reducing the primary deficit, d

   b. increasing the growth rate, γ_y

   c. reducing the interest rate, r

   d. reducing the existing stock of debt, b_{t-1}.

7. Explain the concept of an expansionary fiscal consolidation. Why is consolidation less likely to be expansionary for a country in a common currency area where all the countries are simultaneously undertaking austerity measures? (The second question can be explored using Chapter 14.)

8. Assume an economy with lump-sum taxes is hit by a large negative demand shock (e.g. financial crisis). In response, the government introduces a large fiscal stimulus package to try and boost economic activity and help to stabilize the economy. Assess whether the policy will be successful in each of the following cases:

   a. In the 3-equation model, when stimulus is financed through borrowing.

   b. In the 3-equation model, when the stimulus is financed by raising taxes (i.e. a balanced budget expansion).

   c. In the RE-PIH model, when the stimulus is financed through borrowing.

In which case will output expand the most? Justify your answer.

9. Explain the concept of deficit bias. Use Section 7.5 (and IMF Fiscal monitor and OECD Economic Survey of UK and Greece) and your own knowledge to identify the different sources of deficit bias in the UK and Greek economies between 2001 and 2007.

10. Explain in words what is meant by the prudent fiscal policy rule. What is the main reason for 'tax smoothing'? Under this rule, how should a government react in the following scenarios:
    a. Defence spending is cut for the foreseeable future due to the end of the Cold War.
    b. The government compensates farmers following a disease outbreak.
    c. The Treasury releases a report forecasting that the cost of the tax-funded health service will treble within twenty years.
    d. The government decides to contribute troops to a war that it expects to be over in a matter of weeks.

11. Why was there a resurgence of interest in fiscal policy councils (FPCs) after the onset of the global financial crisis? Can FPCs be seen as a substitute for fiscal rules?

PROBLEMS

1. Use the 3-equation model to discuss whether contractionary fiscal policy should be used in the following situation—the economy is initially at equilibrium and there is a positive shock to aggregate demand from improved consumer confidence.

2. Begin with the scenario in Figure 7.7a. Following the shift to an explosive debt path, assume that the debt ratio has risen further before the government reacts. If its objective is to return the debt ratio to its initial level, explain using a diagram how it could achieve this by using fiscal policy.

3. This question uses the UK Office for Budget Responsibility's (OBR's) 2011 Fiscal Sustainability Report (July 2011). The report can be downloaded from the publications section of the OBR website (https://obr.uk/frs/fiscal-sustainability-report-july-2011/).

   Table 5.1 of the report shows the adjustment to the primary balance needed to ensure the long-term sustainability of the public finances. How do each of the following factors affect the extent of adjustment (i.e. tightening) required to reach the target debt to GDP ratio by 2060? In each case, you must give an explanation of how you think the factor influences the debt dynamics (equation 7.9).

    a. interest rates
    b. productivity

c. migration

d. age structure

e. increased health spending

f. lower morbidity rates.

4. This question uses the Macroeconomic Simulator (available at www.oup.com/he/carlin-soskice) to model the evolution of the public finances. Start by opening the simulator and choosing the closed economy version. Then reset all shocks by clicking the appropriate button on the left-hand side of the main page. Use the simulator and the content of this chapter to work through the following questions [Hint: for all these questions the real interest rate is 3%].

   a. Set long-run economic growth to 'yes' and the growth rate to 2%. Set the initial public expenditures/GDP to 21% (giving a primary budget deficit of 1%) and the initial public debt/GDP to 60%.

   b. Click on the 'public finance figures' button on the top left of the main page. Is public debt sustainable? Justify your answer by using the debt dynamics equation (7.9).

   c. Change the long-run growth rate to 4% and then 6%. Is the debt sustainable in these cases? If so, why?

   d. For each of the three cases, draw a diagram (with the primary deficit on the y-axis and the debt ratio on the x-axis) showing the evolution of the public debt ratio (see Section 7.3).

   e. Do the result for parts (b) and (c) still hold if the initial public expenditures/GDP is set to 25% (giving a primary budget deficit of 5%)? Why?

5. This question uses the Macroeconomic Simulator (available at www.oup.com/he/carlin-soskice) to model fiscal consolidation. Start by opening the simulator and choosing the closed economy version. Then reset all shocks by clicking the appropriate button on the left-hand side of the main page. Use the simulator and the content of this chapter to work through the following questions [Hint: for all these questions the real interest rate is 3%].

   a. Set long-run economic growth to 'yes' and the growth rate to 2%. Set the initial public expenditures/GDP to 23% (giving a primary budget deficit of 3%) and set the initial public debt/GDP to 60%.

   b. Click on the 'public finance figures' button on the top left of the main page. Click on the 'change the time span in figures' button on the left-hand side. Change the timespan to run from 1 to 25 years. Is public debt sustainable in the medium term?

   c. Add a permanent decrease in public expenditure in period 10 of 3%. This is equivalent to a fiscal consolidation. Is public debt sustainable in the medium run after the consolidation package is introduced?

d. Given that the primary budget to GDP ratio is now positive, why does the debt to GDP ratio not fall over time?

e. Click on the 'inflation, income and interest rate figures' button on the left-hand side. What is the short-term impact of the consolidation package on GDP growth? Explain why using the 3-equation model. What does the path of interest rates tell us about the central bank's role in supporting fiscal consolidation?

6. 'An important transmission mechanism of monetary policy is through multiplier effects that arise because of differences in the income and wealth of households across the economy. In principle, fiscal policy instruments are better designed to directly target those worst affected by shocks to aggregate demand.' Provide a justification for this statement by reference to economic models. Do you find this to be a convincing case for giving priority to fiscal policy for stabilization?

INTERESTED IN EXPLORING THESE TOPICS FURTHER?

Visit www.oup.com/he/carlin-soskice to consolidate and extend your learning with the multiple-choice questions and Animated Analytical Diagram accompanying this chapter.

PART

3

FINANCIAL INSTABILITY IN THE MACROECONOMY

CHAPTER

8

SOURCES OF FINANCIAL SECTOR INSTABILITY

8.1 INTRODUCTION

The role of banks in the economy and the relationships between the banking system, the real economy, and monetary policy are set out in Chapter 5. To this point, we have assumed that the financial system functions smoothly and that if households and firms are able to borrow they can implement their spending decisions by using the credit facilities and payment services provided by banks. In this chapter we reassess this assumption and lift the lid on the potentially destabilizing features of the financial system, such as the financial accelerator and asset price bubbles, which can amplify and propagate shocks through the economy. These are examples of a *positive feedback process* whereby some initial change sets in motion a process that magnifies the initial change. Positive feedback processes can have an upward trajectory or a downward one, and beneficial or adverse outcomes. Vicious and virtuous circles are examples of positive feedback processes. The term 'positive' simply refers to the amplifying character of the process.

We introduce the concept of a financial cycle to provide a framework for better understanding the relationship between key financial variables, such as private credit and house prices, and the macroeconomy. Figure 8.1 illustrates the upswing and downswing of a financial cycle centred on banks extending credit to households to finance housing. In the upswing phase, banks are overly optimistic about the future state of the economy, and conditional on these beliefs, they maximize expected profits by increasing lending to households. The increase in credit supply produces a house price boom. This increases the market value of houses, which means households can borrow more from banks based on the increased value of their housing collateral.

This step is shown in the top left box of Figure 8.1, which says 'Household borrowing increases'. The extra borrowing by households, which is based on the higher house prices, in turn allows households to buy more housing, which feeds back into higher house prices, and the upswing of the financial cycle continues. For example, when house prices rise, a family can sell their house and use the capital gain they have made to borrow more and fund the purchase of a yet higher priced house.

The upswing does not continue forever. Following a self-fulfilling positive feedback process, prices are higher than many market participants believe to be sustainable in

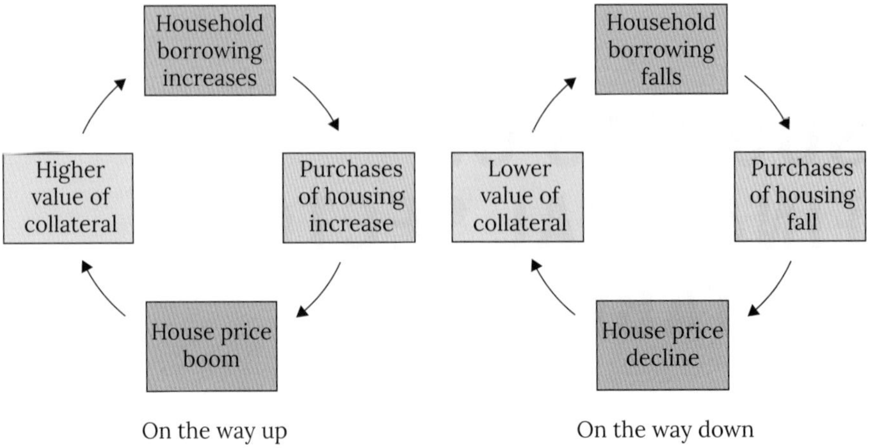

Figure 8.1 Upswing and downswing of a house price cycle.

the long run. Doubts emerge and the belief weakens that such high prices will last. At a certain point, doubts are sufficient to provoke house selling and house prices begin to fall. The right-hand side of Figure 8.1 shows the downswing of the cycle in which price falls are amplified. Lower house prices reduce the collateral of households, constraining their borrowing. As a result of lower borrowing, the demand for housing falls and this triggers a further round of falling house prices.

If the downswing of a financial cycle based on housing illustrated in Figure 8.1 is severe enough, it can turn into a banking crisis through the interconnected balance sheets of households and banks. During the downswing, people lose their jobs and are unable to repay their mortgages. As we saw in Chapter 5, if house prices are falling, the value which banks recover from a defaulted loan may be smaller than the value of the original loan. This reduces the size of assets on the bank's balance sheet (see Figure 5.11 for a reminder of how the balance sheet operates), and if a large number of loans are defaulted on, this may result in the bank becoming insolvent once the value of the bank's assets becomes smaller than the value of its liabilities. The insolvency of a bank can quickly turn into a full-blown banking crisis if the government does not step in to prevent the fear of the collapse of core banking services from spreading.

In turn, the systemic importance of banks in the economy has consequences for their behaviour. Believing that the government would have to bail them out to prevent a banking crisis means that, in effect, banks receive an implicit subsidy as those who lend to them know that the government will ensure they recover their funds. By lowering the cost of borrowing, this encourages banks to take more risks than would be the case in the absence of the implicit subsidy.[1] This is referred to as the 'too big to fail' problem, and the trade-off between protecting the economy from systemic risk and

[1] For more detailed analysis and an overview of empirical estimates of the implicit subsidies to banks, both before and after the financial crisis, see Buch et al. (2021).

avoiding moral hazard from modified bank behaviour is explored in Section 8.2 and at the beginning of Chapter 9.

A banking crisis based on a house price boom and bust is sometimes called a 'plain vanilla' banking crisis. In the 2008–09 global financial crisis, the banking crises in Ireland and Spain were of this kind. But a second, more complex kind of banking crisis with novel features arose with its epicentre in the US. In the plain vanilla crisis, banks lend to households who buy houses. The potential instability centres on the *leverage of households*. In the second type of banking crisis, the borrowing behaviour of banks is an additional source of instability. It is *leveraged banks* that play a key role.

Figure 8.2 looks very similar to Figure 8.1 but introduces a different driving force: the *borrowing by banks to buy financial assets*. The financial assets in question are called *securitized assets* or *financial derivatives*, and include assets based on mortgages. The name for this class of risky assets is asset-backed securities (ABS).

The cycle begins with a rise in the price of these assets. This strengthens the balance sheet of banks through a process called *mark-to-market accounting*. A bank that uses mark-to-market accounting records the price of assets on their balance sheet at their current market value and not at the value at which they were bought. This means that, when asset prices increase, the bank's assets rise in value and its equity increases—this is referred to as a strengthening of its balance sheet. There is an important difference between household and bank behaviour. An increase in collateral permits a credit-constrained risk-*averse* household to increase its borrowing, but only until the household reaches its desired level of borrowing. By contrast, in the model of an investment bank (based on research by Shin and Geanakoplos), a risk-*neutral* bank borrows more whenever it can, as long as the expected return from the new assets it acquires is positive. Consequently, when the value of their equity rises, the banks borrow more, and the additional assets they buy with the new borrowing push asset prices up further.

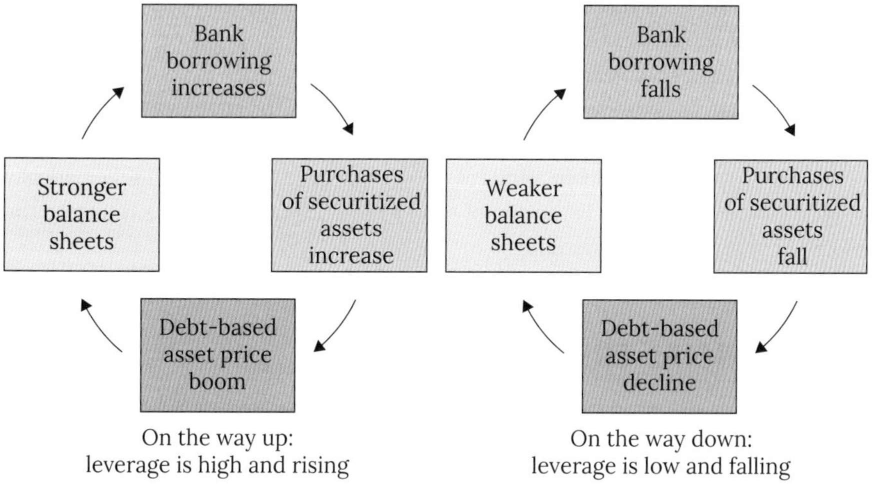

Figure 8.2 The upswing and the downswing of the bank-based financial cycle.
Source: adapted from Shin (2009a).

The downswing of the financial cycle for banks has the same form as the house price one for households. Similarly to the house price case, a change in beliefs among market participants triggers a fall in the price of ABS. When the price falls, the banks lose equity, and may have to deleverage to offset the gap between the unchanged value of their liabilities and the lower value of their assets. As we saw with the Barclays Bank example in Chapter 5, this process involves selling off risky assets such as ABS. If many banks try to do this at the same time, the price of ABS falls further, leading to losses in equity and the downswing continues. Just as in the house price cycle, a banking crisis occurs when the fall in the value of bank assets is sufficient to wipe out the bank's equity: with debts (or liabilities) in excess of the value of their assets, their net worth is negative and the bank is insolvent.

The collapse of a house price cycle brings misery to families as houses are repossessed. A banking crisis, whether caused by a house price cycle (plain vanilla) or by the risky borrowing by banks illustrated in Figure 8.2, can bring down the financial system as a whole and threaten the livelihoods of people throughout the economy. The danger of spillover from a banking crisis to a recession, as jobs are lost and output falls throughout the economy, makes the banking industry special and poses particular problems for the design of economic policy, such as addressing 'too big or systemic to fail'.

Housing and banking crises are less frequent than business cycle recessions. As we shall see in the data, the upswing of a financial cycle with rising house prices and growing leverage can be sustained through a business cycle recession. A financial upswing that poses a threat to financial stability can occur simultaneously with successful management of the business cycle by an inflation-targeting central bank.

Although households and firms suffer impairment of their balance sheets in a normal recession (e.g. as savings are run down during a spell of unemployment), a financial crisis originates from damage to balance sheets and the effects are more acute, and extend to a broader part of the population. As we shall see, the historical evidence shows that recessions that stem from financial crises are especially severe. They are typically followed by weak recoveries as households and firms pay off debt accumulated during the boom years. It should therefore be a priority for policy makers to formulate financial stability policy such that it safeguards the economy from financial crises. The first step in this process is to understand the economic mechanisms that lie behind the upswings and downswings of the financial cycles illustrated schematically in Figures 8.1 and 8.2. That is the aim of this chapter. In Chapter 10, we return to the design of a safer financial system.

8.2 FINANCIAL CRISES AND CYCLES

8.2.1 Bank behaviour and the macroeconomy

Banks and the *IS* curve

The standard modelling of the IS curve in macroeconomics assumes that households and firms can implement their spending and savings plans by interacting with the banking and payments systems. This assumption is brought into question by the occurrence of financial crises.

Banks are a special case for policy makers

The special treatment of the banking industry by policy makers arises for two reasons. The first is that the economy depends on the continuous provision of core banking services (which includes running the payments system). The second is that problems in one bank spill over to fears about the functioning of the system as a whole. This is referred to as contagion. The dramatic and largely unanticipated effects of the collapse of Lehman Brothers in 2008—an investment bank with no depositors—described in Chapter 9 highlight this. Lehman Brothers was allowed to fail, and there were catastrophic effects across the world. The consequences of the bankruptcy of what turned out to be a systemically important bank highlight why the exit of a failing bank is difficult for governments to allow. There is, however, a trade-off for policy makers between protecting the economy from systemic risk on the one hand, and avoiding moral hazard from modified bank behaviour on the other, as guaranteeing support in case of bankruptcy may encourage banks to take more risks. This trade-off is explored at the start of Chapter 10.

The activities of retail or commercial banks, and investment or shadow banks

To understand the threat banks pose to financial stability, and their role in financial upswings and downswings, we need to distinguish between retail or commercial banks, which are regulated, and investment or shadow banks, which are not.

1. A retail bank engages in traditional banking activity and behaves similarly to the model we constructed in Chapter 5. Its key characteristics are that its core business is principally deposit taking, payment services, and lending—to individuals, mainly for mortgages, and to SMEs (i.e. small- and medium-sized enterprises). Retail banks are tightly regulated and are covered by Deposit Guarantee Schemes.
2. We will use the term 'investment bank' (IB) to include the whole range of lightly regulated banks—often referred to as shadow banks or the shadow banking complex or NBFIs (non-bank financial intermediaries)—that trade in a variety of financial products (such as derivatives, fixed income instruments, currencies, and commodities).[2]

Although, in the real world, the activities of some investment banks include the provision of assistance to institutions such as governments and corporations in raising equity and debt finance, giving advice in relation to mergers and acquisitions, and acting as a counterparty to client trades and market-making, from a macroeconomic stability point of view, the important activity of IBs is trading in securitized assets. When we model investment banks, we shall focus entirely on trading in securitized assets and derivatives based on them.

---

[2] The definitions of retail and investment banks that follow are similar to those in the UK's Independent Banking Commission's report, IBC (2011).

The significance of these lightly regulated banks is that, from the early 1980s, they grew from intermediating less than 15% of credit in the US to around 40% just before the financial crisis (Gertler and Gilchrist 2018). As an example, Countrywide Financial, a US non-bank mortgage lender, became the largest mortgage lender in the country in the years prior to the crisis. The company achieved this rapid growth by aggressively expanding loans to households who would normally be denied credit, so-called subprime lending.[3]

We shall see in Chapter 10 that one outcome of the financial crisis was tighter banking regulation and, as a consequence, a more resilient banking sector, which was tested by the Covid-19 crisis. However, weaker bank profitability has prompted the migration of activities away from the retail banking sector toward shadow banks, including the rapidly growing Fintech sector, raising once more the threat of financial instability arising outside the regulated banks.[4]

Many large international banks are universal banks, which means they combine the activities of retail and investment banks, operating related entities that are part of the shadow banking complex. However, when they do this, they separate their accounts into the so-called *banking book*, in which the retail bank assets (like mortgage loans) are reported and the *trading book*, in which the investment bank assets and derivatives are reported.

In this chapter, we set up a highly stylized simple model of investment banks that illuminates an important source of financial instability. The IBs in the model can be taken to include the trading book activities of universal banks and the activities of the shadow banking complex. An important feature of investment banks is that the assets are 'marked-to-market' as illustrated in the financial cycle shown in Figure 8.2. This means that asset values in the balance sheet reflect market prices. We shall see that mark-to-market valuation of financial assets plays an important role in financial fluctuations. We shall also assume that investment banks are risk-neutral and characterized by a business model called Value at Risk (VaR), which we explain below.

Just as we represent household and firm behaviour in a very stylized way in the IS curve in the 3-equation model, we shall do the same for the financial system by setting out simple models to characterize important features of bank behaviour. In Chapter 9, we return to the financial sector of the real world and apply the models developed here to shed light on the part they played in the global financial crisis, the great recession, and in the regulatory reform that followed.

8.2.2 Financial crises and their cost to the economy

Ben Bernanke defines financial crises as extreme disruptions to the normal functioning of financial markets, which often have a significant effect on the real economy.[5] As the

---

[3] See the Reuters article from the October 15th 2010 entitled, *Factbox: Countrywide's subprime lending*.

[4] For an assessment, see Chapter 3 as well as the discussion by Amit Seru in Chapter 5.2 of Carletti et al. (2020).

[5] See Ben Bernanke's speech on June 15th 2007, entitled *The Financial Accelerator and the Credit Channel*. The speech is available on the Federal Reserve website.

book by Reinhart and Rogoff (2009a) reports, financial crises are nothing new. In fact, the authors find that relatively frequent financial crises have characterized developing and advanced economies for at least the last 800 years. The authors focus their more detailed empirical analysis on the period since 1800 (due to data availability) and produce a dataset of all the financial crises in this period. This includes 66 economies, covering a range of levels of development and geographical regions.

The authors find evidence of four broad varieties of crisis; inflation crises, currency crises, sovereign debt crises (domestic and external), and banking crises. This chapter focuses on *systemic banking crises*, which are crises that 'lead to the closure, merging or takeover by the public sector of one or more financial institutions'. These crises are typically associated with the bursting of house price and credit bubbles and the collapse of highly-indebted borrowers (e.g. banks and households). We use the terms 'financial crisis' and (systemic) 'banking crisis' interchangeably.

What impact do systemic banking crises of this nature have on the real economy? In a study focusing primarily on the financial crises in the post-WWII period (but excluding the 2008–09 crisis), Reinhart and Rogoff (2009b) find that financial crises are drawn out affairs and (although they vary considerably) they typically have three key characteristics:

1. Deep and prolonged asset price collapses: declines in real house prices average 35% over a period of six years and declines in share prices average 55% over a period of three to four years.
2. Large and lasting adverse impacts on output and employment: on average, real GDP per capita contracts 9% (from peak to trough) over two years, and unemployment rises seven percentage points over four years.
3. Government debt explodes: in real terms, the government debt stock rises 86% on average in the three years following a banking crisis.[6] This is primarily due to the collapse in tax revenues associated with the deep output contraction and the implementation of counter-cyclical fiscal policy. Bank bailout costs are usually second order.[7]

These characteristics highlight the sheer magnitude of the impact financial crises typically have on the real economy. The IMF (2009) report provides further evidence; analysing 122 recessions in 21 advanced economies they found that recessions associated with financial crises are more severe and long-lasting than those recessions associated with other shocks.

---

[6] The authors use the percentage increase in the government debt stock instead of the debt-to-GDP ratio to avoid steep output drops complicating the interpretation of the debt-to-GDP ratios. The authors index pre-banking crisis government debt at 100 and find that the average government debt stock rises to 186 (i.e. an increase of 86%) in the three years following a banking crisis.

[7] Bank bailout costs in the global financial crisis (which are not considered in the Reinhart and Rogoff data) were, however, very large compared to government tax revenue in some countries (e.g. Ireland). We discuss the case of the Irish bank bail-out in more detail in Chapter 14.

Research conducted using data on 14 high-income economies between 1870 and 2008, confirmed the earlier results that relative to typical recessions financial crisis recessions are costlier (Jorda et al. 2013). The analysis of the data shows that even when a financial crisis does not result, more credit-intensive upswings tend to be followed by deeper recessions than is the case for a normal business cycle upswing. This is an important result because it puts the spotlight on the build-up of excess credit and its damaging consequences for the real economy.

The global recession of 2008–09 was extremely damaging, as it was not only associated with a financial crisis, but was highly synchronized across the high-income economies. GDP contracted by 3.5% in 2009 alone, and the cumulative cost of lost output over the crisis was even larger.[8] For example, for the UK, it took until the first quarter of 2013 for real GDP to return to its pre-crisis peak of 2008 Q1 and it was 14% below the level it would have been had the pre-crisis trend not been interrupted by the crisis and extended recession.[9] We analyse the global financial crisis in more detail in Chapter 9.

8.2.3 **Financial cycles and business cycles**

Chapters 1–5 were all about the business cycle—the fluctuations of the economy from recession to boom to recession. In the earlier chapters we set out a model in which business cycles can be driven by demand and supply shocks, and by policy changes. In business cycle recessions, unemployment goes up and wellbeing goes down—for people who lose their jobs, for those who find it more difficult to find a job and for those in employment who are more anxious about keeping the job they have. In business cycle booms, although unemployment goes down and real wages tend to rise, both of which raise wellbeing, inflation goes up and there is normally a cost to be paid in terms of a subsequent recession for squeezing inflation out of the economy. For these reasons, the policy maker tries to keep the economy close to the medium-run equilibrium.

The business cycle is measured by fluctuations in real GDP, whereas upswings and downswings of financial cycles refer to fluctuations in key financial variables, such as the amount of bank credit to GDP and house prices. Unlike the business cycle, however, there is no widely accepted methodology for measuring the financial cycle. Nevertheless, we can summarize the key features of financial fluctuations and crises using the work of economists and economic historians (see, for example, Reinhart and Rogoff (2009a and 2009b), Jordà, Schularick, and Taylor (2011, 2013), and Mian, Sufi, and Verner (2017)):

1. In the upswing of a financial cycle, banks extend more credit than in a typical business cycle upswing: this is the driving force of the expansion phase. House prices rise more rapidly during the upswing than on average over the long run.

[8] Source: IMF World Economic Outlook database, October 2012.

[9] The pre-crisis trend level of growth was calculated as the compounded average quarterly growth rate for the 15 years prior to the recession (i.e. 1993 Q1 and 2007 Q4). Source: UK Office for National Statistics (data accessed January 2022) and authors' calculations.

Positive feedback processes amplify both rising house prices and rising levels of debt in the banking sector. The upswing of a financial cycle is often associated with both households and banks increasing their borrowing: households borrow to purchase houses, while banks borrow to ensure they have sufficient reserves to manage outflows of new deposits that are created when lending to households.

2. The upswing often ends with a collapse in house prices and a banking crisis.
3. In the downswing of a financial cycle, banks need to rebuild their capacity to absorb losses following the reversal of the boom phase (where they experienced losses on their loans). To do this, they set a higher interest rate spread above the policy rate and are less willing to make loans.
4. Similarly to banks, when a housing boom reverses, borrowing households need to reduce their levels of indebtedness. Some need to recover from negative equity or 'being under-water' due to the collapse of house prices. They do this by reducing consumption.
5. Both aspects of the aftermath of the downturn in the financial cycle imply a deeper recession than is the case in the absence of these balance sheet effects.
6. Public sector debt increases strongly when there is a financial crisis because of the depth and length of the recession that follows and because of government support for failing banks.

Two mechanisms play an important role in the dynamics of a financial cycle: asset price bubbles and financial accelerators. The latter are based on the effect of asset price changes on the balance sheets of households and banks.

Stylized facts about the financial cycle

In this subsection, we present some stylized facts about the financial cycle and contrast them with the characteristics of the more familiar business cycle. We use the research of economists at the Bank for International Settlements (BIS) in Basel led by Claudio Borio in our presentation of the financial cycle. This group was one of the few that had done systematic research on the interaction of macroeconomic policy and financial instability before the global financial crisis, and the BIS economists have been credited with having warned about the dangers of the build-up of leverage (i.e. the shrinkage of capital buffers) in the financial sector ahead of the crisis.[10]

The BIS financial cycle measure reflects fluctuations in three financial variables; private credit, the private credit-to-GDP ratio and residential property prices. The choice of these variables was informed by the historical evidence on financial fluctuations described above and by their behaviour. These variables follow very similar patterns over time and their peaks are often associated with banking crises. By contrast, stock market prices are not included in the financial cycle measure as they exhibit

[10] For an example of the BIS research on financial instability (carried out prior to the crisis), see Borio and White (2004). The two papers we use as the basis for our discussion of the financial cycle are Borio (2014) and Drehmann et al. (2012).

much more short-term volatility than the chosen variables, and their peaks are less frequently associated with banking crises.

The fluctuations in the financial cycle variables are typically longer than the business cycle fluctuations in output. The gap between business cycle peaks is typically five to six years in advanced countries, whereas financial cycles in the major advanced economies can be more than twice or even three times as long.[11]

Three stylized facts about the financial cycle are:

1. Banks play a key role in the cycle through both their lending and their borrowing behaviour (i.e. both the asset and the liability sides of their balance sheets). And the behaviour and role of investment banks is very different from that of retail banks.
2. The housing sector is procyclical and the purchase of new and second-hand housing is often financed by borrowing from banks.
3. The inter-relationship between banks, household debt and housing is central to the financial cycle, and the peak of the financial cycle is often followed by a banking crisis.

Figure 8.3 shows the business and financial cycles for the United States from the 1970s to the end of 2017. The curve labelled financial cycle reflects the behaviour of bank credit and house prices. The more prolonged upswings and downswings of the financial cycle as compared with those of the business cycle are evident in the chart. Note that, although the financial cycles are not derived from data on banking crises, the peaks of the financial cycle in the US coincide almost exactly with the onset of the last two banking crises.

The underlying series for the private credit (as a percentage of GDP) and real house prices are shown in Figure 8.4. The cyclical components of these variables (and of private credit volume) form the financial cycle shown in Figure 8.3. The cyclical

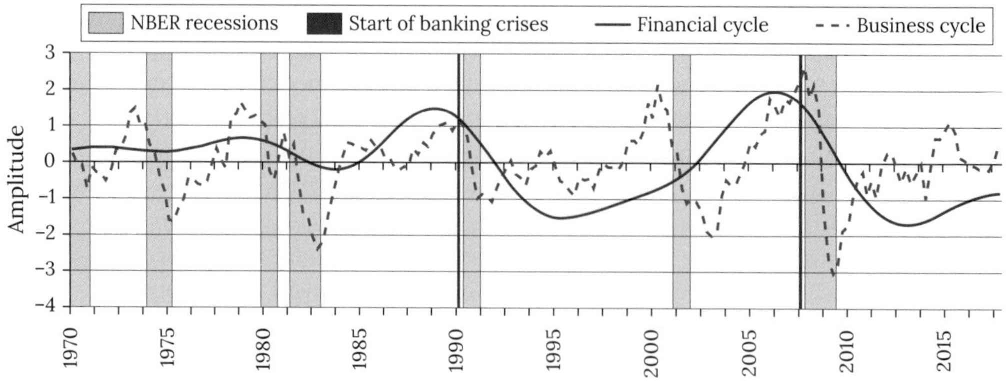

Figure 8.3 The financial and business cycles in the United States: 1970 Q1–2017 Q4.

Source: Drehmann, Borio and Tsatsaronis (2012); updated data provided by the authors.

[11] See Borio (2014).

components are estimated relative to trend (i.e. they are the fluctuations in the series around the long-run trend). The trend in both variables was upward sloping until the financial crisis of the late-2000s.[12]

Reinhart and Rogoff (2009a) provide further evidence for choosing these indicators for measuring financial fluctuations. They use the so-called 'signals approach' to test the relative importance of different indicators as early warning signs for banking crises. They find that real house price growth is close to the top of the list of reliable indicators, whereas real stock price growth is relatively less successful at predicting future banking crises. This is because stock price growth produces more false alarms (i.e. peaks of stock price cycles are less often associated with crises).

The data in Figure 8.4 shows that US house prices rose steadily from the early 1970s to the late 1990s, boomed in the early to mid-2000s, and then fell dramatically between 2006 and 2011. They rose steadily from 2011 to the end of 2021. House prices in 2006 Q1 were almost 2.5 times their 1970 value. Figure 8.4 also shows that (with the exception of a brief fall in the early 1990s) US households and firms continually increased their borrowing in the four decades preceding the financial crisis of the late 2000s. The 2006 peak of the housing and credit cycles were closely associated with both the onset of a banking crisis and a prolonged recession in the late 2000s.

Looking at business cycles and financial cycles together in Figure 8.3 suggests that if policy makers are preoccupied with stabilizing the business cycle, they may overlook the fact that a financial cycle upswing can continue during a recession such as that of the early 2000s. Chapter 10 contains a more extensive discussion regarding the interaction of policies for financial and macroeconomic stability.

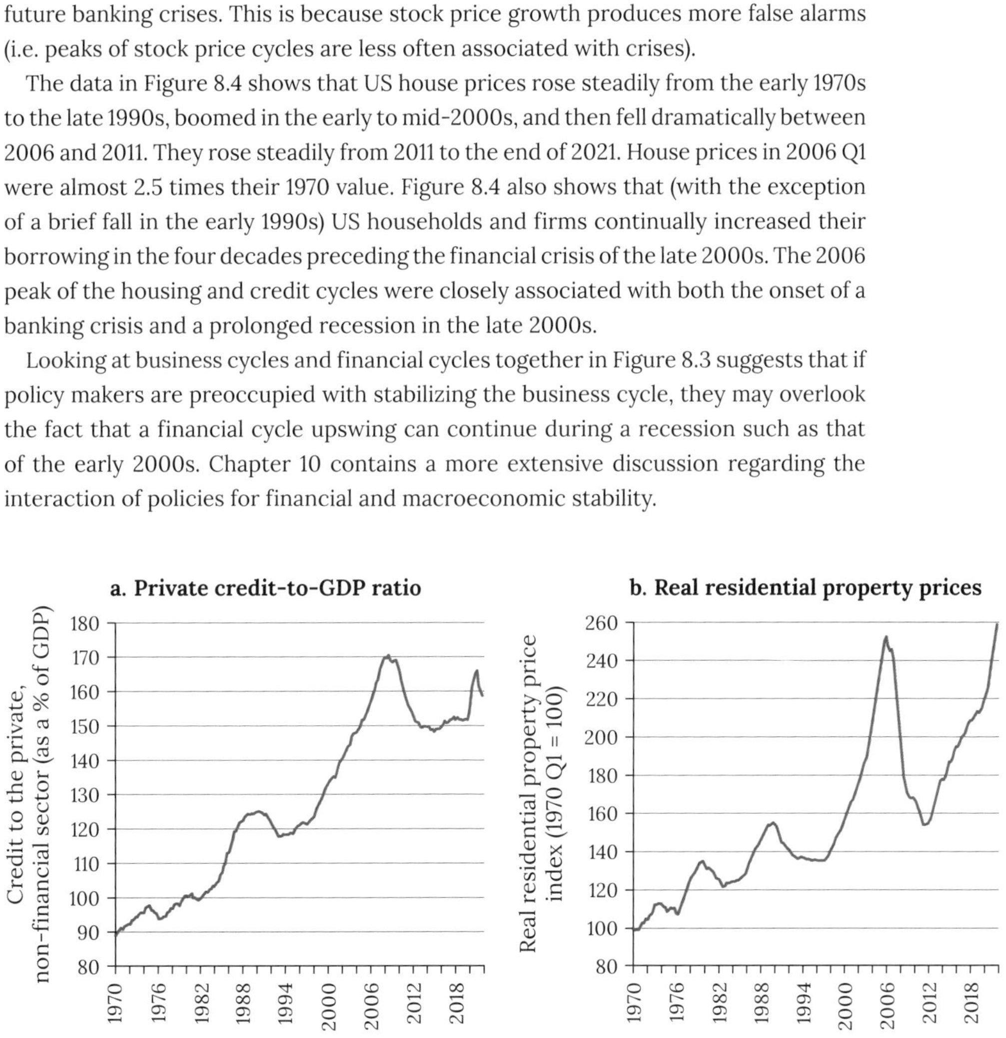

Figure 8.4 Private credit-to-GDP ratio and real residential property prices in the United States: 1970 Q1–2021 Q4.

Source: Bank of International Settlements (accessed July 2022).

[12] The details about how the cycles are extracted from the underlying data are provided in Drehmann et al. (2012).

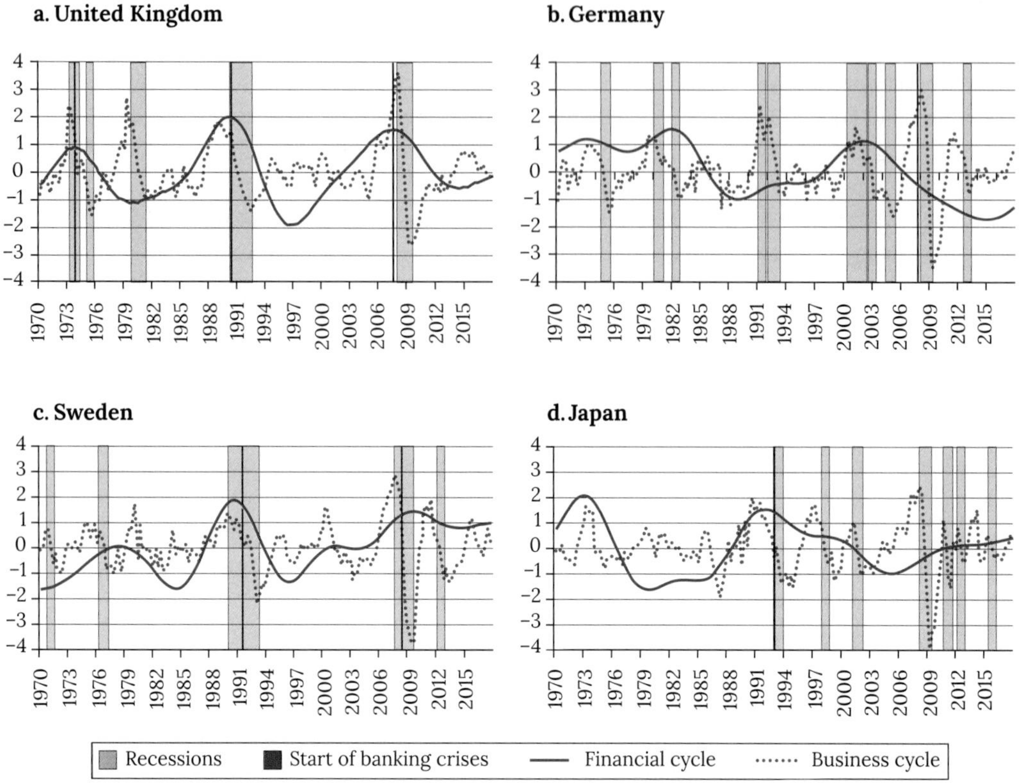

Figure 8.5 The financial and business cycles in selected advanced economies: 1970 Q1–2017 Q4.

Note: We have added recessions onto these graphs based on defining a recession as a period of two or more consecutive quarters of negative growth (i.e. contraction) in real GDP.

Source: Drehmann, Borio and Tsatsaronis (2012); OECD (data accessed July 2020).

Figure 8.5 shows the financial and business cycles for the UK, Germany, Sweden and Japan, which are constructed in the same way as for the US. The picture for the UK looks fairly similar to that of the US, with the upswing in the financial cycle prior to the crisis beginning in the mid-1990s and really taking off in the mid-2000s. However, the other three countries display much more variety. Note that the amplitude of financial cycles can be compared over time and across countries but there is no meaningful comparison between the amplitude of business cycles and financial cycles. However, the relative length of business cycles and financial cycles can be compared.

Both Japan and Sweden experienced large banking sector crashes in the late-80s to early-90s. The adverse effect of this on financial variables in Japan throughout the Great Moderation period is especially notable with a long downswing of the financial cycle.

Germany presents a different picture. The amplitude of its financial cycle is smaller than that of the other three countries and the 2008–09 financial crisis came during the downswing of their financial cycle. This reflects its different housing market, where home ownership rates are low, and where neither high loan-to-value mortgages nor home equity loans are available. In Germany it is not possible to re-mortgage your apartment or house based on its market value. The German case highlights the impact that the institutions a society adopts can have on the amplitude of financial cycles.

For the decade from the mid-1990s, Germany's growth was weak. This is reflected in Figure 8.5 by the frequency of recessions in Germany, which stands in sharp contrast to the UK in the same period, which was recession-free and where a financial cycle built up. Demand for and supply of credit to domestic households by German banks was muted. Germany's banking crisis in 2007 was imported from the US subprime crash through the *overseas* activities of its banks.

By looking at the historical data, and noting the variability of the financial cycle both over time and between different countries, it is clear that economic policy and particular innovations in the financial sector are important for understanding why a financial cycle takes hold. The focus of this chapter is on the mechanisms that led to housing and credit booms in a number of financially liberalized high-income economies in the 2000s (e.g. the UK and the US). These countries were at the core of the global financial crisis. We analyse the crisis in detail in Chapter 9 and discuss the important role played by banks headquartered in countries like Germany where a financial cycle upswing was absent.

8.3 **BASIC MECHANISMS**

We discuss two mechanisms that play an important role in the analysis of financial crises. The first is the asset price bubble and the second is the financial accelerator. An asset price bubble arises when, instead of the usual reduction in demand and fall in price following a positive price shock, a process of self-fulfilling beliefs triggers higher demand and a rising price. The financial accelerator is a specific—collateral-based—mechanism through which changes in asset prices (such as for houses or financial assets) affect the balance sheet of an agent, which in turn leads to a change in borrowing and spending. In this case, a positive price shock to the asset increases spending in the economy because it increases the household's collateral and ability to borrow. As a result of asset price bubbles and financial accelerator processes, the financial sector can amplify and propagate shocks, as illustrated in Figures 8.1 and 8.2.

A famous example of a pure bubble is the Dutch tulip bulb bubble of the 17th century. In the mid-1630s, tulip prices in the Dutch Republic began rising rapidly, which encouraged buyers to offer ever high prices—by early 1637, tulip prices were up to twenty times higher than three months earlier. The prices crashed suddenly in February 1637, and the market for tulips collapsed.[13] Meanwhile, both processes were at play when the house price bubble in Sweden in 1990 was amplified and propagated through the economy by financial accelerator effects as households borrowed more against the rising value of their housing.

---

[13] Alternative, rational, explanations have also been suggested, such as the creation of an options contract market for tulips, see 'Was Tulipmania irrational?', *The Economist*, 4 October 2013. www.economist.com/free-exchange/2013/10/04/was-tulipmania-irrational

8.3.1 Asset price bubbles and self-fulfilling beliefs

Figure 8.6 shows three cases, each of which illustrate price dynamic processes in different kinds of markets. In the diagrams in the upper panels, the price of the good at time t is on the horizontal axis and the price at time t + 1 is on the vertical axis. There is a 45 degree line, which shows a situation of price stability, i.e. where $P_t = P_{t+1}$. The diagrams in the lower panels show the associated supply and demand diagrams for the stable and unstable equilibrium cases.

The market on the left-hand side is the market for a non-durable good, such as fish. The line labelled PDE, which stands for price dynamic equation, shows the relationship between the price this period and next period, and is flatter than the 45 degree line. When there is a positive shock to the price in time t, the PDE shows that the price in the next period begins to fall back to the initial equilibrium. In more detail, once the shock has occurred, the price rises to P_1 as shown in the lower panel, which indicates that there is excess supply. This puts downward pressure on the price next period. The PDE line in the upper panel shows that next period's price will be lower at P_2.

This is just what we would expect in an ordinary market. We show the supply and demand diagram for this case in the lower left-hand panel. When the price rises,

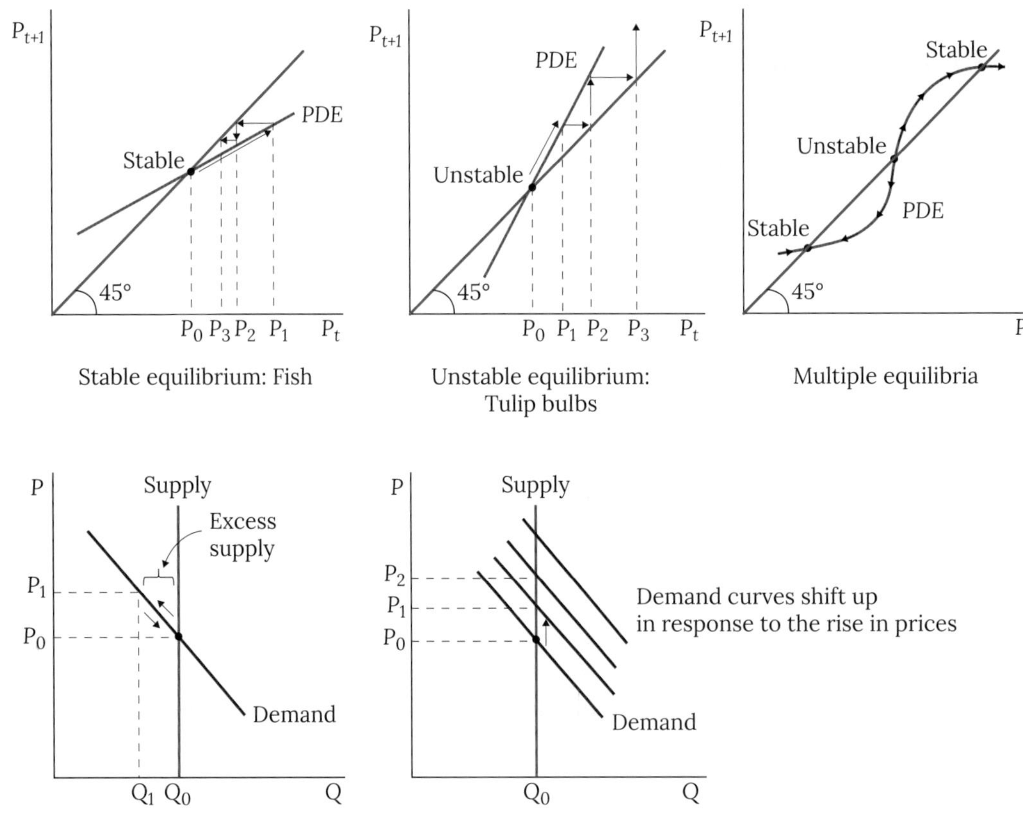

Figure 8.6 Price dynamic processes in different kinds of markets. Visit www.oup.com/he/carlin-soskice to explore price dynamic processes with Animated Analytical Diagram 8.6.

demand falls along the demand curve, to Q1, creating excess supply which depresses the price. Adjustment takes place until demand and supply are once again equal at the initial price (i.e. P_0).

In the second diagram, the PDE line is steeper than the 45 degree line. This reflects the behaviour shown by the lower panel, where the demand curve shifts up in response to the positive price shock. Why does this happen? It can only happen in the market for a durable good or asset that can be stored and we will take the example of the market for tulip bulbs. If the conviction takes hold that the price of tulip bulbs will increase further, then this is represented by the demand curve shifting up. The reason for the upward shift is that agents believe the price of tulip bulbs will go up further. If this happens, then holding more bulbs is a good strategy: there will be a capital gain from holding them because they can be sold later at a higher price than the price paid to acquire them. In the diagram, the initial price rise to P_1 results in an upward shift in the demand curve. The PDE line shows that the following period there will be a higher price, P_2, which in turn leads the demand curve to shift upward again. The price rises get larger and larger, as shown by the widening gap between the PDE line and the 45 degree line.

In a self-fulfilling bubble, the process through which the initial price shock is amplified can continue indefinitely—at least until something happens to change the expectation of continuously rising prices (and of a growing deviation of the price from its initial 'fundamental' value).[14]

The third diagram combines the features of the other two to produce an S-shaped PDE curve. In this case, there are three intersections with the 45 degree line: the one in the middle resembles the unstable (tulip bulb) case; the other two resemble the stable (fish) case. In a market with an S-shaped PDE curve, the economy will be pulled to the stable high or low price equilibrium, and can remain there indefinitely. Since the S-shaped PDE curve has an unstable equilibrium, reflecting a positive feedback process amplifying price changes, it refers to a market with durable goods. Note that although we have drawn the PDE curves in the two left-hand panels as linear, this is just a simplification. What matters is the slope relative to the 45 degree line.

In order to assess the role that expectations play in such markets, we can write the PDE process as $P_{t+1} = f(P_t; A_t)$, where A_t is a variable that shifts the curve. One simple way of thinking about this is for A_t to represent the proportion of the population with a given expectation about next period's price, and the proportion responds to what has happened to the price in the previous period. We show this case in Figure 8.7, where the *position* of the S-shaped curve is pinned down by beliefs and those beliefs can change.

---

[14] For a deeper analysis of bubbles, see the paper by Blanchard and Watson (1982). They have a nice solution to the problem of the tulip case: a bubble requires an increasing price sequence and at some point, this is going to be unsustainable. Their idea is that the bubble can burst at any date with some probability, which means everyone knows it is going to burst eventually, but still find it optimal to go along with the burgeoning bubble.

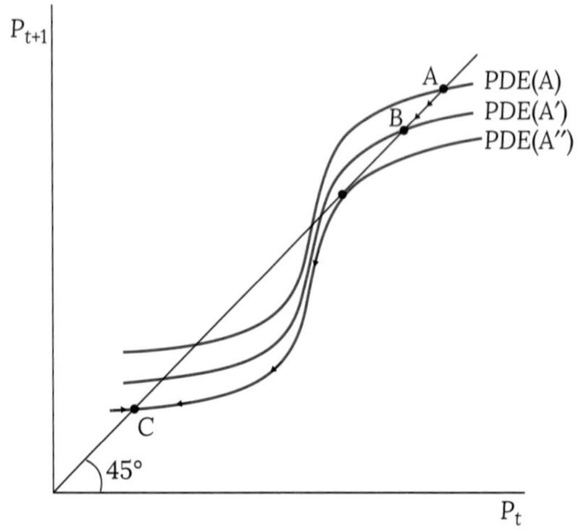

Figure 8.7 The impact of changes in price expectations in a market such as housing with an S-shaped PDE curve. Visit www.oup.com/he/carlin-soskice to explore the S-shaped PDE curve with Animated Analytical Diagram 8.7.

Let us assume the housing market is at the high price equilibrium at point A, which also signifies the initial fraction with those price beliefs. A shock occurs that leads a small fraction of agents to expect a lower price next period (i.e. in the S-shaped function, A falls to A′). The S-shaped PDE curve shifts downward to PDE(A′); those whose expectations have changed sell houses, and the price falls. The new equilibrium is at B. In the following period, the notion of falling house prices is adopted by more people, which shifts the PDE down. As more and more people come to believe the price will fall, the PDE curve will continue to shift down. Eventually, a tipping point is reached at which the PDE has shifted down to PDE(A″), such that it is tangent to the 45 degree line. This is a tipping point because in the following period, the middle equilibrium has disappeared while the top equilibrium is now unstable, and the economy is pulled toward the low price equilibrium at C.

By looking at these three cases, we can see how a process of self-fulfilling price expectations can operate in the market for a durable good. There is no point buying more fish in the hope of making a capital gain on them because the fish will rot. Hence, a process of self-fulfilling expectations cannot get under way in the fish market. In the market for tulip bulbs in the seventeenth century, for office space in Tokyo in the late 1980s or for Bitcoin, however, there is a rationale for paying a higher price in order to get hold of more of the asset so as to benefit from the expected capital gain.

In the left-hand diagram of Figure 8.6 there is a stable equilibrium price, in the middle diagram, there is no stable equilibrium price and in the right-hand one, there are two stable and one unstable equilibria.[15] The diagram with multiple equilibria

[15] How do we tell if an equilibrium is stable or unstable? Imagine that beginning from the equilibrium, there is a small price rise or a small price fall. The PDE can be used to find next period's price given this new price, as was done in Figure 8.6. If next period's price represents a

BOX 8.1 The big ten financial bubbles

As we have seen, financial crises are not a new phenomenon. Historically, crises have frequently, but not always, been preceded by asset price bubbles. Kindleberger and Aliber (2011, p. 11) set out the ten most significant financial bubbles of the last 400 years. Notice that asset price bubbles have occurred across a wide variety of countries and time periods. The bubbles of the last 100 years have predominantly been focused on real estate, stocks and foreign investment.

1636: The Dutch Tulip Bulb Bubble

1720: The South Sea Bubble

1720: The Mississippi Bubble

1927–29: The late 1920s stock price bubble

1970s: The surge in loans to Mexico and other developing economies

1985–89: The bubble in real estate and stocks in Japan

1985–89: The bubble in real estate and stocks in Finland, Norway and Sweden

1990s: The bubble in real estate and stocks in Thailand, Malaysia, Indonesia and several other Asian countries between 1992 and 1997; and the surge in foreign investment in Mexico 1990–99

1995–2000: The bubble in over-the-counter stocks in the United States

2002–07: The bubble in real estate in the United States, Britain, Spain, Ireland and Iceland; and the debt of the government of Greece

captures the possible dynamics of a housing or other asset market where there are repeated booms and busts. The economy will tend to move through a process of self-fulfilling price expectations toward either an upper or a lower equilibrium: a housing boom or a housing bust.

8.3.2 The financial accelerator and collateral

A central feature of household behaviour in the macroeconomic model we are studying in this book arises from the credit constraints they face. For credit-constrained households, an increase in their wealth provides them with more collateral and relaxes the constraint by allowing them to borrow more. We assume that home equity loans are available, such that a household can use the equity in their house as collateral to obtain a loan.[16]

By definition, a credit-constrained household will spend more when the credit constraint is relaxed. This provides a connection between a change in asset price, the

movement back towards the original equilibrium, the equilibrium is stable; if it represents a further movement away from the equilibrium, the equilibrium is unstable.

[16] Home equity loans were available in the UK and the US prior to the 2008–09 crisis. They were not available in France, Germany or Italy.

extent of credit constraints and household spending, that is, between a change in asset price and the IS curve.

As illustrated in Figure 8.1, the financial accelerator is a positive feedback process through which a change in the price of an asset affects the macroeconomy.[17] The asset could be a financial asset such as company stocks (shares) or bonds. We illustrate the mechanics of the financial accelerator using the case of housing because this is where it mainly operates for the household sector.[18] Its operation can be summarized in the following five steps:

1. The credit constraints facing a household depend on the value of the collateral it has. The value of its collateral is its net worth, which is the difference between the value of the house and the size of the mortgage. It is important to highlight that the financial accelerator works because it is the *market* price of the house that establishes its value. When the household's net worth increases, it is able to borrow more. This is referred to as a relaxation of the credit constraints it faces.
2. A positive shock to house prices relaxes credit constraints.
3. Households borrow more. This step rests on the assumption that there is a set of borrower households who have borrowed up to the limit set by the credit constraints. Hence, when the constraint is relaxed by a rise in the value of their housing collateral, they will borrow more.
4. Some of this borrowing is used for consumption and some is used to buy more housing, both existing houses and newly constructed ones. This has a direct effect in shifting the IS curve.
5. The increased demand for housing pushes the price up further and the financial accelerator process begins again at step 2.

The financial accelerator is a positive feedback process because, on the basis of an initial exogenous rise in the price of the asset (in this case, the house), a key constraint limiting the household's desired spending—including on housing—is relaxed, thus pushing the asset's price up further. This has two important effects. First, it *propagates* any positive shock to prices by the positive feedback process. Second, it *amplifies* the business cycle because it stimulates spending by previously credit-constrained people. This shifts the IS curve to the right. The shift will be reinforced by the increase in construction (e.g. new house building) that accompanies the rise in demand for housing (e.g. US, Ireland and Spain in the 2000s).

---

[17] See Bernanke et al. (1999) for a detailed discussion of the financial accelerator. Alternatively, for a high level discussion see Ben Bernanke's speech on June 15th 2007, entitled *The Financial Accelerator and the Credit Channel*. The speech is available on the Federal Reserve website.

[18] For a comprehensive survey of the evidence on what drives house price cycles around the world and on the mechanisms that underlie them (along the lines of the models set out in this chapter), see Duca et al. (2020). Cross-country institutional differences are highlighted, echoing the findings reported in Aron et al. (2012) that the housing collateral channel on consumption (i.e. the financial accelerator) operates in the UK and US household sectors but is absent in Japan.

We can highlight the central role of credit constraints in this process by comparing it to the special case where there are no credit-constrained households. In this case, an exogenous rise in house prices is simply a temporary shock to permanent income. There will be hardly any effect on aggregate demand and there will be no positive feedback process driving house prices up further.

The financial accelerator does not have to rest on bubble behaviour. It is driven by the combination of credit constraints and collateral effects. In the financial accelerator, the demand for the asset is shifted by a change in wealth caused by the change in the asset's price. A rise in price relaxes the credit constraint and drives demand higher because of increased wealth. By contrast, in the case of the bubble based on self-fulfilling expectations, it is the *expectation* of a capital gain (i.e. an expected increase in the price of the asset) that leads the demand curve for housing to shift.

Although these are distinct mechanisms, they can interact with each other. For example, the bursting of a bubble can be the source of a price shock, which will lead the financial accelerator to amplify and propagate the shock further through the economy. The example of a bubble bursting highlights that the financial accelerator operates in both the upswing and downswing stages of the financial cycle.

8.4 HOUSE PRICE CYCLES AND THE 3-EQUATION MODEL

In this section, we draw together the insights from the two mechanisms (asset price bubble and financial accelerator) to describe a positive feedback process for housing, which can drive a financial cycle. We re-introduce the 3-equation model to show the relationship between the house-price driven financial cycle, the business cycle and the inflation-targeting central bank. The specific features of the housing positive feedback process as they played out in the run-up to the global financial crisis are set out in Chapter 9.

The large volume of evidence presented in Reinhart and Rogoff (2009a) suggests that rising house prices (in real terms) and the expansion of private credit go together in the upswing phase of a financial cycle. Reinhart and Rogoff show that house price booms have typically preceded systemic banking crises in both emerging and advanced economies in the post-WWII period. The literature also provides strong evidence that pre-crisis asset price booms are associated with substantial expansions in credit (both domestic and external).[19]

8.4.1 Credit-constrained households, housing collateral, and house price bubbles

In Step 3 above, credit-constrained households are up against their borrowing constraint. The house-price feedback can be set in motion by, for example, an exogenous rise in the price of housing, or by a change in regulation (or in self-imposed guidelines)

[19] See Mendoza and Terrones (2008), Jordà, Schularick, and Taylor (2013) and Mian and Sufi (2018).

of banks related to the loan-to-value ratio they use when making mortgage decisions or collateral rules. The latter is an example of the role of the expansion of credit supply, which has been identified as an important initiating factor in the financial cycle.

A rise in the loan-to-value (LTV) ratio banks are allowed to use in making mortgages leads to a rise in the demand for mortgages. For an individual borrowing to buy a house, the LTV ratio is calculated as the value of the loan received divided by the value of the property purchased. For example, if a borrower took out a loan of $160,000 to buy a house worth $200,000, then the LTV ratio would be 80%. In the US, mortgages with LTV ratios in excess of 100% became widely available in the mid-2000s.[20] This meant that borrowers could receive a loan larger than the value of the property they were buying without providing any down-payment. These looser lending standards made it possible for lower income groups to purchase residential property and consequently boosted mortgage demand.

Bank collateral rules can also influence home equity loan demand. They specify how a change in the market value of a house affects the ability of a household to borrow. If these rules for home equity loans are loosened, it becomes easier for households to borrow against their housing assets. As a result, credit-constrained households increase their borrowing for both consumption and housing.

An example of an exogenous shock unrelated to financial policy that could set in motion the house-price feedback process is population growth. If the population rises in a particular area, assuming that this rise is unrelated to house prices, this will increase the demand for housing which in turn will increase prices. As with the change in regulation, this could then trigger the start of a financial cycle.

Identifying a housing bubble

When the price of houses goes up, a bubble may develop as explained in the previous section. The rise in demand for mortgages pushes up house prices ($\Delta P_H > 0$), which may in turn trigger the expectation that house prices will rise further ($\Delta P_H^E > 0$). When a bubble is formed, the economy is characterized by either a price dynamic equation (PDE) line with a slope of more than 45 degrees (Figure 8.6 central panel), or by the upper part of an S-shaped PDE curve (Figure 8.6 rightmost panel).

However, rising house prices do not necessarily reflect a bubble. Instead, they could reflect changes to the fundamental determinants of price (i.e. supply and demand). We illustrate the difficulty facing policy makers in correctly identifying bubbles by looking at two cases, as shown in Figure 8.8. In the first (shown in the left-hand panel), the supply curve for housing, although inelastic in the short run, is perfectly elastic in the long run; in the second (shown in the right-hand panel), supply is inelastic in the long run as well.

Figure 8.8a could describe a situation in a city surrounded by plenty of space for expansion and where there are no planning impediments to further house building. As an example, imagine that population growth has increased demand, shifting the

[20] See IMF (2011). For comprehensive evidence on the role of housing in the financial accelerator around the world, see Duca et al. (2020).

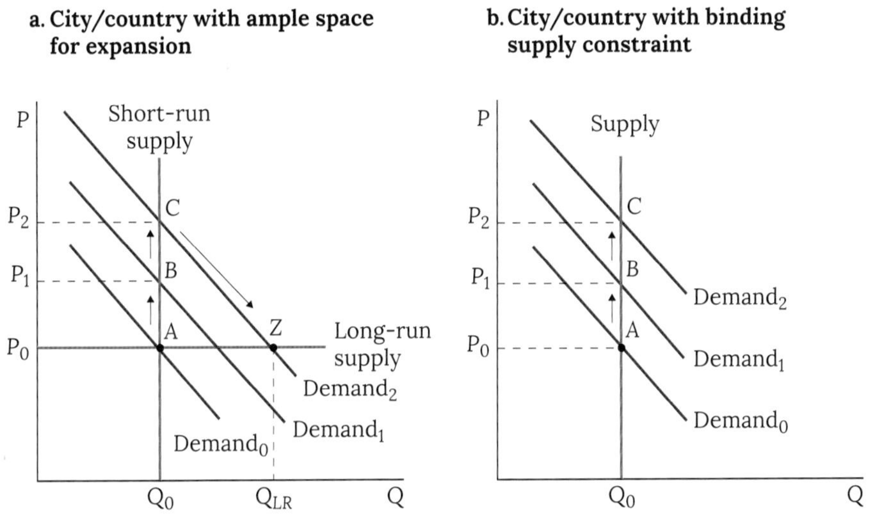

Figure 8.8 The impact of long-run supply constraints on the formation of house price bubbles.

demand curve up to Demand_1. Due to supply being perfectly inelastic in the short run, as new houses cannot be built instantaneously, this pushes prices up to P_1. Despite the fact that prices will eventually return to P_0 when supply increases, this does not represent a bubble, which requires expectations of rising prices. People may expect prices to fall in the long run, but still be prepared to pay a higher price in the short run to secure a house today rather than wait.

However, if one observed persistently rising house prices where these fundamentals were in place, this might be an indication that a bubble is under way. For instance, the rise in prices to P_1 might generate expectations that prices will continue to rise in the short run. The expectation of capital gains from housing would then push the demand curve up to Demand_2, which in turn pushes prices to P_2. This extrapolative expectations process might continue until supply eventually catches up, causing prices to crash back down to P_0. This combination of circumstances—elastic long-run supply and persistently rising house prices—characterized some US cities like Phoenix, Arizona, in the run-up to the financial crisis.

On the other hand, persistently rising house prices would also be consistent with changing fundamentals—the rise in demand to Demand_2 could have been the result of further population pressures, and house buyers could have been purchasing despite knowing that prices will fall. To be able to distinguish between a bubble and a change in fundamentals, a policy maker would need to look at economic data including population growth, the rate of house price changes, and expectations of future prices among house buyers.

By contrast, take a situation where the long-run supply curve is vertical, as shown in Figure 8.8b. This could arise because of binding constraints on building more housing due to a combination of physical and planning reasons. In this case, the initial increase in housing demand from population growth causes prices to shift upwards (from P_0 to P_1), exactly as in the first example, but as there is no supply response, there is no pressure for prices to fall in the long run.

As with panel a, if prices are observed continuing to rise, to P_2, it remains ambiguous whether this is a bubble or not. On the one hand, the original rise in prices to P_1 may have triggered expectations of further price rises, which in turn explains the subsequent rise in demand. The knowledge that supply is inelastic may make it more likely that people will adopt these expectations. On the other hand, the increased demand could have been triggered by fundamentals. This happened in the London property market in 2010, which saw wealthy Eurozone citizens looking for a safe place to put their money during the crisis.[21] In this case, the price of housing rises without a bubble.

We can thus see that in both the elastic long-run supply case, and the inelastic long-run supply case, the policy maker may struggle to identify a bubble. Persistently rising house prices could be triggered by either a bubble, or by changing fundamentals.

One key difference is that when a housing bubble in a country with long-run elastic supply bursts, we would predict there to be lots of empty houses because of the expansion in supply triggered by the high and rising prices. In the aftermath of a crash, banks are reluctant to supply mortgages while households may not be in a position to afford them, leaving many houses unpurchased. This was the case in the US, Ireland, and Spain—in 2014, seven years after the crisis, there were still 3.4 million unoccupied homes in Spain (see Neate, R. 'Scandal of Europe's 11m Empty Homes'. Article published in *The Guardian*, 23 February 2014. www.theguardian.com/society/2014/feb/23/europe - 11m-empty - properties - enough-house-homeless - continent - twice). The problem of over supply is often exacerbated by the fact that new houses take time to build. New supply may continue to come on to the market even after house prices have started to fall.

By contrast, when house prices fell in the UK, which could be modelled as a country with long-run inelastic supply, there were not lots of empty houses—because of planning constraints, supply had responded weakly to rising demand.

8.4.2 The 3-equation model and house price cycles

If home equity loans are available, households enjoying a relaxation of their credit constraints due to the higher market value of their house borrow more in order to spend more on housing, and on consumption of goods and services. This can lead to the construction of new houses, which boosts aggregate demand. In the 3-equation model these effects produce a rightward shift of the IS curve and, holding everything else constant, this will push up inflation and lead to a tightening of monetary policy in the usual way by the central bank. Note, however, that the link to the central

[21] Empirical evidence for these effects in the London housing market is provided by Badarinza and Ramadorai (see Badarinza, C. and Ramadorai, T. (2018), 'Home away from home? Foreign demand and London house prices', *Journal of Financial Economics*, **130**(3), 532–555. https://doi.org/10.1016/j.jfineco.2018.07.010).

bank is *only* via the effect of the increased loans on aggregate demand and the forecast effect on CPI inflation: there is no direct link from the behaviour of house prices per se.[22]

Suppose the central bank successfully shifts the economy on to the *MR* curve and CPI inflation begins to fall. The response of the central bank to the forecast rise in inflation will not necessarily prevent the continuation of the upswing of the financial cycle. This is because there is no mechanism in the model that directly links the stabilizing action of the central bank to the *sources* of the house price feedback process. Higher interest rates would be expected to dampen demand for mortgages, but an interest rate increase designed to get CPI inflation back to target will not necessarily be sufficient to cut off an asset price bubble fuelled by the financial accelerator mechanism. This is illustrated by the continuous upswing in US house prices between the 1970s and the mid-2000s through several business cycles shown in Figure 8.4.

Figure 8.9 summarizes the housing-related financial cycle and its interaction with the business cycle. The top section of the diagram shows how changes in regulation or collateral rules in the retail banking system can lead to a house price boom. A simple formal model of the housing positive feedback process is presented in Appendix 6.8.1. In the appendix model, a fall in the perceived riskiness of housing loans triggers the increase in credit supply.

The bottom section shows the link between the housing market and the 3-equation model. The increased loans for consumption and for investment in new housing increase aggregate demand, which in turn drives up employment and creates inflationary pressure. In the normal way, the central bank policy maker reacts by tightening monetary policy to bring forecast inflation back to target. The diagram highlights the fact that house price increases do not affect either aggregate demand or inflation directly (i.e. there is no direct link between house prices and the 3-equation model).

8.4.3 A plain vanilla financial crisis

We can summarize how a house-price-based boom can turn into a financial crisis as follows:

1. When a property bubble bursts and house prices fall, the net worth of households falls. The financial accelerator reverses, as this fall in collateral reduces borrowing, which in turn causes house prices to fall further, and reduce net worth even more.
2. Some households are also left unable to service their mortgage; for instance, if they lose their job.

---

[22] The measures of inflation targeted by central banks do not typically include house prices directly, but do account for changes in the price of rental accommodation or the imputed costs of owner-occupied accommodation. This includes only the consumption component of owner-occupied housing and ignores the volatile investment component. The elements of housing costs included do not influence the overall price indices that enter the inflation target to a high degree. To see this, plot the US Consumer Price Index against the US Consumer Price Index less Shelter (data available from the US Bureau of Labor Statistics website).

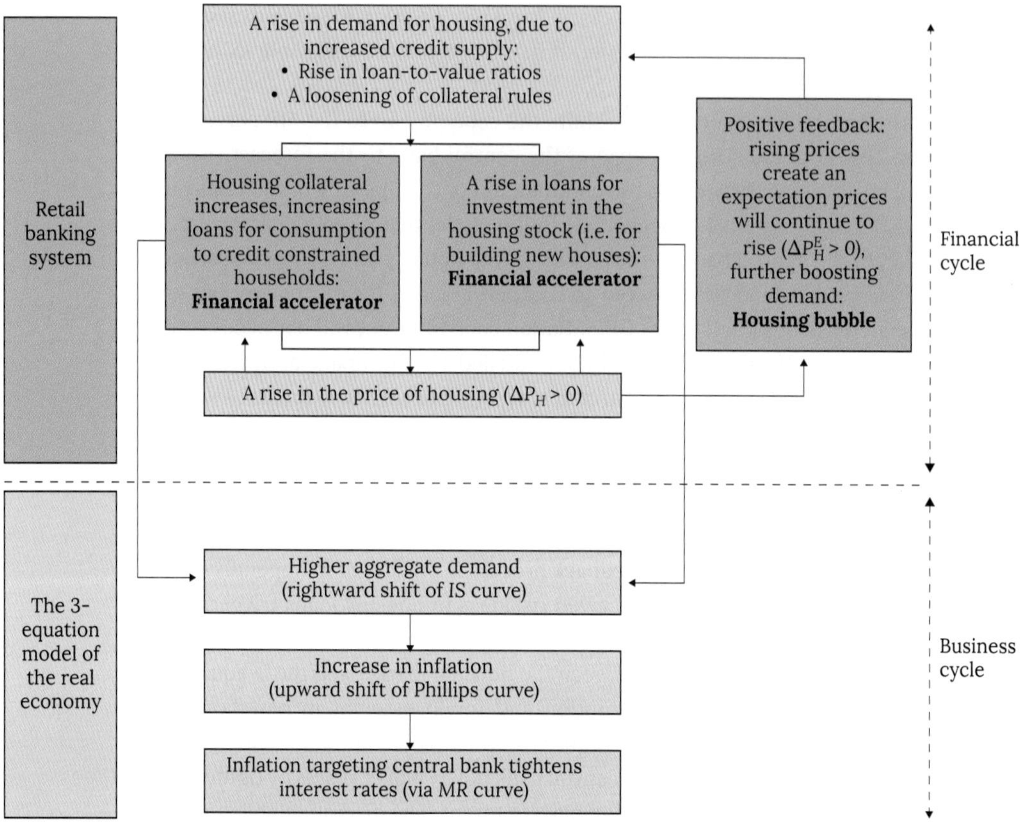

Figure 8.9 The 3-equation model of the macroeconomy and the house price cycle.

3. Houses of borrowers who default are repossessed by the bank (this is called foreclosure) and sold at a loss, i.e. at a price below the balance of the remaining mortgage, due to falling house prices.
4. The net worth of banks falls due to the losses they incur on mortgage loans.
5. If a bank is sufficiently exposed to falling property prices, it can become insolvent: the shrinkage of the value of its assets wipes out its capital buffer.

A plain vanilla crisis does not rely on the more sophisticated behaviour of banks involving novel financial instruments or the investment and shadow banking activities described in the bank-centred positive feedback process in Section 8.5.

Plain vanilla banking crises have occurred frequently in many countries over the years, and governments have been forced to intervene to save and restructure banks so as to prevent contagion and a broader breakdown of the supply of core banking services. Examples are the banking crisis known as the secondary banking crisis in the UK of 1973–77 and the US Savings and Loans crisis of the 1980s. But housing-banking booms and busts of this kind have not gone out of fashion—this is what happened in Ireland and Spain in the 2000s.

8.5 BANK LEVERAGE-CENTRED CYCLES AND THE RISK-CHANNEL

In Chapters 9 and 10, we explain the reasons why, from the perspective of society at large, banks will take on too much risk. In this section, we focus not on the level but on changes in the amount of risk taken on by banks. To do this, we introduce a second positive feedback process. This relates to *bank behaviour* and *financial assets*. It involves a different kind of behaviour by banks from the *retail* banks making housing and consumer loans that we modelled in Chapter 5 and discussed in Section 8.4. We introduce investment banks and as explained in Section 8.2.1, we focus entirely on their asset trading activities.

The model we present is highly stylized. We refer to the main actor as an investment bank. However, it is clear from the experience in the 2000s, discussed further in Chapter 9, that the sort of behaviour captured in the model in the 'investment bank' was observed, not only in some investment banks, but also in some retail banks, universal banks, and other bank-like institutions known as shadow banks. We assume that an investment bank buys mortgages from the retail bank and uses a large number of mortgages as the raw material from which to produce securitized assets. In Chapter 9, we explain the characteristics and origins of the two main types of securitized asset (MBS, mortgage-backed securities, and CDO, collateralized debt obligations) that were central to the upswing of the financial cycle in the 2000s.

Once mortgages are converted into securitized assets, which are the 'F assets' in the model, the forces of demand and supply for the financial asset come into play. These forces are quite separate from the ones in the real economy that underlie the initial demand for loans by households to fund the purchase of a house.

Unlike the plain vanilla banking crises described in Section 8.4, which have been observed since the 19th century, a financial cycle upswing and banking crisis in which a major role is played by investment banks and asset-backed securities is novel (although securitized assets themselves are not new). The details of how the upswing developed in the 2000s combining elements of a familiar plain-vanilla housing-centred cycle with the newer role played by banks borrowing to buy financial assets are described in Chapter 9. Here we concentrate on the mechanisms at work in a bank leverage-centred upswing and downswing.

The key stylized fact that lies behind the model of investment bank behaviour presented here is the dramatic increase in the leverage of banks (i.e. the ratio of their assets to their equity), and especially that of investment banks during the 2000s. Figure 8.10 highlights the increase in leverage in the UK banking system prior to the global financial crisis from 19 to 35 between 2000 and 2008.

8.5.1 Bank-leverage centred cycles and the 3-equation model

In this subsection, we provide an account parallel to the one for the housing feedback process—in this case, for the securitized asset feedback process, which can create a financial cycle as illustrated schematically in Figure 8.2.[23]

---

[23] The analysis in this section is based on a number of papers by Hyun Song Shin (see Shin 2009a, b, Shin 2010a, b, Adrian & Shin 2011) as well as on Geanakoplos (2010).

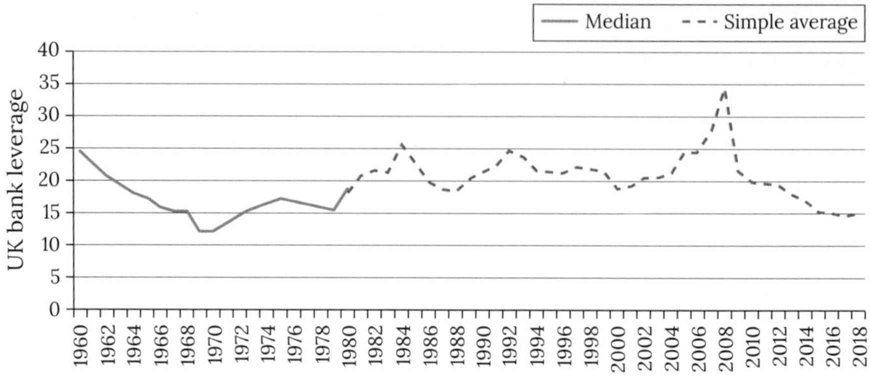

Figure 8.10 Regulated UK banks' leverage (assets/equity): 1960–2018.

Source: Bank of England Financial Stability Report, June 2012, and later data provided directly by the Bank of England.

The upswing of the financial cycle

Figure 8.11 illustrates how an upswing of a financial cycle based on bank behaviour and securitized assets can begin. The assets can also be referred to as risky securities. Three pathways are shown that can lead to a reduction in the perceived riskiness of the securitized assets. Lower risk in turn increases the demand for the securitized asset by both investment banks (IBs) and savers relative to the supply of assets, which for simplicity, we assume is fixed. This produces a rise in its price.

The perception on the part of an individual investor (such as an investment bank or a saver household) that securitized assets are less risky can arise from developments in the macroeconomy, in the housing market or in the financial sector itself as a result of financial innovation. These beliefs are influenced by the ratings given by the credit rating agencies. As we shall see in Chapter 9, each of these appears to have played a role in setting in motion the long upswing of the financial cycle prior to the global financial crisis.

Starting from the bottom of the diagram:

1. The more successful is macroeconomic stabilization policy such as inflation-targeting, and hence the less volatile is the macroeconomy, the lower is the risk of unemployment that would make the repayment of mortgage debt less likely. This makes the securitized asset based on mortgages safer.
2. The second source of lower risk is due to rising house prices: higher house prices reduce the credit risk to the bank since the market value of the asset (i.e. the bank's collateral) rises relative to the associated debt, which is fixed by the historical or purchase price of the house.
3. The third is financial innovation. Financial innovations include a procedure called tranching in which individual mortgages are divided into segments and combined into new financial assets with different levels of risk.[24] Another innovation is the

[24] The process of tranching is explained in more detail in Chapter 9.

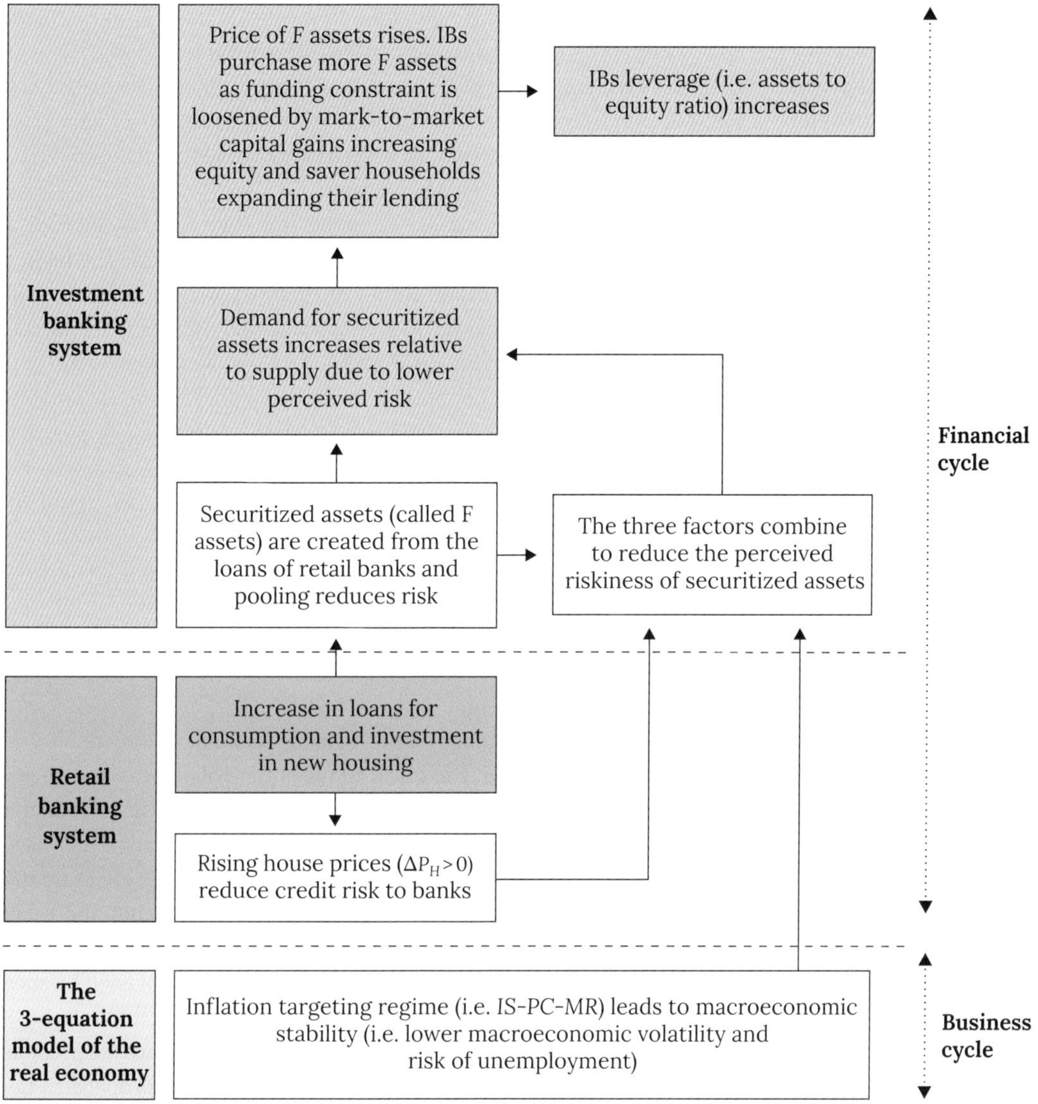

Figure 8.11 The 3-equation model and the bank-leverage based financial cycle

invention of credit default swaps, which are financial contracts that offer protection (i.e. insurance) against the default of securities issued by a borrower (e.g. mortgage based assets).

Each of these channels can lower the risk perceived by the investor. As perceived risk falls demand from all investor types rises and pushes up the price. Savers and investment banks differ in an important respect, however; savers are risk averse while investment banks are risk neutral. It may help to imagine the savers are pension funds although, in our simple model, they are the saver households.

When the price rises, risk-averse savers reduce their demand in response (higher prices mean that financial assets now represent a larger share of the savers' portfolios;

a risk-averse saver will re-balance their portfolio in favour of safer assets such as money), but risk-neutral investment banks do not. Investment banks will want to hold more of the risky asset as long as the expected return is positive, and the price rises therefore result in a significant transfer of financial assets to investment banks. The demand by investment banks to purchase the asset is only limited by their ability to borrow the money from savers (in the money market).

IBs are able to fund increased purchases of assets through both an increased willingess of savers to lend money, due to perceptions of lower risk, and the higher equity associated with mark-to-market valuation of their assets, which as we shall see in Section 8.5.2 relaxes their value at risk constraint. The higher demand can lead to a very large increase in the number of assets held by investment banks and in their leverage. As more assets are purchased, their price continues to rise, which will continue to increase IB equity, and enable them to purchase more assets.

The downswing of the financial cycle and financial crisis

Figure 8.12 shows how the upswing can go into reverse. In the diagram, the trigger is a reversal in the upward trend of house prices (see the middle panel). Risk goes up. This puts the securitized asset feedback process into reverse. The demand for securitized assets falls relative to the supply and the price of the financial asset falls. Given the extent of borrowing by the investment banks, a sufficient fall in the price of the F asset would cause the IB to become insolvent.

Through its effect on the functioning of the banking system, where retail and investment banks are interconnected, the crash reduces the willingness and ability of banks to make new loans. The effect on retail banks stems partially from the contagion effect as fears develop that problems in an investment bank could have ramifications elsewhere in the banking system, partially from the direct effect on the consolidated balance sheet of banks that have both investment banking and retail 'arms', and partially from a reduction of liquidity in the interbank markets.

Banks will sell assets and call in loans in order to strengthen their weakened balance sheets. These actions will dampen aggregate demand and employment through the IS relation as shown by the arrows feeding in to the bottom panel in Figure 8.12. Just as the financial accelerator process fuelled the upswing, it amplifies and propagates the downswing.

The financial cycle can turn down *without* a full-blown financial crisis and insolvent banks—but nevertheless with important effects on the real economy. The reversal of the securitized asset feedback process will impose capital losses on the asset side of the investment bank's balance sheet even if the capital buffer is not eroded entirely.

The lower demand for financial assets will reinforce the weakness in the financial and real estate sectors. Retail banks, IBs and borrower households will all seek to reduce their leverage, i.e. to reduce their debts. This will reduce aggregate demand. As we shall see in Section 8.6, saver households will have no reason to increase aggregate demand to offset this. We also use Section 8.6 to explore whether the policy maker can counteract the impact of the downturn in the financial cycle on the real economy.

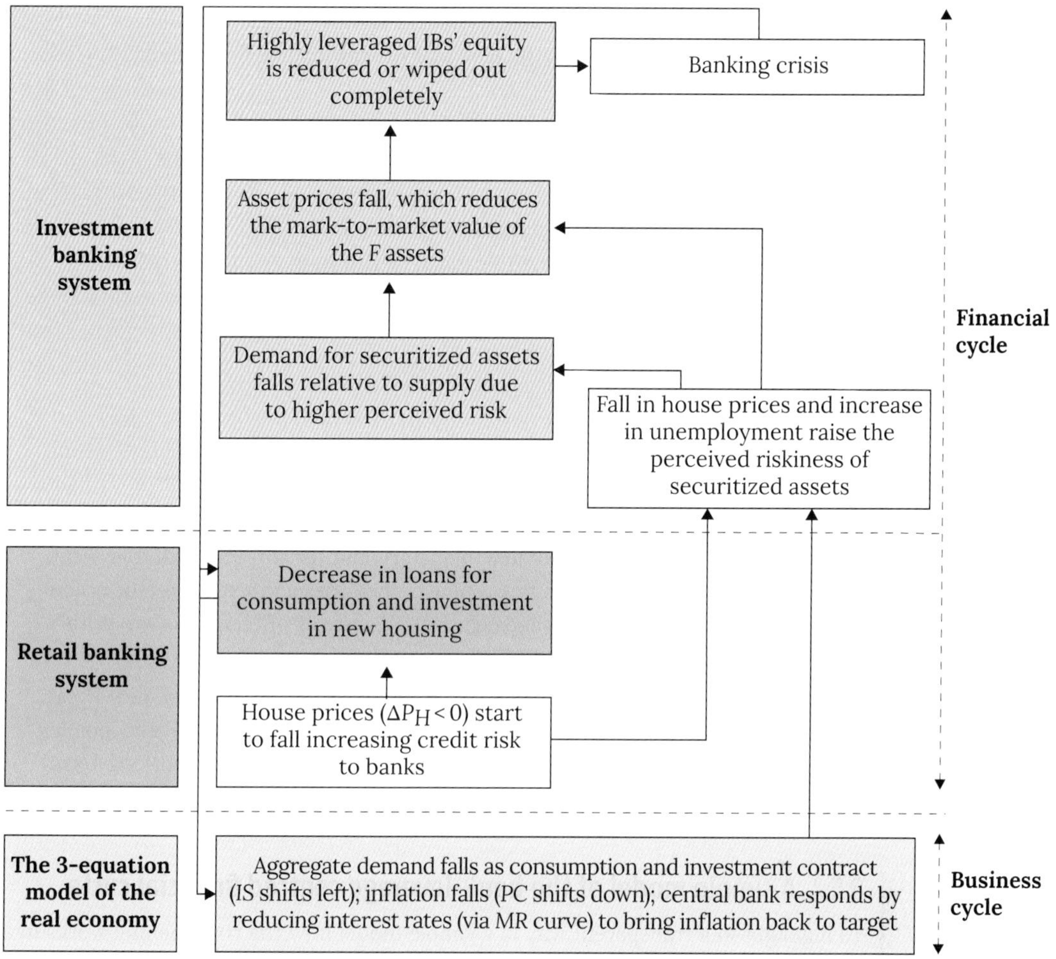

Figure 8.12 The 3-equation model and the financial cycle: a fall in house prices leads to increased perceptions of risk and a financial crisis.

The instability hypothesis

In his explanation of financial crises, the economist Hyman Minsky (1982) highlighted the way in which a benign period in the economy could sow the seeds for a subsequent crisis. When everyone believes risk has gone down, they behave in such a way that makes the system riskier. This logic has also been referred to as a paradox of credibility (Borio and Lowe 2002, Borio and White 2004).

A question that may spring to mind is whether it is satisfactory to model the economy in such a way that in the upswing of the financial cycle everyone is swept up in the belief that risk has fallen—permanently. Economists do not generally like models based on 'false beliefs'. Nevertheless, as Minsky argued, the model appears to provide a useful way of thinking about how a paradox of credibility can create the conditions for a financial crisis. For example, it appears to provide insight to the circumstances that led to the upswing of the financial cycle in the 2000s, which was followed by falling house prices and the bankruptcy of Lehman Brothers, leading to the banking crisis and downswing.

'False beliefs' seems to be a reasonable way of describing the mindset of decision makers—policy makers, managers of banks and individuals—about the lower macroeconomic risk in the 2000s due to the implementation of the inflation-targeting framework, the ever-upward trajectory of house prices and improvements in risk management by more sophisticated financial institutions.

As an example, British chancellor Gordon Brown famously claimed that the new macroeconomic framework would produce stability and put an end to 'boom and bust':

> Every time in recent decades when the British economy has started to grow, governments of both parties have taken short-term decisions which too often have created unsustainable consumer booms, let the economy get out of control and sacrificed monetary and fiscal prudence. And everyone here will remember how quickly and easily boom turned to bust in the early nineties.
>
> So Britain did need a wholly new monetary and fiscal framework that went beyond the crude Keynesian fine tuning of the fifties and sixties and the crude monetarism of the seventies and eighties and, instead, offered a modern British route to stability.[25]
>
> With Bank of England independence, tough decisions on inflation, new fiscal rules and hard public spending controls, we today in our country have economic stability not boom and bust, the lowest inflation in Europe, and long-term interest rates—essential for businesses planning to borrow and invest—lower than for thirty five years.[26]

8.5.2 A simple model of the bank-leverage centred financial cycle

To highlight in a transparent way in a simple model how the risk-channel works in a bank-leverage centred cycle, we make a number of additional assumptions.

Assumptions

We assume that the 'upswing' can be divided into exactly two periods, followed by one period of 'downswing':

1. The first 'upswing' phase begins with the widespread belief that risk has fallen significantly—we assume throughout that the riskiness of assets is a common belief, known to everyone. This pushes up demand for the financial asset, which in turn increases the price. Risk-averse savers will re-balance their portfolios, while risk-neutral investment banks will continue to purchase the asset (we will assume that expected return remains positive). We assume that investment banks are not

---

[25] Excerpt taken from a speech by (then British chancellor) Gordon Brown at the Lord Mayor's Dinner for Bankers and Merchants of the City of London, Mansion House, City of London, June 20th 2001.

[26] Excerpt taken from a speech by (then British chancellor) Gordon Brown at the TGWU 'Manufacturing Matters' conference, March 28th 2002.

deposit-taking so they cannot fund asset purchases through deposits but only with new equity or borrowing. Savers are prepared to lend as long as they perceive their loans to the investment banks as risk free; and that requires that investment bank equity is big enough to cover the worst case scenario. Triggered by the common perception that risk has fallen, the leverage of the investment banks can increase substantially.

2. In the second 'upswing' phase, the rise in the price of the financial asset leads to a capital gain for the investment banks on their holdings of securities. Using mark-to-market valuation, this means that the investment banks have more equity available to cover the worst case risk scenario, so savers are now prepared to lend more. The increase in investment bank holdings of securitized assets will be equal to the rise in equity multiplied by the high leverage level.
3. Given the volume of securitized assets now held by IBs, a completely unexpected reversal of the previous optimistic beliefs about risk and a consequent fall in asset prices leads to major capital losses. These losses can wipe out much IB equity, and put the solvency of some IBs at risk.

In the two upswing periods of the financial cycle we hold conditions in the real economy unchanged. In other words, the dynamics of the upswing of the financial cycle do not depend on spillovers to the real economy. In the modelling, this means we keep the number of financial assets, which we call F, constant. As in the case of the housing cycle, holding the supply of the asset constant focuses attention on the interaction between the price and demand. Moreover, since the repayment schedule of the households with mortgages is based on the loan they took out, it is not affected by the fluctuations in asset prices that take place in the financial sector.

Value at Risk behaviour of the investment bank

Setting out a model using equations and a numerical example helps to clarify the behaviour of a stylized investment bank, which is otherwise unfamiliar. We go through the steps that were summarized above.

The price of an F asset is P. The expected return from the asset is $(1+r)$ per F asset (note that in the VaR model, r refers to the rate of return on the asset; not to the lending rate). Thus, as long as the expected return is greater than the price they have to pay, i.e. $(1+r) > P$, their expected profit is positive $(1+r-P>0)$, which means the investment bank spends PF buying as many of the F assets it can.

The maximum an investment bank can spend on the F assets is equal to their equity, e, plus the amount they can borrow from savers, B. Hence, $PF = B + e$. This tells us the amount they want to borrow.

The next step is to figure out how much the investment banks can borrow. This depends on the behaviour of savers. We assume that savers are prepared to lend to investment banks at the money market rate, r^P, as long as they run strictly no risk of losing the money they have loaned. We assume further that savers who are considering lending to investment banks make the assumption that the maximum possible loss the investment bank can make per F asset is $\bar{z}$. We can think of the ratings agencies (see Chapter 9, Section 9.2.3) being responsible for assessing the degree of risk and assigning a rating (such as AAB), from which savers can infer $\bar{z}$.

Given that the maximum loss per F asset is $\bar{z}$, the lowest possible total return to the investment bank is $(1+r-\bar{z})F$. On that basis, savers are prepared to lend an amount B as long as even in the worst case, the investment bank can pay savers back $(1+r^P)B$. In the worst case, the investment bank gets its lowest total return minus the cost of borrowing, r^P, i.e. $(1+r-\bar{z}-r^P)F$. We can make the notation simpler without altering the logic, by assuming $r^P=0$.

The maximum the investment bank can borrow is

$$\max B=(1+r-\bar{z})F.$$

As we have seen above, as long as the expected return from buying an F asset is positive, i.e. $(1+r)>P$, the risk-neutral investment bank will buy as many as they can. The maximum they can fund is equal to the maximum they can borrow plus their equity:

$$PF=\max B+e=(1+r-\bar{z})F+e.$$

As an example, suppose $r=0.07$, and $\bar{z}=0.04$, then the worst possible outcome is that each securitized asset yields only $1+0.07-0.04=1.03$. If the investment bank held F of these assets, then the least it would have available to pay back the lenders (savers) at the end of the period would be 1.03F. So the most that the investment bank would be able to borrow from the savers would be $B=1.03F$ since the savers would be sure to get that back even in the very worst case scenario. If the investment bank also had equity of 10, it would then have $1.03F+10$ available to buy the assets. If the price of an asset was 1.05, and it spent all it had available to spend, then it would spend $1.05F=1.03F+10$. (And you can solve that equation, as we will do in a more general way below, to see that $F=10/0.02=500$.)

Thus, investment banks spend all they can by borrowing 'up to the hilt' and using their own capital (i.e. equity) for buying F assets as long as $(1+r)>P$ by however small an amount.

From this equation, we can work out how many F assets the investment bank buys:

$$\begin{aligned}PF&=(1+r-\bar{z})F+e\\&\rightarrow(P-(1+r-\bar{z}))F=e\\&\rightarrow F=\frac{e}{(P-(1+r-\bar{z}))}=\frac{e}{\underbrace{\bar{z}}_{\text{risk}}-\underbrace{(1+r-P)}_{\text{return}}}.\end{aligned}\qquad\text{(investment bank demand for F)}$$

If you fill in the values for $r,\bar{z},P$ and e from above, you will see that $F=500$.

This equation highlights that the investment bank's demand for the F asset rises with its equity and rises as risk falls relative to return. Recalling the definition of leverage,

$$\text{leverage}=\lambda=\frac{\text{assets}}{\text{equity}}=\frac{PF}{e}=\frac{\text{price}}{\text{risk}-\text{return to investment bank}},\qquad\text{(leverage of investment bank)}$$

it is clear that leverage will rise when risk falls relative to the return to the investment bank.

Note that the fact that the investment bank's leverage depends on the gap between risk and return does not reflect its attitude to risk. We assume all along that the investment bank is risk-neutral. The role that risk is playing is via the savers: a fall in risk makes savers willing to lend more to the investment bank. Since the worst possible outcome has become less bad, the investment bank can borrow more while respecting the value at risk constraint. Respecting the value at risk constraint means the investment bank can repay the lenders in the worst case. The vital role played by the credit ratings agency in establishing maximum risk is evident from the leverage equation. It is clearly possible for leverage to go very high if risk falls—as long as the return to the investment bank remains positive.

8.5.3 **A numerical example of the bank-leverage centred cycle**

This subsection sets out a simple numerical example of an upswing and a subsequent crash. The formal model behind the example is set out in Section 8.8.2 of the Appendix.

Initial conditions (period 0)

The economy begins with investment bank equity of 10, a rate of return on the financial asset of 0.07, a policy rate of zero, an initial financial asset price of 1 and risk level of 0.12. The second column of Table 8.1 summarizes the initial conditions. We assume that the policy rate and the return on financial assets remain constant throughout the simulation, and note that this implies that $(1+r) > P$ in all periods. From the equation for the investment bank's demand for the F asset, we can calculate:

$$
\begin{aligned}
F_0 &= \frac{e_0}{\underbrace{\bar{z_0}}_{\text{risk}} - \underbrace{(1+r-P_0)}_{\text{return}}} \\
&= \frac{10}{0.12-(1+0.07-1)} = \frac{10}{0.05} = 200; \\
B_0 &= (1+r-\bar{z_0})F_0 = (1+0.07-0.12)200 = 190 \\
F_0P_0 &= B_0 + e_0 = 190 + 10 = 200 \\
\lambda_0 &= \frac{F_0P_0}{e_0} = \frac{200}{10} = 20
\end{aligned}
$$

	Period 0	Period 1	Period 2	Period 3
Policy rate, r^P	0	0	0	0
Rate of return on financial assets, r	0.07	0.07	0.07	0.07
Equity, e	10	10	20	-30 (insolvent)
Risk level, $\bar{z}$	0.12	0.04	0.04	0.12
Price of financial assets, P	1	1.05	1.05	1
Total assets, F	200	500	1000	
Asset value, PF	200	525	1050	
Max borrowing, B	190	515	1030	
Leverage, λ	20	52.5	52.5	

Table 8.1 Numerical example of upswing in the financial cycle and crash.

We use the formulas from the previous subsection to work out F_0, the total amount of financial assets the IB holds, and B_0, the bank's borrowing from households. Note that for the latter we could also have used the identity that equity = assets – liabilities, with equity of 10 and assets of 200, to work out that liabilities are 190.

The penultimate line, F_0P_0, represents the total value of the bank's financial assets, and this representation makes it clear that in this model assets are funded by either borrowing or equity. Alternatively, we could have said that the bank has 200 units of F_0, each priced at $P_0 = 1$, which likewise gives an asset value of 200. Finally, the value of assets together with equity also gives the leverage ratio, λ_0.

Upswing (periods 1 and 2)

The upswing begins as a result of a fall in risk, to $\bar{z}_1 = 0.04$. We assume that everyone in the model economy agrees that risk has fallen because, for example, of the credibility of the credit ratings agencies who have given higher credit ratings to the F asset. The fall in risk leads both IBs and saver households to demand more financial assets, pushing up their price, and we assume that the price rises from 1 to 1.05, or by 5%. As the price increases, the demand from risk-neutral investment banks remains undiminished, while that of the risk-averse holders of assets is reduced due to portfolio re-balancing, thus transferring assets to the investment banks.

We divide the upswing into two periods, 1 and 2. In period 1 we look at the effect of the fall in risk and consequent price change in increasing investment bank holdings of F, which results from an increase in leverage. In period 1, we assume that investment bank capital (equity) does not change. In period 2, we look at the additional effect on the investment bank's demand for assets as a result of the capital gains made in period 1 (i.e. the increase in price in period 1 on the assets held at the start of period 1). This increases investment bank capital via mark-to-market valuation of assets, and the demand for assets now rises because of the higher level of IB capital multiplied by the higher leverage reached in period 1. We assume artificially, but not wholly unrealistically, that this new increased demand for assets does not lead to a further increase in price because the expected return at $P_1 = P_2 = 1.05$ (while positive and therefore attractive to risk-neutral investment banks) is so low that other risk-averse holders of these financial assets require virtually no incentive in the form of higher prices to part with them.

We can now use our simple model and the data from the table to find the leverage and asset holdings of the IB in period 1, after the fall in risk but before a change in capital:

$$F_1 = \frac{e_1}{\underbrace{\bar{z}_1}_{\text{risk}} - \underbrace{(1+r-P_1)}_{\text{return}}}$$

$$= \frac{10}{0.04-(1+0.07-1.05)} = \frac{10}{0.02} = 500;$$

$$B_1 = (1+r-\bar{z}_1)F_1 = (1+0.07-0.04)500 = 515$$

$$F_1P_1 = B_1 + e_1 = 515 + 10 = 525$$

$$\lambda_1 = \frac{F_1P_1}{e_1} = \frac{525}{10} = 52.5$$

In spite of the low expected return of 2% (accounting for a price of 1.05), investment banks are prepared to increase their leverage, which has more than doubled since period 0. Although the return has gone down from 7% to 2%, risk has gone down by more (from 0.12 to 0.04). With the return still positive, investment banks increase their holdings. Savers are prepared to expand their lending because they too believe risk is low. The outcome is a new equilibrium where the bank's total assets have increased to 525, while its total debt has increased to 515, of which 190 is from the original liability.

Now we turn to period 2, the second part of the upswing. In this part, the capital gains made in period 1 increase investment bank capital from $e_0 = 10$ to $e_2 = 20$. This is calculated using the original $F_0 = 200$ assets, and the price of each of these has risen by 0.05, hence an overall capital gain of $200 \times 0.05 = 10$. The initial liabilities B_0 remain unchanged, and as such, this translates into a direct increase in equity of 10. The additional assets purchased in period 1 do not contribute to an increase in equity, as they were purchased at the new price $P_1 = 1.05$, and as such the new liability created to fund them (borrowing of 1.05 per unit) exactly offsets the new asset created on the balance sheet.

Using the rise in capital to $e_2 = 20$, we can calculate the period 2 values:

$$\begin{aligned}
F_2 &= \frac{e_2}{\underbrace{\bar{z}_2}_{\text{risk}} - \underbrace{(1+r-P_2)}_{\text{return}}} \\
&= \frac{20}{0.04-(1+0.07-1.05)} = \frac{20}{0.02} = 1000; \\
B_2 &= (1+r-\bar{z}_2)F_2 = (1+0.07-0.04)1000 = 1030 \\
F_2P_2 &= B_2 + e_2 = 1030 + 20 = 1050 \\
\lambda_2 &= \frac{F_2P_2}{e_2} = \frac{1050}{20} = 52.5
\end{aligned}$$

The increase in equity has therefore led to a further dramatic increase in total assets, from $F_1P_1 = 525$ to $F_2P_2 = 1050$. Intuitively, if the leverage ratio and price are the same as in the previous period, but equity has doubled, holdings of financial assets ($\lambda_2 e_2$) must have also doubled. The final equation shows the funding split between equity and borrowing at the end of the upswing: of 1050 assets, 20 have been funded by equity, and 1030 by borrowing.

Periods 1 and 2 provide a picture of a world in which everyone feels safe—the credit rating agencies have shifted the assessment of risk down—yet it has all the hallmarks of a dangerous situation. As discussed in Chapter 9, it may describe the world Lehman Brothers and the other investment banks were operating in during the 2000s. Investment banks were making very small profits on huge holdings of assets, reflected in very high leverage, and the belief that the assets were almost completely safe. Chapter 9 explains the concentration of the 'very safe' super-senior tranches of securitized assets in the hands of the investment banks.

Figure 8.13 shows the expansion of the IB's balance sheet during the upswing. The figure is drawn to scale and highlights just how small the bank's capital buffer is compared to the size of their balance sheet by the end of period 2. We shall see how this high leverage makes IBs more vulnerable to bankruptcy in the next subsection.

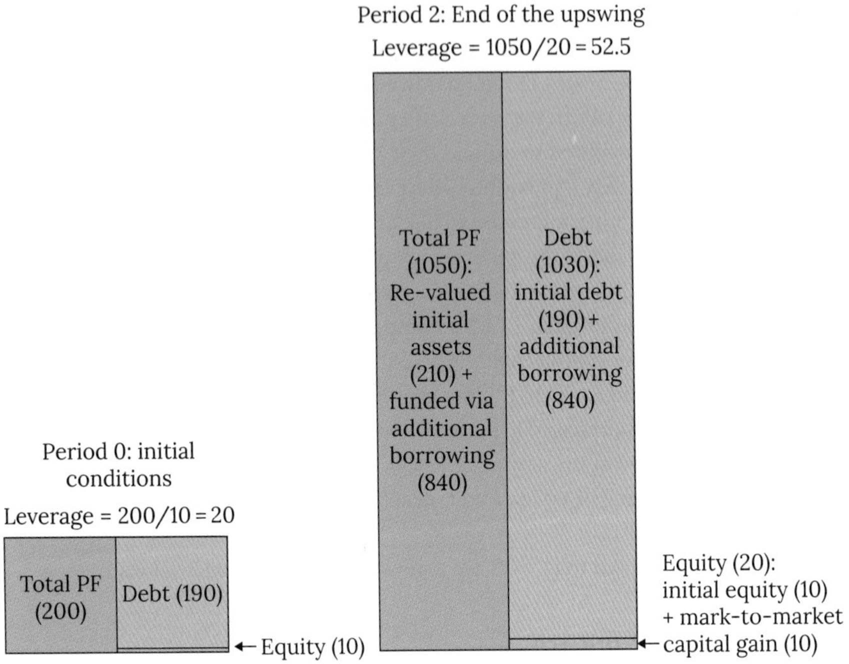

Figure 8.13 The expansion of an IB's balance sheet in response to a fall in risk. Leverage = Assets/Equity.

The important point to take away from this example is that investment banks will always buy as many assets as they can if the expected profit is positive (as they are risk-neutral). The amount they can buy is constrained by their equity and the amount that savers are willing to lend to them. The fall in risk boosts the IB's asset holdings because it loosens their funding constraint by increasing both their equity and the amount they can borrow from savers.

Crash (period 3)

Suppose that in period 3, some 'scary bad news' arrives in the economy and shifts beliefs about risk back to its initial higher level.[27] This could be the result, for example, of a fall in house prices that underlie the securitized assets. If risk is reassessed upwards from 0.04 to 0.12, the demand for securitized assets will fall. If we look at the implications of a fall in price back from 1.05 to 1, then the capital loss on the investment bank's assets is $0.05 \times 1000 = 50$. The investment bank's equity of 20 in period 2 will be wiped out by the capital loss, as shown by the final column in Table 8.1. The investment bank will be insolvent, and we can assume it will cease operations.[28]

---

[27] The term has been used by Fostel and Geanakoplos (2012b), who define 'scary bad news' as news that increases uncertainty and the volatility of asset prices.

[28] Note that although this numerical example shows a case where IB becomes insolvent, this need not always be the case. Whether an IB goes insolvent or not will depend on the size of changes in risk and the degree of responsiveness of price to changes in risk. For example, had risk risen only a small amount in period 3, resulting in a price fall of 0.1, then equity would have fallen by $0.01 \times 1000 = 10$, and the IB would have avoided insolvency.

The threat of insolvency arises because capital gains due to the increase in price during the upswing are made only on the bank's pre-existing assets (F_0), whereas capital losses from the fall in price are made on the entirety of the bank's asset holdings at the top of the upswing (F_2).

Overview

To summarize, there are a fixed number of financial assets that have been created from the mortgage loans and are traded. There are two kinds of investors interested in holding the F assets: the investment bank which is risk-neutral and uses the VaR business model, and the saver households which are risk averse. The behaviour of the investment bank in which it reacts positively to an increase in the price of the securitized asset is a form of financial accelerator, which triggers a process of rising asset prices similar to the tulip bulb case in Figure 8.6. While we have simplified to two upswing periods, in reality the increase in IB holdings between periods 1 and 2 may have boosted the price beyond 1.05, in which case equity would have risen further and thus the increase in IB financial asset holdings would have continued. In this way, the assets will become more concentrated in the hands of the IBs, who will borrow from the savers in order to buy more of the assets.

8.6 BALANCE SHEET RECESSION AND FINANCIAL ACCELERATOR

Balance sheet recessions are those that follow the bursting of large, credit-fuelled, asset price bubbles, such as Japan in the 1990s or the US and many countries in Europe following the global financial crisis. Recessions of this type are different from the usual business cycle downturn because of the effect of the collapse in asset prices on the balance sheets of households and firms. This brings the financial accelerator process into play, which amplifies and propagates the downturn. Households and firms deleverage, that is, they reduce their debt so as to repair their balance sheets. This means they increase their savings. This reduces aggregate demand and unless there is a balancing source of increased aggregate demand, it slows down recovery.[29]

In this section we provide an overview of how a balance sheet recession can be modelled using the tools we have developed in this chapter along with the familiar 3-equation model. We follow the logic of Eggertsson and Krugman (2012), in which the forced repayment of bank loans plays a major part.

We continue to assume that households are of two types—saver and borrower households.[30] Saver households are not credit constrained. They are able to borrow freely and can be modelled using the permanent income hypothesis (PIH) as set out in Chapter 1. They are able to smooth their consumption by lending and borrowing. This

[29] See Koo (2003 and 2011) for a more detailed discussion of balance sheet recessions. For a formal model, see Eggertsson and Krugman (2012). Gertler and Gilchrist (2018) summarize the theory and apply it to the Great Recession.

[30] We use the terms *saver* and *borrower* households to denote non-credit constrained and credit-constrained households respectively, although in some periods saver households will in fact reduce overall savings, while in other periods borrower households will in fact accumulate savings.

also allows them to take advantage of changes in the interest rate to save more when the interest rate is high and vice versa, so as to maximize their utility. In addition to the PIH motivation, we assume saver households save for precautionary reasons. We model this in a simple way by assuming they adjust their savings to achieve a target level of wealth.

Borrower households are credit constrained. This means that their spending depends on the credit they can get from the banks. According to the financial accelerator, the collateral value of housing plays a very important role in the lending decisions of retail banks to households. We assume banks apply a maximum loan-to-value (*LTV*) ratio (i.e. loan value divided by property value) when they extend loans to households. In addition, we assume that the initial value is LTV_{High}, which reflects the loose credit conditions that typically prevail in the years preceding a financial crisis.

We assume that borrower households are fully 'borrowed up' each period, which means that they borrow up to the limit of the prevailing LTV ratio. The maximum amount borrower households can borrow for new housing and consumption is pinned down by the loan-to-value ratio and this period's change in the value of the existing housing stock. However, borrower households may want to save if their net worth in houses is less than their target wealth. As we shall see, this plays a role in a balance sheet recession. The aggregate demand arising from borrower households' expenditure can be calculated as follows: consumption (equal to income after payment of interest to saver households and net of savings required to achieve target wealth) plus expenditure on new housing.

The IS curve in this model economy is the sum of the aggregate demand of saver and borrower households, weighted by the proportion of households in the economy that are credit constrained (i.e. borrower households).

Pre-crash equilibrium

We assume that in the period before the crash, the economy is in equilibrium. This means:

1. both savers and borrowers are exactly achieving their wealth targets;
2. borrowers have borrowed the maximum possible this period, which is the loan to value ratio multiplied by the capital gain on their housing in the previous period;
3. the central bank has set r^P, such that output is at the constant inflation equilibrium, i.e. $y^D = y_e$.

The crash and a balance sheet recession

Given this framework, we are now able to explore the channels through which a collapse in the price of securitized assets and housing affects aggregate demand and shifts the IS curve to the left. We distinguish between (1) a loan-to-value effect and (2) a collateral effect. There are two other effects: (3) the consequence of banks calling in housing loans when borrowers go 'under water', in the sense that the market value of their house is less than the mortgage outstanding; and (4) the increase in savings as both borrower and saver households seek to rebuild target wealth following the fall in the value of houses and financial assets.

(1) Banks lower their loan-to-value ratio, thus $LTV_{High} \rightarrow LTV_{Low}$

Retail banks reduce their loan-to-value ratio for several reasons: loans are considered more risky when house prices have fallen and banks seek to reduce their risk-exposure by reducing their leverage. In turn, this implies a fall in aggregate demand as borrower households face a tighter constraint on how much they can borrow.

(2) Fall in value of housing collateral

When we move from a situation of rising to falling house prices, i.e. from $\Delta P_H > 0$ to $\Delta P_H < 0$, this reduces the value of potential collateral. This has the effect of reducing loans for consumption, and hence, aggregate demand.

(3) Balance sheet effect

A potentially much more important effect is that banks may try and call in loans because the value of the collateral, i.e. the market price of the house, has, for example, fallen below the value of the loan. As we shall see in Chapter 9, some households with negative equity simply walked away from their properties, leaving the bank with an asset (the house) on its balance sheet worth less than the mortgage (which it replaces). This reduces the equity buffer of banks and will lead them to try to re-build the buffer by reducing their outstanding liabilities.

At the level of the aggregate economy, repayment of loans by borrower households transfers income to saver households. Hence, the fall in consumption by the former is partially offset to an extent equal to saver households' increase in permanent income (see Chapter 1). Overall, the marginal propensity to consume of borrower households is higher, which means that this redistribution depresses aggregate demand.

(4) Rebuilding target wealth after a fall in house and financial asset prices

In addition to the effects operating through the constraints placed on aggregate demand as a consequence of falling asset prices as banks reduce loan-to-value ratios and call in loans, households themselves will respond to the fall in the prices of housing and financial assets. The main channel is the desire of borrower households to rebuild their wealth back toward the target level in response to the fall in wealth due to falling house prices. Saver households, which have seen a reduction in the value of their financial assets (F), will also seek to rebuild their wealth. In both cases, aggregate demand will be depressed. In practice, this may be the most important longer run effect.

Unless the deleveraging shock's depressive effect on aggregate demand is counter-balanced by an increase from elsewhere in the economy, a recession is predicted. The ability of monetary policy to stabilize the economy is limited by the zero lower bound, as we discussed in Chapter 3. In the case of a large enough deleveraging shock, the economy can fall into a deflation trap with the twin evils of falling output and prices (see Chapters 3 and 9) in which the paradox of thrift applies so that higher intended savings by households reduce aggregate savings because of the fall in output caused by the lower aggregate demand (see Chapter 1).

The model of a balance sheet recession highlights the following implications for fiscal policy based on Chapter 7.

1. Fiscal stimulus can be effective by boosting aggregate demand in order to give the private sector time to repair their balance sheets.
2. The increase in government debt can then be repaid once the 'deleveraging process' is over.
3. Although fiscal stimulus is called for in a balance sheet recession when the private sector is trying to save more, this increases the burden on fiscal policy, which makes the government's stabilization task more difficult in both economic and political terms.

8.7 CONCLUSIONS

This chapter has focused on financial cycles and financial crises, and their impact on the macroeconomy. A well-functioning banking system allows firms and households to implement their spending plans through borrowing. Banks can, however, take on more risk than is socially optimal because they don't take into account the impact of their actions on system-wide risk. Moreover, the possibility of government bailout reduces the costs to them of downside risk. The financial sector is also an amplifier and propagator of shocks through the economy, due to mechanisms such as the financial accelerator and asset price bubbles. These shocks often spill over into the real economy and can have the devastating effects experienced during financial crises.

In order to better understand the financial sector and its relationship with the real economy, we introduced the concept of the financial cycle, which tracks fluctuations in key financial variables, such as credit and house prices. Upswings and downswings of the financial cycle typically last longer than is the case for the business cycle, and peaks in the cycle are commonly associated with the onset of banking crises. In the inflation-targeting monetary policy framework, financial variables are only considered to the extent that they influence headline inflation. This means potentially dangerous financial imbalances can emerge, even in the face of successful inflation targeting.

At the centre of the models presented in this chapter are two feedback processes similar in structure: the house price and bank-leverage centred feedback processes. The two can also interact with the result that in a (perceived) low-risk environment there are both housing and financial asset price bubbles, and rapid increases in leverage of IBs. The model also shows that any shocks that subsequently increase the perceived level of risk can leave banks vulnerable to large losses and even bankruptcy. This sort of shock and the associated balance sheet recession can have serious implications for the real economy, reducing aggregate demand through several channels.

This framework allows us to answer a number of questions about financial cycles and financial crises and their effect on the economy:

1. What factors can account for a reduction in the perceived level of risk in the economy? Three candidates are: (1) a reduction in macroeconomic volatility increasing the likelihood that households will be able to service their mortgages, (2) rising house prices, which increase the value of housing collateral compared to mortgage loan values, and (3) financial innovation aimed at reducing credit risk. All three were present in the Great Moderation that preceded the global financial crisis.
2. Why does a fall in risk typically lead to a rise in the leverage of IBs? Risk-neutral IBs using a value-at-risk business model want to buy as many financial assets as possible as long as they offer a positive expected return. They are restricted in the amount they can purchase by the size of their equity and their ability to borrow from saver households. It is the saver households' response to the fall in risk that enables the IBs to borrow more and 'lever up' by expanding their balance sheets. Savers are willing to lend more to the IBs after the fall in risk as they believe there is a lower chance of the bad state of the world occurring.
3. Why do rising housing and financial asset prices not dampen the upswing of the financial cycle? This is due to the positive feedback effects when these assets rise in price. When house prices rise, households can take out more loans for consumption (using housing wealth as collateral) and have more incentive to invest in housing (due to the expectation of future house price increases). In terms of financial assets, a rise in price will lead to a capital gain for the IBs as they mark-to-market the value of their assets. They then use this additional equity to fund the purchase of more financial assets (as long as their expected profit is still positive), further pushing up asset prices.
4. What does the term 'balance sheet recession' refer to and what does this mean for the recovery phase of the business cycle? The term refers to recessions that follow the bursting of large credit-fuelled asset price bubbles. Recovery from a balance sheet recession is typically slower than from other recessions as households, firms and banks are 'deleveraging' (i.e. paying down debt). This reduces aggregate demand, and drags on the recovery.
5. What role does household inequality play in the financial cycle? Low-income households are credit-constrained and respond to a rise in credit supply by borrowing more. The increase in value of their collateral when house prices rise, stimulates further borrowing. This leaves them vulnerable to a crash in house prices. As we saw in Chapter 1, they are also more susceptible to unemployment in a recession. Their high marginal propensity to consume amplifies a downturn and this effect is magnified in a balance sheet recession by the need to reduce leverage.

This chapter has provided a theoretical framework for thinking about the financial cycle and financial crises. The following chapter applies the framework to the global financial crisis of 2008–09. This sheds light on the mechanisms that caused the crisis and on the Great Recession that followed.

8.8 APPENDIX

8.8.1 Modelling the housing-centred positive feedback process

In this subsection, we set out a simple mathematical model of the housing-centred feedback process. We collapse the model to just two periods and show how a reduction in risk increases house prices and can fuel a house price cycle as set out in the left-hand panel of Figure 8.1. The key components of the housing cycle model are: $\Delta P_{H,1}$ = the change in house prices between period 0 and period 1; ΔH_1^D = the change in the demand for housing between period 0 and period 1; ΔP_H^E = the change in expected house prices (the change between period 0 expectations of period 1 prices, and period 1 expectations of period 2 prices); L_1 = the amount of loans provided by retail banks in period 1; $\bar{l}$ = the loan-to-value ratio; H_0 = the housing stock in period 0; and z_t = the perceived riskiness of loans in period t.

The model has four equations. The first shows that house price changes are proportional to the change in demand for housing and the change in expected house prices,

$$\Delta P_{H,1} = \alpha \Delta H_1^D + \beta \Delta P_H^E. \tag{8.1}$$

The second shows that the change in expected house prices is proportional to the change in actual house prices,

$$\Delta P_H^E = \gamma \Delta P_{H,1}. \tag{8.2}$$

The intuition behind equation 8.2 is that if prices rise between periods 0 and 1, people's expectations of future prices will also rise by some extent. The third shows that the change in demand for housing is proportional to the new loans that have become available during the upswing,

$$\Delta H_1^D = \delta \Delta L_1. \tag{8.3}$$

The final equation shows that the change in retail bank loans between period 0 and period 1 depends on the loan-to-value ratio, the change in the value of the housing stock, and the change in risk perceptions between period 0 and period 1,

$$\Delta L_1 = \eta \bar{l} \Delta P_{H,1} H_0 - a(z_1 - z_0). \tag{8.4}$$

The first term on the right-hand side has the change in house prices multiplied by the housing stock, giving the increase in the value of housing, multiplied by the loan-to-value ratio, which therefore shows how many new loans can be made based on the change in housing value (i.e. this is the effect of new collateral on loans). This is multiplied by a constant η, as not every house that can be traded will be traded. The second term implies that if risk increases between period 0 and period 1, the amount of loans made by banks will decrease, all else given, and vice versa.

We can immediately see from these equations how a bubble could arise in house prices following a fall in risk. The reduction in risk boosts the amount banks are willing to lend using the loan supply equation (equation 8.4), and credit-constrained borrowers take out additional loans to expand their purchases of housing (equation 8.3). This both increases house prices (equation 8.1) and expectations of future house price rises (equation 8.2), which feeds back into the loan supply equation (as the extra collateral allows households to borrow more). Put another way, the fall in risk and the positive feedbacks produce an upswing in house prices.

We can now substitute equations 8.2, 8.3 and 8.4 back into equation 8.1 and rearrange to find the impact of a change in risk on house prices:

$$\Delta P_{H,1} = \alpha\delta(\eta\bar{l}\Delta P_{H,1}H_0 - a\Delta z_1) + \beta\gamma\Delta P_{H,1}$$

$$\rightarrow \Delta P_{H,1} = -\frac{\alpha\delta}{1-\alpha\delta\eta\bar{l}H_0 - \beta\gamma}a\Delta z_1. \tag{8.5}$$

Equation 8.5 shows that a reduction in risk ($\Delta z_1 < 0$) leads to an increase in the price of housing.[31] This is due to the positive feedback mechanisms outlined above. The equation also shows that if the market perception of risk suddenly increased, then house prices would collapse, potentially leading to a financial crisis.

8.8.2 A model of a bank-leverage centred cycle

This model formalizes the numerical example in the chapter, and it is important to read the example to understand the intuition and underlying assumptions, including periodization, in this Appendix. As in the numerical example, a fall in risk causes the upswing in the market for securitized assets, and an equivalent rise in risk causes the downswing and possible insolvency. Again as there, the problem arises because capital gains due to the increase in price during the upswing are based on a relatively low level of pre-existing assets in period 0, while the capital losses from an equivalent fall in price in the downturn are based on the much larger amount of assets held at the top of the upswing.

We assume that the upswing (initiated by a fall in $\bar{z}$ from $\bar{z_0}$ to $\bar{z_1}$) consists of two periods. In period 1, we look at the effects of the fall in risk (holding IB equity constant): the fall in risk boosts demand for securities by both IBs and passive savers; this pushes up the price of the securities; we assume that (risk-averse) savers are more sensitive to the price increase than IBs, so the rise in price implies the transfer of some securities from savers to IBs. During period 1, leverage increases while equity remains constant.

In period 2 of the upswing, we calculate the effect of the price increase on mark-to-market increase in equity and the effect of the increase in equity on further increasing the demand for securities by IBs (with no such effect on savers). In period 2, we make the simplifying assumption that there is no further increase in prices—the intuition here is that at price P_1 risk-averse savers are making a very low average return so that their supply of securities is now perfectly elastic at that price. This reflects risk-neutral IB demand ‘up to the hilt’ as long as there is *any* positive expected return, up to the

[31] We assume that $1-\alpha\delta\eta\bar{l}H_0 - \beta\gamma$ is positive. Likewise, all constants are also positive.

limits of what IBs can borrow. In the model, F is demand for securities by IBs (we don't explicitly model saver behaviour).

Period 1

We start by calculating the change in IB financial asset holdings between period 0 and 1,

$$\Delta F_1 = F_1 - F_0 = \frac{e_0}{\bar{z_1} - (1+r-P_1)} - \frac{e_0}{\bar{z_0} - (1+r-P_0)} \tag{8.6}$$

We can take a first order linear approximation of F_1. Specifically,

$$\begin{aligned} F_1 = F(\bar{z_1}, P_1) &\approx F(\bar{z_0}, P_0) + F_z(\bar{z_0}, P_0)\Delta\bar{z_1} + F_P(\bar{z_0}, P_0)\Delta P_1 \\ &= \frac{e_0}{\bar{z_0} - (1+r-P_0)} - \frac{e_0}{(\bar{z_0} - (1+r-P_0))^2}(\Delta\bar{z_1} + \Delta P_1) \end{aligned}$$

The final line above uses the quotient rule to collect terms, as we can easily show that $F_z = F_P = -\frac{e_0}{(\bar{z_0}-(1+r-P_0))^2}$. Substituting the approximation for F_1 into equation 8.6, the two F_0 terms cancel, and we are left with,

$$\Delta F_1 \approx -\frac{e_0}{(\bar{z_0} - (1+r-P_0))^2}(\Delta\bar{z_1} + \Delta P_1) \equiv -b(\Delta\bar{z_1} + \Delta P_1) \tag{8.7}$$

Referring to the first term in equation 8.6 as b, it is determined entirely by the period 0 setup. We know that b is positive, as e_0 (initial equity) is assumed positive while the denominator is a quadratic. Equation 8.7 is useful since it clearly shows that $\Delta F_1 > 0$ if and only if prices rise by less than risk falls; in other words, if the return does not fall as much as risk does. Mathematically, given that $\Delta\bar{z_1} < 0$ (risk falls between periods 0 and 1), and $\Delta P_1 > 0$ (prices rise), the equation implies that $\Delta F_1 > 0$ if and only if $|\Delta\bar{z_1}| > |\Delta P_1|$.

Now we assume that the change in price ΔP_1 is proportional to the change in demand, such that,

$$\Delta P_1 = \alpha\Delta F_1 \tag{8.8}$$

where the effect on price of the smaller increase in demand by savers is implicitly included on the right-hand side, as being some proportion of ΔF_1. Substituting equation 8.8 into equation 8.7 and rearranging, we find,

$$\begin{aligned} &\Delta F_1 \approx -b(\Delta\bar{z_1} + \alpha\Delta F_1) \\ \implies &\Delta F_1 \approx -\frac{b}{1+b\alpha}\Delta z_1 \equiv -\gamma\Delta z_1 \text{ with } \gamma > 0. \end{aligned} \tag{8.9}$$

Equation 8.9 allows us to compute the change in IB demand for financial assets determined by a fall in risk (before taking into account mark to-market capital gains).

Finally, substituting equation 8.9 into 8.8 we have,

$$\Delta P_1 = -\alpha\gamma\Delta z_1, \tag{8.10}$$

if we assume that $P_0 = 1$, $P_1 = 1 - \alpha\gamma\Delta z_1 > 1$ whenever $\Delta z_1 < 0$, or in other words prices rise when risk falls.

When $\Delta\bar{z_1}$ is large (as in the numerical example in Section 8.5.3), the linear approximation of equation 8.6 is not accurate, and one should use equation 8.6 instead.

Period 2

In this period, we look at the effect of the increase in capital as a result of the capital gains in period 1:

$$\Delta e_2 = F_0 \Delta P_1. \tag{8.11}$$

The increase in securities demanded as result of e increasing is given by

$$\Delta F_2 = \frac{\lambda_1 \Delta e_2}{P_1}, \tag{8.12}$$

so the bigger the increase in leverage in period 1 the bigger will be ΔF_2.

The total value of security holdings at the end of the upswing is

$$P_2F_2 = P_1(\Delta F_2 + \Delta F_1) + P_0F_0 = \lambda_1 \Delta e_2 + e_0 \Delta \lambda_1 + F_0. \tag{8.13}$$

since we assumed $P_0 = 1$ and $P_1 = P_2$.

Period 3: The downswing

If we assume an equivalent fall in prices during a downswing caused by $\Delta z_3 = -\Delta z_1$, so that $\Delta P_3 = -\Delta P_1$, this causes a capital loss on F_2 and this is much greater than the earlier capital gain on F_0. The capital gain in the upswing was $\Delta e_2 = F_0 \Delta P_1$ and the capital loss on the downswing is $\Delta e_3 = F_2 \Delta P_3 = -F_2 \Delta P_1$. Hence, the net loss over the whole cycle is (note that e_1 and e_0 are equivalent):

$$e_3 - e_0 = \Delta e_2 + \Delta e_3 = F_0 \Delta P_1 - F_2 \Delta P_1 = -(F_2 - F_0)\Delta P_1 = (F_2 - F_0)\alpha\gamma\Delta z_1 \tag{8.14}$$

The last stage uses equation 8.10. This implies insolvency, i.e. $e_3 \leq 0$, when $e_0 + (F_2 - F_0)\alpha\gamma\Delta z_1 \leq 0$, which is true for large enough Δz_1.

QUESTIONS AND PROBLEMS FOR CHAPTER 8

CHECKLIST QUESTIONS

1. Does the problem of moral hazard indicate that insolvent banks should not be rescued? Justify your answer.
2. What are the three key characteristics of systemic banking crises? How would you expect these characteristics to influence the IS curve?
3. Compare and contrast the business and financial cycles on the following measures:
   a. the components of the series;
   b. the length of the cycle.

   Why are equity prices not incorporated into the measure of the financial cycle set out in Section 8.2.3?

4. To what extent is the financial cycle taken into account when inflation-targeting central banks are setting monetary policy?

5. Imagine a city with abundant space for expansion. Are the following statements true, false or uncertain? [Hint: use Figure 8.6 and accompanying text for guidance.]

   a. A spike in demand for housing will see house prices rise in the short run.

   b. An extended period of high demand for housing will lead to a house price bubble.

6. Using the housing market as an example, explain the following concepts:

   a. loan-to-value ratio;

   b. asset price bubble;

   c. financial accelerator.

7. In the bank-leverage centred model of a financial cycle, which factors can contribute to a reduced perception of risk? How does the perceived reduction in risk lead to IBs becoming more highly leveraged? Make sure your answer refers to the Value-at-Risk model.

8. Why does a fall in risk typically lead to a rise in the leverage of IBs?

9. Imagine an investment bank which has equity of 10 and operates in an economy where risk is 0.15, the policy rate is 0, the rate of return on financial assets is 0.05, and the price of financial assets is 1. Use Section 8.5 to answer the following questions:

   a. How many financial assets does the investment bank hold in period 0? What is their leverage?

   b. In period 1, risk falls to 0.04 and price of financial assets rises to 1.03. What happens to the IB's leverage and holdings of financial assets?

   c. In period 2, the IB marks to market its financial assets. How much does this increase their equity? How many financial assets do they hold at the end of this period?

   d. In the next period, risk rises back towards its initial level. Calculate how much asset prices need to fall to bankrupt the IB. What does this tell us about the dangers of leverage in the banking system?

10. What is a balance sheet recession? What factors make these recessions more difficult to recover from than normal recessions? Illustrate a balance sheet recession in the 3-equation model.

11. Discuss the following statement: 'Central banks can offset the fall in borrower demand in a balance sheet recession by reducing interest rates and inducing savers to spend more'. Illustrate your answer using the 3-equation model.

PROBLEMS

1. Pick a high-income economy with an inflation-targeting central bank. Use their national statistical office or other international (e.g. the OECD) sources to find a historical data series for real house price growth, inflation and GDP growth. Did a house price boom precede the most recent recession? Does the central bank in the country you have chosen include house prices (or equivalent) in the measure of inflation which underpins their inflation-targeting regime? If not, then what is their justification? Does the data you have collected suggest their choice (of whether to include house prices or not) has impacted their ability to fulfil their mandate (i.e. keep the economy at the inflation target)?

2. Do arguments presented in Chapter 5 and Chapter 8 explain how information problems lead banks to lend too little to some customers and too much to others? Justify your answer.

3. Adapt Figure 8.9 to show how the economy can experience a plain vanilla financial crisis following a collapse in house prices. [Hint: use Figure 8.12 to see how the equivalent flow diagram was constructed for the bank-leverage centred financial crisis.]

4. Evaluate the following statement: 'Credit ratings agencies and saver households are just as much to blame as investment banks when investment banks go bankrupt during the downswing phase of a financial cycle based on securitized assets'.

INTERESTED IN EXPLORING THESE TOPICS FURTHER?

Visit www.oup.com/he/carlin-soskice to consolidate and extend your learning with the multiple-choice questions and Animated Analytical Diagrams accompanying this chapter.

CHAPTER

9

FINANCIAL SECTOR RISK AND THE GLOBAL FINANCIAL CRISIS

APPLYING THE MODELS

9.1 INTRODUCTION

The recession that swept across the world in 2008–09 was the most severe contraction the global economy experienced since the Great Depression. The Global Financial Crisis seemed to come out of nowhere. At the time, economists were pleased with how well the new macroeconomic policy regime based on inflation-targeting was working. High and volatile inflation of the 1970s and 1980s had been defeated and the calmer macroeconomic environment was sufficiently marked to be called the Great Moderation. Many countries had successfully brought unemployment back down to levels that had prevailed before the big increases of the 1970s.

However, under the conditions of tranquillity of the Great Moderation, levels of debt in households and banks increased dramatically. This did not set off alarm bells among macroeconomists in universities or central banks. The film *The Inside Job* gives a sense of the prevailing complacency among economists.

To understand the global financial crisis, it is necessary to know what preceded it, which can be described using the model developed in Chapter 8 as the upswing of a financial cycle. The model helps explain the reasons for the huge expansion of credit and debt in both the financial and the household sectors of many advanced economies during the 2000s, and to understand why inflation-targeting central banks did not see compelling reasons to intervene in the face of these developments.

Figure 9.1 highlights the increase in debt in the US economy. The accumulation of debt was concentrated in the household and financial sectors. Household debt as a percentage of US GDP rose by 8 percentage points between 1988 and 1998 and 29 percentage points between 1998 and 2008. The equivalent figures for financial sector debt were 30 percentage points and 48 percentage points. Similar patterns were observed in other countries that experienced credit-fuelled booms during the Great Moderation, such as the UK, Spain and Ireland. Household debt as a percentage

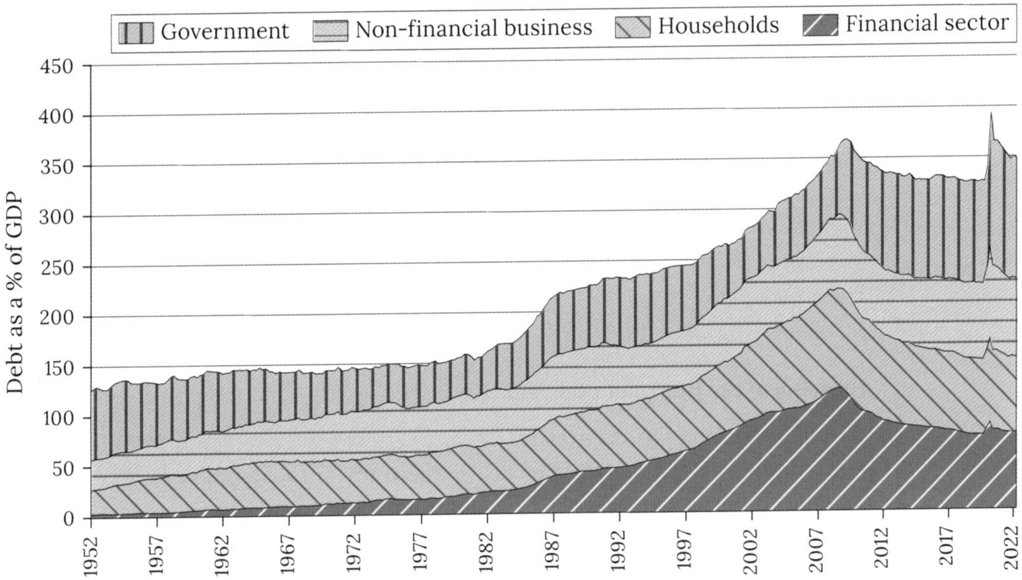

Figure 9.1 Credit market debt outstanding by sector (as a percentage of GDP) in the United States: 1952 Q1–2022 Q2.

Source: Federal Reserve Flows of Funds Accounts, September 2022.

of GDP was 44% in Spain and 69% in the UK in 1999, but rose rapidly to 88% and 105% (respectively) by 2008.[1]

The sharp rise in indebtedness in the 2000s occurred alongside booms in asset prices. For example, US house prices rose by 90% between the first quarter of 2000 and the first quarter of 2006.[2] Central banks predominantly chose not to react to the build-up of debt and rising asset prices in the run-up to the crisis. Alan Greenspan, the Chairman of the Federal Reserve from 1987–2006, was a key proponent of the view that central banks should not lean against asset price bubbles by raising interest rates, but instead should 'focus on policies to mitigate the fallout when it occurs and, hopefully, ease the transition to the next expansion'.[3]

The commonly held view in the pre-crisis period was that central banks should only react to financial developments to the extent that they influenced forecast CPI inflation over the central bank's planning horizon.[4] Well before the crisis, economists at the Bank for International Settlements in Basel pointed out, however, that there have frequently been periods in history where low and stable inflation has coincided with the build-up of private sector debt that sowed the seeds for future banking crises. The

1 Source: Oxford Economics.

2 Source: The S&P/Case-Shiller Home Price Index, Composite US SA.

3 Excerpt taken from Alan Greenspan's Opening Remarks to: *Rethinking Stabilization Policy*: A symposium sponsored by the Federal Reserve Bank of Kansas City, Jackson Hole, Wyoming, August 29th–31st, 2002.

4 See, for example, Bernanke and Gertler (2001).

Director of Research at the IMF, Raghuram Rajan, gave a similar warning at the Jackson Hole meeting of central bankers in 2005.[5]

At the core of the financial crisis in 2008–09 was the behaviour of the financial sector and its interaction with households and their balance sheets through the housing market. We start in Section 9.2 by discussing the possible governance arrangements of a financial system, with a focus on mechanisms designed to reduce solvency risk and liquidity risk. We then see in detail what the pre-2008 financial system looked like, by introducing the relevant incentives, financial instruments and actors (Section 9.3). The remainder of the chapter is organized according to the three phases of the crisis as follows.

Upswing of the financial cycle (Section 9.4)

The deregulation of banks from the 1980s onwards resulted in them becoming more highly leveraged (i.e. with higher debt). There was a proliferation of new financial products created through securitization and tranching. The mis-pricing of these assets was facilitated by the ratings agencies and regulatory authorities.

Household debt levels also increased, mainly as mortgages. Poorer households gained access to credit to buy houses. As we shall see, in the US, government policy encouraged the supply of 'sub-prime mortgages'.

Rising house prices fuelled more borrowing by households, as described by the house-price based cycle set out in Chapter 8. This was amplified by the risk-taking channel as banks increased their leverage. This formed the basis of the upswing of the financial cycle, in which, as we shall see in this chapter, global banks played a central role.

The credit crunch and the financial crisis (Section 9.5)

The collapse of house prices in the US sub-prime housing market revealed the liquidity risk associated with the new ways banks were funding their operations by borrowing short term in the money market. Fear spread through money markets and stock markets, and willing buyers for risky assets of all kinds vanished. This episode, which began in the summer of 2007, was called the *credit crunch*.

In September 2008, US investment bank Lehman Brothers filed for bankruptcy triggering the *global financial crisis*. Fear and uncertainty led to orders for goods and services being cancelled. International trade, investment and consumption spending slumped. This can be represented in the macroeconomic model as a large shift of the IS curve to the left.

Policy intervention in the financial crisis (Section 9.6)

Central banks intervened to provide liquidity so that money markets could function. They slashed policy interest rates to close to zero to try to stimulate spending and they used quantitative easing in an attempt to provide stimulus to the economy once the interest rate was at the zero lower bound.

---

[5] See, for example, Borio and White (2004) and Rajan (2006).

In turn, governments stepped in to save banks from failing and spreading contagion across the financial sector. They could not allow the continuity of core banking services to break down. In addition, they sought to counterbalance the collapse of private sector demand by allowing the economy's automatic stabilizers to work and by increasing spending and cutting taxes.

Policy makers in central banks and government acted fast to stabilize aggregate demand because they were intent on preventing a deflation trap from developing. As set out in Chapter 3, a deflation trap is dangerous because falling prices increase the burden of nominal debt and raise real interest rates. This depresses aggregate demand further and makes stabilization more difficult.

As we saw in Chapter 8, recessions that are preceded by housing booms and are associated with banking crises make rapid recovery difficult. High levels of *private* sector debt take a long time to whittle down. Recession itself worsens the government's fiscal position. A related reason is that saving banks and supporting aggregate demand in the heat of a financial crisis leaves governments with a higher level of debt. When households, banks and government are all trying to reduce their levels of debt, demand in the economy will remain depressed. Austerity policies implemented too soon after a financial crisis can exacerbate the situation.

9.2 GOVERNANCE ARRANGEMENTS FOR FINANCIAL STABILITY

As noted in Chapter 5, when a bank faces a problem of liquidity or solvency, this threatens the provision of core banking services in the economy because of the danger of spillovers and contagion to other banks.

We begin by looking separately at how governments and central banks seek to reduce liquidity and solvency risk. In both cases, reducing risk to the banking sector reduces the potential for spillovers to other parts of the economy. There is, however, a significant trade-off in terms of moral hazard, as guarantees of support for the banking system may increase the likelihood of a crisis happening in the first place. We then examine the division of responsibility between the central bank and government, including the relationship between the central bank and the government.

9.2.1 Liquidity risk and deposit insurance

Liquidity risk is the risk that a bank has inadequate reserves to meet the demand by depositors to withdraw money from their accounts. A shortage of liquidity can happen even at well-run banks, for instance as the result of a banking panic triggering self-fulfilling beliefs that banks will run out of reserves. As we saw in Chapter 5, central banks will act as the Lender of Last Resort facility (LOLR) to provide emergency liquidity when needed, reducing the likelihood of a banking panic.

Government guarantee schemes are likewise designed to prevent liquidity problems, both at an individual bank level and at the level of the banking system (e.g. stopping problems at one bank from spreading fear across the banking sector as a whole). Systems of deposit insurance, for which banks pay, mean that bank deposits below a certain level (e.g. $250,000 in the US and £85,000 in the UK) will be honoured in full in the event the bank is unable to do so.[6]

The classic scenario involving banking panics is the US in the early 1930s.[7] During the Great Depression, about 20% of US banks failed. To get a sense of the scale of what occurred, in the 1920s there were about 600 bank failures per year. Then, between 1930 and 1933 there were about 2,000 failures per year. When mergers and liquidations are taken into account, of the 25,000 US banks in operation at the peak of business in mid-1929, there were only 15,000 left by mid-1933. The crisis led to the establishment of the Federal Deposit Insurance Corporation (FDIC) in 1934. Between 1934 and 1981 on average there were fewer than 15 bank failures per year.

Both liquidity back-stops (LOLR) and deposit guarantee schemes have to be well-designed to tread the fine line between:

1. protecting the public from spillovers and coordination failures arising from 'bad luck' affecting the banking system, which by its nature is very interconnected, and
2. avoiding moral hazard.[8]

The moral hazard problem in this case is that such schemes create incentives for *banks* to avoid taking due care in their loan decisions and more broadly, in their prudential behaviour. For instance the existence of a LOLR facility could induce banks to make more risky long-term loans, knowing that if they run short of liquidity they can borrow from the central bank. This in turn increases the risk of insolvency, as long-term loans have less certainty over repayment.

The schemes can also reduce the incentives for *households* to be prudent. If a household knows their deposits are guaranteed up to a certain amount, they will, for example, be less sceptical of the business model of banks offering very attractive deposit rates. Bad management of banks will escape the attention of depositors who, confident in the belief that any liquidity problem will not affect their savings, feel less incentive to monitor the activities of banks.

So far, this subsection has focused on maturity mismatch on the lending side, between the long-term loans made by banks and short-term demands from depositors. In addition to this, banks also take on liquidity risk on the funding side. This

---

[6] More information on deposit insurance limits and conditions can be found on the websites of the state-backed organizations responsible for deposit insurance; the Federal Deposit Insurance Corporation in the US (https://www.fdic.gov/deposit/deposits/faq.html) and the Financial Services Compensation Scheme in the UK (https://www.fscs.org.uk/what-we-cover/).

[7] There were many serious banking panics in the UK in the past (e.g. in the 1820s), and there were severe banking panics in Argentina in 2002. There were also other US banking crises in 1819, 1837, 1857, 1873, 1884, 1893, 1907 and in the 1980s, but these were all less severe than that of the early 1930s. We discuss the banking panic in the UK bank Northern Rock later in this chapter.

[8] This term originated in the insurance industry to express the problem that insurers face, namely, the person with home insurance may take less care to avoid fires or other damages to his home, thereby increasing the risk above what it would be in absence of insurance. This term now refers to any situation in which one party to an interaction is deciding on an action that affects the profits or wellbeing of the other, but which the affected party cannot control by means of a contract, often because the affected party does not have adequate information on the action. It is also referred to as the 'hidden actions' problem.

most commonly occurs when banks borrow short-term in the money market to fund their longer term lending (e.g. mortgages). Problems with maturity mismatch on the funding side arose in the credit crunch in 2008–09 and will be discussed later in this chapter.

9.2.2 **Solvency and bail-out**

A bank is insolvent or bankrupt when the value of its assets is less than the value of what it owes. If an insolvent bank is not bailed out by the government, it will go out of business. However, the implicit guarantee of government support in the event of insolvency may encourage a bank to take excess risk, which makes the likelihood of requiring government support higher.

The positive probability that an insolvent bank would be bailed out creates a wedge between the private and social cost-benefit calculus of the bank's decisions. The downside risk is partly 'socialized' in the sense that taxpayers normally bear the risk in the case of a bail-out were it to occur. This implicit subsidy would be predicted to affect behaviour and make banks less sensitive to extra risk than would be the case if the bank (owners, managers, bond-holders, depositors) had to face the full cost of bankruptcy. In short, when an individual bank makes commercial decisions, it does not take into account the effect of its decisions on *overall risk* in the financial system, and of the costs to the economy of a financial crisis that might ensue.

This is an example of the problem of externalities that is well-studied in economics, in which the social costs of an individual's actions diverge from the private costs. In the case of pollution, a tax can be levied or bans imposed on emissions of a certain type or scale to bring private and social costs into alignment. The external effects of excessive risk-taking by a bank that is systemically important threaten the continuity of the supply of economy-wide core banking services because of the likelihood of contagion. Governments are afraid to let this happen.

Lying behind the policy problems is an information problem: for example, if the regulator could accurately observe the risks that are being taken on by a bank, it could intervene to keep it at the socially optimal level. One way that a policy maker could mitigate this market failure is to impose capital regulation as a method of inducing the bank to take on less risk (and thereby to operate closer to the socially optimal level of risk taking). This means the policy maker sets the size of the private capital buffer, which is there to absorb losses in the event the bank's assets fall in value. In the wake of the global financial crisis, reforms have been undertaken to make the financial system safer, to which we return in Chapter 10.

The response of the Japanese government to the financial crisis of the 1990s was to avoid banking failures. The approach of the US authorities in the late 1920s and early 1930s was the opposite, as witnessed by the famous suggestion that the banking crisis would 'purge the rottenness out of the system'.[9] As we shall see later in this

---

[9] In 1929, Andrew Mellon, the US Secretary of the Treasury at the time, urged the market to 'liquidate labour, liquidate stocks, liquidate the farmers and liquidate real estate... It will purge the rottenness out of the system.' (Quoted in *The Economist*, 28 Sept.–4 Oct. 2002.)

chapter, in the global financial crisis many banks in a range of different countries were bailed out. But a systemically important bank—Lehman Brothers—was allowed to fail with drastic effects on the world economy. Both responses—governments saving banks and governments letting banks fail—carry dangers.

9.2.3 **Government and central bank responsibilities**

Figure 9.2 shows the broad division of responsibility between the government and the central bank when it comes to dealing with liquidity and solvency problems in the banking system. We have already seen the first two points in the previous subsections, but can now add additional interactions between the central bank and the government.

1. The central bank is the lender of last resort to the banking system and provides liquidity at penalty interest rates in times of market distress. To mitigate liquidity problems, the central bank sets a reserve requirement, a minimum ratio of reserves to deposits that banks have to meet.
2. The government (i.e. the taxpayer) is responsible for the solvency of the banking system. If banks are to be bailed out, this is done by the government ultimately backed up by their tax-raising powers. To mitigate insolvency risk, banking regulators impose a capital ratio requirement on banks to limit their leverage.
3. The central bank is lender of last resort *to the government*. This is easiest to understand if we take the case where the government steps in to bail out failing banks. This leads to a rise in its debt, which is called *sovereign debt*. When there is a large increase in government debt, private sector holders of government bonds may lose confidence in the government's ability to service their debt and to repay the

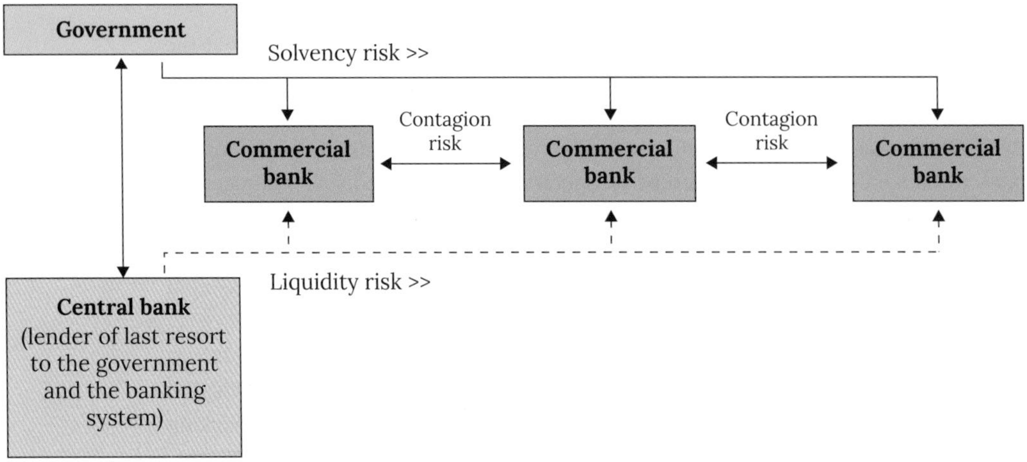

Figure 9.2 Governance arrangements between the government, the central bank, and the banking system. Note that government deposit insurance schemes establish a role for government in the management of liquidity risk.

Source: adapted from Winkler (2011).

principal. As a consequence, they sell the bonds. This leads to a drop in the price of the bond and a rise in the interest rate. The higher interest rate signals the market perception of elevated sovereign default risk. As discussed in Chapter 7, this makes government borrowing more costly, further increasing the risk of default. This is the point at which in countries with their own central bank, the central bank's role of lender of last resort to the government plays a part. The central bank can step in to buy government bonds should the need arise. This action would support the price of bonds and prevent interest rates from rising to reflect sovereign debt risk.

4. A well-functioning governance system requires the private sector to have confidence in both the government and central bank, and in the relationship between the two. From the previous point, we can see that the central bank can always buy government bonds. This is important in circumstances in which the government has to rescue the banking system through bail-outs, leading its own debt to rise. The confidence that the central bank will support the government *in extremis* helps to stabilize expectations of those in the private sector holding government bonds. The central bank needs to be confident that the purpose for which it is providing support to the government is well-defined and limited to the crisis caused by the need for bank bail-outs.

   In a closed economy, the central bank can create all the money it wants in order to buy government bonds, subject to the proviso that the private sector is willing to accept payment in the currency it issues. The pathological situation of hyperinflation arises when this ceases to be the case. The governance structure will disintegrate if the central bank is not confident that the government has controls in place on its expenditure. If it does not, then any independent role for the central bank disappears. In such a case, the government is using 'monetary financing', i.e. direct creation of reserves to fund its spending. This could lead to hyperinflation, as discussed in Section 6.5 of Chapter 6.

   Under less extreme conditions, the system of mutual confidence helps the economy to address the threat of a combined banking and public debt crisis: if the financial markets see the system as credible, a dangerously high sovereign default risk premium will not arise and interest rates on government bonds will remain low.

The different elements of the governance arrangements came into sharp focus during the global financial crisis and the associated Eurozone crisis. In relation to (1), central banks provided liquidity to the banking system in the early part of the financial crisis when markets were not functioning smoothly. Governments had to step in to rescue banks through recapitalization and nationalization once they became insolvent (2). The consequence was a sharp rise in government (i.e. sovereign) debt. The risk of sovereign default and its connection to the function of the central bank as the lender of last resort to government (3) was brought into the spotlight by the Eurozone crisis of 2010.

In the context of a common currency area, there are multiple governments but only one central bank: the European Central Bank is not the lender of last resort to the Eurozone member governments. When confidence in the ability of some Eurozone governments to service their debts fell, the country-specific default risk rose and interest rates on the bonds issued by these governments spiked. This was in contrast to the situation for countries with similar levels of government debt outside the Eurozone and hence, with their own central bank that could buy government bonds (4). See Chapter 14 for further analysis of the Eurozone crisis and a diagram similar to Figure 9.2 depicting the governance arrangements in the Eurozone.

9.3 PRE-CRISIS FINANCIAL SYSTEM: INCENTIVES, INSTRUMENTS, AND ACTORS

9.3.1 Incentives for risk-taking

In Chapter 8, we saw that the special characteristics of the banking industry have important economic consequences. When deciding on how much risk to take on, an individual bank takes no account of the implications of its decision for the risk of contagion across the banking sector as a whole. By neglecting the social costs of spillovers from its own bankruptcy to the rest of the economy, it will take on higher risk than is socially optimal. Moreover, as we saw in the previous section, the fact that for a systemically important bank there is a probability of bail-out by the government means that the individual bank may take on more risk than would be privately optimal in the absence of a possible bail-out.

The phrase 'banking on the state' has been used to describe the way banks took advantage of the fact that banking sector gains are privatized (i.e. accrue to bank shareholders, managers and employees), but the losses are (at least partly) socialized (i.e. the banking system is insured by the state).[10]

In addition to the prediction that retail banks will choose *too low* a capital buffer (that is, choose leverage that is too high) because they ignore the external effects of their decision and they place too little weight on the downside risk because of the possibility of state bail-out, the financial accelerator behaviour of households and investment banks sketched in Figures 8.1 and 8.2 can lead to a process of *rising* leverage. High and rising leverage of systemically important banks raises aggregate risk in the economy and creates vulnerability to a financial crisis as we have seen in Chapter 8—both in the form of a 'plain vanilla' financial crisis and a financial crisis centred on risk-taking by investment banks in their purchase of financial assets.

In the period before the global financial crisis:

1. The existing regulations provided incentives to both retail and investment banks to adopt strategies that added to aggregate risk in the economy.
2. The regulators indirectly encouraged this by allowing banks to use their own models to calculate the riskiness of their portfolios and report their risk-weighted assets.

---

[10] See Alessandri and Haldane (2009).

3. There was a lack of concern for the possibility that the financial system was becoming a risk to the economy as a whole. Small investors such as households no doubt believed regulators and professional investors were managing risk. Deposit insurance schemes encouraged these beliefs.
4. The benign macroeconomic environment and the widely held view that macroeconomic policy making had improved with the implementation of inflation targeting had the effect of encouraging households and banks to believe that aggregate risk in the economy had fallen.

9.3.2 Financial derivatives

There were three financial instruments at the centre of the financial crisis; the mortgage-backed security (MBS), the collateralized debt obligation (CDO) and the credit default swap (CDS). The instruments, which are examples of financial derivatives, were typically constructed using complex mathematical models and ushered in an era in which global finance became all but incomprehensible to those outside the industry. This section aims to cut through the complexity by providing a brief overview of these instruments that helps to illuminate the part they came to play in the pre-crisis global financial system.[11] Figure 9.3 sets out a simplified version of the relationship

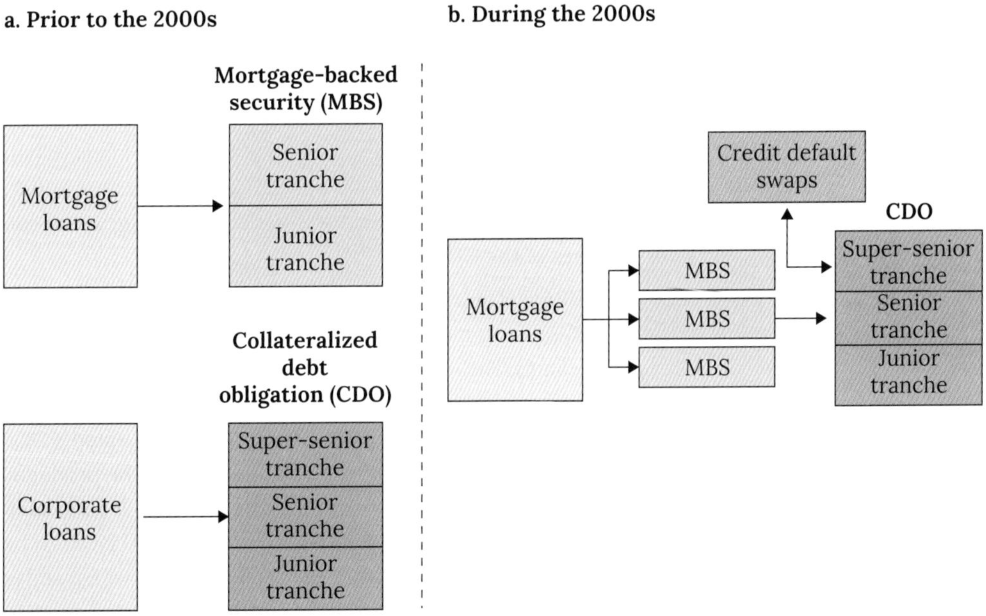

Figure 9.3 A stylized picture of the relationship between three key financial innovations (CDOs, MBSs and CDSs) prior to and during the 2000s.

[11] This section is based on MacKenzie (2009). For a detailed account of the role financial instruments played in the global financial crisis, see Tett (2009), Duffie (2018) as well as Duffie (2019).

between the three key financial instruments (MBSs, CDOs, and CDSs) prior to the year 2000 and then in the upswing phase of the financial cycle after the year 2000.[12]

1. **Mortgage-backed securities (MBSs):** A mortgage-backed security is a financial product secured by a collection of mortgages and referred to as a securitized financial asset. The investor buying the security receives a coupon on their investment that is generated by homeowners paying the interest on their mortgages. The risk of the MBS is the credit risk associated with homeowners not being able to repay their mortgages. The MBS mitigates this risk through two channels. The first is diversification; the mortgages underlying the securities were taken from different geographical regions of the United States. The second involved dividing the securities into '*tranches*'; investors in the lower or 'junior' tranche received a higher return, but were the first investors to lose money if some of the underlying mortgages defaulted. The investors' 'senior' tranche received much lower interest, but also bore less risk. They would only take losses should enough mortgages default to wipe out the entire junior tranche (see Figure 9.3). MBSs predated the crisis by around 20 years. It was thanks to their good track record and lack of defaults prior to the 2000s that they were not commonly talked about.
2. **Collateralized debt obligations (CDOs):** A collateralized debt obligation is similar to an MBS in that it is based on a bundle of underlying loans and is tranched to offer investors a range of products with different risk–return profiles. When CDOs were invented, they were focused on corporate, rather than housing loans. In repackaging and tranching these loans, a key precaution taken to avoid credit risk was to make sure the loans were well diversified across industries. The risk of a CDO comes down to the extent of 'correlation' in the bundle of loans. When correlation is low, defaults are isolated events and only the junior tranche is at risk. In contrast, when correlation is high, defaults are subject to clustering, which can endanger the safer tranches of the CDO.
3. **Credit rating agencies (CRAs):** The risk of financial products is assessed by the credit rating agencies (CRAs) using models and data on past correlations of asset performance (including default). The safest securities are given a rating of Triple A, which means the CRA attaches almost zero probability to default. Only a handful of corporations and governments have a triple A rating. The CRAs rated CDOs by analysing the correlations between the companies underpinning the products. They could do this relatively accurately due to the wealth of available data, such as stock prices and historical default data. When correlation was perceived to be low, the CRAs decided that it was so unlikely that the senior tranche would suffer losses that they awarded the CDO in question a triple A rating.

[12] The diagram is a simplified version of the extremely complex relationship between the three financial innovations. For example, CDOs in the 2000s often also contained corporate and other types of loans. The important thing to take away from the diagram is that CDOs made up of MBSs were not widespread before the 2000s.

4. **CDOs based on MBSs:** It was when banks began to create CDOs formed from MBSs (see Figure 9.3) in the 2000s that they became so dangerous. Evaluating the correlation of the underlying MBSs was intrinsically difficult because there was little historical default data. The CRAs set the correlation at very low levels in their models and senior tranches were awarded triple A ratings. The impeccable credit rating and the high return (relative to other 'safe' assets) on the senior tranches meant they were very attractive to institutional investors (e.g. pension funds, hedge funds, global banks) and were sold all across the globe, with Europe being a particularly strong source of demand. The CRAs, banks and investors, however, failed to take into account the similarity of the MBSs within the CDOs. Paradoxically, it was the geographical diversification of individual MBSs that led to CDOs based on MBSs becoming homogenized and therefore highly correlated. If house prices were to fall across the US, then it was not just some of those MBSs that would suffer losses, they all would. The banks originating the CDOs did not totally eliminate their credit risk, however, as upon generation of a CDO, there was a large tranche left over: the so-called 'super-senior tranche'. This tranche only took losses after the senior tranche was wiped out, and it was viewed as completely inconceivable that the super-senior tranche would take losses. In light of this, the tranche offered such low interest rates that it was difficult to sell to outside investors. Banks therefore largely kept this tranche and bought insurance on it in the form of a credit default swap (CDS).
5. **Credit Default Swaps (CDSs):** The US insurance giant AIG sold insurance in the form of credit default swaps (CDSs) on the super-senior tranches of CDOs held by banks and pledged to repay them in full should the super-senior tranche default. The very small insurance premiums paid by the banks provided AIG with a steady income stream and large profits in good times, but generated staggering losses when the value of CDOs collapsed, leading to a $180bn government-funded bail-out. The AIG bail-out dwarfed the size of the bail-out for any individual bank in the US.

These assets (financial derivatives) were sold in opaque, poorly regulated and understood 'over-the-counter' markets, which contributed significantly to the fragility of the financial system. The main dealers in these markets were the investment banks to which we now turn.[13]

9.3.3 **Actors and the risk-taking channel**

In the wake of widespread financial deregulation, the global financial landscape had changed dramatically from the 1970s. Banks across the developed world increased their return on equity, reduced their capital buffers and moved into higher risk activities, although as we shall see, as reported to regulators, risk had gone down. Implicit subsidies for banks increased because the state safety net for the banking system widened and deepened.

[13] Duffie (2018) provides a brief and accessible explanation of these markets and the problems they caused.

The search for yield

In the upswing prior to the global financial crisis, the process of banks aggressively pursuing strategies to increase their return on equity, also referred to as the 'search for yield', explained in the model in Chapter 8, accelerated. Different parts of the interconnected global financial system went about the search for yield in different ways. The strategies that were followed were influenced by the regulatory framework in which banks were operating. For example, while retail banks in the US and the government-sponsored housing enterprises such as the Federal Home Loan Mortgage Corporation (known as Freddie Mac) and the Federal National Mortgage Association (FNMA, known as Fannie Mae) entered the sub-prime mortgage market, the US investment banks and European banks were taking advantage of the lighter regulation of their leverage to shift their activities to the 'trading book' (see Chapter 8).

The US retail banks and government-sponsored housing agencies

The first half of the 2000s was associated with a rapid expansion of sub-prime mortgages in the United States. The US retail banks were at the heart of this process. Their regulatory framework made it difficult to pursue a strategy of high leverage to boost the return on equity, so they increased the riskiness of their asset pools instead. The banks making sub-prime mortgage loans were effectively removing a proportion of the credit risk from their balance sheets when they sold the mortgages on (via MBSs and CDOs) with the result that they had less incentive to properly assess the creditworthiness of the individuals to whom they were lending.

This strategy was followed by government-sponsored enterprises Fannie Mae and Freddie Mac and shadow banks like Countryside Financial; and insurance giant AIG sold insurance in the form of credit default swaps (CDSs) on the super-senior tranches of CDOs held by banks.

Global banks, the ratings agencies, and the financial regulators

Many of the large continental European banks are *universal banks* that engage in a combination of retail, commercial, wholesale, and investment banking activities. The pre-crisis period also saw the rise in the UK and the US of universal banks. In the US, this was formalized with the repeal in 1999 of the Glass-Steagall Act, which had been introduced in 1933 to improve the safety of the banking system by separating retail from investment banking activities following the experience of the banking crises in the Great Depression. Prominent examples of universal banks include Barclays in the UK and Citigroup in the US.

The global banking data further support the divergence in strategies between US retail and European global banks in the pre-crisis period. The data show that US retail banks' balance sheets had a higher risk per unit of assets than those of the European banks in the run-up to the crisis, but that European banks had much higher leverage.[14]

---

[14] See Alessandri and Haldane (2009). For cross-country data on leverage by type and size of bank using micro data, see Kalemli-Ozcan et al. (2012).

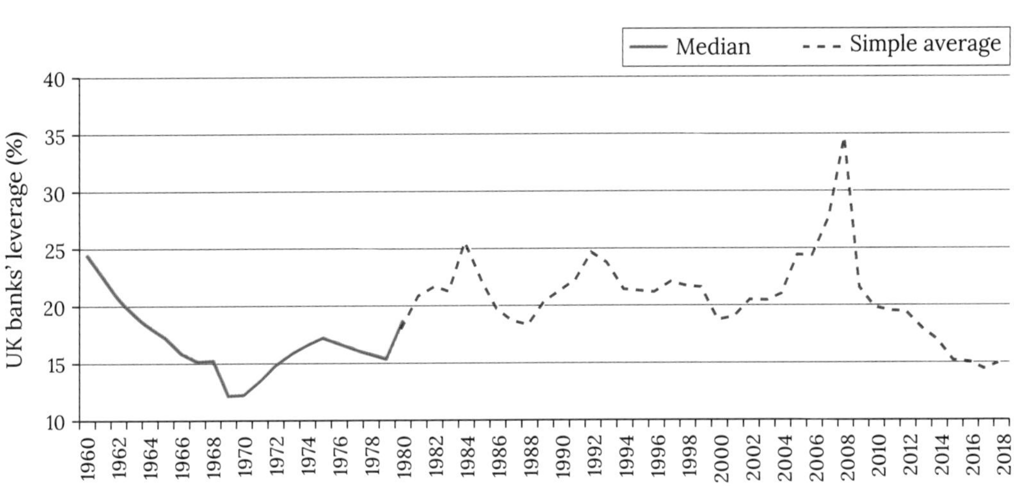

Figure 9.4 Regulated UK banks' leverage: 1960–2018.

Source: Bank of England Financial Stability Report, June 2012, and later data provided directly by the Bank of England.

The lack of regulatory restrictions on simple leverage in Europe meant that the banks could 'lever up' (i.e. expand their assets relative to their equity). Figure 9.4, which is repeated from Chapter 8, shows the dramatic increase in the leverage of UK banks in the years preceding the financial crisis. In terms of the modelling in Chapter 8, the European banks shifted more of their activities onto the trading book in the years before the crisis, where mark-to-market gains on these assets lifted short-term profits and the return to equity. The lax treatment of 'risk-weighted assets' by the regulators played a part in this.

The Basel II regulatory regime under which the European banks operated from 2004 required banks to put a given amount of capital aside (i.e. a minimum capital buffer) for each asset they held, depending on its risk weight. A risk weight is a measure of the abiliy of an asset to absorb losses.

The higher the rating of the asset (i.e. the safer it was perceived to be by the CRAs), the less capital is needed to be held against it (i.e. it received a low-risk weight). For example, triple A sovereign debt (government bonds) received a risk weight of 0%, meaning that no capital had to be held against it.[15] Assets are rated by CRAs, and three of them—Fitch, Moody's and Standard and Poor's—cover around 95% of the world market.[16] They rate both government bonds and privately created assets on a scale from triple A downwards. Under the Basel II regulatory framework, banks were allowed to use their own models to calculate their risk-weighted assets.

---

15 For more information on risk-weights in the Basel II Accord see: Bank for International Settlements (2006), *Part 2 of Basel II: International Convergence of Capital Measurement and Capital Standards: A Revised Framework*, 12–203. https://www.bis.org/publ/bcbs128.htm

16 European Commission (2013), *New rules on credit rating agencies (CRAs)—frequently asked questions*. https://ec.europa.eu/commission/presscorner/detail/en/MEMO_13_13

In the instruments section, we discussed the creation of financial assets with a range of risk profiles from an underlying pool of risky assets (including sub-prime mortgages). The European banks avidly purchased the (supposedly) safest of these assets (i.e. those rated triple A) during the 2000s. In the run-up to the crisis, there were fewer than ten companies in the world in any industry deemed creditworthy enough to warrant a triple A credit rating. In contrast, over 50,000 CDOs were assigned a triple A rating. Banks could use triple A-rated CDOs to increase their total assets without requiring much additional equity to be held. Borrowing to purchase these assets increased the leverage of the European banks.

From the perspective of the economy as a whole, the problem was that risk weights were *falling* due to the proliferation of triple A-rated assets while aggregate risk in the system was *rising*. Purchasers of these assets were often ill-informed about the quality of the assets they were buying and relied too heavily on the ratings agencies, as this quote from Gillian Tett attests:[17]

> The Germans, and the other continental Europeans 'were like the Japanese a decade earlier—the joke [on the trading desks] was that you could stuff them almost anything', one American banker later recalled.

The big five US investment banks

Five systemically important US investment banks were identified as posing the greatest danger to the financial system: Bear Stearns, Lehman Brothers, Merrill Lynch, Goldman Sachs, and Morgan Stanley. Like the IBs in the model of Chapter 8, these five were extremely highly leveraged and were dependent on vast sources of very short-term credit for their high volume small margin operations. In the event, they were revealed to have insufficient liquidity and capital buffers, which meant that when fears arose about their ability to fulfil overnight or within-day contracts, investors withdrew their funds, threatening the entire edifice of interconnected leveraged banking entities around the globe. Because of its central role in the day-to-day supply of liquidity, this flawed financial architecture in the US was key to the vulnerability of the global financial system.[18]

The shadow banking system

In the model presented in Chapter 8, we simplified by assuming that only investment banks borrowed to buy securitized assets. This was in order to keep the model as simple as possible and to draw a conceptual line between the activities of retail and investment banks. As we have seen, universal banks include both retail and investment banking activities. Along with investment banks, they were involved in the creation of the so-called shadow banking system.

The *shadow banking system* is defined by the Financial Stability Board (2012) as 'credit intermediation involving entities and activities outside of the regular banking system'. Shadow banking is the global capital-market based credit system: banks

[17] Excerpt from Tett (2009), pp. 116–17.

[18] See Duffie (2018) for more details about the mechanics of the operations of the big five.

moved activities into associated bank-like entities such as structured investment vehicles (SIVs) to keep these banking activities off their balance sheets and outside the scope of bank regulation. The shadow banking entities became heavily involved in both the demand and supply of securitized assets, as described in the stylized model in Sections 8.4 and 8.5.[19]

The global shadow banking system grew rapidly in the years preceding the financial crisis; it accounted for $65 trillion in 2011, up from $26 trillion in 2002. Put another way, the system was equivalent to 25% of global financial assets in 2011.[20] At the same time as aggregate risk was increasing in the regulated banking sector, for the reasons discussed above, it was being further boosted by the rapid growth of shadow banking.

Bank concentration and interconnectedness

The increases in *concentration* and *interconnectedness* were two key trends in financial systems prior to the financial crisis. The first trend saw the consolidation of national banking systems into the hands of a small number of 'too-big-to-fail' financial giants.[21] For example, the assets of the three largest UK banks exceeded 70% of total UK banking assets just prior to the crisis.[22] The second trend saw banks across the globe become more intertwined and dependent upon one another. For example, up to two-thirds of the huge expansion in banks' balance sheets in the run-up to the crisis was a result of increased claims within the financial system, rather than with non-financial agents.[23]

The nature of modern financial systems has led researchers to model them as networks, much in the same way epidemiologists or statistical physicists model their subject matter. Gai et al. (2011) provide an example of this technique, using a network model of interbank relations to mimic the key structural features of the financial system. The authors use this model to show how higher levels of concentration and interconnectedness in the financial system can increase the chances of systemic liquidity crises when key institutions become distressed.

In the wake of the economic crisis, some economists drew comparisons between ecological food webs and the spread of infectious diseases, and financial networks. This body of work criticizes banks' risk management processes for failing to take account of systemic risk. Haldane and May (2011) use a simple model to show that increasing homogeneity in the financial system—all the banks doing the same thing—increases system-wide risk. If all banks hold a similar set of assets this might minimize their own risk of failure (when considered in isolation) but can potentially make the system much more liable to collapse.

This research led central banks around the world to concentrate on how to design a regulatory framework that minimizes the risk of the system as a whole (referred to as

---

[19] See Claessens et al. (2012), Carletti et. al. (2020).

[20] These figures are taken from Claessens et al. (2012). This paper provides an excellent overview of shadow banking, and the relevant economics and policy.

[21] For a powerful analysis of the problem of 'too-big-to-fail' banks, see Johnson and Kwak (2010), *13 Bankers: The Wall Street Takeover and the Next Financial Meltdown.*

[22] See Gai et al. (2011).

[23] See Gai et al. (2011).

macro-prudential regulation), as opposed to each bank individually (micro-prudential regulation). A key task is to identify and monitor the systemically important banks. We return to this in Chapter 10.

9.4 THE UPSWING OF THE FINANCIAL CYCLE

In the first of the narrative sections, we apply the concept of the financial cycle, and the models of bubbles and the financial accelerator developed in Chapter 8, to help explain the upswing of the financial cycle prior to the global financial crisis. We focus on the United States where the crisis had its roots.

9.4.1 Inequality and sub-prime lending in the US

The US government has been involved in promoting home ownership since the 1930s, when the first housing Government-Sponsored Enterprises such as the FNMA (Fannie Mae) were established. The enterprises were aimed at supporting existing homeowners and keeping credit flowing for new mortgages in the wake of the Great Depression.[24]

These early government policies were focused on boosting home ownership amongst the general population. The mid-1990s saw the government change tack, however, and more aggressively pursue policies aimed at increasing home ownership rates amongst low-income earners, particularly those families that were unable to obtain mortgages through traditional channels. The stated aim of the Clinton Administration's *National Homeownership Strategy* was to ensure that 'working families can once again discover the joys of owning a home' and to 'add as many as eight million new families to America's homeownership rolls by the year 2000'.[25]

This legislation coincided with the beginning of the rapid expansion of sub-prime lending. It is estimated that at the onset of the global financial crisis in mid-2007, sub-prime mortgages accounted for 14% of all first-lien mortgages in the US and that 69% of all US households owned their own homes.[26]

The role of US government policy in encouraging home ownership among low-income earners in the run-up to the global financial crisis can be linked to rising income inequality, macroeconomic stability, and financial fragility (Rajan 2010).[27] Real wages for median workers had stagnated in the US from the 1970s. One way of interpreting the macroeconomic importance of the policy of encouraging higher worker indebtedness (and aspirations for home ownership) is that it helped to sustain

---

[24] For an overview of the history of the housing Government-Sponsored Enterprises, see Federal Home Finance Agency Office of Inspector General (n.d.), 'A brief history of the housing government-sponsored enterprises'. https://www.fhfaoig.gov/Content/Files/History%20of%20the%20Government%20Sponsored%20Enterprises.pdf

[25] The document is available online at https://www.globalurban.org/National_Homeownership_Strategy.pdf

[26] See Ben Bernanke's speech on May 17th 2007 entitled *The Subprime Mortgage Market*.

[27] And, for a formal model of shifts in bargaining power and financial instability, see Kumhof and Ranciere (2010).

aggregate demand following the bursting of the dotcom bubble in 2000 in an economy where real wage growth for the majority of workers had ceased.

In terms of the 3-equation model, weak business investment post 2000 and the longer run weakness in consumption demand threatened to lead to deflation in the recession of 2001. This encouraged policy makers to support the sub-prime housing market as a source of aggregate demand (i.e. to prevent the IS curve from shifting to the left, which could threaten the Fed's mandate for employment and price stability). Little attention was given to the potential risks of financial fragility arising from rising household indebtedness.

There is a lot of evidence that securitization and structured finance had the effect of reducing the cost of funding for banks and reducing the surveillance by banks of their housing loans. Brunnermeier (2009, p.82) summarizes the expansion of this sub-prime lending:

> Mortgage brokers offered teaser rates, no-documentation mortgages, piggy-back mortgages (a combination of two mortgages that eliminates the need for a down payment), and NINJA ('no income, no job or assets') loans.

There is still debate about the direction of causality in the house price bubble and the relative importance of policies encouraging loans to sub-prime borrowers as compared with the role of beliefs that house prices would rise, which generated demand for such loans, along with willing suppliers and the associated proliferation of mortgage-based derivatives.[28]

Consistent with the financial accelerator mechanism of Chapter 8, more lending fuelled rising house prices, and rising house prices in turn increased the willingness of banks to lend without making checks on the ability of borrowers to repay from income because the rising prices increased the value of the banks' collateral. In line with the model of extrapolative price expectations, the expectations of rising house prices also increased the incentive for households to borrow more. In short, households were able and incentivized to increase their leverage. Evidence suggests that this occurred right across the income distribution and was not concentrated in the sub-prime sector of the market.[29]

Leverage is defined as the ratio of an agent's assets to their equity. For example, for a borrower household, its asset is the house it owns, its liability is the mortgage taken out to buy the house, and its equity is the difference between the two. At the time the house is purchased, the household's equity is the downpayment they made. In this case, the household's leverage is the ratio of the value of their house to their equity. The more debt (i.e. the bigger the mortgage) the household has relative to its equity, the higher is its leverage.

When asset prices are rising, higher leverage makes the return on equity higher. If the house price is \$200,000 and the household makes a downpayment of 10%, i.e.

---

[28] Foote et al. (2012) explain how beliefs about house prices explain behaviour in the mortgage market in this period.

[29] See Foote et al. (2021).

\$20,000, it borrows \$180,000. Its initial leverage ratio is $\frac{200}{20} = 10$. Suppose the house price rises to \$220,000, i.e. a rise of 10%. The return to the equity the household invested is 100% (from \$20k to \$40k). Households who are convinced house prices are going to rise will want to increase their leverage—that's how they get a high return. To see this, calculate the return on equity if the downpayment had been only 5%, i.e. an initial leverage ratio of $\frac{200}{10} = 20$.

As discussed in Chapters 1 and 8, the role of a financial accelerator effect in the consumption function is confirmed in empirical research by Aron et al. (2012), who find that growth in housing wealth (i.e. rising house prices) positively affects consumption in the UK and the US. The authors also find that the strength of this relationship increased as these economies became more financially liberalized during the Great Moderation.

Figure 8.1 showed how the house price feedback process can amplify the upswing of a leverage cycle through the collateral effect. The additional leverage increases returns to households when house prices are rising, but as we shall see, if the house price falls, then all of the equity of the household can be wiped out. In our example with a leverage ratio of 10, a fall in the house price by 10% wipes out the equity; if the leverage ratio is 20, a fall of only 5% eliminates the household's equity. Any greater fall in the house price means that they own an asset worth less than the amount they owe on it.

The combination of a long period of rising house prices and easy access to cheap credit encouraged bubbles in the housing market. In Chapter 8, we saw that a bubble can occur when the price of an asset rises beyond what is consistent with the fundamentals (in terms of long-run forces of demand and supply). This is illustrated by the construction boom in the US in the 2000s. In cities like Phoenix or Las Vegas, Arizona, house prices increased by between 75 and 100% from 2003 until their peak in 2006. A look at Phoenix on Google Earth shows that there is virtually unlimited scope for house-building. This suggests that the long-run supply curve for housing is flat and that the higher prices were not sustained by fundamentals (see Figure 8.8).[30]

The global nature of the financial upswing

The financial upswing of the 2000s was different from those that came before it. The size of cross-border banking flows meant this upswing affected more countries across the world and was of a greater magnitude than previous upswings. The financial boom had its roots in the US sub-prime mortgage market, but was transmitted around the world. Some of the mechanisms predated the 2000s such as: (a) European regulatory regimes allowing for high leverage because of low-risk weighting, and (b) the incentives for risk taking provided by the implicit state guarantee for the banking system.

The preexisting factors became salient when they were combined with important developments in the financial system that occurred during the 2000s, such as:

1. financial innovations creating assets from US mortgages and consumer loans that could easily be traded around the world,

[30] See Laibson, D. (2009), 'Bubble Economics' [PowerPoint presentation], Econometric Society Meetings, 4th June 2009, Boston University. https://scholar.harvard.edu/laibson/publications/bubble-economics

2. the growing dominance of 'too big to fail' banks,
3. the rise in importance of and trust in the ratings agencies for bank portfolio decisions, and
4. the prevalence of incentives in banks for 'search for yield' behaviour, which was rewarded with high bonuses.

The global banking system, including the shadow banking complex, became involved in a bank-centred financial accelerator process of the kind set out in Chapter 8. An important component of the steep upswing in the financial cycle between 2000 and the global financial crisis arose because European global banks became heavily involved in borrowing from the US money markets and in using these funds to buy the securitized financial assets from the shadow banking complex. The European banks therefore played an important role in helping to inflate the US sub-prime bubble by indirectly providing credit to US borrowers. The role of cross-border activities is illustrated in a schematic way in Figure 9.5. In the figure, 'banks' refers to US retail banks.

The sheer size of the European lending to the US in the pre-crisis period was staggering. The data reported in Shin (2012) from the Bank of International Settlements shows that European banks reporting to the BIS lent to US counterparties

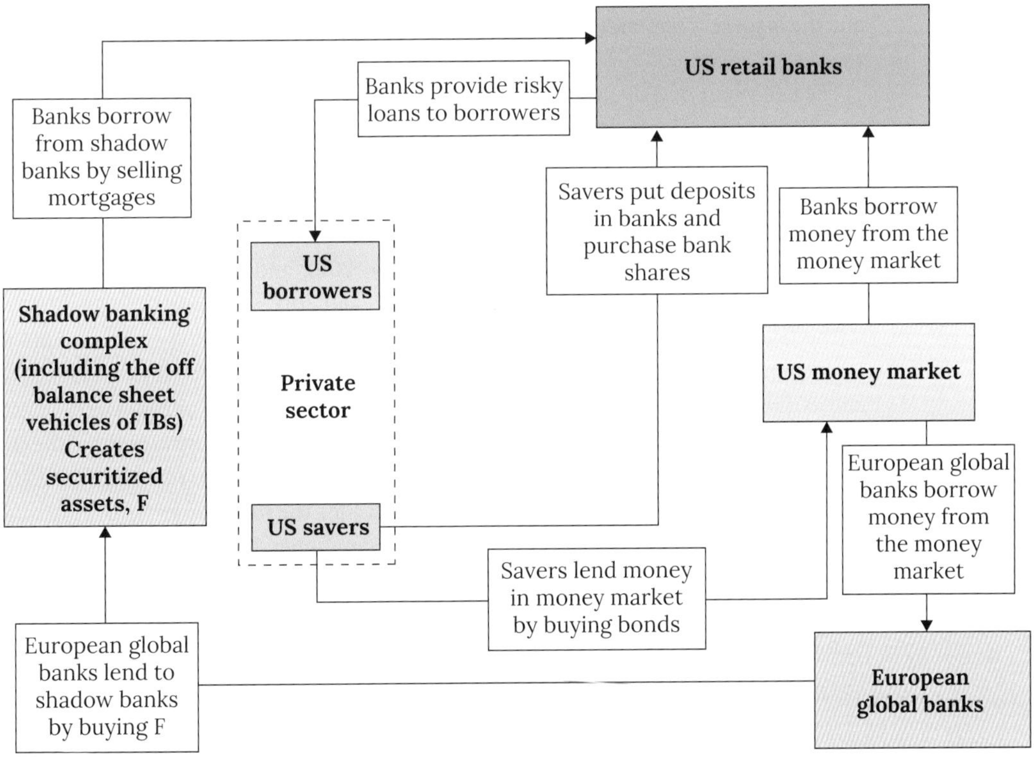

Figure 9.5 The banking system in the upswing of the financial cycle including cross-border banking activities.

Note: F are the securitized assets introduced in Chapter 8. 'Banks' refers to US retail banks.

around \$5 trillion dollars in 2007. The research highlights the large presence of European banks in the market for securitized assets prior to the crisis:[31]

> [T]he picture that emerges is of a substantial amount of credit being extended to US borrowers by the European banks, albeit indirectly through the shadow banking system in the United States through the purchase of mortgage-backed securities and structured products generated by securitization.

In addition, Shin (2012) finds that a high proportion of the money used to purchase these assets came from US prime money market funds (MMFs). In 2008, the short-term liabilities of European banks accounted for roughly half the total assets of US prime MMFs, highlighting the importance of US money markets as a source of funding for global European banks.

9.5 **THE CRISIS**

9.5.1 **The scale of the crisis and nature of the post-crisis recession**

The global financial crisis produced the worst recession since the Great Depression of the 1930s (setting aside the effect on global output of the economic collapse in the defeated countries at the end of the Second World War). The upper panel of Figure 9.6 shows the GDP growth performance of 19 high-income economies (including Japan and the biggest economies from Western Europe, North America, and Australasia) over the last 150 years.

The behaviour of GDP in the crisis was not uniform across different countries—this was a recession that started in the high-income economies and took its largest toll there. This is illustrated in the lower panel of Figure 9.6, which shows that emerging and developing economies managed to avoid a recession. The large, fast growing, emerging economies were also the driving force behind the economic recovery, with India and China expanding by over 10% in 2010, and continuing to markedly outperform the advanced economies in both 2011 and 2012.[32]

The failure of US investment bank Lehman Brothers in the third quarter of 2008 is frequently cited as the pivotal event for the global economic downturn. Figure 9.7 shows the dramatic deterioration of macroeconomic indicators across the G7 that followed this event. The charts separate the United States from the remainder of the G7 (referred to as the G6). To make comparisons easier, in each chart, the index for each measure (except the unemployment rate) is set at 1 for the fourth quarter of 2007 and a vertical line marks the collapse of Lehmans in September 2008.

In April 2009, the IMF pointed out that two features of the recession–its association with deep financial crisis and its highly synchronized nature–suggest that it was likely to be unusually severe and followed by a slow recovery.

---

[31] See Shin (2012), p. 167.

[32] Source: IMF World Economic Outlook database, April 2013.

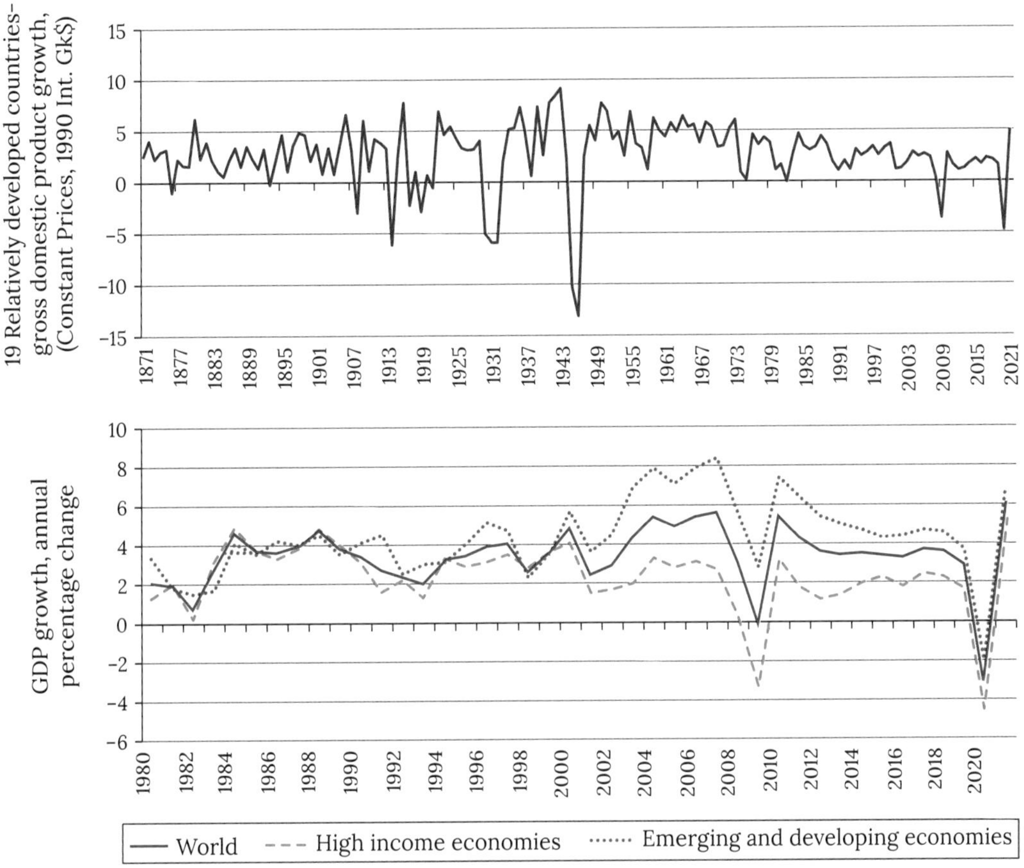

Figure 9.6 Major high-income economies GDP growth 1871–2021 (upper panel) and GDP growth by country group 1980–2021 (lower panel).

Source: Angus Maddison (GGDC); OECD statistics; IMF *World Economic Outlook*, April 2022.

The data in Figure 9.7 show that in line with the IMF forecast:

1. The recovery in GDP was not V-shaped: growth in the recovery was not faster than the previous trend growth rate and did not take economies rapidly back to their previous trend growth path. Instead, growth was at best similar to the trend growth rate (i.e. the post-trough path is roughly parallel with the pre-crisis path). In some countries such as the UK, however, growth did not return to the pre-crisis trend. As noted in Chapter 8, by the first quarter of 2013, UK GDP was still 4% below its pre-crisis peak in Q1 of 2008, and was a full 14% below the level it would have been had the pre-crisis trend not been interrupted by the crisis and extended recession.[33] Elsewhere in Europe, the situation was worse, as the Eurozone crisis compounded the effects of the financial crisis (see Chapter 14).

[33] The pre-crisis trend level of growth was calculated as the average quarterly growth rate for the 15 years prior to the recession (i.e. 1993 Q1 and 2007 Q4). Source: UK Office for National Statistics (data accessed June 2013) and authors' calculations.

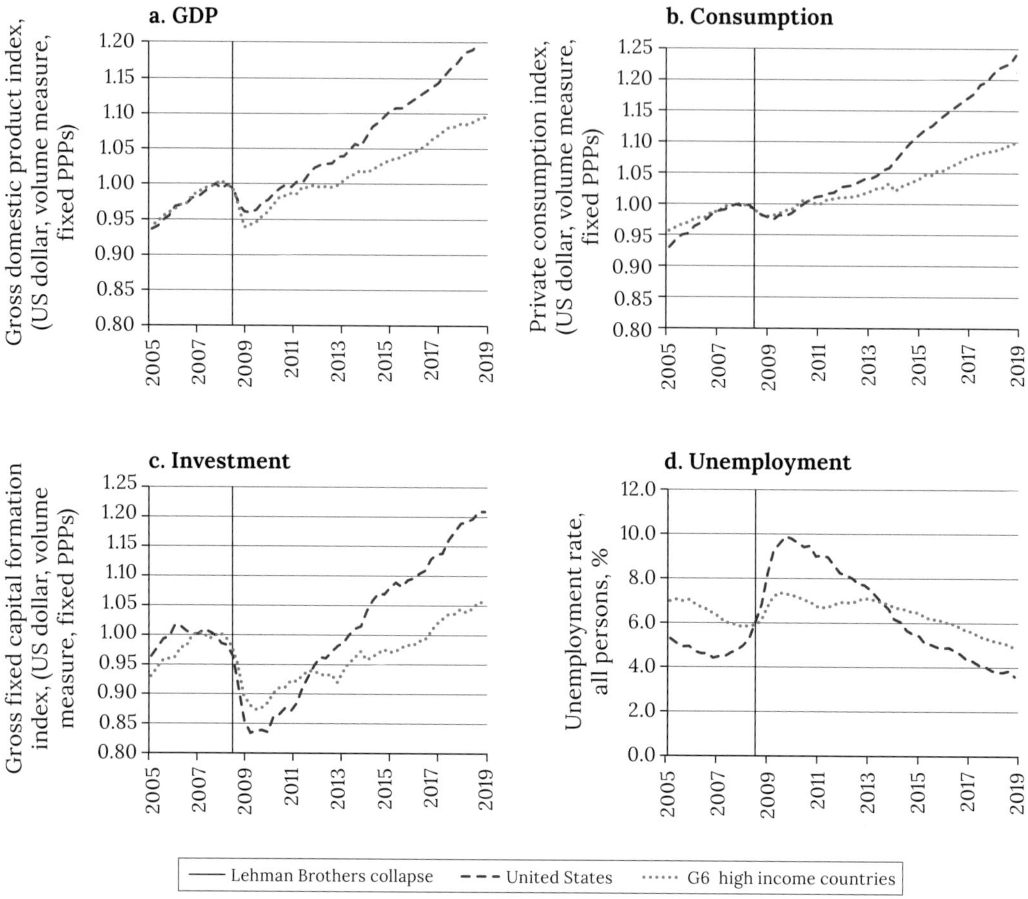

Figure 9.7 Key macroeconomic indicators for the G7 economies between 2005 Q1 and 2019 Q2.

Note: GDP, consumption and investment have been normalized so that 2007 Q4 = 1. The unemployment rate refers to the harmonized unemployment rate for all persons and is seasonally adjusted. The vertical line at 2008 Q3 is to mark the collapse of Lehman Brothers.

Source: OECD, Quarterly National Accounts (data accessed October 2019).

2. As the models of consumption and investment in Chapter 1 would predict, the response of consumption to the crisis was smoother than that of investment.
3. Whereas the behaviour of GDP, consumption and investment were similar in the US and the G6, unemployment was not. For the G6, unemployment was falling prior to the crisis while it was rising in the US. The post-crisis rise in unemployment in the US was much greater than in the G6, with the unemployment rate doubling in the US.

The volatility of the S&P stock index is often used to proxy for 'fear' in financial markets. Figure 9.8 shows that fear reached its highest level since the Great Depression in the autumn of 2008. This was clearly a crisis that emanated in financial markets, but did not end there. It quickly spread to affect real economic activity, plunging the world economy into recession.

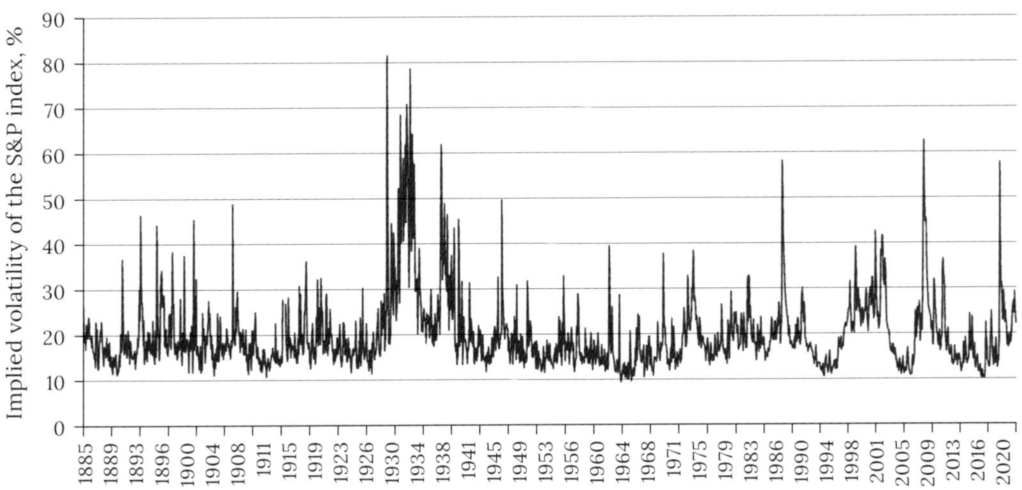

Figure 9.8 The implied volatility of the S&P index between February 1885 and August 2022.
Source: Nicholas Bloom (2009) and Chicago Board Options Exchange.

9.5.2 **The credit crunch**

The credit crunch of 2007–09 was at first largely confined to financial markets. It had three key stages, beginning with the fall in house prices in the US. The second stage was the seizing up of money markets and the third, the collapse and bankruptcy of Lehman Brothers in September 2008.

The collapse of the sub-prime housing market

The Federal Reserve embarked on a cycle of tightening monetary policy from late 2004 onwards in response to mounting inflationary pressures arising from the increase in oil and commodity prices. After a time this started to depress the housing market, as it made it more expensive to borrow, and pushed up the repayments of existing borrowers. The associated fall in house prices meant sub-prime borrowers started to struggle to make their repayments. They could no longer rely on using the rising values of their properties to obtain more loans (to keep up with mortgage repayments) and the financial accelerator mechanism propagated the effects across the economy. Households began to go into negative equity and to default on their housing loans.

The first sign in the financial markets of the growing default rate on home loans came in February 2007 when the index of the value of mortgage credit default swaps dropped sharply.[34] In early August 2007, the problems in the US housing market hit the money markets. Consistent with the arguments above about the role of European banks, the announcement by the French bank BNP Paribas that it could not value its structured financial products, and was therefore stopping redemptions from some of its investment funds, signalled that the crisis was going global. BNP Paribas' investment

[34] See Figure 1 in Brunnermeier (2009).

funds (and others across the world) had bought tranches of the CDOs containing sub-prime mortgages, and suddenly the value of these assets was in doubt.

The seizing up of the money markets

In the course of their normal activities, banks rely on two important money markets to fund themselves when they need short-term liquidity to re-finance their short-term loans. These are:

1. The repo market described in Chapter 5, which operates by banks selling securities and agreeing to buy them back as the loan matures. These loans are secured by collateral.
2. The commercial interbank money market where banks lend to each other short term (from overnight up to three months) unsecured.

Banks had become increasingly dependent on short-term funding, especially the type that used mortgage-backed securities (such as asset-backed commercial paper) as collateral. Short-term funding has to be rolled over frequently. When sub-prime borrowers started defaulting and house prices fell, these securities became hard to value, and hence lenders were reluctant to continue accepting them as collateral for loans. Other collateral was used in repo transactions in the money market but, as solvency questions arose for some banks, bigger haircuts were called for and these markets began to seize up from the autumn of 2007.[35]

An important indicator of the seizing up of the money markets in the credit crunch was the behaviour of interest rates on the interbank market. Before the crisis, the difference between the Bank of England official bank rate and the three-month interbank rate (which is unsecured) was very low, reflecting the prevailing mood of low risk. Once fears developed about liquidity risk, this reduced the supply of interbank loans (which suddenly seemed risky), pushing up the interest rate on them.

Figure 9.9 shows what happened to the three-month interbank rate relative to the Bank of England official bank rates between January 2005 and May 2013. The spread between these two interest rates shows the risk premium attached to interbank lending and is displayed in the lower panel: the jump in August 2007 is clear. Liquidity risk emerged as an important phenomenon in the short-term money market.

Although banks appeared to have shifted all three forms of risk (see Box 9.1 on types of risk) through the creation of so-called special purpose investment vehicles, which were part of the shadow banking complex, the regulated banks themselves were ultimately subject to liquidity risk. When demand for short-term asset-backed commercial paper dried up because households, firms, local government finance offices, and pension funds, etc., did not know how to value it, the bank's special

[35] A bigger haircut means that the loan that can be taken out against a given market value of an asset which is being used as collateral is smaller. For example, in the case of a safe asset, the haircut might be 5%, which means a $1000 US Treasury Bill will be accepted as collateral for a $950 loan.

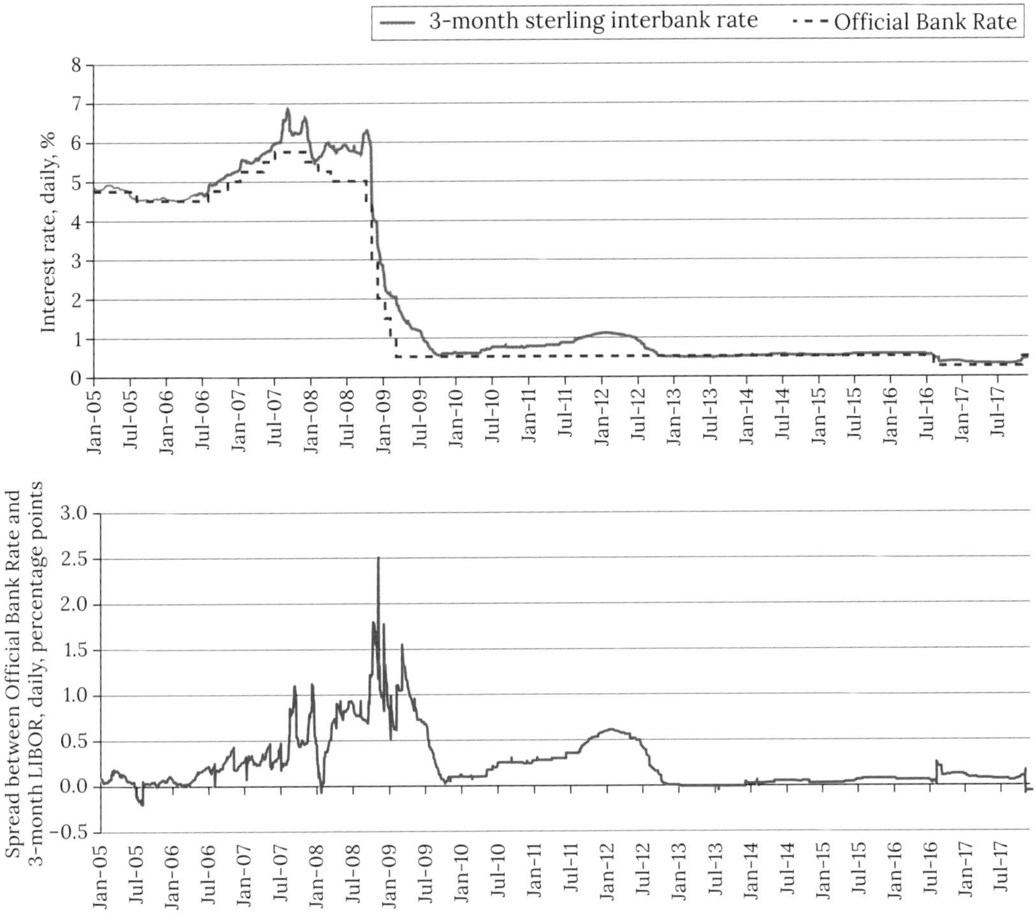

Figure 9.9 UK Official Bank Rates and three-month sterling interbank rates (upper panel), and their spread (lower panel): Jan 2005–Dec 2017.

Source: Bank of England (data accessed October 2019).

investment vehicle (SIV) was not able to fund itself and the parent bank had to provide the required liquidity.

The bank run on the British bank Northern Rock in September 2007 illustrates the role of short-term funding (i.e. liquidity) risk. With Northern Rock, the UK (where, at the time, there was only limited deposit insurance) experienced its first bank run in over 140 years, when depositors nationwide queued to retrieve their savings. The queues started to form in response to the announcement in the media of the Bank of England's emergency liquidity support for the bank.

In this case, the bank run was not a panic-based coordination failure—it was based on the insolvency of the bank arising from its liquidity problems. The bank eventually had to be nationalized. The underlying cause of its failure pre-dates the depositor bank run and reflected a shift in bank funding from deposits to money market funding. In the summer of 2007, only 23% of Northern Rock's liabilities were in the form of

BOX 9.1 Types of risk

Banks are exposed to the following risks:

1. *Liquidity risk*. As we have explained in Chapter 5, the service offered by the bank to instant-access savers is that they can withdraw their deposits at will. An unexpected withdrawal of deposits by savers exposes the bank to liquidity risk and will require the bank to get hold of liquidity (i.e. before loans are due to mature): it has to borrow or sell some assets. Banks can also be exposed to liquidity risk if lenders refuse to roll over short-term debt on maturity (i.e. provide another identical loan).
2. *Credit (or default) risk*. If the borrower fails to meet their mortgage interest payments, this is a default and it means a loss for the bank. A bank is itself subject to credit risk and ultimately to insolvency when the value of its assets falls.
3. *Interest rate risk*. If the bank makes a mortgage loan at a fixed interest rate and pays savers a variable interest rate linked to the central bank's policy rate, then if the central bank increases the policy rate, the spread falls and the bank suffers a fall in its profit margin.

retail deposits, by far the largest component was short-term borrowing from money markets.

This case shows how banks that had not been involved in sub-prime lending directly were nevertheless pulled into the sub-prime crisis through being over-leveraged and relying too much on short-term debt to finance their operations (Shin 2009b). When fear hit the money markets, it became impossible for Northern Rock to fund its loans as they came due to be rolled over: its excessive level of liquidity risk was revealed and depositors rationally sought to withdraw their deposits.

Lehman Brothers: The pivotal event

In Figures 9.8 and 9.9, showing respectively the 'fear index' of stock market volatility and the spread in the interbank market, there is a large spike on September 15th 2008. This marks the day Lehman Brothers declared bankruptcy. This highly leveraged institution became insolvent, as short-term funding dried up and the value of its assets collapsed. Unlike the US investment bank Bear Stearns that was rescued in March 2008, Lehman's was not rescued. The ramifications for the financial markets of letting Lehman's fail were bigger than the US government had expected. The S&P 500 fell nearly 5% that day and the VIX index (which measures the volatility of the S&P 500 and is shown in Figure 9.8) jumped from 25.6 to 31.7. This was not just a one-off shock however, but had wide ranging consequences for financial markets and for the real economy. It was the catalyst that plunged the majority of the world economy into the recession illustrated in Figures 9.6 and 9.7.

9.5.3 The crisis, macroeconomic policy, and the 3-equation model

The credit crunch and recession following the global financial crisis revealed two shortcomings in the widely adopted inflation-targeting monetary policy regime.

1. The first is that the policy interest rate may only weakly affect the lending rate faced by firms and households.
2. The second is that in a crisis, conventional monetary policy loses its effectiveness if the central bank needs to achieve a real interest rate unattainable because the nominal rate cannot be lowered below zero (the ZLB).

The policy rate and the lending rate

In Chapter 5, we saw that (a) the policy rate and the money market rate are virtually identical and (b) the spread between the policy rate, r^P, and the lending rate, r, depends on the riskiness of loans, the risk appetite of the banks, and the capital buffer, all of which in normal times are stable. It is the combination of (a) and (b) along with the interest-sensitivity of aggregate demand that under normal circumstances gives monetary policy its power.

Spread of money market above policy rate

Figure 9.9 shows that the spread between market and policy interest rates rose during the crisis. Providers of funding to banks (e.g. money markets with cash to invest) required a risk premium on loans to take into account the probability that the bank they were lending to went out of business and would be unable to repay. In the wake of the unexpected bankruptcy of Lehman Brothers, this risk premium was substantial, as shown by the jump in the series in mid-September 2008.

Spread of mortgage rate above policy rate

Figure 9.10 relates to (b) and shows that the spread between Bank of England base rate and the mortgage rates being charged by UK banks also increased dramatically after the collapse of Lehman Brothers. The figure shows that UK mortgage rates remained at a high level even after the threat of financial collapse receded and in the face of severe cuts in central bank interest rates. This reflects a rise in funding costs for the banks due to the rise in money market rates, reflecting both increased liquidity risk and increased credit risk, of banks and of borrowers. The model of Chapter 5 would predict a rise in the markup of the lending rate above the cost of funding to reflect the higher credit risk on their loan book. Compared with the benevolent conditions of the Great Moderation, which are likely to have raised the tolerance of risk by banks, the shift to a post-Lehman's world would have been expected to reduce risk tolerance and push the markup over funding costs higher. The risk tolerance term can be interpreted as reflecting the credit risk of banks themselves.

To summarize, a double spread in lending rates emerged in the crisis due to the higher credit risk of the bank itself, as well as of the borrower. The disconnect between the policy rate and the lending rate in the crisis represented a breakdown of a key transmission mechanism of monetary policy in the inflation-targeting framework,

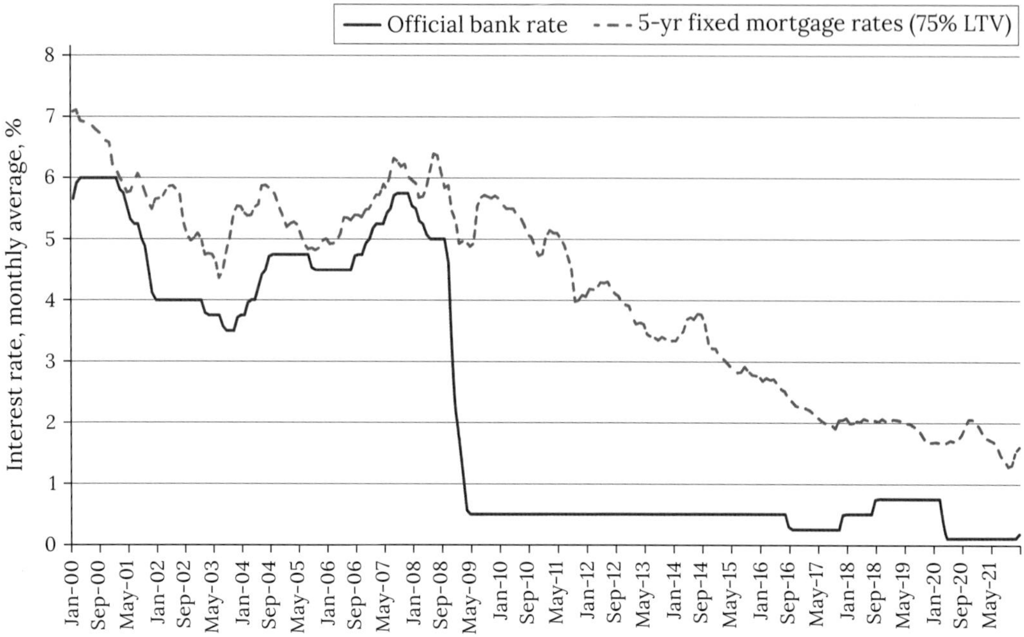

Figure 9.10 UK Official Bank Rates and five-year fixed mortgages rates (75% LTV): Jan 2000 to Dec 2021.
Source: Bank of England (data accessed June 2022).

which relies on changes in the policy rate (r^P) by the central bank to alter the lending rate (r) for households and firms.

The zero lower bound on nominal interest rates

The first step to understanding what happened after the credit crunch requires reintroducing the concept of the zero lower bound (ZLB) on nominal interest rates, which was covered in detail in Chapter 3. We need to rewrite the Fisher equation to reflect the distinction between r and r^P. To reiterate briefly, when we combine the Fisher equation, $i = r^P + \pi^E$, with the fact that nominal interest rates cannot fall below zero, we find the minimum real interest rate that the central bank can set in any period is:

$$\text{Min } r^P = -\pi^E. \tag{9.1}$$

The negative demand shock

According to the S&P/Case-Shiller US National Home Price Index, US house prices began falling in mid-2006. One contributory factor was the rise in interest rates as the Federal Reserve responded to the inflation shock caused by the hike in oil prices in 2005. The smooth return of the economy to target inflation that would normally be expected did not take place. Instead, falling house prices triggered the sub-prime crisis with the national and international ramifications we have described.

We can map the consequences of the sub-prime crisis in the 3-equation model (see Figure 9.11). To make the diagram as clear as possible, we assume the economy begins

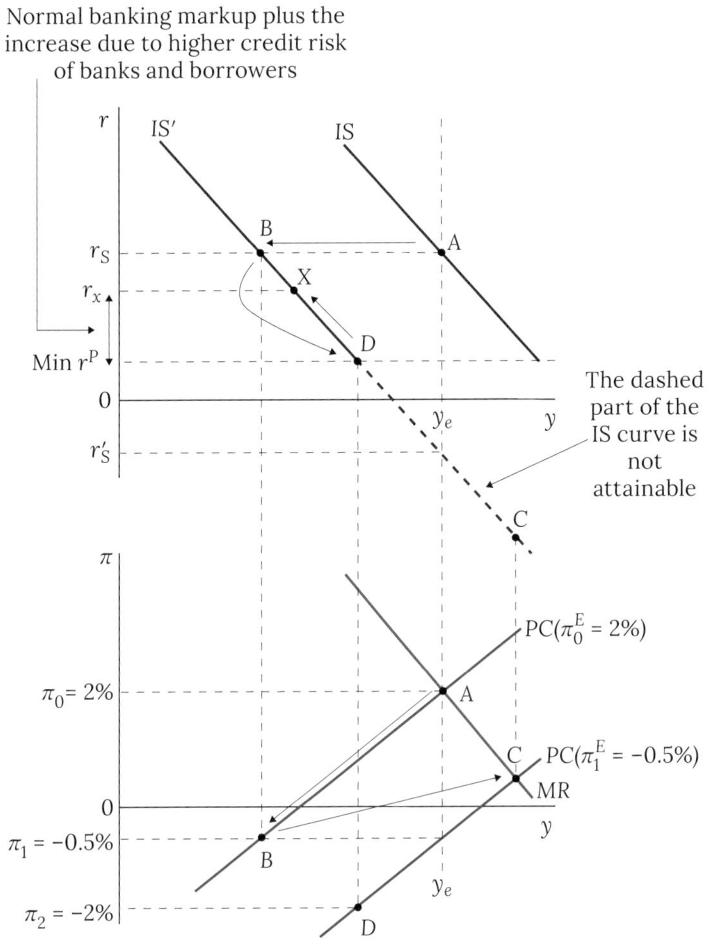

Figure 9.11 The sub-prime crisis and the limits to conventional monetary policy.

in equilibrium with inflation at target. In the autumn of 2007, the credit crunch began. We can model this as follows:

1. The fall in house prices caused a marked reduction in consumption and housing investment. In addition, investment fell due to the increase in uncertainty. These effects combined to cause a severe reduction in aggregate demand, and the IS curve shifts a long way to the left to IS′.
2. The central bank forecasts inflation in the usual way and identifies its target output gap to get the economy on to the MR curve. The desired real interest rate is low (point C), due to the size of the negative demand shock (note that the new stabilizing real interest rate is at r'_S). Since the *nominal* interest rate cannot be negative, we use Min r^P, as defined by Equation 9.1, to check whether the desired real interest rate is attainable.

3. From Figure 9.11, we can see that even when the nominal interest rate is cut to zero, monetary policy is unable to get the economy on to the *MR* line at point C. The dashed section of the IS curve to the right of its intersection with the Min r^P line indicates the points on the schedule that are unattainable: the Min r^P line is pinned down by the fact that expected inflation is −0.5%: this means that the lowest possible real interest rate, given that the nominal interest rate cannot go below zero, is 0.5%. The highest attainable level of output is shown by point D.
4. In fact, in 2008, the situation was worse than shown by point D. Unusually large interest rate spreads above the policy rate emerged so that borrowers were faced with the higher lending rate shown by point X, even further away from the central bank's desired output level at point C.

The debt-deflation trap

In the analysis of the credit crunch in the 3-equation model, the limits to the effectiveness of monetary policy are clear. As interest rates in the major high-income economies were slashed to near zero during the crisis, policy makers feared the economy would enter a deflation trap with a vicious circle of falling prices, rising real interest rates, and contracting output. The case of the economy falling into a deflation trap is shown using the 3-equation model in Chapter 3 (see Figure 3.13).

Once a deflation trap is entered, another channel can depress aggregate demand further. If asset prices in the economy (e.g. property prices) are falling as well as goods prices, then debtors in the economy will not only find that the real burden of their debt is rising (the debt is fixed in nominal terms but prices are falling), but also that the assets that they have used as security or collateral for the debt are shrinking in value. This is the financial accelerator process described in Chapter 8. It will amplify the downward spiral of economic activity. The financial accelerator mechanism shifts the IS curve further to the left. Heightened uncertainty in the economy is likely to make investment less sensitive to the interest rate, thereby steepening the IS and weakening the investment response even if positive inflation expectations and a sufficiently low real interest rate could be generated.

Household debt, inequality, and the transmission of the crisis

Evidence has accumulated for the importance of the household debt-based transmission of the financial crisis to aggregate demand. An important channel through which falling house prices affected household spending in the US and in other countries with elevated household debt ratios was through the deterioration of household balance sheets. This is the crisis counterpart to the boom in house prices stimulated by the expansion of lending, including of sub-prime loans to low-income households.[36] Studies find that consumption fell by more in local areas where household debt had risen the most prior to the crisis. Households with low income and wealth were found to cut back more on consumption for a given fall in housing prices, highlighting the

---

[36] Mian and Sufi (2018) provide an explanation of the empirical methods and results confirming the credit-driven household demand channel for a large number of countries over forty years.

effect on the aggregate economy of their higher marginal propensity to consume out of income and wealth. The spillover from the collapse in consumption to depressing local employment in services—the multiplier in action—was also observed.

9.6 POLICY INTERVENTION IN THE CRISIS

In this section we look first at the lessons that were drawn by policy makers from the Great Depression as to how they should respond to the global financial crisis. Second, we look at the policies that were implemented in the teeth of the crisis in 2008–09. Third, we turn to the policies adopted in the Great Recession that followed the global financial crisis. We shall see that the policies implemented in the crisis phase in 2008–09 were strongly influenced by the economic analysis of the Depression that had accumulated over the years since the 1930s. However, although monetary and fiscal policy were used aggressively to support economic activity, the fiscal stimulus used in the crisis phase was rapidly replaced by fiscal austerity in Europe while economies were still in recession. The special circumstances of the members of the Eurozone, where a sovereign debt crisis emerged in 2010, are discussed in Chapter 14.

9.6.1 Lessons from the Great Depression

The policy response to the Great Depression exacerbated the world's economic woes.[37] There were two key mistakes made by the US authorities, which crippled their economy and reverberated around the world.

1. Contractionary monetary and fiscal policy: The slump in economic output was met with a tightening of policy. The money supply contracted by a third between 1929 and 1933, largely as a result of poor policy from the Federal Reserve and a slew of bank failures. The government also increased tax rates on individuals and businesses. These contractionary policies reinforced the downwards spiral of demand in the economy.
2. A rise in protectionism: In the early stages of the depression, President Hoover introduced the infamous Tariff Act of 1930, which raised import tariffs on over 20,000 products to record levels. This was met with retaliatory measures from the US's main trading partners and world trade plummeted.

The Great Depression was a painful and prolonged period of economic contraction, which saw global stock markets crash, industrial production collapse, and globalization retreat. Figure 9.12 shows the path of key macroeconomic variables during the Great Depression and the financial crisis of 2008–09 and the monetary and fiscal policy responses. The beginning of the two downturns looked ominously similar, but the bounceback was a lot more rapid following 2008–09.

In contrast to the Great Depression, as the financial crisis hit, governments stepped in to support domestic demand by introducing fiscal stimulus packages. Alongside this,

---

[37] For an excellent overview of the Great Depression and its lessons for policy makers and economists, see Crafts and Fearon (2010).

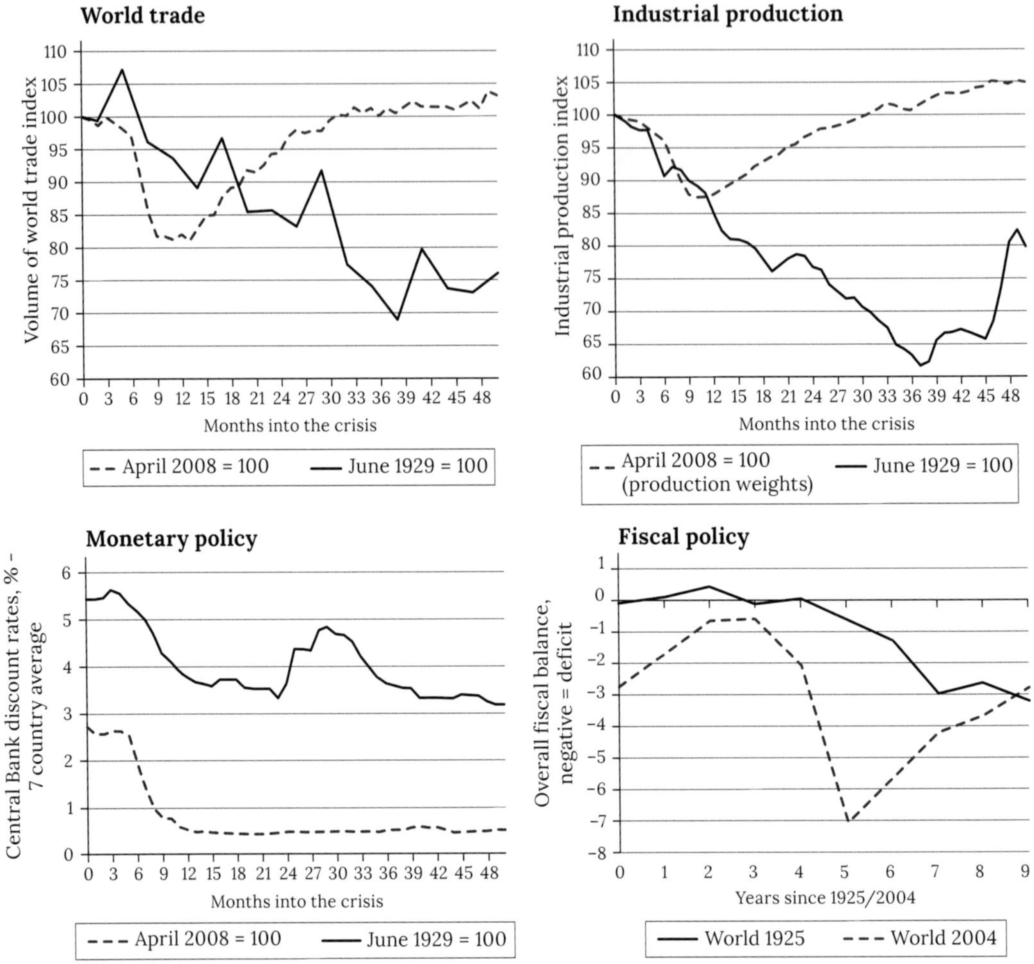

Figure 9.12 Comparison of global macroeconomic indicators and policy response during the Great Depression and the Global Financial Crisis.

Source: Almunia et al. (2010); CPB, Netherlands Bureau for Economic Policy Analysis, World Trade Monitor, May 2013; Bank of England, St Louis Federal Reserve, Bank of Japan, ECB, Riksbank and National Bank of Poland (accessed June 2013); IMF World Economic Outlook, Jan 2009; IMF Fiscal Monitor, April 2013.

central banks slashed interest rates and kept them at historic lows for an extended period of time. In 2008–9, expansionary monetary and fiscal policies were adopted more decisively and applied more consistently, which helped to avoid a repeat of the Great Depression. Economic historians Crafts and Fearon (2010, p. 288) commented on the policy response to the global financial crisis:

> [M]onetary and fiscal policies were pursued on a scale that would have been unacceptable during the 1930s but, crucially, these bold initiatives prevented financial meltdown. . . . the 'experiment' of the 1930s shows only too clearly the likely outcome in the absence of an aggressive policy response.

9.6.2 **Monetary and fiscal policy in the crisis phase**

The lessons from the policy errors of the Great Depression had a marked influence on policy makers in 2008. Ben Bernanke—one of the world experts on the economic analysis of the Great Depression and chairman of the US Federal Reserve during the financial crisis (and awarded the Nobel Prize in 2022)—was acutely aware of the dangers of a deflation trap and took advantage of the numerous policy tools at his disposal to ensure the US economy escaped this fate.

The policy response to the global economic downturn following the financial crisis addressed several problems:[38]

1. *The liquidity problem*: central banks took action to deal with the seizing up of the money markets and associated liquidity problems of banks.
2. *The bank solvency problem*: central banks and governments took action to save failing banks and prevent contagion.
3. *The stabilization of aggregate demand and expectations*: central banks used conventional and unconventional monetary policy, and governments used expansionary fiscal policy.

The liquidity problem: Central bank response

Following the seizing up of the money markets in the credit crunch the central banks of major developed countries were quick to act to provide liquidity to the banks. The Bank of England (BoE) made £10bn of reserves available for three-month loans to banks and widened the list of acceptable collateral. The ECB injected €95bn in overnight credit into the interbank market and the Federal Reserve injected $24bn. These actions provided some respite in the interbank markets, but the spread between LIBOR and base rates remained high (see Figure 9.9).

The Federal Reserve introduced the Commercial Paper Funding Facility, which bought three-month unsecured and asset-backed commercial paper from eligible issuers with money from the New York Federal Reserve. There was also a coordinated response from the ECB, BoE and the Swiss National Bank to provide short-term US dollar funding where requested. These are just a selection of the numerous initiatives central banks employed to ensure that financial institutions could meet their short-term funding needs during these turbulent times.

The solvency problem: Central bank and government responses

The bankruptcy of Lehman Brothers crystallized one fact; this was not just a liquidity crisis, but also a solvency crisis. The write-down of the value of a range of financial assets on banks' books shrunk their asset bases. Due to their high leverage ratios, this was particularly damaging to banks' equity (or net worth). The banks needed capital urgently if they were to plug the gaps in their balance sheets and avoid failure.

---

[38] This subsection was compiled using news reports and press releases from banks and central banks (e.g. the Federal Reserve, the Bank of England, and the ECB). For a high-level overview of the monetary and fiscal response to the crisis, see Mishkin (2011).

The private capital markets and sovereign wealth funds were not willing to provide this additional investment on a sufficient scale, so banks had no choice but to turn to their governments. The US Treasury announced a $700bn bailout plan in October 2008, and similar bailouts took place across Europe.

The support for the financial system over the duration of the crisis came in three main forms:

1. Taking *ownership stakes* in lenders/banks: Governments took equity stakes in financial institutions in exchange for providing capital. The US government took preferred equity stakes in eight major US financial institutions in exchange for $166bn of bailout money, with Bank of America and Citigroup collecting $45bn each. The sturdier of these banks repaid some or all of this money in 2009, freeing them from the federal restrictions that accompanied the funds (e.g. curbs on executive pay).
2. Nationalization: In certain cases, the government took *control* of financial institutions by taking very high equity stakes. This happened with some banks in the UK (e.g. Northern Rock and RBS), Ireland and Iceland, as well as mortgage providers Freddie Mac and Fannie Mae, and insurance giant AIG in the US. In some of these cases, the government became heavily involved in the day-to-day running and strategic decision making of these organizations.
3. Toxic asset purchases: This removed some of the toxic assets from banks' balance sheets. This was most widely used in the US and took place through the Federal Reserve, which set aside $600bn to buy up mortgage-backed securities.

Stabilization policy: Preventing a deflation trap

Conventional monetary policy was used decisively. In November 2008, the Bank of England's Monetary Policy Committee (MPC) cut the policy rate by 150 basis points (from 4.5% to 3%) in one step. This was a much bigger cut than predicted by market commentators. Similar monetary policy responses came in the US, the Eurozone, and other industrialized economies. See Figure 9.12 for the comparison with the response of monetary policy in the Great Depression. The MPC's concern was that inflation would undershoot the target and that the economy would be forced into a deflation trap. The aim was to stimulate aggregate demand, and to keep inflation expectations anchored at 2% in order to prevent a process of deflation becoming entrenched.

Quantitative easing: Unconventional monetary policy

From the 3-equation model (in Chapter 3), the importance of avoiding a deflation trap is clear. In the financial crisis, conventional monetary policy was restricted by the zero lower bound on nominal interest rates, which meant that monetary policy makers had to turn to unconventional policies to stimulate demand and prop up inflation expectations. The main policy used was quantitative easing (often referred to as QE; see Section 6.4.4). When the policy interest rate is as low as it can be, central banks use asset purchases to try to boost asset prices and lower yields. If successful, this should help to boost aggregate demand by encouraging consumption and investment. (Chapter 6 includes a more detailed discussion of QE, including its transmission mechanisms and the impact it has on the central bank's balance sheet.)

Fiscal policy: Automatic stabilizers and fiscal stimulus

The limits of traditional monetary policy were reached in the recession of 2008–09, so to further support the global economy, governments turned to fiscal policy.

The 3-equation model can be used to illustrate the issues facing policy makers. The *MR* line in Figure 9.11 needs to be reinterpreted as the policy rule, and labelled *PR*, so as to include fiscal policy as an instrument as was done in Figure 7.1. Since the best response to the shock is to achieve the positive output gap marked by point C in Figure 9.11, the government would need to introduce a fiscal stimulus to shift the *IS* curve to the right. To achieve the desired output gap, fiscal policy would need to take account of the effect on aggregate demand of the real interest rate, r_x arising from expected deflation, combined with the increase in the margin of the lending rate over the policy rate, due to increased credit risk of banks and borrowers.

This analysis fits well with the policy response of major governments in the wake of the global financial crisis. We can see from Figure 9.12 that fiscal policy was eased much more aggressively during that crisis than in the Great Depression.

Discretionary fiscal policy can be defined by the gap between the current budget deficit and the impact of the automatic stabilizers, as discussed in Chapter 7. This is shown in equation 9.2,

$$\begin{aligned}\text{discret. fiscal impulse at time t} &\equiv \text{budget deficit} - \text{impact of aut. stabilizers}\\ &\equiv [G(y_t) - T(y_t)] - a(y_e - y_t) \qquad (9.2)\end{aligned}$$

where a is a constant and the term $a(y_e - y_t)$ captures the impact on the budget deficit of the automatic stabilizers. When output is at equilibrium (i.e. $y_e = y_t$), the automatic stabilizer term is zero. A budget deficit that persists when output is at equilibrium is therefore discretionary and is referred to as the structural or cyclically adjusted budget deficit.

The first channel of fiscal policy is to allow the *automatic stabilizers*[39] to operate and to accept the associated increase in the deficit. In a recession, without any explicit change of policy, government transfers increase (e.g. more people collect unemployment benefits) and taxes fall as a percentage of income (e.g. if the income tax system is progressive). The greatly increased size of government, including the welfare state, between the 1930s and 2009 meant the automatic stabilizers operated to limit the leftward shift of the IS curve in response to the negative aggregate demand shock following the collapse of Lehman Brothers.

In response to the severity of the fall in aggregate demand, governments in both emerging and high-income economies chose to use discretionary fiscal policy–referred to during the crisis as 'fiscal stimulus'.

---

[39] See Chapter 7 for a more detailed explanation of automatic stabilizers.

The stimulus packages came in many forms, as illustrated by these examples:

1. The UK cut its headline rate of VAT (i.e. sales tax) temporarily from 17.5% to 15%.
2. Many European countries introduced car scrappage schemes, which paid consumers to scrap their existing vehicle upon the purchase of a new one.
3. The Australian government sent out 'tax bonuses' to middle- and low-income individuals, and families (i.e. the government gave cash handouts to the population).

There was considerable variation in the size of the stimulus packages relative to GDP. The UK's fiscal stimulus was much smaller than those in North America, Australia and Germany, for example. Figure 9.13 shows the size of the stimulus packages (announced prior to March 2009) relative to GDP, and splits them between tax cuts and spending increases in a selection of OECD countries. Note that expenditure on bailing out banks is excluded from the calculations of fiscal stimulus and the burden of this for the UK is one reason for its relatively smaller stimulus package.

Unlike the 1930s, the fiscal policy response to the crisis was coordinated across countries. If countries were left to themselves they would not internalize the positive externalities of a stimulus package and the amount of stimulus would be suboptimal. The reason for this is that a proportion of any stimulus will leak abroad through imports, benefiting your trading partners, but without them having to incur any fiscal

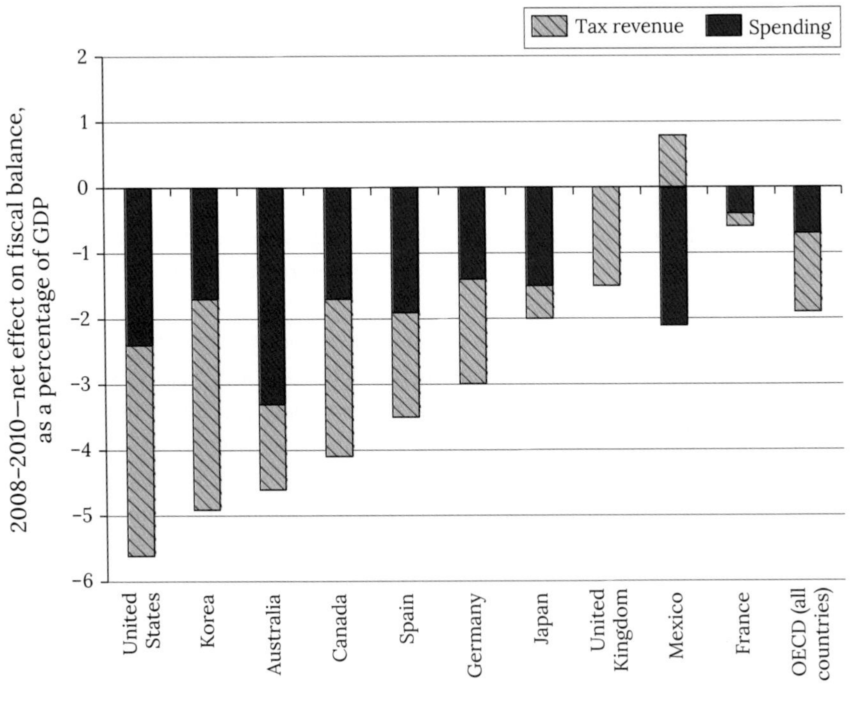

Figure 9.13 The size and mix of the fiscal stimulus packages of selected OECD countries in relation to GDP, 2008–10.

Source: OECD Economic Outlook Interim Report, October 2019.

cost themselves. Without a credible commitment mechanism, every country would attempt to 'free-ride' on the fiscal expansions of others. This was avoided in 2008-09 by world leaders meeting at global summits and committing to each other and their electorates that they would introduce stimulus packages (e.g. the G20 summits in Washington D.C. in late 2008 and London in April 2009). This made backing out politically costly at the domestic and international level.

The working of automatic stabilizers and the implementation of fiscal stimulus measures led to large deteriorations in fiscal balances. The IMF estimated that relative to 2007, fiscal balances as a per cent of GDP worsened by 5.9% across the G20 in 2009 (this does not include any support measures for the banking sector). The crisis-related discretionary measures (i.e. the stimulus packages) were predicted to account for 2% of this change in fiscal balances, and other factors (including automatic stabilizers) accounted for the remaining 3.9%. It is a testament to the depth of the recession that automatic stabilizers played such a significant role.

A country that has a high level of government debt may face constraints on its borrowing. In the financial crisis, Ireland's deficit and debt ballooned because it had to rescue banks, which were very large relative to the size of the economy. Its ability to implement stabilization through fiscal policy was severely constrained. This was also affected by the particular problems faced by a country that needs to borrow to finance fiscal stimulus when it does not have its own currency. Countries in the Eurozone, like Ireland, faced this problem, which is discussed further in Chapters 7 and 14.

Economic theory provides guidance on the conditions under which fiscal stimulus is likely to be effective in boosting aggregate demand and output. The arguments are set out in Chapter 7: fiscal policy effectiveness depends on the state of the economy, the stance of monetary policy (including whether the country has its own currency) and the design of the policy measures. We focus here on the specific case relevant to the aftermath of the financial crisis, that is, following a large negative aggregate demand shock that results in spare capacity in the economy. Fiscal stimulus is more effective in the following instances:

1. When monetary policy supports expansionary fiscal policy by preventing interest rates from rising. This is the case when the reason for using fiscal policy is that conventional monetary policy is ineffective because the economy is at the zero lower bound and QE is being used to lower long-term interest rates.
2. When it takes the form of a temporary rise in government spending. The higher government spending raises demand for goods and services directly. Even when this is accompanied by higher *taxation* to pay for it (a so-called *balanced budget spending increase*), aggregate demand will go up (see Chapter 7).
3. Similar logic applies to the possibility that if the government *borrows* to fund its extra spending, households may anticipate future higher taxation to pay for this. Although any increase in private saving for this purpose will dampen the *multiplier process*, it does not extinguish the positive effect on aggregate demand of the first-round effect (see Chapter 7).
4. When it takes the form of temporary tax cuts and there are credit-constrained households in the economy. If such households would have borrowed more to

smooth their consumption had they had access to credit, then a tax cut will lead to higher spending.

Fiscal expansion is likely to be most effective in a financial crisis when it is timely, temporary and targeted—and as noted above, when it is coordinated across countries. Temporary fiscal measures shift the timing of spending decisions (not only for households, but also for the public sector by, for example, bringing forward infrastructure spending), which is the objective, and help reduce concerns that fiscal intervention will lead to long-run commitments with implications for public debt. This is consistent with the principles of prudent fiscal policy outlined in Chapter 7.

Did expansionary monetary and fiscal policy responses work?

The initial stages of the financial crisis of 2008–09 bore a close resemblance to the Great Depression. The world economy, however, managed to turn itself around much quicker than it did in the 1930s. Part of the reason for this is likely to have been the direct and expectations effects of the coordinated policy response of the world's central banks and fiscal authorities. The highly accommodative policy employed during the global financial crisis prevented a collapse of the global financial system and helped to support demand during a time of particularly low activity and high uncertainty.

A second very important reason was the coordinated commitment to trade and financial market openness (instead of the resort to protectionism that had occurred in the Great Depression). The rapid resumption of strong growth in the increasingly important emerging economies supported growth in the global economy during the lengthy recession in the advanced countries (see the lower panel of Figure 9.6).

9.6.3 Austerity policies in the post-crisis recession

Fiscal stimulus policies introduced in response to the global financial crisis appear to have helped prevent countries from experiencing a deeper output contraction and deflation. Fiscal stimulus was followed, however, by discretionary *contractionary* fiscal policy in many economies *before* they had exited from recession. As explained in Chapter 7, the adoption of tighter fiscal policy with the express aim of reducing the debt to GDP ratio (rather, for example, than to stabilize aggregate demand) is referred to as fiscal consolidation or austerity.

Figure 9.14 shows the discretionary fiscal policy stance of the high-income countries as a whole and the US and UK separately from 2008–2009 until 2013. The indicator is the change in the cyclically adjusted budget balance: a negative value, as is shown for 2008–2009, indicates a rise in the cyclically adjusted budget deficit, that is, a loosening of fiscal policy. Although in the advanced countries as a group and in the US, there was still some fiscal stimulus in 2009–2010, this was not the case in the UK, where austerity policies were introduced as early as 2009–10. The relative harshness of fiscal consolidation in the UK shows up clearly in 2010–2011 with the discretionary withdrawal of demand of more than 2% of GDP. Note that this measure of the discretionary fiscal policy stance shows fiscal policy as tighter if the change is

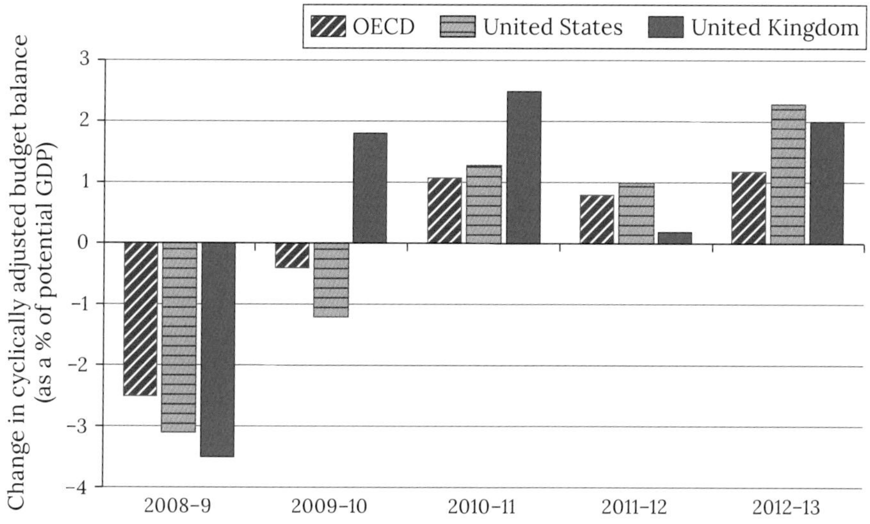

Figure 9.14 The discretionary fiscal policy stance measured by the change in the cyclically adjusted budget balance: 2008–09 to 2012–13.

Source: IMF Fiscal Monitor, October 2019.

positive (represented by positive bars in Figure 9.14), even if a cyclically adjusted deficit remains.

Box 7.2 details the historical experience of the UK in the 1930s to shed light on a very specific policy mix that allowed the economy to recover from the Depression by offsetting the depressing effect of the fiscal austerity imposed at that time. In the UK, unlike the situation post-2008, the Depression of the 1930s did not follow a financial boom and there was no debt hangover.

As we showed in Chapter 8, in a balance sheet recession following a financial crisis there are strong headwinds dragging on aggregate demand because of the legacy of the collapse of the upswing of a financial cycle. Banks, borrower households and governments experience levels of debt above their desired or target levels. Moreover, when many countries are in the same position, demand is reduced not only by the attempt of each of these parties to save more but also by the spillovers through trade links of similar contractionary policies abroad. There is a domestic coordination failure as well as an international coordination failure. Although both failures were avoided in the intense phase of the financial crisis, they characterized the Great Recession that followed.

Experience during the Great Recession led the IMF to revise upwards its estimates of the size of multipliers to a range between 0.9 and 1.7.[40] The factors they list as raising the multiplier under the conditions prevailing in 2012 were the ZLB, the extent of slack (i.e. underutilized resources) remaining in the affected economies, and the synchronized fiscal consolidation across countries.

---

[40] See IMF (2012).

The historical example from the UK in Box 9.2 and the examples from OECD countries in the 1980s and 1990s discussed in Chapter 7 suggest that the negative effects of fiscal austerity can be mitigated, but only under very special conditions.

De Long and Summers (2012) set out a model that analyses the macroeconomic impact of fiscal stimulus when the economy is depressed—i.e. nominal interest rates are at the ZLB and unemployment is above equilibrium. They argue that fiscal stimulus is likely to be self-financing (in the sense that the benefits for future growth outweigh the upfront fiscal cost) when even a small amount of hysteresis takes place in the downturn. As set out in Chapter 4, hysteresis is where high cyclical unemployment has permanent negative effects and raises equilibrium unemployment (as a result, for example, of workers becoming deskilled while unemployed). Hysteresis is discussed further in Chapter 15. De Long and Summers (2012) therefore suggest a strong need for caution when considering premature fiscal consolidation in a depressed (e.g. post-crisis) economy.

The pressure on policy makers to shift from fiscal stimulus to austerity comes from the deterioration in government finances. But the evidence that has accrued suggests that the appropriate response to this is not to attempt to deal with the accumulation of public sector debt by an early tightening of fiscal policy. Unlike an individual household where debt is reduced by saving more, the paradox of thrift explained in Chapter 1 shows that in an economy with spare resources (i.e. with a negative output gap), the attempt by the government as well as the private sector to save more can reduce aggregate demand and output, leaving aggregate saving unchanged but output lower.

The UK's austerity policy and inequality

The UK is a good case study for two reasons: the severity of fiscal austerity relative to other countries as shown in Figure 9.14 and the decision to implement it in spite of the absence of difficulties in the government's ability to finance its deficits. We return in Chapter 14 to the case of Eurozone countries where market access was a constraint on fiscal policy choices.

The theory of 'contractionary fiscal consolidation' had become influential in British policy circles where it was stated in the 2010 Budget: 'These [effects of fiscal consolidation] will tend to boost demand growth, could improve the underlying performance of the economy and could even be sufficiently strong to outweigh the negative effects'. Cross-country research by economists Romer and Romer (2019) identifies the UK alongside Denmark, France, and Austria as countries choosing to implement austerity in the aftermath of the global financial crisis when they did not need to do so.

Following the prescription of the proponents of expansionary fiscal consolidation that austerity should be weighted toward cuts in government spending rather than increased taxation, the British government's policy design was approximately 80 per cent expenditure-cut based and 20 per cent tax-increase based. The theory's advice that spending cuts be concentrated on entitlements was also followed: aggregate real government spending on welfare and social protection was cut by around 16 per cent. In the poorest local authority districts of the country, the cuts in welfare spending per person in real terms were as high as 46.3 per cent.

BOX 9.2 Depression policy mix in the UK

The Depression of the 1930s was far less traumatic in the UK than in the US or Germany.[a] There were no bank failures. Growth resumed and GDP recovered to its pre-crisis level within five years (unlike the longer recession following the global financial crisis in 2008–09). High unemployment was the big problem for the UK in the 1930s: the unemployment rate doubled from 8% in 1929 to peak at 17% in 1932 and was still above 10% in 1938, the year before the start of the second world war.

British experience in the Depression is interesting because it was a unique episode in the UK where a policy of fiscal austerity was implemented in a recession when the interest rate was close to the zero lower bound. How did strong growth return?

The extent of fiscal austerity was considerable: via a combination of spending cuts and tax increases, demand was removed from the economy and the structural budget deficit was reduced by 4% of GDP between 1929–30 and 1933–34, and yet the economy grew reasonably strongly from 1932 onwards. Economic historians agree that fiscal austerity depressed growth during this period. The explanation of why growth resumed depends on the strength of the countervailing policies. The economic historian Nicholas Crafts argues that an important part of the explanation lies with the shift of the control of monetary policy away from the Bank of England to the Treasury, where an explicit policy announced by the Chancellor of targeting an increase in the price level was pursued.

The aim was to end deflation by generating expectations of higher inflation so as to reduce the real interest rate (remember the Fisher equation introduced in Chapter 1).

The mechanism was to be through devaluation of the exchange rate. We explain the relationship between changes in the exchange rate and inflation in detail in Chapter 12. At this stage, all that is needed is an intuitive understanding that a 'cheaper pound', which was possible because the UK had left the Gold Standard, would push up the prices of imported goods. Following a devaluation of about 30%, the Treasury intervened in the foreign exchange market to sell pounds and keep the exchange rate from appreciating. The combination of higher expected prices and high unemployment depressed real wages and the improvement in business profits led to a recovery of investment. There was also a major contribution of house-building to aggregate demand stimulated by the low interest rates, an unimpaired banking system, and the expectation that construction costs would rise. Unlike the current situation in the UK, there were few planning restrictions on house-building in the 1930s.

[a] See Crafts and Fearon (2010) and Crafts (2013).

Contrary to the hypothesis that austerity could stimulate demand, the UK government's austerity measures depressed it through their effects on consumption and investment. Given the concentration of its effects in raising inequality and poverty in the poorest communities, the depressing effect on consumption spending is not surprising. Poor households are credit constrained and could not borrow to sustain consumption (unlike in the theory, where they would anticipate lower future taxes as a result of the government cutting its future commitment to income support payments). Moreover, detailed research using a variety of methods and datasets, including individual level data, shows that the economic consequences of austerity in the UK affected trust in government and voting behaviour, including in the Brexit referendum (Fetzer 2019). The losers from austerity blamed the government and switched their vote to the UK Independence Party (UKIP) and to support for Brexit in the 2016 Referendum. Fetzer's results provide evidence that in the absence of the austerity policy, a 'Remain' victory could have occurred.

9.7 **CONCLUSIONS**

This chapter has applied the models of the financial system and macro economy from the previous chapters to the global financial crisis of 2008–09. The pre-crisis period was associated with the accumulation of private debt in many of these economies, as banks levered-up to increase their returns and households borrowed to consume beyond their means.

The housing-feedback process was driven by the US banks aggressively extending mortgages to people who were less and less able to repay them. The interlinked leveraged-bank centred cycle included the US banks, the global European banks, and the shadow banking complex. They turned mortgages into tradeable assets (through securitization and tranching) and sold them to financial institutions round the world, which borrowed against the mark-to-market value of their assets to purchase them. The safety nets for institutions that had become 'too-big-to-fail' and the regulatory environment that allowed banks to calculate their own risk-weighted assets made possible these strategies, which added to the riskiness of the system as a whole.

These approaches produced high returns in the upswing, but ruinous losses when the sun stopped shining. A downturn in the US housing market and the bankruptcy of systemically important US investment bank Lehman Brothers triggered a set of events that led to the worst recession since the Great Depression. A slump on the scale of the Great Depression was avoided because aggregate demand was stabilized with fiscal and monetary stimulus and governments and central banks acted quickly to shore up the battered financial system. While the lessons of the Great Depression were learned, many governments implemented fiscal austerity policies before private sector indebtedness had been reduced. Lengthy periods of weak growth followed.

The crisis highlighted the inadequecies of the pre-crisis policy framework that combined inflation-targeting central banks with light touch financial regulation. A major theme in the post-crisis policy debate was that measures should be put in place to prevent the upswing of a financial cycle with its pro-cyclical build-up of debt and leverage, which creates the basis for the upswing of a financial cycle, and the vulnerability of the economy to financial crisis. In other words, policy should be designed to prevent a financial *cycle* from taking hold. As we have seen, the root of the problem is a regulatory environment in which banks take excessive risks when measured from society's point of view. This arises because banks do not internalize the impact of their actions on systemic risk. The post-crisis policy debate, which was centred around better protecting modern economies from costly financial crises, is taken up in Chapter 10.

QUESTIONS AND PROBLEMS FOR CHAPTER 9

CHECKLIST QUESTIONS

1. Explain the role of the following factors in the upswing in the financial cycle that preceded the global financial crisis:
   a. The implicit state guarantee for 'too-big-to-fail' institutions
   b. The assumption the MBSs bundled together in CDOs were not highly correlated
   c. Capital regulation based on risk-weighted assets.
2. Why did rising house prices make US retail banks more willing to provide mortgages for low-income earners with poor credit histories?
3. Assess the following statements: S1 and S2. Are they both true, both false or is only one true? Justify your answer.
   S1. The European global banks did not dramatically increase the risk in their loan portfolios in the upswing before the financial crisis
   S2. The European global banks followed a riskier strategy (than previously) in the upswing before the financial crisis.
4. Assume that an investment bank is at its maximum desired leverage of 20: it has $10 million of its own equity (net worth) and has borrowed $190 million to buy assets of $200 million. The price of the bank's assets falls and reduces their mark-to-market value to $195 million. What has happened to the bank's equity and leverage? How much must the bank reduce their assets to restore leverage to its desired level? How will it affect the bank's efforts to return to their desired leverage if other financial institutions are attempting to de-lever at the same time?
5. The following quote about the financial system is taken from Alessandri and Haldane (2009): 'Although *diversification* may purge *idiosyncratic risk*, it simultaneously reduces *diversity* and thereby increases *systematic risk*'. Explain the quote and how it relates to the vulnerability of the financial

system to crises. Make sure your answer fully explains the terms in italics in the quote.

6. Explain the difference between a bank having a liquidity problem and a solvency problem. How does each problem affect a bank's balance sheet?

7. Evaluate the following statement: 'Discretionary fiscal policy should not be used in an economic downturn, because this will lead to tax rises and spending cuts in the future that will damage economic growth.'

8. What policy mistakes were made in the Great Depression? How can these mistakes be shown using the 3-equation model? Show in a diagram how fiscal stimulus could have averted a deflation trap.

9. Discuss the following statement: 'Balance sheet recessions involve a debt overhang, hence the government should impose austerity to reduce the debt burden'.

PROBLEMS

1. Pick three financial institutions, one from the US, one from the UK and one from Continental Europe. Download their annual reports for a pre-crisis year (i.e. before 2008). Use their balance sheets to ascertain whether these banks are best described as retail, investment or universal banks. How do the banks you have chosen vary in regard to the key concepts discussed in this chapter (refer to Chapters 5 and 8)? Your comparison should refer to:
   a. the leverage of each bank
   b. the level of interconnectedness of each bank with governments and foreign banks
   c. the holdings of mortgage-backed securities of each bank
   d. the funding structure of each bank (e.g. debt vs. equity, short vs. long term).

2. Select two economies (outside of the G7 and the Eurozone). Use OECDstat and the IMF World Economic Outlook database to gather data on key macroeconomic variables and policy responses of these two countries during the global financial crisis. Plot this data graphically (as shown for the G7 in Figure 9.7) and compare the path of these series before and after the fall of Lehman Brothers in September 2008. Which economy fared better? Use the data collected and your own knowledge to suggest some reasons why.

3. 'One way of reducing the likelihood of encountering the zero lower bound problem is to have a higher inflation target.' Discuss. In your answer, refer to the role of inflation expectations in the performance of the British economy in the Depression of the 1930s (see Crafts 2013).

4. Making reference to historical precedent, propose and defend a combination of monetary, fiscal and supply-side policies that would have speeded up the exit of the British economy from the Great Recession.

5. Why might a 'balance sheet recession' (i.e. a recession that is preceded by the bursting of an asset price bubble which damages private-sector balance sheets) take longer to bounce back from than a normal recession?

INTERESTED IN EXPLORING THESE TOPICS FURTHER?

Visit www.oup.com/he/carlin-soskice to consolidate and extend your learning with the multiple-choice questions.

CHAPTER 10

FINANCIAL STABILITY POLICY

10.1 INTRODUCTION

Before the financial crisis, macroeconomics textbooks paid little attention to financial stability. The prevailing view was that financial crises were of only historical importance for high-income countries. In this book, the groundwork for understanding the issues surrounding financial stability policy is established in Chapters 5, 8, and 9.

Financial stability is at risk when small shocks to one bank can threaten the stability of the financial system as a whole (systemic risk). This can happen when a bank is so large or interconnected that its failure could cause serious disruption to the banking system and, as a result, to the functioning of the real economy.[1] As we saw in Chapter 9, the failure of a relatively small but highly interconnected bank, Lehman Brothers, produced contagion across banks and financial markets that was transmitted around the world. Suddenly, vulnerabilities in the global financial system were revealed.

The existence of systemically important banks presents governments with a dilemma illustrated spectacularly in the global financial crisis: both the option of saving them, and of letting one fail carry dangers. Since the crisis, governments around the world have—for the first time—introduced regulations directed specifically at systemically important banks, i.e. at the problem of 'too big to fail'. A sustained effort to develop financial stability policy followed.

The chapter begins by summarizing the nature of the financial stability problem before turning to the design of policy, including the relationships between financial stability, monetary, and fiscal policies. The analysis of financial stability policy covers both structural reforms (capital adequacy for banks, resolution regimes for insolvent banks, and the demarcation of retail from investment banks) as well as macro-prudential policy as an ongoing component of financial stability policy. An instrument of macro-prudential policy is a change in the loan to value ratio for mortgages.

The following section looks at the implementation of financial stability policy in practice. Financial innovation, including in response to new financial stability

[1] For comprehensive coverage of regulatory reform around the world and its rationale, see Buch et al. (2021) 'CORE insight too big to fail: lessons from a decade of financial sector reforms' https://www.core-econ.org/insights/too-big-to-fail/text/01.html, and watch this video (https://www.youtube.com/watch?v=S4pwc5oxuRQ). See also Bolton et al. (2019) Sound at last? Assessing a decade of financial regulation. CEPR.

regulations, can create a vulnerability that could trigger the next crisis, so later in the chapter we outline new developments in banking technology and institutions as well as in digital currencies that are on the radar of policy makers concerned with financial stability. Some of these developments were accelerated by the pandemic, including the services offered by FinTech and Big Tech companies, the role of crypto-currencies and stablecoins, and the debate about central bank digital currency and citizen accounts at the central bank.

10.2 FINANCIAL STABILITY: THE PROBLEM AND POLICY DESIGN

10.2.1 The problem of financial stability

The problem of financial stability arises because of the vulnerability of the financial system to contagion from a crisis in a bank of systemic importance. The banking system is essential not only to the economy's payments system but also to the allocation of credit and to providing facilities through which households can save. The linkages between households, firms, and banks through their balance sheets (see Chapter 5) are the conduits for contagion and help to explain the transmission from a crisis in banking to spending, lending and saving decisions and to the macroeconomy. The models in Chapter 8 set out the dynamics of positive feedback processes through which the 'contagion' of a financial market boom and crisis occur.

Financial instability arising from the external effects of risk-taking by banks is a market failure. The magnitude of those external effects creates a moral hazard problem for government: knowing that the failure of a bank of systemic importance will have economy-wide consequences, banks can expect rescue, which incentivizes more risk-taking. The result is that banks enjoy an implicit subsidy from the government, which reduces their cost of funding and increases their volume of risky borrowing and lending. Banks become more leveraged.

The problem of financial stability is summarized in Figure 10.1. In the top row, we see that the risk-taking choices made by banks explained in Chapter 8 and illustrated using the Value at Risk model set out there affect systemic risk and the probability of crisis. This is amplified by the vulnerability of banks to a fall in the value of their assets, summarized by their capital shortfall (a reflection of their choice of leverage). The vertical arrows in both directions between the first and second rows mean that the initial choices by the banks depend on how they expect the government to respond to bank failure. The more likely banks think bail-out is, the greater is the implicit funding subsidy they anticipate, the greater will be their risk-taking and the potential damage to the wider economy (bottom row).

10.2.2 Structural policies for financial stability

One way of reducing the implicit funding subsidy to banks is to control leverage by imposing capital requirements, which increases their capacity to absorb losses. This is a method of reducing the wedge between the private and social cost of borrowing, and thereby internalizing the external effect of the bank's choices. The second approach

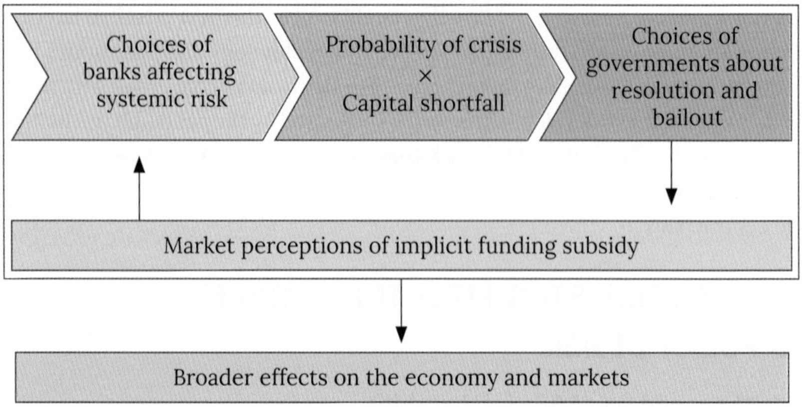

Figure 10.1 The economics of financial instability and policy design
Source: Financial Stability Board (FSB) 2021.

to policy arising from the logic of Figure 10.1 focuses on the bail-out regime. The more successful is the government in dealing with failing banks without bailing them out, the lower will be the implicit funding subsidy, and hence, the lower the systemic risk. The third and complementary approach is to separate the activities of retail banks, which are essential for the economy to function, from those of investment banks, thus ruling out rescue of the latter.

Structural policy—capital adequacy requirements

Requiring banks to be less leveraged by having larger capital (equity) requirements would make them safer and reduce the chance of failure of a systemically important bank, the threat of a financial crisis, and the need for a state bail-out.

The argument that a higher capital ratio makes a bank safer is straightforward and we have seen it already: when a bank (or any other entity like a household or a firm) has high leverage (a low capital ratio), it only takes a small fall in the value of assets for the equity to be wiped out and the bank to be insolvent. For example, if a bank has a capital ratio of 3% (i.e. equity is 3% of assets), then a loss of 1% in the value of assets (due for example to a fall in asset prices by 1%) wipes out one-third of the equity of the bank. By contrast, if equity amounts to 25% of assets, then a 1% fall in the value of assets wipes out only 4% of equity. In the first case the solvency of the bank is clearly threatened by a 1% fall in the price of assets; in the latter it is not.

Figure 9.4 in Chapter 9 shows the leverage of UK banks between 1960 and 2018. The upswing in the financial cycle is clearly shown by the sharp rise in the series in the years preceding the crisis. The series peaks in 2008 at leverage of 35. To put this into the discussion of capital ratios above, a leverage of 50 is equivalent to a capital ratio of 2.9%. The high leverage and low capital ratios of the UK banks meant they were vulnerable to solvency crises once the downswing in the financial cycle took hold. By 2018, the UK banks' leverage ratio was equal to 15, which is equivalent to a capital ratio of 6.7%, more than twice the level in 2008.

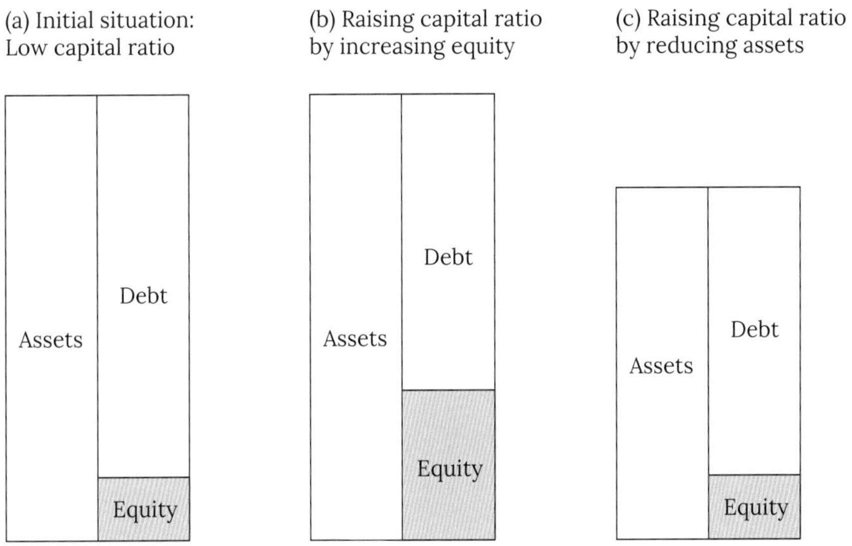

Figure 10.2 Two potential responses to new regulation of a higher capital ratio.

Figure 10.2 illustrates two alternative ways in which a bank can increase its capital ratio. Figure 10.2b shows the bank responding to the new regulation by increasing its equity, leaving the scale of its operation unchanged (total assets). It increases its equity by some combination of:

- selling new shares;
- reducing dividend pay-outs and/or bonuses and salaries.

In panel c, a higher capital ratio is achieved by leaving the amount of equity unchanged and shrinking the bank's assets. The latter method results in a smaller bank.[2] Banks oppose regulation that would require substantially higher capital ratios. One reason banks favour debt finance over equity is because tax systems favour debt.[3] We turn to the theory behind the choice between debt and equity finance.

Does the funding structure between debt and equity matter for companies, including banks?

Having a higher capital ratio means that banks would have to finance a higher proportion of their business with equity (selling shares) rather than with debt (borrowing). We begin by asking whether for a non-financial company, its cost of capital depends on the relationship between debt and equity in its funding. In an important result in the theory of corporate finance, the Modigliani-Miller (MM) (1958) theorem showed

[2] See Jenkins (2011) for a more complete discussion of the tools banks can use to increase equity or shrink assets.

[3] See Vickers (2012) for a further discussion of these issues.

the conditions under which the overall cost of finance to a firm does *not* depend on the balance of financing between debt and equity.[4]

The logic of the result is reasonably intuitive and goes as follows:

- The equity (or share) holders in a company are the residual owners, which means they get any returns to the firm's activities once the parties with contracts with the firm have been paid (i.e. suppliers, workers, tax owed to the government, interest owed to banks, interest owed to bondholders).
- As well as having the chance of upside returns, equity owners bear more risk than the suppliers of debt finance.
- To compensate them for the additional risk, equity owners require a higher return.
- At first sight, this makes it sound as if imposing a higher capital ratio would increase the cost of capital to a company because of the need of the equity owners for a higher return than the suppliers of debt.
- However, this ignores the effect of the change in financing mix on the riskiness of the firm: a firm with higher equity is less risky because it has a larger buffer of capital to absorb any losses.
- Hence, a higher share of equity in the firm's finances lowers risk, which in turn lowers the required return to the equity holders: the overall cost of capital to the firm does not change.

The cost of capital to the firm depends on the value of the firm and underlying risks and not on the financing mix: if it did not, it would be possible to make a profit through arbitrage by either buying debt and selling equity or vice versa.

Does the Modigliani–Miller theorem apply to banks?

The direct application of MM to banks would say that the argument that higher capital ratios would raise the cost of capital to banks ignores the effect of a higher capital ratio in reducing risk: with lower risk, equity holders would require a lower rate of return and overall funding costs would be unchanged. But we know that banks differ from ordinary companies because the government is unlikely to allow a systemically important bank to fail. The different treatment of the bankruptcy of banks from that of ordinary companies affects the interpretation of the MM result.

We have already discussed an important reason why from a social cost perspective, the funding mix of banks is not irrelevant. Acting in their own self-interest, banks will choose a lower than socially optimal capital ratio. The public suffers if the share of equity is too low (leverage is too high) because of the greater risk of financial crisis and of state bail-out. If the capital ratio is raised, this reduces the taxpayer liability (in the event of insolvency) and increases the private cost of capital. By reducing the potential liability of the government, the cost of finance to the government goes down, but goes up for the private bond and shareholders of the bank.

---

[4] See Modigliani and Miller (1958).

John Vickers, who chaired the UK's Independent Commission on Banking, concludes: 'So MM might hold taking the public and private sectors together, while it fails for the private sector in isolation. Again we have a reason why private and social incentives for greater bank capital may diverge'.[5] The results of research are presented in the economist Anat Admati's November 2012 Congressional Testimony (Admati and Hellwig, 2013). The conclusion is that there are few clearly identifiable *social costs* associated with imposing higher capital ratios on banks to offset the substantial social gains associated with reducing the risk of financial crisis.

Is there empirical evidence about the effect of higher capital ratios?

The empirical evidence provided by Miles et al. (2013) suggests that better capitalized banks would reduce the likelihood of financial distress, would be in a better position to make good loans because they will avoid very risky ones, and would probably be smaller because of the reduction in the probability of state support. This points toward substantial net benefits for the economy. An empirical study of German bank lending finds that better capitalized banks do not lend less.[6]

Structural policy—resolution regimes

Increasing the capital ratios of systemically important banks is aimed at reducing the probability of bank failure by reducing the value of the implicit funding subsidy and therefore the incentive for excessive risk-taking. The second policy seeks to reduce the likelihood of bail-out itself, which if successful also reduces the implicit funding subsidy by shifting the costs of restructuring a failing bank from the taxpayer to the owners and creditors of the bank.

Comparing bankruptcy of non-financial firms and banks helps clarify the role of resolution regimes for banks. Among non-financial firms, bankruptcy is commonplace and there is a clear pecking order through which the remaining assets of the firm are distributed to meet its obligations. The firm's resources are distributed in the form of payments to suppliers, wages to workers and taxes owed to the government. Only when these have been paid can bondholders receive something for their bonds: the size of the 'haircut' applied to bonds will depend on the remaining assets of the firm. Equity holders are wiped out when the firm goes bankrupt.

By contrast, if a bank is systemically important and on the verge of bankruptcy, the state steps in and bails out the bank by providing capital in exchange for shares. By preventing bankruptcy because it represents a threat to the continuity of core banking services, the action of the government places costs on the taxpayer and leaves the bank's bondholders unscathed. It would only be in a situation in which the bank actually went bankrupt that the bondholders who had lent to the bank would lose money.

---

[5] Excerpt taken from p. 11 of Vickers (2012). See also Anat Admati's November 2012 Congressional Testimony available at http://financialservices.house.gov/uploadfiles/hhrg-112-ba15-ba04-wstate-aadmati-20121129.pdf. Also see Admati and Hellwig (2013) for a more thorough overview of their research on financial regulation.

[6] See Buch and Prieto (2012).

Resolution arrangements are not credible—i.e. they will not remove the presumption of rescue by the state, and hence of risky behaviour, unless the loss-absorbers in the bank are sufficiently high. To this end, higher capital ratios are augmented by other reforms such as contingent capital, which is debt (bonds) that is converted into equity (and therefore goes to the bottom of the queue for repayment) in a near-bankruptcy situation. More of the losses are absorbed by the private sector and state rescue is avoided (or reduced in size).

Another component of a resolution regime is bail-in, which refers to compulsory haircuts applied to bondholders that write down the value of bonds when the bank is on the point of failing. Bail-in works like this: those first to bear losses are the bank's shareholders. The value of their equity is reduced to reflect the losses that have been incurred. If the amount of capital is not large enough to absorb all the losses, the next in line to bear them are the bank's bondholders. As explained above, the value of these bonds is subject to a haircut or they are converted into equity. Depositors whose deposits are not insured are the next in line to lose. Finally, the deposit insurance scheme may absorb some losses (on behalf of those with insured deposits).

Structural policy—retail versus investment bank activities

For the private resolution of failing banks to be credible, it is also necessary that there is a mechanism to ensure that the provision of core banking services can be maintained while the problematic activities of the bank are wound up or restructured. In our simple modelling framework of two types of bank (retail banks and investment banks) and universal banks that combine both, the retail banks are responsible for the provision of core banking services relating to the payments system, deposits, and lending (including overdrafts) to households and small and medium-sized firms. A policy of structural reform would strictly limit the presumption of government rescue to those parts of the bank that are essential to core banking services. The UK, EU, and US moved in broadly similar directions to alter the institutional structure of banking in pursuit of these aims.

10.2.3 Macro-prudential policy

Recalling the difference between the financial cycle and the business cycle from Chapter 8 and the build-up of financial imbalances during the period of low and stable inflation in the Great Moderation in Chapter 9, it is clear that relying on the central bank's business cycle stabilization policy is not a guarantee of *financial* stability. In addition to the structural reforms, this led to proposals for the introduction of policies to be implemented by a 'financial policy committee' to stabilize the financial cycle. Such policies—intervening to dampen positive feedback processes, including via the financial accelerator in house price bubbles (Chapter 8)—are referred to as macro-prudential policies.

Counter-cyclical macro-prudential regulation

One way of implementing macro-prudential regulation is that in a financial cycle upswing, loan-to-value ratios for housing would be reduced and bank capital adequacy ratios raised. This would help to dampen the boom by interrupting the upswing in the housing and financial sectors. In a downswing, the opposite would happen. By raising loan-to-value ratios, macroprudential intervention would help the economy to recover from the consequences of the downswing of the financial cycle by helping to revive the housing sector.

Aside from time-varying loan-to-value ratios, which are the most commonly used measure, a number of other macroprudential tools have been introduced including caps for mortgage loans, capital requirements and limits to credit growth in specific sectors.[7] The research by Akinci and Olmstead-Rumsey looks at the effectiveness of macroprudential policies in targeting the sources of financial instability, namely, bank credit growth, housing credit growth, and house price appreciation, similar to the variables that constitute the financial cycle indicator presented in Figures 8.3 and 8.5.

Their main findings are that macroprudential policies have been:

- used much more actively since the financial crisis than before and have more often been tightening rather than easing actions;
- mainly targeted at the housing sector;
- effective in reducing bank credit growth and house price appreciation when targeted directly at limiting the rise in house prices.

The interaction of policies for financial and macroeconomic stability

The analytical distinction between the financial cycle and the business cycle is helpful in considering the interaction of policies for financial and macroeconomic stability. The task of a financial policy committee is to find ways of identifying the build-up of a financial cycle. It would implement macro-prudential policies as described above, especially in relation to housing. Macro-prudential policies are counter-cyclical in relation to the upswing of a *financial* cycle.

The financial cycle figures in Chapter 8 (Figures 8.3 and 8.5) indicate that business cycle recessions coincide with many different phases of the financial cycle. Suppose the economy is in a business cycle recession. In the language of the 3-equation model, following its policy rule, the monetary policy committee seeks to boost aggregate demand to get the economy on to the *MR* curve, and it does this by reducing the interest rate. Yet at the same time, the financial policy committee may be worried about the longer-run build-up of a housing-collateral fuelled financial cycle and it would therefore like to see a reduction in loan-to-value ratios. Policies in relation to housing credit are therefore pulling in opposite directions.

Moreover:

> There is often political opposition to macroprudential policy from legislators and the public, who have regularly pushed back on measures to dampen economic growth in an effort to prevent or avoid relatively rare events.
>
> (Elliott, Feldberg, and Lehnert 2013)

---

[7] For an analysis of the measures introduced and their efficacy in 57 high-income and emerging economies, see Akinci and Olmstead-Rumsey (2018).

> It is perhaps for this reason that, for example, no US government agency has authority to impose a maximum loan-to-value ratio on all mortgages–one of the macroprudential tools most often used in other countries.
>
> (Tarullo 2019)

Financial policy committees and the 'growth at risk' criterion

The institutional arrangements for responsibility for financial stability vary across countries. In the UK, macroprudential regulation is the responsibility of the Bank of England, and the Financial Policy Committee sits alongside the better known Monetary Policy Committee. The FPC's responsibility is more difficult to summarize in a loss function of the kind used in the 3-equation model for an inflation-targeting central bank (i.e. the trade-off between minimizing the squared deviations of inflation from target and output from equilibrium).

The trade-off faced by an FPC can be thought of in terms of that between:

- greater safeguarding of the resilience of the financial system; versus
- worsening the terms on which banks provide their core services to households and firms.

Monetary and macroprudential policy makers have different time horizons over which to deliver their results. Our analysis of financial and business cycles in Chapter 8 highlighted the lower frequency of financial cycles and the quote above by Tarullo emphasized that as compared with recessions, financial crises are rare events.

A step toward codifying the remit for macroprudential policy in the form of a trade-off uses the concept of 'growth at risk', also referred to as 'GDP at risk'. This refers to the percentage of GDP that is at risk from financial instability (Cecchetti and Schoenholtz, 2017, Carney, 2020). This concept builds on the idea of risk management introduced in Chapter 8 with the concept of 'value at risk'. Policy makers inevitably face great uncertainty about the future and routinely make forecasts about the distribution of possible out-turns.

- In their routine forecasting to decide on changes in the policy rate (or in QE), the monetary policy maker focuses on the expected outcome in terms of the output gap and forecast inflation of a rise in bank credit to GDP, for example.
- By contrast, the macroprudential policy maker's concern is with the worst, say, 5% of the projected outcomes, which if it materialized would threaten financial stability.

The concept of growth at risk is vividly illustrated in Figure 10.3. The middle red line shows the expected (median) growth, one year ahead. The upper line shows that there is a 5% chance of growth being that much higher than expected, and the lower one the 5% chance of growth being that much below the median. The lower line captures the concept of the growth at risk from the rare event of a financial crisis.

Based on the argument by Cecchetti and Schoenholtz (2017), 'growth at risk' could fulfil for the FPC the role played by the inflation fan chart in the analysis and communications of the monetary policy maker. In the Bank of England's Inflation Report, a fan chart is used to illustrate the central forecast for inflation and the uncertainty around it (see Figure 4.1). Similarly, the FPC could show the growth forecast and the growth at risk at various time horizons. A forecast spike as shown in the chart

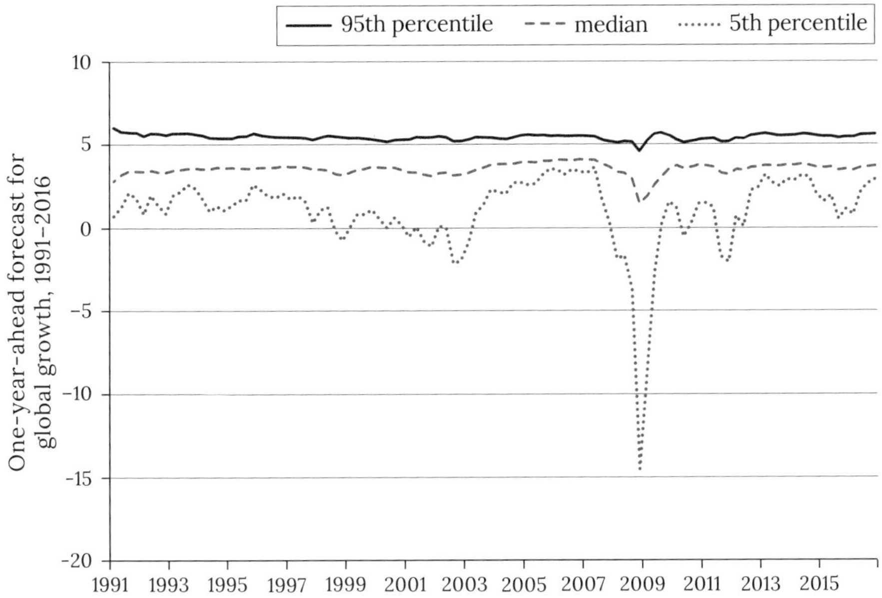

Figure 10.3 One-Year-Ahead forecast for Global Growth, 1991–2016.

Note: The middle line shows the expected (median) growth, one year ahead; the upper line shows that there is a 5% chance of growth being that much higher than expected; the lower line, the 5% chance of growth being that much below the median.

Source: IMF Global Financial Stability Report, October 2017.

for 2009 would be a signal of elevated risk of financial instability and justify prudential policy action.

A major effort would be needed to explain to the public the factors leading the growth at risk from financial instability to rise and fall. For example, what is the role of rising house prices, or household, corporate, or government debt in increasing the probability of a seriously bad outcome for the economy? Whereas there has been a huge investment in the communications strategy of monetary policy makers, awareness of the role of financial stability policy makers is much lower.

Effective management of financial cycles through macro-prudential policy may be very difficult. This highlights the importance of structural reforms to the financial system and, in addition, to the housing market in countries where the latter is an important source of financial instability.

10.3 **IMPLEMENTING FINANCIAL STABILITY REFORM**

The financial crisis was global in scope.[8] The Financial Stability Board (FSB), an international body that was created in 2009 and includes all G20 countries, sets international standards and monitors financial stability. It works with the older institution of the

[8] This section draws heavily on Buch et al. (2021) CORE Insight: Too big to fail (available at: https://www.core-econ.org/insights/too-big-to-fail/text/too-big-to-fail.html#the-reforms), where more detailed evidence is presented.

Basel Committee on Banking Supervision. As explained in Chapter 9, the Basel II standards for the prudential regulation of banks that were in force prior to the crisis allowed banks discretion in determining the risk weights for their assets when calculating how well capitalized they were. This was one of the regulatory failures that contributed to the crisis.

Basel III (2010) tightened up capital adequacy requirements for banks for the reasons explained earlier. Risk-weighted capital ratios were raised and a second capital requirement (measured by the leverage ratio, which is the inverse of the unweighted capital ratio) was introduced. Responding to the key role in the crisis of banks that were 'too big to fail' or 'too inter-connected to fail', the category of a systemically important bank (SIB) was defined. Such banks were required to satisfy additional requirements (reflecting the negative external effects of their activities). The FSB monitors SIBs: at the end of 2018, the largest number of SIBs were in the UK, where 3 of the 14 based there were deemed global SIBs or GSIBs. The largest number of global SIBs were present in the US with 8.[9]

The FSB defines a level of total loss absorbing capacity (such as through bonds that are convertible to equity in order to absorb losses) above the Basel III minimum. This ties in with the design of resolution regimes, for which the FSB sets standards and monitors implementation.

Returning to the framework of Figure 10.1 we can ask how the new regulatory regimes have affected bank and government behaviour in turn.

Banks have increased their capital ratios and the increases have been greater for SIBs, especially global SIBs (see Figure 10.4). The right panel of Figure 10.4 shows that although it has increased, the second measure of capital adequacy (capital/total assets, i.e. the inverse of the leverage ratio) remains lower for the globally systemically important banks. It is possible that this reflects their greater diversification, which reduces risk. By mid-2021, most of the GSIBs had met the requirements for their total loss absorbing capacity by issuing debt that can be bailed in under conditions of bank failure.

As explained earlier, higher bank capital would be expected to be reflected in lower bank profitability as measured by the return on equity. Reducing the implicit funding subsidy for SIBs means higher costs, which *ceteris paribus* would reduce profits. The objective of reducing the riskiness of bank behaviour is consistent with a lower private return on equity for bank shareholders.

Concerns that banks would meet higher capital requirements by shrinking their lending (panel (c) of Figure 10.2) were somewhat allayed by the evidence that the overall availability of credit to the economy did not decline. For individual banks, restructuring that has occurred for example, under public ownership for some failed UK banks (e.g. Royal Bank of Scotland), resulted in smaller (and safer) banks. More generally, the market shares of systemically important banks have fallen as other smaller banks and non-banks have expanded to supply credit. This was the intended effect of the new regulations but there is always the danger that new forms of shadow banking

---

[9] For a full list of countries, see Figure 3 in the Buch et al. (2021) Core Insight: Too big to fail (available at: https://www.core-econ.org/insights/too-big-to-fail/text/too-big-to-fail.html#the-reforms).

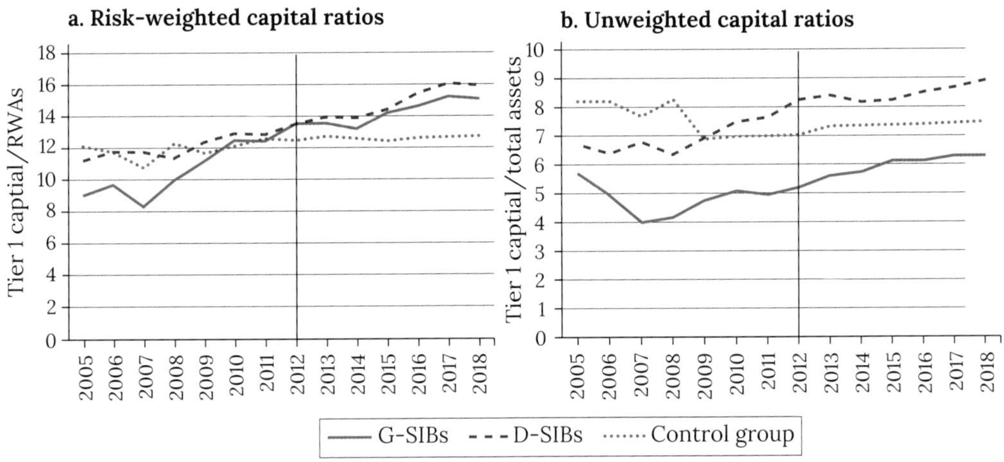

Figure 10.4 Risk-weighted and unweighted capital ratios for systemically important banks (%).

Note: The chart illustrates how risk-weighted (RWAs = risk-weighted assets) and unweighted capital ratios have evolved for domestic and global banks that are systemically important (D-SIBs, G-SIBs), and banks that are not systemically important (the control group). The vertical line at 2012 separates the pre-'too big to fail' reforms period from the post-reforms period.

Source: Financial Stability Board (2021).

will emerge to take advantage of gaps in regulatory coverage. This requires constant vigilance by the regulators at global and national levels.

Better capitalized banks reduce systemic risk but the degree of interconnectedness of banks also matters. After falling sharply in the financial crisis, interconnectedness has moved above the previous peak. Taking this into account, the FSB concludes in its 2021 report that the overall level of systemic risk has not changed much, although the influence of the global systemically important banks has declined somewhat.[10]

The Covid-19 pandemic stressed the world's banking system. However, the rapid intervention by central banks to supply liquidity, and by governments to support households and firms, relieved the pressure on banks and as a consequence, the resilience of the financial system was not fully tested.[11] Regular stress testing of the banking system resumed following the pandemic.[12]

10.4 FINANCIAL INNOVATION AND REGULATION

During the Covid-19 pandemic changes already under way in financial innovation accelerated: the extension of digitalization for consumer transactions, electronic payments and banking services, and the market penetration of both FinTech and Big Tech

[10] See also research by Goodhart et al. (2021) that documents ongoing sources of financial instability: https://cepr.org/voxeu/columns/current-bail-design-does-not-resolve-too-big-fail-problem

[11] See for example Reichlin et al. (2021): https://cepr.org/voxeu/columns/urgent-reform-eu-resolution-framework-needed

[12] See the Bank of England's 2022/23 stress testing (https://www.bankofengland.co.uk/news/2022/ september/key-elements-of-the-2022-stress-test).

in services previously limited to regulated banks. In public debate, cryptocurrencies and stablecoins gained greater prominence, as did central bank digital currency.

To understand the newly emerging landscape, it is useful to recall the functions performed by banks in conventional fractional reserve systems.

- Banks are intermediaries that perform maturity transformation by making long-term loans and taking deposits that must be returned on demand. In many countries, housing loans are a very important segment of this business. The fractional reserve basis of the system makes banks vulnerable to runs.
- In Europe and Japan, banks also provide most of the debt finance for companies through bank loans (market-based debt finance in the form of the sale of corporate bonds is much more important in the US). Given information asymmetries, bank lending relies on long-term relationships between bank and borrower to reduce the extent of credit rationing and credit exclusion.
- Traditionally banks have had a monopoly over retail and wholesale payment services because only they have access to reserve accounts at the central bank, which are required for clearing transactions with other banks.

10.4.1 Regulatory, financial, and technological innovations

The introduction of higher capital adequacy and liquidity requirements for banks was a response to the financial crisis.[13] As we have seen, one way banks met the higher capital requirements–especially in the challenging environment of low interest rates–was by shrinking their lending. A financial system with smaller, safer banks was viewed as an acceptable outcome of the reforms. However, this provided a window for non-banks in the form of FinTech and Big Tech firms to enter the market supplying some bank services. FinTech refers to start-ups that supply financial services using innovations in information and automation technologies, including the use of artificial intelligence to enable more accurate assessments of individual credit risk at low cost. Big Tech refers to platform-based large companies: Alibaba, Amazon, Apple, Baidu, Facebook, Google, and Tencent, for example, which are already or are capable of supplying financial services.

Both types of firm have been very successful in attracting talent, which has enabled rapid innovation combining large data-bases (in the case of Big Tech firms from their social media and search engine businesses) with artificial intelligence and machine learning technology to challenge the fractional reserve-based model of the regulated traditional banks. However, the extent of the challenge across the three functions of banks is not yet clear. For example, to what extent could the big data capabilities of these firms provide a substitute for the accumulation of information through relationship banking in the traditional sector? As of 2023, neither type of entrant has made serious incursion into the deposit-taking business of banks, which probably reflects the regulatory burden that would come with it.

---

[13] This section draws on Carletti et al. (2020) 'Introduction', which is recommended as a source for greater detail.

Another new technology is disrupting the landscape. This is blockchain or the so-called distributed ledger. In Chapter 5, we discussed how the pervasiveness of information asymmetries prevents disintermediated (i.e. direct between borrow and lender) trades with verifiable contracts. Banks sit between borrowers and lenders as the intermediaries that enable transactions to occur that otherwise would not, including at different maturities. And the central bank supplies the trust in the fiat currency in which the disintermediated trades take place. Blockchain is a new technology that its most ambitious proponents see as substituting for the technology and institutions of intermediated finance (through commercial banks), and the services of the central bank.

We discuss different kinds of unregulated currencies below. Aside from cryptocurrencies, the broader promise of the distributed ledger technology is that it can connect borrower and lender directly using blockchain technology and smart (verifiable) contracts, cutting out banks as the intermediary. Its resource-intensive 'mining' technology provided a novel decentralized consensus mechanism to conduct the costly verification of the double-entry ledger of transactions. It is proposed as a substitute for the virtually resource-free trust in fiat money created by a well-functioning central bank. It is useful to distinguish between the following entities:

- **FinTech firms:** FinTech firms are present in lending, payment systems, financial advising and insurance. FinTech credit remains a small share of total credit (including in China, where its footprint is largest), with a larger role in low-income countries with large unbanked populations. These firms are not banks—their funding structure has more equity than banks; they do not have depositors and face a higher cost of capital.
- **Big Tech platforms:** Apart from being nimble, FinTech firms are at a disadvantage as compared with Big Tech. The latter have a huge customer-information base of both businesses and households, brand recognition, and loyalty. The combination creates high switching costs across platforms. If Big Tech firms make serious inroads into the provision of financial services (payments, insurance, lending), they could become dominant players.
- **DeFi (decentralized finance) platforms:** This sector provides a range of financial services using cryptocurrency and stablecoins based on the blockchain (distributed ledger) technology through smart contracts without using intermediaries.
- **Regulated banks:** As a consequence of their charters as regulated banks, they retain access to cheaper funding using the fractional reserve system. This gives them a competitive advantage. They have large and 'sticky' customer bases but also costly legacy assets like branch networks and operate in a more constrained regulatory environment than before the financial crisis.

Table 10.1 distinguishes between physical and digital money in the columns, and between regulated and unregulated currencies in the rows. The final column helps clarify the role of banks, FinTech and Big Tech firms. We return to cryptocurrency and central bank digital currency (CBDC) below.

		Currency format		
		Physical	Digital	Digital 'money' issued/used by
Legal status	Regulated	Banknotes and coins	Electronic bank money (deposits in bank accounts)	Commercial banks, including those without physical branches such as Revolut and Monzo
			E-money such as electronic wallets	FinTech and Big Tech provide payments services—mostly innovating on the 'front end' (customer-business); leaving the back end unchanged through a master bank account
			Central bank digital currency (CBDC)	Central bank
	Unregulated	Some local currencies, e.g. Brixton pound	Cryptocurrency, stablecoins	Anonymous private
			Virtual currency, e.g. Alipay, M-Pesa in Kenya, Libra	Big Tech; FinTech. Mobile phone providers create digital repositories of value that can be used as a form of payment outside the regulated payments system

Table 10.1 Examples of the legal status and currency format of different forms of 'money'.

We have emphasized that the newcomers (FinTech and Big Tech) are not deposit-taking institutions making loans on a fractional reserve basis. To do so, they would have to become banks and accept the regulation that comes with it.

10.4.2 **Cryptocurrencies, stablecoins, and DeFi platforms**

Using the classification introduced in Table 10.1, unregulated digital money takes many different forms. In this section, we focus on unbacked cryptocurrencies and stablecoins. The key difference between them is that unlike stablecoins, cryptocurrencies are not backed by anything. The value of a bitcoin (an unbacked cryptocurrency), for example, depends solely on how much someone is prepared to pay for it at a point in time. Unbacked cryptocurrencies account for more than 90% of crypto assets. Stablecoins make up about 5% and by contrast, as explained below, have a reserve backing, which can be conventional currency. An important factor driving the appeal of cryptocurrencies is that they do not rely on the structures of central banks, governments, and banks.[14] This is also the case for DeFi (decentralized finance) platforms.

[14] A useful resource is the developer documentation on Ethereum's website: https://ethereum.org/en/developer/docs/

Cryptocurrency

Recall that in a modern economy, most money is created by banks. Its ability to satisfy all three properties of money (unit of account, means of exchange, and store of value) derives from well-functioning governance arrangements among central bank, government, and banks (see Figure 9.2). People trust bank money in high-income economies because the government guarantees deposits and will bail out failing banks in extremis. They trust base money because of the governance or constitution, of the central bank, which prevents it from monetizing any arbitrary spending decisions by government.

These reasons for trust in fiat money alert us to the possibility that in many countries, the institutions may not be robust enough to provide the necessary assurances. This explains why the currency of another country can become the 'money' in circulation. The US dollar is legal tender in a handful of independent countries (including Panama, Zimbabwe, Ecuador, El Salvador, and Timor-Leste, according to the IMF).

The supply of crypto does not rely on a central bank or any government body. The 'official' public ledger (basically the blockchain of all transactions) is maintained by a public community of miners, instead of a large, central bank. The production function uses the input of energy to produce the output of crypto. It works like this: miners compete to solve a complex system of mathematical equations using a so-called 'Hashing algorithm'. A mining rig is made up of Graphics Processing Units (GPUs) capable of running up to 30 million maths equations every second. This in turn is an infinitesimal fraction of the number of maths operations happening every second on cryptocurrency networks. Individual miners therefore often join a so-called 'mining pool', cumulating hashing power with thousands of other miners around the world and competing with other mining pools. Transactions in cryptocurrencies are verified through this process, which updates the ledger. Miners who solve the problem first are rewarded with crypto in return for their bookkeeping efforts. Since the Hashing algorithm is common to all miners, profits solely depend on the processing power of their computers and on the amount of electricity consumed.

Such a decentralized system of consensus formation allows for a sense of security amongst its users as there is no need to worry about any governmental or political upheaval that may occur that would devalue certain currencies. For illegal transactions, there is no government oversight. The environmental impact of cryptocurrency mining is substantial; a study by the University of Cambridge estimated that bitcoin mining alone consumes 121.36 terawatt-hours a year.[15] A country consuming this amount of energy per year would be in the top 30 energy users worldwide, just ahead of Argentina. In addition, according to Cambridge's estimates, only 39% of this energy comes from renewable sources.

---

[15] This estimate is updated regularly by the Cambridge Centre for Alternative Finance. Latest data on bitcoin network power demand as well as details on how this is assessed is available at: https://ccaf.io/cbeci/index

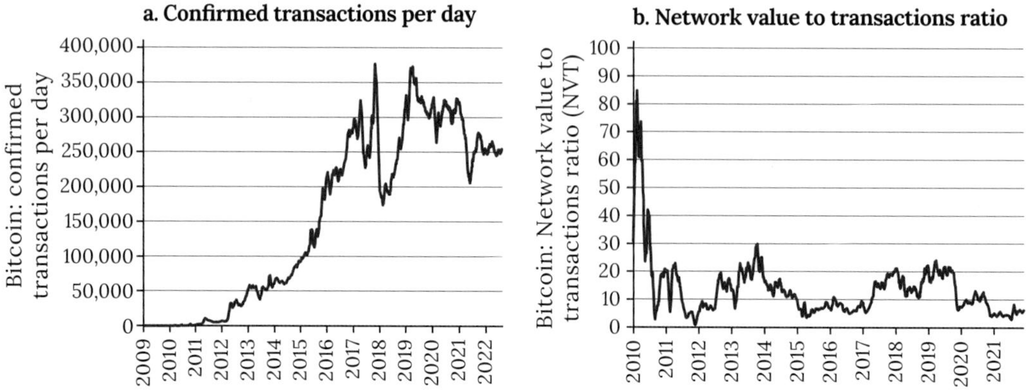

Figure 10.5 Bitcoins: confirmed transactions per day and Network Value to Transaction (NVT) ratio (30 day averages).

Source: Data from Blockchain.com, accessed October 2022.

Charting the use of bitcoin indicates the extent to which it satisfies each of the three necessary conditions for 'money'. Referring to its use as a means of exchange, Figure 10.5a shows the confirmed daily transactions made with bitcoins. Use grew rapidly until late in 2017, since when it appears to have plateaued with high volatility.

The appeal of bitcoin as a risky asset rather than a medium of exchange is illustrated by Figure 10.5b, which shows the ratio of the market value of the stock of bitcoins to the value of transactions financed by them; this is often referred to as 'Network Value to Transaction ratio' (NVT). The ratio has declined but remains above 4 and is volatile. A high NVT indicates that market capitalization remains above utilization of on-chain transaction volume.[16]

Secondly, although growing, the use of bitcoin as a unit of account remains sporadic and limited to very specific environments, such as crowdfunding for blockchain start-ups and on gambling sites (and presumably also for black economy activities).

Thirdly, to serve as a store of value, a currency needs to be stable. Figure 10.6 plots a measure of volatility (the 90-day moving coefficient of variation) for bitcoin and compares it with the volatility of equities proxied by the S&P 500. The far higher volatility of bitcoin is evident from the chart.

Stablecoins

Because of the volatility of cryptocurrencies, another type of unregulated digital money emerged in the form of stablecoins. The key design feature is to maintain a peg (typically one to one) between the stablecoin and an official numeraire (typically the US dollar). Eichengreen (2019) explains the different types of stablecoin and their corresponding limitations as a form of money.

[16] A more detailed discussion on how NVT is computed and its implications is available at: https://academy.glassnode.com/indicators/nvt/nvt-ratio

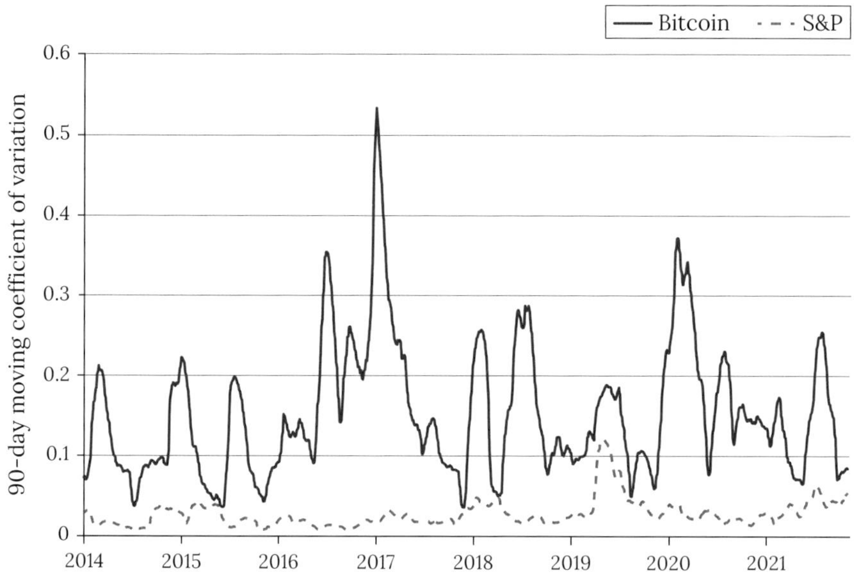

Figure 10.6 Bitcoin volatility compared to the S&P 500, 2014–22.

Note: Volatility is computed as a 90-days moving average coefficient of variation.

Source: Data from Yahoo Finance; https://finance.yahoo.com/quote/BTC-USD/history/, October 2022 and S&P Dow Jones Indices LLC, S&P 500 [SP500], retrieved from FRED, Federal Reserve Bank of St. Louis; https://fred.stlouisfed.org/series/SP500, January 12, 2023. S&P© and S&P 500© are registered trademarks of Standard & Poor's Financial Services LLC, and Dow Jones© is a registered trademark of Dow Jones Trademark Holdings LLC. © 2023 S&P Dow Jones Indices LLC, its affiliates and/or its licensors. All rights reserved.

Type 1 is a *fiat currency fully collateralized stablecoin*. A fully backed stablecoin is costly to operate, as every new unit needs to be funded by commercial bank deposits. Hence, such a currency is not likely to be scalable as there is no real incentive to hold the stablecoin as opposed to deposits at commercial banks. However, in 2021, Tether rapidly expanded its stock of tokens and it has revealed that they are now backed by riskier assets. Regulators are concerned about possible risks for financial stability.[17]

In countries where there is very limited access to accounts at commercial banks, a fully backed stablecoin can play an important role in extending financial inclusion. The most well developed example is M-Pesa in Kenya. Unlike Tether, the assets of M-Pesa are fully collateralized: 'When you purchase e-money units, you deliver Kenyan currency to an agent, who creates fresh M-Pesa units on your behalf with Safararicom/M-Pesa. The exchange of e-money for shillings is free, provided the

[17] See Tett, G. (2021), 'Stablecoin investors may be due a wake-up call'. Article published in *Financial Times*, 14 October 2021. https://www.ft.com/content/b729cf08-6beb-4d75-b19e-779d2d3a14ce

correct cash-collateral (shillings) is delivered, and is something that adds to the M-Pesa money supply.'[18] The shillings are re-invested in a Trust Fund and held in commercial bank accounts approved by the Government of Kenya.

Type 2 is a *crypto collateralized stablecoin* (e.g. Dai). In this case it is another crypto-currency that is held as collateral to back the stablecoin. The obvious drawback of this type of stablecoin is that the collateral value is highly volatile; hence, the stablecoin must be overcapitalized (i.e. over-collateralized) to be a credible store of value.

Type 3 is a *partially collateralized stablecoin*. To maintain a stable value, the platform sells and buys Saga tokens in return for Ethereum (another cryptocurrency) and invests the proceeds in the fiat currencies that make up the IMF's Special Drawing Rights (SDR) basket. As specified in the Saga white paper: '*... inherent value is derived from a combination of factors: market confidence, usefulness as means of exchange, sentiment, and future prospects.*' Hence, if doubt arises about the convertibility of Saga tokens into the currencies in the SDR basket, investors will seek to cash out producing a collapse in the value of the token.

Type 4 is an *uncollateralized stablecoin*. In this case so-called smart contracts are used to manage the supply of the digital coin with the goal of maintaining its value against the dollar. The stablecoin platform issues both digital coins and digital bonds, and the smart contract sells bonds for coins when the price of the latter dips and vice versa in terms of dollars. Clearly, the viability of such schemes depends on success in achieving growth of the platform, since without additional stablecoin holders, there will be nothing with which to pay bondholders.[19]

This overview of crypto and stablecoins highlights their shortcomings as money. A great deal of talent has been attracted into the crypto and stablecoin communities. However limited are the prospects for crypto as 'money', a different use case has emerged. It has spawned the development of non-fungible tokens and the associated digital market places. Work is under way to investigate the potential for blockchain technology and tokenization to enable purchasers of climate-related bonds to track the associated carbon credits 'in real time'. The possibility of attaching future carbon offsets via tokens to green bonds could make such bonds more attractive. Innovations in digital money and blockchain technology have attracted the attention of central banks exploring central bank digital currency as well as green bonds, and also of policy makers concerned about risks to financial stability

---

[18] Quote from Izabella Kaminska's article: Kaminska, I. (2012), 'More on M-pesa and e-money'. Article published in *Financial Times*, 20 July 2012. https://www.ft.com/content/7befd715-be92-34f1-be58-df775e5677a5. For evidence on the impact of M-Pesa on poverty, see Suri, T. and Jack, W. (2016), 'The long-run poverty and gender impacts of mobile money', *Science* **354**(6317), 1288–1292. doi:https://doi.org/10.1126/science.aah5309.

[19] Eichengreen (2019) highlights the similarity between such a financing structure and a Ponzi scheme, which is a fraud in which existing investors in the scheme are paid from the investments of new participants, rather than from the returns to the investment.

Implications for financial stability

1. **Asset price volatility:** Asset price volatility is only a financial stability concern when there are knock-on effects to the financial system and the real economy. To date, banks have limited direct exposure to crypto and this risk is limited.
2. **Leverage and interconnection with the banking system:** However, the spillover from crypto price falls could occur through the liquidity channel as leveraged investors have to sell crypto and other assets quickly to acquire liquidity, sending the prices yet lower. A lack of transparency means it is impossible to know the size of this risk.
3. **Payments system:** This relates to stablecoins because the price volatility of unbacked crypto makes them unsuitable for use as a settlement asset in payment systems. Stablecoins have the potential to create a parallel payments system. There is a risk to financial stability—the payments system—unless the standards that apply to the conventional payments system apply to a stablecoin-based payment system that is, or could become, of systemic importance.
4. **Substitution from banks:** The stability of banks could be at risk if in a nascent banking panic, depositors run to stablecoin.[20]

DeFi (decentralized finance) platforms

In 2022, this was a recent phenomenon attracting the attention of financial stability regulators.[21] These platforms are defined by using both unbacked cryptocurrency and stablecoins to create a variety of financial services. The platform aggregates these services, which are provided through smart contracts on a blockchain without an intermediary. Unlike traditional finance, anyone who can provide the required amount of collateral can use the platform in an automated transaction. Anyone can access the code. In contrast to traditional finance, there is no element of trust involved. Identities and credit-ratings are not checked. This is replaced on DeFi platforms by the requirement that transactions are over-collateralized and the enforcement of the required margins through smart contracts. This emergent decentralized financial services system has no governance structure and there are no 'rules of the game' or disclosure to enable monitoring of systemic risks.

10.4.3 Central bank digital currency

The Bank of England explains what a central bank digital currency is:

> (CBDC) would represent a new form of money in the economy and be available to the public for general use. Unlike banknotes, CBDC would be electronic. And unlike reserves, which are electronic money holdings by financial institutions at the central bank, CBDC would be available to households and businesses. For

[20] See Cunliffe, J. (2021), 'Is 'crypto' a financial stability risk?'. https://www.bankofengland.co.uk/speech/2021/october/jon-cunliffe-swifts-sibos-2021

[21] Financial Stability Board (2022), 'Assessment of risks to financial stability from crypto-assets'. https://www.fsb.org/wp-content/uploads/P160222.pdf

> this reason, CBDC is sometimes described as being similar to a 'digital banknote'. Issued by the Bank of England, CBDC would be the safest form of digital money available for use by the general public.

There are many possible configurations of CBDC under consideration in central banks around the world.[22] One suggestion is that citizens would be able to have their own reserve accounts at the central bank, earning the policy rate (interest on reserves). The implications for commercial banks are one consideration in the design of a CBDC. An important issue is the potential run on commercial banks in a time of financial market stress if households have the option of withdrawing deposits and lodging them in their account at the central bank. This could be mitigated by the central bank lending the commercial banks reserves to replace the deposits.

A survey of 66 central banks on motivations behind the introduction of retail CBDCs shows that the safety and efficiency of domestic payments and financial stability are the most important ones (Boar and Wehrli, 2021). Also, many respondents cited the decreasing use of cash and the need for financial inclusion for those without access to bank accounts for digital transactions. The survey results show that, consistent with the earlier discussion of M-Pesa, the financial inclusion motivation is even stronger in lower income economies.

A related reason for introducing CBDCs is to facilitate the transmission of monetary policy. If retail accounts at the central bank earned the policy rate, then there would be a direct transmission of changes in monetary policy to households. In a world in which banknotes have largely disappeared from use, the central bank could set negative interest rates, releasing it from the zero lower bound constraint. Alternatively, in situations where the government deems it necessary to make direct money transfers to households (such as in a pandemic), the use of CBDC could facilitate this.

With the rapid displacement of banknotes by digital payments, central banks wish to ensure that the payments infrastructure is not run solely by the private sector. In an interesting parallel with debates in the 1980s about privatization of other essential infrastructure services like water, electricity and telecommunications, the aim of policy makers is to take advantage of the innovations arising in the private sector while ensuring that external costs are accounted for. A major concern is that the network character of the payments infrastructure is likely to produce a private monopoly in digital transactions unless there is participation by a CBDC. The spillovers from a failure of the digital payments system to the rest of the economy are very high and not internalized by a private sector provider.

The Bank of England suggests that central banks should provide the minimum level of infrastructure for the digital payments system to be resilient, fast, reliable and efficient but that it should encourage 'diverse participants' including banks, FinTech, and Big Tech firms to respond to the needs of end users.

Issues of anonymity and privacy are under debate in relation to CBDC. One of the attractions of crypto is anonymity. Survey evidence in the US indicates that traditional

[22] See https://cbdctracker.org

financial institutions like banks are ranked more trustworthy with handling data safely than, in order, FinTechs, government agencies, and Big Techs. Traditional financial institutions also rank above FinTechs and non-financial services companies in studies of a large number of high- and middle-income countries (Armantier et al., 2021 and Chen et al., 2021). Although the use of blockchain technology is under discussion in relation to CBDC, there is no necessary connection between the two. CBDC benefits from the 'cheap' technology of the production of trust that is characteristic of fiat money and does not require the extremely costly energy-intensive mining to verify transactions by 'proof of work' on the distributed ledger that is the hallmark of bitcoin. The Ethereum cryptocurrency shifted from 'proof of work' to the less energy-intensive 'proof of stake' method of validating transactions in 2022, but there may be inherent (rather than technological) contradictions in scaling up the transactions that can be handled in the blockchain (i.e. processed and settled) while maintaining decentralization and security.

There are implications for financial stability. Central banks and financial regulators at national and global levels are actively exploring CBDC and its possible implications for financial stability. This work is influenced by the innovations in the private digital currency space and the regulatory issues emerging there. One argument is that a CBDC could play a role in mitigating some of the risks arising from private digital currencies. It could reinforce the traditional role that base money plays in underpinning private money (bank money). However, the following concerns have been identified.[23]

1. **Risks to financial intermediation:** This is the risk that a central bank digital currency could lead to the substitution of deposits at the central bank replacing those in banks, threatening their business model. However, it is noted that banks have responded to such threats repeatedly over history and that given the expected take-up of CBDC, this is unlikely to be a major financial stability threat.
2. **Risks in a banking crisis:** Taken more seriously is the possibility that when a CBDC exists, this could increase the risk of a bank run because, in contrast to banknotes, the CBDC can be held in large volumes. If there was fear of a run on a retail bank, depositors would withdraw their deposits and place them in their CBDC account, exacerbating the run on the bank. However, existing institutional defences against a bank run in the form of banking regulation of capitalization, deposit insurance and resolution regimes are substantial. It has been suggested that a CBDC could assist effective regulation by providing real-time information on deposit flows and enabling the central bank to stabilize expectations rapidly.

[23] Panetta, F., Mehl, A., Newmann, C. M. and Jamet, J. F. (2022), 'Monetary policy and financial stability implications of central bank digital currencies', *VoxEU/Columns* 13 April 2022. https://cepr.org/voxeu/columns/monetary-policy-and-financial-stability-implications-central-bank-digital-currencies

10.5 CONCLUSIONS

The financial crisis shifted the attention of macroeconomic policy makers away from the twin objectives of inflation targeting and public debt management, which had pre-occupied them since the 1980s. It revealed the following:

- Inflation-targeting monetary policy alone cannot be relied on to safely stabilize the economy when it is in the upswing phase of a financial cycle.
- In the upswing, borrowing by the household and banking sectors is too high, and makes the economy vulnerable to a financial crisis. This process is driven by banks, who receive an implicit subsidy for risk-taking.
- In a normal recession, monetary policy relies for its effectiveness on reducing interest rates to induce more borrowing by households and firms (a move down the IS curve to the right). It is therefore especially ill-suited to work well in a recession following a financial crisis when households and firms are seeking to reduce their leverage because of the debt-overhang.
- The state of government finances is flattered by the upswing of a financial cycle because the housing and financial sectors provide strong inflows of tax revenue.
- A financial crisis dramatically worsens the government's fiscal position for three reasons: (a) operation of the automatic stabilizers; (b) discretionary fiscal stimulus in the crisis phase; (c) bailing out banks.
- The desire for de-leveraging by households and banks leads governments to use fiscal policy to support aggregate demand in a post-crisis recession. This further worsens the government's fiscal position, increasing government debt.

In response to these lessons, in the post-crisis world, central banks have seen their remits widen to include more responsibility for banking regulation and financial system oversight. We can summarize the findings of this chapter as follows:

1. Financial stability reforms include structural measures (raising capital adequacy ratios, improving resolution regimes so that bail-in and not bail-out is the default, separating retail from shadow banking activities) and the associated surveillance at national and international level. New institutions such as a Financial Policy Committee have been introduced to implement ongoing macro-prudential regulation including loan-to-value ratios. The concept of 'growth at risk' has the potential to help discipline consideration and communication of policy trade-offs by comparing, for example, short-term gains accruing from lower interest rates (which encourage risk-taking) with the potential long-term threat to financial stability.
2. Reduced bank lending following the global financial crisis brought about a system of somewhat smaller, safer commercial banks, opening a window for Fintech and Big Tech firms to enter the market by providing bank-like services. Moreover, blockchain has garnered attention as a potential substitute for the technology and institutions of commercial banks and, to some extent, the services of central banks. However, unregulated currencies like crypto do not qualify as 'money' due to their

high volatility and very limited use as a medium of exchange. Nevertheless, the appeal of different forms of digital payments has prompted a discussion around the introduction of central bank digital currencies (CBDCs), which many central banks believe could provide more safety and efficiency in domestic payments, address problems of financial inclusion and improve the transparency of monetary policy.

3. The upside of the financial innovation brought about directly by FinTech and Big Tech firms and cryptocurrencies, and indirectly by the response to competition by incumbent banks, is new services and greater financial inclusion. This needs to be evaluated in the light of the implications for financial stability and for competition in the longer term. More efficient and varied financial services can reduce risks. But under the pressure of greater competition, incumbent banks take riskier decisions and the screening of risky entrepreneurial projects may get worse. In China, Big Tech firms are depositing customer funds directly with banks rather than going through the payments system supervised by the central bank, potentially creating an unregulated parallel payment system. Risk-taking may be transferred from banks to the new players, creating systemic risk outside the regulated sector. As we saw in Chapter 9, it was the spillover from the unregulated shadow banking sector to banks that was at the core of the global financial crisis of 2007–09, as had been the case for many earlier financial crises.

QUESTIONS AND PROBLEMS FOR CHAPTER 10

CHECKLIST QUESTIONS

1. What is the relationship between a bank's leverage and its risk-weighted capital adequacy ratio? Refer to the relevant elements of the bank's balance sheet.

2. Evaluate the following claim: 'Higher capital ratios for banks are costly for society as they increase banks' cost of capital'.

3. Explain in your own words what the Modigliani-Miller theorem proves. Is there any difference in applying it to banks and non-banks?

4. Explain how replacing a 'bail-out' regime by a 'bail-in' one could be expected to influence a bank's business model.

5. Use Figure 10.1 to provide a one-paragraph summary of what went wrong in the global financial crisis.

6. Compare how a bank's bondholders fare in a bail-in as compared with a bail-out regime.

7. Justify a scenario in which, for macroprudential reasons, the loan-to-value ratio for home loans is reduced.

8. What is an implicit funding subsidy to banks? Who pays and who receives the subsidy and why?

9. How do stablecoins differ from a cryptocurrency like bitcoin and from a Central Bank Digital Currency? Do they pose different risks to the financial system?

10. How have digital finance technologies contributed to consumer welfare? Provide examples from high- and low-income economies.

PROBLEMS

1. Should central banks burst asset price bubbles? In your answer, specify the asset class you are considering, and refer to analysis of this question by officials in a central bank (other than the US Federal Reserve). Consider how a bubble can be identified, whether all bubbles are bad, and what is the central bank's role in bursting a bubble.

2. What could explain why there was no financial crisis following the loss of $5 trillion in the dotcom crash of the early 2000s but there was one following the loss of $1.2 trillion in the sub-prime crisis of 2008? What would be the estimated loss if the price of bitcoin fell to zero? Would you expect the consequences to be more like the dotcom or the sub-prime crisis?

3. Go to CORE Econ's CORE Insight: *Too big to fail: Lessons from a decade of financial sector reforms* and complete Exercise 1 on the balance sheet of Barclays Bank and how it changed between 2006 and 2020. https://www.core-econ.org/insights/too-big-to-fail/text/01.html#exercise-1-transformation-of-bank-balance-sheet-composition

4. Go to CORE Econ's CORE Insight: *Too big to fail: Lessons from a decade of financial sector reforms* and complete Exercise 2 on the evolution of the funding cost advantages of systemically important banks. https://www.core-econ.org/insights/too-big-to-fail/text/01.html#exercise-2-evolution-of-sibs-funding-cost-advantages

INTERESTED IN EXPLORING THESE TOPICS FURTHER?

Visit www.oup.com/he/carlin-soskice to consolidate and extend your learning with the multiple-choice questions accompanying this chapter.

PART

4

OPEN ECONOMY MACROECONOMICS

CHAPTER 11

THE 3-EQUATION MODEL IN THE OPEN ECONOMY

11.1 OVERVIEW

In this chapter, we extend the macro-model to the flexible exchange rate open economy. How does the openness of the economy to trade and financial flows affect the way an inflation-targeting central bank approaches its stabilization role? In the closed economy, the central bank diagnoses shocks hitting the economy and chooses its interest rate response, taking into account the implications of the shock for future inflation. The main new insight when we extend the discussion to the open economy is that the forward-looking foreign exchange market and the central bank will simultaneously analyse shocks, and their responses will take into account the response of the other party.

Just as a great deal of resources are deployed in central banks to analyse economic developments and forecast inflation based on the diagnosis of the nature of shocks, the same is the case in financial institutions operating in global financial markets. Foreign exchange traders look at what is happening in the domestic and world economy and at how the central bank is likely to respond to economic developments.

The motives of the central bank and the foreign exchange traders for using resources to forecast the future are, however, different. The central bank is attempting to stabilize the economy, whereas the foreign exchange traders are attempting to profit from arbitrage opportunities.

Expectations and the forward-looking foreign exchange market

In Chapter 4, we discussed the pervasiveness of uncertainty in the macroeconomy and how this leads to agents forming expectations about the future so they can make better economic decisions today. In the baseline closed economy 3-equation model, the central bank is forward looking with rational expectations. The central bank has to forecast both the *IS* and *PC* curves in the next period when setting interest rates in the current period. This is due to the assumption that interest rates can only affect economic activity with a one period lag.

When we move to the open economy, we introduce the foreign exchange market, where trades are also assumed to be forward looking and rational. We assume both interest rates and real exchange rates affect the economy with a one period lag. In the open economy 3-equation model, the central bank takes account of the reaction of the foreign exchange market when setting interest rates and the foreign exchange market moves when expectations about future central bank policy change.

Arbitrage opportunities, the foreign exchange market, and the government bond market

When trade in financial assets across borders is possible—referred to as international capital mobility—investors will want to take advantage of differences in rates of return on government bonds. To buy foreign bonds, it is necessary to have the relevant national currency, for example US dollars to buy US Treasury Bills, and euros to buy German government bonds known as Bunds. The exchange rate will depend on supply and demand for currencies in the foreign exchange market as forex traders seek to take advantage of differences in interest rates.

Both the central bank and foreign exchange traders know that the extent of integration of international capital markets means that opportunities to make a profit from a difference in rates of return on bonds issued in different countries will be short-lived. Take the possibility of profiting from an interest rate differential opened up by a decision of one central bank to change its interest rate. This is a form of arbitrage opportunity. If, for example, the Bank of England increased the UK interest rate so that the return on UK bonds was higher than on US bonds, there would be a rush into UK pounds and out of US dollars until the chance of profiting from one rather than the other kind of bond has vanished.

Defining the nominal and real exchange rates

Let's take a step back for a moment and clarify the concept of the exchange rate. We need to define both the nominal and real exchange rates. Home's nominal exchange rate is 'the amount of home currency that can be bought with one unit of foreign currency'. For example, the nominal exchange rate for the UK pound (home economy) is defined in terms of the foreign currency (the US dollar) as the amount of UK pounds that can be bought with one US dollar (i.e. £/$). We use e to denote the nominal exchange rate of the home economy:

$$e \equiv \frac{\text{no. units of home currency}}{\text{one unit of foreign currency}}. \qquad \text{(home's nominal exchange rate)}$$

An increase in e means that one US dollar can buy more UK pounds, so that the pound has depreciated (or weakened). Note that since the nominal exchange rate is defined as the number of home currency units for one foreign currency unit, a depreciation of the pound is the same as $\uparrow e$.

The nominal exchange rate shows the rate at which the currencies of two economies can be exchanged for one another. To measure the rate at which domestic and foreign *goods and services* can be exchanged for each other, we also need to take into account the relative price level between the two economies. This is where we introduce the concept of the *real* exchange rate, which is defined as:

$$Q \equiv \frac{\text{price of foreign goods expressed in home currency}}{\text{price of home goods}} = \frac{P^*e}{P},$$

(home's real exchange rate, price competitiveness)

where P^* is the foreign and P is the home price level. The real exchange rate Q is a measure of price competitiveness between two economies (this Q has no relationship to Tobin's Q). If Q increases, this reflects the fall in the price of home goods relative to the price of foreign goods (when expressed in the same currency). This depreciation of the real exchange rate would make home's exports more attractive to foreigners and discourage the consumption of imports by domestic consumers. We assume throughout our modelling of the open economy that a depreciation of the real exchange rate (i.e. $\uparrow Q$)—an improvement in price competitiveness—will cause an increase in *net exports* (i.e. exports minus imports).[1]

In the open economy model, aggregate demand not only consists of consumption, investment and government spending (as it does in the closed economy), but also net exports. We assume an increase in competitiveness (a real depreciation) boosts aggregate demand through its effect on net exports.

Two stabilization channels in the open economy: Interest rate and exchange rate

Given the central bank's stabilization objective and the way the nominal exchange rate will respond to arbitrage opportunities, the response to a shock will be a combination of a change in the interest rate by the central bank and a change in the exchange rate resulting from the actions of foreign exchange traders. For example, if a shock pushed inflation above target, the response in the closed economy is for the central bank to raise the interest rate in order to depress next period's level of output and bring inflation down.

In the open economy, it is also the case that a negative output gap is required to begin to bring inflation down. However, foreign exchange market operators know that the central bank will raise home's interest rate and this creates an arbitrage opportunity. In this example, we assume that the UK is the home economy and the US is the foreign economy. There will therefore be a rush out of US dollars and into UK pounds, due to the higher return on UK bonds. What happens to the exchange rate between UK pounds and US dollars as a result of this?

In this example, the interest differential in favour of UK bonds results in stronger demand for UK pounds, which forces the currency to appreciate. An appreciated currency will increase the price of the home economy's exports in terms of foreign currency, depressing demand for home-produced goods in foreign markets. It will also reduce the price of foreign-produced goods that are imported to the home economy (in terms of home currency), boosting demand for foreign goods.

In other words, it will make the British economy less competitive and depress aggregate demand for home-produced goods and services. We can therefore see that in addition to the *interest rate channel*, there is a second channel operating to produce the central bank's desired negative output gap: this is the *exchange rate channel*. With the higher interest rate in the UK and the appreciation of the UK pound both bearing down on output, the central bank will know that it needs to raise the interest rate

---

[1] This result will be derived formally when we discuss the Marshall-Lerner condition in Chapter 12.

by less than would be the case in the closed economy to achieve the same negative output gap.

Both parties solve the central bank's stabilization problem—this implies an assumption that both the central bank and the foreign exchange market form expectations rationally, i.e. in a way that is consistent with the model. Together their actions will place the economy on the stabilization path desired by the central bank.

In short, we shall see that the presence of the foreign exchange market means that the work of stabilization is shared between exchange rate and interest rate adjustments. As with any rational expectations assumption, we have to be careful about its relevance for understanding real-world phenomena. In the case of the 3-equation closed economy model, we used the idea of the central bank solving the model in order to make its best judgement about how to respond to a shock; here we are assuming that the profit-seeking motivation of foreign exchange traders will produce an outcome that can be captured by the rational expectations assumption.

This is a more dubious assumption than is the case for the central bank, as we know that financial markets are affected by fads and manias (see Chapters 1, 4, and 8). However, we continue to work with the rational expectations hypothesis for the foreign exchange market as it provides a useful basic model of a very complex situation. In addition to helping us to understand the way interest rate and exchange rate changes interact following a shock to the economy, the open economy model also helps to explain exchange rate overshooting and highlights the trade-off between the contribution of exchange rate changes to stabilization, and the potential for the foreign exchange market to be a source of volatility in the real economy.

11.1.1 How are the key aspects of the open economy reflected in the 3-equation model?

We now explore why central banks in flexible exchange rate economies are active in stabilization. Figure 11.1 shows that central banks frequently change the policy interest rate as they attempt to achieve their inflation target. We can think this through systematically by taking each of the three equations in the 3-equation model in turn.

IS relation

Beginning with the demand side of the economy, the IS, we need to amend the model to recognize that home's households, firms and government spend on imported as well as home-produced goods, and that foreigners buy goods produced at home. Since imports will depend on the level of activity in the home economy, some of the additional demand generated by higher incomes will leak abroad because of purchases of imports. This means the multiplier will be lower, the higher is the marginal propensity to import. The other major change to the IS relationship will come from the impact on imports and exports of changes in the competitiveness of home's production, as noted above. An improvement in home's competitiveness, i.e. a depreciation of the real exchange rate, boosts the demand for exports and dampens the demand for imports as home goods become relatively more attractive both abroad and at home.

In graphical terms, the presence of imports in reducing the multiplier makes the IS curve steeper because a given fall in the interest rate is associated with a smaller

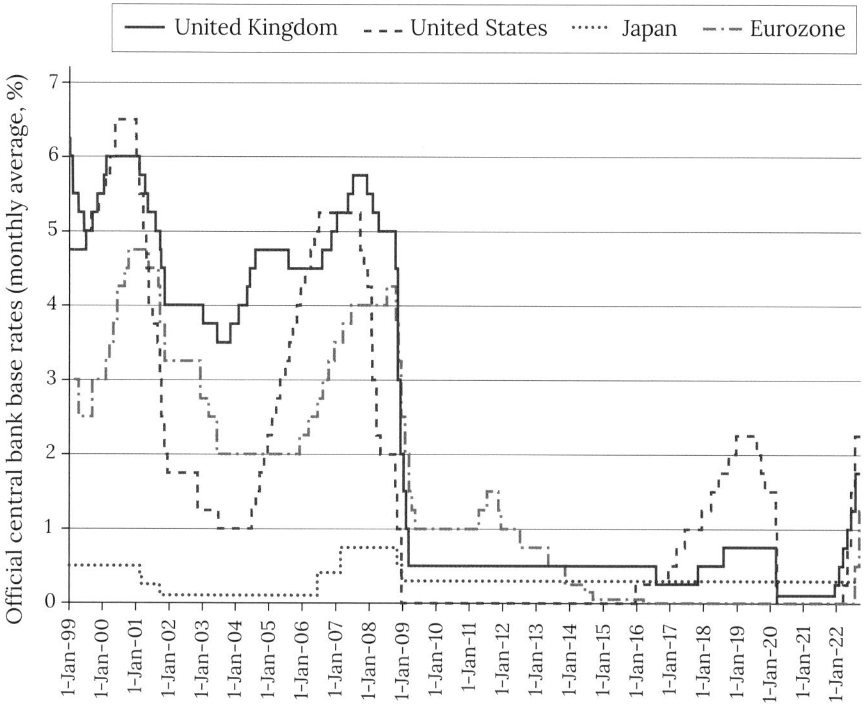

Figure 11.1 Official central bank interest rates, monthly averages, per cent: 1999–2022.

Source: Bank of England; Board of Governors of the Federal Reserve System (US); Bank of Japan; European Central Bank (data accessed September 2022).

increase in output; and a depreciation of the real exchange rate shifts the IS curve to the right. An appreciation of the real exchange rate—a deterioration in home's competitiveness—shifts the IS to the left. These results are derived step by step in Chapter 12.

Phillips curve, *PC*

As in the closed economy, the Phillips curve in the open economy shows the rate of increase of producer prices. In this chapter, we shall assume that households use domestic inflation in their wage-setting calculations.[2]

Central bank behaviour, *MR*

Finally, we turn to the policy maker, which is the central bank. There is no reason why opening up the economy to international trade and capital flows should affect the policy maker's preferences, and hence, the MR curve. We continue to assume that the central bank suffers a loss of utility according to how far away it is from its inflation target and from equilibrium output. But what is the inflation rate the central bank targets? It could target consumer price inflation, which includes the price changes

[2] We shall explore the effects of imports and the exchange rate on wage setting in Chapter 12.

of imported goods or it could target domestic inflation. In this book, we keep to the simple case where the central bank targets *domestic* inflation. We do not, however, ignore the role of so-called imported inflation. It enters the model in Chapter 12, where we assume that the relevant real wage in wage-setting is the real consumption wage, i.e. the nominal wage deflated by the consumer price index. Since import prices are included in the CPI, they influence wage-setting.

To summarize, in the open economy we need to modify the IS curve, making it steeper to reflect the lower multiplier, and noting that it will shift with a change in the real exchange rate. If the central bank targets domestic inflation and wage setters use domestic inflation in their wage-bargaining calculations, we do not need to modify the PC or the determinants of equilibrium unemployment, y_e. Equilibrium employment is determined in the same way as in the closed economy. In the PC-MR diagram, the vertical axis is domestic inflation and the MR curve is derived in the same way as in the closed economy: from the tangencies of the Phillips curves with the loss ellipses, which capture the preferences of the central bank.

11.1.2 How does capital market openness affect stabilization policy?

Two elements of global flows of capital play a crucial role: the foreign exchange market and the ability of home and foreign economic agents to trade home and foreign assets. This ties together the foreign exchange market and the money market where government bonds are bought and sold.

In a world without global financial markets, the supply and demand for foreign exchange and therefore exchange rates are driven by exports and imports (i.e. by the need to finance trade in goods and services). By the late 1980s, values traded in international markets for financial assets far exceeded the value of international trade in goods and services. As a consequence, it is trade in international financial markets that dominates the foreign exchange market. Market participants buy and sell currencies to take advantage of differences in rates of return on financial assets. Just as in the closed economy, we continue to assume there is just one asset, namely government bonds. Foreigners seeking to buy home bonds, need home currency in order to do this and vice versa. As market participants seek to take advantage of differences in interest rates on government bonds issued by different countries, this trading is a key determinant of exchange rate fluctuations. To understand the essential aspects of international financial markets, it is useful to make some simplifying assumptions:

1. There is *perfect international capital mobility*. This means that home residents can buy or sell foreign bonds with the fixed nominal world interest rate, i^*, in unlimited quantities at low transactions costs.
2. The home country is assumed to be *small* in the sense that its behaviour cannot affect the world interest rate.
3. Just as in the closed economy, we assume there are just *two asset types* that households can hold—bonds and money. But now they can hold foreign or home bonds. We assume that they hold only home money.

4. There is *perfect substitutability* between foreign and home bonds. This assumption means that the riskiness of foreign and home bonds is identical, so the only relevant difference between them is the expected return.

The last assumption means we rule out differences in the risk of default of bonds issued by different governments, and we assume that investors do not care about the balance between home and foreign bonds in their portfolio. Cross-country differences in default risk have always been highly relevant for the analysis of emerging and developing economies but much less so in developed economies, where bond yields converged at low levels during the Great Moderation. Default risk, however, reemerged as a pertinent issue for developed economies with the Eurozone crisis in 2010–11, which centred on the diverging default risk on Eurozone government bonds. In this chapter, we assume away issues related to differences in default risk. We return to them when we discuss the Eurozone in Chapter 14.

How do foreign exchange traders respond to interest rate differences? The uncovered interest parity (*UIP*) condition

If home households can hold home and foreign bonds in their portfolio, what will influence their choice? Assumption 4 (above) means there is no difference in risk between the bonds issued by the two governments. In this case, the only difference is the expected return on the two bonds and that will depend on two factors:

1. Any expected difference in interest rates over a specific time horizon; and
2. A view about the likely development of the exchange rate over the same time horizon.

The second of these factors emphasizes the importance of forming expectations about the exchange rate in future periods. When discussing households buying and selling home and foreign bonds, we will refer to this as the actions of foreign exchange market participants. It is reasonable to imagine that foreign exchange traders have a sophisticated understanding of available trades in the market since their success or failure at their job depends on it. In the absence of a more plausible and tractable alternative, following the definitions introduced in Chapter 4, we therefore assume that the foreign exchange market participants have 'model-consistent' or rational expectations. This assumption plays a very important role in the open economy model.

Example

Suppose the UK is the 'home' economy and the US is the 'foreign' economy. As discussed earlier, if the interest rate on home bonds is higher than on foreign ones, that will make home bonds more attractive. This would be followed by appreciation of home's currency (i.e. UK pounds) as people sold US dollars in order to buy UK pounds, which they need to buy the UK bonds. But, we need a model to explain by how much the UK pound appreciates.

Suppose that initially the interest rate on both bonds is 4%. Now let us see what happens if the Bank of England suddenly raised the UK interest rate to 6.5%. This case is shown in Figure 11.2, where e is used to denote the UK pound nominal exchange rate

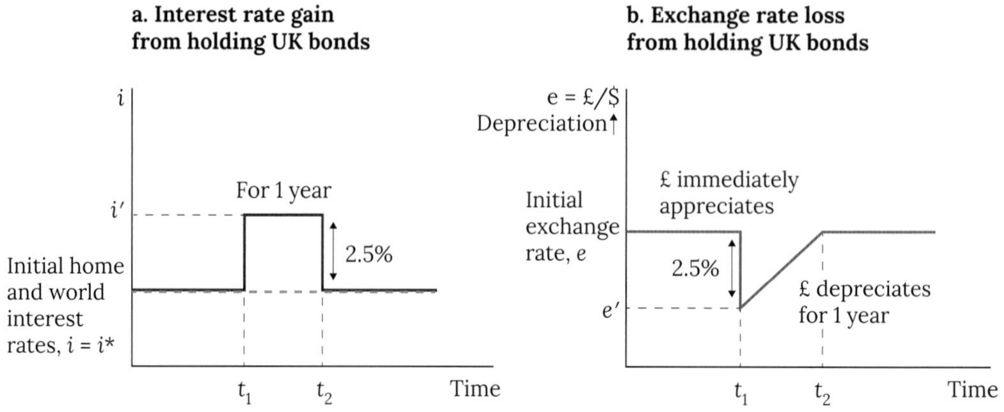

Figure 11.2 Arbitrage in the international bond market. World interest rate (dashed line in the left panel) unchanged throughout.

(i.e. £/$), t is used to denote the time period, i is used to denote the home interest rate and i^* is used to denote the world (or foreign) interest rate. The interest rate change makes UK bonds more attractive and investors will sell US dollars and buy UK pounds in order to take advantage of the higher expected return. But the move out of dollars and into UK pounds leads the US dollar to depreciate (weaken) and the UK pound to appreciate (strengthen).

As investors try to maximize their returns, the UK pound will appreciate by exactly 2.5% so that the expected return on UK and US bonds is identical. An American investor holding UK bonds for the duration of the interest differential (i.e. one year) gets 2.5% more in interest receipts than he would holding US bonds. On the flipside, however, the American investor loses 2.5% as the UK pound depreciates back to its 'normal' level over the course of the year. We assume that the underlying expected level of the exchange rate is exogenous and remains constant. The American investor will have to buy UK pounds at the start of the year in order to purchase the UK bonds, but wants US dollars at the end of the year to spend in the US (Assumption 3). Figure 11.2 shows how this process of arbitrage in the international bond markets works to equalize the expected return on bonds.

A survey of foreign exchange dealers in the UK asked: 'How fast do you think the market can assimilate the new information when the following economic announcements from the major developed economies differ from their market expectations?'[3] For an unexpected interest rate announcement, over 60% of the traders said 'less than ten seconds' with most of the rest saying less than one minute. According to this survey, speedy reaction is most common for news about interest rates, which also has a bigger impact on foreign exchange markets than announcements about inflation, unemployment, the trade deficit, the money supply or GDP. The survey findings suggest that any arbitrage opportunities that arise as a result of interest rate differentials (or expected

[3] See Cheung et al. (2004).

interest differentials) are exhausted extremely quickly. This results in jumps in the exchange rate. In the example shown above, as soon as the interest differential is announced, the UK pound would immediately appreciate by 2.5%.

The result that the exchange rate will jump so as to eliminate differences in expected returns on bonds is called the uncovered interest parity condition (UIP). It is derived in detail in the modelling section (11.2) that follows. We can write it like this:

Interest gain from holding home currency (UK pounds) rather than US dollar bonds	=	Loss from the expected depreciation of home currency (UK pounds) against the US dollar

(UIP condition)

With home's interest rate above the world (US bond) interest rate for one period between t_0 and t_1, the UIP condition states that the exchange rate will jump immediately to eliminate the arbitrage opportunity. Applying this to our example in Figure 11.2, the UIP condition states that: the UK pound exchange rate will appreciate by exactly 2.5% so that the loss from the expected depreciation of the UK pound over this period is equal to the interest gain from holding the higher yielding UK bonds over the same period. All market participants are assumed to believe that the exchange rate will return to its initial level at the end of the period.

The UIP condition tells us that 'unwinding' the initial change in the exchange rate must be equal to the interest rate differential; hence we know that the interest differential pins down the size of the jump. The arbitrage condition also tells us that the exchange rate at any time during the period between t_0 and t_1 will be as shown on the path in the right-hand panel of Figure 11.2. As the time comes closer to when the interest differential will disappear, the size of the interest gain from a UK bond shrinks and hence the matching expected depreciation of the pound must be smaller. The exchange rate must therefore be closer to its expected level of e. If this was not the case, there would be unexploited opportunities for profit-making by buying or selling pounds to buy or sell UK bonds. An important distinguishing characteristic of financial markets (as compared with goods and labour markets) is that *jumps* in prices are commonly observed.

11.1.3 **The reaction of the central bank and the foreign exchange market to an inflation shock**

We have now introduced the key components and mechanisms driving the 3-equation model in the open economy. This allows us to model the adjustment of a small open economy to an inflation shock. Detailed, period-by-period adjustment paths to an inflation shock and a range of other shocks are shown later in the chapter. This initial simple example aims to provide an overview of how the model works and to highlight the key differences from the closed economy model presented in Chapter 3.

We assume that a flexible exchange rate economy, which is initially at equilibrium output and target inflation, is hit by an inflation shock. In this case, just as in the closed economy, the central bank will raise the interest rate in order to reduce output and dampen inflation. However, the foreign exchange market will also react to the knowledge that home's interest rate will be kept above that of the rest of the world for some time. The *UIP* condition tells us that home's exchange rate will therefore appreciate, as there will be increased demand for home's currency. This occurs as investors buy home currency to buy home bonds so as to take advantage of their higher yields.

We know from the *IS* curve that the appreciation of the exchange rate will depress demand by reducing net exports. This means the central bank will not have to raise the interest rate as much as they would in the closed economy, as they correctly anticipate some of the adjustment will take place through the foreign exchange market. In other words, in the open economy, the dampening of demand needed to get the economy back onto the *MR* curve occurs through a combination of a higher interest rate and exchange rate appreciation.

Forward-looking behaviour of central banks and foreign exchange markets—real-world examples

The interaction between a forward-looking central bank and a forward-looking foreign exchange market is at the heart of the model of stabilization policy in the open economy. This is reflected in the publications of central banks and the financial press.

The link between the exchange rate and the monetary policy of the central bank in a flexible exchange rate regime is highlighted in Obstfeld and Rogoff (2009):[4]

> Under the pressure of very loose US monetary policy after the dot-com crash and 9/11, however, the dollar depreciated by more than 16% from early 2002 through the start of 2007, with a significant (but temporary) reversal over 2005 as the Fed tightened.

In the wake of the 9/11 attacks on the US, the Federal Reserve cut interest rates more aggressively than other developed economy central banks (e.g. the European Central Bank; see Figure 11.1). This saw the emergence of an interest rate differential that contributed to the depreciation of the dollar over that period.

In uncertain economic times, such as the UK's stop-start recovery from the 2008–09 financial crisis, it is harder to predict the path of the economy, and consequently of interest rate decisions. Mansoor Mohi-uddin, UBS's managing director of foreign exchange strategy, alluded to this point in early 2011:[5]

> But do not pity the Sterling [i.e. UK pound] bulls. Foreign exchange investors have bolstered the pound this year on expectations interest rates would soon be raised. Yet it remains far from clear whether the Bank's Monetary Policy Committee will take such a step.

Foreign exchange traders make their best estimate with the information they have available in each time period but can be wrong, which might subject the market

[4] See p. 32 of Obstfeld and Rogoff (2009).

[5] Excerpt taken from: Mansoor Mohi-uddin, February 7th 2011, 'Pound remains vulnerable to abrupt reversal of fortune,' article published in the *Financial Times*.

to corrections and jumps in the exchange rate. This could happen if the market anticipated a smaller (or larger) interest rate change than was actually observed. The extra unanticipated change would likely cause a jump in the exchange rate, as the market quickly takes advantage of the unexpected interest rate differential. In short, because the future is uncertain, basing current actions on forecasts and predictions can lead to volatility in the exchange rate.

Foreign exchange markets are complex and are influenced by a whole host of macroeconomic variables. The UIP condition is often hard to observe in exchange rate data, because these other factors influence the future expected exchange rate. During the global financial crisis, the Bank of England kept a close eye on interest rate differentials and the sterling (i.e. UK pound) exchange rate and found a number of other factors contributing to the depreciation of the UK pound over this period:[6]

> Sterling had lost over a quarter of its value since mid-2007. To some degree, that depreciation had probably reflected the need to rebalance the UK economy away from domestic towards external demand. In addition over the past year, the global outlook had deteriorated with resultant downward revisions to interest rate expectations worldwide. But the downward revision to forecasts of the UK economy appeared to have been greater than for some other countries. And those perceptions may have contributed to sterling's decline. Another factor in sterling's decline over the past eighteen months could have been increased risk premia.

As discussed in Chapter 9, the recession of 2008–09 saw the limits of conventional monetary policy reached and central banks had to resort to unconventional monetary policy, such as quantitative easing, to avoid a deflation trap. These policies also affect the foreign exchange market. Quantitative easing aims to influence long-term interest rates and, therefore, to affect interest rate differentials. An article in the *Financial Times* from autumn 2011 attributed moves in the pound exchange rate to changes in expectations about quantitative easing:[7]

> The pound dropped to an eight-month low against the dollar on Wednesday as expectations heightened that the Bank of England would engage in further quantitative easing in an effort to boost the UK economy.

One of the main lessons of this chapter is the way a forward-looking foreign exchange market anticipates the actions of the central bank and facilitates the adjustment of the economy to a shock. On a minute-by-minute basis, the foreign exchange market is assimilating the latest macroeconomic data and making forecasts about how this could affect the interest rates set by the central bank. In light of this, changes in

---

[6] Excerpt taken from: Bank of England, *Minutes of the Monetary Policy Committee Meeting, 4 and 5 March* 2009, published March 18th 2009.

[7] Excerpt taken from: Peter Garnham, September 21st 2011, 'Dovish Bank minutes weigh on Pound,' article published in the *Financial Times*.

interest rate expectations are often built into the foreign exchange market a long time before the interest rate changes actually take place.

Another example of how expectations of future monetary policy affect the behaviour of forex traders is the dramatic appreciation of the US dollar—for the first time since the turn of the century—against all other major currencies between 2014 and 2016. An article in the *Financial Times* from 2015 reads:[8]

> Expectations that the Federal Reserve will raise interest rates in 2015 from historic lows have been a major factor in the dollar's strength, as central banks in other countries including the European Central Bank and the Bank of Japan continue to take an easing stance.

The Fed started to raise rates from the second half of 2015, considerably later than when the appreciation had taken place.

Summary

In this chapter, we extend the core 3-equation model introduced in Chapter 3 to set out a framework for analysing stabilization policy in the flexible exchange rate open economy. This involves opening up the economy to both international trade (i.e. imports and exports) and international capital flows (i.e. home and foreign bonds). The two main effects on the model of introducing the forex market are that:

1. following an economic shock, the central bank and foreign exchange market react to the shock, which means adjustment occurs through both exchange rate and interest rate channels; and
2. the forex market bases its actions partly on its expectations of the future, which can lead to jumps in the exchange rate and increased macroeconomic volatility.

11.2 MODELLING

In Section 11.1, we provided an overview of how the 3-equation model works in the open economy. In this section, we get into the mechanics of the model. The first part of the section formalizes the UIP condition. In the second part, we explain what is meant by medium-run equilibrium in the open economy. We combine these components to build the open economy 3-equation model and use them to analyse the period-by-period adjustment of the economy to shocks. The new RX curve combines the interest rate and exchange rate channels through which the central bank's interest rate decision affects aggregate demand. The RX curve replaces the IS curve as the policy implementation curve in the open economy. Section 11.3 discusses the role of exchange rate overshooting in the open economy.

---

[8] Excerpt taken from: Alice Ross, January 2nd 2015, 'Dollar surges on Fed rate rise expectations', article published in the *Financial Times*.

11.2.1 The foreign exchange market and the *UIP* condition

In Section 11.1, we introduced the concept of the UIP condition, which is central to the behaviour of the foreign exchange market in the open economy 3-equation model. In this subsection, we will set out the equation for the UIP condition and use a graphical analysis to explore the concept in more detail. See the appendix for a comparison between the UIP condition, which we use in the open economy model, and the CIP, covered interest parity condition, which describes a particular kind of financial contract.

The *UIP* condition

The UIP can be represented as:

$$\underbrace{i_t - i_t^*}_{\text{interest gain (loss)}} = \underbrace{\frac{e_{t+1}^E - e_t}{e_t}}_{\text{expected depreciation (appreciation)}} + \underbrace{\rho_t}_{\text{default risk}},$$

where i is the home interest rate, i^* is the foreign interest rate, e is the nominal exchange rate of the home country, e^E is the expected exchange rate of the home country, and ρ_t is a risk premium to insure against the possibility of the government defaulting on its debt obligations. Note that the perfect substitutability assumption ensures ρ_t is equal to zero given that the default risk of home and foreign bonds is the same. The equation says that given the values for i_t, i^* and e_{t+1}^E, we can work out the value to which the exchange rate will jump, e_t.

In the example we introduced in Section 11.1, the initial shock is the rise in i_t. The world (i.e. US) interest rate, i^*, and the view of the exchange market traders about the expected exchange rate in a year's time, e_{t+1}^E, remain unchanged. From the point of view of the UK as the home country, there is an interest gain on the left-hand side, which in the presence of arbitrage must equal the expected depreciation of the pound (on the right-hand side). For the equation to hold therefore, the UK pound exchange rate e_t must immediately appreciate (as people sell US dollars to buy UK pounds): it will appreciate by exactly 2.5% so that its subsequent expected depreciation just offsets the interest gain incurred by holding UK rather than US bonds (see Figure 11.2 in Section 11.1).

So far we do not have a model of what determines the expected exchange rate: we simply assume it is expected to return to its previous value after one period. In Section 11.2.2, we introduce a model that pins down the equilibrium exchange rate, and hence provides an anchor for exchange rate expectations. For the moment, we assume the expected exchange is constant.

We make use of the fact that we can approximate the percentage growth of the exchange rate by the change in the (natural) log of the exchange rate, i.e.

$$\frac{e_1^E - e_0}{e_0} \approx \log e_1^E - \log e_0 \text{ and in our example, } \log e_1^E - \log e_0 \approx 2.5\%.$$

The great advantage of using the log formulation is that we now write the UIP condition as

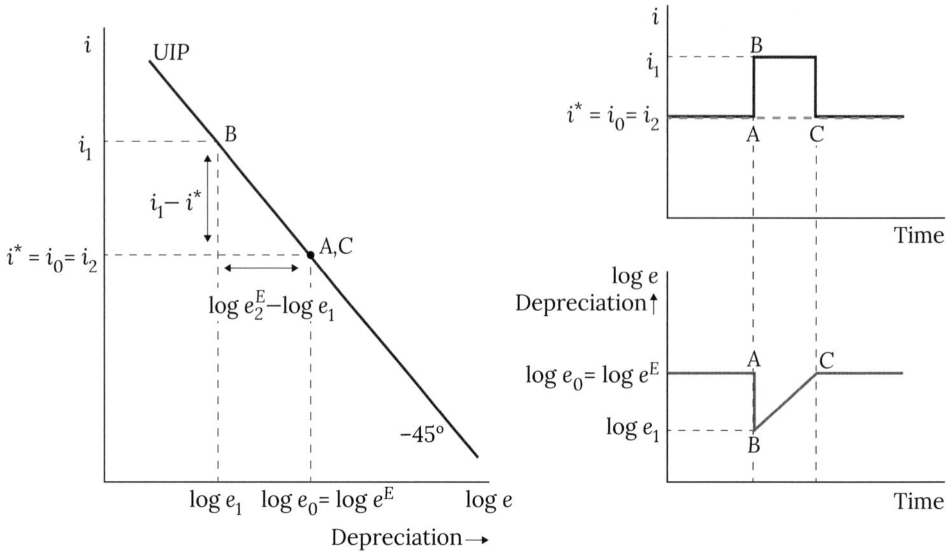

Figure 11.3 The uncovered interest parity condition: $i_t - i^* = \log e^E_{t+1} - \log e_t$. The world interest rate (dashed line) remains unchanged throughout.

$$\underbrace{i_t - i_t^*}_{\text{interest gain (loss)}} = \underbrace{\log e^E_{t+1} - \log e_t}_{\text{expected depreciation (appreciation)}},$$

and we can draw this as a line with a -45° slope as shown in Figure 11.3 with the interest rate on the vertical axis and the log of the nominal exchange rate on the horizontal axis.[9] The *UIP* curve is pinned down by the world interest rate and the expected exchange rate.

Our understanding of the model is helped by looking at two points on the *UIP* curve. The first is point A in Figure 11.3: this is where the home interest rate equals the world interest rate ($i = i^*$) and exchange rate expectations are fulfilled ($\log e_0 = \log e_1^E$), and the exchange rate does not change.

Keeping in mind that our example represents the situation where home's interest rate of i_1 above the world interest rate is expected to prevail for one year, we now look at a second point on this *UIP* curve at B. Assuming the expected exchange rate

[9] Natural logs often allow equations to be displayed and manipulated in a simpler manner. Taking the natural log of a variable is an example of a monotonic transformation, that while changing the values in the series, preserves the order of the underlying variables. This ensures that taking natural logs does not change the meaning of the original data. Another useful property of natural logs is that (when percentages are small) the percentage change between two variables is approximately equal to the difference in the natural logs of those two variables. In the case of the UIP condition, using this property of natural logs allows us to represent the UIP condition as a -45° line, which makes the graphical analysis less complex. In general, this property makes calculating percentages changes or growth rates easier and is often used when analysing time series data. We look at natural logs in more detail in the discussion on long-run growth in Chapter 16.

remains fixed at $\log e_1^E$, then since home's interest rate is now above the world interest rate, there must be a change in the *actual* exchange rate away from $\log e_0$. According to the UIP condition, as soon as the interest rate differential opens up, home's exchange rate will appreciate immediately (jump) to $\log e_1$ so that its expected depreciation over the year is equal to the interest rate differential. In the left-hand panel of Figure 11.3, the two double-headed arrows are equal in length.

In the right-hand panel of Figure 11.3 are shown the time paths of the interest rate at home and abroad (upper) and of the nominal exchange rate (lower). The impulse response function highlights the fact that the interest rate differential persists for one period and that the exchange rate jumps as soon as the news of the interest rate differential arises. During that period, the nominal exchange rate depreciates.

The key features of the UIP diagram with i and $\log e$ on the axes are:

1. each UIP curve has a slope of -45° and must go through the point $(\log e^E, i^*)$;
2. a change in home's interest rate causes a *movement along* the UIP curve (for a given $\log e^E$ and i^*);
3. for a given expected exchange rate, any change in the world interest rate *shifts* the UIP curve;
4. for a given world interest rate, any change in the expected exchange rate *shifts* the UIP curve.

To illustrate how the UIP curve works, suppose there is a fall in the world interest rate that will last for one period. What is the implication for the home country's exchange rate assuming that there is no change in the home interest rate? To answer this question, we assume there is no change in the expected exchange rate. The shift in the UIP curve from UIP to UIP′ due to the fall in the world interest rate is shown in Figure 11.4. The new UIP curve goes through point G: only with $i = i^*$ at that point would there be no change in the exchange rate.

The economy is initially at point A on the UIP curve. With the expected exchange rate equal to $\log e^E$ and with home's interest rate unchanged, and now above the world interest rate of i_1^*, arbitrage in the financial market will lead to an immediate appreciation of the home exchange rate as shown by point B on the new UIP curve, UIP′. At the end of the period, i^* reverts to its initial level (and the UIP curve reverts to the original one). There is no interest differential and the exchange rate is back at its initial level (point C). The impulse response functions in the right-hand panel illustrate the jump appreciation of home's exchange rate and the depreciation over the period during which home's interest rate remains above that of the world.

If the home country is the UK, the UIP condition makes clear, for example, that just before the US interest rate is raised at the end of the period, there is little to be gained by switching to UK bonds: the tiny expected interest gain would be matched by a tiny expected depreciation of the pound: hence e_t would be very close to its expected level.

The diagram also illustrates that there will be no change in the exchange rate at all if the central bank in the home country immediately follows the interest rate move by the foreign central bank. The economy would shift from A to G. At the end of the

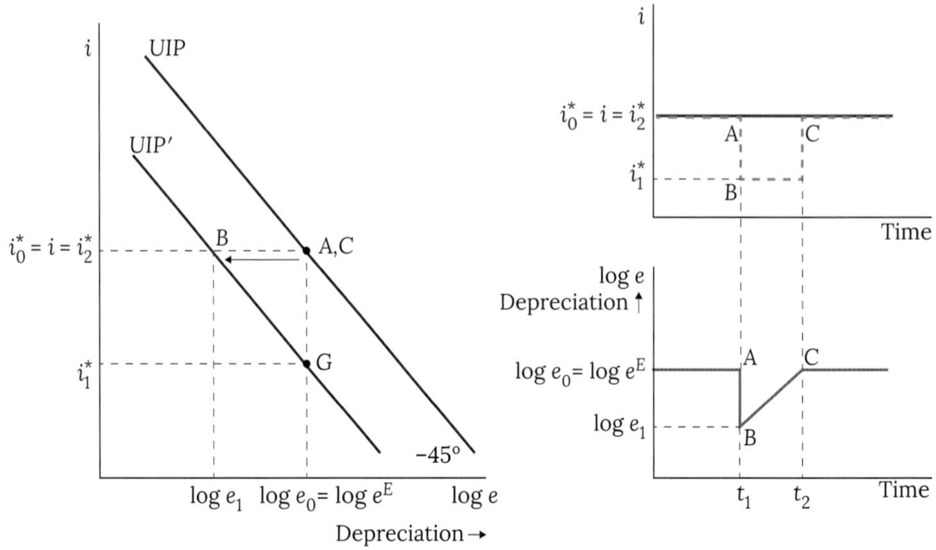

Figure 11.4 The uncovered interest parity condition: a fall in the world interest rate leads to an immediate appreciation of the home exchange rate. Home's interest rate is unchanged throughout. The path of the world real interest rate is dashed. Visit www.oup.com/he/carlin-soskice to explore the UIP and the fall in world interest rate with Animated Analytical Diagram 11.4.

period, if home again follows the interest rate move of the foreign central bank, then the move is from G back to A and the exchange rate does not change.

A final exercise is the analysis of a change in sentiment in the foreign exchange market. If traders suddenly change their view about the likely exchange rate in a year's time, the *UIP* curve will shift. If a depreciated home exchange rate is expected, the *UIP* curve will shift to the right. With the home and world interest rates equal, such a change in sentiment will have the effect of leading to an immediate depreciation of the actual exchange rate to its new expected value (so that the *UIP* condition holds). This illustrates that expectations about future developments are incorporated into today's exchange rate. Drawing the diagrams for the latter two cases (home's central bank immediately follows a move by the foreign central bank; and a change in sentiment in the foreign exchange market about home's exchange rate in a year's time) is left as an exercise for the reader.

11.2.2 **Medium-run equilibrium in the open economy and the *AD-ERU* model**

Before we can bring the foreign exchange market together with the 3-equation model, we need to analyse the characteristics of the constant inflation equilibrium of the open economy.

We saw in Chapter 2 that the closed economy is in medium-run equilibrium when inflation is constant. For inflation to be constant, there must be equilibrium on the supply side, which occurs when wage and price setters have no incentive to change their behaviour—i.e. at the intersection of the WS and PS curves (see Chapter 2). The intersection between the WS and PS curves pins down the *equilibrium rate of unemployment*, which is why we shall call the supply-side curve in the medium-run model the ERU curve. The use of the term ERU is a reminder that the supply side lies behind the determination of the constant inflation equilibrium.

In the open economy, the real exchange rate plays a central role and it is useful to present the medium-run model in a diagram with output on the horizontal axis and the real exchange rate on the vertical axis (see the lower panel of Figure 11.5). Recall the definition of the real exchange rate:

$$Q \equiv \frac{P^*e}{P}. \qquad \text{(home's real exchange rate, price competitiveness)}$$

For reasons that will become clear, we use the log of the real exchange rate rather than its level on the vertical axis in Figure 11.5. We use q to denote the natural logarithm of Q—i.e. $q \equiv \log Q$. The full medium-run model, which includes the trade balance, is introduced in Chapter 12. Here we focus on the supply- and demand-side relationships, and we use the simplest model that allows us to understand stabilization policy problems in the open economy.

As we shall see in this section, the ERU curve in Figure 11.5 captures the supply side, and on the ERU curve, inflation is constant. The demand side in the open economy is

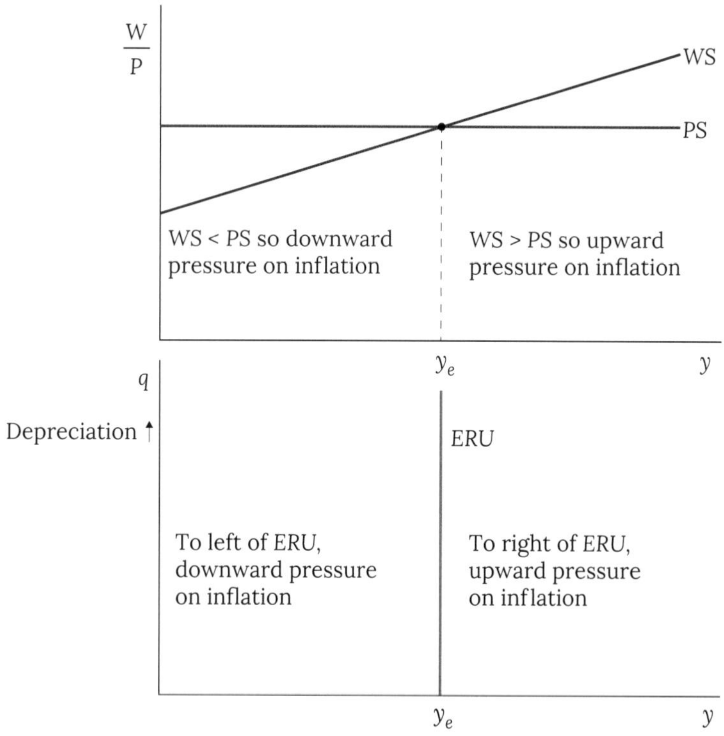

Figure 11.5 Supply-side equilibrium and the ERU curve.

represented by the *aggregate demand* curve (the AD curve) in the same diagram. On the AD curve, the goods market is in equilibrium and the real interest rate is equal to the world real interest rate (i.e. $r = r^*$).

The medium-run equilibrium (MRE) in the open economy is defined by values of output and the real exchange rate. In a MRE, which we shall see is at the intersection of the supply-side (ERU) curve and the demand side (AD) curves, output and the real exchange rate are at their equilibrium levels, and inflation is constant. The medium-run model applies irrespective of the exchange rate regime. The type of exchange rate regime (i.e. fixed or flexible) affects the dynamics of adjustment to shocks, the available policy instruments and how the medium-run inflation rate is determined in Section 12.2.3. We look at the ERU and the AD curves in turn.

Supply-side equilibrium: The *ERU* curve

The ERU curve is defined by the intersection of the wage- and price-setting curves. It shows the combinations of the real exchange rate and output at which there is supply-side equilibrium (i.e. constant inflation). Understanding what is going on when the economy is 'off' a curve that represents equilibria helps to explain the nature of the equilibrium itself: in this case, why inflation is constant *on* the ERU curve.

In this chapter, we continue to work with a single price level, P, which means the WS and PS curves are exactly the same as in the closed economy. Figure 11.5 shows the equilibrium output level, y_e, associated with supply-side equilibrium. At an output level to the right of y_e, the real wage defined by the PS curve is too low for wage setters given that unemployment is below equilibrium. This puts upward pressure on inflation. Similarly, an output level below y_e where unemployment is higher than equilibrium means that the real wage (on the PS) is too high given the relative weakness of workers in the labour market: there is downward pressure on inflation. Although not shown in Figure 11.5, the short-run Phillips curves are derived graphically from the WS and PS curves in exactly the same way as in the closed economy.

The WS-PS intersection defines the ERU curve, which is vertical in the real exchange rate–output diagram at y_e.[10]

We can write the ERU curve as:

$$y = y_e(z^W, z^P), \qquad \text{(ERU curve)}$$

where z^W is the set of supply-side factors that shift the WS curve such as unionization, labour market regulations and unemployment benefits. z^P is the set of factors that shifts the PS curve, such as the tax rate, the level of technology (i.e. labour productivity) and the degree of product market competition. As we saw in Chapter 2, for example, a rise in the reservation wage or in union power shifts the WS curve upwards and reduces equilibrium output. In the open economy diagram, this is represented by a leftward shift in the vertical ERU curve to the new lower level of equilibrium output.

The ERU curve is defined as the combinations of the real exchange rate and output at which the wage-setting real wage is equal to the price-setting real wage. At any

---

[10] In Chapter 12 we shall see why the ERU may be downward sloping.

point on the ERU curve, inflation is constant. Since neither the WS nor the PS curve depends on the real exchange rate, the ERU curve is vertical. In Chapter 12, we will see why the PS curve may depend on the real exchange rate and what that implies for the ERU curve.

Goods market equilibrium: The *AD* curve

The AD curve incorporates both the demand side and the UIP condition in the medium-run equilibrium. To derive the AD curve, we use the version of the IS curve introduced in Chapter 3. For the open economy, this formulation captures the fact that aggregate demand responds negatively to the real interest rate (r) and positively to a depreciation in the real exchange rate (q), both with a one period lag. Hence

$$y_t = A_t - ar_{t-1} + bq_{t-1}, \qquad \text{(open economy IS curve)}$$

where A includes the multiplier and demand shift variables in the open economy, such as world trade, as well as government spending (G) and the variables that shift the consumption and investment functions such as wealth and Tobin's Q. The open economy IS curve is discussed in detail in Chapter 12 (see footnote 18).

The second step in deriving the AD curve is to incorporate financial integration. In medium-run equilibrium, the real exchange rate is constant and equal to its expected value. We shall see that this implies that $r = r^*$. We are considering a small open economy, which cannot affect the world real interest rate. To see why $r = r^*$ in a medium-run equilibrium, we begin by recalling the UIP condition:

$$i_t - i_t^* = \log e_{t+1}^E - \log e_t. \qquad \text{(UIP condition)}$$

From this, we know that for the nominal exchange rate to be unchanged (i.e. $\log e_{t+1}^E = \log e$), then $i_t = i^*$. We can derive the UIP condition in terms of the real rather than the nominal exchange rate (see Section 11.5.3 of the Appendix for the derivation):

$$r_t - r_t^* = q_{t+1}^E - q_t. \qquad \text{(real UIP condition)}$$

The real UIP condition says that if home's real interest rate is higher than the world's, then its real exchange rate is expected to depreciate. For a medium-run equilibrium, we require the real exchange rate to be equal to its expected value, which means it is constant and that $r = r^*$. This produces the aggregate demand equation on which $r = r^*$:

$$y = A - ar^* + bq. \qquad \text{(AD curve, } r = r^*\text{)}$$

We shall see that when home's central bank implements monetary policy in response to a shock, home's r will diverge from r^* and the economy will be 'off' the AD curve during the adjustment process. The AD curve is upward sloping in the exchange rate–output space (as shown in Figure 11.6). This means a more depreciated exchange rate is associated with a higher level of output.

The AD curve shows the medium-run combinations of the real exchange rate, q, and level of output, y, at which the goods market is in equilibrium with the real interest rate equal to the world real interest rate (i.e. $r = r^*$).

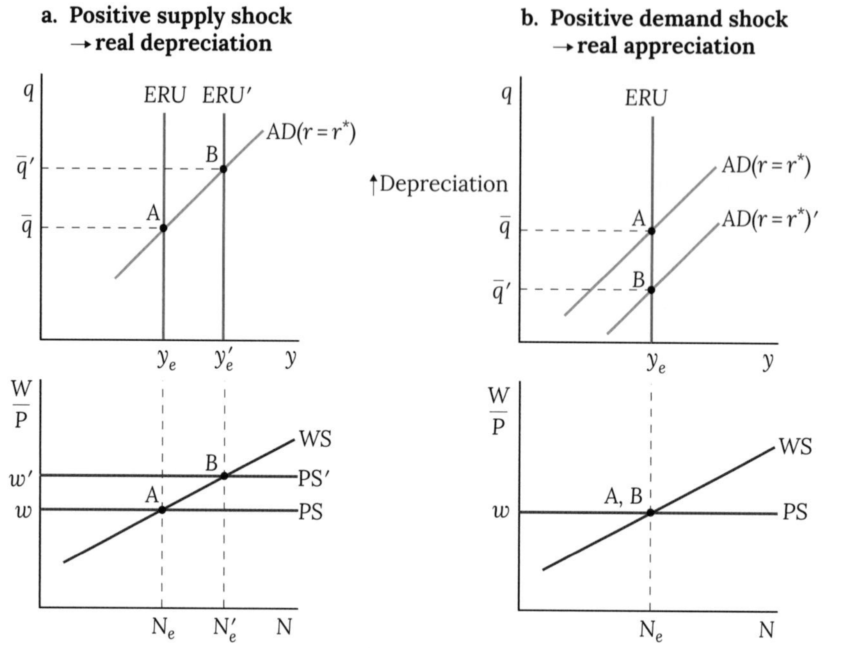

Figure 11.6 What determines the medium-run real exchange rate, $\bar{q}$? Visit www.oup.com/he/carlin-soskice to explore the effect of supply and demand shocks on the medium-run exchange rate with Animated Analytical Diagram 11.6.

The medium-run model (*AD-ERU* model)

The basic medium-run model for analysis in the small open economy consists of:

- The demand side represented by the AD curve. On the AD curve, the goods market is in equilibrium and $r = r^*$.
- The supply side represented by the ERU curve. On the ERU curve inflation is constant.
- In medium-run equilibrium, the economy is at the intersection of an AD curve with the ERU curve: $r = r^*$; $y = y_e$; $q = \bar{q}$; and inflation is constant. Being on the AD curve implies that the real exchange rate is equal to its expected value and hence, constant; being on the ERU curve means $y = y_e$ and hence, inflation is constant.

What determines the medium-run real exchange rate, $\bar{q}$?

At this stage in the chapter, our focus is on understanding the equilibria, i.e. the start and end points for the economy following a shock. We fill in the narrative about how the economy moves from one equilibrium to another in Section 11.2.3. In modelling the UIP condition, exchange rate expectations played a key role. The AD-ERU model helps to explain those expectations by showing how the real exchange rate is determined in the medium-run equilibrium.

In the closed economy, there is a new stabilizing real interest rate at medium-run equilibrium following a permanent demand or supply shock. In the small open economy, the real interest rate is pinned down by the world real interest rate in medium-run equilibrium (i.e. $r = r^*$) and it is therefore the real exchange rate that varies in response to demand and supply shocks.

We assume the economy is initially at medium-run equilibrium on the AD and ERU curves, and look at the implications for the real exchange rate of a supply shock and a demand shock:

- **A supply shock:** A positive supply shock such as a wave of new technology raises productivity and the PS shifts up. This shifts the ERU curve to the right. At the new equilibrium, the real exchange rate has depreciated to $\overline{q}'$. Equilibrium output is higher (see point B in Figure 11.6a). The intuition for this result is that for the level of output demanded to increase to the higher equilibrium level, the real exchange rate must be depreciated. All the other components of aggregate demand are unchanged.
- **A demand shock:** A positive demand shock such as an investment boom shifts the AD curve to the right, and at the new equilibrium, there is an appreciated real exchange rate, $\overline{q}'$ (point B in Figure 11.6b). Output is unchanged in the new equilibrium. In this case, an investment boom raises the value of the variable A in the AD equation; r^* is fixed and therefore an appreciated real exchange rate is required to reduce aggregate demand such that $y = y_e$.

Table 11.1 compares the implications of a variety of permanent supply and demand shocks for unemployment, the real exchange rate and real wages in the new constant inflation equilibrium. To check the implications for the real wage, look for the intersection of the post shock WS and PS curves.

11.2.3 Stabilization under flexible exchange rates

To model stabilization policy in the open economy, we use the AD-ERU model to characterize the medium-run equilibrium and extend the 3-equation model to explain how the central bank responds to a shock. To do this, we introduce a new curve, the RX curve, explained below, which gives the central bank's best interest rate response taking into account the reaction of the foreign exchange market.

	Shock		
	Rise in productivity	Fall in union bargaining power	Increase in autonomous consumption
Equilibrium unemployment	↓	↓	no change
Real exchange rate	depreciation	depreciation	appreciation
Real wage	↑	no change	no change

Table 11.1 Supply and demand shocks: implications for medium-run equilibrium.

Note: ↑ means the variable is higher in the new medium-run equilibrium, ↓ means it is lower and 'no change' means it is unchanged. We assume a flat PS curve throughout.

To simplify the modelling, we assume as noted earlier that the central bank targets domestic inflation. In reality, central banks target consumer price inflation, which includes the effect of changes in import prices.

In the closed economy, the central bank minimizes its loss function, which expresses its objective of keeping inflation close to target, π^T, subject to the constraint from the supply side, which is the Phillips curve (PC). This produces the monetary rule function (MR), which pins down the best response output gap $(y_t - y_e)$. This is in turn implemented through the choice of the real interest rate (r) using the IS equation.

Why should openness of the economy affect the central bank's inflation-targeting behaviour? The answer is that the central bank will need to take account of the forward-looking behaviour in the foreign exchange market and the effect of changes in the exchange rate on aggregate demand. The examples in Section 11.1 highlighted why the central bank will need to build into its decision-making the anticipation of the foreign exchange market response.

In the open economy, the central bank minimizes its loss function, which just as in the closed economy expresses its objective of keeping inflation close to its target, π^T

$$L = (y_t - y_e)^2 + \beta(\pi_t - \pi^T)^2, \qquad \text{(central bank loss function)}$$

1. Subject to the constraint from the supply side, which (again, just as in the closed economy) is the adaptive expectations Phillips curve (PC),

$$\pi_t = \pi_{t-1} + \alpha(y_t - y_e). \qquad \text{(Phillips curve, PC)}$$

2. This produces the monetary rule function (MR), which pins down the best response output gap $(y_t - y_e)$,

$$(y_t - y_e) = -\alpha\beta(\pi_t - \pi^T). \qquad \text{(monetary rule, MR)}$$

3. But now this is implemented through the central bank's choice of r using the *open economy IS curve* and *taking account of the reaction of the forward-looking forex market*,

$$y_t = A_t - ar_{t-1} + bq_{t-1}. \qquad \text{(open economy IS curve)}$$

Earlier in the chapter, we introduced the UIP condition, which showed how the exchange rate jumps in response to any news about home or foreign interest rates. When a shock hits the economy, this is news and both the central bank *and* the foreign exchange market will respond to it (see Figure 11.7, starting at the top, for a summary of the dynamic adjustment of the economy to an inflation shock).

Instead of adjusting back to equilibrium along the IS curve as in the closed economy, the central bank will adjust along a flatter 'interest rate—exchange rate' curve, which we will call the 'RX' curve. The central bank will need to make smaller adjustments to the interest rate when the exchange rate channel operates as well.

Inflation shock: Comparing closed and open economies

The first step is to recall that a temporary inflation shock shifts the Phillips curve for one period. The problem for the inflation-targeting central bank is to get inflation back

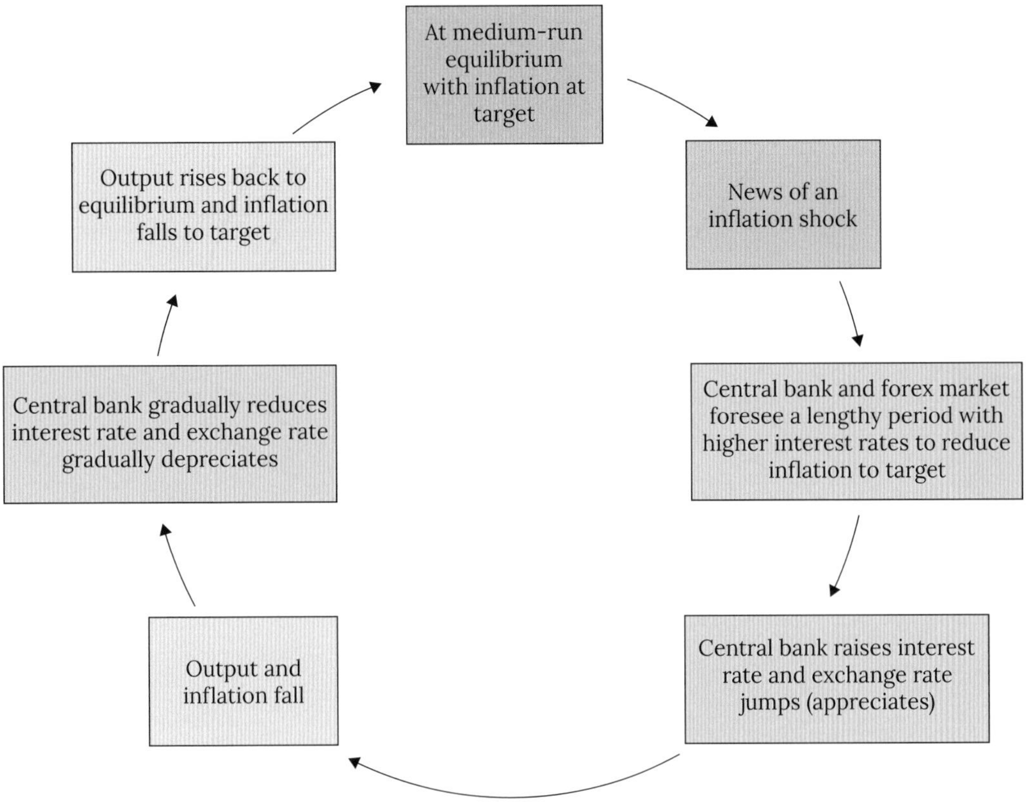

Figure 11.7 Dynamic adjustment to an inflation shock under flexible exchange rates and inflation targeting.

to its target and in order to do that, it must push output below and unemployment above equilibrium by raising the interest rate. This is because of the persistence in the inflation process (indicated by π_{t-1} in the *PC* equation): once inflation has been pushed up by the shock, it is built in to the behaviour of wage and price setters. For example, if food prices were pushed up by the effects of a drought, wage setters will expect in the next round of wage setting to get a wage increase that compensates them for the higher prices they face. In turn, firms will increase their prices to maintain their profit margins in the face of higher labour costs. This feature of inertia in wage and price setting means the central bank faces the constraint of the Phillips curve indexed by the inflation shock even though the shock was a temporary one.

Once inflation is back at target, the economy will be back at the initial equilibrium. This means that in the *AD-ERU* model the new equilibrium coincides with the initial equilibrium—i.e. there is no change in the medium-run equilibrium real exchange rate.

A good way of illustrating the open economy aspects of the problem faced by the central bank is to make a direct comparison with the closed economy. Figure 11.8 shows the *IS* and Phillips curve diagrams for the cases of the open and closed economies following an inflation shock.

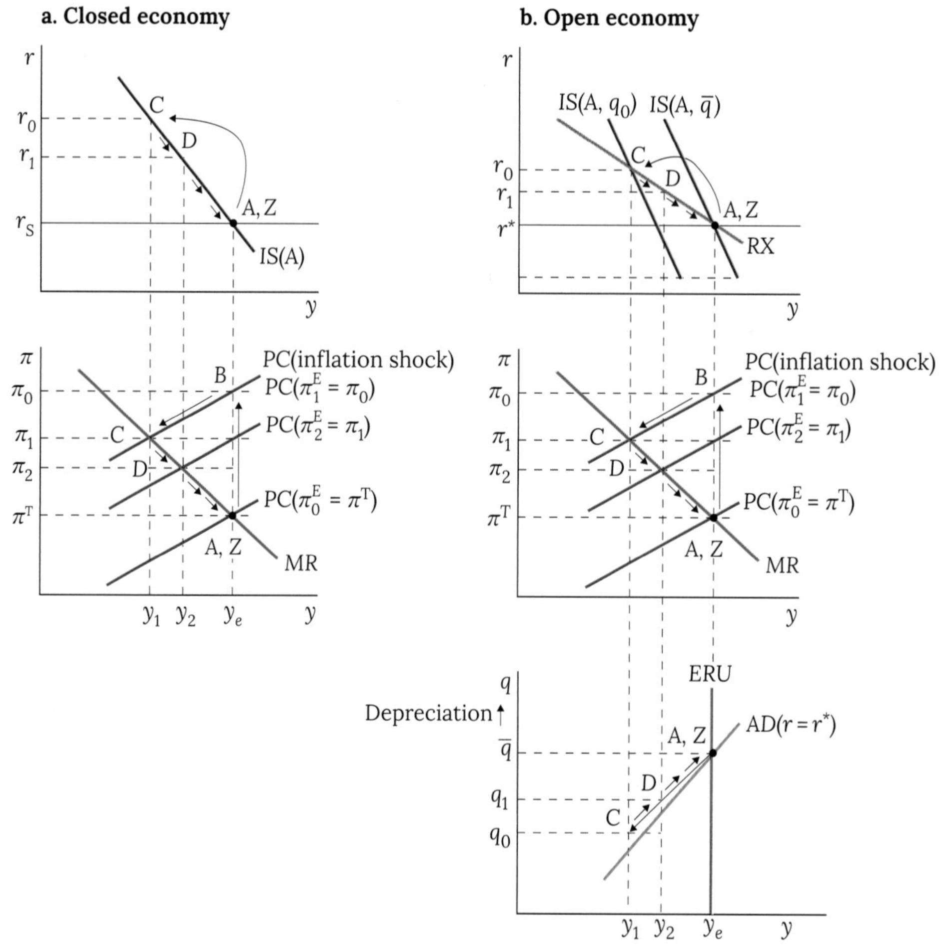

Figure 11.8 Inflation shock: closed and open economies. Visit www.oup.com/he/carlin-soskice to explore inflation shocks in the closed and open economies with Animated Analytical Diagram 11.8. We show there that the long arrow from point A to point C in the bottom right-hand figure is the AD($r = r_t$) curve.

Closed economy

Figure 11.8a (the left-hand panel of Figure 11.8), shows the adjustment of a closed economy to a temporary inflation shock, repeating the analysis from Chapter 3.

Period 0: The economy starts at point A—the central bank's bliss point. The economy is hit by an inflation shock which shifts the PC to PC(inflation shock) and the economy moves from A to B. Point B is not on the central bank's MR curve. The central bank forecasts the PC in the next period. This is PC($\pi_1^E = \pi_0$). Faced with this PC, the central bank would like to locate at point C, back on their MR curve. They therefore set the interest rate at r_0. The interest rate can only affect economic output with a one period lag, however, so the economy ends period 0 with inflation at π_0, output at y_e and interest rates at r_0.

Period 1: The new interest rate has had time to affect aggregate demand. The higher rate of interest dampens investment. This reduces output and the economy moves to point C, with output below equilibrium at y_1 and inflation at π_1. The central bank forecasts the PC in the next period. Based on last period's inflation, the PC it faces is $PC(\pi_2^E = \pi_1)$ and the central bank would like to locate at point D, back on their *MR* curve. They therefore reduce the interest rate to r_1. The interest rate can only affect economic output with a one period lag however, so the economy ends period 1 with inflation at π_1, output at y_1 and interest rates at r_1.

Period 2 onwards: In period 2, the economy moves to point D, as the lower interest rate stimulates demand. This increases output to y_2 and inflation falls to π_2. The same process now repeats itself until the economy is back at equilibrium at Z. The economy will move gradually down the MR curve, as the central bank slowly adjusts the interest rate down from r_1 to r_S. The adjustment to the inflation shock ends when the economy is back at point Z, with output at y_e, inflation at π^T and the interest rate at r_S.

Open economy: Introducing the *RX* curve

Figure 11.8b shows the adjustment of a small open economy to a temporary inflation shock. A compact summary of the open economy 3-equation model is in the Appendix Section 11.5.2.

Period 0: The economy starts at point A and the central bank's reasoning is the same as in the closed economy to locate its best response output gap at point C, on their MR curve. The foreign exchange market foresees that the central bank will keep interest rates above world interest rates for a number of periods in order to squeeze inflation out of the system. The UIP condition implies this will cause an immediate appreciation of home's currency, so that it can depreciate for the *whole period* during which there is a positive interest differential between home and foreign bonds. To get the economy back on the MR curve in the next period, the central bank therefore sets the interest rate at r_0 on the RX curve–taking into account the appreciation in the exchange rate that will occur since the IS curve will shift to the left to $IS(q_0)$. The interest rate and the exchange rate can only affect economic output with a one period lag however, so the economy ends period 0 with inflation at π_0, output at y_e, the interest rate at r_0 and the exchange rate at q_0.

Period 1: The new interest rate and exchange rate have had time to affect aggregate demand. The higher rate of interest dampens investment and the appreciated exchange rate reduces net exports. These forces combine to reduce output and the economy moves to point C, with output below equilibrium at y_1 and inflation at π_1. The IS curve has shifted to the left on account of the more appreciated exchange rate. The central bank forecasts the PC in the next period, $PC(\pi_2^E = \pi_1)$. Faced with this PC, the central bank would like to locate at point D, back on their MR curve. In setting the interest rate, they again take into account the response of the foreign exchange market. The central bank foresees that a depreciation of the exchange rate will follow any reduction in the interest rate, as the UIP condition needs to hold in every period. They therefore reduce the interest rate to r_1 and the exchange rate depreciates to q_1 (point D on the RX curve). The interest rate and the exchange rate can only affect economic output with a one period lag, however, so the economy ends period 1 with inflation at π_1, output at y_1, the interest rate at r_1 and the exchange rate at q_1.

Period 2 onwards: In period 2, the economy moves to point D, as the lower interest rate and depreciated exchange rate stimulate demand. This increases output to y_2 and inflation falls to π_2. The IS curve has shifted to the right (back towards the initial equilibrium), due to the depreciation in the exchange rate. The economy is travelling down the curve labelled RX curve, which is flatter than the IS curve. It shows the adjustment path of a small open economy (with flexible exchange rates) after an economic shock. Along the RX curve the UIP condition always holds—i.e. it shows the central bank the interest rate to set to achieve a given output gap, taking into account the reaction of the forex market. The same process now repeats itself until the economy is back at equilibrium at Z.

The adjustment from D to Z will take a number of periods. The IS curve will gradually shift to the right and the economy will move down the RX and MR curves, as the central bank slowly adjusts the interest rate down from r_1 to r^* and the exchange rate depreciates from q_1 to $\overline{q}$. The interest rate needs to be back at the world interest rate for there to be no pressure on the exchange rate to change and for the economy to be in medium-run equilibrium. The movements in r and q reinforce each other, causing output to rise slowly from y_2 to y_e and inflation to fall slowly from π_2 to π^T. The adjustment ends when the economy is back at point Z, with output at y_e, inflation at π^T, the interest rate at r^* and the exchange rate at $\overline{q}$.

To complete the discussion of the open economy adjustment, the bottom panel of Figure 11.8b shows the AD-ERU diagram. In the case of an inflation shock, the positions of the AD and ERU curves are unaffected by the shock. For the whole of the adjustment process the economy is to the left of the ERU curve and as we saw in Figure 11.5, this leads to downwards pressure on inflation. This causes inflation to fall until the economy is back at target inflation and once again on the ERU curve in medium-run equilibrium. From the top panel, we know that the real interest rate is above the world interest rate during the adjustment process. This means the adjustment along the MR curve from C to Z will lie to the left of the AD curve as shown in the bottom panel. The economy will only be back on the AD($r = r^*$) curve when it is once more in medium-run equilibrium with $r = r^*$. There is a second AD curve (AD($r = r_t$)), which goes through points A, C, and D in Figure 11.8. See the Animated Analytical Diagram of Figure 11.8 for more detail.

11.2.4 Policy implementation curves: *IS* in closed economy and *RX* in flexible exchange rate open economy

For the closed economy, the central bank's best response to a shock is shown by the interest rate on the IS curve and for the open economy by the interest rate on the RX curve. Although for both types of economy, the IS curve shows the goods market equilibrium, this is only the policy implementation curve for the closed economy; the RX is the policy implementation curve for the open economy. It is useful to compare the two curves directly.

Policy implementation curve closed economy:

$$\underbrace{y_t}_{\text{target}} - y_e = -a(\underbrace{r_{t-1}}_{\text{instrument}} - r^S). \qquad \text{(Policy implementation (IS); closed)}$$

Policy implementation curve open (flexible exchange rate) economy:

$$\underbrace{y_t}_{\text{target}} - y_e = -\left(a + \frac{b}{1-\lambda}\right)(\underbrace{r_{t-1}}_{\text{instrument}} - r^*), \qquad \text{(Policy implementation (RX); open)}$$

where $\lambda = \frac{1}{1+\alpha^2\beta}$.

We can summarize the differences between the closed and open economy adjustment paths in Figure 11.8 as follows:

1. The initial interest rate hike (to r_0) in response to the inflation shock is greater in the closed economy. This is because the appreciation of the exchange rate shoulders some of the burden of adjustment in the open economy.
2. The *IS* curve shifts in each period in the open economy but remains fixed in the closed economy. The open economy *IS* curve includes net exports, which are dampened by any appreciation of the real exchange rate and boosted by any depreciation. Net exports are part of the intercept term of the open economy *IS* curve, so the *IS* curve shifts if the real exchange rate changes. In contrast, a change in the real interest rate causes a movement along the *IS* curve (in both the closed and open economies).
3. The closed economy moves along the *IS* curve on its path back to equilibrium. This curve shows the interest rate the central bank must set (its instrument) to achieve its desired output gap on the *MR* curve (its target). The open economy moves along the flatter *RX* curve on its path back to equilibrium. This curve shows the interest rate the central bank must set to achieve its desired output gap, while also taking into account the response of the forex market to any differential between home and world interest rates. The *UIP* condition holds at all points on the *RX* curve.

Figure 11.8 also highlights the important role played by expectations in the adjustment of the economy to an inflation shock in an open economy. The adjustment process relies heavily on the central bank and forex market foreseeing that a lengthy period with higher interest rates will be required to reduce inflation to target (see the third step in the flow diagram in Figure 11.7). The central bank and foreign exchange market solve the forward-looking dynamic adjustment problem simultaneously using the same model, which is an example of rational expectations modelling.

In the Appendix, we show in detail how to derive the *RX* curve mathematically.

To use the *RX* curve, its key features are:

1. It goes through the intersection of r^* and y_e and therefore shifts only when either of these changes.
2. Its slope reflects the interest and exchange rate sensitivity of aggregate demand, the central bank's preferences, and the slope of the Phillips curves:
   a. It is flatter than the *IS* curve;

b. It is flatter, the flatter is the IS curve (i.e. when a is higher indicating higher interest sensitivity of aggregate demand) and the higher is b (i.e. the more sensitive is aggregate demand to the real exchange rate). When there is a larger aggregate demand response to a given change in the interest rate or exchange rate (i.e. a higher a or b), the central bank has to change the interest rate by less, *ceteris paribus*;

c. It is flatter, the steeper is the MR curve (i.e. the lower is α, flatter Phillips curves; or the lower is β, steeper loss ellipses). For example, when the central bank is less 'hard-nosed' the return to equilibrium following a shock will be slower and the central bank will raise the interest rate by less.

The response of the economy and the central bank to an inflation shock in both a small open economy with flexible exchange rates and a closed economy can be shown using the Macroeconomic Simulator (available at www.oup.com/he/carlin-soskice).[11] Figure 11.9 shows the impulse response functions after the economy experiences a 2%

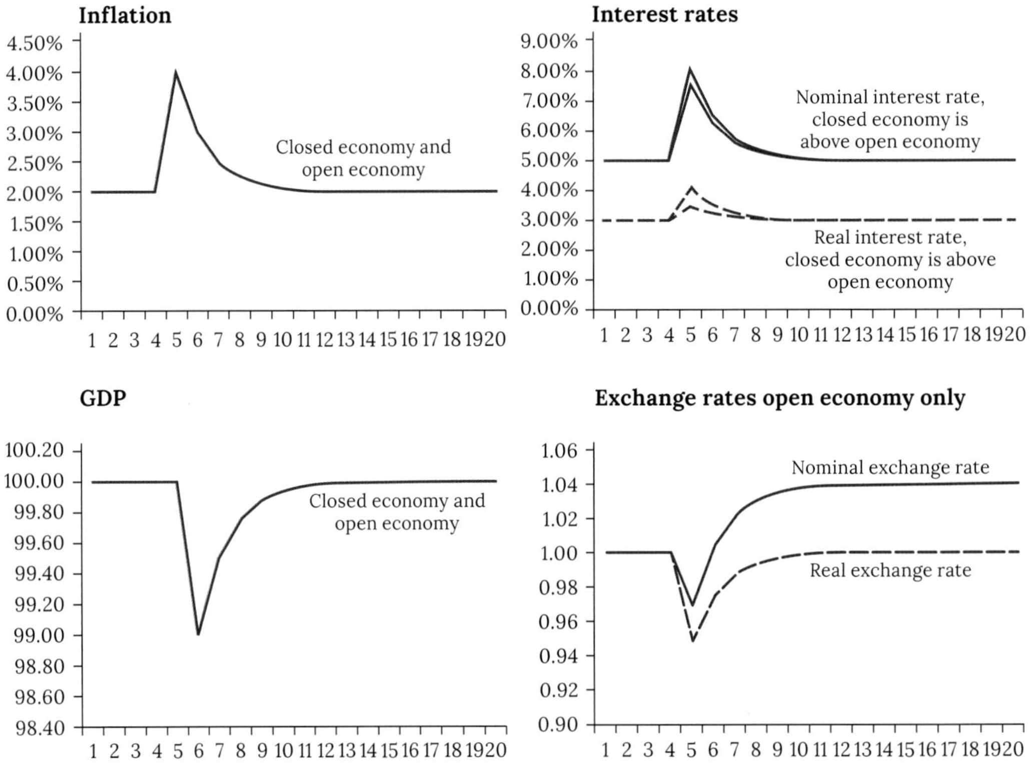

Figure 11.9 Macroeconomic Simulator (see www.oup.com/he/carlin-soskice) example–Impulse response functions after an inflation shock (in period 5) in a closed economy and a small open economy with flexible exchange rates. Where only one path is visible, the paths for the closed and open economies are identical.

[11] The impulse response functions shown in Figure 11.9 show the effect of a 2% positive inflation shock. To re-create these graphs, open the Macroeconomic Simulator (available at www.oup.com/he/carlin-soskice) and choose the closed economy version. Then take the following steps:

inflation shock in period five. We can see that the behaviour of inflation and GDP is the same in both cases, which is analogous to the bottom panels being identical in Figure 11.8. The key difference in the impulse response functions is the behaviour of interest rates. In the closed economy case, the central bank has had to raise the interest rate by more to stabilize the economy after the inflation shock. This is because in the open economy, some of the required reduction in aggregate demand is brought about through the appreciation of the real exchange rate during the adjustment process.

11.3 **APPLICATIONS**

11.3.1 **Demand and supply shocks: The 3-equation and *AD-ERU* models**

From Section 11.2.2 we know that demand and supply shocks change the medium-run exchange rate. The first step is therefore to look at the implications of the demand or supply shock for the medium-run equilibrium using the AD-ERU model in a diagram like the one in Figure 11.10). In the case of a demand shock, the AD curve shifts; for a supply-side shock, the ERU curve shifts.

As our example, we take a permanent negative aggregate demand shock due, for example, to a fall in investment demand, which reduces the term A in the AD equation (shown in Section 11.2.2). This shock shifts the AD curve to AD′.

A permanent negative demand shock

As we have seen in the closed economy (Chapter 3), it is only necessary for the central bank to manage the adjustment of the economy to an aggregate demand shock when it is unable to respond quickly enough to prevent any consequences of the shock for inflation from occurring. If it could act quickly enough by changing the interest rate to offset the effect of the demand shock on inflation, it could avoid the need to get the economy on to the MR curve. This is also the case in the open economy, where we have defined the IS curve such that output in period t depends on the real interest rate, and the real exchange rate in period $t-1$:

$$y_t = A_t - ar_{t-1} + bq_{t-1}. \qquad \text{(open economy IS)}$$

Because it takes one period for the decisions of the central bank and the foreign exchange market to affect the real economy: a shock to y_t cannot be offset by a change in r or in the real exchange rate q within the period. This is taken into account when monetary policy is formulated in practice. For example, the Bank of England's mandate when making interest rate decisions is to target inflation two years ahead.

---

(1) Click on the *reset all shocks* button on the left-hand side of the main page. (2) Set a 2% positive inflation shock and change the sensitivity of expenditure with respect to interest rate to 0.75. (3) Click on the *inflation, income and interest rates figures* button on the left-hand side to view the impulse response functions. (4) Return to the main page and click on the *save* button on the left-hand side. This will store these graphs in memory. (5) Click the *change to a different simulator version* on the main page to switch to the open economy (with flexible exchange rates) version of the simulator and then apply the same shock. (6) Save this data, then click on the *go to saved data* button on the main page to compare the two scenarios.

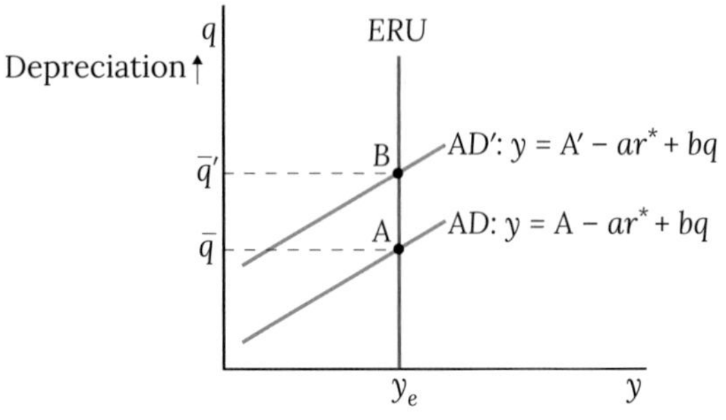

Figure 11.10 Medium-run equilibrium: negative demand shock.

Returning to Figure 11.10, we know that in the small open economy the real interest rate in the new equilibrium is at the world real interest rate, and hence, it is clear that there will be a depreciated *real exchange rate* in the new equilibrium: for output to be equal to y_e, higher net exports must offset the lower investment. This contrasts with the closed economy, where a permanent negative demand shock implies a lower stabilizing *real interest rate* in the new medium-run equilibrium.

Dynamic adjustment to the shock

Next, we analyse the dynamic adjustment of the economy to the shock using the 3-equation model, as shown in Figure 11.11:

Period 0: The economy starts at point A—the central bank's bliss point. The economy is hit by a negative permanent demand shock which shifts the IS curve to IS(A′,$\bar{q}$). Output in the economy falls to y_0 and inflation falls to π_0. The economy moves from A to B. Point B is not on the central bank's MR curve. The central bank forecasts the PC in the next period. This will move to PC($\pi_1^E = \pi_0$) next period. Faced with this PC, the central bank would like to locate at point C, back on their MR curve. At point C, output is above equilibrium, so in order to reach this point, the central bank will need to reduce interest rates to stimulate investment and boost output. The foreign exchange market foresees that the central bank will keep interest rates *below* world interest rates for a number of periods in order to boost demand and return inflation to target. The UIP condition implies this will cause an immediate depreciation of home's currency, so that it can appreciate for the whole period where home's interest rates are below world rates. The central bank therefore sets the interest rate at r_0 taking into account the immediate depreciation in the exchange rate that will occur to get the economy back on the MR curve *in the next period*. The interest rate and the exchange rate can only affect economic output with a one period lag however, so the economy ends period 0 with inflation at π_0, output at y_0, interest rate at r_0 and exchange rate at q_0.

Period 1 onwards: The new interest rate and exchange rate have had time to affect aggregate demand. The lower rate of interest boosts investment and the depreciated exchange rate increases net exports. The economy moves to point C, with output above equilibrium at y_1 and inflation at π_1. The IS curve has shifted to the right to

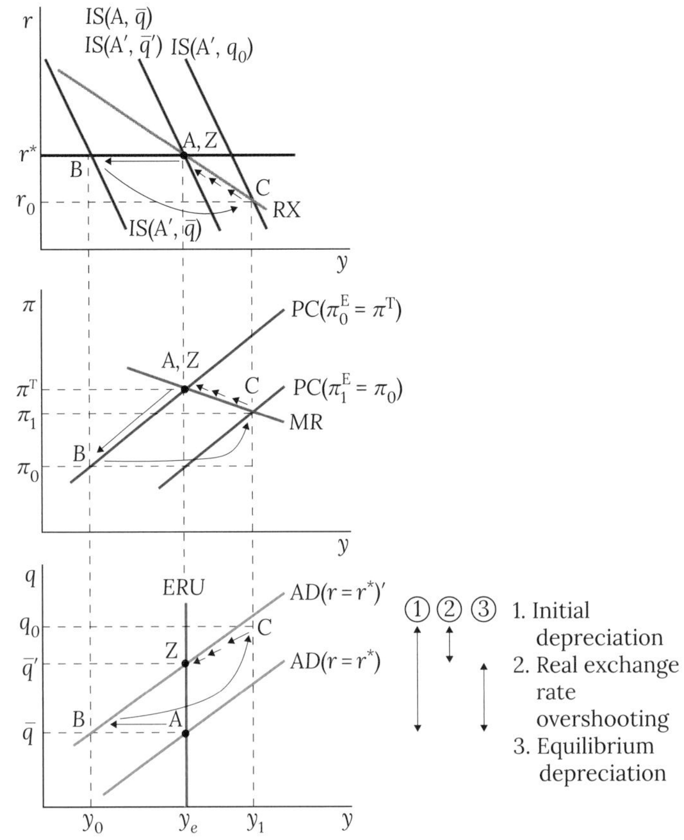

Figure 11.11 Dynamic adjustment to a negative permanent demand shock. Visit www.oup.com/he/carlin-soskice to explore negative permanent demand shock in the open economy with Animated Analytical Diagram 11.11.

IS(A′,q_0) due to the depreciation of the exchange rate. This is further to the right than the original IS curve. The adjustment process from point C back to point Z (not shown in the diagram) follows the process described for an inflation shock in Section 11.2.3 and will take a number of periods. The IS curve will gradually shift to the left and the economy will move up the RX and MR curves, as the central bank slowly adjusts the interest rate up from r_0 to r^* and the exchange rate appreciates from q_0 to $\bar{q}'$. The exchange rate appreciates from period 1 onwards to take account of the fact that home interest rates are below world interest rates. This ensures the UIP condition holds in every period. The interest rate needs to be back at the world interest rate for there to be no pressure on the exchange rate to change and for the economy to be in medium-run equilibrium. Adjustment to the demand shock ends when the economy is back at point Z, with output at y_e, inflation at π^T, the interest rate at r^*, and the exchange rate at $\bar{q}'$.

In the new medium-run equilibrium, the *IS* curve is indexed by lower autonomous demand (as a result of the permanent negative demand shock) and a depreciated real exchange rate (i.e. $IS(A', \overline{q}')$). This is because the permanent fall in autonomous demand needs to be offset by higher net exports for the economy to return to equilibrium output after the shock.

The bottom panel of Figure 11.11 shows the *AD-ERU* diagram. A permanent negative demand shock causes a leftward shift of the *AD* curve. The arrows plot the adjustment path of the economy. They show that the initial depreciation of the real exchange rate (from $\overline{q}$ to q_0) was greater than the equilibrium depreciation (from $\overline{q}$ to $\overline{q}'$). The label ② on the *AD-ERU* diagram shows the difference between the initial and equilibrium movements in the real exchange rate, which is referred to as *real exchange rate overshooting*. We discuss real and nominal exchange rate overshooting in Section 11.3.2.

At point C on the *AD-ERU* diagram, the exchange rate is q_0 and is expected to appreciate back to $\overline{q}'$: this is just what we would expect, given that during the period of expected appreciation, home's interest rate is below the world interest rate. Holders of home bonds are losing out in terms of the interest return on home bonds, but are gaining from the expected appreciation of home's exchange rate.

It is important to note that point C is not on the new *AD* curve, because at this point home's interest rate is below the world interest rate (r must be below r^* to produce the desired boost to demand to offset the shock, whereas r must equal r^* to be on the *AD* curve). Since $r < r^*$, y must be greater than it is on the $AD(r = r^*)'$ line because the lower r will stimulate higher interest-sensitive spending. Hence, point C is to the right of AD'.

Summing up

The examples of an inflation shock (as shown in Section 11.2.3) and an aggregate demand shock (as shown in this section) highlight the similarities and differences between the way the 3-equation model works in the closed and open economies. The analysis of a supply shock is left as an exercise. A quick way to look at the implications of a permanent or temporary supply shock is to experiment with the Macroeconomic Simulator (available at www.oup.com/he/carlin-soskice).

Remember that in the case of a supply shock, the *ERU* curve will shift. In the *AD-ERU* diagram, there will be a new equilibrium real exchange rate and a new equilibrium output level. Just as in the closed economy, a supply shock means the *MR* curve and the Phillips curves shift. In the open economy, the *RX* curve will shift to intersect the new equilibrium output level and r^*. The medium-run outcomes for the real exchange rate and output, as well as the adjustment dynamics, can be checked using the simulator.

The new element in the open economy—whether the shock is an inflation, supply, or demand one—is the way the behaviour of the foreign exchange market interacts with that of the central bank. Table 11.2 contrasts the decision-making process in the central bank and the foreign exchange market in the closed and open economies using the example of a permanent demand shock.

Period	Closed economy	Small open economy
0	CB works out stabilizing interest rate in the new equilibrium, r^S.	CB and forex market work out real exchange rate in the new equilibrium, $\overline{q}$; $r = r^*$. Use AD-ERU model.
	CB works out implications of the shock for the Phillips curve and for its choice of output in period one on the MR curve.	
		CB and forex market work out the path over time of the CB's desired output level along the MR to the new equilibrium.
	CB sets r_0 using the IS curve to achieve its desired output gap in the next period.	CB sets r_0 using the RX curve to achieve its desired output gap in the next q jumps to q_0, as the forex market take advantage of the arbitrage opportunities brought about by the interest rate differential. Both parties take into account the response of the other when formulating their best response.
1	r_0 affects the real economy, shifting output to y_1, which is on the MR curve and minimizes the CB's loss function.	r_0 and q_0 affect the real economy. This shifts output to y_1 on the MR curve, which minimizes the CB's loss function. The IS curve shifts as the real exchange rate affects demand for net exports.
2+	CB adjusts r to move economy along MR (and IS) to equilibrium.	CB adjusts r (and forex market adjusts q) to move economy along MR (and RX) to equilibrium.

Table 11.2 Decision-making process of central bank and foreign exchange market after a permanent demand shock.

11.3.2 Exchange rate overshooting

Exchange rate overshooting refers to the phenomenon of the nominal and real exchange rate jumping by more than the equilibrium adjustment in response to shocks. In the case of an inflation shock, there is no change in the equilibrium real exchange rate, which means that all of the initial jump from $\overline{q}$ to q_0, which shifts the IS curve to the left in Figure 11.8, is overshooting. In the case of a permanent demand shock, the new equilibrium real exchange rate is depreciated, but initially the depreciation overshoots this equilibrium as shown in Figure 11.11.

Overshooting is integral to the 3-equation model of inflation targeting. It exists because of the combination of:

1. an internationally integrated financial market;
2. rational expectations in the foreign exchange market, which leads to jumps in the nominal exchange rate; and
3. sluggish adjustment of wages and prices in the economy, which requires the central bank to keep the interest rate above (or below) the world interest rate until inflation returns to target.

When financial markets are integrated, the real UIP condition,

$$r_t - r^* = q^E_{t+1} - q_t, \qquad \text{(real UIP condition)}$$

holds each period. When $r > r^*$, the real exchange rate, q must jump relative to its expected value. The greater the cumulative deviation of home's interest rate is expected to be above (e.g. in the case of a positive inflation shock) or below (e.g. in the case of a negative demand shock or a positive supply shock) the world interest rate, the more the real exchange rate must overshoot initially in order that it can adjust back to the equilibrium exchange rate during the period of the interest rate differential. Overshooting will be greater when shocks are larger.

We can define the *equilibrium change* as the difference in the real exchange rate between the inital equilibrium and the new medium-run equilibrium. Hence the initial jump in the exchange rate equals the equilibrium change plus the exchange rate overshooting. If the interest rate differential was expected to prevail for just one year, the initial jump will be $[(r_0 - r^*) + \text{equilibrium change}]$; if it is expected to prevail for three years, the initial jump will be $[(r_0 - r^*) + (r_1 - r^*) + (r_2 - r^*) + \text{equilibrium change}]$.[12] In Section 11.3.1, we showed exactly how the initial jump in q is determined in the case of inflation targeting, where the interest rate is gradually adjusted back to the world interest rate. This is shown by point C on the RX curve in Figure 11.11.

Although exchange rate overshooting is an integral part of the modern modelling of a flexible exchange rate economy, this was not always the case. The German-American economist Rudiger Dornbusch developed the theory of exchange rate overshooting as a way of explaining the volatility of exchange rates following the end of the Bretton Woods system of fixed exchange rates at the end of the 1960s.[13]

The idea of overshooting centres on the fact that the nominal exchange rate is a variable that can jump easily—as we discussed when introducing the UIP condition in Section 11.1, within seconds of news arriving that changes the views of traders about the future, transactions take place and the exchange rate jumps. This is also true of the prices of other financial assets like shares and bonds.

By contrast, the prices of most goods and services, and of labour, do not jump. Only the prices of goods that are homogeneous and traded on commodity exchanges, such as oil and wheat, behave like those of financial assets. It is the interaction of prices that jump with those that do not that produces exchange rate overshooting. It is because prices and wages *do not change immediately* to wipe out an inflation shock and return the economy to target inflation, or change to bring about the new equilibrium exchange rate to wipe out an aggregate demand shock, that overshooting via the nominal exchange rate occurs.

---

[12] For example: $(r_0 - r^*) + (r_1 - r^*) + (r_2 - r^*) = (\bar{q}' - q_0)$. Add $(\bar{q} - \bar{q}')$ to both sides: $(r_0 - r^*) + (r_1 - r^*) + (r_2 - r^*) + \underbrace{(\bar{q} - \bar{q}')}_{\text{equilibrium change}} = \underbrace{(\bar{q} - q_0)}_{\text{initial jump}}$.

[13] The initial model of overshooting was developed by Rudiger Dornbusch (1976). For a very readable introduction to the Dornbusch model, see Rogoff (2002), who also describes the atmosphere in Dornbusch's PhD class at MIT when he first explained the model.

BOX 11.1 Dornbusch overshooting and the Thatcher recession

In 1979, Margaret Thatcher became Prime Minister of the UK and her government introduced an anti-inflationary monetary policy referred to as the Medium-Term Financial Strategy. Prime Minister Thatcher announced a reduction in the growth of the money supply with the objective of reducing inflation. Theory suggests that if no overshooting takes place, then a 10% reduction in the money supply produces a 10% fall in prices and output would remain unchanged. The nominal exchange rate would appreciate by 10%, leaving the real exchange rate unchanged.

Dornbusch pointed out that if the foreign exchange market expects that a period with output below its equilibrium level is required to bring prices down, then they will also expect a prolonged period where real interest rates will remain high. This is because the central bank is expected to keep nominal interest rates high until they can see evidence that prices are adjusting downwards. The expectation of higher interest rates leads to an immediate appreciation of home's real exchange rate (i.e. overshooting of the real as well as the nominal exchange rate since the nominal exchange rate appreciates by more than 10%).

Applying this to the Thatcher case, an announcement of a lower money supply growth rate did not produce an immediate fall in inflation. In anticipation

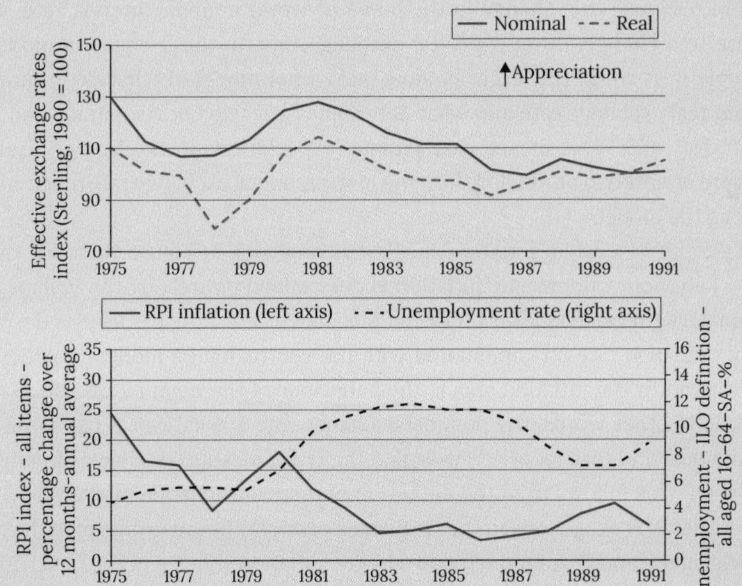

Figure 11.12 UK nominal and real effective exchange rate indices (1990 = 100): 1975–91 (upper panel) and UK unemployment and inflation: 1975–91 (lower panel).

Note: An increase in the effective exchange rate indices represents an appreciation.

Source: Bank of England; IMF International Financial Statistics; UK Office for National Statistics (data accessed October 2011).

(continued)

that a period of high interest rates was needed to push up unemployment and squeeze inflation out of the system, the UK pound appreciated sharply following the announcement of the tight money policy in 1979. Unemployment rose as a consequence of the appreciated real exchange rate and the higher real interest rates. The fall in inflation *followed* the rise in unemployment. Figure 11.12 shows the path of the real and nominal exchange rates, unemployment and inflation over the Thatcher period. Although some of the exchange rate appreciation was attributable to the discovery of North Sea oil, exchange rate overshooting in response to the tight monetary policy was an important part of the story. Exchange rate overshooting was viewed as having led to lasting damage to the UK's manufacturing industry.

What determines the behaviour of the nominal exchange rate?

It is the real exchange rate that affects aggregate demand and output, so that is the focus of attention of the central bank and the foreign exchange market in making their calculations. Nevertheless, the nominal exchange rate is the jump variable, and it is interesting to know how the behaviour of the nominal exchange rate fits into the picture.

In Section 11.2.1, we used the *UIP* condition to see how the nominal exchange rate moved in response to a change in the home or world nominal interest rate, and in response to a change in the expected exchange rate. In the 3-equation model, the same logic is at work. However, we now have a full model of what determines the expected real exchange rate and what determines any gap between home and world real interest rates. This means that rational expectations in the foreign exchange market are oriented to producing the jump in the nominal exchange rate that is implied by solving the model.

We take the case of an inflation shock. Looking back at Figure 11.8b, we can see that the behaviour of domestic inflation is determined entirely by the Phillips curve and monetary rule mechanisms (in the middle panel). Since the model pins down how the real exchange rate (in conjunction with the central bank's monetary policy rule) must respond to the inflation shock, the behaviour of the *nominal* exchange rate is a residual. In other words, the nominal exchange rate is whatever it has to be given that the home and foreign price levels and the real exchange rate have already been determined. This follows from the definition of the real exchange rate: $Q \equiv \frac{P^* e}{P}$. Since we know that P^* is exogenous to the small open economy because it is set in the rest of the world, and P and Q are pinned down by the inflation shock and the best response policy rule, it follows that the nominal exchange rate e is just the residual.

Let us look at an example. Figure 11.13 shows the stylized paths of the domestic price level and the nominal and real exchange rates following an inflation shock using index numbers for each variable set initially at 100. For simplicity, we assume the inflation target and world inflation are both zero. With a target of zero inflation, the price *level* is therefore constant in medium-run equilibrium.

Following the inflation shock (say of 2%), the price level jumps from 100 to 102, and since home's inflation is higher than world inflation on the path back to target

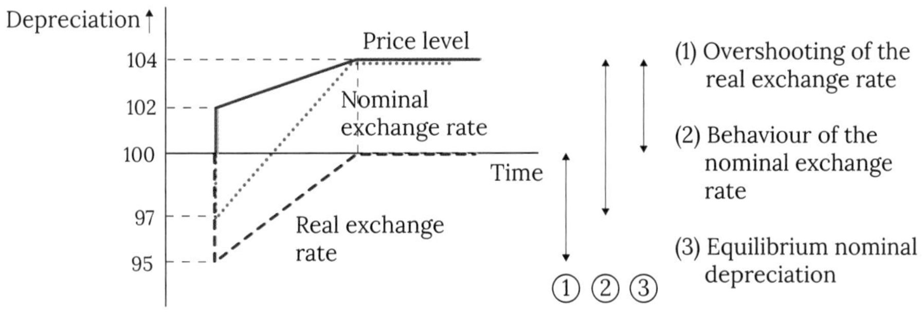

Figure 11.13 Real and nominal exchange rate paths following an inflation shock.

inflation, home's price level continues to rise until the medium-run equilibrium is reached (e.g. at a level of 104). The real exchange rate appreciates immediately and depreciates back to its initial level along the path to the medium-run equilibrium.

The nominal exchange rate depreciates more rapidly than the real exchange rate along the path to the medium-run equilibrium. At medium-run equilibrium, the price level has risen by 4% and the nominal exchange rate has depreciated by 4% relative to their starting levels: the real exchange rate is therefore back at its initial level. This reflects the fact that an inflation shock does not change the medium-run real exchange rate.

Two features of the response of the nominal exchange rate are worth pointing out. The first is that the initial nominal appreciation in period 0 is less than the real appreciation because part of the required real appreciation takes place through the initial inflation shock (and foreign exchange operators can work this out).[14] The second relates to the path back to equilibrium (from point B to Z in Figure 11.8). In this phase, it is clear that home's inflation (although falling) is above world inflation, which would by itself imply an appreciating real exchange rate. However, the real exchange rate must be *depreciating* for two reasons:

1. in order to push the IS curve back to equilibrium (i.e. to the right); and
2. because home's real interest rate is above the world's, i.e. $r > r^*$. The gains from holding home bonds must be offset by the expected real exchange rate loss.

This accounts for the extent of the nominal depreciation, which outstrips the real depreciation, along the path back to equilibrium. See the appendix for an example using the Macroeconomic Simulator (available at www.oup.com/he/carlin-soskice) and for the mathematical derivation of the decomposition of the nominal exchange rate adjustment into the two components of real exchange rate overshooting and the cumulative inflation that occurs at home and abroad.

[14] It can be useful here to rearrange the definition of the real exchange rate to $\overset{\downarrow}{e} = \frac{\overset{\downarrow}{Q}\overset{\uparrow}{P}}{P^*}$ to think about how changes in Q and P affect the nominal exchange rate.

11.3.3 Exchange rate volatility

In this chapter, we have used the open economy AD-ERU model to show that adjustment to demand and supply shocks requires changes in the real exchange rate. Under flexible exchange rates, the 3-equation model tells us that real and nominal exchange rate overshooting are an integral part of the adjustment process. Stabilization of shocks is successful under inflation targeting, but it is necessarily accompanied by exchange rate overshooting.

To this point, we have ignored an important characteristic of the foreign exchange market: its ability to generate shocks. Like other financial markets (see Chapters 1, 4, and 8), the foreign exchange market is subject to panics, waves of optimism and pessimism, and to herd and bandwagon effects. This means that the exchange rate can move—not in response to the mechanisms discussed in this chapter arising from shocks that shift the equilibrium real exchange rate and the overshooting that accompanies the adjustment to shocks—but because of changes in sentiment in the market.

An example occurred in 2011 as the Eurozone crisis took hold and growth prospects in the US weakened. Given its flexible exchange rate, the Swiss franc became a 'safe haven' currency. The Swiss National Bank (SNB) was alarmed at the extent of the inflow of foreign currency and the appreciation of the franc, which was making its manufacturing sector uncompetitive. On September 6th 2011, the SNB took the extremely unusual step of announcing it would buy unlimited quantities of euros to weaken the franc. This amounted to the attempt to fix or peg the exchange rate to the euro. The threat was credible in the market and the pressure shifted to other currencies, creating potential distortions elsewhere in the world.

In Sections 11.3.2 and 11.3.3, we highlighted two features of flexible exchange rate regimes in highly integrated financial markets that complicate efficient resource allocation decisions by households and firms:

1. The presence of exchange rate overshooting due to sluggish adjustment of wages and prices; and
2. The noise arising from unpredictable and uncontrollable features of the forex market.

In Chapter 14, we return to the discussion of the merits of different exchange rate regimes when we analyse the Eurozone.

11.4 CONCLUSIONS

This chapter has set out the basic framework for analysing economic shocks in the open economy. The framework has two key components; the AD-ERU model, which determines medium-run equilibrium and the dynamic open economy 3-equation model, which shows how the central bank stabilizes the economy after an economic shock. The latter model extends the core closed economy 3-equation model of Chapter 3 by opening up the economy to international trade and capital flows. This requires the introduction of the foreign exchange market. In particular, we focus on the behaviour of investors engaged in arbitrage between the bonds issued by different governments.

The open economy framework can be utilized to answer pertinent questions about economic policy and macroeconomic fluctuations in small open economies with flexible exchange rates:

1. What are the key features of the foreign exchange market? How do exchange rates respond to changes in interest rates? In an economy open to international capital flows, households have the option of holding both home and foreign bonds. Assuming there is no difference in default risk between the bonds issued by different governments, the only difference between these bonds is their expected return, which depends on the interest rate and any expected movements in the exchange rate. Households use sophisticated agents (e.g. pension funds) to allocate their investments between home and foreign bonds. These funds buy and sell foreign exchange and are assumed to be both forward looking and rational. Investors see that they can profit from arbitrage opportunities when there is an interest rate differential between home and foreign bonds. Arbitrage means that a movement into home bonds (e.g. as a result of a positive interest differential) causes home's currency to immediately appreciate, so that it can depreciate over the period over which the differential persists. This exchange rate response wipes out any potential gain from holding home bonds over foreign bonds. The relationship between the interest rate differential and the expected change in exchange rates is captured by the *UIP* condition.
2. How does the central bank's response to economic shocks compare in the closed and open economies? In the closed economy, the central bank responds to economic shocks by adjusting the interest rate using the *IS* as the policy implementation curve. In the open economy, the central bank must also take into account the reaction of the forex market to any change in interest rates and uses the *RX* as its policy implementation curve. The central bank and bond investors using the foreign exchange market are rational forward-looking agents who act simultaneously to solve the model after an economic shock. For example, if the central bank raises the home interest rate to squeeze an inflation shock out of the system, then the foreign exchange market will buy home bonds causing the currency to appreciate. This will dampen demand by reducing net exports. We can see from this example that the central bank does not have to change interest rates as much in response to shocks in the open economy, as some adjustment will occur through the real exchange rate channel.
3. How can the open economy model developed in this chapter shed light on the phenomenon of exchange rate overshooting? The overshooting of the exchange rate occurs when the initial jump in the exchange rate as the result of an economic shock is larger than the equilibrium change. This takes place in the model due to our assumption that there are rational expectations in the foreign exchange market, but that wages and prices are sluggish to adjust. The persistence of inflation in our model requires interest rates to diverge from world interest rates for a number of

periods after a shock. The rational forex market responds to the interest differential and the nominal exchange rate jumps. The exchange rate then slowly adjusts to equilibrium while the differential remains. Overshooting can have long-term effects. For example, the over-appreciation of the exchange rate that accompanied the Thatcher disinflation in the UK in the 1980s is said to have done permanent damage to the UK manufacturing sector.

Chapter 12 looks more closely at the demand and supply sides in the open economy, providing the counterpart to the closed economy discussed in Chapters 1 and 2. Chapter 13 analyses the impact of oil price shocks and shows how imbalances can occur between open economies, even when inflation is low and stable. We complete our analysis of the open economy by looking at the economics of the Eurozone in Chapter 14.

11.5 APPENDIX

11.5.1 Comparing the *UIP* condition with the Covered Interest Parity (*CIP*) condition

A comparison between these two concepts can be helpful in highlighting what the UIP is and why we use it in the 3-equation open economy model.[15] The covered interest parity condition refers to a financial market transaction that allows an investor to be fully covered against a future change in the exchange rate.

It works in the following way. If you choose to buy a foreign bond, you need to buy foreign exchange now, receive your return in a year's time in foreign exchange and convert it back into domestic currency. This exposes you to foreign exchange risk if the exchange rate depreciates over the year. To implement what is called the 'exchange rate hedge', you sell dollars in the forward market at the exchange rate f. Because of this sale, in a year's time when you receive $1/e(1+i^*)$ in dollars on your bond, you know what you will get back in £, namely, $1/e(1+i^*)f$. The exchange rate risk is gone.

If we now return to compare our choice between the UK bond and the foreign bond, competition in the financial markets will ensure that the covered interest parity condition holds:

$$(1+i) = \frac{f(1+i^*)}{e_t}. \qquad \text{(Covered Interest Parity Condition, CIP)}$$

If we rearrange and solve for the forward rate, we have:

$$f = \frac{(1+i)}{(1+i^*)}e_t \qquad (11.1)$$

All the variables on the right-hand side are observable and global banks quote forward exchange rates, i.e. 'f', based on this calculation.

[15] This appendix is based on notes from Thomas Michl.

What is the relationship between the forward rate and the expected spot exchange rate in 12 months' time? The UIP condition is based on the hypothesis that they will be equal, i.e. $f = e^E$. It also uses the rational expectations hypothesis that the expected exchange rate is an unbiased estimate of the actual exchange rate, and we assume further, that forex traders have perfect foresight.

This allows us to go from the CIP condition to the UIP condition set out in the chapter.

$$(1+i) = (1+i^*)(e^E_{t+1}/e_t) \tag{11.2}$$

We can write $(e^E_{t+1}/e_t) = 1 + \left(\frac{e^E_{t+1}-e_t}{e_t}\right)$, which implies:

$$i - i^* \approx \left(\frac{e^E_{t+1} - e_t}{e_t}\right). \qquad \text{(UIP condition)}$$

assuming that $i^*\left(\frac{e^E_{t+1}-e_t}{e_t}\right)$ is small.

To summarize, using information on the interest rate on a home and a foreign bond and the current exchange rate, the CIP arbitrage condition tells you the value of the future exchange rate that will completely cover you from exchange rate risk. Hence, this is a theory of the forward exchange rate given the current exchange rate and the interest rates on home and foreign bonds.

By contrast, the UIP condition is a theory about the current exchange rate given interest rates and the expected exchange rate. It describes the arbitrage of an uncovered exposure to exchange rate risk. Since total returns to home and foreign bond have to be equal, the currency of the country with the higher interest rate must be expected to depreciate to wipe out the interest rate advantage.

Prior to the financial crisis, it was said that CIP was true most of the time; this is no longer the case as you can see by googling 'FX swap spread' or 'cross currency basis'.

Our focus is on the UIP condition, since we are interested in a model of the current exchange rate. The UIP condition fails empirical tests of the simplest specifications: the high interest currency rarely depreciates. This means that so-called 'carry trades' are profitable. A carry trade is when you borrow in one currency (say yen) and lend in another (say dollars). According to UIP, this should not be profitable because the dollar is expected to depreciate and will offset the interest advantage. However, this does not seem to happen.

Given the incentives for forex traders to use all information available to succeed at their jobs, it doesn't seem persuasive to blame the assumption of the rational expectations hypothesis. For a useful summary of what is known about exchange rates, the UIP condition and the carry trade, see Burnside (2019). It seems that economists working in the financial markets take the view that UIP works pretty well in capturing the immediate jump as news arrives. However, there appears to be a lot of persistence thereafter with it taking a long time for the exchange rate to settle back to equilibrium.

11.5.2 The 3-equation open economy model—a compact summary

In Section 11.2.3, we showed graphically how the openness of the economy affects the policy of an inflation-targeting central bank. In Section 11.5.3 of the Appendix, we set out in more detail how the model works. In particular, we show how rational expectations and arbitrage in the foreign exchange market (captured by the UIP condition) allow us to pin down precisely the interest and exchange rate responses to different shocks.

It is convenient to repeat the equations for the structure of the economy, because it helps to clarify the origins of the parameters that will be used to derive the RX curve.

We begin with the Phillips curve and the monetary rule equations, which under the assumption of domestic inflation targeting, are the same as in the closed economy. This means the same methodology as Chapter 3 is used here to derive the MR curve.

Persistence in the inflation process is reflected in the Phillips curve, which is:

$$\pi_t = \pi_{t-1} + \alpha(y_t - y_e). \qquad \text{(Phillips curve, PC)}$$

As in Chapter 3, the central bank is modelled as operating under discretion. Each period it minimizes a loss function:

$$L = (y_t - y_e)^2 + \beta(\pi_t - \pi^T)^2, \qquad \text{(central bank loss function)}$$

where $\beta > 1$ characterizes a central bank that places less weight on output fluctuations than on deviations in inflation, and vice versa. The central bank optimizes by minimizing its loss function subject to the Phillips curve. This produces the monetary rule equation (the MR curve), which is the same as in the closed economy:

$$(y_t - y_e) = -\alpha\beta(\pi_t - \pi^T). \qquad \text{(monetary rule, MR)}$$

The demand side of the economy is represented by the open economy IS curve, which captures the fact that demand responds negatively to the real interest rate and positively to a depreciation in the real exchange rate, q:

$$y_t = A - ar_{t-1} + bq_{t-1}. \qquad \text{(open economy IS curve)}$$

The dynamics of the adjustment of the economy to a shock depend on the same aspects of the economy as in the closed economy. The additional open economy factors are the responsiveness of aggregate demand to the real exchange rate, b and the real UIP condition:

$$r_t - r^* = q^E_{t+1} - q_t. \qquad \text{(real UIP condition)}$$

The real UIP condition (derived in Section 11.5.3) says that any positive (negative) real interest differential will be matched by an expected depreciation (appreciation) in the real exchange rate.

The equation for the policy implementation curve, the RX (derived in the section that follows the RUIP) is:

$$y_t - y_e = -\left(a + \frac{b}{1-\lambda}\right)(r_{t-1} - r^*). \qquad \text{(RX equation, policy implementation curve)}$$

$$\text{where} \quad \lambda = \frac{1}{1+\alpha^2\beta}$$

Since a, b and λ are all parameters and r^* is a constant, once y_t (its target) is known, the central bank can calculate r_{t-1}. This is the RX equation. It is clear immediately from

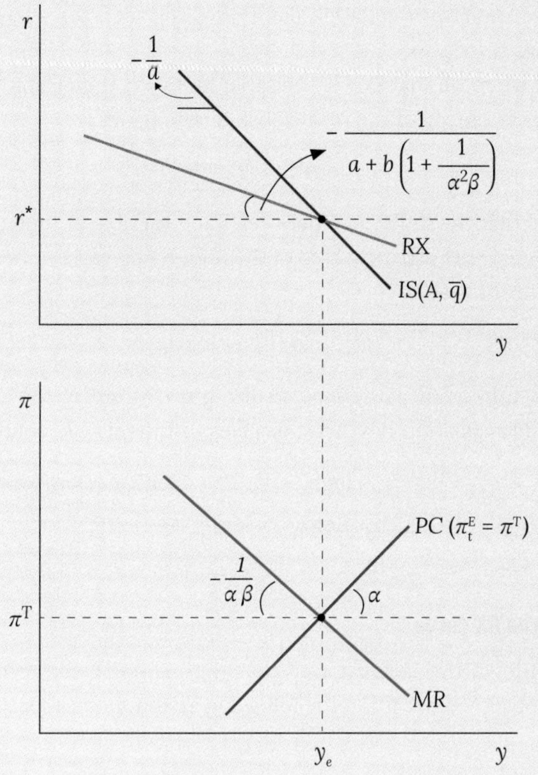

Figure 11.14 The 3-equation open economy model.

this equation that the RX is flatter than the IS line: if we think of an increase in r above r^*, the RX equation tells us that the fall in y below y_e will be greater (since we multiply by $\left(a + \frac{b}{1-\lambda}\right)$) than is the case on the IS, when we multiply by a.

Figure 11.14 shows where the different structural parameters fit into the open economy model. In Chapter 3, we showed how the different parameters affect the curves underlying the core closed economy 3-equation model. In Figure 11.14, we can see where the open economy elements fit in: the lower panel is exactly the same as in the closed economy. In the IS panel, the IS will shift by more in response to a given change in the real exchange rate if b is larger: this flattens the RX curve and implies that a smaller rise in the interest rate is necessary to achieve a given output level on the MR curve.

11.5.3 **The *RX* curve**

A. Derivation of the real *UIP* condition

The first step in deriving the RX curve is to derive the real UIP condition. To do that, we add $-\pi^E_{t+1} + \pi^{*E}_{t+1}$ onto both sides of the nominal UIP condition, which gives:

$$i_t - i^* - \pi^E_{t+1} + \pi^{*E}_{t+1} = \log e^E_{t+1} - \log e_t - \pi^E_{t+1} + \pi^{*E}_{t+1}. \quad (11.3)$$

If we now use the Fisher equation (i.e. $i = r + \pi^E$), then the left-hand side of the equation becomes $r_t - r^*$.

In addition, if we recall that $Q = \frac{P^* e}{P}$ and that $\log Q = q$, then using the properties of logs we can express the log of the real exchange rate (q) as:

$$q = \log P^* + \log e - \log P. \tag{11.4}$$

We also know that the difference between a log variable at time $t+1$ and time t is approximately equal to the growth rate of the underlying variable between those two periods, which means that:

$$\pi^E_{t+1} = \log P^E_{t+1} - \log P_t. \tag{11.5}$$

This is because inflation is defined as the growth rate of the price level. If we substitute back into equation 11.3 then this gives us the real UIP condition,

$$i_t - i^* - \pi^E_{t+1} + \pi^{*E}_{t+1} = \log e^E_{t+1} - \log e_t - (\log P^E_{t+1} - \log P_t) + (\log P^{*E}_{t+1} - \log P^*_t) \tag{11.6}$$

$$r_t - r^* = (\log P^{*E}_{t+1} + \log e^E_{t+1} - \log P^E_{t+1}) - (\log P^*_t + \log e_t - \log P_t)$$

$$r_t - r^* = q^E_{t+1} - q_t. \qquad \text{(real UIP condition)}$$

B. Derivation of the *RX* curve

In order to pin down the interest rate that the central bank needs to set once a shock has been observed, we make the following assumptions about the agents in the model:[16]

- Forward looking with rational expectations: central bank, which targets domestic inflation, and foreign exchange market;
- Backward looking: private sector as represented by IS and PC curves.

Throughout this chapter we have shown that, despite the differences in motives, the presence of the forex market means that the work of stabilization in an open economy is shared between exchange rate and interest rate adjustments. In light of this, the central bank must take into account how the rational forex market will react to an economic shock and pin down the real interest rate to set each period in order to achieve the optimal output gap for the following period. In particular, the optimal policy implementation rule is given by the RX curve, whose equation can be derived in three steps:

Step 1. Find the sequence of optimal output gaps and inflation deviations from target

We first recall the Phillips curve and monetary rule equations which, under the assumptions of domestic inflation targeting, remain identical to the closed economy. In particular, assuming backward-looking inflation expectations:

$$\text{PC}: \pi_t = \pi_{t-1} + \alpha(y_t - y_e). \tag{11.7}$$

[16] This appendix was written by Alessandro Guarnieri and draws on a note by Thomas Michl.

As usual, each period the central bank minimizes its loss function $L = (y_t - y_e)^2 + \beta(\pi_t - \pi^T)^2$ subject to the supply-side constraint (Phillips curve). This produces the monetary rule equation:

$$MR : (y_t - y_e) = -\alpha\beta(\pi_t - \pi^T). \tag{11.8}$$

Note that from equation 11.7, we have:

$$\pi_t = \pi_{t-1} + \alpha(y_t - y_e)$$
$$\rightarrow (\pi_t - \pi^T) = (\pi_{t-1} - \pi^T) + \alpha(y_t - y_e). \tag{11.9}$$

Combining this with the monetary rule equation yields:

$$(\pi_t - \pi^T) = (\pi_{t-1} - \pi^T) - \alpha^2\beta(\pi_t - \pi^T)$$
$$\rightarrow \frac{\pi_t - \pi^T}{\pi_{t-1} - \pi^T} = \frac{1}{1 + \alpha^2\beta} = \lambda = \frac{y_t - y_e}{y_{t-1} - y_e}. \tag{11.10}$$

where $(1 - \lambda)$ is the rate at which the output gap declines on the path along the MR curve.[17] In particular, the last equality follows directly from the MR curve (equation 11.8):

$$(y_t - y_e) = -\alpha\beta(\pi_t - \pi^T)$$
$$\rightarrow \frac{y_t - y_e}{y_{t-1} - y_e} = \frac{-\alpha\beta(\pi_t - \pi^T)}{-\alpha\beta(\pi_{t-1} - \pi^T)} = \lambda. \tag{11.11}$$

It is worth pointing out that none of the open economy elements has been introduced so far.

Step 2. Show that real interest rate deviations decline at the same rate as the output gap

Assume that the central bank reduces the interest rate deviations at a constant rate (i.e. linearly).[18] In particular, let:

$$r_t - r^* = \rho(r_{t-1} - r^*). \tag{11.12}$$

Using the open economy IS curve equation as well as the real UIP condition it is easy to show that $\rho = \lambda$, where λ is as we found above.

From the IS equation:

$$y_{t+1} - y_e = -a(r_t - r^*) + b(q_t - \bar{q}^E). \qquad \text{(Open economy IS curve)}$$

where $\bar{q}^E$ is the expected real exchange rate at medium-run equilibrium. Combining equation 11.12 with the real UIP condition and using recursive substitution:

[17] $\lambda = \frac{y_t - y_e}{y_{t-1} - y_e}$ is, by definition, the growth factor of the output gap. This implies that $\lambda = 1 + g$, where g is the rate of decline of the output gap along the MR curve. Hence, $(1 - \lambda) = 1 - (1 + g) = -g$.

[18] In a closed economy, the assumption of a linear decline of the real interest rate differentials follows directly from the closed economy IS equation: $IS : (y_{t+1} - y_e) = -a(r_t - r^*) \Rightarrow \frac{(y_{t+1} - y_e)}{(y_t - y_e)} = \frac{(r_t - r^*)}{(r_{t-1} - r^*)}$. In the open economy model, we first assume the rate of decline of the interest rate deviations is constant, and then show it must be equal to λ.

$$-(q_t - \bar{q}^E) = \sum_{i=0}^{\infty}(r_{t+i} - r^*) = (r_t - r^*)[1 + \rho + \rho^2 + \rho^3 + ...]. \tag{11.13}$$

We know that (see Chapter 1), since $\rho < 1$, the geometric series $[1 + \rho + \rho^2 + \rho^3 + ...]$ converges to $1/(1-\rho)$. Therefore, $-(q_t - \bar{q}^E) = \frac{1}{1-\rho}(r_t - r^*)$.

Substituting this into the open economy IS curve gives:

$$\begin{aligned} \text{IS}: y_{t+1} - y_e &= -a(r_t - r^*) + b\frac{1}{1-\rho}(r_t - r^*) \\ &= -\left(a + b\frac{1}{1-\rho}\right)(r_t - r^*) \end{aligned} \tag{11.14}$$

$$\rightarrow \frac{y_{t+1} - y_e}{y_t - y_e} = \frac{-\left(a + b\frac{1}{1-\rho}\right)(r_t - r^*)}{-\left(a + b\frac{1}{1-\rho}\right)(r_{t-1} - r^*)} = \frac{(r_t - r^*)}{(r_{t-1} - r^*)}. \tag{11.15}$$

Step 3. The QQ and RX equations

Equation 11.15 proves that $\rho = \lambda$. This allows us to write down the equation of the QQ curve, which gives the exact relationship between real interest rate and real exchange rate in an open economy where the central bank and the forex market are both rational forward-looking agents and solve the model simultaneously. In particular, we showed in step 2 that, assuming $r_t = \rho r_{t-1}$, the RUIP condition gives:

$$-(q_t - \bar{q}^E) = \frac{1}{1-\rho}(r_t - r^*).$$

This implies:

$$\begin{aligned} \frac{1}{1-\lambda}(r_t - r^*) &= (q_t - \bar{q}^E) \\ \rightarrow (r_t - r^*)\left(1 + \frac{1}{\alpha^2\beta}\right) &= (q_t - \bar{q}^E). \end{aligned} \tag{QQ curve}$$

Note that the QQ curve is flatter than the -45° of the RUIP curve. This is because a larger initial jump in the real exchange rate, i.e. q_0, is necessary when $r_t - r^* \neq 0$ for more than one period (overshooting). Simply substituting the QQ equation in the open economy IS curve equation yields:

$$\begin{aligned} y_{t+1} - y_e &= -a(r_t - r^*) + b(q_t - \bar{q}^E) \\ &= -a(r_t - r^*) - b\frac{1}{1-\lambda}(r_t - r^*) \\ \rightarrow y_{t+1} - y_e &= -\left(a + b\frac{1}{1-\lambda}\right)(r_t - r^*). \end{aligned} \tag{RX curve}$$

Or, more completely:

$$\text{RX}: y_{t+1} - y_e = -\left[a + b\left(1 + \frac{1}{\alpha^2\beta}\right)\right](r_t - r^*). \tag{11.16}$$

It is important to note that since $b\left(1 + \frac{1}{\alpha^2\beta}\right) > 0$, the RX curve is always flatter than the IS curve. As explained earlier in the chapter, this is because the presence of the forex market implies that the central bank will need to adjust the real interest rate by less than would be the case in a closed economy, as part of the necessary crowding in/out of expenditure now comes from the real exchange rate channel.

C. Geometry of the *RX* curve: varying the parameters

The RX equation is

$$y_t - y_e = -\left(a + \frac{b}{1-\lambda}\right)(r_{t-1} - r^*), \qquad \text{(RX equation)}$$

where

$$\lambda = \frac{1}{1+\alpha^2\beta}.$$

One way of developing an intuitive understanding of the effect of parameter changes on the central bank's best response to shocks in the open economy is to conduct experiments of varying the parameters. Variations in a and b, the coefficients in the IS curve, have simple graphical representations: an increase in a means that interest-sensitive expenditure responds more to changes in the interest rate, and the IS curve is flatter. This has the effect of reducing the interest rate and exchange rate responses, and a larger share of the output gap is accounted for by the interest rate component (which increases from $(r_{t-1} - r^*)$ to $-a(r_{t-1} - r^*)$). The RX curve is flatter.

If b increases, aggregate demand is more sensitive to changes in the real exchange rate. Geometrically, the line with slope $\left(\frac{1-\lambda}{b}\right)$ becomes flatter. This lowers the initial interest rate chosen by the central bank and the associated exchange rate appreciation, and increases the share of the output gap accounted for by the exchange rate component. The RX curve is flatter.

If α or β decrease, then the MR curve is steeper. This means a lower $(1-\lambda)$ and a slower rate of decline of the output gaps on the path back to equilibrium. For example, the central bank's preferences are weighted less strongly toward reducing inflation—it is a 'wetter' central bank. In the RX equation, a slower rate of decline of the output gap has the same effect on the slope of the RX as a rise in b: i.e. it makes the RX flatter. If we compare two economies identical in every way except that the first has a less hard-nosed central bank (lower β), then in the face of the same inflation shock, the first will be observed to have a smaller output gap and a lower interest rate.

All of these predictions can be tested using the Macroeconomic Simulator (available at www.oup.com/he/carlin-soskice).

11.5.4 The role of the nominal exchange rate in the model

A. The behaviour of the nominal exchange rate; an example using the macroeconomic simulator

In Section 11.3.2 we explained the role of the nominal exchange rate as the residual in the 3-equation open economy model.[19] In Section B of this Appendix we also provide a mathematical derivation to show how to exactly compute the value of the nominal exchange rate in each period. To further clarify the behaviour of the nominal exchange rate, here we go over an example using the Macroeconomic Simulator (available at www.oup.com/he/carlin-soskice).

---

[19] This appendix was written by Alessandro Guarnieri.

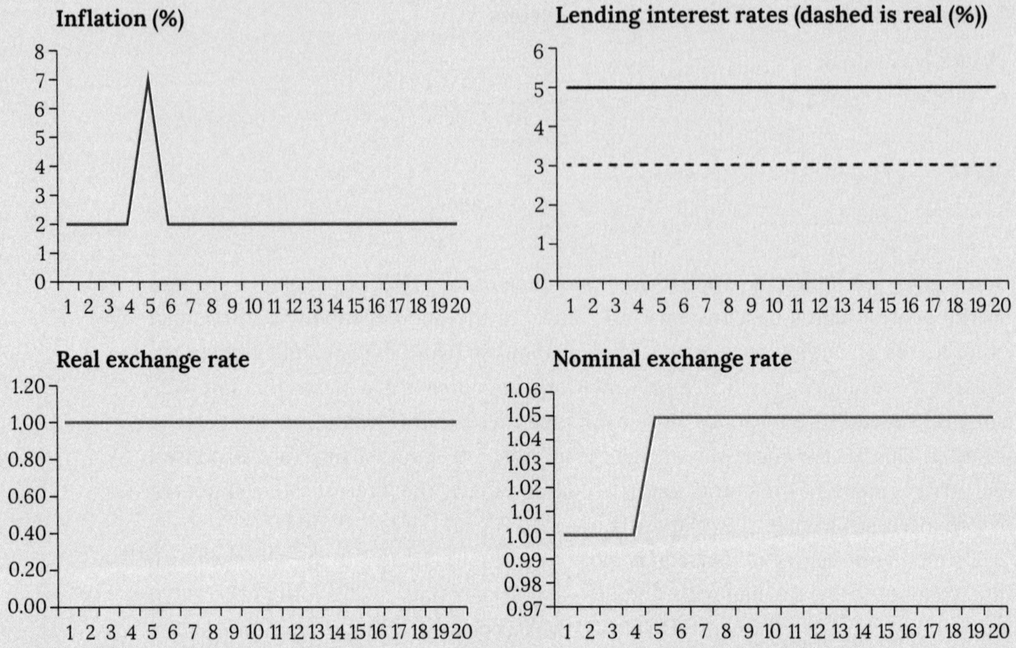

Figure 11.15 Impulse response functions from a 5% inflation shock and fully anchored inflation expectations.

For consistency with Section 11.3.2, we retain the example of an inflation shock; moreover, we set the degree of credibility of the central bank's inflation target in the home economy to be perfect; in other words, agents anchor their inflation expectations at the central bank's target irrespective of the shock hitting the economy.

In the simulator, a 5% inflation shock can be run by setting a temporary negative supply side shock of size 5%. We also set the degree of anchoring to 1 (fully anchored) as this is equivalent to perfect credibility of the inflation target. Figure 11.15 shows the simulation output obtained from running such shock.

As expected given fully anchored inflation expectations, in the period following the shock inflation is back at its pre-shock level. The first thing to notice is that neither the nominal nor the real interest rates have changed. This is because the central bank does not need to create a negative output gap for inflation to fall; agents' expectations are anchored at target and therefore, given the temporary shock, no actual monetary policy response is required to stabilize the economy (see Chapter 4). It might be tempting to think that even though the nominal interest rate is unchanged, the real interest rate should still fall in period 5 given that inflation is higher. However, recall that the Fisher equation is defined by:

$$r_t = i_t - \pi^E_{t+1}. \qquad \text{(Fisher equation)}$$

Perfect credibility implies that inflation expectations never increase, and therefore the real interest rate is unchanged at period 5 despite higher actual inflation.

We now look at the time path of the real exchange rate. As we can see, this remains constant throughout. This has two implications:

1. The expected real exchange rate following the shock is unchanged;
2. There is no real exchange rate overshooting.

The second point is perfectly consistent with the real interest rate being constant. In fact, recalling the real UIP condition:

$$\sum_{t=0}^{\infty}(r_t - r^*) = \bar{q}^E - q_0. \tag{11.17}$$

We see that since $r_t - r^* = 0$ at all times, then $\bar{q}^E$ must be equal to q_0, which is the same as saying that no real exchange rate overshooting occurs.

The first point is explained by the fact that the shock has no consequences for aggregate demand, and thus there is no need for any crowding in/out of expenditure coming from increased/decreased competitiveness of the home economy. On the contrary, any change in expected real exchange rate would effectively be a source of a demand shock rather than an adjustment channel. We can then see how the constant trend of the real exchange rate is fully pinned down by the model.

Finally, we can now make sense of the behaviour of the nominal exchange rate. As we can see, in period 5 the nominal exchange rate depreciates and then stays constant at the depreciated level. This makes perfect sense if we rely on the interpretation, presented in Section 11.3.2, of the nominal exchange rate as the residual in the model. We begin by recalling the definition of real exchange rate:

$$Q \equiv \frac{P^* e}{P}. \tag{11.18}$$

Since inflation increased for one period, the ratio of world prices over home prices $\frac{P^*}{P}$ is permanently lower. But then, since Q is constant, this implies that e must have depreciated (increased) such that the effect of the inflation shock on Q is perfectly offset. In particular:

$$\begin{aligned}\frac{\Delta Q_t}{Q_{t-1}} &\approx \frac{\Delta P_t^*}{P_{t-1}^*} - \frac{\Delta P_t}{P_{t-1}} + \frac{\Delta e_t}{e_{t-1}} \\ &= \pi_t^* - \pi_t + \frac{\Delta e_t}{e_{t-1}}.\end{aligned} \tag{11.19}$$

As explained before, $\Delta Q_t / Q_{t-1} = 0$ at all times.

Now focus on t=5 (period when the shock occurs). We have $\pi_5^* - \pi_5 = -0.05$ since we modelled a 5% inflation shock. Then, in order for $\Delta Q_5 / Q_4$ to equal zero, we must have:

$$\frac{\Delta e_5}{e_4} = \frac{e_5 - e_4}{e_4} = +0.05 \tag{11.20}$$

Table 11.3 shows the numerical results of the simulation. As computed before, the simulation yields:

$$\pi_5^* - \pi_5 = -0.05, \qquad \frac{e_5 - e_4}{e_4} = +0.05, \quad \text{and} \quad \frac{\Delta Q_5}{Q_4} = 0 \tag{11.21}$$

Going through this example should have helped to convey the interpretation of the nominal exchange rate as the residual in the model. Note that this interpretation holds

Period	Inflation	Real exchange rate	Nominal exchange rate
1	2%	1.00	1.00
2	2%	1.00	1.00
3	2%	1.00	1.00
4	2%	1.00	1.00
5	7%	1.00	1.05
6	2%	1.00	1.05
7	2%	1.00	1.05
8	2%	1.00	1.05

Table 11.3 Numerical results from a 5% inflation shock and fully anchored inflation expectations.

for all kinds of shocks. The one used in this example was chosen for the simplicity of its numerical results.

We can also interpret this example using the setup in Figures 11.3 and 11.4. Knowledge of the model by forex participants (as well as in the central bank) means that home's interest rate will not change. The world interest rate is also unchanged. However, the expected nominal exchange rate in period 5 is depreciated by 5%. This shifts the UIP curve to the right. Given the change in expectations, demand for home currency drops and the exchange rate moves immediately to satisfy the UIP condition.

B. The nominal exchange rate as a residual

As Section 11.3.2 shows, since the model pins down the behaviour of the real exchange rate following an economic shock, it follows that the behaviour of the nominal exchange rate is a residual. This is best understood by looking back at the QQ curve equation:

$$\frac{1}{1-\lambda}(r_t - r^*) = (\bar{q}^E - q_t). \qquad \text{(QQ curve)}$$

In particular, the real exchange rate moves in conjunction with the central bank's monetary rule according to the real UIP condition, which is thus integral to the model.

In the absence of interest rate differentials the RUIP condition implies that $\bar{q}^E = q_t$ for all periods, where $\bar{q}^E$ is the expected real exchange rate at medium-run equilibrium. Therefore, any deviation of the real exchange rate from $\bar{q}^E$ must be determined by differentials between the home real interest rate and world real interest rate.

We now look back at the definition of the real exchange rate:

$$Q \equiv \frac{P^* e}{P}. \qquad (11.22)$$

Going back to the example in Section 11.3.2, suppose the economy is hit by an inflation shock; P, and thus inflation, is clearly pinned down by the shock itself.[20] Moreover,

[20] To be more precise, domestic inflation is determined entirely by the Phillips curve and monetary rule equations.

we have just explained Q is pinned down by the model according to the *RUIP* condition under the assumption of rational and forward-looking foreign exchange traders. This implies that, given that P^* is exogenous, the behaviour of the nominal exchange rate, e, must ensure consistency between home inflation and the real exchange rate.

In case of an inflation shock, it can be shown mathematically that, after the immediate real appreciation following the shock, a depreciating real exchange rate (which is expected by the *RUIP* condition) is indeed consistent with home inflation above world inflation throughout the dynamic adjustment process.

We begin by rewriting the real UIP condition:

$$\sum_{t=0}^{\infty}(r_t - r^*) = \bar{q}^E - q_0 \tag{11.23}$$

where q_0 is the real exchange rate after the initial jump (i.e. appreciation).

Letting $\pi^T = \pi^*$, we can use the Fisher equation to rewrite equation 11.23 as:

$$\sum_{t=0}^{\infty}[(i_t - \pi_{t+1}^E) - (i^* - \pi^*)] = \bar{q}^E - q_0.$$

$$\rightarrow \sum_{t=0}^{\infty}[(i_t - i^*) - (\pi_{t+1}^E - \pi^*)] = \bar{q}^E - q_0.$$

Splitting the sum then yields:

$$\sum_{t=0}^{\infty}(i_t - i^*) = (\bar{q}^E - q_0) + \sum_{t=0}^{\infty}(\pi_{t+1}^E - \pi^*). \tag{11.24}$$

Finally, by the *UIP* condition:

$$\sum_{t=0}^{\infty}(i_t - i^*) = \log \bar{e}^E - \log e_0 \tag{11.25}$$

where $\bar{e}^E$ is the expected nominal exchange rate at medium-run equilibrium and e_0 is the nominal exchange rate after the immediate nominal appreciation following the inflation shock.

Combining equations 11.24 and 11.25, we get:

$$(\log \bar{e}^E - \log e_0) = (\bar{q}^E - q_0) + \sum_{t=0}^{\infty}(\pi_{t+1}^E - \pi^*). \tag{11.26}$$

In words, equation 11.26 states that:

(Nominal e.r. overshooting [21]) = (RER overshooting)+
(cumulated sum of inflation deviations).

The inflation shock pushes home inflation above world inflation, hence $\sum_{t=0}^{\infty}(\pi_{t+1}^E - \pi^*) > 0$.

Moreover, since the central bank will raise the real interest rate to achieve a negative output gap, it follows from equation 11.23 that $(\bar{q}^E - q_0) = \sum_{t=0}^{\infty}(r_t - r^*) > 0$.

[21] Here 'overshooting' is used to define the difference between the exchange rate at the new MRE and the exchange rate after its initial jump.

But then, equation 11.26 shows that $(log\bar{e}^E - loge_0) > 0$ and, in particular:

$$(log\bar{e}^E - loge_0) > (\bar{q}^E - q_0) > 0 \quad (11.27)$$[22]

Therefore, this implies that the expected nominal depreciation following the initial jump is bigger than the expected real depreciation. In particular, the nominal exchange rate depreciates more rapidly towards $\bar{e}^E$, thus allowing the real exchange rate to depreciate despite home inflation being above world inflation.

Irrespective of the kind of shock hitting the economy, the main takeaway from the above derivation is the following: the real exchange rate is pinned down by the model according to the *RUIP* condition, and inflation is pinned down by the shock and the subsequent monetary policy response. Using this framework, it is clear that the role of the nominal exchange rate is to behave as a simple residual, i.e. it must behave such as to ensure that the expected variations in Q (expected as they follow from the RUIP condition) are always consistent with the inflation deviations determined by the shock.

[22] Because $q = logQ$, the following comparison between nominal and real depreciation is valid, since the same monotonic increasing transformation was applied to e and Q.

QUESTIONS AND PROBLEMS FOR CHAPTER 11

CHECKLIST QUESTIONS

1. Use a *UIP* diagram to illustrate the following cases. Discuss the adjustment process in each case and show how it relates to the UIP equation.
   - **a.** Home's interest rate falls below the world interest rate for one period.
   - **b.** The world interest rate increases for one period and the home economy raises their interest rate in line.
   - **c.** The foreign exchange market changes their expectation of the exchange rate in a year's time to a more depreciated exchange rate.

2. Answer the following questions about the supply and demand sides in the medium-run model:
   - **a.** What does the ERU curve represent? What would happen to the ERU curve if unemployment benefits were raised? What would you expect to happen to inflation?
   - **b.** What does the AD curve represent? Derive the AD curve graphically from the IS curve. [Hint: draw the IS diagram below the AD diagram and think about how changes in the real exchange rate affect the IS curve. To derive the AD, map the combinations of q and y on each IS curve at $r = r^*$.]
   - **c.** How does a rise in the world real interest rate affect the AD curve? What is the effect on the medium-run real exchange rate?

3. What conditions need to hold for a small open economy to be in medium-run equilibrium?

4. In a small open economy, is a negative supply shock or a negative demand shock more damaging for medium-run output? Explain in words and use AD-ERU diagrams to back up your argument. Describe the effects on the real wage, unemployment and the real exchange rate in medium-run equilibrium of an increase in unemployment benefits.

5. Use the 3-equation open economy model to answer the following questions:

   a. Explain what the following statement means: 'after a demand shock in a small open economy, the exchange rate overshoots'. Use an AD-ERU diagram to help explain your answer.

   b. What causes exchange rate overshooting?

   c. What problems, if any, would you expect exchange rate overshooting to cause?

   d. How could you modify the 3-equation open economy model so that exchange rate overshooting does not occur? Explain in words.

6. Is the following statement true or false? Explain your answer. 'Central banks have to be more aggressive when making interest rate changes in the open economy because the IS curve is steeper than in the closed economy.'

7. Consider a large permanent negative demand shock that hits two small economies. The economies are identical except that one is closed and the other is open. Answer the following:

   a. Briefly explain how a large negative demand shock can lead to a deflation trap.

   b. Which of the economies is more likely to fall into a deflation trap following the shock? Justify your answer.

   c. What initial conditions would make it likely that both economies would experience a deflation trap?

   d. Use the Macroeconomic Simulator (available at www.oup.com/he/carlin-soskice) to check your results.

8. Compare the decision making process taken by the central bank (and forex market in the open economy) in a closed and open economy after a permanent positive supply shock. Create a table similar to Table 11.2. How does the real interest rate in the new medium-run equilibrium compare in the two cases?

9. Explain what is meant by this statement: 'The behaviour of the nominal exchange rate in the model is a residual in the 3-equation open economy model'.

10. This question uses material from Section 11.5.3 of the Appendix. For a benchmark case, draw the PC-MR and the IS-RX diagrams after an inflation shock. Now increase the interest sensitivity of aggregate demand (i.e. a) and redraw the graphs. What has happened to r_0 and q_0? Explain your results.

11. Suppose an economy starts at equilibrium with domestic inflation equal to world inflation.

a. Use the 3-equation open economy model as well as the AD-BT-ERU model to explain the adjustment process in the economy if the inflation target of the home economy is raised (i.e. above the world inflation rate).

b. Comment specifically on the behaviour of the nominal exchange rate.

c. Briefly explain the pros and cons of a higher inflation target. Consider the context to be an open economy with a flexible exchange rate and a recent history of the interest rate at the zero lower bound.

PROBLEMS

1. 'Following an announcement from the Riksbank (the Swedish central bank) of an interest rate increase, an immediate depreciation of the Krona was observed'. How can you explain this outcome? In your answer explain the economics of the UIP condition. Summarize your findings highlighting the role played by expectations and communication by the central bank. You are advised to take the following steps and in each case to draw a UIP diagram:

a. Show the 'normal case' in which the central bank announcement is followed by an immediate appreciation of the Krona.

b. Suppose the rise in the interest rate had been widely expected in financial markets. Show in the UIP diagram that there would be no immediate change in the exchange rate when the Riksbank made its announcement.

c. Finally, show how an immediate depreciation in the Krona can be explained.

2. The Bank of England keeps a directory of the minutes from the monthly meetings of their Monetary Policy Committee online: https://www.bankofengland.co.uk/monetary-policy-report/monetary-policy-report

a. Pick a period following a shock such as after September 11th 2001 or the 2008–09 financial crisis and see how the Bank of England comments on the interaction between the interest rates they set and the UK pound exchange rate. Are interest rate differentials thought to be causing movements in the exchange rate? If not, then does the movement of exchange rates invalidate the UIP condition?

b. Find some news articles from the same period that talk about the reactions of the foreign exchange market (useful sources for market news include the *Financial Times*, Reuters and Bloomberg). Did the forex market anticipate changes in interest rates before they happened? If so, were their predictions proved correct?

c. How does the model fare in the case of the Brexit referendum in 2016 or the Kwasi Kwarteng mini-budget of 2022?

3. Assume you are in a small open economy with flexible exchange rates. The economy experiences a permanent positive demand shock.

a. Draw the PC-MR, the IS-RX and the AD-ERU diagrams to help you explain the path back to medium-run equilibrium.

b. Draw a graph of the real exchange rate over time and give a brief explanation of its path.

c. How does the medium-run equilibrium vary from that which would occur in a closed economy subjected to the same shock?

4. This question uses the Macroeconomic Simulator (available at www.oup.com/he/carlin-soskice) to model supply-side reform in the open economy. Start by opening the simulator and choosing the open economy (flexible exchange rate) version. Then reset all shocks by clicking the appropriate button on the left-hand side of the main page. Use the simulator and the content of this chapter to work through the following questions:

a. Decide on a supply-side reform and describe briefly how it is modelled—i.e. does it affect the WS or PS? What effect does this have on the ERU curve?

b. Apply a permanent 2% positive supply shock. (Note that a positive supply shock is one that reduces equilibrium unemployment; raises equilibrium employment.)

c. Use the impulse response functions from the simulator or from your sketches to help explain the path of the economy following the above shock.

d. Draw the IS-RX and PC-MR diagrams for this scenario. Draw the AD-ERU diagram for this scenario. [Hint: the path of the key variables (output, inflation, real interest rate, real exchange rate) will have to match the impulse response functions from the simulator. Remember that whenever the central bank sets the interest rate different from r^* to get the economy on to the MR curve, the economy will be *off* the AD curve. Once the economy is back at a MRE, then $r = r^*$ and the economy is, once again, *on* the AD curve.]

e. Briefly discuss one aspect of this way of modelling the adjustment of the economy to a supply-side reform that seems to you to be unrealistic. Express your concern in terms of the assumptions of the model.

5. Use the Macroeconomic Simulator (available at www.oup.com/he/carlin-soskice). You will be comparing the results for a closed and an open economy so you will need to change the parameter values to be the same in each case: (i) set the stabilizing interest rate to 3 in the closed economy and the world rate to 3 in the open economy) and (ii) set the sensitivity of expenditure with respect to the interest rate to 0.75. Additionally, in the open economy set the sensitivity of expenditure with respect to the real exchange rate to 1.
   a. Apply a permanent positive demand shock equal to 2.0 per cent. Use the Change y-Axis Scale feature to narrow the window on both real and nominal exchange rate figures to 1.0—0.9. Print your saved data results to incorporate in your answer, including the exchange rate figures and trade balance/current account figures.
   b. Explain why the closed and open economies differ after a demand shock. Explain the behaviour of the real and nominal exchange rates and the real and nominal interest rates. Which changed by more, the real or nominal exchange rate, and why exactly?
   c. Why did the real interest rate behave differently in the two economies?

INTERESTED IN EXPLORING THESE TOPICS FURTHER?

Visit www.oup.com/he/carlin-soskice to consolidate and extend your learning with the multiple-choice questions and Animated Analytical Diagrams accompanying this chapter.

CHAPTER

12

THE OPEN ECONOMY

THE DEMAND AND SUPPLY SIDES

12.1 OVERVIEW

In Chapter 11, we extended the 3-equation model to the open economy to show how an inflation-targeting central bank interacts with the foreign exchange market in response to shocks to the economy. In this chapter, we look more closely at how trade and capital market openness affect the demand and supply sides of the economy.

The world economy has become increasingly integrated since the Second World War. This process of globalization has seen a surge in trade and international capital flows, which has fundamentally changed the way goods and services are produced and consumed. Think for a minute about an item of clothing. In the past, clothing worn in the United States was often manufactured and sold inside the country by American firms. Now, however, even in a large country, the supply chain is likely to be much more international. For example, an item of clothing could use textiles from Bangladesh, be assembled in Vietnam to a French design using machinery manufactured in Germany, and be transported via Hong Kong. And when the clothing finally arrives on the US high street it could be sold by a Spanish clothing retailer. This is a stylized example of a modern day supply chain, which uses the comparative advantages of different countries to ensure goods (of a given quality) are produced as cheaply and efficiently as possible. We could tell an equally globalized story about how the finance was raised for each stage of the production process.

We begin with some data illustrating how the openness of economies to trade and international capital flows has changed over the past decades. Figure 12.1 shows the evolution of external trade and financial flows in the post-World War II period. Trade openness is usually measured by the sum of exports and imports as a percentage of GDP, $((X+M)/GDP)$. Trade in the six major economies shown in Figure 12.1 has steadily increased, albeit experiencing a temporary contraction during the global financial crisis.

The cross-country patterns are interesting: for example, the UK's trade openness remained remarkably stable from the early 1970s at about 40% of GDP. Germany is the most open economy throughout: a dip in the global financial crisis took the indicator of openness from 70% to 60% of GDP but it rebounded and has remained at 70% since. This is a degree of openness characteristic of a small rather than a large economy like Germany. In the run-up to the financial crisis, China's openness was close to Germany's

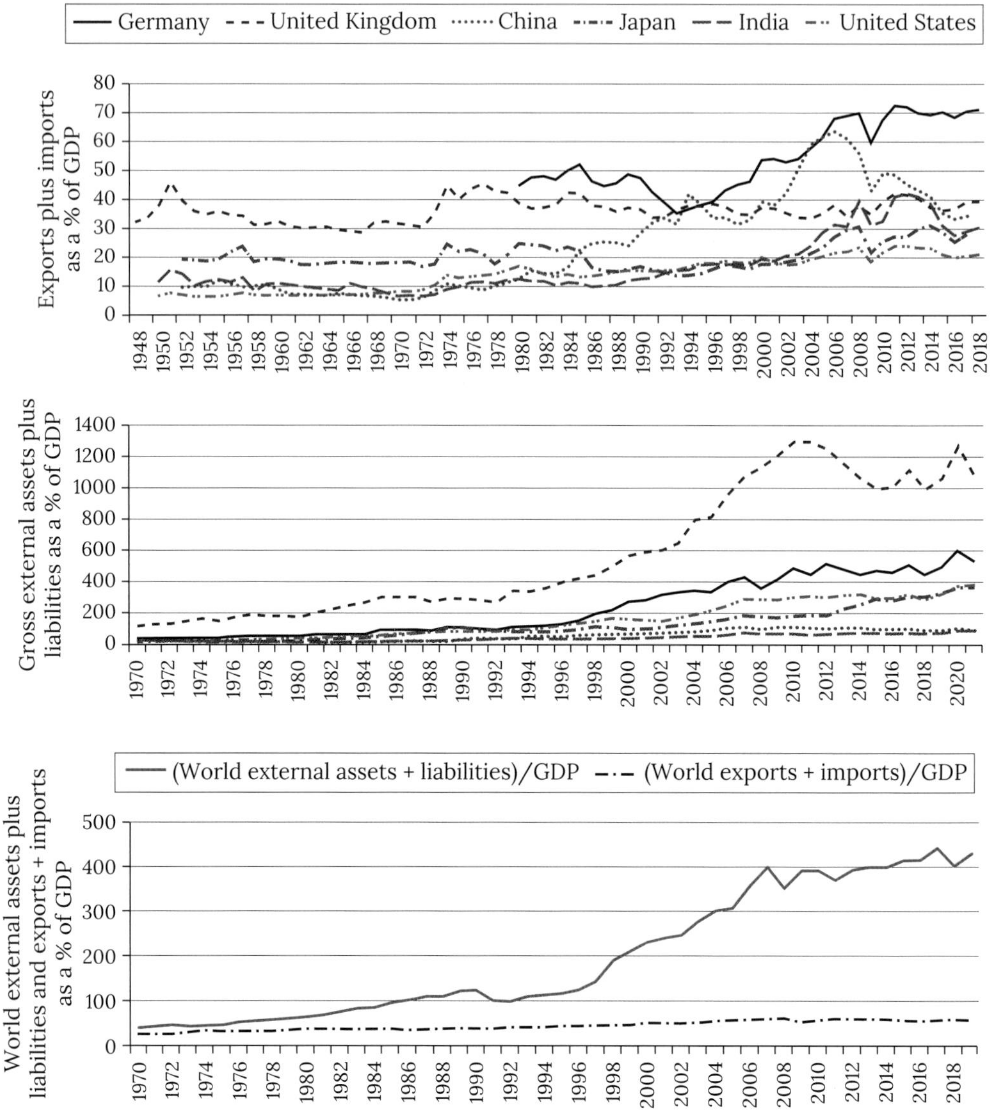

Figure 12.1 Exports plus imports as a percentage of GDP: 1948–2018 (upper panel), gross external assets plus liabilities as a percentage of GDP: 1970–2021 (middle panel), and world financial and trade openness: 1970–2019 (lower panel).

Source: IMF International Financial Statistics (accessed August 2021); Our world in Data–Oxford Martin School; updated version of dataset. Available at Lane, P. R. and Milesi-Ferretti, G.M. (2018), 'The external wealth of nations revisited: international financial integration in the aftermath of the global financial crisis', *IMF Economic Review* **66**, 189–222. https://doi.org/10.1057/s41308-017-0048-y

reflecting a large uptick following its accession to the WTO in 2001. But since the crisis, its trade share has fallen and it looks similar to the other large economies rather than similar to Germany. India was a much more closed economy than China but its openness increased and peaked at around 40% in 2012. Japan and the US are the least open of the major economies. The bottom panel of Figure 12.1 shows that total world trade roughly doubled since the 1970s, going from around 27% of world GDP to around 56%.

The middle panel in Figure 12.1 displays a commonly used indicator of financial globalization: gross external assets plus liabilities as a percentage of GDP. Historically, financial openness in the UK has been higher than elsewhere; however, all the economies in the sample have become more financially open over time, spurred by financial deregulation, which started in earnest in the late 1980s.

The bottom panel shows the opening up of a massive gap between financial openness and trade openness since the 1980s, thus revealing the degree of financial integration in the modern economy. Against the background of the increasingly integrated global economy, we clarify how openness affects the macro model.

12.1.1 The open economy accounting framework

The balance of payments accounts provide a useful way of clarifying important open economy concepts. The open economy accounting framework helps us to understand the sense in which changes in a country's external balance are of interest to a policy maker. The transactions between the home country and the rest of the world are recorded in the balance of payments account, which is divided into the current account and the capital and financial account.

The *trade balance* records the receipts from export sales less payments for imported goods and services, this is $BT \equiv X - M$.

The *current account* consists of the trade balance plus net interest and profit receipts. The current account reflects the fact that home and foreign residents can receive income, such as interest and profit payments, from assets that they own in each other's countries. Specifically, net interest and profit receipts in the home country's balance of payments accounts arise from earnings from foreign assets (e.g. bonds, equities) that are owned by residents of the home country less payments of interest and profit to foreigners who own home country assets.

The *capital and financial account* records changes in the stock of various types of foreign assets owned by home residents, home assets owned by overseas residents, and changes in official foreign exchange reserves of the central bank.

To understand the balance of payments accounts, it is useful to separate the private and official parts of the capital account.

$$
\begin{aligned}
BP \equiv & \underbrace{\left(\underbrace{(X - M)}_{\text{trade balance}} + \text{net interest receipts} \right)}_{\text{current account, CA}} \\
& + \underbrace{(\text{private net capital inflows} - \text{change in official foreign exchange reserves})}_{\text{capital account}} \\
& \equiv (BT + INT) + (F - \Delta R) \equiv 0,
\end{aligned}
$$

where *BT* is the balance of trade and *INT* is net receipts of factor income from abroad. F records private net capital inflows and ΔR is the change in official foreign exchange reserves. We have so far concentrated our open economy analysis on flexible exchange rate economies. To understand the role played by ΔR in the balance of payment accounts, however, we need to think about the two polar exchange rate regimes; *fully flexible* and *fixed*.

At one end of the spectrum of exchange rate regimes is the freely floating, *fully flexible* one (as seen in Chapter 11). In this case, neither the government nor central bank intervenes in the foreign exchange market to influence the price at which one currency trades with another. The exchange rate is then determined by supply and demand for that currency relative to other currencies. As discussed in Chapter 11, supply and demand of different currencies are in turn the outcome of foreign exchange traders' responses to news about interest rates and other economic developments that are viewed as influencing future interest rates and the longer run trajectory of the exchange rate. Under flexible exchange rates, the exchange rate is determined by market forces and there is no official intervention, which means that $\Delta R = 0$.

In a *fixed* exchange rate regime, the nominal exchange rate is kept fixed at a certain level (i.e. $e \equiv \frac{\text{home curr.}}{\text{foreign curr.}} = \text{constant}$) as a result of government policy. The home country's exchange rate is 'pegged' at a fixed rate to another country's currency (e.g. the Hong Kong dollar is pegged to the US dollar) or to a so-called 'basket' of other currencies. In the face of shifts in the demand for and supply of home's currency in the foreign exchange market, the government must actively intervene in the market (i.e. buy and sell foreign exchange) to keep the rate pegged. The purchase of foreign exchange by the home central bank is $\Delta R > 0$ and the sale of foreign exchange is $\Delta R < 0$. A central bank would buy foreign exchange to increase the supply of home currency in the market if excess demand for the home currency in the market is causing pressure for it to appreciate (and vice versa).

An example of this would be the People's Bank of China buying US dollars in order to stop the yuan appreciating against the US dollar. If the government wishes to change the exchange rate peg, it announces the new rate at which it is prepared to buy and sell the home currency. It is a revaluation if it intervenes to support a rate where fewer units of home currency can be bought for one unit of foreign currency; the converse is a devaluation.

The balance of payments records the *sources* and *uses* of foreign exchange and sums to zero.[1] If there is a trade surplus, then exports exceed imports. This means that the home economy's wealth is increasing. The balance of payments identity helps explain this. The current account surplus is a source of foreign exchange. Something must be done with it, and the balance of payments identity highlights that it must either

[1] In practice, the records are incomplete, with the result that an entry for errors and omissions has to be added to make the balance of payments sum to zero.

be used to purchase foreign assets or to increase home's foreign exchange reserves.[2] Both of these represent more wealth for the home economy because the assets can be used at a later date to increase consumption. The converse is true for a country running a deficit: its wealth is falling (or equivalently, its debt to the rest of the world is increasing).

A moment's reflection will suggest that running a trade deficit is not necessarily a problem. For example, a country with a trade deficit may be fast-growing with lots of highly profitable investment opportunities: being able to borrow from abroad allows it to take advantage of these opportunities. Equally, a country with a trade surplus may be slow-growing, and the opportunity to lend abroad enables its residents to take advantage of investment opportunities in other countries, which are better than those at home.

When analysing performance in a particular economy, it is important to bear in mind that trade or current account imbalances may reflect the optimizing behaviour of forward-looking agents, including governments, but they may not. For example, a trade deficit may reflect weak competitiveness, and high levels of private or government consumption (i.e. low savings rather than high investment). These are all reasons for monitoring the trade balance in our analysis of the open economy.

Capital gains and a country's net foreign asset position

The size of the overseas balance sheets of wealthier countries has been growing rapidly since the late 1990s.[3] As illustrated in Figure 12.1, this is especially true in the United Kingdom, where both foreign assets held by UK-registered institutions and foreign claims on the UK increased in value from around 50% of nominal GDP in the late 1960s to 300% in the early 2000s.[4] Expanding gross asset and liability positions have an important implication for the role of exchange rate variations in explaining the behaviour of a country's net international investment position (NIIP), which is a stock measure. In particular, following Obstfeld (2012), the change in NIIP (also referred to as 'Net foreign asset position'), is computed as:

$$\Delta \text{NIIP} \equiv \text{CA} + \text{Capital gains}, \qquad \text{(change in net foreign asset position)}$$

where 'CA' denotes the current account balance—a flow measure—and 'Capital gains' denotes the net change in nominal market value between the pre-existing stocks of foreign assets and liabilities due to changes in the valuation of a country's foreign assets relative to its liabilities. The net asset position is affected by exchange rate variations and changes in asset prices (e.g. stock market appreciation).

---

[2] At first sight it may seem paradoxical that a negative F in the balance of payments represents home's *purchase* of foreign assets—but the purchase of foreign assets is a use of foreign exchange and therefore has a negative value in the balance of payments accounts.

[3] See Obstfeld (2012).

[4] See Broadbent (2014).

The equation for the change in a country's net foreign asset position implies that the interpretation of the current account deficit, and more importantly the extent to which this predicts a country's future ability to borrow in international markets, depends on the size of its overseas balance sheet. Intuitively, a country with a healthier net foreign asset position is less likely to experience so-called 'sudden stops' in overseas funding of its borrowing. In economic terms, the NIIP is the 'constraint' on the present value of net export deficits a country can run in the future.

We saw in Chapter 8 the analogous effect in relation to a household: a change in the valuation of its major asset, namely the owner-occupied house, dramatically affects the ability of the household to borrow to finance current consumption.

The UK provides a great example; despite running a persistent current account deficit for more than 30 years, which adds to its debt, its net foreign asset position deteriorated much less than the cumulative current account balance (see Figure 12.2). This is partially a consequence of exchange rate depreciations; while a current account deficit is expected to deteriorate the NIIP, it also leads to a depreciation of the sterling. This implies that the sterling value of foreign assets held by UK-registered institutions increases. In principle, the effects of current account deficits and capital gains could

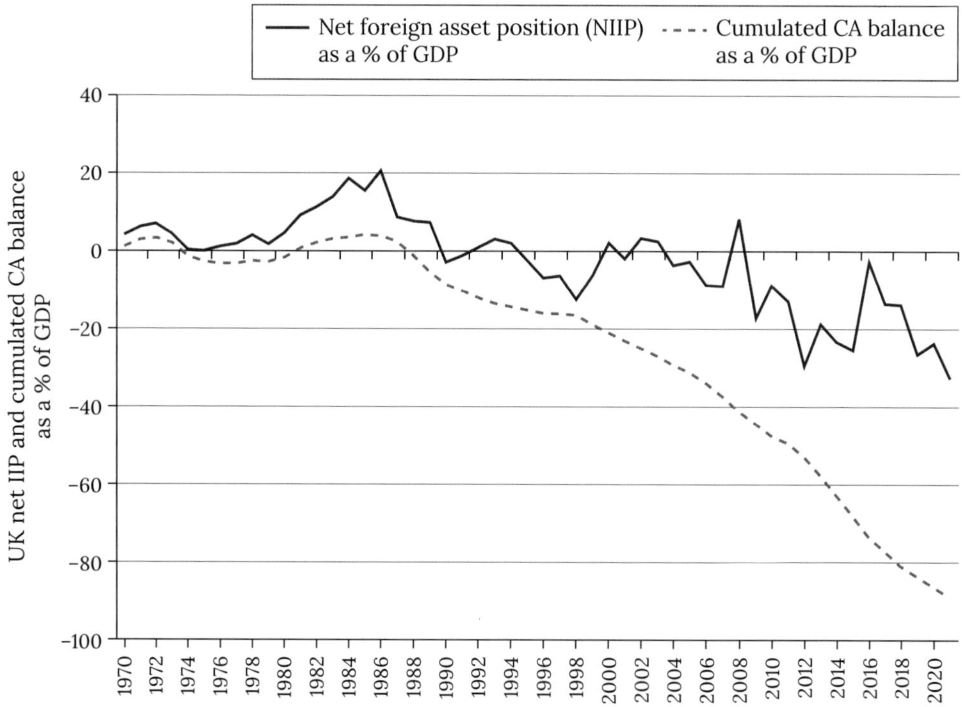

Figure 12.2 UK Net Foreign Asset Position (excluding gold) and cumulated Current Account balance as a % of GDP.

Source: updated version of dataset constructed by Lane, P. R. and Milesi-Ferretti, G. M., 2018 (the data reported here reflects the September 19th, 2022 update).

offset each other, thus leaving the UK net foreign asset position unchanged (note that there is no analogy with this exchange rate effect in the case of a household's balance sheet).

As a consequence, despite the current account deficit, the healthier state of the NIIP suggests there is no significant threat of sudden stops in overseas funding. However, this immediately begs the question of how such conditions can persist without foreign holders of sterling deposits requiring a risk premium to hold sterling given an expectation of depreciation (as was the case in the 1976 sterling crisis). There is an interesting contrast between the current situation and that of 1976 when there was a 'balance of payments crisis'. The 1976 crisis was indeed exacerbated by fears that disorderly sterling depreciation was driving the prevailing double digit inflation higher by raising the prices of imported consumer goods, which were feeding through to wage bargains. By contrast, the credibility of the inflation-targeting monetary framework set in place in the UK in the 1990s appears to have allowed it to benefit from 'the exorbitant privilege' of foreigners' willingness to hold UK assets in spite of the trend deterioration of the current account (Broadbent 2014).

12.1.2 The demand side, trade balance, and the supply side

The demand side and trade balance

What affects our demand for foreign goods and services and the demand of foreign residents for our tradable products? As noted in Chapter 11, one obvious influence is 'relative prices'. If our goods are relatively expensive, then demand for them by foreigners will be reduced and home residents will tend to buy more imported goods. In order to compare prices across countries, we need to convert them to a common currency, producing a measure of price competitiveness, which we call Q. As discussed in Chapter 11, Q is the price of foreign goods expressed in home currency divided by the price of home goods, which are also expressed in home currency, $Q \equiv \frac{P^*e}{P}$.

Higher Q is a real depreciation for home—an improvement in its competitiveness, because its goods are cheaper relative to those of the rest of the world. Just as in the case of the nominal exchange rate, it is safest to avoid using the terms 'rise' or 'fall', or 'high' or 'low', in relation to the real exchange rate. It is better to stick to the terms 'appreciation' or 'depreciation'.

Of particular importance is the relationship between changes in the real exchange rate and the trade balance. In Chapter 11, we assumed that if the home economy's competitiveness improved, i.e. its real exchange rate depreciated, net exports would rise, shifting the IS curve to the right. In this chapter, we will show why it is reasonable to make that assumption. In doing so, we will highlight the two-sided character of exchange rate depreciation. The first is the link from the real exchange rate to competitiveness via the demand for exports and imports. As we saw in Chapter 11, an improvement in home's competitiveness increases exports because forcigners find our goods and services more attractive and it depresses imports, because home residents also switch toward home-produced output. The combination of more exports and less imports improves the trade balance.

However, there is another effect of an exchange rate depreciation. Why does a real depreciation lead home residents to switch away from imports? The answer is because they have become more expensive. Since a given volume of imports will be more expensive, there will be a second influence of the depreciation on the trade balance, one that worsens it. The two effects of a real depreciation on the trade balance go in opposite directions—the first improves it and the second causes a deterioration. The first effect is called the *volume* effect because it relates to how the quantities of imports and exports respond to the change in competitiveness. The second effect is called the *relative price* or *terms of trade effect* because it relates to the effect on a given volume of imports of the change in the relative price between home-produced and foreign goods. Which effect is stronger?

We can think this through intuitively as follows. When the exchange rate depreciates, say, by 10%, this will raise the cost to the home economy of a given volume of imports by 10%. They are 10% more expensive. For the volume effect to outweigh the depressing effect of the higher cost of imports on the trade balance overall, the boost to export volumes and the fall in import volumes must add up to more than 10%. This result is called the Marshall–Lerner condition. Fortunately the empirical evidence of its validity is reasonably clear-cut: the volume effect is strong enough to outweigh the terms of trade effect, so we can be confident that a real depreciation improves the balance of trade. As long as the Marshall–Lerner condition holds—and we will assume it always does—a rise in Q, i.e. a real depreciation or an improvement in home's competitiveness, increases net exports and shifts the IS curve to the right.

The supply side in the open economy

In Chapter 11, we assumed that wage setting was based on real wages defined in terms of the domestic price level, i.e. the prices of goods and services produced at home. In this chapter, we relax that assumption to explore how changes in import prices may affect the supply side and equilibrium unemployment. In the closed economy model, and in the open economy model of Chapter 11 with a vertical ERU curve, the economy can only move to a new medium-run equilibrium with lower unemployment if there are supply shocks or policy reforms that have the effect of shifting the WS curve downwards or the PS curve upwards. We shall see that when wage-setting behaviour is defined by real consumption wages, including the import component of the bundle of goods and services that households consume, the ERU curve is downward sloping.

If the ERU curve is downward sloping, shifts in aggregate demand can move the economy to another constant inflation equilibrium. The intuition is that a positive aggregate demand shock can be associated with a new constant inflation equilibrium at lower unemployment and an appreciated real exchange rate. This is because the lower real cost of imports, due to the appreciation, allows real wages to rise: hence there can be a new WS-PS intersection at lower unemployment, higher real wages, lower import costs and unchanged firm profit margins. The PS curve will shift up showing that workers get higher real consumption wages following a real appreciation. Wage and price setters will be content and there will be no pressure for inflation to change.

The medium-run model: *AD-BT-ERU*

In Chapter 11, we introduced the AD—ERU model to show how shifts in aggregate demand or supply-side shocks affect the real exchange rate in the constant inflation equilibrium. A positive aggregate demand shock is associated with an appreciated real exchange rate and vice versa. We can now include the more general downward-sloping ERU curve.

We shall also include the *BT* curve, to show the trade balance explicitly. The *BT* curve is upward sloping in the diagram (Figure 12.3) with output on the horizontal axis and the real exchange rate on the vertical. At a point above the *BT* line, there is a trade surplus (lower competitiveness and/or higher output to boost imports is needed to get to balanced trade) and below the *BT* line there is a trade deficit (higher competitiveness and/or lower output to dampen imports is needed to balance trade).

We can explain intuitively why the *BT* curve will be flatter than the *AD* curve—we set out the argument systematically in the modelling section (Section 12.2.3). Here is the intuition:

1. A real depreciation boosts net exports and raises aggregate demand so the economy moves to the north-east along the *AD* curve.
2. If the economy is initially in trade balance, it is on both the *AD* and *BT* curves so the question we must answer is whether at the new goods market equilibrium, there is a trade surplus. If so, then the economy—on the *AD*—must be above the *BT* curve and the *BT* must therefore be flatter than the *AD* curve.
3. The boost to net exports caused by the depreciation will raise output through the multiplier process. The additional imports caused by the higher income will be less than the initial rise in net exports, leaving the economy with a trade surplus.
4. The multiplier process will not drive output up by enough to lead to increased imports equal to the boost to net exports due to the depreciation. This is because only a proportion of any increase in output is spent on imported goods.

Figure 12.3 uses the medium-run model to look at the predicted effects of supply shocks and policy reforms, and then at demand shocks. We can see that, in contrast to the model with a vertical *ERU*, if the *ERU* curve is downward sloping, then demand shocks as well as supply shocks are associated with changes in the equilibrium level of output.

From the 1980s onwards, weaker trade unions in some countries and greater coordination among wage setters in others, and increased competition in the product market can be modelled by a rightward shift of the *ERU* curve. If we keep the demand side unchanged, then policies and structural reforms that shift the *ERU* to the right will be associated with lower equilibrium unemployment, a depreciated real exchange rate and an improvement in the trade balance (as shown in Figure 12.3a).

Figure 12.3b shows that a positive demand shock boosts output and appreciates the real exchange rate. Examples where domestic demand shocks and appreciated real exchange rates appear to have been important in the 2000s include countries with private sector demand shocks (such as strong leverage cycles as discussed in Chapter 8, like Spain or Ireland) or with expansionary government fiscal policies (such

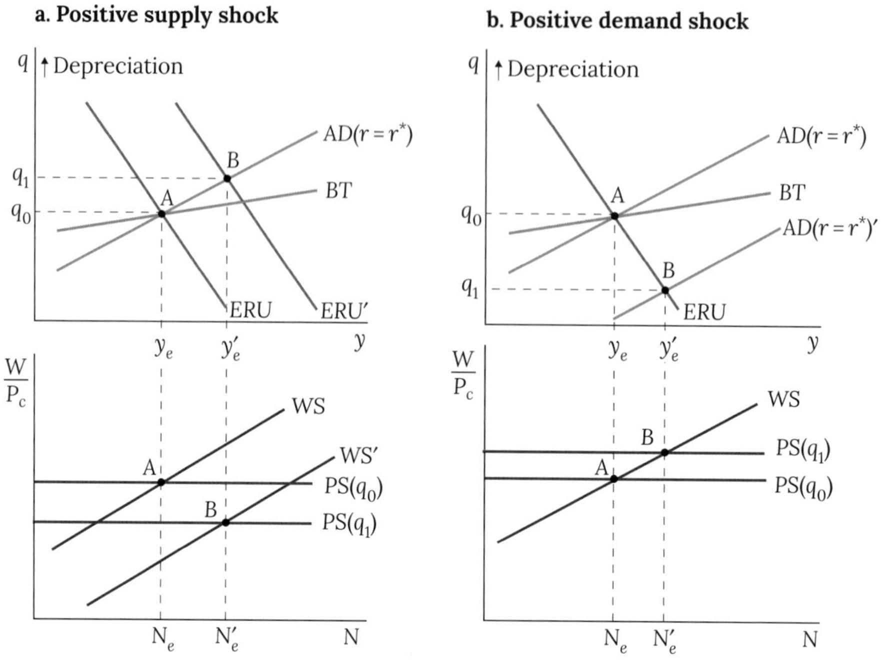

Figure 12.3 The response of an economy with a downward-sloping *ERU* curve to economic shocks
a. Positive supply shock
b. Positive demand shock.

as the UK government's increased spending on health and education under Prime Minister Tony Blair, or the US government's tax cuts and increased military spending under President George W. Bush). If the demand shock is domestic—whether private or public—it will be associated with a deterioration of the country's external balance.

Table 12.1 shows key macroeconomic indicators for Spain and the UK in 1999 and 2007. One interpretation of the evolution of the Spanish economy over this period is that a large property bubble in the pre-recession years was responsible for the

	Spain		UK	
	1999	2007	1999	2007
Unemployment rate (%)	12.5	8.3	5.9	5.3
Inflation rate (%)	2.2	2.8	1.3	2.3
Real exchange rate (1999 = 100); rise in the index is a real appreciation	100	125	100	109
Current account balance (% of GDP)	−2.7	−8.8	−1.8	−2.8

Table 12.1 Macroeconomic indicators for the UK and Spain: 1999 and 2007.
Note: Unlike in the figures, a rise in the real exchange rate index is a real appreciation.
Source: IMF World Economic Outlook, April 2011; OECD Economic Outlook Annex Tables, 2012.

combination of lower unemployment, a more appreciated real exchange rate and a serious deterioration in the current account balance. The indicators for Spain are consistent with it experiencing a positive demand shock as shown in Figure 12.3b. For the UK case, the data also suggest a positive demand shock played a role in the evolution of the economy in the pre-crisis years. In addition, the UK is expected to have benefitted from the lagged effects of supply-side reforms initiated under Prime Minister Thatcher in the 1980s. It is important to note that, even in the face of positive demand shocks, inflation remained low and stable in both economies. This is consistent with the presence of multiple constant inflation equilibria in the medium-run model with a downward-sloping *ERU* curve. The experience of the British economy during the Great Moderation prior to the financial crisis is the subject of a case study in Section 12.3.

12.2 **MODELLING**

This section provides the detail behind the discussion in Section 12.1. We divide the modelling section into three subsections. The first covers the demand side. In this chapter, we derive the open economy *IS* curve, paying particular attention to the relationship between the real exchange rate and the trade balance.

The second subsection covers the supply side and fills in the details behind the derivation of a downward-sloping *ERU* curve. We extend the model presented in the last chapter by setting out the implications of assuming that wage setting is based on the real consumption wage. The real consumption wage is calculated by using the prices of both domestically produced and imported goods. We shall see that this means the *PS* curve shifts with changes in the real cost of imports (i.e. the real exchange rate) and the *ERU* curve becomes downward sloping, which results in multiple levels of output being consistent with constant inflation.

The last subsection combines both the supply and demand sides into a new medium-run model. We use the *AD-BT-ERU* model to show the medium-run implications of supply and demand shocks and why current account imbalances of the kind observed in the years before the global financial crisis can persist in medium-run equilibrium.

12.2.1 **The demand side and trade balance**

Summary

In this subsection, four results about the demand side and the trade balance are explained. These results are used in both the open economy 3-equation model and in the *AD-BT-ERU* model. Readers familiar with these results can skim this section and go on to Section 12.2.2.

1. The open economy *IS* curve is steeper (a given fall in the real interest rate is associated with a smaller increase in output in the open economy). The reason is that the size of the multiplier is reduced in the open economy because of the marginal propensity to import. As income rises, not only do taxation and savings rise, but so does the level of imports. We show the results using a simple Keynesian consumption function. As explained in Chapter 1, due to the presence of credit constraints and uncertainty about whether income shocks are temporary

or permanent, a model that includes permanent income behaviour is also likely to have a sizeable multiplier, which will be dampened by the marginal propensity to import.

2. The open economy IS curve shifts in response to changes in the real exchange rate (Q) and world output (y^*). A depreciation of home's real exchange rate (i.e. an improvement in home's price competitiveness) or a rise in y^* shifts the IS to the right. If the Marshall–Lerner condition holds, this boosts the trade balance and aggregate demand. The Marshall–Lerner condition says that the effects of an exchange rate depreciation in raising the volume of exports and reducing the volume of imports outweigh the terms of trade effect, which will increase the value of the import bill. A rise in world demand increases net exports. For any interest rate, goods market equilibrium will therefore occur at a higher level of output, and the trade balance improves.
3. Although both a real depreciation and a rise in world demand raise output and improve the trade balance (at a given interest rate), there is an important difference between the cases. Depreciation entails a deterioration in home's terms of trade, which means higher import costs and lower living standards in the home economy.
4. Following a depreciation of the real exchange rate, there will be a trade surplus at the new goods market equilibrium. The increase in output at the new goods market equilibrium is equal to the multiplier times the boost to net exports caused by the depreciation. The increase in balanced trade output is equal to the reciprocal of the marginal propensity to import times the boost to net exports. Since the multiplier is smaller than the reciprocal of the marginal propensity to import, the goods market equilibrium is at a lower income level than the new balanced trade level of output: hence there is a trade surplus (see the equations for the goods market equilibrium and the trade balance).

Goods market equilibrium in the open economy

Recall the goods market equilibrium condition from Chapter 1:

$$y = y^D,$$

where y is output and y^D is aggregate demand. In the closed economy aggregate demand is:

$$y^D = c_0 + c_1(1-t)y + I(r) + G.$$

Introducing trade in goods and services has two effects. First, demand for home's output is boosted by demand from abroad, in the form of exports, X. Second, it is dampened by goods imported from abroad, M, which substitute for domestic output. Remember that $(C+I+G)$ measures total spending by home agents on consumption, investment and government purchases *irrespective* of the origin of the goods or services. To calculate *total* demand for *home*-produced goods and services, y^D, we subtract spending on imports, M, and add foreign demand for exports, X:

$$y^D = (C + I(r) + G) - M + X \equiv (C + I(r) + G) + BT,$$

(aggregate demand, open economy)

where the trade balance, $BT \equiv X - M$, is also called net exports.

To begin with, we assume that exports are exogenous and that imports depend only on the level of domestic output or income. We define exports and imports as

$$X = \overline{X} \text{ and } M = my,$$

where m is a constant between 0 and 1 and is called the marginal propensity to import. At this stage, we keep the models as simple as possible so that we can highlight a key difference between the open and closed economy IS curves: the size of the multiplier.

The economy is in goods market equilibrium when output and aggregate demand are equal, $y = y^D$:

$$y = y^D = c_0 + c_1(1-t)y + I(r) + G + \overline{X} - my. \quad (12.1)$$

Collecting the terms in y on the left-hand side and rearranging gives the goods market equilibrium condition in the form: output is equal to the multiplier times the exogenous components of demand plus investment at a given real interest rate. Thus:

$$y = \underbrace{\frac{1}{1 - c_1(1-t) + m}}_{\text{multiplier}} \left(c_0 + I(r) + G + \overline{X}\right), \quad \text{(goods market equilibrium)}$$

If we compare the open economy multiplier to its closed economy counterpart (introduced in Chapter 1), we can see that the open economy multiplier is lower because of the marginal propensity to import, m:

$$\underbrace{\frac{1}{1 - c_1(1-t) + m}}_{\text{open economy multiplier}} < \underbrace{\frac{1}{1 - c_1(1-t)}}_{\text{closed economy multiplier}}. \quad (12.2)$$

When exogenous spending goes up, output rises by less than in the closed economy because some of the demand is satisfied by imports rather than by domestic production. This also means that output reacts less to any given change in the real interest rate in the open economy (all other things held constant)—hence, the open economy IS curve is steeper.

Price-setting behaviour and competitiveness

Price and cost competitiveness

Since relative prices, $Q \equiv \frac{P^* e}{P}$, affect net exports, we need to know how they are set in the open economy and how they are related to costs. Given that firms normally operate under imperfect competition and thus face downward-sloping demand curves, we assume that firms set home prices on the basis of home costs using the price-setting rule for the closed economy explained in Chapter 2.

But when it comes to foreign markets, two alternative pricing rules for exports, expressed in domestic currency, are suggested:

1. The first—*home-cost pricing*—is that firms set export prices in the same way as for goods sold at home, i.e. based on domestic costs (P1);
2. The second—*world pricing*—is that firms set export prices based on the prices of similar products produced abroad (P2).

To see how these differ, imagine there is an increase in costs in the home country but not abroad (and assume that the nominal exchange rate remains unchanged).

1. Under the first pricing hypothesis (P1), home's firms raise export prices relative to the price of the output of firms abroad. By passing on higher home costs in their prices, home is less competitive, which represents a real appreciation for the home country (↓ Q).
2. Under world pricing, home's firms do not change their export prices, because by assumption prices in the foreign market are unchanged. In this case, there is no change in the *price* competitiveness of exports. However, we would expect their higher costs to affect the ability of home firms to compete internationally. If the costs of home firms rise relative to their competitors but prices are unchanged, then the profit margins of home firms are squeezed. This means home firms will be at a relative disadvantage in their access to internal finance to fund future investment, marketing, research and development or after-sales service. Although price competitiveness is maintained, 'non-price competitiveness' is reduced.

This suggests that an alternative way of defining the real exchange rate is based on relative *costs* rather than relative *prices*. One commonly used measure of competitiveness is called relative unit labour costs, or RULC, and is defined as follows:

$$\begin{aligned} RULC &\equiv \frac{\text{foreign unit labour costs expressed in home currency}}{\text{home unit labour costs}} \\ &\equiv \frac{ULC^{*}e}{ULC}. \qquad \text{(cost competitiveness; real exchange rate)} \end{aligned}$$

Higher home costs reduce home's competitiveness: (↓ RULC): this is a real appreciation for home.[5]

The Law of One Price and Absolute Purchasing Power Parity

The two pricing rules can be compared to the so-called Law of One Price (LOP) and to the hypothesis of Purchasing Power Parity (PPP). According to the Law of One Price, the common currency price of a traded good is identical in different countries. For any good, *j*, that is traded,

$$P_j = P_j^{*}e.$$

The logic of the LOP is straightforward: international trade should have the effect of equalizing prices for the same good in different countries, since as long as transport

[5] Just as is the case with the price-based measure of the real exchange rate, conventions vary. Sometimes RULC is defined with home costs in the numerator, in which case a rise in RULC is a deterioration of home's competitiveness and hence a real appreciation.

costs are not too high, profits can be made by transporting a good from a location where the price is low and selling it where the price is high. This process of arbitrage would tend to equalize the prices in the two locations. If the LOP holds for all goods *and* the same basket of goods is consumed in different countries, then this basket of goods will have the same common currency price anywhere in the world. This is referred to as Absolute Purchasing Power Parity: if for all goods j in a basket of goods that is common to consumers in both countries,

$$P_j = P_j^* e \text{ for all goods } j, \text{ then } P = P^* e$$
$$\implies Q = 1. \qquad \text{(Absolute Purchasing Power Parity)}$$

The hypothesis of Absolute Purchasing Power Parity implies that the real exchange rate is always equal to one. If we add the assumption of perfect competition, then since under perfect competition, price is equal to marginal cost, marginal costs will be equalized in all countries and there will be no supernormal (i.e. economic) profits. Hence, unlike the world pricing hypothesis discussed above, where costs can differ across countries and profit margins can expand and contract, in a world of Absolute PPP and perfect competition, neither price *nor* cost competitiveness can vary.

Evidence on price-setting

The empirical evidence is not supportive of the LOP or Absolute PPP. Transport costs and barriers to international trade interfere with the LOP, and the presence of non-traded goods and services in the consumption bundle and differences in consumer tastes across countries prevent the Absolute Purchasing Power Parity hypothesis from holding. In evaluating the accumulated evidence, Obstfeld argues that '[a]pparently consumer markets for tradables are just about as segmented internationally as consumer markets for nontradables'.[6]

The main reason is that international markets are imperfectly competitive. Most tradables—both goods and services—are differentiated products, and producers pursue pricing strategies to maximize their long-run profits. For example, firms set different prices in different markets to take advantage of variations in the elasticity of demand. An extensive survey of pricing strategies is provided by Goldberg and Knetter.[7] They report evidence of the widespread use of so-called pricing to market and of the incomplete pass-through of exchange rate changes into prices: 'world pricing' incorporates both these effects.

In reality, firms' pricing strategies lie between the two alternatives of home-cost based and world pricing presented above. Fortunately, the main results of the macro model do not depend on which of these simple pricing hypotheses is used: the way that shocks and policy responses are transmitted varies, but the qualitative results are similar.

One of the big facts that has emerged since the era of floating exchange rates began in 1973 is that the fluctuations in nominal exchange rates have been accompanied by

---

6 See p. 16 of Obstfeld (2001).

7 See Goldberg and Knetter (1997).

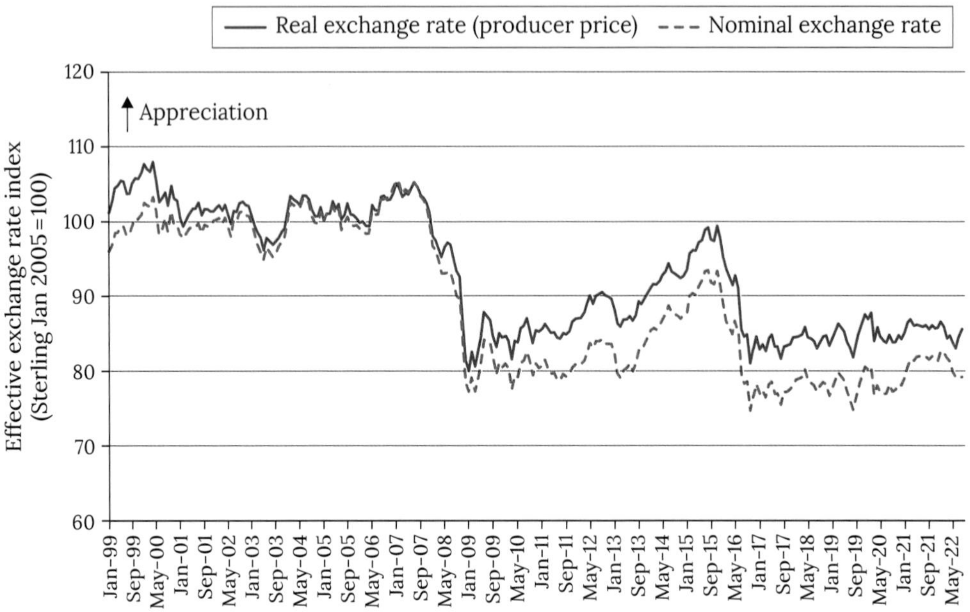

Figure 12.4 UK nominal and real effective exchange rates indices based on producer price index (Jan 2005 = 100: 1999–2022).

Note: An increase in the index is an appreciation.

Source: Bank of England; European Central Bank (data accessed September 2022).

fluctuations in real exchange rates. To quote Obstfeld's evaluation of the evidence: 'Real exchange rate variability tends to be almost a perfect reflection of nominal rate variability, with changes in the two rates highly correlated and independent movements in price levels playing a minor, if any, role'.[8] A simple explanation is that nominal exchange rates are volatile and prices are sticky because they are based on the price-setting strategies of imperfectly competitive firms. Figure 12.4 illustrates this for the UK, where we see that the sharp nominal depreciations of sterling during the financial crisis and following the 2016 Brexit vote were tracked closely by real depreciations.

An appropriate model should accommodate this fact. Either the home-cost or world pricing rule would do (LOP plus perfect competition, i.e. Absolute PPP, will not). We stick to the home-cost pricing rule because it conveniently allows us to use the real exchange rate defined in terms of price competitiveness. The assumption that prices in home currency are set by home costs implies that the price level of home-produced goods sold at home and in the export market is the same, and that the price in home currency of imports is set by the price in the rest of the world (i.e. by costs in those economies). After summarizing the evidence, Obstfeld states: 'These relationships are consistent with a model in which domestic marginal cost (consisting mainly of wages)

[8] See p. 14 of Obstfeld (2001).

is sticky in domestic-currency terms, and export prices are set as a (perhaps somewhat variable) markup over marginal cost.'[9]

Hence we have:

$$P_X = P = (1 + \mu^c) \cdot \text{unit cost} \qquad \text{(export price)}$$

$$P_M = P^* e, \qquad \text{(import price)}$$

where μ^c is the markup. This means that export prices are set as a markup on domestic unit labour costs.

Implications for competitiveness of a change in the nominal exchange rate

Let us now follow through how a change in the nominal exchange rate affects relative prices or costs, and hence competitiveness. Suppose there is a depreciation of home's currency. We continue to assume that labour is the only cost of production and consider each price-setting hypothesis in turn.

1. **Under home-cost pricing (P1),** the depreciation has no effect on the price set for exports in home currency. However, the price in the foreign market falls, which implies a rise in price competitiveness since home's goods are now cheaper in the foreign market relative to the unchanged price of goods produced elsewhere (i.e. ↑ Q). Meanwhile, prices of imports set in the foreign currency are unchanged but are now more expensive in terms of home currency (↑ $P^* e$), reinforcing the overall rise in home's competitiveness.
2. **Under world pricing (P2),** the depreciation has no effect on prices in foreign markets, nor on the price in home currency terms of imports, so price competitiveness, Q, is unaffected. However, home benefits from higher home currency revenues on its exports. This widens profit margins, improving home's non-price competitiveness measure by the fall in home's costs (ULC/e) relative to abroad's, measured in a common currency: ↑ $RULC = \frac{ULC^* e}{ULC}$. For those firms selling into the home (e.g. the UK), prices in sterling are unchanged but the foreign producer gets lower revenue in their own currency. Given unchanged costs, the profit margins of firms exporting to the UK fall, making home more competitive.

As our baseline case, we assume in this book that countries invoice their exports in domestic currency. In the world, however, this is not always the case. An extreme case is Colombia, where 98% of its exports are invoiced in US dollars. To the extent exports of countries outside the US are priced in US dollars, they will gain no benefit in price competitiveness when the dollar appreciates. Since US price competitiveness will decline under these circumstances, there is a depressive effect on global trade associated with dollar appreciation.[10]

---

[9] See p. 24 of Obstfeld (2001).

[10] A study by economists at the IMF in 2020 (Boz et al.) documents that although the share of global exports that goes to the US is 10%, the share of exports invoiced in dollars is more than double, at 23%. The importance of the dollar as a vehicle currency (i.e. used for invoicing in trade that does not involve the US) is highlighted by the comparison with the euro. Whereas 37% of world exports are destined for EU countries, the euro's share of global export invoicing is not

The two sides of exchange rate depreciation

In this section, we set out the details of the two-sided character of changes in the real exchange rate, which was introduced in Section 12.1. On the one hand, a real depreciation makes our goods more attractive in export markets and makes imports less attractive to home consumers. Being more competitive sounds like good news. But on the other hand, a real depreciation means that any volume of imports that we buy is more expensive—this is the bad news. The first effect boosts the export industries and aggregate demand, but the second reduces real wages and living standards. The two effects push the trade balance in different directions: the first effect improves the trade balance but the second worsens it.

By making some assumptions, we can give a definite answer to the question of whether a real depreciation improves the trade balance. As noted in the Overview, this is called the Marshall–Lerner condition. The intuition is straightforward: if the effect of the depreciation in boosting the *volume* of net exports outweighs the fact that the import bill will go up one-for-one with the depreciation, then the trade balance improves. We shall see that another way of putting this is to say that if the sum of the price elasticities of demand for exports and imports is greater than one, the trade balance improves.

To show how the Marshall–Lerner condition works, we need to include the real exchange rate explicitly in the import and export functions. In the home market, home goods with price P compete with imports (in home currency terms) with price P^*e. The relative price is therefore our measure of competitiveness, $Q \equiv \frac{P^*e}{P}$. In export markets, home-produced goods (exports) with price P compete with world goods priced (in home currency terms) at P^*e. Once again, the relative price is our measure of competitiveness, Q.

The nominal value of exports in home currency terms, X_{nom}, is equal to the price index of exports times the volume. The volume of exports can be expressed as a share of world output, where our share σ (sigma) depends positively on competitiveness, and y^* is world output:

$$X_{nom} = P_X \underbrace{\sigma\left(\frac{P^*e}{P}\right)}_{\text{home's share}} \underbrace{y^*}_{\text{world output}}.$$

To get the export function in real terms, we divide each side by the domestic price level, $P = P_X$:

$$X = \sigma\left(\frac{P^*e}{P}\right)y^* = \sigma(Q)y^*. \qquad \text{(export function)}$$

that much larger at 46%. When the dollar is used for invoicing exports between two countries other than the US, changes in the dollar exchange rate are passed through into import prices and affect competitiveness and the volume of imports. What this means is that for the US, a dollar depreciation makes its exports cheaper in foreign markets as explained above, whereas for another country that invoices in dollars, a depreciation of its currency vis-à-vis the dollar has no effect on the price competitiveness of its exports but makes its imports more expensive. For further examples, see this article in *The Economist*, 'Global trade's dependence on dollars lessens its benefits', Schools Brief, August 29th 2020.

The value of imports M_{nom} in home currency terms is the price index, $P_M = P^*e$ times the volume of imports. The volume depends on the marginal propensity to import, which will be a negative function of competitiveness, and on the level of domestic output.

$$M_{nom} = P_M \cdot \underbrace{m(Q)}_{\substack{\text{marginal propensity}\\ \text{to import}}} \cdot \underbrace{y}_{\text{home output}}.$$

To derive the import function in real terms, we divide each side by P.

$$\begin{aligned} M &= \frac{P_M}{P} m(Q)y \\ &= \frac{P^*e}{P} m(Q)y \\ &= Qm(Q)y. \end{aligned} \qquad \text{(import function)}$$

This means that the balance of trade is:

$$\begin{aligned} BT &= X - M \\ &= \underbrace{\sigma(Q)y^*}_{\text{volume}} - \underbrace{Q}_{\text{ToT}} \underbrace{m(Q)y}_{\text{volume}} \\ &= X(Q, y^*) - QM(Q, y). \end{aligned} \qquad \text{(balance of trade)}$$

The good news about a real depreciation for the home economy is the so-called volume effect and the bad news is the relative price, or terms of trade (ToT), effect. The volume effect is the effect on the volume of exports and of imports due to a change in Q. The volume effect is unambiguous: a rise in Q boosts the volume of exports ($\sigma(Q)$ rises as home takes a larger share of world output) and reduces the volume of imports ($m(Q)$ falls as home's marginal propensity to import falls). But, a rise in Q will raise the relative price of a given volume of imports.

Another way of expressing the 'relative price effect' of a change in Q is to use the concept of the *terms of trade*. The terms of trade is defined as the price of exports divided by the price of imports:

$$\frac{P_X}{P_M} = \frac{P}{P^*e} = \frac{1}{Q}, \qquad \text{(terms of trade)}$$

where an increase in $\frac{P_X}{P_M}$ is an improvement in the terms of trade because a greater volume of imports can be bought for a given volume of exports. Conversely, an increase in Q means a rise in the price of imports relative to exports: it is a deterioration in the terms of trade.[11] For a given volume of imports, this will produce a decline in the trade balance.

In summary, given the way that import and export prices are defined, a rise in Q for the home economy is a:

---

[11] Our baseline pricing hypothesis is consistent with the evidence that a nominal depreciation is associated with a deterioration of home's terms of trade. See Obstfeld and Rogoff (2000).

1. rise in price competitiveness, which is the same thing as a depreciation of the real exchange rate
2. deterioration in the terms of trade because it produces a rise in the real cost of imports.

As long as the volume effects are strong enough to outweigh the countervailing terms of trade effect, then a real depreciation (a rise in Q)—i.e. an improvement in home's price competitiveness—improves the trade balance. The converse is true for a real appreciation. This result is the famous Marshall–Lerner condition, which states that as long as the sum of the price elasticity of demand for exports and the price elasticity of demand for imports exceeds one, a depreciation will improve the balance of trade. The simplicity of the Marshall–Lerner condition depends on the assumption that goods are in perfectly elastic supply (i.e. the price does not change as output increases) and that we begin in trade balance, but the central insight of comparing the volume with the terms of trade effects is a general one. There are many ways to prove the Marshall–Lerner condition—one is shown in the Appendix to this chapter.

In the dynamic IS model introduced in Chapter 11, there is a one period lag from a change in the real exchange rate to the effect on output: this reflects the time for new orders to be placed and resources to be reallocated in response to the change in competitiveness.

In our model of the open economy, we assume the trade balance improves with a depreciation of the real exchange rate, given the level of output—i.e. we assume the Marshall–Lerner condition holds.

BOX 12.1 Numerical example of the Marshall–Lerner condition

For example, suppose the home economy begins in trade balance with exports equal to imports, which are equal to 100. The elasticity of demand for exports is 0.75 and for imports is 0.50. Consider the implications of a 1% rise in competitiveness arising for example from a rise of 1% in foreign relative to domestic prices: export volume rises by 0.75 to 100.75; import volume falls by 0.50 to 99.50; the real price of imports rises by 1%, pushing the import bill up to 100.495 (since $1.01 \times 99.5 = 100.495$). In this case, the balance of trade improves because $BT = 100.75 - 100.495 = 0.255$.

If, on the other hand, export demand elasticity was considerably lower at just 0.25, export volume would only rise by 0.25 to 100.25. Everything else stays the same so the balance of trade actually deteriorates ($BT = 100.25 - 100.495 = -0.245$).

The elasticities used in the example are more 'pessimistic' than the consensus estimates from empirical studies. Dornbusch reports estimates for the absolute value of the price elasticity of demand for exports of 1.06 in Germany, 1.31 in the US, and 1.68 in Japan and for imports of 0.50 in Germany, 0.97 in Japan, and 1.35 in the US.[a] The requirement that the sum of the price elasticities of demand is greater than one is easily met for each of these countries.

[a] See Dornbusch (1996).

Empirical studies generally provide support for the Marshall–Lerner condition. The caveat to this result is that in the very short run, when contracts are already in place, the volume effect is minimal but the terms of trade effect operates fully: this means that in the short run a real depreciation typically depresses the trade balance. This is referred to as the J-curve effect. The trade balance can worsen in the short run, for two reasons:

1. The short-run price elasticity of demand for exports and imports is much lower (approximately one half) its long-run value. This means that the volume response to the depreciation is initially weak.
2. To the extent that exports are invoiced in domestic currency, the dollar value of exports falls immediately, while imports invoiced in foreign currency remain unchanged in dollar terms. In home currency terms, export receipts are unchanged while the import bill rises immediately. Hence the trade balance worsens.

Real exchange rate and trade balance

A real depreciation raises net exports via the Marshall–Lerner condition; higher net exports in turn raise output and pull up imports. What is the overall—or general equilibrium—effect on the trade balance once we allow output to adjust?

The trade balance is:

$$BT = X - M \qquad \text{(trade balance)}$$

and we can therefore write the level of output at which trade is balanced (i.e. $BT = 0$), as $y_{BT}(Q, \sigma, y^*, m)$. A rise in price competitiveness increases the level of output at which trade is balanced and a higher level of world demand has the same effect: in each case the y_{BT} line shifts to the right in the IS diagram. To the right of y_{BT} there is a trade deficit and, to the left, there is a trade surplus.

What happens to output and the trade balance when the exchange rate depreciates, boosting net exports? The economy begins in goods market equilibrium and with balanced trade at A in Figure 12.5. The real depreciation from Q to Q′ shifts both the

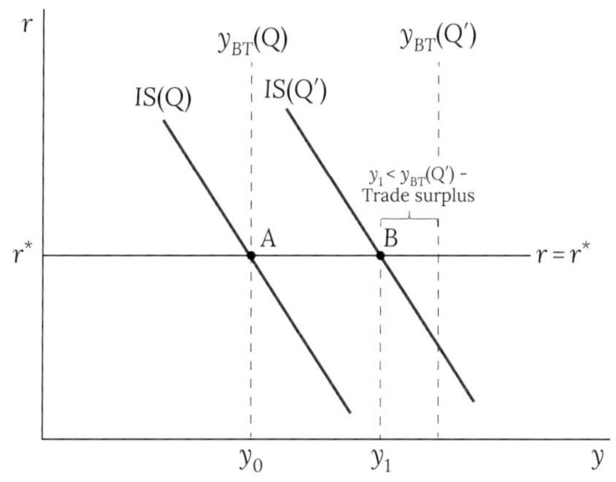

Figure 12.5 Real depreciation (↑ Q): impact on output and the trade balance.

IS curve and the y_{BT} line to the right. We assume the interest rate remains unchanged at r^*. The rise in net exports due to the rise in Q raises aggregate demand (y^D), which pushes up output and income until a new goods market equilibrium is established. This is where the higher savings, taxation *and* imports induced by the rise in exports are equal to the increase in demand: output rises from y_0 to y_1 in Figure 12.5. At the new goods market equilibrium at B, output is to the left of the new y_{BT} line (the level of income at which imports would be equal to exports at the depreciated exchange rate) and there is a trade surplus.

Another way to see this is to note that the increase in output at the new goods market equilibrium is equal to the multiplier times the boost to net exports caused by the depreciation. The increase in balanced trade output is equal to the reciprocal of the marginal propensity to import times the boost to net exports. Since the multiplier is smaller than the reciprocal of the marginal propensity to import, the goods market equilibrium is at a lower income level than the new balanced trade level of output: hence there is a trade surplus (see the equations for the goods market equilibrium and the trade balance). This result is set out in more detail in Section 12.2.3.

12.2.2 The supply side in the open economy

Multiple equilibria: A downward-sloping *ERU* curve

In Section 12.1, we introduced the logic of the existence of a range of constant inflation equilibrium unemployment rates in the open economy. In this section, we set out the derivation of the downward sloping ERU curve, beginning with the question of how workers calculate their real wage in the open economy. In the open economy we can no longer talk about a single price level. Assuming workers buy both home-produced and imported goods, the price level that is relevant in assessing the real value of nominal wages is the nominal wage in terms of consumer prices (i.e. W/P_c, where P_c is the consumer price index). To define the consumer price index, P_c, it is assumed that consumers purchase a bundle of goods and services, where the imported ones have a price of P^*e and the home-produced ones have a price of P. The share of the consumption bundle that is imported we will call ϕ (pronounced 'phi' for 'foreign'). We assume that ϕ is constant for simplicity. The consumer price index is:

$$P_c = (1-\phi)P + \phi P^*e.$$

Note that the standard of living of home households will fall if the prices of imported goods rise, even if the prices of home-produced goods remain fixed. This is because the real consumption wage, W/P_c, falls when P_c increases. In Chapter 11, in order to focus on stabilization, we ignored this effect by assuming that workers defined the real wage relevant to wage setting only in terms of home-produced goods (i.e. W/P). This meant that the WS and PS curves were unchanged from the closed economy and there was a unique equilibrium unemployment rate and a vertical ERU curve.

We now look at the consequences for the medium-run model of taking on board the fact that the WS curve is defined in terms of the real consumption wage (i.e. W/P_c). The y-axis in the WS-PS diagram is defined in terms of W/P_c and not W/P as it was in Chapter 11 (see Figure 12.6b). The wage-setting curve in the open economy is upward sloping just as in the closed economy: as employment rises and the labour market tightens, the expected real consumption wage workers require to supply effort goes up. In this case, the real consumption wage depends on the price of both home-produced goods and imports; this means that employers have to pay a particular real consumption wage (W/P_c) at a given level of employment on the WS curve to get workers to exert effort in the efficiency wage model or to strike a deal with their employees or with the union representing them. The main driver of wage-setting decisions is still the tightness of the labour market. Exactly the same factors as in the closed economy can cause the WS curve to shift in this model, such as changes in union bargaining power or unemployment benefits.

To find equilibrium output, we also need to define the PS curve in terms of the real consumption wage—it is then possible to draw WS and PS curves on the same diagram. When defined in terms of the real consumption wage, we shall see that the PS curve is a function of the real cost of imports, i.e. of the real exchange rate. It will shift up and down as the real exchange rate changes. Why? Depreciation reduces the real wages workers get (i.e. on PS) because the price level of the imported goods they consume goes up.

The simplest way to think about how the PS curve is affected by changes in the real exchange rate is to go through an example step by step. We do this by considering what happens when there is a depreciation of the real exchange rate, Q (as a result of a depreciation of the nominal exchange rate, e).

The PS curve shows the real wage workers get after firms have set their prices, P. To show the PS curve in the labour market diagram with W/P_c on the axis, we have to figure out the real wage workers get after firms set their prices, taking into account the additional effect on W/P_c due to the inclusion of import prices.

A depreciation of the nominal exchange rate, e, causes a depreciation of the real exchange rate, as $Q = \frac{P^* e}{P}$. Depreciation, an increase in Q, is an increase in the *real cost of imports*.

The consumer price index, P_c, is a weighted average of home and imported goods. As we saw above, $P_c = (1-\phi)P + \phi P^* e$. The second term in the consumer price index equation has increased as a result of the increase in e.

We also need to check what happens to the price home firms set, P. Home firms set their price as a markup on their unit labour costs, i.e. W/λ. The real exchange rate does not come into this calculation. This means that home prices, P, remain the same (i.e. the first term in the consumer price index equation is not altered by the depreciation).

Hence, a depreciation will always increase P_c in the model.

The increase in P_c reduces the real consumption wage, W/P_c. Bananas and other imported elements in the consumption bundle become more expensive, making workers worse off. This results in a downward shift of the PS curve.

Summary

A depreciation of the real exchange rate shifts the PS curve down because it reduces the real consumption wage workers get after firms have set their prices. The real consumption wage is reduced because imports become more expensive following the depreciation. The opposite of this logic holds for an appreciation of the real exchange rate.

The example highlights the importance of correctly interpreting the PS curve. The curve shows the real wage that is available to workers after the firm has secured its profit margin, which it does by setting prices for home-produced goods. After a depreciation, workers cannot buy as many goods and services with the nominal wages firms pay them and the PS curve shifts downwards. After an appreciation, workers can buy more goods and services with the nominal wages firms pay them (bananas and other imported goods are cheaper) and the PS curve shifts upwards.[12]

When measuring real wages in terms of W/P_c, a real depreciation shifts the PS curve downwards. The intersection of the WS curve and the new PS curve is therefore at lower output as shown in Figure 12.6b at point B.[13] Translating this result into the real exchange rate–output diagram produces a downward-sloping supply-side equilibrium. This is the downward-sloping *ERU* curve.

With a downward-sloping *ERU* curve, we can now show how a low level of unemployment and the associated high level of output can be sustained without inflationary pressure (point A in the top panel of Figure 12.6b).

Just as in Chapter 2, where we introduced the closed economy WS curve, a low rate of unemployment means a low cost of job loss, which raises the wage-setting real wage (WS is upward sloping). For this to be a supply-side equilibrium (i.e. a WS-PS intersection), the value of the price-setting real wage must be at the same high level. This requires that the real cost of imported consumption goods be sufficiently low (i.e. by a sufficiently appreciated real exchange rate, which shifts the PS curve up). This gives point A at the combination of an appreciated value of q and a high level of output. Exactly the same logic lies behind the location of point B.

Deriving the equation for the downward-sloping *ERU* curve

To derive the downward-sloping *ERU* curve, we need to set out the details of wage and price setting in the open economy. We use the cost-plus pricing rule for home-produced goods sold at home and exported:

$$P = P_X = (1 + \mu^C) \cdot \text{unit cost},$$

[12] Another possibility for modelling would be to think about the impact of imported inputs on firms' costs. We analyse this case when we model an oil price shock in Chapter 13. To make the analysis as simple as possible here, we assume that no intermediate goods (i.e. firm inputs) are imported—i.e. the only imports in the economy are final goods consumed by workers. This assumption means that a depreciation cannot affect firms' costs. This means the only impact of imports on the PS curve in our model is to change P_c and hence the real consumption wage of workers given the price set by firms for home-produced output.

[13] In Figure 12.6 and all the other figures in this chapter we use $q = \log Q$ as our measure of the real exchange rate. This makes the analysis simpler and allows for all the diagrams in the chapter to be compatible with one another.

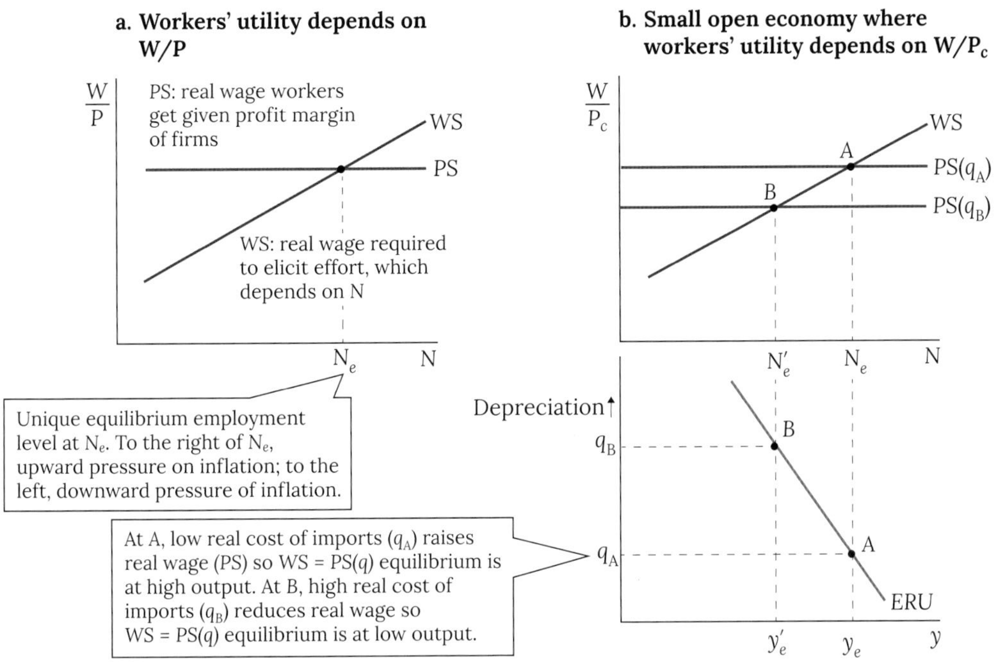

a. Workers' utility depends on W/P
W/P
PS: real wage workers get given profit margin of firms
WS
PS
WS: real wage required to elicit effort, which depends on N
N_e
N
Unique equilibrium employment level at Nₑ. To the right of Nₑ, upward pressure on inflation; to the left, downward pressure of inflation.
b. Small open economy where workers' utility depends on W/P_c
W/P_c
WS
A
PS(q_A)
B
PS(q_B)
N'_e
N_e
N
Depreciation
q_B
B
q_A
A
ERU
y'_e
y_e
y
At A, low real cost of imports (q_A) raises real wage (PS) so WS = PS(q) equilibrium is at high output. At B, high real cost of imports (q_B) reduces real wage so WS = PS(q) equilibrium is at low output.

Figure 12.6 Supply-side equilibrium in the closed and open economy. Visit www.oup.com/he/carlin-soskice to explore deriving a downward-sloping ERU curve with Animated Analytical Diagram 12.6.
Note: For convenience, we assume that $y = N$, i.e. labour productivity is equal to 1.

where μ^C is the markup on costs. As we saw in the previous subsection, the consumer price index is defined as:

$$P_c = (1-\phi)P + \phi P^* e,$$

where we use the fact that $P_M = P^* e$. The real consumption wage is defined in terms of consumer prices:

$$w = \frac{W}{P_c}.$$

Wage setting

Wage-setting behaviour is the same as in the closed economy. The only modification is to make explicit the role of the consumer price index:

$$W = P_c \cdot b(N).$$

The wage-setting curve is defined by

$$w^{WS} = \frac{W}{P_c} = b(N), \qquad \text{(WS, wage-setting real wage equation)}$$

where a rise in employment is associated with a rise in the wage-setting real wage (i.e. the WS is upward sloping).

Price setting

In the absence of any imported inputs into production (e.g. oil), price setting in the open economy is the same as in the closed economy, i.e. prices are set as a markup on unit labour costs:

$$P = P_X = (1+\mu^C)\cdot\frac{W}{\lambda},$$

where P is the price of home goods sold at home and in export markets and λ is the level of labour productivity. To work with the wage- and price-setting curves, both must use the same definition of the real wage. This means that we need to express the price-setting real wage in terms of the consumer price index, i.e. W/P_c.

The first step is to substitute the price equation into the equation for the consumer price index, P_c.

$$\begin{aligned} P_c &= (1-\phi)P + \phi P^* e \\ &= (1-\phi)\left[(1+\mu^C)\frac{W}{\lambda}\right] + \phi P^* e. \end{aligned}$$

In order to find the expression for the price-setting real wage, we need to do some algebra. The next steps are shown in the footnote.[14]

In the final step, we rearrange the equation so that the price-setting real wage is on the left-hand side and the markup is on price, μ:

$$w^{PS} = \frac{\lambda(1-\mu)}{1+\phi(Q-1)}. \qquad \text{(PS, price-setting real wage equation)}$$

By inspecting the equation, it is clear that a rise in Q reduces w^{PS}.[15]

We can see from this that the price-setting real wage in the open economy is equal to the closed economy price-setting real wage (i.e. $\lambda(1-\mu)$) modified by the real exchange rate, Q. If there are no imported goods, the weight of imports in the consumer price index is zero (i.e. $\phi = 0$) and it is easy to see that the price-setting real wage is indeed equal to its closed economy value,

$$w^{PS} = \lambda(1-\mu). \qquad \text{(PS, closed economy)}$$

---

[14] The first line below shows the equation after dividing by $P = (1+\mu^C)\cdot\frac{W}{\lambda}$. Then, we use the definitions of the real wage, $w = \frac{W}{P_c}$ and of the real exchange rate, $Q = \frac{P^*e}{P}$ to simplify the equation. In the third line, we rearrange the equation so that the real wage is in the numerator. Lastly, in the fourth line, we use the equation that $\frac{1}{1+\mu^C} = 1-\mu$.

$$\frac{P_c\lambda}{W(1+\mu^C)} = (1-\phi) + \frac{\phi P^* e}{P} \qquad (12.3)$$

$$\frac{\lambda}{w(1+\mu^C)} = (1-\phi) + \phi Q \qquad (12.4)$$

$$\frac{w(1+\mu^C)}{\lambda} = \frac{1}{(1-\phi)+\phi Q} \qquad (12.5)$$

$$\frac{w}{\lambda(1-\mu)} = \frac{1}{(1-\phi)+\phi Q}. \qquad (12.6)$$

[15] This can be shown using the approximation $w^{PS} \approx \lambda(1-\mu)(1-\phi(Q-1))$ so that the inverse relation between w^{PS} and Q is approximated by $\partial w^{ps}/\partial Q \approx -\lambda(1-\mu)\phi < 0$.

The PS curve also reverts to the closed economy form if $Q = 1$, which is the case when the prices of home- and foreign-produced goods are always identical in a common currency, as would be the case if the Law of One Price held.

The price-setting behaviour of firms means that regardless of the level of Q, nominal wages can purchase the same volume of *home*-produced goods and services as they could in the closed economy. But in the open economy, workers choose to spend some of their wages on imported goods. If imports are more expensive (i.e. $\uparrow P^*$ or $\uparrow e$), then they can afford fewer consumption bundles. This means that a higher cost of imports reduces the real wage of workers: the PS curve shifts down with a rise in Q.

This shows another way of thinking about the case of the vertical ERU case: if wage setters do *not* take into account the effect of changes in the imported component of their consumption bundle in wage setting, then the ERU is vertical.

12.2.3 The medium-run model: *AD-BT-ERU*

The *AD* curve

In Chapter 11, we used the dynamic open economy IS equation to underpin the 3-equation model:

$$y_t = A - ar_{t-1} + bq_{t-1}, \qquad \text{(open economy IS equation)}$$

where q is defined as the log of Q. This version of the open economy IS curve highlights the inverse relationship of output with the real interest rate and the direct relationship with competitiveness.[16] The open economy multiplier is included in each of the terms A, a and b.[17] In the dynamic version, we explicitly show the lagged effects of the interest rate and exchange rate on output.

In turn, the IS curve is the basis for the AD curve in the medium-run model, which was derived in Chapter 11 using the real UIP condition:

$$y = A(\sigma, y^*) - ar^* + bq, \qquad \text{(AD curve, } r = r^*\text{)}$$

where r^* is the world real interest rate. The constant in the AD curve, A, includes both σ and y^* as demand shift variables. For the economy to be on the AD curve, it must be the case that home's interest rate is equal to the world interest rate (i.e. $r = r^*$). This is because the home economy's real exchange rate must be equal to its expected value for the economy to be in a medium-run equilibrium.

The *BT* curve

As we saw in Section 12.2.1, the trade balance is an important factor in modelling the open economy. The final component of the medium-run model is the BT curve. The

---

[16] As discussed in detail in Chapter 11, we use the natural log of the real exchange rate in the IS equation in the 3-equation model. This is because it makes the mathematics easier.

[17] To simplify the model, we use linear functions for investment and consumption, and for exports and imports. $X = x_0 + x_2 q$ and $M = m_1 y - m_2 q$. The term x_0 includes home's share of world trade, σ, and world output, y^*. As usual, the multiplier is k. We can therefore write $A = k(c_0 + a_0 + G + x_0)$, $a = ka_1$ and $b = k(x_2 + m_2)$ in the IS and AD equations.

BT curve shows the combinations of the real exchange rate, q, and the level of output, y, at which trade is balanced: $X = M$. We summarize the BT curve using a simple linear equation as follows:

$$y^{BT} = B(\sigma, y^*) + cq, \qquad \text{(BT curve)}$$

where y^{BT} is the level of output at which trade is balanced, B and c are constants. B depends on the exogenous determinants of exports and imports: σ is home's share of world trade, y^* is world output and m is the marginal propensity to import.[18]

As discussed previously, changes in σ and y^* will shift both the AD and BT curves.

Why is the BT curve flatter than the AD curve?

The BT curve is flatter than the AD curve, i.e. $c > b$. This means that a rise in home's competitiveness (a real depreciation) improves the trade balance. As explained in Figure 12.5 and the associated discussion, this reflects two factors:

- The Marshall–Lerner condition; and
- The fact that the multiplier is less than the reciprocal of the marginal propensity to import.

To see why this is the case intuitively, we start by recalling the definition of both curves.

The AD curve represents goods-market equilibrium: along the AD output y equals aggregate demand, y^D. The BT curve represents balance of trade: at all points net exports $(X - M)$ are equal to zero (a mathematical derivation is provided in Appendix 12.5.2).

Now, consider Figure 12.7. In the figure, there is a real depreciation of size Δq. It is associated with a rise in output of Δy^{AD} and a larger increase in the level of output at which trade would be balanced, Δy^{BT}. The size of Δy^{AD} is equal to the multiplier, k, times the injection of aggregate demand arising from the depreciation, ΔX (for simplicity, we assume the volume effect and terms of trade effect on imports exactly offset each other; this implies $\Delta(X - M) = \Delta X$). The size of Δy^{BT} will be larger than Δy^{AD} because ΔX is multiplied by the reciprocal of the marginal propensity to import, which we know must be larger than the multiplier.

Using the *AD-BT-ERU* model

The medium-run model is formed by combining the AD, BT, and ERU curves in the q–y space, as shown in Figure 12.8. The figure shows how the position of the economy on the diagram can be used to diagnose the trade balance (a position off the BT curve) and whether there is any pressure on inflation to change (a position off the ERU curve).

[18] Using the linear export and import equations, we write $y_{BT} = \frac{1}{m_1}x_0 + \frac{1}{m_1}(x_2 + m_2)q$. Hence, $B = \frac{1}{m_1}x_0$ and $c = \frac{1}{m_1}(x_2 + m_2)$ in the BT equation.

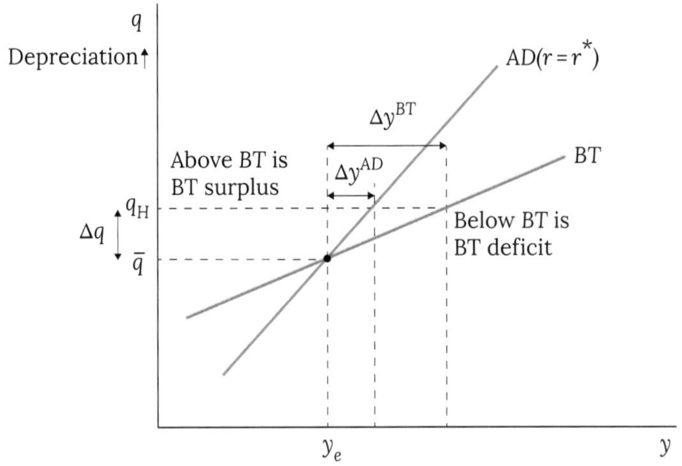

Figure 12.7 The AD and BT curve slope comparison.

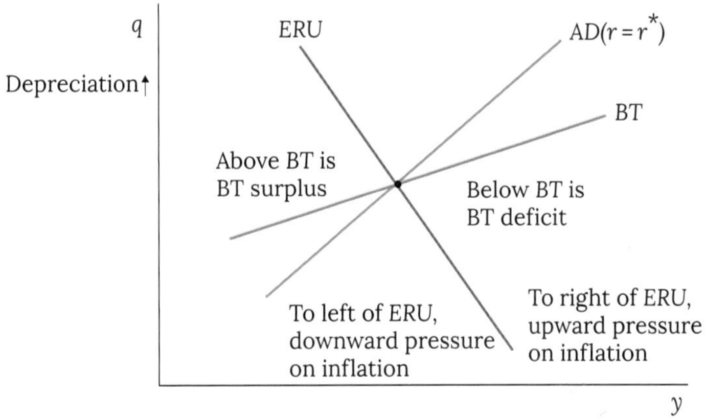

Figure 12.8 The AD-BT-ERU model.

Supply, demand, and external trade shocks in the open economy

As we saw in Section 12.1, the key difference between the model presented here and the one in Chapter 11 is the introduction of a price-setting curve that depends on the real exchange rate, which produces a downward-sloping ERU curve. We have also introduced the BT curve, which can of course be used in the case of a vertical ERU curve.

We analyse how a downward-sloping ERU curve affects the medium-run implications of demand- and supply-side shocks. Figure 12.9 illustrates the AD-BT-ERU and WS-PS diagrams following (a) a positive supply shock and (b) a positive demand shock. We assume the economy is initially at medium-run equilibrium on the AD, BT, and ERU

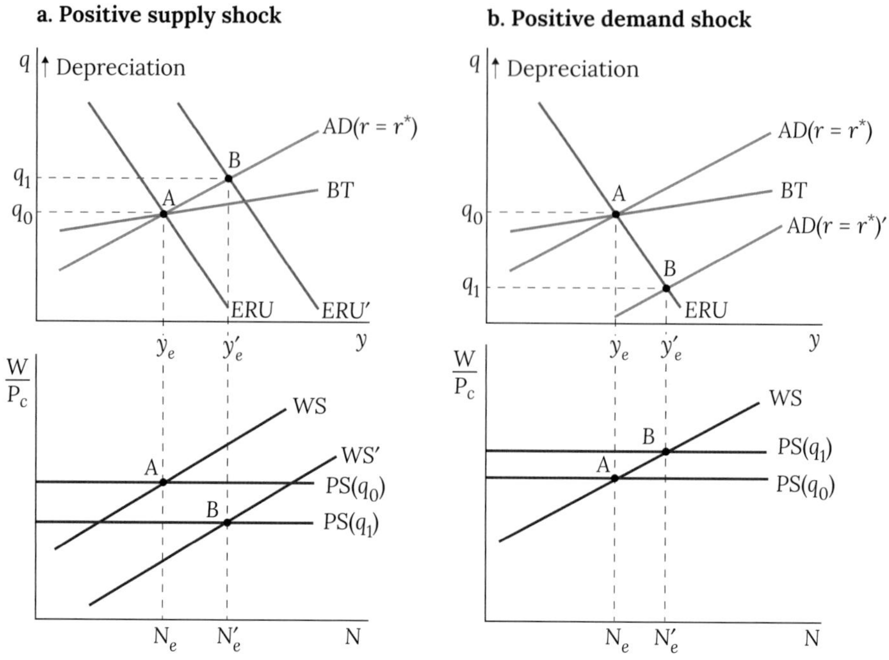

Figure 12.9 What determines the medium-run equilibrium? Visit www.oup.com/he/carlin-soskice to explore effect of supply and demand shocks on medium-run equilibrium with Animated Analytical Diagram 12.9.

curves, and look at the medium-run implications of the shocks for the real exchange rate, equilibrium unemployment, the trade balance and real wages.

A supply shock: A positive supply shock, such as a reduction in union bargaining power, shifts the WS curve downwards. This shifts the ERU curve to the right. There is a depreciated real exchange rate in the new medium-run equilibrium, as well as an increase in equilibrium output (see point B in Figure 12.9a). The economy can operate at a new medium-run equilibrium with higher output. On the demand side, this is because of the higher competitiveness associated with the weaker unions. The depreciated real exchange rate means that real wages measured in terms of the consumer price index are lower. At point B, the economy is above the BT curve, which means the economy has moved into trade surplus.

A demand shock: A positive demand shock, such as a fall in the savings rate because households are able to get access to mortgages more easily, shifts the AD curve to the right, which results in an appreciated exchange rate at the new equilibrium. In light of the downward-sloping ERU, it also leads to a reduction in the equilibrium rate of unemployment (see point B in Figure 12.9b). This is markedly different from the outcome seen in the closed economy and in the open economy in Chapter 9 with a vertical ERU curve, where demand shocks could not affect the equilibrium rate of unemployment. By reducing the real cost of imported consumption goods, the appreciation of the real exchange rate that accompanies this shock shifts the PS(q) curve upwards and results in a higher real wage for workers. The economy moves along the *WS* curve to the north-east. At point B, the economy is below the *BT* curve, which means the economy has moved into trade deficit.

The extension of the model to the open economy means that it is not only domestic shocks to supply and demand that can affect the home economy. Economic shocks such as changes in world demand (y^*) or change in home's share of world exports (σ) can arise from outside the home economy, which will affect the medium-run equilibrium in the home economy. Such shocks are referred to as *external trade* shocks.

A positive trade shock due to higher world demand (y^*) because of a boom in a region of the world which constitutes a significant proportion of world GDP or a rise in home's share of world demand (σ) shifts the *AD* and *BT* curves to the right. An example of an external trade shock would be if France's share of world trade, σ, rises because preferences in the rest of the world shift from beer to wine, benefiting French exports of wine. Another example is where there is a change in the non-price attributes of the products of one country. For example, suppose that at a given price, the quality of cars made in India suddenly increases. This represents a positive external trade shock for India and a negative shock for its foreign competitors in the auto industry.

We show the *AD-BT-ERU* diagram following a positive external trade shock in Figure 12.10:

An external trade shock: The *AD* curve shifts to the right because $A(\sigma, y^*)$ has increased and the *BT* curve shifts to the right because the term $B(\sigma, y^*)$ has increased. The new *AD* and *BT* curves are denoted by *AD′* and *BT′*. We know that medium-run equilibrium is

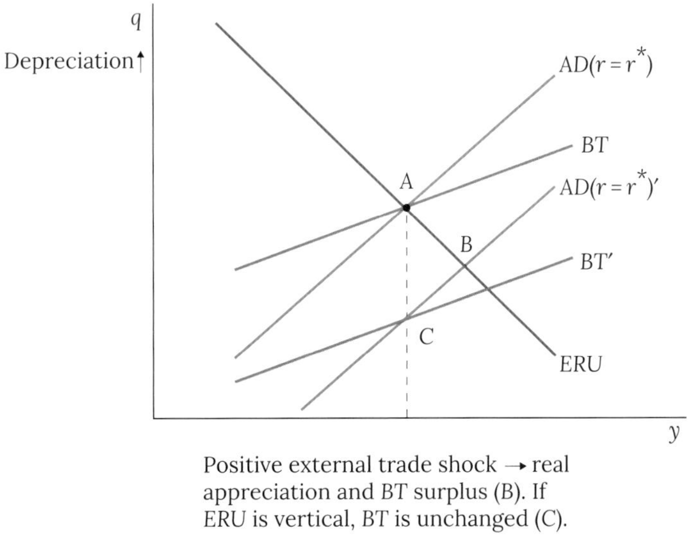
q
Depreciation
AD(r = r*)
BT
A
AD(r = r*)′
B
BT′
C
ERU
y
Positive external trade shock → real appreciation and BT surplus (B). If ERU is vertical, BT is unchanged (C).

Figure 12.10 How does an external trade shock affect medium-run equilibrium? Visit www.oup.com/he/carlin-soskice to explore external trade shocks with Animated Analytical Diagram 12.10.

	Shock			
	Rise in productivity	Fall in union bargaining power	Increase in autonomous consumption	Increase in world output
Equilibrium unemployment	↓	↓	↓	↓
Real exchange rate	depreciation	depreciation	appreciation	appreciation
Trade balance	↑	↑	↓	↑
Real wage (W/P_c)	↑	↓	↑	↑

Table 12.2 Supply and demand shocks: implications for medium-run equilibrium in the AD-BT-ERU model with a downward-sloping ERU curve.

Note: ↑ means the variable is higher in the new medium-run equilibrium, ↓ means it is lower. We assume a flat PS curve throughout. For the trade balance, ↑ represents an improvement in the trade balance.

at point B, where the new AD curve and the ERU curve intersect. At point B, there is an appreciated real exchange rate, higher output and a trade surplus. The economy is in trade surplus as it is above BT′. We can see that AD′ and BT′ intersect at point C, which is vertically below the initial intersection. This is because at point C, an appreciation of the real exchange rate from point A is such that it would cause net exports to fall by the exact amount by which the external trade shock increases them. Trade is therefore balanced at point C and output is unchanged.[19]

In Chapter 11, we analysed how the medium-run equilibrium in the model with a vertical ERU curve is affected by supply and demand shocks. We repeat that exercise here with the downward sloping ERU curve and include an external trade shock. Table 12.2 summarizes the implications for the economy of a variety of permanent shocks. It shows the change in unemployment, the real exchange rate, the trade balance, and real wages between the initial and the new constant inflation equilibria. The results hold for both flexible and fixed exchange rate regimes.

Table 12.2 shows that:

1. the key differences from the model with a vertical ERU curve are that the reduction in union bargaining power leads to a lower real wage since we are defining the real wage in terms of W/P_c and that an increase in autonomous consumption leads to both a higher real wage and a lower level of equilibrium unemployment
2. the introduction of the BT curve allows us to study how the economy reacts to an external trade shock and how different shocks are expected to affect the trade balance. The table shows that positive supply shocks are associated with a

[19] Interestingly, in the case of a vertical ERU (at C), a positive trade shock leaves the trade balance unchanged in the medium-run equilibrium. The reason is that, in this case, output in medium-run equilibrium is solely pinned down by the supply side.

real exchange rate depreciation and hence an improvement in the trade balance, whereas positive demand shocks are associated with an appreciation in the real exchange rate and a deterioration in the trade balance. An external trade shock leads to a real appreciation, but because the BT curve also shifts, the shock improves the trade balance.

Inflation in medium-run equilibrium: Flexible and fixed exchange rates

What determines the medium-run inflation rate? At any medium-run equilibrium—i.e. at the intersection of an AD curve with the ERU curve—the real exchange rate is constant. If Q is constant, i.e. $\frac{\Delta Q}{Q} = 0$, we can use the definition of $Q \equiv \frac{P^* e}{P}$ to write the expression:

$$\frac{\Delta Q}{Q} = \frac{\Delta P^*}{P^*} + \frac{\Delta e}{e} - \frac{\Delta P}{P}$$

$$\text{For } \frac{\Delta Q}{Q} = 0, \ \frac{\Delta P}{P} = \frac{\Delta P^*}{P^*} + \frac{\Delta e}{e}$$

$$\rightarrow \pi^{MRE} = \pi^* + \frac{\Delta e}{e},$$

which implies that home inflation is equal to world inflation plus the depreciation of home's nominal exchange rate.[20]

The intuition is that competitiveness remains constant as long as home and abroad's prices are rising at the same rate in a common currency (since the right-hand side of the equation converts the growth of world prices in foreign currency into their growth in domestic currency terms). If home inflation is 5% and world inflation 2%, home's competitiveness will remain constant if its nominal exchange rate depreciates at a rate of 3% per annum.

What determines the rate of home inflation? In the closed economy, it is the monetary policy regime that fixes the medium-run inflation rate. Specifically, in an inflation-targeting monetary policy regime, the central bank's inflation target sets medium-run inflation.

Likewise, in a small open economy with flexible exchange rates, the inflation rate in the medium run is set by the central bank's inflation target (assuming that the inflation-targeting regime is credible), i.e.

---

[20] In continuous time, we find an expression for the growth rate of Q by first taking logs, then differentiating with respect to time and using the fact that $d\log x/x = 1/x$:

$$\log Q = \log P^* + \log e - \log P$$

$$\frac{d\log Q}{dt} = \frac{d\log P^*}{dt} + \frac{d\log e}{dt} - \frac{d\log P}{dt}.$$

Use $d\log x/dx = 1/x$ to get

$$\frac{dQ/dt}{Q} = \frac{dP^*/dt}{P^*} + \frac{de/dt}{e} - \frac{dP/dt}{P}$$

$$= \pi^* + \frac{de/dt}{e} - \pi.$$

$$\pi^{MRE} = [\pi^T], \qquad \text{(medium-run inflation rate, flexible exchange rate regime)}$$

where *MRE* stands for medium-run equilibrium, and the square brackets are used to indicate an exogenous variable, in this case chosen by the policy maker.

But what does this imply for the nominal exchange rate? Since both home and world inflation are now determined exogenously, the real exchange rate will only be constant if any discrepancy between home and world inflation is offset by a constant rate of change of the nominal exchange rate:

$$\frac{\Delta e}{e} = [\pi^T] - [\pi^*]. \tag{12.7}$$

If home's inflation target is below world inflation, then the exchange rate must steadily appreciate to keep the real exchange rate constant. Conversely, if home inflation is above world inflation, there will be a constant depreciation of home's exchange rate to keep the real exchange rate constant. Note that if home's central bank *chooses* $\pi^T = \pi^*$ then in the medium-run equilibrium, the nominal exchange rate will be constant. This may be one reason that central banks in different countries have chosen very similar inflation targets.

How can we reconcile equation 12.7 with a fixed exchange rate regime, where the nominal exchange rate is not allowed to change? In this case, where $\frac{\Delta e}{e} = 0$, for the real exchange rate to be constant, home inflation must be equal to world inflation:

$$\pi^{MRE} = [\pi^*]. \qquad \text{(medium-run inflation rate, fixed exchange rate regime)}$$

In turn, 'world' inflation will be set by the inflation target of the central bank to which the home economy's exchange rate is pegged. By choosing a fixed exchange rate regime, home loses control over monetary policy. A consequence of this is that its medium-run inflation rate is determined by world inflation.

Establishing a credible low inflation monetary regime: Flexible and fixed exchange rates

The Eurozone provides a real-world example of a fixed exchange rate regime. In 1999, the euro was introduced, irrevocably fixing the exchange rates between 11 European countries. The medium-run rate of inflation in these economies was pinned down by the inflation target of the European Central Bank, the Eurozone-wide institution to which each national government ceded control of monetary policy. Figure 12.11 shows how the inflation rates of four Eurozone economies (Italy, Spain, Germany, and Greece) fell to low and stable levels after the introduction of the single currency. The countries that benefited most from adopting the euro (in terms of reduced inflation) were the countries that had experienced difficulties establishing credible low inflation monetary regimes of their own, such as Italy and Spain.

The establishment of the single currency was signalled as early as 1992, via the provisions of the Maastricht Treaty. One explanation for the pattern observed in Figure 12.11 is that the *expectation* of the establishment of a credible low inflation monetary policy regime helped to anchor inflation expectations in the years before the euro was introduced (in 1999).

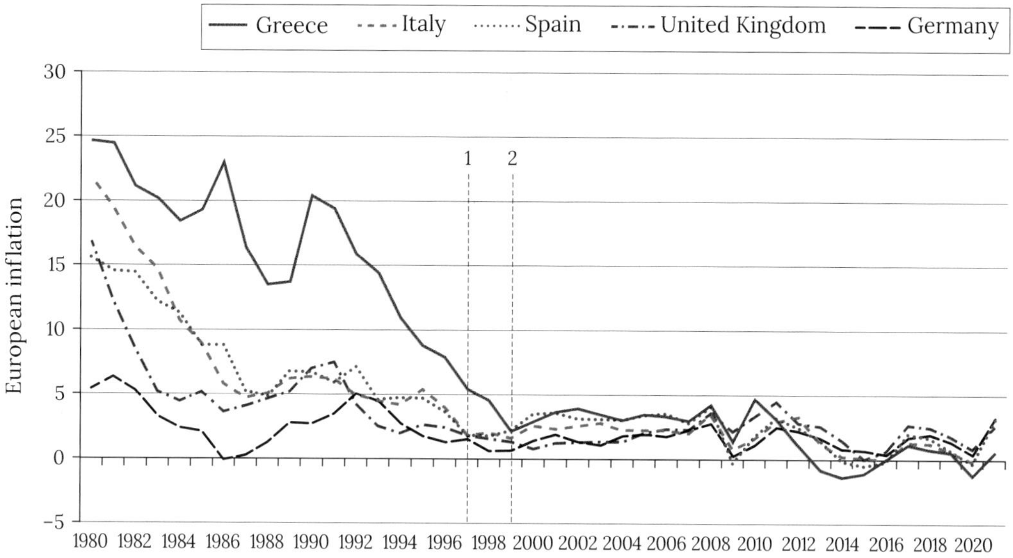

1. UK government establishes the Monetary Policy Committee to independently set interest rates.
2. Introduction of the euro, which fixed the exchange rates of 11 countries.

Figure 12.11 Inflation rates for selected European economies: 1980–2021.

Source: IMF World Economic Outlook, April 2022.

The Eurozone example shows that giving up control of monetary policy to a credible supra-national institution can help to create a low inflation environment. In this way, it can be viewed as a policy alternative to granting the national central bank independence (in a flexible exchange rate regime). Figure 12.11 shows the comparison between the countries acquiring low inflation credibility via membership of the Eurozone with the UK.

In 1992, the UK government chose to hand over responsibility for monetary policy to the Bank of England; in May 1997, it was made independent. The Bank's Monetary Policy Committee (MPC) is independent of political interference and meets on a monthly basis to set interest rates. The inflation target (i.e. π^T) of the MPC is 2% and we can see from Figure 12.11 that inflation was much lower and less volatile in the UK following the transfer of responsibility.[21]

Medium- and long-run equilibrium

A key characteristic of the medium-run equilibrium is that inflation is constant. However, we have also seen that the economy may be in trade imbalance at the medium-run equilibrium. This was the case in Spain and the UK in the run-up to the

[21] The MPC has targeted the year-on-year change in the Consumer Price Index (CPI) since 2003. Prior to that, the MPC targeted the year-on-year change in the Retail Price Index excluding mortgage interest payments (RPI-X) and due to small differences in the baskets of goods used to calculate the two indices, the target for RPI-X was slightly higher, at 2.5%.

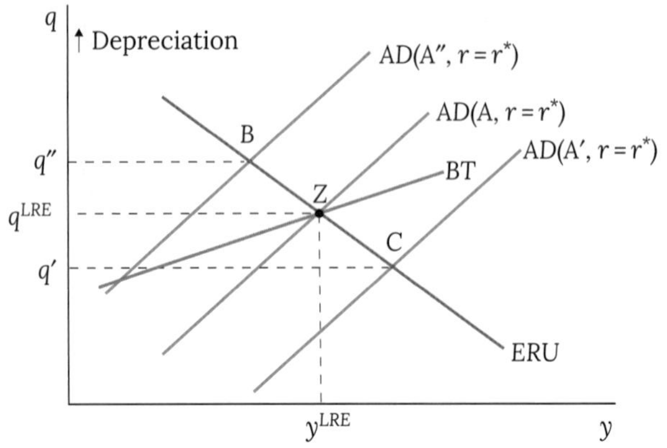

Figure 12.12 Medium- and long-run equilibria in the open economy.

financial crisis (see Table 12.1). We can define the long-run equilibrium as the situation in which the economy is not only at constant inflation, but also at trade balance. The difference between medium- and long-run equilibria in the basic model is illustrated by the example in Figure 12.12. Let us compare the characteristics of points Z, B, and C.

1. Medium-run equilibria with constant inflation are at points such as Z, B and C, where the economy is on the ERU curve, but not necessarily in trade balance. There is a trade surplus at point B, because it is above the BT curve, and a trade deficit at point C. The economy can remain at points like B and C with stable inflation. However, in the longer run, pressures may emerge as a consequence of the external position that tend to push the economy toward point Z.
2. Long-run equilibrium is at point Z—on the AD, ERU, and BT curves—where supply-side equilibrium coincides with the balanced trade level of output. This is likely to be a sustainable long-run position for the economy.

In the long run, there may be pressures that tend to ensure that there is current account balance in the economy. We explore the sustainability of current account imbalances in Chapter 13.

12.3 APPLICATIONS

12.3.1 The UK economy before the financial crisis

This section provides a case study of the British economy between the mid-1990s and the onset of the global financial crisis in 2008. It highlights how the model can provide insights into the factors driving macroeconomic performance when it is used alongside real-world macroeconomic data.

The second half of the 1990s through to the early years of the new century saw the most successful period of macroeconomic performance for the UK in the post-war era.

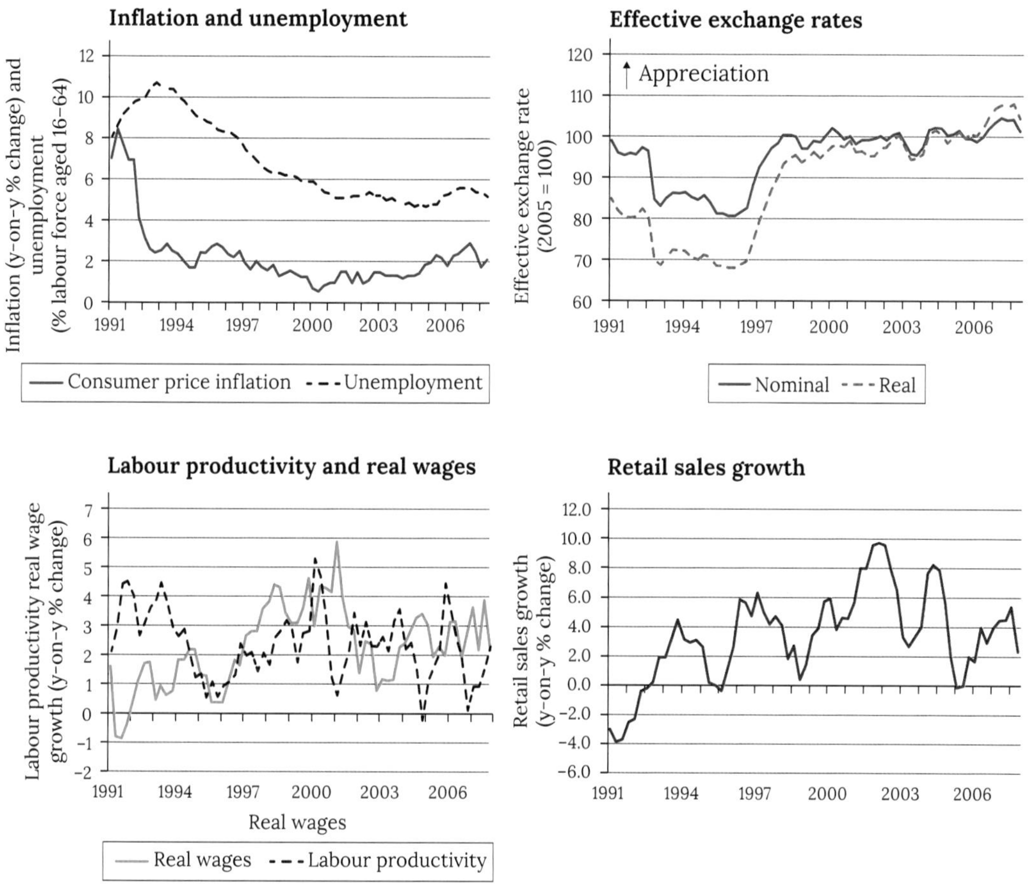

Figure 12.13 UK macroeconomic indicators: 1990–2007.

Source: UK Office for National Statistics; Bank of England; IMF IFS (data accessed January 2012).

Figure 12.13 illustrates the evolution of the UK economy between 1990 Q1 and 2007 Q4. The figures show the following trends:

1. Unemployment declined dramatically over the period. Inflation fell in the early part of the period and stayed low and stable from then on.
2. There was a large nominal and real appreciation in the mid to late-1990s.
3. Real wage growth and productivity moved in a similar manner, although real wage growth exceeded productivity growth for most of the period.
4. Retail sales experienced a strong upwards trend between the early 1990s and the mid-2000s.

The most striking feature of the UK's economic expansion over this period was that it was able to achieve such a marked decline in unemployment combined with low and stable inflation.

Supply-side hypothesis

The model is used in Figure 12.14a to illustrate that supply-side reform in the context of a sensible framework for macroeconomic policy could account for the sustained fall in unemployment without rising inflation from 1997. In 1996–97, the British economy was at a point like A, with balanced trade and inflation at about the level of its trading partners. Let us consider a first scenario in which we assume that the ERU curve shifted to the right due to the lagged effects of supply-side reforms. The economy would be predicted to experience falling unemployment and inflation below its competitors.

Table 12.3 shows that during the 1980s and 1990s the UK saw a dramatic reduction in labour and product market rigidities such as the reduction in the power of unions and the progressive deregulation of product markets (to encourage competition). Each of these supply-side improvements is expected to have affected the ERU curve through their effect on the underlying WS-PS curves (see Chapters 2 and 15 for details of how

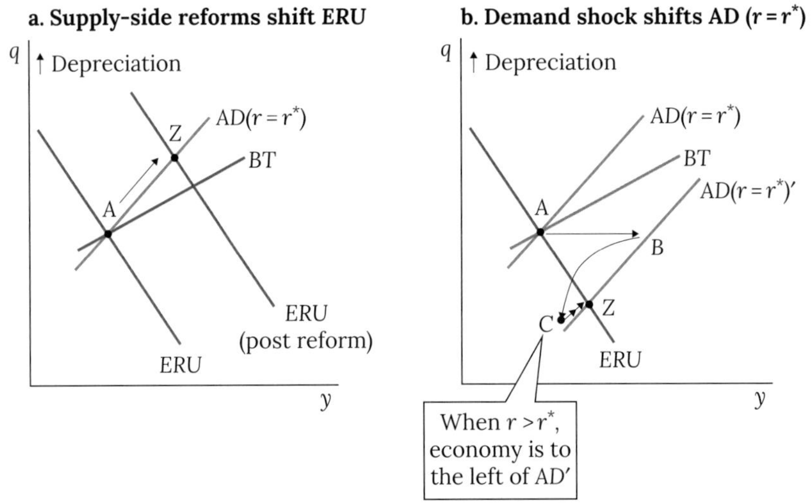

Figure 12.14 Two hypotheses for the UK's shift to lower unemployment without inflationary problems. Visit www.oup.com/he/carlin-soskice to explore two hypotheses for the UK's shift to lower unemployment without inflationary problems with Animated Analytical Diagram 12.14.

	1983	1988	1993	1998	2003
Average replacement rate	21.7	18.1	18.5	17.5	16.5
Tax wedge	26.6	25.1	23.8	24.9	17.4
Product market regulation	4.5	3.8	2.2	1.4	1.0
Union density	48.0	42.6	36.1	31.5	30.5

Table 12.3 UK labour market institutions and government policy: 1983–2003.

Source: OECD Employment Outlook, June 2006.

changes in each variable would be expected to affect equilibrium unemployment). This hypothesis suggests that there are long lags associated with supply-side reforms—reforms that started in earnest in the 1980s are thought to have contributed to the good economic performance of the UK economy in the late 1990s and early 2000s.

In these circumstances, the central bank would accommodate the supply-side improvement and adjust their estimate of the equilibrium rate of unemployment. In the new medium-run equilibrium, the real exchange rate would be depreciated and there would be a trade surplus.

However, it is obvious from the data in the top right-hand panel of Figure 12.13 that there is a problem with this as the sole explanation of British performance because of the behaviour of the real exchange rate. From 1997, there was a large real appreciation, driven by an appreciation of the nominal exchange rate. Yet according to the pure supply-side reform story, the real exchange rate should depreciate.

Demand shocks hypothesis

Let us now consider a different hypothesis to account for falling unemployment and modest inflation. For the sake of this example, suppose that the supply side remains unchanged but there is a boom in aggregate demand (e.g. a consumption boom). In the new medium-run equilibrium at point Z in Figure 12.14b, the real exchange rate is appreciated and there is an external deficit.

As noted above, there was a sharp nominal (and real) appreciation of sterling in 1997. This is consistent with the prediction of the macro model set out in Chapter 11. In a flexible exchange rate regime, a consumption boom would boost output and inflation (A $\longrightarrow$ B in Figure 12.14b). Using the logic of the model, the central bank would respond by raising the interest rate and the exchange rate would appreciate (B $\longrightarrow$ C in Figure 12.14b). The economy shifts to lower output, because of the combined effect of the increase in interest rates and the appreciation.[22] Once inflation falls, the central bank begins to lower the interest rate and the economy adjusts to the new medium-run equilibrium at Z. The economy ends up with lower unemployment, a real exchange rate appreciation and a weaker external balance.[23]

As the diagrams in Figure 12.14 show, both scenarios are consistent with the combination of lower unemployment and stable inflation in the new medium-run equilibrium at Z. Yet they imply very different outcomes for the real exchange rate, real wages and the trade balance. In the first scenario, the real exchange rate depreciates, real wages decline and the trade balance improves. In the second one, real wages rise, the real exchange rate appreciates, and the trade balance deteriorates.

---

[22] Since the *AD* curve is defined for $r = r^*$, if $r > r^*$, then interest sensitive spending is dampened and the economy is to the left of the AD' curve (at C).

[23] To use the dynamic model in the case of a downward-sloping *ERU*, it is necessary to locate the new y_e at the output level of point Z. The new *MR* and *RX* curves would go through this level of output. Adjustment would then take place in the usual fashion. We do not discuss adjustment in the RX-PC-MR diagrams with a downward-sloping *ERU* in order to make the analysis as simple and easily digestible as possible. This is left as an exercise for the reader.

Do either of these stylized pictures fit the UK's experience? As we have seen, the first corresponds poorly with the behaviour of the nominal and real exchange rate. The second entails a real appreciation but ignores the supply-side reforms documented in Table 12.3.

There is some evidence that consumer behaviour was an important part of the post-1997 growth phase. The bottom right-hand panel of Figure 12.13 shows how robust predominantly non-food retail sales growth was over this period, being particularly strong in the first half of the 2000s. A major trigger for the consumption boom was financial liberalization, which had the effect of lifting the liquidity constraints on some households—whereas previously they had been unable to borrow and smooth their consumption, they were now able to do so. This is highlighted by the household savings ratio in the UK, which fell from 11.7 in 1992 to just 2.7 in 2007.[24] Another contributing factor to the reduced savings rate was the perceived higher levels of household wealth that resulted from the stock market and real estate booms that took place over the period, and the ability of credit-constrained households to increase consumption by withdrawing equity from their houses (as discussed in Chapters 8 and 9).

Other factors that are likely to have contributed to the consumption boom were the windfall gains to consumers due to changes in the financial sector (e.g. demutualization of building societies) and the high levels of real wage growth seen during the late 1990s and early 2000s. In this period, real wage growth outstripped productivity gains in the economy, as shown by the bottom left-hand panel of Figure 12.13. This matches the period during which sterling appreciated strongly, thus making imports cheaper to domestic consumers and raising their real wages.

As the consumption boom slackened, public expenditure took over in maintaining the growth of demand. The Labour government elected in 1997 was able to consolidate the public finances during a period of robust private sector growth in its first term, which gave it the scope to introduce major public expenditure programmes in its second term from 2001.

In 1997, the Bank of England was made independent and began using a Taylor-type rule to adjust the interest rate. It raised the interest rate in 1997, but it is unlikely that this can account fully for the appreciation of the nominal exchange rate. One further change to the UK economy that is relevant to nominal exchange rate behaviour in the period from the mid-1990s is the emergence of export strength in knowledge-based services such as banking, finance, consulting, and other business services.[25] This helps to explain the limited deterioration of the current account balance in the face of the large real appreciation. Such a shift in export capability (a rise in net exports at a given real exchange rate) is represented in the model by a rightward shift of the BT curve, and may help to explain the nominal appreciation.

---

[24] Source: OECD Economic Outlook, June 2012. Variable used is household and non-profit institutions serving households gross saving ratio.

[25] For an interesting analysis of the changing structure of the UK balance of payments (in an international perspective), see Rowthorn and Coutts (2004).

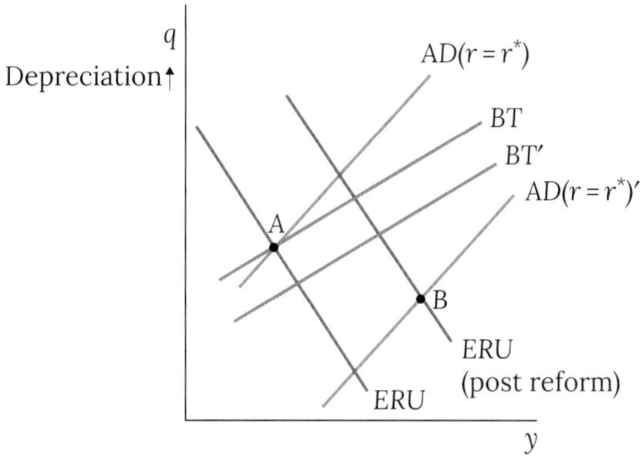

Figure 12.15 UK from 1997—synthetic hypothesis.

By combining the aggregate demand, supply side and *BT* shifts as in Figure 12.15, we have the elements for a systematic consideration of the driving forces behind the evolution of the British economy from the mid-1990s to the eve of the financial crisis.

12.4 CONCLUSIONS

This chapter has extended our understanding of the open economy by providing more detail on how the demand and supply sides operate when economies are open to international trade. On the demand side, we have shown that the open economy *IS* curve is steeper than in the closed economy, due to the diversion of some aggregate expenditure away from home production towards imports in the open economy. We have also shown that exchange rate depreciation improves the trade balance, as long as the Marshall–Lerner condition holds. This assumption forms the backbone of the open economy *IS* and *AD* curves. In addition, we have introduced the concept of the trade balance, which can be modelled by the *BT* curve in the output–real exchange rate diagram.

On the supply side, we have altered a key assumption from Chapter 11, choosing to model wage setting based on workers' real consumption wages (which includes the price of imports). If workers' utility is defined in terms of their real consumption wage, the constant inflation equilibrium will be found by the intersection of the *WS* and the *PS* curves, where the real consumption wage is on the vertical axis. In this modified model of the labour market, changes in the real exchange rate (i.e. the cost of imports), which affect the real wages that workers receive after firms have set their prices, shift the *PS* curve. For example, if the real cost of imports goes up (i.e. a real depreciation), the real consumption wage consistent with firms' pricing behaviour for a given nominal wage, goes down: this shifts the *PS* curve down.

This has an important effect on the medium-run model (i.e. the *AD-BT-ERU* model): the *ERU* curve becomes downward sloping, which means that there is a range of levels of output (and unemployment) consistent with constant inflation. This is in contrast to the medium-run model in Chapter 11, where there was a unique equilibrium rate of unemployment (exactly as in the closed economy) modelled by a vertical *ERU* curve.

The more detailed analysis of the demand and supply sides introduced in this chapter helps to illuminate interesting puzzles in the global economy, such as:

1. Why can real exchange rate depreciation be considered a 'double-edged sword'? There are two sides to a real exchange rate depreciation; the *volume effect* and the *relative price effect*. The volume effect occurs because a depreciation results in an improvement in home's competitiveness, which in turn affects the demand for exports and imports. Home's exports appear cheaper to foreigners after a depreciation, so export demand will increase. In addition, home consumers substitute away from imports and towards home-produced goods as imports rise in price. The volume effect therefore unambiguously improves the trade balance. In contrast, the relative price effect worsens the trade balance, as any volume of imports that home consumers purchase is more expensive following the depreciation. Which effect is bigger? As long as the Marshall–Lerner condition holds, and we assume it always does, then a depreciation of real exchange rate will result in an improvement in the trade balance. Depreciation is a double-edged sword because, although it improves the trade balance and helps the tradables sector, it reduces living standards by raising the real cost of imports.
2. How can we determine whether supply or demand shocks accounted for the good economic performance during the Great Moderation? Both supply and demand shocks can change constant inflation output in the AD-BT-ERU model with a downward-sloping *ERU* curve. Positive supply and demand shocks are both associated with reduced unemployment and stable inflation—but other characteristics of the medium-run equilibria are different. A positive demand shock is associated with an appreciation of the real exchange rate and a deterioration of the external balance, whereas a positive supply shock is associated with the opposite. In the case study of the UK economy in Section 12.3, we ruled out the robust economic performance being a result solely of supply-side policies, because the real exchange rate appreciated and the external balance deteriorated. The macroeconomic data instead seemed to suggest a combination of both supply and demand shocks.
3. How can current account imbalances persist in the medium run? We introduced the *BT* curve in this chapter. It represents the combinations of the real exchange rate and output at which the economy is in trade balance. It is flatter than the *AD* curve: this reflects both the Marshall–Lerner condition and the fact that the multiplier is less than the reciprocal of the marginal propensity to import. The condition for a medium-run equilibrium is that the economy is on both the *AD* and *ERU* curves (i.e. at their intersection). At a medium-run equilibrium the economy does not have to be on the *BT* curve: it can be in trade surplus, trade balance or trade deficit. In the long run however, there are both economic and political forces that may drive the economy back towards external balance. These forces will be explored in Chapter 13.

Chapter 13 applies the tools learnt so far to studying the global economy further, using the open economy macro model to provide a framework for analysing global imbalances, oil shocks and policy interdependence.

12.5 APPENDIX

12.5.1 The Marshall–Lerner condition: A proof

Assume that trade is initially balanced, and that the prices of exports and imports do not change in response to the volume sold. Since $BT = \sigma(Q)y^* - Qm(Q)y$, the change in the trade balance in response to a change in competitiveness is

$$\frac{\partial BT}{\partial Q} = \sigma'(Q)y^* - Qm'(Q)y - my$$
$$= \sigma y^* \frac{\sigma'(Q)}{\sigma} - Qm'(Q)y - my.$$

But by assumption, $BT = 0$, i.e. $\sigma(Q)y^* = Qm(Q)y$, and therefore

$$\frac{\partial BT}{\partial Q} = Qmy\frac{\sigma'(Q)}{\sigma} - Qm'(Q)y - my.$$

Dividing through by my,

$$\frac{1}{my} \cdot \frac{\partial BT}{\partial Q} = \frac{Q\sigma'(Q)}{\sigma} - \frac{Qm'(Q)}{m} - 1.$$

Since $my > 0$, $\frac{\partial BT}{\partial Q} > 0$ if and only if

$$\frac{Q\sigma'(Q)}{\sigma} - \frac{Qm'(Q)}{m} > 1.$$

Now, $\frac{Q\sigma'(Q)}{\sigma}$ is *minus* the elasticity of demand for exports, since Q is the inverse of the real price of exports. Similarly, $\frac{Qm'(Q)}{m}$ is the elasticity of demand for imports. The Marshall–Lerner condition for an improvement in the balance of trade to follow from a rise in competitiveness is that the sum of the absolute values of the demand elasticities is greater than one; i.e.

$$\left|\frac{Q\sigma'(Q)}{\sigma}\right| + \left|\frac{Qm'(Q)}{m}\right| > 1.$$

12.5.2 The *AD* and *BT* curves

A. Why is the *BT* flatter than the *AD*? A mathematical derivation

Recall that exports and imports are defined by the following functions:

$$X = \sigma(Q)y^* \tag{12.8}$$
$$M = Qm(Q)y \tag{12.9}$$

Now suppose the economy experiences a real depreciation (i.e. $\uparrow Q$). According to the Marshall-Lerner condition, this causes net exports to increase by an amount $\Delta(X - M) > 0$. As in Section 12.2.3, we will again assume $\Delta(X - M) = \Delta X$ to simplify the derivation.

Following the exogenous higher foreign demand, it is possible to compare the increase in output necessary to restore the GME condition (on the AD curve) with that necessary to ensure trade is re-balanced (on the BT curve).

Focusing first on the AD curve, the increase in net exports following the real depreciation causes aggregate demand to increase via higher foreign demand. By the GME condition, output needs to increase so that the additional foreign demand is satisfied. Mathematically, we first recall that, assuming no income taxes:

$$\begin{aligned} y^{ADcurve} &= c_0 + c_1 y^{ADcurve} + I + G + (X - Qm(Q)y^{ADcurve}) \\ &= \frac{1}{(1-c_1) + Qm(Q)}(c_0 + I + G + X). \end{aligned}$$

Therefore, the increase in output necessary to ensure the GME condition is satisfied is computed as:

$$\Delta y^{ADcurve} = k\Delta X. \quad (12.10)$$

since output increases by the multiplier times the exogenous increase in foreign aggregate demand to keep $y = y^D$. Recall that the multiplier $k = \frac{1}{(1-c_1)+m}$, where $m = Qm(Q)$.

Moving on to the BT curve, we assume the economy was initially at trade balance (i.e. $X - M = 0$). The increase in net exports implies that imports must increase by the same amount in order for trade balance to be restored. $\Delta M = \Delta X$ is then required for the economy to be back on the BT curve (recall that we assumed $\Delta(X - M) = \Delta X$). From equation 12.9, this implies that:

$$\Delta M = Qm(Q)\Delta y^{BTcurve} = \Delta X.$$

$$\rightarrow \Delta y^{BTcurve} = \frac{\Delta X}{Qm(Q)}. \quad (12.11)$$

Replacing the change in exports with the relationship we derived in equation 12.10 gives:

$$\begin{aligned} \Delta y^{BTcurve} &= \frac{\Delta X}{Qm(Q)} = \frac{\Delta y^{ADcurve}}{kQm(Q)} \\ &= \frac{[(1-c_1) + Qm(Q)]\,\Delta y^{ADcurve}}{Qm(Q)} \end{aligned} \quad (12.12)$$

It is clear from equation 12.12 that the change in output on the AD curve is larger than that on the BT curve. This is because households not only import a fraction of their income (captured by m), but also save some fraction of it, namely $(1 - c_1)$. The multiplier, k, is in fact larger than the reciprocal of the marginal propensity to import.

This implies $\Delta y^{BTcurve} > \Delta y^{ADcurve}$, which proves the BT curve is flatter than the AD curve. Figure 12.7 illustrates the point, where Δq in the diagram causes the exogenous increase in net exports.

B. The *AD* and *BT* curves following an external trade shock

In this section[26] we provide a mathematical derivation to illustrate why the BT and AD curves shift vertically by the exact same amount in response to an external trade shock as the one represented in Figure 12.10. To do so, we first recall that:

[26] This appendix was written by Alessandro Guarnieri.

$$\text{On the AD curve}: y = C + I(r) + G + (X - M). \tag{12.13}$$

$$\text{On the BT curve}: X - M = 0. \tag{12.14}$$

Point A in Figure 12.10 lies on the BT curve, which implies $X^A = M^A$. Substituting in equation 12.13 yields:

$$y^A = C^A + I(r)^A + G^A + (X^A - M^A) = C^A + I(r)^A + G^A \tag{12.15}$$

Suppose that the positive external trade shock increases exports such that, at point C, we have:

X^C (exports at point C after the shock) = X^A (exports at point A before the shock) + ΔX,

where ΔX is positive.[27]

Let $\Delta q = q^A - q^C$ be the real appreciation necessary to re-balance trade; we can think of it as the real appreciation necessary to boost imports by an amount $\Delta M = \Delta X$. We then have:

$$X^C - M^C = X^A + \Delta X - M^A - \Delta M = X^A - M^A = 0. \tag{12.16}$$

If we now compute the level of output after such RER appreciation, and hence at point C, we get:

$$\begin{aligned} y^C &= C^A + I(r)^A + G^A + (X^C - M^C) \\ &= C^A + I(r)^A + G^A + (X^A + \Delta X - M^A - \Delta M) \\ &= C^A + I(r)^A + G^A + (X^A - M^A) \\ &= C^A + I(r)^A + G^A \\ &= y^A. \end{aligned}$$

where y^A is the same output level computed in equation 12.15. Therefore, Δq is necessary to restore net exports equal to zero, and thus keep output unchanged. This is the reason why point C in Figure 12.10 is vertically below point A.

---

[27] Note that this is not necessarily the case. In principle, the real appreciation from A to C could depress exports to an extent that outweighs the effect of the positive external trade shock. In this case, the appreciation is such that the terms of trade effect on imports will be higher than the volume effect, leading to decreased imports at point C compared to point A.

QUESTIONS AND PROBLEMS FOR CHAPTER 12

CHECKLIST QUESTIONS

1. Explain the difference between the closed and open economy IS curves. Which curve is steeper? Explain, both in words and with reference to equations, why this must be the case.

2. Explain the sense in which an improvement in price competitiveness might be considered a 'good thing' for the economy. Might it also be considered a 'bad thing'? Is an improvement in the terms of trade the same as an improvement in price competitiveness?

3. Construct a numerical example to show how the Marshall–Lerner condition works. Why might its predictions not hold in the very short run?

4. How does the price-setting real wage equation differ in the case where you assume (a) a vertical ERU and (b) the downward-sloping ERU curve? Show how the price-setting real wage is derived in case (b).

5. Are real wages higher, lower or unchanged in the new medium-run equilibrium following a cut in unemployment benefits? Explain your answer.

6. Compare an economy with a vertical ERU curve with an otherwise identical economy with a downward-sloping ERU curve. Briefly explain how these economies differ. Consider a government facing an upcoming election. Does a downward-sloping ERU curve affect the policy maker's incentive to be fiscally disciplined ahead of an election?

7. Assume a small open economy with a downward-sloping ERU. There is a permanent rise in productivity. Explain why in spite of a depreciated real exchange rate at the new MRE, the real consumption wage is higher.

8. Assume the home economy is a small open economy. It initially starts in trade balance with output at equilibrium. There is a sudden shift in preferences away from the home country's exports and towards the exports of their competitors (i.e. a reduction of σ in the home economy). Are the following statements about the new medium-run equilibrium true or false? Justify your answers and use AD-BT-ERU diagrams where appropriate.

   a. This shock will increase the level of output in the home economy if you assume a downward-sloping ERU curve.

   b. This shock will have no effect on world output.

   c. This will lead to an improvement in the trade balance in the home economy.

9. Explain in words with the help of a diagram (with a $q-y$ panel) why the BT curve is flatter than the AD curve. Show the result using equations.

10. What is the inflation rate in medium-run equilibrium in a fixed exchange rate economy? How will deviations in inflation from this rate affect the country's competitiveness?

11. A small open economy with flexible exchange rates is having trouble controlling inflation. What options does it have for establishing a credible low inflation monetary regime? Are there any downsides to these options?

12. Explain carefully in words each of the following identities highlighting the differences between them. Give an example for each identity to illustrate its distinct meaning.

a. $CA \equiv X - M + INT$.

b. $\Delta NIIP \equiv CA + \text{Capital gains}$.

13. The value of the UK pound sterling depreciated sharply after the Brexit referendum, with a 'drop' of 12% in just two weeks' time.[28] Despite the sharp nominal depreciation, export prices (in sterling) for sterling-invoiced transactions remained broadly unchanged in the four weeks following the referendum, and increased only marginally from the fifth week. Using the material from this chapter, is this behaviour more consistent with the *home-cost pricing* hypothesis (P1) or the *world pricing* hypothesis (P2)? Do you expect something different for those firms invoicing their exports in US dollars?

PROBLEMS

1. Use the website of *The Economist* magazine and search for the latest version of the 'Big Mac Index'. Answer the following questions:

a. What does the index show and how does it relate to the concept of purchasing power parity?

b. Describe some interesting cross-country comparisons in the data.

c. What does the index tell us about the relative size of the Chinese and US economies?

2. Use the content of this chapter and Chapter 11 to answer the following questions:

a. How would you expect an inflation-targeting central bank to respond to a fall in world trade? Explain the central bank's reasoning.

b. Does the exchange rate overshoot as a consequence of the central bank's actions? Justify your answer.

3. This question uses content from both this chapter and Chapter 11. Read the following excerpt from 'Economic luck that cannot last':[29] 'The governor [of the Bank of England, Mervyn King] emphasizes four underlying causes of the improvement in UK performance: a monetary framework that evolved from inflation-targeting, in 1992, to the Bank's operational independence, in 1997; fiscal consolidation; 20 years of supply-side reforms; and a series

---

[28] See Corsetti et al. (2022).

[29] This excerpt is taken from Martin Wolf's article in the *Financial Times* on October 30th 2003 entitled 'Economic luck that cannot last'. Note that the article was written in 2003 (i.e. before the global financial crisis).

of shocks that averaged out over time, rather than cumulated in either an upward or downward spiral. Yet, as Mr King notes, one beneficent shock did cumulate: to the terms of trade (the ratio of export to import prices), which improved by about 10% after 1996. This generated a substantial increase in real take-home pay without adding to employers' costs.'

How can we use the open economy models to explain the evolution of the UK economy over this period? In answering the question, you are advised to take the following steps:

a. Link supply-side reforms to economic performance using the AD-BT-ERU model.

b. Use the 3-equation model to explain how an inflation-targeting central bank can respond to a shock and return the economy to target inflation.

c. Use the AD-BT-ERU model to explain how a demand shock could have 'beneficent' or good effects on economic performance and relate this to the UK.

d. Identify the reasons why this 'good luck' cannot last (as in the headline of the article).

4. Pick a large Eurozone economy (e.g. France, Spain, Germany or Italy). Perform a short case study on the performance of your chosen economy between the mid-90s and the mid-2000s by following these steps:

a. Use Eurostat to collect data on key macroeconomic indicators over the period (similar to that shown for the UK in Figure 12.13)

b. Use OECD.Stat to collect supply-side data over the period (similar to that shown for the UK in Table 12.3)

c. What were the major macroeconomic developments in your chosen country over the period?

d. Can the evolution of your chosen economy over this period be explained using the AD-BT-ERU framework (similar to that shown for the UK in Figure 12.15)? Concisely summarize any problems you had in doing this.

5. Figure 12.4 plots the UK nominal and real effective exchange rates using the producer price index (PPI) for the latter. For this exercise you are asked to recreate the same figure using the relative unit labour cost (RULC) definition of the real exchange rate, as well as the relative price definition, but based on the consumer price index (CPI) rather than domestic inflation (PPI). For the nominal exchange rate data, go to the Bank of England Database; select 'Interest & exchange rates data', and then '£ Sterling (Jan 2005 = 100)–Month average–XUMABK67–Monthly' from the 'Exchange rate indices' tab. For the real exchange rate data, go to the IMF International Financial Statistics. Under the 'data' menu, select 'International Finance Statistics'; select 'Query', and then choose the UK and the relevant years, with monthly data. For indicators, first select 'Exchange Rates, Real Effective Exchange Rate based on Consumer Price Index, Index', and then

'Exchange Rates, Real Effective Exchange Rate based on Unit Labour Cost, Index'. You will also need to set January of 2005 = 100 before plotting these together with the BoE nominal data (this is done by dividing each value by the Jan-2005 value and then multiplying by 100).

a. Comment on how well each real exchange rate measure tracks the trend of the nominal exchange rate, and compare this with Figure 12.4.

b. Focus on the behaviour of RULC after the 2008 financial crisis. What economic developments in the UK during this period may explain this trend in cost-competitiveness? What are the implications for the profit margins of UK firms?

c. Do the factors you mentioned in point (b) also seem to significantly affect the two relative price definitions of the real exchange rate? If not, why?

INTERESTED IN EXPLORING THESE TOPICS FURTHER?

Visit www.oup.com/he/carlin-soskice to consolidate and extend your learning with the multiple-choice questions and Animated Analytical Diagrams accompanying this chapter.

CHAPTER

13

OPEN ECONOMY EXTENSIONS I

OIL SHOCKS, IMBALANCES, AND INTERDEPENDENCE

13.1 OVERVIEW

In this chapter, we extend the open economy model in a way that helps us to discuss some interesting puzzles. One set of puzzles relates to how economies were operating in the fifteen years that preceded the global financial crisis. This was the era of the Great Moderation. High and volatile inflation appeared to have been eliminated from the high-income economies and there were dramatic reductions in unemployment in many European economies, where it had remained stubbornly high in the 1980s. Whereas the oil price shocks of the 1970s had caused major economic disruption, oil shocks in the 2000s were absorbed relatively easily.

Policy makers and some academic observers were confident that a decade of labour market reforms and a better policy-making environment, exemplified by the kind of inflation-targeting regime discussed in Chapters 3 and 11, had played a part in producing improved performance. Yet, the unfolding of the global financial crisis and the Eurozone sovereign debt crisis from 2008 revealed that beneath the surface of the Great Moderation, imbalances were building and with them, the pre-conditions for crisis. More recently, the consequences for supply chains of the Covid-19 pandemic and of the Ukraine war for global energy prices brought concerns about stagflation into the debate again.

In Chapters 8 and 9, we focused on the build-up of a leverage cycle in a number of high-income economies. In this chapter, we introduce into the macroeconomic framework the tools that are useful in understanding the international dimensions of these crises. Another set of puzzles relate to macroeconomic challenges arising from climate and other environmental shocks, that have international dimensions.

As a first step, we show how shocks to commodity prices, such as oil prices, can be analysed in the *AD-BT-ERU* model. The analysis is motivated by the severe disturbance to the global economy caused by the oil shocks of the 1970s. The two oil shocks in 1973 and 1979 were followed by years of low growth, high inflation and rising unemployment—so-called 'stagflation'. It is striking that when the oil price increased sharply again in the 2000s, the macroeconomic effects were very different. In spite of near-record oil prices (in real terms), inflation remained subdued and unemployment in many countries was at its lowest level for several decades. This raises the question as to why the outcome was different. We shall see that the extended model can help provide insight into this, as well as into the shocks accompanying the climate crisis and the war in Ukraine.

The second extension to the open economy model in this chapter centres on imbalances and the interdependence of countries. Some countries run current account surpluses; others current account deficits. Are these international payments patterns problematic or do they simply reflect benign differences among countries, for example, in investment opportunities or natural resource endowments?

Some observers argue that the very large build-up of global current account imbalances in the years before the financial crisis played a causal role in the crisis. But before tackling that issue, we need to extend the *AD-BT-ERU* and 3-equation models to the two-bloc case. The simplest way of thinking about the interaction between economies is to assume the world is made up of just two large blocs of economies. We assume that in each bloc there is an inflation-targeting central bank. Using the extended model, we can explain how it was possible for inflation-targeting central banks in the two blocs to successfully keep inflation close to target, and yet for there to be persistently rising external imbalances.

13.1.1 How does a commodity price rise affect the macroeconomy?

As far as an oil-importing country is concerned, we shall see that an oil shock is a combination of two different shocks: it is a negative external trade shock (which is also a negative aggregate demand shock) and a negative supply shock. However, in the analysis at the time of the first oil shock in 1973, policy makers concentrated on the first feature of the shock. They were preoccupied with the depressing effects on aggregate demand, employment and the trade balance, and failed to take into account the impact on the supply side of the economy. We provide a more detailed description of the oil crises in Section 13.2.1.

Why does an oil shock depress aggregate demand?

Oil is a key imported input to production and also an important element in the household consumption bundle. When the oil price rises, this depresses aggregate demand in oil-importing countries. Thinking of the definition of aggregate demand, the higher oil price reduces net exports by raising the real import bill. From the perspective of households, when the oil price goes up, the price of petrol at the pump rises. Firms will also pass on the higher price of energy in the prices of their goods. These price rises reduce the real incomes of households. More is spent on imported oil so less is spent on domestic production. Unless they can borrow to smooth this shock, consumption will fall. This reduction in aggregate demand (because of the fall in $(X-M)$ as the real cost of imported oil rises) shifts the *AD* curve to the left in the

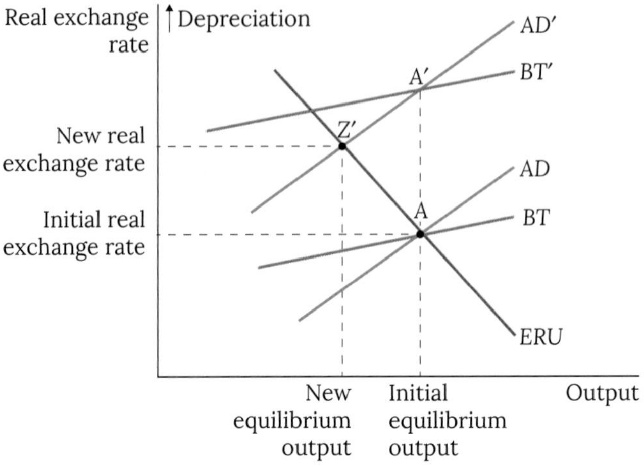

Figure 13.1 The external trade effects of a rise in the price of oil. Visit www.oup.com/he/carlin-soskice to explore the external trade effects of an oil shock with Animated Analytical Diagram 13.1.

AD-BT-ERU model. It also depresses the trade balance and we can show this in the model as a leftward shift in the BT curve. The shifts in the AD and in the BT curves are shown in Figure 13.1.

As we saw in Chapter 12 (Figure 12.10), it is not a coincidence that the new BT curve intersects the new AD curve vertically above the initial equilibrium. If we consider a real depreciation that would fully offset the effect on aggregate demand and the trade balance of the oil price shock, it would leave output unchanged at point B on the shifted AD and BT curves (see also Section 12.5.2B).

From Figure 13.1, we can see that the external trade shock would mean a new medium-run equilibrium at point Z′, with higher unemployment and a trade deficit. It is these aggregate demand and trade balance aspects of the shock that were at the top of policy makers' minds in 1973. They focused on trying to offset the implications of the shock for aggregate demand and the external balance.

Why is an oil shock a negative supply shock?

It turns out that an oil shock is also a negative *supply shock*: this means not only that it raises unemployment as a consequence of the fall in aggregate demand, but that it also shifts the ERU curve to the left. Why is this? Think back to a household faced with a higher cost of living as a consequence of the energy price hike. In Chapter 12, we discussed the fact that households are likely to view their welfare in terms of their real consumption wage, i.e. they will evaluate the value of their nominal wage according to the consumption bundle they can buy with it. If the real value of their nominal wage is reduced by higher energy prices, this shifts the price-setting curve downwards (for a given real exchange rate), opening up a gap between the real consumption wage they require to supply effort on the WS curve at a given rate of unemployment and the real

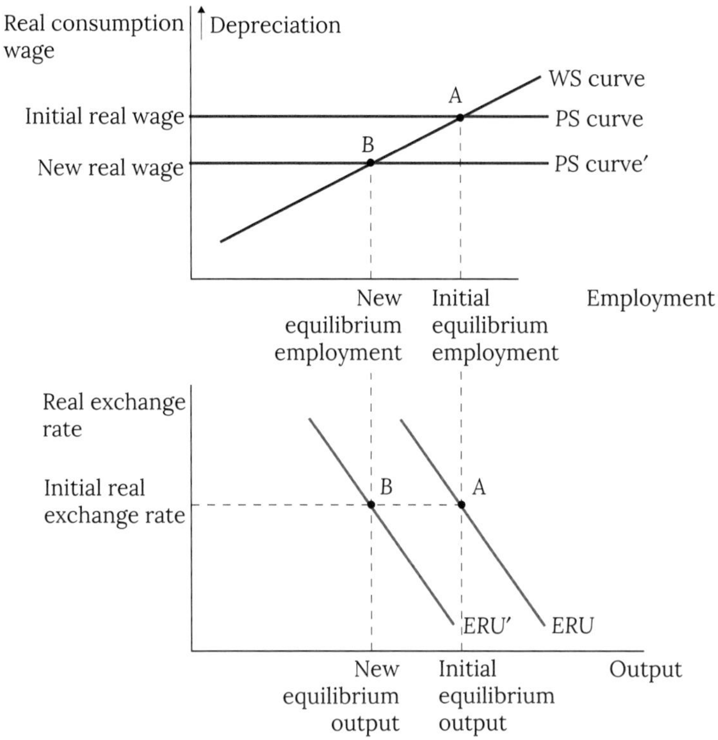

Figure 13.2 A negative supply shock: an increase in the oil price shifts the *ERU* curve to the left.

value of the wage they get. In Figure 13.2, we can see that this downward shift in the PS curve has the effect of shifting the *ERU* curve to the left.

Thinking about an oil price increase as a negative supply shock helps to explain why the oil shock in 1973 led not just to a one-off increase in inflation, but to rising inflation—at a time when unemployment had also risen. There will be upward pressure on inflation as long as there is a gap between the WS curve and the new lower PS curve: unemployment must increase if the economy is to achieve stable inflation. In other words, if the policy maker tries to offset the effect of the fall in aggregate demand by monetary or fiscal stimulus, the economy will experience rising inflation.

What is the role of fiscal policy?

Suppose the policy maker used a fiscal stimulus to shift the aggregate demand curve back to its initial pre-shock position (from *AD′* to *AD* in Figure 13.3) to offset the effect of the shock in depressing aggregate demand. The fiscal stimulus would have restored output and unemployment to their pre-shock levels at A. Would this reversal of the demand effects of the shock restore equilibrium in the economy? The answer is 'no' if the relevant post-shock supply-side equilibrium is on *ERU′*: the new equilibrium unemployment is higher as shown by point B in Figure 13.3. Since at A the real wage has been pushed down by higher energy prices, wage setters will get higher money

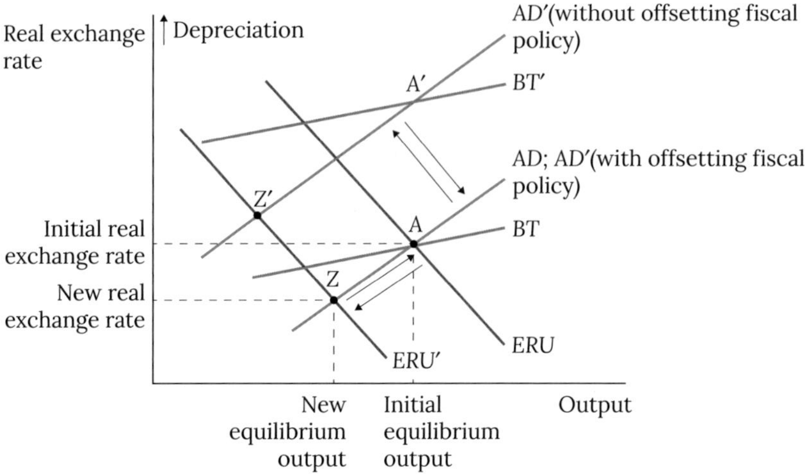

Figure 13.3 Expansionary fiscal and monetary policy in response to a rise in the price of oil.

wages to compensate them, and inflation will no longer be constant (i.e. there is rising inflation at A). This is reflected in the diagram by the fact that point A is to the right of the relevant *ERU* curve labelled *ERU′*. Note also that at A (with the fiscal stimulus), there will be both a trade deficit (the economy is below *BT′*) and a budget deficit.

What is the role of monetary policy?

In the analysis so far, the economy ends up at point Z in Figure 13.3 with constant inflation. Unemployment is higher than it was initially and there is a substantial deterioration in the economy's external balance (note the position of *BT′*).

An alternative to the use of fiscal stimulus is to use monetary policy to stimulate aggregate demand by producing an exchange rate depreciation through a reduction in the interest rate. In a fixed exchange rate regime, the same result could be achieved by a devaluation. Either of these 'accommodative' policies would take the economy from Z′ toward point A′. Note that at A′ following this monetary policy response, there is no external deficit but there is upward pressure on inflation since the economy is to the right of the *ERU′* curve.

By raising import prices across the board, the depreciation caused by looser monetary policy, will provoke higher nominal wage settlements. Higher wage and price inflation will result. As the impact of higher inflation on home's competitiveness kicks in, the economy will move to the south-west toward point Z′. To offset this recession, the government would have to implement another loosening of monetary policy. Another burst of inflation would ensue.

How could a supply-side policy help?

Although many countries experienced the combination of high inflation and unemployment in the 1970s and 1980s, this was not true of all—see Figure 2.1 in Chapter

2 for a comparison of unemployment rates in high-income economies during this period. We can use the model to help provide a possible explanation. If the negative supply-side effect of the shock could be offset by an appropriate supply-side policy, then the stagflationary consequences of the oil shock would be mitigated.

One such policy is a wage accord. A wage accord, or incomes policy as it was sometimes called at the time, is typically a tripartite agreement between the government, employee unions and employer associations. The accord means that employees accept wage restraint in order to maintain higher employment than would be the case otherwise. These accords have the effect of shifting the wage-setting curve downward and hence offsetting (at least partially) the downward shift of the price-setting curve. If the wage accord fully offsets the effect of the oil shock, then the *ERU* curve will not shift to the left. Such a policy would reduce both the rise in unemployment and the rise in inflation associated with the oil shock. The downside of these policies is that they are hard to sell politically, as coupling rising oil prices with wage restraint means workers have to accept a reduction in their real incomes. The discussion in Chapter 15 about differences in institutional structures across countries helps to explain why the oil shocks of the 1970s resulted in stagflation in some countries but not others. Countries with coordinated wage-setting, such as those in the Nordic economies and Austria, kept unemployment low in spite of these shocks.

Why did the oil price hike in the 2000s not lead to stagflation?

Over the course of the period between 2002 and 2008, real oil prices almost doubled, taking them to a level above that of 1980. Yet, inflation remained low and unemployment was falling in many countries. An important reason that the depressive demand effects were muted in the 2000s was the very different behaviour of financial institutions. Banks were very keen to increase their lending and, in the US for example, they allowed households to withdraw equity from their houses to enable them to maintain their consumption in the face of the oil price increases. The behaviour of banks is discussed at greater length in Chapter 9.

On the supply side, it seems that workers were less able or less inclined to get compensation through their wages for the higher oil prices in the 2000s than had been the case in the 1970s. This may be related to the decline in the role of unions in wage setting over this period (see Chapter 15). If this was the case, then in terms of the model, both the aggregate demand curve and the *ERU* curves would have shifted less to the left than was the case in the 1970s due respectively to bank and union behaviour. Finally, with their inflation-targeting mandates, central banks were not inclined to try to offset the effect on demand by loosening monetary policy in the 2000s. Commodity price shocks are modelled in detail in Section 13.2 and climate and pandemic shocks in Section 13.3.

13.1.2 Interpreting an economy's sector financial balances: Does a current account imbalance matter?

To answer this question, it is useful to explain circumstances under which a current account imbalance is benign. The logic is familiar from the discussion of household decisions in Chapter 1. At different stages in their lifecycle, households would ideally like to borrow or lend in order to maintain a fairly smooth consumption path. A phase of borrowing would be expected when income is below its expected longer-term level; a phase of lending would be expected during years of higher than 'permanent' income. The ability to borrow and lend, i.e. access to the capital market, allows the household to improve its welfare relative to a situation in which its consumption is tied to its current income.

The same logic can be applied to a country. A good example is a situation in which a country gets a windfall increase in its wealth and hence in its 'permanent income' because of the discovery of a natural resource. Applying the same logic as in the household case, the country's permanent income has gone up, which means consumption can be higher now and into the indefinite future. If the country has access to borrowing on the international capital market, then current consumption of home residents can go up immediately on the discovery of the natural resource before any of it has been extracted. In practical terms, this means a rise in imports as home residents purchase more goods from abroad to sustain their higher consumption.

If we assume that the initial position was of current account and trade balance, we would observe a deterioration in the current account on discovery of the natural resource. In this example, the current account deficit is not a signal of any weakness in the performance of the economy: indeed, the current account deficit reflects the increase in long-run wealth of the country, which allows residents to improve their living standards immediately because they can borrow from abroad to fund the higher level of imports. Once the revenue from the natural resource comes on-stream, the accumulated debt associated with the years of current account deficits can be repaid.

However, just because we can think through an example in which a current account deficit is benign does not mean this is always the case. Let us take a very different example. Suppose the economy is characterized by a property price bubble. As we have seen, this can lead to a consumption boom as households feel wealthier as a consequence of rising house prices. For the economy as a whole, higher consumption leads to higher imports and to a deterioration in the current account. The country is accumulating debt to the rest of the world for as long as the current account deficit persists. Unlike the resource windfall case in which the means for repaying the debt are 'in the ground', the house-price boom does not create more wealth that can be used to repay the debt as it comes due. When the bubble bursts and house prices fall, the illusion of higher permanent income for the country is shattered and the country will have to find a way of servicing the higher debt it has accumulated. This will normally entail a fall in living standards. Section 13.4 examines external imbalances and resource windfalls in more detail.

13.1.3 **Inflation targeting in a two-bloc world**

One of the striking features of the global economy from the year 2000 in the late phase of the Great Moderation was the mounting external imbalances of a number of large economies. Figure 13.4 shows that the US, Spain, and the UK had rising

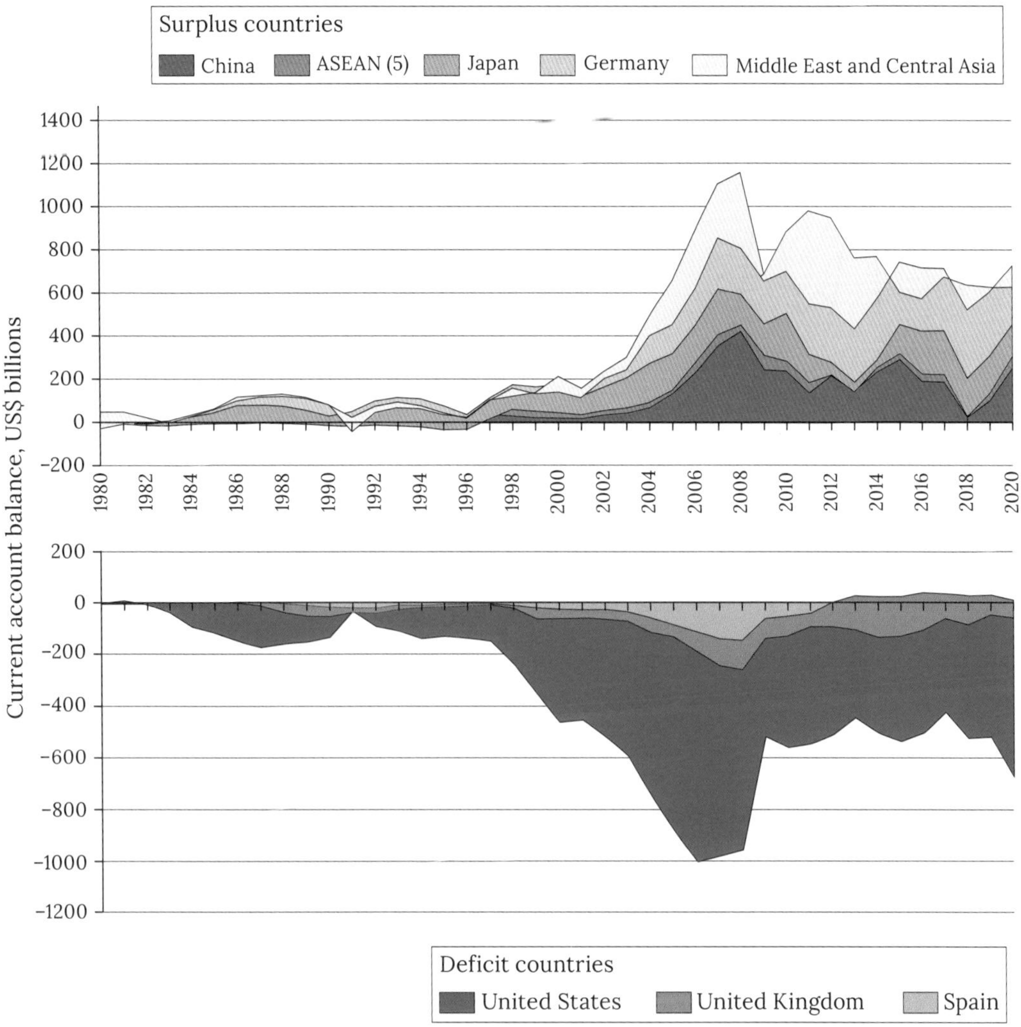

Figure 13.4 Current account balances—countries with large surpluses or CA deficits: 1980–2020.

Source: IMF World Economic Outlook, April 2022.

external deficits of a globally significant size. The counterpart to these deficits were the growing surpluses of China, the oil-producing countries, and Germany. Japan's substantial surplus remained fairly stable over the 2000s.

In the same period, central banks in both developed and emerging economies practiced inflation targeting and were seemingly successful at achieving low and stable inflation. Figure 13.5 shows how inflation in these two country blocs remained low in the 2000s. This is in contrast to previous periods, which were blighted by high and volatile inflation, particularly in emerging economies.

In hindsight, the imbalances that emerged in the 2000s seem unhealthy, a sure sign of the troubles that were to come. In the wake of the financial crisis and Eurozone

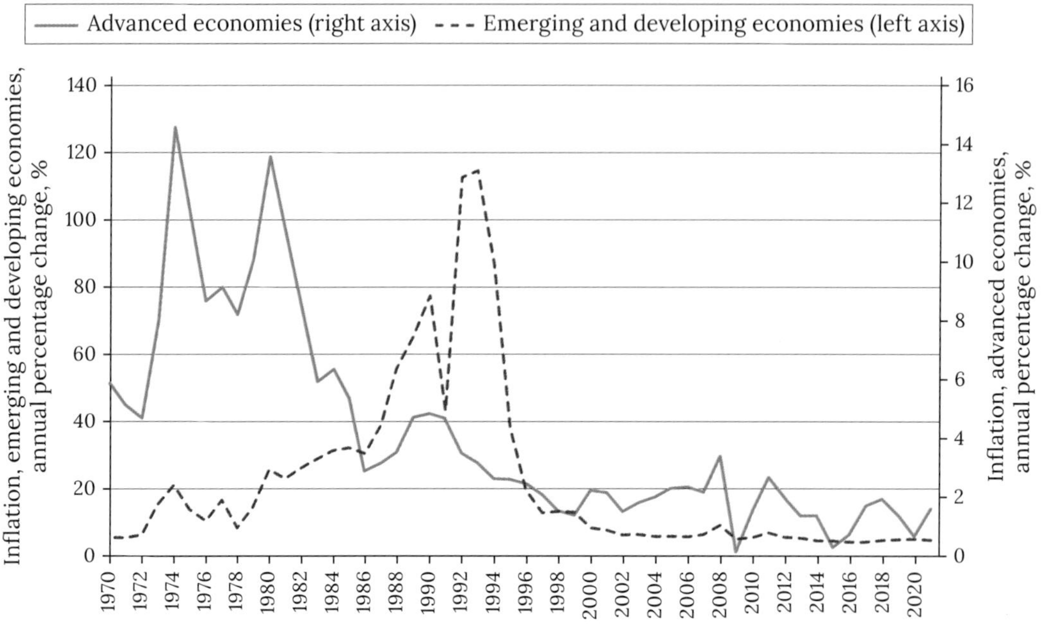

Figure 13.5 Consumer price inflation, annual average percentage change: 1970–2021.

Source: IMF International Financial Statistics, April 2021 WEO.

crisis that followed, politicians and economists were quick to extol the virtues of 'rebalancing'—i.e. countries moving towards more balanced current account positions. We can use a two-bloc version of the 3-equation model to explore interdependence among countries and to show how the response of an inflation-targeting central bank in one bloc to a bloc-specific shock affects the economy and the policy maker in the other bloc. We show that both blocs can achieve their inflation target, but current account and real exchange rate divergences emerge if there are different shocks and/or patterns of demand in the two blocs. The two-bloc model will be set out and used to analyse the dynamic adjustment of two blocs to economic shocks in Section 13.5.2.

13.1.4 **Different medium-run 'growth' strategies can cause global imbalances**

One way of understanding the global imbalances that arose in the pre-crisis period is to see them as the outcome of the choice of different medium-run 'growth' strategies by significant global economies. For example, US economic policy under George W. Bush promoted consumption and housing booms and rising government spending. From the analysis in Chapter 12, we know that a constant inflation equilibrium can be consistent with external imbalance in an open economy. For example, we showed there that a government in an economy (with a downward-sloping *ERU* curve) can encourage higher domestic demand (public or private), which will be associated with lower unemployment and higher real wages (via an appreciated real exchange rate), which in turn, is consistent with stable inflation.

If this were to improve a government's prospects for re-election, then why don't all countries act this way? If they all tried to do so at the same time, then since the world as a whole is a closed economy, this would be modelled by a rightward shift of the world *IS* curve in a closed economy model and it would not be possible to maintain constant inflation.

In Figure 13.6, we provide a simple illustration of the medium-run equilibrium in the global economy in the pre-crisis years. Bloc I represents those economies who adopted a policy of supporting growth through domestic demand, such as the US, UK, and Spain. At the level of the global economy, these expansionary policies were, however, offset by the bloc II economies, who depressed domestic demand in order to keep their real exchange rate depreciated and support their export-led 'growth' strategy. Two

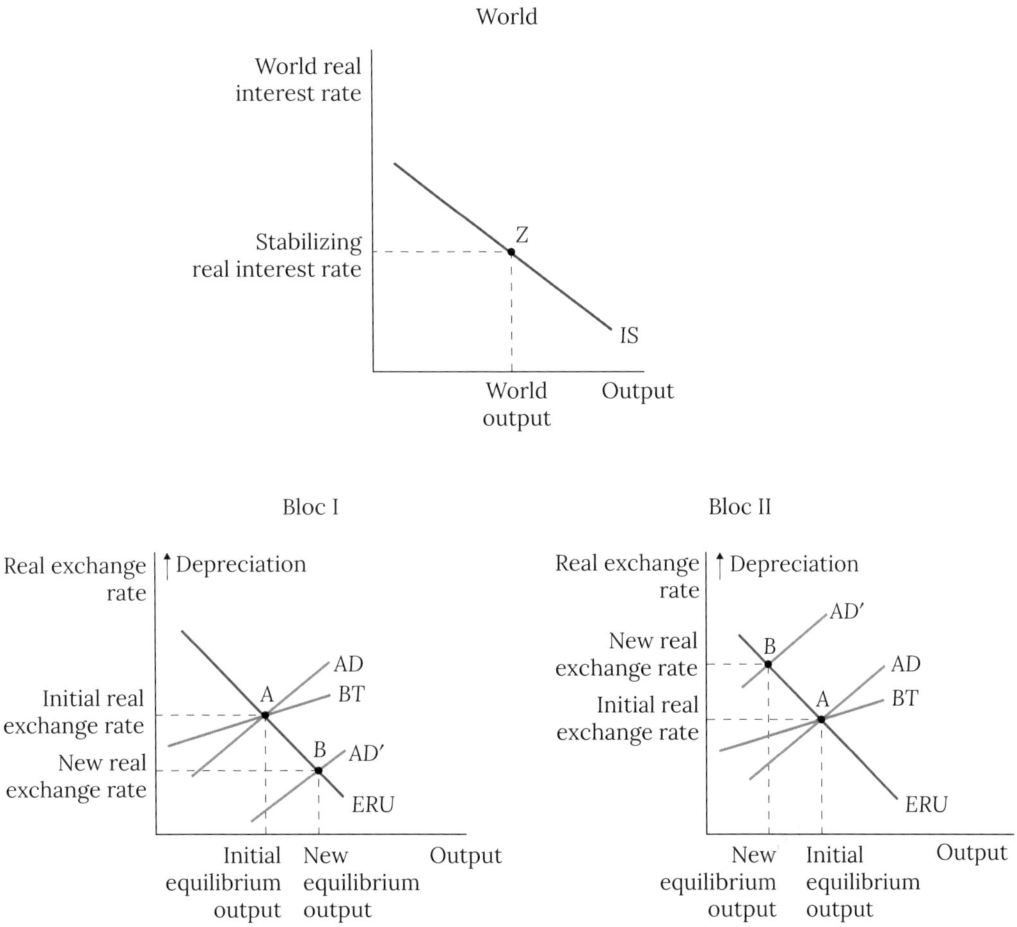

Figure 13.6 Different growth strategies: one bloc pursuing expansionary policies and the other pursuing restrictive policies. Visit www.oup.com/he/carlin-soskice to explore different bloc growth strategies with Animated Analytical Diagram 13.6.

important countries where the attention of policy makers was on restraining domestic demand and promoting net exports in the 2000s were Germany and China.

In the stylized example in Figure 13.6, bloc I is in a constant inflation equilibrium with lower unemployment and an external deficit and bloc II is in a constant inflation equilibrium with higher unemployment and a trade surplus. Assuming that the demand shifts are opposite and symmetric, the world economy remains at the unique constant inflation equilibrium as shown in the upper panel of Figure 13.6 at Z.

We can distinguish between an export-oriented growth strategy of China and Germany and a finance- and consumption-oriented growth strategy of the US, UK, and Spain. These strategies resulted in the emergence of large external imbalances from the beginning of the 2000s, with export surpluses rising sharply in China and Germany, and deficits rising rapidly in the US, and to a lesser extent in the UK and Spain (see Figure 13.4).

As we discussed in Chapter 9, financial deregulation in the US began in the early 1980s and culminated in 1999 with the repeal of the Glass Steagall act. In the UK, it was the 'big bang' policy of 1986 that signalled the start of rapid financial deregulation. In the US, this led to the extension of credit to low-income households for mortgages. Financial deregulation fuelled housing booms in many other countries, including Spain, where the creation of the Eurozone increased access to, and reduced the cost of, loans. In many of the economies with finance-oriented growth strategies, household savings ratios fell to historically low levels in the 2000s.

However, as Figure 13.4 makes clear, not all countries were characterized by the same pattern. In particular, in terms of countries with global impact, China and Germany looked very different. Both countries had rapidly increasing current account surpluses. Looking first at China, in spite of a very high and rising investment share of GDP and rapid growth at rates close to 10% per annum, savings were even higher (reflecting increasing savings by firms offsetting a falling savings rate of households). The Chinese government favoured an export-led growth strategy to create a large globally competitive manufacturing sector. It was prepared to prioritize this over a more balanced growth pattern, which would have allowed the exchange rate to appreciate, and real wages and domestic consumption to rise.

As Germany emerged from its period of financing reconstruction in East Germany following reunification in 1990, the government concentrated on setting policy so as to encourage the restoration of competitiveness in the export sector, which had been eroded during the post-unification boom in the early 1990s. The government kept fiscal policy tight and supply-side reforms focused on increasing the cost of job loss: both had the effect of encouraging wage restraint. Against the background of weak demand at home, German firms sought to take advantage of the opportunities available to reorganize production networks in Central and Eastern Europe and to sell to the rapidly growing markets in China and elsewhere in the emerging economies. Real wage growth was low, consumption depressed and the household savings rate was increasing. Although China was growing very fast and Germany slowly, the common factor of an export-oriented growth strategy meant that in both countries national savings were higher than investment and there was an export surplus.

The third important source of rising current account surpluses was the impact of the rapid economic expansion of emerging economies on the demand for oil and on oil prices and, hence, on the export surpluses of the oil-producing countries.

By the mid-2000s, the magnitude of the surpluses relative to the global economy was unprecedented. Those surpluses were recycled to other regions. This echoed on a global scale the recycling of the surpluses of the oil exporters to Latin America following the OPEC shocks of the 1970s, which created the basis for the subsequent regional debt crisis.

In a very stylized way, we can relate this discussion to Figure 13.6. Bloc I represents the finance- and consumption-oriented countries and bloc II the export-focused countries. Each bloc is assumed to have an inflation-targeting central bank. The boom in demand in bloc I causes an appreciation in the exchange rate and a current account deficit, whereas the opposite macroeconomic policy stance in bloc II ensures a depreciated exchange rate and a trade surplus. The strategies of the two blocs offset each other, which means that world interest rates could be kept low (as shown by the upper panel of Figure 13.6) without causing either bloc to miss their inflation target.

13.2 MODELLING OIL AND OTHER COMMODITY PRICE SHOCKS

As we have seen in Section 13.1, the oil shocks of the 1970s were extremely disruptive to the oil-importing economies, whereas the increase in the 2000s, which was of roughly the same size, was much less so. The impact of the Ukraine war produced another energy price shock. Looking ahead, as economies become heavily reliant on battery technology, their dependence on the import of inputs such as rare earths will rise.

Here we show how to extend the open economy modelling to the case where the economy imports raw materials, which we will call 'oil'. To do this we make a different simplifying assumption about home's economic structure than the one in Chapter 12. Specifically, as shown in Table 13.1, home now imports *only* raw materials whereas in Chapter 12, all of home's imports were of manufactured goods.

A key new variable appears in the model, called tau (pronounced like 'cow')

$$\tau \equiv \frac{P^*_{rm}}{P^*_{mf}} \tag{13.1}$$

which can be interpreted in three different ways as:

1. The relative price of raw materials to manufactures at the global level;
2. The real price of raw materials;
3. The world terms of trade seen from the perspective of oil exporters (or the inverse of the world terms of trade from the perspective of oil importers, who export manufactures). A rise in τ is a terms of trade gain for oil exporters, i.e. a so-called improvement in their terms of trade and the reverse for oil importers.

Home economy	Trade	Prices in home currency	Real exchange rate (producer price based)	Terms of trade, $TOT \equiv \frac{P_X}{P_M}$
Chapters 11 and 12				
Exports	Manufactured goods	$P_X = P$	$Q = \frac{P^*e}{P}$	$TOT = \frac{1}{Q}$
Imports	Manufactured goods	$P_M = P^*e$		
Chapter 13				
Exports	Manufactured goods	$P_X = P_{mf} = P$	$Q = \frac{P^*_{mf}e}{P_{mf}} = \frac{P^*e}{P}$	$TOT = \frac{P_{mf}}{P^*_{rm}e} = \frac{P_{mf}}{\tau P^*_{mf}e} = \frac{1}{\tau Q}$
Imports	Raw materials	$P_M = P^*_{rm}e = \tau P^*_{mf}e$ where $\tau = \frac{P^*_{rm}}{P^*_{mf}}$		

Table 13.1 Trade, prices, real exchange rates, and terms of trade: assumptions used in Chapters 11–13.

Table 13.1 shows the relevant equations for home's prices, real exchange rate and terms of trade, which is useful for reference. In this chapter for simplicity, we assume that *all* imports are raw materials, when of course many will be manufactures. And remember in turn that 'manufactured goods' includes 'services'.

The table highlights two important differences:

1. When all trade is in manufactures as in the earlier chapters, there are no subscripts denoting manufacturing. Given that only one type of good is traded, the terms of trade is the inverse of the measure of the real exchange, Q.
2. In the oil-importing case, the measure of the real exchange rate is the so-called producer price measure defined solely in terms of the goods in which the country competes, namely, manufactures. As a result, the measure of the real exchange rate is the same as before. But because home now imports only raw materials, the terms of trade is no longer equal to the inverse of the real exchange rate and τ as well as q shifts the PS curve.

13.2.1 External supply shocks (e.g. oil shocks) in the *AD-BT-ERU* model

An external supply shock is defined as an unanticipated change in the world terms of trade between manufactured goods and raw materials: a change in the world price of oil is a good example. As explained in Section 13.1.1, this type of shock combines the effects of an external trade shock (as seen in Chapter 12) with a supply-side impact on the price-setting real wage curve. The consequence is that there is a shift in the AD curve, in the *BT* curve, and in the *ERU* curve, with all three curves shifting in the same direction.

The price of imported oil affects the home economy in two ways—by raising the costs of production for firms that use oil directly or indirectly as an input and by directly raising the consumer price index through household petrol and oil use. For simplicity in the derivation to follow, we assume the transmission of oil price changes is only through the latter route. This allows us to continue to assume that labour is the only input to home's production of manufactured goods and gives a simple expression for the price-setting real wage. This simplification does not affect the main insights from the model.

A very simple way to model the impact of oil is therefore to assume that the consumer price index is the price index of home value-added (i.e. marked-up unit labour costs) plus the unit cost of imported oil. Changes in the oil price feed directly into the consumer price index as shown in the second term in the equation below.

$$P_c = P_{mf} + \underbrace{\upsilon\tau P^*_{mf}e}_{\text{unit cost of imported oil}}$$

where $P_{mf} = \frac{W}{\lambda(1-\mu)}$ is the price index of home value added and υ is unit materials requirement. This implies a price-setting real wage:[1]

$$w^{PS} = \frac{\lambda(1-\mu)}{1+\upsilon\tau Q}.$$

Any rise in τ reduces the price-setting real wage. Note that any fall in unit materials requirement through increased energy efficiency, for example, would tend to offset this. We would expect this to occur in the longer run in response to higher oil prices, but we can ignore it in the short- and medium-run analysis.

Figure 13.7 shows how the impact of an oil price rise on the PS curve feeds through to shift the ERU curve to the left. This rests on the assumption that wages are set according to the real consumption wage, where workers require compensation for increases in their cost of living arising from higher oil prices. This is referred to as 'real wage resistance' and is reflected in the presence of the real consumption wage (W/P_C) on the vertical axis of Figure 13.7. This implies that to analyse oil shocks, it is necessary to use the downward-sloping ERU curve. In a more complex model in which oil is an input to the production of home's manufactures, a rise in the price of oil raises costs for firms in the home economy. Assuming they protect their profit margins by passing this increase on to consumers, it reduces the real consumption wage of workers, shifting the PS curve downward (just as in the simpler case).

The new MRE is at point B. The new ERU curve goes through B, with the real exchange rate of q_0 and lower equilibrium output, y'_e. Note that to derive the shift in

---

[1] The derivation is similar to footnote 12 in Chapter 12. We begin by substituting the price-setting equation from Chapter 2 in the equation for P_C:

$$P_C = (1+\mu^C)\frac{W}{\lambda} + \upsilon\tau P^*_{mf}e$$

$$\rightarrow \frac{P_C\lambda}{W(1+\mu^C)} = 1 + \frac{\upsilon\tau P^*_{mf}e}{P_{mf}} = 1+\upsilon\tau Q$$

Therefore writing the price-setting real wage in terms of the markup on price, we have:

$$\frac{W}{P_C} = w^{PS} = \frac{\lambda(1-\mu)}{1+\upsilon\tau Q} \tag{13.2}$$

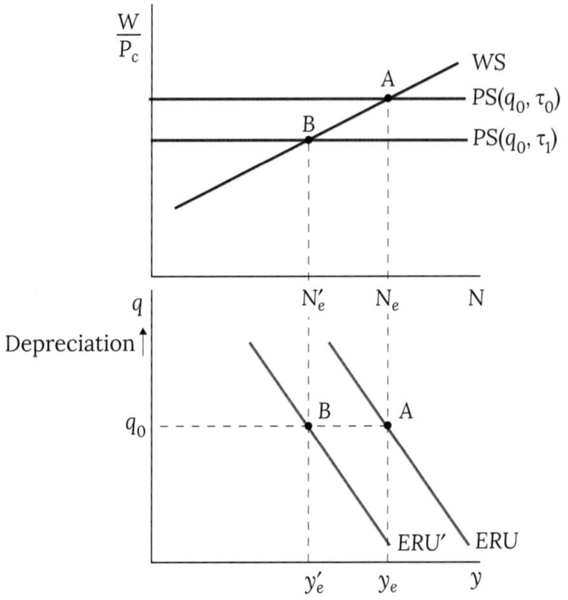

Figure 13.7 A negative supply shock: an increase in the oil price (↑ τ) shifts the ERU curve to the left. Visit www.oup.com/he/carlin-soskice to explore a negative oil supply shock with Animated Analytical Diagram 13.7.

the ERU curve as the oil price varies in the diagram, we have to hold the real exchange rate, q, constant.

13.2.2 **The full model**

Demand side and external balance

As we have seen in Section 13.1, an oil price hike depresses aggregate demand because by increasing the import bill, it reduces home's net exports. Since the price elasticity of demand for oil is very low, we assume that the volume of imports of oil does not change in the short run; paying more for them depresses consumption and with it, the demand for home production. There is no change in home's exports. We assume for simplicity that y^* does not increase as a result of the rise in income in the oil-producing nations. A compact summary of the model is in Appendix 13.7.1.

Net exports are[2]:

$$X - M = X(\sigma(Q), y^*) - \tau QM(Q, y), \tag{13.3}$$

and the rise in τ shifts the AD curve and the BT curve to the left. Both shift by the same amount relative to the y-axis and intersect vertically above the initial output

[2] See Appendix 13.7.1 for the derivation of the relevant equations.

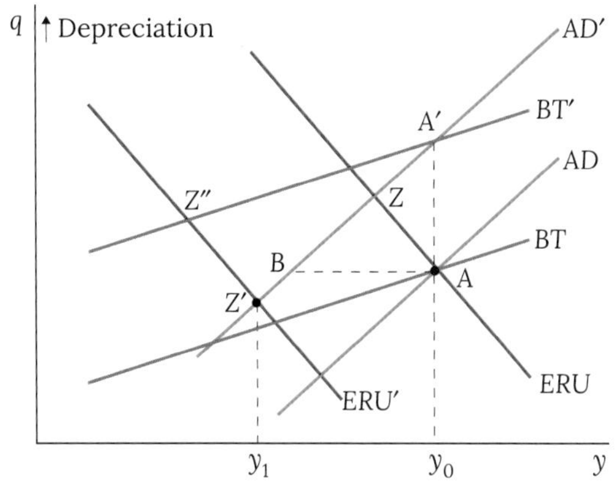

Figure 13.8 A negative external supply shock: the combined effect of an increase in the oil price ($\uparrow \tau$) in the AD-BT-ERU model. The new long-run equilibrium is at point Z″. Visit www.oup.com/he/carlin-soskice to explore negative oil supply shocks (full effect) with Animated Analytical Diagram 13.8.

level in Figure 13.8 at A′ since the same real depreciation would reverse the effect on net exports from the oil price increase.

Demand and supply-side effects; new medium-run equilibrium

Figure 13.8 summarizes the effect on all three curves of an oil shock. The new medium-run equilibrium is at point Z′, where the new AD′ curve intersects the new ERU′ curve. There is lower output and higher unemployment. The new long-run equilibrium, where the economy is also on the BT curve is at Z″, at yet lower output. Note that the extent of the leftward shift of the ERU curve depends on the degree of real wage resistance. If wage-setters were able to ignore the effect of higher oil prices on the CPI, then in Figure 13.7, the WS curve would shift down to intersect the new PS curve at the initial equilibrium output level. In that case, the ERU curve would not shift left and the new equilibrium in Figure 13.8 would be at point Z. There is a wide range of possibilities between these two outcomes. Zero real wage resistance means that workers would provide the same effort at a given unemployment rate before and after the rise in the CPI even though the purchasing power of the nominal wage had fallen.

Alternative policy responses to the shock

The impact effect of the shock is due to the fall in aggregate demand taking the economy from A to B. There are two ways the government could seek to restore output from its depressed level at B to y_0. Expansionary fiscal policy, would shift the AD curve back to the right (to AD), offsetting the impact on aggregate demand of the oil price increase; alternatively, loosening monetary policy would produce a depreciation of the exchange rate, and the economy would move along the AD′ curve to y_0. However, given the shift in the ERU curve, if the government tries to restore aggregate demand and output to its pre-shock level at point y_0, then the inflationary consequences of the commodity price rise are clear. Following the external supply shock, the initial equilibrium point A is *above* the new *ERU* curve labelled *ERU*′. This means that at y_0, the real wage is below the wage-setting real wage because the PS curve has shifted down due to the increase in τ. Point A is no longer a medium-run equilibrium. If, on the other hand, the authorities did not attempt to offset the demand shock, the economy at B is still to the right of the *ERU*′ curve (as it is placed in Figure 13.8) and there would be inflationary pressure until output had fallen to y_1. In the case of a smaller leftward shift in the *ERU* curve (due to less real wage resistance for example), point B could be to the left of Z′. With a negative bargaining gap at B, inflation would be falling and the economy could be steered to the new MRE. The use of accommodative monetary policy is discussed in the context of the OPEC I shock section.

Comparing three oil shocks

This section focuses on the three major global oil shocks since the early 1970s, comparing their causes, their macroeconomic implications and the associated policy responses. Figure 13.9 shows the path of oil prices over the last 50 years—to compare across periods, we show log real oil prices.[3] This approach allows for variations in the series to be interpreted as percentage changes. The shaded grey areas show the oil price shocks that we analyse in this section. The graphs also show the movement of US consumer price inflation and unemployment over the period, providing an insight into the macroeconomic consequences of each shock.

The three oil shocks we are investigating took place in 1973–74, 1979–80 and 2002–08. We will go through each shock in turn, setting out its causes and its macroeconomic effects. We will also investigate the dominant monetary policy response of central banks in developed economies to each episode.

OPEC I: 1973–74

The Yom Kippur War began in the Middle East on October 6th 1973. This did not directly affect oil shipments, but did lead to the Organization of Petroleum Exporting Countries (OPEC) cutting production of crude oil significantly towards the end of 1973. This is thought to have been the main driver of the more than doubling of crude oil prices seen over this period—the nominal oil price rose from \$4.3 to \$10.1 per barrel between 1973 Q4 and 1974 Q1. The overall impact of this event is estimated to have been between a 7% and 9% reduction in world oil supply.[4] In addition to this supply shock, demand pressures are thought to have played a complementary role in the oil price rise. Barsky and Kilian (2002) suggest that general inflation and booming prices for other commodities contributed to the upward pressure on oil prices.

---

[3] This way of presenting data means that an increase in the index from 1 to 2 is (approximately) a doubling of real oil prices. The first step is to produce the series for oil prices in real terms, by deflating nominal oil prices by the US GDP deflator (i.e. 2012 = 100). Next, the natural logarithim of this series is taken. Lastly, the series is multiplied by 100. This method is in line with that used in Blanchard and Gali (2007).

[4] See Hamilton (2009).

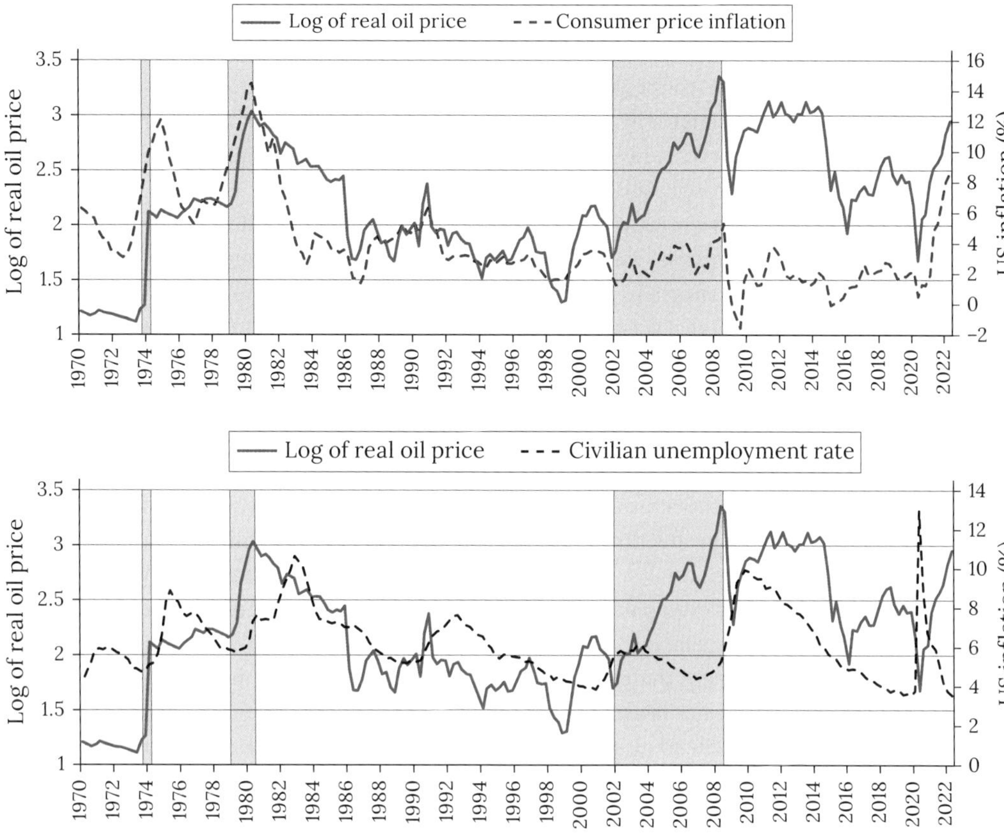

Figure 13.9 Log of real oil prices and US macroeconomic indicators: 1970 Q1–2022 Q2.
Source: Federal Reserve Bank of St Louis, FRED (data accessed September 2022).

Figure 13.9 shows that this shock coincided with a rise in inflation to double digits. In contrast, the unemployment impact was largely felt in the year after the oil price hike, when the unemployment rate in the US nearly doubled.

In response to the first oil shock in 1973, many countries focused on the aggregate demand consequences and sought to offset them via expansionary fiscal and monetary policies. The example of expansionary fiscal policy was used in Section 13.1. We look now at the consequences of an accommodating monetary policy, which would allow the exchange rate to depreciate so as to offset the fall in aggregate demand. Referring back to Figure 13.8, the aim would be to restore output to y_0 and move the economy from B to A′ via a depreciation of the real exchange rate.

At point A′, however, the economy is to the right of the *ERU* curve. This causes inflation to rise, as workers' real wage expectations are not being met (as shown in Figure 12.6 in Chapter 12). The increase in inflation (↑ P relative to P*) results in an appreciation of the real exchange rate, via the equation $Q = \frac{P^*e}{P}$. This leads to a movement leftwards down the AD curve, as net exports fall, until the economy is at Z′, where the new AD and *ERU* curves intersect. This is the new medium-run equilibrium (MRE), where there is no pressure on inflation to change.

The consequence of the adoption of policies like this after 1973 was the onset of so-called stagflation: rising unemployment and rising inflation (as the economy eventually adjusted from A′ to the new medium-run equilibrium at Z′ with unemployment rising and a burst of inflation). Any renewed attempt by the government to keep output at its pre-shock level would prompt a further increase in inflation (as the same process outlined above repeats itself).

In the UK, government policy exacerbated the stagflation. The government negotiated incomes policies during the 1970s to compensate workers for the rising cost of living. As firms sought to protect their profit margins the wage–price spiral continued. By encouraging real wage resistance (i.e. raising money wages to maintain real wages) this added to the sharp rises in actual and equilibrium unemployment and inflation seen in the UK after each of the oil shocks.[5]

OPEC II: 1979–80

The second oil shock was once again the result of largely exogenous geopolitical events disrupting the production of crude oil in the Middle East.[6] This time, production was affected by both the Iranian Revolution in late 1978 and the Iran-Iraq War of 1980. As in 1973, these developments led to sharp rises in oil prices, which affected both US inflation and unemployment in a similar manner as the 1973–74 shock, as shown by Figure 13.9. Again, the unemployment response lagged the inflation response, with unemployment not peaking until 1982, at a rate of over 10%.

When the 1979–80 oil shock struck, the nature of the shock was better understood and many countries attempted to use tight monetary policy to prevent exchange rate depreciation and hence prevent a big upsurge in inflation. For example, average UK official bank interest rates were 10% in 1978 Q3 and continued to rise during the shock, reaching 17% in the first half 1980. From here interest rates gradually fell, but stayed above 10% until the middle of 1983.[7] This shift of monetary policy regime to non-accommodation of inflation coincided with a change of government in the UK, as Thatcher took power in mid-1979. Her economic views were highly influenced by Milton Friedman's 'Monetarist' school of thought and this was reflected in her decision to squeeze inflation out of the system through tight monetary policy (even if it meant unemployment would be above equilibrium for some time). Thatcher's Monetarist experiment is discussed in more detail in Chapter 6.

In terms of Figure 13.8, adoption of tight monetary policy would mean that output would fall from A to B to Z′, but without the additional hike in inflation that accompanied loose monetary policy. The already high rates of inflation and the sluggish adaptation of wage and price setters to tighter monetary policy meant that most countries experienced years of high unemployment before inflation was reduced to low levels in the 1990s. This shows that governments were generally unsuccessful in

---

[5] See David Walton's speech on February 23rd 2006 entitled, *Has Oil Lost the Capacity to Shock?* The speech is available from the Bank of England website.

[6] See Hamilton (2009).

[7] Source: Bank of England (data accessed January 2014).

introducing the types of supply-side policies (e.g. wage accords that accepted real wage cuts) discussed in Section 13.1.1, which would have mitigated the inflation and output responses to the oil shocks.

Oil price rises 2002–08

There was a persistent and marked rise in oil prices between 2002 and 2008, which culminated in a peak real oil price in 2008 Q2 that exceeded that reached in the 1979–80 oil shock.[8] The forces driving this movement in prices were quite different from the episodes in the 1970s, with demand factors in the global oil market playing a much larger role. The 2000s was a period of rapid economic expansion for emerging markets and especially China, whose demand for oil increased exceptionally fast over this period. In addition to this, world oil production stagnated between 2005 and 2007, partially driven by a decline in Saudi Arabian output. These demand and supply factors produced upward pressure on prices, as more nations were actively competing for a finite amount of resources.

A further component of the third oil shock that did not feature in the oil shocks of the 1970s was speculation in financial markets. Hamilton (2009) argues that the excessively high oil prices reached in 2008 were in part influenced by the flow of dollars into commodity futures contracts. The path of the macroeconomy during this pronounced and consistent rise in oil prices was unexpected given past experiences. Instead of stagflation, the third oil shock coincided with a period of falling unemployment and low inflation (for the US, see Figure 13.9).

What factors can account for the very different macroeconomic consequences? Can the model help explain why things were different this time around? On the demand side, two factors appear to have been important. Firstly, greater access to credit meant that households were able to cushion themselves against the increase in energy costs by withdrawing equity from their houses.[9] Secondly, there is some evidence that substitution away from energy-intensive activities was easier.

On the supply side, both labour market reforms and inflation-targeting macroeconomic frameworks appear to have made wage setters less inclined or able to secure compensation in their wages for higher imported energy costs. This would be reflected in a smaller leftward shift of the *ERU* curve. The importance of labour market reform was emphasized by David Walton, a member of the Bank of England's Monetary Policy Committee in a 2006 speech, when he cited the increased flexibility of the UK labour market as a key reason for the oil price rises of the first half of the 2000s not disturbing the UK's low unemployment equilibrium.[10]

Central banks in the high-income countries have learnt through experience of the dangers of oil shocks for the macroeconomy and in particular for inflation. The change

---

[8] There were some brief periods between 2002 Q1 and 2008 Q2 where oil prices fell, but they were small and quickly reversed (see Figure 13.9). In light of this, we treat the whole period as one oil shock.

[9] See Feldstein (2006).

[10] See David Walton's speech on February 23rd 2006 entitled, *Has Oil Lost the Capacity to Shock?* The speech is available from the Bank of England website.

in policy stance since the early 1970s and the increased emphasis on keeping inflation expectations firmly anchored in the face of oil shocks was displayed in a 2004 speech by Edward M. Gramlich, then a member of the Board of Governors of the Federal Reserve:[11]

> I must stress that the worst possible outcome [of an oil shock] is not these temporary increases in inflation and unemployment. The worst possible outcome is for monetary policy makers to let inflation come loose from its moorings.

13.3 CLIMATE AND PANDEMIC SHOCKS

The modelling framework developed in this chapter can be addressed to two other kinds of shock—those associated with the climate crisis and with pandemics. The reason is that both produce effects on the economy that combine negative aggregate demand- and supply-side elements, along with the involvement of international trade. In that sense, the lessons from the analysis of oil shocks are relevant.

13.3.1 Climate shocks

Economists working on climate change and central bank policy identify two different kinds of risk:

1. **Physical risk:** risks associated with damage from climate-change induced 'natural' disasters.
2. **Transition risk:** risks associated with the transition to a zero net carbon emission economy. Such risks characterize the entire transition path but behaviour in financial markets can 'bring forward' the impact of such risks if more certainty develops about the risks themselves as well as about policy to mitigate them. This has the potential to produce financial instability.

Adverse supply-side shock: In the short run, in the case of a physical risk event, economic activity shrinks because supply chains are interrupted and people cannot work as a result of transport disruption, for example. Holding all else constant, this will produce a positive inflation shock, modelled by an upward shift of the Phillips curve. In the longer term, if the disruption is large and persistent, this will reduce productivity (shifting the PS downward), and shifting the *ERU* curve to the left.

In relation to transition risk, the introduction of a carbon tax, for example, has a supply-side effect as it shifts the PS downward (refer back to Chapter 2 for a model of this).

Adverse aggregate demand shock: In the event of a physical risk event, we can assess the implications for each component of aggregate demand. Consumption is affected because the supply shock spills over to aggregate demand as the affected credit-constrained households are unable to smooth their spending. Investment projects will be put on hold due to the uncertainty about the persistence of the effects

---

[11] Excerpt taken from: Edward M. Gramlich's speech on September 16th 2004 entitled, *Oil Shocks and Monetary Policy*. The speech is available from the Federal Reserve website.

of the climate-related event. The uncertainty will depress business investment and household investment in new housing as well as in consumer durables (see Andersson et al. 2020).

External trade: A major climate event in a region strongly integrated in the world economy would depress aggregate demand and, potentially, world trade (see Tamiotti et al. 2009). If the production of important inputs to global manufacturing is disrupted, this has the potential to create a terms of trade shock to trading partners similar to an oil shock.

To summarize, in a diagram like Figure 13.8, a climate-caused natural disaster shifts the *AD* curve left, and for a persistent shock, the *ERU* curve also shifts left. Unlike an oil shock, the effects on aggregate demand, the trade balance and the supply-side come through different channels (as compared with the direct external terms of trade or 'tau' effect on *AD*, *BT*, and *ERU* for an oil shock). Whereas in the oil shock case, the shock is modelled narrowly as a negative external terms of trade shock (i.e. to *BT*), in the climate case, the proximate causes of the shock are considered more broadly. In terms of a diagram, this means that there is no reason for the leftward shifted *AD* and *BT* curves to intersect vertically above the initial MRE.

Financial stability: A climate-related event cuts firms' operating profits, which threatens their solvency; this in turn is a threat to banks who have made loans to firms. Note that the channel in the financial crisis was different in two ways—first, it was households and not firms that saw losses in the value of their equity (in housing) and second, banks themselves were highly leveraged. The financial crisis was a shock emanating from the fragility of the financial system itself. In terms of the transition risk, a change in sentiment about new green technology or regulations, or unanticipated moves in government policy could imply dramatic changes in the valuation of fossil fuel companies and others with so-called stranded assets (e.g. oil and gas reserves not exploited).

The central bank's mandate: For central banks with mandates that include 'supporting overall government policy', this is being interpreted as requiring them to align their policies—both on inflation and on financial stability—with zero net carbon transition impacts and priorities. One example is that of so-called Green Quantitative Easing, which favours the purchase of assets that meet specific 'green' criteria.[12] Equally, the central bank could offer better collateral conditions on its lending to firms that have better green credentials. This means that the composition of QE would be influenced by the climate objective; the size would continue to be determined by the price-stability objective.

13.3.2 **Pandemic shocks**

The disruption to global trade as a consequence of the Covid-19 pandemic can be modelled as a fall in y^* in the model, i.e. as a temporary external trade shock (shifting the *AD* and *BT* curves to the left). Some observers have forecast that the vulnerabilities in supply chains revealed by the pandemic will produce the 're-shoring' of manufacturing,

[12] See Dafermos et al. (2018) for estimates of the effectiveness of a green QE programme.

reversing many decades of off-shoring and globalization of production.[13] To the extent this happens, it would be expected to depress both the productivity of imported materials (increasing υ) and of labour productivity (a λ shock), modelled by a leftward shift in the *ERU* curve. It is also expected that the pandemic would have a scarring effect on the labour market, arising from hysteresis, as discussed in Chapter 4. The supply-side effects of the pandemic would be predicted to produce a temporary inflation shock and a possibly permanent supply-side shock, shifting the *WS* curve upwards, and hence, the *ERU* to the left. Representing this combination of shocks in a diagram like Figure 13.8 is left as an exercise for the reader.

Analysis of the three oil shocks provides a useful lens with which to evaluate the climate and pandemic threats to the macroeconomy. A fourth oil shock is apparent in Figure 13.8 in the 2020s arising from the aftermath of the pandemic and the Ukraine war. The analysis in this section shows the importance of:

1. correctly identifying the nature of the shock,
2. recognizing how different policy frameworks produce different outcomes in the face of the same shock, and
3. understanding wage-setting behaviour in predicting whether a temporary burst of inflation is likely to turn into a wage–price spiral.

13.4 EXTERNAL IMBALANCES

13.4.1 Current account imbalances

Do current account imbalances matter? An intertemporal approach to the balance of payments

Does it matter from an economic perspective if there is a current account or trade deficit or surplus in the economy? To answer this question, it is necessary to recall that any non-zero current account reflects a change in the country's wealth. If the home country has a current account surplus then this means that it is lending abroad—if it has a current account deficit, then it is borrowing from abroad. Since this borrowing will have to be repaid (with interest) in the future, the trade deficit represents a decline in the home country's wealth. A trade deficit will imply a current account deficit unless the home country receives a sufficient net inflow of interest and profit receipts on the foreign assets that it owns. Note that in this chapter, we abstract from the capital gains or losses on a country's stock of foreign assets and liabilities that can affect the relationship between a country's cumulative current account balance and its net foreign asset position as explained in Section 12.1.

[13] See Barbieri et al. (2020). Interested readers may also check the VoxEU article 'Decoupling from global value chains' by Peter Eppinger et al. The 2020 Economist Intelligence Unit report 'The Great Unwinding: Covid-19 and the regionalisation of global supply chains' also provides interesting insights into the topic.

A decline in wealth sounds like a bad thing—but this is not necessarily the case. When a student goes into debt to finance their university studies, their financial wealth falls. The wisdom of this move depends on the extent to which the university education increases the student's human capital and improves their earning capacity.

In the same vein, we can show how countries can rationally use borrowing from abroad to smooth consumption when there is an expectation that future income will exceed current income. Starting from the accounting identities, we can show the link between the current account and consumption.

$$X - M \equiv y - C - I - G$$
$$CA \equiv X - M + INT$$
$$\equiv y + INT - C - I - G = \tilde{y} - C,$$

where $\tilde{y} \equiv y + INT - I - G$.

By defining $\tilde{y} \equiv y + INT - I - G$ i.e. GDP plus net interest from abroad minus investment and government spending, we can see that the current account can be viewed as $\tilde{y} - C$, or savings plus taxes.[14] We shall call $\tilde{y}$ aggregate household disposable income and note that it includes net interest from abroad. The intertemporal model of consumption of Chapter 1 focuses on the objective of consumption smoothing. Using the identity, we can see that in the open economy, fluctuations in the current account can allow aggregate consumption to remain constant in the face of fluctuations in income. Consumption smoothing is a form of 'risk sharing': the ability to borrow or lend enables households (and open economies) to spread the risk of income shocks and thereby to implement preferences for consumption smoothing. This is referred to as risk-sharing and can be seen as an insurance mechanism. It is potentially available to countries who open up their capital markets.

The intertemporal model of the current account (ICA) represents the CA as a forward-looking function of income and asset returns. And the cumulated value of

[14] We can express the current account in a different form by expanding the terms $\tilde{y}$ and C:

$$CA = \tilde{y} - C$$
$$= y + INT - I - G - c_0 - c_1(1-t)y$$

and adding and subtracting taxes yt :

$$= y - yt + INT - I - G - c_0 - c_1 y + c_1 yt + yt$$
$$= y(1 - t - c_1 + c_1 t) + INT - c_0 - I - G + T$$
$$= (1 - c_1)(1 - t)y + INT - c_0 - I - G + T$$
$$= \underbrace{s_1 y^{disp} + INT - c_0 - I - G}_{\text{aggregate household disposable savings}} + \underbrace{T}_{\text{taxes}}. \tag{13.4}$$

The last equation can also be rewritten as:

$$CA = \underbrace{(s_1 y^{disp} + INT - c_0 - I)}_{\substack{\text{private sector} \\ \text{financial balance + INT}}} + \underbrace{(T - G)}_{\substack{\text{Government} \\ \text{financial balance}}}. \tag{13.5}$$

This will be relevant in Section 13.4.2.

past CA balances is defined as the net foreign asset (NFA) position. This model of the current account requires two key assumptions:

1. *Perfect international capital mobility*: home residents can buy or sell foreign bonds with the fixed world interest rate, r^*, in unlimited quantities at low transactions costs.
2. Domestic consumption is set by the infinite horizon *rational expectations permanent income hypothesis*. As discussed in Chapter 1, this amounts to perfect consumption smoothing in expectation when the real interest rate (r) is equal to the subjective discount factor (ρ).

Using the notation introduced in Chapter 1, we can write the ICA model as follows:

$$\mathrm{CA}_t = -\sum_{i=1}^{\infty}\left(\frac{1}{1+r^*}\right)^i \Delta\tilde{y}^E_{t+i},$$

where CA_t is the current account balance at time t, $\sum_{i=1}^{\infty}$ is the sum from period $t+1$ to infinity, r^* is the world interest rate, $\tilde{y}^E_{t+i}$ is aggregate household net income at time $t+i$, expected at the current period, t.

In this framework, just like a household, a country has an intertemporal budget constraint. Consumption smoothing by borrowing and lending makes sense for individuals and the same can be said for countries. If a country experiences a temporary decrease in income this period (i.e. fall in $\tilde{y}_t$ due, for example, to an exogenous fall in exports), then there is an expectation that future income will be higher than current income (i.e. $\Delta\tilde{y}^E_{t+i} > 0$, in future periods, i.e. when $i > 0$).

In this scenario, a current account deficit in period t would simply reflect optimal borrowing at the world interest rate, r^*, to smooth consumption against the adverse income shock. Borrowing from abroad needs to be repaid in the future, so from period $t+1$ onwards, the country would run a series of small current account surpluses as the debt is repaid (and the NFA gradually returns to zero). This illustrates that a country's current account deficit can be a reflection of its 'permanent income' and therefore that the possibility of borrowing from abroad is a rational method of increasing the utility of its citizens. The example shown here is analogous to a household borrowing to smooth their income when they have a bad income shock or when their expected lifetime income increases as was discussed in detail in Chapter 1.

Consider the example of 'good luck' when a country discovers a natural resource, such as oil or diamonds (see Figure 13.10). This raises the country's wealth and therefore its permanent income (i.e. $\Delta\tilde{y}^E_{t+i} > 0$, when $i > 0$). The extraction of the resource commonly takes place some time after the discovery is made. However, the ability to borrow in international capital markets means the country can smooth its consumption, raising living standards even ahead of the first drop of oil being extracted. There are three separate factors that contribute to the emergence of a CA deficit upon the discovery of oil in this scenario:

1. Current consumption rises due to the expectation of higher future income (higher permanent income).

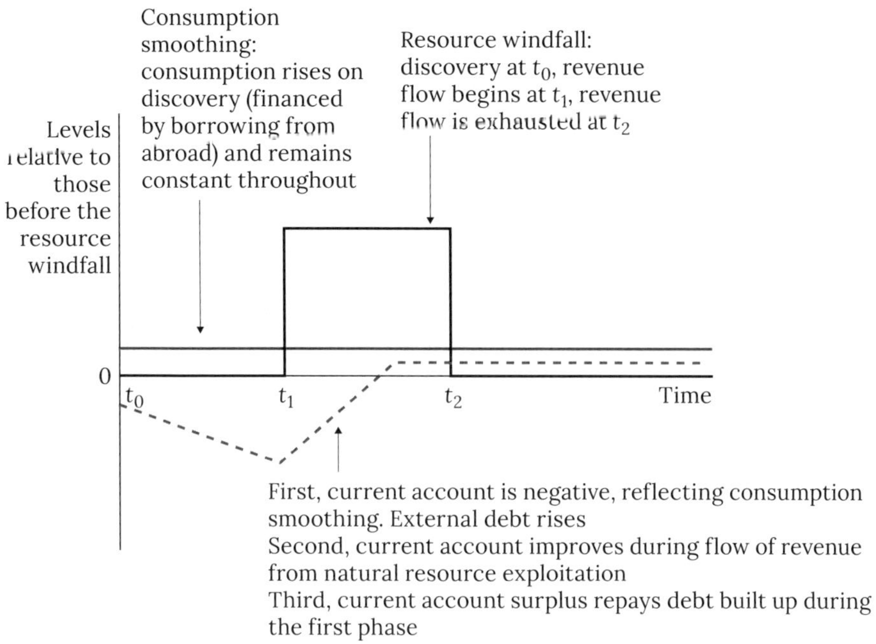

Figure 13.10 Resource windfall and the current account. Visit www.oup.com/he/carlin-soskice to explore resource windfall and the current account with Animated Analytical Diagram 13.10.

2. Domestic investment increases to enable the extraction of the natural resources. The new investment is partly funded through international borrowing.
3. The nominal and real exchange rates appreciate, because the forex market anticipates that the real exchange rate that will balance the current account will be an appreciated one. The discovery is a positive external trade shock (as discussed in Chapter 12).

Figure 13.10 shows the time profile of the discovery of the resource, the period for which revenues are extracted and the period after the natural resource is exhausted. Following the discovery, such a country will have a current account deficit. Its consumption is permanently higher than would have been the case in the absence of the natural resource discovery. Once the revenue from the resource extraction begins to flow the current account balance improves. The current account eventually moves to a small surplus, which continues until the country has repaid the debt built up during the initial phase. This adjustment was observed in the UK in the 1970s with the discovery of oil in the North Sea.

If we think about current account imbalances more generally, for a country that does not have very profitable investment opportunities at home, it makes sense that domestic savings are used for net investment abroad. The purchase of foreign assets that the current account surplus represents may provide a higher return than would investment at home. High saving economies in Asia, such as Singapore, provide examples here.

Causes and consequences of current account imbalances

If there are no credit constraints and all economic agents act rationally by weighing up the relative returns from different investment opportunities, then a current account imbalance simply reflects the differences in preferences, in investment opportunities and in resource windfalls across countries. This is a useful benchmark case, but a persistent current account deficit is not always benign.

For reasons of myopia and political pressures, a current account deficit may not reflect higher investment at home in response to especially attractive investment opportunities or because of a resource windfall—rather, it may reflect low savings because of high private consumption based, for example, on a property price bubble or unsustainably high government consumption, or it may reflect investment in wasteful projects.

We saw in Chapter 12 that a country does not have to be in trade balance to be in medium-run equilibrium. We also alluded to the fact that there are economic and political forces that can push countries back towards trade balance in the long run. These forces are likely to be stronger when the imbalance is viewed as being unsustainable (rather than benign).

There are a number of different channels through which persistent imbalances could come under pressure. To make the discussion as simple as possible, we assume that net interest and profit receipts from abroad are zero so that the current account balance and the trade balance are equivalent (see Chapter 12 for more information on the open economy accounting framework).

Consumption effects of changes in wealth: A trade surplus indicates rising wealth for the home country and a trade deficit, the opposite. We saw from the Permanent Income Hypothesis in Chapter 1 that changes in lifetime wealth can result in changes in consumption in the current period. Applying this idea, consumers in an economy with a persistent trade deficit may think that belt tightening will eventually be required for the home economy to service and repay their foreign debts. This could lead to estimates of permanent income being adjusted down and an associated fall in consumer spending, which would shift the *AD* curve leftwards and move the economy back towards long-run equilibrium.

Willingness of financial markets to fund deficits: If sentiment in financial markets is that a trade deficit reflects high home consumption or wasteful investment, then funds will cease to be available to the home country at the world interest rate. Our assumption that there is perfect international capital mobility would break down. This will dampen private investment and may force the government to tighten demand policy to reduce the deficit.

Exchange rate expectations: In a fixed exchange rate regime, if private counterparties are not willing to purchase the home currency to finance the external deficit, this reduces demand for home currency and puts pressure on it to depreciate. To avoid this scenario, the home country will have to sell foreign exchange reserves to defend its exchange rate peg. Selling foreign exchange reserves will increase the demand for home currency and stop it from depreciating. However, the foreign exchange reserves

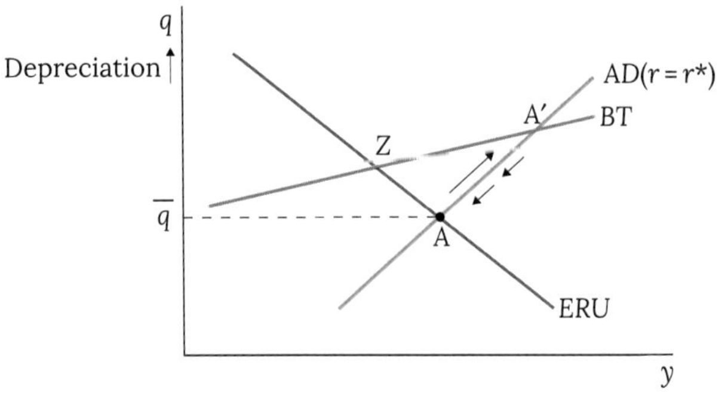

Figure 13.11 Medium-run equilibrium at A (trade deficit) is disturbed by exchange rate depreciation. Long-run equilibrium at Z. Visit www.oup.com/he/carlin-soskice to explore medium-run equilibrium and a trade deficit with Animated Analytical Diagram 13.11.

of the central bank are limited, and borrowing to supplement them may be difficult, meaning the peg cannot be defended *indefinitely* in an economy with a persistent trade deficit. Eventually a currency crisis or the threat of one will lead to some combination of devaluation and fiscal tightening moving the economy back towards trade balance.

When analysing flexible exchange rates, up to this point we have assumed that exchange rate expectations are pinned down by the medium-run equilibrium value of q (e.g. at $\overline{q}$ in Figure 13.11). However, if we assume that the expected exchange rate is influenced by the trade balance, the ability of the central bank to achieve its inflation target is undermined. Let us now assume that the expected exchange rate adjusts immediately to deliver a real exchange rate consistent with trade balance: a trade deficit then becomes destabilizing for the economy. In Figure 13.11 the economy is at medium-run equilibrium at point A with a trade deficit and constant inflation. Under the new assumption, the exchange rate will immediately depreciate, causing a movement along the AD curve to A′ as q depreciates. This movement causes the economy to move to the right of the ERU curve. To the right of the ERU curve, there is a gap between the WS and PS curves and inflationary pressures will emerge. As home's inflation rises relative to that of its competitors, home will become less competitive. This implies a real appreciation for home: and the economy will move back in the direction of point A as net exports fall. We can imagine that such a process could repeat itself. Once exchange rate expectations become unanchored in this way, there can be a spiral of rising inflation and nominal exchange rate depreciation until tighter *fiscal* policy is implemented and the AD curve is shifted to the left.

Political pressures: There could be political pressure to reduce imbalances. This is particularly relevant in surplus countries, where economic and financial market pressures to adjust are weaker than in deficit ones. This pressure can come from within the country, as the population urges the government to boost activity and operate at a lower unemployment rate, or from international trading partners. An example of external pressure to reduce imbalances is the tension between the US and China over China's manipulation of the yuan exchange rate.

As a result of these forces, long-run equilibrium is at a position on the *ERU* curve *and* at current account balance (Z). As we have seen, when the current account is balanced, the country's wealth is constant—in the sense that it is not borrowing from or lending to the rest of the world. To make the exposition as simple as possible, we have ignored the difference between the trade balance and the current account. This allows us to define the long-run equilibrium in the *AD-BT-ERU* model as the intersection of the *ERU* curve and the *BT* curve (as shown by y^{LRE} in Figure 12.12 in Chapter 12 and labelled point Z in Figure 13.11). Although economic pressures are more likely to make deficits unsustainable, external or internal political pressure may also lead a surplus country to adjust to the long-run equilibrium—or at least in the direction of a more balanced external position.

13.4.2 Sector financial balances

A major theme in the discussion of the background causes of the global financial crisis is global imbalances. What are these imbalances and how do they fit into the model? To understand what lies behind the emergence of persistent current account (or trade) surpluses or deficits, it is helpful to see how the goods market equilibrium condition for one economy can be rearranged to show its sector financial balances. We can write the goods market equilibrium condition in terms of sectoral savings and investment balances.

Three sector balances are of interest: the private sector financial balance (private savings net of its investment), the government sector financial balance (taxation net of government expenditure), and the trade balance (net investment abroad). We assume that the economy is in a short-run equilibrium at which $r = r^*$. *Ceteris paribus*, a trade surplus means that stock of foreign assets is increasing in the home economy. This measures the increase in the holdings of foreign wealth in the home economy and is therefore referred to as net investment abroad. Similarly to footnote 14, we rearrange the outflows and inflows version of the goods market equilibrium condition to separate out taxation and show the sector financial balances:[15]

$$(S - I(r^*)) + (T - G) = X - M$$

$$\underbrace{(s_1 y^{disp} - c_0 - I(r^*))}_{\substack{\text{private sector} \\ \text{financial balance}}} + \underbrace{(ty - G)}_{\substack{\text{government} \\ \text{financial balance}}} = \underbrace{X(Q, y^*) - QM(Q, y)}_{BT\text{ = net inv abroad}},$$

where y^{disp} is disposable income, $y^{disp} = (1 - t)y$. Note that adding net interest receipts from abroad, i.e. INT, to both sides gives back equation 13.5 from footnote 14.

This expression is useful because it highlights the flow equilibrium in the economy. One sector, for example, the private sector, can only run a financial deficit if it borrows from another sector: this would mean some combination of borrowing from the government (i.e. a government budget surplus) and borrowing from abroad (a foreign trade deficit). Whenever the goods market is in equilibrium, private savings net of investment (the private sector's financial balance) plus the government budget surplus (the government's financial balance) are equal to the trade surplus.

[15] To see this, note that $S = y^{disp} - C = y^{disp} - (c_0 + (1 - s_1)y^{disp}) = s_1 y^{disp} - c_0$.

How can 'twin deficits' arise?

The sector financial balances provide a useful lens with which to look at a country's macroeconomic developments, but the equation must be used with care. It is a goods market equilibrium condition, so in order to understand the implications of a shock or policy change it is first necessary to identify the shock and to work out the new goods market equilibrium.

In order to do this, we need to use a model. In our first example, we use the AD-BT-ERU model to illustrate the twin deficits that arise following an expansionary fiscal policy. We begin in equilibrium at trade and government budget balance, and in private sector financial balance. As shown in Figure 13.12, a rise in G leads to a new constant inflation equilibrium at higher output (on the ERU curve). Both in the temporary shorter-run equilibrium at point B and in the medium-run equilibrium at Z, there is a trade deficit. In both cases, output is higher than initially, which pushes up imports; in the new medium-run equilibrium, the exchange rate is appreciated, which depresses net exports (both B and Z are below the BT line).

What about the fiscal balance at Z? To pin things down, let us concentrate on the new medium-run equilibrium. Higher output generates higher tax revenues but not by enough to prevent the government's budget balance from deteriorating.[16] Thus, in the new equilibrium, the government's financial balance has deteriorated: there is a budget deficit. Higher y also raises savings and improves the private sector balance (since nothing has happened to s_1, c_0, or I—remember that in the new equilibrium at Z, $r = r^*$). To summarize, the increase in government spending results in a budget deficit. The financial sector balances equation highlights the fact that in the new equilibrium,

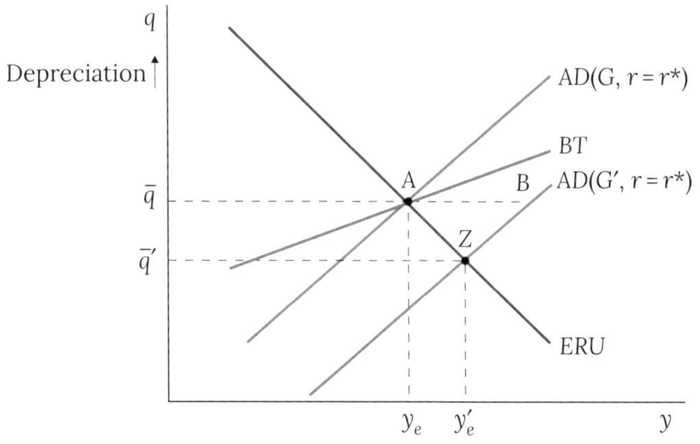

Figure 13.12 Twin deficits arising due to an expansion of government spending.

[16] The rise in G raises income, which raises savings and imports as well as tax revenue. The level of output in the new equilibrium will therefore be lower than the level that would raise taxes by the increase in G. Hence, there is a budget deficit in the new equilibrium. As an exercise, show this algebraically.

this is partly financed by borrowing from the private sector (which goes into financial surplus) and partly by borrowing from abroad (the trade balance goes into deficit). So-called twin deficits (fiscal and trade) have emerged.

Interpreting sector financial imbalances: Examples

Since the early 2000s, twin (or, as we shall see, triple) deficits have consistently been observed in the United States, as shown by Figure 13.13. Earlier, the Clinton presidency witnessed a trend improvement of the government balance to reach a balance just as the Dotcom bubble burst. The public finances under Clinton reflected the prudential fiscal policy view (explored in Chapter 7) that the appropriate time for fiscal tightening is during a private sector upswing. In the last twenty years, the budget deficit reflected a combination of tax cuts and expensive foreign wars. Government spending in the first decade of the 2000s was financed by borrowing from abroad: if the current account deficit exceeds the government deficit, this indicates that the private sector is also

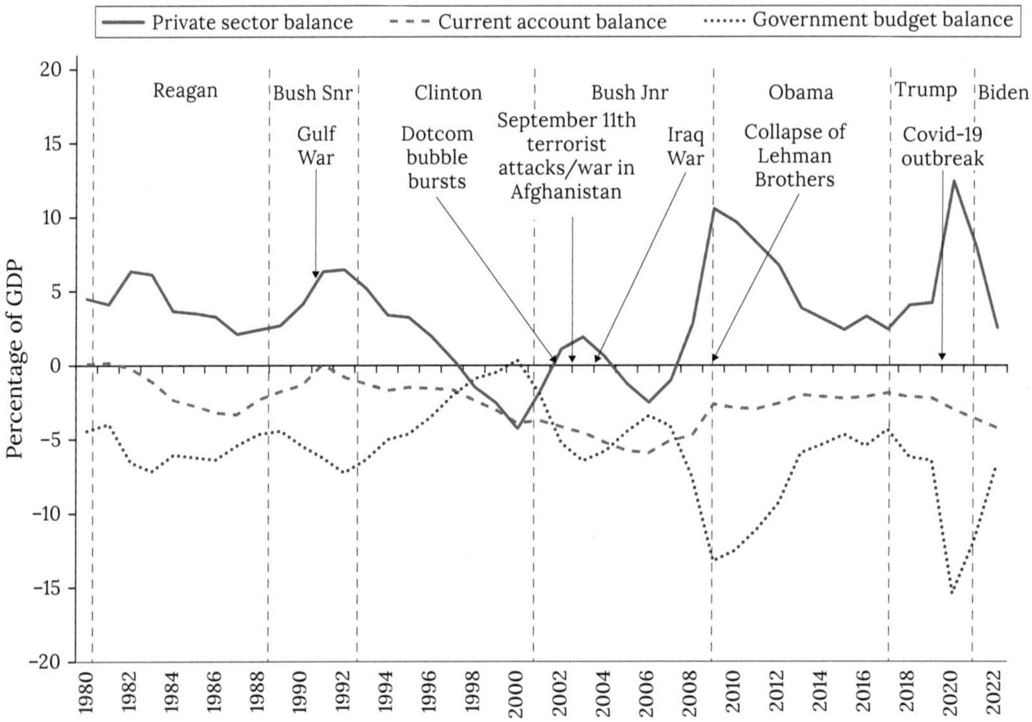

Figure 13.13 United States Sector Financial Balances: 1980–2022.

Note: The private sector balance was computed using the sector financial balances equation (i.e. private sector balance = current account balance less government budget deficit).

Source: OECD (accessed June 2022).

borrowing from abroad, resulting in triple deficits. These occurred in the build-up of both Dotcom and financial crisis bubbles. US borrowing was the mirror image (see Figure 13.4) of Chinese lending (i.e. the purchase of US Treasury bills by the Chinese authorities as part of their intervention in currency markets).

Can the US current account be rationalized by using the intertemporal model of the current account? The future macroeconomic adjustment brought on by such a substantial current account deficit could be thought of as benign if the build-up of debt simply reflected optimal borrowing to smooth consumption. Some economists have pointed to expectations of rapid income growth and the presence of exceptionally low interest rates (which reduces the cost of financing the government debt and encourages consumption in the present) as possible reasons why this might be the case. However, these arguments lost some weight after the onset of the global financial crisis, which showed that the macroeconomic adjustment (i.e. repaying of debt) in the United States indeed had painful economic ramifications. This will be explored in more detail in Section 13.5.1, as will the role of global imbalances in the 2008 crisis.

Further evidence of sub-optimal borrowing can be found in Trump's years. Well before the Covid-19 outbreak, the Trump administration interrupted the efforts toward improving the government's financial balance carried out during Obama's presidency, by implementing tax cuts in spite of low unemployment, and by waging trade wars against China. Such policies resulted in twin deficits and an improved private sector balance as trade wars hindered investment opportunities. Gaining electoral advantage rather than economic logic motivated these policies.

In our second example exploring sector financial balances, we use the intertemporal model and, for simplicity, assume that the exchange rate is fixed. In this case, oil is discovered. We introduce a government sector into the model of a resource windfall discussed above and assume that the rise in the economy's permanent income leads the government to increase its expenditure on education and other infrastructure by borrowing from abroad. In this example, the private sector also goes into deficit as consumption smoothing by households raises consumption when the discovery of oil is announced. Here, there are 'triple deficits' in anticipation of the flow of oil.

A more complicated model would include the likely effect of the oil discovery on the exchange rate. Countries where there has been a natural resources windfall have typically experienced exchange rate appreciation and suffered from 'Dutch disease', named after the Netherlands' experience following the discovery of natural gas in the North Sea. Dutch disease captures the idea that the non-resource tradables sector experiences a loss of competitiveness as a consequence of the exchange rate appreciation. The exchange rate appreciated when gas was discovered, because the foreign exchange market anticipated that the real exchange rate at which there would be current account balance was an appreciated one (as the AD-BT-ERU model predicts when there is a positive external trade shock).

13.5 GLOBAL INTERDEPENDENCE

13.5.1 Global interdependence and imbalances

As Figure 13.4 showed, a notable characteristic of the period of the 2000s—the late phase of the Great Moderation (as discussed in the introduction to this chapter)—was the growth in external imbalances of large countries in the global economy. The US, Spain and the UK had rising external deficits of a globally significant size. The counterpart to these deficits were the increasing surpluses of China, the oil-producing countries and Germany. Japan's substantial surplus remained fairly stable in the 2000s. In the same period, central banks in both developed and emerging and developing economies were using inflation targeting and were successful at achieving low and stable inflation. Figure 13.5 in Section 13.1 shows how inflation in these two country blocs remained low in the 2000s. This is in contrast to previous periods, where inflation, particularly in emerging and developing economies, proved difficult to control.

In hindsight, the imbalances that emerged in the 2000s seem unhealthy, a sure sign of the troubles that were to come. In the wake of the financial crisis, politicians and economists were quick to extol the virtues of 'rebalancing'—i.e. countries moving towards more balanced current account positions. In the years preceding the crisis economists were divided over whether the current account imbalances were benign, reflecting rational optimizing by economic agents, or whether they were unsustainable and posed a threat to medium-run economic stability.

Caballero et al. (2008) presented a unified model which sought to explain how large and rising US current account deficits could be coupled with low long-term interest rates and a rising share of US financial assets in world portfolios in a medium-run equilibrium. They divided the world into three regions: high-growth high-finance 'U' countries (e.g. US, UK, Australia), low-growth high-finance 'E' countries (e.g. Eurozone, Japan) and high-growth low-finance 'R' (i.e. the rest of the world). High finance referred to a high level of financial development.

The core of the model is that there is fast economic growth in the R countries (i.e. emerging markets), but that their underdeveloped financial systems cannot provide enough high-quality savings instruments to satisfy demand. This pushes up demand for savings instruments from the U and E regions. The model assumes that U has higher growth potential than E, so a disproportionate amount of global savings flows into these countries. This model explained how three macroeconomic trends that defined the early and mid-2000s—a worsening of the US current account deficit, low global interest rates and a rising share of US assets in world portfolios—could co-exist.

However, it has been criticized, particularly concerning the fact that the model assumptions better suit the 1990s (with the Asian financial crisis) than the mid-2000s. In the latter period, it could be argued that emerging markets did have the capacity to generate assets that others wanted.[17]

The Caballero et al. (2008) model emphasizes the importance of the US government's ability to create desirable financial assets (such as Treasury Bills). This is also high-

[17] See Frankel (2006).

lighted in a paper by Richard Cooper on the eve of the financial crisis, which concluded that current account imbalances were benign, as they simply reflected rational savings decisions of individuals in economies with ageing populations (e.g. Germany, Japan, China).[18] Given the more favourable demographics in the US, the argument follows that these imbalances could persist until the baby boom generation in the ageing economies reached retirement, at which point the imbalances would naturally unwind as individuals sold these assets to finance consumption during retirement.

Not all economists held the view that these imbalances were sustainable. A number thought that the global imbalances, the vast majority of which were between the US and the major surplus countries (i.e. Japan, Germany, and China), would inevitably lead to a large and potentially destabilizing depreciation in the dollar (Obstfeld and Rogoff 2005; Feldstein 2008). This would make US exports more attractive to foreigners and at the same time, make imports more expensive for US consumers. We know from Chapter 10, that if the Marshall–Lerner condition holds, a depreciation of the dollar would lead to an improvement in the trade balance.

13.5.2 **A 2-bloc model with inflation-targeting central banks**

The aim of this section is to set out a model which can provide a simple explanation of how two country blocs, each with an inflation-targeting central bank, but with different patterns in demand, could produce persistent imbalances in the global economy. We set out a 2-bloc model of the world economy and show how external imbalances can be consistent with successful inflation targeting.

In Section 13.1.4, we introduced the idea of medium-run global imbalances by using the downward-sloping *ERU* curve. It is easier to model the dynamic adjustment of two blocs to a shock, however, if we simplify on the supply-side and revert to a vertical *ERU*. The downward-sloping *ERU* is helpful in bringing out the incentive for a country to allow a domestic demand boom to take hold as discussed in Section 13.1.4. Here, we abstract from the motivation for different patterns of demand and concentrate on how the dynamic interaction takes place between two blocs where the supply-side is identical in each and is captured by a vertical *ERU* (i.e. there is a unique constant inflation equilibrium in each bloc). We return to different patterns of demand in Chapter 14 in the context of the heterogeneous behaviour of members of the Eurozone.

The role of q and r^* in the 2-bloc model

In the model, there are two blocs, I and II. To fix ideas, think of bloc I as being the deficit countries (US, UK, Spain) and bloc II as the surplus countries (China, Germany, Japan, oil exporters). But note that in the model, the two blocs constitute the whole of the world economy and there is an inflation-targeting central bank in each. In each bloc, the medium-run equilibrium is where aggregate demand is equal to equilibrium output (which is the same in each bloc at y_e), with $r = \overline{r}^*$ and $q = \overline{q}$.

[18] See Cooper (2008).

To simplify the notation, we assume that the coefficients on the interest rate and real exchange rate are identical in each economy and equal to one. This means we can write the medium-run equilibrium for each bloc as follows:

$$y_e = A^I - \overline{r}^* + \overline{q} \qquad \text{(bloc I)}$$

$$y_e = A^{II} - \overline{r}^* - \overline{q}. \qquad \text{(bloc II)}$$

We can see why q is positive for I and equal and opposite for II by writing out the definition of q in the 2-bloc case,

$$q = \log\left(\frac{P^{II}e}{P^I}\right) \text{ and } e = \frac{\$_I}{\$_{II}}.$$

A rise in q is a real depreciation for bloc I; a rise in e is a nominal depreciation for bloc I and vice versa for bloc II. We assume that $A^I > A^{II}$ (i.e. that autonomous demand is higher in bloc I).

The first aspect of the model is that if we equate the right-hand side of each equation, we can simplify and get an expression for the real exchange rate, $\overline{q}$:

$$A^I - \overline{r}^* + \overline{q} = A^{II} - \overline{r}^* - \overline{q}$$

$$2\overline{q} = A^{II} - A^I$$

$$\overline{q} = \frac{A^{II} - A^I}{2} < 0.$$

Since $A^I > A^{II}$, bloc I's real exchange rate is appreciated. This is reflected in $\overline{q} < 0$. Now remember that the expression $y = C + I + G + X - M$ can be rearranged to show that $X - M = y -$ (*'domestic absorption'*). In this model, it is clear that bloc I's trade deficit (its net imports from bloc II), which is output minus domestic absorption, is negative ($BT^I = y_e - (A^I - \overline{r}^*) = \overline{q} < 0$) and this is equal to bloc II's trade surplus (its net exports to bloc I), which is positive: $BT^{II} = y_e - (A^{II} - \overline{r}^*) = -\overline{q} > 0$.

Changes in the real exchange rate between blocs ensures that in each bloc, aggregate demand is at equilibrium and hence inflation is constant. If the blocs were symmetric in their levels of autonomous aggregate demand, $\overline{q} = 0$, which means the real exchange rate $Q = 1$ and common currency prices are identical in each bloc. Trade would be balanced.

The second aspect of the model is to note the role of the world real interest rate: this adjusts to ensure that for the global economy (the combination of bloc I and bloc II), aggregate demand is consistent with output at its equilibrium level in the world as a whole. To see this, we write aggregate demand in block I as $y^{D,I}$ and similarly for bloc II. We need to ensure that

$$y^{D,I} + y^{D,II} = 2y_e.$$

$$\text{Hence, } A^I - \overline{r}^* + \overline{q} + A^{II} - \overline{r}^* - \overline{q} = 2y_e$$

$$A^I + A^{II} - 2\overline{r}^* = 2y_e$$

$$2\overline{r}^* = A^I + A^{II} - 2y_e$$

$$\overline{r}^* = \frac{A^I + A^{II}}{2} - y_e.$$

This shows that the world real interest rate adjusts to ensure a constant inflation equilibrium for the world as a whole. This happens as a result of the central banks of bloc I and bloc II adjusting the interest rate to guide inflation back to target in their blocs. Both of these central banks are forward looking and rational and solve the model taking into account the actions of the other central bank.

In the top panel of Figure 13.14, the symmetric equilibrium is shown. In the lower panel, we show the new medium-run equilibrium in the world and in each bloc following a permanent positive demand shock in bloc I, which pushes $A^I > A^{II}$. The result is a higher world real interest rate, an appreciated real exchange rate, and trade deficit in bloc I, and a depreciated real exchange rate and trade surplus in bloc II. Inflation is constant in the new MRE. Next we examine how the economies move from the old to the new equilibrium. (Reading the summary at the end of this section before going through all the details may be helpful.)

A permanent demand shock in bloc I

In Chapter 11, we showed how the central bank and foreign exchange market simultaneously solve the model to work out how the central bank would choose its interest rate response to a shock, and how the exchange rate would change. In the 2-bloc model, there are three parties involved in solving the model: the central banks in each

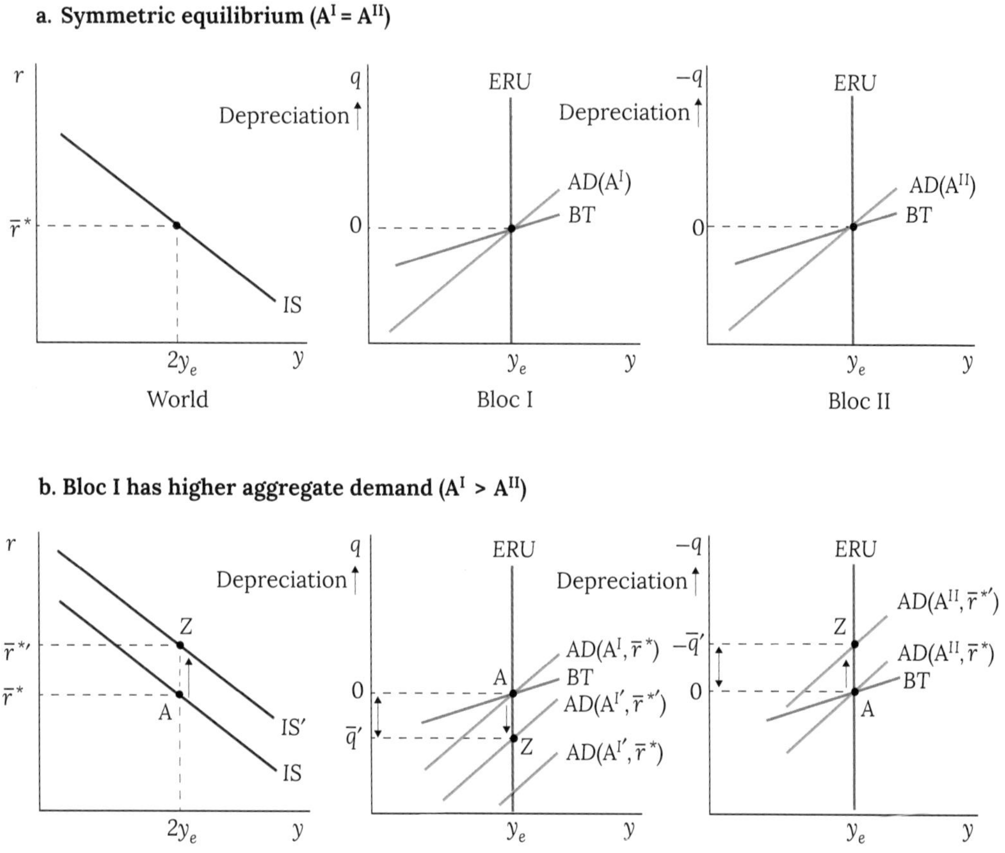

Figure 13.14 The 2-bloc model with (a) a symmetric equilibrium and (b) a permanent positive demand shock in bloc I. Visit www.oup.com/he/carlin-soskice to explore the two-bloc model with permanent higher demand in bloc I with Animated Analytical Diagram 13.14.

bloc and the foreign exchange market. We need to use our imagination to think of these three rational actors playing a game with each other in which they have complete information about the model and about the shock.

To analyse how they react to a demand shock in one of them, we begin in a symmetric equilibrium with the blocs identical in every respect (the top panel of Figure 13.14).

Bloc I: We assume a positive permanent shock to demand in bloc I in period zero. This pushes up output and inflation in bloc I in period zero and, just as in the closed economy, bloc I's central bank will have to respond to this in order to get the economy on the path back to target inflation. As we shall see, the analysis we have used for a small open economy gives good guidance as to what happens in the 2-bloc case. In response to the demand shock in period zero, the central bank in bloc I increases its interest rate to dampen activity. As usual, this is accompanied by an appreciation of the real exchange rate in bloc I and in period one, bloc I is on the MR curve and on the path back to target inflation.

Spillovers to bloc II via *q*: Meanwhile all three actors have to consider the spillovers from the shock to bloc II's economy. In this simple model, spillovers from I to II take place only through changes in the real exchange rate. In reality, there would also be feedback via the effect of changes in income in bloc I on imports from bloc II. In our model, the marginal propensity to import is zero. In a more realistic model, an increase in A^I would not only push up output in bloc I, but also increase their demand for imports. As bloc I's imports are bloc II's exports, the initial increase in A^I would also increase A^{II}. We exclude this feedback mechanism from the model as it complicates the analysis.

In the model, it takes one period for interest and exchange rate changes to have an effect: hence, in period zero, nothing happens to inflation or output in bloc II. However, bloc II's central bank observes the shock to bloc I in period zero and works out that in order to keep to its inflation target, it will need to act. Why? Because the appreciated real exchange rate in bloc I implies a depreciated real exchange rate for bloc II: whatever happens to the real exchange rate in bloc I happens (in reverse) to the real exchange rate in bloc II. Unless the central bank in bloc II raises its interest rate to offset the effect of the depreciation in its real exchange rate on its aggregate demand, there will be an increase in bloc II's inflation in period 1. By working through the model, the three parties will figure out that the central bank in bloc II will be able to fully offset the effects of the shock on inflation in its economy.

Figure 13.15 shows the new medium-run equilibrium (as in the lower panel of Figure 13.14) and sketches the path of adjustment in each bloc. Figure 13.16 shows the adjustment process in the PC-MR and IS-RX diagrams for each bloc, which can be explained period-by-period as follows:

Adjustment to new equilibrium: Period 0: Both economies start at their respective bliss points—point A in Figure 13.16. There is a positive demand shock in bloc I, which is observed by both central banks and the forex market. This moves bloc I to point B with output at y_0 and inflation at π_0. Bloc II has not moved from its original position. The central banks forecast their Phillips curves in the next period. In bloc I, the PC

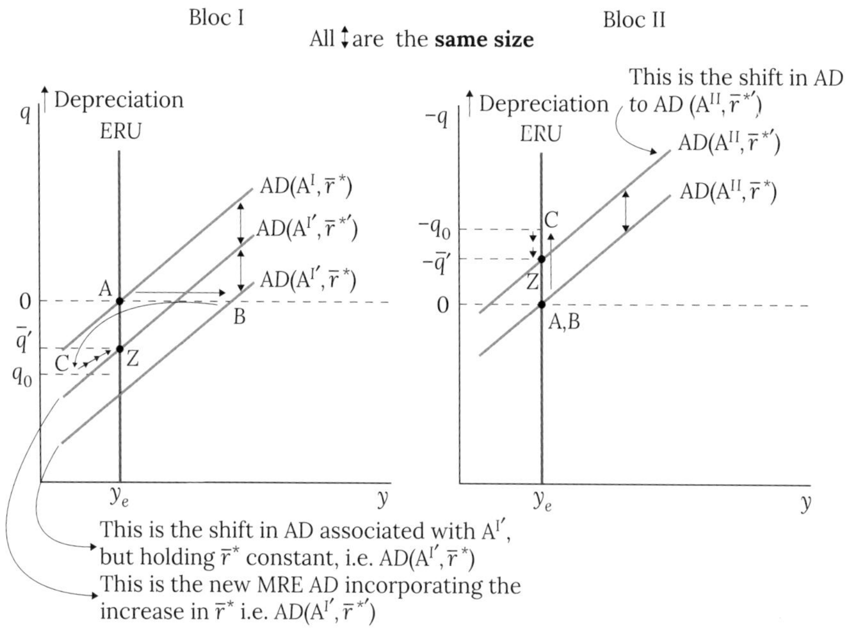

Figure 13.15 The 2-bloc model: the AD–ERU diagrams for bloc I and bloc II using the example of a permanent positive demand shock in bloc I. Visit www.oup.com/he/carlin-soskice to explore the two-bloc model with permanent higher demand in bloc I further with Animated Analytical Diagram 13.15.

will move to $PC(\pi_1^E = \pi_0)$ next period. Bloc I is not on its *MR* curve at point B. Their desired position on next period's *PC* is point C. In order to achieve this, the central bank in bloc I raises the interest rate to r_0^I, taking account of the appreciation of the exchange rate that will occur (so the *UIP* condition holds) and of the reasoning of bloc II's central bank.

Meanwhile, in bloc II, the central bank forecasts that the *PC* will not move next period, as inflation has not changed. They have, however, noted that the actions of bloc I's central bank will lead to a depreciated exchange rate in bloc II (as an appreciation in bloc I is a depreciation in bloc II in this model). To counter this effect and keep the economy at its bliss point, the central bank of bloc II must raise interest rates to r_0^{II}. This rate hike is exactly what is required to offset the boost in output that would occur as the result of the depreciated exchange rate.

The new interest rates and exchange rates can only affect the economy with a one period lag. This means that bloc I ends period 0 with output at y_0, inflation at π_0, the interest rate at r_0^I and the exchange rate at q_0. In contrast, bloc II remains at its bliss point, with a real interest rate of r_0^{II} and an exchange rate of $-q_0$.

Period 1 onwards: The new interest rates and exchange rates have had time to take effect and both blocs have moved to point C. In bloc I, the higher interest rate and the appreciated real exchange rate reinforce each other and dampen aggregate demand,

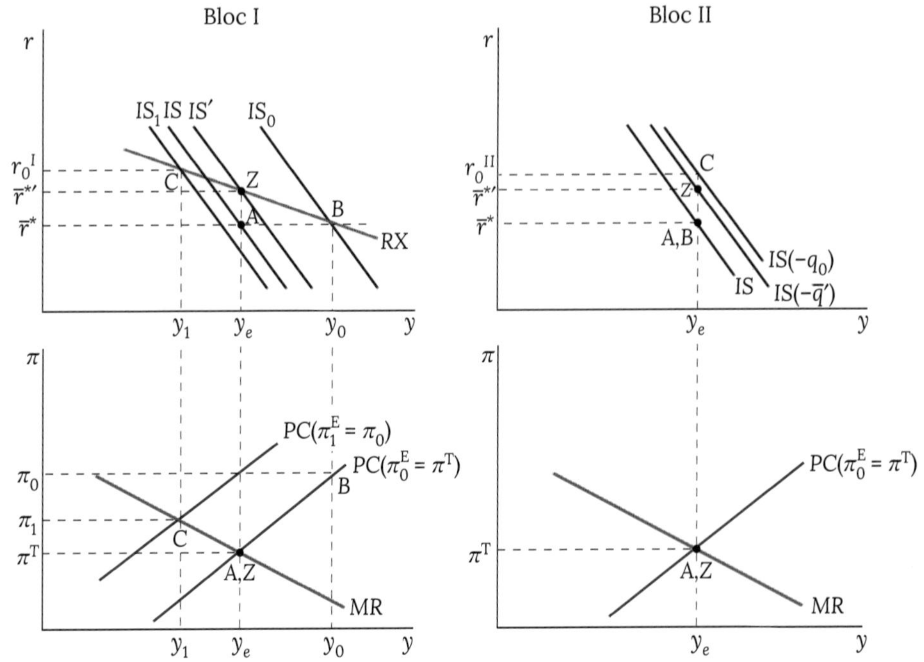

Figure 13.16 The 2-bloc model: the IS-RX and PC-MR diagrams for bloc I and bloc II using the example of a permanent positive demand shock in bloc I. Visit www.oup.com/he/carlin-soskice to explore the two-bloc model with permanent higher demand in bloc I further with Animated Analytical Diagram 13.16.

causing output to fall to y_1 and inflation to fall to π_1. In bloc II, the interest rate and exchange rate effects exactly offset each other and the economy remains at its bliss point.

In bloc I, the adjustment from C to Z is very similar to the demand and supply shock cases in the open economy 3-equation model discussed in Chapter 11. The economy adjusts along the RX curve to the new medium-run equilibrium at point Z. The RX curve has shifted upwards after the demand shock in bloc I. This is because the RX curve is pinned down by the world rate of interest, which changes as a result of the demand shock. During the adjustment from C to Z in bloc I, the central bank slowly reduces the interest rate from r_0^I to $\overline{r}^{*\prime}$ to stay on the MR and RX curves. The path of interest rates takes account of the depreciation that occurs each time the interest rate is reduced. This depreciation means the UIP condition holds in all periods.

In bloc II, the adjustment from C to Z is simpler. The central bank can see that the exchange rate in bloc I is going to slowly depreciate over this period, meaning that bloc II's exchange rate is going to slowly appreciate. To offset the depressing effect from this appreciation, the central bank will slowly reduce interest rates from r_0^{II} to $\overline{r}^{*\prime}$. Throughout the entire adjustment period, bloc II does not move from its bliss point—i.e. where output is at equilibrium and inflation is at target.

The adjustment to the demand shock in bloc I ends when the blocs are at point Z, where inflation is back at target and output is back at equilibrium in both blocs. The new medium-run equilibrium is however characterized by a higher world interest rate (i.e. $\overline{r}^{*\prime} > \overline{r}^{*}$), a more appreciated exchange rate in bloc I and a more depreciated exchange rate in bloc II.

There are a number of important points to highlight from this process:

1. The initial interest rate hike in bloc I is greater than that in bloc II (i.e. $r_0^{I} > r_0^{II}$). This is because the permanent positive demand shock takes place in bloc I.
2. Throughout the adjustment process bloc II remains at equilibrium output and target inflation (i.e. its bliss point): all that the bloc II central bank has to do each period is to adjust its interest rate to offset the effects of the real exchange rate changes arising from bloc I's adjustment path.
3. When the adjustment process is complete, both economies are at equilibrium output with inflation at target and with the same real interest rate. As shown in the bottom left-hand panel of Figure 13.14, the common (i.e. world) real interest rate is higher than in the initial medium-run equilibrium to squeeze out the higher aggregate demand. Bloc I has an appreciated real exchange rate in the new medium-run equilibrium. It also has a trade deficit. Conversely, bloc II's exchange rate is depreciated and it has a trade surplus.

Lastly, Figure 13.17 shows the impulse response functions for the key variables in each bloc. The details of the dynamic adjustment are set out in more detail in Section 13.7.2 of the Appendix.

Summary

The model is very stylized and is based on very strong assumptions about rationality and full information on the part of the three actors. Nevertheless, it brings out an important feature of an interdependent global economy: if economies differ in the kind of shocks they are exposed to—for example, as we saw in Chapters 8 and 9, the scale of financial and leverage cycles was very different in different countries—it is still possible for macroeconomic equilibrium to prevail in the sense of a constant inflation equilibrium in both blocs.

The reason for assuming that the marginal propensity to import is zero is that it allows us to abstract from the spillovers between the two blocs arising from aggregate demand shifts. If we included the marginal propensity to import, then when bloc I has a positive AD shock, that implies higher import demand coming from bloc I as incomes there rise. Imports come from bloc II. From bloc II's perspective, this would impart a positive AD shock on bloc II, shifting its AD curve to the right (like a rise in y^* in bloc II's export function). Bloc II's central bank would then have to respond both to the positive aggregate demand spillover arising from the depreciation of its exchange rate (a movement along the AD curve) and from the higher demand for its exports at a given exchange rate (a shift of the AD curve). The central bank in bloc II would still

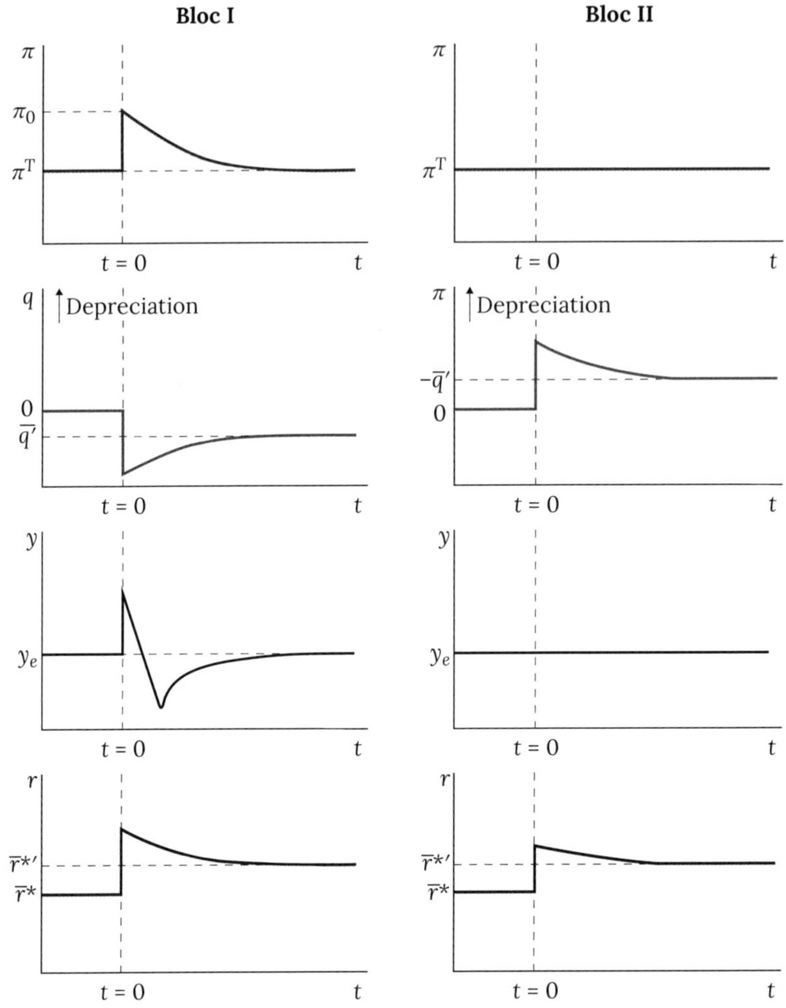

Figure 13.17 The 2-bloc model: the impulse response functions (IRFs) for bloc I and bloc II using the example of a permanent positive demand shock in bloc I.

face the issue of offsetting unwanted demand spillovers coming from bloc I—but now originating from two different sources.

The 2-bloc model illustrates how current account imbalances can arise—when blocs are affected by different shocks and/or have different patterns of demand—and how they can be consistent with stable inflation. As highlighted by the intertemporal approach to the current account presented earlier in the chapter, such imbalances are not necessarily a problem: they may reflect an optimal response to differences in resource endowment (such as a natural resource windfall) or differences in preferences as countries take advantage of international capital mobility to smooth consumption.

13.6 CONCLUSIONS

This chapter has used open economy macro models to improve our understanding of oil shocks and global imbalances. Setting out a framework within which to analyse these shocks and imbalances allows us to better understand their macroeconomic consequences and provides useful lessons for policy making. The lessons apply to the global dimensions of the climate crisis and the pandemic.

We have shown how oil price (i.e. commodity) shocks can be modelled by introducing the world terms of trade between manufactures and raw materials. In this framework, an increase in the oil price is both a demand and a supply shock for an oil-importing economy, resulting in shifts in both the *AD* and *ERU* curves.

We have also introduced two new open economy models—the intertemporal model of the current account (ICA) and the 2-bloc model—which provide valuable insights into the sizeable current account deficits that characterized the global economy during the Great Moderation.

The ICA highlights that current account deficits can be either benign or potentially dangerous, depending on whether they reflect optimizing forward-looking behaviour (e.g. borrowing to develop a newly discovered natural resource) or are not justified by economic fundamentals (e.g. a consumption boom based on an asset price bubble). The 2-bloc model can be used to show how two blocs in the world economy with different patterns of demand can result in both current account and real exchange rate divergences and successful inflation targeting.

This chapter allows us to analyse phenomena such as oil, climate and pandemic shocks:

1. Why did the oil price shock of the 2000s not lead to widespread 'stagflation', such as that experienced as a result of the 1970s oil shocks? The oil shocks of the 1970s were primarily driven by the supply side and reflected exogenous geo-political events disrupting oil supply, whereas an increase in oil demand (particularly in fast-growing emerging markets) played a much more significant role in the 2000s shock. The latter shock coincided with a period of low inflation and falling unemployment, which was in stark contrast to the 'stagflation' of the 1970s. This is due to a combination of factors, including (a) the increased flexibility of labour markets in the 2000s and (b) the easier access to credit and ability to substitute away from energy-intensive activities in the latter period. In addition, inflation-targeting central banks used non-accommodating monetary policy to keep inflation expectations firmly anchored in the latter period, whereas policy makers mistakenly tried to keep output at its pre-shock level in the 1970s. This failure to account for the supply-side implications of the oil shock led to significantly worse economic outcomes in the 1970s than in the 2000s. The less costly impact of the oil price rises of the 2000s helps to place the global supply-chain problems that arose in the pandemic, as well as the energy price shock due to the Ukraine war, and their likely impact on inflation into historical perspective.
2. What were the macroeconomic consequences for economies following different growth strategies during the Great Moderation period? There were two distinct

blocs of economies during the years before the financial crisis; the deficit countries (the US, the UK, and Spain) and the surplus countries (Germany, China, and the oil exporters). The former favoured expansion of the financial sector. An emphasis on the export sector was very important in both China and Germany. Although China was growing rapidly, its growth was unbalanced: very high investment levels were associated with even higher saving rates. Germany grew very slowly: restrained domestic demand complemented restructuring of the export sector as a basis for export-led growth. The macroeconomic consequence of these different strategies was that although inflation targets were met, there was a build-up of large imbalances among countries.

3. Were the large current account imbalances accumulated during the pre-crisis years the result of intertemporal optimization? In the wake of the global financial crisis of 2008–09, it seems clear that the current account imbalances were not mainly the result of rational forward-looking behaviour. Households and banks in the United States, Spain, and the UK borrowed excessively, which resulted in the build-up of a dangerous leverage cycle (see Chapters 8 and 9), and made the global economy vulnerable to a financial crisis.

The analysis of resource windfalls and Dutch disease shows how the behaviour of forward-looking households, firms and financial markets can bring to the present some of the effects of discoveries that take years or even decades to exploit. These effects include the appreciation of the real exchange rate in the case of a natural resource windfall, which has the effect of weakening the competitiveness of industries producing non-resource sector tradeables (Dutch disease).

This analysis can be used to shed light on some of the effects of the climate crisis, including consequences for financial stability (see Chapter 10). Countries rich in fossil fuel resources will find themselves with so-called stranded assets. Given the climate emergency, many of these resources will remain in the ground. This is a negative resource windfall. Exchange rates in fossil fuel rich economies will depreciate and consumption will be reined in as permanent income is projected to be lower than had been anticipated. Nevertheless, this mitigates for Dutch disease and will improve the prospects for industries outside the resource sector from which new sources of comparative advantage can emerge.

Chapters 11, 12, and 13 have primarily focused on open economy macroeconomics in relation to economies with flexible exchange rate regimes. In 2019, however, 16% of world output was accounted for by the Eurozone, a common currency area with irrevocably fixed exchange rates.[19] An economic model of the global economy would therefore not be complete without a proper treatment of the economics of a common currency area (and more broadly, of fixed exchange rate regimes). Chapter 14 fills this gap, investigating how membership of the Eurozone affects macroeconomic adjustment and stabilization policy.

[19] Calculated using the IMF World Economic Outlook Database, October 2021.

13.7 APPENDIX

13.7.1 A compact summary of the oil shock model

A new import function

In the oil shock model presented in this chapter we assume home is a pure raw materials importer and a manufactured goods exporter.[20] Table 13.1 in Section 13.2 shows how export and import prices are affected by this set of assumptions. In particular, the world real price of raw materials τ, now affects the real price of imports.

In Chapter 12 we defined M, the import function in real terms as:

$$M = \textit{Real price of imports} \times \textit{Marginal propensity to import} \times y.$$

When home is a pure raw materials importer, the real price of imports is given by the oil price expressed in home currency terms divided by the price level in the home economy. We use the price of manufactured goods, i.e. P_{mf}, as the baseline price the home economy uses for comparison with its competitors because it is modelled as a manufactured goods exporter. This is the producer price index for the home economy. Hence,

$$\textit{Real price of imports} = \frac{P_M}{P_{mf}} = \frac{P^*_{rm}e}{P_{mf}}.$$

Multiplying and dividing by P^*_{mf} in the equation above we get:

$$\frac{P_M}{P_{mf}} = \frac{P^*_{rm}e}{P_{mf}} = \frac{\left(\frac{P^*_{rm}}{P^*_{mf}}\right)P^*_{mf}e}{P_{mf}} = \tau\frac{P^*_{mf}e}{P_{mf}} = \tau Q. \tag{13.6}$$

As one would expect, a rise in τ causes the real price of imports to increase as a higher bill is now paid by the home economy for any given volume of imports.

However, if no assumptions are made on the elasticity of demand for imports, the effect of a rise in τ is more complex since the marginal propensity to import may also be affected. In particular, it is reasonable to expect the marginal propensity of imports to be negatively related to τ, since importers are intuitively less willing to spend money on a relatively more expensive imported good. Therefore, marginal propensity to import is defined as:

$$MPI = m(\tau Q). \tag{13.7}$$

where $\partial m/\partial\tau \leq 0$ and $\partial m/\partial Q \leq 0$.

We can then write the imports function for the home economy as:

$$M = \tau Q m(\tau Q)y. \tag{13.8}$$

---

[20] This appendix was written by Alessandro Guarnieri and draws on notes from Christopher Lee.

There is no role for τ in the export function given that home is modelled as a manufacturing goods exporter. The balance of trade equation in this model is then:

$$X - M = \sigma(Q)y^* - \tau Q m(\tau Q)y. \tag{13.9}$$

A further assumption on import elasticity of demand

In Section 13.2.2 we assumed that the volume of imports of oil does not change in the short run following a rise in 'the world relative price of oil' τ. The rationale is that demand for oil is price inelastic because of the lack of substitutes for this essential input. Hence, when τ increases, the responsiveness of demand for oil is negligible, thus leaving the terms of trade effect (i.e. a higher import bill for any volume of imports) the only significant source of variation in net exports. For simplicity, we assume the short-run demand is perfectly price-inelastic, which means that the volume of imports is unchanged following a change in τ. A higher import bill is then the only source of variation in net exports, which explains why the *AD* and *BT* curves unambiguously shift left.

Equation 13.9 then becomes:

$$X - M = \sigma(Q)y^* - \tau Q m(Q)y,$$
$$\rightarrow X - M = X(\sigma(Q), y^*) - \tau Q M(Q, y).$$

13.7.2 Dynamic adjustment to a shock in the 2-bloc model

In this section, we will provide the mathematics behind the dynamic adjustment to shocks in the 2-bloc model. We will use the example of the case where there has been a positive permanent demand shock in bloc I (but not bloc II) in period 0. The intuition and explanation for this example is provided in Section 13.5.2 of the main body of this chapter.

We assume that bloc I and bloc II are in equilibrium in $t = -1$. So

$$y^{I}_{-1} = A^{I} - \overline{r}^{*} + \overline{q} = y_e$$
$$r^{I}_{-1} = r^{II}_{-1} = \overline{r}^{*}$$
$$\pi^{I}_{-1} = \pi^{II}_{-1} = \pi^{T}, \text{ and}$$

$$y^{II}_{-1} = A^{II} - \overline{r}^{*} - \overline{q} = y_e, \text{ such that}$$
$$A^{I} = A^{II}.$$

Then in $t = 0$, autonomous demand in bloc I increases permanently to $A^{I'}$. All three actors first work out the changes to equilibrium values. Bloc I and bloc II were identical before the shock, so that $\overline{q} = 0$ and $\overline{r}^{*} = A^{I} - y_e = A^{II} - y_e$. After the permanent demand shock in bloc I, the new medium-run equilibrium becomes:

$$y_e = A^{I'} - \overline{r}^{*'} + \overline{q}'$$
$$y_e = A^{II} - \overline{r}^{*'} - \overline{q}'$$
$$\overline{r}^{*'} = \frac{A^{I'} + A^{II}}{2} - y_e$$
$$\text{and } \overline{q}' = -\frac{A^{I'} - A^{II}}{2}.$$

What happens in period 0?

$$y_0^I = y_e + A^{I'} - A^{II}$$
$$\pi_0^I = \pi^T + (y_0^I - y_e)$$
$$= \pi^T + (A^{I'} - A^{II}).$$

The central bank in bloc I, the central bank in bloc II and the foreign exchange market can now forecast that next period's Phillips curve in I will be

$$\pi_1^I = \pi_0^I + (y_1^I - y_e).$$

It's also common knowledge that the central bank in bloc I has a monetary rule (MR) that defines the trade-off between output and inflation reductions each period—hence also next period, period 1. To simplify the notation, we assume $\alpha = \beta = 1$:

$$y_1^I - y_e = -(\pi_1^I - \pi^T). \qquad \text{(monetary rule; bloc I)}$$

Putting period 1's Phillips curve and monetary rule equations together, all three rational actors can work out the combination of inflation and output in period 1 in bloc I that the central bank of bloc I will want to see. Thus:

$$\pi_1^I = \pi_0^I - (\pi_1^I - \pi^T)$$
$$\pi_1^I = \frac{(\pi_0^I + \pi^T)}{2}$$
$$y_1^I = y_e - \frac{(\pi_0^I - \pi^T)}{2} = y_e - \frac{A^{I'} - A^{II}}{2}.$$

Now all three actors know the output level, y_1^I, which the central bank in bloc I wants to achieve next period. To do so the only instrument bloc I's central bank has at its disposal is r_0^I. This has to be set to solve:

$$y_1^I = A^{I'} - r_0^I + q_0.$$

The problem is that q_0 depends on r_0^I via the UIP condition:

$$r_0^I - r_0^{II} = q_1^E - q_0$$
$$r_1^I - r_1^{II} = q_2^E - q_1^E$$
$$\ldots.$$

The central banks in both I and II must respect this set of equations. Summing both sides we get $\sum_0^\infty (r_t^I - r_t^{II}) = \overline{q}' - q_0$ since $\lim_{t\to\infty} q_t^E = \overline{q}'$. Moreover $r_t^I, r_t^{II} \to \overline{r}^{*'}$. Hence

$$\sum_0^\infty (r_t^I - r_t^{II}) = \sum_0^\infty \left(\left(r_t^I - \overline{r}^{*'}\right) - \left(r_t^{II} - \overline{r}^{*'}\right) \right) = \overline{q}' - q_0.$$

Now assume that r^I and q both converge to their new equilibrium levels $\overline{r}^{*'}$, $\overline{q}'$ at a proportional rate of λ. The derivation of λ follows the same method as in the small open economy (see Appendix 11.5.2 of Chapter 11), so we no longer assume $\beta = 1$. Solving the central bank's loss-minimization problem:

$$\begin{aligned} L &= (y^I - y_e)^2 + \beta(\pi^I - \pi^T)^2 \\ &\Longrightarrow (y^I - y_e) + \beta(\pi^I - \pi^T) = 0 \\ &\Longrightarrow (y_1^I - y_e) = -\beta(\pi_1^I - \pi^T). \end{aligned}$$

From this we derive λ:

$$(y_1^I - y_e) = -\beta(\pi_1^I - \pi^T) \text{ and } (\pi_1^I - \pi^T) = (\pi_0^I - \pi^T) + (y_1^I - y_e)$$

$$\lambda = \frac{(\pi_1^I - \pi^T)}{(\pi_0^I - \pi^T)} = \frac{1}{1+\beta}.$$

Hence $\sum_0^\infty \left(\left(r_t^I - \bar{r}^{*\prime}\right) - \left(r_t^{II} - \bar{r}^{*\prime}\right)\right) = \frac{r_0^I - \bar{r}^{*\prime}}{1-\lambda} - \frac{r_0^{II} - \bar{r}^{*\prime}}{1-\lambda} = \bar{q}' - q_0$.[21] Since $y_1^{II} = y_e$ that implies

$$\begin{aligned} y_1^{II} - y_e &= 0 = -\left(r_0^{II} - \bar{r}^{*\prime}\right) - \left(q_0 - \bar{q}'\right) \\ &\rightarrow \left(r_0^{II} - \bar{r}^{*\prime}\right) = \left(\bar{q}' - q_0\right) \rightarrow \frac{\left(r_0^I - \bar{r}^{*\prime}\right)}{1-\lambda} - \frac{\left(\bar{q}' - q_0\right)}{1-\lambda} = \left(\bar{q}' - q_0\right) \\ &\rightarrow (r_0^I - \bar{r}^{*\prime}) = (\bar{q}' - q_0)(2-\lambda). \end{aligned}$$

This is now substituted into bloc I's IS curve in deviation form to get:

$$\begin{aligned} (y_1^I - y_e) &= -(r_0^I - \bar{r}^{*\prime}) - \left(\frac{r_0^I - \bar{r}^{*\prime}}{2-\lambda}\right) \\ &= -(r_0^I - \bar{r}^{*\prime})\left(1 + \frac{1}{2-\lambda}\right) \\ &= -(r_0^I - \bar{r}^{*\prime})\left(\frac{3-\lambda}{2-\lambda}\right). \end{aligned}$$

This is the RX curve showing the relation along the equilibrium adjustment path—through the relevant points of IS curves with different values of q. Notably the RX curve is flatter than the representative IS curve, implying that a given change in r has a greater impact on y in the open economy than in the closed. This is because the change in r both operates directly on y with coefficient -1 (or more generally a), and operates indirectly on y via its effect on changing q with coefficient $-\frac{1}{2-\lambda}$. Thus a much smaller change in r is needed in the open economy to have the same effect on y as in the closed economy. For example, if $\lambda = 0.5$, then r needs to change by only 3/5 of the amount as in the closed economy.

This is larger than in the small open economy case because of the 'bloc' effect. When q appreciates initially, r^{II} has to rise to keep y^{II} in equilibrium. This requires a bigger change in r^I than would be the case in the small open economy: in effect the rise in r^I has triggered a rise in the world rate of interest, which would have been fixed in the small open economy. The slope of the RX line here is $-\frac{2-\lambda}{3-\lambda}$ and in the small open economy case $-\frac{1-\lambda}{2-\lambda}$. The empirical implication here is that we might expect to see common patterns to interest rate changes across the world if there is a shock in any one big bloc.

---

[21] Note that here we require the rate of deviations in interest rate differentials, i.e. λ, to be the same in both blocs; this is possible even though $r_0^I > r_0^{II}$ given that the difference in interest rates between the two blocs becomes minimal, and hence negligible, as both blocs approach the new equilibrium $\bar{r}^{*\prime}$.

Note that a direct comparison with the small open economy only holds in the case of an idiosyncratic shock to a bloc such as in the example used in this appendix. When both blocs are affected by an economic shock, it makes little sense to compare the adjustment process in one bloc with that in the small open economy model. To understand this, think of the case in which blocs I and II are both affected by a positive aggregate demand shock. There is no direct comparison with the model set out in Chapter 11 since we are simultaneously changing the conditions in the small open economy and the rest of the world.

QUESTIONS AND PROBLEMS FOR CHAPTER 13

CHECKLIST QUESTIONS

1. Explain using words and diagrams how an oil shock can be considered both a demand shock and a supply shock. Illustrate using data from a country affected by the energy price shock caused by the war in Ukraine.
2. Use Section 13.2.1 to answer the following questions about the oil price shocks of the 1970s:
   a. How did the misdiagnosis of the oil shock of 1973/74 affect policy choices and economic performance?
   b. Was the same mistake made following the 1979 oil shock? If possible provide some evidence to support your answer.
   c. Use the AD-BT-ERU diagram to illustrate the basis of the policy error.
3. Oil prices fell dramatically in 1986. Use the WS-PS and ERU diagrams to explain the effect of this supply-side shock on a small open economy. At the initial real exchange rate, what has happened to real wages and the level of employment?
4. Assess the following statement: 'the 2002–08 oil shock had less negative macroeconomic consequences than those in the 1970s due to the success of inflation-targeting central banks at stabilizing their economies'.
5. A small open economy is initially in trade balance. There is a temporary increase in household income for one period (i.e. rise in $\tilde{y}_t$). What effect does this have on the current account in period t and the following periods? Does this story change if the increase in income is permanent?
6. What is meant by the term 'Dutch disease'? How does this relate to the intertemporal model of the current account?
7. Discuss the political and economic forces that could move a small open economy towards trade balance in the long run.

8. Use an AD-BT-ERU diagram and the sector financial balances framework from Section 13.4.2 to show how a country whose government is restricting domestic demand could run 'twin surpluses' (i.e. government and current account surpluses).

9. Use Section 13.5.2 to answer the following questions about macroeconomic imbalances in the 2-bloc model:

a. Use a 2-bloc model to explain in words how there can be constant inflation in each bloc but current account imbalances.

b. Begin with 2 symmetric blocs. Now assume there is a permanent positive demand shock to bloc I and an equal and opposite permanent demand shock to bloc II. Describe the new medium-run equilibrium (MRE). [Hint: draw the AD-BT-ERU diagrams for the world, bloc I and bloc II before and after the shock as in Figure 13.14.] Your answer should focus on the differences between the initial and new MRE. Don't discuss the adjustment path to the new MRE. How could you adjust the nature of the shocks so that there was a lower real interest rate in the new MRE?

10. What is the consequence if all countries follow a demand-focused (i.e. expansionary) growth strategy? How did differing growth strategies across economies with global impact produce current account imbalances in the pre-crisis period?

11. Economist Willem H. Buiter referred to climate change as a 'stagflationary challenge'.[22] Using the materials from Section 13.3, explain in words why the overall effect of a climate shock could lead to higher inflation and lower employment. You may use a diagram to illustrate your point. Do you expect the new AD and BT curves to intersect vertically above the initial equilibrium output?

12. This question uses materials from Section 13.4.1. Consider an example of 'bad luck', opposite to the one presented in the textbook. An example may be one where there is a sudden announcement of environmental restrictions on mining, which will come into effect in the future and last for a specified length of time. Hence, exploitation of a country's natural resource will stop and not resume for a given period of time. Describe what the predictions of the intertemporal approach to the current account would be under such a scenario.

---

[22] See the full article 'When central banks go green', published on Project Syndicate on January 2nd 2020.

PROBLEMS

1. Collect data on real oil prices from the start of the 1970s to the present; Figure 13.9 uses FRED's WTISPLC series ('Spot Crude Oil Price: West Texas Intermediate (WTI)'). Pick an emerging and a developed economy and collect data from their national statistics or an international organization (e.g. IMF, OECD, Eurostat, World Bank) on the unemployment rate and the inflation rate from the start of the 1970s until the present. Do the patterns observed match those of the US in Figure 13.9? If not, propose some potential explanations.

2. Assess the following statement: 'economic policy makers should not directly intervene to reduce current account imbalances because they simply reflect rational savings decisions and comparative advantages in an increasingly globalized world'.

3. Set out the IS-RX and PC-MR diagrams for bloc I and bloc II (as per Figure 13.16) and the associated impulse response functions (as per Figure 13.17) for the case where there is a positive demand shock in bloc I and a negative demand shock in bloc II (assume the shocks are equal and opposite and take place simultaneously).

4. Use the mathematics from Section 13.7.2 of the Appendix to derive the RX curve after a negative demand shock in bloc II.

5. 'The oil-producing countries striving for a larger share of the national income need not necessarily result in a further acceleration of the pace of price rises. Whether this occurs depends in every country very greatly on whether it is made easier or more difficult to pass on higher prices of these imports—in other words, on whether the intensification of the international distribution struggle triggered by the oil-producing countries' price agreement is followed by an intensification of the domestic struggle for the distribution of the national income... The aim of the Bundesbank's policy, in full agreement with the federal government, is to restrict the scope for passing on the higher prices...'

   See page 1 of Deutsche Bundesbank (1974) 'Report of the Deutsche Bundesbank for the year 1973'. (https://www.bundesbank.de/en/publications/reports/annual-and-environmental-reports/annual-report-1973-702870)

   a. Explain the analysis of the West German central bank, the Bundesbank, using the models you have studied.
   b. How did the Bundesbank respond to the first oil shock? Relate this to the model.

c. Summarize the performance of the West German economy in 1974 (unemployment, inflation, current account balance) and compare it with that of the UK. Plot the data yourself and think how best to display it.

d. Compare the response of UK policy makers to the first oil shock with that of West Germany.

6. Read the following quote by the economist Willem Buiter on climate change:

> In recent decades, central banks have faced few significant stagflationary challenges (low economic growth coupled with high inflation) beyond the familiar case of oil shocks. But that could change if the adverse supply- and demand-side effects of climate change become more frequent and severe....Extreme manifestations of climate change could depress aggregate demand and potential output significantly, unpredictably, and over extended periods of time. (Willem Buiter, Former chief economist, Citibank; now, Columbia University.)

Use the models you have studied and your own research to answer these questions:

a. Evaluate the claim that climate change poses a 'stagflationary challenge' to policy makers with similarities to an oil shock. In what sense is it an adverse 'supply' shock; in what sense is it an adverse 'demand shock'? Explain differences as well as similarities.

b. Why does climate change also pose a risk to financial stability and what policies are central banks adopting to manage such a risk?

c. If mitigating climate change itself was added as a monetary policy goal of central banks what policies could they implement in support of this additional mandate?

7. What, if any, relevance is the Bundesbank's 1973 analysis (see Problem 5) to the energy price shock of 2022? Select a country for your case study and justify your answer by reference to models, data, and policy choices.

INTERESTED IN EXPLORING THESE TOPICS FURTHER?

Visit www.oup.com/he/carlin-soskice to consolidate and extend your learning with the multiple-choice questions and Animated Analytical Diagrams accompanying this chapter.

CHAPTER 14

OPEN ECONOMY EXTENSIONS II

FIXED EXCHANGE RATES AND THE EUROZONE

14.1 INTRODUCTION

Among the 38 OECD member countries, 19 have floating exchange rates. Switzerland moved back to floating in January 2015 after a period from September 2011 during which the Swiss National Bank managed the exchange rate. 19 member countries have chosen to give up their own exchange rate and adopt the euro and one member's currency is pegged to the euro via ERM II (Denmark).[1] In Chapters 11 and 13, we concentrated on countries with independent central banks and floating exchange rates. We now turn our attention to the analysis of fixed exchange rates. Our focus is on the Eurozone, the members of which collectively accounted for 16% of global GDP in 2019.[2] We provide a set of tools for understanding the origins, successes and vulnerabilities of the Eurozone—a large-scale experiment in the adoption of irrevocably fixed exchange rates, which began with 11 countries in 1999 and grew to 19 members by 2015.

The Eurozone—successes and imbalances

Before showing how the 3-equation model can be extended to analyse macroeconomic policy with fixed exchange rates, we introduce the Eurozone. Its experience illustrates the role played by the central bank in a common currency area in responding to common shocks as well as highlighting the implications of country-specific shocks. The Eurozone celebrated its first ten years in 2009. In this period of the tranquility of the Great Moderation, the European Central Bank (ECB) functioned successfully, delivering an average inflation rate for the Eurozone just above its target of 2%. It encountered its first crisis in 2010.

---

[1] This information is taken from the IMF's annual report on exchange arrangements and exchange restrictions 2018.

[2] Calculated using the IMF World Economic Outlook Database, April 2021.

In Chapter 13, we used a model to show how low and stable inflation could be achieved in a global economy in spite of imbalances in the blocs that make it up. In this chapter we shall apply this insight to the Eurozone as the 'global' economy, which achieved low and stable inflation during the 2000s, in spite of the emergence of imbalances among member countries. We modify the model to a common currency area where the two constituent blocs do not have independent monetary policy. Different growth patterns were behind the build-up of imbalances in the Eurozone just as they were in the global economy at the time. Figure 13.4 in Chapter 13 shows the evolution of current account balances in a number of large economies: two Eurozone economies feature on opposite sides in the chart. On the surplus side is Germany, with a rapidly growing surplus in the 2000s and on the deficit side is Spain, with a rapidly growing deficit. We shall see how different growth patterns arose in the Eurozone and the role the associated imbalances played in the sovereign debt crisis of 2010. The Eurozone survived the crisis. However, in common with other high-income countries, economic performance in the decade running up to the Covid-19 pandemic was weak. Deflation was a persistent concern.

Common and country-specific shocks

The 3-equation model can be applied to the ECB as the inflation-targeting central bank. The ECB responds to shocks to the common currency area as a whole, referred to as common or symmetric shocks. But there will also be shocks that affect member countries differently. For example, there could be a housing boom in one country but not another: in the Eurozone, there was a housing boom in Spain but house prices fell in Germany during the same period of the 2000s. These are country-specific or asymmetric shocks. An important task in this chapter is to extend the modelling framework to explain the different channels through which adjustment to shocks takes place under fixed exchange rates, and to apply that to the members of the Eurozone.

Since individual countries in the Eurozone do not have an independent monetary policy, national fiscal policy is the obvious stabilization instrument. But in a common currency area, the use of fiscal policy by one member can have negative spillover effects for the currency area as a whole. This possibility led the Eurozone to adopt a fiscal policy framework for its members called the Stability and Growth Pact.

In the run-up to the global financial crisis, the private sector overheated in Ireland and Spain, and inflation was above the Eurozone average. We apply the 3-equation model to show how national fiscal policy could have been used to 'lean against the wind' and dampen the boom. This was not done. We shall also see that self-stabilizing forces arising from the deteriorating competitiveness of the countries with higher inflation in the Eurozone were not strong enough to counteract the overheating. And, just like the US or UK with flexible exchange rates, measures were not taken before the financial crisis to halt the growth of leverage in banks in the Eurozone (as discussed in Chapter 9).

Vulnerability to a sovereign debt crisis

The Eurozone crisis brought to the fore the need to model the vulnerability of a member of a common currency area to a sovereign debt crisis, where financial markets attach very different risk premia to the government bonds issued by different member country governments. This requires an explanation of the relationship between banks, government and the central bank, which extends the analysis of Chapters 5 to 10.

The role of Eurozone membership is highlighted by the contrasting experiences of Spain and the UK. Although the underlying determinants, referred to as 'the fundamentals', of the solvency of the British and Spanish governments in 2011 were quite similar, interest rates on 10-year government bonds diverged sharply, reflecting differences in the market perception of the risk of sovereign default. This divergence demonstrated the vulnerability to a sovereign debt crisis of a country that borrows in a currency it does not issue. As a member of the Eurozone, the Spanish government borrows in euros, but it is the Eurozone central bank, the ECB, which issues euros.

14.1.1 **Origins of the Eurozone and the theory of an optimal currency area**

The political impetus for creating a common currency area in Europe increased as a consequence of German reunification in 1990. The potential for a larger unified Germany to unbalance the achievements of post-war integration was defused by the idea that Germany would be tied more tightly to the European project through economic and monetary union.

In economic terms, German manufacturing firms favoured monetary union as a way of preventing their competitors in France, Italy, and Spain from using exchange rate depreciation as a tool to regain competitiveness, as had happened under previous exchange rate arrangements. The private sector and policy makers in France, Italy, and Spain saw economic and monetary union as a means of acquiring a credible low inflation policy regime through a German-style inflation-targeting central bank at the level of the common currency area.

The themes of competitiveness and the behaviour of wage and price setters under the new rules of the game of a currency union play a big role in this chapter. We will also shine light on the extent to which the different motivations countries had for joining a common currency area affected its operation.

The theory of an optimal currency area points to the costs and benefits of a country giving up independent monetary policy (and an independent exchange rate).

Microeconomic benefits

The microeconomic benefits that arise from using a common currency increase with the degree of economic integration among the countries.

1. It is argued that monetary integration stimulates higher trade and investment because adopting a single currency eliminates foreign exchange rate risk. As we saw in Chapter 12, an unexpected change in the exchange rate affects the profitability of production in different locations. Decisions about location often involve long-lived investment in physical plant and equipment. Where companies would previously have operated in two different countries to hedge the risk of a change in the exchange rate, in a common currency area, they can take advantage of economies

of scale and achieve a more efficient allocation of resources by concentrating production in the best location.

2. Real resource savings arise from eliminating transactions costs that are incurred by currency conversion.
3. Competition in goods and labour markets would be expected to increase due to greater ease of price and wage comparisons. More competition, in turn, would be expected to produce both static and dynamic efficiency gains (as discussed in Chapters 15 and 16).
4. Monetary union is expected to increase the liquidity of financial markets. This is of particular benefit for small member countries. More liquid financial markets can also bring dangers of resource misallocation as explained in Chapters 8 and 9.

Evidence

A meta-analysis of 34 studies concluded that currency unions boost bilateral trade by between 30% and 90%.[3] Following the formation of the Eurozone, trade within it increased more than with non-EMU members.[4] Before EMU, the EU countries that stayed out of the Eurozone (UK, Sweden, Denmark) had lower than average bilateral trade shares with Eurozone members and may have benefited through this channel had they joined.[5]

In relation to the competition effects, Holland (2009) concluded that:

> trade liberalization, both on a global and European scale have reduced markups, and that liberalization has had a clear effect on the sustainable level of employment in European countries. However, it does not appear that the transparency associated with the euro has had a significant impact on the markup.

Macroeconomic costs and benefits

To pin down the macroeconomic costs and benefits of choosing to join a common currency area (CCA), the comparison is with a flexible exchange rate regime where the nominal exchange rate can aid the adjustment of the economy to shocks.

The theory of an optimal currency area highlights the main macroeconomic *cost* incurred by joining one: the policy maker is no longer able to use monetary policy (and the associated change in the nominal exchange rate) to adjust to country-specific shocks. The UK, for example, was able to benefit from a substantial nominal (and real) depreciation when hit by the negative aggregate shock that accompanied the financial crisis.

The cost of losing the ability to rapidly adjust competitiveness via nominal depreciation falls with the degree of integration between a country and the rest of the CCA. The more closely the business cycle of a member is correlated with that

[3] See Rose and Stanley (2005).
[4] See Micco et al. (2003) and Barr et al. (2003).
[5] See Barr et al. (2003).

of other members, the better will be the stabilization performed by the CCA central bank and the less the benefits of monetary policy independence.

There are a number of factors that influence the degree of integration among the members and how quickly they can stabilize against country-specific shocks in the absence of domestic monetary policy.

1. The extent of *wage and price flexibility*. Domestic wage flexibility can substitute for a flexible nominal exchange rate since changes in prices influence the real exchange rate. For example, a period of wage and price growth below that of the other CCA members will make a country more competitive and boost net exports. There are different levels of wage flexibility across Eurozone members. We shall discuss the implications of this in Section 14.4.1.
2. The *mobility of labour*. In principle, closer economic integration makes labour more mobile and migration (temporary or permanent) provides a shock absorber that can help substitute for the loss of the exchange rate instrument. This channel works particularly well in the US, where the movement of workers across state borders is fluid. National differences in language, training and accreditation, and in the flexibility of housing markets are among the reasons for the limited mobility of labour across national borders in the Eurozone.
3. The size of *fiscal transfers*. The bigger the central (i.e. Eurozone level) tax and transfer system, the more automatic stabilization there is for country-specific shocks (see Chapter 7 for an explanation of the way automatic stabilizers work). This channel does not operate well in the Eurozone, as the EU budget is tiny. In comparison, in the United States, the federal tax and transfer system is much more substantial and automatic stabilization therefore greater.

There are a number of *benefits* of giving up flexible exchange rates and joining a CCA:

1. The *reduction in exchange rate volatility* and the absence of nominal and real exchange rate overshooting from economic adjustment. We discussed the negative macroeconomic consequences of these two features of flexible exchange rate economies in Chapter 11.
2. A *credible nominal anchor*. By giving up control of monetary policy to the ECB, countries which had previously proved unsuccessful in managing inflation through their own central bank could 'tie their hands' and establish a low inflation monetary policy regime. This was a key reason for the southern European economies to join the euro. Adopting the euro was seen as an alternative to delegating authority for monetary policy to an independent national central bank (as happened in the UK).
3. No *competitive devaluations*. Ruling out competitive devaluation of the exchange rate was a major selling point of Eurozone membership to the German public, who already had a credible low inflation monetary policy regime implemented by the Bundesbank.

Macroeconomic adjustment in the Eurozone is discussed in detail in Section 14.4, where we set out the channels through which stabilization can occur in the absence of monetary policy and a flexible nominal exchange rate. We also look at the differences in labour market institutions across member states that meant some were more successful at stabilizing against country-specific shocks than others under conditions of monetary union.

14.1.2 The Eurozone's performance

The first 10 years

One way of assessing the Eurozone's macroeconomic performance in its first decade is to use the same criteria we use for countries like the US or the UK: how close was the Eurozone on average to the inflation target set by the European Central Bank and to an output gap close to zero? Figure 14.1 shows the answer: where the horizontal and vertical lines at zero cross shows an average inflation rate of 2% and an output gap of zero. In its first decade and before the global financial crisis, the performance of the Euro area as a whole was close to target for inflation, with most countries displaying a small positive output gap. This suggests that the ECB was successful in managing shocks common to the Eurozone.

However, Figure 14.1 shows very clearly how much variation there was in the performance of Eurozone member countries: at the top are the four countries involved

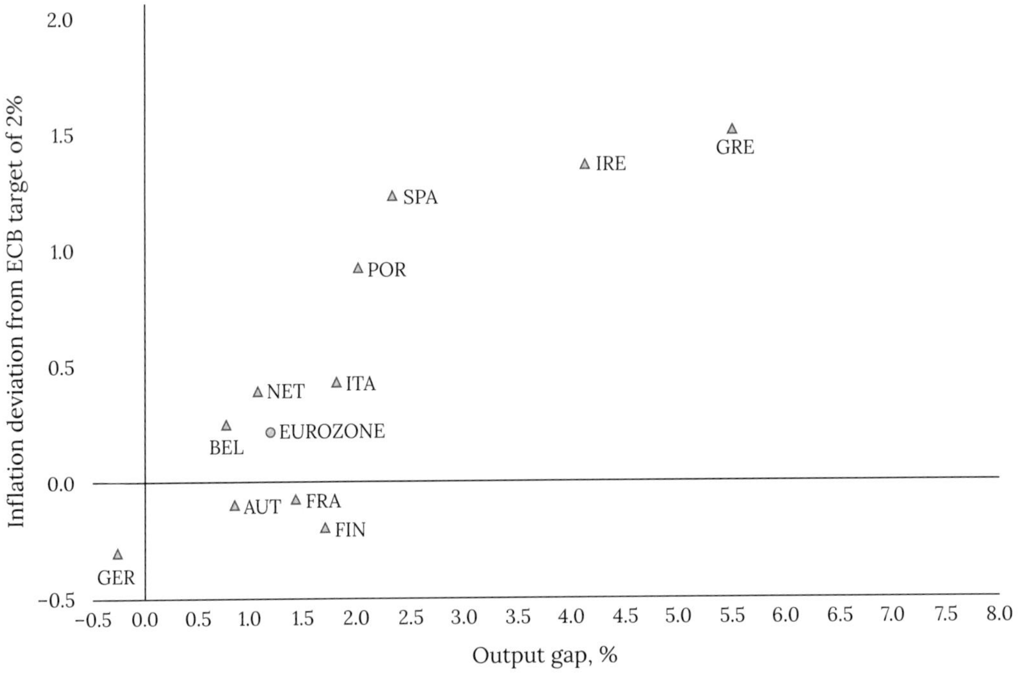

Figure 14.1 Eurozone performance: inflation and output gap, 1999–2008 (average per cent per annum).

Source: OECD Economic Outlook Database (May 2014). Inflation is consumer price index, harmonized, output gap is for total economy. Greece is from year of entry, 2001.

in the Eurozone crisis from 2010, Greece, Spain, Ireland, and Portugal. These countries all had average inflation rates well above the ECB's inflation target of 2% and positive output gaps during the first decade of the euro. In the opposite corner with inflation below the target and with a negative output gap is Germany.

A second way of viewing the variation in country performance is to look at how real exchange rates and current account balances evolved. We introduced the difference between real and nominal exchange rates in Chapter 11. Figure 14.2 shows indexes for the intra-Eurozone real effective exchange rates (REER) and the current account balances for the four largest member countries (by GDP) between 1999 and 2021. The REER index is set at 100 in 1999 when the Eurozone was formed. The nominal exchange rate for each of the four countries is 100 for the whole period, reflecting the fact that nominal exchange rates are fixed between Eurozone members.

In Figure 14.2, the current account balances are shown as a percentage of each country's GDP, where a negative value indicates a current account deficit and vice versa. The real exchange rates are defined in terms of relative unit labour costs and the index rises when the real exchange rate of the economy appreciates and

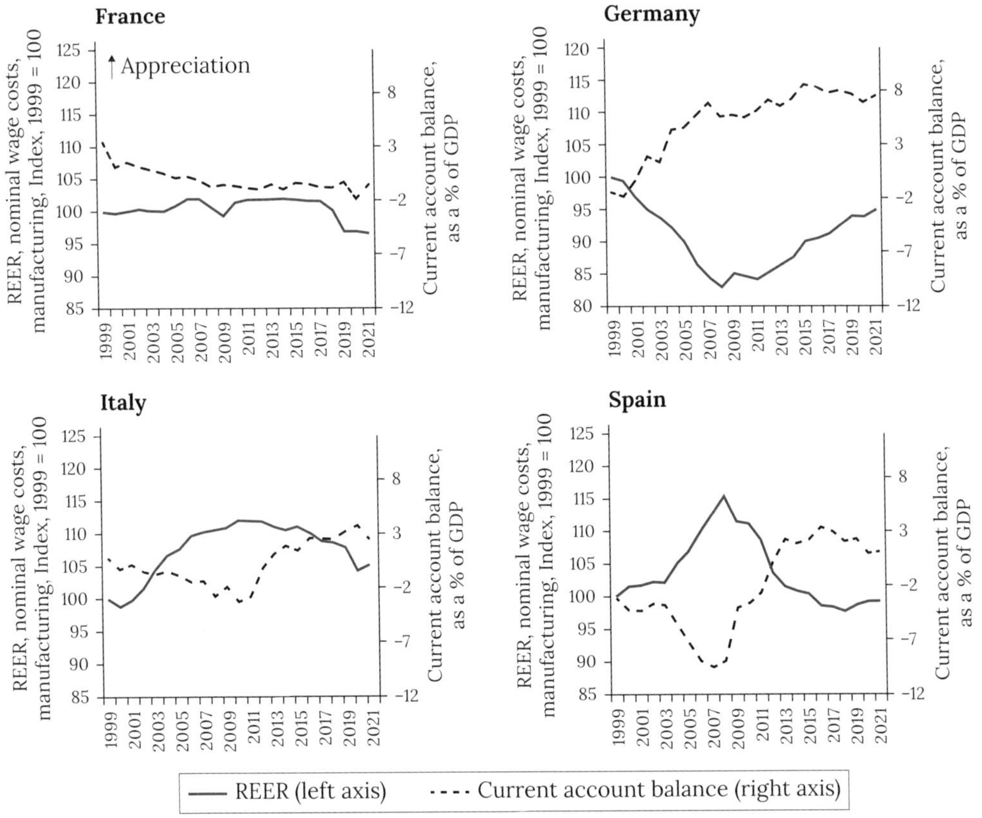

Figure 14.2 Current account balances and intra-eurozone real effective exchange rates (REER)–France, Germany, Italy and Spain: 1999 to 2021. Increase in REER is a real appreciation.

Source: European Commission, July 2022; OECD Economic Outlook, July 2022.

competitiveness falls. This shows vividly how even when the nominal exchange rate is fixed, real exchange rates can move very differently: Spain's competitiveness relative to the Eurozone average fell by 26% over the first decade of the Eurozone, whereas Germany's improved by 17.5%. These divergences in external competitiveness were reflected in the build-up of current account imbalances, as shown in Figure 14.2. We can see that Spain and Italy built up large current account deficits in the first ten years of the single currency, while Germany ran a large surplus.

This development was not anticipated when the formation of a common currency area was being discussed. It was assumed that once the nominal exchange rate had been given up—and with it, the opportunity to regain competitiveness through a nominal depreciation—wage- and price-setting behaviour would adjust. What would adjustment mean? It would mean nominal wages taking the burden of adjustment to ensure that competitiveness evolved in a manner consistent with stability. To keep the real exchange rate unchanged, for example, would require that unit labour costs evolve in line with the Eurozone average, which itself would closely follow the inflation target.

Divergences within the Eurozone

Why might divergences in inflation rates and real exchange rates within a currency union matter? To the extent that expected inflation in a member country differs from the currency union average, the member country's real interest rate is affected as the Fisher equation shows. We shall see that this can be destabilizing: a country with higher than union average inflation (like Spain, Ireland, Portugal, and Greece as shown in Figure 14.1) has a lower real interest rate. If the higher inflation was the result of a country-specific positive demand shock, a lower real interest rate will reinforce rather than offset this shock.

Movements in the real exchange rate will also affect net exports and the trade balance. A member's external indebtedness will rise if it runs persistent current account deficits. Eventually this is likely to affect the terms on which the country can borrow, i.e. their bond yields. In a common currency area, the only way a country can reverse an appreciation in its real exchange rate is by achieving a combination of slower nominal wage growth and faster productivity growth than the union average. In Section 14.4.1, we discuss the particular problems in the Eurozone that have arisen because of the differences among the countries in their wage-setting systems.

Public sector and household debt also evolved differently in member countries. The left-hand side of Figure 14.3 shows the long-run behaviour of the household debt to GDP ratio and the right-hand side the government debt to GDP ratio for the large Eurozone countries. The UK, which remained outside the Eurozone, is also included for comparative purposes. The big differences across member countries in levels of debt when the Eurozone was formed are clear: Italy's public debt was very high but its household debt, relatively low. Public debt levels of Germany, France and Spain were similar in 1999 but evolved completely differently in the years before the global crisis: Spain's public debt ratio fell dramatically and household debt increased. In Germany, public debt increased but household debt fell. Spain's public debt problem arose only after the crisis, showing that fiscal recklessness during the 'good years' was not the

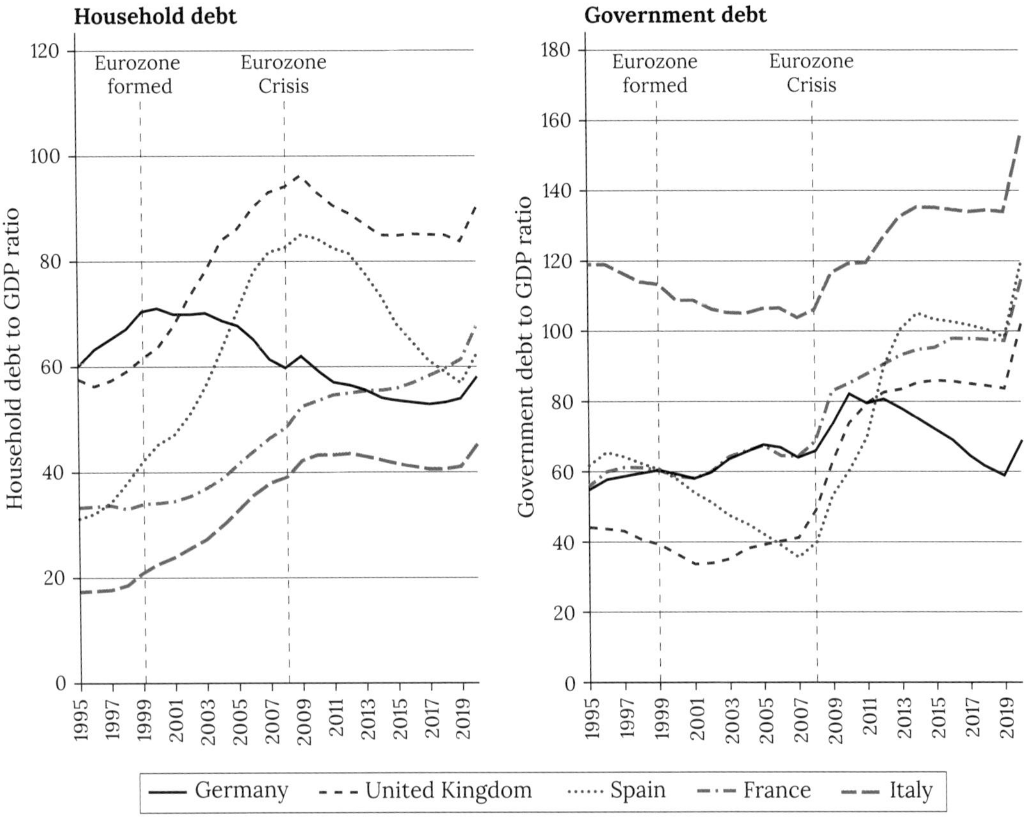

Figure 14.3 Trends in household and public debt to GDP ratios for selected European countries between 1990 and 2020.

Source: OECD Economic Outlook, June 2022; IMF (data accessed July 2022).

root cause of Spain's later sovereign debt problems. In Chapter 7 Section 7.3.3, we use a model of debt dynamics to explain the behaviour of public sector debt in the Eurozone.

We shall see that the diversity of performance of member countries reflected policy choices at national level and differences in private sector behaviour, including the role of labour market institutions.

The financial crisis and Eurozone crisis

The success of the Eurozone prior to the financial crisis was reflected by these indicators:

1. The Euro area was on average close to the ECB's inflation target and output was close to equilibrium (Figure 14.1).
2. Government debt ratios were falling in the high debt countries of Italy and Spain (Figure 14.3).
3. Long-term bond yields on debt issued by Euro area governments were very close to those on the German Bund, indicating that financial markets did not perceive any difference in the risk of default by member governments (Figure 14.4).

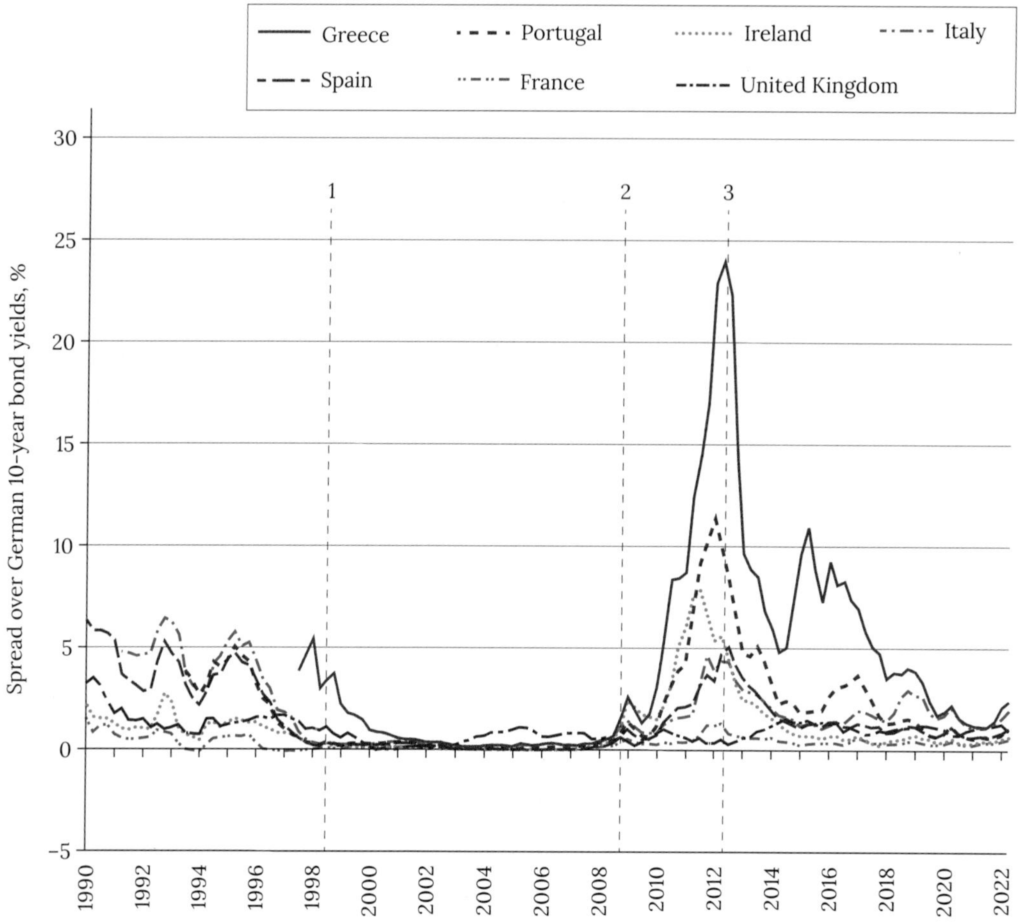

Figure 14.4 Long-term interest rate differentials on 10-year government bonds vis-à-vis Germany between 1990 Q1 and 2022 Q2 for Eurozone members and the UK.

Notes:

1. Introduction of the euro, which fixed the exchange rates of 11 countries (Greece joined in 2001)
2. Lehman Brothers files for Chapter 13 bankruptcy protection (i.e. onset of financial crisis)
3. ECB President Mario Draghi announces 'the ECB is ready to do whatever it takes to preserve the euro'. Shortly after, the ECB announces Outright Monetary Transactions, a programme of government bond buying in secondary markets with the 'aim of safeguarding an appropriate monetary policy transmission and the singleness of monetary policy'.

Source: OECD (accessed September 2022).

Extending the uncovered interest parity condition (UIP) to include the risk of a government defaulting on its debt highlights the exchange rate and default risk:

$$i = i^* + \left(\log e^E_{t+1} - \log e_t\right) \qquad \text{(UIP condition)}$$

$$i = i^* + \underbrace{\left(\log e^E_{t+1} - \log e_t\right)}_{\text{exchange rate risk}} + \underbrace{\rho_t}_{\text{default risk}}, \qquad \text{(UIP condition with default risk)}$$

where ρ_t is the default risk on government debt. The risk-adjusted UIP condition says that a CCA member's interest rate will be above the CCA interest rate to the extent that its nominal exchange rate is expected to depreciate and its risk of default on government debt exceeds that of the benchmark CCA government. In the Eurozone, the benchmark government debt is that issued by Germany (so-called German Bunds) and exchange rate risk is zero (as exchange rates are fixed between members). Hence, the difference between German and, for example, Greek interest rates on ten-year bonds reflects only the difference in default risk.

However, the vulnerability of the Eurozone to a financial crisis was reflected by the following indicators:

1. There was a lot of heterogeneity in member country inflation and output gap performance in the years after the formation of the Eurozone.
2. Household debt ratios were rising fast in some members.
3. The presence of large, highly leveraged banks, which were revealed in the crisis as systemically important, including in small countries such as Ireland.

The ECB responded rapidly and effectively to the credit crisis in 2007 that preceded the global financial crisis (discussed in Chapter 9). As credit dried up and panic spread in financial markets, the ECB played the role of lender of last resort to the banks of member countries. Just like the Bank of England and the Federal Reserve, the ECB made liquidity available to banks in unlimited amounts, as highlighted by (then President of the ECB) Jean-Claude Trichet in a speech in April 2009:[6]

> Our primary concern was to maintain the availability of credit for households and companies at accessible rates. We significantly adapted our regular operations in the crisis. Since then, we have followed a new 'fixed rate full allotment' tender procedure and we have significantly expanded the maturity of our operations. This means that banks have been granted access to essentially unlimited liquidity at our policy interest rate at maturities of up to six months.

The financial crisis revealed the importance of the relationship between the central bank and the government, and exposed fault lines in the design of the Eurozone, in which a single supra-national central bank existed alongside national fiscal authorities. Integrated global financial markets created the opportunity for any differences in perceived riskiness of bonds issued by member governments to be priced and to threaten the stability of the Eurozone.

The Eurozone crisis culminated in the intervention of ECB President, Mario Draghi, announcing in July 2012 that the Bank would do *whatever it takes* to save the Eurozone—including purchasing government bonds.

14.2 THE EUROZONE STABILIZATION POLICY REGIME

14.2.1 The Maastricht policy assignment

The Maastricht Treaty of 1992 set out the basis for European Monetary Union. The first Chief Economist of the European Central Bank, Otmar Issing, used the term

---

[6] Excerpt taken from Jean-Claude Trichet, April 27th 2009, *The financial crisis and our response so far*, keynote address at the Chatham House Global Financial Forum.

'Maastricht policy assignment' to describe how the responsibility for economic policy was to be divided between the supra-national ECB and the national governments.[7]

1. The ECB is responsible for using monetary policy to respond to Eurozone-wide shocks and for delivering low and stable inflation in the euro area.
2. National governments are responsible for fiscal sustainability and subject to that, for providing stabilization for country-specific shocks and for the asymmetric effects of common shocks, which occur when common shocks have different effects in different member countries).
3. The aim of the European Union's Stability and Growth Pact was to prevent governments from pursuing policies that might threaten the ECB's inflation objective.
4. National labour and product markets, and national supply-side policies would determine equilibrium unemployment. However, supply-side reforms would be supported by the European Union's 'Lisbon strategy'. The Lisbon strategy was a European Union programme for the 10 years from 2000 aimed at making the EU 'the most competitive and dynamic knowledge-based economy in the world capable of sustainable economic growth with more and better jobs and greater social cohesion' (Lisbon European Council, March 2000). In 2010, the Lisbon strategy was replaced by the EU's 'Europe 2020' programme.[8]

14.2.2 **Monetary policy in the Eurozone**

The European Central Bank began work as the single monetary policy maker in the Eurozone in 1999. The Eurozone is a unique structure. It has one central bank for the whole currency bloc, but independent national fiscal authorities and distinct labour market arrangements for each member. The ECB is politically independent of governments—its constitution reflects the legacy of the German central bank, the Bundesbank, and as a result it is more independent than either the Federal Reserve in the US or the Bank of England. It sets its own monetary policy in terms of its target (price stability, defined until 2021 as an inflation rate of close to but below 2%). It uses its policy instrument, the interest rate, to achieve this target, considering both economic and monetary 'pillars' discussed below.

The economic pillar uses forecasts of the output gap and the deviation of inflation from target to inform the interest rate decision. The arguments set out in Chapters 3 and 4 about the credibility of an independent inflation-targeting central bank suggest the ECB is likely to have delivered a lower inflation bias than some members could have achieved with a national monetary policy.

The monetary pillar reflects the influence of the legacy of the German central bank, the Bundesbank. Unlike many central banks, the Bundesbank had considerable success in targeting the growth of the money supply as part of its price stability mandate.

---

[7] Issing, O. (2004) 'A framework for stability in Europe'. https://www.bis.org/review/r041130h.pdf

[8] Pisani-Ferry, J. and Sapir, A. (2006) 'Last Exit to Lisbon'. https://www.bruegel.org/policy-brief/last-exit-lisbon-0

This contrasts with the failure of monetary targeting elsewhere.[9] For this purpose, it uses a reference growth rate of a broad monetary aggregate. Its reference for the growth rate of the money supply (the broad monetary aggregate, M3) is 4.5%. This number is consistent with a growth rate of nominal GDP of approximately 4% (e.g. inflation of less than 2% and output growth of 2–2.5%) and with prevailing estimates of a trend decline in the velocity of circulation at a rate of decline of 0.5–1% p.a.).[10]

Although much of the Anglo-American commentary about the behaviour of independent central banks has been critical of the ECB's 'second pillar', monetary economist (and former member of the Bank of England's Monetary Policy Committee) Charles Goodhart (2006) argued that if inflation expectations come to be more closely anchored to target inflation, current inflation may no longer be a good signal of future inflationary pressure. Under these circumstances, relying only on the economic pillar could be misleading and the growth rate of a money aggregate may be a more relevant indicator of future inflation.

An episode of faster than target monetary growth from 2005 was accompanied by higher bank lending. The ECB viewed this as signalling a potential inflationary problem in the future (a possibility not reflected in the well-anchored inflation expectations) and pointing toward the need to tighten monetary policy. In view of the subsequent credit-related crisis, this is an interesting example of how the ECB's second pillar could potentially play a useful role.

A second example is the sharp increase in the growth of monetary aggregates in 2020. According to the ECB, the main reason behind this was a rise in the annual growth in deposits held by non-monetary financial institutions as well as non-financial corporations. This reflects the transmission through the economy of the QE purchases by the ECB designed to address deflation fears (discussed at the end of Chapter 5).

The ECB's performance in monetary policy is judged as having been broadly successful in its first decade. Its constitution is viewed as strong on independence but weaker on transparency and accountability and its asymmetric target (inflation close to but below 2%) was criticized because it left the Eurozone more vulnerable to deflation (see Chapter 3 for the analysis of a deflation trap) than would be the case with a symmetric target.

14.2.3 **Fiscal policy in the Eurozone**

Together with the Maastricht Treaty, the Stability and Growth Pact (SGP) set the macroeconomic framework for the Eurozone as a whole. The SGP specified that national budget deficits be kept below 3% and that the ratio of government debt to GDP be kept below 60%. The choice of these particular numbers can be rationalized by noting that a debt ratio of 60% was the average of the EU members in the years

---

[9] For a comparison with the UK, see Carlin and Soskice (2006), Chapter 8 pp. 273 and 277.

[10] The calculation uses the Quantity Equation: $MV = Py$, where V is the velocity of circulation. Hence $\Delta M/M = \pi + \Delta y/y - \Delta V/V$ so we have $2 + 2 - (-0.5) = 4.5$. See Chapter 6 for more detail on the Quantity Theory of Money.

preceding the formation of the Eurozone; and with a debt ratio of 60%, the debt to GDP ratio will remain constant if the nominal growth rate is 5% and the budget deficit is 3% of GDP.[11]

Why should the state of a member country's deficit and debt levels be of any concern to the EU or the ECB? Is this not simply a matter of national policy? The reason for supra-national concern about the deficits and debt levels in member countries arises because of fears of spillovers from national policy decisions to the Eurozone. Arguments about possible spillovers include the following:

1. For any one small country, there may be an incentive to run a budget deficit in order to boost aggregate demand (shift the *AD* curve to the right) and move along a downward-sloping *ERU* curve to a lower equilibrium unemployment rate. Of course if all members of the Eurozone were to do this, then this rightward shift in the IS curve for the Eurozone as a whole would lead to higher inflation and the ECB would have to raise the interest rate to dampen demand. The SGP seeks to prevent individual members from behaving like this.
2. A second source of spillover relates directly to government debt. In principle, the market should price any differential risk of default on government debt across Eurozone members into the price of that country's bonds. Until the Greek crisis of May 2010, the differences in the cost to different Eurozone governments of borrowing were very small. This is shown in Figure 14.4. The problem is that once the risk of default rises in one member, contagion can occur to other members. This is clearly a source of spillover from the fiscal policy of one member to others.

According to its own criteria for success, the Eurozone's record on fiscal policy in the Eurozone's first decade is not as satisfactory as that of monetary policy. See Figure 7.10 for the record of breaches of the deficit and debt targets between 1999 and 2021. But a second question is whether fiscal policy in the Eurozone was stabilizing or not. Figure 14.5 illustrates the much smaller countercyclical fiscal response of the Eurozone to the global financial crisis as compared with the US, Japan, and the UK. The Euro area was in primary surplus by 2015, with member governments withdrawing stimulus in contrast to the other economies, where fiscal policy continued to be more supportive of aggregate demand.

The SGP was revised in 2005. The aim was to discourage pro-cyclical fiscal policy by defining the fiscal rule for deficits in terms of the budget balance adjusted for the state of the economic cycle (the cyclically adjusted budget balance, see Chapter 7). There was greater emphasis on the sustainability of public debt and on structural issues such as the impact of future pension obligations. In addition, country-specific medium-term objectives were introduced, which ranged from a 1% of GDP deficit for countries with low debt and high potential growth to budget balance or surplus for countries with high levels of debt or with low potential for growth. Unlike the original

[11] In Chapter 7, we set out the mathematics behind government debt dynamics, which provides a simple way of checking this calculation.

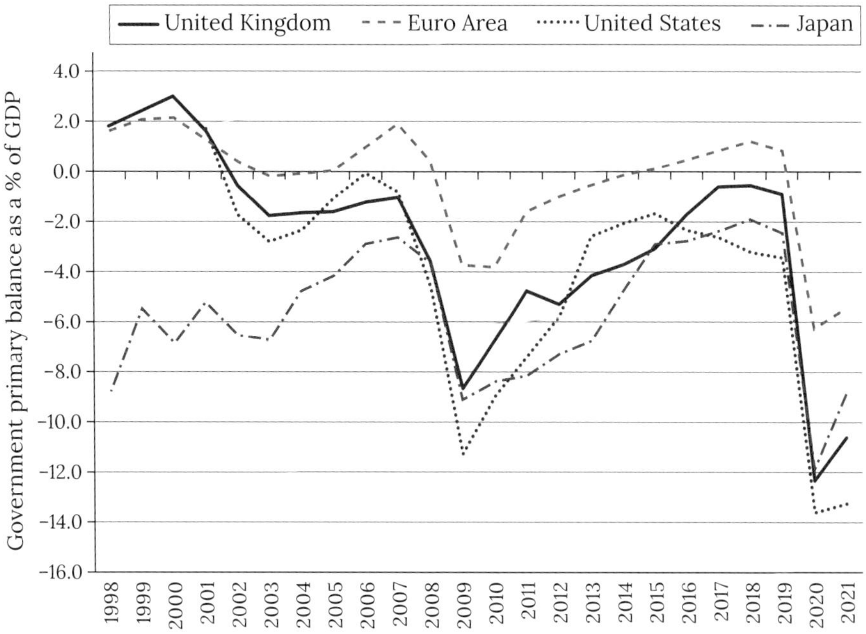

Figure 14.5 Government primary balance as a percentage of GDP in the Euro Area, Japan, UK, and US: 1998 to 2021.

Note: Government primary balance is defined as the difference between tax revenues and government spending in goods and services.

Source: Data extracted from IMF World Economic Outlook, April 2021.

formulation of the SGP, these amendments are broadly consistent with the principles of a prudent fiscal policy rule set out in Chapter 7.

14.3 MODELLING FISCAL STABILIZATION POLICY UNDER FIXED EXCHANGE RATES

In the modelling section, we look first at the stabilization of shocks to the entire Eurozone and then at stabilization of idiosyncratic shocks at the member country level. In view of the additional complexities introduced in this section, we make a simplifying assumption and assume that the *ERU* curve is vertical, i.e. that wage-setting takes place in terms of producer and not consumer prices. Although the case of a common currency area where the nominal exchange rate is irrevocably fixed is used, the modelling applies to fixed exchange rate regimes more generally.

14.3.1 Stabilization in a common currency area: Common shocks

In the Eurozone, monetary policy is set by the ECB and the member states have no control over their own nominal interest or exchange rates. The ECB responds to common shocks, that is, those that affect all members, by choosing the interest rate

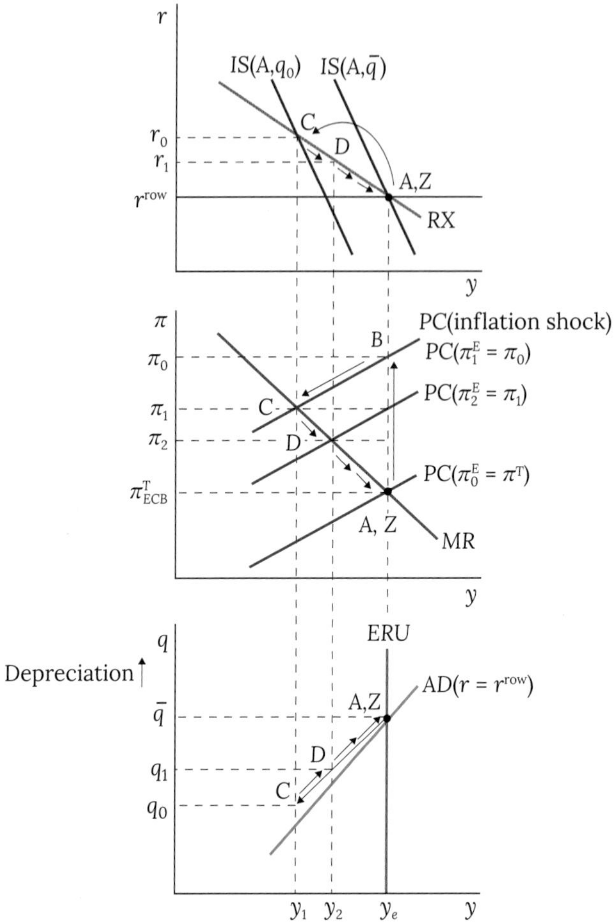

Figure 14.6 Adjustment by the ECB to a common inflation shock to the Eurozone.

to achieve its inflation target. Taking the example of an inflation shock that increases prices in the Eurozone as a whole, the ECB reacts in a similar fashion to a national central bank in a flexible exchange rate regime.

Figure 14.6 shows the adjustment of the economy to an inflation shock. Note that the interest rate in the rest of the world is indicated by r^{row}. We do not go through the period-by-period adjustment as it is exactly the same as the inflation shock example in Chapter 9, but the figure highlights some important points:

1. Although exchange rates are fixed between members, the Eurozone has a freely floating exchange rate with the rest of the world.
2. Adjustment to common shocks is therefore the same as for a country with a flexible exchange rate. In the case of an inflation shock in Figure 14.6, the ECB is modelled as raising its interest rate above the world interest rate, r^{row}, to get the economy on to the MR curve and return the Eurozone economy to target inflation.

3. The tool that helps return the economy to equilibrium after a common shock is the ECB's ability to influence aggregate demand by altering the interest rate, which in turn influences the exchange rate via the UIP condition.

The response of a national central bank in a flexible exchange rate regime to a range of macroeconomic shocks (e.g. inflation, supply, and demand shocks) is analysed in detail in Chapters 11 and 12. When studying particular episodes of ECB policy-making, it is useful also to keep in mind the two-bloc model studied in Chapter 13. The Eurozone is a large economy and its monetary policy decisions will have implications for the rest of the world.

14.3.2 **Stabilization under fixed exchange rates or in a common currency area: Country-specific shocks**

Is stabilization policy necessary?

Before considering the case of a country with a fixed exchange rate such as a Eurozone member, it is useful to recall the way that stabilization policy works using monetary policy. One of the main results about stabilization in the closed economy and in the flexible exchange rate economy (set out in Chapter 3, 11, and 6) is the so-called Taylor principle. This says that the central bank should respond to forecast inflation by raising the *real* interest rate. This result was built into the operation of inflation-targeting central banks around the world and has been credited with helping to keep inflation low and stable. In the case of an inflation shock, unless the central bank raises the nominal interest rate more than one-for-one with the expected increase in inflation, the real interest rate falls and the economy will move further away from equilibrium. The Taylor principle is discussed in detail in Chapter 6.

Is a policy intervention of this kind to stabilize aggregate demand also needed in a CCA? Not necessarily. The reason is that when the nominal exchange rate is fixed as is the case for a member of the Eurozone, if inflation goes up, it makes the economy less competitive and this will dampen net exports and pull the economy back toward equilibrium without the need for policy intervention. This is called the 'real exchange rate' channel of adjustment. If this mechanism can be relied on, we would need to worry much less about how fiscal policy could be used to stabilize the economy. But can it be relied on? The example below from the history of the Eurozone suggests it cannot.

Destabilization in the Eurozone

An example of a country-specific inflation shock comes from the case of Ireland in the initial phase of the Eurozone. Following the adoption of the euro, the euro depreciated against both the US dollar and the pound sterling. Because Ireland has much stronger trade relations with the US and the UK than is typical in the Eurozone, the euro depreciation had a bigger effect in raising inflation in Ireland (as imported goods increased in price, which in turn triggered domestic wage increases) than was the case in other members. This represented a country-specific inflation shock for Ireland.

The Irish example highlights that there is another channel that can operate in a CCA to *destabilize* the economy and may prevent the 'no intervention' strategy via the appreciation of the real exchange rate from working to keep inflation in a member country close to the Eurozone target. This is the 'real interest rate' channel.

When a member country's inflation is above the Eurozone average, this may affect *expected* inflation in that economy. If expected inflation rises, then the real interest rate falls and this boosts output, putting additional upward pressure on inflation as output rises above equilibrium. Instead of moving back to equilibrium as happens through the real exchange rate channel, the economy will move further away from equilibrium with rising output and rising inflation.

This helps to explain what happened in Ireland and Spain in their post-euro property booms: the combination of the low nominal interest rate set by the ECB with high domestic inflation (relative to the Eurozone average) pushed down the real interest rate. In conjunction with the operation of the financial accelerator and bubble mechanisms studied in Chapter 8, this stimulated investment in construction projects and consumption in those economies. It is said that 60% of Europe's concrete was being used in Spain in 2006. The real interest rate in Ireland and Spain was actually negative for much of the period from euro entry until 2007.

Under these circumstances, the model indicates that the national government has to intervene with a sufficiently contractionary fiscal policy to ensure that the economy returns to equilibrium. As noted above, the failure to do so fuelled the house price bubbles and construction booms in Spain and Ireland before the crash of 2007–08.

The Taylor principle and the Walters critique

In a flexible exchange rate regime, the Taylor principle is incorporated in the 3-equation model. For a member of a CCA, unless a similar principle is applied so that the required negative output gap is created to dampen inflation (through the combination of tighter fiscal policy and the operation of the real exchange rate channel), instability can arise. This is referred to as the Walters critique. British economist Alan Walters argued against UK membership of the euro on the grounds of this kind of instability.

In the analysis of stabilization under *flexible* exchange rates, we did not mention the government's financial balance, i.e. whether it was in budget deficit or surplus. This is because under normal conditions, stabilization against a private sector shock is carried out by the central bank using the interest rate and once the economy has returned to medium-run equilibrium, the government's financial balance excluding interest payments, which is called its primary balance, will be back at its initial level. We shall see that the result is different when fiscal policy is used as the stabilization policy by a member of a CCA. This draws attention to whether fiscal policy is a good substitute for monetary policy.

Figure 14.7 summarizes the stabilization issues that arise for a member of a CCA because they do not have their own monetary policy. The government can choose to do nothing in response to a shock (the left-hand side of Figure 14.7) or to use fiscal policy (the right-hand side). We look at the real exchange rate and real interest rate channels in turn, and then show why fiscal policy is not a perfect substitute for monetary policy in stabilization because of its consequences for the budget balance.

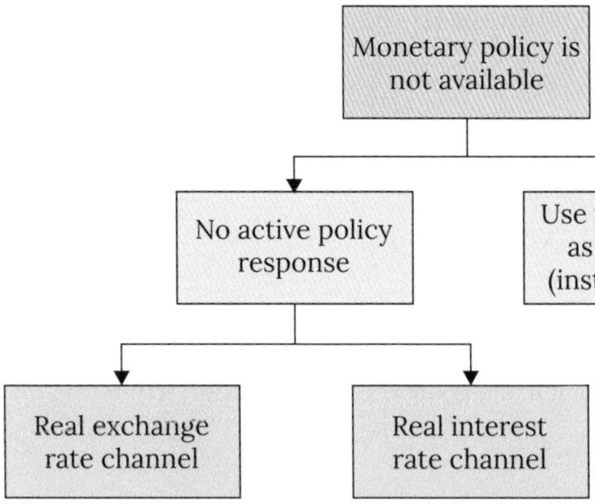

Figure 14.7 Stabilization policy options under fixed exchange rates, e.g. as a member of a CCA.

14.3.3 The real exchange rate (competitiveness) and real interest rate channels

As noted above, if the government decides not to use policy to respond to a shock, two adjustment processes arise automatically. These are the real exchange rate and real interest rate channels. Inflation in medium-run equilibrium in a member of a CCA is pinned down by the inflation target of the CCA's central bank, i.e. $\pi^{MRE} = [\pi^{T}]$. In the Eurozone, this is the ECB's inflation target.

The simplest way of explaining the two channels is by making different assumptions about how inflation expectations are formed. In Chapter 11, we saw that in a fixed exchange rate economy, home's nominal interest rate is equal to the world nominal interest rate ($i = i^*$). In the case of a CCA, the 'world' nominal interest rate refers to the interest rate set by the CCA's central bank. Throughout this section, we shall refer to variables at the CCA level with a star and variables at a member level without a star ($[\pi^{T}_{ECB}] = [\pi^*]$) and we ignore the rest of the world. If inflation expectations in a CCA member are firmly anchored to the CCA's inflation target, i.e. $\pi^E = [\pi^T]$, then from the Fisher equation, the real interest rate remains constant at the CCA real interest rate (i.e. r^*):

$$r = i - \pi^E \qquad \text{(Fisher equation)}$$

$$\text{If } \pi^E = \pi^* \text{ and since } i = i^*$$

$$\text{then } r = i^* - \pi^* = r^*.$$

Using the definition of the real exchange rate, $Q \equiv P^*e/P$ and taking logs, we have $q = p^* + \log e - p$, where q, p, and p^* indicate the log of the variable. In a CCA, we can see that a CCA member's competitiveness improves (its real exchange rate depreciates) when its inflation is below CCA inflation and vice versa:

$$\Delta q = \Delta p^* - \Delta p = \pi^* - \pi.$$

The real exchange rate (competitiveness) channel

The real exchange rate channel works like this: if we take the case of a positive inflation shock as our example, a rise in a CCA member's inflation reduces its competitiveness and depresses output via the IS relation:

$$y_t = A_t - ar_{t-1} + bq_{t-1}.$$

The causal chain for the real exchange rate channel is:

$$\uparrow \pi \rightarrow \downarrow q \rightarrow \downarrow y \rightarrow \downarrow \pi \ldots \text{ until } \pi < \pi^* \text{ when } \uparrow q \rightarrow \uparrow y.$$

$$\text{Eventually, } y = y_e \text{ and } \pi = \pi^*.$$

In Figure 14.8a the upward shift in the Phillips curve due to the inflation shock is shown. As a consequence of the impact of the shock in reducing the CCA member's

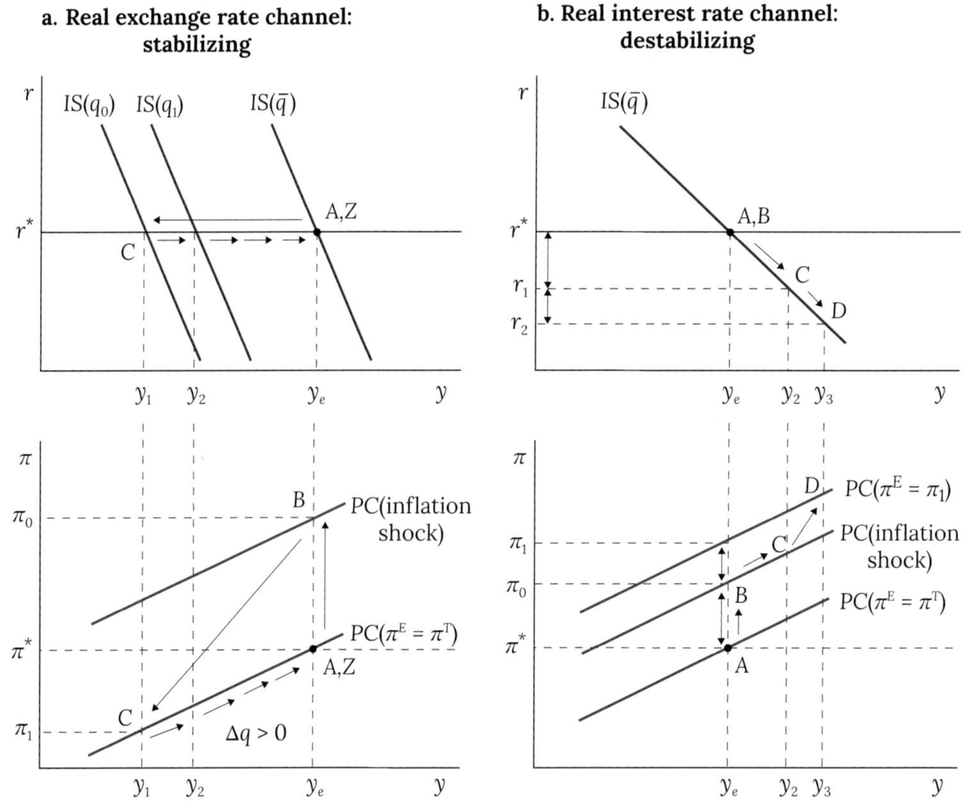

Figure 14.8 Inflation shock: comparing the stabilizing real exchange rate channel with the destabilizing real interest rate channel. Visit www.oup.com/he/carlin-soskice to explore stabilizing real exchange rate and destabilizing real interest rate channels with Animated Analytical Diagram 14.8.

Note: the role of the inflation expectations assumption. In (a), expected inflation remains anchored at target; in (b), expectations are adaptive.

competitiveness, the IS curve shifts to the left and the economy is at lower output (at point C on the $r = r^*$ line because of our assumption that $\pi^E = \pi^*$). What happens to inflation? As usual, this depends on inflation expectations. Because of our assumption that inflation expectations are firmly tied down to the CCA's inflation target, in the period after the inflation shock, the Phillips curve reverts to the one indexed by $\pi^E = \pi^*$. The fall in output caused by the CCA member's loss of competitiveness pushes inflation below π^* and as we can see from the definition of the real exchange rate, this boosts their competitiveness. The following period, the IS curve shifts to the right ($IS(q_1)$) and the economy begins to recover. Eventually, it is back at equilibrium with the initial real exchange rate.[12] Nothing has happened to government spending or taxation, so the economy remains in fiscal balance.

The real interest rate channel

Let us now see what happens when inflation expectations are not firmly anchored to the CCA's inflation target. When there is a backward-looking element in inflation expectations, the Fisher equation indicates that a CCA member's real interest rate can deviate from the CCA real interest rate. This will be the case if agents believe that inflation will continue to behave as it has in the past. To make the explanation of this channel as clear as possible, we shut down the real exchange rate channel by assuming the IS curve does not shift with a change in the real exchange rate. Figure 14.8b illustrates how the real interest rate channel works. Inflation expectations are formed in a backward-looking way with $\pi^E = \pi_{-1}$. The inflation shock shifts the Phillips curve up as usual. This now raises *expected* inflation, which reduces the CCA member's real interest rate (to r_1). This leads to a rise in output and inflation (point C). Inflation expectations are updated and the Phillips curve shifts up again. Output rises further.[13]

The causal chain for the real interest rate channel works like this:

$$\uparrow \pi \rightarrow \uparrow \pi^E \rightarrow \downarrow r \rightarrow \uparrow y \rightarrow \uparrow \pi \ldots, \text{ which is destabilizing.}$$

In a more realistic model, the real exchange rate effect will operate alongside the real interest rate effect. But as long as the real interest rate effect is stronger, the problem of instability identified by Walters exists.[14]

The rationale for discretionary fiscal policy as stabilization policy

Why might the government in a common currency area use fiscal policy for stabilization? This is a good point at which to return to the reasons central banks around the world adopted inflation-targeting monetary policy: they did it in order to reduce the costs associated with stabilizing aggregate demand and other shocks. We have seen how the real exchange rate channel operates under flexible exchange rates via

---

[12] For simplicity, we assume the economy moves smoothly to the new equilibrium and does not oscillate around it.

[13] The Macroeconomic Simulator (available at www.oup.com/he/carlin-soskice) can be used to show the destabilizing real interest rate channel in action (see Problem 4).

[14] See T. Kirsanova, D. Vines and S. Wren-Lewis (2006), 'Fiscal policy and macroeconomic stability within a Monetary Union', CEPR DP, 5584.

jumps in the nominal exchange rate. Recall that it is the sluggishness of wage and price adjustment that produces exchange rate overshooting. It is not surprising therefore that members of a CCA—also characterized by sluggish wage and price adjustment—would consider using fiscal policy to stabilize country-specific shocks.

As we have seen an important reason for the failure of the real exchange rate channel to swiftly stabilize in a CCA is the presence of unanchored inflation expectations (Orphanides 2020). Until July 2021, the ECB's inflation target was expressed as 'close to but below 2%'. This is likely to have contributed to downward bias in inflation expectations, i.e. expected inflation drifts below 2%, becoming unanchored. Figure 14.9 illustrates the persistence of this problem throughout the Eurozone's existence using a measure of long-term inflation expectations.

Since fiscal policy is not available at the level of the Eurozone, these results emphasize the importance of member countries being able and willing to use fiscal policy. Evidence from earlier chapters shows that fiscal multipliers are likely to be higher under zero lower bound conditions, which was likely the case for Eurozone members.[15] Expansionary fiscal policy can help to raise inflation expectations. This reduces the real interest rate and stimulates interest-sensitive spending.

Consider fiscal spillovers. An interesting case study arises in the Covid-19 pandemic: this was a common shock to the Eurozone and the interest rate was at the zero lower bound (see Figure 6.1). Under these conditions, there are strong arguments

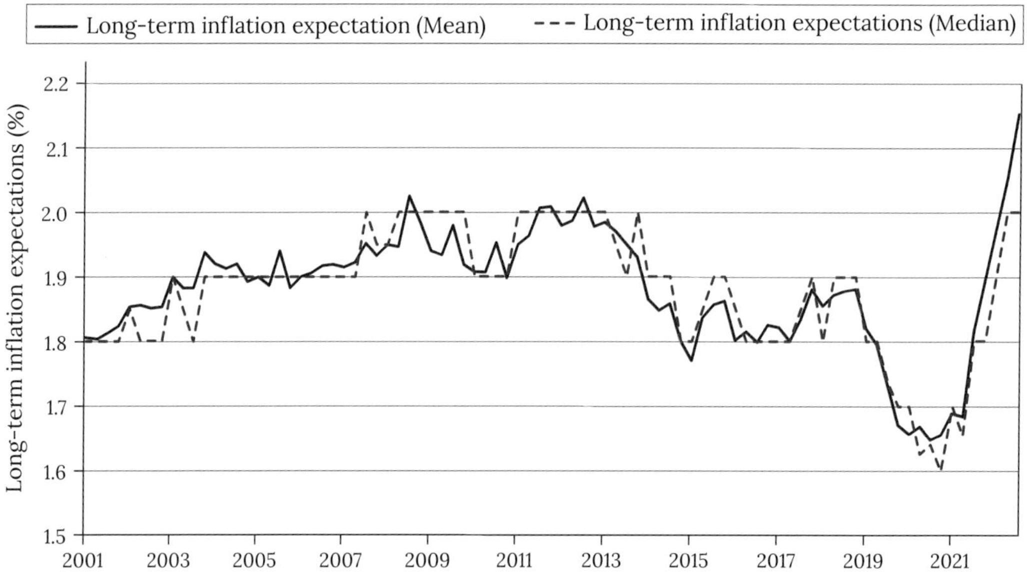

Figure 14.9 Long-term inflation expectations of professional forecasters in the Eurozone—percentage annual change.

Note: long-term expectations here are the five-year-ahead expected annual inflation.

Source: Extended chart from Orphanides, 2020. Data extracted from ECB Survey of Professional Forecasters, 2022 Q3.

[15] See Pappa (2020).

for a common fiscal policy response among Eurozone member countries. As noted above, with a commitment from the ECB that monetary policy would remain loose, the conditions were conducive to strong fiscal multiplier effects. This episode brings into focus how spillovers from national fiscal policy can make a positive contribution to stabilization.

In Section 14.2.3, the possibility of negative spillovers to other members from 'irresponsible' fiscal policy decisions in one country was discussed. The experience following the financial crisis when the Eurozone suffered from low growth and inflation persistently below target, and also during the pandemic has shown the opposite case: restrictions on the use of fiscal policy at national level can hamper recovery of aggregate demand.

An example illustrates how a positive spillover to aggregate demand can arise: if the largest member, Germany, implements a fiscal expansion, then this leads to higher demand by residents of Germany for imports from other countries. Moreover, higher demand might stimulate prices and lead to a real appreciation in Germany relative to other Eurozone countries, stimulating demand further by the real depreciation experienced elsewhere. Beetsma et al. (2006) estimate that a spending-based fiscal expansion of 1% of GDP in Germany would lead to an average increase in the output of other EU economies by 0.15% after two years. The pandemic illuminated the potential benefits from coordination, for example, around German leadership in fiscal expansion.

Summarizing, a government could turn to fiscal policy as a substitute stabilization tool when monetary policy is unavailable for two reasons:

1. It may be necessary in order to prevent the instability of the Walters' critique effect.
2. Sluggish wage and price adjustment may make the real exchange rate channel slow and costly in terms of a period of elevated unemployment.

Even in an economy where the exchange rate channel dominates the interest rate channel, inflation expectations may adjust only slowly to the CCA's inflation target. Looking at Figure 14.8a, if instead of jumping back to its original position in the period after the inflation shock, the Phillips curve shifts downward only a little, then inflation will remain above the CCA's inflation target and the CCA member's competitiveness will continue to deteriorate. The process will be stabilizing in the end, because eventually, the combination of the downward drift of the Phillips curve and the rise in the output gap will push the CCA member's inflation below the CCA's inflation target, and its competitiveness will begin to improve. In such a case, relying on the competitiveness channel may impose heavy costs on the economy in the form of inflation and output deviations from π^T and y_e respectively.[16]

[16] The Macroeconomic Simulator (available at www.oup.com/he/carlin-soskice) can be used to model the speed of adjustment to a negative demand shock in CCA member and flexible exchange rate economies (see Problem 5). This highlights the costs imposed when fiscal policy is not used to stabilize country-specific shocks in a CCA.

14.3.4 **Modelling fiscal stabilization policy**

There are two different ways of thinking about the role of fiscal policy in stabilization. The first is discretionary policy, where the government chooses some combination of spending increase and tax cut (or the reverse) to deliver the best response output gap. Problem 5 leads you through an exercise in which discretionary fiscal policy is used to stabilize a permanent negative aggregate demand shock.

The second approach is to think about the design of fiscal policy in a parallel way to monetary policy, namely as a problem of minimizing the costs of deviations from equilibrium output and the inflation target, which in the case of a member of a CCA, is the inflation target of the CCA central bank.

Instead of altering fiscal policy (represented by a shift in the *IS* curve in the model) by using the judgement of government officials at the time, in the second approach, there is a policy rule or *PR* curve that pins down the government's best-response output gap. Fiscal policy is adjusted so as to deliver the output gap shown by the *PR*.

Using a fiscal stabilization policy rule (equivalent to the *MR*)

To apply the lessons from the 3-equation model to the use of fiscal policy for stabilization under fixed exchange rates or for a member of a CCA, we begin by assuming that the policy maker has the same utility (i.e. loss) function as the monetary policy maker in a flexible exchange rate regime (or a closed economy) and faces the same constraints. In other words, the policy maker minimizes its losses subject to the constraint of the Phillips curve. To make the comparison with the flexible exchange rate economy as direct as possible, we use the same loss function and the same Phillips curve.

The policy maker is modelled as minimizing this loss function:

$$L_t = (y_t - y_e)^2 + \beta(\pi_t - \pi^T)^2, \qquad \text{(government loss function)}$$

where π^T is the CCA's inflation target and $\beta > 1$ characterizes a government that places less weight on output fluctuations than on deviations in inflation, and vice versa. The only difference from the flexible exchange rate economy is that the government wants to minimize deviations from the CCA's inflation target and not a national inflation target. In the general case of a fixed exchange rate economy the inflation target is that of the central bank in the country to which the exchange rate is fixed, e.g. the ECB for Denmark and the Federal Reserve for countries that fix to the dollar.

The Phillips curve is the same as in the flexible exchange rate economy:

$$\pi_t = \pi_{t-1} + \alpha(y_t - y_e). \qquad \text{(Phillips Curve, PC)}$$

The government optimizes by minimizing its loss function subject to the Phillips curve. This produces the policy rule equation (the *PR* curve), which differs from the *MR* curve only in the replacement of a national-level inflation target with a CCA-level inflation target, π^T_{ECB}, which is assumed to be equal to π^*:

$$(y_t - y_e) = -\alpha\beta(\pi_t - \pi^*). \qquad \text{(Policy Rule, PR)}$$

Inflation shock

Figure 14.10 provides a direct comparison between the use of fiscal policy in a CCA member and monetary policy in a flexible rate economy in response to an inflation shock. We see immediately that because of our assumptions about the policy maker's loss function and the Phillips curve, the lower panel is virtually identical in each economy—the only differences are in the labelling of the policy rule curve, and the fact that at equilibrium, inflation is equal to the CCA's inflation target in the CCA member (labelled π^*) and equal to the national inflation target in the flexible exchange rate economy (labelled π^T).

The lower panels show that the optimizing policy maker in each type of economy chooses the same sequence of output gaps on the path back to equilibrium. However, how policy is used to implement those output gaps differs. The central bank in the flexible rate economy gets the economy on the path back to equilibrium by raising the interest rate and taking advantage of the exchange rate appreciation that will

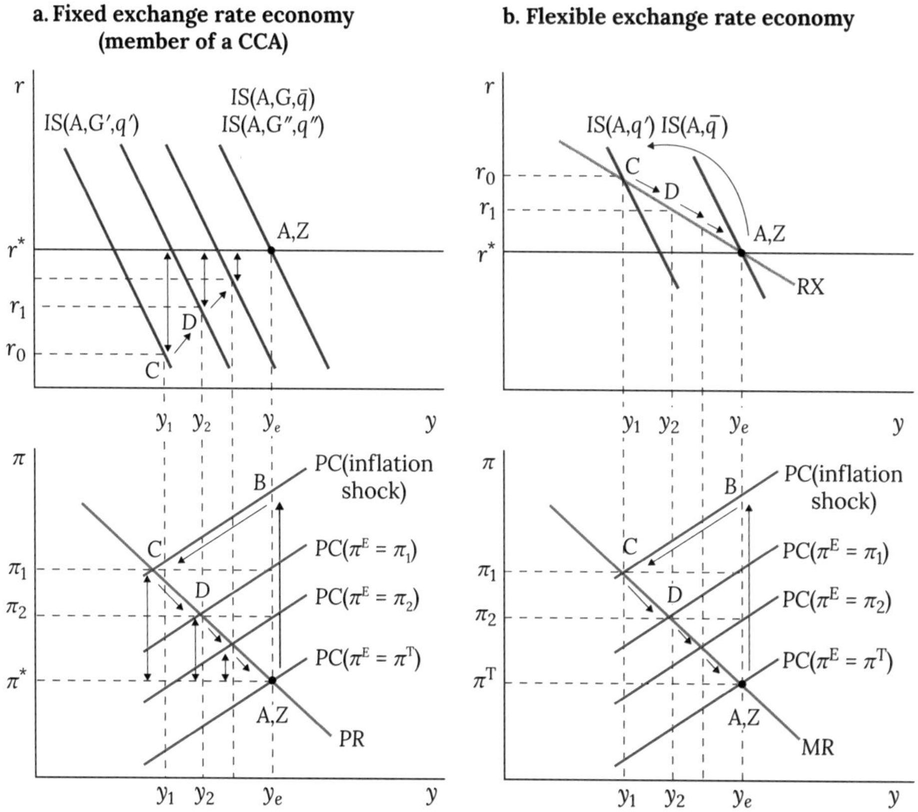

Figure 14.10 Inflation shock: comparison between the use of fiscal policy to stabilize (fixed exchange rates) and monetary policy (a flexible exchange rate economy). Note the CCA central bank's inflation target π^*. Visit www.oup.com/he/carlin-soskice to explore inflation shock further with Animated Analytical Diagram 14.10.

	Fixed exchange rates (member of a CCA)	Flexible exchange rates
Initial equilibrium	$\pi = \pi^T_{ECB} = \pi^*; y = y_e; q = \overline{q}; G = G$	$\pi = \pi^T; y = y_e; q = \overline{q}; G = G$
New equilibrium	$\pi = \pi^T_{ECB} = \pi^*; y = y_e; q = q'' \downarrow; G = G'' \uparrow$	$\pi = \pi^T; y = y_e; q = \overline{q}; G = G$

Table 14.1 Characteristics of the initial and new equilibria in the case of an inflation shock in a fixed exchange rate economy (e.g. CCA member) and a flexible exchange rate economy.

accompany it (right upper panel). The IS curve is shifted to the left by the appreciation and goes through point C.

In a CCA member, the government will decide on its initial fiscal policy stance, G', (to achieve the output gap at point C) taking into account the fact that higher expected inflation reduces the real interest rate to r_0 and higher actual inflation reduces competitiveness to q'.

The crucial point to note is that once the CCA member is back at equilibrium with inflation at target, its real exchange rate will have appreciated. The reason is clear from the left-hand lower panel of Figure 14.10: its inflation is above the CCA's inflation target throughout the inflation shock episode. Hence, its price level will have risen relative to the other members of the CCA and with a fixed nominal exchange rate, e, its real exchange rate will have appreciated. In the flexible rate economy, the real exchange rate is back to its initial level $\overline{q}$: the burst of higher inflation at home is offset by the appropriate nominal depreciation to leave the real exchange rate unchanged. The appreciated real exchange rate (q'') at equilibrium in the CCA member means that net exports are lower and therefore for the level of demand to be sufficient for output of y_e, government spending must be higher ($G'' > G$).

Table 14.1 shows the characteristics of the initial and new equilibria for the case of an inflation shock. Under flexible exchange rates, π^T is the national inflation target and monetary policy is used to stabilize. In a CCA member, $\pi^T_{ECB} = \pi^*$ is the CCA's inflation target and fiscal policy is used to stabilize.

Summary

In a *flexible* rate economy following an inflation shock, the central bank uses changes in the nominal interest rate to stabilize and it leaves no trace once the economy is back at equilibrium. However, in a CCA member, if fiscal policy has to be used to stabilize (because the real exchange rate channel is insufficiently effective), there is a fiscal deficit when the economy is back at equilibrium. Indeed, because net exports are lower and government spending is higher, the economy is characterized by twin deficits, a budget deficit and an external trade deficit.

In an AD-ERU diagram (not shown, see Checklist question 9), the flexible exchange rate economy returns to its starting point with budget balance. But the CCA member for which fiscal policy has been used to stabilize will be at a medium-run equilibrium with an appreciated real exchange rate and on a new AD curve indexed by the higher level of government spending. There is a budget deficit at the new medium-run equilibrium.

Aggregate demand shock

If the economy is hit by a country-specific negative aggregate demand shock, the central bank in a flexible exchange rate economy will cut the interest rate. The exchange rate will depreciate and the economy will move on to the MR line at point C in the right-hand panel of Figure 14.11. At the new equilibrium at point Z, the flexible exchange rate economy is characterized by $r = r^*$ with a depreciated real exchange rate ($\overline{q}''$) and unchanged government expenditure. The primary fiscal deficit is unchanged.

In a common currency area, the PR line in the left hand panel of Figure 14.11 shows the output gap the government has to choose in order for the economy to move back to equilibrium following the same path as the flexible rate economy. It raises G to G′ at point C taking into account the fact that their real interest rate has been pushed up by lower inflation. To shift the economy to the new equilibrium at Z, the government adjusts government expenditure each period. Once the economy is at Z, the real exchange rate is depreciated (to $\overline{q}'$). The depreciation is not as large as in the flexible rate economy because it only reflects the cumulative inflation differential vis-à-vis the rest of the world: in the flexible exchange rate case, the depreciation

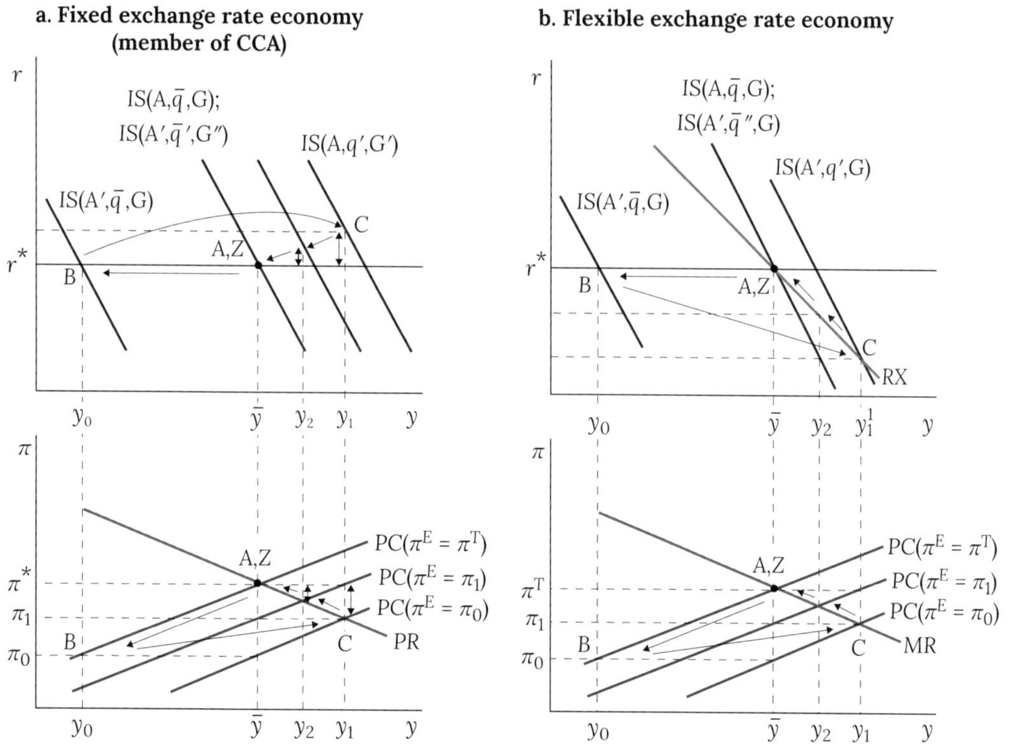

Figure 14.11 Permanent negative aggregate demand shock: comparison between the use of fiscal policy (fixed exchange rates or CCA member) and monetary policy (flexible exchange rates). Visit www.oup.com/he/carlin-soskice to explore further with Animated Analytical Diagram 14.11.

consists of the same cumulative inflation differential plus some nominal depreciation. Hence, once the member of the common currency area is at the new equilibrium at Z, $r = r^*$, $\overline{q}' < \overline{q}''$ and $G'' > G$.

The bottom line is that in the face of a permanent negative demand shock, a CCA member that uses exactly the same policy rule as in the flexible exchange rate economy to return inflation to the CCA inflation target—but implements the desired output gaps by using fiscal rather than monetary policy—ends up with a primary budget deficit when it is back in equilibrium, whereas the flexible exchange rate economy does not.

Supply-side shock

Suppose a member economy experiences a negative supply-side shock. This could be a fall in trend productivity growth due, for example, to the failure to implement new information and communications technology throughout the economy as it emerges. In the 3-equation model, we capture this shock by a permanent downward shift of the PS curve. This reduces equilibrium output. The Policy Rule curve shifts to the left.

The shock pushes up inflation at the initial level of output since it creates a positive bargaining gap. The government has to take two factors into account when calculating the fiscal contraction needed to get the economy on to the new PR curve at point C, which is to the left of the new equilibrium output level. The first is the effect of higher inflation in appreciating the real exchange rate and the second is its effect in reducing the real interest rate below r^*. These effects on aggregate demand go in opposite directions and are relatively minor as you can check using the Macroeconomics Simulator (available at available at www.oup.com/he/carlin-soskice). The bulk of the stabilization is done by the fiscal contraction (which shifts the IS and the AD curves to the left).

From point C, the government steadily eases the contractionary policy stance as it guides the economy along the PR curve to the new equilibrium at Z. The cumulative effect of inflation higher than elsewhere in the CCA leaves the home economy with an appreciated real exchange rate and an external deficit. The government's budget will be in surplus at the new lower level of medium-run output.

Under flexible exchange rates, the new medium-run level of output, real interest rate and exchange rate are the same as in the CCA member. Recall that the adjustment path under flexible exchange rates involves exchange rate overshooting via a jump in the nominal exchange rate producing an initial appreciation greater than the equilibrium one, and the combination of the appreciation of the real exchange rate and a higher real interest rate dampening aggregate demand to deliver the best response output gap at point C. The government does not adjust its fiscal stance in response to the shock.

Summary

In response to country-specific shocks, policy makers in a fixed exchange rate regime or in a common currency area can choose not to intervene and rather, to rely on the stabilizing mechanism of the real exchange rate channel. But this may not produce rapid stabilization because of the countervailing operation of the destabilizing real

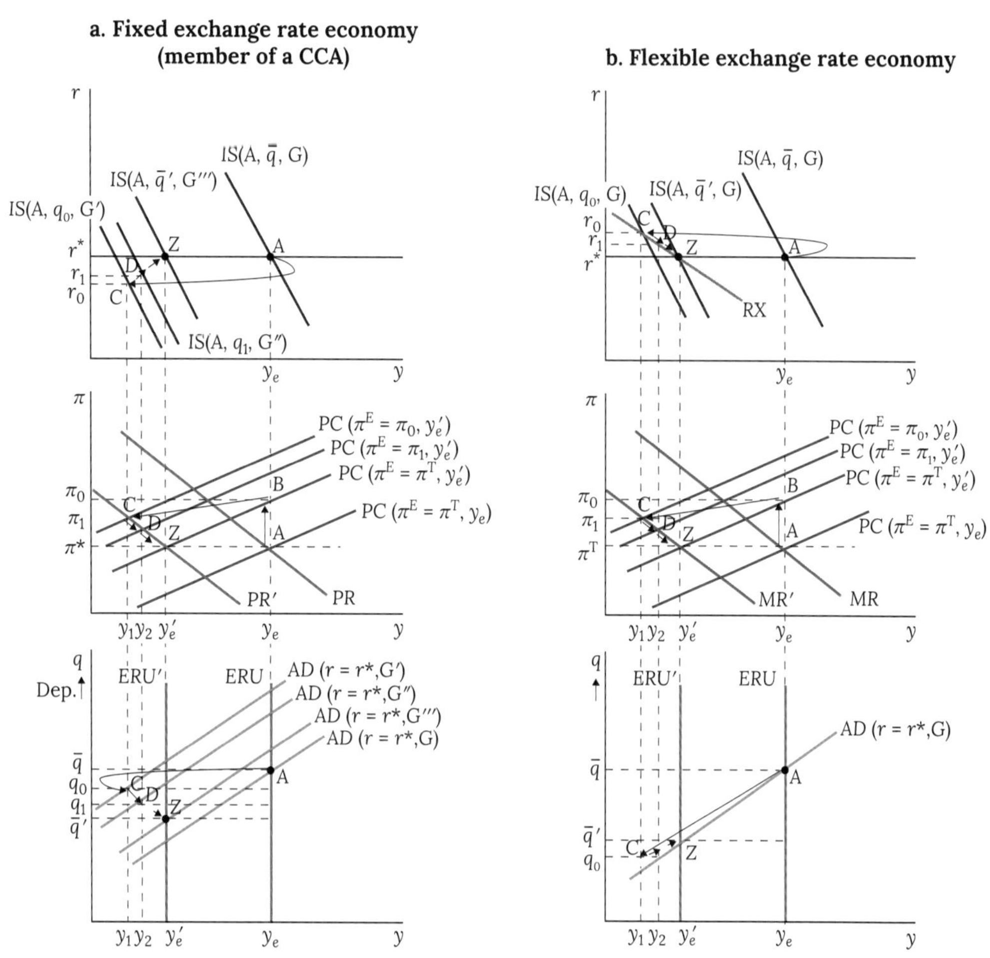

Figure 14.12 Permanent negative supply-side shock: comparison between the use of fiscal policy (CCA member) and monetary policy (flexible exchange rates).

interest rate channel and/or because the operation of the real exchange rate channel is sluggish. Hence, the government may use fiscal policy to stabilize. But fiscal policy is not a panacea.

Our results show the following:

1. A fiscal stabilization policy rule can be used to stabilize output and inflation under fixed exchange rates or in a CCA. However, although using the same loss function as in the flexible rate economy will return the economy to a medium-run equilibrium with inflation at the CCA's inflation target, the economy will not in general return to an equilibrium in which the government budget is balanced.
2. If the government wishes to ensure budget balance at medium-run equilibrium, then its stabilization task is more complex. The nub of the problem is that deviations from the inflation target of the CCA central bank during adjustment to a shock

cumulate, producing persistent effects on the real exchange rate, which do not occur under flexible exchange rates. In a common currency area, it is not only the deviation of inflation from target (i.e. from π^*) that brings welfare losses but also the deviation in the price level from that of other members, which is manifested in trends in real exchange rates.

This characteristic of how a common currency area operates points to the importance of heterogeneity in the way wages are set across member states, to which we now turn.

14.4 RISKS IN A HETEROGENEOUS COMMON CURRENCY AREA

At the beginning of the chapter, the heterogeneity in inflation and output gap performance of member countries before the financial crisis was displayed in a scatter plot (Figure 14.1). Differential inflation rates between countries reflect wage-setting behaviour and in turn are reflected in the evolution of real exchange rates. Figure 14.13 shows the trend real depreciation in Germany over the years before the financial crisis; the trend reversed after the crisis but its competitiveness gain was not fully eroded 13 years later even with low unemployment. The trends in two other large members—Spain and Italy—help explain why. Spain's pre-crisis boom saw its real exchange rate appreciate; the very high unemployment then unwound this. Italy showed slow progress in recovering its lost competitiveness in the decade and a half from the mid-2000s in spite of unemployment substantially higher than Germany's.

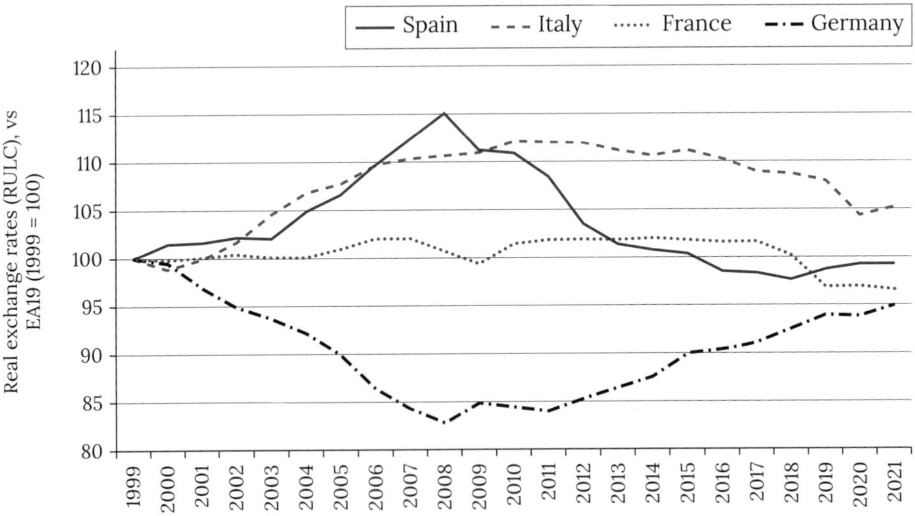

Figure 14.13 RER Intra-Eurozone real exchange rates measured by relative unit labour costs, 1999–2021.

Source: European Commission, *Price and Cost Competitiveness* report, data accessed July 2022.

14.4.1 The real exchange rate channel: Wage-setting and internal devaluation

Differences in wage-setting systems in the Eurozone

The role that fiscal policy plays in macroeconomic stabilization in a currency union could be shared with or substituted by wages policy or by the kind of coordinated wage-setting behaviour discussed in detail in Chapter 15. This possibility depends on institutional arrangements for collective bargaining and is relevant in the Eurozone because of the use made of it by Germany as documented in the case study of Germany and France in Chapter 15. In particular, we shall see that Germany's wage-setting system means that the real exchange rate channel explained in Section 14.3.3 operates there. This poses particular difficulties for some other member countries in which the real exchange rate channel does not operate as effectively.

As we have seen in Section 14.1.1, from a macroeconomic perspective, one attraction for a country on joining a common currency area with Germany is to acquire a credible commitment to low inflation. However, as noted in Section 14.1.2, divergent real exchange rates arose because inflation rates did not converge rapidly to the ECB's target *and* Germany's inflation was below the target. Remember that any cumulated difference in price levels is reflected in real exchange rates.

Figure 14.2 shows that from 2000, Germany experienced a substantial real depreciation within the Eurozone. This took place through a combination of restraint in nominal wage growth and more rapid productivity growth than was the case in member countries in the southern Eurozone. Although this partly reflected the recovery of Germany's competitiveness, which had been depressed by the consequences of German reunification in the early 1990s, more importantly, it demonstrated the country's ability to engineer a real depreciation inside the Eurozone when required.

German wage coordination

While it does not have a classical flexible labour market, Germany, like some other northern Eurozone members (and some EU countries outside the Eurozone like Sweden and Denmark), has wage-setting institutions that enable nominal wage growth to be coordinated so as to achieve a real exchange rate target. The way in which different wage-setting institutions (coordinated, industry-level and firm-level) can be modelled is set out in Chapter 15. In the 2000s, unions in Germany agreed to modest nominal wage increases in multi-year deals, and works councils that represent workers in large companies negotiated over wage and hours flexibility in exchange for investment by firms in fixed capital and training.[17]

Germany's model of export-led growth relies on skilled workers in its core manufacturing industries. This places such workers in a strong bargaining position. As a

[17] See, for example, Carlin and Soskice (2009) and Dustmann et al. (2014).

result, unions and employers' associations in the export sector are important in wage setting. They play two roles in keeping the export sector competitive. First, agreements between unions and employers' associations restrain the bargaining power of skilled workers in those industries. Second, unions and employers in the export sector lead the wage-setting round in the economy as a whole so as to ensure that the pace of wage increases is pinned down by the competitiveness requirements of the export sector and not by the wage bargains in the non-tradeables parts of the economy, such as the public sector, where external pressure to contain cost increases is absent. Coordinated wage setting in Germany is primarily the outcome of private sector behaviour—not the result of government policy.

The German model allows coordinated wage restraint to substitute for stabilizing fiscal policy. To see how coordinated wage setting works, we can use the example shown in Figure 14.8. The left-hand panel can be thought of as representing Germany and the right-hand panel, a member country such as one in the periphery, where inflation expectations are not anchored to the ECB's inflation target. If there is an inflation shock to each country, the response in Germany is a reduction in wage increases, so that they are below the ECB's inflation target in order to restore the real exchange rate to its initial level. This restores competitiveness and the economy returns to equilibrium. Coordinated wage setting can make the real exchange rate channel work effectively.

A country without this kind of wage behaviour may experience destabilization as shown in the right-hand panel of Figure 14.8. Weak and sluggish wage adjustment and inflation expectations that are backward looking and not anchored to the ECB's inflation target bring the destabilizing real interest rate channel into play. To return to equilibrium at the initial real exchange rate, such a country would have to use tight fiscal policy to implement the large negative output gap associated with the relevant Phillips curve (labelled $\pi^E = \pi_{-1}$) sufficient to bring inflation *below* the target. Only a period with elevated unemployment and inflation below π^* will see the economy return to equilibrium without an appreciated real exchange rate.

To take another example, in the face of a negative aggregate demand shock, Germany is able to achieve a response similar to that implemented under flexible exchange rates whereby demand is stabilized by a real depreciation achieved via *wage restraint*. Under *flexible* exchange rates, the real depreciation takes place via a nominal depreciation triggered by a cut in the interest rate. By contrast, as we saw in Figure 14.11, even if a Eurozone member without wage coordination uses fiscal policy to stabilize along the PR curve it will need to manage the consequences that arise for the government deficit because of the change in the real exchange rate in medium-run equilibrium.

For countries like Germany where the export sector is the dynamic part of the economy, it can be argued that it is important to limit the use of discretionary fiscal policy for stabilization since it weakens the incentive of wage setters to exercise wage restraint and to coordinate around the required real exchange rate.

Living in the Eurozone with Germany

For Eurozone members that do not have wage-setting institutions that make the real exchange rate an effective stabilization mechanism, there are serious problems with achieving satisfactory macroeconomic performance. For example, a country entering the Eurozone with a higher growth rate of unit labour costs than the average will suffer from falling competitiveness. An attempt to offset the negative effects of this on aggregate demand by using expansionary fiscal policy will produce problems of fiscal imbalance; on the other hand, allowing a credit-fuelled housing boom to sustain growth (reflected in the trends in household debt shown in Figure 14.3) brings the problems of potential instability explained in Chapters 8 and 9. The divergence of real exchange rates that characterized the Eurozone in its first decade (as shown in Figure 14.2) reflects both the failure of domestic unit cost growth to adjust to the Eurozone inflation average of just above 2% and the success of Germany in achieving unit cost growth below 2% p.a.

Given the variation in institutional characteristics among members and Germany's export-oriented growth strategy, this problem is likely to remain a source of tension for the Eurozone.

In summary, labour market institutions matter for the ability of member states to adjust without the use of fiscal policy. The presence of coordinated wage bargaining that increases the flexibility of wages improves the operation of the real exchange rate channel. These institutions are typical in Germany and the other Northern European economies, which is beneficial for *their* adjustment, but can cause detrimental spillover effects reflected in real exchange rates and current accounts at the Eurozone level.

14.4.2 **Heterogeneity and the Eurozone crisis**

The build-up of imbalances in the Eurozone prior to the financial crisis was discussed in terms of the different growth strategies of member countries in Chapter 13. One way of highlighting the role of those imbalances is to note the common characteristics of the countries that were at the heart of the Eurozone crisis, the so-called PIIGS—Portugal, Ireland, Italy, Greece, and Spain. Members of the Eurozone are ranked in Table 14.2 by the size of the government bond spread over the German Bund: this is an indicator of the intensity of the Eurozone crisis shown in Figure 14.14.

As shown in Table 14.2, the crisis countries (at the top of the table) had current account deficits over the pre-crisis period and with the exception of Ireland, a substantially appreciated real exchange rate. Real interest rates were low relative to the other Eurozone members, reinforcing domestic-demand led growth strategies and opening up the possibility of a destabilizing interest rate channel. Note that in terms of pre-crisis *fiscal balance*, there was nothing distinctive about the PIIGS.

These data underscore the need to keep in mind the role of wage-setting and the different institutional arrangements across countries when looking at the susceptibility of members to crisis.

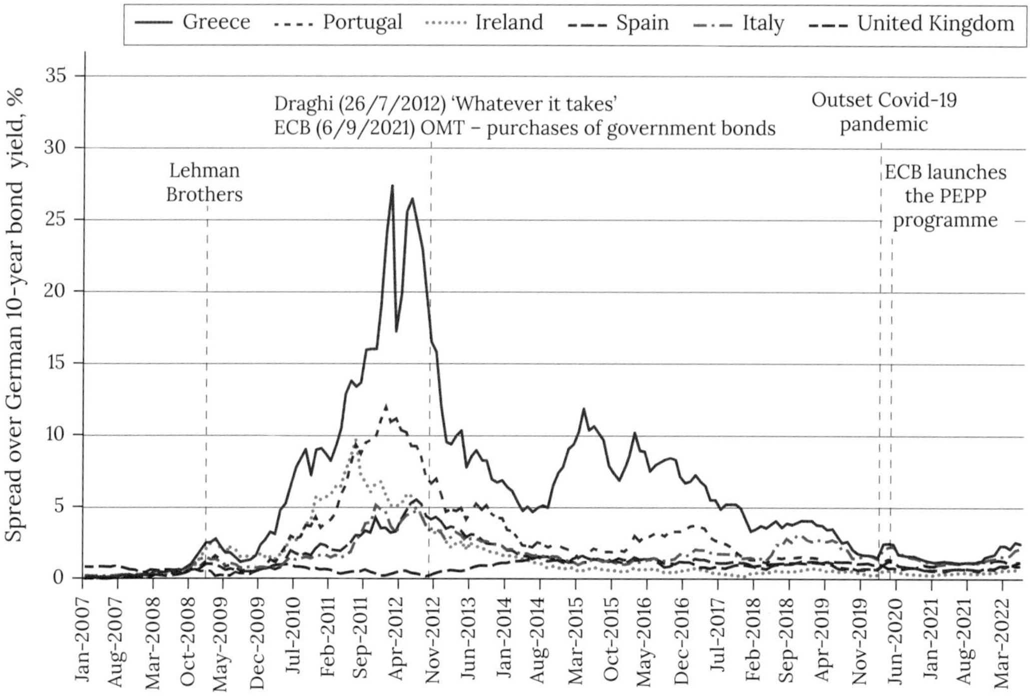

Figure 14.14 The Eurozone crisis: sovereign debt spreads, 2007–22.

Source: OECD stats (accessed July 2022).

	Current account (% GDP)	Real exchange rate (manuf.)	Real interest rate	General government balance (% GDP)
Greece	−8.1	129.9	0.9	−5.8
Ireland	−1.6	97.0	0.3	1.6
Portugal	−9.2	107.6	1.2	−3.6
Spain	−5.5	123.0	0.2	0.1
Italy	−1.1	123.6	2.0	−2.8
Belgium	3.6	104.0	2.4	−0.5
Austria	1.3	92.6	2.9	−1.8
France	0.8	98.7	2.5	−2.6
Finland	6.2	79.1	3.1	3.7
Netherlands	5.3	101.1	1.6	−0.5
Germany	2.7	85.1	3.5	−2.1

Table 14.2 Eurozone member countries' economic performance indicators, 1999–2007. Countries ranked from the top by interest rate spread over German Bund Q2 2011 (a measure of the extent of EZ sovereign debt crisis).

Note: RER: 1999=100; increase is appreciation. European Commission, Economic and Financial Affairs, Economic Databases and Indicators Price and Cost Competitiveness.
RIR: 10 year government bond yields and spread over German bonds deflated by GDP deflator.

Source: OECD.

14.5 EUROZONE GOVERNANCE, SOVEREIGN RISK, AND THE BANKING SYSTEM

In this chapter, we have seen that a CCA member loses access to the nominal exchange rate as a mechanism for adjustment to shocks and that neither adjustment via domestic wages and prices (the real exchange rate channel) nor via the use of fiscal policy is problem-free. On the other hand, the economy avoids the disturbances that can come from the foreign exchange market itself. Until 2010, this was a reasonable summary of the issues facing a country deciding whether to join the Eurozone.

Although familiar to observers of emerging economies, a sovereign debt crisis—the inability of the government to honour the repayment of bonds it has issued—was new to those whose expertise was limited to high-income countries like Eurozone members. The first market signal of a problem of sovereign debt in the Eurozone came from the appearance of large interest rate differentials between bonds issued by Germany (and France) and those issued by the periphery countries (Greece, Portugal, Spain, and Ireland). This followed the collapse of Lehman Brothers in 2008 (see Chapter 9).

As noted in the introduction, during the Eurozone's first decade, interest rate spreads on government bonds among Eurozone members shrank dramatically. Prior to the formation of the Eurozone, the interest rate differentials reflected both the exchange rate risk and the government default risk. Once inside the Eurozone, the exchange rate risk (e.g. the risk that the Italian lira would depreciate against the German D-Mark) vanished because all members used the euro, leaving only differences in government default risk to account for the variation in interest rates on long-term (e.g. ten-year) government bonds.

Figures 14.4 and 14.14 show the differential between the interest rate on long-term government bonds issued by a number of European countries and the German Bund rate.[18] The full time series from 1990 (shown in Figure 14.4) includes the period before the Eurozone was formed (in 1999). The countries shown include those caught up in the Eurozone crisis of 2010 along with France and the UK. The UK is not a member of the Eurozone: its interest differential therefore reflects both the exchange rate risk and the default premium throughout the period. For the countries that joined the Eurozone when it began, the sharp fall in the interest differential with Germany when the exchange rate parities with the euro were announced in 1998 is clear. The same happened with Greece prior to its entry in 2001.

During the Eurozone's first decade, interest differentials with Germany on long-term government bonds were very small. Explanations include the following:

1. The markets viewed the likelihood of a default by a Eurozone government as being very low. For example, they considered the risk of a systemic banking crisis in a Eurozone member that would require a government rescue of banks as a very low probability event.

---

[18] See Section 14.5.3 for a list of sources for the ECB quotes in Figure 14.4.

2. The markets did not connect the divergent performance among Eurozone members with the possible implications for government solvency.
3. The markets did not believe the Eurozone's 'no bail-out clause' and took the view that any problem in one member government's ability to service its debts would be solved by the ECB and/or by the other Eurozone governments.

When the global financial crisis took hold in 2008 and large banks in small countries (like Ireland) began to fail, this market perception changed dramatically. Markets suddenly began to differentiate between the bonds issued by different Eurozone member governments. The emergence of very large interest rate spreads indicated that the markets were not confident that national governments that got into difficulty as a result of increases in national public debt due to bank failures and recession would be supported by other Eurozone governments, the European Commission or the ECB. The lack of confidence was justified given the governance arrangements in the Eurozone.

14.5.1 **Governance arrangements: Banks, governments, and central bank**

The nature of the governance problems in the Eurozone arises from the following facts:

- Citizenship is of member countries.
- Governments have tax raising powers with the consent of their citizens.
- Governments have responsibility for insolvency crises of banks headquartered in their country.
- The ECB has responsibility for addressing bank liquidity crises in member countries.

At the root of the Eurozone's vulnerability to a sovereign debt crisis were the relationships put in place when it was created among banks, national governments and the ECB. A coherent set of relationships among these three groups that was robust to a financial crisis was not established. In the Maastricht policy assignment discussed in Section 14.2.1, banks were not mentioned. This was a key omission. In terms of the relationships among member governments and between them and the ECB, the central elements were as follows:

1. **Government to government:** the 'no bail-out' clause stated that other member governments could not be called upon to bail out a government in trouble.
2. **ECB to government:** the 'no monetary financing' clause stated that the ECB would not provide credit to governments (i.e. it would not be the lender of last resort to governments).
3. **The fiscal rules:** the entry rules for deficits and debt and the Stability and Growth Pact, which were designed to support (1) and (2).

Prior to 2010, this governance structure was believed to be sufficient. In particular, it was believed to make a supra-national *government* redundant. To highlight the problems that have arisen, it is useful to review the relationships among banks, government and central bank in a nation state with an independent central bank.

The features of banks headquartered in Eurozone countries that made bank failure especially problematic are the following:

1. The size of banks relative to GDP and their holdings of government debt.
2. The fact that national governments were responsible for dealing with insolvent banks.
3. The cross-border banking relationships involving different regulatory authorities and rules—for deposit insurance, resolution mechanisms such as 'bail-in' of creditors of failing banks and fiscal support.

Comparison between the Eurozone and US

Both for understanding the problems in the Eurozone and for thinking about reforms, it is helpful to compare the governance arrangements in the US and the Eurozone before the crisis. The US is a federal system, and parallels can be drawn between the US states and the member countries of the Eurozone. In the US, the:

- Federal Reserve stabilizes common shocks, is responsible for financial stability and is the lender of last resort to the federal government and to the banking system
- federal budget provides stabilization to the states in the face of asymmetric shocks (e.g. federal contributions to unemployment benefit and federal taxes). In the US, stabilization of state-specific aggregate demand shocks through federal taxes and transfers lies between 10 and 20%[19]
- states have balanced budget rules
- failure of a bank headquartered in a state is not the responsibility of the state but of the federal regulators and the federal government
- federal government does not bail out delinquent states—they are allowed to default

In the Eurozone prior to the sovereign debt crisis, the following measures were in place:

- The ECB stabilized common shocks and, as was demonstrated by its actions in the financial crisis, was the lender of last resort to the banking system (although this was not explicitly part of the Maastricht Treaty). However, it was not responsible for financial stability and was not the lender of last resort to member governments.
- There was no federal government and no stabilization through the EU budget (it is too small).
- Member countries had national fiscal autonomy subject to rules (i.e. the SGP).
- The failure of a bank headquartered in a member country was the responsibility of the country and not of Eurozone or European Union regulators or a Eurozone government (there is no Eurozone government).

---

19 See Melitz and Zumer (2002).

- The Maastricht Treaty included a 'no bail-out clause' that stated that member governments would not be bailed out.

In conjunction with Figures 14.15 and 14.16, this comparison between the US and the Eurozone highlights the incoherence of the Eurozone governance structure prior to the sovereign debt crisis. In addition, the analysis presented in this section so far suggests that the problems brought to the fore by the financial crisis involve three key parties: banks, governments, and the central bank. We discuss the changes the Eurozone has made to the governance structure in the wake of the sovereign debt crisis in Section 14.5.3. At this stage, we focus on the original governance structure of the Eurozone and show why it left the currency union vulnerable to a sovereign debt crisis.

Figure 14.15 illustrates the relationships among commercial banks, the government and the central bank in a nation state. We begin with the *commercial banks*. In Figure 14.15, which was introduced in Chapter 9, the *central bank's role of lender of last resort* (LOLR) *to the banking system* is represented by the dashed arrows labelled 'liquidity risk'. As we have seen in Chapter 9, a key role of the central bank is to provide liquidity in a situation where a bad shock to the economy has raised the possibility that banks may become insolvent (i.e. that their assets are worth less than their liabilities). Under such circumstances, there can be a run on banks as depositors do not want to be the last in line to turn their potentially risky deposits into safe cash.

The institutional response to this source of fragility was to create a lender of last resort to the banking system in the form of a central bank. The central bank's LOLR role to the banking system rests on its judgement that the panic in the market is misplaced: i.e. that the problem is in fact not one of solvency, but of liquidity (i.e.

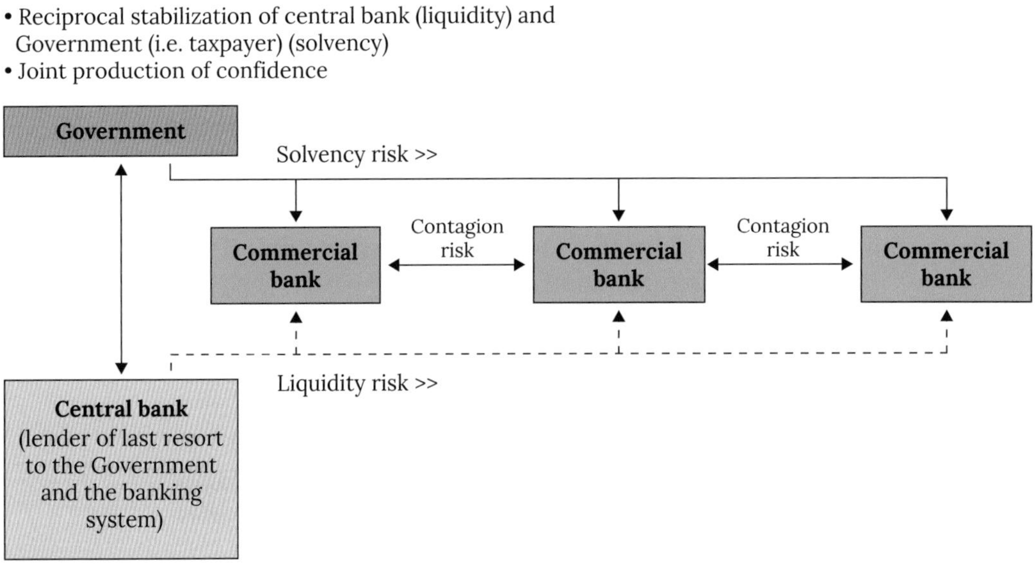

Figure 14.15 Governance arrangements in a nation state.

Source: adapted from Winckler (2011).

a bank has insufficient liquid assets to cover its due liabilities). In the case where a bank is insolvent, the central bank and government work together. The central bank controls the panic by providing liquidity and the government, with its access to tax revenue (current and future), is responsible for the restructuring, recapitalization or orderly closure of the bank. This role is captured in Figure 14.15 by the arrows labelled solvency risk.

We turn now to the role of the *government as borrower*. Households and firms make use of banks and the bond market to finance long-term investment projects using shorter-term loans. Governments also borrow shorter-term in the bond market to finance long-term projects. The service provided by banks and the bond markets that allows this is called maturity transformation, and whether the borrower can service the debt is called rollover risk. When the government is the borrower, it is relying on its ability to raise tax revenue to provide confidence to the bond market that it will service its debts. It is clear that if the government is being called upon to use tax revenue to support failing banks (or there is a possibility it will have to do so), its ability to service its debt via tax revenue is reduced. This highlights the interconnection between the banks, the government and the bond market. We can see the parallel with the 'last in line' liquidity problem for banks (Chapter 9): if fear emerges that the government will not be able to service its debts, holders of bonds will sell them, prices will fall and, reflecting the rise in the risk premium, interest rates will rise.

How can this be prevented? If the *central bank is the lender of last resort to the government*, it can be relied upon to step in and buy government bonds. How is this possible and why would the central bank do this? The parallel with the case of banks is again useful. If we assume that the flight from government bonds is consistent with the underlying ability of the government to service its debts (i.e. the government is solvent) then the government is suffering from a liquidity problem. The central bank can step in by creating reserves (just as it does when dealing with the liquidity problem of the banking system) and buying government bonds. The central bank would end up with more government bonds on its balance sheet and the counterpart on the liability side is an increase in reserves (i.e. base money). The mutual support of the government and central bank for each other—the taxpayer base is the ultimate guarantee of the solvency of the government and the central bank's commitment to buy government bonds in unlimited quantities (LOLR)—is shown by the double-headed arrow in Figure 14.15. This means that even when the market has doubts about the solvency of the government, the existence of the LOLR prevents runs on government bonds. If this structure of mutual confidence completely breaks down, reflected for example in the unwillingness of citizens to hold home's money, the economy can plunge into hyperinflation (see Chapter 6).

14.5.2 **The Eurozone crisis and the doom loop**

Figure 14.16 illustrates the governance structure of the Eurozone prior to the financial crisis. As discussed in 14.1.2, when the financial crisis began, the ECB responded promptly in its role of lender of last resort to banks to prevent liquidity-driven

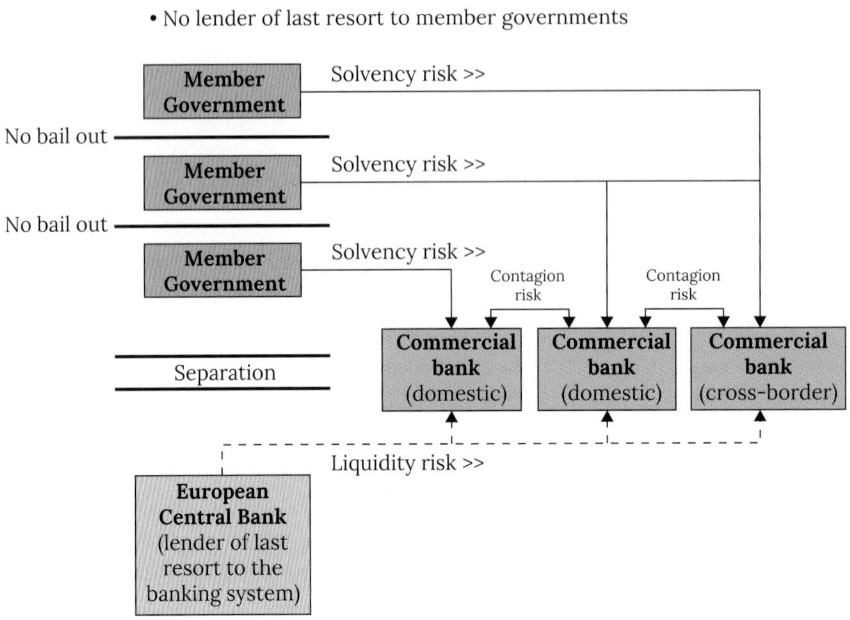

Figure 14.16 Governance arrangements in the Eurozone prior to the crisis.

Source: adapted from Winckler (2011).

bank runs. When the crisis shifted from liquidity to solvency problems of banks, the fractures illustrated in Figure 14.16 emerged with force.

In the Eurozone, responsibility for dealing with insolvent banks rested with member country governments (see Figure 14.16). This meant that governments had to use national borrowing to pay for the recapitalization of banks headquartered in their country during the global financial crisis. The burden on governments increased (just as it did in the US and the UK, for example). However, the big difference is that for a Eurozone member, it could not rely on a lender of last resort to support its bond sales if required. There was no central bank that would—in extremis—purchase its bonds. There are three aspects to this: first, the member countries were issuing bonds in a currency (the euro) that they did not control; and second, they had no central bank that could 'print money' in order to purchase government bonds. Moreover, the central bank that issues the euros (the ECB) was prevented by its mandate from acting as lender of last resort to the governments of member states.

This created the fear of illiquidity of the government, i.e. that it would not be able to roll over its debts as they became due. As a result, interest rates on government bonds increased. We can see the same element of self-fulfilling prophecy here as arises in the case of a bank run: even if the bank is solvent, once doubts emerge about its liquidity, panic begins and depositor behaviour can produce insolvency. The circuit can be interrupted by the existence of a LOLR which quashes liquidity fears. Similarly, in the bond market, a LOLR to the government can prevent the damaging positive feedback loop from taking hold.

BOX 14.1 Spain and the UK: sovereign risk inside and outside the Eurozone

To highlight the difference between the risk of sovereign default for a country inside and outside the common currency area it is useful to compare Spain and the UK. In this box, we show that on the basis of the determinants of government solvency, there was little to separate these two countries. However, interest rates on ten year government bonds in Spain at the end of November 2011 were 6.5% while they were 2.3% in the UK.

Table 14.3 compares the two countries and shows that the UK government was more indebted than that of Spain in 2010. GDP growth forecasts in the two countries were broadly similar at that point in time, with Spain expected to grow slightly more slowly in 2012 and 2013.

Given these figures, we would expect both countries to have had similar ten year government bond yields (i.e. default risks), but this was not the case. We can see from Table 14.3 that Spanish bond yields were higher than the UK's for 2010. We can also see that the UK's cost of borrowing fell in 2011, while Spain's continued to rise, culminating in interest rates on Spanish bonds being 2.3 percentage points higher than those on UK bonds (on average) over 2011. This apparent inconsistency between government solvency and perceived sovereign default risk is summed up by Pisani-Ferry (2012):

> This comparison is prima facie evidence that the fiscal situation per se fails to explain tension in the euro-area government bond markets. Or, to put it slightly differently, although their levels of deficit and public debt are the same, euro-area countries seem to be more vulnerable to fiscal crises than non-euro area countries.

As we saw in Chapter 12, in the 1990s, Spain and the UK both solved their high inflation problem by adopting a new monetary policy regime: the UK chose

Variable	Year	Spain	UK
General government underlying primary balances (as a % of potential GDP)	2010	−5.6	−5.5
Maastricht definition of general government gross public debt (as a % of nominal GDP)	2010	61.0	79.9
Real GDP growth (%, Dec 2011 forecast)	2012f	0.3	0.5
Real GDP growth (%, Dec 2011 forecast)	2013f	1.3	1.8
10-year government bond yields (%, average)	2010	4.3	3.6
10-year government bond yields (%, average, Dec 2011 forecast)	2011f	5.4	3.1

Table 14.3 Macroeconomic and government finance indicators for the UK and Spain.

Source: OECD Economic Outlook, December 2011.

(*continued*)

to establish a credible monetary policy through inflation-targeting and an independent central bank and Spain chose to borrow a credible monetary policy by giving up its exchange rate and joining the Eurozone. Both countries enjoyed buoyant domestic economies in the 2000s, and both suffered bank failures and a subsequent deterioration of the public finances in the global financial crisis. Yet, Spain faced much higher interest rates on government borrowing than the UK and was identified in 2011 as one of the so-called PIIGS. PIIGS refers to Portugal, Ireland, Italy, Greece and Spain and became a synonym for the Eurozone economies threatened by a sovereign debt crisis.

De Grauwe (2011) suggested that this was a consequence of Spain entering the European Monetary Union and the UK not doing so. The argument is that when Spain adopted the euro, it lost control over the currency it issued debt in, which meant that the financial markets could force the Spanish sovereign into default (or at least cause a sovereign liquidity crisis). De Grauwe highlights two important factors that make the UK less vulnerable to being forced into default by financial markets than a Eurozone country (in a similar fiscal situation). Firstly, the UK has a freely floating exchange rate, which will depreciate if government bonds are sold off. This should help to raise growth and increase inflation, both of which are positive for debt dynamics. Secondly, if the UK cannot roll over its debts at a reasonable interest rate, then it could force the Bank of England (in its role as LOLR) to buy government securities. In summary, the governance structure of the Eurozone prior to the crisis (and particularly the lack of a credible LOLR to member governments) helps to explain the reason for seemingly solvent Eurozone governments (e.g. Spain and Italy) ending up in liquidity crises.

The diabolic or doom loop is an expression coined in the Eurozone crisis to describe the interconnection between problems in the banking system, government financial balances, market reactions and the real economy.[20]

Figure 14.17 captures the positive feedback processes constituting the doom loop. It is best to begin with the balance sheets of banks in Eurozone countries, where on the asset side, two factors played a key role. Banks are major holders of government bonds in Eurozone countries and the financial crisis was initiated by a fall in house prices. Falling house prices threatened the solvency of banks and increased the probability that governments would have to bail them out. At the same time, the recession caused by the collapse of the housing bubbles worsened government finances through the automatic stabilizers (as well as a result of discretionary government stimulus), further worsening government deficits.

Financial markets responded by targeting bonds issued by vulnerable Eurozone governments. Given the large size of banks relative to national economies, the prospect of bail-out was low, raising fears of great damage to the real economy. The result was an increase in sovereign debt default risk (falling bond prices; rising risk premia) in Eurozone countries with failing banks because unlike countries with their own central

[20] See Brunnermeier and Reis (2023).

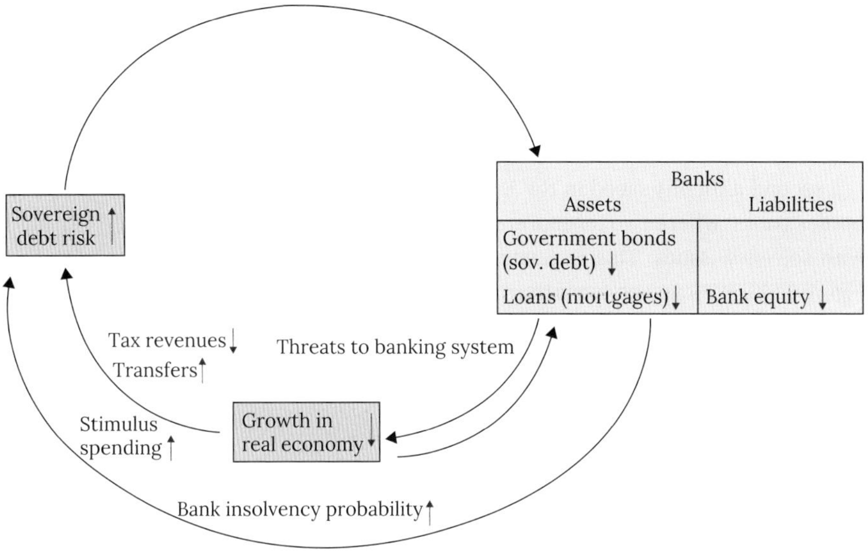

Figure 14.17 Doom loop: the positive feedback processes connecting the value of bank assets and government solvency with the real economy.

bank, they did not have a lender of last resort to the government who could purchase government bonds and support the price. Falling bond prices fed back to worsen further the value of bank assets, raising the risk of bank insolvency and the probability of bail-out, turning the screw once more on the doom loop.

Bank problems

In the Eurozone, banks are major holders of government bonds. For example, the percentage of national government bonds that were held by domestic banks in Spain, Italy and Germany was 28.3%, 27.3%, and 22.9% respectively in mid-2011. The equivalent figure for the UK was 10.7% and for the US was just 2%. The close ties between the governments and the banks in the Eurozone add to the vulnerability of the system. When government bond prices fall, bank solvency is called into question; in turn, when banks are more likely to be insolvent, the contingent liabilities of the government (to recapitalize and restructure them) rise and government solvency comes into question.

The reason European banks held a lot of government bonds is that they were deemed 'risk-free' by financial regulators, accepted as collateral by the ECB and used for repo operations. The ECB did not distinguish between the default risk of different member governments, which gave banks strong incentives to hold these bonds.

The absence of a pan-European or Eurozone bank resolution scheme during the crisis meant countries were faced with dealing with bank solvency on their own. The fact that banks were often large relative to the size of the country helped turn the bank solvency issue into a sovereign debt problem.

For example, the Irish commercial bank, Bank of Ireland, had total assets that were equal to 99% of Irish GDP in 2007. This can be compared to Bank of America that had total assets that were equal to only 12% of US GDP in the same year. This meant that the

US government could bail out Bank of America (BoA) and other financial institutions without the government finances becoming unsustainable. This was not the case in Ireland and would not have been the case had North Carolina (the US state where BoA is headquartered) been responsible for bailing out BoA—BoA had total assets equal to 431% of North Carolina's GDP in 2007.[21]

A second difficulty faced in the Eurozone arose because of the presence of cross-border banks, where two (or more) national governments are responsible for dealing with solvency issues. This is illustrated by the inclusion of a cross-border bank in Figure 14.16. We can see from the figure, that two member governments are jointly responsible for the restructuring, recapitalization or orderly closure of the cross-border bank (as indicated by the 'solvency' arrows).

By contrast, in the US, managing bank failure is the responsibility of the federal government. So although the ECB provided liquidity support to banks in the crisis, unlike in the US, it was unable to follow this up with recapitalization of banks. There was no equivalent to the US TARP (Troubled Asset Relief Program).

Government problems

The doom loop that took hold in some Eurozone countries was not caused by levels of government debt to GDP much higher than in the US. In fact as the upper panel of Figure 14.18 shows, Spain's public debt ratio in 2010 was substantially lower than in the US. The lower panel of the figure points to the key difference in fiscal arrangements: public sector debt in the Eurozone is held at member country level; in the US, it is mainly held at federal level.

The upper panel of Figure 14.18 compares the debt to GDP ratios of the US and the Eurozone member countries in 2010. In contrast, the lower panel shows how the debts of the individual Eurozone countries compare to Eurozone GDP and how the debts of the individual US states compare to US GDP just before the onset of the financial crisis.

This difference in fiscal arrangements has it roots in the political structure of the Eurozone. This has major consequences for the resilience of the governance mechanism. If a US state—even a large one like California—defaults, this represents a small shock to US GDP. As the lower panel of Figure 14.18 shows, this is not the case in the Eurozone. To summarize, collapse of a housing bubble in California's economy that brought down a bank headquartered there would trigger fiscal support for the state from the operation of automatic stabilizers (federal unemployment benefits and taxes) and the federal government would also be responsible for bailing out the bank.

The interconnection of banks and sovereigns (i.e. governments) in the Eurozone crisis can be measured by the correlation of sovereign and bank default risk. In Figure 14.19 the risks are measured using the credit default swaps (CDS) spread, which

[21] These figures were calculated by the authors in March 2012 using data from the 2007 annual reports of Bank of Ireland (BoI) and Bank of America (BoA), the IMF World Economic Outlook Database, and the US BEA. The figures for total assets for BoI are as of March 31st 2007 and for BoA are as of December 31st 2007. GDP data for all regions are in current prices and for 2007.

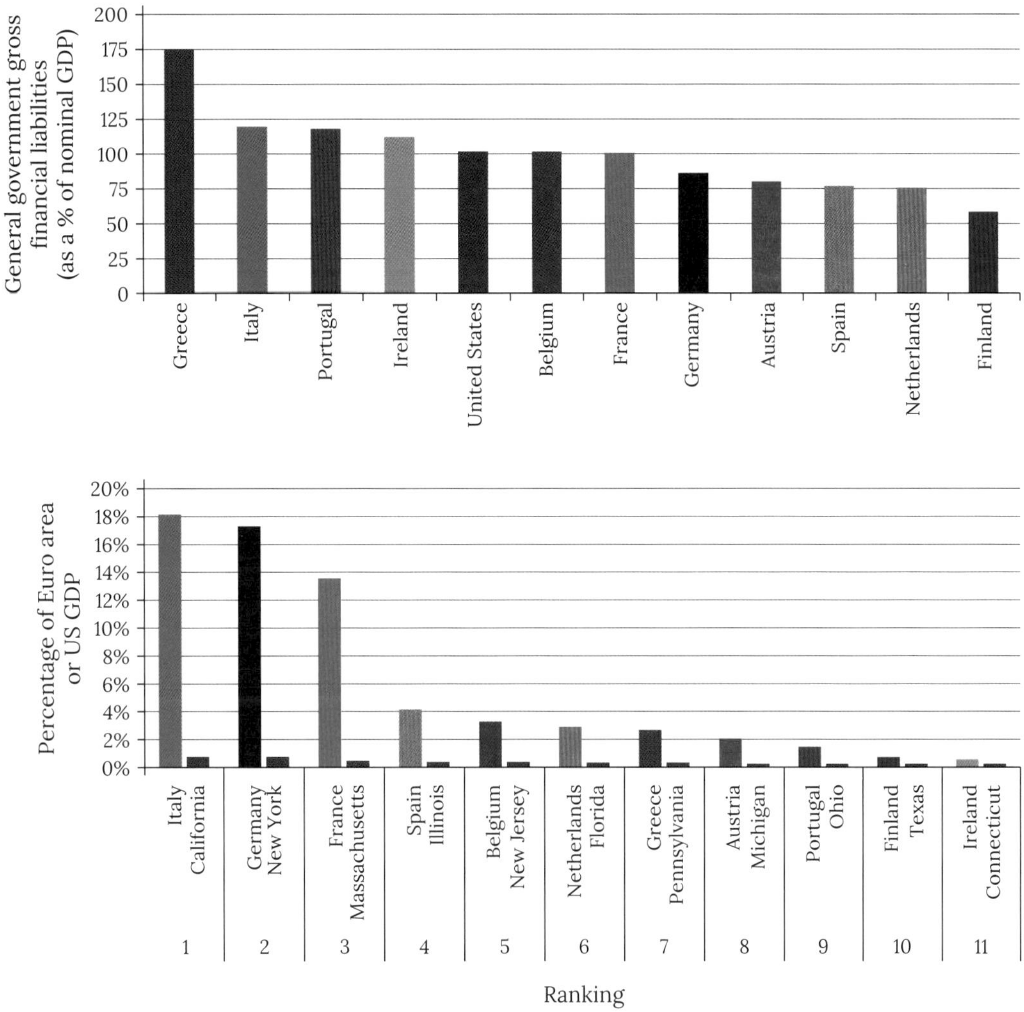

Figure 14.18 Upper panel: gross general government financial liabilities (as a % of nominal GDP) in 2010. Lower panel: Eurozone government debt (as a % of Eurozone GDP) and US state debts (as a % of US GDP) in 2007.

Source: OECD Economic Outlook, December 2011; Eurostat (data accessed March 2012), US Census Bureau, 2007 Census of Governments.

reflects the insurance premia against default implied in holding different bonds. The default risk variable for banks is the average of the measure for the largest banks in the country.

The data for Greece and the US are shown for the period of the financial crisis and running up to the Eurozone crisis. The Italian data for 2014–17 illustrate that although sovereign default risk was lower (see also Figure 14.14), the association between bank and sovereign default risk remains strong, signalling the continued presence of the doom loop phenomenon.

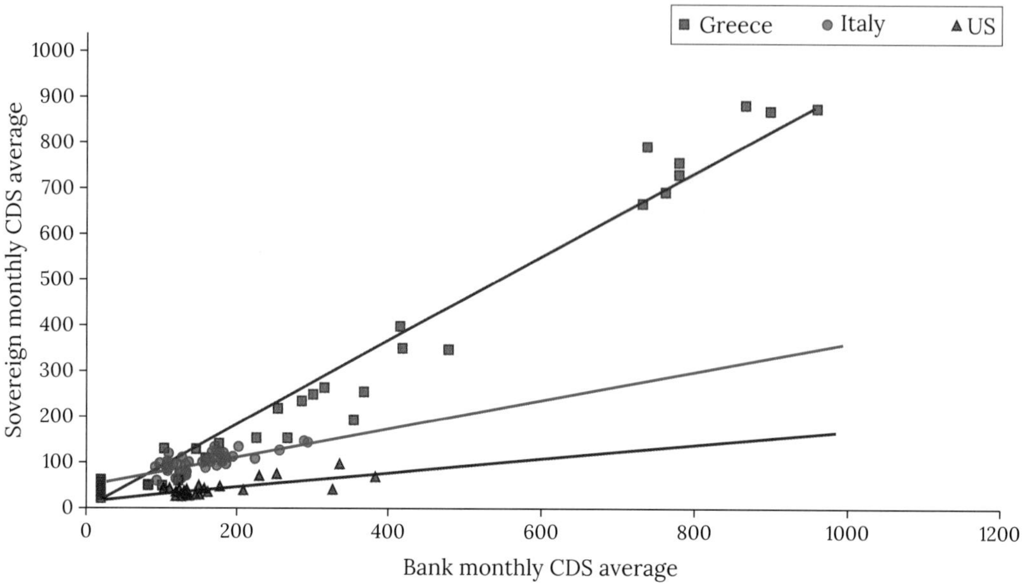

Figure 14.19 Riskiness of banks and of governments.

Source: Datastream. The data extends the chart from Brunnermeier and Reis, 2020.

Notes: Data for Greece and the US is for the period between 2007 and 2010, while the Italian data reflects the period between 2014–17. The data series are obtained from Datastream splicing the 'CMA' and 'Refintiv' series based on availability.

14.5.3 **Governance solutions**

In a speech in July 2012, the President of the ECB, Mario Draghi, stated: 'the only way out of this present crisis is to have more Europe, not less Europe. A Europe that is founded on four building blocks: a fiscal union, a financial (i.e. banking) union, an economic union and a political union.'

This statement can be interpreted by looking at Figures 14.15 and 14.16. A true fiscal union would introduce stabilizing fiscal flows via the operation of automatic stabilizers at Eurozone level as in a national economy or in a federal economy like the US. A banking union would allow orderly resolution of failing banks, including cross-border ones and ones that are large relative to the size of the member country. And an economic and political union would provide the legitimacy for the fiscal and banking unions, including formalizing the ECB as the lender of last resort to governments. The problems arising from the tension between the 'national citizen taxpayer' and the supra-national central bank and common currency of the Maastricht model would be resolved.

Draghi's statement referred to the logic of the situation and was not a forecast of future policy actions. Creating a coherent governance structure for the Eurozone requires addressing the interconnection among banks, governments and the central bank. European policy makers have been trying to tackle these problems since the onset of the sovereign debt crisis in 2010, with varying degrees of success. This subsection sets out some of the governance solutions that have been implemented or are still being negotiated, and relates them to our analytical framework. We also discuss some of the problems with the proposed solutions and the challenges still facing the Eurozone if it wishes to be sustainable in the long run.

Government to government: Fiscal policy reform

The Eurozone governments broke the 'no bail-out' clause that separates member governments in the governance structure of the Eurozone (see Figure 14.16). At the height of the crisis in 2010–11, Greece, Ireland and Portugal were all bailed out and forced into pursuing austerity policies by the creditor nations.[22]

In order to avoid getting into a situation where governments require bail-outs at the expense of Eurozone taxpayers, European policy makers introduced a series of fiscal policy reforms 'making the best use of the flexibility within the existing rules of the Stability and Growth Pact' (2015).[23] The European Stability Mechanism (ESM) would provide loans to troubled member governments but only under strict conditionality, typically entailing austerity measures (to make this approach consistent with the 'no bail-out' clause). The scale of the ESM's resources is small—only about 4% of Eurozone GDP. The combination of small-scale loans (not grants) and conditionality strictly limits cross-border stabilization. Chapter 7 covers the Eurozone crisis and the danger of premature austerity, especially in the presence of hysteresis.

The ECB to government: Establishing a LOLR to member governments

The turning point in the sovereign debt crisis came in the second half of 2012, as shown by the reduction in peripheral bond yields after point 3 in Figure 14.4. Two actions by the ECB prompted the turnaround. First, in the same speech referred to above (July 2012), ECB President Mario Draghi publicly stated that 'within our mandate, the ECB is ready to do whatever it takes to preserve the euro. And believe me, it will be enough'.[24] Second, the ECB announced the Outright Monetary Transactions (OMT) programme, which promised to buy peripheral country bonds on secondary markets until pressure in the bond markets eased off (subject to some conditionality clauses i.e. promises for structural reform).[25]

---

[22] See Lane (2012) for a good summary of the Eurozone sovereign debt crisis.

[23] European Union: European Commission (2015) 'Communication from the Commission to the European Parliament, the Council, the European Central Bank, the Economic and Social Committee, the Committee of the Regions and the European Investment Bank: Making the best use of the flexibility within the existing rules of the Stability And Growth Pact', COM/2015/012 final, Document 52015DC0012. https://eur-lex.europa.eu/legal-content/EN/TXT/?uri=celex:52015DC0012 See also Thygesen, N., Santacroce, S., Orseau, E., Eliofotou, P., Cugnasca, A. .and Beetsma, R. (2018) 'Reforming the EU fiscal framework: A proposal by the European Fiscal Board', VoxEU/VoxEU Column. https://cepr.org/voxeu/columns/reforming-eu-fiscal-framework-proposal-european-fiscal-board

[24] Excerpt taken from a speech by Mario Draghi, President of the European Central Bank, at the Global Investment Conference in London on July 26th 2012.

[25] The details of the OMT programme are available from the ECB website: https://www.ecb.europa.eu/press/pr/date/2012/html/pr120906_1.en.html

In 2012 and 2013, the ECB did not actually use OMT, but bond yields fell substantially regardless. This is because the ECB's actions removed the 'separation' between the central bank and the member governments in the governance structure of the euro (see Figure 14.16). By effectively changing the role of the ECB to be a lender of last resort to member governments, the ECB lowered the default risk for the PIIGS and their borrowing costs fell accordingly.

The conditionality attached to OMT is one possible cause for concern in the future, as it could impede the ECB's role as the lender of last resort to governments. National central banks, by contrast, are unconditional lenders of last resort. The persistent correlation between bank and sovereign risk illustrated for Italy in Figure 14.19 is likely to reflect the incompleteness of the ECB's commitment to the role of lender of last resort to member governments. Consistent with this is the fact that sovereign spreads increased very sharply for the vulnerable Eurozone members at the outset of the pandemic but they fell sharply when the ECB's PEPP bond-buying programme was launched.

Banks to governments: The banking union

The dangerous interconnectedness of banks and sovereigns in the Eurozone—the doom loop—played a significant part in the sovereign debt crisis. One solution to this governance problem is to create a banking union, where member countries are jointly responsible for the solvency of banks located in the Eurozone.

At the end of 2013, the EU Council agreed on a general approach for the Single Resolution Mechanism (SRM). The SRM is the EU's banking union, which will raise resolution funds from national bank levies and use them to resolve failing banks across the EU.[26]

The mutualization of resolution funds will be phased in over a ten-year period, however, which poses a short-term problem for the banking systems in vulnerable peripheral economies. In the short term, responsibility for national banking systems ultimately resides with national governments. If they cannot afford to provide solvency to their banking systems, then they will again have to seek bail-outs from other Eurozone members and endure the harsh conditionality (i.e. austerity and structural reform) that accompanies the loans. The phasing in of the SRM may therefore delay the clean-up of bad banks in the peripheral economies and, as a consequence, their economic recovery. These design problems were evident in the early functioning of the SRM, which was tested by the failure of one Spanish and two Italian banks in 2017.[27]

Some elements of the new resolution mechanism were implemented. For example, in the Spanish case, in line with the principles of the SRM, there was no taxpayer bail-out and the equity owners and bond-holders in the bank were bailed in, which means they lost their assets. But in the case of the Italian banks, although the claims of share- and

---

[26] For a summary of the Council's agreed general approach on the Single Resolution Mechanism, see https://www.consilium.europa.eu/en/policies/banking-union/single-resolution-mechanism/

[27] For a review of these cases, see Beck, T. (2017) 'The European Banking Union at three: A toddler with tantrums', VoxEU/VoxEu, 4 July 2017. https://cepr.org/voxeu/columns/european-banking-union-three-toddler-tantrums

junior bond-holders were wiped out, heavy involvement by the Italian government in taking the risk on bad bank assets contravened the SRM; as did the fact that the senior bond-holders in the banks were not penalized.

Because the underlying problems in the Italian banking system have not been resolved, national involvement in banking failures remains. Equally, a move to a full banking union is hampered by the legacy problems. An important step is to create a Eurozone-wide deposit insurance scheme but for that to happen, the Germans need to be convinced that they will not be bailing out Italian depositors. Italy remains the Achilles heel of the banking union because the conditions for the doom loop—loss-making banks with many bad loans in their portfolio and a government with high public debt—persist.

14.5.4 Progress in governance reform under pressure of the pandemic

We use the framework set out in the preceding sections to analyse the response of the ECB and the European Union to the pandemic. It has produced important changes in governance.[28]

The ECB sought to:

- stabilize financial markets so as to prevent a new sovereign debt crisis from arising,
- support the supply of credit by banks to firms and households, and
- steer inflation back up towards the 2% target.

In support of the first two objectives, the ECB expanded its existing asset purchase programme (QE via the Pandemic Emergency Purchase Programme, PEPP) and used its targeted longer-term refinancing operations (TLTRO) to incentivize banks to lend to the non-financial private sector.

The asset purchase programme targets the yield curve in order to loosen monetary policy and at the same time stabilizes the markets. This helped to reverse the increases in yields especially on the bonds issued by the governments of Spain, Italy, Greece and Portugal that occurred early in the pandemic. As we know from the doom loop model, rising sovereign default risk impairs the balance sheets of banks holding government debt so cutting this feedback process was important for the success of the ECB's policy.

Banks can only get cheap credit from the ECB in the TLTRO programme if the money is actually passed on to households and firms in the form of loans. In contrast to the usual funding that a central bank offers banks, which is very short term, TLTROs offer loans that only have to be paid back after four years. This provides banks with stable and dependable funding. Survey evidence indicates that banks took up the loans and used them to lend at near historically low rates to households and firms. This is an example of the central bank directly targeting the lending rate in a situation in which the policy rate is stuck at the lower bound.

---

[28] This subsection draws on Philip R. Lane's speech 'Monetary policy in a pandemic: ensuring favourable financing conditions', at the Economics Department and IM-TCD, Trinity College Dublin, November 26th 2020.

The ECB emphasizes the importance of its commitment to favourable financing conditions for shoring up the confidence of households, firms, banks, governments and financial markets. If confidence falls, the large multipliers in play in the pandemic (due to the greater prevalence of credit constraints) imply an adverse feedback loop as risk premia rise and spending falls. Avoiding a sovereign debt crisis and triggering the doom loop was a priority.

Against the background of halting fiscal policy reform since the financial crisis, the Covid-19 pandemic catapulted the EU into emergency measures, which have elements of a fiscal union.

Exceptional stimulus measures were implemented by national governments—as the constraints of the Stability and Growth Pact were lifted—and were complemented by unprecedented action at the level of the EU,[29] creating what has been referred to as the 'embryo of a federal fiscal policy' (Pappa 2020, p. 27). When the EU agreed a new budget (for 2021–27), 'July 2020' joined 'July 2012' as a turning point in EU governance. The new budget:

- raised revenue from international financial markets for the first time,
- foresaw future green taxes to service the debt, and
- introduced the Next Generation EU funds (NGEU) to provide grants and loans to member states to support both recovery from the pandemic and investment in the transition to a green digital economy.

In contrast to the ESM, the NGEU arrangements do not entail conditionality. This marks a major change in policy. The largest component of the package is the Recovery and Resilience facility, which was specifically designed to reduce pressure on national budgets, particularly for the countries disproportionately affected by the pandemic so as to enable an appropriately counter-cyclical fiscal stance.

The credibility of these fiscal measures in supporting economic activity (and the complementary monetary policy actions of the ECB) saw a *reduction* in sovereign debt spreads, even in the presence of dramatically increased government deficits and debt.

From the perspective of the Maastricht policy assignment, the pandemic response was unorthodox both on the monetary and fiscal side. In the same speech referenced in footnote 29, ECB board member Isabel Schnabel summarized: 'The policy response to the pandemic is a remarkable showcase for the power of monetary and fiscal policy interaction to boost confidence, stabilize aggregate demand and avoid a persistent destabilization of medium to long-term inflation expectations'. Nevertheless, this is not a permanent commitment to a greater role for fiscal stabilization and coordination of monetary and fiscal policy. The rapid change in the global economic environment during 2022 revealed the fragility of the confidence of financial markets in the level of commitment to European integration as bond yields on debt issued by the different EU programmes discussed above rose above those on French government bonds.[30]

---

[29] See the keynote speech by Isabel Schnabel, 'High Debt, Low Rates and Tail Events: Rules-based Fiscal Frameworks under Stress', Frankfurt am Main, February 26th 2021.

[30] See Bonfanti, G. and Garicano, L. (2022) 'Do financial markets consider European common debt a safe asset?', *Bruegel*. https://www.bruegel.org/blog-post/do-financial-markets-consider-european-common-debt-safe-asset

14.6 CONCLUSIONS

This chapter has focused on the economics of fixed exchange rate regimes, and in particular the Eurozone economy; the largest common currency area of nation states in the world. The introduction of the euro had both microeconomic benefits, such as increased trade and investment, and macroeconomic benefits, such as the provision of a credible low inflation monetary regime. However, relinquishing exchange rate flexibility and monetary policy also created problems for stabilization against country-specific economic shocks and produced increased vulnerability to a sovereign debt crisis.

The thrust of this chapter has been to think about macroeconomic policy under fixed exchange rates, and particularly the Eurozone, in the framework of the 3-equation model. We can use the 3-equation model to answer interesting questions about macroeconomic adjustment under fixed exchange rates:

1. How does a member of a common currency area stabilize against *common* shocks to the currency zone? The central bank of the CCA (the ECB in the case of the Eurozone) will stabilize against common shocks through the use of monetary policy and the associated changes in the nominal exchange rate (against the rest of the world). In other words, adjustment is the same as in a flexible exchange rate economy (discussed in Chapter 11).
2. How does a country with a fixed exchange rate or a CCA member stabilize against *country-specific* shocks? The model can be used to compare policy responses when a member country is hit with a country-specific shock: to do nothing, or to use fiscal policy to stabilize. If it decides to do nothing, there are two channels that operate automatically. The first is the real exchange rate channel, which arises because inflation differentials between members affect their external competitiveness. The second is the real interest rate channel, which arises because inflation differentials between members can affect their real interest rates. The first channel is stabilizing and the second is destabilizing. If the economy is put on a destabilizing path after a shock, the government can use fiscal policy to guide it back to equilibrium. The use of fiscal policy can help to limit deviations from equilibrium output and target inflation, but unlike monetary policy, it can also leave the government in deficit when back at equilibrium.
3. Why do wage-setting institutions matter in the adjustment to shocks? Highlighted in the literature on an optimal currency area and the costs and benefits of a flexible exchange rate, this issue is evident in the Eurozone. Wage-setting institutions, such as the coordinated wage bargaining that takes place in Germany, affect how well the real exchange rate channel works for a member of a CCA. The more flexible are wage and price setting, the better the channel works at stabilizing the economy. Members with these institutions will have to do less active stabilization using fiscal policy, and hence are less likely to build up government and external deficits.

The euro was adopted at the start of 1999. By a number of measures its first ten years were successful; average inflation was kept close to the ECB's 2% target and member states became more economically and financially integrated. Beneath the surface, however, the picture was not quite so rosy. Large imbalances arose in real exchange rates and current accounts between the northern and southern parts of the currency bloc. The peripheral economies became very externally indebted; Greece's government borrowed excessively and Spain and Ireland had wild, credit-fuelled construction and consumption booms.

In a nation state, the external imbalances and indebtedness might not have led to a sovereign debt crisis. However, the unique governance structure that was put in place at the inception of the euro made it vulnerable to a government debt crisis after a large negative demand shock. The global financial crisis provided that shock, and the responsibility of members to stand behind the banks headquartered in their countries combined with the lack of a credible lender of last resort to governments contributed to the sovereign debt crisis.

The Eurozone sovereign debt crisis did huge damage to the economies of its members, but the currency union survived. The ECB's decision to act as lender of last resort to member governments was crucial. But the harsh conditionality imposed on the bail-outs of the crisis countries produced a decade of poor performance. Policy was in its own 'doom loop' summarized at the European summit in 2018 by the agreement to create:

- a Eurozone deposit insurance system and provide more resources for the ESM *but only after successful banking reform* (in particular, through the resolution of the bad loans plaguing the Italian banks);
- greater Eurozone fiscal capacity *but only after the high government debt levels in some members were brought down.*

Ironically, as we have shown, the catastrophe of the pandemic broke this loop and brought forward some of the steps toward the fiscal union component of Draghi's four building blocks (banking union, fiscal union, economic union, political union). Yet underlying governance problems remain and were revealed in the Ukraine-war induced energy price shock.

QUESTIONS AND PROBLEMS FOR CHAPTER 14

CHECKLIST QUESTIONS

1. What are the microeconomic benefits of a currency union?
2. Germany had a credible central bank before the introduction of the euro. What was their macroeconomic incentive to join the currency union? Was this incentive shared by the countries in Southern Europe?

3. Explain the factors that contributed to the difference in inflation rates between Germany and Spain between 1999 and 2008. What effect did this differential have on the external competitiveness of these two economies?

4. What are the two pillars of the ECB's monetary policy? Discuss the pros and cons of the ECB's strategy.

5. Use your knowledge of common currency areas (CCAs) to assess whether the following statements (S1 and S2) are both true or whether only one of them is true. Justify your answer:

   S1. If country A in a CCA undertakes an expansionary fiscal policy then they can reduce the unemployment rate.

   S2. The rate of unemployment in country A will be reduced even more should the other countries in the union also undertake expansionary fiscal policy.

6. Consider a country with a fixed exchange rate. Explain the difference between the real exchange rate channel and the real interest rate channel. Which of these channels has to dominate for the economy to revert to equilibrium after a shock without any active policy response?

7. What is the Walters critique and why was it used as an argument for the UK not joining the single currency?

8. Use the 3-equation model to show how fiscal policy can be used to stabilize the economy after a positive demand shock in a country that is a member of a CCA. What effect does this have on the budget balance?

9. Use an AD-ERU diagram with a vertical ERU curve to show the new medium-run equilibrium of a flexible exchange rate economy and a member of a CCA following a negative demand shock. Assume that the CCA member uses fiscal policy as a stabilization tool. What are the differences in y, q and G between the two economies in the new medium-run equilibrium?

10. How could the 2-bloc model from Chapter 13 be used to shed light on the economic divergence between the Northern and Southern European countries during the first ten years of the single currency? Explain in words.

11. Describe why the following factors made the Eurozone vulnerable to a sovereign debt crisis:

    a. Member countries issued debt in a currency they did not control.

    b. National governments were responsible for the solvency of their banks.

PROBLEMS

1. 'The ECB's success in achieving low and stable inflation during the Eurozone's first decade disguised the build-up of dangerous imbalances among the members.'

   Provide an explanation and assessment of the claims in this statement. Use the models presented in Chapters 11–14 to

   a. Discuss reasons why countries that wish to achieve low inflation may join a common currency area. Discuss how the ECB achieved its inflation objective.
   b. Explain what could be meant by 'dangerous imbalances' among the members.
   c. Use the *AD-BT-ERU* model to explain how imbalances could occur consistent with the ECB achieving its inflation target. Relate this to the performance of specific countries.

2. When joining a common currency area a country relinquishes the use of monetary policy.

   a. Explain how fiscal policy can be used as a substitute when undertaking stabilization policy. Use the 3-equation model to provide an example.
   b. Are there any drawbacks to stabilizing using fiscal policy?
   c. What advantages have euro area economies gained by having an independent monetary authority? Give an example of a country where this has been particularly important.

3. Take either the Covid-19 pandemic or the Ukraine war as an exogenous shock to the Eurozone. Use the modelling in this chapter along with policy makers' commentary and relevant data to characterize the nature of the shock and to evaluate the policy responses at supra-national and national levels.

4. This question uses the Macroeconomic Simulator (available at www.oup.com/he/carlin-soskice). to show the destabilizing real interest rate channel. Begin by opening the simulator and selecting the open economy (fixed exchange rates without endogenous fiscal policy) version. Then reset all shocks by pressing the appropriate button on the left-hand side of the main page. Use the simulator and the content of this chapter to work through the following:

   a. Apply a 2% inflation shock.
   b. Use the impulse response functions to describe the path of the economy after the shock.
   c. Is the economy self-stabilizing in this scenario?
   d. Use the model to explain how the real interest rate channel can lead to this outcome.

5. This question uses the Macroeconomic Simulator (available at www.oup.com/he/carlin-soskice) to compare the effects of a negative demand shock in two economies; one with a fixed exchange rate regime and one with a flexible exchange rate regime. Begin by opening the simulator and selecting the open economy (flexible exchange rate) version. Then reset all shocks by pressing the appropriate button on the left-hand side of the main page. Use the simulator and the content of Chapters 11–14 to work through the following:

a. Apply a permanent 2% negative demand shock (i.e. –2%). Save your data.

b. Switch to the open economy (fixed exchange rates without endogenous fiscal policy) version of the simulator by pressing the relevant button on the left of the main page. Set the degree of inflation inertia to 0.2. Apply a permanent 2% negative demand shock (i.e. –2%). Save your data.

c. How long does it take for the economy to return to medium-run equilibrium in each case? Why is the speed of adjustment different?

d. Can fiscal policy be used in the fixed exchange rate (i.e. CCA) case to speed up the adjustment? Are there any disadvantages of doing this? Suggest a real-world setting in which you could apply this analysis. [Hint: what happens to the adjustment of the economy in the simulator if public expenditure is permanently increased by 1.5%?]

INTERESTED IN EXPLORING THESE TOPICS FURTHER?

Visit www.oup.com/he/carlin-soskice to consolidate and extend your learning with the multiple-choice questions and Animated Analytical Diagrams accompanying this chapter.

PART

5

THE SUPPLY SIDE, TECHNOLOGY, AND GROWTH

CHAPTER

15

SUPPLY-SIDE INSTITUTIONS, POLICIES, AND PERFORMANCE

15.1 INTRODUCTION

Understanding the causes of the unemployment patterns shown at the start of Chapter 2 in Figure 2.1 (reproduced here in Figure 15.1) for the rich countries of the world is a challenge for economists and policy makers. The economist Richard Layard emphasizes the research results on the consequences of unemployment for human wellbeing[1]:

> From the new science of happiness we now know enough of the causes of human happiness to make some quite firm statements. When a person becomes unemployed his welfare falls for two reasons–first the loss of income, and second the loss of self-respect and sense of significance (the psychic loss).
>
> Layard, 2004

The data in Figure 15.1 provide a graphic illustration of the dispersion of unemployment rates across the OECD countries in the last fifty years by showing the five-yearly average unemployment rates for selected countries. The OECD's standardized measure of unemployment based on labour force surveys is used, which allows cross-country comparisons to be made. Although not all countries are shown in the chart, the patterns are as follows:

- Unemployment was low virtually everywhere in the 1960s.
- There is a cloud of countries with unemployment rates below the US up to the early 1980s, which moves above the US thereafter until the global financial crisis in 2008.
- Several European countries had spectacular improvements in their unemployment performance in the 1990s: the UK, Ireland, the Netherlands and Denmark are said to have experienced 'employment miracles' over this decade.

---

[1] This excerpt is taken from p. 1 of Layard (2004).

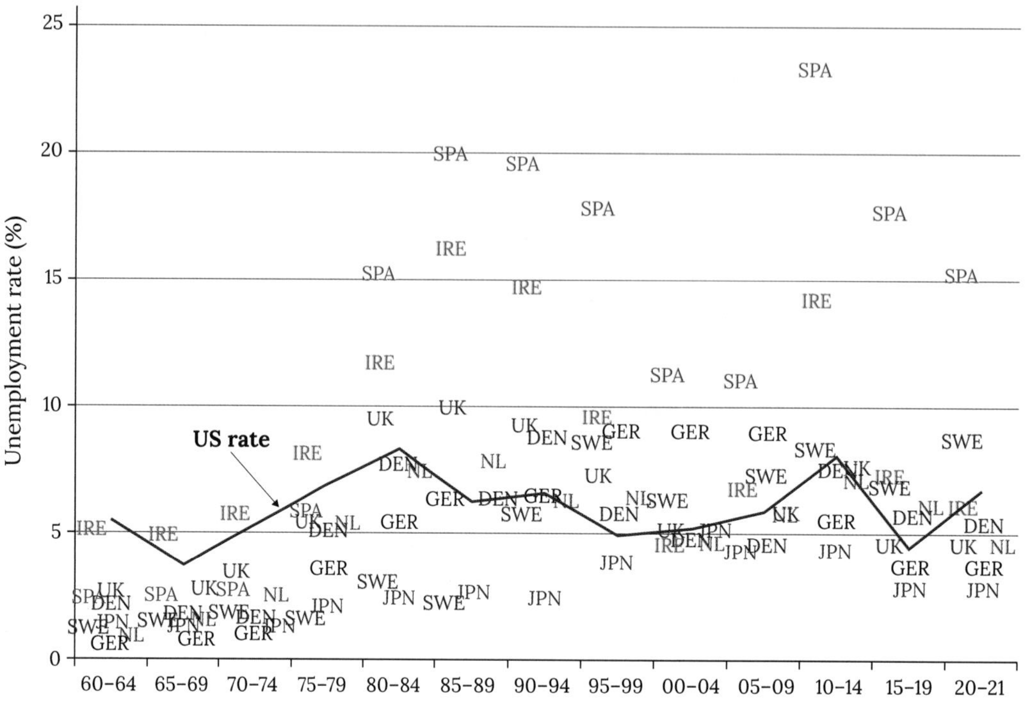

Figure 15.1 Trends and heterogeneity in unemployment for selected OECD economies, 1960–2021.

Source: Howell et al. (2007), Figure 1.1, used until 1995. Updated to 2021 using OECD harmonized unemployment rates (data accessed June 2022).

- Austria, Norway and Japan have very low rates throughout. Sweden and Finland had very low unemployment until the early 1990s.
- Spanish unemployment has been the highest in the sample in every period since the start of the 1980s. It has also fluctuated substantially, for example, it fell from over 20% in the late 1990s to under 10% by 2005–08.
- The heterogeneity in the unemployment experience of European countries, where some highly unionized countries with high taxation have *low* unemployment, and where in some others there were major changes in labour market policy, has been used to test theories linking unemployment to policy and institutions.
- Eurozone countries Spain and Ireland were badly affected by the Eurozone crisis (Chapters 9 and 14) and saw their employment miracles rapidly unravel during the Great Recession. Germany stands out as a country where the labour market performed relatively well during the financial crisis, with the unemployment rate falling to levels not seen since before German unification in the early 1990s.
- The Covid-19 pandemic affected the demand for labour in similar ways across countries but the outcomes for unemployment were different. Many European countries protected the employment relationship by introducing furlough schemes while other countries like the US provided enhanced and extended unemployment benefits.

The variation in experience of unemployment from the 1970s onwards—and again, following the financial crisis—produced major research efforts to uncover the underlying causes of the trends and cross-country patterns. The research has highlighted differences in institutions for wage setting, changes in the efficiency of the labour market in matching job seekers and vacancies, and evidence on the prevalence of monopsony power and hysteresis.

In Chapter 2, we introduced the basic supply-side model of the economy and showed that supply-side equilibrium is defined by the intersection of the wage- and price-setting (WS and PS) curves. In this framework, there is a unique rate of unemployment at which inflation is constant. At equilibrium, there is involuntary unemployment. Factors shifting the equilibrium rate of unemployment can be divided into wage-push factors that shift the WS curve and price-push factors that shift the PS curve.

Equilibrium unemployment rises with a downward shift of the price-setting or an upward shift of the wage-setting curve. From Chapter 2, we write the equation for the price-setting curve:

$$\frac{W}{P_c} = \lambda F(\mu, \mathbf{z_p}), \qquad \text{(PS curve)}$$

where P_c is the consumer price index and $\mathbf{z_p}$ is a set of price push variables including the tax and oil price wedges. The PS curve shifts down when there is a rise in the mark-up, μ, due, for example, to a weakening in the enforcement of competition policy, a fall in productivity, λ, or a rise in the tax or oil price wedge.

We write the WS equation:

$$\frac{W}{P_c^E} = B(N, \mathbf{z_w}) \qquad \text{(WS curve)}$$

where $\mathbf{z_w}$ is a set of wage push variables. The $\mathbf{z_w}$'s include institutional, policy, structural and shock variables. The WS curve shifts up when there is a rise in the reservation wage due, for example, to higher or longer duration unemployment benefits or if it becomes more difficult to monitor effort or to fire workers who shirk. Stronger unions may shift the WS curve up; as does the withdrawal of bargaining restraint in the context, for example, of the collapse of a wage accord between unions and government.

The chapter begins in Section 15.2 by extending the wage-setting model in Chapter 2 to deal with a second problem faced by the employer when workers differ in the net utility of unemployment. In this case, in addition to motivating the worker to supply effort, the employer has to recruit workers to the firm. In this model, employers have labour market power, called monopsony. There is growing evidence of its prevalence across the economy. A source of monopsony power is that job seekers find it costly to search for work outside their locality, which implies there are few available employers when they seek a vacancy. Because job seekers place different values on the net utility of unemployment, there is an upward sloping reservation wage curve facing the employer. Increasing the size of the firm means paying a higher wage to all workers.

After explaining the recruitment problem we combine the recruitment and the motivation problems to derive the *firm's* wage-setting curve. By varying the unemployment rate we then derive the *economy's* WS curve. We also use the model of wage-setting to analyse the effects a minimum wage has on a firm's employment decision.

Section 15.3 uses the 'flow' or 'search and matching' approach to the labour market in a different way from the focus on wage setting in the monopsony model in the previous section. Attention is on how well the labour market achieves the matching of unemployed workers with unfilled job vacancies rather than on how the wage is set. From this we develop a model of the Beveridge curve, which shows the relationship between the unemployment rate and the vacancy rate in the economy. We then show how the insights of the flow approach for the efficiency with which job seekers and vacancies are matched can be integrated with the WS-PS framework. Both business cycle fluctuations and structural changes in the labour market as occurred, for example, as a consequence of the pandemic, can be represented in the combined Beveridge curve and WS-PS model.

Section 15.4 enriches the supply-side model further by introducing the variety of ways labour unions are organized, which have different predictions for the WS curve, and hence for equilibrium unemployment. Some features of the variation in unemployment across countries and over time in Figure 15.1 can be interpreted through the lens of the models presented in this section.

Section 15.5 develops the analysis of the interaction between aggregate demand shocks and the supply side—'hysteresis'—introduced in Chapter 4. Three models provide some micro-foundations for the phenomenon. Two of these relate to labour market scarring, which influenced the design of responses to the pandemic.

15.2 A MICRO-FOUNDED *WS* CURVE: COMBINING SEARCH AND MATCHING AND LABOUR DISCIPLINE

In the model of the labour market set out in Chapter 2, the key characteristic is the fact that effort is unobservable. This creates the incentive for the employer to set a wage above the reservation wage so the worker expects to experience a cost if they were to lose their job and hence chooses not to shirk. Involuntary unemployment in equilibrium is the outcome.

We now broaden our modelling to include heterogeneity among workers and jobs.[2] When job seekers value jobs differently, they will have to search for jobs and both unemployed workers and vacancies will always be observed in the economy.

In this section, we explain the flows that occur in the labour market and set out a model of the firm in which the employer faces twin problems of recruitment and motivation. We introduce the new problem of how to set the wage when recruiting workers who differ in the value to them of unemployment. In the WS curve to this point, we have only incorporated the problem of how the employer motivates workers

[2] This model was developed for CORE Econ's *The Economy* 2.0. The main authors are Margaret Stevens, Samuel Bowles, and Wendy Carlin, with contributions from Suresh Naidu, Arin Dube, and the CORE Econ team. A more extensive presentation can be found in *The Economy* 2.0, *Microeconomics*, Unit 6.

to provide the required level of effort. In that model, all workers are identical—and so are jobs. This implies that although the employer has the power to get the worker to exert effort (because of the threat of job loss if caught shirking), they have no labour market power. The labour market is competitive because there are many employers offering jobs; the reason the labour market does not clear is because the contract is incomplete.

In the combined recruitment and motivation model, the recruitment problem produces an upward sloping reservation wage curve in contrast to the horizontal one in Chapter 2. Having recruited a worker, a wage above the reservation wage must be paid to solve the motivation problem. This is the firm's no-shirking wage curve. To derive the WS curve for the economy as a whole, we look at how the wage changes as the unemployment rate changes.

The benefits of introducing the monopsony component are to provide in a single model,

- A more complete and realistic description of how wages are set when there are flows into and out of the different labour market states.
- A treatment of monopsony power in the labour market, in which the employer marks down the wage below the contribution of the marginal worker to the firm's revenue. This markdown of the wage is somewhat offset by the employment rent the firm has to pay to incentivize the worker to exert adequate effort.
- A way of modelling the effect of changes in the minimum wage on the firm's wage and employment decision.

15.2.1 **Labour market flows**

Figure 15.2 shows the flows that occur in the labour market. Workers search for jobs and firms for workers. Matches between them are created and then destroyed. Employers post vacancies and fill them from 'job to job' moves, from the pool of unemployed and from those who are out of the labour market.

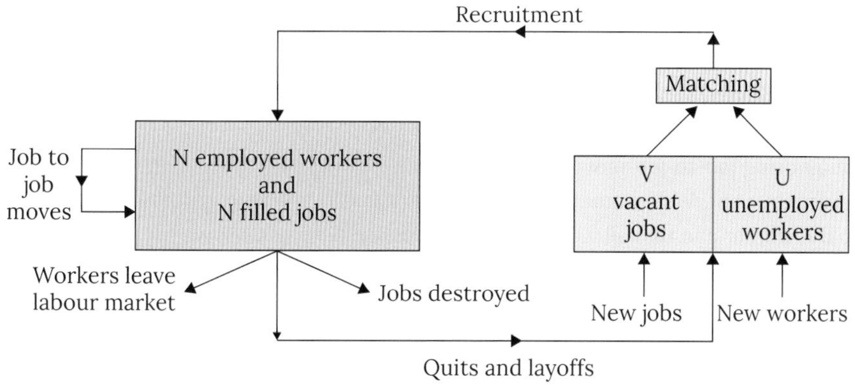

Figure 15.2 Search, flows and matches in the labour market.

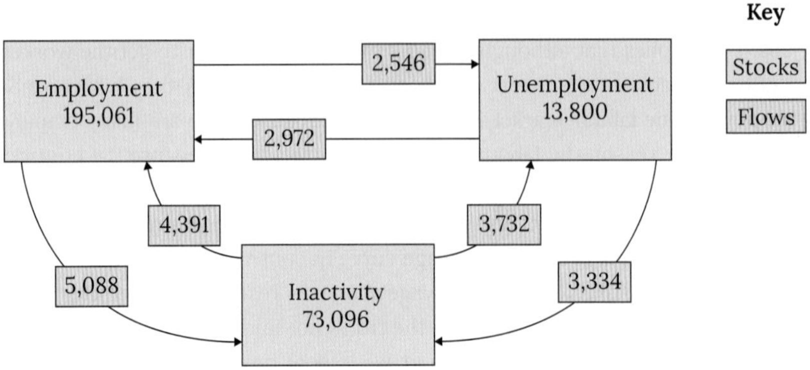

Figure 15.3 Labour market flows between employment, unemployment and inactivity (in thousands) in the European Union: 2022 Q1.

Source: Labour Force Survey, Eurostat, data accessed September 2022.

If an unemployed worker applies and gets the job, this is a 'match' (a move along the recruitment arrow). The worker moves into a job on the left-hand side of Figure 15.2 and both the number of vacancies and of unemployed workers falls. If, later, the worker finds a better job, they move 'job to job' and the number of filled jobs remains unchanged.

The continuous flux of the labour market is reflected in the data in Figure 15.3 showing the flows in the European Union in the first quarter of 2022. Roughly 74% of the working age population were active in the labour market at the end of 2021. Most had jobs but around 6.6% were unemployed and actively searching (the right-hand side of Figure 15.2). Looking 3 months later, millions of workers had changed their labour market status (e.g. over two and a half million workers had transitioned from employment to unemployment, and over five million joined the inactive pool; at the same time, almost three million had taken jobs from unemployment and over four million from inactivity). Note that the flows in Figure 15.3 do not capture job to job moves.

15.2.2 **The firm's recruitment problem and wage-setting**

As illustrated in Figures 15.2 and 15.3, the labour market is always in motion.[3] In this model, the employer seeks to hire workers from the pool of job seekers. We simplify by ignoring job to job moves and just consider flows of workers between jobs and unemployment. We assume that the employer makes a 'take it or leave it' wage offer to the worker and that all workers in the firm are paid the same wage.

[3] A famous early book on modelling the labour market in this way is Alan Manning's *Monopsony in Motion: Imperfect Competition in Labor Markets* published in 2003.

For a worker considering taking a job with this firm, we assume that she has a planning horizon of h, which you can think of as weeks or months. To be concrete, we will use 'weeks'. Her decision about accepting the offer depends on her next best alternative, which is her reservation wage, comprising:

- Her income while unemployed, which will be the unemployment benefit plus any family support or other sources of income. We will assume this income is unemployment benefit, b per week.
- Her additional weekly net utility while unemployed. This can be positive or negative—she may have savings and use the time without a job to acquire further skills but on the other hand, it might be demoralizing and erode her ability to compete for jobs. Being unemployed may make it easier to manage care responsibilities and it cuts out commuting time and costs. It is immediately obvious that the net utility of remaining unemployed rather than accepting the job offer will vary across individuals according to their personal circumstances and their tastes. The individual-specific net utility of unemployment is called α^M with M denoting this particular individual. In the simpler model in Chapter 2, α is the same for all job seekers.
- The average net utility in jobs that are available in the labour market as the job seeker compares the current job offer with other opportunities. This is the wage minus the cost of effort required in the job, and is v per week.
- How long she would expect to stay unemployed looking for a better job opportunity. We call this j weeks.The job seeker is making a forward-looking decision over a 'planning horizon' of h weeks.

As shown in Figure 15.4, this means that there is an upward sloping 'hiring' line showing that the number of hires the employer could make each week increases as the wage offered is at or above the reservation wage of those who see the vacancy and are interested in the job. Each week there will also be quits and a simple assumption is that quits are proportional to the size of the firm.

Where the quits line intersects the hiring line shows the wage that is consistent with maintaining the firm at a particular level of employment. This tells us that if the firm wants to expand its employment, it must pay a higher wage to attract the applicants who have a higher reservation wage. An important implication is that when increasing the size of the firm, the employer has to pay a higher wage to all its workers. The combinations of the wage and the *size of the firm*, N, in the upper panel map into points A and C in the lower panel to produce the upward sloping reservation wage curve.

We can derive an equation for the worker's reservation wage as follows. Over the planning horizon, h, the job seeker:

- gets weekly unemployment benefit, b
- receives the idiosyncratic (i.e. individual-specific) utility, α^M, for the weeks they are unemployed

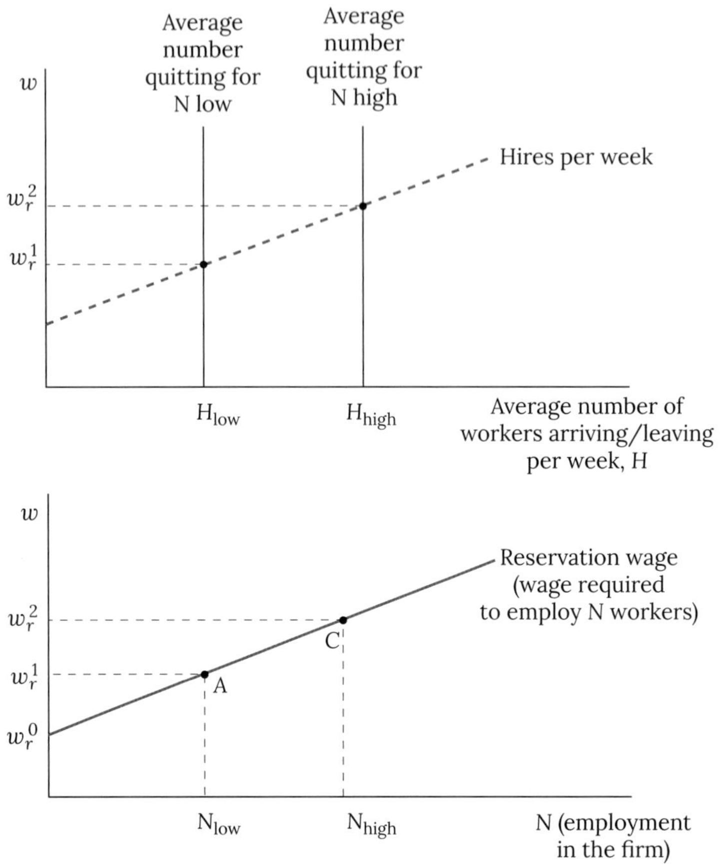

Figure 15.4 Deriving the reservation wage curve from weekly quits and hires for firms of different sizes.

- compares the job offer with the expected utility from other jobs of v per week, which is the wage minus the cost of effort, and
- expects to remain j weeks in unemployment before finding another job.

This implies that they expect to receive $(b+\alpha^M)$ for j weeks and v for the remaining $(h-j)$ weeks. The reservation wage is therefore:

$$\begin{aligned} w_r &= \frac{\text{total value of reservation option}}{h} \\ &= \frac{j(b+\alpha^M)+(h-j)v}{h} \\ &= \tau(b+\alpha^M)+(1-\tau)v, \qquad \text{(reservation wage)} \end{aligned}$$

$$\text{where } \tau = \frac{j}{h} \text{ and } j < h.$$

The 'total value of reservation option' is the expected present value of future income, shown explicitly in the equation. The final expression for the reservation wage is a weighted average of what the job seeker gets now ($b+\alpha^M$) plus what they expect to get when they find a job (the wage net of effort, v). The weights are the expected weeks in each state as a proportion of the planning horizon, i.e. in unemployment, $\tau = j/h$, and in employment, $(1-\tau)$.

Note that so far, the employer knows the reservation wage, which is the lowest wage that has to be offered to get a worker to apply for a job and turn up. This wage is referred to as satisfying the worker's participation constraint. We turn to the next problem the employer faces which is how to get the worker to exert the required effort to make production profitable. This is the labour discipline problem and introduces the incentive compatibility constraint.

15.2.3 **The firm's motivation problem: Labour discipline**

The problem the employer faces—as we saw in Chapter 2—is that effort, which is costly to the worker, is not observable by the employer. The employer cannot write a complete contract with the employee that specifies the effort required and would stand up to the scrutiny of a court. This means setting a wage sufficiently high that the employee chooses not to shirk. The employer will have to pay more than the reservation wage with the result that the employee receives an employment rent, which they would lose were they to shirk and be caught and fired.

The employer and the job seeker interact in a forward-looking game as 'principal' and 'agent'. At the crux of this principal-agent problem is a difference of interest between them. The employer wants the required effort at minimum cost and the worker wants to maximize the wage if they are to exert effort. The employer chooses a wage (above the reservation wage) given the knowledge of how workers will respond to the wage, i.e. whether they will work or shirk. The employee takes account of the wage and the likelihood that were she to shirk, she would be caught and fired. For simplicity, we assume that a worker caught shirking is fired.

The employer's payoff is the profit from production if the employee works hard. The worker's payoff if she exerts the required effort is the utility she receives from the wage (after subtracting the cost of effort).

The employer decides on the wage to set by thinking through the employee's decision—will she take or leave the job offer? As in Chapter 2, the worker chooses between exerting the effort required by the employer or not doing so:

- If she exerts effort this week, she will stay in her job and her utility is the wage minus the cost of effort, $w - c$.
- If she shirks, then she gets utility of w since she doesn't incur the cost of effort but she may be caught and fired.

So, she thinks ahead over her planning horizon of h weeks:

- If she shirks, she will get w for s weeks and if caught and fired, will be unemployed for $h - s$ weeks with income of w_r.

Hence, the employer must set a wage so that the employee's payoff from not shirking is at least as high as the payoff from shirking. This is the 'no-shirking wage'.

$$\underbrace{h(w-c)}_{\text{payoff from not shirking}} \geq \underbrace{sw}_{\text{payoff from shirking}} + \underbrace{(h-s)w_r}_{\text{payoff after being fired}} \tag{15.1}$$

or, equivalently

$$\underbrace{h(w-c-w_r)}_{\text{net payoff from not shirking}} \geq \underbrace{s(w-w_r)}_{\text{net payoff during weeks shirking}} \qquad \text{(no-shirking condition (NSC))}$$

The wage that satisfies the no-shirking condition is called the no-shirking wage and this is the wage the employer will offer and that will be accepted. This is referred to as the worker's incentive compatibility constraint. The second way of expressing the NSC highlights that the wage must be high enough above the reservation wage to deter shirking.

Solving the no-shirking condition equation for the wage, w, gives

$$w = w_r + c + \underbrace{\left(\frac{s}{h-s}\right)c}_{\text{rent to deter shirking}} \qquad \text{(no-shirking wage)}$$

$$= w_r + c + \text{rent}(s,c)$$

The rent to deter shirking is increasing in the cost of effort, c, and also in s because poorer monitoring and therefore a longer expected time before being detected increases the wage the employer has to pay; it can be written as $\text{rent}(s,c)$. It is also decreasing in h because the longer is the job seeker's planning horizon, the lower is the incentive to shirk.

15.2.4 **The wage-setting model combining recruitment and motivation problems**

It is straightforward to move from the reservation wage of a particular job seeker, labelled 'M', to the reservation wage curve for the employer seeking to recruit N workers. The idiosyncratic net utility of the Nth worker is α^{N} and the reservation wage curve is:

$$w_r = \tau(b+\alpha^{\text{N}}) + (1-\tau)v. \qquad \text{(reservation wage)}$$

Each employee has a no-shirking wage that is above their reservation wage by the same amount, i.e. by the cost of effort, c, plus the employment rent, $\text{rent}(s,c)$, so the no-shirking wage curve is drawn above the reservation wage curve.

The equation for the no-shirking wage curve is:

$$w = \underbrace{\tau(b+\alpha^{\text{N}}) + (1-\tau)v}_{\text{reservation wage of N}^{\text{th}}\text{ worker}} + c + \underbrace{\left(\frac{s}{h-s}\right)c.}_{\text{rent to deter shirking}} \qquad \text{(no-shirking wage curve)}$$

Figure 15.5 shows the reservation wage and the no-shirking wage curve faced by the firm. For a firm of size N_1, the firm must pay w_2 to both attract and motivate the workers. At this wage, there are other workers who would apply for an advertised job shown by the horizontal distance to the reservation wage curve. But the no-shirking wage for these applicants is above w_2, which means they would shirk on the job. This explains why the firm will carefully screen and interview applicants. The horizontal double-headed arrow indicates the involuntarily unemployed—they would accept a

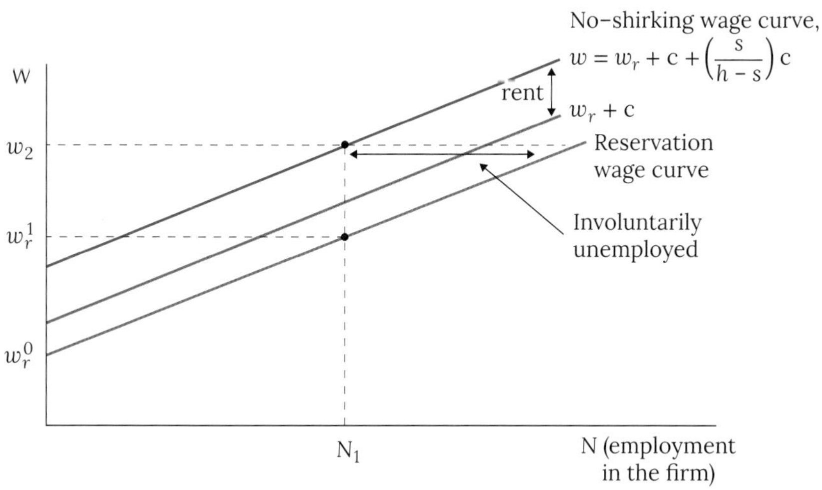

Figure 15.5 The combined search and matching and labour discipline model showing the reservation wage curve, the no-shirking wage curve, the employment rent, and involuntary unemployment.

job at this wage but, having screened them, the employer would not offer the job. This assumption means the employer only hires non-shirking workers.

To summarize, the model tells us that as the size of the firm increases, the firm pays a higher wage because the marginal worker hired has a higher reservation wage than the last one hired. This stems from the idiosyncratic component of the reservation wage, which reflects the variation in net utility of unemployment across job seekers. At each employment level, the employer pays a wage higher than the reservation wage to cover the cost of effort and to provide a rent to the employee that will deter shirking.

The no-shirking wage curve shifts down if the capacity to monitor effort rises (lower s), if morale improves in the firm, reducing the cost of effort (lower c) and if competitors reduce their demand for labour (lower v).

15.2.5 **Deriving the economy-wide *WS* curve from the recruitment and motivation model**

In the analysis of the firm's decision, we have held constant the unemployment rate in the economy. When deriving the reservation wage for the job seeker's planning horizon of h weeks, we found that it depended on j the expected number of weeks before getting a job offer. From the perspective of the economy as a whole, j increases with the unemployment rate, u. This interpretation of j allows us to connect wage-setting by the employer to the economy-wide wage-setting curve.

To derive the economy's wage-setting curve, WS, from the firm's no-shirking wage curve, we assume that all firms are identical and that each sets the same wage (at any employment level). The rent to deter shirking is the same in all firms. Since they are all identical, $v = w - c$, which means that:

$$w = w_r + c + \left(\frac{s}{h-s}\right)c$$

Using the reservation wage equation to substitute for w_r and doing some rearrangements[4] we obtain:

$$\begin{aligned} w &= b + \alpha^N + c + \frac{1}{\tau}\left(\frac{s}{h-s}\right)c \\ &= b + \alpha^N + c + \frac{1}{\tau(u)} \underbrace{\left(\frac{s}{h-s}\right)c}_{\text{employment rent}} \end{aligned} \quad \text{(wage-setting equation, identical firms)}$$

where u is the unemployment rate.

In the last line, we have expressed τ as a function of the unemployment rate in the economy, u, because when the unemployment rate falls, the expected weeks in unemployment as a fraction of the planning horizon falls. This gives us a negative relationship between the wage and the unemployment rate in the economy, or equivalently, a positive relationship between the wage and employment. Hence, the WS curve slopes up. Moreover, as $j \to 0$, $w \to \infty$, which tells us that as the pool of unemployed job seekers is drained, it is not possible to set a wage high enough to deter shirking because the employment rent is zero. A new job just as good as the old one can be found instantly. The WS curve is convex.

There are two processes increasing the wage along the WS curve in the economy as employment increases:

1. Every firm pays more because (holding the economy-wide unemployment rate constant) the marginal worker has a higher reservation wage than the previous one hired because α^N rises with the firm's employment. This is shown by a movement along a no-shirking wage curve for the firm (e.g. along the solid wage curve in the upper panel of Figure 15.6).
2. For every firm, when the economy wide unemployment rate is lower, the cost of job loss falls and this raises the no-shirking wage of all workers and shifts the firm-level wage function up. This is shown in Figure 15.6 by the dashed wage curves (the one

---

[4] Below is the full derivation of the wage-setting equation for identical firms:

$$\begin{aligned} w &= w_r + c + \left(\frac{s}{h-s}\right)c \\ &= \tau(b + \alpha^N) + (1-\tau)v + c + \left(\frac{s}{h-s}\right)c \text{ and, using } v = w - c, \\ &= \tau(b + \alpha^N) + (1-\tau)(w - c) + c + \left(\frac{s}{h-s}\right)c \\ &= \tau(b + \alpha^N + c) + w - \tau w - c + c + \left(\frac{s}{h-s}\right)c \\ &\rightarrow \tau w = \tau(b + \alpha^N + c) + \left(\frac{s}{h-s}\right)c \\ &\text{Hence,} \quad w = b + \alpha^N + c + \frac{1}{\tau}\left(\frac{s}{h-s}\right)c. \end{aligned}$$

Dividing through by τ we obtain the final wage-setting equation in the text.

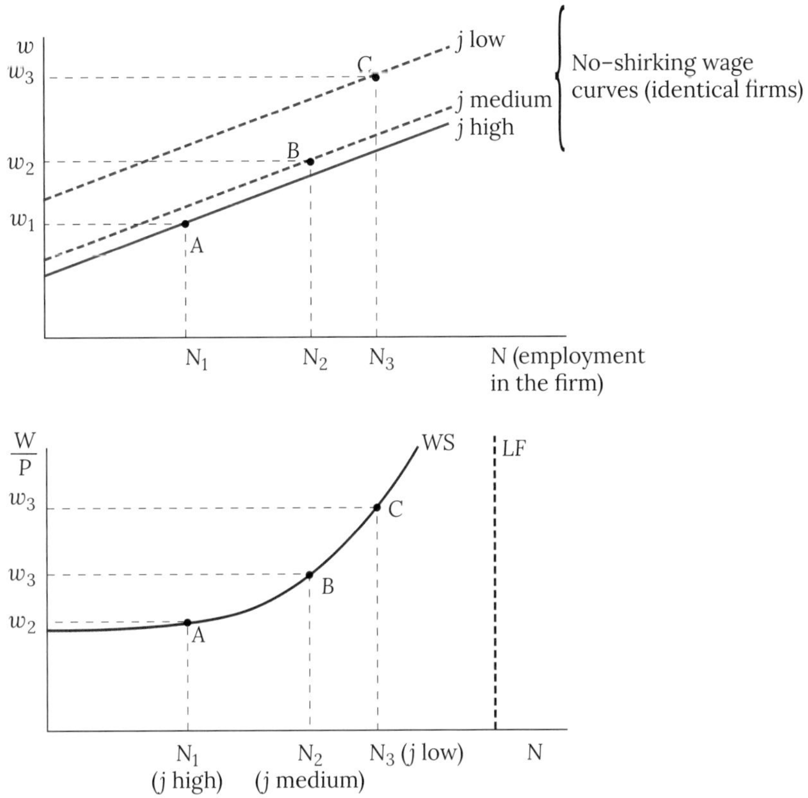

Figure 15.6 Deriving the WS curve from firm level wage setting.

through B, for example, is shifted by the fall in the unemployment rate from high to medium).

As unemployment falls toward zero (shown by the vertical labour force line), the WS curve steepens (lower panel of Figure 15.6).

From the combined search and matching and labour discipline model, the following results arise for the economy's WS curve:

- As the unemployment rate falls, the wage rises along the WS curve; the WS curve is convex.
- A rise in the unemployment benefit, b, and other determinants of the net utility of unemployment, α, shift the WS curve up.
- A higher cost of effort, c, shifts the WS curve up, as does a change in technology that makes the detection of shirking more difficult, higher s.
- If, for example, unions reduce the cost of effort (c) or reduce the net utility of unemployment (α) by making working life more pleasant, then this shifts the WS down; if they make it harder for employers to fire workers (increasing $\frac{s}{(h-s)}$), then this pushes the WS up.

15.2.6 **Labour market power, monopsony, and the minimum wage**

To determine the wage and level of employment in the aggregate economy, we use the economy-wide WS-PS model. However, in this section we narrow the focus to a single firm and use the model of wage-setting to explain how a single employer, who has labour market power, sets the firm's wage and employment to maximize profits.

An employer facing an upward sloping average cost of labour curve (the no-shirking wage curve from Figure 15.5) has labour market power. Remember that the curve is upward sloping because the reservation wage of job seekers varies: attracting an additional worker requires offering a higher wage, which has to be paid to all workers. This is referred to as monopsony[5] power.

To understand what this type of power amounts to it is useful to draw the analogy with the product market, where a firm has *monopoly* power when facing a downward sloping demand (average revenue) curve. In the product market, a firm with market power faces customers who have few easily substitutable goods available to them. The elasticity of the firm's demand curve is therefore low and it maximizes profits by restricting quantity and raising the price. The parallel in the labour market is that job seekers have few easily substitutable job openings (e.g. in their local labour market) and the employer with market power maximizes profits by restricting employment and lowering the wage. The more inelastic is the firm's average cost of labour curve, the more market power it has. Remember that just as the firm with monopoly power has to charge the same price to all customers regardless of their individual willingness to pay, the employer has to pay workers the same wage regardless of their individual no-shirking wage.

To take the simplest case of a single monopoly producer, the profit-maximizing price is set on the demand curve where the marginal revenue is equal to the marginal cost. The monopolist restricts output and raises the price to maximize profits.

In the labour market, the monopsony employer sets the wage where the marginal cost of labour is equal to the marginal revenue product. To focus attention in our discussion on labour market power (monopsony), we simplify by assuming the firm can sell its output at a fixed price of one and that productivity is constant (i.e. the marginal revenue product is constant and equal to the marginal and average product).

Figure 15.7 illustrates the profit-maximizing choice of wage and employment by the firm with monopsony power. Any of the factors discussed in Section 15.2.5 that shift the no-shirking wage curve up will lead to a higher profit-maximizing wage and lower employment. In this model, the difference between the marginal revenue product of labour and the no-shirking wage, w^*, indicates the markdown.

15.2.7 **Examples of employers' wage-setting power (monopsony)**

As we have seen, the key to understanding the employer's wage-setting power in their labour market is the upward sloping average cost of labour curve. Evidence

---

[5] Pioneering work in this area was done by the Cambridge economist, Joan Robinson, who coined the term 'monopsony' in her 1932 book *The Economics of Imperfect Competition* (London: Macmillan).

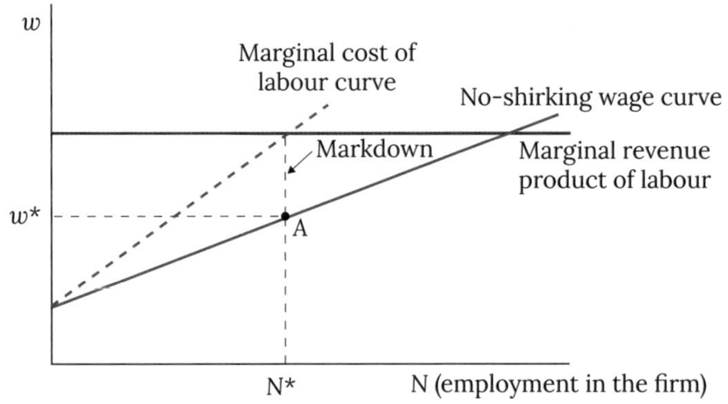

Figure 15.7 The profit-maximizing wage and employment level, monopsony firm (note that the output price is set at 1).

of monopsony is found in studies that estimate the extent to which firm-specific employment is sensitive to the wage—this is referred to as the labour supply elasticity. If the firm sets the wage too low, it will fail to attract workers; if it sets it too high, it loses profits as illustrated for the monopsonist in Figure 15.7, where there is a single employer. The lower is the elasticity, the less sensitive is employment to the wage and the less the employer needs to worry about recruitment when it offers a lower wage.[6] Krueger (2018) summarizes: '[f]irms with more inelastic labor supply pay lower wages, suggesting that they exploit their monopsony power' (p. 4).

In the competitive labour market model, by contrast, the elasticity of the labour supply to the firm is infinite: their hiring does not affect the wage. Many studies find an elasticity of approximately 4, which means that wages are marked down relative to the marginal revenue product by about 20% (Card 2022).

Using different data and methodology from those reported by Card, Yeh et al. (2022) estimate the markdowns in US manufacturing plants from 1976 to 2014. They find that US manufacturing is characterized by significant markdowns, which rise with firm size (its employment share). The degree of employer power measured this way fell between the late 1970s and 2000s but increased sharply thereafter. The authors suggest that this may be related to the decline in US business dynamism from the start of the millennium measured by declining rates of job and worker flows and of entrepreneurship and start-up activity (Decker et al. 2016). They estimate that a worker earns 65 cents of each dollar generated at the margin. They find some evidence of a negative correlation between the degree of unionization at industry level and the average markdown.

From the perspective of the worker, in the absence of wage-setting power in the labour market, any given job seeker faces a very large number of potential employers.

[6] Sokolova and Sorensen (2021) provide a meta-analysis of estimates of the elasticity of labour supply. For an alternative interpretation of monopsony power in terms of the firm's problem of deterring quits rather than in recruitment, see Naidu and Carr (2022).

A second source of evidence on monopsony power shows, however, that in many local labour markets, there are relatively few potential employers. Azar et al. (2020), whose study covers online job listings for the entire US, finds that for local labour markets for narrowly defined occupations, there is the equivalent of 2.3 employers. They also find that wages are lower where concentration is higher. Other studies show that where the consolidation of employers takes place through a merger of firms, the outcome is a negative effect on wages (Card 2022).

A third kind of evidence arises from arrangements by employers that suppress competition for workers. An early example from the Silicon Valley market for high tech workers began in the mid-1980s with an arrangement between Pixar and Lucasfilm in relation to animation engineers. It only ended in 2008, with payouts to affected engineers and wage increases elsewhere in the industry (Card 2022). Such coordination among employers is the wage-fixing equivalent of price-fixing in the product market.

At the other end of the labour market are examples of how competition is suppressed through the use of non-compete clauses in fast food companies, which restrict the ability of workers to apply for jobs in other franchises of the same company. In McDonalds, for example, an employee could not be employed by another McDonalds within 6 months of leaving their job. Importantly, workers do not get a higher wage to compensate them for foregoing future employment opportunities. Non-compete clauses apply to about one quarter of US workers and prevent them from applying for many jobs for which they are qualified (Krueger 2018). Ashenfelter and Krueger (2021) report that 58% of franchise companies have a 'no-poaching of workers' clause. Even more blatant are examples of collusion among employers to keep pay down, for example in the nursing sector (Krueger 2018).

15.2.8 **Minimum wages, employment, and inequality**

In a labour market where the employer has some monopsony power, if they are forced to pay a wage above the profit-maximizing level, employment can increase because the imposed minimum wage eliminates the incentive to restrict hiring that arises from the upward sloping average cost of labour. When a binding minimum wage is imposed, marginal and average cost of labour are equal so that hiring more workers has no effect on the wage paid.

It is easy to illustrate the pro-employment effect of a minimum wage. In Figure 15.8, if a minimum wage above the monopsony wage, w^*, is set, then this flattens the average cost of labour curve as shown. The firm maximizes profits at point B where both employment and the wage are higher. The firm will never pay a wage above the marginal revenue product because that would be loss making. This highlights the importance of correctly characterizing the nature of the labour market when evaluating the likely impact of a change in the minimum wage.

Minimum wage policies have been one response to the increase in inequality in market incomes since the 1980s. In a traditional model of a labour market that clears at the wage where the labour supply and labour demand curves intersect, a minimum wage above the market-clearing wage would reduce employment. However, as we have seen, a realistic model of the labour market with an upward sloping average

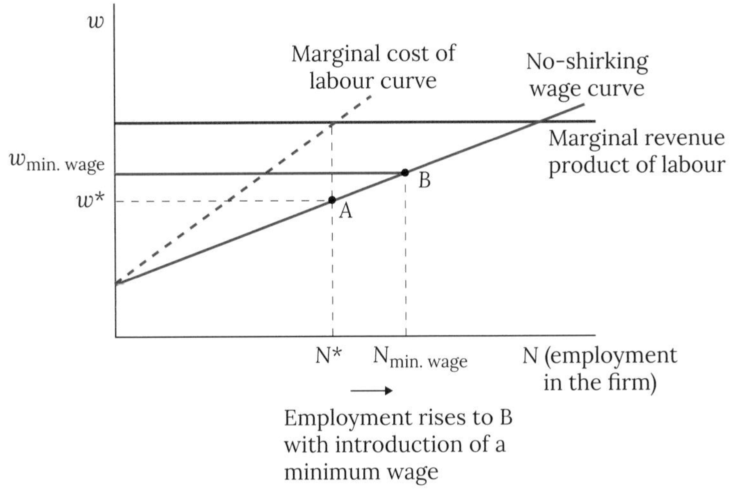

Figure 15.8 The effect of a rise in the minimum wage in a monopsonistic labour market.

cost of labour is one in which a higher minimum wage can increase earnings as both employment and the wage rise.

Carefully designed studies of the minimum wage in the US[7] found that for those with low incomes, the positive effect on earnings from a higher minimum wage was much greater than any negative effect of the minimum wage in depressing employment. Indeed, studies found that employment rose in some cases (as predicted by Figure 15.8).[8] The 2019 report by Arindrajit Dube for the UK government reviews the international evidence on the impact of minimum wage policies and concludes:

> Overall the most up to date body of research from US, UK and other developed countries points to a very muted effect of minimum wages on employment, while significantly increasing the earnings of low paid workers.

Giupponi and Machin (2022) show that the introduction of the national minimum wage in the UK in 1999 played a crucial role in stopping and reversing the upward trend in inequality at the bottom of the earnings distribution. By 2019, 7% of all workers were covered by the minimum wage. Earnings inequality was undergoing long-run structural change that benefited college educated workers in the wake of the ICT revolution (see Chapter 17). In the 2010s, low-paid workers in the UK gained relative to those in the middle and top of the income distribution because of above inflation increases in the minimum wage.

---

[7] The famous difference-in-difference study by David Card and Alan Krueger (1994) is an early example.

[8] See for example Cengiz et al. (2019), who find a positive yet statistically insignificant effect. See also Dube (2019) for a more comprehensive review of the international evidence. For an accessible database with the estimates from many studies, see Dube and Zipperer (2022).

15.3 SEARCH AND MATCHING: THE BEVERIDGE CURVE AND INFLATION

Figure 15.2 draws attention to vacancies alongside unemployment, i.e. 'jobs looking for workers' as well as 'workers looking for jobs'. Whereas the focus in the search and matching model in Section 15.2 was on how the firm sets the wage, we turn now to how well the labour market achieves matching between vacancies and job seekers. The Beveridge curve plots the relationship between the vacancy rate in the economy and the unemployment rate. We show how to integrate the Beveridge curve with the WS-PS model to analyse inflation as well as unemployment and vacancies. This is followed by a comparison of Beveridge curves for different countries using the model to shed light on how different labour markets responded to the global financial crisis and the pandemic.

15.3.1 A model of the Beveridge curve

To model the aggregate relationship between vacancies and unemployment, we focus on how well workers are matched to vacancies in the economy as a whole. With a constant labour force, labour market equilibrium in the flow approach means that hires, H, are equal to separations, S, from employment. Separations cover job losses due to the closure of firms as well as quits. An important aspect of how the labour market works is how well it achieves the matching of unemployed workers with unfilled job vacancies.

A simple version of the matching function can be explained as follows. It is assumed that U is the number of unemployed, V is the number of vacancies and α is the parameter that describes the efficiency of the matching process in the economy. We can write the matching function as

$$H = \alpha \cdot m(U, V),$$

where a higher number of new hires is associated with higher matching efficiency ($\alpha > 0$). It is important to note that H and S are flows per period and that the period can be of any length as long as hires and separations are measured consistently. The matching function describes how the unemployed are matched with the vacancies. Holding the matching efficiency and the number of vacancies constant, higher unemployment is associated with more matches since there are more applicants for each job. Similarly, holding unemployment constant, more vacancies are associated with more matches. If we assume that the flow of workers from employment to unemployment is $S = sN$ where s for 'separation rate' is the proportionate exit rate from employment, then the labour market will be in a flow equilibrium when the flow *into* unemployment, sN is equal to the flow *out of* unemployment into jobs:

$$sN = \alpha \cdot m(U, V).$$

Using the assumption that matching takes place under constant returns to scale and assuming for simplicity that the separation rate, is an exogenous constant (e.g. firms are randomly affected by shocks that result in separations), we can divide through by N, which gives us:

$$s = \alpha \cdot m(\frac{U}{N}, \frac{V}{N}).$$

If we draw a diagram with the 'unemployment rate' ($u \equiv U/N$) on the horizontal axis and the vacancy rate ($v \equiv V/N$) on the vertical axis, the labour market equilibrium can be plotted as shown in Figure 15.9. The vacancy/unemployment curve depicting labour market equilibrium in the flow model is called the Beveridge curve. The curve is downward sloping because at high unemployment, with a given matching technology, it will be necessary for vacancies to be low to deliver the constant number of matches required to balance the fixed separation rate, s. Conversely at low unemployment with fewer people looking for work, more vacancies are required to ensure that the number of those taking jobs is equal to the separation rate.

In Figure 15.9a the Beveridge curve and two rays from the origin are shown labelled by the level of aggregate demand. When aggregate demand is high, the economy is in goods market equilibrium shown by the 'High aggregate demand' ray: the buoyant labour market has high vacancies as employers seek to hire more workers and low unemployment (point A). In a recession, the reverse situation holds (point B). As aggregate demand fluctuates over the course of the business cycle, the economy moves along the Beveridge curve from A to B and back again. Figure 15.9b shows two Beveridge curves. With the vacancy rate shown by point A, if the match between

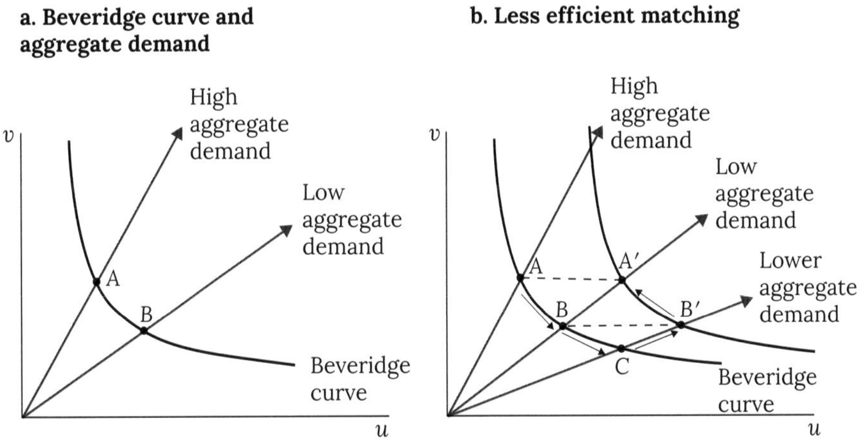

Panel a illustrates how the relationship between the vacancy rate and the unemployment rate is traced out by the Beveridge curve over the business cycle: as aggegate demand falls, the economy moves from A to B.
Panel b shows an example of how the interaction between fluctuations in aggregate demand and changes in matching efficiency traces out a path on two Beveridge curves (A, B, C, B′, A′)

Figure 15.9 The Beveridge curve model.

vacancies and the unemployed is worse, then the unemployment rate will be higher. The second right-shifted Beveridge curve reflects a lower efficiency of matching, i.e. a lower value of α. In the example illustrated in Figure 15.9b, the economy moves along the Beveridge curve from A to B to C as a recession takes hold. In the recession, suppose that the process of matching vacancies and workers deteriorates leading to point B′: both unemployment and vacancies rise. As the cyclical recovery takes place, the economy moves from B′ to A′ tracing out a new Beveridge curve.

15.3.2 Integrating the *WS-PS* model and the Beveridge curve

To relate the WS-PS model to the Beveridge curve model, we introduce the vacancy rate into the WS curve. Holding all the other determinants of the wage- and price-setting curves constant, for a given unemployment rate, higher vacancies in the economy increase the wage workers can bargain for, or that employers need to set to attract good workers. The WS equation written in terms of the unemployment rate is:

$$\frac{W}{P_c^E} = b(u, v, \mathbf{z}_w),$$

where, v is the vacancy rate and u is the unemployment rate. Holding everything else constant, the WS curve shifts up when the vacancy rate increases since it increases the probability of exit from the unemployment pool. As Figure 15.10a shows, a higher rate of vacancies implies a lower equilibrium employment rate and hence higher equilibrium unemployment: there is a positive relationship between vacancies and equilibrium unemployment (at which WS and PS are equal). In the Beveridge curve diagram, we now include the positively sloped line showing the wage- and price-setting equilibrium (Figure 15.10b). In the Beveridge curve diagram, full equilibrium

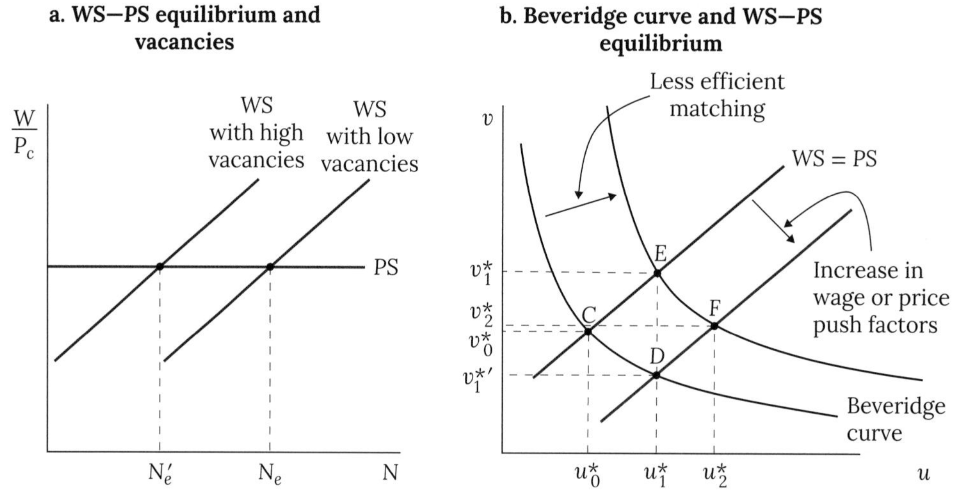

Figure 15.10 Reconciling the flow approach and the WS–PS model:
a. The WS–PS equilibrium and vacancies
b. The Beveridge curve and the WS–PS equilibrium.
Visit www.oup.com/he/carlin-soskice to explore the WS-PS with the Beveridge curve with Animated Analytical Diagram 15.10.

in the labour market is shown by the intersection of the Beveridge curve and the WS = PS line.

It is clear from the diagram that there will be higher unemployment in equilibrium if the ability of the economy to match workers to jobs worsens (an outward shift of the Beveridge curve) as can be seen by comparing the initial equilibrium at point C with the new one at E. Note that in this case, both unemployment and vacancies will be higher in the new equilibrium (at E, u_1^*, v_1^*).

The adjustment of the economy to the new equilibrium at E can be explained as follows: if a deterioration in matching occurs, vacancies rise, thereby pushing the WS curve upwards. This opens up a bargaining gap at u_0^*, raising inflationary pressure (as shown in Figure 15.10a at N_e). Equilibrium unemployment has gone up (the new equilibrium employment is N_e'): an inflation targeting central bank would tighten monetary policy and guide the economy to the higher unemployment rate consistent with constant inflation at its target, i.e. at point E, u_1^* (in Figure 15.10b).

Alternatively, if there is a rise in wage (or price) push in the economy (a negative supply shock) but the Beveridge curve remains unchanged, then the WS = PS curve shifts to the right and equilibrium occurs at higher unemployment (at u_1^*) but with a lower vacancy rate at point D, ($v_1^{*'}$). The intuition in the second case is that higher unemployment is associated with a lower vacancy rate in equilibrium (for matching reasons) and this somewhat offsets the effect of higher wage pressure, leaving equilibrium unemployment lower than would be the case if the vacancy rate did not fall.

Finally, if we observe that equilibrium unemployment goes up with little change in the vacancy rate, this suggests that there has been a shift in the WS or PS curve and in the Beveridge curve (as in the move from point C to point F).

By introducing the flow approach to the labour market, we have widened the set of factors that can account for changes in equilibrium unemployment. In addition to those that shift the WS or the PS curves, we now include features of the way the labour market brings workers and jobs together, for example:

1. Barriers to occupational and geographic mobility imply weaker matching and will shift the Beveridge curve outward; similarly policies to overcome these barriers by improving the efficiency of employment and training agencies or the operation of the housing market or transport infrastructure can have the opposite effect.
2. Forms of employment protection legislation may affect the ability of employers to hire workers, weakening the matching process.
3. Some factors will in principle shift both curves: for example, an increase in unemployment benefit duration weakens search intensity and shifts the Beveridge curve to the right and, as a wage-push factor, also shifts the WS upwards shifting the WS = PS curve in the Beveridge curve diagram to the right. These effects reinforce each other, worsening equilibrium unemployment.

15.3.3 **Empirical Beveridge curves**

The combined Beveridge curve and WS-PS model helps explain interesting aspects of labour market performance in the financial crisis, the Covid-19 pandemic and the Ukraine war shock.

Elsby et al. (2010) find that the labour market response to the global financial crisis initially bore distinct similarities to other postwar recessions. The demographic groups that suffered most were young, male, less-educated and ethnic minority workers. The impact on youth unemployment was particularly acute, with youth unemployment averaging nearly 18% between 2009 and 2011. Applying the flow approach, they find that the composition of separations from employment shifted from quits toward layoffs; workers laid off typically moved into unemployment and not straight into another job. This was a major driver of the rise in unemployment during the crisis.

However, as the recession progressed, the labour market response diverged from the recessions of the early 1990s and early 2000s. The exit rate of unemployed workers from joblessness dropped to historically low levels. The level of unemployment during the recession was higher than that implied by the historic Beveridge curve, which signifies a loss of efficiency in matching workers with vacancies.

This contributes to long-term unemployment (see Figure 15.12). The problem of long-term unemployment was new and particularly acute in the United States, where as a percentage of total unemployment it jumped from 10% in 2007 to over 31% in 2011.

The persistent effects of the financial crisis on the US labour market are illustrated by the Beveridge curve (Figure 15.11). Note that the Beveridge curve shifts out following

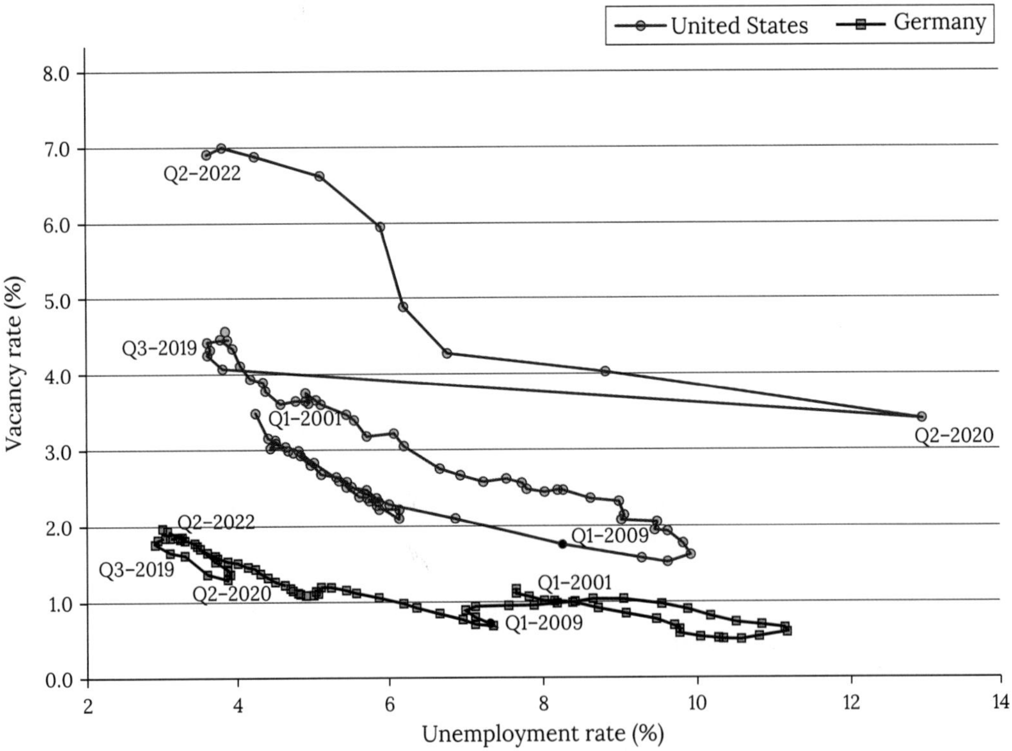

Figure 15.11 Beveridge curves in the US and Germany: 2001 Q1–2022 Q2.

Note: Rates are expressed as a percentage of the active population (15 and over, all persons).

Source: OECD Stats.

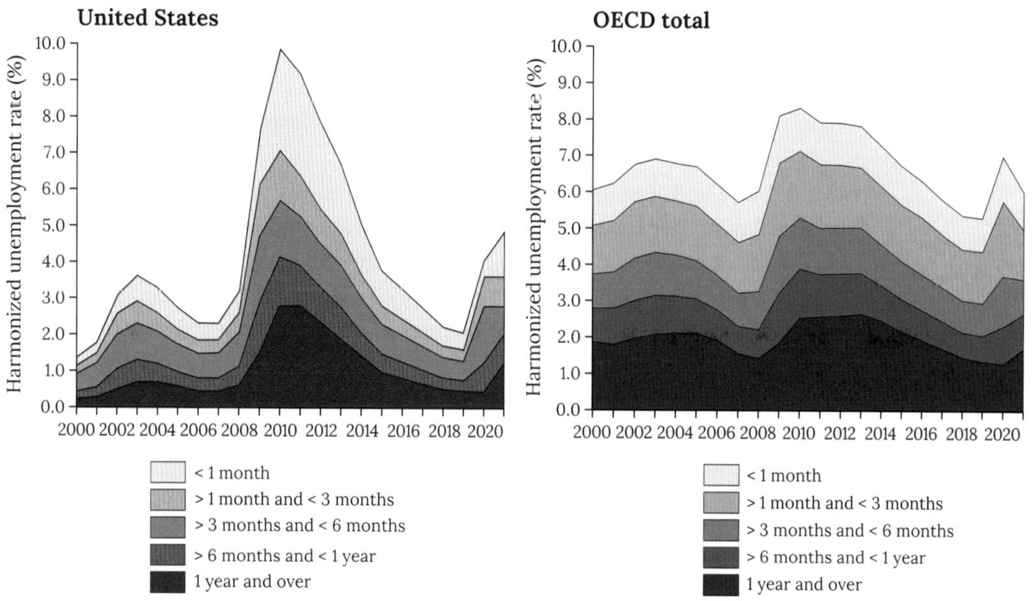

Figure 15.12 Unemployment rate by duration—US and OECD total: 2001–2021.

Note: Data was calculated by multiplying the harmonized rate of unemployment by the percentage shares of total unemployment by duration.

Source: OECD (data accessed September 2022).

the financial crisis, indicating an increase in mismatch in the labour market. The contrast with Germany is vivid, where the Beveridge curve shifted inwards around the time of the financial crisis.

Both the pandemic and energy shock caused by the war in Ukraine revived interest in using the Beveridge curve to help interpret unusual events and their likely impact on the labour market, including the implications for inflation and monetary policy.[9]

Covid-19 effect. The specific nature of the pandemic saw the shutdown of much economic activity requiring face-to-face interactions by a combination of government orders and the response to the disease outbreak by households and firms. In the recovery phase, vacancies were high relative to the unemployment rate as compared with the pre-pandemic situation. Workers withdrew from the labour market during the pandemic and did not return promptly, many taking early retirement. For the US, this is illustrated in Figure 15.11. This is not observed for Germany.

In both the US and the UK, the central bank hoped that matching efficiency would improve as job markets readjusted. In the absence of this being purely transitory, the outward shift observed in the Beveridge curve in the UK as well as the US implies a higher equilibrium unemployment and vacancy rate. In Figure 15.10b, for example, an economy with an initial equilibrium at point C, would face higher equilibrium unemployment at point E if the matching deterioration persists. The model predicts

[9] See Blanchard, Domash, and Summers (2022) and Haskel (2021).

that this puts upward pressure on inflation until unemployment rises to the higher equilibrium level. However, if vacancies fall without unemployment rising this suggests the Beveridge curve is shifting back to its earlier position, which would reduce inflationary pressure. To visualize this, you can superimpose an upward sloping WS = PS curve in Figure 15.11.

War in Ukraine. The supply-side effect of the oil and gas price shock of 2022 arising from the Ukraine war can be modelled by a downward shift in the PS curve (Chapters 2 and 13), which implies a rightward shift of the WS = PS curve in Figure 15.10b, and, as a consequence, a new equilibrium at point D with higher unemployment. Moreover, if either the mismatch effects of the pandemic persist or new ones emerge because of lasting supply-chain disruption due to the war, a move along the Beveridge curve (C to D) and a move to the new curve (D to F) would be predicted.

Monetary policy makers facing these bad shocks would have to raise the interest rate sufficiently so as to increase unemployment above the new, higher, equilibrium rate in order to bring inflation down.

15.4 LABOUR MARKET INSTITUTIONS, UNEMPLOYMENT, AND INEQUALITY

15.4.1 Union organization and equilibrium unemployment

In this section, we move in a new direction by focusing on how the different ways in which wage-setting is organized by unions, employers and governments can affect the WS curve, and hence equilibrium unemployment. An influential article written by Lars Calmfors and John Driffill in the late 1980s argued that there was a hump-shaped relationship between the degree of centralization of wage setting and the equilibrium rate of unemployment.[10]

The Calmfors-Driffill model showed low unemployment is consistent with either very decentralized wage setting or with very centralized wage setting; the worst institutional arrangement was a so-called intermediate level. This is interesting because it provides a possible explanation for the persistence of very low unemployment rates in a number of highly unionized Nordic countries and Austria in the 1970s and 1980s, when unemployment rose elsewhere as illustrated in Figure 15.1. The model retains relevance as we try to explain changes in unionization, inequality and unemployment across countries before and after the global financial crisis.

The insights of the Calmfors-Driffill model can be explained intuitively. The model assumes that all workers are unionized and compares three different contexts for wage setting: at firm level, at industry level and at the level of the economy as a whole.

1. 'Firm level' or 'decentralized' means a situation in which there is a union specific to each firm that sets the wage in the firm.

[10] Calmfors and Driffill (1988).

2. 'Industry level' or 'intermediate' means there is a union that sets the wage for all workers in an industry (e.g. the engineering industry union or the banking industry union).
3. 'Economy-wide' or 'centralized' means there is a single union that sets the wage for all workers in the economy. As we shall see, wage setting does not have to be literally centralized for the economy-wide outcome to prevail: what matters is the extent to which wage setters take into account the economy-wide implications of their wage-setting decision. For this reason, the term 'coordinated' is often preferred to 'centralized'.[11]

To be able to compare the predictions for unemployment across the different wage-setting structures, it is important to rule out other possible influences on the outcome. For this reason, we assume that the union's utility function is the same for each of the cases we look at. One way of modelling the union's utility function is that it simply mirrors the preferences of its members. This will give a utility function where wellbeing increases with employment and with the real wage. For simplicity, we also assume that the wage is chosen by a monopoly union rather than by bargaining between the union and the employer. The union unilaterally sets the wage and the employer chooses the level of employment.

There are two different forces for wage moderation:

1. How does the union expect employment of its members to respond to a change in the wage?
2. To what extent does the union take into account the impact of its decisions on the economy-wide price level and hence, on the macroeconomic equilibrium?

In relation to the first, as wage setting becomes more decentralized, the union becomes more concerned about the effect on the employment of its members if it increases the wage. If we think of the case where there is one union per firm, the union will worry that a wage increase in the firm will make the firm less competitive than others producing similar goods. As a consequence, the firm will lose market share and decrease employment, which will have a negative impact on the utility of union members. This acts to limit the exercise of union power when wages are set by the union at firm level.

By contrast, when wages are set by an industry union, the union will view the impact of its wage increase on the demand for industry output and hence on industry employment as limited. This is because the degree of substitutability between the products of different industries (e.g. between engineering equipment and textiles) is much less than between the products of different firms in the same industry (e.g. between the fork-lift trucks produced by firm A and firm B). Hence, the industry union will exercise less restraint and choose a higher wage than the firm-level union.

The second force for wage moderation is of a quite different kind. It arises from consideration of the general equilibrium or economy-wide effects of the wage increase.

---

[11] For further discussion about how coordination in wage setting takes place see below and Soskice (1990).

A union that is operating at the level of the firm takes as given the economy-wide price level and, when setting the money wage, assumes that this sets the real consumption wage for the workers in the firm (i.e. $\frac{W_i}{P_c}$, for firm i), which is what its members care about. Its decision on W_i does not affect P_c. However, if the union is setting the wage for all workers in the economy, the impact of its decision on the economy-wide consumer price level cannot be ignored. The union will therefore recognize that any increase in the wage it sets (e.g. a 4% increase) will generate an increase in the price level in line (i.e. by 4%) as costs in the economy rise by 4%. Since its decision on W affects P_c, the outcome will be that the real consumption wage does not rise.

The Calmfors-Driffill model in a diagram

To see the above argument graphically, we begin with the union indifference curves (see Figure 15.13a). These comprise two components: on the one hand, workers are interested in maximizing the wage bill and this produces a downward sloping indifference curve in the real wage–employment diagram. The second component is that there is a disutility of work so eventually the indifference curve slopes upward. We assume that the indifference curves of the individual workers form the basis of the union's indifference curves.[12] The labour supply curve, N^S is derived by taking any real wage and finding the amount of labour supplied so this goes through the minimum points of the indifference curves. As argued in Chapter 2, the labour supply curve is very inelastic and the WS curves lie to the left of it.

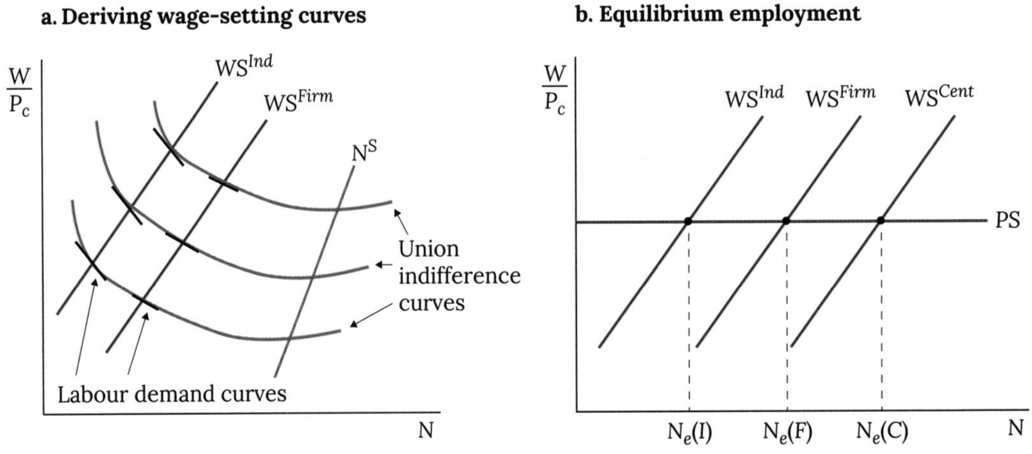

Figure 15.13 The Calmfors–Driffill model.
a. Deriving wage-setting curves under different institutional arrangements.
b. Equilibrium employment with a centralized union, firm-level unions and industry-level unions.

[12] See Chapter 15 of Carlin and Soskice (2006) for the derivation of the formal model.

Centralized (or coordinated) wage setting: A single union

The centralized union takes into account the fact that the economy will end up on the price-setting curve after wages and prices have been set. The centralized union realizes that it cannot achieve a real wage higher than that on the PS curve. In the simple case of a horizontal PS curve, the real wage is constant so when the centralized union picks its best point along the PS curve, it will choose to maximize employment. This implies that the centralized union chooses not to exercise its monopoly power in wage negotiations: its utility is maximized at the employment level where the WS curve determined by efficiency wages in the absence of unions cuts the PS curve. This WS curve is labelled '*Cent*'.

Industry-level wage setting

If unions are organized at industry level, then as explained above, they believe that their wage decision will have little impact on employment since the degree of substitutability between the products of different industries is low. This is reflected in the rather steep downward sloping industry-level labour demand curves. The industry-level union optimizes by choosing the highest indifference curve subject to the constraint of the labour demand curve. Three labour demand curves for different levels of aggregate demand in the economy are shown. By joining up the points of tangency, the wage-setting curve for the case of wage setting by industry-level unions is derived, WS^{Ind} (see Figure 15.13a).

Firm-level wage setting

As we move to a more decentralized context for wage setting, the union becomes more concerned about the impact of its wage decision on employment of its members: if it raises its wage, the firm will raise its price and consumers will switch to other suppliers. The greater elasticity of demand produces flatter labour demand curves as shown in the diagram, with the consequence that the wage-setting curve for decentralized wage setting lies below that for industry-level wage setting, WS^{Firm}.

Macroeconomic equilibrium

To draw out the implications for equilibrium unemployment, we note that once wages are set, firms set prices. Returning to the level of the economy as a whole, we therefore have the PS curve as shown in Figure 15.13b. Equilibrium employment for the case of industry-level wage setting is shown by the intersection of the WS^{Ind} and the PS. This is below that for the case of firm-level wage setting.

As argued above, the centralized case brings in the second element in the Calmfors-Driffill story: the wage decision affects prices and as the coverage of wage setting increases, it becomes impossible for the union to ignore the consequences of its wage decision for the economy-wide price level and hence for the real consumption wage, which enters its utility function. Given that the centralized union knows it cannot achieve a higher real wage than determined by the PS curve, it maximizes utility by going for the highest possible level of employment. This is at the intersection of the PS curve and the non-union WS curve labelled WS^{Cent} (since this shows the minimum real wage the employer would set consistent with workers exerting effort). Hence equilibrium employment in this case is at $N_e(C)$.

These results predict a hump-shaped relationship between the centralization of wage setting and equilibrium unemployment. Soskice (1990) focuses on the nature of wage-setting that occurs at different levels rather than the level itself. His argument is that *if* wage-setters take into account the external effect of their behaviour on employment (for example, because of the anticipated reaction of the central bank, or because of the implications for the real exchange rate and employment in an open economy), their behaviour is *coordinated* irrespective of whether the formal location of wage-setting is for example, the firm, the industry or economy-wide. This version of the C-D model is referred to as the Calmfors-Driffill-Soskice model below.

As we saw in Chapter 14 when discussing the performance of the Eurozone, this characterization of wage-setting and how it differs across Eurozone members helps explain the contrasting trends in competitiveness (the real exchange rates) between the formation of the Eurozone and the EZ crisis. In Germany, by leading wage-setting and with the objective in common of sustaining the competitiveness of the sector, the employers and unions in the engineering industry (Gesamtmetall and IG Metall) effectively coordinated the wages set across the economy. This more complex institutional structure is able to mimic the centralized outcome modelled by Calmfors and Driffill (Visser 2016).[13]

The longstanding German model of coordination enabled it to emulate the 'centralized' format typical of wage-setting in the Scandinavian countries in the 1960s and 1970s. But then in Norway, Denmark and Sweden, centralized bargaining began to disappear from the 1980s and gave way to German-style 'trend-setting'. Wage-setting in these countries along with Austria, Finland, Belgium, the Netherlands, and Japan continues to be rated as highly coordinated. In some countries, like the Netherlands, the government plays a role whereas in Japan, neither the government nor unions are involved—wage coordination is carried out by the employers (Visser 2016; see Table 4 for coordination scores).

While the decline in union density and the decentralization of wage setting has been widely observed across the OECD, the group of countries in north-west Europe (and Japan) remains distinctive. Elsewhere coordination among wage setters is largely absent.

15.4.2 Evidence on labour market institutions for OECD countries: Unemployment and inequality

Within-country changes in unemployment over periods longer than business cycles, cross-country patterns and well-documented differences in labour market institutions can be brought together using the frameworks of the WS-PS, wage coordination and Beveridge curve models.

[13] See Aidt and Tzannatos (2006) for a review of the evidence on the 'hump-shaped' relationship.

As we have seen, the model of the determinants of equilibrium unemployment centres on factors shifting the wage-setting and/or price-setting curves or the unemployment/vacancy (Beveridge) curve:

a. The WS curve shifts up with a rise in union bargaining power and with a fall in the cost of job loss (e.g. a rise in the unemployment benefit replacement rate). The degree of coordination of wage setting also affects the WS curve.

b. The PS curve shifts down with a rise in the tax wedge; an unanticipated fall in trend productivity growth; a fall in the pressure of competition in the product market; or a rise in the oil price.

c. The unemployment-vacancy (Beveridge) curve shifts to the right in unemployment-vacancy space when there is a rise in the mismatch between jobs available and potential employees (see Figure 15.9).

Although changes in institutions have been observed as reported, for example for union density in the US, such changes are often slow-moving. Given institutional inertia, this raises the question of how a shock that is common across countries (such as an oil shock) interacts with the supply-side institutions in different countries. For example, a supply-side shock such as an oil shock or a slowdown in productivity growth shifts the PS curve down: the impact of this on equilibrium unemployment depends on the slope of the WS curve, i.e. on how sensitive are real wages (of wage setters) to unemployment. One way of characterizing a flexible labour market is one in which the WS curve is very steep—i.e. real wages are very responsive to changes in unemployment. If the WS is very flat, then for a given negative external terms of trade shock, a much larger rise in unemployment is required to bring about the necessary downward adjustment of real wage claims (see Figure 15.14 for an illustration). When wage-setting is highly coordinated as in the Nordic economies, for example, the wage-setting curve is steep as in the flexible wage case illustrated.

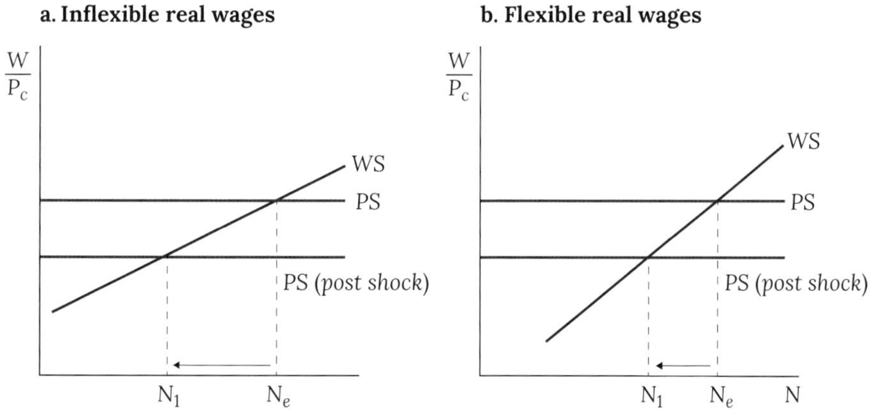

Figure 15.14 Common shock: interaction with flexible and inflexible real wages.
a. Inflexible real wages: large fall in N.
b. Flexible real wages: small fall in N.

A decade after the financial crisis (and before the pandemic), it is instructive to look at the state of employment and inequality in the high-income economies through the lens of the models in this chapter. Table 15.1 collects summary evidence on performance as well as on institutional and policy variables.

	Six 'liberal' economies	Five high unemployment European countries	Six low unemployment European countries	Germany
1. Unemployment rate (2018) %	4.9	9.7	5.1	3.2
2. Employment rate (2018) %	73.3	64.5	76.3	74.9
3. Unemployment benefits: Net replacement ratio (2019) %	66.9	81.6	82.0	81.6
4. Employment protection legislation (2019) index	1.8	2.6	2.2	2.3
5. Trade union membership (2016) % of employees	19.3	35.0	40.6	17.0
6. Collective bargaining coverage (2016) % of employees	30.6	92.7	77.2	56.0
7. Coordination of bargaining (2019) index	1.5	3.2	3.8	4.0
8. Tax revenue (2019) % of GDP	28.8	41.4	39.8	38.6
9. Active labour market policies (2018) % of GDP	0.2	0.7	0.9	0.7
10. Wage differentials; median gross earnings to 10th percentile (2018)	1.8	1.5	1.5	1.8
11. Gini coefficient: Disposable income (2019)	0.35	0.34	0.31	0.37
12. Top 1 percent share: Disposable income (2019) %	10.1	7.4	7.4	9.7
13. Gini coefficient: Net wealth (2019)	0.77	0.72	0.72	0.75
14. Top 1 percent share: Net wealth (2019) %	25.1	21.0	24.6	29.1

Table 15.1 Employment, inequality, and labour market institutions across country groups (2018–19).

Data are mean values for country groups. *Liberal economies*: Australia, Canada, Ireland, New Zealand, UK, USA; *High unemployment euro countries*: Belgium, Finland, France, Italy, Spain; *Low unemployment euro countries*: Austria, Denmark, Netherlands, Norway, Switzerland, Sweden.

Note: Data are for the year indicated in the left column or the latest available if missing for some countries.

Source: For earlier data, see Table 2 in Baker, Howell, and Schmitt (2007);

Rows 1–2: OECD Employment Outlook 2021. Row 3: OECD Benefits, Taxes and Wages. Row 4: OECD Employment Protection database. Rows 5–6: OECD Trade unions and collective bargaining. Row 7: OECD/AIAS ICTWSS database. Row 8: OECD Global revenue statistics database. Row 9: OECD Public expenditure and participant stocks on Labour Market Programmes. Rows 10: OECD Decile rations of gross earnings. Rows 11–14: World Inequality Database.

Varieties of capitalism

Following the lead of the literature on the 'varieties of capitalism' (Hall and Soskice, 2001),[14] countries in Table 15.1 are organized into three groups (chosen by Howell et al. 2007). Updating the results to around the year 2019 suggests that the country groupings are still relevant, reinforcing the conjecture that institutional change is often slow. Nevertheless, we make one important change, removing Germany from the 'high unemployment' European group. This is consistent with the analysis in Chapter 14 of the important changes in Germany (a combination of labour market deregulation policies and flexibility of the wage-setting structure itself) in the years following the formation of the Eurozone and discussed at the end of this section.

Applying the Calmfors-Driffill-Soskice model, the prediction of low unemployment in the liberal economies, the 'coordinated' European economies, and in this period, in Germany stands out. Moreover, not only is unemployment nearly twice as high elsewhere in Europe, but the employment rate is markedly lower. The countries with low unemployment are achieving that result not by dampening participation in the labour market, but the opposite.

Note the sharp contrast between the 'liberal' economy and European model of low unemployment: in Europe, unemployment benefits are much more generous—replacing more than 80% of previous salary—and employment protection legislation is stronger. Read in the light of the predictions of the models surveyed in this chapter, the ability of wage-setters to coordinate their behaviour is playing a substantial role: according to the index in Table 15.1, wage coordination is highest in Germany, with a high level also characteristic of the other European low unemployment economies. Coordination is not relevant for wage-setting in the 'liberal' economies. However, the high unemployment European economies appear to suffer in terms of labour market outcomes because the high coverage of union wages does not bring wage coordination.

The WS-PS model predicts that a high tax wedge raises equilibrium unemployment. This prediction breaks down when looking across European economies—the share of tax revenue in GDP is high right across Europe and markedly higher than in the liberal ones. Yet once again, it appears that wage coordination succeeds in enabling high taxation to co-exist with low unemployment. In terms of the model, although the tax wedge pushes the PS curve downward *ceteris paribus*, all else is not equal across Europe. The economies with coordinated wage setting would be modelled by a downward shift in the PS curve, reflecting a high tax wedge, together with wage

[14] Hall and Soskice divided high-income economies into 'coordinated market economies' and 'liberal market economies'. In the former group were Nordic, Germanic, and East Asian countries with long-termist finance, training- and research-oriented companies, and coordinated wage setting. In the latter were Anglo-Saxon countries with opposite characteristics. Two other equally influential classifications are: the three worlds of capitalism (Esping-Anderson 1990) and the contrast between the highly redistributive proportional representation electoral systems of northern Europe and the majoritarian systems of the Anglo-Saxon countries, with low redistribution (Iversen and Soskice 2006).

moderation arising from coordination, which shifts the WS curve down in line, and therefore leaves equilibrium unemployment low.

Europe and the liberal economies also differ in the resources devoted to active labour market policies aimed at better matching workers looking for jobs with jobs looking for workers. The model in Figure 15.10 predicts that if higher active labour market spending reduces the mismatch between unemployed workers and vacancies, it will shift the Beveridge curve inwards and produce lower unemployment and vacancies holding other determinants of the WS and PS curves unchanged. This fits the low unemployment European economies, including Germany.

Cross-country studies of unemployment, policies, and institutions

Although the results of studies that attempt to confirm the role of the factors in Table 15.1 are disputed, it is useful to explain briefly the three main strategies that have been undertaken in the empirical work. Policy makers continue to refer to studies of this kind to justify labour market reform measures:

1. The simplest kind of study attempts to explain the cross-country variation in unemployment rates across the OECD countries. Studies of this type focus on the relative *position* of the WS and PS curves in different countries. A widely cited cross-sectional study is that of Nickell (1997), which uses data for 20 OECD economies for two five-year periods to investigate the impact of a range of labour market institutions on unemployment.
2. The second type of study, pioneered by Blanchard and Wolfers (2000), tests the hypothesis that it was the interaction between different (stable) institutions and common shocks to which countries were subjected that accounts for cross-country variation in employment over time. The idea is that some institutions translated bad shocks (e.g. to productivity) into more persistent unemployment problems than others. This can be illustated using the WS-PS model by considering a common shift in the PS curve that interacts with WS curves of differing slopes, as shown in Figure 15.14. Testing this hypothesis requires using panel data—i.e. data that varies across both countries and time—and introducing interaction terms between time dummies and a set of institutional variables into the regression model.
3. The last type of widely used study design attempts to identify the role of institutional *change* in accounting for the time-series variation in unemployment across the OECD countries: i.e. *within country* shifts in the WS or PS curve due to institutional changes. This requires a panel dataset. A prominent example of this type of analysis was published in the OECD Employment Outlook 2006.[15] The analysis took advantage of OECD efforts to harmonize (i.e. make comparable) the data on labour market institutions across countries, using data from 1982–2003 for 20 OECD economies.

[15] See OECD (2006). In this vein, Soskice and Iversen (2000) show that non-accommodating central banks reinforce coordinated wage bargaining to reduce equilibrium unemployment.

	Nickell (1997)	Blanchard and Wolfers (2000)	OECD EO (2006)
Institutions:			
Employment protection (+ 1 unit)	No effect	0.24	No effect
Unemployment benefit replacement ratio (+ 10 pp)	0.88	0.70	1.20
Unemployment benefit duration (+ 1 yr)	0.70	1.27	–
ALMP (+10 pp)	-1.92	No effect	–
Union density (+ 10 pp)	0.96	0.84	No effect
Union bargaining coverage (+ 10 pp)	3.60	No effect	–
Bargaining coordination (+1 unit) (scale 1–3)	−3.68	−1.13	−1.42
Taxes (+ 10 pp)	2.08	0.91	2.80

Table 15.2 Estimated effects of institutions on unemployment: three studies.

Note: For detailed discussion see Howell et al. (2007). pp means percentage points. 'No effect' means not statistically significant. The–symbol means a variable not included in the study.

Source: Howell et al. (2007). Table 3.

Table 15.2 summarizes the results of the three studies. The first thing that is immediately clear is that for some of the labour market institutions (e.g. employment protection and active labour market policies (ALMP)) there is no robust evidence for their effect on unemployment. In other cases, there seems to be more consensus. For example, the studies find that increases in the tax wedge and the level of unemployment benefits exert a statistically significant and positive effect on the unemployment rate (i.e. they increase it). In contrast, they find that bargaining coordination reduces unemployment. Table 15.2 was constructed using Howell et al. (2007), which provides a wider comparison of ten studies.[16] The most notable lesson from the comparison of cross-country studies is that even for variables where there is more consensus, the studies do not appear to give precise answers to the question of the likely *magnitude* of the effect of institutional and policy differences on unemployment outcomes. These results are a warning to policy makers who believe that there are 'off-the-shelf' recipes for labour market reforms that reduce equilibrium unemployment.

Inequality

Before moving to a comparison between high unemployment France and low unemployment Germany, it is interesting to note the differences in a number of indicators of inequality across the country groups.

Using the Gini coefficient for disposable income, the lowest inequality is in the low unemployment European countries—note that Germany's Gini is higher even than

[16] The study by Howell et al. (2007) provides a systematic comparison of the cross-country empirical evidence and provides results for ten studies. Heckman (2007) comments on this paper and other literature investigating the impact of labour market institutions on unemployment.

the average for the liberal economies, where the Gini is close to that of the high unemployment European countries.

Wealth concentration is very high right across these high-income countries, with most Gini coefficients above 0.7. The variation in wealth inequality is lower than for pre-tax income. Across the 17 high-income countries in Table 15.1, the minimum (i.e. least unequal) Gini for wealth is 0.64 for the Netherlands and the maximum is 0.83 for the US but 13 of the 17 countries have values between 0.7 and 0.77. And the top 1 per cent hold at least one-quarter of net wealth—except in the high unemployment European countries where the share in one-fifth.

Germany and France—a case study

A comparison of the Beveridge curves for France and Germany in Figure 15.15 reveals a similar starting point in the early 2000s but a divergence of performance from the middle of the decade. Germany's Beveridge curve shifts inwards in the years after the financial crisis, which reflects improved functioning of the labour market in a structural sense. By contrast, mismatch appears to have worsened in France following the financial crisis and rising vacancies have accompanied stubbornly high unemployment.

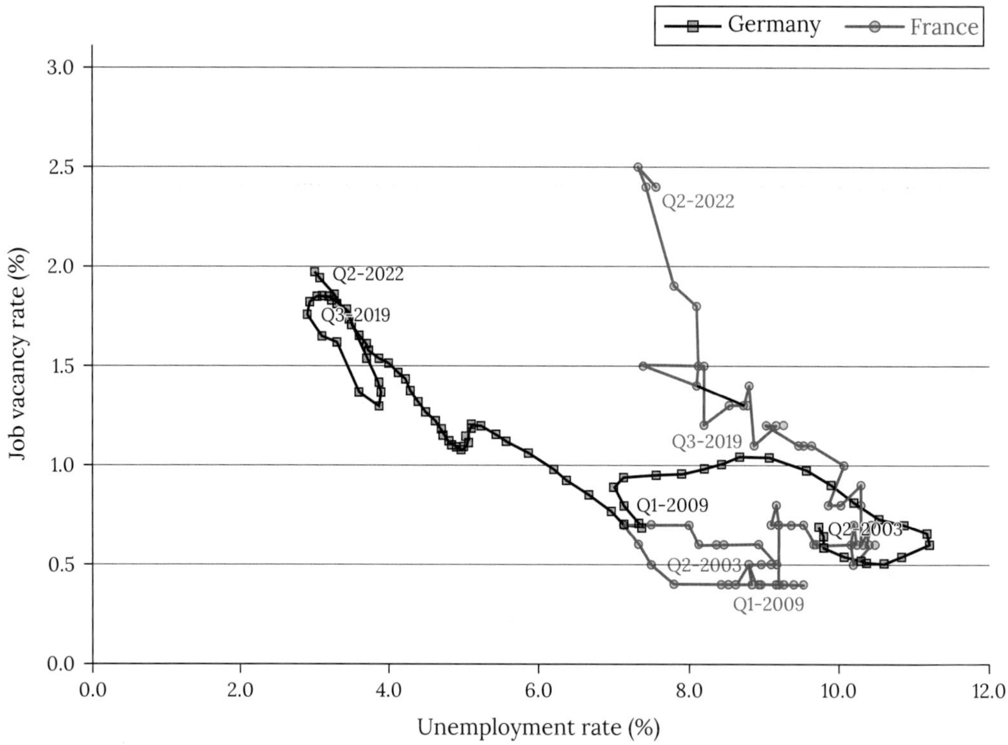

Figure 15.15 France and Germany Beveridge curves: 2003 Q2 to 2022 Q2.

Source: OECDStats and Eurostat (data accessed October 2022).

Figure 15.16 illustrates a number of relevant contrasts between France and Germany.[17] The top panel shows the growth of GDP per capita from 1995 to 2016 together with the growth of real hourly compensation. The real wage series show the growth of the real consumption wage (earnings deflated by the CPI) and the real product wage (earnings deflated by GDP). The three series show very similar trends in France, which indicates that workers benefited from productivity growth and the profit share remained constant. In terms of earnings as shown in the lower panel, France maintained distributional stability or even some gains for the lowest paid. In Germany, it is a story of two halves: the period up to the financial crisis and the period thereafter. In the first period, workers did not share in productivity growth (top left panel). However, from 2010 onwards, real wages grew faster than productivity. The bottom left panel shows that low-wage workers lost out in the first period but the trend was reversed in the second. Impressive gains were made in rising employment rates and falling unemployment in Germany from 2005, which contrasts sharply with the French record.

15.5 HYSTERESIS, SCARRING, AND COORDINATION PROBLEMS

In Section 4.4.2, we introduced the concept of hysteresis, which describes how a prolonged recession can lead to a deterioration of the supply side of the economy, raising its equilibrium unemployment rate. Sometimes referred to as 'scarring', the potential for hysteresis mechanisms to damage the supply side was of sufficient concern to policy makers that it influenced the design of policies to mitigate the consequences of the Covid-19 pandemic. The objective was not only to support the incomes of those involuntarily excluded from working as a result of the pandemic but also to do it in ways that sustained the attachment of temporarily idle workers to the work-place.

In the benchmark closed economy 3-equation model of Chapter 3, the equilibrium rate of unemployment is shifted by a range of supply-side factors. The policy implication is twofold:

1. Aggregate demand shocks have a short-run effect on unemployment but no effect in the medium run.
2. While aggregate demand policies have a role to play in stabilizing the economy around equilibrium unemployment, they cannot influence its level.

However, as set out in Section 4.4.2, if unemployment stays above equilibrium for an extended period, it could have a damaging effect on the supply side of the economy resulting in higher equilibrium unemployment. This is an example of hysteresis or 'path dependence'.

Hysteresis was first widely used in macroeconomics to help explain European unemployment in 1970s and 1980s, where the recessions associated with the oil shocks seem to have permanently increased unemployment. As noted in Chapter 4, it returned to the spotlight following the global financial crisis, however, as a large number of OECD economies experienced high and persistent unemployment.

[17] This discussion draws on Kugler et al. (2018).

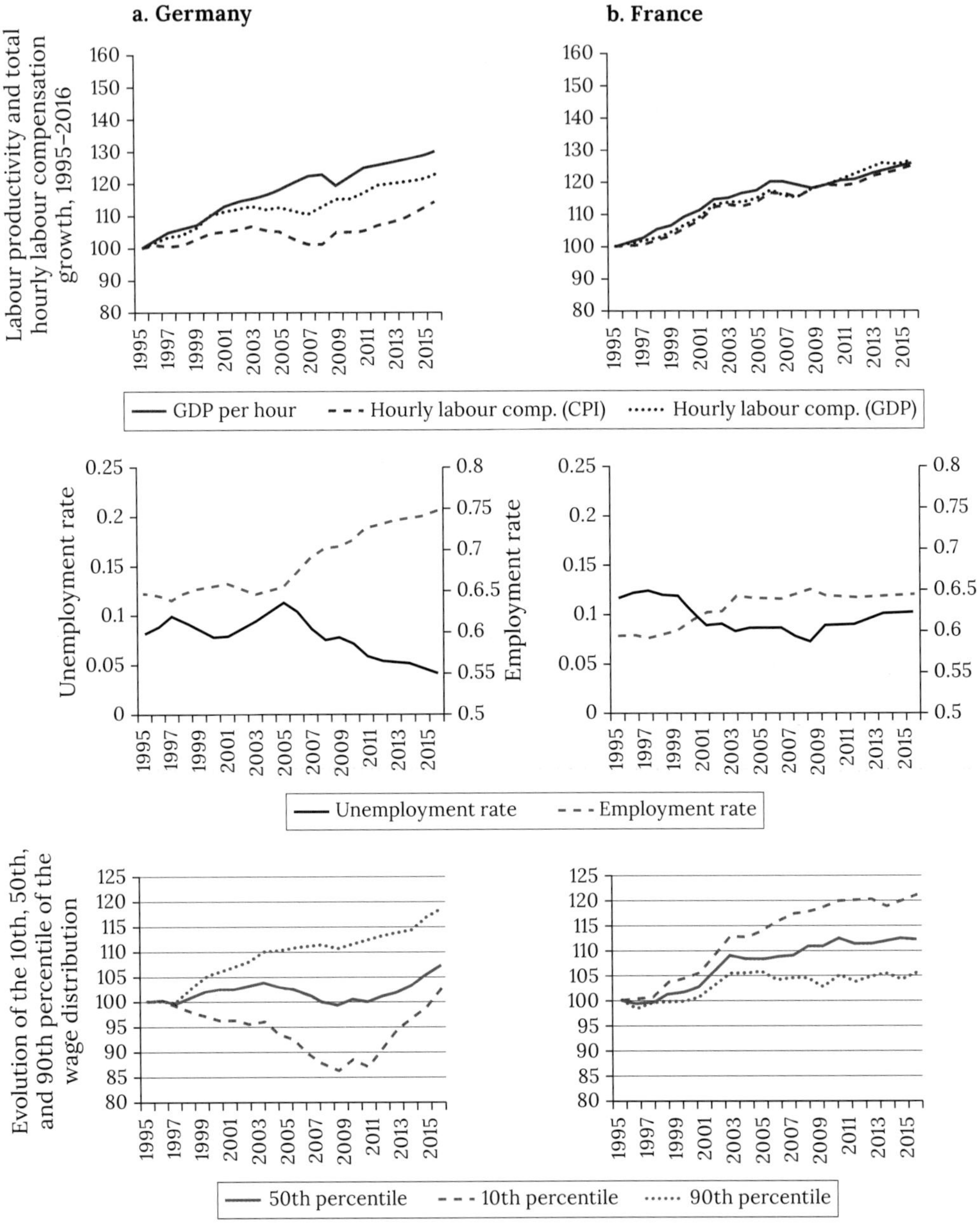

Figure 15.16 Productivity, employment, and inequality trends in Germany and France.

Source: Data provided directly by Kugler et al. (2018).

In this section, we provide examples of unemployment persistence stemming from mechanisms that work through the WS or PS curve:

1. The insider-outsider effect, where wages are set to benefit those in work, i.e. the insiders (WS effect);[18] and
2. The long-term/short-term unemployment effect, where the long-term unemployed (the outsiders) lose touch with the labour market and cease to influence wage setting (WS effect);
3. The investment coordination-productivity effect, where a level of aggregate demand above a threshold raises the confidence of firms sufficiently to produce a high level of investment and an associated rise in productivity (due to new technology embodied in new machinery, equipment and structures) (PS effect).

15.5.1 **The insider-outsider model (*WS* curve)**

We assume the economy is initially at equilibrium employment, N_e in Figure 15.17 and that there is a fall in aggregate demand that reduces employment to N_1. Our usual assumption is that the falling inflation at N_1 leads the central bank to cut the interest rate and boost aggregate demand so that the economy returns to $N = N_e$. If, however, the central bank is inactive, or the economy is at the zero lower bound (ZLB) after a balance sheet recession (see Chapter 8), and if the impact of falling inflation on aggregate demand is weak, then the economy may remain for some time at N_1.

Two groups of workers may then be identified: (1) the unemployed outsiders; and (2) the insiders who remain employed at N_1.

The insiders are in a strong bargaining position because, for example, their firm-specific skills mean that the firm cannot simply sack them and replace them with new workers. Insiders are presumed to be interested in maintaining their own employment and increasing their real wage; they attach no importance to the creation of employment for those currently unemployed.[19]

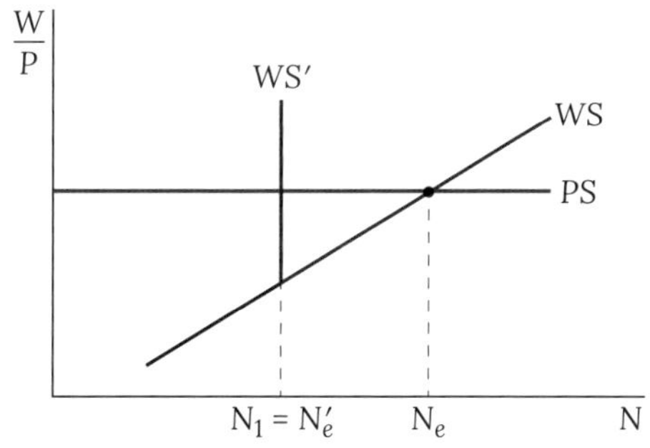

Figure 15.17 Hysteresis: the insider-outsider model.

[18] The original articles on the insider-outsider effect were: Lindbeck and Snower (1986) and Blanchard and Summers (1986).

[19] Note that implicitly in our usual discussions of wage setting, the utility function of workers (and unions) is based on a representative (or average) worker's preferences before they know whether they are employed or unemployed.

The consequence is that the WS curve becomes vertical at N_1 as shown in Figure 15.17. Any increase in aggregate demand will simply be reflected in a rise in the real wage until the $w^{WS} = w^{PS}$, after which, higher aggregate demand will produce rising inflation: equilibrium employment has fallen to $N_1 = N_e'$. This is a model of pure hysteresis in the sense that once unemployment has risen and insiders have emerged with wage-setting power, equilibrium unemployment goes up and remains at the new level. Although the rise in equilibrium unemployment originated with a fall in aggregate demand (that was not offset), only a supply-side change, which alters wage-setting arrangements can reduce equilibrium unemployment.[20]

15.5.2 **Long-term unemployment and unemployment persistence model (*WS* curve)**

As an example of the interaction between aggregate demand and equilibrium unemployment, we look at the phenomenon of long-term unemployment in the labour market.[21] The long-term unemployed are viewed as having in effect withdrawn from participation in the labour market because of a progressive loss of skills and erosion of psychological attachment to working life. They are therefore only poor substitutes for those in work and exert little competitive pressure in the labour market. The higher is the proportion of the long-term unemployed in the overall pool of unemployment, the less impact will any given level of unemployment have on wage setting.

If this is the case, then since a long period of high unemployment is likely to eventually push up the proportion of the long-term unemployed, equilibrium unemployment will rise. In the WS–PS diagram, the WS curve shifts upwards. This in turn weakens the self-equilibrating process through which high unemployment dampens wage inflation. The objective of reducing the scarring effects of unemployment lies behind 'welfare-to-work' programmes. The aim of such programmes is to reconnect unemployed workers with the labour market by using combinations of sticks (e.g. loss of benefits if active search is not undertaken) and carrots (e.g. grants for travel to job interviews, training for interviews).

To explain how the emergence of long-term unemployment can lead to a prolonged period of high unemployment, we take as an example the case of an economy initially in equilibrium with constant inflation at point A in Figure 15.18. Let us assume that inflation is stable but high at point A and a newly elected government wishes to reduce inflation to π_L or adopts a policy of austerity aimed at reducing the level of government debt.

This leads it to reduce aggregate demand to N_1 and to keep activity low until inflation has been reduced to π_L. However, with high unemployment at N_1, the share of long-term unemployment begins to rise: it rises to LTU_H, at which point it stabilizes. With a large pool of long-term unemployed, the WS curve shifts upward as explained above: this is WS(LTU_H). As is clear from the diagram, disinflation is slowed down by

[20] The microeconomic working of the model is set out in more detail in Chapter 15 of Carlin and Soskice (2006).

[21] See Layard and Nickell (1986).

- Begin at A. Government cuts N to N_1 in order to reduce inflation.
- At B, *LTU* rises to LTU_H (equilibrium *LTU* associated with N_1); WS shifts up (B to C) and disinflation is weaker.
- New equilibrium employment at D.
- At D, *LTU* begins to fall to LTU_M (equilibrium *LTU* associated with N_2) and WS shifts down.
- Initial equilibrium at A is attainable as *LTU* is reduced.

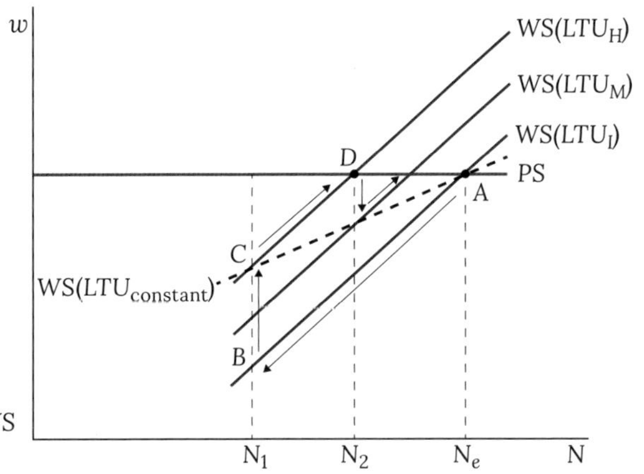

Figure 15.18 Hysteresis: the long-term unemployment model.

the upward shift of the WS curve. If we assume that inflation is brought down to π_L then the government will want to move the economy back to N_e. However, because of the presence of higher share of long-term unemployed, equilbrium unemployment is now at N_2. But unlike the insider-outsider model, in this case, the economy will eventually return to equilibrium at A. The reason is that at point D, the share of long-term unemployed will begin to decline since unemployment is lower than at N_1 and the WS(*LTU*) curve will shift down.

Gradually, as employment recovers, the share of long-term unemployed will shrink and the economy will return to A. If the 'scarring' effect of long-term unemployment is very serious, specific policies targeted at reintegrating the long-term unemployed back into jobs may be necessary in order for the equilibrium at A to be attained. Once back at A, the government will have achieved its objective of reducing inflation but the process will be protracted if workers become disconnected from the labour force during the phase of high unemployment. The flatter WS curve (dashed) in the diagram shows the wage-setting curve when the long-term unemployment share is unchanging. It is the intersection of the dashed WS curve and the PS curve that fixes the 'long-run' equilibrium rate of unemployment: the shifting WS curve slows down the return to A and the economy will be observed at 'medium-run' constant inflation equilibria such as at point D.

15.5.3 **Investment coordination-productivity model (*PS* curve)**

A hysteresis mechanism that operates through the PS curve can be illustrated using Figure 15.19. The model assumes that investment is a coordination game in which the economy can get stuck at a low investment equilibrium if each firm believes that other firms will keep investment low. High investment by other firms will provide the firm with confidence that the market for its products will be buoyant; low investment by

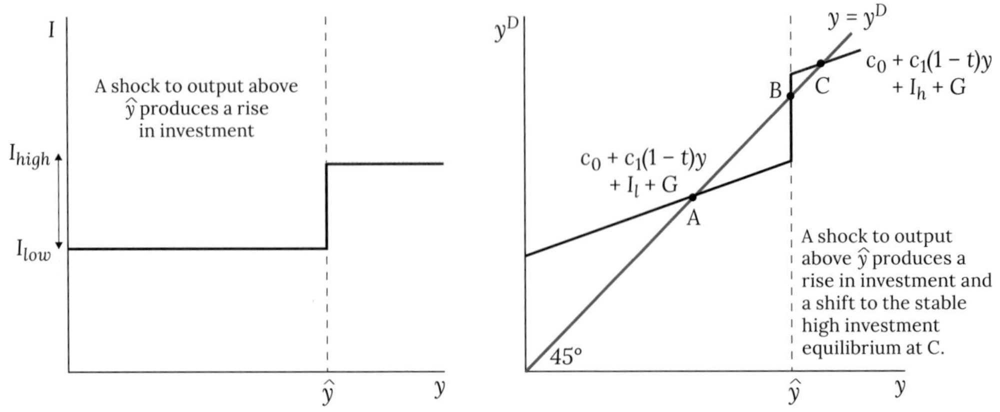

Figure 15.19 Hysteresis: the investment coordination model.

other firms will sap that confidence and the firm will invest little itself. If all firms reason the same way, two stable equilibria exist.

The left panel of Figure 15.19 shows the two investment levels, 'high' and 'low'. If output in the economy is higher than $\hat{y}$, which we call the threshold, firms coordinate on the high investment equilibrium; otherwise, investment is low. The right-hand panel uses the Keynesian cross (45-degree) diagram to illustrate the two stable equilibria at low and high investment. The AD curve is piece-wise linear: small temporary shocks around the low investment equilibrium result in convergence back to point A in the usual way via the multiplier process. A large temporary shock that shifts output above the threshold will lead the economy to converge to the new, high investment equilibrium at C.

If we introduce the assumption that new higher productivity technology is incorporated in investment, then productivity at point C will be higher than at point A. This will shift the PS curve upwards, leading to a new medium-run equilibrium at lower unemployment. If the economy is persistently in the low equilibrium state at point A, its productivity is lower and medium-run unemployment, higher.

This channel through which hysteresis can operate underscores the costs of prolonged recession and highlights the importance of the central bank or government's role in keeping the level of aggregate demand in the economy appropriately high.

Hysteresis: Empirical studies

In a series of papers, Lawrence Ball (1999, 2009, 2014) tests for evidence that macroeconomic policy choices by governments and central banks influence unemployment by virtue of their effect on actual unemployment. His first claim in his 1999 paper is that some countries pursued excessively tight macroeconomic policies in the early 1980s, which led to prolonged recessions and produced more long-term unemployment. As we have seen in the previous subsection, if the long-term unemployed are ineffective in dampening wage pressure, equilibrium unemployment is pushed up. 'Over-tight' policies became a self-fulfilling prophecy because the upward shift in the WS curve then requires tighter macro policy to stabilize inflation.

His second claim is that countries where unemployment fell substantially in the 1990s were those that undertook expansionary macro policies, i.e. hysteresis operated in reverse with strong aggregate demand reducing unemployment, which in turn brought down equilibrium unemployment.

The third claim is that the 'great recession' following the financial crisis produced substantial hysteresis effects. He shows that the cumulated output loss varied greatly across countries from close to zero for Switzerland and Australia to between 30% and

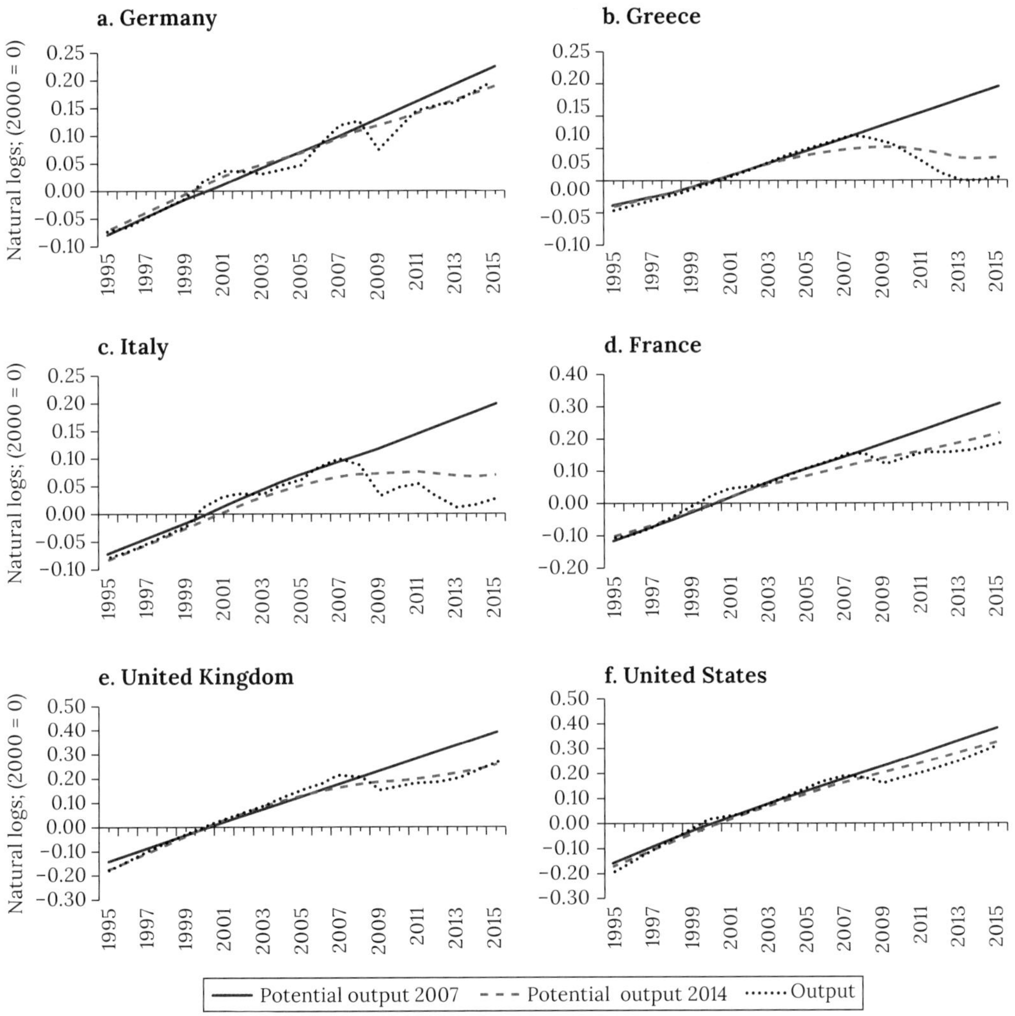

Figure 15.20 Long-term hysteresis effects in six countries.

Source: This replicates six panels of Figure 2 from Ball (2014). Data on potential output from the 2007 and 2015 *OECD Economic Outlook* was used to measure actual output. The charts use the log of potential output, normalizing the year 2000 to 0. The 2007 projections were extended beyond 2009 by using average growth of log potential output in previous years, as in Ball (2014).

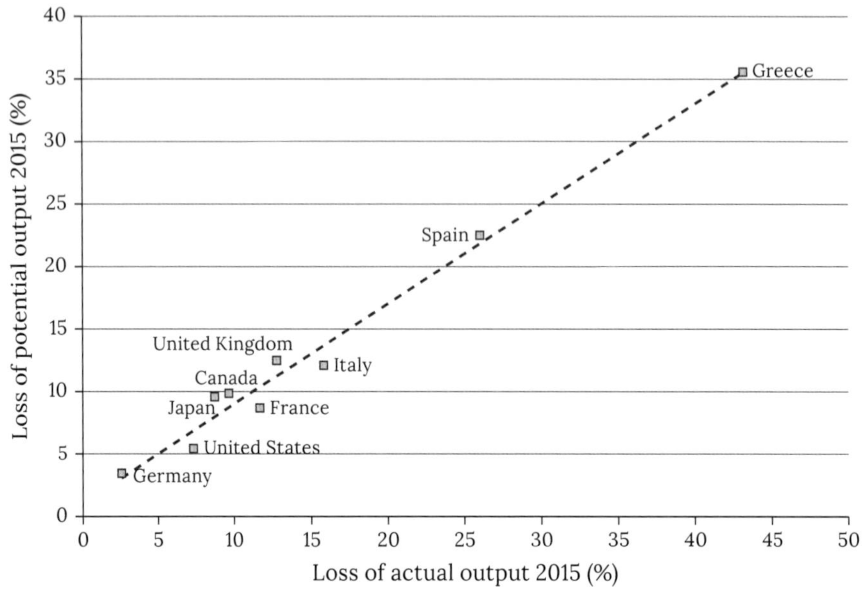

Figure 15.21 Long-term hysteresis effects in six countries.

Source: This replicates Figure 4 from Ball (2014) for eight countries. Data sources are the same as in Figure 15.20.

35% of GDP (Greece, Hungary, Ireland) when the level in 2015 is compared with the level for that year based on the forecast growth rate of output between 2001–09 (see Figure 15.20) for other examples. The effect of this for the high-income countries as a whole, and given their significance for global trade for the world as a whole, was considerable. Weighted by country size, the cumulated loss was 8.4% of potential GDP.

Hysteresis or scarring mechanisms are explored in a quantitative economic model by Heathcote et al. (2020) in a paper with the evocative title 'Does the cycle cause the trend?' Their focus is on the way that scarring effects are concentrated on specific groups in the economy with consequences for inequality—and, via inequality, for the persistence of the recession. They use data for the US on business cycles from the late 1970s onwards and show that if a recession hits the economy, the following hysteresis and inequality effects arise:

- Low-skilled workers are more likely to experience unemployment.
- They lose skills while unemployed because the 'learning by doing' on the job is undone; the skill premium in wages for skilled v. unskilled workers rises.

The combined effect of spells of unemployment, the cost of job search, lower job finding probabilities, declining skills and the fall in relative wages is to produce withdrawal from the labour force on an increased scale. The non-participation decision becomes optimal for the worker. Interpreted using the WS-PS model, the effect for the economy as a whole is an upward shift in the WS curve, raising equilibrium unemployment.

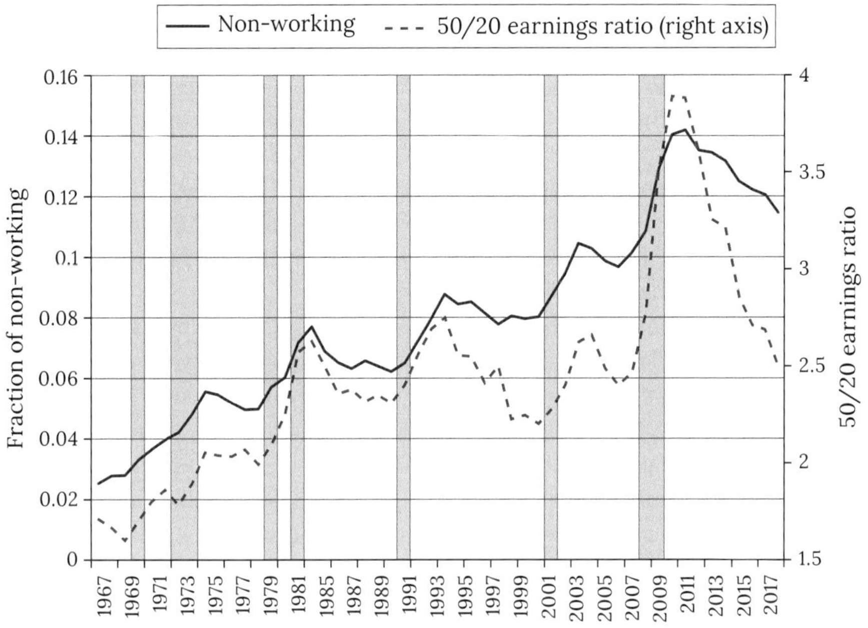

Figure 15.22 Fraction of non-working households and earnings inequality at the bottom.

Source: Figure 4, reprinted from Heathcote, J., Perri, F., and Violante, G. L. (2020). The rise of US earnings inequality: Does the cycle drive the trend? *Review of Economic Dynamics*, **37**(1), S181–S204. https://doi.org/10.1016/j.red.2020.06.002. With permission from Elsevier.

Figure 15.22 shows the upward ratcheting of the fraction of those not participating in the labour market with each successive recession and the associated upward ratchet in the inequality of earnings at the bottom of the distribution. The long recoveries in the 1990s and after the financial crisis in which unemployment fell to low rates reduced the wage gap but did not take non-participation back to its pre-recession level.

15.6 **CONCLUSIONS**

This chapter builds on the foundations set out in Chapter 2 to provide a more detailed picture of the supply side of the economy. The models presented provide hypotheses for exploring the cross-country differences and time trends in unemployment in the high-income countries over the past five decades:

- **Benchmark WS-PS model:** Any wage-push factors ($\mathbf{z_w}$) that shift the WS curve can influence the equilibrium level of unemployment, such as the bargaining power of unions or the generosity or duration of unemployment benefits. Any price-push factors ($\mathbf{z_p}$) that shift the PS curve can influence both the equilibrium level of unemployment and the real wage, such as productivity, the tax wedge and the level of product market competition. Empirical evidence on the evolution of markups was presented in Chapter 2.

- **The combined search and matching and labour discipline model of wage-setting:** The model tells us that the larger is the employer's desired firm size, the higher is the wage that has to be offered to attract each additional worker. A higher unemployment benefit and any alteration in the job seeker's circumstances that increases their net utility of unemployment will raise the reservation wage, shifting the curve up. To deter shirking, the employer must pay a wage above the reservation wage to cover the cost of effort and to provide the employee with an employment rent, which will be lost if the worker is fired. By varying the unemployment rate in the economy, the aggregate WS curve can be derived.

  The employer has monopsony power because given their location and other characteristics, job seekers face a limited number of potential employers. This provides an incentive for the firm to restrict employment and lower the wage to maximize profits. Empirical evidence supports the existence of markdowns, reducing the wage below the revenue produced by the marginal worker hired. In this model, supported by empirical evidence, a minimum wage may increase earnings and employment as the employer's incentive to restrict hiring is eliminated.
- **Beveridge curve model:** An important aspect of the labour market is how well it matches individuals who are out of work with unfilled vacancies. A simple matching function produces a negative relationship between the vacancy rate and the unemployment rate in the economy. The curve is shifted by factors that influence *matching efficiency*, such as barriers to occupational and geographic mobility including home ownership, and the disruption to the functioning of the labour market caused by the pandemic.
- **Calmfors–Driffill–Soskice model:** This famous modelling approach provides richer insights into the impact of different forms of union wage setting on equilibrium unemployment. It sheds light on the observed differences in institutions and labour market outcomes in some key OECD countries (see Table 15.1). A particularly interesting comparison comes from looking at labour market trends in Germany and France since the mid-1990s.

- **Hysteresis models:** The central insight of these models is that changes in aggregate demand that lead to persistently high unemployment can influence equilibrium unemployment. This is different from the benchmark WS-PS model where only supply-side factors matter. Three models of hysteresis are presented; insider-outsider, long-term unemployment, and the investment coordination-productivity model. In the first, insiders (i.e. those in employment) set wages to benefit only themselves and force up equilibrium unemployment. In the second, the long-term unemployed become detached from the labour market, their skills atrophy and they cease to influence wage-setting, which also pushes up equilibrium unemployment. The last model illustrates the role played by firms' coordination in their investment decisions; if each firm believes that other firms will coordinate on a 'low' ('high') level of investment, then expectations become self-fulfilling and the economy is stuck at a low (high) equilibrium output.

QUESTIONS AND PROBLEMS FOR CHAPTER 15

CHECKLIST QUESTIONS

1. In the WS–PS model, use diagrams to show what happens following:
   a. A rise in the tax wedge
   b. A reduction in union bargaining power
   c. A tightening in the enforcement of competition policy

   In each case, briefly explain the implications for the real wage and the equilibrium level of employment.

2. Give two explanations for why the hiring curve in Figure 15.4 is upward-sloping. Use examples from labour markets with which you are familiar.

3. Redraw Figure 15.7 to include the reservation wage curve and show the markdown, cost of effort and the employment rent. Explain your reasoning.

4. Why is unemployment referred to as a 'worker discipline device' in the Shapiro-Stiglitz efficiency wage model? Refer back to Chapter 2 and find out what fulfils this role in Akerlof's model of efficiency wages.

5. Use the equations for the reservation wage and the no-shirking wage to explain the effect of the following on the wage the employer sets, and also on equilibrium unemployment.
   a. A reduction in unemployment benefits
   b. Flexible working, including working from home
   c. A new camera system is installed that improves monitoring

6. Use the matching functions and the Beveridge curve shown in Section 15.3 to explain the assertion in Elsby et al. (2010) that the fall in the exit rate from unemployment contributed to the build-up of long-term unemployment in the US during the global financial crisis.

7. Use the Calmfors-Driffill model tó determine whether the following statements are true, false or uncertain. Briefly explain your answer.
   a. Industry-level unions face more inelastic product demand than firm-level unions
   b. Industry-level unions take into account their effect on the economy-wide price level when negotiating wages
   c. Centralized wage setting secures the lowest level of unemployment because centralized unions have the most bargaining power
   d. The hump-shaped (inverse U) relationship between centralization of wage setting and unemployment would be more pronounced in an open economy than in a closed one

8. Explain what is meant by coordinated wage setting and use the Beveridge curve and WS-PS model to assess the impact of the breakdown of coordination on an economy's vacancy and unemployment rates.

9. Discuss three reasons why the Spanish and German unemployment trends were so different in the aftermath of the global financial crisis. Could the Spanish government have done anything different to mitigate the rise in unemployment?

10. How can the insider-outsider model explain persistently high levels of unemployment? Can this form of hysteresis be prevented by increasing aggregate demand?

11. Use the long-term unemployment model to explain how the OECD economies could have seen a rise in *equilibrium* unemployment as a consequence of the global financial crisis.

PROBLEMS

1. Use the matching functions, Beveridge curve and WS–PS model from Section 15.3 to discuss how the following events and policies could affect the labour market:
   a. An extension of unemployment benefit duration during a downturn
   b. Increasing expenditure on active labour market policies
   c. A cap on skilled immigration
   d. Joining a single currency (e.g. the Eurozone)
   e. A policy to encourage home ownership
   f. A pandemic

2. Take the position of either Agell or Heckman and defend your position and what it implies for labour market reform in Europe following the global financial and Eurozone crises.
   - 'Labour market reforms failing to distinguish between good and bad rigidities will do more harm than good.' Jonas Agell (2003) CESifo Forum
   - 'A substantial portion of European unemployment is a symptom of the deeper problem that incentives to innovate, to acquire skills, and to take risks have been thwarted by the welfare state and regulation.' James Heckman (2003) CESifo Forum

3. Use Figure 15.1 to pick two economies with contrasting unemployment trajectories between the mid-80s and the global financial crisis. Following that, download data from the OECD on the harmonized rate of unemployment for your two countries between 1985 and 2007. Use the OECD data on labour market institutions referred to in Table 15.1 to discuss whether the different paths of unemployment in these two countries are consistent with the changes in labour market institutions. What other factors might

have influenced the employment outcomes in the two countries over this period?

4. Concisely contrast Sweden's Covid-19 public health strategy with that of another Nordic economy. Find the data to construct Beveridge curves for both economies. What insights are provided by the modelling in Section 15.3 for the labour market outcomes during and post-Covid? (To gain an understanding of the spread of a virus and its economic consequences, use CORE Econ's interactive visualization tool: https://www.core-econ.org/covid-simulation/.)

5. How do (a) monopsony and (b) monopoly power of employers, and (c) union power of employees affect inequality? For each, first explain the mechanisms linking the type of power to inequality. Then comment on the predictions for inequality in each case in the WS-PS model (using the Lorenz curve model from Chapter 2). Illustrate each case with an example from a country of your choice.

6. Choose a model in this chapter as the organizing framework for investigating the likely effects on labour market outcomes of a 4-day week in which a firm pays employees their 5-day salary for 4 days work. Pilots began in 2022 (see https://www.4dayweek.com).

INTERESTED IN EXPLORING THESE TOPICS FURTHER?

Visit www.oup.com/he/carlin-soskice to consolidate and extend your learning with the multiple-choice questions and Animated Analytical Diagrams accompanying this chapter.

CHAPTER

16

GROWTH AND INNOVATION

16.1 INTRODUCTION

In this chapter, we bring together the short- and medium-run modelling of the macroeconomy developed in the earlier parts of the book with the analysis of long-run growth. The aim is to understand how the more or less continuous process of rising living standards experienced in some parts of the world for more than 200 years depends on the process of accumulation of physical and human capital and technological progress.

As we shall see, continuously rising living standards have not always been characteristic of human societies and they have been experienced very unevenly across the countries of the world. In most, but not in all cases where it has been observed, we see a subtle mixture of competitive pressure and some protection for innovators that allows them to reap rewards of their costly investment in new products or processes. Planned economies represent an exception, where private rewards for innovation are absent.

16.1.1 Capitalism transforms the world

Figure 16.1 plots estimates of global GDP per capita since the year 1000 for five countries in different regions of the world. Taking such a long-run view brings into focus the extraordinary character of economic development in the last 250 years. The figure is shaped like an ice hockey stick. Average living standards in these different parts of the world were fairly stagnant for a very long sweep of human history. The UK, where the Industrial Revolution began around 1750, was the first place where a long period of sustained and rapid growth of living standards occurred. Other countries followed at different times.

With growth of more than 2% per annum, living standards were doubling every generation in the countries where capitalism was firmly established. The result of this uneven development was that entire countries fell behind, and the world came to be made up of the rich nations and poor ones. Figure 16.1 reveals a rapidly widening gap between the UK and China until late in the twentieth century.

The world economy has not always seen vast differences in living standards across countries. Research results in Figure 16.2 show estimates of GDP per capita for England, Italy (the centre and north of the country), Japan, China and India for the period from the year 1000 until 1850. The data are in real terms and are comparable across countries. The research shows that from the middle of the seventeenth century,

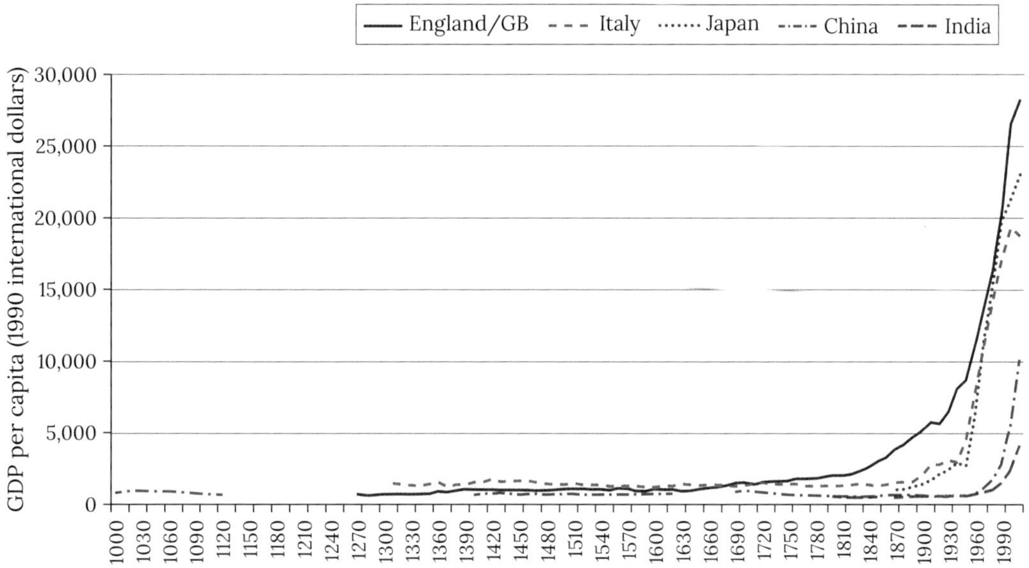

Figure 16.1 GDP per capita (1990 international dollars): 1000–2010.

Source: Broadberry (2022).

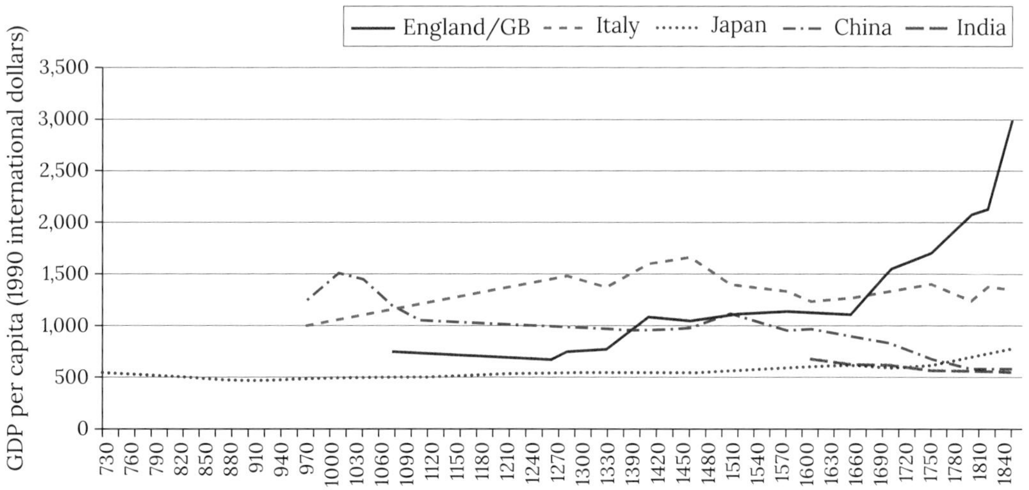

Figure 16.2 GDP per capita (1990 international dollars): 730–1850.

Note: All series have been linearly interpolated to create annual series.

Source: Broadberry et al. (2015).

England and the Low Countries (not shown in the figure) diverged from the Asian countries. Japan, China and India had living standards between 60 and 70% of those of England in 1600, but by 1850, they were between 20 and 30% as high. Strikingly, in this period, North West Europe pulled away from Southern Europe. In 1600, living standards in the north and centre of Italy were comparable with those in England, but by 1850, the average Italian was only half as well off as the average English person.

The interconnection of great changes in technology with the emergence of capitalism as the dominant economic system in Europe in the nineteenth century marked the beginning of the transformation of the way of life of humans across the globe.

Capitalism is an economic system in which the capital stock is privately owned and where employers hire workers to produce goods and services with the aim of making a profit. Figure 16.1 vividly captures the uniquely productive character of this economic system. The hallmark of capitalism is that individuals who are wealthy or are creditworthy and are therefore able to borrow can take big risks in introducing new products and organizational methods. The combination of individuals reaping the rewards of successful risk-taking in large-scale ventures but—within limits—bearing the costs of failure distinguishes capitalism from other economic systems; as summarized by Bowles (2006):[1]

> For the first time in history, competition among members of the economic elite depended on one's success in introducing unprecedented ways of organizing production and sales, new technologies, and novel products.

A large-scale experiment with a different economic system—that of the planned economy—was implemented by communist regimes in the Soviet Union and Eastern Europe, China and in a number of other countries. The Soviet Union introduced its first five-year plan in 1928. A second wave of countries operated planned economies from the late 1940s. Under central planning, production takes place in state-owned enterprises, and resources are allocated to different sectors according to the decisions of planning bureaucrats. There is no incentive for people to take the risk of introducing new products, services or methods of production since they would not reap the rewards if the venture was successful. The potential for large gains from innovation in a capitalist economy was absent in a planned economy. There was also no penalty for failure. Enterprises operated with what has been described by the Hungarian economist Janos Kornai as *soft budget constraints*, which means that running at a loss did not lead an enterprise to cease operation.

Figure 16.3 shows the evolution of living standards across a selection of emerging and developing economies between 1928 and 2010. The former USSR (i.e. the Soviet Union) could not match the growth in living standards observed in capitalist South Korea in the post-WWII period. Planning was abandoned in Eastern Europe and the Soviet Union in the early 1990s, and a major factor in its collapse was the failure of the planning system to deliver parity in living standards with peer market economies. Figure 16.3 also shows that the collapse of planning and the embrace of the market in the former Soviet bloc was followed by a lengthy transitional recession. Living standards fell, and in many countries it was over a decade before they were restored to their pre-transition levels. This experience was a surprise to many observers and highlighted the need to understand the pre-conditions for the successful operation of a market economic system. As we shall see later in this chapter, rapidly rising living standards and a process of catching up to the world technology frontier has

[1] This excerpt is taken from p. 335 of Bowles (2006).

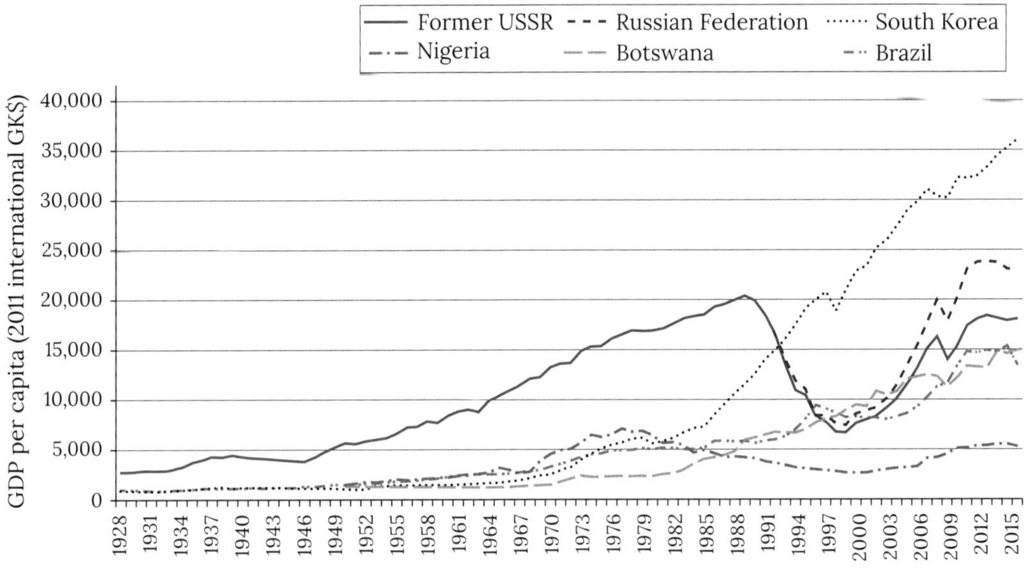

Figure 16.3 GDP per capita (2011 international Geary-Khamis dollars): 1928–2016.

Note: Where data are missing, series have been linearly interpolated to create annual series.

Source: New Maddison Project Database (2018 version).

been the exception rather than the rule for most countries for most of the period since capitalism took root, first in north-west Europe and soon after in the countries where European migrants settled. Figure 16.3 provides examples of market economies in Africa and South America where growth in living standards across the twentieth century was weaker than in the planned Soviet Union.

Looking back at the experience of the planned economies in the former Soviet Union and Eastern Europe and comparing them with the rest of the countries in the world suggests that planning allowed poor countries to industrialize by introducing large-scale electrification and widespread education. For poor countries, the benefits of planning in these important dimensions of modernization appear to have outweighed its weakness in dampening market incentives. For countries that had already industrialized and introduced schooling for their populations before planning was introduced, the costs of planning in hampering innovation outweighed the benefits, and these economies lagged further and further behind the world technology frontier.[2] The weakness of the planned economies in innovation is highlighted by their absence from the top 100 innovations made in the world after the experiment with planning began.[3]

16.1.2 Fundamental and proximate sources of growth

The discussion of the successes and failures of the planned and the capitalist economic systems suggests that the *proximate* or immediate sources of the growth of living

[2] For more detail, see Carlin, Schaffer, and Seabright (2013).

[3] See Table 1 in Kornai (2013).

standards are first, the accumulation of capital—both physical and human—and second, the development and diffusion of new technology. Unlike previous economic systems, both planning and capitalist systems succeeded in mobilizing resources to raise the human and physical capital intensity of production required for industrialization. With more equipment, including infrastructure such as electrification, and with better skills, more output per worker could be produced. However, the capitalist system proved superior to planning in generating continuous technological progress in the form of new methods of production and new products that raised living standards.

The *fundamental* causes of growth are those that explain what lay behind the accumulation of capital and the development of technology that have transformed human lives. What explains why capitalism emerged in one part of the world—north-west Europe—and not elsewhere (for example, in the Yangzi Delta in China or in southern Europe) and what explains why some countries and regions have benefited from the accumulation of capital and dynamism capitalism offers and some have not?

Research by economic historians has attempted to shed light on troubling questions such as the roles of colonialism and slavery in accounting for the 'great divergence' of fortunes among regions of the world around the time of the British Industrial Revolution.[4] British colonization of India began with the commercial activities of the East India Company (rather than the government) and the mercenary armies they assembled at the beginning of the 17th century. The British state had full control by the middle of the 19th century and ruled until independence in 1947. India had supplied textiles to the world before the British Industrial Revolution but by 1870 its world-leading industry was in permanent decline (Parthasarathi 1998, and Broadberry and Gupta 2009).

A body of work is accumulating that pins down mechanisms that produced the decline in GDP per capita in India under British colonial rule. An important one (Banerjee and Iyer 2005) was the empowerment of local land-owning elites to collect taxes for the colonial power, initially through its 'agent', the East India Company. Moreover, research has found that the legacy of this anti-modernization policy can still be observed today in the lower economic development of the districts affected than in those that were not, underlining colonialism's persistent effects.

India was a source of tax revenue and markets for British textiles. To produce textiles in the mills of northern England, British factory owners relied on the import of the raw material, cotton, and of calories to feed the industrial workers. Cotton was produced by enslaved workers in North America and sugar came mainly from slave plantations in the British West Indies. Access to these inputs enabled Britain to specialize in textile manufacture with the attendant benefits of learning by doing and economies of scale.

Whether there was an alternative path to rapid growth that did not involve colonies, cotton, and calories—and enslaved people—is difficult to answer. Existing counterfactuals examined by economic historians suggest this is unlikely. For example, replacing the calories from sugar would have required 11–15% of Britain's arable land

---

[4] This section draws on work for the CORE Econ project for *The Economy* 2.0 (2023) by Samuel Bowles, Wendy Carlin, Tzvetan Moev, Suresh Naidu, and Kevin O'Rourke.

(Pomeranz 2000).[5] Higher food prices would have increased costs for British firms and slowed down expansion. Similar calculations suggest that a wool-based textile industry on the scale of cotton would have required more than Britain's crop and pasture land.

There is not scope in this book to investigate the fundamental causes of growth but research can be grouped into broad hypotheses on the role of geography (for example, location in tropical or temperate climate zones), culture (for example, protestant or catholic Christianity, or Islam) and institutions (such as property rights).[6]

In this chapter, we focus on the proximate causes: factor accumulation and technological progress. We begin, in Section 16.2, by showing the connection between short- and medium-run models of the business cycle and a very widely used model of economic growth based on factor accumulation; the Solow-Swan model. The model was independently developed by Robert Solow (in the USA) and Trevor Swan (in Australia) in 1956.[7] For brevity, we will refer to the Solow model from now on. It shows how, if we abstract from the fluctuations in aggregate demand that produce business cycles, the willingness of a society to save and invest more of annual output (and consume a smaller share) will lead it to adopt a more capital-intensive method of production with higher output per head. We show the connection between this result and the predictions of the models studied earlier in the book.

As well as describing the role of capital accumulation in growth in a single economy, the Solow model provides a set of predictions about the convergence of poor economies to the living standards of rich ones. We use data from the real world to weigh up the empirical support for these predictions. Technological progress is introduced in the Solow model in a purely mechanical way that is consistent with the growth in living standards observed in developed economies since the Industrial Revolution.

We show how growth accounting can be used as part of the description of the role of technological progress in long-run economic performance, and investigate how well the Solow model can explain the cross-country distribution of living standards observed in the world.

The Solow model with technological progress does not, however, address the structural role of innovation in the economic system. The centrality of innovation to the market economy relies on the pursuit of temporary profits by the entrepreneur who is the first mover bringing a new product or service to the market. The economist Joseph Schumpeter, who wrote in the first half of the twentieth century, explained that the creative role of the entrepreneur brought with it the destruction of methods

---

[5] See also the published 2019 lecture by economic historian Gavin Wright, available at Wright, G. (2020) 'Slavery and Anglo-American capitalism revisited', *The Economic History Review*, **73**, 353–383. https://doi.org/10.1111/ehr.12962

[6] See Acemoglu, Johnson and Robinson (2005), Acemoglu and Robinson (2012), North (1991) and Sokoloff and Engerman (2000).

[7] See Solow (1956) and Swan (1956). For a fascinating discussion of the sophistication of Swan's model, his associated work and why Swan has little name recognition, see Dimand and Spencer (2008).

and products rendered unprofitable by the innovation. The term 'creative destruction' is identified with this feature of a market economy.[8]

To pursue these ideas, we introduce endogenous technological progress and the way endogenous growth models work in Section 16.4, and in Section 16.5 we present insights from the Schumpeterian growth model developed by Aghion and Howitt. This model has proved a very rich source of insights about growth and inequality that can be tested using cross-country and industry data. Questions that are addressed include the role of competition in growth and whether macroeconomic stabilization policy is good for long-run growth.

In the appendix, we set out the basic concepts and tools that are essential for studying growth theory, such as calculating growth rates and using log and exponential functions.

16.2 EXOGENOUS GROWTH: THE SOLOW MODEL

As we shall see later in the chapter, the Solow model is limited in its ambition to uncover the dynamics of the growth and innovation process. Nevertheless, it has proved to be a reliable workhorse model of the role of capital accumulation in growth. Much more comprehensive expositions of the Solow model are set out in specialized growth textbooks, such as Weil (2012) and Jones and Vollrath (2013). Here we select the aspects of the model that are essential to understanding why the Solow model has played such a central role in empirical studies of growth.

16.2.1 The model

The production function

We begin with production in a one-good economy. The single good is something like corn or wheat, which can either be consumed or invested, i.e. used as a capital input, so as to produce more goods next period. Labour is also used in production, which takes place according to the *production function* $Y = AF(K, N)$, where the production function is smooth and where the marginal products of capital and labour are positive and diminishing. All variables are in real terms.

Additionally we shall assume that the production function exhibits *constant returns to scale* (CRS). This refers to the idea that duplicating production facilities doubles output. It allows us to define output and capital in *intensive form* (i.e. per worker) as $y = Y/N$ and $k = K/N$.

In practice economists often use a particular production function for the Solow model. It is the Cobb-Douglas production function given by

[8] Creative destruction and the role of the entrepreneur were central to Schumpeter's 1934 work; in his later writings (1942), he focused on coordination of research in large corporations.

$$Y = AK^{\alpha}N^{1-\alpha} \tag{16.1}$$

$$\frac{Y}{N} = A\frac{K^{\alpha}}{N}\frac{N}{N^{\alpha}} \tag{16.2}$$

$$y = Ak^{\alpha}, \qquad \text{(Intensive production function)}$$

where we divide through by N to get it in the intensive form shown in the final equation. A is referred to as total factor productivity, or *TFP*. The parameter α is between 0 and 1 and is capital's share of income. Labour's share is $(1-\alpha)$.

Writing the production function in intensive form highlights the meaning of *TFP*: it says that output per worker (that is, labour productivity) will depend on capital per worker, k, and *TFP*. *TFP* captures all the reasons apart from the amount of capital the worker has to work with that affect their productivity. This will include the technology in use, the efficiency with which technology and capital are used, and management quality.

The intensive form of the production function is shown in Figure 16.4. The function is concave, which reflects the assumption of diminishing returns to capital. As production becomes more capital intensive (i.e. a movement to the right along the x-axis), output per capita increases, but by a smaller amount with each additional increase in capital intensity. The figure also shows how the average product of capital (APK) and the marginal product of capital (MPK) are calculated. At any point on the production function, the APK is simply calculated as $y/k = (Y/N)(N/K) = Y/K$, and the MPK is derived as the slope of the tangent to the production function at a given level of capital per worker. When using a Cobb-Douglas production function of Ak^{α}:

$$\text{MPK} = \frac{d[Ak^{\alpha}]}{dk} = A\alpha k^{\alpha-1}. \tag{16.3}$$

It is plain to see from Figure 16.4 that APK > MPK for any point on the production function. This is always the case when the production function exhibits diminishing returns.

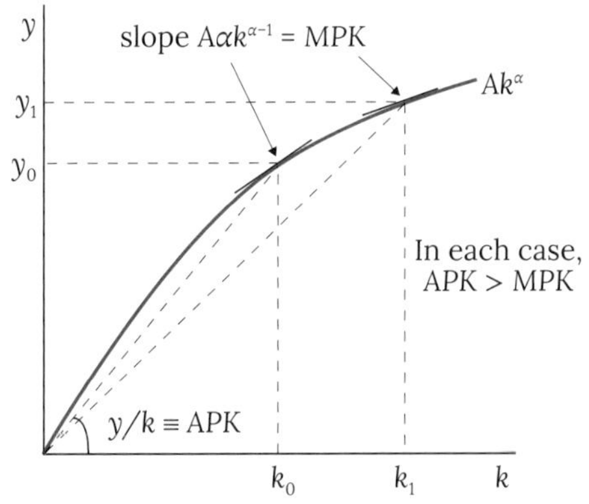

Figure 16.4 The production function.

Growth as capital accumulation

How does the labour input grow?

We shall assume that the labour force grows at a constant rate n. If we work in continuous time, it is natural to define this growth rate as:

$$n = \frac{\dot{N}}{N} = \frac{dN/dt}{N}, \qquad \text{(growth rate of labour)}$$

which implies that the labour force grows exponentially and for any initial level N_0, at some time, t, in the future the level of the labour force is $N_t = N_0 \exp(nt)$. Throughout the chapter we will make use of the dot notation to denote rate of changes (i.e. $\dot{x} = dx/dt$ for any macroeconomic variable x). Section 16.7.1 in the Appendix contains details on this and other tools and terms used when presenting growth models.

How does the capital input grow?

To see how the capital stock changes, i.e. dK/dt (or $\dot{K}$), we need to deduct depreciation from gross investment, i.e.

$$\dot{K} = I - \delta K, \qquad \text{(change in capital stock)}$$

where I is gross investment and δ is the rate at which capital depreciates.

We assume that we are dealing with a closed economy, which means that no borrowing from abroad is possible and hence, assuming there is no government sector, savings are equal to investment. In addition, the economy has a constant exogenously given savings rate s out of current income Y. Together, these imply that

$$I = sY.$$

Next, we incorporate the condition that savings is equal to investment and substitute in the production function to get:

$$\dot{K} = I - \delta K = sY - \delta K = sAK^{\alpha}N^{1-\alpha} - \delta K. \qquad (16.4)$$

By dividing through by K, we have

$$g_K = \frac{\dot{K}}{K} = s\frac{Y}{K} - \delta = s \cdot \text{APK} - \delta, \qquad \text{(growth rate of capital stock)}$$

which says that the growth of the capital stock depends on the average product of capital, APK, and is therefore a declining function of the capital–labour ratio (k) (see Figure 16.5). In the Cobb-Douglas case, $g_K = s \cdot Ak^{\alpha-1} - \delta$.

16.2.2 Steady state growth and levels of GDP per capita

Steady state or balanced growth is defined by a situation in which output and capital grow at the same rate, i.e. the capital to output ratio is constant. In the model without technological progress, capital and output grow at the rate given by the rate of population growth:

$$g_Y = g_K = n. \qquad \text{(Steady state growth)}$$

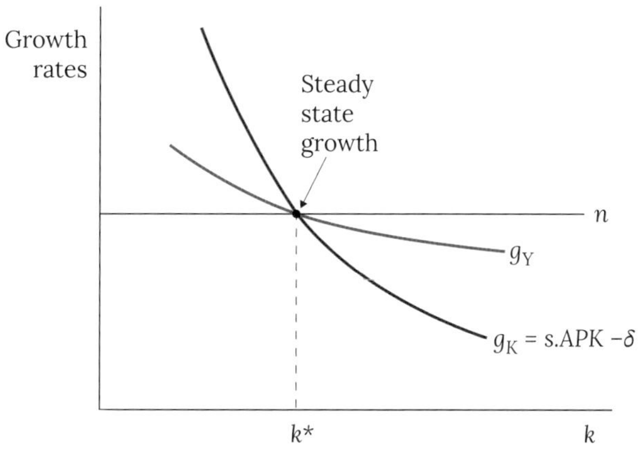

Figure 16.5 Steady state growth rates in the Solow model: g_Y is a weighted average of g_K and n. Visit www.oup.com/he/carlin-soskice to explore steady state growth rates in the Solow model with Animated Analytical Diagram 16.5.

In steady state growth, since output and labour are growing at the same rate, the capital–labour ratio will be constant. The concept of steady state growth is a specific type of equilibrium in which the growth rate is constant.[9] This is called the steady state capital–labour ratio k^*. The capital–output ratio is often called v and the steady state value of v is v^*. From the equation for the growth rate of the capital stock, steady state growth requires

$$g_K = s\frac{Y}{K} - \delta = n$$

which implies:

$$v^* = \left(\frac{K}{Y}\right)^* = \left(\frac{k}{y}\right)^* = \frac{s}{n+\delta}. \qquad \text{(Harrod-Domar formula)}$$

The Harrod-Domar formula is useful because it provides an explicit expression for the steady-state capital–output ratio in terms of the exogenous variables s, n and δ, which does not depend on the particular form of the production function. We can summarize the results of the Solow growth model so far:

1. In steady state growth, output and capital grow at the same rate as the exogenously given growth rate of the labour force. There is no growth in output per capita in the steady state.
2. The capital–output ratio in the steady state is higher, the higher is the savings rate and the lower are the labour force growth rate and depreciation.

---

[9] An equilibrium is defined as a model outcome that is self-perpetuating. In this case, something of interest does not change unless an outside or external force is introduced that alters the model's description of the situation.

In Figure 16.5, we show steady state growth in a diagram with the capital labour ratio on the horizontal axis and growth rates on the vertical axis. The horizontal line shows the growth rate of labour, n. There is a downward-sloping line showing the growth rate of capital, labelled $g_K = sAPK - \delta$. This is downward sloping because as we have already seen, the APK is a decreasing function of the capital–labour ratio. The line showing the growth rate of output labelled g_Y lies between the growth rate of capital and of labour.[10] This is intuitively clear: output will grow at the rate of a weighted average of the growth rates of the two inputs, capital and labour. In steady state growth, all three curves intersect since $n = g_K$.

The diagram showing steady state growth rates (as in Figure 16.5) is very useful for analysing the *growth of output*, whereas the standard Solow diagram, which we shall derive next and is shown in Figure 16.6, is useful for analysing the *growth of output per capita*.

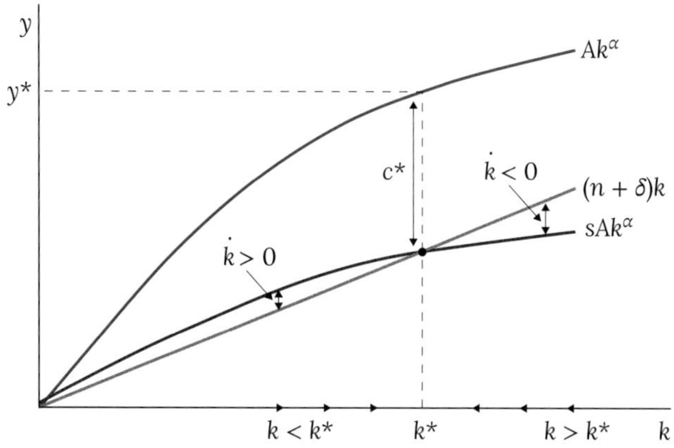

Figure 16.6 The dynamics of capital and output in the Solow model. Visit www.oup.com/he/carlin-soskice to explore the dynamics of capital and output in the Solow model with Animated Analytical Diagram 16.6.

---

[10] To derive g_Y we start with the Cobb-Douglas production function, $Y = K^{\alpha}N^{1-\alpha}$ (assuming A is one for simplicity). We then take logs and differentiate it to get:

$$\frac{d\log Y}{dt} = \alpha\frac{d\log K}{dt} + (1-\alpha)\frac{d\log N}{dt}$$
$$\frac{d\log Y}{dY}\frac{dY}{dt} = \alpha\frac{d\log K}{dK}\frac{dK}{dt} + (1-\alpha)\frac{d\log N}{dN}\frac{dN}{dt}$$
$$\frac{\dot{Y}}{Y} = \alpha\frac{\dot{K}}{K} + (1-\alpha)\frac{\dot{N}}{N}$$
$$g_Y = \alpha g_K + (1-\alpha)n.$$

Hence, the growth rate of output is a weighted average of the growth rate of the capital stock and population growth. A similar derivation works for a general production function with constant returns to scale; see Chapter 13 in Carlin and Soskice (2006) for details.

There is a second way of characterizing the steady state growth path, in which we use the intensive form of the production function. From above, we have

$$\dot{K} = sAK^{\alpha}N^{1-\alpha} - \delta K \text{ and, dividing through by K and rearranging} \quad (16.5)$$

$$\frac{\dot{K}}{K} = sAk^{\alpha-1} - \delta. \quad (16.6)$$

Since

$$\frac{\dot{k}}{k} = \frac{\dot{K}}{K} - n,$$

we subtract n from equation 16.6 to get the equation for the growth rate of the capital–labour ratio

$$\frac{\dot{k}}{k} = sAk^{\alpha-1} - (n+\delta)$$

and multiplying both sides by k, we obtain the *Fundamental Solow Equation of Motion*, which describes how capital per worker varies over time:

$$\dot{k} = sAk^{\alpha} - (n+\delta)k. \quad (16.7)$$

It is worth exploring in some detail what equation 16.7 tells us. The first term on the right-hand side shows the extent to which investment is adding to the capital stock per worker. The second term shows the amount of investment needed to offset depreciation (δk) and to equip additions to the labour force at existing levels of capital per head (nk). Note that if there were no savings in the economy ($s = 0$) then $\dot{k} = -(n+\delta)k < 0$, that is, capital per head would be falling under the pressures of an increasing population, $n > 0$ and capital depreciation, $\delta > 0$.

We present this result in a standard Solow diagram (Figure 16.6) by plotting the two parts of the right-hand side of equation 16.7. This is similar to Figure 16.13a above. The capital labour ratio, k, is on the horizontal axis and output per worker, y, is on the vertical one. sy is a curve shaped like the production function but shrunk by the fraction, s. The line from the origin is labelled $(n+\delta)k$. This line shows what is required to keep the capital labour ratio fixed and it reflects the need to replace capital stock as it depreciates at rate δ, and the need to equip with capital new entrants to the labour force arriving at rate n. The difference between the two curves at any level of k determines $\dot{k}$. For example, if $sAk^{\alpha} > (n+\delta)k$, capital per worker increases because investment per head is greater than the reduction in capital per head due to an increasing population and depreciation.

The point where the two curves intersect is given by the level of capital per worker (k^*) where $sA(k^*)^{\alpha} = (n+\delta)k^*$. At this point $\dot{k} = 0$ and $\dot{y} = 0$, which means that the level of capital per worker and output per worker are constant. This defines a *steady state* in the Solow model: at k^*, Y, K and N grow at the same constant rate n.

In Figure 16.6, the steady state levels of output per head (y^*) and of consumption per head (c^*) are shown. We can easily see that the steady state level of output per head is given by

$$y^* = A(k^*)^{\alpha}$$

while the steady state level of consumption per head is a fraction of steady state income. It is given by

$$c^* = A(k^*)^\alpha - sA(k^*)^\alpha = (1-s)A(k^*)^\alpha.$$

It is possible to solve for the steady state values of k^* and y^* explicitly. The equilibrium property $\dot{k} = 0$ implies $sA(k^*)^\alpha = k^*(n+\delta)$, where we can rearrange for k^* and obtain the steady state value of capital and output per unit of labour:

$$k^* = \left(\frac{As}{\delta+n}\right)^{\frac{1}{1-\alpha}} \quad \text{(steady state capital labour ratio)}$$

$$y^* = A(k^*)^\alpha = A^{\frac{1}{1-\alpha}}\left(\frac{s}{\delta+n}\right)^{\frac{\alpha}{1-\alpha}}. \quad \text{(steady state output per capita)}$$

Does a higher savings/investment ratio always raise welfare?

In the Solow model, a higher savings rate will always raise output per capita. If welfare were measured in GDP per capita, then a higher savings/investment rate would always raise welfare. We can see from Figure 16.7 that China's investment rate has increased markedly over the past 50 years, whereas investment rates elsewhere are lower. There is much discussion among observers of the Chinese economy about the need to reduce the investment share and the Solow model helps clarify the reasoning.

A preferable measure of welfare to GDP per capita is consumption per capita, denoted as cy in the Solow model, where c is the 'consumption rate' or the marginal propensity to consume. If this were taken as the yardstick for welfare, we can ask how a hypothetical social planner whose aim is to maximize welfare would set the savings

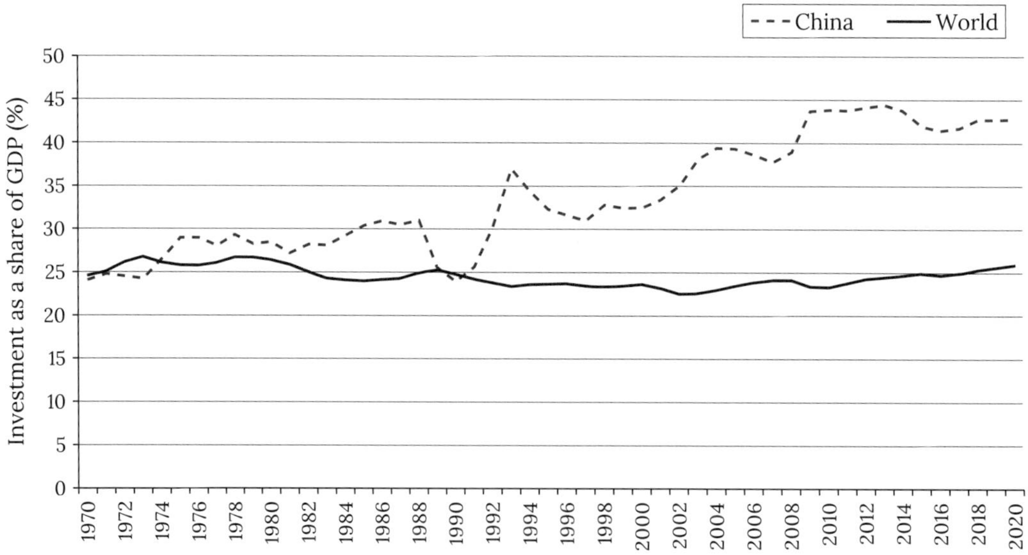

Figure 16.7 Investment as a share of GDP: 1970–2020.

Source: World Bank, Gross fixed capital formation (% of GDP), June 2022.

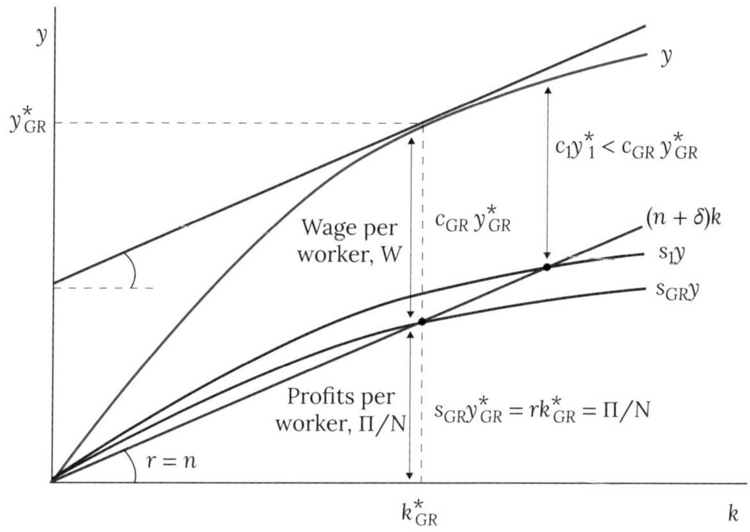

Figure 16.8 The Golden Rule. Visit www.oup.com/he/carlin-soskice to explore the Golden Rule with Animated Analytical Diagram 16.8.

rate to maximize welfare. The saving rate that would be chosen is called the Golden Rule saving rate.

It is very intuitive to illustrate the concept of the Golden Rule graphically, as is done in Figure 16.8. The figure shows that consumption per worker (the gap between the production function and the savings function) is maximized at the steady state marked k^*_{GR} at which the tangent to the production function has the same slope as the line $(n+\delta)k$. With competitive markets, the slope of the tangent to the production function, which is the marginal product of capital, is equal to $r+\delta$. The marginal product of capital has to cover the rental cost of capital, r, plus depreciation, δ. As shown in the diagram, consumption per head is maximized when $r+\delta = n+\delta$, i.e. where $r = n$. The function $s_{GR}y$ will go through this point.

$$f'(k) = n+\delta = r+\delta$$
$$\rightarrow r = n. \qquad \text{(condition for the Golden Rule savings rate)}$$

Using the Harrod-Domar formula, we can calculate the Golden Rule savings rate. For the Cobb-Douglas production function, the Golden Rule savings rate is equal to capital's share:

$$\begin{aligned} s_{GR} &= \frac{(n+\delta)k^*_{GR}}{f(k^*_{GR})} = \frac{(r+\delta)k^*_{GR}}{f(k^*_{GR})} = \frac{f'(k^*_{GR})k^*_{GR}}{f(k^*_{GR})} \\ &= \frac{\Pi}{Y^*_{GR}}. \\ &\rightarrow s_{GR} Y^*_{GR} = S_{GR} = \Pi \\ &\rightarrow s_{GR} y^*_{GR} = \frac{\Pi}{N}. \end{aligned}$$

Two interesting results come from this. First, it says that at the Golden Rule, total savings, S, are equal to total profits, Π, and hence, total wages are equal to total consumption. Wages per worker and profits per worker are shown in Figure 16.8 and the geometry of the result that savings are equal to profits is shown. Second, for the Cobb–Douglas production function, since $\alpha = \frac{f'(k)k}{f(k)}$, then it follows that the Golden Rule savings rate is equal to α, capital's share of output.[11]

It is clear from Figure 16.8 that an increase in the savings rate above s_{GR} actually reduces consumption per worker. It therefore also reduces welfare in this framework. The figure highlights an interesting point: if welfare is measured in terms of consumption per worker, then although it raises output per worker, raising the savings rate will not necessarily raise welfare.

A reduction in the saving/investment rate

Let us now consider the following policy experiment: at time t_1, there is an exogenous fall in the savings rate. For example, a fall that takes China's investment share (savings rate) down toward levels observed elsewhere in the world. In Figure 16.9, we trace the impact of this shock and show how k and y adjust as the economy moves to a new steady state. We assume that $A = 1$ for simplicity in the diagram. In the top left panel this experiment is represented by a downward shift in the sy curve corresponding to the decrease of the savings rate from s_0 to s_1. The economy slowly adjusts from the old steady state k_0 to the new steady state k_1, where capital per worker is lower than at t_0.

The transition dynamics are better illustrated in the bottom left panel, where we can inspect growth rates directly. The shock is shown by the downward shift of the g_K curve. Immediately after the exogenous shock occurs at t_1, the growth rate of capital drops down to the rate illustrated on the new curve. Output growth drops as well. As the economy slowly converges to the new capital per worker long-run steady state k_1^*, the growth rate g_K (and hence g_Y too) rise back to their steady state values of n. The economy converges to point B. The paths of output and capital growth are shown explicitly in the top right panel.

The last panel (bottom right) shows how the level of output per capita is permanently lower after the exogenous fall in the savings rate. As we have shown, however, if the economy began with a savings rate above the Golden Rule level, consumption per capita is higher in the new steady state if the new savings rate is closer to the Golden Rule level.

---

[11] A 'mechanical' derivation of this result follows from solving the constrained optimization problem below:

$$\max_s (1-s)y \quad \text{subject to} \quad y = A(k^*)^{\alpha} \tag{16.8}$$

$$\rightarrow \max_s (1-s)A^{\frac{1}{1-\alpha}}\left(\frac{s}{\delta+n}\right)^{\frac{\alpha}{1-\alpha}} \tag{16.9}$$

Taking the first order conditions:

$$\frac{\alpha}{1-\alpha}A^{\frac{1}{1-\alpha}}\frac{1}{(\delta+n)^{\frac{\alpha}{1-\alpha}}}s^{\frac{\alpha}{1-\alpha}-1} - \frac{1}{1-\alpha}A^{\frac{1}{1-\alpha}}\frac{1}{(\delta+n)^{\frac{\alpha}{1-\alpha}}}s^{\frac{\alpha}{1-\alpha}} = 0 \tag{16.10}$$

$$\rightarrow s = \alpha \tag{16.11}$$

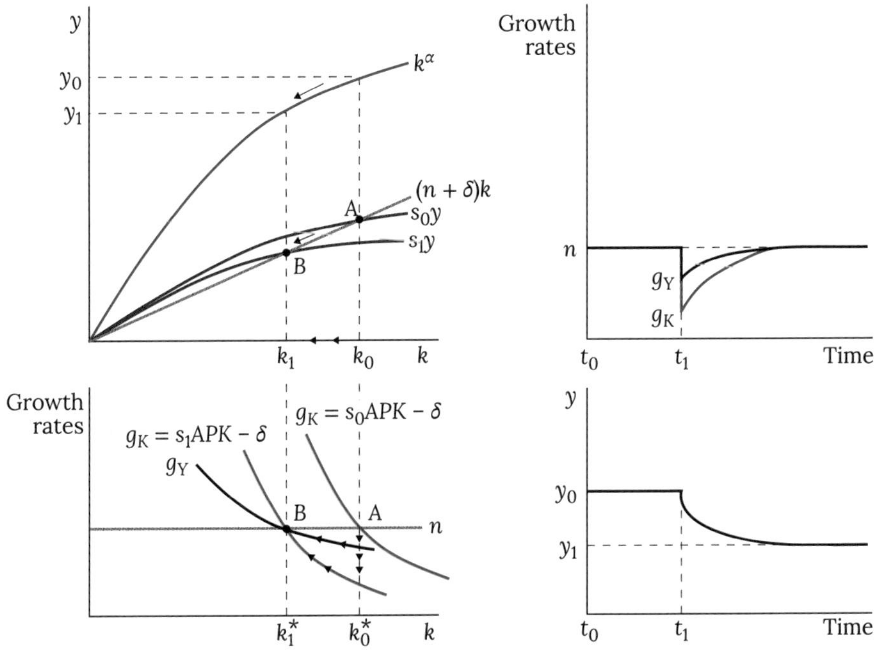

Figure 16.9 How does a fall in the savings rate affect growth in the Solow model? Visit www.oup.com/he/carlin-soskice to explore how a fall in the savings rate affects growth in the Solow model with Animated Analytical Diagram 16.9.

The explanation for what at first may seem to be a surprising result—namely, that a lower investment share does not reduce *growth* permanently—lies once again in the assumption of diminishing returns to capital accumulation in the Solow model. This means that the initial fall in the growth rate of the capital stock does *not* bring a proportionate decrease in output. Thus, along with the fall in capital per worker and productivity, there is an initial fall in the capital–output ratio. This means that the slower capital stock growth generated by the lower savings rate fades away as reduced depreciation eventually counterbalances the reduction in investment.

Population growth and the saving/investment rate

At the start of the chapter (in Figure 16.1), we saw that there have been periods of history where living standards have significantly diverged between countries (e.g. East and West during the Industrial Revolution), but that there have also been periods of noticeable convergence (e.g. East and West since 1980). In this section, we will more systematically compare the predictions of the Solow model to the real-world data, paying special attention to the concept of convergence.

We can use the equation derived earlier for output per worker in the steady state to set out the predictions of the Solow model.

$$y^* = A^{\frac{1}{1-\alpha}}\left(\frac{s}{\delta+n}\right)^{\frac{\alpha}{1-\alpha}}. \qquad (16.12)$$

The model predicts that when the economy is in long-run steady state, output per head is: (1) increasing in the level of total factor productivity, A; (2) increasing in the savings rate (investment share) of the economy, s; (3) decreasing in the rate of population growth, n; and (4) decreasing in the depreciation rate, δ.

Figure 16.10 uses statistics from the Penn World Table to construct scatter plots of GDP per capita in 2019 and population growth and investment share over the last 59 years. The predictions of the Solow model suggest that there should be a negative association between population growth and GDP per capita, signalling that those countries that experienced slower population growth between 1960 and 2019 should be richer today. We can see from Figure 16.10a that there is only weak evidence for this relationship in the data. It appears to be true that richer countries generally have slower population growth, but the relationship is far from perfect, especially for the poorer countries in the sample. For example, Jamaica and Jordan have almost identical GDP per capita today, but population growth has been substantially higher in Jordan since 1960.

When applied to cross-country performance, the Solow model also predicts that those countries that save more should have higher GDP per capita. We can use

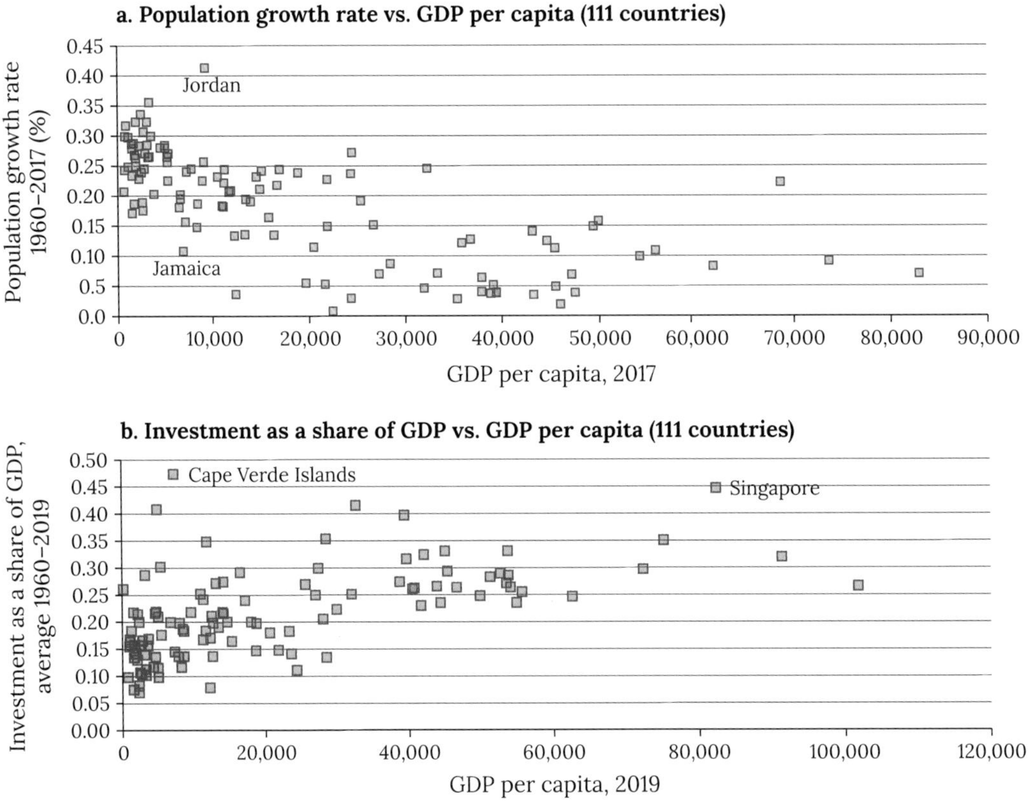

Figure 16.10 Current levels of GDP per capita vs. population growth and investment as a share of GDP over the last 59 years.

Source: Penn World Table 10.1, June 2022.

investment data to see if this prediction matches the cross-country data, as the Solow model assumes all savings are invested. Figure 16.10b shows a similarly weak relationship. Richer countries have had higher investment on average, but there is still a lot of unexplained variation in the data. For example, Cape Verde and Singapore have invested a similar proportion of GDP over the past half century, but the former is one of the poorest countries in the world and the latter one of the richest.

The cross-country scatter plots provide some weak evidence for the predictions of the Solow model, but the model cannot explain the large variation in living standards seen in the world today. It is also important to note that even if correlations in the data are consistent with the model's predictions, they do not provide evidence for the causal story provided by the model. For example, it is likely that richer countries are able to afford a higher saving rate than very poor ones; equally, families in richer countries may choose to have smaller families than in poor countries because they do not need to rely on their children to provide for them in old age.

Human capital

Up to this point, we considered the raw amounts of capital and labour across economies. To better reconcile the theory and the cross-country data, we need to include an additional source of productivity. If the productivity source is more abundant in rich economies then this would help to explain the lack of evidence for convergence seen in the empirics. One possibility is that more education increases the marginal product of labour for all given levels of raw physical capital and labour. In other words, more education enables workers to produce more with the same inputs.

Figure 16.11 plots GDP per capita in 2019 against average educational attainment over the past half century for 104 countries. The figure shows a clear upwards trend, with richer countries having higher educational attainment.

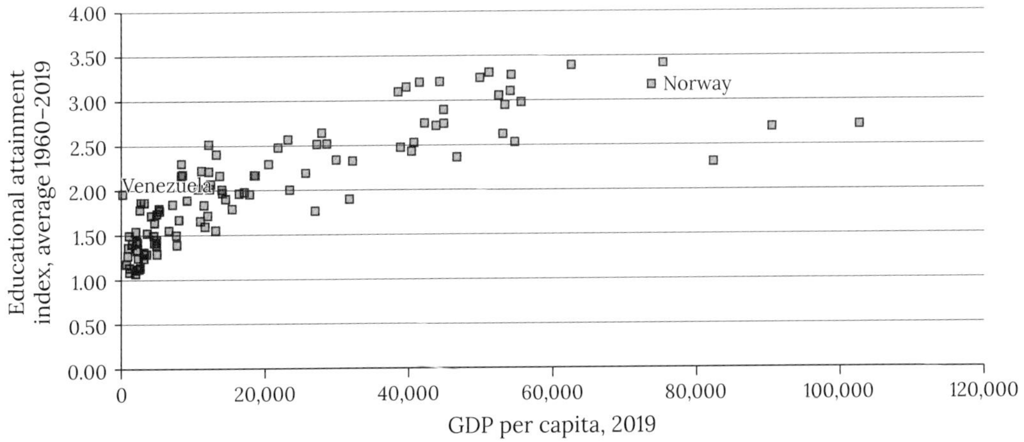

Figure 16.11 Current levels of GDP per capita vs. educational attainment, 1960–2019.

Source: Penn World Table 10.1, June 2022.

Setting the causality issue (i.e. is more education driving higher incomes or do rich countries simply spend more on education?) to one side, the Solow model can be extended to include human capital. In this context we can think of education as a proxy for human capital. Other components of human capital might include the health of the workforce and the quality of education. Once we have decided how to measure human capital the next question is how to incorporate it in the production function. In the standard Solow model, labour input is assumed to be the same for each worker across countries. We now relax this assumption and allow labour input per worker, h, to be different across countries. The augmented Cobb–Douglas production function is:

$$Y = AK^{\alpha}(hN)^{1-\alpha},$$

where h is a measure of the level of educational attainment in a country.

By taking $h^{(1-\alpha)}$ outside the bracket, the production function is now the same as that used in Section 16.2, except the A in front of the production function has been replaced with $h^{(1-\alpha)}A$.

$$Y = h^{(1-\alpha)}AK^{\alpha}N^{1-\alpha}.$$

Following the same steps as the derivations in Section 16.2, we solve for the steady state level of output per head in the augmented Solow model.

$$\begin{aligned} y^{*} &= (h^{(1-\alpha)}A)^{\frac{1}{1-\alpha}}\left(\frac{s}{n+\delta}\right)^{\frac{\alpha}{1-\alpha}} \\ &= hA^{\frac{1}{1-\alpha}}\left(\frac{s}{n+\delta}\right)^{\frac{\alpha}{1-\alpha}}. \end{aligned}$$

The important thing to take away from this version of the Solow model is that it predicts that countries with higher levels of educational attainment will have higher levels of output per head in steady state (all other factors held constant). The model therefore provides a potential explanation for the persistence of the gap in living standards between poor and rich economies.

Technological progress and steady state growth in the Solow model

Figure 16.22 in Appendix 16.7.1 shows a remarkably steady long-run growth rate of output per capita in the USA. Long-run growth since 1870 has been at the rate of 2.4% per annum. This fact provides the motivation for the modelling of technological progress in the Solow model. The Solow model does not attempt to explain the determinants of technological progress. But it pins down the form technological progress would have to take if it was to be consistent with the phenomenon of balanced or steady state growth.

Once we pose the problem like this, the answer is quite intuitive. Technological progress will have to be of the form that does not use up any resources in the economy (all investment is used to replace and increase the size of the capital stock) and that increases the productivity of labour. This is called exogenous Harrod-neutral (or labour-augmenting) technological progress.[12] It is usually described as a process that involves steady technological improvement, which raises output per worker by a constant rate, of x% per annum.

With exogenous technological progress at rate x, the Solow model requires only minor, mechanical adjustment. The Cobb-Douglas production function for output, Y, becomes,

$$Y = K^{\alpha}(A_t N)^{(1-\alpha)}$$
$$\text{where } A_t = A_0 \exp(xt).$$

It is important to note the difference between A in the standard Solow model from Section 16.2 and the A_t introduced here. Up to this point, A has represented the *level* of TFP in an economy, which could affect the level of steady state output per capita in the standard Solow model, but not the growth rate. The A_t introduced in this section is an exponential growth process (see Section 16.7.1) that represents the growth of the technological frontier over time, hence it can affect steady state growth rates.

The model implies that the rates of growth of output and capital in actual and per capita terms on the balanced growth path are

$$g_Y = g_K = n + x, \text{ and}$$
$$g_y = g_k = x,$$

which means there is constant growth of output per worker in the steady state.

We can reconcile the Solow model with technological progress with the standard Solow model by introducing the concept of efficiency units, such that

$$\hat{y} = \frac{Y}{A_t N} = \frac{y}{A_t} \text{ and } \hat{k} = \frac{K}{A_t N} = \frac{k}{A_t},$$

where $\hat{y}$ is output per efficiency unit of labour and $\hat{k}$ is capital per efficiency unit of labour. When working in efficiency units, it is useful to remember that y and k can be retrieved by multiplying the corresponding values in efficiency units by A_t. Using these definitions we take the same steps as in the basic Solow model to arrive at the fundamental law of motion for the Solow model with technological progress. It is left to the reader to work through this derivation:

$$\dot{\hat{k}} = s(\hat{k})^{\alpha} - (n + \delta + x)\hat{k}$$

As illustrated in Figure 16.12, the economy is in the steady state when there is no change in capital per efficiency unit. As before, we derive the steady state levels of capital per efficiency unit and output per efficiency unit, where asterisk indicates steady-state level:

---

12 Harrod-neutral technological progress is necessary for steady state growth with a general production function. If the production function is Cobb-Douglas, however, the three forms of technological progress (augmenting labour, capital, or both factors) are identical and consistent with steady state growth. See the appendix to Chapter 13 of Carlin and Soskice (2006).

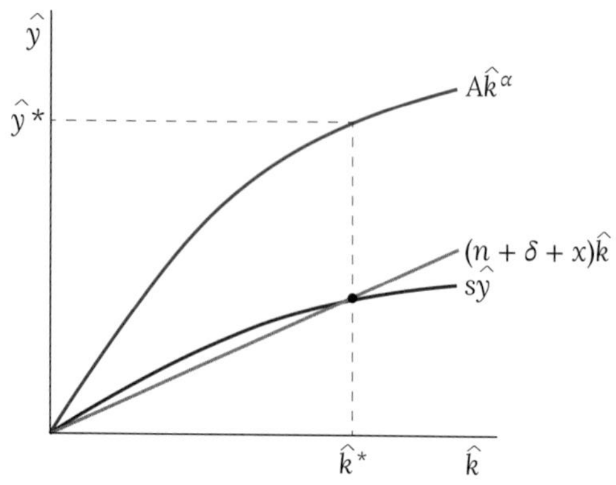

Figure 16.12 The Solow model with technological progress.

$$s(\hat{k}^*)^{\alpha} = (n+\delta+x)\hat{k}^*$$

$$\hat{k}^* = \left(\frac{s}{n+\delta+x}\right)^{\frac{1}{1-\alpha}}$$

$$\hat{y}^* = (\hat{k}^*)^{\alpha} = \left(\frac{s}{n+\delta+x}\right)^{\frac{\alpha}{1-\alpha}}.$$

We use this last expression to solve for the steady state value of output per worker:

$$y_t^* = A_t\left(\frac{s}{n+\delta+x}\right)^{\frac{\alpha}{1-\alpha}}.$$

This equation shows that at time t after the economy has reached its long-run steady state growth path, output per head is: (1) increasing in the level of technological development A_t at time t; (2) increasing in the savings rate of the economy, s; (3) decreasing in the rate of population growth, n; and (4) decreasing in the depreciation rate, δ.

Consistent with our intuition, this shows that economies that save more, have lower fertility and are advanced technologically will have higher GDP per capita. But note that while higher savings and lower population growth mean a higher level of living standards, only faster technological progress (higher x) can raise the steady state *growth rate* of living standards.

Figure 16.12 shows the Solow diagram with exogenous technological progress. It is very similar to the standard diagram except that it is in efficiency units and the line from the origin–$(n+\delta+x)\hat{k}$–includes the rate of technological progress x and now shows what investment is required to keep capital per efficiency unit of labour fixed. In this model, a rise in the exogenous rate of technological progress raises output and creates new capital investment opportunities. It also puts the economy onto a higher growth path, permanently increasing the rate of growth of output per worker.

16.2.3 Solow model meets the 3-equation model

To connect the Solow model to the 3-equation model, we note that the short- and medium-run macroeconomic model developed in this book is organized around the concept of the output gap $(y_t - y_e)$. We have looked at how shocks to aggregate demand or supply shift current output and/or equilibrium output, the implications for unemployment, and how the policy maker responds to the forecast inflation or deflation that arises.

One way of thinking about a growth model is that it pins down the growth rate of equilibrium output—it abstracts from deviations of output from trend caused by shocks to either aggregate demand or supply. Growth models ignore inflation by conducting all of the analysis in real terms. Problems of aggregate demand are ignored as well by assuming that all savings are automatically invested. This means that attention is focused on the determinants of the growth of equilibrium output.

The simplest way to bring the Solow model together with the 3-equation model is to focus on the assumption in the Solow model that all savings are invested. By relaxing this assumption, fluctuations in aggregate demand can cause deviations of output from potential, which in turn opens up the possibility that there is a role for the central bank in stabilization.

In order to make the comparison between the 3-equation and Solow models clear, we use the notation of this chapter, where Y is output in real terms; y is output per capita. For the comparison, we assume there is no population growth so we do not need to use the intensive production function. Figure 16.13 shows in the left panel, the short-run model illustrating the paradox of thrift. The economy begins at point A. A rise in the propensity to save (steeper savings function) implies a lower level of

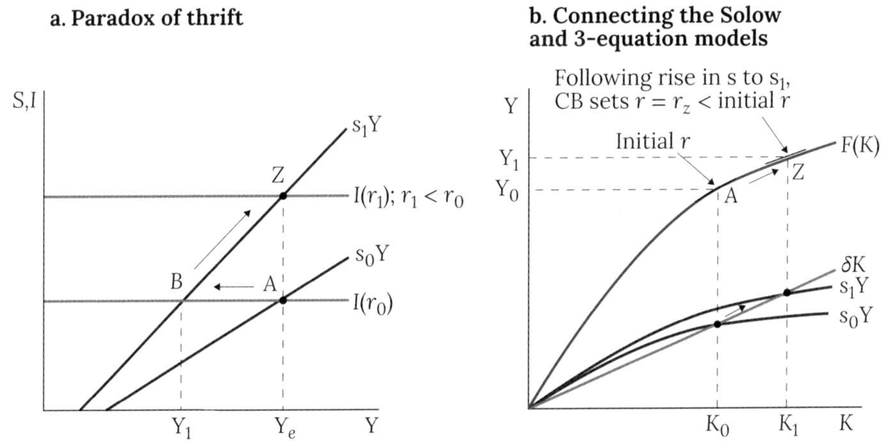

Figure 16.13 A rise in the savings rate: the Solow model and 3-equation model. Visit www.oup.com/he/carlin-soskice to explore a rise in the savings rate, the Solow model, and 3-equation model with Animated Analytical Diagram 16.13.

output. The result of the attempt to save more is that total savings are unchanged and output is lower, i.e. there is a negative output gap at point B.

An inflation-targeting central bank would respond to the fall in inflation below target at B by cutting the interest rate. This would stimulate investment, shifting the investment function upward and the economy would end up back in medium-run equilibrium at Z.

We now turn to showing the models in the Solow diagram (in the right-hand panel of Figure 16.13). A simplified version of the Solow model is used with zero population growth and omitting technological progress; it is otherwise unaltered. The initial steady state is at point A. The saving rate goes up. Since this is also the investment rate in the Solow model, capital is accumulated and output rises. Due to diminishing returns to capital accumulation, eventually the additional investment is exactly equal to the depreciation of the existing capital stock ($s_1 Y = \delta K$) at the capital stock, K_1, and a new steady state is reached at higher output, point Z.

If we now drop the 'all savings are invested' assumption and introduce a policy maker who understands both the paradox of thrift and the Solow model, the central bank understands that given the higher propensity to save, a higher level of output is possible at a higher capital labour ratio. Productivity would also be higher. But in order for this to be achieved, higher investment must be stimulated and this requires a lower interest rate.

The slope of the production function is equal to the marginal product of capital since it shows the change in output associated with a change in capital. The central bank therefore uses the production function to identify the lower marginal product of capital associated with the new equilibrium: in this simple model, the marginal product of capital is equal to the real interest rate plus the rate of depreciation. Hence it sets the interest rate at the lower rate r_Z, so that $r_Z + \delta = MPK_Z$ shown by the slope of the production function at point Z in Figure 16.13b. Because of the intervention of the central bank, investment rises in response to the lower interest rate and the economy moves to the new equilibrium at higher output and a more capital intensive method of production (point Z).

16.3 CROSS-COUNTRY GROWTH

16.3.1 Convergence between rich and poor countries

The Solow model predicts *absolute* convergence: poor countries will grow faster than rich countries and eventually catch up to their per capita GDP through the process of capital deepening. To illustrate the idea of absolute convergence, we return to the Fundamental Solow Law of Motion,

$$\dot{k} = sAk^{\alpha} - (n + \delta)k,$$

and divide through by k to find the growth rate of the capital–labour ratio:

$$g_k = \frac{\dot{k}}{k} = sAk^{\alpha-1} - (n + \delta). \tag{16.13}$$

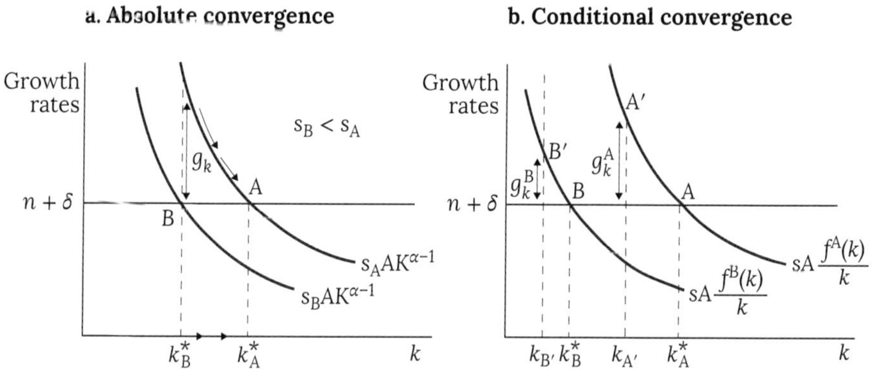

Figure 16.14 Absolute and conditional convergence in the Solow model. Visit www.oup.com/he/carlin-soskice to explore absolute and conditional convergence in the Solow model with Animated Analytical Diagram 16.14.

Figure 16.14a shows the balanced growth paths for a rich country, A, and a poor country, B, which differ only in their savings rates. The poor country has a lower capital–labour ratio (i.e. $k_B^* < k_A^*$) and consequently has a lower output per capita than the rich country. In steady state, both economies are growing such that:

$$g_K = g_Y = n$$
$$g_k = g_y = 0,$$

hence output per capita growth is zero in both the poor and rich countries.

Is there anything the poor country can do to boost their capital–output ratio and increase their living standards to those of the rich economy? According to this simple version of the Solow model, an increase in the savings rate of the poor country will lead to a period of positive growth of capital per worker. In the left panel of Figure 16.14, the rich and poor countries now have identical parameters but the poor country is out of equilibrium. Given the rise in its saving rate, it is away from steady state. The model predicts that the poor economy will converge from its low output per capita level to that of the rich country: the doubled-headed arrow at point B shows the growth rate of the capital labour ratio (equation 16.13) triggered by the rise in the savings ratio. The economy transits as shown in Figure 16.14a to point A because the increase in the saving rate allows the poor country to take advantage of the high marginal product of capital at the low initial level of capital intensity.

This brings us to the idea of *conditional convergence*, which is where countries converge to their own steady states and more similar economies have steady states closer to one another. Let us consider the case in which the production functions differ between rich and poor countries. To this point we have assumed that poor and rich countries have the same Cobb-Douglas production function, $Y = AK^{\alpha}N^{1-\alpha}$. In other words, that poor and rich countries can produce the same amount of output from a given amount of labour and capital. This may well not be true; for example, richer economies could have more efficient production processes.

To illustrate the concept of conditional convergence, imagine there are a set of poor countries with intensive form production functions of $f^B(k)$ and a set of rich countries with $f^A(k)$. Figure 16.14b shows this example in a graphical form. The growth rate of capital per worker for each country depends on their distance from the steady state of their country group. For example, we can see that a poor country located at point B′ will experience capital per capita growth of g_k^B and converge to the steady state capital per capita of the poor set of countries. The equivalent is true of a rich country at point A′. In this example, the rich country is actually predicted to grow faster, as it is further away from its own steady state. This highlights the key feature of conditional convergence: it is the distance away from your own steady state that dictates the speed of output per capita growth.

The weaker proposition of conditional convergence predicts that countries with similar steady states will converge, but that fundamentally different economies will not. The lack of convergence between rich and poor economies in this framework could be because poorer countries have inferior production functions, lower TFP or for other reasons, such as lower levels of savings or higher rates of population growth.

Mankiw, Romer, and Weil (1992) test for conditional convergence using the Solow model framework and find that the data shows evidence of it but convergence is much slower than the model would predict. This suggests that the production function is less concave, i.e. the returns to the accumulation of capital decline more slowly. By including the accumulation of human as well as physical capital, returns to total capital decline more slowly. Estimating this model from data for GDP per capita for a sample of 98 countries they find that the model accounts much better for the variation in GDP per capita across countries than does the model without human capital. They find strong evidence for conditional convergence, with the convergence rate close to that predicted by the Solow model augmented with human capital.

Including human capital narrows the gap between theory and empirical analysis. The model focuses on *broad* capital accumulation—of human as well as physical capital—as the engine of catch-up growth.

Absolute convergence—recent decades

At the core of catch-up by poor countries according to the Solow model is the mechanism of diminishing returns to capital accumulation. If countries differ in their 'fundamentals' of population growth, the saving/investment rate, human capital and production function, there is only the weaker prediction of convergence to the country's own steady state. This is also referred to as 'club' convergence: economies converge to the level of GDP per capita of their peers with similar fundamentals.

While the Solow model provides a framework for interpreting cross-country growth performance using the concepts of absolute and conditional convergence (Figure 16.14), it is not the only lens as we shall see when we look at the model of Schumpeterian growth later in the chapter. Irrespective of the model one has in mind, it is interesting to examine the data on cross-country growth and its correlates.

The very long run data presented in the introduction to the chapter provide a story of divergence as a set of northern European countries transited from the so-called

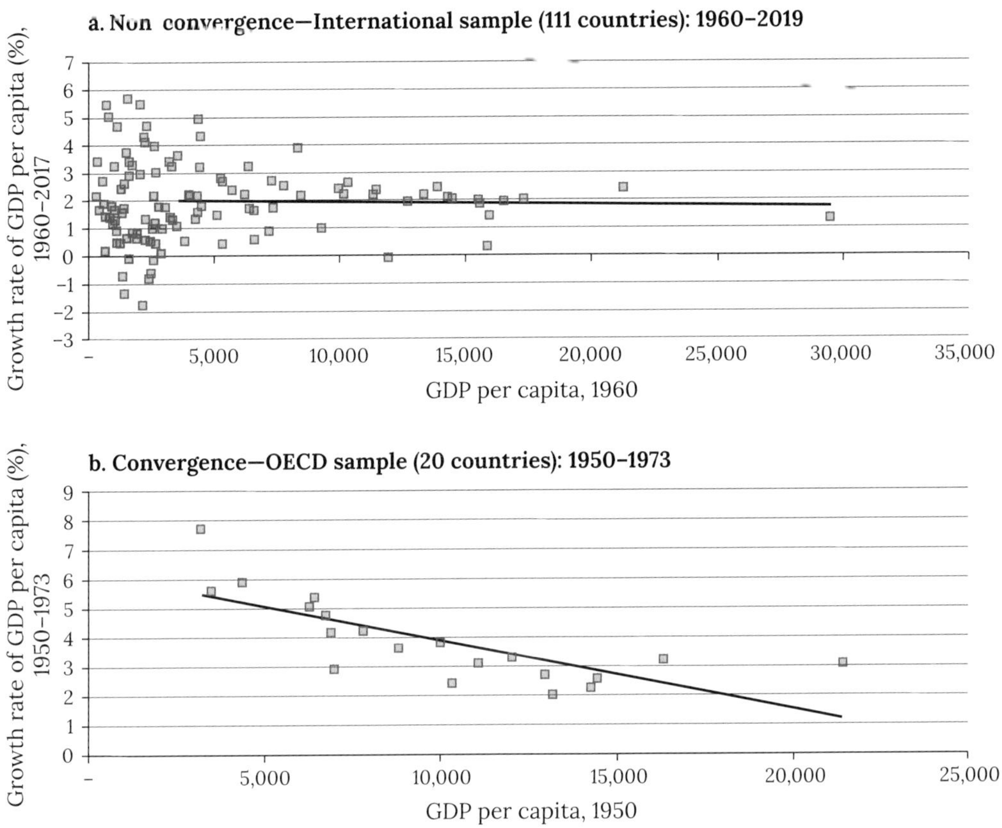

Figure 16.15 Do we see economic convergence in the real world?

Source: Penn World Table 10.1, June 2022.

Malthusian trap with stagnant living standards into a phase of continuous growth. Many countries had not begun a process of continuous growth by the middle of the 20th century. Large datasets covering all of the world's economies are available from 1960 and it is from 1960 to the present that we now look at the relationship between initial GDP per capita and subsequent growth (Figure 16.15).

The conclusion of the large literature on cross-country growth that peaked around 1990 was that poor countries did not on average catch up with richer ones between 1960 and 1985; absolute convergence was absent.[13] It was found, however, in studies confined to a sample of economies in a convergence 'club' like the states of the US or OECD countries (see Figure 16.15b).

However, adding another three decades of data provides a somewhat different result. Low-income countries grow faster than high-income ones from around the

[13] Note that in this literature, country observations are not weighted by population size so that for example, the contribution to the 'average' of El Salvador with 6.5 million is the same as that of China with 1.4 billion.

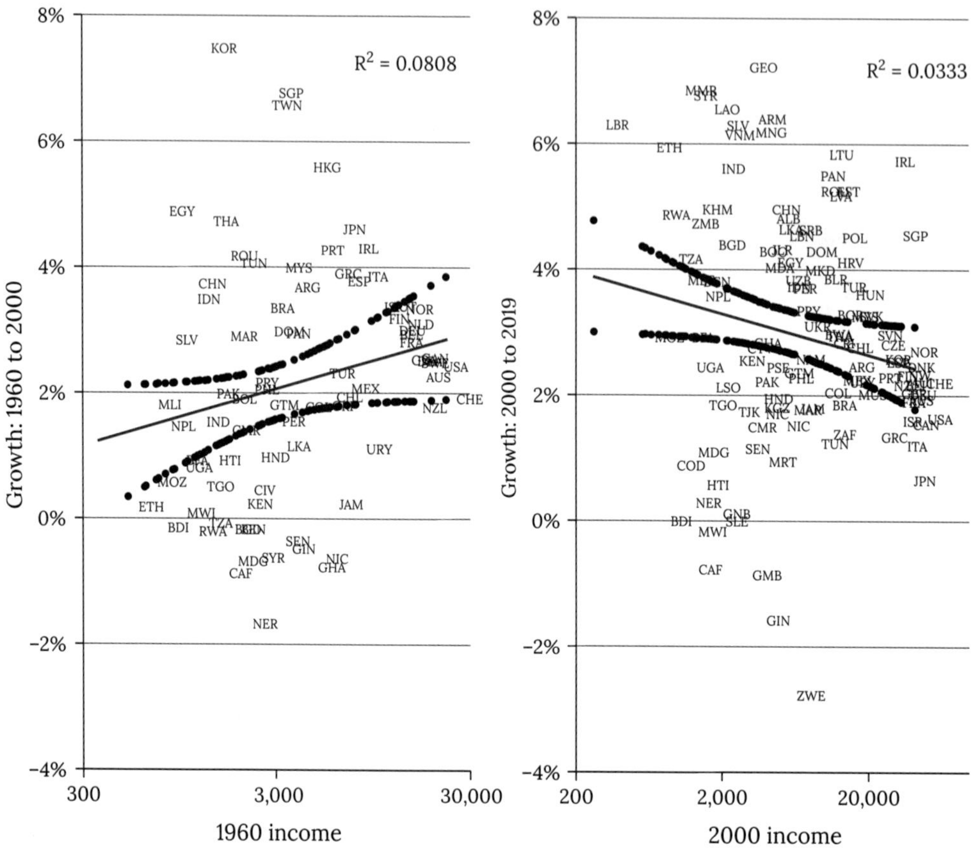

Figure 16.16 Changing patterns of convergence: two non-overlapping periods.

Note: The horizontal axis shows the natural log of real per capita GDP from the Penn World Tables version 10.0 in the initial year, and the vertical axis shows average annual real per capita growth over the period listed. For clarity of interpretation, the labels of the horizontal axes show actual income (i.e. not in logarithmic form). The area within the black dots represents a 95% confidence interval around the regression line. The country corresponding to the code in the scatter can be found by googling 'country code SLV'.

Source: Recreated from Figure 3 in Patel, D., Sandefur, J., & Subramanian, A. (2021). The new era of unconditional convergence. *Journal of Development Economics*, 152, 102687. https://doi.org/10.1016/j.jdeveco.2021.102687. With permission from Elsevier.

mid-1990s (see Figure 16.16) but the size of the convergence parameter, often referred to as 'beta', is much smaller than 2%.[14] As the 'Rule of 70' tells us (see Section 16.7.1 in the Appendix), with a beta parameter of 2%, a country would close half the gap between its

[14] The convergence parameter beta gives the constant rate at which the gap between current output per worker in efficiency units and its steady state value disappears. For a detailed explanation of how beta is derived in theory and measured from the data see Chapter 13 in Carlin and Soskice (2006).

		1960	1970	1980	1990	2000	2010
Average growth rate	Low	2.01	1.04	0.26	1.29	3.31	2.84
	Middle	2.98	2.08	0.57	0.11	4.70	2.82
	High	3.52	2.79	1.99	2.40	1.82	2.19
Share negative	Low	0.24	0.24	0.42	0.37	0.16	0.16
	Middle	0.14	0.30	0.41	0.28	0.00	0.13
	High	0.00	0.00	0.07	0.18	0.07	0.05
Number of countries	Low	21	33	36	41	50	38
	Middle	42	44	37	46	46	45
	High	21	23	28	34	28	41

Table 16.1 Growth patterns by country income group (low, middle, high).

Note: Table shows summary statistics based on the Penn World Tables version 10.0. All growth rates are calculated at the decadal level. 'Share negative' shows the share of countries within each group with a negative decadal growth rate in that period. In 1960, low-income countries are those with per capita income below the 25th percentiles and high-income are those above the 75th percentiles. In years since 1960, the relative position of these original cut-offs to the United States is calculated and those thresholds are applied dynamically. This is not a fixed sample; the income classifications are defined contemporaneously at the start of each decade. The sample ends in 2019.

Source: Recreated from Table 1 in Patel, D., Sandefur, J., & Subramanian, A. (2021). The new era of unconditional convergence. *Journal of Development Economics*, 152, 102687. https://doi.org/10.1016/j.jdeveco.2021.102687. With permission from Elsevier.

current and the steady state GDP per capita in (70/2 =) 35 years, the beta coefficient on the sample of 124 countries for 2000–19 is 0.45%, which implies it would be 170 years before half the gap to the steady state was closed.

Table 16.1 provides information on the pattern of per capita growth of low, middle and high-income countries. Average growth in the high-income countries is higher than elsewhere in the first four decades after 1960. Although the 1980s was a low growth decade for all three groups, it was especially bad for low and middle-income countries, where over 40% of the economies in each group had negative average growth. The contrast with the 2000s and 2010s, especially for those with middle incomes, is stark: very few low- and middle-income countries experienced negative decadal growth and average growth rates were comparable to the so-called 'golden age' growth rates of high-income countries in the 1950s and 1960s. The lacklustre growth of high-income countries from the 2000s contributes somewhat to the degree of catch-up. As noted in Chapter 9, the effects of the global financial crisis were largely confined to the high-income group.

The in-between decade of the 1990s is interesting: the Soviet Union disintegrated in 1989, which added 15 new countries to the sample. Countries in this group as well as the other former Eastern bloc economies experienced a more or less prolonged period of output decline before growth recovered, which is reflected in the weak decadal average growth of middle-income countries in the 1990s.

Convergence of Solow fundamentals

A plausible reason for the emergence of (weak) absolute convergence from around 2000 is a narrowing of the gap between countries in the determinants of steady state GDP per capita.[15] When the fundamentals converge, absolute convergence is more likely, or to put it a different way, absolute and conditional convergence 'converge'. Kremer et al. use data from 1985 to 2015 to document convergence in the Solow fundamentals of population growth, saving/investment share, and human capital, and reach the following conclusions:

- **Population growth:** Population growth has fallen faster in countries with the highest population growth rates in 1985.
- **Saving/investment rate:** Countries with higher investment shares in 1985 saw them decrease more strongly, and some low-income countries increased investment (e.g. Mozambique, Ethiopia, and Angola).
- **Human capital:** Poor countries have gradually caught up in years of schooling to rich ones, which means there has been some convergence in human capital per capita.

The narrowing between the Solow fundamentals in low- and high-income countries from the year 2000 is associated with the absolute convergence observed in this period. Nevertheless, the speed of convergence is much slower than experienced in the post-war decades by the high-income countries.

16.3.2 Convergence in policy reforms

Macroeconomic policy reforms considered essential for growth were tied to so-called structural adjustment aid provided to countries in the 1980s and 1990s by the IMF. They are summarized in a statement published in 1990 and were known as 'The Washington Consensus'. These reforms came under the umbrella of 'structural adjustment', 'globalization' and 'neoliberalism' and were targeted at countries in Latin America and Africa in the 1980s. They also influenced policy design in post-Soviet economies in the 1990s. However, weak growth in these regions through to the mid-1990s in combination with rapid growth in East Asian economies that did not follow the reform orthodoxy cast doubt on their role in growth.[16]

This raises the question of whether in parallel with the Solow fundamentals, some measures of policy reform improved in the years during which a degree of absolute convergence was observed.

Using the Washington Consensus, Easterly (2019) identifies five indicators of bad and extremely bad policy outcomes:

---

[15] This section and Section 16.5.2 draw on the results presented in Kremer et al. (2021).

[16] See, for example, Rodrik (2006), and earlier papers by Easterly published in 2001 and 2005. He wrote: 'Repeated [structural] adjustment lending ... fails to show any positive effect on . . . growth' (Easterly 2005).

- **High inflation:** The share of countries with inflation greater than 20% increased from the late 1960s, peaked in 1995 and fell precipitously thereafter. Such dysfunctional inflation rates virtually disappeared in the new millennium.
- **Black market premium on foreign exchange:** Premia of above 20% were common especially in Africa until 1995. Just like high inflation, this phenomenon largely disappeared.
- **Currency overvaluation:** Rates of overvaluation (measured using purchasing power parity data and corrected for the relative cheapness of nontraded goods in low-income countries) of more than 50% peaked with more than half of all countries affected in 1980. Prevalence fell to around 10% of countries by 1995, although it reappeared in the later 2000s.
- **Negative real interest rates on bank savings deposits:** The share of countries with real interest rates of below minus 5% fell from a peak of 50% in 1980 to about 10% after the mid-1990s (with the exception of a spike around the time of the financial crisis).
- **Abnormally low trade shares in GDP:** A downward trend characterizes the prevalence of an economy more closed to trade than would be expected—from half of all countries in 1961 to 20% by 1990 and 10% by the early 2000s.

The 92 countries with at least one extremely bad policy in the 1980–98 period, improved them over the 1999–2015 period, and experienced higher average growth (2.1% as compared with 0.7% in the first period). This documentation of declining pathologies contributes new evidence to the correlates of cross-country growth and is less unfavourable to the relevance of Washington Consensus reforms than the data to the early 1990s had suggested. It does not, however, by itself support a causal role for orthodox reforms in improved performance.

16.3.3 Growth accounting: Measuring and interpreting TFP

At the start of Section 16.2, we introduced the idea of total factor productivity, or *TFP*. *TFP* growth is a label for the contribution to economic growth that is unaccounted for by the growth of factor inputs (e.g. labour and capital). It captures the intangible aspects of human progress, such as efficiency gains and management quality, that improve the productivity of factor inputs (i.e. the amount of output that can be produced with a given amount of inputs).

Solow's method of calculating total factor productivity growth is known as *growth accounting*. To see how this works we can start from our standard Cobb-Douglas production function:

$$\mathrm{Y} = \mathrm{A}\mathrm{K}^{\alpha}\mathrm{N}^{1-\alpha}.$$

We then take logs and differentiate with respect to time to get:

$$\frac{\dot{\mathrm{Y}}}{\mathrm{Y}} = \frac{\dot{\mathrm{A}}}{\mathrm{A}} + \alpha\frac{\dot{\mathrm{K}}}{\mathrm{K}} + (1-\alpha)\frac{\dot{\mathrm{N}}}{\mathrm{N}}$$

$$g_{\mathrm{Y}} = g_{\mathrm{TFP}} + \alpha g_{\mathrm{K}} + (1-\alpha)n.$$

TFP growth (also known as the Solow residual) is the difference between output growth and a weighted sum of the growth of factor inputs where the weights are given by the factor shares, i.e. it is the growth that is not attributed to the growth of either labour or capital inputs. Using national accounts data it is possible to calculate TFP growth.

$$\text{TFP growth} = g_Y - \alpha g_K - (1-\alpha)n.$$

In empirical analysis, it is often illuminating to work in per capita terms and we can rearrange this equation as follows:

$$\begin{aligned}\text{TFP growth} &= (g_Y - n) - \alpha g_K + \alpha n \\ &= g_y - \alpha g_k,\end{aligned}$$

where as usual, $y \equiv Y/N$ and $k \equiv K/N$. We can also turn the equation around and decompose the growth of labour productivity into the contribution from the growth of capital intensity, i.e. capital-deepening, and the contribution of TFP growth:

$$g_y = \alpha g_k + \text{TFP growth}.$$

Over the years economists have come up with many objections to Solow's attempt to use a simple accounting decomposition based on the Cobb-Douglas production function to measure technological progress,[17] but as a way of organizing the data, the technique is widely viewed as valuable.

Table 16.2 shows how growth accounting can provide useful insights for understanding the within- and cross-country evolution of GDP and of hourly labour productivity. Coverage of the period from 1960 to 2019 for a set of high-income countries produces interesting findings. Cette and coauthors constructed a database for growth accounting in which the growth of output per hour is split between the contribution of capital of three types and the contribution of TFP. The three types of capital are:

- ICT (information and communication technology) capital,
- robots,
- non-ICT, non-robots capital.

In a further step, TFP growth is itself split between the contribution of

- education (with one additional year of education assumed to raise the level of average productivity by 5%)
- robotization (the contribution of robots is split with 24% attributed to its effect through the stock of capital referred to as 'robots', above, and 76% to an increase in TFP referred to as 'robotization').

The table contains a large amount of information, and it is left for the reader to explore at greater depth, including consulting the tables for other countries that can be found in the article. Here are some highlights:

---

[17] For a wide-ranging, critical assessment, see Lipsey and Carlaw (2004).

GDP growth (in %) and contributions (in pp) United States	Period 1 1960–75	Period 2 1975–95	Period 3 1995–2005	Period 4 2005–19	Total period 1960–2019
GDP (1)	3.66	3.16	3.39	1.70	2.99
Hours (2)	1.38	1.88	1.01	0.71	1.33
Productivity (3) = (1)-(2)	2.28	1.28	2.38	1.05	1.66
Capital deepening (4)	0.67	0.25	0.58	0.40	0.45
ICT capital total (5)	0.11	0.27	0.43	0.20	0.24
Robots (6)	0.00	0.01	0.03	0.03	0.02
Non ICT capital and non robots capital (7) = (4)-(5)-(6)	0.56	−0.03	0.12	0.17	0.19
TFP (8) = (3)-(4)	1.61	1.03	1.79	0.65	1.22
Education (9)	0.45	0.27	0.20	0.17	0.28
Robotization (10)	0.01	0.03	0.08	0.10	

GDP growth (in %) and contributions (in pp) Eurozone	Period 1 1960–75	Period 2 1975–95	Period 3 1995–2005	Period 4 2005–19	Total period 1960–2019
GDP (1)	4.60	2.44	2.12	1.09	2.61
Hours (2)	-0.71	-0.22	0.93	0.37	-0.01
Productivity (3) = (1)-(2)	5.31	2.66	1.19	0.72	2.62
Capital deepening (4)	2.03	0.97	0.43	0.42	1.02
ICT capital total (5)	0.17	0.23	0.24	0.14	0.19
Robots (6)	0.00	0.03	0.08	0.05	0.04
Non ICT capital and non robots capital (7) = (4)-(5)-(6)	1.86	0.71	0.11	0.23	0.79
TFP (8) = (3)-(4)	3.28	1.69	0.76	0.30	1.60
Education (9)	0.59	0.38	0.21	0.31	0.39
Robotization (10)	0.01	0.08	0.24	0.15	0.12
Residual (11) = (8)-(9)-(10)	2.68	1.23	0.31	-0.16	1.09

GDP growth (in %) and contributions (in pp) United Kingdom	Period 1 1960–75	Period 2 1975–95	Period 3 1995–2005	Period 4 2005–19	Total period 1960–2019
GDP (1)	2.35	2.28	3.05	1.36	2.21
Hours (2)	-0.70	-0.23	0.89	0.91	0.11
Productivity (3) = (1)-(2)	3.05	2.51	2.16	0.45	2.10
Capital deepening (4)	1.69	0.79	0.41	0.32	0.84
ICT capital total (5)	0.11	0.24	0.35	0.08	0.19
Robots (6)	0.00	0.01	0.01	0.01	0.01

Table 16.2 Contributions to growth of real output in the market economy, United States, Eurozone, United Kingdom, and Germany: 1960–2019.

Source: Reproduced from Cette et al. (2022).

Non ICT capital and non robots capital (7) = (4)-(5)-(6)	1.58	0.54	0.05	0.23	0.64
TFP (8) = (3)-(4)	1.36	1.72	1.75	0.13	1.26
Education (9)	0.76	0.42	0.06	0.10	0.37
Robotization (10)	0.00	0.03	0.04	0.02	0.02
Residual (11) = (8)-(9)-(10)	0.60	1.27	1.65	0.01	0.87

GDP growth (in %) and contributions (in pp) Germany	Period 1 1960–75	Period 2 1975–95	Period 3 1995–2005	Period 4 2005–19	Total period 1960–2019
GDP (1)	3.68	2.47	1.20	1.52	2.33
Hours (2)	-1.41	-0.42	-0.67	0.86	-0.41
Productivity (3) = (1)-(2)	5.09	2.89	1.87	0.65	2.74
Capital deepening (4)	2.16	0.96	0.80	0.23	1.07
ICT capital total (5)	0.19	0.24	0.26	0.07	0.19
Robots (6)	0.01	0.05	0.17	0.10	0.08
Non ICT capital and non robots capital (7) = (4)-(5)-(6)	1.97	0.68	0.37	0.05	0.80
TFP (8) = (3)-(4)	2.93	1.93	1.06	0.42	1.68
Education (9)	0.69	0.20	0.03	0.01	0.25
Robotization (10)	0.02	0.15	0.53	0.32	0.24
Residual (11) = (8)-(9)-(10)	2.22	1.58	0.50	0.09	1.19

Table 16.2 Continued

1. **Trends in productivity and TFP growth:** The post-WWII period was characterized by countries in continental Europe catching up to US productivity levels; this was echoed in the TFP growth comparisons. The US 'tech boom' from 1995 stands out in the data for the period 1995–2005 with higher productivity growth than before but there was no sign of this in the data for Europe. Performance in the Eurozone was weak vis-à-vis both the UK and the US. In all regions, productivity and TFP growth were at their lowest in the final period, 2005–2019. We return to discussions about the productivity puzzle in Chapter 17.
2. **ICT:** Consistent with the pattern in (1), capital deepening was much greater in Euro area countries in the 1960–75 period than in the US. However, for 1995–2005, ICT capital (one component of capital-deepening) contributed twice as much to average productivity growth in the US as in the Eurozone.
3. **Robots:** Given the concentration of robot use in the engineering industries in which Germany has a comparative advantage, it is unsurprising that they contribute more to productivity growth (via TFP and capital accumulation) than is the case elsewhere, especially from 1995. Robots are virtually nowhere to be seen in the UK data. In the data for Japan (not shown), the contribution of robots and robotization is at its peak in the 1975–95 period.

4. **Education:** The contribution of education to productivity growth almost disappears in the UK after 1995, whereas increasing years of schooling continue to add modestly to TFP growth in the US, and somewhat more so in the Euro area (but not Germany) throughout.

16.4 ENDOGENOUS GROWTH

Using the Solow model, we obtained insight into the role of capital accumulation as a mechanism through which a society raises GDP per capita and how the presence of diminishing returns to factor accumulation implies that changes in the saving/investment rate or in policies or institutions cannot affect the rate of productivity growth in the long run. This is determined outside the model by the rate of exogenous technological progress. Nevertheless, the 'Solow fundamentals' along with the policies and institutions that determine them can affect the *level* of GDP per capita in a Solow world, and as a result, the rate at which poorer countries catch up to richer ones.

We shall see that the defining feature of a model with endogenous growth is a production function in which there are constant returns to the accumulation of a factor. With constant returns to accumulation at the level of the economy as a whole (be it of physical capital, human capital or ideas), the growth rate of GDP per capita in the steady state no longer depends on an assumed rate of exogenous technological progress.

This result begs the question: what is it that offsets diminishing returns and produces constant returns to the factor that is accumulated? Irrespective of the factor that is accumulated, the common characteristic of models of endogenous growth is that there are spillovers to the economy as a whole from the individual producer's decision to accumulate. As we shall see, there are three implications of this:

1. Technological progress itself is endogenous because it is the outcome of decisions made by economic agents.
2. The spillovers to the aggregate economy imply there is a market failure because the individual producer takes no account of the external effect of their decision, and hence there is scope for welfare-improving economic policy to increase the investments that produce public goods (knowledge). The social marginal return to accumulation exceeds the private return.
3. If technological progress takes the specific form of producing constant returns to the accumulation of capital, human capital, or ideas at the aggregate level, then there is endogenous growth, and long-run productivity *growth* will depend on the resources devoted to accumulation.

For example, a model based on physical capital accumulation (Frankel 1962; see Section 16.7.2 in the Appendix) creates constant returns at the level of the economy as a whole as follows: investment by a firm with a conventional production function with diminishing returns, spills over to increase the stock of knowledge in the economy as a whole, which is available to all firms. This can be described as a process of learning by doing at the level of the aggregate economy with the implication in (2) above that too little investment will occur if this is left to private sector decision-making. A version of Frankel's model is set out in the appendix to illustrate the 'micro-macro' combination that highlights the difference between endogenous technological progress and endogenous growth.

16.4.1 Research and development

This section introduces the role of ideas and technological innovation as the engine of capitalist economic growth. The approach to technological progress in the Solow model places the process outside the realm of economic forces. Improvements in productivity appear like manna from heaven at no resource cost. Models with endogenous innovation centre on purposeful innovation activities undertaken with the aim of securing innovation rents because, at least for a time, the productivity enhancement is not freely available to imitators.

The ideas that form the output of the innovation process are different from many of the other goods we encounter in everyday life, and economists refer to them as possessing the properties of *non-rivalry* and *non-excludability*. By contrast, most goods are both rivalrous and excludable. Non-rivalry refers to the use of an existing idea at zero marginal cost. It is the rivalrous nature of most natural resources that lies behind much human conflict. More generally, your consumption of the additional food resources used in your meals today comes at a marginal cost and you can prevent others from eating the food.

Economists often visualize the ideas that result from innovation as blueprints. These blueprints are instructions on how to build the latest solar panel or how to produce the MRNA Covid-19 vaccine. Once a blueprint becomes available (many patents last for 20 years), anyone who understands it can use it and market their own products based on it. This explains why we have generics pharmaceutical companies producing drugs that are chemically identical to their most famous branded cousins.

Hence ideas in the context of innovation are non-rivalrous. However, at least for some time period, they are excludable. The excludability property of ideas in the process of innovation naturally leads to an imperfect market structure in the market for blueprints.

The legal institution of patents is one method that allows firms to make their blueprint public and at the same time earn supernormal profits (or, equivalently innovation rents) for a limited period of time. In exchange for making the knowledge public, the inventor has the right to exclude others from making, using or selling their invention for 20 years. Pharmaceutical companies invest billions of dollars in developing new drugs. If new drugs were marketed immediately at the marginal cost of manufacture (think of how low the marginal cost of producing one pill is) firms would soon go out of business and innovation would slow. Setting prices above the zero marginal cost in the market for ideas is entailed by the intrinsic properties of ideas as blueprints. On the other hand, the non-rivalrous nature of ideas promises social benefits as everyone can benefit from them without diminishing their availability to others. Before we return to the role in innovation of the extent of competition in the product market and of spillovers, we establish the relationship between endogenous growth and endogenous technological progress based on the production of ideas.

16.4.2 Endogenous growth and endogenous technological progress: The Romer model

The nature of endogenous growth

At its most basic, as described by Frankel, a model of endogenous growth requires that the production function for the economy as a whole exhibits exactly constant returns to a factor that can be accumulated—for example, capital, human capital or ideas. This contrasts with the production function in the Solow model, where there are diminishing returns to capital, or to human and physical capital.

Taking the example of capital as the factor that can be accumulated, in Figure 16.17, a production function with constant returns to capital is shown. It is linear rather than concave. In this case, where the sY line coincides with the δK line, saving (and investment) is just equal to depreciation and, whatever level the capital stock is at, it will remain constant at that level, K_0 in Figure 16.17. If the savings rate rises to s_1 then unlike the case with diminishing returns (illustrated in Figure 16.13a), the capital stock will continue growing without limit; as will output. This is a model of 'endogenous growth'.

Endogenous technological progress consistent with endogenous growth

To incorporate the production of ideas into a simple growth model, we begin with a production function using capital and labour, but with a twist: we distinguish between workers who are employed in production and those employed in research. The population is assumed to be constant. We denote by N_t^Y the total number of workers employed in the final goods market. These are the workers who use the blueprints in conjunction with physical capital and raw labour to produce final goods. We also denote by N_t^R the number of workers employed in R&D. These are the researchers who increase the stock of knowledge in the economy through innovation. They create blueprints that will be used later on in production by workers in the final goods sector.

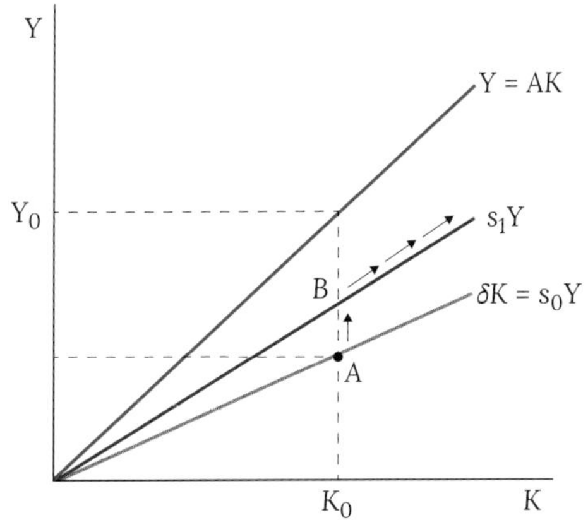

Figure 16.17 A rise in the savings rate in the endogenous growth model. Visit www.oup.com/he/carlin-soskice to explore a rise in the savings rate in the endogenous growth model with Animated Analytical Diagram 16.17.

We use a Cobb-Douglas production function for final goods:

$$Y_t = K_t^{\alpha}(A_t N_t^Y)^{1-\alpha},$$

where A_t now stands for ideas. This does not represent exogenous technological progress as in the Solow model, but is an integral component of the model. Total labour in the economy at time t is given by $N_t = N_t^Y + N_t^R$, that is, the sum of the labour employed in the manufacturing sector producing final output and the labour employed in the research sector producing blueprints.

What can we say about the accumulation equation for blueprints or ideas, A? The source of endogenous growth in this model is the *constant returns* to the *accumulation of blueprints*. We begin with a general specification for endogenous technological progress and then show the constant returns case:

$$\dot{A}_t = cA_t^{\eta} N_t^R,$$

which says that ideas accumulate proportionally to the number of workers N_t^R employed in R&D and in a way that is related to the current stock of ideas A_t, where c is a constant. The size of the parameter η is important for the accumulation of ideas equation. As long as $\eta > 0$, the equation captures the notion that the economy benefits from positive spillovers or external effects from the existing stock of ideas. If $\eta = 1$, there are constant returns to the accumulation of ideas and this will be a source of endogenous growth. This version of the model is often referred to as the Romer model.[18]

Since we are especially interested in the possibility of endogenous growth, we concentrate on the special case where $\eta = 1$. In this case the accumulation equation for ideas is given by

$$\dot{A}_t = cA_t N_t^R,$$

where we divide both sides by A_t to obtain the growth rate of ideas

$$g_A = cN_t^R.$$

Note that only with $\eta = 1$ do we get steady state endogenous growth: it requires constant returns to the accumulation of ideas. The growth rate of the factor that can be accumulated can be expressed entirely in terms of the exogenous variables. This gives a constant rate of technological progress in the steady state, $g_A \equiv \dot{A}_t/A$.

In the Solow model with exogenous technological progress (where $g_A = x$), the steady state growth rate of per capita output is equal to the growth rate of ideas, where x is given exogenously. The difference here is that under the assumption that $\eta = 1$, $g_A = cN_t^R$, which means that the steady state growth rate of the economy is higher the more people are employed in the research sector.

To summarize, this is called a model of *endogenous growth* because unlike the Solow case, where an increase in the rate of technological progress, x, was exogenous, here a permanently higher growth rate of productivity can be achieved by a policy of increasing the number of R&D workers.

---

[18] This is an outline of the model developed by Paul Romer (1990). See Carlin and Soskice (2006) Chapter 14 for an extended presentation.

16.5 SCHUMPETERIAN GROWTH: THE AGHION-HOWITT MODEL

Innovation works through entrepreneurs who implement new discoveries and bring them successfully to the market. Writing in the first half of the 20th century, Joseph Schumpeter identified the entrepreneur as the key agent in the process of innovation, which extends well beyond the idea of inventing a new product.[19] Innovations include developing a new route by which existing factors of production are channelled into the production process; a new product or improving the quality of an existing product; a completely new production process for an existing product; or a completely new market, where there previously was none.

Schumpeter's concept of creative destruction encapsulates the dual nature of technological progress: in terms of 'creation', entrepreneurs introduce new products or processes in the hope that they will enjoy temporary monopoly profits, known as innovation rents, as they capture markets. In doing so, they make old technologies or products obsolete—this is the 'destruction'. The size of the market plays a very important role in the Schumpeterian model because it affects the scale of innovation rents that can be enjoyed.

The motivation for innovators to make risky investments in new products is to make a temporary profit by stealing a march on other producers. This requires that the innovation cannot immediately be copied by an imitator. Formal patents are only one method of protecting the temporary monopoly profits of the entrepreneur, trade secrets are another and being the first mover into a market is a third. The first mover method for capturing innovation rents highlights the important role in market economies of the emergence of new firms. One reason for the weakness of innovation in planned economies was the control by the state over new business activities.

For the process of creative destruction, it is also necessary that institutions are in place to ensure that the rents from innovation go to the entrepreneur and are not confiscated by the government or other powerful groups like organized crime.

Linking the Solow model to the Schumpeterian model

The insights of Schumpeter and Solow can be brought together to discuss appropriate growth-enhancing policies. Schumpeter's insight that the prospect of a larger market spurs innovation is complementary to Solow's insight that faster technological progress reduces the amount of capital required per efficiency unit of labour. We take each element in turn and present them in Figure 16.18.

In the Solow model, we can compare different steady state growth paths for different rates of exogenous technological progress, x. Given the savings rate, population growth rate, and depreciation in the economy, a higher rate of technological progress implies a lower level of capital per efficiency unit of labour on the steady state growth path (the line labelled $(n+\delta+x)\hat{k}$ in Figure 16.12 rotates to the left). This allows us to derive a downward-sloping relationship between the level of capital per efficiency unit of labour, $\hat{k}$, and x, the rate of technological progress, which in turn defines the growth

[19] Schumpeter (1934; 1961 edition: p. 66).

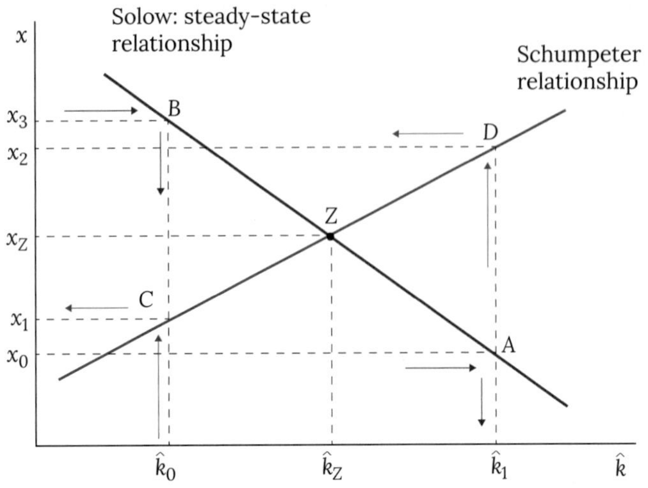

Figure 16.18 Bringing Solow and Schumpeter together: the interaction of technological progress and capital accumulation. Visit www.oup.com/he/carlin-soskice to explore the Solow and Schumpeter relationships with Animated Analytical Diagram 16.18.

rate of output per capita in the steady state. This downward-sloping line is shown in Figure 16.18 and labelled the 'Solow steady state relationship'.

In the Solow relationship, the causality goes from the rate of exogenous technological progress to the steady state level of capital per efficiency unit. Faster technological progress means that at the initial steady state, less capital is now needed to equip new entrants to the labour force (since the newly arrived technology raises their productivity using the existing capital). This shifts the economy to a faster rate of growth with lower capital intensity measured in efficiency units. In Figure 16.18, we can compare the initial equilibrium at point A with the new equilibrium at point B associated with the higher rate of technological progress.

Next, a Schumpeterian element is introduced by modelling the determinants of x, the rate of technological progress, as a function of innovative activities. In a model of endogenous growth based on endogenous technological progress, steady state growth will depend on the expected returns to innovative effort which are greater with higher capital (and output) per efficiency unit of labour, as depicted in the upward-sloping Schumpeter relationship. Schumpeter stressed the importance of the size of the market for the incentive to innovate, and a simple way of capturing this is to assume that a higher level of output or of capital per efficiency unit of labour implies a larger market for the innovator.

This gives a second relationship between the rate of technological progress, x, and capital intensity per efficiency unit, $\hat{k}$. This positively sloped relationship is labelled the 'Schumpeter relationship' in Figure 16.18. Compare point C in Figure 16.18 with point D. In the Schumpeter relationship, the causality goes from the size of the market, which is taken as given by the innovator and is proxied by the economy's capital per efficiency unit, to the rate of technological progress.

On the steady state growth path, the economy where both these forces are at work is characterized by the combination of capital per efficiency unit and rate of technological progress where the two relationships intersect. In the example shown in Figure 16.18, the growth rate at point Z is x_Z.

Policies to raise long-run productivity growth

We now consider how policy could be used to shift either of these relationships and promote higher steady state growth:

1. **An increase in the savings (and investment) rate:** Governments can use tax policy to stimulate saving and investment and shift the Solow relationship outward. At a given rate of technological progress, higher saving leads to an increase in capital per efficiency unit through the Solow (capital accumulation) mechanism.

   In the combined model, this increases the size of the market for innovators and prompts more R&D activity via the Schumpeter relationship. The economy moves to a new steady state growth path fixed by a point to the north-east of point Z at point A in Figure 16.19.

   In contrast to the standard Solow model, this means that higher saving produces a permanently higher growth rate. It is interesting to note as well that to the extent there is a causal link of this kind from capital per efficiency unit to R&D and via R&D to growth as suggested by the Schumpeter relationship, a regression framework based on the Solow model will overestimate the direct contribution of capital to growth by ignoring the fact that part of its contribution is via the R&D that it stimulates.
2. **An improvement in the expected returns to innovation:** Typical policies to stimulate R&D and shift the Schumpeter relationship upwards are taxes and subsidies

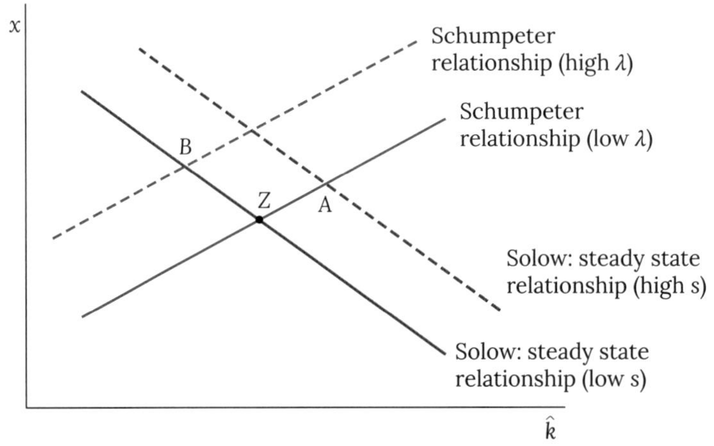

Figure 16.19 Policy experiments and endogenous growth: rise in savings; rise in the intensity of R&D. Visit www.oup.com/he/carlin-soskice to explore policy experiments and endogenous growth with Animated Analytical Diagram 16.19.

that reduce the marginal cost of R&D. Policies to increase investment in higher education, and as argued in Section 16.5.1, well-designed competition policies could also have this effect. Policies that help to expand the size of the market are also relevant. In the second experiment, we assume that the policy environment becomes more supportive of R&D, i.e. high λ.[20] As a result, R&D intensity rises, which shifts the Schumpeter line upwards. The more rapid technological progress takes the economy to a higher growth path at lower capital per efficiency unit along the Solow relationship. The new steady state growth equilibrium is to the north-west of point Z at point B.

Similarly, better protection of innovation from imitators through, for example, more effective enforcement of property rights, shifts the Schumpeter line upwards and raises the steady state growth rate. Conversely, the Schumpeter line is shifted down by a higher interest rate as this depresses the present value of expected profits from the innovation. Complementary policies could be adopted that would act on both relationships, raising the growth rate of productivity.

16.5.1 **The model**

To move from a broad framework for discussing Schumpeterian growth to one in which the process of creative destruction itself is modelled requires specifying in more detail how innovation takes place. The fundamental relationship that we need to introduce is a so-called research arbitrage condition in which the marginal cost of R&D is equated to the expected marginal benefit. This pins down how labour is allocated between R&D and production.

In order to show how to derive the arbitrage condition in a way that can be easily grasped, Aghion and Howitt provide a stripped-down version of their basic model. In this simplified model, there is no capital. There are two goods in the economy: final goods and intermediate goods. Innovation only takes place in the intermediate goods sector. The final good, Y, is produced using the intermediate good only (i.e. no labour is used in the production of the final good) and as quality improvements in intermediate goods take place, this raises the output of final goods. The production function for final goods is therefore written as:

$$Y = Am^{\alpha}, \tag{16.14}$$

where m is the intermediate good and α is a constant less than one. A is the productivity parameter and in this model, it reflects the quality of the intermediate good. Any quality improvement of the intermediate good due to innovation will raise A.

The key assumption necessary for the model of endogenous *technological progress* to produce endogenous growth is that each innovation raises the quality of the intermediate good from A to γA, where $\gamma > 1$ and n is the nth innovation:

[20] See Bloom, Van Reenen, and Williams (2019).

$$A_{n+1} = \gamma A_n. \tag{16.15}$$

This is where the 'constant returns' assumption that we have seen to be necessary to deliver endogenous growth appears in this model.[21] The production function for the *intermediate good* is very simple: one unit of labour produces one unit of m. This means that m also measures the amount of labour used in the production of the intermediate good so the total labour force is split between the production of the intermediate good and R&D activity directed toward improving its quality:

$$N = m + q, \tag{16.16}$$

where q is the amount of labour devoted to R&D. It is assumed that the market for the final good is perfectly competitive. But in the intermediate goods sector, anyone who innovates has a monopoly for one period before the quality improvement is imitated by the other producers. Figure 16.20 provides a schematic illustration of how the different elements of the model fit together.

Each individual in this economy lives for just one period and aims to maximize their consumption at the end of the period. The decision they face is how to maximize their consumption by making a choice between on the one hand, working in the intermediate goods sector and receiving a wage of w and, on the other hand, engaging in risky R&D in the hope of innovating and making monopoly profits. The return from engaging in R&D depends on the probability of success and it is assumed that the investment of q units of labour in R&D leads to a quality improvement with probability λq.

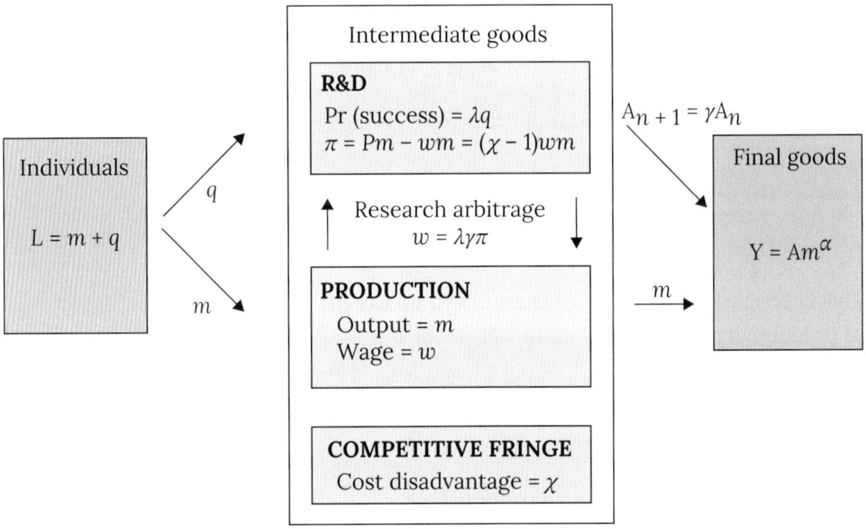

Figure 16.20 Schematic illustration of the Aghion–Howitt model of Schumpeterian growth.

---

[21] As Solow points out, if the effect of innovation on output takes a different form such as $A_{n+1} = A_n + \gamma$ instead of $A_{n+1} = A_n\gamma$, where n is the nth innovation, then growth will not be endogenous (Solow 2000, p. 177).

Although a successful innovator has a monopoly in the production of the higher quality intermediate good, there is a so-called competitive fringe of producers who can produce the lower quality version of the good. The presence of the competitive fringe limits the price the innovator can charge and hence, the innovation rents. The unit cost of production of the competitive fringe is higher because they have not innovated and they can produce good m at a cost of χ units of labour, where $\chi > 1$ as compared to the one unit of labour required by the firm that has innovated.

If the cost disadvantage of the competitive fringe is very large, i.e. $\chi \geq 1/\alpha$, then the monopolist is able to charge the monopoly price and the extent of competition plays no role. In order to rule this out, it is assumed that $\chi < 1/\alpha$. In this case, the maximum price that the innovator can charge is χw: at this price, the competitive fringe will not produce the intermediate good because they prefer to receive the wage, w. The profit for a successful innovator is equal to total revenue minus total cost and is higher, the higher is χ:

$$\begin{aligned}\pi &= Pm - wm \\ &= (\chi - 1)wm.\end{aligned}$$

The two key equations are for the clearing of the labour market and the research arbitrage condition. Labour market clearing is, as we have seen:

$$\mathrm{N} = m + q.$$

We now have all the ingredients for the research arbitrage condition:

$$\begin{aligned}w &= \lambda\gamma\pi \\ &= \lambda\gamma(\chi - 1)wm.\end{aligned}$$

Substituting for m using the labour market-clearing equation gives:

$$\begin{aligned}\frac{1}{\lambda\gamma(\chi - 1)} &= \mathrm{N} - q \\ &\rightarrow q = \mathrm{N} - \frac{1}{\lambda\gamma(\chi - 1)}.\end{aligned}$$

This determines the amount of labour devoted to R&D in the steady state. The growth of productivity in the steady state will be equal to

$$x = \lambda q(\gamma - 1). \tag{16.17}$$

In words, productivity will grow according to:

- the incremental size of the innovation, i.e. $\gamma - 1$,
- the amount of resources devoted to R&D, q, and
- the probability that R&D delivers an innovation, λ.

By substituting the steady state equation for q, we can see the set of determinants of the growth rate:

$$g_y = x = \lambda(\gamma - 1)\left[N - \frac{1}{\lambda\gamma(\chi - 1)}\right]. \tag{16.18}$$

Growth in output per capita in this economy is permanently higher, the higher is the probability that R&D delivers an innovation (λ), the bigger is the incremental size of the innovation, γ, the larger is the size of the labour force, N, and the larger is χ. The role of the first two factors is clear.

However, the idea that a larger labour force per se or a larger number of R&D workers can increase the rate of growth forever does not accord with the facts: the fivefold increase in the number of R&D workers in the USA since the 1950s has not been accompanied by a change in the rate of productivity growth. Aghion and Howitt show how their model of Schumpeterian growth can be modified to eliminate this so-called scale effect while retaining the feature of endogenous growth. First of all they extend the simple model to allow for the existence of many varieties of the intermediate good. They then argue that the number of varieties proliferates as the economy grows and that in steady state growth, extra R&D input is dissipated by being spread across all varieties so that there is no relationship in the steady state between the size of the labour force and the growth of productivity. This produces a modified equation for steady state growth:

$$g_y = f[\lambda, (\gamma - 1), (\chi - 1)], \tag{16.19}$$

in which the size of the labour force plays no role but in which the other determinants remain in place.[22] Policies that impinge on the research arbitrage equation so as to increase the share of resources devoted to R&D will raise the growth rate in this model.

Aghion and Howitt provide some evidence from the USA for the post-war period to suggest that the data is consistent with the prediction of their endogenous growth model that productivity growth should track the ratio of R&D expenditure to GDP (q in the model).

Finally, we turn to the role of χ in the Schumpeterian model. The higher is χ, the higher is the cost disadvantage of the non-innovating competitive fringe in the intermediate goods sector and, as we have seen, this raises the profits for an innovator and hence is associated with a higher growth rate. χ can be interpreted as an inverse measure of product market competition in the intermediate goods sector: in a more competitive economy, χ will be closer to one and the monopoly profits available to a successful innovator are lower. This captures Schumpeter's insight that stronger product market competition may blunt the incentive for innovation. However, Schumpeter also stressed the pro-innovation role of the competitive struggle to be the first to innovate. We turn next to providing an introduction to the debate about the role competition plays in innovation.

---

[22] This is explained in more detail in Aghion and Howitt (2005), in *Handbook of Economic Growth*, Volume 1A. Chapter 2, Section 5.

16.5.2 **Competition**

The Aghion-Howitt model provides a way of explaining two opposite effects of competition on innovation and has been used to test whether they are found in the data.[23]

Figure 16.21 shows the relationship between the innovation activities of British firms as measured by patents and a measure of the degree of competition in the product market. As product market competition increases to the right of the figure, innovation first increases but at high levels of competition, innovation falls. This inverse U-shaped relationship in the data suggests that both of the Schumpeterian effects can be in operation. For sectors where competition is low, more intense rivalry appears to stimulate patenting; whereas in sectors where competition is already intense, an increase in competition sees innovation fall off.

When modelling the inverse U-shaped relationship, the economy is divided into three sectors according to whether the sector begins the period with technology at the frontier, one step behind or two steps behind. Innovation is always 'step-by-step', which means that a firm can only upgrade its technology by one step as a result of innovation activity: there is no leapfrogging. Moreover, it is impossible for a sector to be more than two steps behind the frontier because it is assumed that there is an automatic spillover from innovation in the one step behind sector after one period. These assumptions mean that there are three sector types.

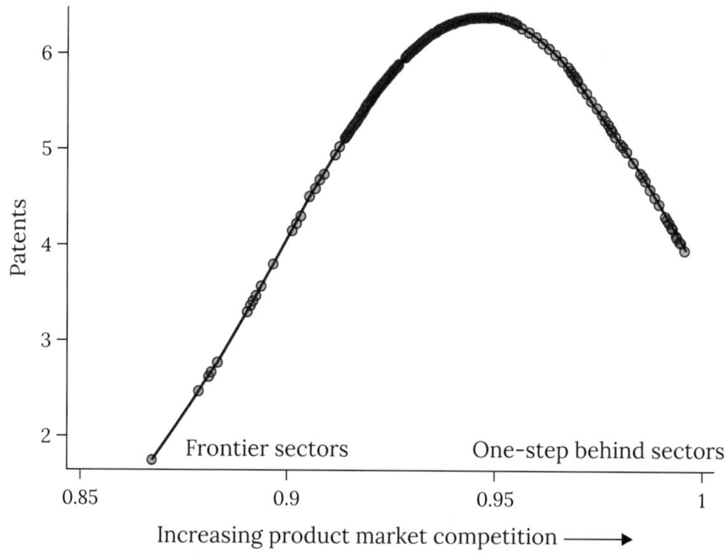

Figure 16.21 The relationship between innovation and competition: UK firms.

Source: Aghion et al. (2005); data kindly provided by Nick Bloom.

[23] This work is based on Aghion et al. (2001). It is presented in Aghion and Howitt (2009) and Aghion et al. (2014).

1. In frontier sectors, large or radical innovations are possible, which improve quality (cut costs) by so much that they confer temporary monopoly pricing power on the innovating firm. For such firms, more competition makes more attractive the carrot of monopoly rents that would follow a successful innovation. Hence, at the frontier, *more competition boosts innovation*. This is referred to as the 'escape competition' effect.
2. For the one-step behind sectors, it is assumed that the size of innovation these firms could make is sufficiently modest that an innovator is unable to charge the monopoly price. The reason is that the modest innovation does not force the other firms in the industry (referred to as the competitive fringe), which do not innovate, out of business. Since there is no chance to escape the competitive fringe, *more competition dampens innovation* by lowering the successful innovator's markup. With more competition, more firms can innovate and the markup for each of them will be lower.
3. For the two-step behind sectors, there is no incentive to innovate at all—they automatically gain from the spillover of innovation from the one-step behind sectors after one period.

As shown in Figure 16.21, there is interesting empirical support for the existence of these effects. Aghion et al. (2005) use firm-level data from the UK on patents as a measure of innovation and on the price-cost margin as an inverse measure of the extent of competition in the product market. The relationship is plotted using a quadratic estimator (which allows a non-linear relationship). The data suggest that at lower levels of competition, which are characteristic of frontier sectors, an increase in competition would stimulate innovation because firms have more incentive to escape the competition and seek the monopoly rents. In the more competitive environment inside the frontier, where only incremental innovations are possible and therefore the prize of monopoly rents is not available, the effect of an inverse relationship between competition and innovation dominates: more competition lowers innovation.

The idea that more intense competition boosts innovation in frontier firms but may discourage it among non-frontier firms is reflected in the results of another empirical test. Aghion et al. (2009) use UK firm-level data and measure the extent of competition by the entry of foreign firms into an industry. They find that as the entry rate of foreign firms rises (pushing up competition), a measure of innovation (TFP growth) rises for firms near the frontier but falls for firms far away from the frontier. This suggests that for frontier firms, policies to boost competition (for example, by encouraging entry of foreign firms) promote innovation through the incentives they create for firms to get a step ahead. But for firms far from the frontier, the additional competition is discouraging for innovation.

For frontier firms, policies that promote competition and policies favouring innovation are *complementary* for boosting growth. The reinforcing effect of greater competition and policies to raise the expected return from R&D, including stronger temporary protection of innovators' intellectual property, brings to the fore the subtle balance between the private incentives to take risky R&D decisions and the social benefits of the spread of new ideas.

Evidence of this complementarity comes from the European Union. Researchers found that innovation in member countries with stronger protection of intellectual property rights increased more following the implementation of the European Single Market than in members with weaker IP protection (Aghion et al. 2014).

16.5.3 **Creative destruction and inequality**

As we have seen, the Schumpeterian model of growth relies on the carrot of higher profits (innovation rents) to stimulate improvements in quality. With high levels of competition, the receipt of innovation rents is temporary as new entrepreneurs emerge to displace the incumbents. Successful innovation is rewarded, which raises inequality at the top of the income and wealth distributions. But success in protecting those rents and inhibiting the operation of the 'stick' of creative destruction restricting new entry and firm turnover will dampen growth and entrench high levels of inequality. The hump-shaped relationship between competition and innovation lies behind the hypotheses that have been put to the empirical test in recent decades. We provide some of the evidence that backs up the Schumpeterian model's predictions, beginning with the channel from innovation to inequality.[24]

Innovation via creative destruction leads to inequality; persistence is the problem

Two very different kinds of study highlight the contribution to the very top incomes in the economy of an individual's direct participation in successful innovations by private firms. In data on Finnish firms, 45% of the rents from innovation go to entrepreneurs, only 8% to inventors, 22% to white collar workers and 26% to blue collar workers.

Using US state-level data for the period from 1976 to 2009 on top 1% income shares and measures of patents as proxies for innovation, and implementing a research design that enables causal effects to be identified, Aghion et al. (2019) found that higher levels of innovation caused greater inequality at the top of the income distribution. However, there is no relationship between the innovativeness of a state in the US (measured by patents) and the extent of inequality among the bottom 99%. The same study found that the most innovative commuting zones in the US were those that had the highest level of social mobility as measured by the probability of an individual with parents from the bottom 20% of the income distribution reaching the highest 20% in adulthood. This suggests that innovation is indeed associated with very high incomes but also with higher social mobility and not with higher overall inequality (Aghion et al. 2019).

The danger is that innovation rents would be used to protect innovating firms from competition and by preventing the social mobility that comes with new entrants, would undermine the temporary nature of the 'good' inequality arising from innovation incentives. The same US state-level data is used to provide evidence of this effect by interacting a measure of the extent of spending by firms on lobbying government

---

[24] This section draws on Blundell, R., Jaravel, X., and Toivanen, O. (2022) 'Inequality and creative destruction', Institute for Fiscal Studies. doi:https://doi.org/10.1920/wp.ifs.2022.0822.

officials with the innovation indicator: where lobbying is greater, the innovation by entrant firms is lower and there is a weaker association with the top income share.

Turning to the downward-sloping part of the hump-shaped relationship between competition and innovation, unlike at the frontier where more competition stimulates innovation, far from the frontier, more competition depresses it as lagging firms give up on the effort to catch up. Such firms are likely to be geographically concentrated in low productivity, low wage, low growth areas. Monopsonistic labour markets (see Chapter 15) in which the access of workers to competing job offers (e.g. due to costs of commuting) depress wages and allow a long tail of low innovation firms to survive.

The effect of inequality on innovation

To the extent that the creative destruction process is inhibited by the success of incumbents in defending their market positions, top income inequality ceases to reflect innovation. There is less innovation and less social mobility.

From research on Italian firms comes evidence that income inequality associated with the rents accruing from creating barriers to entry has a detrimental effect on innovation (see Akcigit et al. 2020). The top twenty firms are ordered by their rank in the market. Researchers show that the market leading firms innovate less and invest more in political lobbying (designed to reinforce the barriers to effective competition).

The Schumpeterian model also points to the role of inequality in affecting the direction that innovation takes, which can in turn affect living standards across the income and wealth distributions. As we have seen, the scale of innovation rents and hence, the size of the market is an important determinant of the incentive for the development of new products. When the distribution of income is strongly skewed toward the very rich, innovation will become pro-rich in nature. Studies in the US display a positive feedback process in which growing income inequality produces higher relative demand for income-elastic products, which leads to greater product variety and lower relative prices for goods and services purchased by the rich than would otherwise be the case. This reinforces inequality in living standards (Jaravel 2019).

Growing evidence documents the consequences for the pace of innovation and its direction arising from the misallocation of talent because the opportunity to participate in the risky business of invention and innovation is not open to the children of less educated parents. This is documented in cross-country data on the subsequent education and careers of participants in the international Mathematical Olympiad (Agarwal and Gaule 2020). In the US, children of parents in the top 1% of the income distribution are ten times more likely to become inventors than children whose parents' income is below the median. Engaging in invention is also disproportionately concentrated among male and white children. Research using quantitative modelling to include the general equilibrium effects across the economy of this pattern of participation indicates that the effects restricting access to innovation has a substantial effect in reducing growth. If all the barriers were eliminated, then it is estimated that economic growth could double from 2% p.a. in the baseline to 4% p.a. (Einio, Feng, and Jaravel 2022).

Policy implications

Policy priorities arising from the Schumpeterian model are to protect the incentives for private sector innovation that arise from the prospect of innovation rents and at the same time to promote competition to prevent entrenched incumbency and to open access to participation in innovation from across the population. This suggests that a focus on both competition policy and education is justified. For the latter, policies to provide children from low-income families with the exposure to inventors that they lack in their families and neighbourhoods, is essential for stimulating innovation that benefits society broadly. Complementary policies are those that enhance the ability of people with lower wealth to engage in risky innovation such as via the redistribution of wealth and policies that reduce the riskiness of using existing wealth, for example in one's home, as collateral.

16.5.4 Business cycle fluctuations and innovation

Earlier in this chapter, we took a look at how models of long-run growth can be related to short- and medium-run models of business cycle fluctuations. The Schumpeterian model provides additional insights about the connection between growth and volatility. As we have seen, sustained growth in per capita GDP in the Schumpeterian model is due to purposeful investment in R&D and other productivity-enhancing activities. This prompts the question of how business cycle booms and recessions may affect investment in R&D, and whether this mechanism should influence the way macroeconomic stabilization policy is conducted.

Creative destruction—the positive role of firm-level volatility

Creative destruction means that higher quality products and methods of production displace inferior ones. This suggests that a particular kind of volatility related to the entry and exit of activities within and between firms themselves plays a crucial role in sustaining dynamism. Both incumbent firms and new entrants innovate: evidence from the USA suggests that about 25 percent of productivity growth comes from new entrants.[25] The pervasiveness of a 'soft budget constraint' for enterprises in planned economies, which meant that they could survive irrespective of their performance, was linked with the absence of dynamism in economies operating under central planning's 'rules of the game'.[26]

Business cycle volatility and growth

We turn next to consider the impact on long-term growth of business cycle fluctuations caused, for example, by shocks to aggregate demand and supply. In the 3-equation model, the policy maker uses monetary and fiscal policy to keep the economy close to equilibrium output, and to reduce the damage caused by fluctuations in unemployment. The Schumpeterian model of growth provides additional reasons for active counter-cyclical policy intervention that would see governments increasing

---

[25] See Bartelsmann and Doms (2000) and Foster, Haltiwanger, and Krizan (2001).

[26] See Kornai (2013).

public deficits and central banks cutting real interest rates in recessions and doing the converse in booms.

The argument rests on the fact that the availability of credit to firms is tightened in recessions as firms appear less creditworthy to lenders. When firms are credit constrained, inadequate access to funding forces them to cut down on productivity enhancing investment in innovative activities. Moreover, the prospect that funding for innovation may dry up in a downturn is also likely to dampen long-term growth-enhancing investments. This creates a role for government stabilization policy. Another channel through which stabilization policy is growth enhancing, suggested by the Schumpeterian approach, is its role in stabilizing the size of the market.

Studies using cross-industry cross-country data show that countries with more countercyclical fiscal and monetary policies ease the credit constraints on firms in industries that are especially credit or liquidity constrained. This provides evidence supportive of the mechanism through which countercyclical policy enhances growth by reducing the extent to which recessions depress access to finance for innovation.[27]

If we bring together the argument about creative destruction with the one about recessions exacerbating credit constraints and inhibiting innovation, we have the implication that in a dynamic economy, economic policy should promote micro volatility in the sense of firm entry and exit, but should control macro volatility by aiming to keep the economy close to equilibrium output.

16.5.5 **Climate crisis, growth, and innovation**

The 'hockey stick' pattern in GDP per capita over the past two hundred years (Figure 16.1) is an example of a so-called phase transition: some economies exited a world in which there was virtually no long-run growth in living standards to one in which it was continuous with living standards doubling each generation. Taking a closer look at the long flat section of the hockey stick reveals the Malthusian pattern in which growth of average living standards leads to higher population growth, which eventually drives them down again. The Malthusian trap was sprung when, in a Schumpeterian fashion, entrepreneurs responded to the possibility of making innovation rents by introducing new energy intensive methods of production when the price of coal fell relative to wages in England (see CORE Econ's *The Economy* 2.0 Microeconomics Unit 2 for further details and data).[28]

A second hockey stick showing the rise in global temperature paralleled the first as a result of fossil-fuel intensive economic growth: the emission of carbon dioxide into the atmosphere.[29] And it is now indisputable that the stock of carbon dioxide is causing the rise in global temperatures that threatens future living standards across the globe (2021 IPCC report).

---

[27] For example, see Chapter 14 of Aghion and Howitt (2009), Aghion et al. (2012), and Aghion et al. (2014).

[28] For a more detailed presentation of how the model of Schumpeterian growth provides guidance on 'Green innovation and sustainable growth', see Chapter 5 in Aghion et al. (2021).

[29] See CORE Econ's *The Economy* 2.0 Microeconomics Unit 1 Figure 1.2 for data.

Carbon-based economic growth was responsible for reducing the share of the world population living in extreme poverty from 76% in 1820 (just as the Industrial Revolution was getting under way) to 10% in 2018. The question arises as to how the one in ten people in the world (i.e. over 700 million) who now live in extreme poverty can escape it consistent with the radical decarbonization that is required for a sustainable planet. Extreme poverty refers to the inability to meet basic needs including minimal nutrition and adequately heated shelter. Using the prices of locally available goods and services, this is set at a level of $1.90 per day. The scale of the task remaining is highlighted by the fact that in 1820, there were 964 million people in extreme poverty: that number has since fallen by less than one-fifth. Moreover, 44 per cent of people in the world live on less than the equivalent of $5.50 per day.[30]

Putting together the two hockey sticks and the data on global poverty pinpoints the challenge facing humanity: is it possible to move to a sustainable environment and achieve a substantial reduction in global poverty? For those in countries where high levels of poverty persist, replicating the carbon-intensive path out of poverty followed by today's middle- and high-income countries is not consistent with environmental sustainability. Just as it was innovation that enabled economies to escape the logic of the Malthusian trap, innovation is an essential part of solving the climate crisis and enabling broad-based escape from poverty without reliance on fossil fuels.

Government policy has to play an important role in the green transition for the following reasons:

1. **External effects.** Policy: carbon taxes, subsidies for renewables. The external effects of the emission of greenhouse gases do not directly enter the decision-making of firms, which means government policies to tax carbon or subsidize renewables, for example, are necessary to alter innovation as well as production and consumption decisions.
2. **Path dependence.** Policy: directed innovation such as green R&D subsidies. Research shows that the choice by a firm of innovations—whether green or brown—depends on their previous innovation experience. Government incentives are required to shift the choice from brown (which is lower cost because of past experience) to green by providing subsidies for innovation in green technologies. Once experience builds up in green innovation, subsidies are no longer required and a virtuous circle of green innovation arises. Once the virtuous circle is under way at the frontier, firms in low-income countries will find it profitable to adapt it for local use.
3. **Social preferences.** Policy: support for social movements and education. These interventions can change people's preferences and shift the pattern of demand toward decarbonization. Such changes are complementary to (1) and (2) because they reduce the magnitude of relative price changes that are needed to achieve a

[30] For data see Hasell, J., Roser, M., Ortiz-Ospina, E., and Arriagada, P. (2022) 'Poverty'. (https://ourworldindata.org/poverty).

given reduction in carbon emissions and accelerate the switch from brown to green innovation.

4. **Creative destruction.** Competition policy. Just like the escape from the Malthusian trap in the Industrial Revolution, the path to net zero is innovation-intensive and the Schumpeterian growth model as well as historical experience highlights the importance for its success of policies to enhance competition and foster the entry of new firms, as well as to compensate the losers.

These policies are mutually reinforcing as illustrated by the study of dirty and clean (green) patents in the automotive industry around the world.[31] The authors found that a greening of consumer values in favour of sustainable technology (of a magnitude observed over the past two decades) along with increased competition enforced by the government would account for a greening of innovation of the same magnitude as would have resulted from a forty percent increase in fuel prices. Higher fuel prices will tilt innovation toward lower carbon technologies but unless accompanied by offsetting transfers, and until the growth of the market reduces the price of renewable energy production, they are regressive. This is a good example of how pro-poor decarbonization can occur with smaller changes in relative prices (and less political opposition) than would otherwise be the case.

16.6 CONCLUSIONS

This chapter has focused on the *proximate* causes of growth: factor accumulation and technological progress. The proximate causes of growth lie at the heart of why the capitalist system has achieved sustained growth in living standards across the Western economies since the Industrial Revolution. In short, this economic system succeeded both in mobilizing resources to raise the amount of physical and human capital employed in production and in providing the incentives for continuous technological innovation. The models presented in this chapter can help explain growth patterns across economies and assist in developing policies to promote fairer and greener growth for the future:

1. **Does capital accumulation raise living standards in the long term?** Can governments set ambitious targets of steady state growth? We have based our discussion of long-run economic growth around the most widely used models of growth; the Solow model and endogenous growth models. The Solow model shows how broad capital accumulation produces higher living standards in the long-run steady state. It suggests that there is a limit to the extent to which changes in policy or institutions can influence long-run growth, due to the assumption of diminishing returns to capital. Although the Solow model can be adapted to include technological progress, it can only account for long-run productivity growth in a mechanical way. It falls to the endogenous growth models to provide a framework for thinking about the central role of purposeful innovation in economic growth.

---

[31] See Aghion et al. (2020).

2. **Can a higher saving rate produce permanently higher growth? Is competition positively or negatively correlated with innovation?** The key difference between the Solow model and endogenous growth models is that the latter assume there is some mechanism which offsets the diminishing returns to capital. Economists have explored a number of potential mechanisms that could achieve this, such as investment in human capital or research and development or knowledge spillovers from the accumulation of physical capital. The mechanisms open the door to the possibility that policy can affect long-run growth. The Schumpeterian model puts the concept of 'creative destruction' at the centre of the expansion of the technological frontier in successful economies. Innovation is driven by the promise of excess profits, and new products and production methods making old products and firms obsolete is integral to that process. In order to turn the Schumpeterian framework into a tractable growth model, Aghion and Howitt introduce an arbitrage condition between the marginal cost of innovation and its expected marginal benefit. A large and growing empirical literature corroborates the predictions of the model connecting innovation (creative destruction), competition and inequality.
3. **How does innovation affect inequality?** Are there policies that sustain incentives to innovate arising from the expected rewards without distorting the direction of technological progress to benefit those with high incomes, which entrenches inequality? Can creative destruction help produce growth consistent both with planetary boundaries and with a substantial reduction in global poverty? The insights from Schumpeterian growth theory provide guidance for policy consistent with these objectives. Important are policies to enable the widest possible participation in innovation across the population, to sustain entry and exit of firms and to limit opportunities for incumbents to use their rents to stifle newcomers.

16.7 **APPENDIX**

16.7.1 **Growth concepts and useful tools**

In order to set out the main concepts and tools used in growth theory, we consider the path of GDP per capita in the United States in the post-war period. Table 16.3 shows the real GDP per capita of the US for selected years between 1950 and 2019.

	Real GDP per capita (2017 US$)	Log of real GDP per capita
1950	15,854	9.671
2018	61,537	11.027
2019	62,491	11.043

Table 16.3 Real GDP per capita for the United States, 1950–2019.
Source: Penn World Table 10.0, June 2021.

We use these statistics to calculate a number of different growth rates. Mastering these simple techniques is essential for understanding growth theory and will also come in handy when examining any economic time series data.

Annual growth rates

The annual growth rate is calculated in discrete time using the following formula:

$$\gamma_y = \frac{y_{t+1} - y_t}{y_t} = \frac{\Delta y}{y}.$$

We can now calculate the annual growth rate of US GDP per capita between 2018 and 2019 by inserting the relevant figures from Table 16.3 into the formula:

$$\frac{y_{t+1} - y_t}{y_t} = \frac{62,491 - 61,537}{61,537} = \frac{954}{61,537} = 0.0155 = 1.55\%.$$

It is useful to note that when national statistics agencies (e.g. the US BEA) release national accounts data on GDP or GDP per capita and they quote a headline figure for annual growth, this is the calculation they are making. For example, the growth rate of US real GDP per capita in 2019 was 1.55%.

The annual growth rate can also be calculated a slightly different way. It gives exactly the same result, but is often easier to use in spreadsheet programmes:

$$\frac{y_{t+1} - y_t}{y_t} = \frac{y_{t+1}}{y_t} - 1 = \frac{62,491}{61,537} - 1 = 0.0155 = 1.55\%.$$

The log difference method for computing annual growth rates

Economic statistics can often be easier to manipulate using logs. Transforming a time series into logs can seem like an unnecessary complication, but once you get to grips with the basic mathematical properties of logs it opens up a range of useful tools. A prime example of this is using the log difference method to approximate annual growth rates, as shown by the following formula:

$$\gamma_y \approx \log(y_{t+1}) - \log(y_t).$$

We can now once again use the figures from Table 16.3 to calculate the annual growth rate:

$$\gamma_y \approx \log(62,491) - \log(61,537) = 11.043 - 11.027 = 0.016 = 1.6\%.$$

The growth rate almost exactly matches that calculated in the previous subsection. The log difference method gives a good approximation of the annual growth rate when growth rates are relatively small (i.e. when $\log(1 + \gamma_y) \approx \gamma_y$).

Compound annual growth rates

The compound annual growth rate (or CAGR) provides the trend rate of growth over multiple periods. It is necessary to have a formula that takes into account the fact that y_0 (i.e. the base year for calculating the annual growth rate) is rising in each period. If we ignored 'compounding' and just calculated the percentage growth for the whole period and divided it by the number of years in the sample, then this would overstate the annual growth rate. We will give an example of this shortly.

The formula for the compound annual growth rate for discrete time periods is

$$\bar{\gamma}_y = \left(\frac{y_t}{y_0}\right)^{1/t} - 1,$$

where y_0 is GDP per capita in the first year of the time series, y_t is GDP per capita in the last year of the time series and t is the number of periods in the time series. To see why this is correct, we can start by noting that:

$$\begin{aligned}
&y_t = y_0 \left(1+\bar{\gamma}_y\right)^t \\
&\rightarrow \left(1+\bar{\gamma}_y\right)^t = \left(\frac{y_t}{y_0}\right) \\
&\rightarrow \left(1+\bar{\gamma}_y\right) = \left(\frac{y_t}{y_0}\right)^{\frac{1}{t}} \\
&\rightarrow \bar{\gamma}_y = \left(\frac{y_t}{y_0}\right)^{\frac{1}{t}} - 1
\end{aligned}$$

We can now use the figures from Table 16.3 to calculate the trend rate of growth for US GDP per capita between 1950 and 2019:

$$\bar{\gamma}_y = \left(\frac{62,491}{15,854}\right)^{1/69} - 1 = (3.94)^{1/69} - 1 = 2\%.$$

On average, between 1950 and 2019, US real GDP per capita grew by 2%.

It is easy to use the US data to illustrate the inaccuracy of calculating the trend rate of growth without taking compounding into account. The percentage change in GDP per capita between 1950 and 2019 was $(62,491/15,854) - 1 = 294\%$. If we divide this by the number of periods in the sample then we get a trend rate of growth of $294\%/69 = 4.26\%$. The 'naive' method of computing the trend rate of growth gives an answer more than twice as high as the correct answer, which shows the dangers associated with using a formula that neglects compounding.

The exponential method of calculating compound growth rates

There is another method of calculating compound growth rates that involves using exponentials and logs. This method is particularly useful when we are dealing with continuous time and not discrete time as in the previous subsection. The formula for calculating the compound growth rate in continuous time, $\bar{g}_y$, is derived from the following relationship:

$$y_t = y_0 e^{\bar{g}_y t} \quad \text{or alternatively,}$$
$$y_t = y_0 \exp(\bar{g}_y t).$$

We can use the figures from Table 16.3 to show that this formula produces the same trend rate of growth for the US economy as does the CAGR. We first need to take logs of the equation shown above and then rearrange to get $\bar{g}_y$ in terms of the other variables.

$$\log y_t = \log(y_0 \exp(\bar{g}_y t))$$
$$\log y_t = \log y_0 + \bar{g}_y t$$

$$\bar{g}_y = \frac{\log(y_t/y_0)}{t}$$

$$\bar{g}_y = \frac{\log(62,491/15,854)}{69} = 2\%.$$

The relationship between exponential growth and logs

We have shown that logs and exponentials possess properties that can be useful when manipulating economic data, but how do economic time series relate to their log series (i.e. the time series created when we take logs of the original series)? We answer this question by looking at a time series of US GDP per capita growth from 1870 through to 2016.

Figure 16.22a (the left-hand panel) shows the raw data and Figure 16.22b shows the log series. It is immediately noticeable that the underlying series shows exponential growth, whereas the log series shows an upwards linear trend. This is no coincidence. It has to do with the relationship between series that exhibit exponential growth and their log series, which was set out in the previous subsection. If we go back to the equation that shows how $\log y_t$ relates to time, then we can see that it is a linear relationship with an intercept of $\log y_0$ and a slope of $\bar{g}_y$ (or the trend rate of growth):

$$\log y_t = \log y_0 + \bar{g}_y t.$$

In general, any economic time series which has a constant rate of growth over many years will appear to increase exponentially. This is due to the effect of compounding. When the log of the series is taken then it will become a linear series with a slope equal to the trend rate of growth.

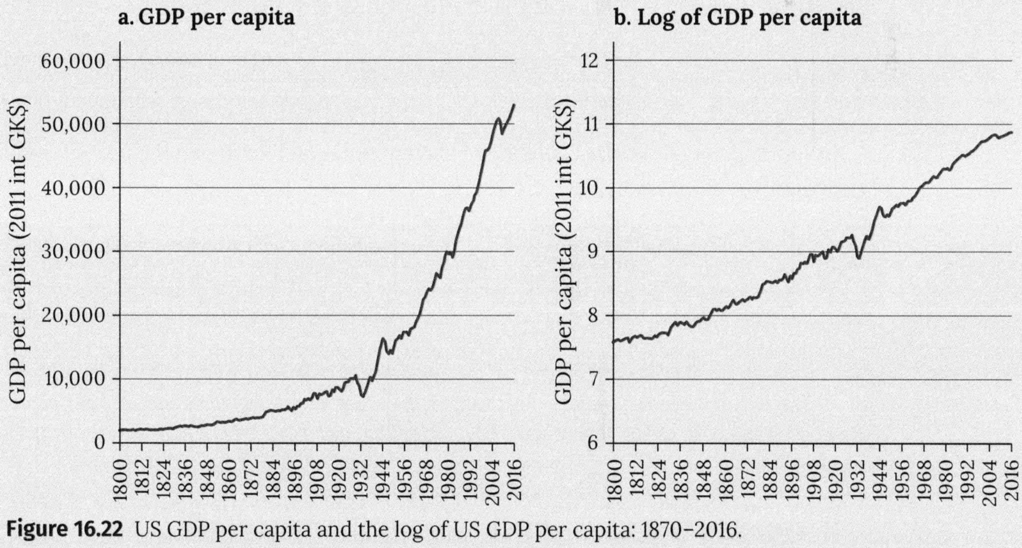

Figure 16.22 US GDP per capita and the log of US GDP per capita: 1870–2016.

Source: New Maddison Project Database (GGDC) 2018 version, October 2019.

The rule of 70 and years to convergence

The relationship between GDP per capita and time that is shown in the exponential growth model leads us to a neat rule. The rule allows us to calculate approximately how long it takes for GDP per capita to double if an economy is growing at a constant rate of growth.[32]

$$\text{doubling time} = \frac{70}{\text{percentage growth rate}}.$$

In the previous subsections, we saw that the trend rate of US GDP per capita growth was 2% between 1950 and 2019. This leads to a doubling time of $70/2\% = 35$ years. If the rate of GDP per capita growth was faster than this, say 5%, then it would double roughly every 14 years. In contrast, a rate of growth at 1% would see GDP per capita taking 70 years to double.

The use of continuous time in growth models

In the book thus far we have worked mainly in discrete time, where there are set time periods that are usually assumed to be equally spaced—i.e. period t, period $t+1$, etc. In growth theory, however, it is easier and requires less cumbersome notation to derive the results in continuous time. Continuous time is not split into discrete periods of a year or a quarter, but instead runs along a continuum. In our GDP per capita example, this would mean that the difference in GDP per capita could be observed at any two points in time and not solely between set time periods.

Throughout this chapter we use the so-called dot notation to refer to the rate of change of key variables. $\dot{y}$ or 'y dot' is the rate of change of GDP per capita and is closely related to the familiar concept of the change in GDP per capita between period t and period t+1, $y_{t+1} - y_t$, which is often abbreviated to Δy. $\dot{y}$ is the continuous time equivalent of Δy and is defined as the time derivative of y, that is dy/dt. To summarize:

$$\Delta y \equiv y_{t+1} - y_t \qquad \text{(rate of change, discrete time)}$$

$$\dot{y} \equiv dy/dt. \qquad \text{(rate of change, continuous time)}$$

In addition, we can divide each rate of change equation by y to find the proportional growth rate of GDP per capita:

$$\gamma_y = \frac{y_{t+1} - y_t}{y_t} = \frac{\Delta y}{y} \qquad \text{(proportional growth rate, discrete time)}$$

$$g_y = \frac{\dot{y}}{y} = \frac{dy/dt}{y}. \qquad \text{(proportional growth rate, continuous time)}$$

[32] The rule of 70 comes from the fact that $\log 2 \approx 0.7$. If we take y_0 to be the GDP per capita in period 0 and t_d to be the time it takes to double, then using the exponential growth formula, we have:

$$2y_0 = y_0 \exp \bar{g}_y t_d.$$

We can then take logs of both sides and rearrange to derive the rule of 70:

$$t_d = \frac{\log 2}{\bar{g}_y}.$$

In each case, the growth rate, e.g. 0.02, is multiplied by 100 to produce a *percentage* growth rate.

16.7.2 **Knowledge spillovers and Frankel's model of growth**

In this section we set out the model of endogenous growth developed by Marvin Frankel in 1962. As anticipated in Section 16.4, Frankel's framework models endogenous economic growth while allowing trends in productivity at the firm level to be dependent on growth in the capital stock.

The model starts at the micro level, by assuming an economy populated by many firms characterized by a Cobb-Douglas production function of the following form:

$$Y_i = K_i^{\alpha}(AN_i)^{1-\alpha}. \tag{16.20}$$

where A is no longer an exogenous multiplicative factor, but instead enters the production function through labour; this reflects the idea that knowledge, through the acquisition of new skills, is translated into higher labour productivity at the micro level of the individual firm.

The 'learning by doing' phenomenon is thus integral to the model, and it takes place through the accumulation of capital. In other words, endogeneity of technological progress results from modelling A as proportional to aggregate capital accumulation. At the firm level, this implies:

$$A_i = A_0 K_i^{\eta}. \tag{16.21}$$

Suppose there is a number S of firms in the economy, we can express the economy-wide knowledge A as:

$$A = \sum_{i=1}^{S} A_0 K_i^{\eta} = A_0 K^{\eta}. \tag{16.22}$$

Where K is the aggregate level of capital accumulation in the economy. Because knowledge is modelled as a public good, each firm benefits from positive externalities (spillovers) from investment by all other firms. Consequently, aggregate, or more properly, common knowledge A enters an individual firm's production function as shown in equation 16.20.

Aggregate production in the economy is then given by:

$$Y = K^{\alpha}(AN)^{1-\alpha} = K^{\alpha}(A_0 K^{\eta} N)^{1-\alpha} = A_0{}^{1-\alpha} K^{\eta(1-\alpha)+\alpha} N^{1-\alpha}. \tag{16.23}$$

Equations 16.20 and 16.23 imply that:

1. For the firm (i.e. equation 16.20), there are constant returns to scale ($\alpha + 1 - \alpha = 1$) and diminishing returns to capital ($\alpha < 1$). Note that this relies on A being constant for the individual firm.

2. For the economy (i.e. equation 16.23), there are increasing returns to scale ($\eta(1-\alpha) + \alpha + 1 - \alpha > 1$). Returns to capital are (1) constant if $\eta = 1$, (2) increasing if $\eta > 1$, and (3) decreasing if $\eta < 1$. In other words, returns to capital for the economy depend on the size of the knowledge spillovers from capital accumulation, η.

If we look at the case where $\eta = 1$, i.e. where knowledge is just a linear function of capital accumulation, equation 16.23 becomes of the form:

$$Y = {A_0}^{1-\alpha} K N^{1-\alpha}. \tag{16.24}$$

Let us return to the capital accumulation equation:

$$\dot{K} = sY - \delta K = s{A_0}^{1-\alpha} K N^{1-\alpha} - \delta K,$$
$$\rightarrow g_k = \frac{\dot{K}}{K} = s{A_0}^{1-\alpha} N^{1-\alpha} - \delta. \tag{16.25}$$

Which, contrary to the case where output follows a Cobb-Douglas production function, is independent of the capital stock. In particular, as the capital stock expands, its growth rate no longer declines. The implication in terms of long-run growth is that an endogenous increase in the savings rate now increases long-run growth permanently since the subsequent expansion in the capital stock does not put downward pressure on its growth rate.

The nice feature of this model is that endogenous growth at the economy level is consistent with the presence of a neoclassical (concave) production function at the level of the firm.

Moreover, there are interesting insights from the knowledge spillovers model that go beyond its role in providing a microeconomic based story for the possibility of endogenous growth.

- First, it makes clear that a model of endogenous technological progress does not necessarily entail endogenous growth. If $\eta < 1$, then the economy grows at a rate independent of the savings/investment rate (unlike the AK model) but its output per capita does grow (unlike the Solow model). To see this, we take the production function: ${A_0}^{1-\alpha} K^{\eta(1-\alpha)+\alpha} N^{1-\alpha}$ and look for a common exponential growth rate for output and capital. This requires us to take logs and differentiate with respect to time:

$$\log Y = (1-\alpha)\log A_0 + (\eta(1-\alpha)+\alpha)\log K + (1-\alpha)\log N,$$
$$\rightarrow g_y = (\eta(1-\alpha)+\alpha) g_K + (1-\alpha)n. \tag{16.26}$$

and then to set $g_y = g_K$, to get:

$$g_y = g_K = \frac{(1-\alpha)n}{1-\eta+\eta\alpha-\alpha} = \frac{(1-\alpha)n}{(1-\alpha)(1-\eta)} = \frac{n}{1-\eta}. \tag{16.27}$$

The growth rate of output *per capita* in the steady state is $g_y - n = \frac{n}{1-\eta} - n$ and therefore:

$$g_y = \frac{\eta}{1-\eta} n. \tag{16.28}$$

This contrasts both with the Solow model without technological progress, where $g_y = 0$ and the model with technological progress, where $g_y = x$, where x is exogenous. In our new model, growth of per capita output is due entirely to technological progress but this is now endogenous, in the sense that it arises from knowledge spillovers associated with capital accumulation. However, a higher savings/investment share does not raise the growth rate. This will only be the case when $\eta = 1$, i.e. in the AK case. Frankel's model highlights perfectly the difference between endogenous technological progress and endogenous growth

- Second, the knowledge spillovers model raises an interesting policy issue. Since decision makers at the level of the firm take no account of the impact of their investment decisions on knowledge available throughout the economy, there is a difference between the optimal amount of investment from the perspective of a firm and from the perspective of the economy as a whole. A social planner looking from the perspective of the economy as a whole takes into account the externalities that arise from capital accumulation. In this context the actions taken by a firm may not be Pareto optimal from the social point of view. This means that there are actions available that would make everyone better off without harming anyone. The reason they are not chosen is because firms fail to recognize an aspect of the decision process that is only properly internalized in the decision once we adopt the perspective of the social planner. In particular, firms pay a marginal cost per unit of investment given by the real interest rate. Hence, each profit-maximizing firm chooses an *optimal* level of capital, say K^*_{it}, by equating the marginal revenue product (MRP_{K_i}) from installing an extra unit of capital with the real interest rate. From the social planner's perspective, the optimal capital stock will be chosen where the *social* marginal revenue product (MRP_K) is equal to the real interest rate. The presence of positive externalities from capital accumulation implies that $MRP_K > MRP_{K_i}$ and hence that the social planner would choose a higher level of capital stock compared to the firms. This provides a rationale for the government to introduce subsidies for investment.

QUESTIONS AND PROBLEMS FOR CHAPTER 16

CHECKLIST QUESTIONS

1. Assess the following statements S1 and S2. Are they both true, both false or is only one true? Justify your answer.

   S1. A rise in the saving rate will cause a recession.

   S2. A rise in the saving rate is good for growth.

2. How will an inflation-targeting central banker react to a fall in the savings rate? Answer very briefly using the 3-equation model and then extend your analysis using the standard Solow diagram to show what happens to the interest rate.

3. Using the data in Table 16.3, calculate the following:

   a. The CAGR for US GDP per capita between 1950 and 2019

   b. The time it would take for US GDP per capita to double if it grew at the rate calculated in part a.

4. Use equation 16.7 to derive the steady state values of capital per worker and output per worker in the standard Solow model. Interpret these equations.

5. Discuss the following statement: 'increasing the savings rate in the economy always increases welfare as it leads to an increase in output per capita'.

6. Assume we are in a Solow world in which the population is growing at a constant rate (and there is no technological progress). Suppose from an initial steady state, there is a sudden fall in the growth rate of the population. Would you predict a rise or a fall in output growth? How about in the growth of output per head? Describe how and why the economy adjusts to a new steady state and how the new steady state differs from the old one. Show the time paths for the growth rates of output, output per head, the capital stock and the capital intensity of production. To help in answering the question, produce a set of diagrams similar to those in Figure 16.9.

7. In the course of answering this question, explain the concepts of absolute and conditional convergence.
   a. Explain the mechanism(s) through which, according to the Solow model, an initially poor country would be predicted to catch up to the living standards of a rich country. Set out carefully the assumptions that you are making to derive this result.
   b. Now use the model to explain why catch-up may not take place.
   c. Comment on the likely validity of the assumptions in (a) and (b) when applying the model to the real world.

8. How do endogenous growth models explain the persistence of differences in living standards among economies? Explain the role played by the production function for goods and the accumulation function for ideas in coming to your conclusion.

9. What does the term 'creative destruction' mean? In a Schumpeterian growth model, what determines the growth rate of productivity? How does this compare to the mechanism driving growth in the Solow model with technological progress?

10. Does accepting that new technology is deliberately produced, and that a larger or smaller share of GDP may be devoted to it, imply that the long-run growth rate is endogenously determined?

11. Assess the following statements S1 and S2. Are they both true, both false or is only one true? Justify your answer making reference to the objectives of the policy maker.

S1. Economic policy should aim to limit firm-level volatility.

S2. Economic policy should aim to limit macro-level volatility.

12. Choose three models covered in this chapter and contrast the mechanisms through which they may explain cross-country heterogeneity in long-run economic performance.

13. What is Total Factor Productivity (TFP)? How can it be measured?

14. Can both Arrow and Schumpeter be right?

- *Arrow* (1962): 'Product market competition spurs innovation.'
- *Schumpeter* (1942): 'The prospect of market power and large scale spurs innovation.'

15. Is there any support in the models studied in this chapter for the statement that inequality is good for growth?

16. Use Figure 16.18 and consider how an increase in trade or globalization would affect the rate of technological progress, x, and capital per efficiency unit, $\hat{k}$.

PROBLEMS

1. In an economy characterized by a Cobb-Douglas production function (without technical progress), labour's share of income is 70% and the depreciation rate is 3% per annum. The economy is in a steady state with GDP growth at 4% per year and with a capital output ratio of 2. Find the savings rate and the marginal product of capital. At time t the savings rate in this economy increases to a new constant level, with the outcome that the economy converges to the Golden Rule steady state. What are the new savings rate, capital output ratio and marginal product of capital? Use diagrams with time on the horizontal axis to sketch the path of the capital-output ratio, the marginal product of capital and of consumption per unit of labour.

2. Download data on GDP per capita between 1960 and the latest available year for two countries of your choosing (other than the USA) from the Penn World Table. Plot the data on a log scale. Calculate / plot the following and comment briefly on your findings:

a. The annual growth rate for the period from 2007 to the most recent year available (using both the normal and log difference methods).

b. The CAGR for the whole period and for the periods before and after 2007. Extrapolate GDP per capita from 2007 using the first period's CAGR and plot the data.

c. The time it would take for GDP per capita to double if growth was equal to the trend rate for the period before 2007 calculated in part (b).

3. Consider an economy which experiences civil war. How will this affect the short-run performance of the economy? Describe the steady state to which the economy returns after the end of the civil war. Are there any long-run effects of civil war that may affect the economy many years after the war has ended? [Hint: use the Solow model and discuss the effects of civil war on human capital.] For background reading on the effects of civil wars, see Blattman and Miguel (2010).

4. Study Table 16.2. Use the information in the table (and the paper it is taken from) to write a two page note on the role of innovation in the evolution of the Euro Area and US economies since 1980. Your note should include an explanation of how innovation is measured.

5. 'More competition and stronger protection of IPR (intellectual property rights) will speed up technological progress.' Is this a recommendation you would take to a policy maker? You have 700 words to make your case.

6. Consider the model of economic growth with spillovers by Marvin Frankel introduced in the Appendix (16.7.2). Explain why we need to have many firms with an identical production function. Do you find the functional form for the firms' production function realistic? Explain. Assume that the economy with $\eta = 1$ experiences an unexpected increase in A to A′. Describe its effect. Can this model explain cross-country heterogeneity? Does this model imply conditional or unconditional convergence?

INTERESTED IN EXPLORING THESE TOPICS FURTHER?

Visit www.oup.com/he/carlin-soskice to consolidate and extend your learning with the multiple-choice questions and Animated Analytical Diagrams accompanying this chapter.

CHAPTER

17

THE ICT REVOLUTION, PRODUCTIVITY PUZZLE, AND POLITICAL ECONOMY OF UNEVEN GROWTH

This chapter has been co-authored by Wendy Carlin, Andrew McNeil, and David Soskice.

17.1 INTRODUCTION

Chapter 16 introduced economic growth models where technological progress was a parameter that was exogenous (the Solow model) or captured endogenously so that there is some mechanism which offsets the diminishing returns to capital. In this chapter, we introduce the concept of 'technological revolutions', and focus on the fourth—the ICT or digital—revolution. We use political economic arguments to explain why the breakthrough innovations were in a small number of research clusters in the US. We argue that the political and institutional environment in the United States enabled private firms to compete for potential economic profits arising from the development of new innovative digital products and processes. The 'rules of the game' in the US originated in its economic and political history and were further aligned with the potential of the ICT revolution through the adoption of what are referred to as neo-liberal policies. Among the unique set of institutions that together supported the ICT revolution were decentralized and widely available finance, large research universities, a relatively high-skilled pool of graduate labour, a well-defined set of property rights and legal institutions, and a large domestic market.

Other high-income economies lagged the United States in the amount and importance of radical innovation taking place. However, in the early period of the ICT revolution they were able to adopt many of the products and processes that needed little customization (such as word processing and spreadsheet software). They thus converged to the United States' level of GDP per capita, or at least remained a constant distance from the frontier. This is in line with earlier technological revolutions, where new management practices and product innovations were relatively straightforward to copy and diffuse. This was reflected in the absolute convergence of high-income countries during the 1950s and 1960s (see Chapter 16).

In more recent years, however, the new technology requires much greater levels of customization and other countries have 'followed' the United States in different ways, and with varying degrees of success. We take four case studies, the United Kingdom, Germany, Sweden, and China, where each country's ability to diffuse technology is influenced by factors including firm ownership structure, spatial variation (particularly in labour markets), and existing industry structure. We highlight different types of diffusion which exist to a greater or lesser extent in each country. The three major types are 'simple prepackaged diffusion', customized systems software for services, and integrating ICT software services into industrial products (known as servitization). We aim to highlight the importance for macroeconomists of these different diffusion processes complementing their understanding of growth with insights from political economy.

In Section 17.5, we consider a puzzle as to why the ICT revolution seems to be having a limited positive effect on measured productivity growth over the last couple of decades. Even the country that we argue is the technological 'leader', the United States, has only grown at 1.76% annually from 2005–19. Of this, total factor productivity contributes a rather meagre 0.65 percentage points (Cette et al. 2022). The lack of productivity growth seems puzzling given the importance we place on the fourth technological revolution. There is no consensus as to why productivity growth has been so weak; we outline four potential explanations.

Finally, we consider one consequence of the ICT revolution, which was the dramatic polarization of society. There are clear 'winners' and 'losers' from the technological revolution. Whole swathes of middle class routinized jobs have disappeared and been replaced by automated processes, computers, and robots. In some cases, individuals have been able to upskill and capture the associated premium of high-skilled jobs, but large groups have lost out and found themselves in the low-skilled service occupations that are difficult to automate. Moreover, these 'losses' have been felt most intensely in certain regions. Often a few technological, graduate-intensive, hubs take nearly all the gains from productivity increases. This matters not only for growth and income distribution, but also for political outcomes. There is an expansive literature documenting how those who are 'left-behind' because of individual-level factors (such as intergenerational downward social mobility) or socio-tropic effects (the 'geography of discontent') (McCann 2020) vent their disappointment by turning to anti-system, or populist, parties. Despite the increased populist vote, high-income democracies have so far trod this thin line successfully, negotiating what some would argue is an inherent conflict between capitalism and democracy (Iversen and Soskice 2019).

17.2 TECHNOLOGY REGIMES OVER TWO CENTURIES

Most economic historians see the process of industrialization as having gone through four major technological revolutions, the last being the contemporary ICT or digital revolution.[1] Each of these revolutions were based on one or a collection of intersecting

---

[1] The leading contemporary theorists are Dosi (1982) and Perez (2003), in turn much influenced by Freeman (2002) and Nelson and Winter (1985). Acemoglu and Johnson (2023) contribute an important recent analysis.

new technologies which were applied to a wide range of different sectors and activities. Now, the combination of computers, smartphones and the internet is applied to just about everything and is called a *general purpose technology*. These four technological revolutions disrupted existing technologies and activities. *Creative destruction* (Schumpeter) was evident across virtually all sectors of the economy because of the emergence of a new general purpose technology.

17.2.1 The first three technological revolutions

The first, the Industrial Revolution was centred on the north of England from the late 18th century to the middle of the 19th century. The general purpose technology was steam power, itself powered by coal, which generated the energy to run multiple spindle machines (largely invented in northern England by self-educated engineers). These massively increased the productivity of cottage workers who had previously used a single spinning wheel; the most famous machine was the 'spinning Jenny' of Arkwright and Hargreaves. The steam generating machines could not be moved, leading to the development of the factory with the steam engine centrally located. Through multiple pulleys, the steam engine powered a large number of spinning Jennies within the factory building. Steam production required iron (to contain the intense pressures), as well as coal. And from the early 19th century, steam, iron and coal enabled the development of railways. Railways were developed, again in the north of England, their engines or locomotives being called 'iron horses'. And (only a bit later) ocean-going steamships were developed, from the UK.

The second, the Scientific Revolution began in the last quarter of the 19th century in Germany and the US. Electric power was the general purpose technology, eventually covering every sector of the economy and indeed society. But the scientific revolution proper was at its core an organizational revolution, centred on the concept of the giant corporation, analysed by Alfred Chandler in his famous book *Scale and Scope* (1994). Largely based on the great American and German companies across the sectoral board, these companies had research divisions which applied scientific developments to new products, marketing and sales, training, human resources, finance, distribution and so on. They relied on universities to teach basic science to the researchers they hired; and their research departments did high level research. This was particularly the case in chemicals, pharmaceuticals, telephony and wireless, and metallurgy. The US pushed faster ahead than Germany in developing economies of scale, and created multidivisional conglomerates to exploit their ability to do this.

The third, the Fordist Revolution. The internal combustion engine was invented in the 1880s (mainly) in Germany, as gasoline was becoming available. But building autos was expensive. Fordism was the brilliant idea of assembly line production. If goods (despite their complexity) were built up based on many individual operations, then assembly line production made them cheap to produce. For the first time large volumes of relatively cheap cars could be manufactured. The 'Fordism' period was most concentrated from the end of the First World War to the 1970s and 1980s. Until the First World War, few people had cars; they were owned by the wealthy; travel was by train and bus; most people lived in cities close to where they worked or in inner suburbs.

Now, at least in the US, a whole new pattern of life developed. Living in the suburbs, with standardized building techniques, workers and their families could have houses with garages and yards; electricity and water were built into houses; working class families could access the increasing range of consumer durables which were being developed and produced at low cost. As in the scientific revolution, much of which continued under Fordism, new products were developed and modified in-house. Workers, at least in the US, from the mid-1920s on, were unionized; and because production depended on the assembly line moving, Fordism gave production workers considerable power. What are often referred to as large Fordist corporations, now with assembly lines as well as the other characteristics of the scientific revolution dominated high-income countries. Innovation and modification took place inside Chandlerian conglomerates, which had major research departments.

17.2.2 **ICT, the fourth technological revolution**

The ICT (Information and Communications Technology) Revolution has been with us, growing increasingly rapidly and evolving over the past four decades. Nearly all the main innovations originate from the United States (see Section 17.4.1 as to why we think this is so). Within the United States, innovation was concentrated around a few large clusters, particularly Cambridge (Massachusetts) and Silicon Valley. The brilliant Nobel-laureate scientist William Shockley raised money to develop semi-conductor technology in the 1950s, with a laboratory in Palo Alto (reputedly to be near his ailing mother). He was an impossible manager and a group of his top scientists broke away to form Fairchild, which spawned many spinoffs, notably including Intel (in 1968). Intel became the dominant semi-conductor company for 3 decades. All these activities were clustered in the area, with increasingly close links to Stanford University and then the University of California at Berkeley. Via a different but related route, the internet was developed, initially to communicate between universities, as a defence department initiative (DARPA).[2]

To take a step back, we can say the ICT revolution is based on two 'machines', computers and the internet. The computer is a device in which data is stored and programs resident in the computer give instructions as to how the data is to be transformed. The internet transfers data from one computer to another, wirelessly or via cables. It was really the discoveries in the 1940s and 1950s in the US of the semi-conductor and the miniaturized integrated circuit that enabled computing at enormous speeds and in increasingly small computers. In relation to the internet, packet-switching, and then (in the late 1980s), the URL, enabled anyone to access any document in the system from anywhere. Through the 1990s optic fibres with integrated amplifiers enabled internet users costless and almost instantaneous communication with internet users anywhere else.

By the 2000s, a large proportion of the population in the high-income world had access to personal computers and the internet. Search engines had become established by the mid 2000s, notably Google, Yahoo, and MSN Search, together with Wikipedia. Using the internet anyone had access to an incredible amount of exponentially growing information and knowledge. Moreover, nearly 50% of young people were going through some form of tertiary education. The term, the 'Knowledge Economy', caught on to describe the high-income world and how it was transforming.

---

[2] Isaacson has a very readable history of this complex intertwined history (Isaacson 2014).

In the earlier phase of the ICT revolution, technology was often highly sophisticated and revolutionary but could be used by a wide audience without highly specialized knowledge (think word processing). By the turn of the millennium, such technology had largely been rolled out in the high-income economies. There would of course be continual improvements, for example in usability and speed, but from then onwards, we think of a shift in the ICT revolution to technology which was often customizable and adapted to specific purposes by firms. This becomes important for how countries diffuse technology (Section 17.4).

The political economy foundations of the ICT revolution

Like each of the previous technological revolutions, the ICT revolution required supportive changes in the 'rules of the game' set by the government in order for the disruptive new technologies to be commercialized. These changes were among those that produced what is sometimes referred to as the neo-liberal paradigm. The move towards neo-liberalism in the 1980s and 1990s reflected the perceived failure of the post WWII social contract (Bowles and Carlin 2021). The rapid growth and full employment of the 1950s and 1960s had ceased by the 1970s. Instead, there was a paradigmatic shift which emphasized deregulated labour markets and a shrinking state. Inevitably this gave a more dominant role to firms. At least in part, there was an underlying belief that the lack of competition in markets had restricted incentives for private enterprise and inhibited risk-taking. Adoption of the neo-liberal framework explicitly weakened unions and opened up many markets to competition that were previously dominated by large publicly owned enterprises such as telecommunications. The neo-liberal framework hastened the decline of the Fordism-based industrial world and set up a world that was destined to be changed by ICT.

Thus, a key role in driving innovation was assigned to private sector competition (modelled in the Schumpeterian growth process discussed in Chapter 16). The state was seen as too powerful an actor with close ties to large established corporations, and politicians potentially incentivized to use the state to support loss-making companies and their workforces. Along with the push for more competition came privatization. In addition, the belief that innovation required risk-taking, and entrepreneurship was seen as necessitating lower taxation, especially on high incomes. This coincided with the perceived need for more disciplined macroeconomic management, and for control of inflation, particularly after the major scare of inflation in the 1970s and start of 1980s.

Disciplined macroeconomic management led to central bank independence and the use of interest rates for inflation targeting; it also led to controls on fiscal policy, which, since lower taxation was seen as important, implied constraints on government expenditure and targeting of public sector deficits and public debt in relation to GDP (as set out in Chapters 6 and 7). A major problem with the neo-liberal policy mix was that suspicion of public expenditure got baked into policy-making, as well as by the electorate. Indeed, we believe this may have had a major detrimental impact on innovation and productivity growth in the current century (see Section 17.5.4).

In the modelling of growth in Chapter 16, no attention is paid to the location of economic activity. However, knowledge competences and innovation capacities are embedded in geographical clusters in the high-income economies. Thus, while company ownership (and financial assets generally), as well as patents, are mobile, innovation skills and competences are tacit and locationally embedded (Iversen and Soskice 2019). And, contrary to the view that the internet has made the earth 'flat' (Friedman 2006), tacit knowledge is typically attached to a location (Leamer 2007).

It is difficult to argue that it was either incumbent firms or new high tech entrants that drove the adoption of the neo-liberal rules of the game. Prima facie, firms stand to benefit from the opportunity for increased markets and profits. However, companies compete fiercely in technologically innovative markets and cannot easily collude to pressure the state to deregulate and shift the balance of power towards capital over labour. Thus, unable to collude against the state, and unable to relocate without losing the skilled workforces which create much of their value-added, high-income capitalist companies are not able to over-ride the autonomy of the advanced democratic sovereign state. Although it is possible that the push for deregulation was an interest shared by both capital and the state, we are not convinced that dominant firms necessarily pursued this agenda. Certainly, the state agenda contrasts to earlier periods where the state prioritized full employment, often through greater state intervention.

The role of government in the ICT revolution relates to the importance of co-location of assets, which implies that firms are not footloose in the manner often assumed. This contrasts with the Fordist revolution. For example, as many European countries caught up to United States in the 1950s and 1960s, the roll-out of Fordism was less dependent on locationally embedded assets. The practices of the factory assembly line could be adopted with a semi-skilled workforce that undertook mostly routine and semi-routine tasks. Such a labour force was readily available or could be relatively easily trained up across regions and countries. By contrast, the roll-out of highly sophisticated ICT requires a workforce with high level skills, and commonly a university degree. Graduates are themselves more attracted to 'cosmopolitan' hubs where partners, with often diverse but equally highly skilled occupations, can locate together. These areas are to be found where there is a pool of suitable labour. In the headquarters of a large multinational, they require many ICT literate employees with diverse professional backgrounds, from lawyers, to accountants, to HR professionals. For a wider discussion of the growing incentive for co-location see Soskice (2021). As we develop later in the chapter, there are dramatic consequences for spatial polarization (Section 17.6.2).

We see a further persuasive argument that the move towards a neo-liberal framework did not reflect the power of companies over governments. The neo-liberal emphasis on increased competition often broke incumbents' market dominance. This is epitomized in the US and the UK, where advanced capitalism is seen at its most powerful, most shareholder-oriented, and least socially responsible. With some exceptions, the top US and UK companies which had dominated the Fordist era were largely broken up by 2010, mainly by the radical opening of corporate governance markets and the transformation of financial institutions. They were replaced in the US by the FAANG (Facebook, Amazon, Apple, Netflix, and Google) companies. Those large corporates, 'goliaths' in Bessen's language, which did survive were able to manage the transition to the ICT era by integrating software across their organization to effectively create a 'winner takes all' market share (e.g. Walmart), blocking new entrants (Bessen 2022).

In the case of the UK, British industry (the employers' organization, the CBI) and much of the financial establishment had been deeply hostile to Thatcher's proposals in the late 1970s and 1980s. In fact, Thatcher was not appealing to the established conglomerates in the UK or those dominant financial institutions in the City of London (most of the largest companies in FTSE100): on the contrary—not to put too fine a point on it—she broke them up.

Political parties and electoral success—convergence on the 'neo-liberal' settlement

We have argued above that an important dimension of the neo-liberal paradigm was a response to the perception of a lack of enterprise and risk taking in the economy. Adoption of these ideas across countries varies in intensity and timing but what is clear is that there was a shift in high-income democracies towards this ideology, which included a new brand of centre-leftism, 'The Third Way', across Europe and the United States (Mudge 2008). This Third Way of politics epitomized by Clinton and Blair (and articulated by Giddens 1999), distilled five key ideas: transcending the distinction between left and right, advancing equality of opportunity, employing mutual responsibility, strengthening community, and embracing globalization (Leigh 2003).

The shift towards a neo-liberal consensus was spearheaded by the Republicans in the US with Ronald Reagan and later, the Democrat, Bill Clinton. In the UK, Thatcher's Conservative Party appealed to a large part of the aspirational electorate who wanted upgraded education and careers for their children, and were worried as industry was gradually collapsing. Labour and some of the unions initially responded to Thatcher by swinging—electorally disastrously—to the left under Michael Foot; but under successive leaders, from Kinnock to Blair, they ended up supporting most of her changes including legislation to weaken unions. And Blair aimed explicitly at the aspirational electorate Thatcher had captured.

There is also evidence of a shift within Continental Europe. Despite the persistence of clear differences in the variety of capitalism (see the respective cases of Germany and Sweden later in Section 17.4), there were moves to reform labour markets across Europe, most notably with the Hartz IV reforms in Germany, which passed in 2003 (see Chapter 15). These were implemented by the centre-left SPD, and ultimately ended up toughening welfare support, such as the conditions under which one could claim unemployment insurance.[3]

There were also regional and international institutions and incentives which encouraged, or compelled, countries to follow the neo-liberal consensus. One was in the form of a set of conventional wisdom policy choices that dictated 'good' policy known as the Washington Consensus (see Chapter 16). While these structural reforms were only enforced for countries requiring IMF bailout funds, they influenced policy design around the world (particularly in post-Soviet countries). Similarly, with many European countries joining the Eurozone in the late 1990s, as discussed in Chapter 14,

---

[3] For more detail, see Carlin et al. (2015).

these countries were locked into decisions made by the European Central Bank, which tended to follow a German preference for low inflation rates at the expense of other goals, and fiscal restraints that produced pro-cyclical policy.

One of the consequences of the ICT revolution has been to increase inequality. The winners (mostly graduates) and the losers (mostly non-graduates) from the knowledge economy have become increasingly polarized in terms of their earning outcomes, where they live, and opportunities for their children. This will be developed in detail later (Section 17.6.3). Perhaps unsurprisingly, therefore, this settlement on a neo-liberal consensus has been challenged. In the wake of the financial crisis, several 'populist' or 'anti-system' parties and movements have been established across Europe, ranging from UKIP in the UK advocating for Brexit, to the Five Star Movement and then the Brothers of Italy party forming a government in Italy, to the development of the far-right Vox in Spain. In short, the electoral process has switched from producing governments in a relatively narrow spectrum from the centre-left and centre-right (in one form or another depending on the electoral system) to one in which 'populist' and 'progressive' forces can dominate the outcome. Despite these gains for anti-system movements and parties, we argue that high-income democracies remain remarkably resilient (Section 17.6.3).

17.3 **AMERICA'S ICT REVOLUTION**

As described in Chapter 16, evidence regarding GDP per capita convergence or non-convergence of countries varies somewhat depending on the timeframe and grouping of countries one studies. Here, we take a narrower view and consider a group of high-income democracies plus China[4] over the timespan of the ICT revolution (very loosely from 1980 onwards), which we follow up in case studies. The United States remains the leader in GDP per capita throughout the period (Figure 17.1). However, when we analyse GDP per hour worked as shown in Figure 17.2, we get a more accurate measure of relative productivity since individuals in the United States work more hours than in other countries. We can see that relative to the other large economies, the US has led but during the 1980s there was some convergence of the follower countries, the United Kingdom and Germany. Although Germany was back at US levels of hourly productivity before the pandemic, over the last decade or so, relative to the UK and the broader OECD group, the United States maintained its technological dominance with the gap to the frontier roughly constant. The exception is Sweden, which has kept pace with the US throughout the entire period from 1980 (see our case study, Section 17.4.4.).

One explanation of this pattern of growth between countries is participation in the fourth industrial revolution, i.e. the adoption of ICT. As mentioned in the introduction, rather than a steady process taking place evenly over roughly four decades, we can think of the ICT revolution in two parts. The first part is led by US innovations that were relatively straightforward to diffuse to the followers—we will later call this 'simple

[4] We include China here as it will later form part of our case study analysis.

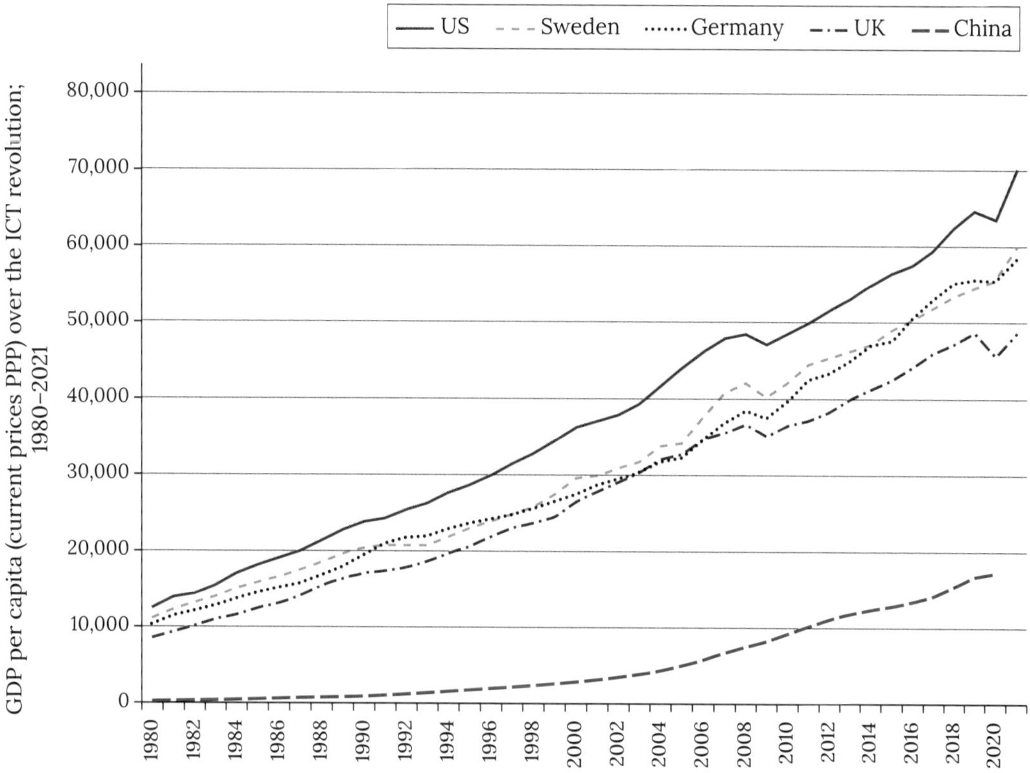

Figure 17.1 GDP per capita (Euro PPP) over the ICT revolution.

Note: GDP per capita in Euros, PPP.

Source: OECD Statistics (data accessed November 2022).

prepackaged diffusion' in Section 17.4.1. One can think of office software packages. They require some upfront skills but little in the way of customization.

The second phase involves a much higher level of skill, which would tend to be thought of as graduate level, and customization of technology (for further refinement see Section 17.4.1). We see this reflected in the decomposition of the productivity data using growth accounting, which was presented in Chapter 16, and in abbreviated form in Table 17.1 (Cette et al. 2022). To recap, TFP growth slowed down in the latest period (see Section 17.5 for potential explanations as to why). We also see variation between countries, TFP contributed more towards economic growth in the Eurozone, UK, and Germany in the initial phase of the ICT revolution, captured here by 1975–95, when compared to the United States. However, in the latest period, 2005–19, the United States once again diverges from its peers.

This pattern is explained, at least in part, by US leadership in the ICT revolution. In the earlier periods, these technologies were much more straightforward to diffuse across countries. However, due to the complementary assets required in the latter stages of the ICT revolution, other countries cannot so easily replicate these

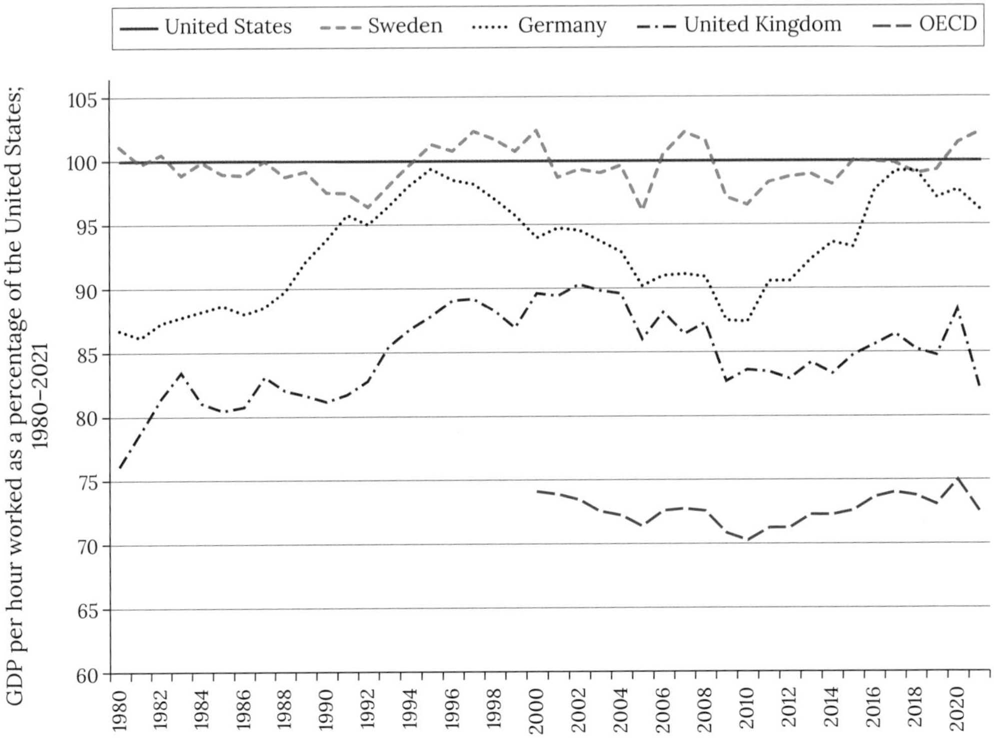

Figure 17.2 GDP per hour worked as a percentage of the United States.

Source: OECD Statistics (data accessed September 2022).

	1975–95	1995–2005	2005–19
United States	1.03	1.79	0.65
Eurozone	1.69	0.76	0.3
United Kingdom	1.72	1.75	0.13
Germany	1.93	1.06	0.42

Table 17.1 TFP contribution to GDP growth by country and time-period during the ICT revolution.

Source: Cette et al. (2022), extracted from full Table 16.2 in Chapter 16.

technologies and converge to the frontier. Moreover, even in the US, the breakthrough innovations took place in a small number of research clusters (most notably Silicon Valley, Seattle, LA, Cambridge/Boston, NY, DC, N Carolina Research Triangle); this is discussed shortly. Diffusion from these areas to the rest of the US was often difficult.

17.3.1 **Evidence of the US as technology leader in the ICT revolution**

The US is identified as the driver of innovation in the knowledge economy because most of the breakthrough innovations have come from there. Aghion and co-authors theorize this in terms of economies that are frontier establishers, and those behind the frontier. In relation to the OECD, we argue that the US is the frontier establisher with the other high-income economies behind the frontier, but at a constant distance (Aghion et al. 2021).

From the input side, the extent of the difference between the United States and 'the rest' is clear when measured either in terms of high-profile innovations or regular patents. Urquiola (2020) shows the dominance of the United States in Nobel Prize winners (see Figure 17.3, where high profile innovations are proxied through mentions in Nobel Prize winners' biographies). Similarly, patents filed under the Patent Cooperation Treaty (PCT) (OECD data), show how the United States dwarfs European countries (Figure 17.4). Interestingly, Japan has started to catch up over recent years. Given the United States is more populous than the other countries in the chart, some of this is a population effect. However, as we will go on to describe, we believe the American technological dominance goes well beyond population and market size.

The most technologically productive institutions tend to emanate from the United States. Five of the world's ten universities with the most highly cited researchers are based there (Clarivate 2021). Likewise, the United States has over 200 privately owned start-ups valued at more than $1bn (unicorns), which is double that of China and more than 8 times that of the United Kingdom in third place (Hammond and Ruehl 2020). It is not just the start-ups where American firms lead the way. McKinsey's (Manyika et al.

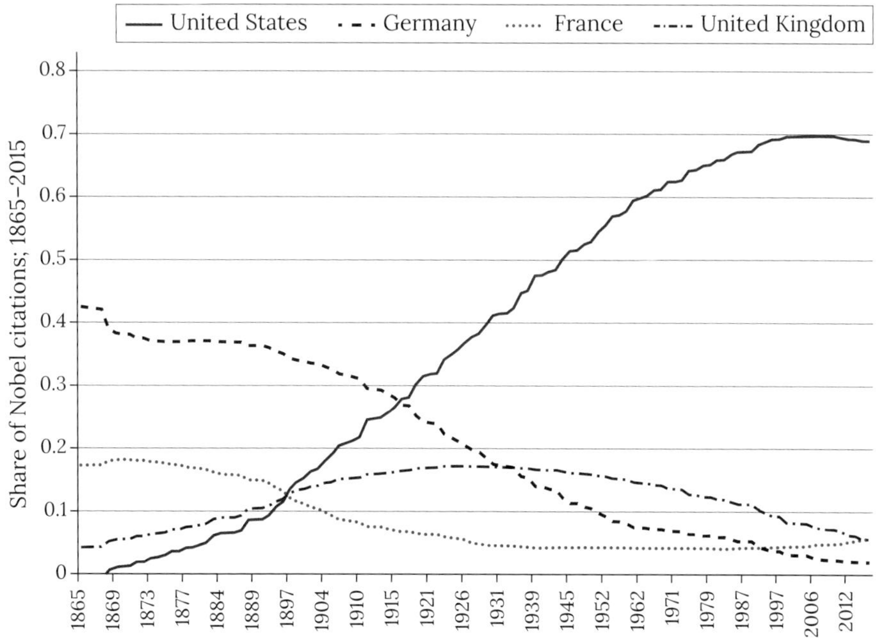

Figure 17.3 Share of Nobel Prize Mentions at pre-Nobel Institutions.

Note: data is a weighted average of university country locations up to the Nobel Prize award; it captures the contribution of the countries' universities to the research involved in the award, rather than the capacity of universities to hire Nobel Prize winners after the award.

Source: Urquiola (2020) Table 1.2.

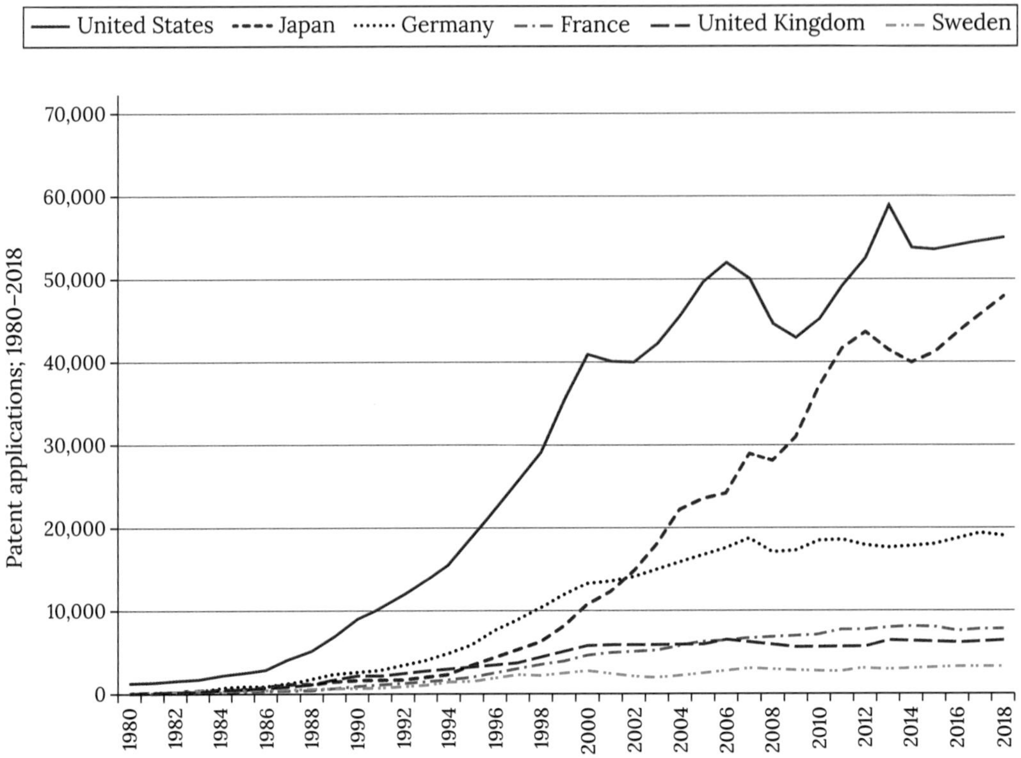

Figure 17.4 Patent applications under the Patent Cooperation Treaty by inventor's country of residence.
Source: OECD Statistics.

2018) report shows how of the largest 5,750 companies in the world, those 'superstar' firms who capture the largest economic profit are predominantly from the US.[5]

17.3.2 US leadership in radical innovation

American institutions

American success in establishing the technological frontier in the ICT revolution is a consequence of its particular constellation of decentralized and quasi-deregulated institutions. The decentralized complex of relationships is between finance, the top research universities, major innovation 'eco-systems' and major city administrations (Soskice 2021).

Placing it in prime position for the ICT revolution was the United States' long dominance since the late 19th century of major breakthrough innovations. At that time, institutions supportive of radical innovation and unique amongst the emerging high-income economies took shape. On these foundations, four sets of institutions are of particular importance:

[5] See details of how McKinsey calculates economic profit in their report (Manyika et al. 2018).

1. Highly flexible, decentralized, open, and competitive systems of research and higher education, largely at university level, and/or in the research laboratories of large corporations. Competition between many universities tended to produce a drive for performance to attract students and grants. In turn, there was a sorting effect, whereby those universities which emerged as the best performers (according to metrics such as citations) would then go on to attract the best future staff. For some of the 'winner' universities, this turned into a virtuous circle. The result in the aggregate was that the United States developed a group of universities which attracted global talent (student and staff), and would be world leading (MacLeod and Urquiola 2021).
2. Equally flexible and decentralized systems of finance, widely geographically distributed, informal small networks of wealthy individuals, which became venture capitalist and private equity partnerships, with relatively little regulation, and substantial capacity for investment in high-risk ventures as well as ones potentially disruptive to existing corporations (Neal and Davis 2007).
3. Companies capable of scaling sales (referred to as scalability), as well as a legal competition system that both ensures reasonably competitive product markets and allows scalability. Historically, there were three key conditions enabling great scalability for companies in North America. First was the extraordinary size of the market as European immigrants came in great numbers to populate the Midwest and the West; second, was the condition of free trade within North America imposed by the Supreme Court (implying that states or cities could not adopt local protectionism); and third was the imposition of tariffs on European goods to keep them out of the market. In addition, unions in manufacturing were de facto repressed (with the exception of the 'stable' Fordist period from the late 1930s to the 1970s) further increasing the power of the giant industrial corporations.
4. Finally, a deep and liquid high-level (professional and technical) labour market in the major research agglomerations that allows easy movement across professions (via professional schools) enables talented individuals to form spin-offs from existing (advanced technology) companies, and allows them to recover status after unsuccessful innovative projects (Klepper 2010; Klepper and Thompson 2010).

In addition to these decentralized and deregulated 'market institutions' is a second set of factors, 'legal and political institutions' characterizing the relationships between the political system, the court system and the business and wealth sectors.

Recent research (Hacker et al. 2022) explains the decentralized and porous business/money system, which enabled business to move to different environments. Those multiple venues include counties, cities, states, as well as the federal level, with courts, elections, and parties at each level. These 'legal and political institutions' are also decentralized and functionally deregulated. Absent at all these venues is a centralized established bureaucracy (Hacker et al. 2022; Soskice 2021). The vacuum is filled, not overtly by corruption but, by lobbying and investment in politicians by companies. To have a 'pliant' not to say mildly corrupt local legal, political, and administrative system makes life much easier for successful start-ups who need to quickly shape their physical environments. To a greater extent than in other countries, growing companies can operate in flexible environments (particularly within research-intensive agglomerations).

Unlike the other large high-income countries, the innovative ideas from leading research universities, their academics and their networked diasporas can be easily financed, teams of able managers, lawyers, research software engineers easily assembled to join (ostensibly) high-risk entrepreneurial teams. Within the US, scalability of sales (especially initially) is straightforward, and city and county governments are pliable through lobby-able political and legal systems.

American management characteristics (Bloom et al. 2012)

Highly complementary to and permitted by these factors, are US management practices especially in relation to personnel policies, which proved to be particularly well-suited to rapid decentralized decision-making in highly ICT-based companies. The result is that US companies had moved to decentralized operations much earlier than in Europe employing a larger percentage of graduates, particularly ICT-skilled graduates (software engineers, etc) (Bloom et al. 2012). As can be seen in Figure 17.5 the US tertiary expansion was far earlier than other high-income countries. In fact, for

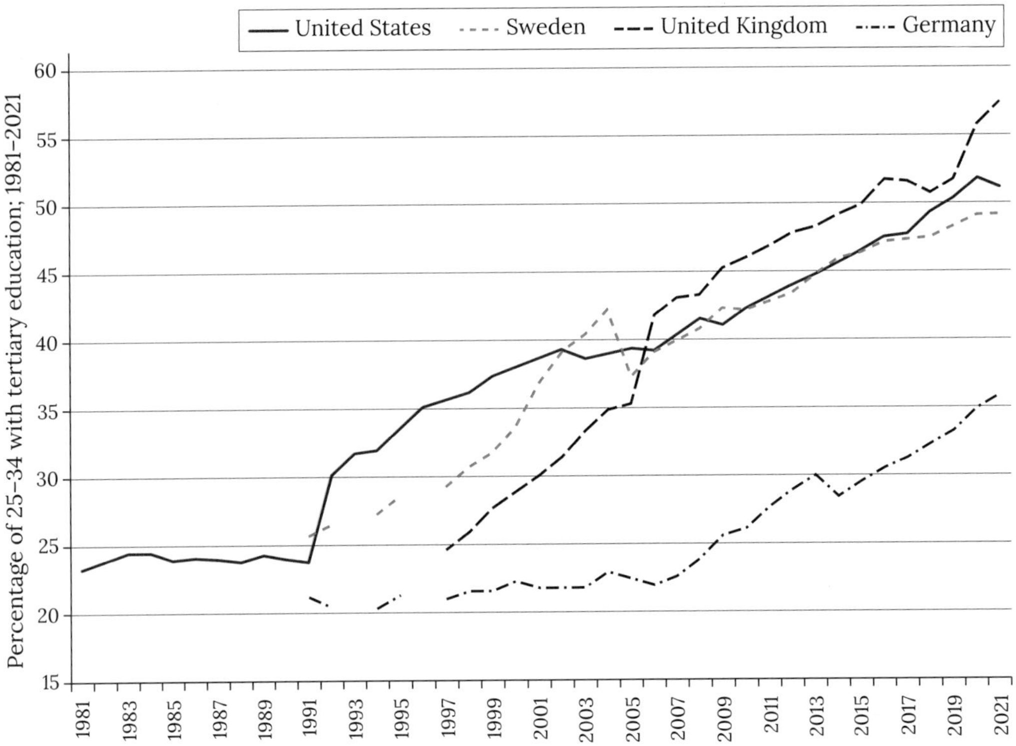

Figure 17.5 Tertiary expansion during the ICT revolution—percentage of 25–34 with tertiary education.

Source: OECD data (OECD 2022).

the early 1990s, the percentage of graduates in the US labour force was roughly double that in the UK. The UK share of graduates has only recently caught up. These workers had performance-related incentives and managers would act quickly to promote good performers. The decentralized organizational structure meant it was easier to identify the able performers.

17.3.3 **Innovation and diffusion within the United States**

We have argued that the United States is in a unique position to dominate radical technological innovation. While true in the aggregate this does not preclude the role within the US of another of our core arguments, co-location of assets. To briefly recap, the most innovative firms will want to locate in a few technological hubs, which are generally in big cities. Here, there will be a large skill cluster of graduates. Graduates are attracted to these cosmopolitan centres where partners, with different high-skilled occupations, can both pursue careers. This is increasingly important with a higher tendency for graduates to marry other graduates (assortative mating). Thus, there is a spatial concentration of human capital.

The importance of co-location of human capital for the dispersion of innovation is clear across regions in the United States. Figure 17.6 shows that states such as California and Massachusetts produce vastly more patents per person than other states. Indirectly, this affects regional GDP per capita, with those states that tend to have higher patenting rates also having higher incomes than others (see Table 17.2). Moreover, many of the richest states have seen the highest productivity growth over the latter part of the ICT revolution (in this case we have data from 2008 to 2021,

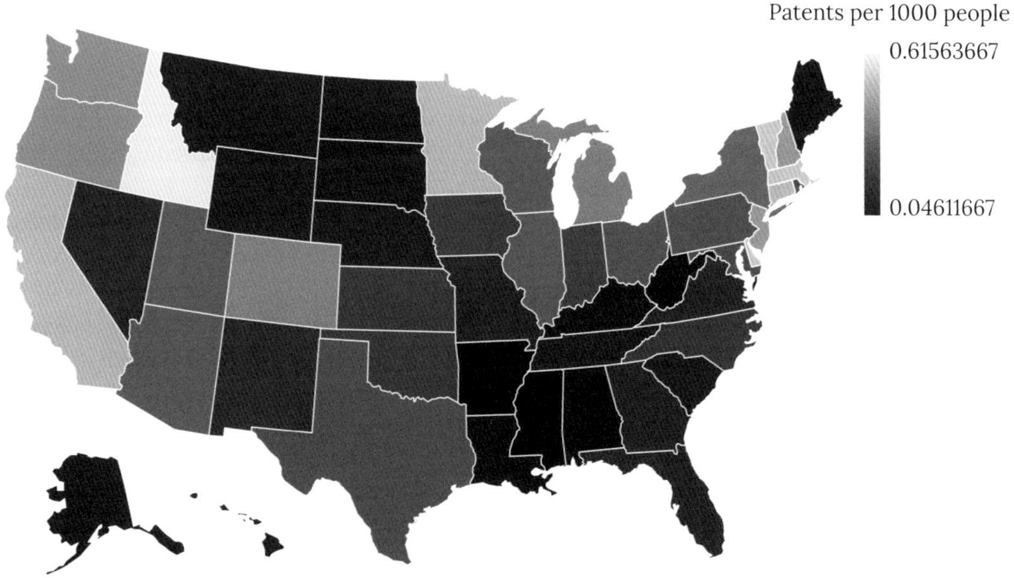

Figure 17.6 Average patents per 1000 people (1985–2015).
Source: United States Patent and Trademark Office open data portal.

Highest		Lowest	
State	2019 GDP per capita	State	2019 GDP per capita
Massachusetts	75,258	Alabama	41,389
New York	75,131	Idaho	40,566
Alaska	74,422	West Virginia	40,265
North Dakota	70,991	Arkansas	39,580
California	70,662	Mississippi	35,015

Table 17.2 US state GDP per capita in 2019.

Note: Per capita Real Gross Domestic Product (GDP) of the United States in 2019, by state (in chained 2012 US dollars).

Source: Bureau of Economic Analysis and Statista.

Highest		Lowest	
State	Av. labour prod. growth (%)	State	Av. labour prod. growth (%)
North Dakota	3.4	Nevada	0.7
Washington	2.7	Alaska	0.2
California	2.6	Connecticut	0.1
Oregon	2.1	Louisiana	0.0
Massachusetts	1.9	Wyoming	-0.4

Table 17.3 US state GDP per capita growth in 2008–21.

Note: Calculated as arithmetic average of 2008 to 2021 annual labour productivity growth rates.

Source: US Bureau of Labor Statistics.

Table 17.3). Massachusetts, California, and North Dakota[6] make the top 5 for both GDP per capita and productivity growth (in addition, New York is 7th in productivity growth and 2nd in GDP per capita).

A limited number of technological hubs (innovation clusters) are centres for innovation in the US, which highlights the question of how new products and processes are diffused throughout the country and across industries. The next sections focus on different patterns of international diffusion and some of the analysis also applies to the US. As in the other countries, there is a wide dispersion of firms within narrowly defined industries with the frontier firms being significantly more productive than the rest (see Section 17.5.3 for more details). Human capital rich, graduate-intensive, cities are more likely to be able to disseminate technological breakthroughs effectively.

There are some advantages for domestic US technological diffusion over international innovation transfer, but we still expect large differentiation and spatial polarization (Section 17.6). Most importantly, many firms have branches throughout the United States and thus management practices and processes can diffuse quicker.

[6] The data for North Dakota reflects the massive boom in fracking and oil and gas extraction, which is not related to the ICT revolution.

We also know that physical mobility of individuals is much higher within the United States than internationally or even across countries in Europe. Individuals tend to move between firms, move locations, and move between academia and industry more frequently than in Britain or Europe (Soskice 2021). To quote Morris's early case study of the British and American microelectronics industry:

> A specific case where labour mobility greatly assisted the early growth of semiconductor manufacture in America, is the well-known example of the diffusion of technical expertise from Bell Laboratories to an extremely large number of firms. In this respect, Bell was unique in providing a technical stimulus. In general, movement between academia and industry has been much more frequent within the United States, and a higher proportion of goal-oriented work is carried out within the universities. (Morris 1994, p. 247)

17.4 VARIETIES OF ICT REVOLUTION: LEADER AND FOLLOWERS

In this section, we explain how the ICT revolution that originated in the high tech clusters in the US diffused across high-income countries (as well as within the US). We set up an analytical framework to distinguish five 'varieties of diffusion', illustrating each by reference to case studies of the UK, Germany, Sweden, and China.

17.4.1 Varieties of ICT diffusion: A typology

The characteristics of the US that led to its leading role in the ICT revolution include the exceptional nature of American institutions, in particular, the extent of decentralization and lack of regulation of parts of the planning, financial and research systems, the early achievement of high rates of graduate education and the numbers concentrated in the nascent innovation hub areas, as well as the match between decentralized US management practices and breakthrough innovations.

How do American breakthrough innovations spread to other high-income economies? Our starting point is that it depends on the type of ICT diffusion. We outline five broad categories (summarized in Table 17.4). The first three are the most common: in abbreviated versions they are 'simple' diffusion, diffusion in services, and diffusion in manufacturing. The latter two types are more specific, respectively, where diffusion takes place in multinational market-dominating corporates (typically with a US HQ), and in national financial empires.

Simple prepackaged diffusion. Technology is easily transferred from one region to another. Usually, such technology would be directly diffused in its original form without customization, although there may be imitators. We think of examples such as smartphones, standalone office software, platform based-apps (e.g. Zoom, Whatsapp, Uber). Much of this technology was developed during the earlier part of the ICT revolution, but not exclusively so, particularly in relation to some of the platform-based apps. As argued in Section 17.3, we see this as a reason why high-income countries were able to converge (or stay at a constant distance to the frontier) to the US in the first decades of the ICT revolution.

In order to access 'simple prepackaged diffusion' technology the workforce should have some form of ICT literacy without the necessity to be highly educated or trained.

Type of ICT diffusion	Competences	Corporate governance / ownership	Geography	Workplace organization	Examples
Simple prepackaged	Secondary education	Any (often individual ownership of technology)	Anywhere	No participation in a workplace needed	Standalone software (MS Word); Facebook membership
Customized systemic services software	Graduates with social skills, creativity, management skills, ICT engineers	Corporate environment. Often with ownership stake or bonus structure	Graduate-intensive cities, often linked to research universities	Relational decision-making, highly educated, group-working, substantial training/retraining	Fintech; Medtech
Integrating software into industrial products (servitization)	Skilled engineering workers now need integrated engineering and ICT engineering skills; combined with social skills, creativity, and strong management skills	Patient capital—For example, foundations or block holders; take long-run perspective	Hub-spoke system with plants, typically in smaller cities, close to big cities with knowledge-intensive business services (KIBS), and research institutions	Relational decision-making, group-working, substantial training/retraining	Automobile manufacturing
Complex pre-packaged customized services software	Graduates with social skills, creativity, strong management skills, ICT engineers	Cooperative environment, stake in ownership, bonuses for HQ employees (tight financial management in branches)	Graduate-intensive cities, research universities for HQs	Relational decision-making, highly educated, group-working, substantial training/retraining	Walmart, McDonalds, Hilton
Financial empire	Graduates with social skills, creativity, strong management skills, ICT engineers	Concentrated ownership across multiple firms and industries. Cooperative environment, stake in ownership, bonuses; strong cooperation with skilled employees and their union	Graduate-intensive cities, research universities	Relational decision-making, highly educated, group-working, substantial training/retraining	Wallenberg / Investor AB

Table 17.4 Summary of 'types' of ICT diffusion.

In most high-income countries where the vast majority of the labour force have a secondary school education, this should be sufficient. When using the technology, it can generally be operated by a single user without any need for significant adaptation. Thus, tasks in firms do not need significant cooperation and individuals need few relational skills to complete tasks effectively. Moreover, if an individual has access to the technology, there is no restriction as to where the task can be done.

Customized system services software. High value-added software for professional services or institutional groups. The software cannot just be rolled out but rather requires high levels of customization. Competition between providers is based on product quality (and reputation) rather than cost. Examples include software for start-ups in a variety of '-Tech' industries such as FinTech, MedTech, EdTech and LawTech.

Diffusing customized system services software requires a highly skilled graduate workforce. Some workers will be ICT specialists, but we think of most employees being 'ICT engineers' in the broader sense that they are able to incorporate technology into their everyday working life. The technology is key to workers' productivity. Individuals need strong social and relational skills to work within a creative team-based logic. Strong management practices are essential for dissemination of the technology, at both the top and in middle management. This should encourage a cooperative environment, where workers will often have an ownership stake and there will be performance-related pay based on department or overall firm performance (given individual performance alone is often difficult to measure with the collaborative nature of work). This technology is mostly found within graduate-intensive cities, often in close proximity to research-based universities.

Research oriented companies integrating ICT software services into industrial products (servitization). High tech manufacturers integrate ICT into the manufacturing process. They use technology in management processes and final goods production to compete on product quality and remain competitive in the face of low-cost competition (especially since the China shock, and its WTO accession in 2001). Increasingly, sophisticated software is integrated with the final industrial goods and not just in the production process itself (for example, for cars, the computer with GPS, multimedia, information on performance of the car etc. and robots and automated systems in manufacturing and inventory management).

Skilled engineering workers now need integrated engineering and ICT engineering skills. Hence, we are seeing the switch to Universities of Applied Science from apprenticeships (see more details in the Germany case study). Workers need to combine engineering and ICT abilities with social skills, creativity, and strong management skills. Workers will continue to have firm-specific skills as the software is highly customized and requires understanding of firm-specific information and relationships. Firms must train their workers to implement and customize new technology. Given this long-run perspective, firms are still often owned by foundations or block holders (patient capital), and there is strong cooperation with works councils. However, in contrast to earlier periods, because product competition with other similar companies is very strong, coordination between companies has weakened, just as social partnership has declined.

Often, we will see a hub-spoke system with plants typically in smaller cities, close to big cities with KIBS (knowledge-intensive business services) and research institutions. Those smaller towns are thus typically higher skilled, higher income places than comparable size towns in countries which operate more intensely in the system services software field.

Complex pre-packaged customized services software. Large multinational corporations that are dominant in an industry can develop a software system that is so wide-ranging and complex that it is too difficult for others to copy, and hence provides significant barriers to entry (Bessen 2022). Walmart is the widely used example; they have a large presence in the United States and often expanded organically or via acquisitions into other countries. In 1999 in the UK, they bought the already large supermarket chain ASDA.[7] We could also think of large hotel chains e.g. Hilton or food retailers e.g. McDonalds. These non-traded service sector firms can boost productivity outside technological hubs by diffusing a centrally devised process out to regional branches (Hsieh and Rossi-Hansberg 2019). The process is typically as follows. Technology innovation is managed by a central headquarters (predominantly in the US) and then diffused to other regional offices (in say London, Paris, or Singapore). The regional headquarters will require some customization but mainly integration. Branches within regions will have almost no customization with processes and products dictated by a central strategy. In fact in the Walmart case much of the complex software is developed in Silicon Valley, and is then diffused to branches where further but simpler customization may be required.

For the regional headquarters, in general the workforce will need to employ graduates, and social and relational skills are particularly important for interacting with the central HQ. The workforce will need creativity and be able to adapt to new management practices diffused by the HQ. Again, we would expect stakes in ownership and bonuses based on divisional performance. The regional offices will be placed in graduate-intensive cities, maybe with research institutions nearby. Workers will generally have long tenure in these firms due to the complexity of the ICT; they will require frequent training and there is an emphasis on work sustaining relationships.

US principles of decentralized management apparently diffuse well to other countries in Europe. For example, when US multinationals bought foreign companies they increased their productivity—this effect was larger than when non-US multinationals were the acquirer. The research by Bloom, Sadun, and Van Reenen (2012) goes on to show that this 'productivity miracle' is a result of people management practices in US-owned companies.

Financial-empire-wide ICT integrated development. As we show in our Swedish case study below, many modern Swedish companies are owned by one of two financial empires. The basic goal of the financial empires is to provide expertise and a governance push to transform key areas of the Swedish economy. While Sweden may be one of a kind, we think there are parallels and lessons to be learned in other countries. The model may be relevant to sovereign wealth funds, which own a large national share of assets or to some large global asset managers that now have a share in virtually all large publicly traded companies, e.g. BlackRock. Likewise, some asset managers have a similar position within a country, such as Legal and General or abrdn (the result of mergers between Scottish Widows, Aberdeen, and Standard Life) in the UK, Axa or Amundi in France, and Allianz or DWS in Germany.

Given their large diverse assets, investors have a much wider interest than in a specific company or industry; they have an incentive to encourage innovation and to dif-

[7] Walmart would later go on to sell ASDA in 2021.

fuse it across the entire economy. It promotes alignment between government, workers (trade unions) and the large investors. Workforces need to be highly skilled and adapt quickly to ICT advances, with high relational skills, creativity, and strong management practices. Again, firms will tend to situate themselves in graduate-intensive cities. Given the patient capital and long-term focus of thc financial empires and their individual companies, we would also expect high levels of training and re-training.

Next, we develop our country case studies using the framework of varieties of diffusion that we have developed and knowledge of the political economy of each country. Although China does not neatly fit our paradigm above, nor is it yet a high-income country, given its global importance we have added a tentative case study drawing on the same conceptual framework.

17.4.2 The United Kingdom: Knowledge hub imitator

The UK is a service based economy (Hutton and Ward 2021): 79% of employment is in services and only 10% in manufacturing. In some ways the UK has been very successful at implementing two of the methods of diffusion above. First, there are pockets of the economy which have diffused technology using the customized system software we have previously described. In these sectors, locally frontier firms emerged within the relevant sector. Second, there are a number of US multinationals which have introduced their (globally) frontier model to the UK, creating large hubs (e.g. Amazon and Google).

Both models are based on a 'graduate world', with organizational decentralization. Employees are expected to take more initiative; with the ability to access massive knowledge through ICT they need a high level of analytic skills; and since they will need to solve problems together, they also require social skills.

The UK was well set up to exploit this new paradigm as university participation expanded dramatically from the early 1990s to the present (Figure 17.5). In 2018 half of the school leaving age population would go on to tertiary education (a faster expansion for women than men).[8]

What explains the expansion of university participation in the UK parallel to that of organizational decentralization, and what does this have to do with prior US experience? There are three possibilities according to Blundell et al. (2022): (1) That the decentralization of organizational structures in firms was exogenous and that the percentage of graduates responded to this endogenously; this possibility is rejected because participation in higher education is decided independently of (typically well before and in the absence of knowledge about) decentralization. (2) That both are exogenous, so that UK companies invested in developing appropriate ICT-based organizational structures coincidentally with the expansion of higher education; but this is not very plausible given that the graduate wage premium is observed to remain constant (rather than to fall, as larger graduate cohorts entered the labour market). (3) The percentage of graduates coming on to the job market is exogenous; and UK companies can choose at low cost to adopt the already developed US decentralized organizational technologies utilizing ICT.

---

[8] Statistics are based on Department for Education predictions on school leavers going on to higher education before they are 30, rather than the OECD measure quoted earlier.

Blundell et al. provide evidence in support of the third hypothesis, which would suggest the diffusion model. The argument is as follows: it is de facto low cost to adopt the US-developed ICT-enabled decentralized management technology when establishing a new facility in which employees (now more highly skilled) are differently organized. Next, given constant returns to scale in production, there is a 'world' price for services produced with the 'decentralized organization plus graduates' package. Hence, the graduate wage is in principle independent of the *number of graduates*. Put another way, *ceteris paribus*, there would be a 'world real wage' for graduates employed in firms organized this way in these advanced technology sectors. There is an analogy here to the factor price theorem in international trade. This explains why, despite the mass increase in UK higher education, there has remained a relatively constant wage premium between graduates and non-graduates (Blundell et al. 2022).

Critically, what this tells us is that the UK, as a follower country, can increase growth relative to the baseline by moving non-graduates via university education into the US-developed organizational technology, with the presumptively attached productivity. For simplicity, assume that each new graduate replaces a non-graduate worker who has retired or alternatively the new graduate was previously a non-graduate worker. *Ceteris paribus*, if the productivity level elsewhere in the economy is constant and with a constant population, the change in output in the UK is then equal to the increase in graduates multiplied by the (growing) productivity difference.

While many, mainly graduates, have profited from diffusion of services software and management, diffusion has been limited by the absence in many sectors, firms, and regions of the competences needed. Half of school leavers will go on to become graduates, half do not. Moreover, graduates tend to flock to a few technological hubs, especially London (Britton et al. 2021). Those places without the stock of graduates fail to attract finance or multinational companies. Unlike Germany or Sweden, in the UK there is little family ownership or block private holders of large enterprises to provide patient capital outside the major cities. Political power in the UK is centralized to Westminster so there is little that local governments can do to foster incentives for ICT diffusion.

Thus, unsurprisingly there is a wide dispersion of productivity between firms in the UK with a fat tail of unproductive firms, so much so that modal productivity is around 50% lower than mean productivity (Haldane 2017). Firms that are the least productive tend to export less, be domestically owned, have fewer employees, and are based in specific areas (Haldane 2017).

In the UK case, technological diffusion, and hence movement towards the frontier, happens to a great extent in US-owned firms and in a few industries, such as finance, law, and pharmaceuticals. To reiterate, these are graduate industries based in a few large technological hubs. Diffusion is limited, and there are consequences for polarization as we develop in Section 17.6.

17.4.3 **Germany: Research-oriented and manufacturing-based**

According to the EU's 2021 Regional Innovation Scorecard (European Commission 2021), in the top 25 leading research areas, there are just 2 in the UK (London and the SE), and there are no French, Spanish, or Italian regions. But there are 7 German regions, of which four are in Southern Germany.

Germany's use of US developed ICT is quite different from that in the UK. In Germany, deindustrialization (the fall in the share of employment in industry) has been much slower than in the other high-income economies. It successfully adapted to the collapse of the Soviet Union by developing supply chains incorporating skilled workers in former eastern bloc countries on its borders. This helped it retain its comparative advantage in technologically advanced engineering products, including vehicles, as the Chinese market expanded rapidly, and to continue its successful system of incremental innovation. The ICT revolution produced challenges to that system. For example, how was ICT to be integrated into a system built on non-graduate apprentices?

The integration of the major radical innovations in software from the US into product and service innovation was seen as necessary to preserve competitiveness in German exports. This has been most successful in Southern Germany. Although Southern Germany has a large and effective services economy, and although manufacturing there has declined significantly since the 1980s, in relative terms it has remained a substantial manufacturing area. In fact, the decline in employment in manufacturing is misleading, since a large part of the transformation has consisted in the de facto integration of advanced digital services into manufactured products, via so-called knowledge-intensive business services (KIBS). KIBS take knowledge and information from outside the company and integrate it into a company of which they have detailed knowledge to improve its performance and productivity. This fits into our second model where technical diffusion is predominantly through research oriented companies integrating ICT software services into industrial products. Thus, the way in which radical innovations, mainly from the US, were spread contrasts sharply with diffusion in the UK.

Southern Germany is an extraordinarily dense, autobahn-connected region with many of the most research-oriented large companies in contemporary Germany. Unlike in the radical innovation clusters in the US, 'old' large companies continue to have dominant positions. There are a number of very large research and export-oriented companies with well-trained workforces, most notably Siemens, Daimler, BMW, SAP, Bosch, LIDL, BASF; also Porsche and Audi (relatively independent parts of the VW group). In addition, it is home to a large number of leading Mittelstand (medium-sized, typically family-owned) companies, equally research- and export-oriented and with highly skilled workforces.

Focusing on the most innovative region of Southern Germany highlights four main problems (partially in common with other parts of Germany) in the current millennium:

1. The major need for skills has been in ICT. While the German workforce was generally well-trained, ICT skills were not initially strong; this in part as a result of the apprenticeship system. The economic driver of Southern Germany has been successful exporting; but export markets have become increasingly competitive, especially in manufacturing, reflecting the combination of modularization of manufacturing parts and globalization. Software-based services have equally been

increasingly modularized and globalized, largely to India (Branstetter et al., 2019). To maintain competitiveness, the innovation-based products which are needed for success in export markets require bundling with ICT-intensive software services (technically called 'servitization').

2. These problems were compounded—especially for Baden-Württemberg and Bavaria where the auto industry is largely based—with the pressure to switch from internal combustion to electric (hence software-intensive) vehicles.
3. Until the early 2000s, federal rules governing vocational training, co-determination, and works councils and corporate governance partially underwrote long-term decision-making as well as wage moderation, workforce cooperation and investment by companies in vocational training. These German 'rules of the game' limited poaching of skilled workers, unilateral collective and individual dismissals, and short-term decisions for example in closing temporarily loss-making subsidiaries. Then, with the Social Democrat, Gerhard Schroeder as Chancellor (1998–2005) many of these rules were substantially liberalized. The major banks (Deutsche, Commerz, and Dresdner) had been major block-holders, but ceased to be so when Schroeder ended high capital gains tax on their holdings in 2000.
4. Related to (3): until the late 20th century, research-oriented (advanced) companies in the private sector had enjoyed relatively close relations with each other, under the aegis of business associations, especially at the sectoral level. This was reinforced by sectoral unions. A great deal of information was exchanged directly and indirectly between companies, including about directions of research. But competition in export markets increased through the 2000s; and this put the strongly business 'coordinated' system under pressure; highly competitive innovating companies were nervous about exchanging information about their research directions. This led to a loosening of the integration of business associations and sectoral unions distancing them from strategic discussions (e.g. in supervisory boards); and reduced joint/coordinated research with competitors.

How did the Southern German economy resolve these problems? There are both external and internal drivers of change. The external driver has been first and foremost, the need to integrate the ICT revolution (especially software) into the high quality products (themselves research-driven) of Baden-Wurttemberg and Bavaria. The massive problem has been the transformation of highly skilled engineering workforces without ICT education into ICT-skilled workforces, while maintaining a consensus environment within companies.

- **Corporate governance and long-termism:** In the period we are looking at, the research- and export-oriented companies played increasingly independent roles (both the very large companies such as Daimler or Siemens, and also Mittelstand exporters).

  They in turn were increasingly driven by their owners. Here there is a paradox: despite measures liberalizing corporate governance in Germany at the start of the

2000s (under the SPD-led Schroeder government), exporting companies maintained long-term perspectives. Why? First, most big exporting companies were made up of a bundle of 'implicit' long-term contracts, notably between highly skilled workforces which accepted technological and strategic change and (sometimes radical) retraining, in exchange for employment security (or perhaps early retirement). Companies had strong incentives not to break such implicit understandings. Second, even though the large banks were allowed by Schroeder's new rules to sell their shares (which they did), owners remained long-term oriented. Combined with the continuing role of ownership by private (often founder family) foundations, shareholder blocks remained. Ironically, although a significant proportion of the DAX was owned by BlackRock, State Street, and Vanguard (largely via passive ETFs), these funds happily saw such long-term-oriented German corporations as a key part of their portfolio (as Larry Fink, Chairman and CEO of BlackRock, often explained).

- **Rethinking unions:** Industrial, largely sectoral, unions play a less important role than previously. In the past they had important representatives on the Supervisory Boards (Aufsichtsräte) of companies of any significance. That gave them wide knowledge from participating in strategic discussions, of competitive strategy and research developments across the relevant sector. This was also true of business associations. In our view (partly based on ongoing research with Frieder Mitsch), highly competitive research-oriented companies were nervous of these information flows; and the traditional role of sectoral corporatist institutions (both business associations and national/sectoral unions) has declined.

  But this has not meant that the role of employee representation of skilled, educated employees has declined: far from it. The employee-elected chairs of works councils (themselves largely unionized) are increasingly integrated into corporate decision-making. The interests of works councils, so long as both sides stick to the implicit contract, are aligned to the long-term interests of the company and its owners. This arrangement plays a large part in enabling the integration of ICT skills in the existing workforce, and accepting a shift from (over time) an apprentice-based system of training new employees to one based increasingly on graduates.

- **ICT-skilled employees: from apprentices to graduates:** In the 1990s, skilled employees in German manufacturing were largely trained as apprentices, becoming Facharbeiter, technicians or Meisters, as well as lower level managers; engineers and higher level managers were/are graduates. The 21st century has seen a major decline in apprenticeships and a corresponding increase in graduates (Figure 17.7a): this switch has been most marked in the more research-oriented companies. In addition, a new type of (lower-level) university had been established in the 1980s called Fachhochschulen (Universities of Applied Science) in Germany and Austria. These are more vocational (especially engineering and software engineering and business) universities, and in Southern Germany operated close to bigger companies. Students doubled in number between 2000 and 2021 (Figure 17.7b).

  This move into Universities of Applied Science (UAS) was done in close collaboration with the research-oriented company sector, and the UAS operate informally

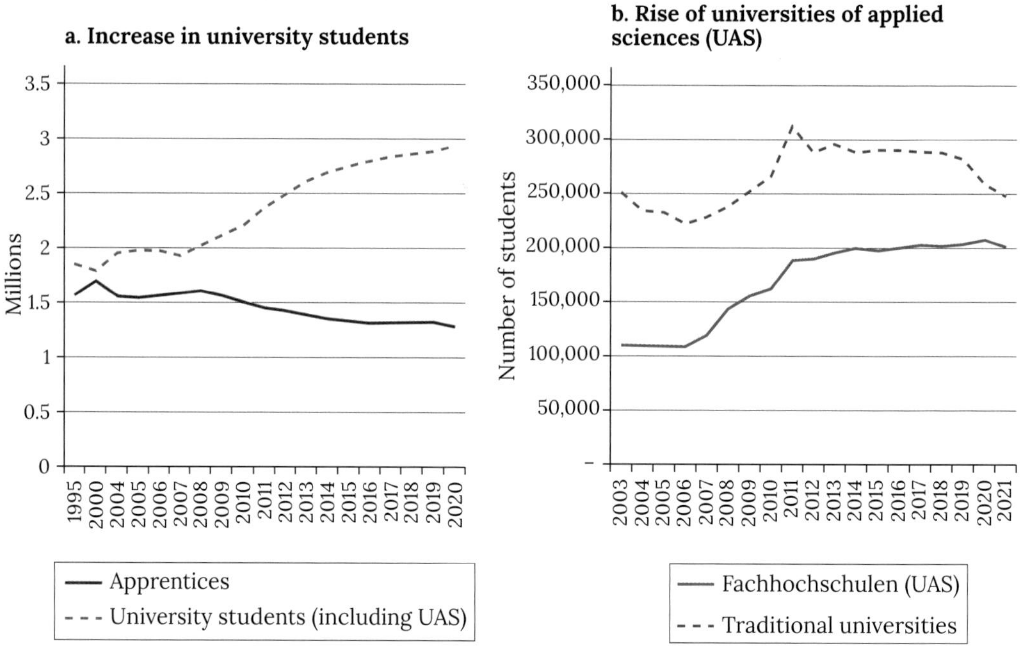

Figure 17.7 The German decline of apprenticeships and rise of the Universities of Applied Science.
Note: Provided by Frieder Mitsch.
Source: BMBF, BIBB, Statistisches Bundesamt.

with the businesses close by.[9] Some larger companies (including Daimler) have established 'Dual study' degree courses. In addition, students who do apprenticeships in advanced companies will often then do a degree course while maintaining a close connection with the company. Advanced technology companies have also established retraining and upskilling facilities/schools within the company, often concerned to upgrade ICT skills for existing employees without sufficient prior training or qualifications.

- **The role of Federal, regional and city government:** Finally, regional and city governments play a central role especially in setting up and augmenting Universities of Applied Science; in this they work with local companies. Land (i.e. state) governments have primary political responsibility for all universities, and the Southern German governments have played a major role in their development. While Universities of Applied Science have been crucial in spreading competencies in ICT, the long-established Technical Universities (especially Munich, Karlsruhe, Stuttgart) have provided world class research, not of radical breakthrough innovations, but of leading-edge capacities in transforming those radical innovations for

[9] As shown in Figure 17.5, the higher education expansion occurred much later than most high-income countries. Despite the recent expansion, it remains at a much lower level compared to the UK, USA, and Sweden.

research-oriented companies in Southern Germany. The employer demand for graduates from Universities of Applied Science has grown as Germany has adapted to this model of research-oriented manufacturing-based diffusion. The alignment between firms' needs (and firms often fund particular programmes in UAS) and the Federal and regional government's role in setting up and funding Universities of Applied Science has helped the transition towards this model.

17.4.4 Sweden: Research- and financial empire-based

From the late 1940s to the early 1970s, the Swedish economy adopted an increasingly egalitarian wage policy with centralized bargaining, an active (retraining) labour market policy, together with a strongly compensatory welfare state. With the OPEC crises in the mid and late 1970s productivity growth declined, the state greatly expanded subsidized employment, and post-tax wage equality became increasingly tight, both at the bottom and top ends of the distribution. In 1990, a banking crisis led to a major recession. All these factors contributed to limited incentives for individuals to invest in new skills, a low rate of company formation, falling export market shares, and ultimately low productivity growth. Under long-term Social Democratic governments, Sweden had become very attractive from a social perspective; but it was clear that it was failing to meet the challenge of the developing ICT revolution.

As the centre-right coalition entered government in 1991, there was a recognition of the underlying tensions between the new coalition and key firms. The unique feature of Swedish large business is the high concentration of ownership. The top 15 families hold 70% of the Stockholm Stock Exchange (Thelen 2019). Of these, the Wallenbergs, predominantly through Investor AB, and Industrievarden are by far the most significant, having controlling shares in 13 of the top 25 companies (Thelen 2019). Figure 17.8 highlights the contrast between the high concentration of wealth in Sweden (a similar Gini coefficient to that of the UK and Germany; lower than the US) and its much lower inequality in pre- and especially post-tax income).

The role of these giant multi-sector (finance, services, manufacturing) conglomerates in Sweden differs from that of the large German manufacturing companies. The interests of the German firms lay in retaining their dominance in their existing markets (especially abroad) by integrating ICT into sophisticated manufacturing. The relevant broadly supportive policies were the Hartz reforms of 2003, which, for example, toughened rules on eligibility of individuals for unemployment benefits. By contrast, the interests represented in the diversified portfolio of the Wallenberg family and Industrievarden led the Swedish government to adopt supply side policies to ease the transition away from traditional manufacturing across the economy to both advanced manufacturing and services. The Swedish emphasis was on active labour market policies and re-skilling.

The underlying issues facing the Swedish economy as a result of the ICT revolution (and increased global competition) were clear to both the SAF (employers association) and to the respective trade unions: LO (blue collar), TCO (professional, engineering etc), and SACO (white collar). They were supportive of the need for deep-seated

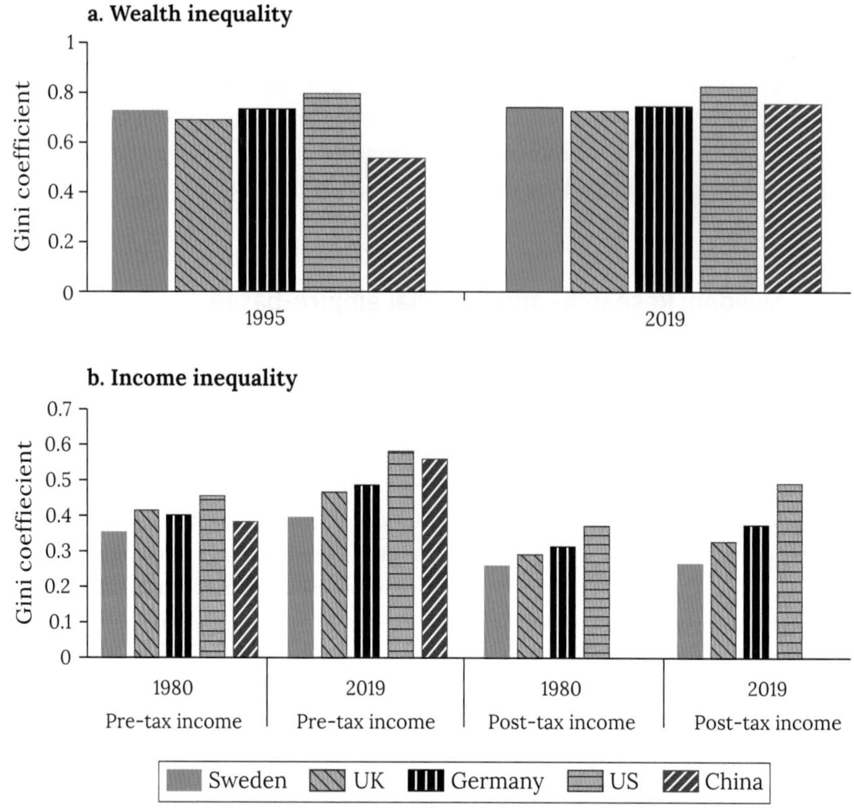

Figure 17.8 Inequality throughout the ICT revolution.

Note: Earliest available wealth inequality data is for 1995.

Source: World inequality database.

changes to the existing model following the centre-left re-entering government in 1994.

The major changes in the model are as follows:

1. Decentralization of wage bargaining, based on sectors and then companies. This preserved the long-standing feature of the 'Swedish model' that a constraint on wage settlements is required to sustain international competitiveness. This can be summarized as price-setting using 'world pricing' (Chapter 11) and 'real exchange rate–oriented wage setting' (Chapters 14 and 15) and required coordination between sectors open to trade and those sheltered from it including the public sector. However, within decentralized wage bargaining, sectoral minimum wages were established. Crucially, the new wage-setting system enabled much bigger increases for graduates and highly skilled workers.
2. At the same time the government encouraged the expansion of higher education, increasing spending from 1% of GDP in 1990 to 2% in 2000, resulting in a dramatic increase in participation (Figure 17.5). There was a corresponding increase in education spending more generally. For those 'left-behind' by the ICT transition,

there was a large increase in the other traditional bulwark of the Swedish model, active labour market policy (Chapter 15) and re-skilling (Thelen 2019).

3. With strong government and business group backing, there was a strategy of supporting university research into digitalization, especially in the main universities, spreading this regionally and into teaching, as well as promoting PhDs abroad (in the US especially), and with strong links to the life sciences. Personal computers were also rolled out as part of 'home' life, as tax breaks were given to companies who gave them to their employees.
4. Business groups developed their strategic directions both in transformation of relevant companies and skill upgrading; and in acquisition and research-investment in areas with strong digital possibilities.
5. While strong pre-existing labour market rules still governed 'permanent' workers (e.g. protection against dismissal, and retention of the need for union agreements at company level for the relevant group of workers), companies were now enabled to employ a margin of flexible and temporary workers. This made founding of new companies easier and big companies such as Ericsson were supportive of graduates forming agreed start-ups with a career in Ericsson if the start-up failed. Recent well-known start-ups from Sweden include Spotify and Klarna.
6. The welfare state became increasingly supportive of the ICT revolution and experimented with opening the provision of education and health to private initiatives. There were also wider regional initiatives governing establishment of colleges and research linkages. For example, see Etzkowitz and Klofsten's (2005) study of Linköping, where the university, government, and businesses complemented each other in innovation. Universities would be focal points for science parks, which would often accommodate businesses spun out of the university, and the state could provide support to business through financing.

These changes have transformed the Swedish economy and have also been widely accepted by the employers' association and the unions. Sweden integrated ICT technology into both highly specialized manufacturing and services. It succeeded in creating a highly skilled workforce while maintaining its core values of equality (notably of disposable income and in relation to gender). The next challenge for Sweden (as with other high-income countries) is to respond to the green transition. As we have argued the financial empire model has adapted well to the ICT revolution, yet it could be that this dominance inhibits the next transition. While patient capital, and long-standing companies with large blockholder positions equip Sweden well for this eventuality, Aagaard et al. (2022) ask whether the lack of 'new' companies may result in a lack of dynamism.

17.4.5 China: From copier to constrained radical innovator

As with much else in this chapter, there is no settled agreement on what is happening in response to the ICT revolution in China; this is in no small part because the Chinese technological and political economy, as well as leadership strategies, are still changing. There is no question, however, that Chinese growth has been remarkable since Deng's famous Southern Tour via Shanghai to Shenzhen and Guangdong gave free rein to cities and regions to open up to FDI, to promote innovation and to promote both private and municipal enterprises (SOEs). Xi Jinping has made striking claims about Chinese success in radical innovation and new technologies. What explains this remarkable growth and how does radical innovation in China compare to that in the US?

A rather obvious point is that China is not yet a high-income country; but nor is it yet obviously caught in a so-called middle-income trap. Economically it operates on broadly capitalist principles. Politically it is not a democracy. And while its extraordinary growth record has faltered in the last two or three years, and whatever anxieties its pursuit of Asian hegemony may give the high-income world, it is an amazing phenomenon.

So how does China work? The Standing Committee (7 members) of the Politburo (25 members) of the Chinese Communist Party (CCP) is where power lies; Xi is the General Secretary of the CCP and runs the Standing Committee. Yet China has a population of 1.5+ billion individuals who, de facto, have the freedom to operate in a (relatively) freewheeling capitalist economy, and it covers a huge land mass with many regions and giant cities. So, Xi has little power to lay down anything in detail. All he can really do is to make general statements about directions and hope they will be broadly carried out by the bureaucrats with real power, who are the mayors of cities and party secretaries in the regions. Yet he also has the power of appointing and removing officials, more or less at will if he so chooses. And this power of appointment and dismissal cascades down through the whole country.

The broad incentive structure can be summarized like this, at least at the key mayoral and party secretary levels:[10]

> You will be moved every 5 or 10 years (so you do not build up a regional power base). And you will be promoted—moved to a more important city/region—if you have been economically successful in your existing locality. How you achieve success is broadly up to you.

Two major elements in this are foreign direct investment (FDI) and the support/foundation of state-owned enterprises (SOEs) with the aid of state banks, sometimes in tandem. In the current millennium, a great emphasis has been put on the acquisition and/or building up of technology (starting from a rather low level).

Incentives for cities and regions

China is almost impossible to govern centrally, especially if Beijing were to control the myriad of place- and sector-based policies needed to give individual companies and local officials the tailored incentives and freedom to promote innovative enterprises. As argued in this chapter, success in the ICT world or 'knowledge economy' works effectively through giving power to decentralized organizations.

---

[10] See Ang (2016, 2020) and Bardhan (2020) for explanations of how the system works.

The central government's answer is initially to recruit academically able young people into public sector administrations (in cities, regions, ministries, or other agencies). When they achieve positions of power (notably a city mayor or regional party secretary), further promotion depends on three factors:

1. First and foremost, the economic growth of the area for which they are responsible,
2. Second, the extent to which popular protests are avoided; this includes ensuring employment, and holding down the cost of living; and in particular the need to minimize petty corruption by public officials, including the police (Ang 2016, 2020),
3. Third, patronage from higher up in the Party—eventually in the Central Committee, the Politburo or highest in the Standing Committee of the Politburo.

Take as an example the mayor of a big city (almost certainly male): he has a very strong incentive to support start-ups and successful growth companies, with land and with finance from the municipal bank; and he will likely retain shares in the company. He will also benefit from (and therefore need to have) patronage higher up in the Party, who will be able to promote the companies he is supporting (and have shares in them).

Given the prevailing low level of public sector salaries, at every level, successful firms in a city can be used to increase public sector salaries there and hence reduce the temptation for low level corruption (Ang 2020). Thus, *if* this system of rewards to successful communist party entrepreneurs works well, and although it may be seen as high-level corruption, it is not necessarily so different from much of the system of rewards in parts of American capitalism. It gives major incentives for well-organized Chinese cities and their administrations to bid for, provide infrastructural support for and benefit from successful companies. In turn, this may well attract FDI.

One major element of infrastructural support (which we will refer to shortly) is for education and training of engineers and software programmers in city higher education.

Radical innovation institutions in China and the US compared

Behind the US, China is the next most successful economy in the world in radical innovation; this is most obviously the case judged by the number of unicorns (Hammond and Ruehl 2020). We will see that in a few areas, China is ahead of the US—for a comprehensive analysis of the evidence see Chen et al. (2021). We discuss the reasons for this below. As in the US, innovation activities are located in a small number of knowledge-intensive cities, most notably Beijing, Shanghai, Shenzhen, Hefei, Wuhan, Hangzhou, and Guangzhou. Our explanation of US success in specific cities is based on a range of relevant institutions. What is interesting is that Chinese institutions—while formally very different—are functionally similar to the corresponding innovation-promoting institutions of the US (with two important qualifications, in the last two bullet points below):

- **People management:** Chinese knowledge-intensive companies have been moving in the US direction (e.g. with Tencent copying Google), although they still may have further to go (World Bank 2019).

- **Large pools of relevant highly qualified labour (engineers, managers, programmers etc) and knowledge-intensive business services (KIBS):** Similar to the US.
- **Flexible decentralized and deregulated risk financing:** managed by mayors with municipal banks, but also via the major presence of US venture funds in China during the last decade: Functionally equivalent to the US.
- **Scalability across huge internal markets:** Similar to the US.
- **Porous business-city relations:** while the mechanisms may not be quite the same, in China a network of lobbyists and business lawyers have relations with city politicians and the court system to help successful companies. Mayors and their subordinate networks also stand to gain from business success, often through direct shareholdings in the Chinese case. Note however that businesses as well as mayors and party secretaries operate under conditions of 'strategic uncertainty' from Beijing. There is the constant small threat that Beijing might intervene and punish behaviour it was worried about (Breznitz and Murphree 2011). This happened to a number of Big Tech companies, notably Alibaba and Ant; and mayors and regional and Beijing bosses live under the threat of possible prosecution for corruption (as happened with Bo-Xilai in 2012), bringing down whole subsidiary networks.
- **Cross-disciplinary open research universities:** the Chinese have certainly developed top universities quite rapidly. However, the major difference from the US is that Chinese universities have significantly less freedom (or alternatively their academics are more careful) when venturing into areas to do with social or psychological analysis, clearly a problem for developing innovations in a whole range of social and business areas. This also inhibits the ability of universities to foster flexible and open relations between academics and business start-ups, critical to the US radical innovation system. Moreover, the Chinese authorities have made plain their concern about high externality software-based companies such as Alibaba, Ant, and Didi. The areas of Chinese frontier technology success are in AI, including surveillance software like face recognition, 5G and other technologies such as smart cities, which benefit from state imposition of standards within China.

17.5 THE ICT REVOLUTION AND PRODUCTIVITY PUZZLE

In Chapter 16 the data in Table 16.2, and the discussion earlier in Section 17.3, showed the secular decline in productivity growth rates since 1960 in high-income countries. The US—the technological leader—was the partial exception with somewhat slower growth of hourly productivity in the initial 1960–75 period than in the 'catching up' economies and faster growth than them post 1995. As discussed in detail above, this is consistent with our thesis of an innovative leader and a group of followers under different phases of the ICT revolution. However, an interesting question arises: given the ICT developments over the past two decades, why was productivity growth so low? There is no settled answer to this question.

17.5.1 Mismeasurement

Goldin et al. (2021) examines the hypothesis that mismeasurement accounts for part of the slowdown in productivity growth recorded in the statistics. The main sources of potential mismeasurement are the price deflator (e.g. handling quality change associated with ICT) and so-called boundary issues in defining GDP (such as the sale of intellectual property by a company in the US to a subsidiary in a tax haven at a low price). Other boundary problems relate to intangibles and to free goods and services. A striking statistic that highlights measurement issues is that despite the massive increase in the presence of information in our daily lives, the share of the information sector in GDP of 4–5% has not changed over the past 35 years (Brynjolfsson et al. 2019). Although these issues create a downward bias in measured productivity levels, the impact on measured productivity growth is less clear-cut. According to Goldin et al.'s estimates, some 13% of the slowdown in productivity in the US after 2005 can be attributed to mismeasurement.

17.5.2 **'Technology' factors**

From the perspective of technology and innovation, the following facts contribute to explaining the coexistence of the ICT revolution and productivity slowdown.

1. Robert Gordon's 2017 book makes the case for the exhaustion of 'low-hanging fruit' innovations, which implies that it is increasingly costly to innovate (Gordon 2017). Gordon's argument is that technological revolutions are not all equal in their potential for lasting productivity growth. In his view, the large ICT gains from 1995–2004 are not repeatable, and future gains will be somewhat incremental as most sectors have incorporated the technology already. Moreover, innovations outside of ICT will be limited. Gordon also places potential future productivity gains in the context of external headwinds. To take just one of these headwinds, even with productivity gains, the demographic shift of a generation of baby boomers retiring will lead to hours per capita declining. Thus, the net effect will be output per capita growing more slowly than output per worker hour.

   Supporting Gordon's hypothesis, Bloom et al. (2020) find that research productivity has fallen. They provide evidence that exponential growth (Chapter 16) in productivity is getting harder to achieve and that sustaining exponential growth appears to require (at least) exponential growth in research effort. One of the examples they use is Moore's Law, which is at the heart of the ICT revolution. Moore's Law is the empirical regularity that states that there has been a doubling around every two years in the number of transistors that can be placed on an integrated circuit that serves as the computer processing unit (CPU). Their finding is that the effective number of constant-quality researchers worldwide devoted to pushing Moore's Law forward is much greater (18 times) in 2014 than it was in 1975.
2. Although R&D effort has remained roughly constant, its composition has changed. Government R&D spending plateaued after 2010; it was replaced by increased business R&D leaving the share of GDP spent on R&D broadly unchanged across the OECD. However, there was a shift in composition toward health R&D, which may have lower spillovers to other industries (Goldin et al. 2021).
3. With a fall in the ratio of patents to innovation effort (consistent with (1)), there would be a predicted fall in entry of new firms. Across the OECD, there has been a fall in business dynamism measured by the entry of new firms (Goldin et al. 2021, Figure 3) and by the falling share of young firms in economic activity (Akcigit

and Ates 2021). Decker et al. (2020) show that declining business responsiveness to shocks has reduced the reallocation of labour to jobs and has been a drag on aggregate productivity.

4. Linked to (3), some large corporations, or 'goliaths', have integrated software in such a complex way that it makes new entry infeasible (Bessen 2022). Firms such as Walmart have huge technological leadership, extending through numerous functions, that effectively creates a 'winner takes all' market share. In turn, their incentive to innovate, given their market dominance, is low.

17.5.3 **Within-country barriers to diffusion**

Much of the above discussion focused on the slow growth of productivity across countries. However, we also know that within many OECD countries there has been an increase in the labour productivity gap between frontier (top 5%) and

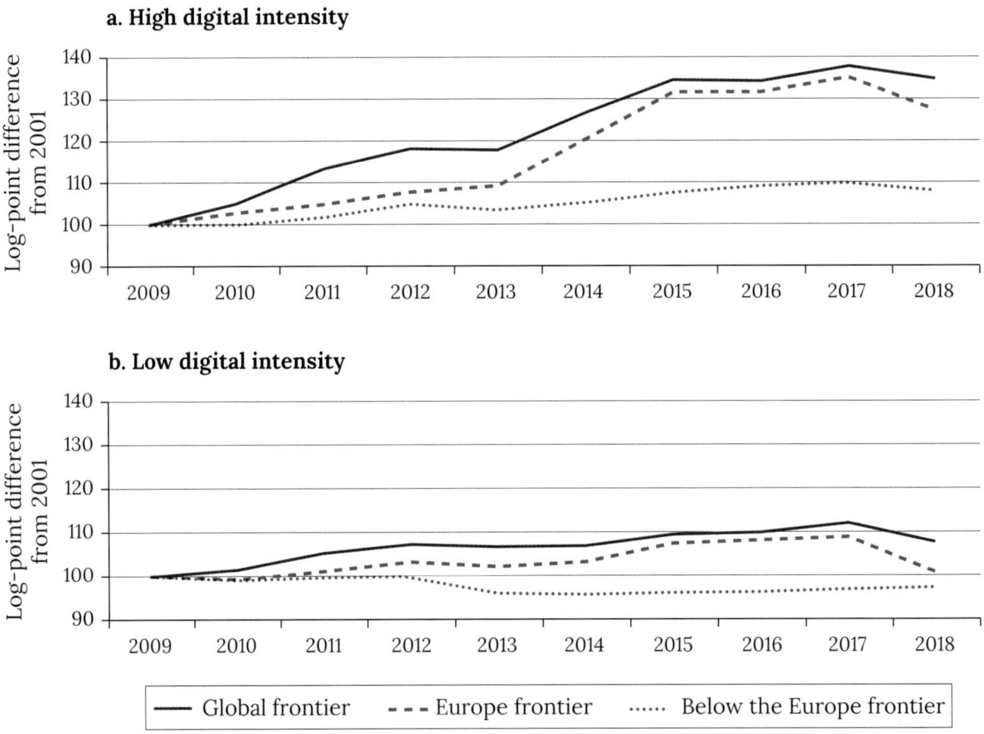

Figure 17.9 Frontier versus laggard firms.

Note: Europe refers to Austria (AT), Belgium (BE), Finland (FI), France (FR), Germany (DE), Ireland (IE), Italy (IT), Luxembourg (LU), Netherlands (NL), Portugal (PT), Spain (ES), Greece (EL), Slovenia (SI), Cyprus (CY), and Malta (MT). The frontier is the average of log productivity for the top 5% of companies with the highest productivity levels within each two-digit industry. The y-axis captures log-point differences from 2001.

Source: Data is from Criscuolo (2021).

laggard firms (Criscuolo 2021; Andrews et al. 2019) (Figure 17.9). That is, within a country, there are large differentials between firms. For example, the ICT revolution made it possible for superstar firms to establish market dominance by applying the technology of 2-sided platforms (for an introduction to the economics of 2-sided platforms see Unit 21 of CORE Econ's *The Economy* (available at https://www.core-econ.org/the-economy/book/text/21.html#215-matching-two-sided-markets)) to create new products like Airbnb. These have the character of winner-take-all markets with economies of scale based on network externalities. Despite many of the new dominant technologically innovative firms relying on general purpose ICT (and then customizing it with great skill), the scale achieved by companies such as Uber, AirBNB, Amazon online retail, Apple online music, and Netflix creates a near winner-take-all market. The gulf between the most productive (frontier) firms compared to the laggards is much greater in high digital intensity sectors (Figure 17.9).

Often superstar firms have further consolidated their position by acquiring start-ups that could have grown to compete with them (e.g. Facebook (Meta) purchases Instagram and WhatsApp). Across industries, market concentration has risen. The market share of top 4 and top 20 firms increased sharply from 2000 (Autor et al. 2020). As discussed in Chapter 16, this would weaken pressure to innovate at the frontier.

Andrews et al. (2019) provide two explanations to support this hypothesis. First, it may be that laggard firms are not able to catch up to the frontier because of missing complementary intangible assets. For example, they may be unable to recruit appropriate managers or implement the cultural change required to integrate new technologies. As discussed in Section 17.4.3, most types of diffusion require particular competences. One possibility is that graduates tend to live in the most successful cities. Metropolitan areas are also the areas with the highest growth rates (OECD 2020). Further evidence is provided by the example of the UK, where there are large regional differences in the percentage of firms which are laggards (Figure 17.10). Here, one can see the possibility of a low innovation trap in which firms in 'left-behind' areas have fewer resources to draw upon, i.e. a graduate workforce. In turn, they are unable to catch up to the technological frontier, and thus are unable to attract sufficient graduates to the area.

A second possibility is that there are rising barriers to entry and low product market competition. We have explored this phenomenon from two somewhat opposing angles (but both can happen at the same time in different industries). Older 'goliath' firms may protect their position through integrating ICT, and new start-ups are able to dominate new markets by quickly building scale and creating a winner-take-all market. As shown in Chapter 16 with low market contestability firms may have little incentive to innovate (Aghion et al. 2005).

17.5.4 **Faltering growth expectations**

In the Carlin-Soskice growth expectations model,[11] we try to explain three phenomena across the high-income economies in the post-financial crisis period:

[11] For a more detailed treatment and model, see Carlin and Soskice (2018).

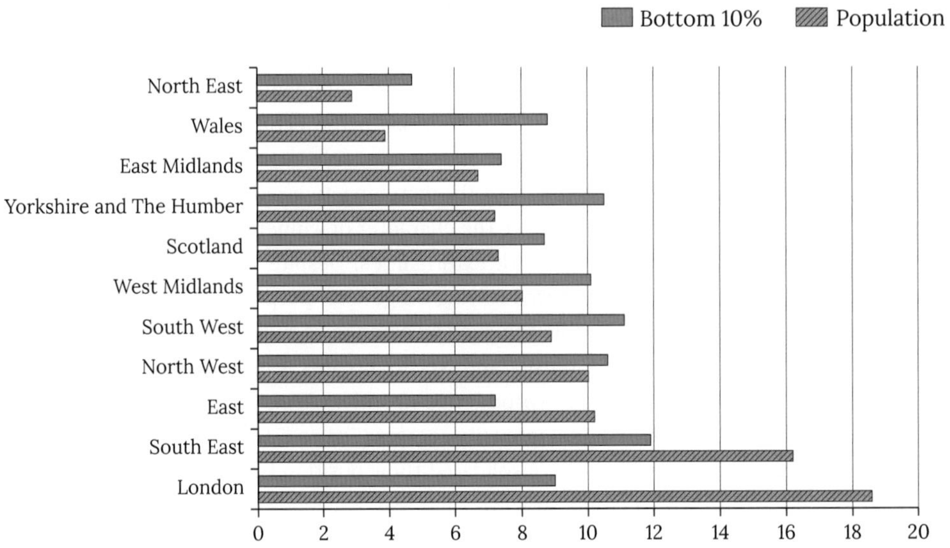

Figure 17.10 UK Regional share of local firms in bottom 10% compared with regional share of local firms in population (ONS).

Note: Based on ONS analysis, with data from Annual Business Survey, Inter-Departmental Business Register and ONS.

Source: Data from Great Britain in 2014. For a description of how firms are apportioned to each region see https://www.ons.gov.uk/economy/economicoutputandproductivity/productivitymeasures/articles/understandingfirmsinthebottom10ofthelabourproductivitydistributioningreatbritain/jantomar2017

- The decline in labour productivity growth ($g_Y - n$)
- The associated decline in investment per worker ($g_K - n$)
- The decline in the rate of (embodied) technological progress (x)

We build a simple model in which businesses are initially optimistic about the growth of markets relative to population, and hence have the confidence to invest in fixed capital. Unlike the models in Chapter 16, we assume that new technology is embodied in fixed investment. As a result, optimism produces higher investment (growth of the capital stock) per worker, which raises the rate of embodied technological progress, producing higher productivity growth in the steady state. Markets grow faster than population and the optimistic expectations are fulfilled.

As discussed in Chapter 9, in spite of robust profits and widening profit margins (Chapter 2) firms in high-income economies have undertaken less business fixed investment as a percentage of GDP since the financial crisis. One interpretation is the entrenchment of more pessimistic expectations about the discounted present value of their after-tax profits due to intertwined concerns about the future growth of markets and of new technology.

Once pessimism sets in, firms are pushed away from the optimistic world, becoming nervous about making investment decisions because of the profound uncertainty felt

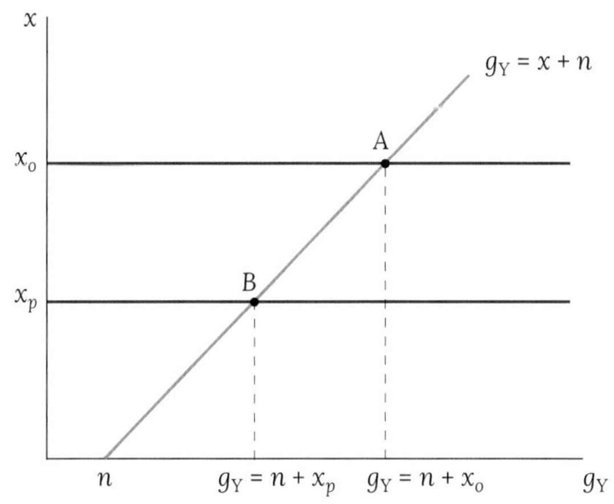

Figure 17.11 Carlin-Soskice expectations model.

by owners and managers. Among reasons for the change of sentiment is, very directly, the 'shock effect' of a deep financial crisis in the high-income world. Second, the rapid changes in advanced technology taking place created nervousness on both the supply and demand side of producing and selling goods and services in the future. And third, the increasingly sunk nature of some investment costs, in which a large proportion goes into specific software that is difficult to reuse increases the option value of waiting (see Chapter 1).

The model used here goes back to Chapter 16 and extends the Solow model. The production function is:

$$Y_t = K_t^{\alpha}(A_t N_t)^{1-\alpha},$$

where we use Harrod labour-saving technological progress (as earlier) to allow a steady state capital-labour ratio.

This can be put in growth rate terms:

$$g_Y = \alpha g_K + (1-\alpha)d\log(A) + (1-\alpha)n.$$

So, in a steady state:

$$g_Y = d\log(A) + n.$$

Assuming a constant rate of technological progress, x, then $g_Y = x + n$ or $x = g_Y - n$, which is shown in Figure 17.11 by the upward-sloping line with a slope of 45°.

Next, we introduce in the model, the idea that businesses may be optimistic or pessimistic about future technological progress, x, equal to output growth relative to the growth of the labour force.

We can break this down into two components:

1. A confident or a pessimistic belief by individual companies about future technological progress, x, or aggregate market growth in excess of workforce growth. Behind this is the assumption that expectations of pessimism (or of optimism) are

usually widespread across the business community; this assumption of common expectations comes from social psychology (Tuckett 2012).

2. We assume that the necessary investment per worker consistent with the optimistic or pessimistic beliefs $x = g_Y - n$ is implemented. Optimistic beliefs go with high investment per worker, and pessimistic beliefs with low investment per worker.

Diagrammatically, the two steady state 'expectational' equilibria are illustrated in Figure 17.11. Taking the case of optimistic expectations, given $g_Y = x_{opt} + n$, the economy will move up to the horizontal line $x = x_{opt}$ so that the economy is at the 'high' productivity growth and innovation equilibrium. And mutatis mutandis for the pessimistic expectations case. The optimistic one at point A corresponds to the pre-financial crisis world in the high income economies. Businesses feel confident about market growth relative to employment growth, and equally confident that their planned investment per head will generate the innovations needed to produce the relevant increases in productivity. Correspondingly, a pessimistic sentiment leads to cutbacks in investment per head and in consequence a reduction in innovations and technological change producing the equilibrium at B. Both equilibria are stable. Thus, the model helps illustrate the phenomena observed in the last decade or so.

17.6 WINNERS AND LOSERS

17.6.1 Polarization: Jobs

In this section we dig deeper into the theme of *creative destruction*. As a result of the ICT revolution, automation and robots eliminated many routine jobs in manufacturing and industry as well as in clerical and quasi-routine white-collar sectors. A widely used example is the 'bank manager' who was once pivotal in approving loans to local businesses, a job which has now been replaced largely by sophisticated software. These jobs were medium productivity, and often unionized and/or in large companies with established career-based pay-scales. Through the last three decades, this led some of those displaced to up-skill and move into 'graduate' employment (by gaining a degree), or to leave the labour market through early retirement, or more likely to find employment in less-skilled service sectors.

The 'hollowing out' of the labour market and the decline of 'middle-class' employment (see Goos et al. 2014) has been associated with the broader phenomenon of the *polarization* of society. These developments are reflected in the increase in inequality of market, i.e. pre-tax and transfer incomes. A substantial effort by researchers around the world to collect data on market and post-tax and transfer incomes was stimulated by Piketty's (2014) work and is available from the World Inequality Database. Using that data, we can see how market income inequality, measured by the Gini coefficient, has increased in all of the case study countries (Figure 17.12; see also Figure 17.8). That said, there is large variation in the starting points and extent of the increase in inequality. Sweden was significantly more equal in 1980 than Germany, the UK, and the US, and market inequality changed little after the early 1990s.

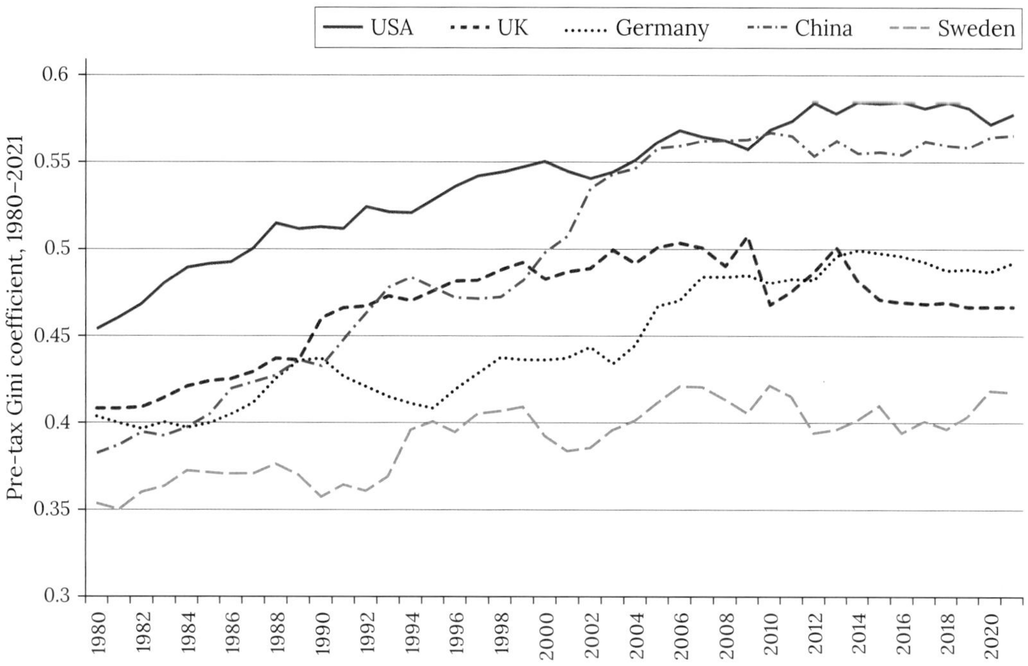

Figure 17.12 Increased pre-tax and transfers inequality during the ICT revolution, measured by Gini coefficients (1980–2021).

Note: Gini coefficients are pre-tax and transfers.

Source: World Inequality Database.

From a political economy perspective, an important question is whether the hollowing out of the labour market and rising market inequality has been translated into rising inequality of post-tax and transfer incomes. People's living standards depend on their income after paying taxes and receiving cash transfers, and on the transfers in kind they receive from public services. If political power shifts with economic power, then one would predict that the middle and lower parts of the income distribution would have lost out over the course of the ICT revolution. Recent evidence using the WID database referred to above suggests to the contrary that in most high-income countries the middle class, defined as the middle 20% of the pre-tax and transfer income distribution, have succeeded in getting compensation through transfers. Those individuals in the middle of the distribution have kept up with the overall growth of the economy much more than would have been expected from pre-tax and transfer incomes. Despite the middle-income earners' share of pre-tax income going down over time, they are able to use their political power to demand redistribution, and share in the gains of growth. To take European countries overall, for both the poorest (bottom 20%) and middle (20%) income earners, their income growth defined the same way is within 5% of the growth of average incomes.

Figure 17.13 shows the evolution of low and middle incomes using the broadest definition (post tax and including transfers in kind and public goods) relative to average incomes for Germany, Sweden, the UK and the US. The country trajectories

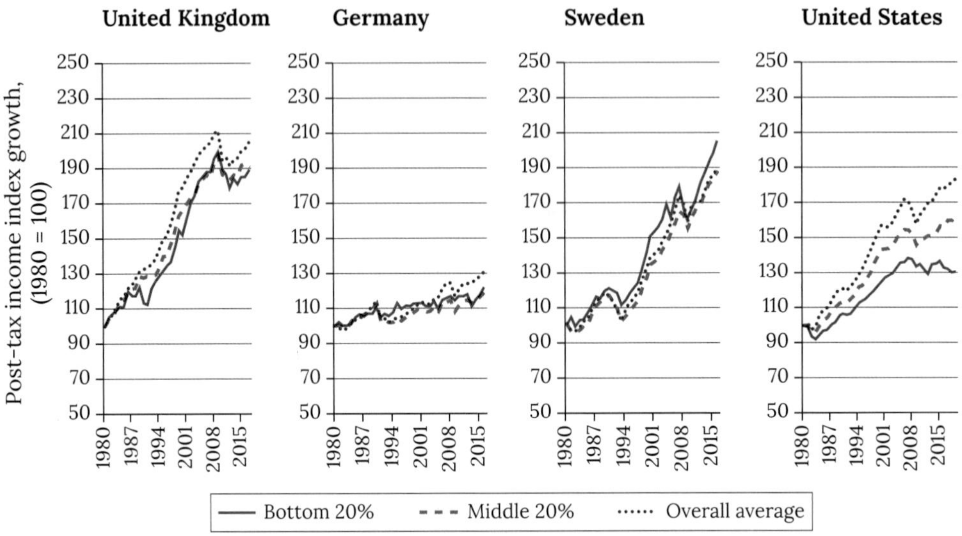

Figure 17.13 The evolution of low and middle incomes (post-tax) since 1980.

Note: The figure shows the evolution of real post-tax income (including in-kind transfers and public goods) for the bottom 20% and middle 20% compared with the mean income. The base of 100 is 1980.

Source: Four panels of Figure 3 in Elkjær, M. A. and Iversen, T. (2022). The democratic state and redistribution: whose interests are served? *American Political Science Review*, 1–16. doi:10.1017/S0003055422000867.

of the three European countries vary but in each case, redistribution has remained reasonably intact for middle and low earners over the course of the ICT revolution. A significant outlier is the United States, where the middle classes and particularly the bottom quintile have fared badly compared to their richer peers (Elkjær and Iversen 2022).

However, even with this evidence that the change in the distribution of post-tax income distribution growth is not as unequal as the distribution of pre-tax income growth, there remain huge societal implications from polarization in the job market. The decline in social status associated with moving down the jobs ladder or being pushed out of the labour force can lead to individuals feeling a sense of loss. Those who lose out become 'strangers in their own land' as eloquently described by Hochschild (2016). As we will discuss below, it can also have serious political implications as individuals who feel let down by societal changes vent their disappointment through anti-system, and particularly, far-right political parties (Gidron and Hall 2020).

For the reader who would like a formal application of this fall of 'old middle class' jobs and its implications for the productivity slow-down and polarization, we recommend Acemoglu and Restrepo (2019).

17.6.2 **Polarization: Places**

Job polarization is frequently associated with geographical polarization, where previously thriving manufacturing-based communities declined economically and socially, complemented by downwards multiplier effects on many other activities in the affected areas. In the US, local government depends to a high degree on local taxation so that the public sector was also depressed. This led to the term 'places that don't matter' (Rodríguez-Pose 2018). To an extent, this maps on to the urban/rural divide. Cities tend to be the most productive places where graduates flock and are the innovation epicentres. However, even across cities there is a major divide between those most successful places, such as New York, London, and Paris, and those areas that have declined over generations. Rodríguez-Pose (2018) maps out how regions have experienced divergent fortunes in employment and GDP growth since 1990.

These areas in persistent economic decline may affect not only the current residents, but impact families for generations. Evidence from the United States and the Moving to Opportunity project shows how children who have longer exposure to worse neighbourhoods have lower adulthood earnings, less chance of going to college, and higher rates of teenage pregnancies (Chetty and Hendren 2018).

Place polarization has the character of a low-level equilibrium trap. For example, recent evidence highlights the importance of social networks. Chetty et al. (2022) show that having a large network of high socio-economic status friends is strongly associated with upward social mobility for those with low socio-economic origins. Of course, building such networks is more difficult in areas in decline, with lower graduate populations, and where segregation by income is prevalent. We also have evidence that graduates tend to flock to areas with better labour market opportunities (Britton et al. 2021). Thus, not only do those areas in decline have fewer graduates, but any children who do go on to university are more likely to leave in search of opportunity—compounding the problem.

17.6.3 **Polarization: Politics**

Given our description of the polarization of society through jobs and place, it is perhaps not surprising that we have seen the venting of the resultant disappointment through politics. We see a continuing political conflict conducted in the electoral battlefield in each of the high-income economies between what had become by the early 2000s distinct progressive and populist electorates (Iversen and Soskice 2019). Those individuals 'left-behind' through individual characteristics, such as a low status job, or living in a 'place that doesn't matter' show a greater tendency to express their frustration by turning to populist parties.

Political differences go beyond the political sphere to affect every day social relationships, as illustrated in Figure 17.14, based on V-Dem data.[12] In what is referred to as 'affective polarization', individuals form judgements towards others based purely on partisanship, resulting in often crude stereotypes and prejudices. Beyond partisanship, Hobolt et al. (2020) show that Brexit identities, for example, were prevalent

[12] The V-Dem interviewers asked, 'Is society polarized into antagonistic, political camps?', if asked for clarification, they would respond, 'Here we refer to the extent to which political differences affect social relationships beyond political discussions. Societies are highly polarized if supporters of opposing political camps are reluctant to engage in friendly interactions, for example, in family functions, civic associations, their free time activities and workplaces.'

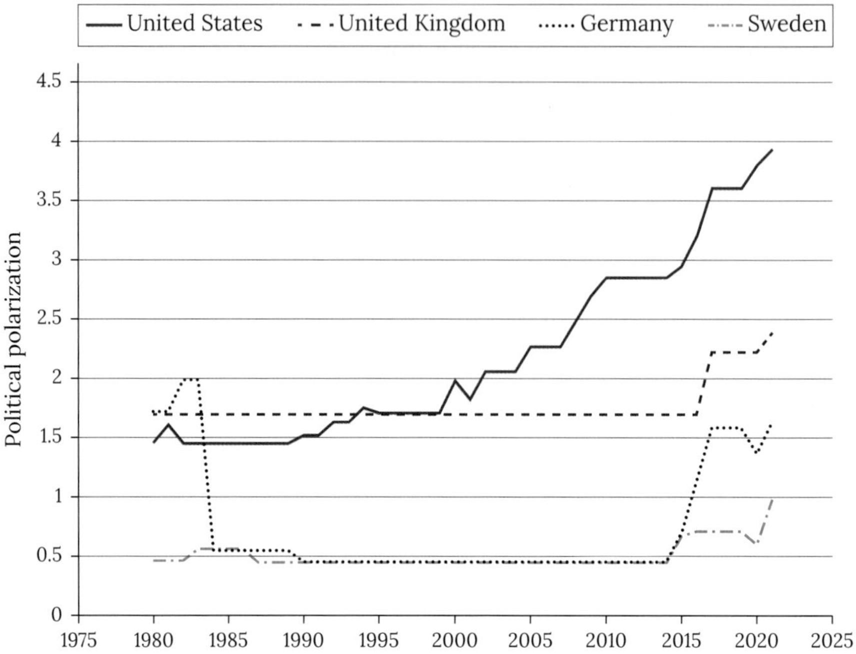

Figure 17.14 Political polarization (V-Dem).

Note: Political polarization measures to what extent political differences affect social relationships beyond political discussion. 4-point scale from 0 'Not at all', to 4 'to a large extent'.

Source: V-Dem 2022.

in the wake of the 2016 EU membership referendum, becoming an important part of personal identity and leading to societal division. Moreover, groups on either side of the political divide have become more divided over time. Those most unequal countries in terms of places and outcomes, the United States and the United Kingdom, are also the ones where there is most political polarization.

In spite of the increased polarization over the previous decades and the conflict between 'progressive' and 'populist conservative' parts of the electorate, the advanced capitalist democracies have so far somehow managed to remain remarkably stable (Iversen and Soskice 2019). As outlined above, Elkjær and Iversen (2022) (see also Glyn 2007) show that redistribution has remained broadly intact (with the significant outlier of the United States) and many governments have continued to promote openness, competition, public sector support for R&D and to the research environment more generally. At the same time, the pre-redistribution income gap is wider than in the past and there is huge inequality of status and esteem. Moreover, we know that we are reaching a generation where fewer people are upwardly socially mobile and more are downwardly mobile (Bukodi and Goldthorpe 2019; Chetty et al. 2017), undermining the implicit social promise that not only will each generation be better off than the last but also have better opportunities to move up the income distribution. This is a topic that will remain at the forefront of research. For a much fuller discussion of this complex interaction between capitalism and democracy, and the resilience of advanced capitalist democracies see Iversen and Soskice (2019).

17.7 CONCLUSIONS

This chapter has argued that we have been experiencing the fourth industrial revolution over the last four decades, promoted by the new general purpose technology, ICT. As with Chapter 16, productivity gains are core to growth and living standards. This chapter opens the black box of productivity growth through the ICT revolution. We explain how there are varieties of this technological revolution, and in our view only one leader, the United States. As explained, even in the US, the real innovation took place in a limited number of innovation clusters, most notably Silicon Valley and Massachusetts.

We provide a framework to distinguish between types of ICT diffusion and develop these models in depth through five case studies. Despite the importance of ICT as a general purpose, transformative technology, productivity growth over the past two decades has been below long-term trends and distributed unequally between people and places.

To summarize the explanation presented in this chapter:

1. There has been widespread 'creative' adoption of the new technology as it gradually spreads across more and more sectors. This is driven by private sector firms and competition, which we argued were enabled by the neo-liberal political economy consensus. As with other industrial revolutions, this is accompanied by 'destruction' of existing sectors and ways of life. Graduates become central to the application of ICT. Thus, mass higher education builds up; at the same time graduate-intensive city agglomerations grow (with growing individual-level and spatial inequality).
2. The United States was, and remains, the leader, at the technological frontier. The varieties of technological adoption across other countries vary widely. We have identified five models that we think can be generalized. The UK diffuses technology on system software for services, which has worked effectively but only for select groups in and around a few technological, graduate focused, hubs. Germany has adapted in many ways over the past twenty years but at its core remains dominated by a highly specialized manufacturing sector, where customization of technology is key. Sweden has a very concentrated ownership structure of its largest firms, which allowed ICT to be at the core of its strategy in the early 1990s. It is now a small open 'ICT focused' country. China started the ICT revolution as a 'copier' and is now transitioning into a constrained innovator.
3. Given our argument that ICT is central to innovation and is a transformative technology, it is puzzling that productivity growth has been low over the course of the ICT revolution, and especially in the period since the financial crisis. We offer a summary of what we believe are the four most convincing arguments: 1) Mismeasurement, 2) Technology factors, 3) Within-country diffusion, and 4) Expectations (based on the Carlin-Soskice 2018 model).

4. The neo-liberal economy has had several unintended consequences. Financial instability builds up (Chapter 8) and leads to the global financial crisis (Chapter 9), which produced prolonged recessions as deleveraging takes place, and as eventually (consistent with the neo-liberal disciplined concern with public debt) governments and their independent central banks withdraw from reflationary macroeconomic policy (Chapter 7). This combines with the asymmetric benefits of the ICT revolution. Some jobs are displaced by technology. Groups of individuals with high skills, especially graduates, tend to benefit from the ICT revolution. Moreover, some places, predominantly big cities, tend to capture most of the gains. There is a clear set of 'winners' and 'losers', which has led to an anti-system backlash. Despite this polarization of society, advanced democratic capitalist societies have so far successfully sustained continued innovation within a democratic political structure.

QUESTIONS AND PROBLEMS FOR CHAPTER 17

CHECKLIST QUESTIONS

1. What were the general purpose technologies in each of the four Technological Revolutions?
2. How has the United States maintained its position at the technological frontier?
3. If we can explain the US leadership in technological innovation, why can other countries not replicate their strategy?
4. Explain the difference between the competences required for 'simple' diffusion and 'customized systems service software'? Why do these differences exist?
5. Reconcile the rhetoric surrounding the fourth technological revolution and the lack of productivity growth across high-income countries over the last two decades.
6. Evaluate the following statement: 'Low productivity growth since the financial crisis is a result of pessimism'.
7. If evidence exists that middle-income workers can 'force' redistribution from the rich, why does polarization still exist? Does job polarization matter even if income is redistributed?
8. How does spatial polarization differ between countries with different varieties of diffusion? Why?

PROBLEMS

1. 'Germany's productivity advantage over the United Kingdom is because manufacturing technology is easier to diffuse than service software innovations.' Document the claim about relative levels of productivity and assess the argument about diffusion.

2. Choose a country not discussed in this chapter and apply to it the analytical framework introduced in the 'varieties of technological diffusion'. Does the framework explain the success of technological diffusion effectively? How about societal polarization across jobs, places, and politics?

3. 'In the past when productivity growth was strong, society could justifiably be aspirational expecting their children to have a higher standard of living than themselves, with slow productivity growth this is no longer the case. It will therefore become impossible to continue to navigate the inherent conflict between capitalism and democracy.' Evaluate the factual basis of the claim in the first sentence. Explain how you understand the phrase 'inherent conflict between capitalism and democracy' in the context of this question.

4. 'China is no longer a constrained innovator but a serious competitor to the United States as a technological leader.' Discuss.

5. Describe the data on Sweden and the US in Figure 17.2 on GDP per hour worked and in Figure 17.12 on market income inequality during the ICT revolution. Do the case studies of these countries shed light on the relationship betweem a country's ability to stay at the technology frontier and economic inequality?

INTERESTED IN EXPLORING THESE TOPICS FURTHER?

Visit www.oup.com/he/carlin-soskice to consolidate and extend your learning with the multiple-choice questions accompanying this chapter.

PART

6

MACROECONOMICS WITH INEQUALITY

CHAPTER 18

HETEROGENEOUS AGENT MACROECONOMICS

ORIGINS, PROGRESS, AND CHALLENGES

This chapter has been co-authored by Wendy Carlin and James Cloyne.

18.1 INTRODUCTION

The goal of this chapter is to provide a bridge to the research frontier in macroeconomics. Evolution in macroeconomics has often been influenced by historical events and the pressing policy issues of the day. The Great Depression marked the birth of macroeconomics and Keynesian thinking. The Great Inflation of the 1970s led to a fundamental change in mainstream methodology, with a focus on 'microfoundations' and rational expectations. And, in the 15 years since the 2008 Global Financial Crisis, macroeconomics has undergone a further revolution.

The Global Financial Crisis brought heterogeneity and inequality into sharp relief. Household debt rose rapidly in many countries prior to 2008 (Jordà, Schularick, and Taylor 2016). The crash that followed the boom illustrated how fragility in household balance sheets can amplify fluctuations (see Chapters 8 and 9 and, for instance, Mian, Rao, and Sufi 2013). The distributional consequences of the boom, the bust, and the sluggish recovery featured heavily in the economic policy debate. Macroeconomic policy itself may generate winners and losers, and how to target interventions remains a key policy question. Distributional issues may also matter for the effectiveness of policy if some households are more responsive than others. Good policy advice therefore demands an understanding of the various ways in which it may affect different households, firms and the economy. The political economy of macroeconomic policy requires an understanding of who benefits and who pays the costs.

The last few decades have seen a concerted effort to bring this heterogeneity back into macroeconomic analysis, and to harness new data to inform theory. An important part of the research frontier—under the umbrella term 'heterogeneous agent macroeconomics'—has further integrated microeconomics and macroeconomics, and provides an attractive framework for harnessing both macro and micro data sources. Without heterogeneity, there can be no inequality and this modelling effort has also provided a framework for understanding the drivers and consequences of inequality in macroeconomics.

What types of questions can be examined using 'heterogeneous agent' macroeconomics? As motivation, we consider three examples from the literature.

First, can fiscal transfers support household spending in times of crisis and how should this stimulus be targeted? Kaplan and Violante (2014) tackle these questions by integrating intuition from the permanent income hypothesis introduced in Chapter 1—that households may save any additional transfers they receive from the government—with the Keynesian insight that some households may be 'hand to mouth' and will spend the extra cash. Which households have a higher marginal propensity to consume is a *prediction* of the model, not an assumption. And households can be wealthy yet highly responsive if their wealth is 'illiquid' (e.g. tied-up in housing). In the data nearly 1/3 of US households may exhibit 'hand to mouth' behaviour. One prediction from the model is that a fiscal transfer designed to stimulate consumption (e.g. in the form of a tax rebate) should be targeted at the bottom 50% of households to generate the largest 'bang for the buck'. After one year, around 50% of the cash will have been spent on average. A more narrowly targeted transfer would miss a large share of highly responsive households and a larger amount per household increases the risk that part of the additional money might be saved.

Second, what are the trade-offs between health outcomes and economic outcomes during the Covid-19 crisis? Kaplan, Moll, and Violante (2020) combine an epidemiology model with an economic model featuring different types of workers, occupations and sectors. The model predicts that the economic costs are always sizable and unevenly shared. With or without lockdowns, the largest costs are felt by households in the middle of the income distribution. Lower income workers depend more on government transfers; those at the top have more flexible jobs. US fiscal policy in Spring 2020 succeeded in lowering economic welfare losses by around 20% on average. Alternative policy options that avoid blunt lockdowns might also lead to a more favourable trade-off between 'lives and livelihoods'. But different policy options have different distributional impacts depending on which workers are most affected.

Third, how might automation have affected income and wealth inequality over time? Moll, Rachel and Restrepo (2022) show that improvements in automation not only benefit high-skilled workers, but also create rising income inequality at the very top by generating higher income from the ownership of capital. Automation raises the return to wealth, but it may also generate stagnant or falling labour income for households lower down the income distribution. The model is used to interpret the fall in the overall share of GDP going to labour since 1980 in the US. As a result of automation, workers in the bottom half of the income distribution experience income declines of around 5–10%, while income remains stagnant for households in the upper-middle part of the distribution. Those in the top 1–0.5% experience a rise in total income of around 20%. For the top 0.1% the increase is even more dramatic.

The origins of the mainstream approach to macroeconomic modelling can be found in the New Classical revolution in the 1970s, which we introduced in Chapter 4. This approach argued that macroeconomic models should be based on rigorous microeconomic foundations and should incorporate forward-looking optimizing agents with rational expectations. In Section 18.2 we cover the seminal real business cycle (RBC) model, where business cycles are driven by fluctuations in technology.

These technology 'shocks' are propagated through the economy as households and firms adjust consumption, investment and hours worked in response to changing production possibilities. Economic fluctuations are efficient and there is no role for government intervention.

Early RBC models were criticized on many grounds, such as the lack of information about the source and nature of the 'technology shocks' driving the model and of their reliance on rational and forwarding-looking behaviour. Nevertheless, this work refocused macroeconomics on investigating the supply-side causes of business cycles (such as productivity shocks, oil shocks) and provided a new methodology for conducting macroeconomic analysis.[1]

New Keynesian (NK) macroeconomics attempted to integrate Keynesian elements, such as imperfect competition and nominal rigidities, into the RBC framework. Like the 3-equation model, the NK model has three main equations: an *IS* curve, a Phillips curve and a monetary policy rule. Firms face price-setting constraints, which gives monetary policy short-run effects over the economy. When interest rates fall, households save less and consume more, leading to a rise in aggregate demand and output. But, unlike the 3-equation model, the NK model assumes all agents have rational expectations and are purely forward-looking.

The NK model allows us to understand why monetary policy might affect the economy, how policy should be set to maximize welfare and the role of policy in shaping expectations. This model provides insights into how policy should be conducted at the zero lower bound, and provides a rationale for the forward guidance policies implemented by various central banks in recent years. Over time, NK models started to incorporate more and more features and became larger and larger. These models were designed to capture the behaviour of a range of macroeconomic variables, and new methods were developed to allow them to be used for forecasting and for giving quantitative policy advice.

While RBC and NK-style models have dominated macroeconomics for several decades, the modelling assumptions, the plausibility of the underlying mechanisms and the restrictiveness of the methodology have been questioned. For example, Blanchard's review (2018) of the 'state of macroeconomics' is sympathetic to but also critical of the NK model, noting that 'its implications, with respect to both the degree of foresight and the role of interest rates in twisting the path of consumption, are strongly at odds with the empirical evidence. Price adjustment is characterized by a forward-looking inflation equation, which does not capture the fundamental inertia of inflation' (Blanchard 2018 p. 45).

In pedagogic terms, these models do not necessarily provide an intuitive understanding of macroeconomics because the mechanisms underlying transmission of shocks and policy can be opaque, a problem that was more pronounced as the models became more complex. As we will see, one reason is that while some of the NK predictions look Keynesian, the mechanisms generating the results are actually

[1] These became known as Dynamic Stochastic General Equilibrium (DSGE) models, as we will explain.

very different. After the Global Financial Crisis, many criticized larger NK models for failing to forecast the Global Financial Crisis, for oversimplifying the transmission mechanisms in the pursuit of rigorous 'microfoundations', and for omitting important mechanisms by focusing on a 'representative agent' under rational expectations.

Newer theories, such as those mentioned above, increasingly start from the view that households and firms are heterogeneous. For example, households may earn different amounts at different points in time and there may be productivity differences across firms. Households and firms may face a range of financial market imperfections. Various models now deviate from the assumptions of perfect information and rational expectations. These models can address a broader set of research questions, can consider a much wider set of transmission mechanisms, and can be evaluated using richer data sets such as household-level surveys or information on household and firm balance sheets. This growing literature has helped shape interest in the distributional implications of macroeconomic policies, and a broader focus on inequality in macroeconomics. This more recent literature is the focus of Section 18.4.

The rest of the chapter is structured as follows. In Section 18.2 we first introduce the real business cycle model and discuss its predictions, strengths and weaknesses. Section 18.3 moves on to discuss the New Keynesian approach and examines how monetary policy works in this model, and what the model implies for optimal monetary policy. Section 18.4 builds on these earlier sections and introduces the Heterogeneous Agent New Keynesian model, focusing on how heterogeneity and inequality change the predictions of earlier representative agent models. Section 18.5 broadens the discussion and provides a high-level overview of the rapidly growing recent literature in heterogeneous agent macroeconomics.

18.2 THE REAL BUSINESS CYCLE MODEL

18.2.1 Introduction

Against the background of dissatisfaction with the empirical performance of the dominant large-scale forecasting models of the economy in the 1970s and the vulnerability of models with backward-looking expectations to the Lucas critique, a completely new research programme in macroeconomics was established, as noted above and in Chapter 4. The real business cycle (RBC) model was developed from New Classical macroeconomics and the early developers were Robert Lucas, Thomas Sargent, Finn Kydland, and Edward Prescott.[2]

The RBC approach started from a number of 'business cycle facts' to be explained. For example, why are output, consumption, investment and hours worked so highly correlated in the data? Why is consumption less volatile ('smoother') than output, yet investment is more volatile than output? The goal was to show that these facts could, in fact, be rationalized by a relatively traditional neoclassical model with utility maximizing households, profit maximizing firms, perfect competition, flexible prices and no role for government intervention.

[2] See Lucas (1972); Sargent and Wallace (1975); Kydland and Prescott (1977, 1982).

One of the methodological aims of the RBC research agenda was therefore to realign macroeconomics more closely with Walrasian microeconomics. In doing so, it sought to unify macroeconomics with a separate literature on economic growth and intertemporal optimization, which was still regarded as part of microeconomics (Prescott 2004). It should be possible, reasoned the RBC modellers, to construct a business cycle model that unified long-run growth and short-run fluctuations.

In Chapter 16 we introduced the Solow growth model, and the RBC model starts from the Ramsey version, i.e. where a constant savings ratio is replaced by optimizing households who optimally choose consumption and savings to maximize utility. To allow for variation in employment, households make a 'labour supply' choice about how many hours to work. As in the Solow model, firms produce output using capital and labour and the model will converge to a steady state over time. To allow for a source of aggregate fluctuations, the RBC model then adds temporary 'shocks' to technology. All firms and households have rational expectations. The behaviour of all agents is governed by so-called 'deep parameters' that characterize the production and utility functions. These deep parameters are intended to be invariant to policy changes, which addresses the Lucas critique discussed in Chapter 4. The name real business cycle comes from the source of the fluctuations, which is on the supply side.

How does the RBC model account for the observed behaviour of key macroeconomic variables? The key propagation mechanism in the RBC model, which turns random shocks to technology into business cycle fluctuations, is the way that households respond to movements in the real interest rate and the real wage. Household consumption and labour supply behaviour are at the core of the model because households care about their utility now and in the future. To maximize their utility over their planning horizon, households will make decisions about both savings and consumption, and work and leisure.

In Chapter 1, we modelled how households conforming to the permanent income hypothesis choose consumption by optimizing subject to their intertemporal budget constraint. They look ahead and make a calculation about their permanent income in order to choose between consumption today and consumption in the future. This idea is at the core of the RBC model. A temporarily higher level of productivity allows the economy to produce more and generate more income. But to ensure higher consumption can be sustained and smoothed over time, households undertake additional saving today.

The RBC model then adds a consumption/leisure choice, in which households decide how many hours to work today and in the future. The model assumes that the labour market is perfectly competitive and households can freely choose between leisure and consumption each period.[3] A temporarily higher level of productivity will raise the real wage and the real interest rate. It is therefore a good time to work. Each additional hour worked earns a higher wage, and any additional income that is saved and invested will earn a higher return. Households therefore work more hours,

[3] The microeconomic foundations of the labour market are like the hiring hall case explained in Appendix 2.5.1 to Chapter 2.

which leads to further increases in output. This labour supply channel is crucial for translating relatively small temporary technology shocks into large movements in output.

Following a negative technology shock, households work less, consume less and save less and these choices are the 'best response' to the technology shock. In this sense, the reduction in employment is 'voluntary'.[4] Given the shock, it is not possible to make someone better off without making someone else worse off. As a result, there is no role for demand-side stabilization policy. An important feature of the RBC model is that business cycles are equilibrium cycles (as we will discuss in more detail in Section 18.2.6) and Pareto efficient.

18.2.2 **Business cycle facts**

In seeking to document a range of stylized business cycle facts, the RBC approach developed a methodology for characterizing business cycles. Business cycles are economic fluctuations around a longer term trend. But this trend is not directly observed in the data, so the first question is how to measure it. The approach takes quarterly macroeconomic data, such as GDP, and uses a statistical procedure called filtering to separate trend growth from business cycle fluctuations. Figure 18.1 shows an example of this using the most commonly used filter, the H-P or Hodrick-Prescott filter, for the US for the period from 1952 Q1 until 2022 Q2.[5] The H-P filter is a more sophisticated method of detrending a logged data series than using a linear trend as it solves a minimization problem that takes into account both the 'goodness of fit' and the 'smoothness' of the detrended series.[6] The RBC literature is concerned with explaining the cyclical component of macroeconomic time series isolated from long-run trends in this way.

As shown in Figure 18.1, this method of estimating the cyclical component in the GDP data shows that output is up to 4% above trend in the peaks and typically up to 5% below trend in the troughs. We can also see that the magnitude of fluctuations in output and consumption are similar, although consumption tends to be somewhat smoother than output. Investment, on the other hand, is much more volatile (note the difference in the scale used to compare output and consumption in panel (a) with that used to compare output and investment in panel (b)). The shaded bands are the recessions as defined by the National Bureau of Economic Research (NBER).

Using the filter procedure to remove the trend from the various series, the RBC modellers begin their analysis by presenting a set of business cycle facts. They focus on the *volatility* of the key variables, the extent to which the variables move together over the cycle (this is called *co-movement*) and how *persistent* are the series. The initial aim

---

[4] Of course, the household is still worse-off than they would have been without the shock. But the outcomes for hours worked, consumption, investment and GDP are all still the best attainable given the level of technology.

[5] The business cycle facts shown in this subsection have been compiled based on the methodology used in King and Rebelo (1999).

[6] A linear trend would be completely 'smooth', but it is not likely to provide a very good 'fit'.

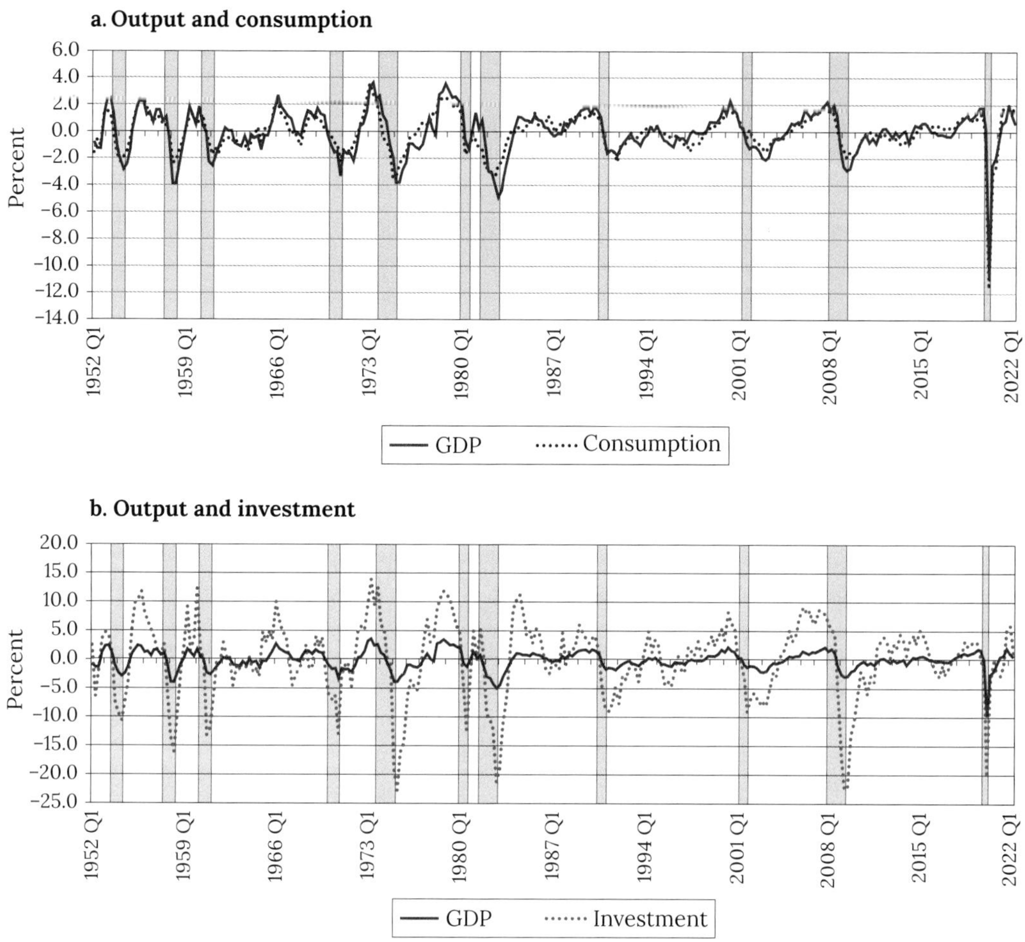

Figure 18.1 Cyclical components of US macroeconomic indicators: 1952 Q1–2022 Q2.
a. Output and consumption
b. Output and investment

Note: All variables have been detrended using a Hodrick-Prescott filter. Output, consumption and investment are in per capita terms. Grey shaded areas represent recessions as defined by NBER.

Source: FRED (data accessed October 2022).

of RBC modellers was to build a model based on microfoundations that was capable of replicating the business cycle facts seen in the aggregate level data (see Section 18.2.4).

Table 18.1 shows the facts that motivate the modelling. In the first column is the standard deviation of GDP, consumption, investment, hourly productivity, hours per worker, real wages, and employment. The second column shows the standard deviation of each variable relative to that of GDP. This matches the facts we saw in Chapter 1, namely, that consumption is less volatile than output and investment is much more volatile. In addition, we see that the real wage is much less volatile than GDP, whereas employment is as volatile as GDP.

	Volatility		Comovement	Persistence
	Standard deviation	Relative standard deviation	Contemporaneous correlation with output	First-order autocorrelation
Output	1.62	1	1	0.76
Consumption	1.43	0.88	0.90	0.72
Investment	6.48	4.07	0.88	0.80
Output per hour	1.02	0.63	0.32	0.70
Hours per worker	0.50	0.31	0.69	0.79
Real wages	1	0.62	0.03	0.66
Employment	1.52	0.94	0.82	0.80

Table 18.1 Business cycle statistics for the US economy.

Note: All variables are in logarithms and have been detrended using a Hodrick-Prescott filter. Output, Consumption and Investment are in per capita terms.

Source: FRED (data accessed October 2022).

Lastly, we see that hours per worker are much less responsive to changes in output than employment (see also Figure 18.2). This business cycle fact is not supportive of one of the key propagation mechanisms summarized earlier: that workers adjust their hours in response to exogenous technology shocks.

The third column shows the co-movement (or correlation) of each series with GDP. Consumption, investment, employment and hours of work are pro-cyclical (positive co-movement with output). Output per hour is also pro-cyclical, but real wages are only weakly (positively) correlated with GDP. The final column reports the persistence of each series. In all series, there is a strong correlation between the variable in period t and in period $t-1$. Growth above trend in one year is typically followed by growth above trend the following year: the economy does not jump from boom to bust year by year.

18.2.3 The RBC model and its properties

It is important to keep in mind that the RBC modellers did not work backwards from the facts or from apparently important features of the real world to make their modelling decisions. Instead of such an inductive approach, they deliberately began with a very simple (and manifestly unrealistic) model and wanted to see how well such a model was able to match the business cycle facts described above. Viewing the RBC approach as one of explicitly adopting a deductive method makes it easier to understand (a) the rationale for the very unrealistic assumptions and (b) the focus on whether an economy with these features can generate fluctuations that match those in a real economy. It contrasts with the inductive approach in the 3-equation model where the microfoundations are based on incomplete contracts and imperfect competition to reflect the presence of involuntary unemployment in equilibrium and the response of output and employment to shocks to aggregate demand.

At its simplest, an RBC model makes the following assumptions (see the web appendix):

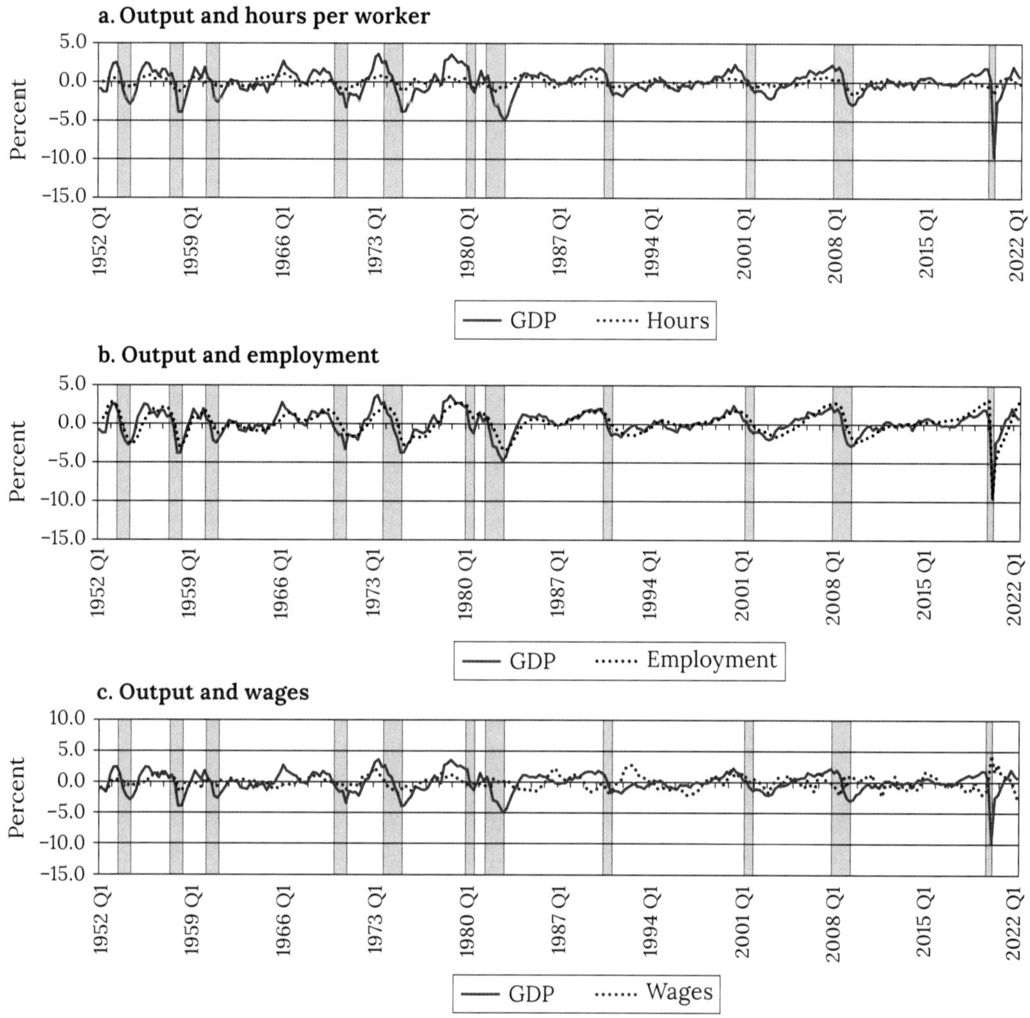

Figure 18.2 Cyclical components of US macroeconomic indicators: 1952 Q1–2022 Q2.
a. Output and hours per worker
b. Output and employment
c. Output and real wages

Note: All variables have been detrended using a Hodrick-Prescott filter. Output is in per capita terms. Grey shaded areas represent recessions as defined by NBER.

Source: FRED (data accessed October 2022).

1. The economy is made up of a large number of identical agents who are assumed to live forever. Each agent is referred to as a 'representative agent'. These agents are referred to as households because they make consumption decisions and choices about how much to work.[7]

[7] One rationale for the representative agent assumption is the existence of complete asset markets that allows households to fully insure against household-specific shocks. The models we discuss later in Section 18.4 will depart significantly from these assumptions.

2. When saving goes up, it is invested and this results in a larger capital stock the following period. A common way to capture this is to assume that households directly own the capital stock.
3. There is a large number of identical firms that produce output using capital and labour under perfect competition.
4. There is full flexibility of nominal wages and prices. We shall therefore work entirely in real terms.
5. Expectations are formed rationally and all agents have perfect information.
6. The economy is disturbed by temporary unforeseen shocks to technology that temporarily and randomly shift the production function. These shocks have inbuilt persistence, which means that they die out slowly. We introduced the concept of total factor productivity in the production function in the Solow model in Chapter 16. As a result, these technology shocks are sometimes called Total Factor Productivity (TFP) shocks or simply productivity shocks.

Long-run properties

It is useful to begin by briefly describing how the economy evolves over the long run in the RBC world. At the heart of the model is the famous Solow growth model (from Chapter 16), modified to include optimizing households. In Solow's model, the economy is characterized by a production function, a constant saving rate and a constant growth rate of the population. In the simplest case, the economy grows along a steady state balanced growth path with a constant real wage and real interest rate. Solow then introduced a special form of technological progress into the model. This exogenous technological progress appears like manna from heaven to raise output per worker hour every period.

In the Solow model with technological progress, output per head and the real wage in the economy therefore grow in steady state at a constant rate fixed by the rate of exogenous technological progress. As noted above, when optimizing households are introduced to the Solow model, it is called the Ramsey or neoclassical growth model. Instead of a constant saving ratio, the saving rate is decided by households in the same way as in the permanent income model of Chapter 1 and depends on the real interest rate and the subjective discount rate.

Figure 18.3 summarizes steady state balanced growth in the RBC model. As in the Solow model, in the long run with a constant rate of population growth, the employment rate (defined here as hours worked per head of the population) is also constant. This is shown by the vertical dashed line in Figure 18.3. The labour demand curve shifts upward each period at the rate of exogenous technological progress. Labour productivity and real wages rise at this constant rate. The predictions of the long-run growth model accord with the fact that in the US, productivity grew at approximately 2–2.5% per annum over the long run and from 1950, there was no trend in hours worked per worker.[8]

[8] Note that the latter did not characterize other high-income countries, where hours worked per worker fell substantially.

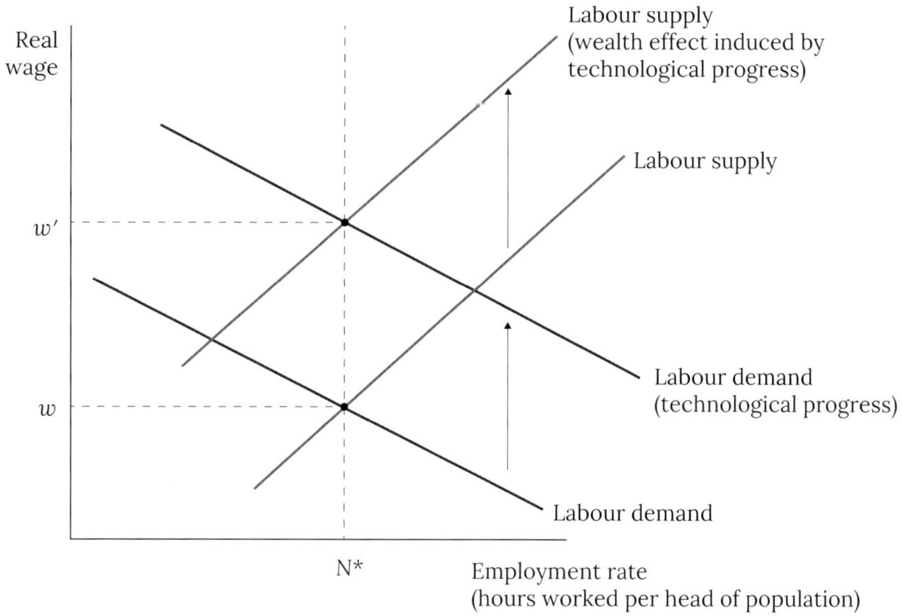

Figure 18.3 Steady state growth in the RBC model.

To the basic version of the Ramsey model, the RBC model adds a consumption-leisure choice for the household. Households dislike working, but working allows the household to increase consumption. As the real wage rises along the steady state growth path there are two competing forces. First, households find working more attractive when the real wage is higher. This is the substitution effect and is reflected in the upward-sloping labour supply curve in Figure 18.3. The slope of the labour supply curve is governed by the *intertemporal elasticity of labour supply* (also known as the Frisch elasticity), defined as the percentage change in hours that arises as a result of a given percentage change in wages (holding constant the marginal utility of wealth).

The second effect is that, as the economy grows households become richer and their *lifetime wealth* increases. Households would therefore like to enjoy more consumption and leisure. This 'wealth effect' shifts the labour supply curve to the left. In the long run, if household preferences and the production function are appropriately restricted then these two forces offset each other. The RBC model therefore features a constant long-run employment rate.[9] This can be seen in Figure 18.3: long-run technological progress leads to a steady rise in labour demand and the real wage. But the shifting labour supply curve leaves the long-run employment rate equal to N*.

Short-run properties

We now consider how a temporary technology shock can generate a business cycle in the RBC model. Technology shocks produce business cycles for two main reasons:

1. The shock itself is assumed to hit the economy and then to die out gradually over time. This in-built persistence is important in making the shock last. This helps

[9] These restrictions ensure that the model has a balanced growth path.

generate persistent cycles rather than simply causing the economy to jump around the long-run growth trend in a seemingly random manner.

2. Forward-looking households take action to maximize their utility by responding to the effect of the technology shock on the interest rate and the wage rate. They are motivated to respond because they prefer a smooth path of consumption. This behaviour helps to sustain the effects of the technology shock on output, employment and the capital stock.

The economy begins in the steady state and on the long-run growth path. The economy is then disturbed by an unexpected improvement in technology that is a shock to the economy's production function. This shifts the production function in a way that increases both the marginal product of labour and the marginal product of capital. In this perfectly competitive model, this means a higher real wage and a higher real interest rate (which in this model is the same as the rate of return on capital).

As discussed above, there are potentially both wealth effects and substitution effects. The wealth effect will tend to raise consumption and leisure. The household is making decisions based on the fact that there is an infinite future and in Chapter 1 we showed that a permanent income hypothesis household will consume an amount equal to the annuity value of expected lifetime wealth. That said, a short-lived temporary technology shock only has a small effect on lifetime wealth, so the initial increase in consumption is relatively muted and consumption is smoothed over time. So as to sustain a smooth consumption path, even after the shock has dissipated, savings and investment will increase on impact.

Turning to the substitution effects, the representative household makes its choices in response to the change in the real interest rate and the real wage, taking into account the way the shock affects its future choices. Because households value a smooth consumption path, the agent will want to optimize on two margins. The household will ensure that the last unit of consumption today provides the same utility as the last unit of consumption *tomorrow* is expected to provide, by responding to the higher interest rate (adjusting savings) and to the higher real wage (adjusting hours).

First, working is now more attractive because the technology shock has increased the marginal product of labour and the real wage. To take advantage of this, households are willing to shift their hours worked from the future to today. Because the wealth effects of the shock are small, this substitution effect dominates and hours worked increase (unlike in the long-run case discussed earlier). The intertemporal elasticity of labour supply plays a key role in governing the strength of this mechanism.

Second, the technology shock increases the marginal product of capital which, in a perfectly competitive model, raises the real interest rate. This makes saving more attractive and signals that it is a good time to do investment. The high return on capital means it is also a good time to work because additional income can be invested and will earn a higher return.

In short, the *technology shock* has (a) increased the marginal product of labour and, hence, the real wage, making working relatively more attractive in this period and (b) increased the marginal product of capital and, hence, the real rate of interest. This makes the returns from saving increase.

Consumption smoothing is therefore at the heart of the RBC model, and it leads to an increase in savings in the current period. In the RBC model, savings are entirely transformed into investment. This is different from the important feature of the 3-equation model that decisions about savings are made by different agents in fundamentally different ways from decisions about investment (see Chapter 1). In a Keynesian model, an important problem for the macroeconomy is that market imperfections mean that there is no automatic mechanism that transforms savings into investment. In the RBC model, an increase in savings as a result of the shock to technology also increases investment, leading to an expansion of the capital stock. The higher capital stock further boosts labour demand. In the RBC model, the high volatility of investment therefore comes from the optimizing decisions of agents who value consumption smoothing not from the fluctuations in animal spirits or sentiment that are at work in the investment function in Chapter 1.

Summary

In Figure 18.4, we show a stylized picture of how a positive shock to technology produces a real business cycle. To build on the intuition from Figure 18.3, we illustrate these effects through the lens of the labour market. The shock has the following effects. In each case the effect is measured relative to the steady state:

1. Output goes up because of the positive technology shock, shown by the shift in the labour demand curve, (1), (even for the same level of labour and capital, there is higher output).

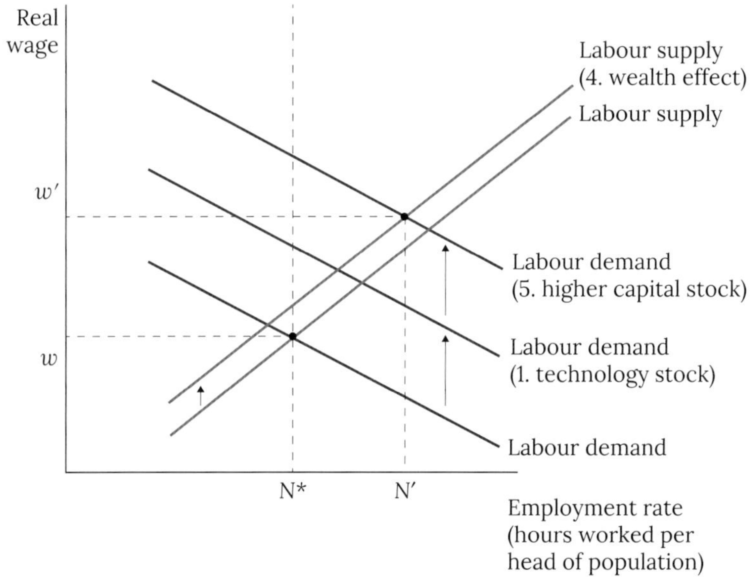

Figure 18.4 The real business cycle model: an exogenous positive technology shock (see the Summary above and below for the interpretation of the numbers).

2. The wage and interest rate go up (because the technology shock raises the marginal products of labour and capital).
3. Consumption goes up but not by as much as output (households smooth the temporary shock over all future periods). Saving and therefore investment go up (the rise in saving is the other side of the coin of consumption smoothing).
4. Hours of work rise to N′. The real wage rises and, because this is a temporary shock, the substitution effect dominates the wealth effect, shown by the shift in the labour supply curve (4).
5. The savings are automatically invested in new capital stock, which shifts the labour demand curve the following period helping to propagate the initial shock, as shown by the shift in the labour demand curve (5).
6. As the technology shock peters out, the economy gradually returns to the steady state growth path.

Steps 1–3 and 5 and their unwinding over time generate a cycle for output, consumption and investment as a result of the technology shock. Step 4 generates fluctuations in employment (hours) and is important for generating amplification in the response of output. It is worth noting the importance of the labour supply elasticity in this model. A higher labour supply elasticity would imply a flatter labour supply curve and generate an even larger effect on hours worked and output.[10]

Figures 18.5a and 18.5b illustrate the outcomes from the RBC model using impulse response functions following a temporary increase in technology. We introduced the concept of an impulse response function in Chapter 3. It plots the response of the economy over time to a particular shock. As can be seen from Figure 18.5a, the response of consumption is very small and extremely smooth in response to a technology shock. The flip side of this is the large response of saving and investment. To maintain consumption as the technology improvement dies out, dis-saving occurs further out. Investment is therefore volatile: it jumps on impact and falls below its long-run value as households dis-save. Figure 18.5b illustrates the effects in the capital and labour markets. Hours worked increase on impact. This drives the amplification of the GDP effect in Figure 18.5a on impact. Hours worked respond strongly to the increase in the real wage, which can also be seen in Figure 18.5b. Figure 18.5b also shows that higher investment, encouraged by the rise in the real interest rate, leads to an increase in the capital stock over time. As the household dis saves the capital stock declines again back to its long-run value. The persistent rise in the capital stock means the effects of the technology shock last longer than the increase in technology.

18.2.4 **Producing quantitative results**

One important aspect of the RBC approach to macroeconomics was a focus on using the model to provide quantitative, numerical, predictions about how the economy responds to shocks over time. These predictions can then be compared with the data.

[10] Some models also remove the wealth effect channel, which would prevent the upwards shift in the labour supply curve, also amplifying the hours worked response.

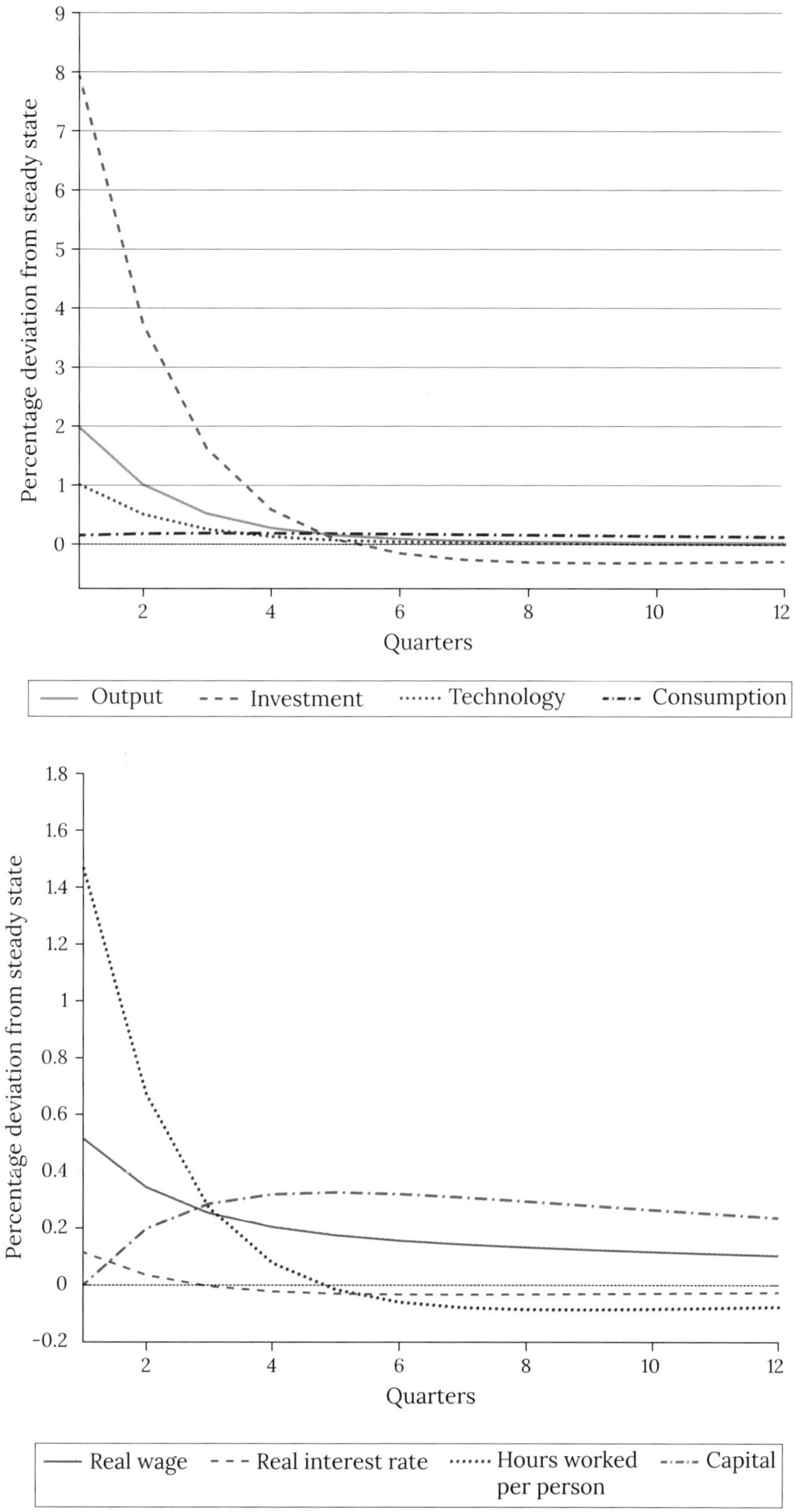

Figure 18.5 Response of the economy to a one-period increase in technology in the RBC model.

In richer models these quantitative exercises are also the basis of evaluating the effects of changes in macroeconomic policy.

To examine how well the RBC model 'fits the data', the output of the solved model is used to create a set of business cycle statistics. This table can then be compared to the actual US business cycle data from Table 18.1 to ascertain the extent to which fluctuations in the US economy are consistent with those predicted by the model.

The process involves restricting the model to match long-run growth facts or other microeconomic evidence about the model's deep parameters (such as the labour supply elasticity). This process is referred to as calibration and has been used extensively in many areas of economics over the last few decades.

Calibrating and solving the model to build a table of business cycle statistics entails a number of steps:[11]

1. Choose functional forms for the equations that underpin the basic neoclassical model (such as the production function and the utility function of households). These choices fix the important parameters in the model that need to be calibrated.
2. Calibrate the model by assigning values to these parameters (e.g. as we shall see below, capital's share, α, in the Cobb–Douglas production function) based on their long-run values from actual data or estimates from studies using, for example, microeconomic data in the economy being studied.
3. Use historical data to find the Solow residual, which is taken as a proxy for the technology shocks to be fed into the model (see below).
4. Use data on the Solow residual to shock the *calibrated* model and produce *simulations* of the path of the *model economy* over time.
5. Detrend the simulations from the model economy using the HP filter. This splits out each macroeconomic variable into a cyclical and a trend component.
6. Use the cyclical components of the simulations from the model economy to create a table of business cycle statistics. Compare the moments (e.g. standard deviations and correlations) produced by the simulated model economy with those calculated from the actual economy (see Table 18.1).

The basic business cycle model produces outcomes that are viewed as matching many aspects of the data, as stated in the conclusion to King, Plosser, and Rebelo (1988):[12]

> When driven by highly persistent technology shocks, the basic neoclassical model is capable of replicating some stylized facts of economic fluctuations. First, the model generates procyclical employment, consumption and investment. Second, the model generates the observed rankings of relative volatility in investment, output and consumption.

[11] This set of steps follows the methodology used in King and Rebelo (1999).
[12] See p. 231 of King, Plosser, and Rebelo (1988).

The ability of this very simple model to fit the fluctuations observed in the macroeconomy has been part of its lasting appeal among an influential group of macro-economists. It seemed to provide a new way of doing macroeconomics that was immune to the Lucas critique. It was also welcomed as offering the possibility of rigorous analysis of government intervention because the building blocks of the model reflect the optimizing decisions of the micro-agents not empirical correlations that could be policy dependent. After setting out the model we discuss its shortcomings in Section 18.2.5.

Measuring technology shocks using the Solow residual

The key impulse mechanism for business cycles in RBC models arises from technology shocks. The Solow residual is the most commonly used proxy for technology shocks in the RBC tradition. We introduced the concept of the Solow residual when we discussed growth accounting in Chapter 16.

This subsection will elaborate on step 3 of the process described above and show how the Solow residual can be calculated from historical macroeconomic data. This will also allow us to see how the US Solow residual has evolved over the past 60 years. The calculation of the Solow residual begins with the production function. In the RBC model, a Cobb-Douglas production function is typically used:

$$y_t = A_t K_t^{\alpha} N_t^{1-\alpha}, \qquad \text{(production function)}$$

where y_t equals output, K_t is the capital input, N_t is the labour input and A_t is total factor productivity or the *Solow residual*. The α in the production function is a constant between zero and one. We can rearrange the production function to find an expression for the Solow residual:

$$A_t = \frac{y_t}{K_t^{\alpha} N_t^{1-\alpha}}. \qquad \text{(Solow residual)}$$

The Solow residual is a measure of output per weighted factor input; a measure of productivity. The growth in the Solow residual is the portion of economic growth that cannot be accounted for by changes in measurable factor inputs (e.g. labour and capital), hence it is often referred to as total factor productivity growth.

The next stage is to find macroeconomic data corresponding to the variables and to the parameter α on the right-hand side of the equation. In a competitive equilibrium (which the RBC model assumes), α is the share of national income that goes to the capital input and $1-\alpha$ is the share that goes to the labour input. In the postwar US data, labour's share of national income is on average around two-thirds. We therefore set $1-\alpha$ at 64% (i.e. 0.64), which is the value used by Prescott (1986). This means α is set at 0.36 and that the equation becomes:

$$A_t = \frac{y_t}{K_t^{0.36} N_t^{0.64}}. \qquad \text{(Solow residual)}$$

We can use macroeconomic data to find the Solow residual in any given year in the past. We use real GDP as a measure of y_t, the real net stock of private fixed assets as a measure of K_t and total employment as a measure of N_t. Figure 18.6 shows the path

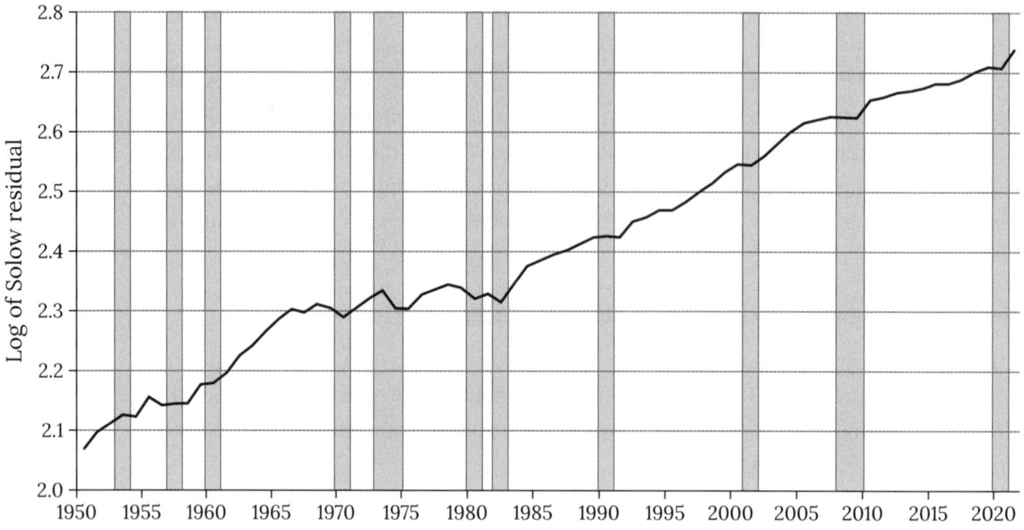

Figure 18.6 Natural log of the US Solow residual (total factor productivity): 1950–2021. NBER-defined recessions are shaded.

Source: US Bureau of Economic Analysis; FRED (data accessed October 2022).

of the natural log of the Solow residual between 1950 and 2021. We can see from the figure that:

1. total factor productivity has trended upwards over time (a long-run trend rate of TFP growth of around 0.90% p.a.);[13]
2. recessions are typically associated with falls in TFP (as shown by the shaded grey bars in Figure 18.6); and
3. from the late 1960s through the early 1980s, there was a period of substantial productivity slowdown.

18.2.5 Criticisms of the RBC model

The impulse and propagation mechanisms

In the RBC model, it is exogenous shocks to technology that are the principal impulses driving business cycles, but what are these technology shocks? Little evidence is provided in the literature on the source or nature of these shocks. As we have seen, for lack of a better alternative, the 'Solow residual' is often used by RBC proponents to proxy for technology. The Solow residual is the portion of economic growth that cannot be accounted for by changes in measurable factor inputs (e.g. labour and capital).

Researchers in the comparative growth and growth accounting literature, where the Solow residual had its origins, are sceptical of the RBC theorists' use of the Solow

[13] The long-run trend rate of TFP growth is calculated as the compound annual growth rate of TFP between 1950 and 2020.

residual as a measure of short-run technology shocks, as perfectly summed up by King and Rebelo (1999):[14]

> The stated goal of that [growth accounting] literature was to measure the long-run evolution of disembodied technical progress, not the short-run behavior of productivity. Its hidden agenda was to make the Solow residual negligible, that is, to measure production inputs well enough that all growth in output could be accounted for by movements in factors of production. For this reason the residual was often referred to as a 'measure of our ignorance'. Growth accountants were horrified when they saw the measure of their ignorance recast as the main impulse to the business cycle.

Another important criticism of using this proxy is that movements in the Solow residual might not just reflect technological change, but also market imperfections, such as labour hoarding and monopoly power.[15] These imperfections produce problems of measurement error, where the Solow residual implies a change in total factor productivity when in fact none has taken place. Labour hoarding, for example, is the name given to the phenomenon when labour is underutilized during a recession. Labour hoarding occurs when firms expect a recession to be temporary and are reluctant to lay off expensively trained staff. If the Solow residual is calculated using employment (as we have in Figure 18.6), then underutilization of labour during a recession will imply that TFP has fallen, when in fact the reduction in output is simply the result of employees working less hard (or fewer hours) than they did before the downturn.[16] An increase in resource misallocation in the economy can also show up as a decline in TFP.

The model requires there to be periods of technological regress to produce business cycles. It is hard to imagine periods since WWII where technology went backwards. To address this, RBC modellers widened the scope of what they consider to be technology shocks. Hansen and Prescott (1993) argue that changes in regulatory and legal systems within a country can be considered as technology shocks and could be negative. The plausibility of this interpretation of technology shocks as a good fit is disputed by Calomiris and Hanes (1995), who believe it is incompatible with the long-run macroeconomic data. They cite the fact that regulatory and legal interventions in the US economy were much smaller before the First World War but business cycles were much larger.[17] If regulatory and legal shocks were in fact causing business cycles, you would expect business cycles to be larger *after* the First World War.

An alternative approach to make the model more realistic is to adjust the model itself. King and Rebelo (1999) formulate an RBC model with variable capital utilization, which can produce realistic business cycles (judged by the behaviour of the moments from the simulated model economy) from small, nonnegative changes in technology.

---

[14] See pp. 962–63 of King and Rebelo (1999).

[15] See Summers (1986).

[16] See Chapter 12 of Williamson (2011).

[17] See Hartley et al. (1997).

Lastly, and very importantly, the propagation of the technology shock through the economy requires the initial impulse to be very persistent. The 'memory' coefficient on the productivity shock must be very high (typically around 0.9) to produce the business cycles we see in the data. There is no economic justification or theory for this assumption. Without a persistent shock the model produces very weak dynamics and does not fit the data well.

The labour market

The original form of the RBC model relies on the intertemporal substitution between labour and leisure to help drive business cycles. To match the model in this regard, we would expect the actual data to show that aggregate hours and productivity vary closely with output, which would imply that hours per worker vary closely with output and that the real wage would be strongly procyclical, as this is one of the mechanisms that induces agents to substitute between labour and leisure.

In the data for the US economy presented in Kydland and Prescott (1982), aggregate hours worked are much more variable than productivity, which is not supportive of the model. What is driving the observed variability in aggregate hours if it is not movements in hours per worker? Figure 18.2 shows that employment varies more with output than does hours per worker, suggesting that changes in employment are the key factor driving changes in aggregate hours.

Again, the RBC model can be modified to better fit the data in this regard. As an example, Hansen (1985) uses a model of indivisible labour (where workers can either work a set amount of hours or not at all) and Christiano and Eichenbaum (1992) allow government consumption shocks to influence labour market dynamics. The output of these models is capable of replicating the actual US labour market data much more closely than the original RBC model.

The second labour market prediction of the model is for a strongly procyclical real wage. The real wage is shown to be acyclical or mildly procyclical in the data. An acyclical or mildly procyclical real wage is consistent with the imperfect labour market model introduced in Chapter 2. In such a model, shocks are mainly demand shocks and the economy moves around the equilibrium rate with the real wage lying in between the upward-sloping wage-setting and the fairly flat price-setting curve. The inconsistency between the RBC model and the data could be rectified by modifying the model, by using indivisible labour (see above) or by including labour supply shocks in addition to productivity shocks.[18]

The key labour market propagation mechanism in the model is the intertemporal (or Frisch) elasticity of labour supply, which indicates how readily workers are willing to substitute labour and leisure over time. Microeconomic studies have shown little evidence that workers carry out enough intertemporal substitution to justify the

---

[18] See Holland and Scott (1998).

fluctuations in aggregate hours shown in the data.[19] This point is emphasized in Chetty et al. (2011), who conduct a review of existing studies and find that:[20]

> micro estimates of intertemporal substitution (Frisch) elasticities are an order of magnitude smaller than the values needed to explain business cycle fluctuations in aggregate hours by preferences.

The problem can be seen in Figure 18.4. A low labour supply elasticity would imply a very steep labour supply curve. Productivity shocks that raise labour demand would then have relatively limited effects on hours worked. On impact, output fluctuations are driven by movements in productivity and labour (because new investment only raises the capital stock next period). If hours worked are relatively unresponsive, the model will generate little amplification of the shock: the movement in output would then be largely driven by the shock itself.

A model with indivisible labour (such as Hansen 1985 and Rogerson 1988) can also help address this issue. In these models households work a fixed shift and do not adjust hours worked in response to real wage changes on the intensive margin. As a result, individual labour supply elasticities can be low, but in the aggregate hours worked is still highly responsive to technology shocks as households move in and out of work (the extensive margin).

18.2.6 RBC's lasting impact and the rise of DSGE modelling

RBC modelling has had a huge impact since its introduction in the early 1980s, which was reflected in Kydland and Prescott winning the Nobel Prize for Economics in 2004. Macroeconomic theories based on the RBC modelling approach became known as *Dynamic Stochastic General Equilibrium* (DSGE) models and this approach has dominated macroeconomics in recent decades.

In a broader sense, DSGE is a style of analysis and should not necessarily be conflated with a particular model (e.g the RBC model). Both the New Keynesian model (Section 18.3 below) and the newer heterogeneous agent macroeconomic models (Section 18.4 below) are built on DSGE methods. The word dynamic refers to the study of how the economy evolves over time, stochastic refers to the introduction of uncertainty and shocks, and *general* equilibrium refers to the fact that, in fully specifying the optimization problems of different agents and how they interact, these models look for equilibrium outcomes across multiple markets (goods, capital, labour).

The term equilibrium therefore has a particular meaning in this tradition of macroeconomics research. In DSGE models, equilibrium simply means the outcomes for quantities and prices that are consistent with the optimizing choices of agents, the production technologies and any resource constraints. And, in this context, market clearing simply means that prices and quantities can be explained by the optimizing choices of agents in the model. In these models, the business cycle itself

---

[19] See Ashenfelter (1984).

[20] See p. 471 of Chetty et al. (2011).

is an *equilibrium outcome*. It is also worth stressing that in richer models with other imperfections and market failures, the equilibrium outcomes are not necessarily the first-best perfectly competitive outcomes produced by the RBC model.

This approach is closely related to the goal of building macroeconomic models from microfoundations. New Classical economists criticized earlier Keynesian approaches for imposing certain relationships without allowing agents in the model to make choices that internalized these imperfections. For example, even if wage contracts prevent the continuous adjustment of nominal wages, 'it would be mutually advantageous for workers and firms to determine levels of employment in an efficient manner' and employment outcomes may not necessarily be that different from the flexible wage equilibrium (Barro 1979). This is particularly important if we want to evaluate the costs and benefits of a change in government policy, a point that echos the Lucas critique we discussed in Chapter 4.

The DSGE approach more generally, and the RBC model in particular, has both supporters and detractors. But to summarize, agreement may be possible on the following contributions that RBC modelling has made to the development of academic macroeconomics:

1. Macroeconomic models now try to focus on microfoundations. In other words, they attempt to pin down how the reaction of these agents to shocks generates aggregate fluctuations. This was influenced by the desire of macroeconomists to build models that were more robust to the Lucas critique. Still, the choice of microfoundations remains open to dispute.
2. While we may reasonably disagree about different microfoundations, assumptions and shocks, macroeconomics is about general equilibrium. Blanchard (2018) believes there is wide agreement on this point, but also notes that not all macroeconomic research needs to start with a general equilibrium model. It is informative to look at particular markets or the behaviour of particular agents in isolation, although ultimately macroeconomists will still be interested understanding the overall aggregate outcomes.
3. Since DSGE models are micro-founded structural models, they are better able to analyse the causal effects of policy–assuming the behaviour incorporated in the structural equations is a good representation of the economy under study—than are ad hoc empirical models. Recent econometric developments where DSGE models are estimated have allowed for proper shock decompositions to be carried out to determine what has driven changes in the data.
4. The RBC literature refocused macroeconomics on real causes of business cycles. Modern DSGE models now include a range of shocks, both from the supply and demand sides.
5. The device of building a model economy is a potentially valuable methodology. More realistic microeconomic foundations can be introduced, which is what the widely used New Keynesian models have tried to do (see Section 18.3). Dynamic macroeconomic models (i.e. quantitative laboratories) can be useful tools for quantifying

the welfare implications of economic policy or changes in society such as ageing (as shown by, for example, Heathcote et al. 2010).

18.3 THE NEW KEYNESIAN MODEL AND MONETARY POLICY

18.3.1 Introduction

The RBC model produces business cycles that are efficient and there is no role for macroeconomic stabilization policy. This result is not specific to the technology shock and the RBC model can be enlarged to include a range of other shocks. For example, shocks can be introduced that make consumption today more desirable. These are referred to as demand shocks but differ from Keynesian-type aggregate demand shocks. Another feature of the RBC model, and many first-generation DSGE models, is that all variables are in real terms. There is no money or nominal prices and monetary policy cannot affect real output. In Chapter 6 we discussed the classical dichotomy and the neutrality of money: an increase in the money supply only leads to higher prices. The RBC model is an example of a classical, perfectly competitive model, where the classical dichotomy holds.

The New Keynesian (NK) model attempts to bring Keynesian insights into a real business cycle style model. To tackle the Lucas critique, NK models start from the RBC modelling approach. The NK model maintains the focus on microfoundations, optimization by households and firms and rational expectations. It then introduces Keynesian elements such as imperfect competition, nominal rigidities and a role for monetary policy. The NK model became the workhorse model for monetary policy analysis in the literature. The core elements of the NK model exist in many more advanced macroeconomic models, including many of the heterogeneous agent New Keynesian models that we will cover in Section 18.4.

This section focuses on the so-called 3-equation NK model, and compares it with the 3-equation model in this book. We cover this at a relatively high level, with some additional technical detail in the web appendix. Textbook treatments can be found in Galí (2015) and Walsh (2010), and in the seminal paper of Clarida, Galí, and Gertler (1999). We discuss how monetary policy works in this model and how monetary policy can be conducted to maximize welfare.

18.3.2 The 3-equation New Keynesian model

The New Keynesian (NK) model has relatively complicated microfoundations but it can eventually be simplified to three key equations (IS/PC/MR): an IS curve that captures the relationship between the output gap and the real interest rate, a Phillips curve relating inflation to the output gap, and a monetary policy rule that explains how interest rates are set relative to inflation. At a high level, these equations appear broadly similar to the main equations of the 3-equation model presented earlier in this book. There are, however, some important differences and a number of core mechanisms are closer in spirit to the RBC model.

The demand side

The demand side of the NK model is very close to the RBC model. There is a representative household who makes choices about consumption and leisure to maximize their lifetime utility. The simple NK model does not include capital or investment, instead households can potentially save using one-period bonds. As in the RBC model, households want to smooth consumption over time and look at lifetime income when considering consumption decisions. In Chapter 1 we explained that, in such a model, the relationship between consumption today and consumption tomorrow is governed by the Euler equation.

Recall, when the household's utility function is logarithmic, the Euler equation relates consumption today to expected consumption tomorrow, the real interest rate and the household's subjective discount factor. In the context of a constant real interest rate, the Euler equation is (see Appendix 1.5.2 to Chapter 1):

$$C_t = \frac{1+\rho}{1+r} C^E_{t+1}$$

The Euler equation forms the basis for the NK IS curve. The basic NK model does not have investment or capital accumulation. There is also no government and the economy is closed. As a result, all output must be consumed ($Y_t = C_t$). The Euler equation can then be seen as relating output today to expected output tomorrow and the real interest rate.

To write this expression in a linear form, it is common to take logs and assume the long-run steady state inflation target is equal to zero. As shown in the web appendix, the Euler equation above can be transformed into an equation describing the demand-side of the NK model:

$$y_t = y^E_{t+1} - \frac{1}{\sigma}(r_t - \bar{r}) \tag{18.1}$$

where y_t is (log) output and y^E_{t+1} is expected (log) output tomorrow. The real interest rate is now allowed to vary over time, r_t, and, as discussed in Chapter 1, the real interest rate is equal to the nominal interest rate set by the central bank minus expected inflation ($r_t = i_t - \pi^E_{t+1}$). It is common to consider more general utility functions than log utility (studied in Chapter 1), in which case the coefficient $\frac{1}{\sigma}$ appears in front of the real interest rate. This comes from households' preferences and is often called the *elasticity of intertemporal substitution*, which is defined as the percentage change in consumption growth relative to a one percent change in the real interest rate. Finally, the term $\bar{r}$ is the long-run steady state real interest rate. Expected output growth is therefore related to the deviation of the real interest rate from its long-run value.

This already looks like an IS curve in the sense that it relates output to real interest rates. Note, however, that this equation is *forward looking* because expected output appears on the right-hand side. The IS curve from the 3-equation model introduced in Chapter 1, does not have this expected output term. The NK dynamic IS curve relates (expected) output *growth* to the real interest rate. The IS curve in Chapter 1 relates current output to the lagged real interest rate.

The other important difference with the IS curve introduced in Chapter 1 is that interest rate changes directly affect households' desire to consume vs. save. In Chapter 1, the real interest rate affected aggregate demand via investment. In Chapter 1, household consumption is only *indirectly* affected via multiplier effects since we assume (on empirical grounds) that the net effect of the income and substitution effects of an interest rate change on consumption are limited. We will return to this distinction between the direct and indirect effects of interest rates on consumption in Section 18.4 when we discuss the latest research in models with heterogeneous agents.

As in the 3-equation model, the NK model features nominal rigidities and prices do not adjust immediately in response to short-run economic shocks.[21] As in the 3-equation model, output will deviate from the outcome that would have been obtained under flexible prices. It is therefore conventional to express the IS equation in terms of the output *gap*, x_t. In the NK model the output gap, x_t, is defined as the difference between actual output, y, and what it would have been in the absence of nominal rigidities. The flexible price level of output is sometimes called the *natural rate of output* or *potential output*. One way to think about potential output is as the level of output that would have been generated by an RBC-style model with flexible prices. Part of the business cycle in the NK model can therefore be attributed to 'real' fluctuations. That said, potential output here differs from the RBC model because the simple NK model does not have capital and there is monopolistic competition. The NK steady steady levels of output and employment are therefore lower than in a model with perfect competition.

We can now express equation 18.1 in terms of the output *gap*. We obtain the following expression:

$$x_t = x^E_{t+1} - \frac{1}{\sigma} r_t + u_t \tag{18.2}$$

where u_t is a 'shock' that is driven entirely by changes in potential output. u_t could be driven, for example, by technology shocks. If we introduce demand shocks that affect a household's desire to consume, these will also show up in u_t. Note that if output equals potential output ($x_t = x^E_{t+1} = 0$), $r_t = \sigma u_t$. This is sometimes called the *real natural rate of interest* because it is the level of the real interest rate that would occur with flexible prices. We will denote this as r^n_t below. In Chapter 3 the counterpart is the stabilizing rate of interest, r_S.

In Chapter 1 we also noted that real interest rates are nominal interest rates adjusted for expected inflation. This is the Fisher equation. Using this in equation 18.2 produces the NK *dynamic IS curve*:

$$x_t = x^E_{t+1} - \frac{1}{\sigma}(i_t - \pi^E_{t+1} - r^n_t) \tag{DIS}$$

---

[21] The 3-equation model in this book focuses on nominal wage rigidity, but it is also possible to write a version of the NK model with nominal wage rigidity. In this chapter we focus on the simple 3-equation NK case with sticky prices.

The supply side

The NK model deviates more significantly from the RBC model in terms of how output is produced and how prices are determined. The RBC model features perfect competition where firms are price-takers. In such a model, price equals marginal cost and the real wage is equated to the marginal product of labour, as discussed in Chapter 2. The main objective in the NK model is to introduce price stickiness in a model with profit maximizing firms. Price stickiness is needed for monetary policy to have real effects, and for output to be 'demand determined' in the short run. But to incorporate price stickiness with profit maximizing firms, these firms need to be able to *set* prices, which is inconsistent with perfect competition. The production structure of the NK model is very detailed. Here we sketch the main assumptions:

1. There are a large number of firms who each produce a slightly differentiated good using workers. Each of these goods can be imperfectly substituted for one another and the *elasticity of substitution* between any two of these goods is the same. As a result, this type of model is called *monopolistic competition*. Firms make profits and set a price that is higher than marginal cost. Each firm faces a downward-sloping demand curve, as in Chapter 2, and demand for their product depends on: their own price relative to the average of all other firms, the substitutability between varieties and the level of aggregate demand. The steady state flexible price equilibrium is characterized by a price setting curve that looks very similar to the price setting curve in Chapters 2 and 3.
2. Firms face nominal rigidities when setting prices. Price stickiness is often modelled via the assumption introduced by Calvo (1983) that firms can change their price if they get the 'green light', which occurs randomly for each firm. Hence only a fraction of firms are able to adjust their price in each period. Nominal rigidity is therefore *an assumption*, although the Calvo mechanism is intended to be a short-cut for a more 'micro-founded' theory of price stickiness.[22]
3. Firms live forever, are forward looking and have rational expectations. When they do reset their prices, they take account of the possibility that they will have to maintain this price in the future. Firms also commit to meet any demand at the chosen price. As a result, they consider the implications for lifetime profits when they reset their prices. Although prices are sticky, firms are always making profit maximizing choices about how much labour to hire and which price to set (when they are able to adjust price).
4. All the different varieties of goods are bundled together into a single basket, C, that is consumed by households. The price of final consumption is therefore the economy's average consumer price level.

Using the first order conditions from the representative firm's optimization problem, it is possible to derive a Phillips curve that describes the evolution of inflation. This

[22] An alternative approach, that also leads to a New Keynesian Phillips curve, is to assume that firms face quadratic costs of adjusting their price, following Rotemberg (1982).

is the *New Keynesian Phillips curve*, and a simplified derivation from first principles is provided in the web appendix to this chapter.

This derivation produces the equation for the New Keynesian Phillips (NKPC) curve:

$$\pi_t = \psi E_t \pi_{t+1} + \frac{\delta(1-(1-\delta)\psi)}{1-\delta}\alpha x_t. \qquad \text{(NKPC)}$$

When prices are set on the Calvo basis, inflation in period t can be expressed as a function of two terms: (a) the rate of inflation that is expected to prevail *next period*, i.e. $E_t \pi_{t+1}$ multiplied by the discount factor, $\psi = \frac{1}{1+\rho}$ and (b) the output gap term, αx_t, multiplied by a constant that depends on the share of firms that are able to change their price, δ, and the discount factor. The output gap x_t is defined as above.

Why does the output gap affect inflation in the New Keynesian Phillips curve? In the NK model, the output gap is proportional to time variation in the real marginal costs of firms. When demand is high, some firms cannot adjust price and therefore increase output, leading to a positive output gap. Higher production requires more workers, so the real wage—and hence real marginal cost—increases. When firms do reset the price, they consider the entire path of future real marginal costs when setting the price that will maximize lifetime profit.

Interestingly, this way of modelling price rigidities has the consequence that when a firm gets the green light, it will take a forward-looking view and adjust its price, taking into account the expected future sequence of output gaps. This will produce a jump in the prices set by the firms who are able to adjust: only being able to adjust price infrequently produces jumps in the price when adjustment is allowed. Hence inflation in the economy as a whole jumps in response to shocks. We shall see that the NKPC has some strange features, which have led Robert Solow to comment that although it might be new, it is neither Keynesian, nor a Phillips curve.[23]

Monetary policy

The final equation of the baseline NK model is a monetary policy rule. The simplest rule often used relates interest rates to inflation. This is a simplified version of the famous Taylor Rule discussed in Chapter 6:

$$i_t = \bar{r} + \phi_\pi \pi_t \qquad (18.3)$$

Note that we are still assuming that long-run steady state inflation is zero, so the inflation term can be thought of as the deviation of inflation from a zero long-run target rate of inflation. For monetary policy to successfully generate a single stable path for inflation back to target, policy has to follow the Taylor Principle and use a rule with $\phi_\pi > 1$.

The form of this rule is very similar to the 'best response' Taylor Rule derived in Chapter 6. In the NK model, however, this rule is not generally optimal. But Taylor Rules are often thought to broadly capture the empirical behaviour of the Federal Reserve during Chair Alan Greenspan's tenure, so it is common to assume a rule of this form.

---

[23] See Carlin et al. (2012).

BOX 18.1 Comparing the NKPC and the adaptive expectations Phillips curve

Although the NKPC has the broad characteristics of a traditional Phillips curve—that inflation is related to expected inflation and the output gap—the forward-looking nature of the NKPC means it is quite different to the adaptive expectations PC.

First consider the adaptive expectations (i.e. backward-looking) Phillips curve rewritten using the same notation as this section to facilitate comparisons:

$$\pi_t = \mathrm{E}_t\pi_t + \alpha x_t \tag{18.4}$$

$$= \pi_{t-1} + \alpha x_t \qquad \text{(adaptive expectations Phillips curve)}$$

where, $\mathrm{E}_t\pi_t = \pi_{t-1}$.

Unlike the standard Phillips curve discussed in Chapters 2 to 4, the expected inflation term in the NKPC relates not to the expected value of current inflation, but to next period's inflation. Because the NKPC includes expected future inflation and the adaptive expectations PC includes last period's inflation, very different predictions arise.

To help with the intuition, we compare the response of inflation to a temporary positive output gap using the standard adaptive expectations Phillips curve and the NKPC in Figure 18.7. Note that, for illustrative purposes, this is a mechanical exercise and we are taking the output gap as given and focusing on the properties of these two Phillips curves. These are not the outcomes from the full model including monetary policy and where the output gap is also a prediction of the model.

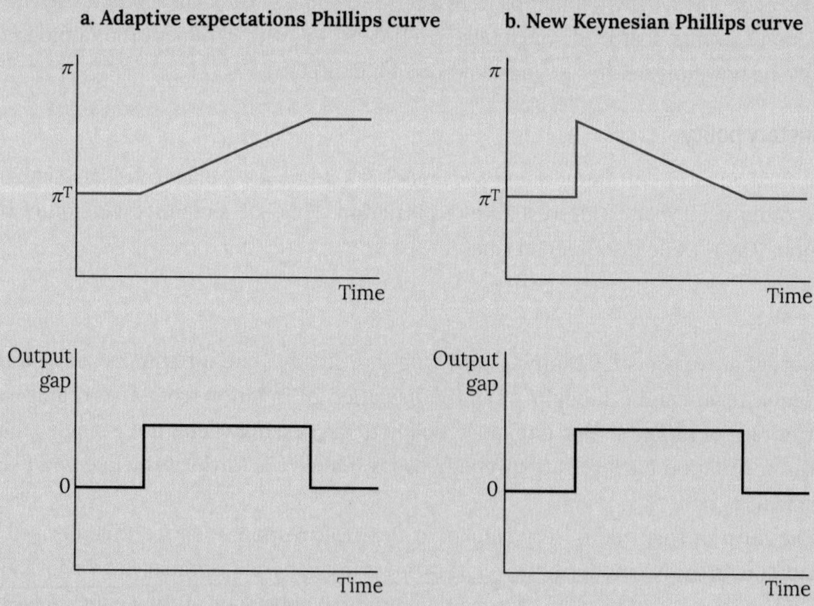

Figure 18.7 The response of inflation to a temporary output gap.
a. Adaptive expectations Phillips curve
b. New Keynesian Phillips curve

A positive output gap is associated with rising inflation with the standard adaptive expectations Phillips curve. The change in inflation is related to the level of the output gap, so inflation rises as long as the output gap is positive. Inflation only falls when the output gap is negative.

In the NKPC, because firms set prices based on their expectations about the future, the level of inflation today is proportional to the sum of all the future expected output gaps. Inflation therefore jumps initially as some firms reoptimize their price, but inflation is then *falling* over time. Put another way, it is optimal for the firm's initial price increase to be more aggressive the longer the output gap is expected to persist. This gives rise to the downward-sloping section of the inflation impulse response function in Figure 18.7b, which coincides with the period when there is a positive output gap. Conversely, a negative output gap would lower inflation on impact, but inflation would then be rising back towards the long-run steady state rate of inflation.

There is a parallel between this logic and the arbitrage behaviour in the foreign exchange market studied in Chapter 11. The behaviour of inflation and the output gap in the NKPC model is analogous to the uncovered interest parity (UIP) condition discussed. In that case, when agents take the view that there will be an interest rate differential vis-à-vis the rest of the world for a period of time, home's nominal exchange rate jumps. If there is a positive interest differential, home's exchange rate appreciates and then depreciates over the period the interest differential prevails. This reflects arbitrage behaviour in a market (for foreign exchange) where prices jump to ensure that the expected return from holding home and foreign bonds (where the default risk is assumed to be identical) is the same. In the NKPC model, firms are forward-looking and predict that the output gap will only last for a set amount of time.

The contrast between the way the two types of Phillips curve work can be highlighted by writing the NKPC in an alternative way, which brings out the fact that inflation depends on the entire future sequence of expected output gaps.[a] The NKPC relates current inflation to expected future inflation and the current output gap. As explained in the main text in Section 18.3.3, it is possible to re-write the equation NKPC as

$$\pi_t = \kappa \sum_{j=0}^{\infty} \psi^j E_t x_{t+j}, \text{ where we write} \qquad \text{(NKPC, alternative form)}$$

$$\alpha \frac{\delta(1-(1-\delta)\psi)}{1-\delta} \text{ as } \kappa \text{ to simplify the notation.} \qquad (18.5)$$

This expression makes it very clear that inflation in period t will jump in response to any news about future output gaps. It also gives us some insights about the role of central bank credibility: if the central bank can *promise* a zero output gap forever, inflation will never deviate from target. We will return to this later when we discuss optimal monetary policy.

[a] See Rudd and Whelan (2007). This paper also provides a useful critical assessment of the NK model and tests its ability to fit the inflation data.

18.3.3 The effects of changes in monetary policy

To illustrate how the NK model works, we now consider a surprise cut in the central bank's nominal interest rate (i_t).[24] For illustrative purposes, in this example we will assume that the unexpected movement in the interest rate persists for a number of quarters, so the nominal interest rate is unexpectedly lower for a period of time.[25]

Figure 18.8 shows the impulse response functions for the output gap and inflation following a surprise reduction in the nominal interest rate of around 0.5 percentage points. The movement in the output gap can also be seen as the movement in actual

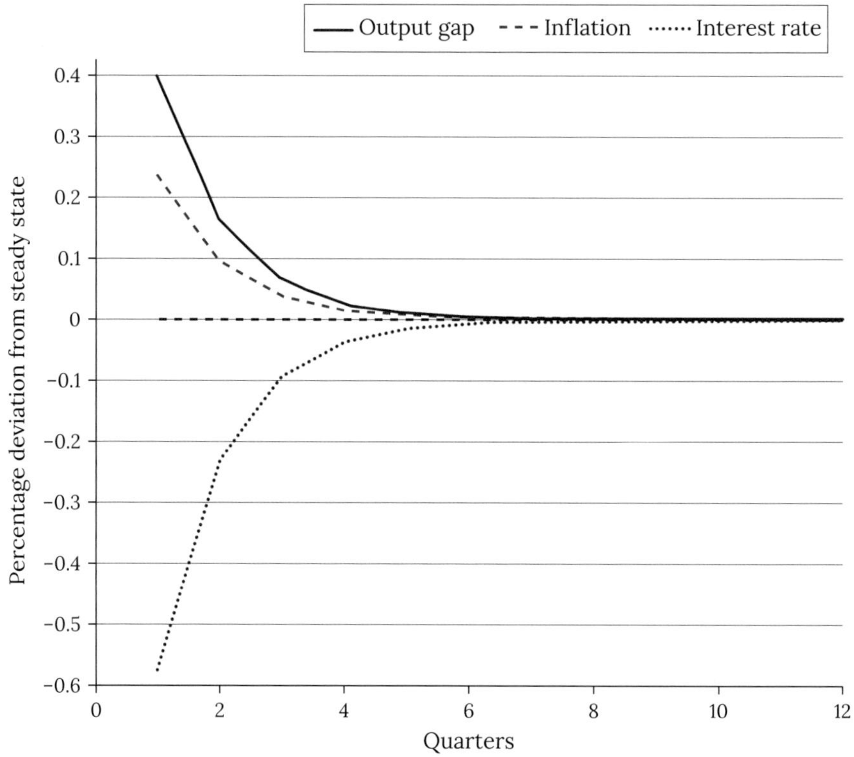

Figure 18.8 Response of inflation, the output gap and interest rates to a surprise reduction in the nominal interest rate in the simple 3-equation New Keynesian model.

[24] This can be achieved by adding an additional term to equation 18.3 that randomly moves interest rates around today. This additional term is often called a 'monetary policy shock' and is designed to capture unexpected movements in the policy rate.

[25] A slightly more general monetary policy rule is used to create this example. This rule includes the level of interest rates last period, where γ controls the *persistence* of nominal interest rates: $i_t = \gamma i_{t-1} + (1-\gamma)(\bar{r} + \phi_\pi \pi_t + \phi_x x_t)$.

output y.[26] In this experiment, interest rates fall on impact and remain below the long-run value $\bar{r}$ for around 6 quarters. The output gap—and hence output—and inflation rise immediately, and remain above their long-run steady state levels for around 6 quarters.

Why does the output gap and inflation rise? Because some firms cannot adjust their price today, inflation does not respond as much as it would under flexible prices. Nominal interest rate changes then lead to movements in the real interest rate (via the Fisher equation). From the NK dynamic IS curve, a change in the real interest rate changes the incentive to consume today vs. consume tomorrow. Lower real interest rates discourage saving and encourage consumption. This leads to a rise in aggregate demand.

What happens next? If a firm cannot adjust price, it will respond to the extra demand by increasing production. The only way firms can increase production is by employing more workers. But for the workers to be willing to work more, the real wage must rise. Firms that do adjust their price today understand that they may not be able to adjust prices in the future. They therefore consider the future path of revenue and costs implied by their choice of price today.[27] Output jumps on impact (because some firms cannot adjust prices) and inflation jumps (because some firms do adjust prices). The central bank responds to the additional inflationary pressure and guides the economy back to the steady state. The chosen policy rule will influence the exact quantitative magnitudes shown in Figure 18.8.

There are several differences in the transmission mechanism in this model relative to the 3-equation model studied earlier in the book. First, in this model, the core mechanism is the household's consumption response to the real interest rate, which Blanchard (2018) refers to as interest rates 'twisting the path of consumption'. The elasticity of intertemporal substitution $\frac{1}{\sigma}$, that controls how consumption growth is affected by real interest rates, is therefore a key element of this model. As a result, Cochrane (2015) notes that this model would be better referred to as the 'sticky-price intertemporal substitution model'. By contrast, in the 3-equation model in this book, interest rates affect investment and consumption spending, especially through the housing channel; and then indirectly via the multiplier.

Second, all variables jump on impact in the NK model. In the 3-equation model with an adaptive expectations Phillips curve, the output gap would rise and as long as the output gap is positive, inflation will be steadily rising. The role of the monetary policy rule would then be to react and generate a negative output gap in order to bring inflation back to target. In the NK model, the output gap and inflation remain positive for the whole period in Figure 18.8.

---

[26] This would not be the case if we were considering the responses to a technology shock, for example. A technology shock would also move potential output, as it does in the RBC model.

[27] One implication of Calvo style price stickiness is that the economy's average price markup, and hence firm profits, goes down when the economy expands. Some have argued that this is at odds with the data, which may cast doubt on the transmission mechanisms in the NK model. See, for example, Nekarda and Ramey (2020).

The NK model is also based on purely forward-looking behaviour. The effect of this can be seen by writing the IS curve and the NKPC in a different form using the method of repeated substitution explained in the footnote:[28]

$$x_t = -\frac{1}{\sigma}\sum_{j=0}^{\infty} E_t(r_{t+j} - r^n_{t+j}) \tag{18.6}$$

and

$$\pi_t = \kappa \sum_{j=0}^{\infty} \psi^j E_t x_{t+j} \tag{18.7}$$

where, to keep notation concise, $\kappa = \alpha\frac{\delta(1-(1-\delta)\psi)}{1-\delta}$.

Focusing on the rewritten IS equation 18.6, the output gap today negatively depends on the difference between the real interest rate and the natural real interest rate from now to the infinite future. The purely rational and forward-looking nature of the model is clearly unrealistic, but incorporating these features into how we think about monetary policy produces at least three important insights:

1. It is not just the current real interest rate that matters, but the entire future expected path of real interest rates. In reality, we tend to think that people's expectations about the future path of the central bank policy rate matters for outcomes today. For example, if a household takes out a mortgage with a fixed interest rate for the next 5 years, the lender will decide this interest rate based on where they think policy rates will be over the next 5 years.
2. Policy makers may be able to influence outcomes today by shaping expectations about the future path of interest rates even if they do not actually change interest rates, which Guthrie and Wright (2000) refer to as Open Mouth Operations. Central banks therefore invest a lot of resources in effective communication. This rationale

---

[28] Here we illustrate the process for the NKPC. The same steps can be followed for the IS curve as well. The first step is to take the original NKPC:

$$\pi_t = \psi E_t \pi_{t+1} + \kappa x_t.$$

We can then use this relation to move the equation forward by one period and find an expression for π_{t+1}:

$$\pi_{t+1} = \psi E_{t+1}\pi_{t+2} + \kappa x_{t+1}.$$

This is then substituted back into the original NKPC, such that:

$$\pi_t = \psi E_t(\psi E_{t+1}\pi_{t+2} + \kappa x_{t+1}) + \kappa x_t.$$

The process then carries on, hence the term 'repeated substitution'. The next stage is to get an expression for π_{t+2} (using the original NKPC) and to substitute that into the equation above. This process is repeated an infinite number of times. We can then use a summation to get an expression for π_t in terms of the entire future sequence of output gaps:

$$\pi_t = \kappa \sum_{j=0}^{\infty} \psi^j E_t x_{t+j}.$$

Note that this derivation is based on the rule of iterated expectations, which implies that $E_t E_{t+1} = E_t$ etc.

also underpins so-called forward guidance policies that we discussed in Chapter 6. Even if a policy maker is unable to influence real interest rates today, they can still impart stimulus by changing expectations about future real interest rates. This forward-looking aspect of policy is, however, unrealistically powerful in this model. Changes in real interest rates in the distant future can still have a large effect today. This is sometimes called the Forward Guidance Puzzle (Del Negro, Giannoni, and Patterson 2012) and has led researchers to try and dampen the effect, for example by incorporating imperfect information or departures from rational expectations.

3. Whether monetary policy is tight or loose depends on the real interest rate *relative* to the natural real interest rate. Just as in the 3-equation model, lower interest rates may not be evidence of loose policy if the natural real rate is very negative. This was the rationale for still providing substantial additional monetary stimulus in 2009 even after interest rates reached historic lows.

What about the response of inflation? Equation 18.7, which is examined in more detail in Box 18.1, shows that inflation today is purely a function of the expected future path of output gaps. In the context of monetary policy changes, roughly speaking, whatever monetary policy delivers for the path of the output gap will be mirrored in the inflation outcomes via equation 18.7.

18.3.4 **Optimal monetary policy**

One advantage of studying a model that starts from utility maximization is that the model has an explicit concept of welfare. Given that NK business cycles contain an inefficient component, we can therefore examine whether monetary policy can restore output to potential, stabilize inflation, and whether this will improve welfare.

The most important imperfection that drives a gap between actual output and potential output is price stickiness. In principle, the model's steady state is also inefficient because of distortions introduced by market power in the goods sector. The baseline analysis of optimal policy usually proceeds by assuming that fiscal policy is able to offset this long-run steady state distortion. The discussion in this section therefore implicitly follows this approach.[29] It is possible to show that the welfare losses due to sticky prices depend on the output gap and inflation. The loss function has a similar form to the central bank loss function introduced in Chapters 3 and 6. Specifically:

$$L = E_0 \sum_{t=0}^{\infty} \frac{1}{2} \psi^t \left(\pi_t^2 + \beta x_t^2 \right) \tag{18.8}$$

There are two main differences from the baseline model of optimal monetary policy in Chapter 3. First, losses are dynamic: there are potentially losses today and in all future periods.[30] Households care about this because they are infinitely lived. Second,

[29] Further interesting results occur when this assumption is relaxed (see Galí 2015 for more detail).

[30] In Chapter 3 the implications of dynamic losses are set out in Appendix 3.5.2.

the coefficient β is a specific function of all the parameters of the model, rather than a reflection of the subjective preferences of the central bank.

What does optimal monetary policy look like in this model? By inspecting the loss function 18.8 we can see that optimal policy would like to set the output gap and inflation to zero: policy should aim to restore full employment and set inflation to target (zero in this case).

Equations 18.6 and 18.7 offer some insights into how this can be achieved. In equation 18.6, if the central bank can set $r_t = r_t^n$ in all periods, the output gap will be zero. And, as can be seen from equation 18.7 if the output gap is always zero, inflation will never deviate from the long-run steady state target (assumed to be zero in this model). The optimal policy is for the central bank to target the natural real interest rate. This logic underpins why central banks often discuss the natural real interest rate (sometimes referred to as r^* in the world of central banking) when describing their policy objectives.

What monetary policy rule might implement this in the NK model? A policy that sets the nominal interest rate equal to r_t^n will only deliver the optimal policy if it successfully delivers zero inflation. The central bank therefore needs to explain how it will respond to inflation deviations from target. This provides a rationale for strict inflation targeting and the following policy rule would deliver full stabilization of the output gap and inflation in this model:

$$i_t = r_t^n + \phi_\pi \pi_t \tag{18.9}$$

where again $\phi_\pi > 1$.

Note that it is not necessary to target the output gap specifically. This is because the output gap and inflation are intrinsically linked in this model. One policy instrument is therefore sufficient to hit both the output gap and inflation targets. Blanchard and Galí (2007) refer to this property as the 'Divine Coincidence', although this result is not necessarily true in more complex NK models.

Monetary policy under discretion and commitment

The Divine Coincidence is a special result that relies, in part, on all economic shocks showing up in the IS curve.[31] But policy makers often feel they face a 'trade off' when stabilizing inflation: it may not be possible to stabilize inflation and the output gap at the same time.

In the 3-equation NK model, this situation occurs when there are shocks that directly affect the Phillips curve. In Chapter 3 we referred to this as an inflation shock. In this case, the NKPC now includes a final term, e_t which can move around:

$$\pi_t = \psi E_t \pi_{t+1} + \kappa x_t + e_t \tag{18.10}$$

A number of shocks might be captured by e_t including changes in wage bargaining power or certain movements in taxes that have supply-side effects. This is sometimes

[31] This is not the case in the textbook 3-equation model because of the lag structure in the IS and PC equations.

also referred to as a cost-push shock because it can capture anything that puts pressure on the marginal costs of firms.

In such circumstances the policy maker cannot simultaneously deliver zero inflation and a closed output gap. Optimal policy will tend to require higher interest rates to offset the inflationary pressure, but a lower level of inflation can only be achieved by generating a negative output gap. The policy maker therefore has to trade off controlling inflation with holding the economy below potential. This trade-off is central to understanding monetary policy in the 3-equation model in the book.

The forward-looking nature of the NKPC curve, however, allows us to investigate the benefits of the central bank being able to *commit* to a given adjustment path following an inflation shock. In the cases we have looked at in earlier chapters of this book, the policy maker has been characterized by *discretion*. Monetary policy makers in contemporary central banks practise discretion: they are able to re-optimize their policy stance (i.e. readjust interest rates) in each period.

Discretionary policy in the NK model is suboptimal relative to a policy that can commit to deliver certain outcomes in the future. To explore this, we focus on two related results that arise in the NK model:

1. Both the rise in inflation and the size of the negative output gap required to counteract an inflation shock are smaller under commitment than under discretion. This is called the *stabilization bias* of a policy of discretion. The response of the policy maker is 'too harsh' because it is unable to commit not to change the policy once the private sector sets prices.
2. The optimal policy rule under discretion is one that targets inflation (and produces stabilization bias), whereas the optimal rule with commitment targets the price level. This suggests that one reason we do not observe price-level targeting is that in the real world of policy making, achieving commitment is difficult. But the policy debate has been characterized by attempts to introduce a form of price-level targeting. For example, some have suggested targeting nominal GDP instead of inflation. And the Federal Reserve has recently emphasized *average* inflation targeting, which means that periods of below target inflation will be offset by periods of above target inflation later. Since inflation is the growth rate of prices, this should replicate a price-level target.

The full analysis of optimal policy in the NK model is set out in Galí (2015) Chapter 5 and Walsh (2010) Chapter 11. Here we sketch more detail on the intuition, emphasizing the two results above.

The simplest way to see both the welfare benefits of commitment (price-level targeting) and the difficulty of achieving it is to consider a temporary (i.e. one period) inflation shock. We assume, as before, that the central bank has an inflation target of zero. This implies a constant price level in the steady state and is used for convenience.

We first consider the situation of discretion, where the central bank re-optimizes each period. The central bank responds to the inflation shock by 'leaning into the wind' and choosing its optimal response, which will entail a negative output gap. If the policy maker could announce its plan of minimizing its losses over a lengthy period of adjustment to the shock and could commit to sticking to it, it is able to respond to the shock with a smaller deviation of inflation from target and a smaller negative output gap. We can see this in Figure 18.9, by comparing points A and A′ and noting that $\pi_1 > \pi_1' > \pi^T (= 0)$ and $x_1 < x_1' < 0$.

What such a policy maker would do is to take advantage of its commitment to the least cost policy plan in order to influence private sector expectations. The policy maker would rather experience a sequence of smaller deviations in the output gap and inflation than a one-off larger loss today. The policy maker therefore uses the power of commitment to promise a sequence of small output gaps over time. Because the NKPC is forward looking, this entire path of negative output gaps has an effect on inflation outcomes today (see, again, equation 18.7). As shown in Figure 18.9 the optimal plan under commitment sees inflation falling below target and gradually returning to target as the output gap is reduced.

Figure 18.9 highlights the differences in the outcomes under discretion and commitment. We can see the following:

1. The costs associated with the adjustment paths are smaller under commitment. The more muted response under commitment highlights the stabilization bias that arises under discretion. Welfare is lower in the case of discretion because the higher costs in the first period outweigh the discounted value of the deviations in output and inflation over the adjustment period under commitment.
2. The price level is permanently higher in the case of discretion, whereas it returns to its initial level in the case of commitment. Only by having some time with inflation below target, which is possible with commitment but not discretion, can the price level return to its starting point (shown by P = 100 in the figure).
3. The commitment plan is, however, time inconsistent. Because the shock only lasts one period, the central bank has an incentive to make promises about negative future output gaps, reap the benefit of lower inflation today but then abandon this

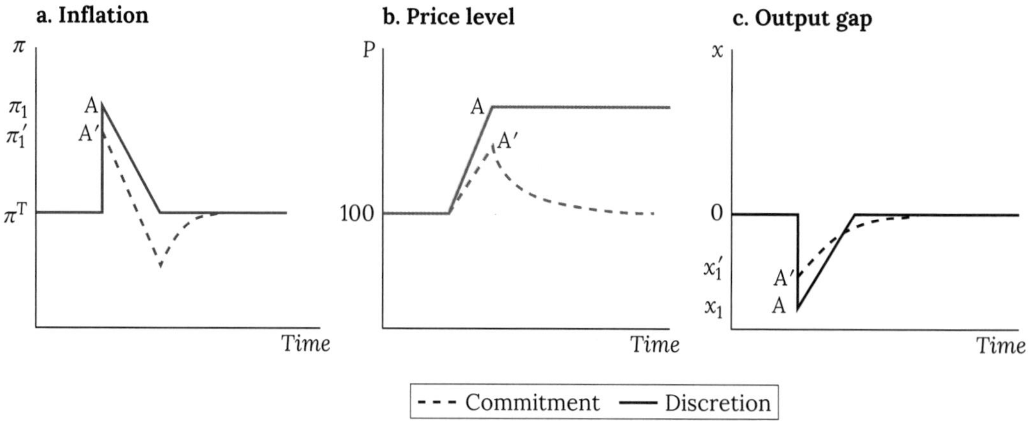

Figure 18.9 Stabilization bias: commitment vs discretion—impulse response functions after an inflation shock.

plan in the future when the shock is gone (and restore the output gap to zero). Still, this exercise illustrates the potential benefits if commitment could be achieved. This is also why central banks may wish to build up a reputation, minimize surprise deviations from a pre-announced plan and to try and follow rules that reinforce trust that the central bank will 'stay the course'.

18.3.5 **Beyond the baseline model**

The simple 3-equation NK model is very stylized, but successfully showed how to produce some Keynesian predictions (albeit without Keynesian transmission mechanisms) from a real business cycle modelling framework. Goodfriend and King (1997) refer to this as the New Neoclassical Synthesis because it brings together the real business cycle framework in the neoclassical tradition with Keynesian insights. The NK model therefore forms the basis of many modern business cycle and macroeconomic policy models. A vast literature has built on this model over the last few decades. It is not possible to provide a full review of this literature. Here we simply mention a few notable developments. In Section 18.4 we will cover the latest extensions to models with heterogeneous agents.

An important development from the baseline NK model was to devise a richer framework that could capture key aspects of the data. Christiano, Eichenbaum and Evans (2005) developed a larger version of the NK model with a range of additional mechanisms. Their goal was to match empirical evidence on how changes in monetary policy affect the economy. Empirical evidence, which started to accumulate in the 1980s and 1990s, found delayed effects of changes in interest rates. In fact these effects build up in a 'hump shaped' fashion (as in the modelling in earlier chapters), which is clearly at odds with the sharp jumps in Figure 18.8.

Smets and Wouters (2003, 2007) developed a similar model that could be fully estimated using empirical data. This model could then be used to examine which types of shocks (demand, monetary, fiscal, financial, investment-specific technology, markup and exchange rate shocks, in addition to the RBC-style technology shock) might have been responsible for the business cycle seen in the data. These models were used for macroeconomic forecasting and policy analysis.[32] Such medium-scale New Keynesian models became the workhorse DSGE models prior to the Global Financial Crisis. Many central banks adopted variants of the Smets and Wouters (2003, 2007) framework. Some of the key additions to the simple NK model are:

1. the addition of investment and capital accumulation, usually with investment adjustment costs to capture the hump-shaped response of investment often seen in the data;
2. mechanisms to allow capital to be utilized to different degrees over the business cycle, which helps add amplification and persistence;

[32] For a critical view of the suitability of these estimated medium-scale DSGE models for policy analysis see Chari, Kehoe, and McGrattan (2009).

3. partial indexation of prices and wages, which introduces lagged inflation into the *Phillips* curve (see Box 18.2 for more discussion about this hybrid Phillips curve);
4. habit formation in consumption which introduces a role for lagged consumption in the IS curve and adds a humped-shaped profile to the consumption response;
5. wage stickiness which helps amplify the effects of nominal rigidities and (together with capital utilization) help dampen the response of price markups;
6. lags in the Taylor rule, which introduces the lagged interest rate in the Taylor rule.

Christiano, Eichenbaum, and Evans (2005) show that this type of medium-scale NK model captures the empirical evidence on the dynamic effects of a change in monetary policy. Smets and Wouters (2003, 2007) argued these models 'combine a sound, microfounded structure suitable for policy analysis with a good probabilistic description of the observed data and good forecasting performance' (Smets and Wouters 2007, p. 587).

The literature has enriched the NK environment in numerous other directions. Here we summarize a few common themes:

- Financial market imperfections and the role of banks have been increasingly brought into the NK model. Early examples of DSGE models with financial frictions include Bernanke, Gertler, and Gilchrist (1999) who introduced a financial accelerator where asset price responses to monetary policy changes can amplify the effects of monetary policy on the economy by affecting the health of firms' balance sheets. Other important examples include Kiyotaki and Moore (1997) who focus on the role of borrowing constraints tied to the collateral value of assets (but in a real model) and Iacoviello (2005) who introduces Kiyotaki-Moore style frictions in a NK model of the housing market. Post-global financial crisis, research on financial frictions exploded, including much more focus on the banking sector (for example, see Gertler and Kiyotaki 2015, and Gertler, Kiyotaki, and Prestipino 2016).
- Various papers depart from the perfectly competitive labour market of the baseline model by introducing wage bargaining power, sticky wages and involuntary unemployment. Wage stickiness is considered by Erceg, Henderson, and Levin (2000) and has been subsequently integrated by many others. Many New Keynesian papers focus on the output gap and fluctuations in hours worked, but do not have a separate concept of unemployment. Various papers have therefore sought to incorporate unemployment explicitly into the New Keynesian framework. Prominent examples 'incorporating search and matching frictions' (where workers have to search for jobs and are matched with employers, see Pissarides 2000) include Walsh (2003, 2005), Trigari (2009), Blanchard and Galí (2010), and Ravenna and Walsh (2011). See also Christiano, Trabandt, and Waletin (2010) and Christiano, Eichenbaum, and Trabandt (2016), among many others.
- After 2009 many economies hit the zero lower bound and short-term nominal interest rates could no longer be used to stimulate the economy. Many papers have therefore studied how to conduct monetary policy at the zero lower bound, Eggertsson and Woodford (2003) being a prominent example. A number of insights from the NK model that we discussed above, such as the role of commitment policy

and price-level targeting, have informed the ZLB debate in recent years (see, for example, Woodford 2012).

- There is a very large New Open Economy Macroeconomics literature based on open economy DSGE models that integrate various New Keynesian insights. Early contributions included Obstfeld and Rogoff (1995) and Corsetti and Pesenti (2001). The baseline small open economy version of the NK model was introduced by Galí and Monacelli (2005). Corsetti, Dedola, and Leduc (2010) provide an overview of this literature from a monetary policy perspective.
- The increased interest in fiscal policy as a stabilization tool after 2009 also led to an explosion in fiscal policy research (Ramey 2019). The modelling of fiscal policy was very limited in models such as Smets and Wouters (2007). In the years since 2009, the modelling of fiscal policy has been greatly expanded to include a range of different fiscal policy instruments, the role of debt, the interaction of monetary and fiscal policy and an examination of the fiscal multiplier both at and away from the zero lower bound. Leeper, Traum, and Walker (2017) provide an extensive evaluation of the government spending multiplier in a variety of medium scale New Keynesian models.
- A number of papers have introduced more complex production structures, for example by including multiple sectors or allowing for an input-output structure where, as in the real world, the output of some firms is used as an intermediate input into the production of other goods. Some examples include Basu (1995), Nakamura and Steinsson (2010), Carvalho, Lee, and Park (2021) and Pastern, Schoenle, and Weber (2020). La'O and Tahbaz-Salehi (2022) study optimal monetary policy in a production network.
- There has also been increasing interest in imperfect information and departures from rational expectations, especially in recent years. Contributions based on incomplete information of some form include Morris and Shin (2002, 2006), Mankiw and Reis (2002), Woodford (2003), Nimark (2008), Angeletos and La'O (2009) and Angeletos and Lian (2018). These papers tend to maintain rational expectations but incorporate incomplete information or lack of common knowledge across agents. Other approaches explicitly depart from rational expectations and there are various ways of capturing non-rational behaviour, informed by a rapidly growing literature in experimental and behavioural microeconomics. Examples include Sims (2003) ('rational inattention'), Farhi and Werning (2019) ('Level-k Thinking'), García-Schmidt and Woodford (2019) ('Reflective Equilibrium') and Gabaix's Behavioral New Keynesian Model (2020) (based on so-called Cognitive Discounting).

18.4 HETEROGENEOUS AGENT NEW KEYNESIAN MACROECONOMICS

18.4.1 Introduction

Until the Global Financial Crisis in 2008, medium-scale New Keynesian models were often the main workhorse model for business cycle research. These models were also used in numerous central banks around the world for forecasting and analysing the impact of policy. By and large these were still representative agent models, or

BOX 18.2 The hybrid Phillips curve

The hybrid Phillips curve is an example of how models used in the policy arena (for example Smets and Wouters (2003, 2007) seek to overcome unsatisfactory features of both the adaptive expectations Phillips curve (it is empirically successful, but is subject to the Lucas critique; lacks microfoundations and rational expectations; and lacks a channel for credibility to affect inflation) and the NKPC (which is forward looking and therefore not subject to the Lucas critique; has microfoundations and rational expectations with a role for credibility, but counterfactual empirical predictions). The hybrid includes forward-looking inflation expectations but acknowledges that inflation appears to be persistent or inertial, i.e. that it depends on lagged values of itself.

$$\pi_t = \lambda \pi_{t-1} + (1-\lambda)E_t \pi_{t+1} + \Lambda \alpha x_t. \qquad \text{(hybrid PC)}$$

The hybrid Phillips curve can be rationalized by the assumption that some proportion, λ, of firms use a backward-looking rule of thumb to set their inflation expectations while the remainder use forward-looking expectations. This parallels the consumption function discussed at the end of Chapter 1, where a proportion of households are assumed to use rule of thumb behaviour and base their consumption decisions on current income, while the rest are modelled as using the forward-looking permanent income hypothesis. Another frequently used rationalization is the idea of habit formation in consumption, which produces slow adjustment to income shocks. These sources of persistence are necessary for NK DSGE models to fit the data. They considerably complicate the models and make it difficult to uncover the role played by the microfoundations that stem from the origins of the model in the RBC modelling tradition.

included only a limited degree of heterogeneity.[33] On the policy front, during the Great Moderation from the 1990s until 2007 macroeconomic stabilization policy was in the hands of central banks, and there was little discussion about the distributional implications of policy, or how inequality might affect the way different policies operate.

The early generation of RBC models focused on a representative agent in part because economists did not have the tools or the computing power to solve models with meaningful heterogeneity. In part fuelled by new solution methods for DSGE models and improvements in computing power, a range of heterogeneous agent models started to be developed, building on important contributions by, for example, Bewley (1986), Imrohoroğlu (1989), Huggett (1993) and Aiyagari (1994).

---

[33] Examples include models with borrowers and lenders/savers (e.g. Bernanke, Gertler, and Gilchrist 1999, and Iacoviello 2005), and models that include a certain proportion of non-optimizing households who consume all their income each period (e.g. Galí, López-Salido, and Vallés 2007).

Although the production side of these models often still resembled the RBC model, households now face uncertainty about their own individual income, and incomes will differ across households. In these models, households are not able to fully insure themselves against income fluctuations, such as spells of unemployment. As a result, consumption cannot be fully smoothed as the permanent income hypothesis would predict.

The inability to fully insure against income fluctuations is usually captured by some form of financial market imperfection like a credit constraint. These models are therefore known as 'incomplete markets' models because, as in this book, it is not possible to write contracts that deliver full income insurance. These models usually still assumed flexible prices and perfectly competitive firms. While a large literature has developed studying issues of inequality, redistribution, retirement, social security, welfare and tax policy (see, for example, Heathcote, Storesletten, and Violante 2009 for a review) this literature often proceeded independently of New Keynesian macroeconomics.

Macroeconomists have, therefore, been interested in heterogeneity and inequality for many decades but two challenges prevented the unification of these different strands of research. First, business cycle models with nominal rigidities, aggregate fluctuations and heterogeneous agents are technically demanding to solve. Second, it was not clear to what degree heterogeneity would quantitatively affect aggregate outcomes. Krusell and Smith (1998), for example, showed that a heterogeneous agent model with aggregate technology shocks (in the style of the RBC model) produced very similar macroeconomic dynamics as the representative agent model. This is because, in their model, aggregate dynamics are dominated by households who hold the majority of the economy's wealth. These households are able to smooth consumption optimally. Borrowing-constrained households, on the other hand, only account for a small share of aggregate wealth and consumption in their model.

The Global Financial Crisis brought inequality and distributional issues to the forefront of the policy debate. The collapse in the housing market, and the subsequent recession, had very different effects across the population. Inequality exacerbated the crisis, but the crisis also produced very unequal outcomes. Pre-crisis differences in income and wealth were reflected in big differences in the composition of household balance sheets. This led to sharp and unequal declines in consumer spending through large and heterogeneous marginal propensities to consume (see Mian, Rao, and Sufi 2013). The fall in economic activity also produced very different labour market outcomes depending on occupation, skills and income. Monetary and fiscal policy affected some groups more than others.

A new revolution in macroeconomic modelling has therefore taken place over the last 15 years. The research frontier has sought to unify the following: (i) the methodological innovations of the RBC revolution, in particular the focus on optimization and general equilibrium discussed in Section 18.2, (ii) an explicit consideration of heterogeneity, inequality and incomplete markets and (iii) Keynesian business cycle elements such as sticky prices and wages, inefficient recessions and booms, and a role for monetary and fiscal stabilization policy, as discussed in Section 18.3. But keeping track of the entire distribution of income and wealth, and how these evolve with aggregate shocks and macroeconomic policy is challenging. Progress has been greatly advanced by new solution techniques and improvements in computational power (see, for instance, Ahn, Kaplan, Moll, Winberry, and Wolf (2018), Reiter (2009) and Auclert, Bardóczy, Rognlie, and Straub (2021) for examples).

This section provides a high-level overview of the resulting Heterogeneous Agent New Keynesian literature. These models generate an interaction between the distribution of income and wealth and the business cycle. As a result, numerous important questions about the relationship between inequality and macroeconomic policy can now be explored. There are various important early examples in this field, which we touch on again later.[34] But as a prominent example that closely relates to the NK model from Section 18.3, we first discuss the Heterogeneous Agent New Keynesian (HANK) model of Kaplan, Moll and Violante (2018).

18.4.2 The Heterogeneous Agent New Keynesian model

In this section we describe the main elements of the Heterogeneous Agent New Keynesian (HANK) model by Kaplan, Moll, and Violante (2018) (KMV). We then discuss some of the main mechanisms and the role of, and implications for, inequality in the following section.

This model incorporates the main elements of household behaviour from the earlier heterogeneous agent incomplete markets literature, and combines this with the production structure from the New Keynesian model with sticky prices. The 'heterogeneous agent' part of the model refers to households; the firm side of the model is similar to the NK model we discussed in Section 18.3 although, like the RBC model and medium-scale NK models, the KMV model also includes capital and investment. In this section we therefore focus on the household side.[35]

The household block of the KMV HANK model is based on Kaplan and Violante (2014), which we discussed in the introduction to this chapter. The main assumptions on the household side are as follows:

1. As in the RBC and NK models, households consume and work (supply labour). Households are ex-ante identical (e.g. they have the same preferences and face the same constraints in principle) but have different experiences over time. In particular, households face idiosyncratic variation in their labour income, for example due to unemployment. As a result, different households earn different amounts at different points in time. There is persistence in how much a household earns over time, but earnings are also subject to jumps that occur randomly. The earnings distribution is designed to match key aspects of US Social Security Administration

[34] This include papers by Oh and Reis (2012), Werning (2015), McKay and Reis (2016), McKay, Nakamura, and Steinsson (2016), Gornemann, Kuester, and Nakajima (2016), Den Haan, Rendal, and Riegler (2018) and Guerrieri and Lorenzoni (2017), Auclert (2019), Bayer, Lutticke, Pham-Dao, and Tjaden (2019), Luetticke (2021), Ravn and Sterk (2021).

[35] As we will discuss later, there is also a growing literature focusing on firm heterogeneity and monetary policy. Examples include models by Ottonello and Winberry (2020) and Jeenas (2019).

data on household income. In short, the model features an empirically relevant distribution of income, and this distribution is a key input into the model.

2. Households cannot fully insure themselves against variation in their income. When household income falls, households cannot fully smooth consumption. A large body of empirical work supports the idea that consumption is relatively responsive to unexpected changes in income (see Chapter 1 and Jappelli and Pistaferri 2010 for a review).
3. Consumption may be highly responsive to unexpected temporary income fluctuations because financial markets are incomplete. Households can save in two ways: (a) using a low-return liquid asset, like cash, money in a bank account or government bonds, and (b) a high-return but illiquid asset that is hard to access, like housing wealth or a pension. If the household wants to withdraw money from the illiquid asset, they have to pay a transaction cost. The liquid asset is useful for consumption smoothing, but the illiquid asset cannot be used for this purpose without incurring costs. The illiquid asset is, however, useful for longer-term wealth accumulation. Households can borrow in liquid assets, but only up to a borrowing limit. An example of this is credit card borrowing or an (unsecured) personal loan, where there is typically a maximum credit limit.[36] The distinction between liquid and illiquid assets is designed to capture an important aspect of household balance sheets in the data. Table 18.2 for example—drawn from Kaplan, Violante, and Weidner (2014)—shows that in many countries even the median household has very little liquid wealth. But they still have sizable illiquid wealth, often related to housing.
4. The interest rate on borrowing is higher than the savings rate. One rationale for this would be intermediation costs in the banking sector (as explained in Chapter 5).
5. Because households have different income experiences, their balance sheets also have different compositions (of liquid and illiquid assets) over time. The model is calibrated to match inequality in the US wealth distribution using US household level data on household balance sheets from the Survey of Consumer Finances.

The production side of the model is very similar to the NK model outlined in Section 18.3. The main difference is the inclusion of capital in production. The supply side of the model can still be characterized by a New Keynesian Phillips curve.

On the fiscal side, the government taxes household labour income at a proportional income tax rate. The government uses taxes to buy government goods and services, pay interest on government debt and finance transfers to households. Monetary policy follows a Taylor Rule very similar to equation 18.3 in the NK model in Section 18.3.

[36] In this model borrowing only occurs in the liquid asset, i.e. debt is unsecured. Other papers in the literature (that we will discuss in more detail in Section 18.5) have also incorporated secured borrowing, for example where debt is secured against collateral like housing. This can introduce other channels if looser monetary policy raises asset prices and therefore relaxes borrowing constraints as explained in the discussion of the financial accelerator in Chapter 8.

	United States		United Kingdom		Germany		France	
	Median	Percent positive	Median	Percent positive	Median	Percent positive	Median	Percent positive
Income (age 22–59)	47040	94.8	29340	97.9	35444	99.4	31518	99.9
Net worth	56721	88.3	187157	88.0	46798	94.9	108976	96.6
Net liquid wealth	1714	75.0	2111	63.2	1319	85.3	1453	92.5
Cash & transaction accounts	2640	92.3	2639	76.6	1154	87.6	1255	95.3
Directly held stocks	0	14.2	0	16.0	0	11.0	0	15.1
Directly held bonds	0	1.4	0	15.4	0	5.0	0	1.5
Revolving credit card debt	0	38.2	0	40.5	0	22.5	0	7.6
Net illiquid wealth	52000	76.1	174999	84.3	39306	87.6	104214	92.2
Housing net of mortgages	29000	62.9	81400	67.7	0	47.6	86372	60.7
Retirement accounts	1508	52.6	58560	76.6	0	24.5	0	3.9
Life insurance	0	18.6	0	11.0	0	49.3	0	37.8

Table 18.2 Household income, liquid and illiquid wealth holdings, and portfolio composition, sample of countries.
Note: All values are reported in local currency units.
Source: Reproduced and adapted from Kaplan, Violante, and Weidner (2014).

18.4.3 Key features and 'wealthy hand to mouth' households

Although KMV is not the only paper to consider incomplete markets and nominal rigidities, this particular setup allows for an empirically realistic model of the distribution of both household earnings and wealth in the economy. In fact, this interaction of household-specific income fluctuations, together with the two asset structure plays a central role in this HANK model and allows the model to generate many more households with a high marginal propensity to consume (MPC). Broadly speaking, a number of different types of households emerge, as outlined in Violante (2021).

First, there is a group of households with very low liquid assets and who derive most of their income from labour and possibly government transfers. They are more likely to exhibit a high marginal propensity to consume. These are often called 'hand to mouth' households.

Second, a group of richer middle class households who choose to hold little wealth in liquid assets, but have a sizable amount of illiquid assets. We could think of these as younger and middle-aged households who own a house (usually with a mortgage, see Cloyne, Ferreira, and Surico 2020) and/or who may be saving for retirement using an illiquid retirement account like a pension plan. These households face a trade-off: to exploit the benefits of the high-return asset, they will then have relatively few liquid assets for consumption smoothing. These households end up choosing to save little in the liquid asset and act in a hand to mouth manner in response to unexpected income changes. These households are still relatively wealthy and Kaplan and Violante (2014) refer to these as 'wealthy hand to mouth' households.

Third, a group of richer households who do not act in a hand to mouth manner. But these households still fear hitting a borrowing constraint if their income falls in the future. These households still want to save 'for a rainy day'. This motive is called precautionary savings, a concept we introduced in Chapter 1.

Fourth, a group of wealthy households. For these households the precautionary savings motive is small. These households also have a low marginal propensity to consume and act more like the representative agent permanent income consumer in the NK model from Section 18.3. For these households capital and savings income is also very important.

The NK model in Section 18.3 heavily relied on an 'intertemporal substitution' mechanism: the direct incentive to save less and consume more when interest rates fall. Relative to the NK model, the HANK model features various other channels, which vary in strength across households. The relative importance of all the different channels will depend on the distribution of income and wealth in the economy. For example, when calibrated to US data, the model generates a sizable proportion of hand to mouth households, and this plays a particularly important role.

The earlier NK literature had incorporated some degree of heterogeneity using two types of agents (what Kaplan, Moll, and Violante (2018) call two agent NK models or TANK for short). For example, Galí, Lopez-Salido, and Vallés (2007) extend the NK model from Section 18.3 to include hand to mouth alongside fully optimizing households. But hand to mouth agents in this framework are simply assumed to consume all their labour income. These households have a marginal propensity to consume equal to one by assumption. By contrast, in KMV's model, the distribution of MPCs arises as an implication of income inequality and balance sheet heterogeneity.

Earlier (non-NK) heterogeneous agent macroeconomic models had also considered how to generate higher MPCs through borrowing constraints and income risk. But many of these models only include a single liquid asset, so there was no role for the asset composition of the household's balance sheet. This turns out to make a big difference. For example, Kaplan and Violante (2018) note that, in a one asset variant of the KMV model, the average MPC is only 4%, which means that for an unexpected $100 income windfall, the average household only consumes $4.[37] Common solutions to raise the MPC in one asset heterogeneous agent models often generated more 'poor' households than there are in the data.

By introducing more realistic balance sheet heterogeneity and the concept of the wealthy hand to mouth, Kaplan and Violante (2014) and Kaplan, Moll, and Violante (2018) are able to generate large and heterogeneous MPCs with a realistic income and wealth distribution. The KMV model generates an average quarterly MPC of 15–20%. This lines up with empirical evidence from Johnson, Parker, and Souleles (2006), Misra and Surico (2014) and Kaplan and Violante (2014) on the consumption effects of temporary tax rebates in the United States. Misra and Surico (2014) also document

[37] In the representative agent model the MPC is even lower because households are permanent income consumers, as discussed in Chapter 1. Kaplan and Violante (2018) note that, assuming a 0.5% quarterly real interest rate, the representative agent model's MPC is only around 0.5%.

	Liquid wealth		Illiquid wealth	
Moment	Data	Model	Data	Model
Top 0.1 percent share	17	2.3	12	7
Top 1 percent share	47	18	33	40
Top 10 percent share	86	75	70	88
Bottom 50 percent share	−4	−3	3	0.1
Bottom 25 percent share	−5	−3	0	0
Gini coefficient	0.98	0.86	0.81	0.82

Table 18.3 Wealth shares generated by KMV HANK model and corresponding empirical data from the Survey of Consumer Finances.

Note: The authors used data from the 2004 Survey of Consumer Finances (SCF) to obtain empirical statistics. The table shows how well their model matches wealth shares observed in the population.

Source: Reproduced from Table 5 in Kaplan, G., Moll, B., and Violante, G. L. (2018). Monetary policy according to HANK. *American Economic Review*, **108**(3), 697–743. https://doi.org/10.1257/aer.20160042. Reproduced using the replication package of Kaplan, Moll, and Violante (2018). Copyright American Economic Association; reproduced with permission of the *American Economic Review*.

significant heterogeneity in the MPC across households. Mian, Rao, and Sufi (2013) showed that large and heterogeneous MPCs played an important role in the Great Recession. Wealthy hand to mouth households are also an important share of the population in the data. Kaplan, Violante, and Weidner (2014) show that around 1/3 of households in the US may be hand to mouth, with two-thirds of these being wealthy.

The KMV model is calibrated to capture the US income and wealth distribution. Table 18.3 from KMV shows the shares of liquid and illiquid wealth at different points of the wealth distribution in the United States in 2004, together with the associated statistics produced by the model. The model is able to replicate key aspects of the data for most of the distribution. Based on this empirically realistic distribution of wealth, Figure 18.10 shows heterogeneity in the marginal propensity to consume across households with different liquid and illiquid asset holdings. The highest MPCs occur for households with zero liquid wealth, and the MPC remains high even when these households have sizable illiquid wealth. There is also a second spike in the MPC for households who are at the borrowing constraint, although this is only relevant for a relatively small number of households. The model can therefore generate a sizable number of hand to mouth households with a high marginal propensity to consume, consistent with the data.

It is worth noting that, in this model, hand to mouth behaviour is the optimal response of households given their income risk and the structure of their balance sheets. Hand to mouth behaviour is not a fixed assumption (e.g. by assuming that some households consume all their labour income each period). This helps address the Lucas critique discussed in Chapter 4 and earlier in this chapter. If we *assume* that a household is hand to mouth, they will *always* consume the same amount from an income windfall. Instead, in these heterogeneous agent models, the MPC is not

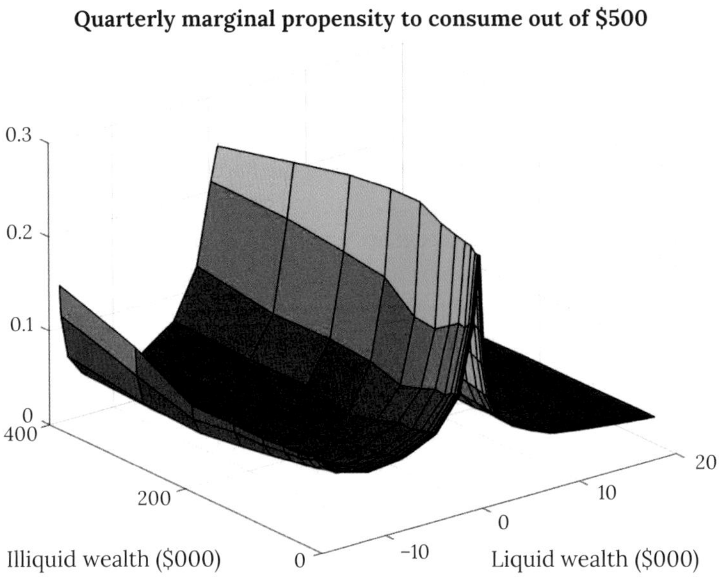

Figure 18.10 The distribution of marginal propensities to consume in the HANK model.

Source: Figure 2(b) from Kaplan, G., Moll, B., and Violante, G. L. (2018). Monetary policy according to HANK. *American Economic Review*, **108**(3), 697–743. https://doi.org/10.1257/aer.20160042. Reproduced using the replication package of Kaplan, Moll, and Violante (2018). Copyright American Economic Association; reproduced with permission of the *American Economic Review*.

invariant to the policy intervention. For example, as noted earlier, in Kaplan and Violante (2014), a larger tax cut per household increases the chance that a household might save some of the windfall. More generally, changes in the income and wealth distribution will also change the economy's average marginal propensity to consume.

18.4.4 **Inequality and the effects of monetary policy**

How does the transmission of monetary policy change in KMV's HANK model relative to the NK model from Section 18.3? The model now features a range of possible transmission channels, and the importance of these mechanisms is closely related to the distribution of income and wealth in the economy. KMV identify two broad types of effects: direct and indirect effects from an interest rate change. Direct effects include the direct incentive to adjust consumption vs. savings in response to interest rate changes, what we called 'intertemporal substitution' in Section 18.3 and also any direct income effect from the interest rate change. But, in this model, monetary policy also leads to a number of indirect channels, as in Chapter 1. For example, cuts in interest rates lead to higher demand and output. To produce more, firms will demand more labour and household income will increase. This rise in income makes it possible to consume more, and the strength of this effect is governed by the marginal propensity to consume, as in the IS curve in Chapter 1. We now explore these direct vs. indirect channels in more detail.

Inequality matters for the way monetary policy works

When interest rates are cut, do households consume more because saving is now relatively less attractive (the intertemporal substitution effect) or because they have more money to spend (an indirect effect)? KMV show that in the representative agent NK model, the direct effect accounts for 99% of the impact of an interest rate cut on consumption.

In HANK models with richer heterogeneity in income and wealth, many other channels come into play. Figure 18.11, from Violante (2021), shows that different mechanisms matter for different parts of the liquid wealth distribution.

Interest rate cuts may stimulate consumption directly for some households, but this will also lead to higher aggregate demand, more production and increased labour income overall. For households with relatively low liquid assets (poor and wealthy hand to mouth households), the marginal propensity to consume is high. Households with a high MPC consume this additional income, leading to further increases in aggregate

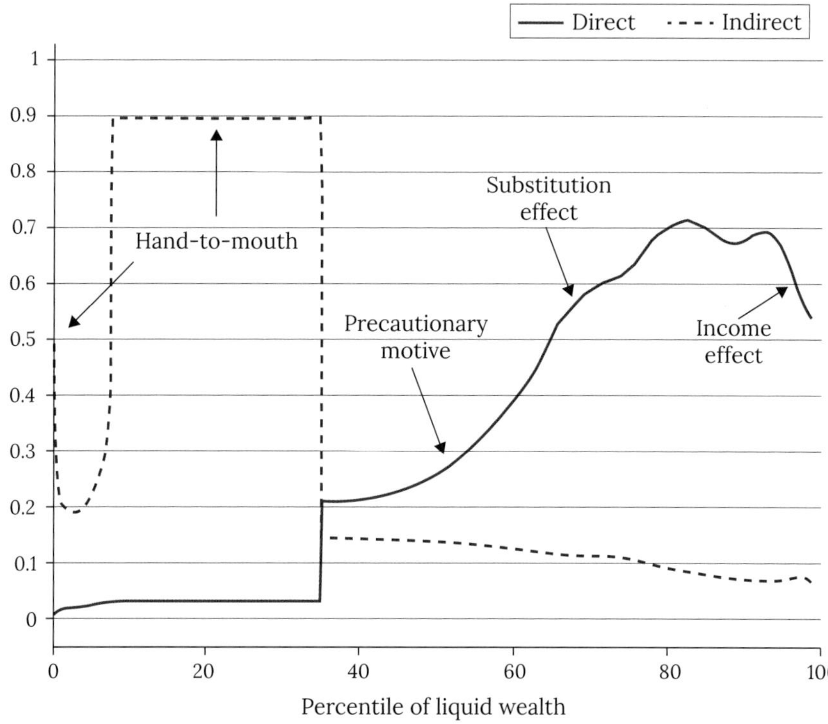

Figure 18.11 Strength of different mechanisms by household liquid wealth. The figure shows the response of consumption to a monetary policy change decomposed into direct effects (e.g. intertemporal substitution) and indirect effects (e.g. via changes in labour earnings).

Source: Violante, G. (2021). What have we learned from HANK models, thus far? (conference presentation). *Proceedings of the ECB Forum on Central Banking*, 29 October 2021. https://www.ecb.europa.eu/pub/conferences/html/20210928_ecb_forum_on_central_banking.en.html.

demand and output. We now have a Keynesian multiplier effect that is absent from the NK model in Section 18.3. This can be seen in the left-hand side of Figure 18.11. The indirect effects via higher labour earnings are large and the direct effects via, for example, intertemporal substitution, are small. In short, just as in the 3-equation model earlier in this book, these households consume more because they have more income, not because saving is less attractive.

As liquid wealth rises, the direct effects start to kick in. But in the middle of the distribution the desire to save less and consume more (the intertemporal substitution channel) is offset by a rise in the precautionary motive. These households may not be constrained today, but they still fear a bad shock to their income that might make them constrained in the future. As a result, these households do not want to reduce savings too much as interest rates fall. As households become wealthier, intertemporal substitution effects start to dominate. For the very richest, who derive more income from capital and savings, lower interest rates may have a *negative* effect.

What is clear from Figure 18.11 is that the transmission of monetary policy to consumption is much more complex than in Section 18.3. The ultimate outcomes of an interest rate change will depend on the relative strength of all these effects which, in turn, depend on the particular distribution of income and wealth in the economy at any point in time.

One strength of the overall modelling approach, which dates back to the original RBC methodology discussed in Section 18.2, is that the model can be calibrated to real world data and quantitative predictions can be generated. In the case of KMV, the model is calibrated to match the US distribution of income and wealth. Figure 18.12 then shows the impulse response function for overall household consumption. Overall, interest rates fall by around 0.5–0.75 percentage points and remain lower than the long-run level for around 8 quarters. Aggregate consumption increases by around 0.4 percent on impact. But, unlike the representative agent results in Section 18.3, this average effect is driven by a number of different mechanisms. The red dotted line shows the contribution of the direct effects, such as the intertemporal substitution channel. This accounts for around 20% of the overall effect on consumption over the first year.[38]

The other lines decompose different indirect effects. First, the dashed light blue line shows the effect coming from the rise in labour income. This accounts for around 50% of the overall consumption effect. This makes a sizable contribution because, as household income expands, high MPC households consume more. Second, the red dot-dashed line shows a 'portfolio reallocation effect' which comes from the relative movements in the return on illiquid vs. liquid assets and the change in stock prices, although this effect is small overall.

The third type of indirect effect relates to the interaction of monetary and fiscal policy. In the main version of the KMV model, lower interest rates lower interest payments on government debt. The government has to decide what to do with

[38] In contrast, a similar figure for the representative agent model would show that the overwhelming majority of the effect would be driven by direct effects. The majority of the effects in the 3-equation model from earlier in the book are also indirect effects.

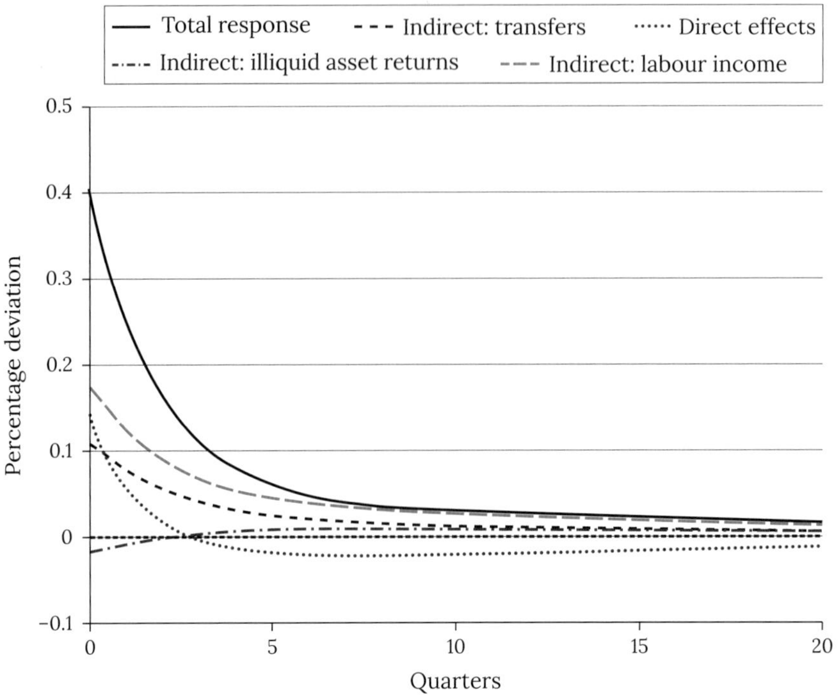

Figure 18.12 The response of average consumption to an interest rate cut that lowers interest rates by around 0.5–0.75 percentage points on impact. The interest rate path looks similar to the example in Figure 18.8. The figure above shows the effect on average consumption decomposed into direct and indirect effects.

Source: Figure 4(b) from Kaplan, G., Moll, B., and Violante, G. L. (2018). Monetary policy according to HANK. *American Economic Review*, **108**(3), 697–743. https://doi.org/10.1257/aer.20160042. Reproduced using the replication package of Kaplan, Moll, and Violante (2018). Copyright American Economic Association; reproduced with permission of the *American Economic Review*.

these additional resources. In the model this is captured by a fiscal policy rule. The assumption in the baseline KMV model is that the government automatically redistributes these savings to households as additional transfers.[39] The effect of this is shown in the dashed dark blue line in Figure 18.12. HANK models like KMV therefore feature a breakdown of Ricardian equivalence. One implication of Ricardian equivalence, as discussed in Chapter 7, is that temporary transfers to households should not affect consumption for permanent income hypothesis consumers. But, in this model, additional fiscal transfers affect consumption because some consumers have a high MPC. HANK models therefore feature a much more complex interaction

[39] In the model this happens as a result of the chosen fiscal policy rule, although in reality the fiscal response is not necessarily automatic.

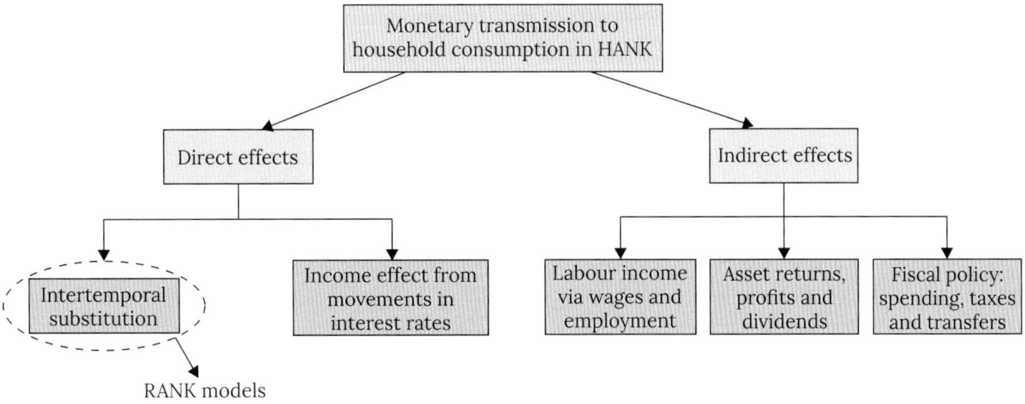

Figure 18.13 A stylized representation of the various direct and indirect effects in the representative agent NK model (RANK) and KMV's heterogeneous agent New Keynesian model (HANK).

between monetary and fiscal policy.[40] The indirect effect on consumption from this interaction is relatively large in Figure 18.12.

How the government chooses to use the additional resources generated by the fall in interest rates therefore matters for the transmission of monetary policy. Instead of raising transfers, we could assume that government spending increases, proportional tax rates fall or that some government debt is repaid. When taxes or spending adjust, the total indirect effects remain around 80%. When the government repays debt, these indirect effects are somewhat lower at around 60%. Why is this the case? When taxes fall or government spending rises, the fiscal authority is reinforcing the rise in aggregate demand. But this is not the case when government debt is repaid.

Figure 18.13, based on Moll (2020), shows a stylized representation of the different channels at play. As can be seen the main direct channel in the representative agent NK (RANK) model is intertemporal substitution. The other parts of the figure capture the various other mechanisms that are decomposed in Figure 18.12 and discussed above.

Does heterogeneity amplify or dampen the effects of monetary policy?

Given all these different mechanisms, are the effects of monetary policy larger or smaller in HANK models relative to representative agent models? The answer is: it depends. A greater role for indirect effects does not necessarily mean the model generates larger effects overall. For example, a larger share of hand to mouth households

[40] The assumption that savings on debt interest are distributed to households as lump-sum transfers is usually made for simplicity. Alternative options such as adjustments to government spending or distortionary taxes would lead to a variety of additional effects. Kaplan, Moll, and Violante (2018) and Alves, Kaplan, Moll, and Violante (2020) also consider a number of additional fiscal policy rules and show that the choice of fiscal policy rule has important implications for the quantitative size of the indirect effects. This highlights the importance of considering the interaction of monetary and fiscal policy in these models.

will increase the indirect effect, but will also potentially dampen the direct effect. In general, whether monetary policy is amplified or dampened depends on the mechanisms in the model, the distribution and composition of income and wealth, and how different sources of income are exposed to business cycle fluctuations.

One of the key determinants of whether the effects of an interest rate change are amplified (relative to the representative agent model) is whether the income of high MPC households is more exposed to aggregate fluctuations. Intuitively, amplification will occur if income is redistributed towards households who also have a higher marginal propensity to consume. Empirical evidence supports this notion that household income may be unequally exposed to macroeconomic shocks, for example low-income households may be more likely to become unemployed during a recession (Guvenen, Schulhofer-Wohl, Song, and Yogo 2017, and Patterson 2022). A number of papers show that this unequal exposure of earnings can amplify the effects of monetary policy in HANK models if income is redistributed towards high MPC households (for example Auclert 2019, Bilbiie 2020, Alves, Kaplan, Moll, and Violante 2020, and Slacalek, Tristani, and Violante 2020).[41] Households may also differ in risk attitudes, for example in their marginal propensity to save in risky capital, as explored by Kekre and Lenel (2022). The response of investment will then be influenced by whether income is redistributed towards or away from households with a higher propensity to take risk.

The nature and composition of household income also matters for macroeconomic outcomes in HANK models. Alves, Kaplan, Moll, and Violante (2020) show that the overall effects of monetary policy depend on how profits are distributed across the population, and how these are reinvested. If dividends are reinvested in illiquid assets, monetary policy changes may have a smaller effect on the economy relative to the representative agent case. Bilbiie, Känzig, and Surico (2022) show that capital inequality across households reinforces the macroeconomic effects of income inequality in response to aggregate demand shocks. Broer, Hansen, Krusell, and Öberg (2020) show that the source of nominal rigidity is important for the redistributional effects between capitalists and workers when interest rates are cut. For example, when prices are sticky, capitalists lose out and workers gain. This is because when some firms cannot adjust price, their price-cost markups fall as the economy expands and wages rise.[42]

Finally, whether HANK models generate amplification crucially depends on the interaction with fiscal policy, as noted earlier. When interest rates fall, it matters how the government chooses to distribute the benefits of lower interest payments on government debt. Alves, Kaplan, Moll, and Violante (2020) examine this using a number of different scenarios and show that the overall consumption response to monetary policy changes can be amplified by a factor of two depending on how fiscal policy reacts.

[41] Werning (2015) and McKay, Nakamura, and Steinsson (2016, 2017) also discuss related points in the context of forward guidance policies.

[42] This response of firm profits also occurs in the simple 3-equation NK model when prices are sticky, as mentioned in Section 18.3. Broer, Hansen, Krusell, and Öberg (2020) also regard this mechanism as 'implausible' and therefore view a mechanism based on rigid wages as more consistent with the data.

An important implication of all these points is that the conduct of monetary stabilization policy may now be considerably more complex, especially if much of the effect works through indirect channels that are not directly under the influence of the central bank. HANK models show that there are many potential channels of transmission. The effects can be larger or smaller than representative agent models and, in reality, these effects could vary over time with the distribution of income and wealth in the economy. While this complexity may make monetary policy harder to conduct, it underscores the need to understand different sources of heterogeneity and inequality in the economy when assessing the likely impact of an interest rate change.

Monetary policy has distributional consequences

The distribution of income and wealth is a key input into the model. But inequality is also an outcome. As we have seen, in HANK models like KMV, different households react in different ways to changes in monetary policy. In KMV, this heterogeneity is closely linked to pre-existing inequality in income, wealth and the composition of household balance sheets. But a further implication of this is that monetary policy itself will potentially have an effect on the distribution of consumption, income and wealth.

As an example, Kaplan and Violante (2018a) look at how consumption responds to an interest rate rise across the wealth distribution. Households lower down in the wealth distribution are most exposed to the indirect effects coming from labour income. These households see the largest drop in consumption when monetary policy tightens. The consumption response of the bottom 25% is more than double the consumption response of the top 25%. The very wealthy see very little movement in consumption, partly because higher interest rates actually increases their consumption. Tighter monetary policy raises consumption inequality. Empirical evidence from Coibion, Gorodnichenko, Kueng, and Silvia (2017) also shows that increases in interest rates tend to raise consumption inequality, although the effect is relatively modest.

Further empirical evidence on the distributional effects of monetary policy comes from Cloyne, Ferreira, and Surico (2020). This paper shows that whether a household owns their home outright or owns with a mortgage is a useful proxy for the composition of the household's balance sheet. In particular, mortgagors tend to have little liquid assets but are still relatively wealthy: they tend to be wealthy hand to mouth. Outright homeowners have sizable liquid and illiquid assets and may be closer to the standard unconstrained permanent income consumer.

As shown in Figure 18.14, mortgagors make a much larger adjustment in consumption expenditures when interest rates are cut by 0.25 percentage points. In both the UK and the US, mortgagor non-durable consumption rises by 0.2% after three years and durable expenditure rises by over 1%. Outright homeowners see a much smaller effect and it is not statistically significant. The non-durable consumption response is even negative. These empirical estimates broadly line up with the predictions of HANK models and show that monetary policy has important distributional implications in theory and in the data. Other related work includes Wong (2021), who examines the

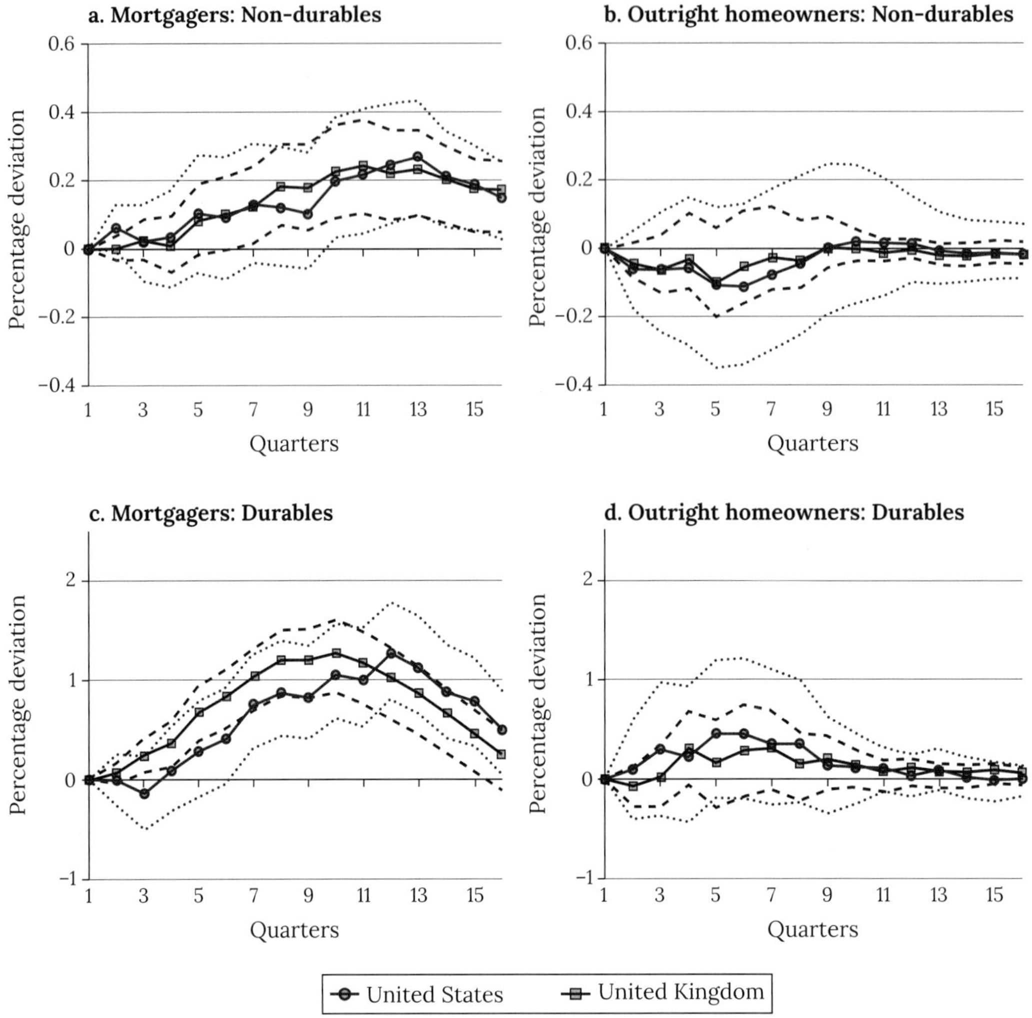

Figure 18.14 The response of non-durable and durable expenditure to a 0.25 percentage point reduction in the interest rate. The responses are split by housing tenure status and shown for the United States (red circles) and the United Kingdom (blue squares). Figure reproduced using the replication package from Cloyne, Ferreira and Surico (2020).

role of mortgage refinancing, and Holm, Paul, and Tischbirek (2021) who explore the transmission channels using administrative data from Norway.

By generating movements in asset prices monetary policy may also affect the gains from holding capital and therefore wealth inequality, as mentioned above. On the empirical side, as discussed in Chapter 6 for example, Bartscher, Kuhn, Schularick, and Wachtel (2021) study the effects of monetary policy on employment and wealth and, in particular, examine the distributional consequences of monetary policy for racial inequality. They find that loose monetary policy raises the employment of Black households by more than white households, but that this is by far outweighed by the larger wealth gains of white households.

18.5 AN ACTIVE RESEARCH AGENDA

Once we move beyond the representative agent framework, there are potentially many channels through which macroeconomic fluctuations and policies might affect the economy and the distribution of consumption, income and wealth. In Section 18.4 we used the model of Kaplan, Moll, and Violante (2018) as a prominent example of how heterogeneity might influence the transmission of monetary policy.

Heterogeneity, inequality and business cycles is a lively and active area of macroeconomic research. The wider literature has, for example, been considering other macroeconomic policies such as quantitative easing, forward guidance and fiscal policy, and has also broadened the focus towards firm heterogeneity. Depending on the focus, not all papers in this wider literature necessarily incorporate price stickiness or the full set of New Keynesian features. Furthermore, while households in Section 18.4 are heterogeneous 'ex-post' (they have different experiences over time), other papers in the literature also allow households to be ex-ante heterogeneous (e.g. because of different preferences, behavioural traits and so forth), which may also be important for inequality.

This section provides a flavour of some of the interesting questions tackled by recent academic research. It is, however, a large and rapidly growing field and this section is not intended to be a full review of the state of the literature.

18.5.1 The macroeconomic consequences of debt and leverage

Should policy makers worry about the strength and composition of household balance sheets? For example, should policy makers worry about household leverage and the distribution of debt in the economy? The Global Financial Crisis starkly illustrated how weak household balance sheets can amplify economic crises (see Chapters 8 and 9 and, for instance, Mian, Rao, and Sufi 2013). HANK models are well suited to understanding these issues. The distribution of mortgage debt, the differential exposure of different borrowers to house price and inflation movements and the correlation of these factors with marginal propensities to consume have all featured heavily in research and policy debates in the last 15 years.

Recent research on the role of housing and mortgage debt in the heterogeneous agent tradition, which reflects the large body of empirical work on the housing channel of monetary policy (surveyed in Duca, Muellbauer, and Murphy 2020), includes: Hedlund, Karahan, Mitman, and Ozkan (2017) (monetary policy has an important house price channel and is more powerful in a highly levered economy); Garriga, Kydland, and Šustek (2017), Calza, Monacelli and Stracca (2013) and Guren, Krishnamurthy, and McQuade (2021) (monetary policy is more powerful when mortgages have adjustable rather than fixed interest rates, a key policy issue in 2009); Beraja, Fuster, Hurst, and Vavra (2019) (limited housing equity restricts refinancing ability and may dampen the power of monetary policy); Wong (2021), Eichenbaum, Rebelo, and Wong (2022) and Berger, Milbradt, Tourre, and Vavra (2021) (mortgage refinancing behaviour can account for why the spending of younger households is more sensitive to monetary policy, and why monetary policy may have weaker effects after a period of low interest rates) and Guren, McKay, Nakamura, and Steinsson (2021) (the household consumption response to house price fluctuations is sizable, but somewhat smaller in the 2000s than earlier periods).[43]

Aside from housing market specific channels, Auclert (2019) highlights two further channels related to household balance sheets. First, surprise inflation—for example generated by expansionary monetary policy—can redistribute wealth from savers to borrowers, which could have aggregate implications if borrowers have a higher MPC (Auclert 2019, Doepke and Schneider 2006). Furthermore, Auclert (2019) shows that there could be an interest rate exposure channel, for example, for households who tend to have long-term borrowing contracts.

18.5.2 **Does income risk matter for macroeconomic outcomes?**

Households may face different income *risks* over the business cycle. For example, the risk of unemployment tends to rise in recessions, especially for some types of workers. Because heterogeneous agent macroeconomic models typically feature a precautionary savings motive (households 'save for a rainy day'), they are well-suited to understanding the consequences of changes in risk.

In terms of the business cycle, an increase in income risk might lead to greater precautionary savings, which could depress aggregate demand. Bayer, Luetticke, Pham-Dao, and Tjaden (2019) show this can lead to hoarding of liquid assets, lowering capital returns. Ravn and Sterk (2021) and Acharya and Dogra (2020) consider models where the economy can get stuck in a high unemployment trap and where recessions can become self-fulfilling. Intuitively, when income risk is negatively correlated with the business cycle, fear of weak economic conditions in the future implies higher income risk, which can depress demand today as precautionary savings increase. Gornemann, Kuester, and Nakajima (2021) show that wealthier households tend to prefer (in terms of welfare) a monetary policy that targets inflation, while wealth-poor households prefer unemployment-focused policies.

18.5.3 **Understanding the effects of unconventional monetary policy**

Unconventional monetary policies such as forward guidance and quantitative easing were widely used around the world after interest rates hit the zero lower bound in many countries after 2009. HANK models also help us understand how these new policy measures may work.

As mentioned in Section 18.3, the simple NK model produces a sizable so-called 'Forward Guidance Puzzle', where announcements about interest rate changes in the distant future can have implausibly large effects today.

HANK models may potentially weaken this effect helping to resolve the puzzle. Important contributions include, Werning (2015), McKay, Nakamura, and Steinsson (2016) and Hagedorn, Luo, Manovskii, and Mitman (2019). McKay, Nakamura, and Steinsson (2016), for example, show that the precautionary savings motive can dampen

---

[43] Iacoviello (2005) provides an early influential example of a (TANK) New Keynesian model with groups of savers and borrowers and where movements in house prices amplify the effects of monetary policy and other shocks.

the Forward Guidance Puzzle because it dampens the incentive to consume vs. save (as discussed earlier). Hagedorn, Luo, Manovskii, and Mitman (2019) show that, in a model with various other extensions, the puzzle can be completely resolved.

Quantitative easing (QE) policies are also very naturally analysed in the heterogeneous agent environment. QE was used around the world many times after 2009 and involved purchasing long-term assets (such as long-term government bonds or private sector assets) but, being a newly deployed policy intervention, the transmission mechanisms are less well-understood than for interest rate changes (see Chapters 5 and 6). QE naturally involves buying particular types of assets, and from particular agents. In many representative agent models QE is ineffective. This can change in models with different types of agents; see Cui and Sterk (2021) and Kaplan, Moll, and Violante (2016) for examples where QE can have powerful effects with heterogeneous agents.

18.5.4 The role of fiscal stabilization policy

Sections 18.3 and 18.4 focused primarily on monetary policy, but an important aspect of the policy debate in the last 15 years has been around the role for fiscal policy for stabilization purposes.

Early seminal contributions in the heterogeneous agent New Keynesian tradition focused on the role of automatic stabilizers, for example social insurance programmes and fiscal transfers, which are naturally targeted towards particular groups, often the poorest. HANK models offer a very natural way to understand these policies and examine their potential for providing stabilization. Oh and Reis (2012) show that targeted transfers can be very effective in a model with nominal rigidity and idiosyncratic uninsurable risk about income and health. McKay and Reis (2016) show that automatic stabilizers reduce output volatility less through aggregate demand channels and more through redistribution and social insurance effects. Den Haan, Rendahl, and Riegler (2018) study the role of unemployment insurance policies in helping dampen the business cycle and raise average employment.

Other papers have focused more specifically on fiscal stimulus programmes. As discussed in the introduction, Kaplan and Violante (2014) examine how introducing wealthy hand to mouth agents can greatly increase the average MPC in the economy, leading to a much larger effect of tax rebates on consumption. Their motivating evidence comes from the large tax rebate programmes introduced in the United States in 2001 and 2008. On the spending side, Hagedorn Manovskii, and Mitman (2019) show that the government spending multiplier can be larger than one in a HANK model featuring a realistic distribution of marginal propensities to consume. Kaplan, Moll, and Violante (2020) study, as noted in the introduction, the effects of lockdown during the Covid-19 pandemic and the distributional and aggregate consequences of the fiscal response.

One implication of this literature on fiscal policy is that targeting a fiscal intervention could be very important for generating effective stabilization. In many HANK models, it makes sense to target households with low liquid assets and high marginal propensities to consume. With a sizable share of wealthy hand-to-mouth households, this group is not necessarily only the poorest households. In general, any stimulus should be targeted towards those households that are most exposed to macroeconomic fluctuations. For example, Kaplan and Violante (2014) show that a fiscal transfer (such as a tax rebate) will have the largest aggregate impact if it is targeted on the bottom 50% of the income distribution.

18.5.5 How *should* monetary and fiscal policy be conducted?

Much of the research mentioned above focuses on the effects of policy interventions or shocks. There are, however, important normative questions about how policy *should* be set to maximize welfare. We examined this in the context of the NK model in Section 18.3 and in the 3-equation model starting in Chapter 3. There is an active and growing literature on optimal policy in HANK models. Welfare was, however, much easier to characterize with a representative agent. Moreover, with so many additional mechanisms and distributional issues, optimal policy potentially becomes much more complex. But, in HANK models, new important questions can now be asked. For example, should central banks consider inequality when designing policy? And should fiscal and monetary policies be coordinated to raise welfare?

As discussed in Section 18.4 monetary policy can have various distributional effects, but interest rate changes—being a single policy instrument—may be a blunt tool for addressing these. A combination of monetary and fiscal policies may be able to strike the right balance between macroeconomic stabilization and redistribution objectives. Given that not all households are affected equally by recessions, a targeted fiscal intervention could be more effective at stabilizing income and consumption. With a cost-push inflationary shock (e.g. of the type seen during 2021–22 in the face of rising world oil prices and supply chain disruptions), coordination may be required to achieve optimal stabilization of inflation and any distributional objectives.

Bilbiie, Monacelli, and Perotti (2021) note that 'stabilization and redistribution are intertwined in a model with heterogeneity, imperfect insurance, and nominal rigidity—making fiscal and monetary policy inextricably linked for aggregate-demand management'. For example, in their model, changes in fiscal policy can reduce inequality but it may also lead to redistribution of resources towards households with a higher MPC, thereby exerting inflationary pressure and complicating the central bank's task of stabilizing inflation. Le Grand, Martin-Baillon and Ragot (2021) show that, under certain conditions when fiscal policy has enough policy instruments, monetary policy can focus on price stability but there 'is an active role for redistribution over the business cycle' using fiscal policy.

Other recent examples focus specifically on optimal monetary policy in the face of inequality and redistribution objectives. For example, Bhandari, Evans, Golosov, and Sargent (2021) show that an inflationary shock due to rising firm markups shifts income from workers to owners of capital and an optimal monetary policy might need to lower interest rates, in contrast to the standard argument that interest rates should increase in the face of cost-push inflation. In Acharya, Challe, and Dogra (2020) reductions in inequality can lead to improvements in welfare. In their model, under certain circumstances the Divine Coincidence result (discussed in Section 18.3) no longer holds. In recessions, inequality is high and the benefit of reducing inequality by stabilizing output is also high. Monetary policy should therefore be more accommodative than in the standard representative agent model, even if this leads to higher inflation.

McKay and Wolf (2023a, 2023b) study optimal monetary policy rules in a HANK model. In contrast to the other papers above, they show that optimal monetary policy is, at best, only moderately affected by concerns about inequality. This is because, in their model, monetary policy is a relatively blunt tool for dealing with distributional issues. Fiscal policy, however, is much more effective at dealing with the distributional consequences of the business cycle.

18.5.6 **Non-rational expectations and heterogeneous agents**

Many of the papers above still assume rational expectations and modelling efforts have been directed more towards understanding heterogeneity and inequality. But a number of papers have also started to incorporate non-rational expectations in heterogeneous agent models. For example, Farhi and Werning (2019) show that HANK features interact with non-rational behaviour (so-called 'level-k' thinking which constrains agents' ability to understand the behaviour of others) to potentially help resolve the Forward Guidance Puzzle. Auclert, Rognlie, and Straub (2020) show how incorporating 'sticky information' helps HANK models match the humped-shaped behaviour of various macro variables in the data, a key objective of earlier Smets and Wouters (2007) style models mentioned in Section 18.3. Laibson, Maxted, and Moll (2022) incorporate agents with present bias and examine how it interacts with the mortgage market. The model features much larger MPCs (as estimated, for example, by Ganong and Noel 2019, discussed in Chapter 1) and the effects of monetary and fiscal policy are amplified.[44]

18.5.7 **What about firm heterogeneity?**

We end this section noting that, although the last 15 years has seen intense focus on household heterogeneity, there is a growing literature on firm heterogeneity in a New Keynesian style model. Chapter 1 discussed why credit constraints might make investment more sensitive to current cash flows. Many of these heterogeneous firm models connect to these issues and study the potential role of financial frictions and credit constraints in firm behaviour. This work builds on a deep literature studying firm heterogeneity in other contexts, usually in models with flexible prices.[45] These models are designed to answer questions like: are financial frictions important for the behaviour of investment? Which firms are most exposed to changes in monetary policy?[46]

---

[44] Ganong and Noel (2019) also interpret their empirical findings on the high sensitivity of consumption to income changes using a model of present-biased consumers.

[45] See, for instance, Cooley and Quadrini (2001), Albuquerque and Hopenhayn (2004), Cooper and Haltiwanger (2006), Khan and Thomas (2013), and Senga, Thomas and Khan (2016).

[46] Empirical evidence suggests that there is considerable heterogeneity in the response of firms to interest rate changes; see, for example, Gertler and Gilchrist (1994), Crouzet and Mehrotra (2020), Ottonello and Winberry (2020), Jeenas (2019), and Cloyne, Ferreira, Froemel, and Surico (2018).

Bernanke, Gertler, and Gilchrist (1999) (BGG) is a seminal reference on financial frictions in the New Keynesian model. In this model, firms need to borrow but also experience idiosyncratic fluctuations in their productivity. Due to imperfect information lenders cannot observe this and the cost of borrowing ends up depending on net worth. This leads to a financial accelerator because an interest rate cut stimulates the economy, raises asset prices and boosts firms' net worth. The BGG model is designed to be aggregated and the focus is on overall macroeconomic effects. Ottonello and Winberry (2020) and Jeenas (2019) are more recent examples in a new and growing literature studying firms, investment and monetary policy in a full heterogeneous firm model. For example, Ottonello and Winberry (2020) examine the importance of heterogeneity in risk and show that firms who are more likely to default may respond less to monetary policy changes because they face a steeper marginal cost curve for investment finance.

BOX 18.3 **Toolkits for solving macroeconomic models**[a]

The widespread adoption of DSGE models has been enabled by free and open-source toolboxes that solve, simulate, and estimate these models. The most popular toolbox to solve models with a representative agent (or distinct types of agents, such as borrowers and savers) is Dynare. It takes as inputs the equations describing the model and returns the solution of the model with many options for further analysis. Various policy institutions (central banks, ministries, international organizations) and some private financial institutions use Dynare for performing policy analysis and as a support tool for forecasting. In the academic world, Dynare is used for research and teaching purposes in graduate macroeconomics courses.

The RBC and NK models in Sections 18.2 and 18.3 are non-linear. For example, the production function takes a Cobb-Douglas form with exponents. But a popular set of solution techniques approximates the model as a set of linear equations, as we have done to create equations DIS and NKPC in Section 18.3, for example.[b]

In 1990, a special issue in the *Journal of Business and Economic Statistics* handled by Taylor and Uhlig investigated the (non) linear properties of the RBC model. The contributors found the dynamics of the RBC model to be close to linear, which opened the possibility to work with linear solutions and connect to the empirical literature. Linearization methods have been very popular for solving a wide class of RBC and NK models, including the larger models mentioned in Section 18.3.5. Still, whether 'linearization' works well depends on the specific research question and must be answered time and again for new models.

In addition to being able to solve and simulate a wide range of DSGE models, Dynare is also very efficient at estimating DSGE models using macroeconomic data and conducting a range of quantitative and forecasting exercises. The medium-scale NK models such as Christiano, Eichenbaum, and Evans (2005) and Smets and Wouters (2007) discussed in Section 18.3.5 can be easily solved and estimated using Dynare.

More recently, similar toolboxes have been developed to estimate heterogeneous agent macroeconomic models. Examples include Auclert et al. (2021) and Bayer et al. (2019). Similar to the KMV HANK model discussed in Section 18.4, these models feature a distribution of households or firms over productivity, wealth, or any other dimension that is of interest. Both toolboxes follow the pioneering work by Reiter (2009) and rely on a combination of linear approximation for aggregate variables and a non-linear solution at the household level. Again, there has been a debate about whether a linear solution for aggregate variables is a good approximation for this class of models. But Den Haan, Judd, and Juillard (2010)'s special issue in the *Journal of Economic Dynamics and Control* finds this to be the case for the Krusell and Smith (1998) model mentioned earlier in the chapter.

Importantly, HANK models imply a correlation between the business cycle and cross-sectional data, as discussed in Section 18.4. The inclusion of cross-sectional data in the estimation of macroeconomic models is a new and active area of research: Do cross-sectional data improve our understanding of the drivers of the business cycle? Do business cycle fluctuations drive inequality and does the policy response matter? The advent of new toolboxes to solve and estimate models with heterogeneous agents greatly enhances our ability to answer these and other interesting questions.

---

[a] We thank Ralph Luetticke for contributing this box.

[b] Dynare uses 'perturbation theory' to approximate the dynamics of the model by a Taylor expansion of chosen order. In the web appendix we made use of the Taylor expansion to derive equation *DIS* in the text. In practice, a first order—i.e. linear—approximation is often sufficient to describe the dynamics locally well. Some research questions may require 'higher order' approximations. Dynare is able to handle first order and higher order approximations of many DSGE models.

Read the web appendix to this chapter to learn more about the RBC and New Keynesian models (available at www.oup.com/he/carlin-soskice).

18.6 CONCLUSIONS

The goal of this chapter has been to provide a bridge between the rest of the book and contemporary mainstream macroeconomics research. Many of the issues and mechanisms discussed extensively in earlier chapters are alive and well at the research frontier. Macroeconomists continue to grapple with issues of macroeconomic stability, control of inflation, the role of the financial system and, more recently, issues of inequality and heterogeneity in our understanding of the business cycle.

The last 15 years has seen an intense focus on issues of heterogeneity and inequality catalysed, in part, by the 2008 Global Financial Crisis. With the help of recent research efforts, important questions about how the distribution of income and wealth interacts with the business cycle and macroeconomic policy can now be tackled. And these issues were, once again, at the heart of the policy debates during the Covid-19 economic crisis.

To understand mainstream macroeconomic research, its contributions and the ongoing challenges, requires an understanding of the origins of the modern mainstream approach. This chapter has provided an overview of 40 years of business cycle research, from the development of the early RBC model, to the New Neoclassical Synthesis and New Keynesian macroeconomics, to the recent revolution in heterogeneous agent New Keynesian macroeconomics. The objective in this chapter has been to focus on the types of questions macroeconomists can answer with these methods, on the economic lessons learned and on the intellectual development of the approach.

The work of Lucas and his contemporaries fed directly into the real business cycle (RBC) models of the 1980s, which still form the basis for the modelling approach that dominates macroeconomics research today. The RBC revolution sought to refocus macroeconomics towards microfoundations, dynamically optimizing agents, rational expectations and the potential 'real' causes of business cycles, such as technology shocks.

Recent macroeconomic models, as we have seen, are much more varied and complex than the earlier RBC contributions. For example, the next generation of macroeconomic models sought to bring Keynesian insights back into an RBC type modelling framework. These New Keynesian models showed how imperfect competition and nominal rigidities could be incorporated into a macroeconomic model with microfoundations, optimizing households and firms and rational expectations. Taking the Lucas critique seriously, important questions could now be asked about the role of macroeconomic stabilization policy and the design of monetary policy institutions.

These NK models became more complex and various additional issues could then be addressed. As a result, the New Keynesian research agenda has had a huge influence on modern macroeconomics. Many mainstream business cycle models start from a variant of the New Keynesian model. Medium and larger scale New Keynesian models can be found in numerous policy institutions and central banks where they are used to aid with forecasting and policy analysis.

But the workhorse medium-scale New Keynesian model prior to the Great Recession was still one featuring a representative agent, or a limited degree of heterogeneity, rational expectations and various transmission mechanisms that were relatively classical. The simple 3-equation NK model, for example, predicts that interest rate cuts stimulate the economy because households find it less attractive to save, and more attractive to spend. The 3-equation NK model does not, for example, feature a Keynesian multiplier of the form seen in Chapter 1, although larger versions of the NK model have included various further channels of policy transmission.

As we have seen, incorporating heterogeneity into business cycle analysis has greatly enriched our understanding of economic fluctuations and how macroeconomic policy works. This body of work has shown that many of the mechanisms through which shocks are transmitted and policy affects outcomes that were incorporated in the 3-equation and financial accelerator models developed earlier in this book are now at the centre of contemporary research. In turn, macroeconomists have sought greater use of microeconomic and disaggregated data on households and firms. In these heterogeneous agent New Keynesian models, the distribution of income, consumption and wealth play a central role in determining how the macroeconomy behaves. Macroeconomic fluctuations and policy also now have important distributional implications. This chapter has attempted to provide an accessible overview of this exciting research agenda.

QUESTIONS AND PROBLEMS FOR CHAPTER 18

CHECKLIST QUESTIONS

1. List the key assumptions behind the RBC model. Are these assumptions realistic? To justify your answer, provide some real-world examples where these conditions do not hold. Is this an objection to the modelling strategy adopted?

2. Explain in words how exogenous technology shocks produce business cycles in the RBC model.

3. Use a diagram (as per Figure 18.4) to explain the movements of the labour supply and demand curves after a negative technology shock. What might constitute a negative technology shock?

4. Explain in words what the *Solow residual* is. Use the production function to derive an equation for the Solow residual. Are there any problems with using the Solow residual as a proxy for technology shocks in the RBC model?

5. What are some common criticisms of the RBC model? Suggest how the model could be modified to deal with these problems.

6. Write out the equations for the adaptive expectations and New Keynesian Phillips curves. What are the main differences between the two? Use the equations to explain the costs associated with disinflations.

7. This question requires using the 3-equation (Chapter 3) and New Keynesian models to analyse the adjustment of the economy after a negative demand shock. Assume the economy is initially in equilibrium and the negative output gap lasts for a set amount of time.
   a. Draw the impulse response functions for inflation and the output gap for each model (as per Figure 18.7).
   b. Explain why the paths of inflation are different in each model.
   c. How would the adjustment path change for the 3-equation model if a proportion of households exhibit permanent income behaviour and have rational expectations?

8. Assess the following statements S1 and S2. Are they both true, both false or is only one true? Justify your answer.

   S1. A monetary policy maker will achieve stabilization at least cost by committing to a price-level target.

   S2. When a monetary policy maker has discretion to choose the interest rate in each period, they will follow the same adjustment path as under commitment because this minimizes the cost of adjustment to shocks.

9. Discuss the following statement: 'the 3-equation (Chapter 3) model is just a simple version of the NK model'. When comparing the two different models make sure you discuss:
   a. How different agents interact to 'solve the model'.
   b. The propagation mechanisms driving business cycles.
   c. The implications for inflation and the output gap of economic shocks.
   d. The link between the labour market and inflation.
   e. The impact of business cycles on unemployment.
10. Discuss the following statement: 'in the 3-equation NK model, the main way in which monetary policy affects the economy is through intertemporal substitution'.
11. Is the following statement true or false: 'If a household is wealthy, they will always have a low marginal propensity to consume?'. Discuss your answer with reference to the heterogeneous agent macroeconomic models discussed in Section 18.4.
12. In heterogeneous agent New Keynesian models, what do we mean by 'direct' and 'indirect' effects in the transmission of monetary policy? Discuss two different ways in which monetary policy might have indirect effects on household consumption.
13. Is the following statement true or false: 'In heterogeneous agent New Keynesian models, the distribution of income and wealth is irrelevant for the effects of monetary and fiscal policy on macroeconomic outcomes like GDP and inflation'. Discuss your answer with reference to Section 18.4.

PROBLEMS

1. Choose a large developed European economy (e.g. Germany, UK, France etc.). Use the OECD.Stat website to gather a quarterly economic time series of macroeconomic indicators (see the list of variables used in Table 18.1). Take the natural logarithm of each series and then pass it through an H-P filter (an Excel add-in for this can be downloaded from https://web-reg.de/webreg-hodrick-prescott-filter/). The difference between the actual and detrended log series is equivalent to the cyclical component of each series. Create graphs comparing the cyclical component of each variable to the cyclical component of GDP (as per Figures 18.1 and 18.2). Use the STDEV.P and the CORREL functions in Excel to compute the volatility and co-movements with GDP of each of your series (as per Table 18.1). Answer the following questions:
   a. How far does the business cycle data of your chosen country match the predictions of the original RBC model (as shown in Kydland and Prescott 1982)?

b. What do your findings suggest about the success of the original RBC model at mimicking business cycles outside of the United States?

2. Use Section 18.2 and other relevant academic literature to assess the following statement: 'real business cycle models are preferable to traditional Keynesian macroeconomic models as they are not based on ad hoc assumptions, but rather solid microfoundations, such as intertemporal optimizing individuals and perfectly competitive markets'.

3. This question focuses on the predictions of the 3-equation (Chapter 3) and NK models and how they compare to the real-world data. Use Section 18.3 and your own analysis to answer the following questions:

   a. What do the two models predict should have happened to inflation during the global financial crisis (i.e. a large negative output gap that is expected to persist for a number of periods)?

   b. Choose two OECD economies and use the OECD.Stat website to download inflation data from 2006 to the end of 2011. Plot this data on a graph. Describe the path of inflation for each of these economies over the period.

   c. Does the data more closely match the predictions of the 3-equation model or the NK model? Are there significant differences across the two countries?

   d. What other factors might have influenced the path of inflation in these countries over this period?

4. Macroeconomic policy is about controlling the economy in the sense of keeping it close to a constant inflation target. Read the following statement and answer the accompanying questions: 'when thinking of controlling a classroom full of children, one would probably think it wise to base classroom rules on the actual behaviour of children rather than on how they would behave if they solved a forward-looking problem'.

   a. Does the line of reasoning in the statement have any implications for the RBC and NK DSGE models? [Hint: think about the assumptions behind the models.]

   b. Are there any insights from the microeconomic literature on behavioural economics that would suggest that the RBC and NK DSGE models place too much weight on agents solving complicated problems forward over distant time horizons? [Hint: a useful starting point is the work of Nobel Prize winners Daniel Kahnemann and Amos Tversky.]

5. Use Section 18.4 and any other relevant academic literature to discuss the following statement: 'the conduct of macroeconomic stabilization

policy is considerably more complex once we consider heterogeneity and inequality'.

INTERESTED IN EXPLORING THESE TOPICS FURTHER?

Visit www.oup.com/he/carlin-soskice to consolidate and extend your learning with the multiple choice questions and the web appendix accompanying this chapter.

BIBLIOGRAPHY

Aagaard, P., Andersen, J. R., Dahlqvist, F., and Nauclér, T. (2022), 'Nordic companies are uniquely positioned to lead the world in combating climate change, potentially creating a nordic silicon valley of sustainability'. Article published by McKinsey. **URL:** *https://www.mckinsey.com/capabilities/sustainability/our-insights/playing-offense-to-create-nordic-sustainability-champions*

Abbas, S., Belhocine, N., El Ganainy, A., and Horton, M. (2010), 'A Historical Public Debt Database'. *IMF Working Paper WP/10/245.*

Acemoglu, D. and Johnson S. (2023), *Power and Prosperity: Our Thousand Year Struggle over Power and Prosperity*, Hachette.

Acemoglu, D. and Restrepo, P. (2019), 'Automation and new tasks: How technology displaces and reinstates labor', *Journal of Economic Perspectives* **33**(2), 3–30.

Acemoglu, D. and Robinson, J. (2012), *Why Nations Fail: The Origins of Power, Prosperity and Poverty*, Profile Books, London.

Acemoglu, D., Johnson, S., and Robinson, J. (2005), Institutions as the fundamental cause of long-growth, *in* P. Aghion and S. Durlauf, eds, *Handbook of Economic Growth*, North Holland, Amsterdam.

Acharya, S., Challe, E., and Dogra, K. (2020), 'Optimal monetary policy according to HANK', *Federal Reserve Bank of New York Staff Report* (916).

Acharya, S. and Dogra, K. (2020), 'Understanding HANK: insights from a PRANK', *Econometrica* **88**(3), 1113–1158.

Admati, A. and Hellwig, M. (2013), *The Bankers' New Clothes: What's Wrong with Banking and What to Do about It*, Princeton University Press.

Adrian, T. and Shin, H. (2011), Financial intermediaries and monetary economics, *in* B. M. Friedman and M. Woodford, eds, *Handbook of Monetary Economics*, Vol. 3, Elsevier, Amsterdam, 601–650.

Agarwal, R. and Gaule, P. (2020), 'Invisible geniuses: Could the knowledge frontier advance faster?', *American Economic Review: Insights* **2**(4), 409–424.

Agell, J. and Lundborg, P. (1995), 'Theories of pay and unemployment: Survey evidence from swedish manufacturing firms', *The Scandinavian Journal of Economics* **97**(2), 295–307.

Aghion, P., Akcigit, U., Bergeaud, A., and Blundell, R. (2019), 'Innovation and top income inequality', *Review of Economic Studies* **86**, 1–45.

Aghion, P., Akcigit, U., and Howitt, P. (2014), What do we learn from Schumpeterian growth theory?, *in* P. Aghion and S. N. Durlauf, eds, *Handbook of Economic Growth*, Vol. 2, North Holland, New York.

Aghion, P., Antonin, C., and Bunel, S. (2021), *The Power of Creative Destruction Economic Upheaval and the Wealth of Nations*, Harvard University Press, Cambridge, MA.

Aghion, P., Bloom, N., Blundell, R., Griffith, R., and Howitt, P. (2005), 'Competition and innovation: An inverted-u relationship', *The Quarterly Journal of Economics* **120**(2), 701–728.

Aghion, P., Blundell, R., Griffith, R., Howitt, P., and Prantl, S. (2009), 'The effects of entry on incumbent innovation and productivity', *Review of Economics & Statistics* **91**(1), 20–32.

Aghion, P., Bénabou, R., Martin, R., and Roulet, A. (2020), 'Environmental preferences and technological choices: is market competition clean or dirty?', *NBER Working Paper* (26921).

Aghion, P., Farhi, E., and Kharroubi, E. (2012), 'Monetary policy, liquidity, and growth', *NBER Working Paper* (18072).

Aghion, P., Frydman, R., Stiglitz, J., and Woodford, M. (2003), *Knowledge, Information, and Expectations in Modern Macroeconomics: In Honor of Edmund S. Phelps*, Princeton University Press, Princeton.

Aghion, P., Harris, C., Howitt, P., and Vickers, J. (2001), 'Competition, imitation and growth with step-by-step innovation', *The Review of Economic Studies* **68**(3), 467–492.

Aghion, P. and Howitt, P. (1998), *Endogenous Growth*, MIT Press, Cambridge, MA.

Aghion, P. and Howitt, P. (2005), Growth with quality-improving innovations: An integrated framework, *in* P. Aghion and S. N. Durlauf, eds, *Handbook of Economic Growth*, Vol. 1A, North Holland, 68–107.

Aghion, P. and Howitt, P. (2009), *The Economics of Growth*, MIT Press, Cambridge, MA.

Aghion, P., Howitt, P., and Prantl, S. (2014), 'Patent rights, product market reforms, and innovation', *Journal of Economic Growth* **20**, 223–262.

Ahn, S., Kaplan, G., Moll, B., Winberry, T., and Wolf, C. (2018), 'When inequality matters for macro and macro matters for inequality', *NBER Macroeconomics Annual* **32**.

Aidt, T. S. and Tzannatos, Z. (2006), 'The cost and benefits of collective bargaining', *Cambridge Working Papers in Economics* (0541).

Aiyagari, S. R. (1994), 'Uninsured idiosyncratic risk and aggregate saving', *Quarterly Journal of Economics* **109**(3), 659–684.

Akcigit, U. and Ates, S. T. (2021), 'Ten facts on declining business dynamism and lessons from endogenous growth theory', *American Economic Journal: Macroeconomics* **13**(1), 257–298.

Akcigit, U., Baslandze, S., and Lotti, F. (2020), 'Connecting to power: Political connections, innovation, and firm dynamics', *FRB Atlanta Working Paper* (2020-5).

Akerlof, G. (1982), 'Labor contracts as partial gift exchange', *Quarterly Journal of Economics* **97**, 543–569.

Akinci, O. and Olmstead-Rumsey, J. (2018), 'How effective are macroprudential policies? An empirical investigation', *Journal of Financial Intermediation* **33**, 33–57.

Albuquerque, R. and Hopenhayn, H. A. (2004), 'Optimal lending contracts and firm dynamics', *The Review of Economic Studies* **71**(2), 285–315.

Alesina, A. and Ardagna, S. (1998), 'Tales of fiscal adjustment', *Economic Policy* **13**(27), 489–585.

Alesina, A. and Ardagna, S. (2010), 'Large changes in fiscal policy: Taxes versus spending', *in* J. R. Brown, ed., *Tax Policy and the Economy*, Vol. 24, Cambridge, Massachusetts: National Bureau of Economic Research.

Alessandri, P. and Haldane, A. G. (2009), 'Banking on the state', Bank of England.

Almunia, M., Benetrix, A., Eichengreen, B., O'Rourke, K., and Rua, G. (2010), 'From Great Depression to Great Credit Crisis: similarities, differences and lessons', *Economic Policy*, **25**(62), 219–265.

Altig, D. E., Baker, S., Barrero, J. M., Bloom, N., Bunn, P., Chen, S., Davis, S., Leather, J., Meyer, B., Mihaylov, E., Mizen, P., Parker, N., Renault, T., Smietanka, P., and Thwaites, G. (2020), 'Economic uncertainty in the wake of the Covid-19 pandemic'. Article in VoxEU. Accessed September 2020. **URL**: https://voxeu.org/article/economic-uncertainty-wake-covid-19-pandemic

Álvarez, L., Dhyne, E., Hoeberichts, M., Kwapil, C., Bihan, H. L., Lünnemann, P., Martins, F., Sabbatini, R., Stahl, H., Vermeulen, P., and Vilmunen, J. (2006), 'Sticky prices in the euro area: A summary of new micro-evidence', *Journal of the European Economic Association* **4**(2/3), 575–584.

Alves, F., Kaplan, G., Moll, B., and Violante, G. L. (2020), 'A further look at the propagation of monetary policy shocks in HANK', *Journal of Money, Credit and Banking*. **52**(S2).

Amendola, A., Serio, M. D., Fragetta, M., and Melina, G. (2020), 'The euro-area government spending multiplier at the effective lower bound', *European Economic Review* **127**(103480).

Anbil, S., Anderson, A., and Senyuz, Z. (2020), 'What happened in money markets in September 2019?'. **URL:** *https://www.federalreserve.gov/econres/notes/feds-notes/what-happened-in-money-markets-in-september-2019-20200227.htm*

Andersson, M., Baccianti, C., and Morgan, J. (2020), 'Climate change and the macro economy', *European Central Bank* **Occasional Paper Series** (243).

Andrews, D., Criscuolo, C., and Gal, P. N. (2019), 'The best versus the rest: Divergence across firms during the global productivity slowdown', *CEP Discussion Paper* (1645).

Ang, Y. Y. (2016), *How China Escaped the Poverty Trap*, Cornell University Press.

Ang, Y. Y. (2020), *China's Gilded Age: The paradox of economic boom and vast corruption*, Cambridge University Press.

Angeletos, G. M. and La'O, J. (2009), 'Incomplete information, higher-order beliefs and price inertia', *Journal of Monetary Economics* **56**, S19–S37.

Angeletos, G. M. and Lian, C. (2018), 'Forward guidance without common knowledge', *American Economic Review* **108**(9), 2477–2512.

Antras, P. (2020), 'De-globalisation? Global value chains in the post-Covid-19 age', *ECB Forum on Central Banking*. Sintra.

Armantier, O., de Bruin, W. B., Topa, G., van der Klaauw, W., and Zafar, B. (2015), 'Inflation expectations and behavior: Do survey respondents act on their beliefs?', *International Economic Review* **56**(2), 505–536.

Armantier, O., Doerr, S., Frost, J., Fuster, A., and Shue, K. (2021), 'Whom do consumers trust with their data? US survey evidence', *BIS Bulletin* (42).

Aron, J., Duca, J. V., Muellbauer, J., Bauer, J., Murata, K., and Murphy, A. (2012), 'Credit, housing collateral, and consumption: Evidence from Japan, the UK and the US', *Review of Income and Wealth* **58**(3), 397–423.

Ashenfelter, O. (1984), 'Macroeconomic analyses and microeconomic analyses of labor supply', *Carnegie-Rochester Conference Series on Public Policy* **21**(1), 117–156.

Ashenfelter, O. and Krueger, A. B. (2021), 'Theory and evidence on employer collusion in the franchise sector', *Journal of Human Resources* **57**(Special Issue 1), S324–S348.

Ashraf, N., Karlan, D., and Yin, W. (2006), 'Tying Odysseus to the mast: Evidence from a commitment savings product in the Philippines', *The Quarterly Journal of Economics* **121**(2), 635–672.

Attanasio, O. and Pistaferri, L. (2016), 'Consumption inequality', *Journal of Economic Perspectives* **30**(2), 3–28.

Auclert, A. (2019), 'Monetary policy and the redistribution channel', *American Economic Review* **109**(6), 2333–67.

Auclert, A., Bardóczy, B., Rognlie, M., and Straub, L. (2021), 'Using the sequence-space jacobian to solve and estimate heterogeneous-agent models', *Econometrica* **89**(5), 2375–2408.

Auclert, A., Rognlie, M., and Straub, L. (2020), 'Micro jumps, macro humps: Monetary policy and business cycles in an estimated HANK model', *NBER Working Paper* (26647).

Auerbach, A. J. and Feenberg, D. (2000), 'The significance of federal taxes as automatic stabilizers', *The Journal of Economic Perspectives* **14**(3), 37–56.

Auerbach, A. J. and Gorodnichenko, Y. (2012), 'Measuring the output responses to fiscal policy', *American Economic Journal: Economic Policy* **4**(2), 1–27.

Auerbach, A. J. and Gorodnichenko, Y. (2013), Fiscal multipliers in recession and expansion, *in* A. Alesina and F. Giavazzi, eds, *Fiscal Policy after the Financial Crisis*, National Bureau of Economic Research: University of Chicago Press, 63–98.

Autor, D., Dorn, D., and Hanson, G. (2013), 'The China Syndrome: Local Labor Market Effects of Import Competition in the United States', *American Economic Review* **103**(6), 2121–2168.

Autor, D., Dorn, D., Katz, L. F., Patterson, C., and Van Reenen, J. (2020), 'The fall of the labor share and the rise of superstar firms', *The Quarterly Journal of Economics* **135**(2), 645–709.

Azar, J., Marinescu, I., Steinbaum, M., and Taska, B. (2020), 'Concentration in US labor markets: Evidence from online vacancy data', *Labour Economics* **66**(101886).

Bachmann, R. and Zorn, P. (2020), 'What drives aggregate investment? Evidence from German survey data', *Journal of Economic Dynamics and Control* **115**, 103873.

Ball, L. (1994), What determines the sacrifice ratio?, *in Monetary Policy*, University of Chicago Press, 155–193.

Ball, L. (1999), 'Efficient rules for monetary policy', NBER *Working Paper* (14818).

Ball, L. (2009), 'Hysteresis in unemployment: Old and new evidence', *International Finance* **2**(1), 63–83.

Ball, L., Furceri, D., Leigh, D., and Loungani, P. (2019), 'Does one law fit all? Cross-country evidence on Okun's Law', *Open Economies Review* **30**(5), 841–874.

Ball, L., Leigh, D., and Loungani, P. (2017), 'Okun's Law: Fit at 50?', *Journal of Money, Credit and Banking* **49**(7), 1413–1441.

Ball, L. M. (2014), 'Long-term damage from the Great Recession in OECD Countries', *European Journal of Economics and Economic Policies: Intervention* **11**(2), 149–160.

Banerjee, A. and Iyer, L. (2005), 'History, institutions and economic performance: The legacy of colonial land tenure systems in india', *American Economic Review* **95**(4), 1190–1213.

Bank of England (2021), 'Responses to the Bank of England's March 2020 Discussion Paper on CBDC'. **URL:** *https://www.bankofengland.co.uk/paper/2021/responses-to-the-bank-of-englands-march-2020-discussion-paper-on-cbdc*

Bank of Japan (2013), 'The "Price Stability Target" under the Framework for the Conduct of Monetary Policy'. Document published 22 January 2013. Accessed August 2020. **URL:** *https://www.boj.or.jp/en/announcements/release_2013/k130122b.pdf*

Barattieri, A., Basu, S., and Gottschalk, P. (2014), 'Some evidence on the importance of sticky wages', *American Economic Journal: Macroeconomics* **6**(1), 70–101.

Barbieri, P., Boffelli, A., Elia, S., Fratocchi, L., and Kalchschmidt, M. (2020), 'What can we learn about reshoring after Covid-19?', *Operations Management Research* **13**, 131–136.

Bardhan, P. (2020), 'The Chinese governance system: Its strengths and weaknesses in a comparative perspective', *Chinese Economic Review*, 1, June.

Barr, D., Breedon, F., and Miles, D. (2003), 'Life on the outside: Economic conditions and prospects outside euroland', *Economic Policy* **18**(37), 573–613.

Barro, R. J. (1974), 'Are government bonds net wealth?', *Journal of Political Economy* **82**(6), 1095–1117.

Barro, R. J. (1979), 'Second thoughts on Keynesian economics', *The American Economic Review* **69**(2), 54–59.

Barsky, R. B. and Kilian, L. (2002), 'Do we really know that oil caused the great stagflation? A monetary alternative', *NBER Macroeconomics Annual 2001* **16**, 137–198.

Bartelsman, E. J. and Doms, M. (2000), 'Understanding productivity: Lessons from longitudinal microdata', *Journal of Economic Literature* **38**(3), 569–594.

Bartscher, A., Kuhn, M., Schularick, M., and Wachtel, P. (2021), 'Monetary policy and racial inequality', *Federal Reserve Bank of New York Staff Reports* (959).

Basu, D. (2013), 'Guest post: The time series of high debt and growth in Italy, Japan, and the United States', *Next New Deal: The Blog of the Roosevelt Institute*.

Basu, S. (1995), 'Intermediate goods and business cycles: Implications for productivity and welfare', *The American Economic Review* **85**(3), 512–531.

Baum, A., Checherita-Westphal, C., and Rother, P. (2013), 'Debt and growth: New evidence for the euro area', *Journal of International Money and Finance* **32**(0), 809–821.

Bayer, C., Luetticke, R., Pham-Dao, L., and Tjaden, V. (2019), 'Precautionary savings, illiquid assets, and the aggregate consequences of shocks to household income risk', *Econometrica* **87**(1), 255–290.

Bean, C. (2005), 'Monetary Policy in an Uncertain World'. Speech by the Chief Economist of the Bank of England, to The Oxford Institute of Economic Policy, on 22 February 2005. Accessed August 2020. **URL:** *https://www.bankofengland.co.uk/speech/2005/monetary-policy-in-an-uncertain-world*

Beck, T. (2017), 'The European banking union at three: A toddler with tantrums'. Article

published on VoxEU. **URL:** *https://voxeu.org/article/european-banking- union-three*
Beetsma, R., Giuliodori, M., Klaassen, F., and Wieland, V. (2006), 'Trade spill-overs of fiscal policy in the European union: A panel analysis', *Economic Policy* **21**(48), 639–687.
Beetsma, R., Thygesen, N., Cugnasca, A., Orseau, E., Eliofotou, P., and Santacroce, S. (2018), 'Reforming the EU fiscal framework: A proposal by the European fiscal board'. Article published on VoxEU. **URL:** *https://voxeu.org/article/reforming-eu-fiscal-framework-proposal-european-fiscal-board*
Beraja, M., Fuster, A., Hurst, E., and Vavra, J. (2019), 'Regional heterogeneity and the refinancing channel of monetary policy', *The Quarterly Journal of Economics*, **134**(1), 109–183.
Berger, D., Milbradt, K., Tourre, F., and Vavra, J. (2021), 'Mortgage prepayment and path-dependent effects of monetary policy', *American Economic Review* **111**(9), 2829–2878.
Bernanke, B., Gertler, M., and Gilchrist, S. (1999), The financial accelerator in a quantitative business cycle framework, *in* J. Taylor and M. Woodford, eds, *Handbook of Macroeconomics Vol. 1*, Elsevier Science, Amsterdam, 1341–1393.
Bernanke, B. S. (2003), "Constrained Discretion" and Monetary Policy'. Speech by a Member of the Board of Governors of the Federal Reserve System, New York University, on 3 February 2003. Accessed November 2020. **URL:** *https://www.federalreserve.gov/boarddocs/speeches/2003/20030203/*
Bernanke, B. S. (2016), 'What tools does the fed have left? Part 3: Helicopter money'. Article published on Brookings on 11 April 2016. **URL:** *https://www.brookings.edu/blog/ben-bernanke/2016/04/11/what-tools-does-the-fed-have-left-part-3-helicopter-money/*
Bernanke, B. S. (2020), 'The new tools of monetary policy', *American Economic Association Presidential Address* (Lecture).
Bernanke, B. S. and Gertler, M. (2001), 'Should central banks respond to movements in asset prices?', *The American Economic Review* **91**(2), 253–257.
Bessen, J. (2022), *The New Goliaths: How corporations use software to dominate industries, kill innovation, and undermine regulation*, Yale University Press.
Bewley, T. (1999), *Why Wages Don't Fall During A Recession*, Harvard University Press, Cambridge, MA.
Bewley, T. F. (1986), Stationary monetary equilibrium with a continuum of independently fluctuating consumers, *in* W. Hildenbrand and A. Mas-Colell, eds, *The New Palgrave Dictionary of Economics: 2nd edition*, North Holland, 79–102.
Bewley, T. F. (2007), Fairness, reciprocity and wage rigidity, *in* P. Diamond and H. Vartiainen, eds, *Behavioral Economics and Its Applications*, Princeton University Press, 157–194.
Bhandari, A., Evans, D., Golosov, M. and Sargent, T. J. (2021), 'Inequality, business cycles, and monetary-fiscal policy', *Econometrica* **89**(6), 2559–2599.
Bilbiie, F. O. (2020), 'The new Keynesian cross', *Journal of Monetary Economics* **114**, 90–108.
Bilbiie, F. O., Känzig, D. R., and Surico, P. (2022), 'Capital and income inequality: An aggregate-demand complementarity', *Journal of Monetary Economics* **126**, 154–169.
Bilbiie, F. O., Monacelli, T., and Perotti, R. (2021), 'Stabilization vs. redistribution: The optimal monetary-fiscal mix', *CEPR Discussion Paper* (DP15199).
Bivens, J. and Irons, J. (2010), 'Government debt and economic growth', *Economic Policy Institute Briefing Paper* (271).
Blanchard, O. (2018), 'On the future of macroeconomic models', *Oxford Review of Economic Policy* **34**(1-2), 43–54.
Blanchard, O., Domash, A., and Summers, L. (2022), 'Bad news for the Fed from the Beveridge space', *Peterson Institute For International Economics* (22–7).
Blanchard, O. and Gali, J. (2007), 'The macroeconomic effects of oil shocks: Why are the 2000s so different from the 1970s?', *NBER Working Paper* (13368).
Blanchard, O. and Gali, J. (2010), 'Labor markets and monetary policy: A New Keynesian model

with unemployment', *American Economic Journal: Macroeconomics* **2**(2), 1–30.

Blanchard, O. and Summers, L. (1986), 'Hysteresis and the European unemployment problem', *NBER Macroeconomics Annual* 1986(1), 15–90.

Blanchard, O. J. and Watson, M. W. (1982), Bubbles, rational expectations and financial markets, *in* P. Wachtel, ed., *Crises in the Economic and Financial Structure*, D.C. Heathand Company, Lexington, MA, 295–316.

Blanchard, O. and Wolfers, J. (2000), 'The role of shocks and institutions in the rise of european unemployment: The aggregate evidence', *The Economic Journal* **110**(462), 1–33.

Blanchflower, D. G. and Oswald, A. J. (1995), 'An introduction to the wage curve', *The Journal of Economic Perspectives* **9**(3), 153–167.

Blanchflower, D. G. and Rauner, B. V. (2003), *The Wage Curve*, MIT Press.

Blattman, C. and Miguel, E. (2010), 'Civil war', *Journal of Economic Literature* **48**(1), 3–57.

Blinder, A. S. (1999), *Central Banking in Theory and Practice (Lionel Robbins Lectures)*, MIT Press, Cambridge, MA.

Blinder, A. S., Canetti, E. R., Lebow, D. E., and Rudd, J. B. (1998), *Asking About Prices: A New Approach to Understanding Price Stickiness*, Russell Sage Foundation.

Blinder, A. S., Ehrmann, M., Fratzscher, M., de Haan, J., and Jansen, D. (2008), 'Central bank communication and monetary policy: A survey of theory and evidence', *Journal of Economic Literature* **46**(4), 910–945.

Blinder, A. S. and Reis, R. (2005), 'Understanding the Greenspan Standard', *Paper presented at the Federal Reserve Bank of Kansas City symposium, The Greenspan Era: Lessons for the Future, Jackson Hole, Wyoming, 25–27 August*, 2005.

Bloom, N. (2009), 'The impact of uncertainty shocks', *Econometrica* **77**(3), 623–685.

Bloom, N. (2014), 'Fluctuations in uncertainty', *Journal of Economic Perspectives* **28**(2), 153–176.

Bloom, N., Bond, S., and Van Reenen, J. (2007), 'Uncertainty and investment dynamics', *Review of Economic Studies* **74**(2), 391–415.

Bloom, N., Jones, C. I., Van Reenen, J., and Webb, M. (2020), 'Are ideas getting harder to find?', *American Economic Review* **110**(4), 1104–1144.

Bloom, N., Van Reenen, J., and Williams, H. (2019), 'A toolkit of policies to promote innovation', *Journal of Economic Perspectives* **33**(3), 163–184.

Bloom, N., Sadun, R., and Van Reenen, J. (2012), 'The organization of firms across countries', *The Quarterly Journal of Economics* **127**(4), 1663–1705.

Blundell, J. and Machin, S. (2020), 'Self-employment in the Covid-19 crisis', *CEP Covid-19 Analysis* **003**.

Blundell, R., Bond, S., Devereux, M., and Schiantarelli, F. (1992), 'Investment and Tobin's q: Evidence from company panel data', *Journal of Econometrics* **51**(12), 233–257.

Blundell, R., Dias, M. C., Cribb, J., Joyce, R., Waters, T., Wernham, T., and Xu, X. (2022), 'Inequality and the Covid-19 crisis in the United Kingdom', *Annual Review of Economics* **14**, 607–636.

Blundell, R., Green, D. A. and Jin, W. (2022), 'The UK as a technological follower: Higher education expansion and the college wage premium', *The Review of Economic Studies* **89**(1), 142–180.

Blundell, R., Jaravel, X., and Toivanen, O. (2022), 'Inequality and creative destruction', *CEPR Discussion Papers Series* (DP16867).

Boar, C. and Wehrli, A. (2021), 'Ready, steady, go? Results of the third BIS survey on central bank digital currency', *BIS Papers* (114).

Bolt, J. and van Zanden, J. L. (2013), 'The first update of the Maddison Project; re-estimating growth before 1820', *Maddison Project Working Paper* (4).

Bond, S. and Cummins, J. (2001), 'Noisy share prices and the q model of investment', *IFS Working Paper* **W01/22**.

Bonfanti, G. and Garicano, L. (2022), 'Do financial markets consider European common debt a safe asset?'. Blog post published on Bruegel on 08 December 2022. Accessed December 2022. **URL:** *https://www.bruegel.org/blog-post/do-financial-markets-consider-european-common-debt-safe-asset*

Borio, C. (2014), 'The financial cycle and macroeconomics: What have we learnt?', *Journal of Banking and Finance* **45**, 182–198.

Borio, C. (2021), 'The distributional footprint of monetary policy', *BIS Annual Economic Report* 2021.

Borio, C. and Lowe, P. (2002), 'Asset prices, financial and monetary stability: Exploring the nexus', *BIS Working Papers* (114).

Borio, C. and White, W. (2004), 'Whither monetary and financial stability? The implications of evolving policy regimes', *BIS Working Papers* **147**.

Boucinha, M. and Burlon, L. (2020), 'Negative rates and the transmission of monetary policy', *ECB Economic Bulletin* **Issue 3/2020**.

Bowles, S. (1985), 'The production process in a competitive economy: Walrasian, neo-Hobbesian, and Marxian models', *The American Economic Review* **75**(1), 16–36.

Bowles, S. (2006), *Microeconomics: Behaviour, Institutions and Evolution*, Russell Sage Foundation. Princeton University Press, New Jersey.

Bowles, S. and Carlin, W. (2020*a*), 'Inequality as experienced difference: A reformulation of the Gini coefficient', *Economics Letters* **186**(2020), 1087–89.

Bowles, S. and Carlin, W. (2020*b*), 'What students learn in economics 101: Time for a change', *Journal of Economic Literature* **58**(1), 176–214.

Bowles, S. and Carlin, W. (2021), 'Shrinking capitalism: Components of a new political economy paradigm', *Oxford Review of Economic Policy* **37**(4), 794–810.

Bowles, S. and Halliday, S. D. (2022), *Microeconomics Competition, Conflict, and Coordination*, Oxford University Press, Oxford.

Boz, E., Casas, C., Georgiadis, G., Gopinath, G., Mezo, H. L., Mehl, A., and Nguyen, T. (2020), 'Patterns in invoicing currency in global trade', *IMF working paper* (No 20/126).

Brainard, L. (2021), 'Full employment in the new monetary policy framework', *Inaugural Mike McCracken Lecture on Full Employment* **13 January 2021**.

Branstetter, L. G., Glennon, B., and Jensen, J. B. (2019), 'The IT revolution and the globalization of R&D', *Innovation Policy and the Economy* **19**(1), 1–37.

Brayton, F., Levin, A., Lyon, R., and Williams, J. C. (1997), 'The evolution of macro models at the Federal Reserve Board', *Carnegie-Rochester Conference Series on Public Policy* **47**, 43–81.

Breznitz, D. and Murphree, M. (2011), *Run of the Red Queen: Government, innovation, globalization, and economic growth in China*, Yale University Press.

Briotti, M. G. (2004), 'Fiscal adjustment between 1991 and 2002: Stylised facts and policy implications', *ECB Occasional Paper Series* (9).

Brittle, S. (2010), 'Ricardian equivalence and the efficacy of fiscal policy in Australia', *Australian Economic Review* **43**(3), 254–269.

Britton, J., van der Erve, L., Waltmann, B., andXu, X. (2021), 'London calling? Higher education, geographical mobility and early-career earnings', *Institute for Fiscal Studies*.

Broadbent, B. (2014), 'The UK Current Account'. Speech given by Ben Broadbent, Deputy Governor for Monetary Policy, Bank of England, At Directors Breakfast, Chatham House, London on 29 July 2014. Accessed June 2021. **URL:** *https://www.bankofengland.co.uk/speech/2014/the-uk-current-account*

Broadberry, S. (2013), 'Accounting for the great divergence', *London School of Economics and Political Sciences, Economic History Working Papers* (184/13).

Broadberry, S., Campbell, B., Klein, A., Overton, M., and Van Leeuwen, B. (2015), *British Economic Growth, 1270–1870*, Cambridge University Press, Cambridge, UK.

Broadberry, S. and Gupta, B. (2009), 'Lancashire, India, and shifting competitive advantage in cotton textiles 1700–1850: The neglected role of factor prices', *Economic History Review* **62**(2), 279–305.

Broer, T., Hansen, N. J. H., Krusell, P., and Öberg, E. (2020), 'The new Keynesian transmission mechanism: A heterogeneous-agent perspective', *Review of Economic Studies* **87**, 77–101.

Brunnermeier, M. K. (2009), 'Deciphering the liquidity and credit crunch 2007–2008', *Journal of Economic Perspectives* **23**(1), 77–100.

Brunnermeier, M. K. and Reis, R. (2023), *A Crash Course on Crises*, Princeton University Press, Princeton.

Brynjolfsson, E., Collis, A., and Eggers, F. (2019), 'Using massive online choice experiments to measure changes in wellbeing', *Proceedings of the National Academy of Sciences* **116**(15), 7250–7255.

Buch, C., Dominguez-Cardoza, A., and Ward, J. (2021), 'Too big to fail: Lessons from a decade of financial sector reforms'. CORE Insight. **URL**: *https://www.core-econ.org/insights/too-big-to-fail/text/01.html*

Buch, C., Dominguez-Cardoza, A., and Völpel, M. (2021), 'Too-big-to-fail and funding costs: A repository of research studies'. **URL:** *https://www.bundesbank.de/resource/blob/850252/ef3d9f2716b5912dcbda4b9e20e6a134/mL/2021-01-technical-paper-data.pdf*

Buch, E. M. and Prieto, E. (2012), 'Do better capitalized banks lend less? Long-run panel evidence from Germany', *CESifo Working Paper Series* (3836).

Buiter, W. H. (2001), 'Notes on a code for fiscal stability', *Oxford Economic Papers* **53**(1), 1–19.

Buiter, W. H. and Grafe, C. (2004), 'Patching up the pact', *Economics of Transition* **12**(1), 67–102.

Buiter, W. H. and Miller, M. (1981), 'The Thatcher experiment: The first two years', *Brookings Papers on Economic Activity* **1981**(2), 315–379.

Buiter, W. H. and Miller, M. (1983), 'Changing the rules: Economic consequences of the Thatcher regime', *Brookings Papers on Economic Activity* **1983**(2), 305–379.

Bukodi, E. and Goldthorpe, J. H. (2019), *Social mobility in Britain: Research, politics and policy*, Cambridge University Press.

Burnside, C. (2019), Exchange rates, interest parity, and the carry trade, In *Oxford Research Encyclopedia of Economics and Finance*, Oxford University Press.

Burret, H., Feld, L. and Köhler, E. (2013), 'Sustainability of public debt in Germany: Historical considerations and time series evidence', *Jahrbücher f. Nationalökonomie u. Statistik*, **233**(3).

Button, R., Pezzini, S., and Rossiter, N. (2010), 'Understanding the price of new lending to households', *Bank of England Quarterly Bulletin* **Q3**.

Caballero, R. (1999), Aggregate investment, *in* J. B. Taylor and M. Woodford, eds, *Handbook of Macroeconomics*, Vol. 1B, Elsevier Science, Amsterdam, 813–862.

Caballero, R. J., Farhi, E. and Gourinchas, P. O. (2008), 'An equilibrium model of "global imbalances" and low interest rates', *The American Economic Review* **98**(1), 358–393.

Cagan, P. (1956), The monetary dynamics of hyperinflation, *in* M. Friedman, ed., *Studies in the Quantity Theory of Money*, University of Chicago Press, Chicago, 25–117.

Calmfors, L. (2010), 'The Swedish fiscal policy council-experiences and lesson', *Paper for Conference on Independent Fiscal Policy Institutions, Budapest, 18–19 March 2010.*

Calmfors, L. and Driffill, J. (1988), 'Bargaining structure, corporatism and macroeconomic performance', *Economic Policy* **3**(6), 13–61.

Calmfors, L. and Wren-Lewis, S. (2011), 'What should fiscal councils do?', *Economic Policy* **26**(68), 649–695.

Calomiris, C. W. and Hanes, C. (1995), Historical macroeconomics and macroeconomic history, *in* K. D. Hoover, ed., *Macroeconometrics: Developments, Tensions, and Prospects*, Dordrecht: Kluwer, Dordrecht, pp. 351–416.

Calvo, G. A. (1983), 'Staggered prices in a utility-maximizing framework', *Journal of Monetary Economics* **12**(3), 383–398.

Calza, A., Monacelli, T., and Stracca, L. (2013), 'Housing finance and monetary policy', *Journal of the European Economic Association* **11**(S1), 101–122.

Campbell, C. M. and Kamlani, K. S. (1997), 'The reasons for wage rigidity: Evidence from a survey of firms', *The Quarterly Journal of Economics* **112**(3), 759–789.

Campbell, J. Y. and Mankiw, N. G. (1989), 'Consumption, income, and interest rates: Reinterpreting the time series evidence', NBER *Macroeconomics Annual* **4**, 185–216.

Card, D. (2022), 'Who set *your* wage?', *American Economic Review* **112**(4), 1075–1090.

Card, D. and Krueger, A., (1994), 'Minimum wages and employment: A case study of the fast-food industry in New Jersey and Pennsylvania', *American Economic Review* **84**(4), 772–793.

Carletti, E., Claessens, S., Fatás, A., and Vives, X. (2020), 'The bank business model in the post-covid-19 world', *Centre for Economic Policy Research.*

Carlin, W., Gordon, R. J., and Solow, R. M. (2012), Round table discussion: Where is macro going?, *in* R. M. Solow and J. Touffut, eds, *What's Right with Macroeconomics?*, Cheltenham, UK and Northampton, MA, USA: Edward Elgar.

Carlin, W., Hassel, A., Martin, A., and Soskice, D. (2015), The transformation of the German social model, *in* J. E. Dølvik and A. Martin, eds, *European Social Models from Crisis to Crisis. Employment and Inequality in the Era of Monetary Integration*, Oxford University Press, 49–104.

Carlin, W., Schaffer, M., and Seabright, P. (2013), 'Soviet power plus electrification: What is the long-run legacy of communism?', *Explorations in Economic History* **50**(1), 116–147.

Carlin, W. and Soskice, D. (2005), 'The 3-equation new keynesian model: A graphical exposition', *Contributions to Macroeconomics* **5**(1).

Carlin, W. and Soskice, D. (2006), *Macroeconomics: Imperfections, Institutions, and Policies*, Oxford University Press, Oxford.

Carlin, W. and Soskice, D. (2009), 'German economic performance: disentangling the role of supply-side reforms, macroeconomic policy and coordinated economy institutions', *Socio-Economic Review* **7**(1), 67–99.

Carlin, W. and Soskice, D. (2015), *Macroeconomics: Institutions, Instability, and the Financial System*, Oxford University Press, Oxford.

Carlin, W. and Soskice, D. (2018), 'Stagnant productivity and low unemployment: Stuck in a Keynesian equilibrium', *Oxford Review of Economic Policy* **34**(1-2), 169–194.

Carney, M. (2020), 'The grand unifying theory (and practice) of macroprudential policy'. Speech by Mark Carney, former Governor of the Bank of England, at Logan Hall, University College London. **URL:** *https://www.bankofengland.co.uk/-/media/boe/files/speech/2020/the-grand-unifying-theory-and-practice-of-macroprudential-policy-speech-by-mark-carney.pdf*

Carroll, C. D. (1997), 'Buffer-stock saving and the life cycle/permanent income hypothesis', *The Quarterly Journal of Economics* **112**(1), 1–55.

Carvalho, C., Lee, J. W., and Park, W. Y. (2021), 'Sectoral price facts in a sticky-price model', *American Economic Journal: Macroeconomics* **13**(1), 216–56.

Castro, V. (2011), 'Can central banks' monetary policy be described by a linear (augmented) Taylor rule or by a nonlinear rule?', *Journal of Financial Stability* **7**(4), 228–246.

Cecchetti, S. G., Mohanty, M. S., and Zampolli, F. (2011), 'The real effects of debt', *BIS Working Papers* (352).

Cecchetti, S. G. and Schoenholtz, K. L. (2017), 'GDP at risk'. Money and Banking blog post 21 November 2017. **URL:** *https://www.moneyandbanking.com/commentary/2017/11/26/gdp-at-risk*

Cengiz, D., Dube, A., Lindner, A., and Zipperer, B. (2019), 'The effect of minimum wages on low-wage jobs', *The Quarterly Journal of Economics* **134**(3), 1405–1454.

Cette, G., Devillard, A., and Spiezia, V. (2022), 'Growth factors in developed countries: A 1960-2019 growth accounting decomposition', *Comparative Economic Studies* **64**, 159–185.

Chandler, A. D. and Hikino, T. (1994), *Scale and Scope: The dynamics of industrial capitalism (1st Harvard University Press pbk. ed)*, Belknap Press.

Chari, V. V., Kehoe, P. J., and McGrattan, E. R. (2009), 'New Keynesian models: Not yet useful for policy analysis', *American Economic Journal: Macroeconomics* **1**(1), 242–66.

Chen, J., Yin, X., Fu, X., and McKern, B. (2021), 'Beyond catch-up: Could China become the global innovation powerhouse? China's innovation progress and challenges from a holistic innovation perspective', *Industrial and Corporate Change* **30**(4), 1037–1064.

Chen, S., Doerr, S., Frost, J., Gambacorta, L., and Shin, H. S. (2021), 'The Fintech gender gap', *BIS Working Papers* (931).

Cheng, J. and Wessel, D. (2020), 'What is the repo market, and why does it matter?'. **URL:** *https://www.brookings.edu/blog/up-front/2020/01/28/what-is-the-repo-market-and-why-does-it-matter/*

Chetty, R., Grusky, D., Hell, M., Hendren, N., Manduca, R., and Narang, J. (2017), 'The fading American dream: Trends in absolute income mobility since 1940', *Science* **356**(6336), 398–406.

Chetty, R., Guren, A., Manoli, D., and Weber, A. (2011), 'Are micro and macro labor supply elasticities consistent? A review of evidence on the intensive and extensive margins', *American Economic Review* **101**(3), 471–75.

Chetty, R. and Hendren, N. (2018), 'The impacts of neighborhoods on intergenerational mobility I: Childhood exposure effects', *The Quarterly Journal of Economics* **133**(3), 1107–1162.

Chetty, R., Jackson, M. O., Kuchler, T., Stroebel, J., Hendren, N., Fluegge, R. B., Gong, S., Gonzalez, F., Grondin, A., Jacob, M., Johnston, D., Koenen, M., Laguna-Muggenburg, E., Mudekereza, F., Rutter, T., Thor, N., Townsend, W., Zhang, R., Bailey, M., Barberá, P., Bhole, M. and Wernerfelt, N. (2022), 'Social capital I: Measurement and associations with economic mobility', *Nature* **608**(7921), 108–121.

Cheung, Y.-W., Chinn, M. D., and Marsh, I. W. (2004), 'How do UK-based foreign exchange dealers think their market operates?', *International Journal of Finance & Economics* **9**(4), 289–306.

Chirinko, R. S. (1993), 'Business fixed investment spending: Modeling strategies, empirical results, and policy implications', *Journal of Economic Literature* **31**(4), 1875–1911.

Christiano, L., Eichenbaum, M., and Rebelo, S. (2011), 'When is the government spending multiplier large?', *Journal of Political Economy* **119**(1), 78–121.

Christiano, L. J. and Eichenbaum, M. (1992), 'Current real-business-cycle theories and aggregate labor-market fluctuations', *The American Economic Review* **82**(3), 430–450.

Christiano, L. J., Eichenbaum, M., and Evans, C. L. (2005), 'Nominal rigidities and the dynamic effects of a shock to monetary policy', *Journal of Political Economy* **113**(1), 1–45.

Christiano, L. J., Eichenbaum, M. S., and Trabandt, M. (2016), 'Unemployment and business cycles', *Econometrica* **84**(4), 1523–1569.

Christiano, L. J., Trabandt, M., and Walentin, K. (2010), 'Involuntary unemployment and the business cycle', *NBER Working Paper* (15801).

Chung, H., Laforte, J. P., Reifschneider, D., and Williams, J. C. (2012), 'Have we underestimated the likelihood and severity of zero lower bound events?', *Journal of Money, Credit and Banking* **44**, 47–82.

Claessens, S., Pozsar, Z., Ratnovski, L., and Singh, M. (2012), 'Shadow banking: Economics and policy', *IMF Staff Discussion Note* **SDN/12/12**.

Clarida, R., Galí, J., and Gertler, M. (1999), 'The science of monetary policy: A new Keynesian perspective', *Journal of Economic Literature* **37**(4), 1661–1707.

Clarivate (2021), 'Clarivate identifies the one in 1,000 citation elite with annual highly cited researchers list'. Article published by Clarivate on 16 November 2021. **URL:** *https://clarivate.com/news/clarivate-identifies-the-one-in-1000-citation-elite-with-annual-highly-cited-researchers-list/*

Clark, A. E. and Oswald, A. J. (1994), 'Unhappiness and unemployment', *The Economic Journal* **104**(424), 648–659.

Clark, A. E. and Oswald, A. J. (2020), 'A simple statistical method for measuring how life events affect happiness', *International Journal of Epidemiology* **36**(6), 1139–1144.

Cloyne, J. (2013), 'Discretionary tax changes and the macroeconomy: New narrative evidence from the United Kingdom', *American Economic Review* **103**(4), 1507–1528.

Cloyne, J., Ferreira, C., Froemel, M., and Surico, P. (2018), 'Monetary policy, corporate finance and investment', *NBER Working Paper* (25366).

Cloyne, J., Ferreira, C., and Surico, P. (2020), 'Monetary policy when households have debt: New evidence on the transmission mechanism', *The Review of Economic Studies* **87**(1), 102–129.

Cochrane, J. (2012), 'Austerity, stimulus, or growth now?'. Blog post published 21 March 2012. **URL:** *https://johnhcochrane.blogspot.*

com/2012/03/austerity-stimulus-or-growth-now.html

Cochrane, J. (2015), 'Whither inflation?'. The Grumpy Economist blog post 31 August 2015. **URL:** *https://johnhcochrane.blogspot.com/2015/08/whither-inflation.html*

Coibion, O., Gorodnichenko, Y., Kueng, L., and Silvia, J. (2017), 'Innocent bystanders? Monetary policy and inequality', *Journal of Monetary Economics* **88**, 70–89.

Commission, E. (2021), 'Regional innovation scoreboard 2021'. European Commission, Directorate-General for Internal Market, Industry, Entrepreneurship and SMEs. **URL:** *https://data.europa.eu/doi/10.2873/674111*

Cooley, T. F. and Quadrini, V. (2001), 'Financial markets and firm dynamics', *American Economic Review* **91**(5), 1286–1310.

Cooper, R. N. (2008), 'Global imbalances: Globalization, demography, and sustainability', *The Journal of Economic Perspectives* **22**(3), 93–112.

Cooper, R. W. and Haltiwanger, J. C. (2006), 'On the nature of capital adjustment costs', *The Review of Economic Studies* **73**(3), 611–633.

Corsetti, G., Crowley, M., and Han, L. (2022), 'Invoicing and the dynamics of pricing-to-market: Evidence from UK export prices around the Brexit referendum', *Journal of International Economics* **135**(7), 103570.

Corsetti, G., Dedola, L., and Leduc, S. (2010), Optimal monetary policy in open economies, *in* B. Friedman and M. Woodford, eds, *Handbook of Monetary Economics*, Vol. 3B, Elsevier, 861–933.

Corsetti, G. and Pesenti, P. (2001), 'Welfare and macroeconomic interdependence', *The Quarterly Journal of Economics* **116**(2), 421–445.

Cottarelli, C. and Jaramillo, L. (2013), 'Walking hand in hand: Fiscal policy and growth in advanced democracies', *Review of Economics and Institutions* **4**(2).

Crafts, N. (2013), 'Long-term growth in Europe: What difference does the crisis make?', *National Institute Economic Review* **224**.

Crafts, N. and Fearon, P. (2010), 'Lessons from the 1930s Great Depression', *Oxford Review of Economic Policy* **26**(3), 285–317.

Crafts, N. and Mills, T. C. (2013), 'Rearmament to the rescue? New estimates of the impact of "Keynesian" policies in 1930s' Britain', *The Journal of Economic History* **73**(4), 1077–1104.

Criscuolo, C. (2021), 'Productivity and business dynamics through the lens of Covid-19: The shock, risks and opportunities', *Beyond the Pandemic: The Future of Monetary Policy* **117**.

Crouzet, N. and Mehrotra, N. R. (2020), 'Small and large firms over the business cycle', *American Economic Review* **110**(11), 3549–3601.

Crowley, M., Han, L., and Corsetti, G. (2019), 'Dollars and sense: The sterling depreciation and UK price competitiveness'. Article published in VoxEU / Columns, 26 August 2019. URL: https://cepr.org/voxeu/columns/dollars-and-sense-sterling-depreciation-and-uk-price-competitiveness

Cui, W. and Sterk, V. (2021), 'Quantitative easing with heterogeneous agents', *Journal of Monetary Economics* **123**, 68–90.

Cœuré, B. (2019), 'Inflation expectations and the conduct of monetary policy'. Speech by a Member of the Executive Board of the ECB, to the SAFE Policy Center (Frankfurt), on 11 July 2019. Accessed September 2020. **URL:** *https://www.ecb.europa.eu/press/key/speaker/bm/html/index.en.html*

Dafermos, Y., Nikolaidi, M., and Galanis, G. (2018), 'Climate change, financial stability and monetary policy', *Ecological Economics* **152**, 219–234.

de Grauwe, P. (2011), European monetary union, *in* S. N. Durlauf and L. E. Blume, eds, *The New Palgrave Dictionary of Economics*, Palgrave Macmillan, Basingstoke, UK.

De Mello, L., Kongsrud, P. M., and Price, R. W. R. (2004), 'Saving behaviour and the effectiveness of fiscal policy', *OECD Economic Department Working Paper* (397).

Deaton, A. (1992), *Understanding Consumption*, Clarendon Press, Oxford.

Decker, R. A., Haltiwanger, J., Jarmin, R. S., and Miranda, J. (2016), 'Decline business dynamism: What we know and the way forward', *American Economic Review* **106**(5), 203–207.

Decker, R. A., Haltiwanger, J., Jarmin, R. S., and Miranda, J. (2020), 'Changing business dynamism and productivity: Shocks versus responsiveness', *American Economic Review* **110**(12), 3952–3990.

Dell'Ariccia, G., Rabanal, P., and Sandri, D. (2018), 'Unconventional monetary policies in the euro area, Japan, and the United Kingdom', *Journal of Economic Perspectives* **32**(4), 147–172.

Del Negro, M., Giannoni, M., and Patterson, C. (2012), 'The forward guidance puzzle', *Federal Reserve Bank of New York Staff Reports* (574).

De Loecker, J. and Eeckhout, J. (2018), 'Global market power', *NBER Working Paper* (24768).

DeLong, J. B. and Summers, L. (2012), 'Fiscal policy in a depressed economy', *Brookings Papers on Economic Activity* 233–297.

Demertzis, M. and Hughes Hallett, A. (2007), 'Central Bank transparency in theory and practice', *Journal of Macroeconomics* **29**(4), 760–789.

Den Haan, W. J., Judd, K. L., and Juillard, M. (2010), 'Computational suite of models with heterogeneous agents: Incomplete markets and aggregate uncertainty', *Journal of Economic Dynamics and Control* **34**(1), 1–3.

Den Haan, W., Riegler, M., and Rendahl, P. (2018), 'Unemployment (fears) and deflationary spirals', *Journal of the European Economic Association* **16**(5), 1281–1349.

Dewatripont, M., Reichlin, L., and Sapir, A. (2021), 'Urgent reform of the EU resolution framework is needed'. Article published on VoxEU on 16 April 2011.

Diamond, D. W. and Dybvig, P. H. (1983), 'Bank runs, deposit insurance, and liquidity', *Journal of Political Economy* **91**(3), 401–419.

Dimand, R. W. and Spencer, B. J. (2008), 'Trevor Swan and the neoclassical growth model', *NBER Working Paper* (13950).

Dincer, N. N. and Eichengreen, B. (2014), 'Central Bank transparency and independence: Updates and new measures', *International Journal of Central Banking* **10**(1), 189–259.

Dixit, A. (1992), 'Investment and hysteresis', *The Journal of Economic Perspectives* **6**(1), 107–132.

Doepke, M. and Schneider, M. (2006), 'Inflation and the redistribution of nominal wealth', *Journal of Political Economy* **114**(6).

Dolls, M., Fuest, C. and Peichl, A. (2011), *Automatic Stabilizers, Economic Crisis and Income Distribution in Europe*, Vol. 32, Emerald Group Publishing Limited.

Dornbusch, R. (1976), 'Expectations and exchange rate dynamics', *Journal of Political Economy* **84**(6), 1161–1176.

Dornbusch, R. (1996), 'The effectiveness of exchange-rate changes', *Oxford Review of Economic Policy* **12**(3), 26–38.

Dosi, G. (1982), 'Technological paradigms and technological trajectories', *Research Policy* **11**(3), 147–162.

Drehmann, M., Borio, C., and Tsatsaronis, K. (2012), 'Characterising the financial cycle: don't lose sight of the medium term!', *BIS Working Papers* (380).

Du Caju, P., Gautier, E., Momferatou, D., and Ward-Warmedinger, M. (2008), 'Institutional features of wage bargaining in 23 European countries, the US and Japan.', *IZA Discussion Paper* **No. 3867**.

Dube, A. (2013), 'Guest post: Reinhart/Rogoff and growth in a time before debt', *Next New Deal: The Blog of the Roosevelt Institute*.

Dube, A. (2019), 'Impacts of minimum wages: review of the international evidence'. An independent report on the impacts of minimum wages, to inform the UK government's decisions on the remit of the Low Pay Commission beyond 2020. **URL:** *https://www.gov.uk/government/publications/impacts-of-minimum-wages-review-of-the-international-evidence*

Dube, A. and Zipperer, B. (2022), 'Minimum wage own-wage elasticity database'. A collection of estimates from minimum wage research studies. Accessed December 2022. **URL:** *https://economic.github.io/owe/*

Duca, J. V., Muellbauer, J., and Murphy, A. (2020), 'What drives house price cycles? International experience and policy issues', *Journal of Economic Literature* **59**(3), 773–864.

Duffie, D. (2018), 'Post-crisis bank regulations and financial market liquidity', *Thirteenth Paolo Baffi Lecture on Money and Finance, Banca d'Italia, Eurosystem* **March 2018**.

Duffie, D. (2019), 'Prone to fail: The pre-crisis financial system', *Journal of Economic Perspectives* **33**(1), 81–106.

Durlauf, S. N. and Hester, D. D. (2008), 'IS-LM', *in* S. N. Durlauf and L. E. Blume, eds, *The New Palgrave Dictionary of Economics: 2nd edition*, Vol. 4, Palgrave Macmillan, London, 3303–3309.

Dustmann, C., Fitzenberger, B., Schönberg, U., and Spitz-Oener, A. (2014), 'From sick man of Europe to economic superstar: Germany's resurgent economy', *Journal of Economic Perspectives* **28**(1), 167–188.

Easterly, W. (2005), 'What did structural adjustment adjust? The association of policies and growth with repeated IMF and World Bank adjustment loans', *Journal of Development Economics* **76**(1), 1–22.

Easterly, W. (2019), 'In search of reforms for growth: new stylized facts on policy and growth outcomes', NBER *Working Paper* (26318).

Eeckhout, J. (2021), 'Book review: The great reversal by Thomas Philippon', *Journal of Economic Literature* **59**(4), 1340–1960.

Eggertsson, G. B. and Woodford, M. (2003), 'The zero bound on interest rates and optimal monetary policy', *Brookings Papers on Economic Activity* (1), 139–211.

Eggertsson, G. and Krugman, P. (2012), 'Debt, deleveraging, and the liquidity trap: A Fisher-Minsky-Koo approach', *The Quarterly Journal of Economics*, **127**(3), 1469–1513.

Eichenbaum, M., Rebelo, S., and Wong, A. (2022), 'State-dependent effects of monetary policy: The refinancing channel', ECB *Forum on Central Banking* (June 2018).

Eichengreen, B. (2019), 'From commodity to fiat and now to crypto: What does history tell us?', NBER *Working Paper* (25426).

Eichengreen, B., El-Ganainy, A., Esteves, R. P., and Mitchener, K. J. (2021), *In Defense of Public Debt*, Oxford University Press, Oxford.

Eichengreen, B., Feldman, R., Liebman, J., von Hagen, J., and Wyplosz, C. (2011), *Public Debts: Nuts, Bolts and Worries (Geneva Reports on the World Economy*, No. 13), Centre for Economic Policy Research, London.

Einio, E., Feng, J., and Jaravel, X. (2022), 'Social push and the direction of innovation', *Centre for Economic Performance Discussion Paper* (1861).

Elkjær, M. A. and Iversen, T. (2022), 'The democratic state and redistribution: Whose interests are served?', *American Political Science Review*, 1–16.

Elliott, D. J., Feldberg, G., and Lehnert, A. (2013), 'The history of cyclical macroprudential policy in the United States', *Finance and Economics Discussion Series, Board of Governors of the Federal Reserve System* (US) (2013-29).

Elsby, M. W., Hobijn, B., and Şahin, A. (2010), 'The labor market in the great recession', *Brookings Papers on Economic Activity* **Spring 2010**.

Ennis, H. M. and Wolman, A. L. (2010), 'Excess reserves and the new challenges for monetary policy', *Richmond Fed Economic Brief* (10-03).

Erceg, C. J., Henderson, D. W., and Levin, A. T. (2000), 'Optimal monetary policy with staggered wage and price contracts', *Journal of Monetary Economics* **46**, 281–313.

Esping-Andersen, G. (1990), *The Three Worlds of Welfare Capitalism*, Princeton University Press.

Estrella, A. and Fuhrer, J. C. (2002), 'Dynamic inconsistencies: Counterfactual implications of a class of rational-expectations models', *The American Economic Review* **92**(4), 1013–1028.

Etzkowitz, H. and Klofsten, M. (2005), 'The innovating region: Toward a theory of knowledge-based regional development', *R and D Management* **35**(3), 243–255.

Farber, H. (2005), 'What do we know about job loss in the United States? Evidence from the displayed workers survey, 1984–2004', *Federal Reserve Bank of Chicago Economic Perspectives* **QII**, 13–28.

Farber, H. S., Herbst, D., Kuziemko, I., and Naidu, S. (2021), 'Unions and inequality over the twentieth century: New evidence from survey data', *The Quarterly Journal of Economics* **136**(3), 1325–1385.

Farhi, E. and Werning, I. (2019), 'Monetary policy, bounded rationality, and incomplete markets', *American Economic Review* **109**(11), 3887–3928.

Farmer, J. D., Goodhart, C., and Kleinnijenhuis, A. (2021), 'The current bail-in design does not resolve the too-big-to-fail problem'. Article published on VoxEU on 1 October 2021.

Fatás, A. (2018), 'Self-fulfilling pessimism: The fiscal policy doom loop'. Article published on VoxEU on 28 September 2018.

Fatás, A. and Mihov, I. (2012), 'Fiscal policy as a stabilization tool', *CEPR Discussion Papers* (8749).

Fazzari, S. M., Morley, J., and Panovska, I. (2012), 'State-dependent effects of fiscal policy', *Australian School of Business* (27).

Feldstein, M. (2006), 'The 2006 economic report of the president: Comment on chapter one (the year in review) and chapter six (the capital account surplus)', *Journal of Economic Literature Internet* **44**(3), 673–679.

Feldstein, M. (2008), 'Resolving the global imbalance: The dollar and the US saving rate', *The Journal of Economic Perspectives* **22**(3), 113–126.

Fetzer, T. (2019), 'Did austerity cause Brexit?', *American Economic Review* **109**(11), 3849–3886.

Financial Stability Board (2021), 'Evaluation of the effects of too-big-to-fail reforms: Final report'. **URL:** *https://www.fsb.org/2021/03/evaluation-of-the-effects-of-too-big-to-fail-reforms-final-report/*

Fischer, S., Sahay, R., and Vegh, C. A. (2002), 'Modern hyper- and high inflations', *Journal of Economic Literature* **40**(3), 837–880.

Fisher, P. (2009), 'The Bank of England's Balance Sheet: Monetary Policy and Liquidity Provision during the Financial Crisis'. Speech by the Executive Director for Markets and Member of the Monetary Policy Committee of the Bank of England, given at the Professional Pensions Show, Excel Centre, London, on 19 November 2009. Accessed November 2020. **URL:** *https://www.bankofengland.co.uk/-/media/boe/files/speech/2009/the-bank-of-englands-balance-sheet*

Fleisher, B. and Wang, X. (2001), 'Efficiency wages and work incentives in urban rural China', *Journal of Comparative Economics* **29**(4), 645–662.

FOMC (2012), 'Statement on Longer-Run Goals and Monetary Policy Strategy'. Announced January 25 2012, effective January 24 2012. Accessed August 2020. **URL:** *https://www.federalreserve.gov/monetarypolicy/files/FOMC_LongerRunGoals.pdf*

Foote, C., Gerardi, K., and Willen, P. (2012), 'Why did so many people make so many ex post bad decisions? The causes of the foreclosure crisis', *NBER Working Paper* (13950).

Foote, C., Loewenstein, L., and Willen, P. (2021), 'Cross-sectional patterns of mortgage debt during the housing boom: Evidence and implications', *Review of Economic Studies* **88**, 229–259.

Fostel, A. and Geanakoplos, J. (2012*a*), 'Debt, deleveraging, and the liquidity trap: A Fisher-Minsky-Koo approach', *The Quarterly Journal of Economics* **127**(3), 1469–1513.

Fostel, A. and Geanakoplos, J. (2012*b*), 'Why does bad news increase volatility and decrease leverage', *Journal of Economic Theory* **147**(2), 501–525.

Foster, L., Haltiwanger, J., and Krizan, C. (2001), Aggregate productivity growth. lessons from microeconomic evidence, *in* C. R. Hulten, E. R. Dean, and M. Harper, eds, *New Developments in Productivity Analysis*, University of Chicago Press, Chicago.

Foster, L. and Rosenzweig, M. (1994), 'A test for moral hazard in the labor market. Contractual arrangements, effort, and health', *The Review of Economics and Statistics* **76**(2), 213–227.

Frankel, J. A. (2006), 'Global imbalances and low interest rates: An equilibrium model vs. a disequilibrium reality', *KSG Working Paper* (RWP06-035).

Frankel, M. (1962), 'The production function in allocation and growth: A synthesis', *The American Economic Review* **52**(5), 996–1022.

Freeman, C. and Louca, F. (2002), *As Time Goes By: From the Industrial Revolutions to the Information Revolution*, Oxford University Press.

Friedman, M. (1957), *A Theory of the Consumption Function*, Princeton University Press, Princeton.

Friedman, M. (1968), 'The role of Monetary Policy', *The American Economic Review* **58**(1), 1–17.

Friedman, M. (1969), *The Optimum Quantity of Money and Other Essays*, Aldine Publishing Company, Chicago.

Friedman, M. (1970), *The Counter-Revolution in Monetary Theory* (*First Wincott Memorial Lecture*), Institute of Economic Affairs.

Friedman, T. L. (2006), *The World is Flat: The globalized world in the twenty-first century (Updated and expanded)*, Penguin Books [u.a.].

Fuhrer, J. and Moore, G. (1995), 'Inflation persistence', *The Quarterly Journal of Economics* **110**(1), 127–159.

Gabaix, X. (2020), 'A behavioral new Keynesian model', *American Economic Review* **110**(8), 2271–2327.

Gagnon, J., Raskin, M., Remache, J., and Sack, B. (2011), 'The financial market effects of the federal reserve's large-scale asset purchases', *International Journal of Central Banking* **7**(1), 1–41.

Gai, P., Haldane, A., and Kapadia, S. (2011), 'Complexity, concentration and contagion', *Journal of Monetary Economics* **58**(5), 453–470.

Galí, J. (2015), *Monetary Policy, Inflation, and the Business Cycle: An Introduction to the New Keynesian Framework and Its Applications: Second Edition*, Princeton University Press.

Galí, J., López-Salido, J. D., and Vallés, J. (2007), 'Understanding the effects of government spending on consumption', *Journal of the European Economic Association* **5**(1), 227–270.

Galí, J. and Monacelli, T. (2005), 'Monetary policy and exchange rate volatility in a small open economy', *The Review of Economic Studies* **72**(3), 707–734.

Ganong, P. and Noel, P. (2019), 'Consumer spending during unemployment: Positive and normative implications', *The American Economic Review* **109**(7), 2383–2424.

García-Schmidt, M. and Woodford, M. (2019), 'Are low interest rates deflationary? A paradox of perfect-foresight analysis', *American Economic Review* **109**(1), 86–120.

Garriga, C., Kydland, F. E., and Šustek, R. (2017), 'Mortgages and monetary policy', *The Review of Financial Studies* **30**(10).

Geanakoplos, J. (2010), The leverage cycle, *in* D. Acemoglu, K. Rogoff, and M. Woodford, eds,

Gonçalves, C. E. S. and Carvalho, A. (2009), 'Inflation targeting matters: Evidence from OECD economies' sacrifice ratios', *Journal of Money, Credit and Banking*, Vol. 24, NBER, 1–65.

Gerlach, S. (2018), 'The dollar-euro exchange rate, 2016–2018', VoxEU CEPR.

Gertler, M. and Gilchrist, S. (1994), 'Monetary policy, business cycles, and the behavior of small manufacturing firms', *The Quarterly Journal of Economics* **109**(2), 309–340.

Gertler, M. and Gilchrist, S. (2018), 'What happened: Financial factors in the great recession', *Journal of Economic Perspectives* **32**(3), 3–30.

Gertler, M. and Kiyotaki, N. (2015), 'Banking, liquidity, and bank runs in an infinite horizon economy', *American Economic Review* **105**(7), 2011–2043.

Gertler, M., Kiyotaki, N., and Prestipino, A. (2016), Wholesale banking and bank runs in macroeconomic modeling of financial crises, *in* J. Taylor and H. Uhlig, eds, *Handbook of Macroeconomics*, Vol. 1B, Elsevier, 1345–1425.

Giavazzi, F. and Pagano, M. (1990), 'Can severe fiscal contractions be expansionary? Tales of two small European countries', NBER *Macroeconomics Annual* **5**, 75–111.

Giddens, A. (1999), *The Third Way: The renewal of social democracy*, Polity Press.

Gidron, N. and Hall, P. A. (2020), 'Populism as a problem of social integration', *Comparative Political Studies* **53**(7), 1027–1059.

Giupponi, G. and Machin, S. (2022), 'Labour market inequality', IFS *Deaton Review of Inequalities*.

Glyn, A. (2007), *Capitalism Unleashed: Finance, globalization, and welfare*, Oxford University Press, Oxford.

Goldberg, P. K. and Knetter, M. M. (1997), 'Goods prices and exchange rates: What have we learned?', *Journal of Economic Literature* **35**(3), 1243–1272.

Goldin, I., Koutroumpis, P., Lafond, F., and Winkler, J. (2021), 'Why is productivity slowing down? *Journal of Economic Literature*. **URL:** *https://www.aeaweb.org/articles?id=10.1257/jel.20221543*

Gonçalves, C. E. S. and Carvalho, A. (2009), 'Inflation targeting matters: Evidence from OECD economies' sacrifice ratios', *Journal of Money, Credit and Banking* **41**(1), 233–243.

Goodfriend, M. and King, R. G. (1997), 'The new neoclassical synthesis and the role of monetary policy', *NBER Macroeconomics Annual* **12**.

Goodhart, C. (1986), 'Financial innovation and monetary control', *Oxford Review of Economic Policy* **2**(4).

Goodhart, C. (1989), 'The conduct of monetary policy', *The Economic Journal* **99**(396), 293–346.

Goodhart, C. (2006), 'The ECB and the conduct of monetary policy: Goodhart's law and lessons from the euro area', *Journal of Common Market Studies* **44**(4), 757–778.

Goos, M., Manning, A., and Salomons, A. (2014), 'Explaining job polarization: Routine-biased technological change and offshoring', *American Economic Review* **104**(8), 2509–2526.

Gordon, R. J. (2017), *The rise and fall of American growth: The US standard of living since the Civil War*, Princeton University Press.

Gornemann, N., Kuester, K., and Nakajima, M. (2016), 'Doves for the rich, hawks for the poor? distributional consequences of monetary policy', *International Finance Discussion Papers* (1167).

Gornemann, N., Kuester, K., and Nakajima, M. (2021), 'Doves for the rich, hawks for the poor? distributional consequences of systematic monetary policy', *Institute Working Paper* (50).

Gross, D. B. and Souleles, N. S. (2002), 'Do liquidity constraints and interest rates matter for consumer behavior? Evidence from credit card data', *The Quarterly Journal of Economics* **117**(1), 149–185.

Guajardo, J., Leigh, D., and Pescatori, A. (2011), 'Expansionary austerity: New international evidence', *IMF Working Paper* (11/158).

Guajardo, J., Pescatori, A., and Leigh, D. (2014), 'Expansionary austerity? International evidence', *Journal of the European Economic Association* **12**(4), 949–968.

Guerrieri, V. and Lorenzoni, G. (2017), 'Credit crises, precautionary savings, and the liquidity trap', *The Quarterly Journal of Economics* **2017**, 1427–1467.

Guren, A. M., Krishnamurthy, A., and McQuade, T. J. (2021), 'Mortgage design in an equilibrium model of the housing market', *The Journal of Finance* **76**(1), 113–168.

Guren, A. M., McKay, A., Nakamura, E., and Steinsson, J. (2021), 'Housing wealth effects: The long view', *The Review of Economic Studies* **88**(2), 669–707.

Guthrie, G. and Wright, J. (2000), 'Open mouth operations', *Journal of Monetary Economics* **46**, 489–516.

Guvenen, F., Schulhofer-Wohl, S., Song, J., and Yogo, M. (2017), 'Worker betas: Five facts about systematic earnings risk', *American Economic Review* **107**(5), 398–403.

Hacker, J. S., Hertel-Fernandez, A., Pierson, P., and Thelen, K. (2022), 'The American political economy: Markets, power, and the meta politics of US economic governance', *Annual Review of Political Science* **25**(1), 197–217.

Hagedorn, M., Luo, J., Manovskii, I., and Mitman, K. (2019), 'Forward guidance', *Journal of Monetary Economics* **102**, 1–23.

Haldane, A. G. (2017), 'Productivity puzzles'. Speech given by Andrew G Haldane, Chief Economist, Bank of England. **URL:** *https://www.bankofengland.co.uk/-/media/boe/files/speech/2017/productivity-puzzles.pdf?la=en&hash=708C7CFD5E8417000655BA4AA0E0E873D98A18DE*

Haldane, A. G. and May, R. M. (2011), 'Systemic risk in banking ecosystems', *Nature* **469**, 351–355.

Hall, G. J. and Sargent, T. J. (2010), 'Interest rate risk and other determinants of post-WWII US government debt/GDP dynamics', *NBER Working Paper* (15702).

Hall, P. and Soskice D. (eds) (2001), *Varieties of Capitalism: The Institutional Foundations of Comparative Advantage*, Oxford University Press.

Hall, R. E. (1978), 'Stochastic implications of the life cycle-permanent income hypothesis:

Theory and evidence', *Journal of Political Economy* **86**(6), 971–987.

Hall, R. E. and Mishkin, F. S. (1982), 'The sensitivity of consumption to transitory income: Estimates from panel data on households', *Econometrica* **50**(2), 461–481.

Hamilton, J. D. (2009), 'Causes and consequences of the oil shock of 2007–08', *Brookings Papers on Economic Activity* **40**(Spring), 215–284.

Hammond, G. and Ruehl, M. (2020), 'Why Hong Kong is failing to produce more tech start-ups'. Article published in the *Financial Times*, 3 February 2020. **URL:** *https://www.ft.com/content/458bc9d0-3e79-11ea-a01a-bae547046735*

Hansen, G. D. (1985), 'Indivisible labour and the business cycle', *Journal of Monetary Economics* **16**, 309–327.

Hansen, G. D. and Prescott, E. C. (1993), 'Did technology shocks cause the 1990–1991 recession?', *The American Economic Review* **83**(2), 280–286.

Hansen, S. and McMahon, M. (2016), 'The nature and effectiveness of central-bank communication'. Article published on VoxEU on 3 February 2016. **URL:** *https://voxeu.org/article/nature-and-effectiveness-central-bank-communication*

Hartley, J. E., Hoover, K. D., and Salyer, K. D. (1997), 'The limits of business cycle research: Assessing the real business cycle model', *Oxford Review of Economic Policy* **13**(3), 34–54.

Haskel, J. (2021), 'Inflation now and then'. Remarks given by Jonathan Haskel, External Member of the Monetary Policy Committee, Bank of England, and Imperial College Business School, Imperial College, London.

Hauser, A. (2019), 'Waiting for the exit: QT and the Bank of England's long-term balance sheet'. Speech given by Bank of England's Executive Director for Markets, at the European Bank for Reconstruction and Development, on 17 July 2019. Accessed August 2021. **URL:** *https://www.bankofengland.co.uk/speech/2019/andrew-hauser-speech-hosted-by-the-afme-isda-icma-london*

Heathcote, J., Perri, F., and Violante, G. L. (2020), 'The rise of us earnings inequality: Does the cycle drive the trend?', *Review of Economic Dynamics* **37**(s1), S181–S204.

Heathcote, J., Storesletten, K., and Violante, G. L. (2009), 'Quantitative macroeconomics with heterogeneous households', *Annual Review of Economics* **1**, 319–354.

Heathcote, J., Storesletten, K., and Violante, G. L. (2010), 'The macroeconomic implications of rising wage inequality in the United States', *Journal of Political Economy* **118**(4), 681–722.

Heckman, J. J. (2007), 'Comments on are protective labor market institutions at the root of unemployment? A critical review of the evidence by David Howell, Dean Baker, Andrew Glyn, and John Schmitt', *Capitalism and Society* **2**(1).

Hedlund, A., Karahan, F., Mitman, K., and Ozkan, S. (2017), 'Monetary policy, heterogeneity, and the housing channel', 2017 *Meeting Papers* (1810).

Hicks, J. R. (1937), 'Mr. Keynes and the "classics"; a suggested interpretation', *Econometrica* **5**(2), 147–159.

Hobolt, S., Leeper, T., and Tilley, J. (2020), 'Divided by the vote: Affective polarization in the wake of the Brexit referendum', *British Journal of Political Science* **51**(4), 1476–1493.

Hochschild, A. R. (2016), *Strangers in their own land: Anger and mourning on the American right*, New Press.

Hohberger, S., Priftis, R., and Vogel, L. (2017), 'The macroeconomic effects of quantitative easing in the euro area: Evidence from an estimated dsge model', *European University Institute* EUI Working Paper ECO 2017/04.

Holland, A. and Scott, A. (1998), 'The determinants of UK business cycles', *The Economic Journal* **108**(449), 1067–1092.

Holland, D. (2009), 'The impact of European and global integration on the mark-up of prices over costs', *National Institute Economic Review* **208**(1), 118–128.

Holm, M. B., Paul, P., and Tischbirek, A. (2021), 'The transmission of monetary policy under the microscope', *Journal of Political Economy* **129**(10), 2861–2904.

Holmes, M. J. (2006), 'To what extent are public savings offset by private savings in the OECD?', *Journal of Economics and Finance* **30**(3), 285–296.

Howell, D., Baker, D., Glyn, A., and Schmitt, J. (2007), 'Are protective labor market institutions at the root of unemployment? A critical review of the evidence', *Capitalism and Society* **2**(1).

Howitt, P. (2009), Inflation targeting in Canada: Optimal policy or just being there? *in* R. Leeson, ed., *Canadian Policy Debates and Case Studies in Honour of David Laidler*, Springer, 41–79.

Hsieh, C. T. and Rossi-Hansberg, E. (2019), 'The industrial revolution in services', *NBER Working Paper* (25968).

Huggett, M. (1993), 'The risk-free rate in heterogeneous-agent incomplete-insurance economies', *Journal of Economic Dynamics and Control* **17**(5-6), 953–69.

Hutton, G. and Ward, M. (2021), *Business Statistics*, House of Commons Library.

Iacoviello, M. (2005), 'House prices, borrowing constraints, and monetary policy in the business cycle', *The American Economic Review* **95**(3), 739–764.

ICB (2011), 'Final report recommendations'. The Independent Commission on Banking released its Final Report on 12 September 2011.

Ihrig, J. and Wolla, S. (2020), 'Let's close the gap: Revising teaching materials to reflect how the federal reserve implements monetary policy', *FEDS Working Paper* **No. 2020-92**.

Ilzetzki, E., Mendoza, E. G., and Végh, C. A. (2013), 'How big (small?) are fiscal multipliers?', *Journal of Monetary Economics* **60**(2), 239–254.

IMF (2009), 'World economic outlook: From recession to recovery: How soon and how strong?'. Technical Report.

IMF (2010), Chapter 3: Will it hurt? macroeconomic effects of fiscal consolidation, *in World Economic Outlook: Recovery, Risk and Rebalancing*, 93–124.

IMF (2012), 'World economic outlook: Coping with high debt and sluggish growth'. Washington, DC, October.

IMF (2020), 'World economic outlook: A long and difficult ascent'. Washington, DC, October.

Imrohoroğlu, A. (1989), 'Cost of business cycles with indivisibilities and liquidity constraints', *Journal of Political Economy* **97**(6), 1364–1383.

Irons, J. and Bivens, J. (2010), 'Government debt and economic growth: Overreaching claims of debt "threshold" suffer from theoretical and empirical flaws', *EPI Briefing Paper* (271).

Isaacson, W. (2014), *The Innovators: How a group of hackers, geniuses, and geeks created the digital revolution*, Simon & Schuster, New York.

Issing, O. (2004), 'A framework for stability in Europe'. Speech by Professor Otmar Issing, Member of the Executive Board of the European Central Bank, at the University of London, European Economics and Financial Centre, London, 19 November 2004.

Iversen, T. and Soskice D., (2006), 'Electoral Institutions and the Politics of Coalitions: Why Some Democracies Distribute more than Others', *American Political Science Review*, **100**(2), 165–181.

Iversen, T. and Soskice, D. (2019), *Democracy and prosperity: Reinventing capitalism through a turbulent century*, Princeton University Press.

Jácome, L. and Lönnberg, Å. (2010), 'Implementing official dollarization', *IMF*.

Jappelli, T. (1990), 'Who is credit constrained in the US economy?', *The Quarterly Journal of Economics* **105**(1), 219–234.

Jappelli, T. and Pistaferri, L. (2010), 'The consumption response to income changes', *Annual Review of Economics* **2**(1), 479–506.

Jaravel, X. (2019), 'The unequal gains from product innovations: Evidence from the US retail sector', *The Quarterly Journal of Economics* **134**(2), 715–783.

Jeenas, P. (2019), 'Firm balance sheet liquidity, monetary policy shocks, and investment dynamics', *Job Market Paper*.

Jenkins, R. (2011), 'Why banks must think carefully before they shrink their assets'. Article by a Member of the Bank of England's Financial Policy Committee, published in *The Times* on 14 December 2011.

Johnson, D. S., Parker, J. A., and Souleles, N. S. (2006), 'Household expenditure and the income tax rebates of 2001', *The American Economic Review* **96**(5), 1589–1610.

Johnson, S. and Kwak, J. (2010), 13 *Bankers: The Wall Street Takeover and the Next Financial Meltdown*, Pantheon Books, New York.

Jones, C. I. and Vollrath, D. (2013), *Introduction to Economic Growth: Third Edition*, W. W. Norton & Company, New York.

Jordà, O., Schularick, M., and Taylor. A. (2011), 'Financial crises, credit booms, and external imbalances: 140 years of lessons', *IMF Economic Review*, **59**(2), 340–378.

Jordà, O., Schularick, M., and Taylor, A. M. (2013), 'When credit bites back', *Journal of Money, Credit and Banking* **45**(s2), 3–28.

Jordà, O., Schularick, M., and Taylor, A. M. (2016), 'The great mortgaging: housing finance, crises and business cycles', *Economic Policy* **31**(85), 107–152.

Joyce, M., Tong, M., and Woods, R. (2011), 'The United Kingdom's quantitative easing policy: Design, operation and impact', *Bank of England Quarterly Bulletin*, 2011 **Q3**.

Kalemli-Ozcan, S., Sorensen, B., and Yesiltas, S. (2012), 'Leverage across firms, banks, and countries', *Journal of International Economics* **88**(2), 284–298.

Kaminska, I. (2012), 'More on m-pesa and e-money'. Article published in the *Financial Times* on 20 July 2012. **URL:** *https://www.ft.com/content/7befd715-be92-34f1-be58-df775e5677a5*

Kapetanios, G., Mumtaz, H., Stevens, I., and Theodoridis, K. (2012), 'Assessing the economy-wide effects of quantitative easing', *Bank of England Working Paper* (443).

Kaplan, G., Moll, B., and Violante, G. L. (2018), 'Monetary policy according to HANK?', *American Economic Review* **108**(3), 697–743.

Kaplan, G., Moll, B., and Violante, G. L. (2020), 'The great lockdown and the big stimulus: Tracing the pandemic possibility frontier for the US', *National Bureau of Economic Research* (27794).

Kaplan, G. and Violante, G. L. (2014), 'A model of the consumption response to fiscal stimulus payments', *Econometrica* **82**(4), 1199–1239.

Kaplan, G. and Violante, G. L. (2018), 'Microeconomic Heterogeneity and Macroeconomic Shock', NBER *Working Paper* (24734).

Kaplan, G., Violante, G. L., and Weidner, J. (2014), 'The wealthy hand-to-mouth', *Brookings Papers on Economic Activity* **48**(Spring), 77–153.

Kekre, R. and Lenel, M. (2022), 'Monetary policy, redistribution, and risk premia', *BFI Working Paper* (2020-02).

Keynes, J. M. (1921), *A Treatise on Probability*, Macmillan, London.

Keynes, J. M. (1936), *The General Theory of Employment, Interest and Money*, Palgrave Macmillan, London.

Keynes, J. M. (1937), '*The general theory of employment*', *The Quarterly Journal of Economics* **51**(2), 209–223.

Khan, A. and Thomas, J. K. (2013), 'Credit shocks and aggregate fluctuations in an economy with production heterogeneity', *Journal of Political Economy* **121**(6), 1055–1107.

Kindleberger, C. and Aliber, R. (2011), *Manias, Panics and Crashes: A History of Financial Crises, Sixth Edition*. Palgrave Macmillan, London.

King, M. (1997*a*), 'Changes in UK monetary policy: Rules and discretion in practice', *Journal of Monetary Economics* **39**(1), 81–97.

King, M. (1997*b*), 'The Inflation Target five years on'. Lecture delivered by the Chief Economist of the Bank of England, at the London School of Economics, on 29 October 1997. Accessed August 2020. **URL:** *https://www.bankofengland.co.uk/-/media/boe/files/speech/1997/the-inflation-target-five-years-on.pdf*

King, R. G., Plosser, C. I., and Rebelo, S. T. (1988), 'Production, growth and business cycles: I. The basic neoclassical model', *Journal of Monetary Economics* **88**(21), 195–232.

King, R. G. and Rebelo, S. T. (1999), Chapter 14 resuscitating real business cycles, *in* J. B. Taylor and M. Woodford, eds, *Handbook of Macroeconomics*, Vol. 1, Part B, Elsevier, Amsterdam, 927–1007.

Kiyotaki, N. and Moore, J. (1997), 'Credit cycles', *Journal of Political Economy* **105**(2), 211–248.

Klepper, S. (2010), 'The origin and growth of industry clusters: The making of Silicon Valley and Detroit', *Journal of Urban Economics* **67**(1), 15–32.

Klepper, S. and Thompson, P. (2010), 'Disagreements and intra-industry spinoffs', *International Journal of Industrial Organization* **28**(5), 526–538.

Klomp, J. and de Haan, J. (2010), 'Inflation and Central Bank independence: A meta-regression analysis', *Journal of Economic Surveys* **24**(4), 593–621.

Knight, F. H. (1921), *Risk, Uncertainty, and Profit*, Houghton Mifflin, New York.

Koo, R. C. (2003), *Balance Sheet Recession: Japan's Struggle with Uncharted Economics and Its Global Implications*, John Wiley & Sons, Singapore.

Koo, R. C. (2011), 'The world in balance sheet recession: Causes, cure, and politics', *Real-world economics review* **58**, 19–37.

Kornai, J. (2013), *Dynamism, Rivalry, and the Surplus Economy: Two Essays on the Nature of Capitalism*, Oxford University Press, Oxford.

Kremer, M., Willis, J., and You, Y. (2021), 'Converging to convergence', *NBER Working Paper* (29484).

Krueger, A. (2018), 'Luncheon address: Reflections on dwindling worker bargaining power and monetary policy', *Proceedings of the Jackson Hole Economic Policy Symposium, Changing Market Structures and Implications for Monetary Policy* Jackson Hole, Wyo(23–25 August).

Krugman, P. (2009), 'Depression multipliers'. Article published on *The New York Times* on 10 November 2009. **URL:** *https://krugman.blogs.nytimes.com/2009/11/10/depression-multipliers/*

Krugman, P. (2010), 'Reinhart and Rogoff are confusing me'. Blog post published on *The New York Times* on 11 August 2009.

Krusell, P. and Smith, A. A. (1998), 'Income and wealth heterogeneity in the macroeconomy', *Journal of Political Economy* **106**(5), 867–896.

Kügler, A., Schönberg, U. and Schreiner, R. (2018), 'Productivity growth, wage growth and unions', *Journal of Political Economy* **114**(6).

Kumar, M. S. and Woo, J. (2010), 'Public debt and growth', *IMF Working Paper* (10/174).

Kumhof, M. and Ranciere, R. (2010), *Inequality, leverage and crises*, IMF Working Paper (WP/10/268).

Kuttner, K. N. (2018), 'Outside the box: Unconventional monetary policy in the great recession and beyond', *Journal of Economic Perspectives* **32**(4), 121–146.

Kydland, F. E. and Prescott, E. C. (1977), 'Rules rather than discretion: The inconsistency of optimal plans', *Journal of Political Economy* **85**(3), 473–492.

Kydland, F. E. and Prescott, E. C. (1982), 'Time to build and aggregate fluctuations', *Econometrica* **50**(6), 1345–1370.

Laibson, D., Maxted, P., and Moll, B. (2022), 'Present bias amplifies the household balance-sheet channels of macroeconomic policy', *NBER Working Paper* (29094).

Lane, P. R. (2012), 'The European sovereign debt crisis', *Journal of Economic Perspectives* **26**(3), 49–68.

Lane, P. R. (2020*a*), 'The ECB's monetary policy response to the pandemic: Liquidity, stabilisation and supporting the recovery'. Speech by a Member of the Executive Board of the ECB, at the Financial Center Breakfast Webinar, on 24 June 2020. Accessed August 2020. **URL:** *https://www.ecb.europa.eu/press/key/speaker/bm/html/index.en.html*

Lane, P. R. (2020*b*), 'Monetary policy in a pandemic: Ensuring favourable financing conditions'. Speech by Philip R. Lane, Member of the Executive Board of the ECB, at the Economics Department and IM-TCD, Trinity College Dublin. **URL:** *https://www.ecb.europa.eu/press/key/date/2020/html/ecb.sp201126 c5c1036327.en.html*

Lane, P. R. and Milesi-Ferretti, G. M. (2007), 'The external wealth of nations Mark ii: Revised and extended estimates of foreign assets and liabilities, 1970–2004', *Journal of International Economics* **73**(2), 223–250.

Lane, P. R. and Milesi-Ferretti, G. M. (2018), 'The external wealth of nations revisited: International financial integration in the aftermath of the global financial crisis', *IMF Economic Review* **66**, 189–222.

La'O, J. and Tahbaz-Salehi, A. (2022), 'Optimal monetary policy in production networks', *Econometrica* **90**(3), 1295–1336.

Lavoie, M. (2013), 'The monetary and fiscal nexus of neo-chartalism: A friendly critique', *Journal of Economic Issues* **47**(1), 1–32.

Layard, R. (2004), 'Good jobs and bad jobs', *CEP Occasional Papers* (19).

Layard, R. and Nickell, S. (1986), 'Unemployment in Britain', *Economica* **53**(210), s121–s169.

Lazear, E. P., Shaw, K. L., and Stanton, C. (2016), 'Making do with less: Working harder during recessions', *Journal of Labor Economics* **34**(1), S333-S360.

Leamer, E. E. (2007), 'A flat world, a level playing field, a small world after all, or none of the above? A review of Thomas I Friedman's "The world is flat"', *Journal of Economic Literature* **45**(1), 83–126.

Leeper, E. M., Traum, N., and Walker, T. B. (2017), 'Clearing up the fiscal multiplier morass', *American Economic Review* **107**(8), 2409–54.

Le Grand, F., Martin-Baillon, A., and Ragot, X. (2021), 'Should monetary policy care about redistribution? Optimal fiscal and monetary policy with heterogeneous agents', **URL:** https://francois-le-grand.com/docs/research/LMR_OptimalMonetaryFiscal.pdf

Leigh, A. (2003), 'The rise and fall of the third way', *Australian Quarterly* **75**(2), 10.

Lerner, A. (1943), 'Functional finance and the federal debt', *Social Research* **10**(1), 38–51.

Lindbeck, A. and Snower, D. J. (1986), 'Wage setting, unemployment, and insider-outsider relations', *The American Economic Review* **76**(2), 235–239.

Lipsey, R. G. and Carlaw, K. I. (2004), 'Total factor productivity and the measurement of technological change', *Canadian Journal of Economics/Revue Canadienne d'économique* **37**(4), 1118–1150.

Ljungqvist, L. (2008), Lucas critique, *in* S. N. Durlauf and L. E. Blume, eds, *The New Palgrave Dictionary of Economics: 2nd edition*, Vol. 5, Palgrave Macmillan, London, 3810–3812.

Lloyd, S. and Marin, E. (2020), 'Uncovering uncovered interest parity: Exchange rates, yield curves and business cycles'. Published on *Bank Underground* on 13 July 2020.

Lorenzoni, G. and Werning, I. (2023), 'Inflation is conflict', *NBER Working Paper* (31099).

Lucas Jr, R. E. (1972), 'Expectations and the neutrality of money', *Journal of Economic Theory* **4**(2), 103–124.

Lucas Jr, R. E. (1976), 'Econometric policy evaluation: A critique', *Carnegie-Rochester Conference Series on Public Policy* **1**, 19–46.

Luetticke, R. (2021), 'Transmission of monetary policy with heterogeneity in household portfolios', *American Economic Journal: Macroeconomics* **13**(2), 1–25.

MacFarlane, I. (2005), 'Monetary policy'. A statement by the Governor of the Reserve Bank of Australia, 2 March 2005. Accessed August 2020. **URL:** *https://www.rba.gov.au/media- releases/2005/mr-05-04.html*

MacKenzie, D. (2009), 'All those arrows', *London Review of Books* **31**(12), 20–22.

MacLeod, W. B. and Urquiola, M. (2021), 'Why does the United States have the best research universities? Incentives, resources, and virtuous circles', *Journal of Economic Perspectives* **35**(1), 185–206.

Mankiw, N. G. (2020), 'A skeptic's guide to modern monetary theory', *AEA Papers and Proceedings* **110**, 141–144.

Mankiw, N. G. and Reis, R. (2002), 'Sticky information versus sticky prices: A proposal to replace the new Keynesian Phillips curve', *The Quarterly Journal of Economics* **117**(4), 1295–1328.

Mankiw, N. G., Romer, D., and Weil, D. N. (1992), 'A contribution to the empirics of economic growth', *The Quarterly Journal of Economics* **107**(2), 407–437.

Manning, A. (2003), *Monopsony in Motion: Imperfect Competition in Labor Markets*, Princeton University Press.

Manyika, J., Ramaswamy, S., Bughin, J., Woetzel, J., Birshan, M., and Nagpal, Z. (2018), 'Superstars: The dynamics of firms, sectors, and cities leading the global economy', *McKinsey Global Institute Discussion Paper* (October 2018).

Mariger, R. P. (1986), *Consumption Behaviour and the Effects of Government Fiscal Policies*, Harvard University Press, Cambridge, MA.

Martin, A., McAndrews, J., and Skeie, D. (2016), 'Bank lending in times of large bank reserves', *International Journal of Central Banking* **12**(4), 193–222.

Martínez-García, E., Coulter, J., and Grossman, V. (2021), 'Fed's new inflation targeting policy seeks to maintain well-anchored expectations', *Federal Reserve Bank of Dallas*.

Masciandaro, D. and Romelli, D. (2019), Peaks and troughs: Economics and political economy of central bank independence cycles, *in* D. G. Mayes, P. L. Siklos and J. Sturm, eds, *The Oxford Handbook of the Economics of Central Banking*, Oxford University Press.

Mason, J. W. and Jayadev, A. (2018), 'A comparison of monetary and fiscal policy interaction under "sound" and "functional" finance regimes', *Metroeconomica* (69), 488–508.

Mayes, D. G., Siklos, P. L., and Sturm, J. (2019), *The Oxford Handbook of the Economics of Central Banking*, Oxford University Press, Oxford.

McCann, P. (2020), 'Perceptions of regional inequality and the geography of discontent: Insights from the UK', *Regional Studies* **54**(2), 256–267.

McKay, A., Nakamura, E., and Steinsson, J. (2016), 'The power of forward guidance revisited', *American Economic Review* **106**(10), 3133–3158.

McKay, A., Nakamura, E., and Steinsson, J. (2017), 'The discounted Euler equation: A note', *Economica* **84**, 820–831.

McKay, A. and Reis, R. (2016), 'The role of automatic stabilizers in the US business cycle', *Econometrica* **84**(1), 141–194.

McKay, A. and Wolf, C. (2023a), 'Monetary Policy and Inequality', *Journal of Economic Perspectives* **37**(1), 121–144.

McKay, A. and Wolf, C. (2023b), 'Optimal Policy Rules in HANK', *Working Paper*.

McLeay, M., Radia, A., and Thomas, R. (2014), 'Money creation in the modern economy', *Bank of England Quarterly Bulletin* **Q1**.

McLeay, M. and Tenreyro, S. (2019), 'Optimal inflation and the identification of the Phillips curve', *National Bureau of Economic Research*.

Meghir, C. (2004), 'A retrospective on Friedman's theory of permanent income', *The Economic Journal* **114**(496), F293–F306.

Melitz, J. and Zumer, F. (2002), 'Regional redistribution and stabilization by the center in Canada, France, the UK and the USA: Reassessment and new tests', *Journal of Public Economics* **86**(2), 263–286.

Mendoza, E. G. and Terrones, M. E. (2008), 'An anatomy of credit booms: Evidence from macro aggregates and micro data', *International Finance Discussion Papers* (936).

Mian, A., Rao, K., and Sufi, A. (2013), 'Household balance sheets, consumption, and the economic slump', *The Quarterly Journal of Economics* **128**(4), 1687–1726.

Mian, A. and Sufi, A. (2018), 'Finance and business cycles: The credit driven household demand channel', *Journal of Economic Perspectives* **32**(3), 31–58.

Mian, A., Sufi, A., and Verner, E. (2017), 'Household debt and business cycles worldwide', *The Quarterly Journal of Economics* **132**(4), 1755–1817.

Micco, A., Stein, E., and Ordoñez, G. L. (2003), 'The currency union effect on trade: Early evidence from EMU', *Economic Policy* **18**(37), 315–356.

Michl, T. R. and Oliver, K. M. (2019), 'Combating hysteresis with output targeting', *Review of Keynesian Economics* **7**(1), 6–27.

Miles, D., Yang, J., and Marcheggiano, G. (2013), 'Optimal bank capital', *The Economic Journal* **123**(567), 1–37.

Mishkin, F. S. (1999), 'International experiences with different monetary policy regimes', *Journal of Monetary Economics* **43**(3), 579–605.

Mishkin, F. S. (2011), 'Over the cliff: From the subprime to the global financial crisis', *The Journal of Economic Perspectives* **25**(1), 49–70.

Misra, K. and Surico, P. (2014), 'Consumption, income changes, and heterogeneity: Evidence from two fiscal stimulus programs', *American Economic Journal: Macroeconomics* **6**(4), 84–106.

Mitchell, W., Wray, L. R. and Watts, M. (2019), *Macroeconomics*, Red Globe Press, London.

Modigliani, F. and Brumberg, R. H. (1954), Utility analysis and the consumption function: An interpretation of cross-section data, *in* K. K. Kurihara, ed., *Post-Keynesian Economics*, Rutgers University Press, New Brunswick, 383–436.

Modigliani, F. and Miller, M. H. (1958), 'The cost of capital, corporation finance and the theory of investment', *The American Economic Review* **48**(3), 261–297.

Moessner, R. and Takáts, E. (2020), 'How well-anchored are long-term inflation expectations?', *BIS Working Papers* **No 869**.

Moll, B. (2020), 'Research agenda: The rich interactions between inequality and the macroeconomy', *EconomicDynamics Newsletter, Review of Economic Dynamics* **21**(2).

Moll, B., Rachel, L., and Restrepo, P. (2022), 'Uneven growth: Automation's impact on income and wealth inequality', *Econometrica* **90**(6), 2645–2683.

Morris, P. R. (1994), 'The growth and decline of the semiconductor industry within the UK 1950–1985', *PhD thesis The Open University*.

Morris, S. and Shin, H. S. (2002), 'Social value of public information', *American Economic Review* **92**(5), 1521–1534.

Morris, S. and Shin, H. S. (2006), 'Inertia of forward-looking expectations', *American Economic Review* **96**(2), 152–157.

Mourre, G. and Poissonnier, A. (2019), 'What drives the responsiveness of the budget balance to the business cycle in EU countries?', *Intereconomics* **54**(4), 237–249.

Mudge, S. L. (2008), 'What is neo-liberalism?', *Socio-Economic Review* **6**(4), 703–731.

Muellbauer, J. (2022), 'Real estate booms and busts: Implications for monetary and macroprudential policy in Europe', ECB *Forum on Central Banking*, Sintra. **URL**: https://www.ecb.europa.eu/pub/conferences/ecbforum/shared/pdf/2022/Muellbauer_paper.pdf.

Muellbauer, J. and Aron, J. (2022), 'The global climate accelerator and the financial accelerator: Clarifying the commonalities, and implications from Putin's war'. Article published on VoxEU on 24 March 2022. **URL:** *https://cepr.org/voxeu/columns/global-climate-accelerator-and-financial-accelerator-clarifying-commonalities-and*

Naidu, S. and Carr, M. (2022), 'If you don't like your job, can you always quit?', *Economic Policy Institute* **May 2022**.

Nakamura, E. and Steinsson, J. (2010), 'Monetary non-neutrality in a multisector menu cost model', *The Quarterly Journal of Economics* **125**(3), 961–1013.

National Bank of Canada (2017), 'The Phillips curve still holds!', *Special report: Economics and strategy*, September 15 2017.

Neal, L. and Davis, L. E. (2007), Why did finance capitalism and the second industrial revolution arise in the 1890s?, *in* N. R. Lamoreaux and K. L. Sokoloff, eds, 'Financing Innovation in the United States, 1870 to the Present', The MIT Press, 129–162.

Nekarda, C. J. and Ramey, V. A. (2020), 'The cyclical behavior of the price-cost markup', *Journal of Money, Credit and Banking* **52**(S2).

Nelson, R. and Winter, S. (1985), *An Evolutionary Theory of Economic Change*, Harvard University Press.

Nickell, S. (1997), 'Unemployment and labor market rigidities: Europe versus North America', *The Journal of Economic Perspectives* **11**(3), 55–74.

Nickell, S. and van Ours, J. (2000), 'Why has unemployment in the Netherlands and the United Kingdom fallen so much?', *Canadian Public Policy* **26**(s1), S201–220.

Nickell, S., van Ours, J., and Huizinga, H. (2000), 'The Netherlands and the United Kingdom: A European unemployment miracle?', *Economic Policy* **15**(30), 135–180.

Nijkamp, P. and Poot, J. (2005), 'The last word on the wage curve?', *Journal of Economic Surveys* **19**(3), 421–450.

Nimark, K. (2008), 'Dynamic pricing and imperfect common knowledge', *Journal of Monetary Economics* **55**(2), 365–382.

North, D. C. (1991), 'Institutions', *The Journal of Economic Perspectives* **5**(1), 97–112.

Obstfeld, M. (2001), 'International macroeconomics: Beyond the Mundell-Fleming model', *NBER Working Paper* (8369).

Obstfeld, M. (2012), 'Does the current account still matter?', *The American Economic Review* **102**(3), 1–23.

Obstfeld, M. and Rogoff, K. (1995), 'Exchange rate dynamics redux', *Journal of Political Economy* **103**(3), 624–660.

Obstfeld, M. and Rogoff, K. (2000), 'New directions for stochastic open economy models', *Journal of International Economics* **50**(1), 117–153.

Obstfeld, M. and Rogoff, K. (2009), 'Global imbalances and the financial crisis: Products of common causes', *CEPR Discussion Paper* (7606).

Obstfeld, M. and Rogoff, K. S. (2005), 'Global current account imbalances and exchange rate adjustments', *Brookings Papers on Economic Activity* (1), 67–123.

OECD (2006), 'Employment outlook: Boosting jobs and income'. Report published on the responsibility of the Secretary-General of the OECD. **URL:** *https://doi.org/https://doi.org/10.1787/empl_outlook-2006-en*

OECD (2020), 'OECD regions and cities at a glance 2020'. OECD Statistics; Accessed September 2022. **URL:** *ttps://www.oecd-ilibrary.org/content/publication/959d5ba0-en*

OECD (2022), 'Population with tertiary education'. OECD Statistics; Accessed September 2022. **URL:** *https://doi.org/10.1787/0b8f90e9-en*

Oh, H. and Reis, R. (2012), 'Targeted transfers and the fiscal response to the great recession', *Journal of Monetary Economics* **59**, S50–S64.

O'Rourke, K. and Eichengreen, B. (2010), 'What do the new data tell us?'. Article published on VoxEU on 8 March 2010.

Orphanides, A. (2020), 'The fiscal-monetary policy mix in the euro area: Challenges at the zero lower bound', *Economic Policy* **35**(103), 461–517.

Orphanides, A. and Williams, J. C. (2005), Imperfect knowledge, inflation expectations, and monetary policy, *in* B. S. Bernanke and M. Woodford, eds, *The Inflation-Targeting Debate*, National Bureau of Economic Research, 201–246.

Orszag, P. R., Rubin, R. E., and Stiglitz, J. E. (2021), 'Fiscal resiliency in a deeply uncertain world: The role of semiautonomous discretion', *Peterson Institute For International Economics* **Policy Brief 21-2**.

Oswald, A. J. (1997), 'Happiness and economic performance', *The Economic Journal* **107**(445), 1815–1831.

Ottonello, P. and Winberry, T. (2020), 'Financial heterogeneity and the investment channel of monetary policy', *Econometrica* **88**(6), 2473–2502.

Owyang, M. T., Ramey, V. A., and Zubairy, S. (2013), 'Are government spending multipliers greater during periods of slack? Evidence from twentieth-century historical data', *American Economic Review* **103**(3), 129–134.

Pappa, E. (2020), 'Fiscal rules, policy and macroeconomic stabilization in the euro area', *ECB Forum on Central Banking*. Paper presented at the ECB Forum on Central Banking, Sintra.

Parthasarathi, P. (1998), 'Rethinking wages and competitiveness in the eighteenth century: Britain and South India', *Past & Present* **158**(1), 79–109.

Pasten, E., Schoenle, R., and Weber, M. (2020), 'The propagation of monetary policy shocks in a heterogeneous production economy', *Journal of Monetary Economics* **116**, 1–22.

Patel, D., Sandefur, J., and Subramanian, A. (2021), 'The new era of unconditional convergence', *Journal of Development Economics* **152**(102687).

Patterson, C. (2020), 'The matching multiplier and the amplification of recessions', *The Washington Center for Equitable Growth* **040820-WP**.

Patterson, C. (2023), 'The matching multiplier and the amplification of recessions', *American Economic Review*. **113**(4), 982–1012.

Perez, C. (2003), *Technological Revolutions and Financial Capital: The Dynamics of Bubbles and Golden Ages*, Edward Elgar.

Perotti, R. (2013), Fiscal policy after the financial crisis, *in* A. Alesina and F. Giavazzi, eds, *The 'Austerity Myth': Gain without Pain?*, University of Chicago Press, 307–354.

Phelps, E. S. (1967), 'Phillips curves, expectations of inflation and optimal unemployment over time', *Economica* **34**(135), 254–281.

Piketty, T. (2014), *Capital in the Twenty-first Century*, The Belknap Press of Harvard University Press.

Pisani-Ferri, J. and Sapir, A. (2006), 'Last exit to Lisbon', *Bruegel Policy Contribution* (March 2006).

Pisani-Ferry, J. (2012), 'The euro crisis and the new impossible trinity', *Bruegel Policy Contribution* (January 2012).

Pissarides, C. A. (2000), *Equilibrium Unemployment Theory: Second Edition*, MIT Press, Cambridge.

Pomeranz, K. (2000), *The Great Divergence: China, Europe, and the Making of the Modern World Economy*, Princeton University Press, Princeton.

Prescott, E. (1986), 'Theory ahead of business cycle measurement', *Federal Reserve Bank of Minneapolis Quarterly Review* **Fall**, 9–22.

Prescott, E. C. (2004), 'The Transformation of Macroeconomic Policy and Research', Nobel Prize in Economics documents 2004-7, Nobel Prize Committee.

Raff, D. M. G. and Summers, L. H. (1987), 'Did Henry Ford pay efficiency wages?', *Journal of Labor Economics* **5**(4), S57–S86.

Rajan, R. (2010), *Fault Lines*, HarperCollins Publishers.

Rajan, R. G. (2006), 'Has finance made the world riskier?', *European Financial Management* **12**(4), 499–533.

Ramey, V. A. (2011), 'Can government purchases stimulate the economy?', *Journal of Economic Literature* **49**(3), 673–85.

Ramey, V. A. (2019), 'Ten years after the financial crisis: What have we learned from the renaissance in fiscal research?', *Journal of Economic Perspectives* **33**(2), 89–114.

Ravenna, F. and Walsh, C. E. (2011), 'Welfare-based optimal monetary policy with unemployment and sticky prices: A linear-quadratic framework', *American Economic Journal: Macroeconomics* **3**(2), 130–62.

Ravn, M. O. and Sterk, V. (2021), 'Macroeconomic fluctuations with HANK & SAM: An analytical approach', *Journal of the European Economic Association* **19**(2), 1162–1202.

Read, D. and van Leeuwen, B. (1998), 'Predicting hunger: The effects of appetite and delay on choice', *Organizational Behavior and Human Decision Processes* **76**(2), 189–205.

Reinhart, C. M. and Rogoff, K. S. (2009a), *This Time is Different: Eight Centuries of Financial Folly*, Princeton University Press, Princeton, NJ.

Reinhart, C. M. and Rogoff, K. S. (2009b), 'The aftermath of financial crises', *The American Economic Review* **99**(2), 466–472.

Reinhart, C. M. and Rogoff, K. S. (2010), 'Growth in a time of debt', *The American Economic Review* **100**(2), 573–578.

Reinhart, C. M. and Rogoff, K. S. (2013), 'Does high public debt consistently stifle economic growth? A critique of Reinhart and Rogoff', *Cambridge Journal of Economics* **38**(2), 257–279.

Reis, R. (2021), 'Losing the inflation anchor', *Brookings Papers on Economic Activity* **Fall 2021**.

Reiter, M. (2009), 'Solving heterogeneous-agent models by projection and perturbation', *Journal of Economic Dynamics and Control* **33**(3), 649–665.

Riksbank (2010), *Monetary Policy in Sweden*, Sveriges Riksbank Stockholm.

Rodrik, D. (2006), 'Goodbye Washington consensus, hello Washington confusion? A review of the World Bank's economic growth in the 1990s: Learning from a decade of reform', *Journal of Economic Literature* **44**(4), 973–987.

Rodríguez-Pose, A. (2018), 'The revenge of the places that don't matter (and what to do about it)', *Cambridge Journal of Regions, Economy and Society* **11**(1), 189–209.

Rogerson, R. (1988), 'Indivisible labor, lotteries and equilibrium', *Journal of Monetary Economics* **21**(1), 3–16.

Rogoff, K. (2002), 'Dornbusch's overshooting model after twenty-five years', *International Monetary Fund's Second Annual Research Conference Mundell-Fleming Lecture*.

Röhn, O. (2010), 'New evidence on the private saving offset and Ricardian equivalence', OECD *Economics Department Working Papers* (762).

Romer, C. D. and Romer, D. H. (2010), 'The macroeconomic effects of tax changes: Estimates based on a new measure of fiscal shocks', *American Economic Review* **100**(3), 763–801.

Romer, C. D. and Romer, D. H. (2019), 'Fiscal space and the aftermath of financial crises: How it matters and why', *Brookings Papers on Economic Activity* **Spring**, 239–331.

Romer, P. M. (1990), 'Endogenous technological change', *Journal of Political Economy* **98**(5), s71–s102.

Rose, A. K. and Stanley, T. D. (2005), 'A meta-analysis of the effect of common currencies on international trade', *Journal of Economic Surveys* **19**(3), 347–365.

Roser, M. (2021), 'How much economic growth is necessary to reduce global poverty substantially?'. Article published on Our World in Data on 15 March 2021. **URL:** *https://ourworldindata.org/poverty-minimum-growth-needed*

Rotemberg, J. J. (1982), 'Sticky prices in the United States', *Journal of Political Economy* **90**(6), 1187–1211.

Rowthorn, R. and Coutts, K. (2004), 'De-industrialisation and the balance of payments in advanced economies', *Cambridge Journal of Economics* **28**(5), 767–790.

Rowthorn, R. E. (1977), 'Conflict, inflation and money', *Cambridge Journal of Economics* **1**(3), 215–239.

Rudd, J. and Whelan, K. (2007), 'Modeling inflation dynamics: A critical review of recent research', *Journal of Money, Credit and Banking* **39**(1), 155–170.

Rule, G. (2015), 'Understanding the central bank balance sheet', *Bank of England CCBS*.

Sargent, T. J. and Wallace, N. (1975), '"Rational" expectations, the optimal monetary instrument, and the optimal money supply rule', *Journal of Political Economy* **83**(2), 241–254.

Schembri, L. L. (2018), 'Anchoring expectations: Canada's approach to price stability'. Speech by the Deputy Governor of the Bank of Canada, to the Manitoba Association for Business Economists, on 15 February 2018. Accessed September 2020. **URL:** *https://www.bankofcanada.ca/2018/02/anchoring-expectations-canadas-approach-to-price-stability/*

Schnabel, I. (2021), 'Unconventional fiscal and monetary policy at the zero lower bound'. Keynote speech by a member of the Executive Board of the ECB at the Third Annual Conference organized by the European Fiscal Board entitled 'High Debt, Low Rates and Tail Events: Rules-Based Fiscal Frameworks under Stress'. **URL:** *https://www.ecb.europa.eu/press/key/date/2021/html/ecb.sp210226 ff6ad267d4.en.html*

Schumpeter, J. A. (1934), *The Theory of Economic Development: 1961 Edition*, OUP Galaxy, New York.

Schumpeter, J. A. (1942), *Capitalism, Socialism and Democracy: 2003 Edition*, George Allen and Unwin, London.

Seabright, P. (2010), *The Company of Strangers: A Natural History of Economic Life*, Princeton, NJ.

Seater, J. J. (1993), 'Ricardian equivalence', *Journal of Economic Literature* **31**(1), 142–190.

Senga, T., Thomas, J., and Khan, A. (2016), 'Default risk and aggregate fluctuations in an economy with production heterogeneity', *https://tatsuro-senga.net/uploads/3/5/4/0/35400463/kstdefaultoct2016afull.pdf*

Shapiro, C. (2012), Competition and innovation: Did Arrow hit the bull's eye?, *in* J. Lerner and S. Stern, eds, *The Rate and Direction of Inventive Activity Revisited*, University of Chicago Press, 361–404.

Shapiro, C. and Stiglitz, J. E. (1984), 'Equilibrium unemployment as a worker discipline device', *The American Economic Review* **74**(3), 433–444.

Sheets, N. and Sockin, R. (2012), 'Escaping the zero lower bound–are bulging central bank balance sheets a good substitute for rate cuts?', *Citigroup, Global Economics, Empirical and Thematic Perspectives.*

Shiller, R. J. (1997), Why do people dislike inflation?, *in* C. D. Romer and D. H. Romer, eds, *Reducing Inflation: Motivation and Strategy*, University of Chicago Press, 13–70.

Shin, H. (2009*a*), 'Discussion of the leverage cycle by John Geanakoplos', NBER *Macroeconomics Annual* **24**, 75–84.

Shin, H. (2009*b*), 'Reflections on Northern Rock: The bank run that heralded the global financial crisis', *The Journal of Economic Perspectives* **23**(1), 101–119.

Shin, H. (2010*a*), 'Financial intermediation and the post-crisis financial system', *BIS Working Papers* (304).

Shin, H. (2010*b*), *Risk and Liquidity: Clarendon Lectures in Finance*, Oxford University Press, Oxford.

Shin, H. (2012), 'Global banking glut and loan risk premium', *IMF Economic Review* **60**(2), 155–192.

Sims, C. A. (2003), 'Implications of rational inattention', *Journal of Monetary Economics* **50**, 665–690.

Sims, E. and Wu, J. (2020), 'Wall Street vs. Main Street QE', NBER *Working Paper* (27295).

Slacalek, J., Tristani, O., and Violante, G. L. (2020), 'Household balance sheet channels of monetary policy: A back of the envelope calculation for the euro area', *Journal of Economic Dynamics & Control* **115**(C).

Smets, F. and Wouters, R. (2003), 'An estimated dynamic stochastic general equilibrium model of the euro area', *Journal of the European Economic Association* **1**(5), 1123–1175.

Smets, F. and Wouters, R. (2007), 'Shocks and frictions in US business cycles: A Bayesian DSGE approach', *The American Economic Review* **97**(3), 586–606.

Sokoloff, K. L. and Engerman, S. L. (2000), 'History lessons: Institutions, factors endowments, and paths of development in the new world', *The Journal of Economic Perspectives* **14**(3), 217–232.

Sokolova, A. and Sorensen, T. (2021), 'Monopsony in labour markets: A meta-analysis', *ILR Review* **74**(1), 27–55.

Solow, R. (2000), *Growth Theory: An Exposition: 2nd Edition*, Oxford University Press, Oxford.

Solow, R. M. (1956), 'A contribution to the theory of economic growth', *The Quarterly Journal of Economics* **70**(1), 65–94.

Solow, R. M. (1998), *Monopolistic Competition and Macroeconomic Theory: Federico Caffé Lectures*, Cambridge University Press.

Song, Z., Storesletten, K., and Zilibotti, F. (2012), 'Rotten parents and disciplined children: A politico-economic theory of public expenditure and debt', *Econometrica* **80**(6), 2785–2803.

Soskice, D. (1990), 'Wage determination: The changing role of institutions in advanced industrialized countries', *Oxford Review of Economic Policy* **6**(4), 36–61.

Soskice, D. (2021), The United States as radical innovation driver: The politics of declining dominance?, *in* J. S. Hacker, A. Hertel-Fernandez, P. Pierson, and K. Thelen, eds, *The American Political Economy*, Vol. 1, Cambridge University Press, 323–350.

Soskice, D. and Iversen, T. (2000), 'The non-neutrality of monetary policy with large price or wage setters', *Quarterly Journal of Economics* **115**(1), 265–284.

Stevens, G. R. (1999), 'Six years of inflation targeting'. Speech by the Assistant Governor of the Reserve Bank of Australia, to the Economic Society of Australia, on 20 April 1999. Accessed August 2020. **URL:** *https://www.rba.gov.au/publications/bulletin/1999/may/pdf/bu-0599-2.pdf*

Sturm, J. E. and de Haan, J. (2011), 'Does central bank communication really lead to better forecasts of policy decisions? New evidence based on a Taylor rule model for the ECB', *Review of World Economics* **147**(1), 41–58.

Summers, L. H. (1986), 'Some skeptical observations on real business cycle theory', *Federal Reserve Bank of Minneapolis Quarterly Review* **10**(4), 23–27.

Swan, T. W. (1956), 'Economic growth and capital accumulation', *Economic Record* **32**(2), 334–361.

Tamiotti, L., Teh, R., Kulaçoğlu, V., Olhoff, A., Simmons, B., and Abaza, H. (2009), 'Trade and climate change', *Report by United Nations Environment Programme and the World Trade Organization.*

Tarullo, D. K. (2019), 'Financial regulation: Still unsettled a decade after the crisis', *Journal of Economic Perspectives* **33**(1), 61–80.

Taylor, J. B. (1982), 'The Swedish investment funds system as a stabilization policy rule', *Brookings Papers on Economic Activity* **13**(1), 57–106.

Taylor, J. B. (1993), 'Discretion versus policy rules in practice', *Carnegie-Rochester Conference Series on Public Policy* **39**(0), 195–214.

Taylor, J. B. (1999), A historical analysis of monetary policy rules, *in* J. B. Taylor, ed., *Monetary Policy Rules*, National Bureau of Economic Research, 319–348.

Tett, G. (2009), *Fool's Gold: How Unrestrained Greed Corrupted a Dream, Shattered Global Markets and Unleashed a Catastrophe*, Little Brown, London.

Tett, G. (2021), 'Stablecoins investors may be due a wake-up call'. Article published on the *Financial Times* on 14 October 2021. **URL:** *https://www.ft.com/content/b729cf08-6beb-4d75-b19e-779d2d3a14ce*

The Federal Reserve Board (1999), 'Monetary policy report to the congress'. Report given on July 22 1999. Accessed August 2020. **URL:** *https://www.federalreserve.gov/boarddocs/hh/1999/July/FullReport.htm*

Thelen, K. (2019), 'Transitions to the knowledge economy in Germany, Sweden, and the Netherlands', *Comparative Politics* **51**(2), 295–315.

Thiel, C. E., Bonner, J., Bush, J. T., Welsh, D. T., and Garud, N. (2021), 'Stripped of agency: The paradoxical effect of employee monitoring on deviance', *Journal of Management* 1–32.

Tobin, J. (1969), 'A general equilibrium approach to monetary theory', *Journal of Money, Credit and Banking* **1**(1), 15–29.

Tobin, J. and Brainard, W. C. (1977), Asset market and the cost of capital, *in* B. Balassa and R. Nelson, eds, *Economic Progress, Private Values and Public Policy: Essays in Honor of William Fellner*, North-Holland, New York, 235–262.

Treasury, H. (2010), 'Economic and fiscal strategy report and financial statement and budget report', HC 61. Ordered by the House of Commons to be printed 22 June 2010. **URL:** *https://www.gov.uk/government/publications/budget-june-2010*

Trigari, A. (2009), 'Equilibrium unemployment, job flows, and inflation dynamics', *Journal of Money, Credit and Banking* **41**(1), 1–33.

Tucker, P. (2004), 'Managing The Central Bank's balance sheet: Where monetary policy meets financial stability'. Speech by an Executive Director and Member of the Monetary Policy Committee of the Bank of England, to mark the fifteenth anniversary of Lombard Street Research, on 24 July 2004. **URL:** *https://www.bankofengland.co.uk/-/media/boe/files/speech/2004/managing-the-central-banks-balance-sheet.pdf*

Tuckett, D. (2012), 'Financial markets are markets in stories: Some possible advantages of using interviews to supplement existing economic data sources', *Journal of Economic Dynamics and Control* **36**(8), 1077–1087.

Urquiola, M. (2020), *Markets, minds, and money: Why America leads the world in university research*, Harvard University Press.

Vickers, J. (1986), 'Signalling in a model of monetary policy with incomplete information', *Oxford Economic Papers* **38**(3), 443–455.

Vickers, J. (2012), 'Some economics of banking reforms', *University of Oxford Department of Economics Discussion Paper Series* (632).

Vines, D., Kirsanova, T., and Wren-Lewis, S. (2006), 'Fiscal policy and macroeconomic stability within a currency union', CEPR *Discussion Papers* (5584).

Violante, G. (2021), 'What have we learned from HANK models, thus far?', *Proceedings of the ECB Forum on Central Banking* **2021**.

Visser, J. (2016), 'What happened to collective bargaining during the great recession?', IZA *Journal of Labor Policy* **5**(9).

Vlieghe, G. (2020), 'Monetary policy and the Bank of England's balance sheet'. Speech given by an External Member of the Bank of England's Monetary Policy Committee, at an online webinar, on 23 April 2020. Accessed August 2021. **URL:** *https://www.bankofengland.co.uk/speech/2020/gertjan-vlieghe-speech-monetary-policy-and-the-boes-balance-sheet*

Vlieghe, G. (2021), 'Revisiting the 3D perspective on low long-term interest rates'. Speech given by an External Member of the Bank of

England's Monetary Policy Committee, at an online public event, on 26 July 2021. Accessed July 2021. **URL:** *https://www.lse.ac.uk/Events/2021/07/202107261200/rates*

Wakker, P. P. (2008), Uncertainty, *in* S. N. Durlauf and L. E. Blume, eds, *The New Palgrave Dictionary of Economics: 2nd edition*, Vol. 8, Palgrave Macmillan, London, 6784–6795.

Walsh, C. (2003), Labor market search and monetary shocks, *in* S. Altug, J. Chadha and C. Nolan, eds, *Elements of Dynamic Macroeconomic Analysis*, Cambridge University Press, Cambridge, 451–486.

Walsh, C. (2005), 'Labor market search, sticky prices, and interest rate policies', *Review of Economic Dynamics* **8**, 829–849.

Walsh, C. E. (2010), *Monetary Theory and Policy, Third revised edition*, MIT Press, Cambridge.

Weil, D. N. (2012), *Economic Growth: International Edition, Third Edition*, Pearson Education, Harlow.

Welch, J. and Byrne, J. A. (2003), *Jack: Straight from the Gut*, Grand Central Publishing, New York.

Werning, I. (2015), 'Incomplete markets and aggregate demand', *NBER Working Paper* (21448).

Williamson, S. D. (2011), *Macroeconomics: Fourth Edition*, Pearson Education, Inc.

Winckler, A. (2011), 'The joint production of confidence: Lessons from nineteenth-century US commercial banks for twenty-first-century euro area governments', *Financial History Review* **18**(3), 249–276.

Wong, A. (2021), 'Refinancing and the transmission of monetary policy to consumption', **URL:** *https://economics.princeton.edu/working-papers/refinancing-and-the-transmission-of-monetary-policy-to-consumption/*

Woodford, M. (2003), *Interest and Prices: Foundations of a Theory of Monetary Policy*, Princeton University Press, Princeton.

Woodford, M. (2008), 'Forward guidance for monetary policy: Is it still possible?'. Article published on VoxEU on 17 January 2008.

Woodford, M. (2012), 'Methods of policy accommodation at the interest-rate lower bound', *Proceedings–Economic Policy Symposium–Jackson Hole, Federal Reserve Bank of Kansas City*, 185–288.

World Bank Group, and the Development Research Center of the State Council, P. R. China (2019), *Innovative China: New Drivers of Growth*, World Bank, Washington, DC.

Wright, G. (2020), 'Slavery and Anglo-American capitalism revisited', *Economic History Review* **73**(2), 353–383.

Yagan, D. (2019), 'Employment hysteresis from the Great Recession', *Journal of Political Economy* **127**(5), 2505–2558.

Yeh, C., Mancuso, C., and Hershbein, B. (2022), 'Monopsony in the US labor market', *American Economic Review* **112**(7), 2099–2138.

INDEX

Note: Tables, figures, and boxes are indicated by an italic *t*, *f*, and *b* following the page number.

A

C

F

G

H

I

N

O

P

T

U

V

W

X

Y

Z